MUSEUM OF BROADCAST COMMUNICATIONS

Encyclopedia of

TELEVISION

SECOND EDITION

MUSEUM OF BROADCAST COMMUNICATIONS

Encyclopedia of

TELEVISION

SECOND EDITION

Volume 4
S–Z
INDEX

Horace Newcomb
EDITOR

FITZROY DEARBORN
New York • London

Published in 2004 by
Fitzroy Dearborn
An imprint of the Taylor & Francis Group
270 Madison Avenue
New York, New York 10016

First published by
Fitzroy Dearborn Publishers
70 East Walton Street
Chicago, Illinois 60611
U.S.A.

Library of Congress Cataloging-in-Publication Data:

Encyclopedia of television / Museum of Broadcast Communications ; Horace
Newcomb, editor.—2nd ed.
        p. cm.
    Includes bibliographical references and index.
    ISBN 1-57958-394-6 (set : alk. paper) -- ISBN 1-57958-411-X (v. 1 :
alk. paper) -- ISBN 1-57958-412-8 (v. 2 : alk. paper) -- ISBN
1-57958-413-6 (v. 3 : alk. paper) -- ISBN 1-57958-456-X (v. 4 : alk.
paper)
    1. Television broadcasting--Encyclopedias. I. Title: Encyclopedia of
television. II. Newcomb, Horace. III. Museum of Broadcast
Communications.
    PN1992.18.E53 2005
    384.55'03--dc22
                                2004003947

Contents

Advisory Board

Alphabetical List of Entries

Volume 1

Volume 2

Volume 3

Volume 4

Tabloid Television in the United States
Taiwan
Talk Show in the United States
Talking Heads
Tarses, Jay
Tartikoff, Brandon
Taxi
Teaser
Technology, Television
Teenagers and Television in the United States
Telcos
Telecommunications Act of 1996
Telefilm Canada
Telemundo
Telenovela
Teleroman
Teletext
Telethon
Television Studies
Terrorism
That Girl
That Was the Week That Was
Thaw, John
Theme Songs
thirtysomething
This Hour Has Seven Days
This Is Your Life
Thomas, Danny
Thomas, Tony
Thorn Birds, The
Three's Company
Thunderbirds
Tiananmen Square
Till Death Us Do Part
Tillstrom, Burr
Time Shifting
Time Warner
Tinker, Grant
Tinker, Tailor, Soldier, Spy
Tisch, Laurence
Tiswas
Tommy Hunter Show, The
Tonight
Tonight Show, The
Top of the Pops
Touched By an Angel
Tour of the White House with Mrs. John F. Kennedy, A
Trade Magazines
Translators and Boosters
Tribune Broadcasting
Trodd, Kenith
Troughton, Patrick
Turkey

Turner Broadcasting Systems
Turner, Ted
20th Century, The
20/20
24-Hour News
Twilight Zone, The
Twin Peaks
2000 Presidential Election Coverage
227

Uncounted Enemy: A Vietnam Deception, The
Undercurrents
Unions/Guilds
United States Congress and Television
United States Presidency and Television (Historical Overview)
Universal (NBC-Universal, Vivendi Universal)
University Challenge
Univision
Untouchables, The
UPN Television Network
Upstairs, Downstairs

Valour and the Horror, The
Van Dyke, Dick
Variety Programs
Very British Coup, A
Victory at Sea
Video Editing
Videocassette
Videodisc
Videotape
Videotex and Online Services
Vietnam: A Television History
Vietnam on Television
Violence and Television
Voice of Firestone, The
Voice-Over

W (formerly Women's Television Network)
Wagon Train
Wales
Walking with Dinosaurs
Wallace, Mike
Walsh, Mary
Walt Disney Programs (Various Titles)
Walters, Barbara
Waltons, The
War Game, The
War on Television
Warner Brothers Presents
Watch Mr. Wizard
Watch with Mother

S

St. Elsewhere

U.S. Serial Medical Drama

St. Elsewhere was one of the most acclaimed of the up-scale serial dramas to appear in the 1980s. Along with shows such as *Hill Street Blues, L.A. Law,* and *thirty-something, St. Elsewhere* was a result of the demographically conscious programming strategies that had gripped the networks during the years when cable TV was experiencing spectacular growth. Often earning comparatively low ratings, these shows were kept on the air because they delivered highly desirable audiences consisting of young, affluent viewers whom advertisers were anxious to reach. Despite its never earning a seasonal ranking above 49th place (out of about 100 shows), *St. Elsewhere* aired for six full seasons on the National Broadcasting Company (NBC) from 1982 to 1988. The series was nominated for 63 Emmy Awards and won 13.

Set in a decaying urban institution, *St. Elsewhere* was often and aptly compared to *Hill Street Blues,* which had debuted a season and a half earlier. Both shows were made by the independent production company MTM Enterprises, and both presented a large ensemble cast, a "realistic" visual style, a profusion of interlocking stories, and an aggressive tendency to break traditional generic rules. While earlier medical dramas such as *Dr. Kildare, Ben Casey,* and *Marcus Welby, M.D.* featured godlike doctors healing grateful patients, the staff of Boston's St. Eligius Hospital exhibited a variety of personal problems, and their patients often failed to recover.

St. Elsewhere's content could be both controversial and surprising. In 1983, for instance, it became the first prime-time series episode to feature an AIDS patient. Six years before *NYPD Blue* began introducing nudity to network television, *St. Elsewhere* had shown the naked backside of a doctor (Ed Flanders) who had dropped his trousers in front of his supervisor (Ronny Cox) before leaving the hospital and the show. It was also not uncommon for principal characters to die unexpectedly, which happened on no fewer than five occasions during the run of the series.

As a medical drama, *St. Elsewhere* dealt with serious issues of life and death, but every episode also included a substantial amount of comedy. The show was especially noted for its abundance of "in jokes" that made reference to the show's own ancestry. In one episode, for example, an amnesia patient comes to believe that he is Mary Richards from *The Mary Tyler Moore Show,* MTM Enterprises' first production. Throughout the episode, the patient makes oblique references to MTM's entire program history. Later, in the series' final episode, a scene from the last installment of *The Mary Tyler Moore Show* is restaged, and the cat that had appeared on the production logo at the end of every MTM show for 18 years dies as the final credits roll.

St. Elsewhere proved to be a fertile training ground for many of its participants. At the start of the 1992–93 season, creators John Falsey and Joshua Brand had a

St. Elsewhere, William Daniels, Ed Begley, Jr., Mark Harmon,
Ed Flanders, 1982–88.
Courtesy of the Everett Collection

critically acclaimed series on each of the three major
networks: *Northern Exposure* (Columbia Broadcasting
System [CBS]), *I'll Fly Away* (NBC), and *Going to Extremes* (American Broadcasting Company [ABC]).
Writer-producer Tom Fontana became the executive
producer of *Homicide: Life on the Street* with
Baltimore-based film director Barry Levinson. Other
St. Elsewhere, producers and writers went on to work
on such respected series as *Moonlighting, China
Beach, L.A. Law, Civil Wars, NYPD Blue, ER,* and
Chicago Hope. Actor Denzel Washington, virtually
unknown when he began his role as Dr. Phillip Chandler, had become a major star of feature films by the
time *St. Elsewhere* ended its run.

St. Elsewhere also exerted a significant creative influence on *ER,* the hit medical series that debuted on
NBC in 1994. While the pacing of *ER* is much faster,
both the spirit of the show and many of its story ideas
have been borrowed from *St. Elsewhere.*

ROBERT J. THOMPSON

See also **Marcus Welby, M.D.; Medic; Melodrama;
Workplace Programs**

Cast

Dr. Donald Westphall	Ed Flanders
Dr. Mark Craig	William Daniels
Dr. Ben Samuels (1982–83)	David Birney
Dr. Victor Ehrlich	Ed Begley, Jr.
Dr. Jack Morrison	David Morse
Dr. Annie Cavanero (1982–85)	Cynthia Sikes
Dr. Wayne Fiscus	Howie Mandel
Dr. Cathy Martin (1982–86)	Barbara Whinnery
Dr. Peter White (1982–85)	Terence Knox
Dr. Hugh Beale (1982–83)	G.W. Bailey
Nurse Helen Rosenthal	Christina Pickles
Dr. Phillip Chandler	Denzel Washington
Dr. V.J. Kochar (1982–84)	Kavi Raz
D. Wendy Armstrong (1982–84)	Kim Miyori
Dr. Daniel Auschlander	Norman Lloyd
Nurse Shirley Daniels (1982–85)	Ellen Bry
Orderly Luther Hawkins	Eric Laneuville
Joan Halloran (1983–84)	Nancy Stafford
Dr. Robert Caldwell (1983–86)	Mark Harmon
Dr. Michael Ridley (1983–84)	Paul Sand
Mrs. Ellen Craig	Bonnie Bartlett
Dr. Elliot Axelrod (1983–98)	Stephen Furst
Nurse Lucy Papandrao	Jennifer Savidge
Dr. Jaqueline Wade (1983–88)	Sagan Lewis
Orderly Warren Coolidge (1984–88)	Byron Stewart
Dr. Emily Humes (1984–85)	Judith Hansen
Dr. Alan Poe (1984–85)	Brian Tochi
Nurse Peggy Shotwell (1984–86)	Saundra Sharp
Mrs. Hufnagel (1984–85)	Florence Halop
Dr. Roxanne Turner (1985–87)	Alfre Woodard
Ken Valere (1985–86)	George Deloy
Terri Valere (1985–86)	Deborah May
Dr. Seth Griffin (1986–88)	Bruce Greenwood
Dr. Paulette Kiem (1986–88)	France Nuyen
Dr. Carol Novino (1986–88)	Cindy Pickett
Dr. John Gideon (1987–88)	Ronny Cox

Producers

Bruce Paltrow, Mark Tinker, John Masius, John
Falsey, Joshua Brand

Programming History

NBC

October 1982–August 1983	Tuesday 10:00–11:00
August 1983–May 1988	Wednesday 10:00–11:00
July 1988–August 1988	Wednesday 10:00–11:00

Further Reading

Barker, David, "*St. Elsewhere:* The Power of History," *Wide Angle,* (1989)

Feuer, Jane, Paul Kerr, and Tise Vahimagi, editors, *MTM—"Quality Television,"* London: British Film Institute, 1984

Paisner, Daniel, *Horizontal Hold: The Making and Breaking of a Network Television Pilot,* New York: Birch Lane Press, 1992

Schatz, Thomas, "St. Elsewhere and the Evolution of the Ensemble Series," in *Television: The Critical View,* edited by

Horace Newcomb, New York: Oxford University Press, 1976; 4th edition, 1987

Tartikoff, Brandon, and Charles Leerhsen, *The Last Great Ride,* New York: Random House, 1992

Thompson, Robert J., *Good TV: The St. Elsewhere Story,* New York: Syracuse University Press, 1996

Tinker, Grant, and Bud Rukeyser, *Tinker in Television: From General Sarnoff to General Electric,* New York: Simon and Schuster, 1994

Turow, Joseph, *Playing Doctor: Television, Storytelling, and Medical Power,* New York: Oxford University Press, 1989

Sagansky, Jeff (1952–)

U.S. Television Executive

From his humble beginnings as an entry-level intern for the National Broadcasting Company (NBC) in 1977, Jeff Sagansky quickly rose through the ranks of the entertainment industry to hold some of the most powerful executive positions in television and film during the latter part of the 20th century and into the 21st. From director of dramatic development at NBC to president of production at TriStar, from president of production at the Columbia Broadcasting System (CBS) to executive copresident of Sony Pictures Entertainment, he progressed from programming boy genius to well-established chief executive officer. As one reviews his professional history, it is clear that Sagansky has been a major player in the business of American popular culture.

Shunning the more conventional vocational paths of his fellow Harvard Business School alumnae, Sagansky began his career at NBC in 1977 and soon was working with industry veterans such as Stephen Cannell (who was producing *The Rockford Files* at the time). By 1978, he had been promoted to manager of film programs and in 1979 was named director of dramatic development. When Fred Silverman arrived at NBC in 1978, however, Sagansky became concerned about his role at the network, and he eventually left to become vice president of development for a television production firm, the David Gerber Company. After three years at this position, Sagansky returned to NBC after Silverman was fired and began to work closely with the very successful new NBC entertainment chief Grant Tinker. From 1982 to 1985 as senior vice president in charge of series programming, Sagansky was part of team that developed tremendously popular programs such as *Family Ties* (1982–89), *Cheers* (1982–93), *The Cosby Show* (1984–92), *Miami Vice* (1984–89), and *Highway to Heaven* (1984–89), programs that propelled the network to the top of the ratings.

Despite his success at NBC, Sagansky was too ambitious to stay at the network for too long, and he left television for the motion picture business becoming the president of production at TriStar Pictures from 1985 to 1989. Working closely with longtime producer Ray Stark, Sagansky's tenure at TriStar was inauspicious at best, and while there he oversaw the production of films such as *About Last Night* (1986), *Peggy Sue Got Married* (1986), *Steel Magnolias* (1989), *Glory* (1989), and *Look Who's Talking* (1989). Although he was promoted to president of TriStar pictures in 1989, when the Sony Corporation purchased TriStar and Columbia Pictures and placed Jon Peters and Peter Guber at the helm, Sagansky may have sensed that his job was in jeopardy. Therefore, it was no surprise when he leapt at the opportunity to return to his television roots soon after this change in management.

In 1990, Sagansky became the president of CBS Entertainment and working together with broadcast president Howard Stringer, he oversaw a quick ratings turnaround at CBS as the network moved from third place to first place during the first 18 months of his tenure. With shows such as *Northern Exposure* (1990–95), *Picket Fences* (1992–96), *The Nanny* (1993–99), *Dr. Quinn, Medicine Woman* (1993–98), *Touched by an Angel* (1994–2003), and *Chicago Hope* (1994–2000), CBS gained audience share but continued to attract an older and therefore less attractive (to advertisers) demographic.

Continuing his pattern of relatively brief periods of employment at any one company, Sagansky left CBS in 1994 to return to the Sony Corporation of America as executive vice president, working there until 1998. While at Sony, he was deeply involved in the company's purchase of the Spanish-language entertainment company Telemundo as well as the merger of Sony Theatres with Cineplex Odeon Theatres and the launch of the PlayStation video game platform. Once again, however, new opportunities beckoned, and in 1998 he took the position of president and chief executive officer of Paxson Communications and oversaw the launch of the family-friendly PAX channel in 1998. During his time with the company, the channel's network distribution grew from 60 to 90 percent of American households, but PAX was never able to develop a genuine hit show. Sagansky's position at Paxson Communications changed in 2002, when he was named vice chairman of the company's board of directors and relinquished his role as president and chief executive officer. He stayed at Paxson for one more year before abruptly resigning from his position in August 2003. As of January 1, 2004, Sagansky was currently exploring other opportunities in the entertainment industry.

ANDREW C. MILLER

Jeff Sagansky. Born in Wellesley, Massachusetts, January 26, 1952. B.A., Harvard University, 1972; M.B.A, Harvard Business School, 1974. Held numerous posts at NBC from 1977 (left for three years to work at a television production firm, the David Gerber Company). President of Production at TriStar Pictures, 1985–89. President of TriStar Pictures, 1989. Named president of CBS Entertainment, 1990. Left CBS to return to the Sony Corporation of America as executive vice president, 1994–98. Named president and chief executive officer of Paxson Communications, 1998. Oversaw the launch of the PAX channel, 1998. Appointed vice chairman for the board of directors at Paxson, 2002. Resigned, August 2003.

Salant, Richard S. (1914–1993)

U.S. Media Executive

Richard S. Salant started in television in 1952 as vice president of the Columbia Broadcasting System (CBS) and corporate officer to Frank Stanton, who was president of CBS. A Harvard-educated lawyer, Salant worked in government and private practice for 12 years before switching industries. His corporate experience was fueled by his lifetime commitment to such issues as freedom of the press, ethics in news production, and the relationship of government, corporate broadcast management, and news production. His longevity in the television industry stemmed from such intangible qualities as skillful conflict resolution that minimized public debate, the ability to isolate issues from complex events, and verbal clarity in articulating his position.

Salant served almost a decade as vice president and corporate officer, with no experience or training as a journalist, before Stanton appointed him president of the CBS News division in 1961. The appointment drew immediate and strong protest from Walter Cronkite, Charles Collingwood, and Eric Sevareid, who were distressed at the unprecedented appointment of a lawyer and feared constant legal scrutiny of news judgments. However, Stanton, reacting to CBS President William S. Paley's impatience at the second-place standing of the news division, believed that the ap-

pointment would bring positive change. When that failed to materialize by 1964, Salant was moved back to his previous position, only to be reappointed by Stanton in 1966 after Fred Friendly's sudden resignation as president of the news division. By the end of 1967, CBS News was in first place, remaining there for Salant's tenure. The strength of his advocacy for the news division earned Salant the title "patron saint of broadcast journalism."

Years before he rose to lead the news division, Salant used his legal knowledge, from 1953 through 1959, to represent CBS in Washington, D.C., in congressional hearings and forums pertaining to broadcast regulation and rights. He learned the structure of the industry for his speeches and testimony on issues such as subscription television, UHF (ultrahigh frequency)/VHF (very high frequency) allocations, monopoly rulings, coverage of House hearings by broadcasters, and the barriers constructed to free expression by section 315 (the "equal time rule") of the Communications Act. He argued that Congress's ban on the journalistic use of cameras and microphones in its chambers relegated broadcasters to second-class status, and he posited that section 315 prevented the free pursuit and airing of information. From his participation in the complex discussions of these legal is-

Richard S. Salant.
Courtesy of the Everett Collection/CSU Archives

sues, Salant slowly derived the position that news should be based on information the public needs to know to participate in a democratic system, not on what they would like to know. On that principle, Salant made the controversial decision to introduce the *CBS Morning News* with a serious, hard-news format, in opposition to the entertainment format of the morning shows of the American Broadcasting Company (ABC) and the National Broadcasting Company (NBC). Even when the CBS program lagged far behind its competition, Salant adamantly refused a change in program content.

Salant had a passion for the potential of television news, and starting in 1961 he brought a meticulous set of policies to the news division so that the ethics and credibility of news remained unscathed. These policies ranged from the sweeping change that separated sports and other entertainment projects from the news division to detailed guidelines for editing interviews. His directives banished music and sound effects from any news or documentary program. They stopped the involvement of news personnel in entertainment ventures. They terminated the news division's practice of providing outtakes of news stories to the Central Intel-

ligence Agency or any other government bureau. They both limited the use of and marked all occurrences of simulations. In 1976, these guidelines and policies were compiled in a handbook, *CBS News Standards.* Responding to changes in the world, on April 15, 1979, Salant added guidelines on covering terrorists and hostage situations. News division employees are required to read the handbook and sign an affidavit agreeing to comply with the guidelines.

In 16 years as president, Salant looked at small and large policies for their potential contribution toward building a credible public image for CBS News. He spoke out against the news division creating "personalities" to market programs. He was especially concerned for the potential harm of docudramas, which, if not consistently marked and explained as fictionalizations, might be taken as news products by the public. Most troubling to Salant was the network's lack of supervision over news emanating from CBS-owned stations. Integrity and credibility came in a package under the CBS name, and the package extended, in his view, to the local level. Even when CBS affiliates vehemently objected to the *CBS Evening News'* critical perspective on the Vietnam War and the government, Salant refused to alter journalistic judgments.

Throughout three critical periods in American history (the Vietnam War, the civil rights era, and Watergate), Salant's continuous examination of broadcast ethics and news judgment set the pace for other networks and the industry. When Friendly resigned as president of CBS News in 1966 because network executives declined to preempt regular daytime programming in order to air the Senate Foreign Relations Committee Hearings on Vietnam, Salant reiterated the importance of news judgment under the criterion of selective coverage. Congress, Washington, and the president would not, he argued, control airways with a selective coverage policy. The networks were responsible for alternative ways of reporting, such as evening news specials, half-hour news summaries, and the provision of alternative voices.

Salant realized that his background in the CBS corporate arena would always cast doubt on his decisions. His record of wrestling more broadcasting time for news in prime time as well as daytime eventually changed that. In fact, Salant's inside knowledge of CBS helped the news division to move from a 15-minute newscast to a 30-minute one, and he led the network to institute weekend editions of the *CBS Evening News.* Under his guidance, CBS started a full-time election unit; created additional regional news bureaus outside New York and Washington; launched *60 Minutes, Magazine, 30 Minutes, Calendar,* and the children's series *In the News;* began a regular one-hour documentary series called *CBS Reports;* produced many investigative and controversial documentaries; and covered the Watergate affair with more than 20 one-hour specials on the events. During Salant's reign, the CBS News division jumped from 450 employees to 1,000, and the annual budget increased to $90 million in 1979, up $70 million since 1961.

These accomplishments were not Salant's most difficult. He succeeded, with great pain, in insulating news division personnel from the wrath of corporate criticism and deflected movements against the division's autonomy. In two documentaries where CBS business interests were criticized in a manner that could have potentially created serious repercussions, Salant deflected pressure from CBS executives. "The Trouble with Rock" (*CBS News Special,* 1974) accused Columbia Records of payola, drug use by executives, and paying organized crime figures to protect artists. "You and the Commercial" (*CBS Reports,* 1973), revealing the questionable persuasive strategies of advertisements aimed at children, angered executives at the highest levels of the network. When CBS President Paley vehemently objected to Cronkite's *Evening News* report on Watergate, the first by a network, and demanded the story never appear again, Salant defied Paley, airing a second part although reducing the number of issues covered. Whereas this action is open to multiple interpretations, Salant's decisions in 1973 are clearer. He supported CBS News journalists in a protest against Paley's call for the elimination of instant specials after presidential speeches or news conferences.

Salant continually addressed the volatile connection between news and corporate management in a pragmatic manner. He did not see the relationship as strictly adversarial, nor did he see it as polarized between two opposing sides. Every conflict was a path toward new strategies to apply in the future. Salant's brilliance as division president was grounded in the attitude and communication skills he brought to conflicts. He diverted escalating personal attacks and swung discussions back to issues.

Not everyone appreciated this strategy. When Friendly resigned, Salant referred to his action as a misunderstanding and explained CBS's strategy on the congressional hearings. When local affiliates called for less Watergate coverage and when they demanded Dan Rather's reassignment after talking back to the president at a news conference, Salant did denounce defiance and arrogance in any news division. But he turned the argument so that affiliates had to examine the central issue as a matter of news judgment: network news needed its independence, even if it was dependent on affiliates.

In one of the most widely discussed controversies of his tenure, the findings reported in the CBS documentary *The Selling of the Pentagon* (1971) put Salant in a difficult and complex position. The government called congressional hearings and subpoenaed CBS documents, accusing the news division of manipulative editing and false claims. Again, Salant simplified the matter, accusing the government of infringing on the freedom of speech. He argued that a network has the right to be wrong and, even when wrong, the right not to be judged by the government. To support this view, he pointed to an issue with ramifications for the entire television industry: the government had the power to jeopardize free speech by its power to intimidate affiliates that carried controversial programs. Even in the midst of his defense, however, Salant was not afraid to criticize CBS or network news, and his attitude provided credibility to his position. After the confrontation with Congress, when CBS did something questionable—such as paying H.R. Haldeman $50,000 for an interview on *60 Minutes*—an admission of wrongdoing was forthcoming.

On mandatory retirement from CBS, Salant immediately went to NBC, serving two uneventful years as a vice president and general adviser in the network. Only one Salant proposal for NBC received extensive coverage. He recommended development of a one-hour evening news program, from 8:00 to 9:00 P.M., freeing the earlier prime-time slot for local news and saving networks the expense of an hour of dramatic programming. Salant finished his career as president and chief executive officer of the National News Council. This independent body, recommended in 1973 by a Twentieth Century Fund panel on which Salant served, was created in 1983 to make nonbinding decisions on complaints brought against the press or by the press. Faced by a hostile industry that wanted no monitor looking at its work, the council disbanded after one year. This attitude on the part of the industry was discouraging to Salant, especially considering the increased government attacks on media credibility that also functioned to maintain government credibility. Potentially, the council could do what Salant did at CBS: protect news standards and press freedom. But the networks had changed radically. By the mid-1980s, news was a profit center, noted Salant, and these larger issues were irrelevant. Although Salant did not succeed in having the standards of broadcast journalism maintained, he set historical precedent with CBS News programming.

RICHARD BARTONE

See also **Columbia Broadcasting System;** **Cronkite, Walter;** *News, Network;* **Paley, William S.;** *Selling of the Pentagon; 60 Minutes;* **Stanton, Frank**

Richard Salant. Born in New York City, April 14, 1914. Educated at Harvard College, A.B., 1931–35; Harvard Law School, 1935–38. Married: 1) Rosalind Robb, 1941 (divorced, 1955); children: Rosalind, Susan, Robb, and Priscilla; 2) Frances Trainer, 1955, child: Sarah. Served in U.S. Naval Reserve, 1943–46. Worked as attorney for the National Labor Relations Board, 1938–41; attorney in the Solicitor General's Office, U.S. Justice Department, 1941–43; associate, Roseman, Goldmark, Colin, and Kave, 1946–48, partner, 1948–51; vice president, special assistant to the president, CBS, Inc., 1952–61, 1964–66; president, CBS news division, 1961–64, 1966–79; member, board of directors, CBS, Inc., 1964–69; vice chair, NBC, 1979–81; senior adviser, 1981–83; president and chief executive officer, National News Council, 1983–84. Died February 16, 1993.

Publications

"He Has Exercised His Right—To Be Wrong," *TV Guide* (September 28, 1969)

"TV News's Old Days Weren't All That Good," *Columbia Journalism Review* (March–April 1977)

"When the White House Cozies Up to the Home Screen," *New York Times* (August 23, 1981)

"Clearly Defining Fact from Fiction on Docudramas," *Stamford Advocate* (February 24, 1985)

"CBS News's 'West 57th': A Clash of Symbols," *Broadcasting* (October 28, 1985)

Salant, CBS, and the Battle for the Soul of Broadcast Journalism: The Memoirs of Richard S. Salant (edited by Susan Buzenberg and Bill Buzenberg), 1999

Further Reading

Auletta, Ken, *Three Blind Mice: How the TV Networks Lost Their Way,* New York: Random House, 1991

Beaubien, Michael P., and John S. Wyeth, Jr., editors, *Views on the News: The Media and Public Opinion,* New York: New York University Press, 1984

Bleiberg, Robert M., "Salanted Journalism," *Barron's* (June 21, 1976)

Brogan, Patrick, *Spiked: The Short Life and Death of the National News Council,* New York: Priority Press, 1985

Brown, Les, "Salant Defends Coverage of Watergate," *New York Times* (May 16, 1974)

Brown, Les, "Salant Talks About His Plans for NBC News," *New York Times* (April 17, 1979)

Collins, Thomas, "Salant: Calm Before the Storm," *Newsday* (March 3, 1971)

"Dick Salant and the Purity of the News," *Broadcasting* (September 19, 1977)

Friendly, Fred, *Due to Circumstances Beyond Our Control,* New York: Random House, 1967

Gardella, Kay, "CBS News Prexy Salant Declares War on Past," *New York News* (June 7, 1967)

Gates, Gary Paul, *Air Time: The Inside Story of CBS News,* New York: Harper and Row, 1978

Gould, Jack, "Salant, CBS's Man Behind the 'Selling of the Pentagon,'" *New York Times* (March 1, 1971)

Hammond, Charles Montgomery, Jr., *The Image Decade: Television Documentary 1965–1975,* New York: Hastings House, 1981

Leonard, Bill, *In the Storm of the Eye: A Lifetime at CBS News,* New York: Putnam, 1987

Midgley, Leslie, *How Many Words Do You Want?,* New York: Birch Lane Press, 1989

"Never a Newsman, Always a Journalist," *Broadcasting* (February 26, 1979)

Schaefer, Richard, "The Development of the CBS News Guidelines During the Salant Years," *Journal of Broadcasting and Electronic Media* (Winter 1998)

Shayon, Robert Lewis, "The Pragmatic Mr. Salant," *Saturday Review* (March 11, 1961)

Williamson, Lenora, "Salant Tackles Problems at National News Council," *Editor and Publisher* (June 4, 1983)

Sale of the Century

Australian Game Show

Sale of the Century is the most successful game show ever produced and shown on Australian television. The series began on the Nine Network early in 1980 and, apart from the short four-week summer break each year, has been transmitted in the same prime-time access slot of 7:00 P.M. five nights a week ever since. Apart from the historical ratings dominance of the Nine Network in the Australian television market place, the reasons for the success of *Sale* have much to do with the format of the program, its pace, and its prizes. The game consists of three rounds in which three contestants compete for the right to buy luxury prizes at low prices. The first to sound a buzzer gains the opportunity to answer a general knowledge ques-

Sale of the Century.
Photo courtesy of Grundy Television Pty Ltd.

tion. Each contestant begins with a bankroll of $25, receiving $5 for a correct answer and losing $5 for an incorrect one.

At the end of each round, the contestant with the highest score is offered the opportunity to buy a luxury item, such as a color TV set, with some of the points. At the end of the program, the overall winner goes to a panel where he or she tries to guess the location of a particular prize behind a set of panels. Whether lucky or not, the contestant returns to the next episode of *Sale.* From time to time, the producers have varied the format as *Celebrity Sale of the Century,* using television personalities and other celebrities as contestants, playing for either home viewers or charity.

The program succeeds because it is a blend of general knowledge, luck, and handsome prizes. The question-and-answer format, combined with the time factor, draws in the home viewer, while guesses at the panels and whether to buy items offered involve luck and risk. This combination gives *Sale of the Century* a pace and interest that make it a bright, attractive game show.

Sale of the Century originally ran on the National Broadcasting Company (NBC), the American television network, from 1969 to 1973. The Australian-based Grundy Organization had since 1961 been a very frequent licensee/producer of American game show formats, but it had decided in the early 1970s to develop or buy in formats of its own. Grundy bought the format for *Sale of the Century* in 1979 and later the same year sold the program to the Australian Nine Network. By this time, the Grundy Organization was the biggest program packager in Australian television and had decided that the only way to continue to expand was to internationalize its operation. However, because of differing licensing arrangements, Grundy was aware that many of the American game-show-format license rights were not available to the company in other territories—hence the decision to buy format copyrights on programs such as *Sale.* The outstanding rating success of *Sale* in the Australian television market made it easier to sell the format elsewhere. Thus, since 1982, the company has reversioned *Sale of the Century* in five other territories: Hong Kong (RTV, 1982), United States (NBC, 1982/1988), United Kingdom (Sky, 1989/1991), New Zealand (TVNZ, 1989/1993), and Germany (Telos/DSP, 1990/1993).

Some of the program's hosts in different countries have included Tony Barber (Australia), Joe Garagiola (United States), Jack Kelly (United States), Steve Parr (New Zealand), Nicholas Parsons (United Kingdom), Jim Perry (United States), and Glen Ridge (Australia).

ALBERT MORAN

See also **Quiz and Game Shows**

Programming History
Nine Network
3,460 episodes
July 1980–   Weeknights 7:00–7:30

Sandford, Jeremy (1934–)

British Writer

Jeremy Sandford is the writer of *Cathy Come Home* and *Edna the Inebriate Woman;* his oeuvre may be one of the smallest yet most famous in the history of British television drama. *Cathy Come Home* is surely the most-talked-about television play ever, an iconic text in the radical canon of the 1960s *Wednesday Play,* which has become overshadowed by the association with its director, Ken Loach, and producer, Tony Garnett. Following *Cathy Come Home,* Sandford intended to write a trilogy on homelessness titled *In the Time of Cathy,* but *Edna the Inebriate Woman* was the only play completed. This story of an itinerant "down-and-out" moved the focus from the cruelty inflicted on families to the lives of the single homeless—the sort of person, Sandford suggested, that Cathy had become as she walked away from the railway station, stripped of her family.

After more or less disappearing from television, Sandford surfaced in 1980 with a play commissioned for the series *Lady Killers* and then in 1990, as the homeless population in Britain began once again to be a topic of public debate, with a documentary for the British Broadcasting Corporation (BBC), *Cathy, Where Are You Now?*

When *Cathy Come Home* was reshown in 1993 as part of a season commemorating the establishment of the housing charity Shelter, Sandford wrote to the *Independent,* taking issue with a claim that doubts had been raised over the accuracy of the homelessness and family-separation statistics given at the end of the play. "I work as a journalist as well as an author," he wrote, "and it would be professional suicide to be inaccurate." Sandford has never wholly identified himself as a television dramatist. At one time a poet and artist, he had nursed an early ambition to be a professional musician and played the clarinet in an Royal Air Force band during his national service. One of his first plays, *Dreaming Bandsmen,* broadcast by BBC Radio in 1956 and later staged in Coventry, seemed to confirm his early reputation as a surrealist, but at the same time he was recording radio documentaries about working-class life in the East End, and it was as a journalist and activist that he began writing about homelessness in the early 1960s. As he told an interviewer in 1990, he had always sought to play his role on the stage of life

rather than simply reflecting it. Thus, he not only submerged himself in the netherworld of the down-and-out for his research on *Edna* but also went on to arm himself with his written work as part of an active crusade on behalf of the dispossessed. A special showing of *Cathy Come Home* was arranged for Parliament, and Sandford himself toured the country screening and talking about both plays at public meetings.

Homelessness, itinerancy, and housing policy have been particular obsessions of Sandford. His Anglo-Irish grandmother, Lady Mary Carbery, was a member of the Gypsy Lore Society, and he has campaigned on behalf of gypsies as well as editing their newspaper, *Romano Drum.* A play about gypsies, *Till the End of the Plums,* was to complete a trilogy about the homeless but was never produced.

Born of wealthy parents (his father owned a private printing press) and educated at Eton and Oxford, Sandford was brought up in a stately Herefordshire home. In the late 1980s, after a long association with the alternative communities of folk festivals and camps, he moved into a large country house and opened it up as a study center for New Age travelers.

A further play, *Smiling David,* about the case of a Nigerian drowned in a Leeds river and the agencies implicated in the events, was commissioned for radio and broadcast in 1972 but never made it to the television screen. Sandford's often-noted status as a documentarist and social advocate rather than a natural television dramatist is emphasized by the fact that the scripts for *Cathy* and *Edna* are published in a series of political and social treatises. His polemical and factual writing, such as *Down and Out in Britain,* which accompanied *Edna,* far exceeds the amount he has written for television. However, the importance of his two major works in defining the cultural role of television drama in Britain as an intrinsic part rather than simply a mirror of sociopolitical actuality cannot be ignored. *Cathy Come Home* remains a landmark in this sense. "If any writer ever hoped that an idea of his would be accepted by the public as valid and taken to their hearts," Sandford wrote in 1968, "then he would have hoped for the reaction that has followed my *Cathy Come Home.*" Sandford's exchange with Paul Ableman in the pages of *Theatre Quarterly* over the ethics of fictional form in *Edna the Inebriate Woman* set the agenda for a debate about the aesthetics and politics of drama-documentary that was to dominate television drama criticism through the 1970s and 1980s.

JEREMY RIDGMAN

See also **Cathy Come Home; Garnett, Tony; Loach, Ken; Wednesday Play**

Jeremy Sandford. Born 1934. Attended Eton Public School, Berkshire; Oxford University. Married: 1) Nell Dunn, 1956 (divorced, 1986); three sons; 2) Philippa Finnis, 1988. Worked initially as a journalist; established reputation as socially committed writer for television and radio with *Cathy Come Home*, 1966; editor, *Romano Drum* (gypsy newspaper); director, Cyrenians; executive, Gypsy Council; sponsor, Shelter. Recipient: Screen Writers Guild of Great Britain Awards, 1967 and 1971; Prix Italia for Television Drama, 1968; Critics' Award for Television Drama, 1971.

Television Plays

1966	*Cathy Come Home*
1971	*Edna the Inebriate Woman*
1980	*Don't Let Them Kill Me on Wednesday* (*Lady Killers*)

Television Documentary

1990	*Cathy, Where Are You Now?*

Radio

Dreaming Bandsmen, 1956; *Smiling David*, 1972.

Stage

Dreaming Bandsmen, 1956.

Publications (selected)

Dreaming Bandsmen, 1956
Cathy Come Home, 1966
Synthetic Fun: A Short, Soft Glance, with Roger Law, 1967
Edna the Inebriate Woman, 1971
Down and Out in Britain, 1971; revised edition, 1972
In Search of the Magic Mushrooms: A Journey Through Mexico, 1972
"Edna and Cathy: Just One Huge Commercial" (Production Casebook No. 10), *Theatre Quarterly* (April–June 1973)
Gypsies, 1973; new edition as *Rokkering to the Gorjios*, 2000
Tomorrow's People, 1974
Smiling David: The Story of David Oluwale, 1974
Prostitutes: Portraits of People in the Sexploitation Business, 1975; revised edition, 1977
Virgin of the Clearways, 1978
Songs from the Roadside, Sung by Romani Gypsies in the West Midlands, 1995

Further Reading

Ableman, Paul, "Edna and Sheila: Two Kinds of Truth," *Theatre Quarterly* (July–September 1972)
Banham, Martin, "Jeremy Sandford," in *British Television Drama*, edited by G.W. Brandt, Cambridge: Cambridge University Press, 1981
Dunn, Elizabeth, "Gimme Shelter," *Sunday Telegraph* (July 8, 1990)
Rosenthal, Alan, *The New Documentary in Action: A Casebook in Film Making*, Berkeley: University of California Press, 1971
Shubik, Irene, *Play for Today: The Evolution of Television Drama*, London: Davis and Poynter, 1975; revised edition, Manchester: Manchester University Press, 2000
Worsley, T.C., *Television: The Ephemeral Art*, London: Alan Ross, 1970

Sandrich, Jay (1932–)

U.S. Director

The career of Jay Sandrich, a leading director of American situation comedies, covers much of the first few decades of the sitcom. His programs have been characterized by wit, a supportive working environment, and care for his actors.

The son of film director Mark Sandrich, Jay Sandrich began his television work in the mid-1950s as a second assistant director with Desilu Productions, learning to direct television on *I Love Lucy, Our Miss Brooks,* and *December Bride.* Later he worked on both *The Danny*

Jay Sandrich.
Photo courtesy of Jay Sandrich

Thomas Show and *The Dick Van Dyke Show.* In 1965, Sandrich put in his only stint as a producer, serving as associate producer for the first season of the innovative comedy *Get Smart.* He enjoyed the experience but vowed to stick to directing in future. He told Andy Meisler of *Channels* magazine, "I really didn't like producing. I liked being on the stage. I found that, as a producer, I'd stay up until four in the morning worrying about everything. As a director, I slept at night."

In 1971, he signed on as regular director for the relationship-oriented, subtly feminist *Mary Tyler Moore Show,* beginning a long-term partnership with the then-fledgling MTM Productions. Directing two-thirds of the episodes in the program's first few seasons, he won his first Emmys and worked on the pilot for the program's spin-off, *Phyllis.* In an interview for this encyclopedia, he spoke glowingly of the MTM experience: "[MTM chief] Grant [Tinker] created this wonderful atmosphere of being able to have a lot of fun at your work—plus you were working next door to people who were interesting and bright. And there was this feeling of sharing talent."

Sandrich went on to work as a regular director on the satirical *Soap* and eventually created another niche

for himself as the director of choice for *The Cosby Show* from 1985 to 1991. Meisler's article paints an appealing portrait of the director's relationship with the star and with other *Cosby* production personnel, quoting co–executive producer Tom Werner on the show's dynamics: "Although we're really all here to service Bill Cosby's vision, the show is stronger because Jay challenges Bill and pushes him when appropriate." Sandrich was proud of the program's pioneering portrayal of an upper-class black family and of its civilized view of parent–child relations.

During and following *Cosby*'s run, Sandrich directed pilots and episodes for a number of successful programs, including *The Golden Girls, Benson, Night Court,* and *Love and War.*

Although he ventured briefly into the field of feature films, directing *Seems Like Old Times* in 1980, Sandrich decided quickly that he preferred to remain in television. "The pace is much more interesting," he explained. "In features you sit around so much of the time while lighting is going on, and then you make the picture, and you sit around for another year developing projects. I like to work. I like the immediacy of television." Asked whether there was a Jay Sandrich type of program, Sandrich ruminated, "I don't know if there is, but I like more human-condition shows, not really wild and farcy, although *Soap* gave me really a bit of everything to do....Basically, I like men–women shows....I go more for shows that have more love than anger in them." Certainly most of his programs have evinced this inclination.

For many of his colleagues, Sandrich has defined the successful situation-comedy director. "I think it was Jay who first made an art form of three-camera film," said producer Allan Burns (quoted in Meisler), referring to the shooting technique most often used for sitcoms. Although he is modest about his own accomplishments and quick to note that good writing is the starting point for any television program, Sandrich has asserted that he cherishes his role as director in a medium often viewed as the domain of the producer. "If there's a regular director every week," he has stated,

> [television] should be a major collaboration between the director and the producer—if the director's any good—because he is the one who sets the style and the tone of the show. He works with the actors. And a good director, whether he is rewriting or not, he is always making suggestions...and in many cases knows the script a little bit better than the producer because he's been seeing each scene rehearsed and understands why certain things work and why they don't....So when it's a regular director on a series, I think it's not a producer's medium. It is the creative team [that shapes a series].

In a 1998 interview in *DGA Magazine,* the veteran director expressed concern about the state of contemporary television production. "Years ago, television wasn't determined by so many people's opinions," he explained. "You didn't have to get the immediate ratings. Shows were given time to build." Nevertheless, Sandrich still works frequently on projects he believes meet his high standards, although he denies that he is still the king of pilots for American comedies. "I think Jimmy Burrows is the king," he has said of his former protégé. "He's gotten so many shows on the air. No, I think I'm the dowager queen or something by now."

TINKY "DAKOTA" WEISBLAT

See also **The Cosby Show; The Danny Thomas Show; The Dick Van Dyke Show; Director, Television;** *Get Smart; I Love Lucy; The Mary Tyler Moore Show; Our Miss Brooks;* **Tinker, Grant**

Jay Sandrich. Born in Los Angeles, California, February 24, 1932. Educated at the University of California, Los Angeles, B.A. 1953. Married 1) Nina Kramer, 1953 (divorced, 1974); two sons and one daughter; 2) Linda Green, 1984. Started career as second assistant director, *I Love Lucy,* Desilu Productions, 1955, then first assistant director, *I Love Lucy* and *The Danny Thomas Show;* director, MTM Productions, from 1971; currently director, primarily for television. Recipient: Emmy Awards, 1971, 1973, 1985, and 1986; Directors Guild of America Awards, 1975, 1984, 1985, and 1986.

Television Series (selected)

1965–70	*Get Smart* (producer)
1967–70	*He and She*
1971–77	*The Mary Tyler Moore Show*
1972–78	*The Bob Newhart Show*
1975–77	*Phyllis*
1976–78	*The Tony Randall Show*
1977–79	*Soap*
1979–86	*Benson*
1984–92	*The Cosby Show*
1985–92	*The Golden Girls*
1988–95	*Empty Nest*
1992–95	*Love and War* (pilot only)
1993–94	*Thea*
1995	*The Office*
1995–96	*The Jeff Foxworthy Show*
1997	*Style and Substance*
1997	*The Tony Danza Show*
2001–02	*Three Sisters*

Television Specials

1996	*London Suite*
2000	*The Man Who Came to Dinner* (on Great Performances)

Films

Seems Like Old Times, 1980; *For Richer, For Poorer,* 1992.

Further Reading

Kuney, Jack, *Take One: Television Directors on Directing,* New York: Greenwood, 1990

Meisler, Andy, "Jay Sandrich: Ace of Pilots," *Channels* (October 1986)

Ravage, John W., *Television: The Director's Viewpoint,* Boulder, Colorado: Westview, 1978

Schindler, Arlene, "Jay Sandrich," *DGA Magazine* (September 1998)

Sanford and Son

U.S. Domestic Comedy

The 1972–76 National Broadcasting Company (NBC) program *Sanford and Son* chronicled the adventures of Fred G. Sanford, a cantankerous widower living with his grown son, Lamont, in the notorious Watts section of contemporary Los Angeles, California. Independent producers Norman Lear and Bud Yorkin licensed the format of a British program, *Steptoe and Son,* which featured the exploits of a Cockney junk dealer, and created *Sanford and Son* as an American version. *Sanford and Son, The Jeffersons,* and *Good Times,* all produced by Lear and Yorkin, featured mostly black casts—the first such programming to appear since the *Amos 'n' Andy* show was canceled in a hailstorm debate in 1953.

The starring role of *Sanford and Son* was portrayed by actor-comedian Redd Foxx. Born John Elroy San-

Sanford and Son, Demond Wilson, Redd Foxx, 1972–77.
Courtesy of the Everett Collection

ford in St. Louis, Missouri, Foxx was no newcomer to the entertainment industry. He began a career in the late 1930s performing street acts, and during the 1950s he achieved a measure of success as a nightclub performer and recorder of bawdy joke albums, with his racy routines influencing generations of comics to the present time. By the 1960s, he was headlining in Las Vegas. In 1969, he earned a role as an aging junk dealer in the motion picture *Cotton Comes to Harlem,* a portrayal that brought him to the attention of Lear and Yorkin.

It was Foxx's enormously funny portrayal of 65-year-old Fred G. Sanford that quickly earned *Sanford and Son* a place among the top-10 most-watched television programs to air on NBC television. He was supported by Lamont, his 30ish son, and a multiracial cast of regular and occasional characters who served as the butt of Sanford's often bigoted jokes and insults. Fred's nemesis, the "evil and ugly" Aunt Esther (portrayed by veteran actor LaWanda Page), often provided the funniest moments of episodes as she and Fred traded jibes and insults. The trademark routine of the series occurred when Fred feigned a heart attack by clasping his chest in mock pain. Staggering drunkenly, he would threaten to join his deceased wife Elizabeth, calling out "I'm coming to join you, Elizabeth!"

Although *Sanford and Son was* enormously successful, Foxx became dissatisfied with the show, its direction, and his treatment as star of the program. In a *Los Angeles Times* article, he stated, "Certain things should be yours to have when you work your way to the top." At one point he walked off the show, complaining that the white producers and writers had little regard or appreciation of African-American life and culture. In newspaper interviews, he lambasted the total lack of black writers or directors. Moreover, Foxx believed that his efforts were not appreciated, and in 1977 he left NBC for his own variety show on the American Broadcasting Company (ABC). The program barely lasted one season.

Sanford and Son survived some five years on prime-time television. It earned its place in television history as the first successful, mostly black cast television sitcom to appear on a U.S. network in prime time since the cancellation of *Amos 'n' Andy.* It was an enormously funny program, sans obvious ethnic stereotyping. "I'm convinced that *Sanford and Son* shows middle-class America a lot of what they need to know," Foxx said in a 1973 interview. "The show... doesn't drive home a lesson, but it can open up people's minds enough for them to see how stupid every kind of prejudice can be." After Foxx left the show permanently, a pseudo-spin-off called *Sanford Arms* proved unsuccessful and lasted only one season.

PAMALA S. DEANE

See also **Amen;** *Amos 'n' Andy;* **Comedy, Domestic Settings;** *Good Times;* **Lear, Norman; Racism, Ethnicity and Television;** *227*

Cast

Fred Sanford	Redd Foxx
Lamont Sanford	Demond Wilson
Grady Wilson (1973–77)	Whitman Mayo
Aunt Esther (1973–77)	LaWanda Page
Woody Anderson (1976–77)	Raymond Allen
Bubba Hoover	Don Bexley
Janet Lawson (1976–77)	Marlene Clark
Roger Lawson (1976–77)	Edward Crawford
Donna Harris	Lynn Hamilton
Officer Swanhauser (1972)	Noam Pitlik
Officer Hopkins ("Happy") (1972–76)	Howard Platt
Aunt Ethel (1972)	Beah Richards
Julio Fuentes (1972–75)	Gregory Sierra
Rollo Larson	Nathaniel Taylor
Melvin (1972)	Slappy White
Officer Smith ("Smitty") (1972–76)	Hal Williams
Ah Chew (1974–75)	Pat Morita

Producer
Norman Lear

Programming History
136 episodes
NBC

January 1972–September 1977	Friday 8:00–8:30
April 1976–August 1976	Wednesday 9:00–9:30

Further Reading

Bogle, Donald, *Blacks in American Television and Film: An Encyclopedia*, New York: Garland, 1988

Bogle, Donald, *Blacks, Coons, Mulattoes, Mammies, and Bucks: An Interpretive History of Blacks in American Film*, New York: Viking Press, 1973; 4th edition, New York: Continuum, 2001

Friedman, Lester D., *Unspeakable Images: Ethnicity and the American Cinema*, Urbana: University of Illinois Press, 1991

Gray, Herman, *Watching Race: Television and the Struggle for "Blackness,"* Minneapolis: University of Minnesota Press, 1995

MacDonald, J. Fred, *Blacks and White TV: Afro-Americans in Television Since 1948*, Chicago: Nelson-Hall Publishers, 1983; 2nd edition, 1992

Marc, David, and Robert J. Thompson, *Prime Time, Prime Movers: From I Love Lucy to L.A. Law—America's Greatest TV Shows and the People Who Created Them*, Boston: Little, Brown, 1992

Taylor, Ella, *Prime-Time Families: Television Culture in Postwar America*, Berkeley: University of California Press, 1989

Sarnoff, David (1891–1971)

U.S. Media Executive

A pioneer in radio and television, David Sarnoff was an immigrant who climbed the rungs of corporate America to head the Radio Corporation of America (RCA). Born on February 27, 1891, in Uzlian, in the Russian province of Minsk, Sarnoff's early childhood years were spent studying to be a rabbi, but when he emigrated to the United States in 1900, he was forced to work to feed his mother, ailing father, and siblings.

Learning early the value of self-promotion and publicity, Sarnoff falsely advanced himself both as the sole hero who stayed by his telegraph key for three days to receive information on the *Titanic*'s survivors and as the prescient prophet of broadcasting who predicted the medium's rise in 1915. While later described by others as the founder of both RCA and the National Broadcasting Company (NBC), Sarnoff was neither. These misconceptions were perpetuated because Sarnoff's later accomplishments were so plentiful that any myth was believable. Indeed, his foresight and corporate savvy led to many communication developments, especially television.

Sarnoff began his career at age nine, selling Yiddish-language newspapers shortly after arriving in New York. To improve his English, he picked up discarded English-language newspapers. By the time he was ten, he had a fairly passable vocabulary. He also soon had his own newsstand. During the day he attended grade school, while at night he enrolled in classes at the Educational Alliance, an East Side settlement house. At age 15, with his father's health deteriorating, Sarnoff was forced to seek a full-time job.

He became a messenger for the Commercial Cable Company, the American subsidiary of the British firm that controlled undersea cable communication. The telegraph key lured him to the American Marconi Company a few months later, where he was hired as an office boy. Once there, he began his corporate rise, including the job of being Marconi's personal messenger when the inventor was in town. With Marconi's endorsement, Sarnoff became a junior wireless telegraph operator, and at age 17 he volunteered for wireless duty at one of the company's remote stations. There he studied the station's technical library and took correspondence courses. Eighteen months later, he was appointed manager of the station in Sea Gate, New York. He was the youngest manager employed by Marconi. After volunteering as a wireless operator for an Arctic seal expedition, he became operator of the Marconi

David Sarnoff, founder of RCA, in his office, circa 1930s.
Courtesy of the Everett Collection

wireless purchased by the John Wanamaker department stores. At night he continued his studies.

Then, on the evening of April 14, 1912, he heard the faint reports of the *Titanic* disaster. One of a number of wireless operators reporting the tragedy, Sarnoff would later claim he was the only one to remain on the air after President Taft ordered others to stay silent. Another controversial claim concerns Sarnoff's assertion that he wrote his famous "Radio Music Box Memo" in 1915. While the version often cited was actually written in 1920, Sarnoff did correspond in 1916 with his superior, E.J. Nally, about protecting American Marconi's interests from others investigating the potential of wireless technology, including "music box" uses.

As his career thrived, Sarnoff's personal life also grew. On July 4, 1917, he married Lizette Hermant, following a closely supervised courtship. Their 54-year marriage survived Sarnoff's occasional philandering and proved the bedrock of his life. They had three sons, Robert, Edward, and Thomas. Robert succeeded his father as RCA's president. In 1919, when British Marconi sold its American Marconi assets to General Electric (GE) to form RCA, Sarnoff came on board as commercial manager. Under the tutelage of RCA's chair, Owen D. Young, Sarnoff was soon in charge of broadcasting as general manager of RCA and was integral in formation of NBC in 1926. As Young's protégé, he also negotiated the secret contracts with American Telephone and Telegraph (AT&T) that led to NBC's development. With acquisition of AT&T's broadcasting assets, RCA had two networks, the Red and the Blue, and they debuted in a simulcast on November 15, 1926.

In 1927, Sarnoff was elected to RCA's board, and during the summer of 1928, he became RCA's acting president when the company's president, General James G. Harbord, took a leave of absence to campaign for Herbert Hoover. Sarnoff's eventual succession to that position was assured. At the end of the decade, Sarnoff negotiated successful contracts to form Radio-Keith-Orpheum (RKO) motion pictures, to introduce radios as a permanent fixture in automobiles, and to consolidate all radio manufacturing by the Victor company under RCA's banner. On January 3, 1930, the 39-year-old Sarnoff became RCA's president.

The next two years were pivotal in Sarnoff's life, as the U.S. Department of Justice sued GE and RCA for monopoly and restraint of trade. Sarnoff led industry efforts to combat the government's suits, which would have destroyed RCA. The result was a consent decree in 1932 calling for RCA's divestiture from GE and the licensing of RCA's patents to competitors. When GE

freed RCA, Sarnoff was at the helm, and for nearly the next three decades, he would oversee numerous communications developments, including television.

Sarnoff's interest in television began in the 1910s, when he became aware of the theory of television. By 1923, he was convinced that television would be the next great step in mass communication. In 1929, Westinghouse engineer Vladimir Zworykin called on Sarnoff to outline his concept of an electronic camera. Within the year, Sarnoff underwrote Zworykin's efforts, and Zworykin headed the team developing electronic television. As the Depression deepened, Sarnoff bought television patents from inventors Charles Jenkins and Lee De Forest, among others, but he could not acquire those patents held by Philo Farnsworth. These he had to license, and in 1936, RCA entered into a cross-licensing agreement with Farnsworth. This agreement solved the technological problems of television, and establishing television's standards became Sarnoff's goal.

The Federal Communications Commission (FCC) would set those standards, but within the industry, efforts to reach consensus failed. Other manufacturers, especially Philco, Dumont, and Zenith, fought adoption of RCA's standards as the industry norm. In 1936, the Radio Manufacturers Association (RMA) set up a technical committee to seek agreement on industry standards, an action blessed actively by Sarnoff and silently by the FCC. For more than five years, the committee would fight over standards. Sarnoff told the RMA that, standards or not, he would initiate television service at the opening of the New York World's Fair on April 20, 1939, and he did. Skirmishes continued for the next two years over standards, but in May 1941 the FCC's National Television System Committee (NTSC) finally set standards at 525 lines, interlaced, and 30 frames per second. Rapid television development stalled, however, as World War II intervened. Sarnoff's attention then turned to devices, including radar and sonar, that would help win the war.

During World War I, Sarnoff had applied for a commission in naval communications, only to be turned down, ostensibly because his wireless job was considered essential to the war effort. Sarnoff suspected anti-Semitism. Now as head of the world's largest communication's firm, Sarnoff was made a brigadier general and served as communication consultant to General Dwight Eisenhower. After the war, with the death of RCA chair of the board General J.G. Harbord in 1947, General Sarnoff, as he preferred to be called, was appointed chair, and he served in that capacity until his death in 1971.

After the war, RCA introduced monochrome television on a wide scale to the American population, and the race for color television with the Columbia Broadcasting System (CBS) was on. CBS picked up its prewar experiments with a mechanical system that Sarnoff did not see initially as a threat because it was incompatible with already approved black-and-white standards. When CBS received approval for its system in 1951, Sarnoff challenged the FCC's decision in the courts on the grounds that it contravened the opinions of the industry's technical leaders and threatened the $2 billion investment the public had already made in television sets. When the lower courts refused to block the FCC ruling, Sarnoff appealed to the U.S. Supreme Court, which affirmed the FCC action as a proper exercise of its regulatory power.

Sarnoff counterattacked through an FCC-granted authority for RCA to field-test color developments. Demonstrations were carefully set for maximum public exposure, and they were billed as "progress reports" on compatible color. By then, the Korean War intervened in the domestic battle over color television and blunted introduction of CBS's sets on a large scale. Monochrome still reigned, and Sarnoff continued pressing the compatibility issue. In 1953, CBS abandoned its color efforts as "economically foolish" in light of the 25 million incompatible monochrome sets already in use. The FCC was forced to reconsider its earlier order, and on December 17, 1953, the commission voted to reverse itself and adopt standards along those proposed by RCA. During the 1950s and 1960s, Sarnoff's interests included not only television but also satellites, rocketry, and computers.

At the same time he was battling CBS over color, Sarnoff's feud with Edwin Howard Armstrong over FM radio's development and patents continued. Sarnoff and Armstrong, once close friends, were hopelessly alienated by the end of World War II. Their deadly feud lasted for years, consumed numerous court challenges, and ended with Armstrong's suicide in 1954.

Sarnoff died in his sleep on December 12, 1971, of cardiac arrest. At his funeral, he was eulogized as a visionary who had the capacity to see into tomorrow and make his visions work. His obituary, which began on page 1 and ran nearly one full page in the *New York Times,* aptly summed up his career in these words: "He was not an inventor, nor was he a scientist. But he was a man of astounding vision who was able to see with remarkable clarity the possibilities of harnessing the electron."

LOUISE BENJAMIN

See also **American Broadcasting Company; Color Television; Columbia Broadcasting System; Farnsworth, Philo; Goldenson, Leonard; National Broadcasting Company; Paley, William S.; Radio Corporation of America; Sarnoff, Robert; United States: Networks; Zworykin, Vladimir**

David Sarnoff. Born near Minsk, Russia, February 27, 1891. Attended public schools, Brooklyn, New York; studied electrical engineering at Pratt Institute. Married: Lizette Hermant, 1917; three sons: Robert, Edward, and Thomas. Joined Marconi Wireless Company, 1906–19, telegraph operator, 1908, promoted to chief radio inspector and assistant chief engineer when Marconi was absorbed by RCA, 1919; commercial manager, then elected general manager, RCA, 1921, vice president and general manager, 1922, executive vice president, 1929, president, 1930, chair of board, RCA, 1947–70; oversaw RCA's manufacture of color television sets and NBC's color broadcasts. Received 27 honorary degrees, including doctoral degrees from Columbia University and New York University. Died in New York City, December 12, 1971.

Publication

Looking Ahead: The Papers of David Sarnoff, 1968

Further Reading

Benjamin, Louise, "In Search of the Sarnoff 'Radio Music Box' Memo," *Journal of Broadcasting and Electronic Media* (Summer 1993)

Benjamin, Louise, "In Search of the Sarnoff 'Radio Music Box' Memo: Nally's Reply" *Journal of Radio Studies* (Summer 2002)

Bilby, Kenneth M., *The General: David Sarnoff and the Rise of the Communications Industry,* New York: Harper and Row, 1986

"David Sarnoff of RCA Is Dead; Visionary Broadcast Pioneer," *New York Times* (December 13, 1971)

Dreher, Carl, *Sarnoff, An American Success,* New York: Quadrangle/New York Times Books, 1977

Lyons, Eugene, *David Sarnoff: A Biography,* New York: Harper and Row, 1966

Sobel, Robert, *RCA,* New York: Stein and Day, 1986

The Wisdom of Sarnoff and the World of RCA, Beverly Hills, California: Wisdom Society for the Advancement of Knowledge, Learning, and Research in Education, 1967

Sarnoff, Robert (1918–1997)

U.S. Media Executive

Robert Sarnoff, eldest son of broadcasting mogul David Sarnoff, followed in his father's professional footsteps through his career at the National Broadcasting Company (NBC) and the Radio Corporation of America (RCA). Contemporaries attributed the son's corporate promotions to nepotism and constantly drew comparisons between his executive performance and style and that of his father. During his years as company head, Robert Sarnoff practiced decision making by consensus, displayed an obsession with corporate efficiency, and constantly sought to implement modern management techniques. David Sarnoff's aggressive, imperial, dynamic manner of command often overshadowed his son's practical yet increasingly mercurial character.

After a short stint in the magazine business, Robert Sarnoff joined NBC as an accounts executive in 1948, at a time when David Sarnoff had recently assumed chairmanship of electronics giant RCA, the parent company of NBC. Robert Sarnoff served in a variety of positions over the next few years, working his way up the business ladder. As vice president of NBC's film unit, he oversaw the development of *Project XX* and *Victory at Sea*—the latter a pioneer in the documentary series format that traced the naval campaigns of World War II through compilation footage. Passing as educational programming, the series was well attuned to Cold War patriotism and earned Sarnoff a Distinguished Public Service Award from the U.S. Navy.

NBC Television programming strategies during the first half of the 1950s were determined largely by the flamboyant Pat Weaver. RCA funded Weaver's extravagant experiments in the medium since it wished to establish NBC's reputation as a "quality" network and was realizing a return on its investment through increased sales of television receivers. By mid-decade, however, RCA policy was modified: NBC was now expected to achieve economic self-sufficiency and advertising sales parity with the archrival Columbia Broadcasting System (CBS). Weaver was first promoted to the NBC chair in 1955 and then forced to resign from the company several months later. In turn, Robert Sarnoff ascended to fill that vacant position.

Sarnoff assumed leadership of the network's financial interests and general policy decisions. Robert Kintner, who had shown a propensity for budget-conscious scheduling at the American Broadcasting Company (ABC), took over as head of NBC-TV programming and was elevated to the rank of NBC president in 1958. Together, the "Bob and Bob Show" (as it was known in the industry) stabilized network operations and routinized programming. Sarnoff established a clear chain of command by streamlining NBC's staff, increasing middle-management positions, and delegating more operating responsibilities to department heads. In order to cut overhead expenses, in-house production was curtailed, and links with several dependable suppliers of filmed programming were created. Program development and series renewal became subject to ratings success and spot-advertising sales. Toward the end of the decade, westerns, action shows,

Robert W. Sarnoff, 1955.
Courtesy of the Everett Collection/CSU Archives

sitcoms, and quiz shows were regular prime-time features. Gone, for the most part, were the costly "spectaculars" and live dramas of the Weaver years. NBC profits improved steadily.

Sarnoff's most public phase came in the late 1950s and early 1960s, when he defended NBC programming policies against critics in the press and in Congress. He argued that the public interest was best served by popular programming, and although he espoused the benefits of a "well-rounded schedule," he clearly practiced a policy of programming to majority tastes. Sarnoff insisted that competition for advertisers, audiences, and affiliate clearance would ensure that the networks would remain receptive to the multiple demands of the market. Ratings were the economic lifeblood of the medium; "high-brow" interests would have to remain secondary to "mass-appeal" shows in the NBC schedule. Critics who lamented the disappearance of "cultural" programming were elitist, he claimed. Neither the Federal Communications Commission nor Congress should interfere in network operations or establish program guidelines, according to Sarnoff, since this government oversight would encourage political maneuvering and obstruct market forces. More effective industry self-regulation and self-promotion, spearheaded by the networks, would ensure that recent broadcasting transgressions (symbolized by the quiz show scandals and debates over violence on television) would not reoccur.

Sarnoff's agenda did not dismiss "public service" programming entirely. Kintner had turned NBC's news department into a commercially viable operation, most notably with *The Huntley-Brinkley Report*. During these years, NBC undertook various educational projects, including *Continental Classroom* (the first network program designed to provide classes for college credit) and several programs on art history (a particular passion of Sarnoff). Sarnoff extolled television's ability to enlighten through its capacity to channel and process the diverse fields of information, knowledge, and experience that characterized the modern age. He touted television's ability to generate greater viewer insight into the political process, and he is credited with bringing about the televised "Great Debates" between John Kennedy and Richard Nixon during the 1960 presidential campaign.

In general, NBC's public service record during the Sarnoff years was disappointing. NBC did, however, become a serious ratings and billings competitor to CBS. In marked contrast to the dismal results of the previous decade, NBC's color programming in the 1960s helped to dramatically boost color set sales and, consequently, RCA coffers.

On the first day of 1966, again thanks largely to his father's influence, Robert Sarnoff became president of RCA. Two years later, he assumed also the role of chief executive officer. David Sarnoff remained chairman of the board until 1970, when ill health forced him to relinquish that position to his son. At RCA, Robert Sarnoff inherited—and exacerbated—problematic developments that would result in his forced resignation in 1975. The younger Sarnoff continued to diversify the corporation, but with some ill-chosen investments that yielded poor returns. Most significantly, he overcommitted company resources in an abortive attempt to achieve competitiveness in the mainframe computer market. During Sarnoff's tumultuous time at RCA, he continued to oversee operations at NBC. There he found little solace, as the network lost ground to CBS and ABC in the early 1970s. NBC's weakened performance contributed to declining RCA stock prices—a state of affairs that resulted in Robert Sarnoff's displacement from the company that had been synonymous with the Sarnoff name over the previous half century.

MATTHEW MURRAY

See also **Kintner, Robert; National Broadcasting Company; Radio Corporation of America; Sarnoff, David; United States: Networks;** *Victory at Sea;* **Weaver, Sylvester "Pat"**

Robert Sarnoff. Born in New York City, July 2, 1918. Educated at Harvard University, B.A. 1939; Columbia Law School, 1940. Worked in office of coordinator of information, Washington, D.C., 1941; U.S. Navy, 1942; assistant to publisher Gardner Cowles, Jr., 1945; staff member, *Look,* 1946; president, NBC, 1955–58; board of directors, RCA, 1957; chair of board, NBC, 1958; chair of board, chief executive officer, NBC, 1958–65; president, RCA, 1966; chief executive officer, 1968; chair of board, 1970–75. Member: Television Pioneers, 1957 (president, 1952–53); International Radio and Television Society; Broadcasters Committee for Radio Free Europe; American Home Products, Inc.; director, Business Committee for the Arts; chair and former president of council, Academy of Television Arts and Sciences; vice president and member of board of directors, Academy of Television Arts and Sciences Foundation. Died February 23, 1997.

Publications

"What Do You Want from TV?" *Saturday Evening Post* (July 1, 1961)

"A View from the Bridge of NBC," *Television Quarterly* (Spring 1964)

Further Reading

Bilby, Kenneth, *The General: David Sarnoff and the Rise of the Communications Industry,* New York: Harper and Row, 1986
Kepley, Vance, Jr., "From 'Frontal Lobes' to the 'Bob-and-Bob' Show: NBC Management and Programming Strategies, 1949–50," in *Hollywood in the Age of Television,* edited by Tino Balio, Cambridge, Massachusetts: Unwin Hyman, 1990
"Sarnoff of NBC: The Decision Makers, Part 5," *TV Guide* (February 2, 1963)
Sobel, Robert, *RCA,* New York: Stein and Day, 1986

Satellite

Television could not exist in its contemporary form without satellites. Since July 1962, when technicians from the National Aeronautics and Space Administration (NASA) in Maine transmitted fuzzy images of themselves to engineers at a receiving station in England using the *Telstar* satellite, orbiting communications satellites have been routinely used to deliver television news and programming between companies and to broadcasters and cable operators. Since the mid-1980s, they have been increasingly used to broadcast programming directly to viewers, to distribute advertising, and to provide live news coverage. More recently, they have become the key tool of a handful of giant media conglomerates to reach a global audience. Increasingly, as with Robert Murdoch's News Corporation, the leading program makers also control both satellite and cable program distribution systems in almost every corner of the globe.

Arthur C. Clarke, the British engineer turned author, is credited with envisioning the key elements of satellite communications long before the technical skill or political will to implement his ideas existed. In 1945, he published a plan to put electronic relay stations—a radio receiver and retransmitter—into space at 23,000 miles above the Earth's equator. At this altitude, the satellite must complete a full rotation around the Earth every 24 hours in order to sustain orbit (countering the pull of the Earth's gravity). Given the rotation of the Earth itself, that keeps the satellite in the same relative position (or "parking space"). This "geosynchronous orbit" is where communications satellites sit today, providing telephone and data communications but mostly relaying television signals (television is the largest user of satellite bandwidth).

An "uplink" transmitter on Earth, using a "dish" antenna pointed toward the satellite, sends a signal to one of the satellite's "transponders." The transponder amplifies that signal and shifts it to another frequency (so as not to interfere with the incoming signal) to be transmitted back to Earth. A "downlink" antenna and receiver on Earth then captures that signal and sends it on its way. The essential advantage of the satellite is that the uplink and downlink may be 8,000 miles apart. In practice, satellite communications is more efficient over a shorter distances than that, but the advantages over terrestrial transmissions—cable, fiber optics, and microwave—are profound, particularly across oceans. As with direct broadcast satellites (DBSs), satellites can transmit to an unlimited number of ground receivers simultaneously, and costs do not increase with distance or number of receivers.

Each satellite has a distinct "footprint," or coverage area, that is meticulously shaped and plotted. In 1971, the first communications satellites carrying "spot beam" antennas were launched. A spot beam antenna can be steered to focus the satellite's reception and transmission capabilities on a small portion of the Earth, instead of the 40 percent of the Earth's surface a wider antenna beam could cover. Spot coverage is crucial in international broadcasting when neighboring

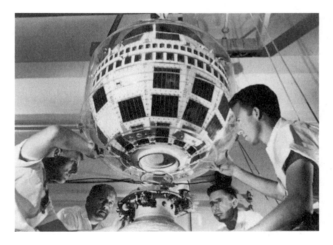

Technicians attaching the Telestar satellite to a Delta rocket for launch.
Property of AT&T Archives. Reprinted with permission of AT&T

countries may object to signal "spillover" into their territory. South Korea, for example, has demanded limitations on satellite broadcasts into its territory from Japanese companies.

Communications satellites since the 1960s have received uplink signals in a range of frequencies (or "bandwidth") near 6 GHz (gigahertz, or a billion cycles per second) and downlinked signals near 4 GHz. This range of frequencies is known as "C-band." Each range of frequencies is subdivided into specific channels, which, in the case of C-band, are each from 36 to 72 MHz wide. In the past, a single analog television transmission would occupy enough bandwidth to fully utilize a single 36-Mhz channel, though hundreds or thousands of voice or data signals requiring far less bandwidth would fit on the same channel. More recently, the use of digital compressed transmissions and higher frequencies has allowed far more television channels per satellite and cut the cost of satellite use.

For decades, many developed and developing countries have used satellite-delivered television to provide useful information to portions of their populations out of reach of terrestrial broadcasting. In 1975, an experimental satellite communications project called SITE (Satellite Instructional Television Experiment) was used to bring informational television programs to rural India. The project led to Indian development of its own satellite network. China has also embarked on a ambitious program of satellite use for development, claiming substantial success in rural education. Many countries, including India, China, Japan, Russia, and Mexico; the European and Asian satellite consortiums; and at least two private companies now launch satellites. During the 1990s, satellite communications shifted from mostly public hands—dominated by the multilateral Intelsat organization—to mostly private hands, with governments auctioning off or giving away their valuable satellite orbital allocations to private companies.

In the late 1970s, with the satellite distribution of Home Box Office (intended only for cable television companies to receive and relay movies to paying customers), "television receive only" (TVRO) dishes became popular for people out of reach of cable television and anyone wishing to avoid the cost of a cable subscription. The large dishes of that era still litter the backyards of rural America. Later, DBS to small home dishes became possible through the use of higher frequencies. Since 1988, with the launch of British Sky Broadcasting, DBS has been heavily used in Europe and, around the same time, eastern Asia; it continues to gain popularity in the United States but still has less than one-quarter of the subscribers of cable television.

In the 1980s, satellites using bandwidths of 11 to 12 GHz (uplink) and 14 GHz (downlink) came into use. This "Ku-band" does not require as much power to be transmitted clearly, thereby permitting the use of small (and less expensive) Earth stations. With the introduction of the Ku-band, television entered the era of live news—satellite news gathering (SNG)—as Ku-band satellites made it easy to uplink television signals with a portable dish from the scene of a breaking news story. Overuse of the C and Ku bandwidths and the desire for even greater signal strength is leading to new satellites that use other areas of the radio spectrum. Television news has also made some use of another satellite technology, remote sensing, using pictures taken by satellites to illustrate or verify news stories. In the 2003 Iraq war, television networks often combined satellite imagery with elaborate animated graphics to illustrate the war, but the U.S. government purchased all the best commercially available satellite imagery to prevent the media from using it.

Encryption, or scrambling, of satellite television signals has become common to ensure that only customers who have bought or rented a decoder can receive transmissions. Even intercompany television feeds via satellite (traditionally known as "backhauls"), such as daily feeds to broadcasters from television news agencies, are encrypted to prevent unauthorized use. With increasing frequency, international television companies now shift production work from one part of the world to another using compressed video files transmitted via private satellite links. A news agency's Chinese bureau, for instance, might transmit masses of unedited video of a major story to London to be edited and sent out to global broadcasters, shifting the burden—and, potentially, control of the story—from local areas of expertise to a few global production centers.

Like other communications technologies, the satellite industry has also embraced digitalization and signal compression as a means of maximizing the use of limited bandwidth, and DBS and intra-industry services are expanding rapidly as a result. By converting analog signals to digital signals, less bandwidth is required, and digital signals can be broken into smaller pieces for transmission through bits of available bandwidth and reassembled at the point of reception. Compression eliminates otherwise redundant portions of a television transmission, allowing for a signal to be sent using far less bandwidth and for the transmission of video as computer files moving from one computer or database anywhere in the world to another. Compression technology now permits hundreds of television channels on a single satellite. Telephony and television use roughly equivalent portions of available satellite capacity, but the demand for DBS has led to a number of satellites dedicated to TV transmission. Currently, well over 200 commercial geostationary communications satellites are in use, but with constant new launches and removals from orbit of old satellites, the number changes frequently.

STAR-TV, controlled by media mogul Rupert Murdoch, transmits television programming over much of Asia and has forced governments worldwide to re-evaluate their stance on issues of national sovereignty and control of incoming information. STAR reaches over 50 countries and potentially half the world's population—far more than any other satellite television service (though it is technically not DBS, still requiring larger dishes). A slew of contentious political and cultural issues have resulted. Murdoch dropped the British Broadcasting Corporation (BBC) World Service Television from his STAR-TV program lineup as a concession to the Chinese government. Other governments have complained about the unrestricted importation of news presented from an Anglo-American viewpoint, though their concerns about political consequences are often couched in terms of protecting local culture. Reports of disruptions to local cultures stemming from international satellite broadcasting are widespread. Also during the 1990s, Africa, the one continent long neglected by the satellite television industry, finally saw widespread availability of satellite television services, dominated by the South African company M-Net.

By 2004, over 20 million U.S. homes subscribed to one of two DBS services: DirectTV or EchoStar (most recently using the brand name "Dish Network"). In 1995, EchoStar launched its own satellite and by 2004 had eight satellites in orbit over the United States, broadcasting digital television, audio, and data channels. DirectTV is a division of Hughes Electronics, a manufacturer and (through PanAmSat) operator of satellites. After a long regulatory battle, at the end of 2003 Rupert Murdoch's News Corporation was given permission to buy DirectTV and take a controlling interest in Hughes—positioning them to be the leading satellite TV provider on five continents (Australia, Asia, Europe, South America, and North America). A friendly Federal Communications Commission allowed Murdoch to avoid the long-standing requirement that DBS operators carry the local stations of their viewers, which is likely to hasten audience erosion at the local level. News Corporation's ability to drive up the cost of cable TV through the pricing of its many channels (to bring customers to DirectTV) also poses a new threat to the U.S. cable industry. Before this merger, the top four commercial satellite operators ran nearly half the world's satellites; this concentration of control will now increase.

In all these instances, satellite technology has called into question conventional notions of the nation-state. Geographic borders may be insufficient definitions of culture and nationality in an era of electronic information, beamed from multiple sources into the sky and down again into almost any location. International TV journalists, for example, no longer needed the permission of local authorities to transmit television news stories to the world—by 2003, briefcase-size satellite uplinks and laptop computer video editing had made such transmissions common from an embattled Iraq and from the remotest conflict zones in Africa. However, the rapid and unrelenting commercialization of space and nearly absolute control of satellites by a just a few large nations and corporations is increasingly perceived as a threat to the global majority, living in developing countries, to communicate freely and influence their own cultures.

CHRIS PATERSON

See also **Ancillary Markets; Association of Independent Television Stations; British Sky Broadcasting; Cable Networks; Cable News Network; Cable Television: United States; Channel One News; Copyright Law and Television; Communication Satellite Corporation; Development Communication; Digital Television; Direct Broadcast Satellite; Distant Signal; European Broadcast Union; European Commercial Broadcasting Satellite; European Union: Television Policy; Federal Communications Commission; First People's Television Broadcasting in Canada; Geography and Television; Home Box Office; Midwest Video Case; International Telecommunication Union; Knowledge Network; Medical Video; Microwave; Movies on Television; Murdoch, Rupert; Narrowcasting; National Cable Television Association; News Corporation, Ltd.; Olympics and Television; Pay Cable; TV; Space Program and Television; Telcos; Technology, Television; Telecommunications Act of 1996; Translators; Turner Broadcasting Systems**

Further Reading

Akwule, R., *Global Telecommunications: Their Technology, Administration, and Policies,* New York: Free Press, 1992

Boeke, C., "Space Segment Supply—Fewer Players, Further Questions," *Via Satellite* (April 2002)

Breeds, J., editor, *The Satellite Book: A Complete Guide to Satellite TV Theory and Practice,* Cricklade, Wilts, United Kingdom: Swift Television Publications, 1994

Clarke, N., and E. Riddell, *The Sky Barons,* London: Methuen, 1992

Collins, R., *Satellite Television in Western Europe,* London: John Libbey, 1992

Frederick, H., *Global Communication and International Relations,* Belmont, California: Wadsworth, 1993

Lacy, S., "Use of Satellite Technology in Local Television News," *Journalism Quarterly* (Winter 1988)

Long, M., *World Satellite Almanac,* Howard W. Sams, 1987; Phillips Publishing Company, 1997

Miller, M., B. Vucetic, and L. Berry, editors, *Satellite Communications: Mobile and Fixed Services,* Boston, Massachusetts: Kluwer Academic Publishers, 1993

Paterson, C., "Reform or Re-Colonization? The Overhaul of African Television," *Review of African Political Economy,* Vol. 78 (1998)

Stilson, J., "Man with a Plan; Rupert Murdoch Hasn't Revealed His Plans for DirecTV, but His Dominating Satellite Strategy Overseas Provides Insights into His Best Practices—Cable Operators, Beware!" *Mediaweek* (December 4, 2003)

Thussu, Daya, *International Communication: Continuity and Change,* London: Arnold, 2000

Saturday Night Live

U.S. Comedy Variety Program

Saturday Night Live (*SNL*) first aired on October 11, 1975, on the National Broadcasting Company (NBC) and has continued since to hold that network's late-night Saturday time slot despite major cast changes, turmoil in the production offices, and variable ratings. A comedy-variety show with an emphasis on satire and current issues, *SNL* has been a staple element of NBC's dominance of late-night programming since the program's inception.

SNL was developed by Dick Ebersol with producer Lorne Michaels in 1975 in response to NBC's search for a show for its Saturday late-night slot. The network had long enjoyed dominance of the weekday late-night slot with *The Tonight Show* and sought to continue that success in the unused weekend time period. With the approval of Johnny Carson, whose influence at the network was strong, Ebersol and Michaels debuted their show, which was intended to attract 18- to 34-year-old viewers.

The regulars on the show have almost always been relative unknowns in the comedy field. The first cast (the Not Ready for Prime Time Players) included Chevy Chase, Dan Aykroyd, John Belushi, Jane Curtin, Gilda Radner, Laraine Newman, and Garrett Morris, all from the New York and Toronto comedy scenes. Featuring a different guest host each week (comedian George Carlin was the first) and a different musical guest as well, *SNL* reflected a nontraditional approach to television comedy from the start. The cast and writers combined the satirical with the silly and nonsensical, not unlike *Monty Python's Flying Circus,* one of Michaels's admitted influences.

The program is produced live from NBC's studio 8-H for 90 minutes. This difficult schedule and pressure-filled production environment has resulted in some classic comedy sketches and some abysmally dull moments over the years. Creating comedy in such a situation is difficult at best, and the audience is always aware when the show is running dry (usually in the last half hour). However, this sense of the immedi-

Saturday Night Live, (Standing) John Belushi, Dan Aykroyd, Bill Murray, Laraine Newman. (Seated) Gilda Radner, Jane Curtin, Garrett Morris, 1975–80 cast.
Courtesy of the Everett Collection

ate and the unforeseen also can give the show its needed edge. By returning to TV's live roots, *SNL* gives its audiences an element of adventure with each program. It has acquainted the generations who never experienced live television programming in the 1950s with the sense of theater missing from prerecorded programming.

For the performers, crew, and writers, the show is a test of skill and dedication. The show has undergone several major changes since its beginning. The most obvious of these have been cast changes. *SNL*'s first "star," Chevy Chase, left the show in the second season for Hollywood. Aykroyd and Belushi followed in 1979. The rest of the original cast, including Bill Murray, who replaced Chase, left when producer Michaels decided to leave the show after the 1979–80 season. Michaels's departure created widespread doubt about the viability of the show without him and his cast of favorites. Jean Doumanian was chosen as producer, but her tenure lasted less than a year. With the critics attacking the show's diminished satirical edge and the lackluster replacement performers, NBC enticed Ebersol to return as producer in the spring of 1981. Ebersol managed to attract some of the original staff for the 1981–82 season, particularly writer Michael O'Donoghue. With the addition of Eddie Murphy, the show began to regain some of its strength, always based in its focus on a young audience and the use of timely material.

Michaels rejoined the show as producer in 1985 and oversaw a second classic period of *SNL*. With talented performers such as Dana Carvey, Jon Lovitz, Jan Hooks, and Phil Hartman, the program regained much of its early edge and attitude. However, the nature of the program is that the people who make it funny (the performers and writers) are the ones who tend to move on after a few years of the grind of a weekly live show. The steady turnover of cast and writers continues to affect *SNL*'s quality, for better and for worse. However, Michaels's presence as producer has established a continuity that reassures the network and provides some stability for the audience.

From its inception, *SNL* has provided U.S. television with some of its most popular characters and catchphrases. Radner's Roseanne Roseannadana ("It's always something") and Emily Litella ("Never mind"), Belushi's Samurai, Aykroyd's Jimmy Carter, Murphy's Mr. Robinson, Billy Crystal's Fernando ("You look mahvelous"), Martin Short's Ed Grimley, Lovitz's pathological liar, Carvey's Church Lady ("Isn't that special?"), Carvey and Kevin Nealon's Hans and Franz, and Mike Myers's "Wayne's World" and Dieter all left marks on popular culture of the late 20th century. In the 1990s and early 2000s, cast members con-

tinued to add new voices to the *SNL* pantheon. In particular, political humor has been among the greatest strengths of recent seasons, with Darrell Hammond's caricature of a leering Bill Clinton during the Monica Lewinsky scandal and Will Ferrell's imitation of a befuddled George W. Bush continuing a tradition of presidential satirization established by earlier *SNL* performers, such as Chase (as Gerald Ford), Phil Hartman (Ronald Reagan and Bill Clinton), and Carvey (most notably, George Bush, Sr.).

The program's regular news spot, *Weekend Update,* has been done by Chase, Curtin, Aykroyd, Nealon, Dennis Miller, Norm MacDonald, Hammond, Tina Fey, and Jimmy Fallon, among others, and, at its best, the mock newscast has provided sharp comic commentary on current events.

SNL has seen many of its cast members move on to other venues. Chase, Aykroyd, Murray, Murphy, Crystal, Myers, Chris Rock, and Adam Sandler have all enjoyed considerable success on the big screen, with many other former cast members also making films, including many based on *SNL* characters. Indeed, at times it has seemed that nearly every character from the *SNL* roster has been featured in a Hollywood feature. However, for every *SNL*-based box office (or home video release) winner, such as *The Blues Brothers* or *Wayne's World,* there have been several busts (*The Coneheads, It's Pat, Stuart Saves His Family, Blues Brothers 2000, A Night at the Roxbury,* and *The Ladies Man*).

Among the *SNL* alumni who have moved from late-night to prime-time sitcoms are Curtin (*Kate and Allie* and *Third Rock from the Sun*), Julia Louis-Dreyfus (*Seinfeld* and *Watching Ellie*), Hartman (*News Radio*), MacDonald (*Norm*), and Jim Belushi (*According to Jim*). Still others have, with varying degrees of success, tried their luck with other TV genres. Rock won critical acclaim and an Emmy for his Home Box Office (HBO) talk show *The Chris Rock Show,* whereas Carvey tried but failed to revive the prime-time variety show format, and Miller fared poorly both as late-night talk show host and as a commentator on *Monday Night Football.*

As a stage for satire, few other American programs match *Saturday Night Live*. As an outlet for current music, the show has featured acts from every popular musical genre and has hosted both established and new artists (from Paul Simon, the Rolling Stones, and George Harrison to R.E.M., Sinead O'Connor, Britney Spears, and Eminem). Because of its longevity, *SNL* has crossed generational lines and made the culture of a younger audience available to their elders (and the opposite is also true). Ultimately, *Saturday Night Live* must be considered one of the most distinctive and significant programs in the history of U.S. television.

GEOFFREY HAMMILL

Announcers
Don Pardo (1975–81, 1982–)
Mel Brand (1981–82)

Casts by Season

1975–76
Dan Aykroyd
John Belushi
Chevy Chase
George Coe
Jane Curtin
Garrett Morris
Laraine Newman
Michael O' Donoghue
Gilda Radner

1976–77
Dan Aykroyd
Chevy Chase
John Belushi
Jane Curtin
Garrett Morris
Bill Murray
Laraine Newman
Gilda Radner

1977–78
Dan Aykroyd
John Belushi
Jane Curtin
Garrett Morris
Bill Murray
Laraine Newman
Gilda Radner
Tom Davis
Al Franken

1978–79
Dan Aykroyd
John Belushi
Jane Curtin
Garrett Morris
Bill Murray
Laraine Newman
Gilda Radner
Tom Davis

Al Franken
Don Novello

1979–80
Jane Curtin
Garrett Morris
Bill Murray
Laraine Newman
Gilda Radner
Harry Shearer
Peter Aykroyd
Tom Davis
Jim Downey
Al Franken
Brian Doyle-Murray
Don Novello
Tom Schiller
Paul Shaffer
Alan Zweibel

1980–81
Denny Dillon
Robin Duke
Gilbert Gottfried
Tim Kazurinsky
Gail Matthius
Eddie Murphy
Joe Piscopo
Ann Risley
Charles Rocket
Tony Rosato
Yvonne Hudson
Mitchell Kriegman
Matthew Laurance
Laurie Metcalf
Emily Prager
Patrick Weathers

1981–82
Robin Duke
Christine Ebersole
Mary Gross
Tim Kazurinsky
Eddie Murphy
Brian Doyle-Murray
Joe Piscopo
Tony Rosato

1982–83
Robin Duke
Mary Gross
Brad Hall

Gary Kroeger
Tim Kazurinsky
Julia Louis-Dreyfus
Eddie Murphy
Joe Piscopo

1983–84
Jim Belushi
Robin Duke
Mary Gross
Brad Hall
Gary Kroeger
Tim Kazurinsky
Julia Louis-Dreyfus
Eddie Murphy
Joe Piscopo

1984–85
Jim Belushi
Billy Crystal
Mary Gross
Christopher Guest
Rich Hall
Gary Kroeger
Julia Louis-Dreyfus
Harry Shearer
Martin Short
Pamela Stephenson

1985–86
Joan Cusack
Robert Downey, Jr.
Nora Dunn
Anthony Michael Hall
Jon Lovitz
Dennis Miller
Randy Quaid
Terry Sweeney
Danitra Vance
A. Whitney Brown
Al Franken
Don Novello
Dan Vitale
Damon Wayans

1986–87
Dana Carvey
Nora Dunn
Phil Hartman
Jan Hooks
Victoria Jackson
Jon Lovitz

Dennis Miller
A. Whitney Brown
Kevin Meaney
Kevin Nealon

1987–88
Dana Carvey
Nora Dunn
Phil Hartman
Jan Hooks
Victoria Jackson
Jon Lovitz
Dennis Miller
Kevin Nealon
A. Whitney Brown
Al Franken

1988–89
Dana Carvey
Nora Dunn
Phil Hartman
Jan Hooks
Victoria Jackson
Jon Lovitz
Dennis Miller
Kevin Nealon
A. Whitney Brown
Al Franken
Mike Myers
Ben Stiller

1989–90
Dana Carvey
Nora Dunn
Phil Hartman
Jan Hooks
Victoria Jackson
Jon Lovitz
Dennis Miller
Mike Myers
Kevin Nealon
A. Whitney Brown
Al Franken

1990–91
Dana Carvey
Phil Hartman
Jan Hooks
Victoria Jackson
Dennis Miller
Mike Myers
Kevin Nealon

A. Whitney Brown
Chris Farley
Al Franken
Tim Meadows
Chris Rock
Adam Sandler
Rob Schneider
David Spade
Julia Sweeney

1991–92
Dana Carvey
Chris Farley
Phil Hartman
Victoria Jackson
Mike Myers
Kevin Nealon
Chris Rock
Julia Sweeney
Beth Cahill
Ellen Cleghorne
Siobhan Fallon
Al Franken
Melanie Hutsell
Tim Meadows
Adam Sandler
Rob Schneider
Rob Smigel
David Spade

1992–93
Dana Carvey
Chris Farley
Phil Hartman
Mike Myers
Kevin Nealon
Chris Rock
Rob Schneider
Julia Sweeney
Ellen Cleghorne
Al Franken
Melanie Hutsell
Tim Meadows
Adam Sandler
Rob Smigel
David Spade

1993–94
Ellen Cleghorne
Chris Farley
Phil Hartman
Melanie Hutsell

Michael McKean
Tim Meadows
Mike Myers
Kevin Nealon
Adam Sandler
Rob Schneider
David Spade
Julia Sweeney
Al Franken
Norm Macdonald
Jay Mohr
Sarah Silverman

1994–95
Morwenna Banks
Ellen Cleghorne
Chris Elliott
Chris Farley
Janeane Garofalo
Norm Macdonald
Michael McKean
Mark McKinney
Tim Meadows
Mike Myers
Kevin Nealon
Adam Sandler
David Spade
Al Franken
Laura Kightlinger
Jay Mohr
Molly Shannon

1995–96
Jim Breuer
Will Ferrell
Darrell Hammond
David Koechner
Norm Macdonald
Mark McKinney
Tim Meadows
Cheri Oteri
Molly Shannon
David Spade
Nancy Walls
Chris Kattan
Colin Quinn
Fred Wolf

1996–97
Jim Breuer
Will Ferrell
Ana Gasteyer

Darrell Hammond
Chris Kattan
Norm Macdonald
Mark McKinney
Tim Meadows
Tracy Morgan
Cheri Oteri
Molly Shannon
Colin Quinn
Fred Wolf

1997–98
Jim Breuer
Will Ferrell
Ana Gasteyer
Darrell Hammond
Chris Kattan
Norm Macdonald
Tim Meadows
Tracy Morgan
Cheri Oteri
Colin Quinn
Molly Shannon

1998–99
Will Ferrell
Ana Gasteyer
Darrell Hammond
Chris Kattan
Tim Meadows
Tracy Morgan
Cheri Oteri
Colin Quinn
Molly Shannon
Jimmy Fallon
Chris Parnell
Horatio Sanz

1999–2000
Jimmy Fallon
Will Ferrell
Ana Gasteyer
Darrell Hammond
Chris Kattan
Tim Meadows
Tracy Morgan
Cheri Oteri
Chris Parnell
Colin Quinn
Horatio Sanz
Molly Shannon
Rachel Dratch
Maya Rudolph

2000–01
Jimmy Fallon
Will Ferrell
Ana Gasteyer
Darrell Hammond
Chris Kattan
Tracy Morgan
Chris Parnell
Horatio Sanz
Molly Shannon
Rachel Dratch
Tina Fey
Jerry Minor
Maya Rudolph

2001–02
Rachel Dratch
Jimmy Fallon
Will Ferrell
Tina Fey
Ana Gasteyer
Darrell Hammond
Chris Kattan
Tracy Morgan
Chris Parnell
Maya Rudolph
Horatio Sanz
Dean Edwards
Seth Meyers
Amy Poehler
Jeff Richards

2002–03
Rachel Dratch
Jimmy Fallon
Tina Fey
Darrell Hammond
Chris Kattan
Tracy Morgan
Chris Parnell
Amy Poehler
Maya Rudolph
Horatio Sanz
Fred Armisen
Dean Edwards
Will Forte
Seth Meyers
Jeff Richards

2003–04
Fred Armisen
Rachel Dratch
Jimmy Fallon

Tina Fey
Will Forte
Darrell Hammond
Seth Meyers
Finesse Mitchell
Chris Parnell
Amy Poehler
Jeff Richards
Maya Rudolph
Horatio Sanz
Kenan Thompson

Executive Producers

Lorne Michaels (1975–80, 1985–), Jean Doumanian (1980–81), Dick Ebersol (1981–85)

Programming History

NBC

October 1975–	Saturday 11:30 P.M.–1:00 A.M.
October 1979–March 1980	Wednesday 10:00–11:00
March 1980–April 1980	Friday 10:00–11:00

Further Reading

Barol, Bill, and Jennifer Foote, "Saturday Night Lives!" *Newsweek* (September 25, 1989)

Beatts, Anne, and John Head, editors, *Saturday Night Live,* New York: Avon, 1977

Cader, Michael, editor, *Saturday Night Live: The First Twenty Years,* Boston, Massachusetts: Cader Books, 1994

Corliss, Richard, "Party on, Wayne—from TV to Movies," *Time* (March 2, 1992)

Cullingford, Elizabeth Butler, "Seamus and Sinead: From 'Limbo' to *Saturday Night Live* by Way of Hush-A-Bye-Baby," *Colby Quarterly* (March 1994)

Greenfield, Jeff, "Live from New York," *New York Times* (April 19, 1993)

Harkness, John, "Out of the Joke Box," *Sight and Sound* (March 1994)

Hill, Doug, and Keff Weingrad, *Saturday Night: A Backstage History of Saturday Night Live,* New York: Beech Tree, 1986

Myers, Mike, and Robin Ruzan, *Wayne's World: Extreme Close-Up,* New York: Hyperion, 1991

Partridge, Marianne, editor, *Rolling Stone Visits Saturday Night Live,* Garden City, New York: Dolphin, 1979

Saltzman, Joe, "The Agony and the Ecstasy: Live Television Comedy," *USA Today Magazine* (November 1987)

Shales, Tom, and James Andrew Miller, *Live from New York: An Uncensored History of Saturday Night Live, as Told by Its Stars, Writers and Guests.* London: Little, Brown, 2002

Saunders, Jennifer (1958–)

British Actor

Since the early 1980s, Jennifer Saunders has been a popular and influential figure in British television comedy. Her success stems from her involvement as both a performer in and a writer of several comedy shows that have been heralded as innovative by critics and received as hugely entertaining by audiences.

Saunders established her career as part of a double act with Dawn French on the live comedy circuit in the late 1970s. She and French, who have remained collaborators on many projects since, made their initial impact while on tour in 1981 with the Comic Strip, a group consisting of several young comedians performing an alternative, innovative form of comedy. The group were rapidly transferred to television, appropriately making their debut on Channel 4's opening night in November 1982. Throughout the 1980s, the original members appeared in *The Comic Strip Presents...*, in which they wrote, directed, and performed a series of narratives satirizing a variety of genre themes. The program set a precedent for the so-called alternative comedy of the 1980s, won critical approval, and was awarded a Golden Rose at the Montreux Festival.

Saunders and French's role within this group was particularly significant in that the two succeeded in providing much more complex and interesting female characters than had hitherto been offered by television comedy. They placed their characters in opposition to the traditional representations of women in British television comedy—such as the sexual accessories of *The Benny Hill Show;* the domesticated, subservient wife of *The Good Life;* and the nag of *Fawlty Towers.* Saunders and French's very presence in *The Comic Strip Presents...* was a timely intrusion into a realm of comedy that had previously been the exclusive domain of male performers, from *Monty Python* to the double

Jennifer Saunders.
Photo courtesy of Jennifer Saunders

acts of the 1970s: *Morecombe and Wise* and *Little and Large*.

The autonomy that women were gaining was confirmed in *French and Saunders*. This show, the first series of which was screened on the British Broadcasting Corporation (BBC) in 1987, presented the pair as partners combining stand-up and sketches. *French and Saunders* offered a uniquely feminine version of British comedy (unique, with the notable exception of *Victoria Wood: As Seen on TV,* first screened in 1985). Their writing and acting focused directly, and with hilarious results, on female experience. Many of the scenes worked to reinforce the centrality of women's talk and to parody the position and representations of women in the media.

It was out of a *French and Saunders* sketch that Saunders conceived of and developed her most prolific work, *Absolutely Fabulous*. Saunders has written and starred in four six-part series of *Absolutely Fabulous* (BBC, 1992, 1994, 1995, 2001, with a fifth season commencing in 2003), which have achieved uniformly high viewing figures as well as critical acclaim. In some respects a domestic sitcom, *Absolutely Fabulous* satirizes the matriarchal household of fashion public relations executive Edina Monsoon (Saunders) and the women around her, including her unruly best friend, Patsy (Joanna Lumley), and long-suffering daughter, Saffron (Julia Sawalha). Because *Absolutely Fabulous* remains an unusual example of a peak-time situation comedy written by women, with a predominantly female cast and a specific address to a female audience, it provides rare viewing pleasures of self-recognition and humor to women. In addition to having feminist concerns at the core of its structure and themes, it stresses the artificiality surrounding "womanliness" and celebrates gender as a complex social and cultural construction.

In terms of her writing and performance, Saunders helped to raise the profile of female comedians in television, leading the way for others, such as Jo Brand and Dawn French, the latter in her solo series *Murder Most Horrid.* Saunders took on her first noncomedy role for a BBC drama, *Heroes and Villains* (1995), a period piece based on the true life of Lady Hester Stanhope, an eccentric 19th-century traveler. As well as revealing a further talent for dramatic acting, the show crystallized Saunders's TV persona and arguably her role in British television as an independent and powerful woman.

NICOLA FOSTER

See also **Absolutely Fabulous; British Programming; French, Dawn; Lumley, Joanna; Wood, Victoria**

Jennifer Saunders. Born in Sleaford, Lincolnshire, England, July 12, 1958. Attended Central School of Speech and Drama. Married: Adrian Edmondson; children: Ella, Beattie, and Freya. Formed cabaret partnership with comedian Dawn French, the Comedy Store, London; appeared in the *Comic Strip* series, early 1980s, and subsequently in *French and Saunders* sketch show and, without French, in *Absolutely Fabulous.*

Television Series

1982–92	*The Comic Strip Presents (Five Go Mad in Dorset; Five Go Mad on Mescalin; Slags; Summer School; Private Enterprise; Consuela; Mr. Jolly Lives Next Door; Bad News Tour; South Atlantic Raiders; G.L.C.; Oxford; Spaghetti Hoops; Le Kiss; Wild Turkey; Demonella; Jealousy; The Strike)*
1985	*Happy Families*
1985–86	*Girls on Top (also co-writer)*

<table>
<tr><td>1987–</td><td>French and Saunders</td></tr>
<tr><td>1992–</td><td>Absolutely Fabulous</td></tr>
</table>

Films

The Supergrass, 1985; *In the Bleak Midwinter,* 1995; *Muppet Treasure Island,* 1996; *Spice World,* 1997; *Fanny and Elvis,* 1999; *Shrek 2,* 2004 (voice only).

Publication

Absolutely Fabulous, 1995

Further Reading

Putterman, Barry, *On Television and Comedy: Essays on Style, Theme, Performer, and Writer,* Jefferson, North Carolina: McFarland, 1995

Sawyer, Diane (1945–)

U.S. Broadcast Journalist

Diane Sawyer, cohost of ABC News' *Good Morning, America* and co-anchor of *PrimeTime Live,* is one of broadcast journalism's most prominent and successful female presences. Sawyer began her career as a weather reporter on a Louisville, Kentucky, television station. In 1970, she took a job at the White House on the staff of Presidential Press Secretary Ron Ziegler. She continued her career as a press aide during Richard Nixon's administration until 1974 and then assisted the former president with the preparation of his memoirs. She made her transition to broadcast journalism in 1978, when she joined CBS News as a reporter in its Washington bureau. When Sawyer accepted the job of State Department correspondent for CBS News (1978–81), she began a career as a popular figure in television journalism; she was the co-anchor of *CBS Morning News* (from 1981), the co-anchor of *CBS Early Morning News* (1982–84), and the first woman on the network's flagship public affairs program, *60 Minutes* (1984–89), before signing in 1989 a multiyear contract to co-anchor with Sam Donaldson *PrimeTime Live* on the American Broadcasting Company (ABC). In 1999, she took on another job with ABC, in addition to her duties at *PrimeTime:* cohosting *Good Morning, America* with Charles Gibson, who also has joined Sawyer as an anchor for the Thursday edition of *PrimeTime.* Sawyer also has co-anchored *20/20* since 1998 and contributed to many other ABC News programs since joining the network.

In addition to her impressive résumé, Sawyer is known for a variety of individual characteristics. Her intelligent reporting and tenacious coverage of the Three Mile Island crisis assisted her in garnering heavy journalistic assignments that, at the time, were considered a challenge to male colleagues working in early morning news. At *CBS Morning News,* she earned a reputation for skilled reporting as well as her ability to help increase ratings. Her commanding delivery helped edge the network's program closer to its rivals in the Nielsen ratings. Her presence and teamwork with Bill Kurtis gave the Columbia Broadcasting System (CBS) its first healthy ratings in this time slot in three decades. High-profile assignments as correspondent of *60 Minutes* established her as a national figure; viewers admired her equally for her personality and her talents as an investigative reporter. Sawyer's skill has contributed to *PrimeTime Live*'s success and its distinct style, and since joining *Good Morning, America,* she has continued to deliver increased ratings. *Washington Post* critic Tom Shales remarks that, even though *Good Morning, America* remains similar to other morning programming, "Sawyer has unquestionably brought . . . a grace and eloquence that elevate the entire program to a level above and beyond the competition."

In the fall of 1994, Sawyer signed a contract granting her a $7 million annual salary, making her one of the highest-paid women in broadcast news. In 2001, her salary remained one of the highest paid to any journalist, an estimated $13 million per year. Although one critique characterized her as "the warm ice maiden," such views may reflect forms of professional jealously. Margo Howard, entertainment critic of *People Weekly* magazine, contends that Sawyer "got to the top with a formidable blend of smarts, drive, [warmth], and earnestness." Another characterization of Sawyer as "a girl who is one of the boys" points to her authoritative, intelligent, enterprising manner.

Observers frequently refer to Sawyer's willingness to move between two styles—that of a tabloid journal-

Diane Sawyer, 2003.
©CJ Contino/Everett Collection

ist and that of the "legitimate" journalist. She oscillates between pieces involving diligent reporting, such as her coverage of the Iranian hostage crisis, and celebrity interviews, such as her interview with the then-married Michael Jackson and Lisa Marie Presley. Her "softball" questions to Tonya Harding during the 1994 Olympics, her low-camp interview with Marla Maples (asking whether Donald Trump was "really the best sex" Maples ever had), her interview with the wife of a convicted Central Intelligence Agency spy, and her brief, heavily promoted and news-free encounter with Boris Yeltsin in the Kremlin during the 1987 coup contribute to the "tabloid" label.

Although the critiques are valid to some degree, Sawyer's distinctive personality has helped *PrimeTime Live* and *Good Morning, America* move toward unqualified success and produce millions of dollars in profits for ABC. All four major networks have sought her services, and she has become a "brand name," a

person the viewers remember, and a television personality who can deliver ratings. She remains one of the most visible news figures in U.S. television.

Lynn T. Lovdal

See also **Morning Television Programs; News, Network;** *Primetime Live; 60 Minutes*

(Lila) Diane Sawyer. Born in Glasgow, Kentucky, December 22, 1945. Educated at Wellesley College, Wellesley, Massachusetts, B.A., 1967. Married: Mike Nichols, 1988. Reporter, WLKY-TV, Louisville, Kentucky, 1967–70; administrator, White House press office, 1970–74; researcher for Richard Nixon's memoirs, 1974–78; general assignment reporter, then U.S. State Department correspondent, CBS News, 1978–89; with ABC News, since 1989, co-anchor *PrimeTime Live* since 1989, cohost *Good Morning, America,* since 1999. Member: Council on Foreign Relations. Recipient: two Peabody Awards; Robert F. Kennedy Award; ten Emmy Awards; duPont Award; Lifetime Achievement Award, International Radio and Television Society. Inducted into Broadcast Hall of Fame.

Television Series (selected)

1978–81	*CBS Evening News* (correspondent)
1981–84	*CBS Morning News* (co-anchor)
1982–84	*CBS Early Morning News* (co-anchor)
1984–89	*60 Minutes* (correspondent and co-editor)
1989–	*PrimeTime Live* (co-anchor)
1993–95	*Day One* (co-anchor)
1994	*Turning Point*
1998–	*ABC News 20/20* (co-anchor)
1999–	*Good Morning, America*

Further Reading

Auletta, Ken, "Promise Her the Moon," *The New Yorker* (February 14, 1994)

Exley, Frederick, "If Nixon Could Possess the Soul of This Woman, Why Can't I? The Decade's Last Piece About Diane Sawyer," *Esquire* (December 1989)

Shales, Tom, "Recent Ratings Slip a Wake-Up Call for *Today* Show," *Washington Post* (November 29, 2001)

Unger, Arthur, "Diane Sawyer: 'The Warm Ice Maiden'" (interview), *Television Quarterly* (Spring 1992)

Zoglin, Richard, "Star Power: Diane Sawyer, with a New Prime-Time Show and a $1.6 Million Contract, Is Hot. But Are Celebrity Anchors Like Her Upstaging the News?" *Time* (August 7, 1989)

Zoglin, Richard, "Good Morning, Diane," *Time* (January 18, 1999)

Scales, Prunella (1932–)

British Actor

Prunella Scales is an established star of British situation comedy, although she has also won praise in a wide range of other productions, including drama for television and stage. Television viewers are most likely to associate her, however, with the classic John Cleese comedy *Fawlty Towers,* in which she played the unflappable Sybil to Cleese's appallingly inept hotelier Basil Fawlty.

As Sybil Fawlty, the archetypal gossipy and battle-hardened nagging wife who in her husband's eyes was more of a hindrance than a help (though in truth she spent much of her time smoothing, with carefully rounded vowels, the ruffled feathers of guests her husband had offended), Scales was deemed perfect. Employing all the skills she had acquired from her early experience in repertory theater and subsequently with the Royal Shakespeare Company and other leading troupes, she easily countered the manic ranting of her screen husband, ensuring that life—such as it was—could carry on at Fawlty Towers. When not seeing to her monstrous coiffure, Sybil took desultory pleasure in providing her husband with new irritations, usually guaranteed to send him into paroxysms of helpless rage. As a mark of the degree to which the performances of Scales and Cleese were essential to the success of the series—widely judged a classic of television comedy—an attempt to make a U.S. version under the title *Amanda's,* with a cast headed by Bea Arthur of *Golden Girls* fame, was a total failure (even though, in desperation, some episodes were duplicated word for word).

Scales had previously performed as bus conductress Eileen Hughes in *Coronation Street* and also as costar of the series *Marriage Lines,* a relatively conventional husband-and-wife situation comedy in which she was paired with Richard Briers. As Kate Starling in the latter production, she charted the ups and downs experienced by typical newlyweds in the 1960s, wrestling with a range of more or less mundane financial and domestic problems (later complicated by the arrival of their baby).

In the wake of the huge success of *Fawlty Towers,* Scales enjoyed further acclaim from critics and audiences alike in the role of the widowed Sarah in Simon Brett's *After Henry,* a compassionate and often hilarious comedy that was equally successful as a series for radio and subsequently on television. When not contemplating the future course of her life as the widowed mother of a teenage daughter, she indulged in entertaining sparring with "mother," played by the redoubtable Joan Sanderson.

Other highlights of Scales's career have included her performance as Elizabeth Mapp in the television version of E.F. Benson's Edwardian *Mapp and Lucia* stories, in which she was cast opposite the equally distinguished Geraldine McEwan. Another triumph was her enthralling impersonation of Queen Elizabeth II in a much-acclaimed television version of Alan Bennett's celebrated play *A Question of Attribution,* which concerned the relationship between the monarch and her art adviser Anthony Blunt, who was fated to be ex-

Prunella Scales.
Photo courtesy of Snipe Productions, Ltd.

posed as a spy for communist Russia. On the stage, meanwhile, she added another monarch to her list of credits when she impersonated Queen Victoria in her own one-woman show.

Considered one of the most technically proficient actresses of stage and screen of her generation as well as an accomplished occasional director, Scales has continued to divide her time between television and the theater throughout her career, sometimes appearing in partnership with her real-life husband, actor Timothy West. In 1996, in recognition of her skills, she was invited to share some of her secrets concerning acting as part of a short series of master classes on the art of comedy performance.

DAVID PICKERING

Prunella Scales (Prunella Margaret Rumney Illingworth). Born in Sutton Abinger, Surrey, England, June 22, 1932. Attended Moira House, Eastbourne; trained for stage at the Old Vic Theatre School, London, and the Herbert Berghof Studio, New York. Married: Timothy West, 1963; children: Samuel and Joseph. Started in repertory theater in Huddersfield, Salisbury, Oxford, Bristol Old Vic, and elsewhere; performed in theater seasons at Stratford-upon-Avon and Chichester Festival Theatre, 1967–68; also acted on London stage; had greatest success on television as Sybil in *Fawlty Towers*, 1975; subsequently appeared in numerous sitcoms and plays; also teaches and directs theater. President, Council for the Protection of Rural England, 1997. Commander of the British Empire, 1992.

Television Series

1963–66	*Marriage Lines*
1975, 1979	*Fawlty Towers*
1977	*Mr. Big*
1985–86	*Mapp and Lucia*
1988, 1990	*After Henry*
1994	*The Rector's Wife*
1995	*Searching*
1995	*Signs and Wonders*
1997	*Emma*

Television Specials

1973	*One Mom's Meat*
1976	*Escape from the Dark*

1977	*The Apple Cart*
1979	*Doris and Doreen*
1982	*A Wife Like the Moon*
1982	*Grand Duo*
1982	*Outside Edge*
1983	*The Merry Wives of Windsor*
1985	*Absurd Person Singular*
1987	*The Index Has Gone Fishing*
1987	*What the Butler Saw*
1991	*A Question of Attribution*
1994	*Fair Game*
1995	*Signs and Wonders*
1997	*Lord of Misrule*
1997	*Breaking the Code*

Films

Laxdale Hall, 1952; *Hobson's Choice*, 1953; *The Crowded Day*, 1954; *Room at the Top*, 1958; *The Waltz of the Toreadors*, 1962; *The Hound of the Baskervilles*, 1978; *The Boys from Brazil*, 1978; *The Wicked Lady*, 1982; *The Lonely Passion of Judith Hearne*, 1987; *Consuming Passions*, 1988; *A Chorus of Disapproval*, 1989; *Howards End*, 1992; *Second Best*, 1994; *Wolf*, 1994; *An Awfully Big Adventure*, 1995; *Stiff Upper Lips*, 1997; *Mad Cows*, 1998; *An Ideal Husband*, 1999; *The Ghost of Greville Lodge*, 1999.

Radio

After Henry; Smelling of Roses.

Stage (selected)

The Promise, 1967; *Hay Fever*, 1968; *It's a Two-Foot-Six-Inches-Above-the-Ground-World*, 1970; *The Wolf*, 1975; *Breezeblock Park*, 1978; *Make and Break*, 1980; *An Evening with Queen Victoria*, 1980; *The Merchant of Venice*, 1981; *Quartermaine's Terms*, 1981; *Big in Brazil*, 1984; *When We Are Married*, 1986; *Single Spies*, 1988; *The School for Scandal*, 1990; *Long Day's Journey into Night*, 1991; *Mother Tongue*, 1992; *Happy Days*, 1993; *The Matchmaker*, 1993; *Staying On*, 1997; *The Birthday Party*, 1999; *The Cherry Orchard*, 2000.

Schaffner, Franklin (1920–1989)

U.S. Director

Franklin Schaffner, one of several prominent directors during U.S. television's "golden age," worked on such prestigious anthology series as *Studio One* (Columbia Broadcasting System [CBS]), *The Kaiser Aluminum Hour* (National Broadcasting Company [NBC]), *Playhouse 90* (CBS), and *The DuPont Show of the Week* (NBC) as well as Edward R. Murrow's *Person to Person* (CBS) and the drama series *The Defenders* (CBS). Schaffner later became known as an "actor's director," but his television work is known primarily for his unique use of the camera.

Schaffner attended Franklin and Marshall College in Lancaster, Pennsylvania, where he majored in government and English. A prize-winning orator, Schaffner appeared in several university productions and also worked part time as an announcer at local radio station WGAL. His plans to attend Columbia Law School were interrupted when he enlisted in the U.S. Navy during World War II. During the war, he served with amphibious forces in Europe and North Africa and, later, with the Office for Strategic Services in the Far East.

After the war, Schaffner first sought work as an actor. He was eventually hired as a spokesperson and copywriter for the peace organization Americans United for World Government. During this period, Schaffner met ABC Radio vice president Robert Saudek and worked as a writer for Saudek's radio series *World Security Workshop*. For that series, Schaffner wrote "The Cave," which was the series' final broadcast (May 8, 1947), and his experience on the series encouraged him to pursue a career in broadcasting.

Schaffner was hired as an assistant director on the radio documentary series *The March of Time* for $35 per week. His work brought him to the attention of Robert Bendick, director of television news and special events for CBS. Bendick hired Schaffner in April 1948 as director of Brooklyn Dodgers baseball as well as other sporting events and public service programs. Schaffner's experience with the spontaneity and immediacy of live special events made him a logical choice as one of three directors for the 1948 Democratic and Republican political conventions held in Philadelphia.

By 1949, Schaffner was ready for the challenge of directing live dramatic programs. After directing *Wesley* (CBS, 1949), a live situation comedy produced by Worthington Miner, Schaffner alternated directing assignments with Paul Nickell on Miner's live anthology series *Studio One*. On that series Schaffner directed adaptations of classics as well as original productions, including the series' first color telecast, *The Boy Who Changed the World* (October 18, 1954). At a time when other directors used static cameras, Schaffner utilized a moving camera with long, graceful tracking shots. In addition to masking the limitations of the studio set, Schaffner's camera work drew audiences into the action of the play. In *Twelve Angry Men* (September 20, 1954), Schaffner designed a 360-degree shot

Franklin Schaffner.
Photo courtesy of Wisconsin Center for Film and Theater Research

that required orchestrated moves of the set's walls during the shot. Schaffner won a 1954 Emmy for his directorial work on *Twelve Angry Men*.

While working on the *Studio One* series, Schaffner drew on his news and public affairs experience to serve as producer and studio director for Edward R. Murrow's interview program *Person to Person* (CBS, 1953–61). Although the initial episodes utilized static camera setups for the remote interviews, Schaffner later incorporated tracking cameras that moved with guests to show their home and activities. Schaffner worked on the series until 1957, when more of his work originated from Los Angeles.

Schaffner drew on his news experience once again for *A Tour of the White House with Mrs. John F. Kennedy* (NBC, February 14, 1962). Schaffner's moving camera and unique camera angles provided viewers with an intimate look at the White House renovation. He won a 1962 Directorial Achievement Award from the Directors Guild of America for his work on the program.

One of Schaffner's best-known works is the production of *The Caine Mutiny Court Martial* (*Ford Star Jubilee*, CBS, November 19, 1955), which was broadcast from the new, state-of-the-art CBS facilities at Television City in Los Angeles. The static action of the play is kept moving by Schaffner's mobile camera and dramatic crane shots. Schaffner was awarded two Emmys for his work on the teleplay: one for Best Director and another for Best Adaptation (with Paul Gregory). The show was originally broadcast in color, but only black-and-white kinescopes survive.

After years as a director of live television dramas, Schaffner directed various episodes of the dramatic series *The Defenders* (CBS, 1961–65), produced by Herbert Brodkin and written by Reginald Rose. The series originated as a two-part episode on *Studio One* in 1957, directed by Robert Mulligan. Schaffner used film editing to create montages of busy New York scenes and unusual camera angles to concentrate on the characters. Schaffner won his fourth Emmy for his work on the series.

Schaffner left television to direct and produce feature films. His film work includes *Planet of the Apes* (1968); *Patton* (1970), for which he received the Academy Award and Directors Guild Award for Best Director; *Nicholas and Alexandra* (1971); *Papillon* (1973); and *The Boys from Brazil* (1978). In 1977, Schaffner's alma mater, Franklin and Marshall College, established the Franklin J. Schaffner Film Library and presented the director with an honorary Doctor of Humane Letters. Schaffner died of cancer in Santa Monica, California, on July 2, 1989.

SUSAN R. GIBBERMAN

*See also **Defenders; "Golden Age" of Television; Person to Person; Playhouse 90; Studio One; Tour of the White House with Mrs. John F. Kennedy***

Franklin J. Schaffner. Born in Tokyo, Japan, May 30, 1920. Graduated from Franklin and Marshall College, Lancaster, Pennsylvania, 1942; studied law at Columbia University. Married Helen Jean Gilchrist, 1948; children: Jenny and Kate. Served in U.S. Navy, 1942–46. Began television career as assistant director, *March of Times* documentary series, 1947–48; television director, CBS, including such programs as *Studio One, Ford Theater,* and *Playhouse 90,* 1949–62; formed Unit Four production company with Worthington Miner, George Roy Hill, and Fielder Cook, 1955; directed *Advise and Consent* on Broadway, 1960; signed three-picture deal with 20th Century-Fox and directed first feature, 1961; TV counselor to President Kennedy, 1961–63; president, Gilchrist Productions, 1962–68; president, Franklin Schaffner Productions, 1969–89. Member: Directors Guild of America (president 1987–89); National Academy of Television Arts and Sciences; Phi Beta Kappa; board member: Center Theater Group of the Music Center, Los Angeles; Academy of Motion Pictures Arts and Sciences, National Council of the Arts, Presidential Task Force on the Arts and Humanities; chairman, executive committee, American Film Institute. Recipient: Sylvania Award, 1953, 1954; Emmy Awards, 1954, 1955, 1962; Best Direction Award, Variety Critics Poll, 1960; Trustee Award (shared with Jacqueline Kennedy) for documentary *A Tour of the White House with Mrs. John F. Kennedy,* American Academy of Television Arts and Sciences, 1962; Academy Award for Best Director, 1970; Directors Guild Award, 1970. Died in Santa Monica, California, July 2, 1989.

Television Series (selected)

1949	*Wesley*
1949–56	*Studio One*
1950–51	*Ford Theater*
1953–61	*Person to Person*
1955–56	*Ford Star Jubilee*
1956–57	*Kaiser Aluminum Hour* (also producer)
1957	*Producer's Showcase*
1957–60	*Playhouse 90*
1959	*Ford Startime*
1961–65	*The Defenders*
1962–64	*DuPont Show of the Week* (also producer)

Television Special

1962	*A Tour of the White House with Mrs. John F. Kennedy*

Films

A Summer World (incomplete), 1961; *The Stripper,* 1963; *The Best Man,* 1964; *The War Lord,* 1965; *The Double Man* (also actor), 1967; *Planet of the Apes,* 1968; *Patton,* 1970; *Nicholas and Alexandra* (also producer), 1971; *Papillon* (also coproducer), 1973; *Islands in the Stream,* 1977; *The Boys from Brazil,* 1978; *Sphinx* (also executive producer), 1981; *Yes, Giorgio,* 1982; *Lionheart,* 1987; *Welcome Home,* 1989.

Radio

World Security Workshop; The March of Time.

Stage

Advise and Consent, 1960.

Publications

"The Best and the Worst of It," *Films and Filming* (October 1964)

"The TV Director: A Dialog," with Fielder Cook, in *The Progress in Television,* edited by William A. Bluem and Roger Manvell, 1967

Worthington Miner: Interviewed by Franklin J. Schaffner, 1985

Further Reading

Applebaum, R., "Interview," *Films and Filming* (February 1979)

Castelli, D. "Interview," *Films Illustrated* (May 1979)

Cook, B., "The War Between Writers and the Directors: Part II: The Directors," *American Film* (June 1979)

Feiden, R., "Interview," *Interview* (March 1972)

"Franklin J. Schaffner," *Kosmorama* (Autumn 1977)

"Franklin J. Schaffner," *Variety* (July 5, 1989)

Geist, Kathe, "Chronicler of Power," *Film Comment* (September/October 1972)

Kim, Erwin, "The Film and Television Career of Franklin J. Schaffner," Ph.D. diss., University of Southern California, 1983

Kim, Erwin, *Franklin J. Schaffner,* Metuchen, New Jersey: Scarecrow Press, 1985

Lightman, Herb, "On Location with *Islands in the Stream,*" *American Cinematographer* (November 1976)

Pratley, Gerald, "Interview," *Cineaste* (Summer 1969)

Sarris, Andrew, "Director of the Month—Franklin Schaffner: The Panoply of Power," *Show* (April 1970)

"TV to Film: A History, a Map, and a Family Tree," *Monthly Film Bulletin* (February 1983)

Wilson, David, "Franklin Schaffner," *Sight and Sound* (Spring 1966)

Schorr, Daniel (1916–)

U.S. Broadcast Journalist

Daniel Schorr is an American television newsman whose aggressive investigative style of reporting made him, at various times in his career, the bane of the KGB, U.S. presidents from Dwight D. Eisenhower to Gerald Ford, Central Intelligence Agency (CIA) chiefs, television executives, and his fellow TV newsmen and women. In 1976, he himself became "the story" when he published a previously suppressed congressional report on CIA assassinations.

Schorr was born and brought up in New York City and did his apprenticeship in print journalism on his high school and college newspapers. During his college years, he also worked on a number of small New York City papers, among them the *New York Journal-American.* Drafted in World War II, he served in Army intelligence. Following the war, he became a stringer for a number of U.S. newspapers and the Dutch news agency ANETA. His radio reports on floods in the Netherlands brought him to the attention of Edward R. Murrow, who hired him for CBS News in 1953.

In 1955, Schorr was assigned to open the first Columbia Broadcasting System (CBS) bureau in Moscow since 1947. His refusal to cooperate with Soviet censors soon earned him their disapproval, and when he returned home for a brief period at the end of 1957, the Soviets refused to permit him to return. For the next few years, Schorr was a roving diplomatic correspondent. In 1959, he provoked the first in a long series of incidents that aroused the ire of various presidents. Schorr's report of the impending resignation of Secretary of State John Foster Dulles so irked President Eisenhower that he denied the report, only to have it confirmed by his press secretary a week later.

During the Kennedy administration, the president asked CBS to transfer Schorr, then the station's correspondent in West Germany, because he felt that

Daniel Schorr.
Courtesy of the Everett Collection/CSU Archives

Schorr's interpretations of U.S. policy were pro-German. During the 1964 election, Schorr's report that the Republican presidential nominee Senator Barry Goldwater had formed an alliance with certain right-wing German politicians and was thinking of spending some time at Adolf Hitler's famous Berchtesgaden retreat caused a furor, and Schorr was ordered to make a "clarification."

In 1966, Schorr returned to the United States without a formal assignment. He created his own beat, however, by investigating the promise and reality of the "Great Society" for the *CBS Evening News.* In this role, he turned in excellent reports on poverty, education, pollution, and health care. His interest in health care led to a provocative 1970 contribution to the documentary series, *CBS Reports.* That same year, the program "Don't Get Sick in America" appeared as a book from Aurora Publishers.

Schorr's muckraking reporting during the Nixon administration earned him a prominent place on Nixon's so-called enemies list. In addition, Schorr's subsequent reporting on the Watergate scandal garnered him Emmys for Outstanding Achievement within a Regularly Scheduled News Program in 1972, 1973, and 1974.

Following Nixon's resignation, Schorr was assigned to cover stories involving possible criminal CIA activities at home and abroad. He soon achieved a scoop based on a tip he received about an admission by President Ford regarding CIA assassination attempts. The comment had come in an off-the-record conversation with the editors of the *New York Times.* Schorr's report forced the Rockefeller Commission investigating the CIA to broaden its inquiry and prompted an exclamation from former CIA chief Richard Helms, referring to him as "Killer Schorr."

Commenting on his journalistic method, more akin to print journalism than conventional television journalism, Schorr has said,

> My typical way of operating is not to stick a camera and a microphone in somebody's face and let him say whatever self-serving thing he wants to say, but to spend a certain amount of time getting the basic information, as though I was going to write a newspaper story.... [I] may end up putting a mike in somebody's face, but it is usually for the final and hopefully embarrassing question.

Soon after making these remarks, Schorr found himself at the center of a huge controversy involving both journalistic ethics and constitutional issues. Schorr came into possession of the Pike Congressional Committee's report on illegal CIA and Federal Bureau of Investigation activities. Congress, however, had voted not to make the report public. In hopes of being able to publish the report, Schorr contacted Clay Felker of the *Village Voice,* who agreed to pay him for it and to publish it. To Schorr's surprise, instead of supporting him, many of his colleagues and editorialists around the country excoriated him for selling the document. Making matters worse was Schorr's initial reaction, which was to shift suspicion from himself as the person who leaked the documents to his CBS colleague Lesley Stahl.

Schorr managed to turn opinion around when, after being subpoenaed to appear before a House Ethics Committee, he eloquently defended himself on the grounds that he would not reveal a source. While this put off the congressional bloodhounds, it certainly did not satisfy some of the wolves at CBS, among whom was Chairman William S. Paley, who wanted Schorr fired. Schorr and CBS news executives resisted until the story of the internal dissension over Schorr's conduct broke during an interview he did with Mike Wallace on *60 Minutes.* As a result, Schorr resigned from CBS News in September 1976. A year later, he wrote about it in his autobiographical account *Clearing the Air.*

Subsequently, Schorr toured on the lecture circuit, taught journalism courses, and wrote a syndicated newspaper column. In 1979, hoping to give his new Cable News Network (CNN) instant journalistic credibility, Ted Turner hired Schorr as a commentator.

However, in 1985, CNN refused to renew his contract. Schorr commented at the time that he had been "forced out" because "they wanted to be rid of what they considered a loose cannon." Since 1985, Schorr has been a senior news analyst for National Public Radio. His reporting and commentary are heard on *All Things Considered* and *Weekend Edition*. In 2001, he wrote a second volume of autobiography, *Staying Tuned: A Life in Journalism*.

Schorr represents the traditions of investigative print journalism transferred to the world of TV reporting. His work, though it has sometimes overstepped boundaries, is in vivid contrast to the often image-conscious attitudes of contemporary TV news.

ALBERT AUSTER

See also **Cable News Network; Columbia Broadcasting System; News, Network**

Daniel Schorr. Born in New York City, August 31, 1916. Educated at the College of the City of New York, B.S. 1939. Married: Lisbeth Bamberger, 1967; children: Jonathan and Lisa. Served in U.S. Army, stationed at Camp Polk, Louisiana, and at Fort Sam Houston, Texas, 1943–45. Worked as a stringer for the Bronx *Home News,* the *Jewish Daily Bulletin,* and several metropolitan dailies, 1930s; assistant editor, Jewish Telegraphic Agency, 1939; worked for the *New York Journal-American,* 1940; New York news editor, ANETA (Dutch news agency), 1941–43, 1945–48; freelance journalist, 1948–53; Washington correspondent and special assignments, CBS News, Latin America and Europe, 1953–55; reopened CBS Moscow Bureau, 1955; roving assignments, United States and Europe, 1958–60; chief, CBS News Bureau, Germany, Central Europe, 1960–66; CBS News Washington correspondent, 1966–76; Regents professor, University of California at Berkeley, 1977; columnist, *Des Moines Register-Tribune* Syndicate, 1977–80; senior Washington correspondent, CNN, 1979–85; senior analyst, National Public Radio, since 1985. Member: American Federation of Radio-TV Artists; New York City Council on Foreign Relations. Recipient: Emmy Awards, 1972–74; Peabody Award for Lifetime of Uncompromising Reporting of Highest Integrity, 1992; inducted into the Society of Professional Journalists Hall of Fame, 1991.

Television
Various CBS News programs, 1953–76 (correspondent)
CNN news programs, 1979–85 (senior Washington correspondent)

Radio
National Public Radio shows, 1985– .

Publications

Don't Get Sick in America!, 1970
Clearing the Air, 1977
"Introduction," *Taking the Stand: The Testimony of Lieutenant Colonel Oliver L. North,* 1987
Within Our Reach: Breaking the Cycle of Disadvantage, with Lisbeth B. Schorr, 1988
Forgive Us Our Press Passes: Selected Works by Daniel Schorr, 1972–1998, 1998
Staying Tuned: A Life in Journalism, 2001

Further Reading

Boyer, Peter J., *Who Killed CBS? The Undoing of America's Number One News Network,* New York: Random House, 1988
Carter, Bill, "Daniel Schorr Wins Top DuPont-Columbia Journalism Award," *New York Times* (January 26, 1996)
Smith, Sally Bedell, *In All His Glory: William S. Paley, the Legendary Tycoon and His Brilliant Circle,* New York: Simon and Schuster, 1990

Schwartz, Sherwood (1916–)

U.S. Producer, Writer

Sherwood Schwartz began his professional writing career in radio in 1939, working for *The Pepsodent Show Starring Bob Hope,* where his older brother Al was also a writer. During World War II, Schwartz served with the Armed Forces Radio Service, writing for a variety of programs. Following the war, he returned to California and radio, writing for *The Adventures of Ozzie and Harriet* and *The Beulah Show.* During the 1950s, when many radio performers and programs migrated to television, Schwartz joined the move, working on *I Married Joan* and *The Red Skelton Show*. His work on the latter was recognized annually by the Writer's Guild from 1955 to 1960 and included the only writing award ever given for pantomime, for "Freddie's Thanksgiving," in which not a single word was spoken. The guild again recognized his work in 1963–64 for the *Lucille Ball Comedy Hour*. Schwartz was also honored by the National Academy of Television Arts and Sciences. Nominated for Emmy Awards in 1961 and 1962 for Outstanding Writing Achievement in Comedy, he received the award in 1961.

In the early 1960s, in addition to writing for *Skelton*, Schwartz also worked on the first season of *My Favorite Martian*. It was during this time that he developed and pitched the concept for *Gilligan's Island,* his first foray as a series creator/producer. The Columbia Broadcasting System (CBS) was interested, and the series became a joint production of CBS, United Artists, and Phil Silvers's Gladasya Productions. The pilot was shot in Hawaii in November 1963 (and interrupted by the assassination of President Kennedy), but three different versions were rejected by CBS. Having disavowed himself from the original cut of the pilot, Schwartz persisted and received permission (but no funding) from United Artists to use the footage and re-cut the pilot yet a fourth time. This was the only version to include the opening theme, for which Schwartz wrote the lyrics. In 60 seconds, the song provided exposition—which Schwartz had argued all along was crucial to the program—to explain why the castaways remained on the island week after week. This version of the pilot was delivered to CBS the Friday before the network was to announce its fall 1964 schedule; CBS executives were sufficiently impressed with Schwartz's version to run audience tests over the weekend, and as a result of those tests, *Gilligan's Island* was added to the CBS schedule. In each of the next three seasons the program aired in a different time period and on a different night, but it always won its time slot and was often in the top ten of the national Nielsen ratings. Although renewed for a fourth season, *Gilligan's Island* was later dropped to make room for *Gunsmoke*, which had originally been cut from CBS's 1967–68 schedule. Since the end of its prime-time network run, *Gilligan's Island* has been one of the most successful programs in the history of television syndication. Constantly in reruns, it was first a staple on local broadcast stations as after-school fare for children and later on cable channels. The show spawned two animated series (*The New Adventures of Gilligan,* American Broadcasting Company [ABC], 1974–77 and *Gilligan's Planet*, ABC, 1982–83) and three television movies.

Schwartz's second major series contribution to television came two years after *Gilligan*. With an idea springing in part from an article he read in 1966, indicating that more than 20 percent of all marriages included children from a previous marriage, he created *The Brady Bunch*. Once again Schwartz wrote the theme song lyrics, this time for the story of "a lovely lady" and "a man named Brady" and their two sets of kids. He pitched the program to all three networks, and it was rejected. Following the box office success of the Henry Fonda/Lucille Ball film *Yours, Mine and Ours* in 1968, however, (a film developed after Schwartz created his TV concept), the show became part of ABC's 1969 fall schedule. The program was not a huge ratings success, generally falling in the 20 to 30 range in the national Nielsen ratings, but it did attract the young viewers ABC was seeking.

While Schwartz's programs were dismissed as typical lowbrow television, recent critical views have cast his work in a more favorable light. At a time when the family was the basis for the typical TV sitcom, *Gilligan's Island* offered a different sort of family (Schwartz called it a "social microcosm" in his pitch to CBS) years before the celebrated ensemble/workplace sitcoms of the 1970s, such as *M*A*S*H* and *The Mary Tyler Moore Show*. Schwartz also pioneered the sitcom reunion movie concept, used to great success with both *Gilligan's Island* (three movies) and *The Brady Bunch*. The characters/series concept of the latter proved to be very resilient, extended to a range of follow-ups on all four major networks, including a variety series (*The Brady Bunch Hour,* ABC, 1977), a "life after" series (*The Brady Brides*), a holiday special (*A Very Brady Christmas*), an hour-long dramatic series (*The Bradys*), and a made-for-TV movie (*The Brady Bunch in the White House*) as well as a stage adaptation (*The Real Live Brady Bunch,* 1990–94), and feature films (*The Brady Bunch Movie* and *A Very Brady Sequel*). Schwartz's *Big John, Little John* series was also notable for bringing the nonanimated/filmed sitcom to Saturday morning children's television well before *Pee-Wee's Playhouse* and *Saved by the Bell*.

J.C. TURNER

See also **Brady Bunch, The; Red Skelton Show, The**

Sherwood Schwartz. Born in Passaic, New Jersey, November 14, 1916. Married sculptor Mildred Seidman, 1941. Children: Don (M.D.), Lloyd (writer, producer, frequent collaborator), Ross (entertainment attorney), Hope Juber (actress, producer, writer). Brothers: Al Schwartz (writer) and Elroy Schwartz (writer, producer). Bachelor's degree (premed), New York University; master's degree (biological sciences), University of Southern California. Writer in Television from 1952; producer in television from 1963. Emmy Award, Outstanding Writing Achievement in Comedy, *The Red Skelton Show,* 1961; nominated for the same program again in 1962; Writer's Guild Awards, 1955–60, 1963–64; Lifetime Achievement Award from DeWitt Clinton High School (New York); R.P. Vision Award and the Spotlight Award from the Beverly Hills Theatre Guild. Member: Writers Guild of America, Dramatists Guild of the American Society of Composers, Authors and Publishers (ASCAP).

Television Series
1952–55	*I Married Joan* (writer)
1951–70	*The Red Skelton Show* (writer)
1963–66	*My Favorite Martian* (writer)
1964–67	*Gilligan's Island* (creator, executive producer, writer, theme lyrics)
1966–67	*It's About Time* (executive producer, writer, theme lyrics)
1969–74	*The Brady Bunch* (executive producer, writer, theme lyrics)
1972–74	*The Brady Kids,* animated (executive producer)
1973–74	*Dusty's Trail,* syndicated (executive producer, writer, theme lyrics)
1976–77	*Big John, Little John* (executive producer, writer, theme song)
1981	*Harper Valley PTA/Harper Valley* (executive producer, writer)
1981	*The Brady Girls Get Married/The Brady Brides* (executive producer, writer)
1986–87	*Together We Stand/Nothing Is Easy* (executive producer, writer)
1990	*The Bradys* (executive producer, writer)

Pilots and Television Specials
1959	*The Red Skelton Chevy Special* (writer)
1963	*Lucille Ball Comedy Hour* (writer)
1974	*Kelly's Kids* (executive producer, writer)

1983	*The Invisible Woman* (executive producer, writer, theme)
1982	*Scamps* (executive producer, writer)

Made-for-Television Movies
1978	*Rescue from Gilligan's Island* (executive producer, writer)
1979	*The Castaways on Gilligan's Island* (executive producer, writer)
1981	*The Harlem Globetrotters on Gilligan's Island* (writer)
1988	*A Very Brady Christmas* (executive producer, writer)
2002	*The Brady Bunch in the White House* (executive consultant)

Films
The Brady Bunch Movie, 1995 (producer); *A Very Brady Sequel,* 1996 (producer)

Stage
Mr. & Mrs., 1962 (producer); *Gilligan's Island: The Musical,* 1992–94 (producer, writer); *Rockers,* 1993 (producer); *The Trial of Othello,* 2000 (producer)

Publications
Inside Gilligan's Island, 1988, 1994

Further Reading
Marc, David, and Thompson, Robert J., "Sherwood Schwartz," in *Prime Time, Prime Movers: From I Love Lucy to L.A. Law—America's Greatest TV Shows and the People Who Created Them,* Boston: Little, Brown, 1992
Moran, Elizabeth, *Bradymania!,* Holbrook, Massachusetts: Adams Publishing, 1995
Schwartz, Sherwood, *Inside Gilligan's Island,* New York: St. Martin's Press, 1994

Science Fiction Programs

Although not one of television's predominant genres in terms of overall programming hours, science fiction nonetheless spans the history of the medium, beginning in the late 1940s as low-budget programs aimed primarily at juvenile audiences and developing, by the turn of the 21st century, into a genre particularly important to syndication and cable markets. For many years, conventional industry wisdom considered science fiction to be a genre ill suited to television. Aside from attracting a very limited demographic group for advertisers, science fiction presented a problematic genre in that its futuristic worlds and speculative story-

Captain Midnight, Richard Webb (1954–56), Sid Melton; series ran 1954–58.
Courtesy of the Everett Collection

lines often challenged both the budgets and the narrative constraints of the medium, limitations especially true in television's first decades. Over the years, however, producers were to discover that science fiction could attract an older and more desirable audience and that such audiences, although often still limited, were in many cases incredibly devoted to their favorite programs. As a consequence, the 1980s and 1990s saw a tremendous increase in science fiction programming in the United States, especially in markets outside the traditional three broadcast networks (American Broadcasting Company [ABC], Columbia Broadcasting System [CBS], and National Broadcasting Company [NBC]).

As a children's genre in the late 1940s and early 1950s, science fiction programming most often followed a serial format, appearing in the afternoon on Saturdays or at the beginning of prime time during the weeknight schedule. At times playing in several installments per week, these early examples of the genre featured the adventures of male protagonists working to maintain law and order in outer space. These early "space westerns" included *Buck Rogers* (ABC, 1950–51), *Captain Video and His Video Rangers* (Dumont, 1949–54), *Flash Gordon* (syndicated, 1953),

Space Patrol (ABC, 1951–52), and *Tom Corbett, Space Cadet* (CBS/ABC/NBC, 1950–52). Each series pitted its dynamic hero against a variety of intergalactic menaces, be they malevolent alien conquerors, evil mad scientists, or mysterious forces of the universe. All these programs were produced on shoestring budgets, but this did not stop each series from equipping its hero with a fantastic array of futuristic gadgetry, including radio helmets, ray guns, and Captain Video's famous "decoder ring." Viewers at home could follow along with their heroes on the quest for justice by ordering plastic replicas of these gadgets through popular premium campaigns. Of these first examples of televised science fiction, *Captain Video* was particularly popular, airing Monday through Friday in half-hour (and, later, 15-minute) installments. One of the first "hits" of television, the program served for many years as a financial lynchpin for the struggling Dumont network and left the air only when the network itself collapsed in 1954.

As was typical of much early programming for children, *Captain Video* concluded each episode with its hero delivering a lecture on moral values, good citizenship, or other uplifting qualities for his young audience to emulate. Such gestures, however, did not spare Captain Video and his space brethren from becoming the focus of the first of many major public controversies over children's television. In a theme that would become familiar over the history of the medium, critics attacked these shows for their "addictive" nature, their perceived excesses of violence, and their ability to "overexcite" a childish imagination. In this respect, early science fiction on television became caught up in a larger anxiety over children's culture in the 1950s, a debate that culminated with the 1954 publication of Dr. Fredric Wertham's *Seduction of the Innocent,* an attack on the comic book industry that eventually led to a series of congressional hearings on the imagined links between popular culture and juvenile delinquency.

In early television, science fiction programming aimed at older audiences was rarer, confined almost entirely to dramatic anthology series such as *Lights Out* (NBC, 1949–52), *Out There* (CBS, 1951–52), and *Tales of Tomorrow* (ABC, 1951–53). As with other dramatic anthologies of the era, these programs depended heavily on adaptations of preexisting stories, borrowing from the work of such noted science fiction writers as Jules Verne, H.G. Wells, and Ray Bradbury. *Tales of Tomorrow* even attempted a half-hour adaptation of Mary Shelly's *Frankenstein.* When not producing adaptations, these anthologies did provide space for original and at times innovative teleplays. Interestingly, however, as science fiction became an increasingly important genre in Hollywood during the mid- to late 1950s, especially in capturing the burgeoning teenage market, its presence on American television declined sharply. One exception was *Science Fiction Theater* (1955–57), a syndicated series that presented speculative stories based on contemporary topics of scientific research.

Science fiction's eventual return to network airwaves coincided with the rising domestic tensions and Cold War anxieties associated with the rhetoric of the Kennedy administration's "New Frontier." As a response to the Soviet launch of *Sputnik,* for example, CBS's *Men into Space* (1959–60) participated in the larger cultural project of explicitly promoting interest in the emerging "space race" while also celebrating American technology and heroism that had been threatened by the Soviets' success. Other series were more complex in their response to the social and technological conflicts of the New Frontier era. In particular, *The Twilight Zone* (CBS, 1959–64) and *The Outer Limits* (ABC, 1963–65), programs that would become two of the genre's most celebrated series, frequently engaged in critical commentary on the three pillars of New Frontier ideology: space, suburbia, and the superpowers.

Hosted and for the most part scripted by Rod Serling, a highly acclaimed writer of live television drama in the 1950s, *The Twilight Zone* was an anthology series that, while not exclusively based in science fiction, frequently turned to the genre to frame allegorical tales of the human condition and the national character of the United States. Some of the most memorable episodes of the series used science fiction to defamiliarize and question the conformist values of postwar suburbia as well as the rising paranoia of Cold War confrontation. Of these, "The Monsters Are Due on Maple Street" was perhaps most emblematic of these critiques. In this episode, a "typical" American neighborhood is racked with suspicion and fear when a delusion spreads that the community has been invaded by aliens. Neighbor turns against neighbor to create panic until at the end, in a "twist" ending that would become a trademark of the series, the viewer discovers that invading aliens *have* actually arrived on Earth. Their plan is to plant such rumors in every American town in order to tear these communities apart, thus laying the groundwork for a full-scale alien conquest.

More firmly grounded in science fiction was *The Outer Limits,* an hour-long anthology series known primarily for its menagerie of gruesome monsters. Much more sinister in tone than Serling's *Twilight Zone, The Outer Limits* also engaged in allegories about space, science, and American society. However, in an era marked by the almost uniform celebration of

American science and technology, this series stood out for its particularly bleak vision of technocracy and the future, using an anthology format to present a variety of dystopic parables and narratives of annihilation. Of the individual episodes, perhaps most celebrated was Harlan Ellison's award-winning time-travel story "Demon with a Glass Hand," an episode that remains one of the most narratively sophisticated and willfully obtuse hours of television ever produced.

While *The Twilight Zone* and *The Outer Limits* remain the most memorable examples of the genre in this era, science fiction television of the mid-1960s was dominated, in terms of total programming hours, by the work of producer Irwin Allen. Allen's series, aimed primarily at juvenile audiences on ABC, included *Voyage to the Bottom of the Sea* (ABC, 1964–68), *Lost in Space* (CBS, 1965–68), *Time Tunnel* (ABC, 1966–67), and *Land of the Giants* (ABC, 1968–70). Each series used a science fiction premise to motivate familiar action-adventure stories. Of these, *Lost in Space* has been the most enduring in both syndication and national memory. Centering on young Will Robinson and his friend the Robot, the series adapted the Swiss Family Robinson story to outer space, chronicling a wandering family's adventures as they tried to return to Earth.

Many other television series of the 1960s, while not explicitly science fiction, nevertheless incorporated elements of space and futuristic technology into their story worlds. Following the success of *The Flintstones,* a prime-time animated series about a prehistoric family, ABC premiered *The Jetsons* (1962–63), a cartoon about a futuristic family of the next century. The sitcom *My Favorite Martian* (CBS, 1963–66), meanwhile, paired an Earthling newspaper reporter with a Martian visitor, while *I Dream of Jeannie* (NBC, 1965–70) matched a NASA astronaut with a beautiful genie. The camp hit *Batman* (ABC, 1966–68) routinely featured all manner of innovative "bat" technologies that allowed its hero to outwit Gotham City's criminals. Also prominent in this era was a cycle of spy and espionage series inspired by the success of the James Bond films, each incorporating a variety of secret advanced technologies. Of this cycle, the British-produced series *The Prisoner* (CBS, 1968–69) was the most firmly based in science fiction, telling the Orwellian story of a former secret agent stripped of his identity and trapped on an island community run as a futuristic police state.

By far the best-known and widely viewed science fiction series of the 1960s (and probably in all of television) was *Star Trek* (NBC, 1966–69), a series described by its creator, Gene Roddenberry, as "*Wagon Train* in space." Although set in the 23rd century, the world of *Star Trek* was firmly grounded in the concerns of 1960s America. Intermixing action-adventure with social commentary, the series addressed such issues as racism, war, sexism, and even the era's flourishing hippie movement. A moderately successful series during its three-year network run, *Star Trek* would become through syndication perhaps the most actively celebrated program in television history, inspiring a whole subculture of fans (known variously as "trekkies" or "trekkers"), whose devotion to the series led to fan conventions, book series, and eventually a commercial return of the *Star Trek* universe in the 1980s, 1990s, and 2000s through motion pictures and television spin-offs.

Like *Star Trek,* the British Broadcasting Corporation (BBC) serial *Doctor Who* also attracted a tremendous fan following. In production from 1963 to 1989, *Doctor Who* stands as the longest-running continuous science fiction series in all of television. A time-travel adventure story aimed primarily at children, the series proved popular enough in the United Kingdom to inspire two motion pictures pitting the Doctor against his most famous nemesis—the Daleks: *Doctor Who and the Daleks* (1965) and *Daleks: Invasion Earth 2150 AD* (1966). The series was later imported to the United States, where it aired primarily on Public Broadcasting Service (PBS) affiliates and quickly became an international cult favorite.

While most television science fiction in the 1950s and 1960s had followed the adventures of Earthlings in outer space, increasing popular interest in unidentified flying objects (UFOs) led to the production, in the late 1960s and into the 1970s, of a handful of programs based on the premise of secretive and potentially hostile aliens visiting Earth. *The Invaders* (ABC, 1967–68) chronicled one man's struggle to expose an alien invasion plot, while *UFO* (syndicated, 1972) told of a secret organization dedicated to repelling an imminent UFO attack. Veteran producer Jack Webb debuted *Project UFO* (NBC) in 1978, which investigated, in Webb's characteristically terse style, unexplained UFO cases taken from the files of the U.S. Air Force. Such series fed a growing interest in the early 1970s with all manner of paranormal and extraterrestrial phenomena, ranging from Erich von Daniken's incredibly popular speculations on ancient alien contact in *Chariots of the Gods* to accounts of the mysterious forces in the "Bermuda Triangle." Such topics from the fringes of science were the focus of the syndicated documentary series *In Search Of* (syndicated, 1976), hosted by *Star Trek*'s Leonard Nimoy.

For the most part, however, science fiction once again went into decline during the 1970s as examples

of the genre became more sporadic and short lived, many series running only a season or less. Series such as *Planet of the Apes* (CBS, 1974) and *Logan's Run* (CBS, 1977–78) attempted to adapt popular motion pictures to prime-time television but with little success. A much more prominent and expensive failure was the British series *Space: 1999* (syndicated, 1975). Starring Martin Landau and Barbara Bain, the program followed a group of lunar colonists who are sent hurtling through space when a tremendous explosion drives the moon out of its orbit. The series was promoted in syndication as the most expensive program of its kind ever produced, but despite such publicity, the series went out of production after only 48 episodes.

Two of the more successful science fiction series of the era were *The Six Million Dollar Man* (ABC, 1975–78) and its spin-off *The Bionic Woman* (ABC/NBC, 1976–78). The "six million dollar man" was Lt. Steve Austin, a test pilot who was severely injured in a crash and then reconstructed with cybernetic limbs and powers that made him an almost superhuman "bionic man." Austin's girlfriend, also severely injured (in a separate incident) and rebuilt (by the same doctors), debuted her own show the following season (complete with a "bionic" dog). The moderate success of these two series sparked a cycle of programs targeted at children featuring superheroes with superpowers of one kind or another, including *The Invisible Man* (NBC, 1975–76), *Gemini Man* (NBC, 1976), *Man from Atlantis* (NBC, 1977–78), *Wonder Woman* (ABC/CBS, 1976–79), and *The Incredible Hulk* (CBS, 1978–82).

Also moderately successful in the late 1970s were a pair of series designed to capitalize on the extraordinary popularity of George Lucas's 1977 blockbuster film *Star Wars*. Both *Battlestar Galactica* (ABC, 1978–80), starring *Bonanza*'s patriarch Lorne Greene, and *Buck Rogers in the 25th Century* (NBC, 1979–81) spent large amounts of money on the most complex special effects yet seen on television, all in an attempt to re-create the dazzling hardware, fast-paced space battles, and realistic aliens of Lucas's film. Less successful in riding *Star Wars*' coattails was the parodic sitcom *Quark* (NBC, 1978), the story of a garbage scow in outer space.

In England, the 1970s saw the debut of another BBC-produced series that would go on to acquire an international audience. *Blake's Seven* (BBC, 1978–81) was created by Terry Nation, the same man who introduced the Daleks to the world of *Doctor Who* in the early 1960s. Distinguished by a much darker tone than most television science fiction, *Blake's Seven* followed the adventures of a band of rebels in space struggling to overthrow an oppressive regime.

Alien invasion was once again the theme on American television in 1983, when NBC programmed a high-profile miniseries that pitted Earth against a race of lizard-like creatures who, though friendly at first, were actually intent on using Earth's population for food. *V* (NBC, 1984–85) proved popular enough to return in a sequel miniseries the following year, which in turn led to its debut as a weekly series in the 1984–85 season. More provocative was ABC's short-lived *Max Headroom* (1987), television's only attempt at a subgenre of science fiction prominent in the 1980s known as "cyberpunk." "Max," who through commercials and a talk show became a pop cult phenomenon in his own right, was the computerized consciousness of TV reporter Edison Carter. Evoking the same "tech noir" landscape and thematic concerns of such cinematic contemporaries as *Blade Runner, Robocop,* and *The Running Man,* Max and Edison worked together to expose corporate corruption and injustice in the nation's dark, cybernetic, and oppressively urbanized future.

Less weighty than Max but certainly more successful in their network runs were two series that, while not necessarily true "science fiction," utilized fantastic premises and attracted devoted cult audiences. *Beauty and the Beast* (CBS, 1987–90) was a romantic fantasy about a woman in love with a lion-like creature who lived in a secret subterranean community beneath New York City, while *Quantum Leap* (NBC, 1989–93) followed Dr. Sam Beckett as he "leapt" in time from body to body, occupying different consciousnesses in different historical periods. The series was less concerned with the "science" of time travel, however, than with the moral lessons to be learned or taught by seeing the world through another person's eyes.

By far the most pivotal series in rekindling science fiction as a viable television genre was *Star Trek: The Next Generation* (syndicated, 1987–94), produced by Paramount and supervised by the creator of the original *Star Trek,* Gene Roddenberry. Already benefiting from the tremendous built-in audience of *Star Trek* fans eager for a spin-off of the old series, Paramount was able to bypass the networks and take the show directly into first-run syndication, where it quickly became the highest-rated syndicated show ever. In many ways, *Next Generation* had more in common with other dramatic series of the 1980s and 1990s than it did with the original series. In this new incarnation, *Star Trek* became an ensemble drama structured much like *Hill St. Blues* or *St. Elsewhere,* featuring an expanded cast involved in both episodic and serial adventures. Broadcast in conjunction with a series of cinematic releases featuring the original *Star Trek* characters, *Next Generation* helped solidify *Star Trek* as a major economic and cultural institution in the 1980s and 1990s.

After a seven-year run, Paramount retired the series in 1994 to convert the *Next Generation* universe into a cinematic property, but not before the studio debuted a second spin-off, *Star Trek: Deep Space Nine* (syndicated, 1993–99), which proved to be a more claustrophobic and less popular reading of the *Star Trek* universe. A third spin-off, *Star Trek: Voyager* (United Paramount Network [UPN], 1995–2001), served as the anchor in Paramount's bid to create its own television network in 1995.

The success of the *Star Trek* series in first-run syndication reflected the changing marketplace of television in the 1980s and 1990s. As the three major networks continued to lose their audience base to the competition of independents, cable, and new networks such as FOX, The WB, and UPN, the entire industry sought out new niche markets to target in order to maintain their audiences. The *Star Trek* franchise's ability to deliver quality demographics and dedicated viewership inspired a number of producers to move into science fiction during this period. These series ranged from the literate serial drama *Babylon 5* (syndicated, 1994–98) to the bizarre police burlesque of *Space Precinct* (syndicated, 1994). Also successful in syndication were "fantasy" series such as *Highlander* (syndicated, 1992–97) and *Hercules: The Legendary Journeys* (syndicated, 1995–99).

For the most part, the three major networks (ABC, CBS, and NBC) stayed away from science fiction in the 1990s, the exceptions being NBC's *Earth 2* (1994–95) and *Seaquest DSV* (1993), the latter produced by Steven Spielberg's Amblin Entertainment. By far the most active broadcaster in developing science fiction in the 1990s was the FOX network, which used the genre to target even more precisely its characteristically younger demographics. FOX productions included *Alien Nation* (1989–91), *M.A.N.T.I.S.* (1994–95), *Sliders* (1995), *VR.5* (1995), and *Space: Above and Beyond* (1995–96). FOX's most successful foray into science fiction, however, was *The X-Files* (1993–2002). A surprise hit for the network, *The X-Files* combined horror, suspense, and intrigue in stories about two FBI agents assigned to unsolved cases involving seemingly paranormal phenomena. Although the series originally centered on a single "spook" of the week for each episode, it eventually developed a compelling serial narrative line concerning a massive government conspiracy to cover up evidence of extraterrestrial contact. Like so many other science fiction programs, the series quickly developed a large and organized fan community. After the departure in May 2001 of series colead David Duchovny and a failed attempted at a spin-off in *The Lone Gunmen* (FOX, 2001), *The X-Files* faltered into cancellation at the end of the 2001–02 season. FOX, however, remains the only U.S. network to include science fiction as a significant component in its marketing strategy. Working with *The Simpsons* creator Matt Groening, the network has enjoyed success with the animated sci-fi comedy *Futurama.* FOX also tapped the futuristic talents of director James Cameron for the postapocalyptic action series *Dark Angel* (2000–02). The only other network with a continuing interest in science fiction has been UPN, courting younger viewers with the teen-centered *Roswell* (which debuted on The WB in 1999 before transferring to UPN for its third and final season, 2001–02) and a revamped version of the *Star Trek* franchise, *Enterprise* (2001–).

At the end of the 20th century, television science fiction had amassed a sizable enough program history and a large enough viewing audience to support a new cable network. A product of the entertainment industry's overall move toward niche marketing, The Sci-Fi channel debuted in 1992. Although the network began with only a library of old movies and television reruns, it soon became a significant source of production for both cable series and made-for-cable movies. Balancing its schedule with original productions, "classics" such as *Star Trek* and *The Twilight Zone,* and series in the related genres of horror and the supernatural, the Sci-Fi channel has quite successfully transformed its ratings and demographics to become a major network in basic cable.

JEFFREY SCONCE

See also **Captain Video and His Video Rangers; Dark Shadows; Doctor Who; Hitch-Hiker's Guide to the Galaxy, The; Max Headroom; Nation, Terry; Pertwee, John;** *Prisoner, The;* **Roddenberry, Gene; Serling, Rod;** *Star Trek;* **Troughton, Patrick;** *Twilight Zone, The*

Further Reading

Bellafante, Ginia, "Out of This World," *Time* (April 3, 1995)

Coe, Steve, "Networks Take a Walk on Weird Side: Programmers Tap into Taste for Fantasy, Sci-Fi, and the Bizarre," *Broadcasting & Cable* (October 30, 1995)

Fulton, Roger, *The Encyclopedia of TV Science-Fiction,* London: Boxtree, 1995

Jenkins, Henry, *Textual Poachers: Television Fans and Participatory Culture,* New York: Routledge, 1992

Lentz, Harris M., *Science Fiction, Horror, and Fantasy Film and Television Credits,* Jefferson, North Carolina: McFarland, 1994

Littleton, Cynthia, "First-Run Faces Unreality: Fantasy, Sci-Fi and the Unexplained Have Proved Fertile Field for Syndication," *Broadcasting & Cable* (October 30, 1995)

Menagh, Melanie, and Stephen Mills, "A Channel for Science Fiction," *Omni* (October 1992)

Okuda, Denise, Debbie Mirek, and Doug Drexler, *The Star Trek Encyclopedia,* New York: Pocket Books, 1994

Peel, John, *Island in the Sky: The Lost in Space Files,* San Bernardino, California: Borgo, 1986

Phillips, Mark, and Frank Garcia, *Science Fiction Television Series: Episode Guides, Histories, and Casts and Credits for 62 Prime Time Shows, 1959 Through 1989,* Jefferson, North Carolina: McFarland, 1996

Rigelsford, Adrian, and Terry Nation, *The Making of Terry Nation's Blake's 7,* London: Boxtree, 1995

Schow, David, *The Outer Limits: The Official Companion,* New York: Ace Science Fiction Books, 1986

Sconce, Jeffrey, "The *Outer Limits* of Oblivion," in *The Revolution Wasn't Televised: Sixties Television and Social Conflict,* edited by Lynn Spigel and Michael Curtin, New York: Routledge, 1995

Spigel, Lynn, "From Domestic Space to Outer Space: The 1960s Fantastic Family Sit-Com," in *Close Encounters: Film Feminism, and Science Fiction,* edited by Constance Penley et al., Minneapolis: University of Minnesota Press, 1991

Tulloch, John, and Henry Jenkins, *Science Fiction Audiences: Watching Dr. Who and Star Trek,* London: Routledge, 1995

Van Hise, James, *Sci Fi TV: From The Twilight Zone to Deep Space Nine,* New York: Harper, 1993

Van Hise, James, *New Sci Fi TV from The Next Generation to Babylon 5,* Las Vegas, Nevada: Pioneer, 1994

White, Matthew, and Jaffer Ali, *The Official Prisoner Companion,* London: Sidgwick and Jackson, 1988

Wright, Gene, *The Science Fiction Image: The Illustrated Encyclopedia of Science Fiction in Film, Television, Radio, and the Theater,* New York: Facts on File, 1983

Zicree, Marc Scott, *The Twilight Zone Companion,* New York: Bantam, 1982

Science Programs

When most people consider the history and development of scientific television programming in the United States, they are quick to mention the popular 1950s show *Watch Mr. Wizard,* one of the first attempts to bring science to the general public through the medium of television. Forty-three years later, in 1994, Don Herbert, creator of the *Mr. Wizard* series, launched a new show titled *Teacher to Teacher with Mr. Wizard.* The enduring image of Herbert as "Mr. Wizard" is a testament to the presence of science-oriented programming throughout the history of television.

Early growth in the area of scientific television programming closely paralleled increasing public awareness of science and technology in everyday life. In an era defined by both the Cold War and the growth of mass media, issues of science and public policy played out on the public airwaves. Eventually, television was seen as the perfect vehicle through which to promote widespread scientific knowledge among the public. Over the years, scientific television programming evolved to serve three primary goals—to entertain, to educate, and, ultimately, to bridge the gap between the general public and the scientific community. In order to achieve such goals, however, sustainable funding had to be secured.

In the United States, scientific television was a key element in early initiatives of the National Science Foundation (NSF) to promote a public understanding of science. Through station by station syndication, the NSF funded several short programs that aired on commercial television. In the 1970s, *Closeups,* produced by Herbert, introduced children to scientific concepts through everyday objects. During this same period, Herbert also developed *How About,* a syndicated scientific news report aimed at adults. More recently, syndication has facilitated the entry of independently funded and produced scientific programs into commercial formats.

In the realm of public television, the NSF invested in the series *Nova.* However, the controversial subject matter engaged in early *Nova* programs tested the NSF's funding procedures. In an attempt to balance the interests of a free press and those of the scientific community, the NSF established a grant-approval system mediated by outside advisers, most often experts in the field addressed in the program. With "balanced, objective, and accurate" programming in mind, the outside adviser has become a standard feature of most scientific television production regardless of funding sources.

The success of *Nova* sparked an ongoing relationship between the NSF and public broadcasting, one that positioned public television at the forefront of scientific programming. This coalition was responsible for the development of several science based specials, such as *The Mind,* and a myriad of children's shows, including *3-2-1 Contact* and *Square One TV.* In many ways, the Public Broadcasting Service (PBS) has forged its identity around science programs, and it shows every indication of continuing its commitment to scientific television in the future.

Alongside the ongoing efforts of the NSF, today's multifaceted television market has led to the development of scientific programming in unanticipated arenas, most notably cable. Cable networks have capitalized on the entertainment value of science and technology to become prolific purveyors of both episodic and news-oriented scientific television shows, such as *Science and Technology Week* (Cable News Network [CNN]) and *Crocodile Hunter* (Animal Planet). Recently, the profusion of cable channels has allowed for high degrees of specialization in programming. While the Discovery channel continues to provide a broad spectrum of science programming, its related channels—including Animal Planet, The Learning Channel, and Discovery Wings—are more narrowly focused in terms of content and format. Such specialization reveals how cable has directed its attention to professionals, offering focused "edutainment" that can cultivate audiences among scientists and non-scientists alike.

Current scientific television programs in the United States can be divided into three basic categories: commercial programming, children's programming, and PBS programming. These categories often overlap. For example, many children's science programs are produced by and aired on PBS. While such categories are useful in providing basic understanding of the focus of certain programs, they are by no means a definitive description of their content.

Most commercial science programming is developed by either network or syndicated sources. The majority of programs target adult audiences, and the topics of the episodes vary greatly. Most of the programs in this category are series, with each episode focusing on a specific topic, such as new technology, the universe, aeronautics, zoology, or genetic engineering. A few, such as the *NASA Space Films* (1990), are dedicated to one specific topic. Almost all entries in this category include a focus on "science and technology" in their program description. In addition to several already mentioned, programs in this category include *Universe* (1979), *Introducing Biology* (1980s), *Omni: Visions of Tomorrow* (1985), *Eye on Science* (Columbia Broadcasting System [CBS], 1981–85), *The Science Show* (1990–93), *World of Discovery* (American Broadcasting Company [ABC], 1990–94), *A View of the World* (1993), *Quantum* (1993), *Sci-Tech TV* (1994), *Hard Wired* (2001), and *Science Daily* (2001).

Although it has been outstripped by recent growth in adult programming, children's scientific television programming continues to be a central focus of the public understanding movement. Since the implementation of the Children's Television Act of 1990, U.S. programmers have been required to air a certain amount of educational material during daytime slots, when children are prime viewers. Several shows, such as Walt Disney's *Bill Nye the Science Guy* (1993–94), were a direct response to this act. Other science programs targeting children and/or teens have included, of course, *Watch Mr. Wizard* (1951) as well as *Newton's Apple* (1982–88), *The Voyage of the Mimi* (1984), *Beakman's World* (1992), and *Timehoppers* (1992). Increasingly, programming is developed specifically for educational settings. For example, the NSF, PBS, and IBM have funded *A Science Odyssey,* a series of five two-hour programs about the history of scientific discovery in the 20th century.

Science television programming produced and aired by PBS also encompasses a wide range of topics. Popular series such as *Nova, Nature,* and *Scientific American Frontiers* focus on a variety of topics, including nature, medicine, and technology. A plethora of specials or short-term programs, such as *Future Quest, Evolution, Savage Earth,* and *Stephen Hawking's Universe,* anchor the remainder of PBS science programming.

Clearly, cable is positioned to become a front-runner in future scientific programming by virtue of cable's resources, funding, and widespread distribution. While PBS has traditionally set the standard in science television, its leadership may be weakened by the continued assault on federal funding of public broadcasting. Of particular note in both cable and PBS science programming is the trend toward "reality-based" TV. A significant proportion of programming on The Learning Channel consists of real-life drama about science. The success of Animal Planet can be attributed in part to such long-running, "real action" shows as *Crocodile Hunter* and *Real Vets.* PBS increasingly includes the drama of "real science" in perennial favorites such as *Nova, Frontline,* and *Scientific American Frontiers.* In the United Kingdom, the British Broadcasting Corporation (BBC) has made an interesting contribution with *Rough Science.* Additionally, many cable systems now offer the Science Channel, which draws on a substantial existing library of science oriented documentaries and specials. Topics range from the usual

perennial favorites—more explorations of the *Titanic* or *The Language of Dogs* to original programming such as *Young Scientist Challenge: 2003* and regular features such as *Science This Week.*

New technology will also undoubtedly play a role in the future development of scientific television programs. Following a trend set by science museums, scientific television will likely move toward interactive programming. Many channels and programs now maintain websites that provide viewers with links to related programming, merchandise, educational materials, interactive games, online chat rooms, or fan websites.

In the final analysis, the future of science television resides with its audiences, particularly as the first generations of viewers raised on science-based children's programming reach maturity and reach for the remote control.

JOANNA PLOEGER AND ROBBIE POLSTON

See also **Discovery Channel;** *Watch Mr. Wizard*

Further Reading

Banks, Jane, "Science As Fiction: Technology in Prime Time Television," *Critical Studies in Mass Communication* (March 1990)

Barinaga, Marcia, "Science Television: Colleagues on Cable," *Science* (1991)

Bib Television Programming Source Books, 1994–95.

Goldsmith, Donald, "Two Years in Hollywood: An Astronomer in Television Land," *Mercury* (March–April 1991)

Hornig, Susanna, "Television's *Nova* and the Construction of Scientific Truth," *Critical Studies in Mass Communication* (March 1990)

Jansson, Rowena, *Getting It Together: A Genre Analysis of the Rhetorical Structure of Open University Television Progammes in Science and Technology,* Lund, Sweden: Lund University Press; Stockholm: Almqvist and Wiksell, International, 2001

Jerome, Fred, "A Retreat—and an Advance—for Science on TV," *Issues in Science and Technology* (Summer 1988)

Jones, Glyn, "New Directions for Science on TV," *New Scientist* (October 13, 1990)

Tressel, George, "Science on the Air: NSF's Role," *Physics Today* (1990)

Scotland

Scotland is a small country located on the geographical periphery of Europe. Its television service reflects many of the key issues surrounding broadcasting in minority cultures. Politically part of the multination

state of the United Kingdom along with the other "Celtic" countries of Wales and Northern Ireland, Scotland's legal, educational, and religious institutions remain separate from those of England, the dominant partner. Its broadcasting systems, like much of its cultural organization, display a mixture of autonomy and dependence, which reflects Scotland's somewhat anomalous position.

Scotland's current programming reflects the evolution of Britain's broadcasting ecology, offering viewers a choice of four channels and a mix of British networked television and Scottish national and local productions. A brief history of its development sets in context both the present state of television in Scotland and some of the prevailing debates about its nature.

The first television service in Scotland was introduced by the British Broadcasting Corporation (BBC) in 1952. To a large extent, the constitution and character of this new medium was determined by its existing radio system. John Reith, the architect of the BBC and himself a Scot, was determined that the BBC should provide an essentially British service. The consequent emphasis placed on the centralization of public service broadcasting led to a downgrading of other forms of more local production as well as to the BBC's oxymoronic categorization of Scotland as a "national region." This decision was not simply an organizational choice but, as McDowell suggests, reflected the dominant ideological belief in the superiority of "metropolitan culture." The BBC's early television broadcasts consisted of largely the same programs as those of London. What was produced in Scotland received considerable criticism in terms of its nature and quality; the Pilkington Report of 1962 noted that the few programs produced by BBC Scotland often "failed to reflect distinctive Scottish culture."

The arrival of independent, or commercial, television in Scotland offered a new source of programming. Like the BBC, the independent companies broadcast a mix of network provision and more local, opt-out, productions. Franchises were awarded to Scottish Television, covering central Scotland; Border Television, covering the Scottish and English borders; and Grampian Television, serving the north of Scotland. The enthusiasm of some for the new medium can be gauged by the notorious comment of Scottish's first proprietor, Canadian magnate Roy Thomson, that an independent franchise was "a license to print money." In these early years, perhaps unsurprisingly, Scottish program schedules, too, were heavily criticized for their poor quality and parochial outlook. The 1970s and 1980s saw both the BBC and Scottish Television upping the level of their local programming, improving its quality and diversity, and beginning to form a stronger presence on the network through programs such as the long-running police drama *Taggart* and the popular soap *Take the High Road*.

The past 25 years have brought significant changes, diversifying the type and origins of programs produced in Scotland. The introduction of Channel 4 in 1982 and quotas for independent production in the 1990 Broadcasting Act have led to the emergence of numerous independent companies, as is the case across the United Kingdom as a whole. While they have undoubtedly broadened the production base and often pioneered innovative forms of programming, the vast majority of these companies are relatively small and powerless in their ability to affect broadcast policy.

In the 1990s, extensive lobbying has brought governmental support of £9.5 million for the production of television programs in Scotland's minority indigenous language, Gaelic. Unquestionably a welcome move, it nonetheless demonstrates (as does the support of Sianal Pedwar Cymru, the Welsh Channel 4) that it is easier to gain recognition for linguistic than for cultural differences.

These moves in television are indicative of wider cultural shifts. For some years, debate has been growing over Scotland's constitutional position in the United Kingdom, manifested in some quarters by demands for political change in the form of self-government or independence. More widespread, however, has been a transformation in cultural activity in Scotland over the past two decades—most notably in literature but also in theater, music, and film—which many see as a form of cultural nationalism.

This climate of cultural and political contention has led to a new attention to questions of representation and national identity. In *Scotch Reels* (1982), critics Colin McArthur and Cairns Craig exposed and deconstructed the dominant representations of Scottishness, identifying two central rhetorics that have informed representations of Scotland—the associated discourses of tartanry and kailyard. While tartanry harks back to a romantic celebration of lost Scottish nationhood and draws on the emblems of a vanished (and imagined) premodern Highland way of life, kailyard celebrates the virtues of small-town life through genial homilies. These discourses are seen to run through heterogeneous productions from Hollywood cinema and *Brigadoon* to indigenous programs such as *Dr. Finlay's Casebook* and *The White Heather Club*.

This deconstruction of what Murray Grigor terms "Scotch myths" has become widely circulated, and indeed parodying the clichés of Scottishness has become something of a trope in contemporary Scottish television productions (although it has yet to penetrate a Hollywood increasingly enamored of Highland heroes such as Braveheart and Rob Roy). Scottish television offers its audiences antiheroes such as Ian Pattison's comic creation Rab C. Nesbitt, a gloriously loudmouthed Glaswegian drunkard and member of the underclass who exaggerates to comic excess accepted notions of nationality and class. A more sophisticated and ambiguous demonstration of this parodic process is to be found in BBC Scotland's police series *Hamish Macbeth.* Set in a picturesque Highland village populated by bizarre characters, it simultaneously sends up the stereotypes of Highland life while embracing their more marketable forms.

Much of the debate about television in Scotland, in academic and popular circles, has concerned itself with analyzing and often attacking the dominant images of Scottishness that have been produced, while comparatively little attention has been paid to questions of production and policy. In Scotland, questions of cultural identity and diversity and of independence and control reverberate through television production at both a symbolic and a material level.

JANE SILLARS

See also **Ireland; Wales**

Further Reading

Caughie, J., "Questions of Representation," in *From Limelight to Satellite: A Scottish Film Book,* edited by E. Dick, London: British Film Institute and Scottish Film Council, 1990

McArthur, C., editor. *Scotch Reels: Scotland in Cinema and Television,* London: British Film Institute, 1982

McDowell, W.H., *A History of the BBC in Scotland,* Edinburgh: Edinburgh University Press, 1992

Nairn, T., *The Break-Up of Britain,* London: Verso, 1977

Sendall, B., and J. Potter, *A History of Independent Television, Volumes 1–4,* London: Macmillan, 1982

Scrambled Signals

The term "scrambled signals" refers to the encryption of programming data streams by television program providers to prevent the unauthorized reception, duplication, or use of their signals. Originally designed in the 1980s to prevent signal theft by home satellite dish owners, scrambling has become an important component of copyright protection from unauthorized use.

With the relaxation of satellite broadcast and reception regulations by the U.S. Federal Communications Commission in 1979 and the tremendous reduction in the cost of satellite receiving equipment due to advances in technology, a booming market developed for home satellite dish receivers in the early 1980s. These satellite dishes were known as television receive-only satellite Earth stations, or TVRO. Essentially, TVRO dish owners were able to intercept, free of charge, cable television programming distributed over C-band satellites. Although most early adopters of TVRO dishes were located in rural areas where cable television was unavailable, cable system operators were nevertheless concerned about the actual and potential loss of subscribers who opted to receive programming for "free." When Congress passed the Cable Communications Policy Act of 1984, which specified that it was indeed lawful to receive unencrypted satellite signals for private viewing, cable system operators convinced program suppliers to scramble their satellite uplink feeds. Although they sought to protect the system operators (their clients) by scrambling, program suppliers also realized the profit potential in selling programming directly to the TVRO owners.

By early 1985, therefore, most major cable program suppliers (led by Home Box Office [HBO] and Showtime) had begun scrambling. As a result, TVRO owners were required to purchase a signal descrambler (also called a converter box) and pay a monthly fee to receive scrambled programming. This move eventually led to the development of direct broadcast services (DBS)—such as DirecTV, Primestar (later purchased by DirecTV), and EchoStar—that supply programming direct to consumers' homes via satellite dishes. DBS has become the most significant competition to local cable companies for the supply of cable programming. By 2001, 16 million U.S. households subscribed to the leading DBS systems.

In the mid-1980s, many TVRO owners worried that they would have to deal with several different encryption systems. The industry, however, adopted as the standard for scrambling the Videocipher II (VC II), a product of M/A-Com (which was later purchased by General Instrument Corporation, itself later purchased by Motorola). The industry was confident that VC II would reduce satellite programming "theft," but the system was plagued with problems. A black market developed relatively quickly for altered descramblers. To receive free programming, dish owners could simply purchase a descrambler with one of the chips in the unit replaced, enabling the unit to descramble all programming. After six years of program scrambling, it was estimated that only 10 percent of the three million dish owners were paying subscribers.

To correct this flaw, General Instrument released an updated version of the descrambler called Videocipher II Plus (VC II1) in late 1991. The new units replaced the multiple chips in the unit with a single chip. Any effort to copy or replace the chip would disable the unit entirely. Shortly thereafter, companies enhanced the system with a renewable encryption system (VCRS) through the use of a TVPassCard (similar to a credit card). Should a breach in security occur, the encryption information on the cards could be changed quickly and inexpensively. Major programmers switched to the upgraded system with due speed.

While the scrambling of signals was initially the concern of cable programmers and operators, the U.S. broadcast networks (Columbia Broadcasting System [CBS], National Broadcasting Company [NBC], and American Broadcasting Company [ABC]) also began to scramble the transmission of programs to their affiliates (in 1986, 1988, and 1991, respectively). In defending his network's move to scramble such transmissions, one network executive contended that network feeds are "private property" and encouraged viewers instead to watch their local affiliates for local news, weather, and commercials. Although obviously directed at protecting the advertising revenues of its affiliates, such reasoning ignores the lack of local reception for many rural owners of satellite dishes.

With the arrival of digital technology, the industry now relies on the MPEG-2 compression format for digital video- and audio-signal distribution to cable headends. MPEG-2 (the digital compression standard developed by the Moving Pictures Experts Group) allows for more programming in the same amount of bandwidth, as multiple channels are multiplexed into a single data stream. The two industry standards for program transmission are DVB (Digital Video Broadcast) and DigiCipher II, Motorola's MPEG-2-based distribution system, which is used by about 70 percent of cable channels in the United States and Canada.

The scrambling of program signals occurs when each MPEG-2 packet is encrypted during uplink to the satellite. The scrambled packets are processed through a conditional access module (CAM) in each decryption device, where the CAM then takes the decryption key from an inserted smart card and descrambles the signal. The encryption code is obviously secret, and various scrambling services exist around the world, including companies such as PowerVu CA, Nagravision, Cryptoworks, Video-Guard, Mediacypher, and IRDETO.

With the continued convergence of digital technologies and telecommunications, the (perceived) threat of such technologies to the economic interests of television, movie, and record producers increases. Digital technologies may allow for improved delivery of multiple media products into the home (as MPEG-2 video compression does for interactive systems, such as high-speed Internet and video-on-demand), but they also allow users to capture, manipulate, duplicate, store, and disseminate digital media products with great ease (dissemination over the Internet being of particular concern to the media industries). What was once a somewhat simple issue of scrambling analog signals has become a much more complicated concern involving copy protection for a myriad of media products via the encryption of digital information.

JEFFREY P. JONES

See also **Satellite**

Further Reading

Graf, Rudolf F., and William Sheets, *Video Scrambling and Descrambling for Satellite and Cable TV,* 2nd edition, Boston, Massachusetts: Newnes, 1998

Hsiung, James C., "C-Band DBS: An Analysis of the U.S. Scrambling Issue," *Telecommunications Policy* (March 1988)

Long, Mark, *Digital Satellite TV Handbook,* Boston, Massachusetts: Newnes, 1999

Mead, Donald C., *Direct Broadcast Satellite Communications: MPEG Enabled Service,* New York: Prentice Hall, 1999

"Unscrambling Pay TV's New Descramblers," *Discover* (May 1986)

Second City Television

Canadian Comedy Program

Second City Television (*SCTV*) was a popular comedy television show originating from Canada that ran in the late 1970s and early 1980s in a variety of incarnations. Pulling much of its talent and ideas from the Chicago and Toronto Second City comedy clubs, the show became an important pipeline for comedians, especially Canadians, into the mainstream of the U.S. entertainment market. Popular performers who moved from *SCTV* into U.S. television and movies include John Candy, Martin Short, Dave Thomas, Catherine O'Hara, Andrea Martin, Rick Moranis, Harold Ramis, Robin Duke, Tony Rosato, Joe Flaherty, and Eugene Levy. Their training in live improvisational comedy allows them to appear in a variety of capacities, but they have worked primarily as writers and performers.

SCTV's early opening-credit sequence set the tone for the show. As the announcer declared, "*SCTV* now begins its programming day," a number of television sets were thrown out of an apartment building's windows, smashing on the pavement below. Using impersonations of well-known celebrities and ongoing original characters, *SCTV* presented a parody of every aspect of television, including programs, advertising, news, and network executives. In effect, *SCTV* was a cross between a spoof of television and a loose satirical soap opera about the running of the fictional Melonville television station. The station's personnel included the owner, Guy Caballero (Flaherty); the station manager; and Moe Green (Ramis), to be replaced by Edith Prickley (Martin), whose sister, Edna Boil (also Martin), advertised her Organ Emporium with husband, Tex (Thomas), in a send-up of cheap late-night commercials. Other recurring figures were the bon vivant and itinerant host, Johnny LaRue (Candy), and the endearingly inept Ed Grimley (Short). Over the years, the *SCTV* programming lineup included the local news, read by Floyd Robertson (Flaherty) and Earl Camembert (Eugene Levy); "Sunrise Semester"; "Fishin' Musician"; and "The Sammy Maudlin Show," hosted by Maudlin (Flaherty) and his sidekick, William B. (Candy), with regular guest appearances from Bobby Bittman (Levy) and Lola Heatherton (O'Hara). Other spoofs included Yosh and Stan Shmenge's polka show (Levy and Candy); Count Floyd's "Monster Chiller Horror Theatre," whose host was played by the news anchor Floyd Robertson (Flaherty); the ersatz children's show "Captain Combat" (Thomas); "Farm Film Report" (Flaherty and Candy); and the improvised editorials of Bob and Doug Mackenzie's "Great White North" (Moranis and Thomas).

SCTV's trademark was the use of complex intertextual references to produce original hybrid comic sketches. A parody of Francis Ford Coppola's 1972 film *The Godfather* became the story of the Mafia-like operations of television networks. "Play It Again, Bob" took Woody Allen's *Play It Again, Sam* (1972) and paired Woody Allen (Moranis) with Bob Hope (Thomas). Brooke Shields (O'Hara) and Dustin Hoffman (Martin) were guests on the "Farm Film Report," where they "blew up real good." In the station owner's attempt to capture a youth audience, the Melonville station tried to mimic *Saturday Night Live,* with guest host Earl Camembert, a ridiculously overenthusiastic studio audience, and setups based around humorless references to drug use. *SCTV*'s continual use of *mise en abyme* devices produced an intricate, layered text in addition to a knowing fan culture. Further, this program, with its markedly satirical view of television and North American culture in general, was an important contribution to the notion that Canadian humor is ironic and self-deprecatory.

The show's history began in 1976, when Andrew Alexander, Len Stuart, and Bernie Sahlins produced the first half-hour episodes, called *Second City TV,* for Global Television Network in Toronto, where it ran for two seasons. Filmways Productions acquired the syndication rights for the U.S. market in 1977.

A deal was struck in 1979 with the Canadian Broadcasting Corporation (CBC) and Allarcom Ltd in which the show would move to Edmonton, Alberta, for broadcast on the national CBC network. In 1981, the National Broadcasting Company (NBC) bought the program, shifted it to a 90-minute format, and moved the show back to Toronto. At NBC, *SCTV* became part of the "late-night comedy wars" between the renamed *SCTV Network 90* on Fridays from 12:30 A.M. to 2:00 A.M., the American Broadcasting Company's (ABC's) *Fridays* on the same night from 12:30 A.M. to 1:30 A.M., and NBC's *Saturday Night Live.* When NBC did not renew *SCTV Network 90* in 1983, Cinemax took it

Second City Television, cast shot, (top) John Candy, Martin Short, (front) Andrea Martin, Joe Flaherty, Eugene Levy, 1983–84.
Courtesy of the Everett Collection

over. Over the years, *SCTV* produced 72 half-hour shows, 42 90-minute shows, and 18 45-minute shows as well as numerous spin-offs and specials. With 13 Emmy nominations, *SCTV* won two for best writing. The show has since been reedited and repackaged into a half-hour "best of" format for syndication. It is now a mainstay on comedy cable channels and a regular choice for late-night network programming.

CHARLES ACLAND

Cast

Guy Caballero	Joe Flaherty
Moe Green	Harold Ramis
Edith Prickley	Andrea Martin
Earl Camembert	Eugene Levy
Floyd Robertson	Joe Flaherty
Count Floyd	Joe Flaherty
Dr. Tongue	John Candy
Bruno	Eugene Levy
Johnny LaRue	John Candy
Bob MacKenzie	Dave Thomas
Doug MacKenzie	Rick Moranis
Tex Boil	Dave Thomas
Edna Boil	Andrea Martin
Mayor Tommy Shanks	John Candy
The Schmenge Brothers	John Candy and Eugene Levy
Perini Scleroso	Andrea Martin
Ed Grimley	Martin Short
Lin Ye Tang	Dave Thomas
Sammy Maudlin	Joe Flaherty
William B.	John Candy
Bobby Bittman	Eugene Levy
Lola Heatherton	Catherine O'Hara
Big Jim McBob	John Candy
Billy Saul Hurok	Joe Flaherty
Harry, the Guy with the Snake on His Face	John Candy
Rockin' Mel Slurp	Eugene Levy
Jackie Rogers, Jr.	Martin Short
Rusty van Reddick	Martin Short

Producers
Andrew Alexander, Ben Stuart, Bernie Sahlins

Programming History
72 half-hour episodes; 42 90-minute episodes; 18 45-minute episodes
Global Television Network
1976–78
CBC
1979–80
NBC
1981–83   12:30–2:00 A.M.
Cinemax Cable
1983–84   Various times

Further Reading
McCrohan, Donna, *The Second City: A Backstage History of Comedy's Hottest Troupe*, New York: Perigree, 1987

Secondari, John H. (1919–1975)
U.S. Documentary Producer

John Secondari played a major role in the early growth of television news at the American Broadcasting Company (ABC) during the 1960s. As executive in charge of the network's first regular documentary series, Secondari forged a coherent house style that featured a heavy emphasis on visualization and dramatic voice-over narration. He later carried these qualities over to a series of occasional historical documentaries that earned him wide recognition and numerous national broadcasting awards.

Born in Rome in 1920, Secondari was educated in the United States and served in the army during World War II. Afterward, he worked in Europe, first for the Columbia Broadcasting System (CBS) and then as the chief of information for the Marshall Plan in Italy. He quit in 1951 to devote himself to fiction writing on a full-time basis. Over the next six years, he authored four books, one of which was turned into the popular Hollywood feature film *Three Coins in the Fountain*. During this period, he also wrote scripts for television anthology dramas, such as *The Alcoa Hour* and *Playhouse 90*. Both his background as a fiction writer and his fondness for Italy would figure prominently in his documentary career at ABC.

John H. Secondari.
Courtesy of the Everett Collection

Secondari joined the network's Washington news bureau in 1957 and started producing documentaries toward the end of the decade. At the time, ABC's news operation was tiny by comparison to its rivals, and its output was therefore quite limited. In the early 1960s, as television news expanded rapidly and as network news competition escalated, the smallest of the three major networks relied heavily on its documentary unit in order to sustain its stature as a bona fide news organization. ABC's major contribution to prime-time information fare during this period was the weekly *Bell and Howell Close-Up!* series, which Secondari took charge of shortly after its launch in 1960.

Underfunded by comparison to his network rivals and lacking a seasoned staff of broadcast news workers, Secondari nevertheless mounted a creditable series and even made some significant contributions during documentary's television heyday. He accomplished this in part by tapping freelance contributors such as producers Robert Drew and Nicholas Webster. Drew's *cinéma vérité* style offered dramatic glimpses of Castro's Cuba, the Kennedy White House, and the cockpit of an X-15. Similarly, Webster provided first-person accounts of racism in New York City, the school system in Moscow, and the revolving door in the U.S. penal system. In these and many other *Close-Up!* documentaries, the camera escorted the protagonist through the routines and challenges of everyday life. The style emphasized intimacy and visual dynamism, qualities explicitly requested by the series sponsor Bell and Howell, a major manufacturer of amateur motion picture equipment. The same qualities could be seen in the output of regular staff members in the ABC documentary unit. A critic for *Variety* once commented on the house style of each network's flagship series, noting that *CBS Reports* could be described as the *Harper's* of television documentary, *NBC White Paper* as the *Atlantic,* and *Bell and Howell Close-Up!* as the *Redbook.* Indeed, the emphasis on dramatic visualization at ABC was accompanied by a commitment to florid voice-over narration that sometimes seemed excessive. Several critics noted that at the end of "Comrade Student" (a profile of Soviet schools), Secondari's commentary turned self-consciously propagandistic. Similarly, a documentary about the Italian Communist Party—on which he collaborated with his wife, Helen Jean Rogers—closes with a paean to the spirit of republican Rome that reputedly dwells in the souls of all Italians and serves as the last bulwark against leftist revolution.

This penchant for the dramatic continued to mark Secondari's work as he moved to historical topics with a series titled the *Saga of Western Man.* Coproduced with Rogers, it began in 1963 with each episode focusing on a particular year, person, or incident that Secondari believed had significantly influenced the progress of Western civilization. Using the camera "as if it were the eyes of someone who had been present in the past," Secondari transported the viewer to historical locations while voice-over narrators read authentic journal entries or letters from the period. For example, Secondari outfitted historical ships in Spain and put to sea with his camera crew in order to capture the sensations of Columbus's transoceanic voyage. These historical reenactments were then edited together with close-up shots scanning the canvases of period paintings. Meanwhile, the audio track featured music and actor Frederic March's dramatic readings from the navigation logs of Columbus. These techniques—which were also being developed by National Broadcasting Company (NBC) producers Lou Hazam and George Vicas—generated widespread critical acclaim and numerous awards for the series, thereby encouraging ABC to sign on for a second season. By year's end, however, some critics began to complain that the method was wearing thin. *The Saga of Western Man* was scaled back and continued on an occasional basis until the end of the 1960s, when Secondari and Rogers left ABC to form their own production company.

Secondari died in 1975 at the age of 55. In all, he garnered some 20 Emmy and three Peabody awards. Perhaps most important, however, was his contribution to the development of the historical television documentary. Secondari's style not only anticipated the later efforts of such producers as Ken Burns but also laid the groundwork for the emergence of the television docudrama in the 1970s.

MICHAEL CURTIN

See also **Documentary; Drew, *Robert; Tour of the White House with Mrs. John F. Kennedy***

John H. Secondari, Born in Rome, Italy, November 1, 1919. Fordham University, New York, B.A. 1939; Columbia University, M.S. in journalism 1940. Married: 1) Rita Hume, 1948 (died); 2) Helen Jean Rogers, 1961. Enlisted in U.S. Army, 1941; appointed to staff of Cavalry School; commanded a reconnaissance unit and a tank company in combat in France, Germany, and Austria; served on staff of General Mark Clark in Vienna; left army with rank of captain, 1946. Worked as a newspaper reporter for the Rome *Daily American,* 1946; foreign correspondent for CBS, 1948; deputy chief, information division of the Economic Cooperation Administration's Special Mission to Italy, 1948–51; freelance writer, 1951–56; chief, ABC's Washington news bureau, 1956; executive producer, ABC's special projects division, 1960–68; formed own production company, 1968. Recipient: *Radio Television Daily's* Television Writer of the Year, 1963; Italy's Guglielmo Marconi World Television Award, 1964; 20 Emmy Awards; three Peabody Awards. Died February 8, 1975.

Television Series

1957–58 *Open Hearing* (moderator)
1960–63 *Bell and Howell Close-Up!*
1963–66 *The Saga of the Western Man* (coproducer)

Television Specials (selected)

1958 *Highlights of the Coronation of Pope John XXIII*
1960 *Japan: Anchor in the East*
1960 *Korea: No Parallel*
1963 *Soviet Women*
1963 *The Vatican*
1970 *The Golden Age of the Automobile*
1970 *The Ballad of the Iron Horse*
1972 *Champions*

Publications (selected)

Coins in the Fountain (novel), 1952
Temptation for a King (novel), 1954
Spinner of the Dream (novel), 1955

Further Reading

Bluem, A. William, *Documentary in American Television,* New York: Hastings House, 1965
Curtin, Michael, *Redeeming the Wasteland: Television Documentary and Cold War Politics,* New Brunswick, New Jersey: Rutgers University Press, 1995
Einstein, Daniel, *Special Edition: A Guide to Network Television Documentary Series and Special News Reports, 1955–1979,* Metuchen, New Jersey: Scarecrow, 1987
Hammond, Charles Montgomery, Jr., *The Image Decade: Television Documentary, 1965–1975,* New York: Hastings House, 1981

See It Now

U.S. Documentary Series

See It Now (1951–58), one of television's earliest documentary series, remains the standard by which broadcast journalism is judged for its courage and commitment. The series brought radio's premier reporter, Edward R. Murrow, to television, and his worldly expertise and media savvy helped to define television's role in covering and, more important, analyzing the news.

The genesis of *See It Now* was a series of record albums that Murrow created during the late 1940s with Fred W. Friendly, a former radio producer at a Rhode Island station. The *I Can Hear It Now* records, which interwove historical events and speeches with Murrow narration, became such a commercial success that the partnership developed a radio series for the Columbia Broadcasting System (CBS) that also creatively used

See It Now, Edward R. Murrow, David Ben-Gurion, 1951–58; 1956 interview in Israel.
Courtesy of the Everett Collection

taped actualities. The weekly *Hear It Now* was modeled on a magazine format, with a variety of "sounds" of current events, such as artillery fire from Korea and an atom smasher at work, illuminated by Murrow and other expert columnists.

After his World War II experience, Murrow had assiduously avoided television, having been overheard stating, "I wish goddamned television had never been invented." Friendly was eager to test the new technology, however, and in 1951 the team agreed to transfer the *Now* concept yet again, this time emphasizing the visual essence of the television medium and calling their effort *See It Now.* Murrow never desired to anchor the evening newscast, and he wanted *See It Now* to be not a passive recitation of current events but an active engagement with the issues of the day. To implement this vision, Murrow and Friendly radically transformed the fundamental nature of news gathering on television.

Unlike other news programs that used newsreel companies to record events, *See It Now* maintained its own camera crews to coordinate filming on location, using 35-millimeter cameras to record the most striking images. Murrow and Friendly also deviated from standard practice by mandating that all interviews would not be rehearsed and that there would be no background music to accompany the visuals. Although *See It Now* relied on CBS correspondents around the world, Murrow, serving as editor in chief, and Friendly, as managing editor, organized the first autonomous news unit, whose ranks included reporter-producers Joe Wershba and Ed Scott, director Don Hewitt, production manager Palmer Williams, and former newsreel cameramen Charlie Mack and Leo Rossi.

"This is an old team trying to learn a new trade," intoned Murrow to inaugurate *See It Now* on November 18, 1951. Murrow, as in all the programs that followed, was ensconced in Studio 41, exposing the tricks of the electronic trade—the monitors, the microphones, and the technicians were all in view. To underscore this new technological undertaking, Murrow summoned up a split screen of the Brooklyn Bridge in New York City and the Golden Gate Bridge in San Francisco, the first live coast-to-coast transmission.

See It Now was the first newsmagazine series on television, alternating live studio commentary with reports from such seasoned correspondents as Howard K. Smith and Eric Sevareid. The series was initially scheduled in the intellectual ghetto of Sunday afternoon. By its third outing, *See It Now* gained a commercial sponsor, Alcoa (the Aluminum Company of America), which sought prestige among opinion makers to offset antitrust troubles. As the half-hour series became the most influential news program on television, it moved into prime time, first on Sunday evenings and then for three years on Tuesday evenings at 10:30.

See It Now established its voice by covering the campaign rituals throughout the 1952 presidential year. Two early pieces were also emblematic of what Murrow and Friendly wanted to accomplish for the new venture: simulated coverage of a mock bomb attack on New York City (a segment that addressed the tensions of the nuclear age) and a one-hour report on the realities from the ground of the Korean War during the 1952 Christmas season. The latter special evoked the frustrations and confusions of everyday soldiers and was described by one critic as "the most graphic and yet sensitive picture of war we have ever seen."

Despite the laudatory reviews and the respectability that *See It Now* brought to television news, a question plagued the partnership: how to cover the anti-Communist hysteria that was enveloping the nation. The team first searched for what Friendly called "the little picture," an individual story that symbolized a national issue. In October 1953, Murrow and reporter Wershba produced "The Case of Milo Radulovich," a study of an Air Force lieutenant who was deemed a security risk because his father, an elderly Serbian immigrant, and sister supposedly read subversive newspapers. Because of the report, for which Murrow and Friendly used their own money to advertise, the secretary of the Air Force reviewed the case and retained Radulovich in the service. In "Argument in Indianapolis," broadcast one month later, *See It Now* investigated an American Legion chapter that refused to book its meeting hall to the American Civil Liberties Union. Again, Murrow and staff succeeded in documenting how McCarthyism, so called because of the demagogic tactics of Senator Joseph McCarthy, had penetrated the heartland.

Having reported discrete episodes on the Cold War, Murrow and Friendly decided to expose the architect of the paranoia, McCarthy himself. On March 9, 1954, *See It Now* employed audiotapes and newsreels to refute the outrageous half-truths and misstatements of the junior senator from Wisconsin. In his tailpiece before the signature "Good Night and Good Luck," Murrow explicitly challenged his viewers to confront the nation's palpable fears. A month later, McCarthy accepted an invitation to respond, and his bombastic rhetoric, calling Murrow "the leader and cleverest of the jackal pack," coupled with the later failure of the senator's televised investigation into the Army, left McCarthy's career in a shambles. The McCarthy program also produced fissures in the relationship between Murrow and the network. Again, CBS did not assist in promoting the broadcast; but this time CBS executives suggested that Murrow had overstepped the boundaries of editorial objectivity. In the process, he had become controversial and, therefore, a possible liability to the company's business opportunities.

Provocative programs, targeting the most pressing problems of the day, continued during the 1954–55 season. Murrow conducted an interview with J. Robert Oppenheimer, the physicist who was removed as adviser to the Atomic Energy Commission because he was accused of being a Soviet agent. *See It Now* documented the effects of the U.S. Supreme Court's 1954 *Brown v. Board of Education* desegregation decision on two southern towns. Murrow, a heavy smoker, examined the link between cigarettes and lung cancer. By the end of the season, Alcoa, stung by *See It Now*'s investigation into a Texas land scandal where the company was expanding operations, ended its sponsorship. Because of the profitability of other entertainment shows, most notably the bonanza in game shows, CBS also decided that *See It Now* should yield its regular time slot and become a series of specials. Many insiders thought the series should be retitled *See It Now and Then*.

During the final three seasons of specials, the tone of *See It Now* became softer. Despite exclusive interviews with Chinese Premier Chou En-lai and Yugoslavian strongman Marshal Josip Tito, the most memorable programs were almost hagiographic profiles of American artists, including Louis Armstrong, Marian Anderson, and Danny Kaye. Controversy for Murrow was now reserved for outside the studio; his 1958 speech to radio and news directors was an indictment of the degrading commercialism pervading network television. The final broadcast, "Watch on the Ruhr," on July 7, 1958, surveyed the mood of postwar Germany. After *See It Now*'s demise, CBS News made sure to split the Murrow–Friendly team. Friendly was named executive producer of *Now*'s public affairs successor, *CBS Reports.* Murrow was a contributor to the series; his most significant investigation was *Harvest of Shame.*

Murrow and Friendly invented the magazine news format, which became the dominant documentary form on network television. The most esteemed inheritor of its legacy, *60 Minutes,* was conceived by integral *See It Now* alumni: Don Hewitt (as *60 Minutes'* executive producer), Palmer Williams (as managing editor), and Joe Wershba (as producer). *See It Now* was also a seminal force in establishing how most television documentaries convey a national issue: illuminating the individual story, immediately and directly, so that it resonates with deeper implications. If Murrow and Friendly created the model for the documentary for both form and content, they also tested the limits of editorial advocacy. Although the series of McCarthy programs have been lionized as one of television's defining moments, Murrow and Friendly exposed as well the inherent tension between the news and the network and sponsor. How to deal with controversy in a commercial medium has remained controversial ever since.

RON SIMON

Host
Edward R. Murrow

Producers
Fred W. Friendly, Edward R. Murrow

Programming History
CBS

November 1951–June 1953	Sunday 6:30–7:00	
September 1953–July 1955	Tuesday 10:30–11:00	
September 1955–July 1958	Irregular schedule	

Further Reading

Barnouw, Erik, *Tube of Plenty: The Evolution of American Television,* New York: Oxford University Press, 1975; 2nd revised edition, 1990

Bliss, Edward J., *Now the News: The History of Broadcast Journalism,* New York: Oxford University Press, 1975

Bliss, Edward J., editor, *In Search of Light: The Broadcasts of Edward R. Murrow, 1938–1964,* New York: Knopf, 1967

Boyer, Peter J., *Who Killed CBS? The Undoing of America's Number One News Network,* New York: Random House, 1988

Cloud, Stanley, and Lynne Olson, *The Murrow Boys,* Boston: Houghton Mifflin, 1996

Friendly, Fred W., *Due to Circumstances Beyond Our Control...,* New York: Vintage, 1967

Gates, Gary Paul, *Air Time: The Inside Story of CBS News,* New York: Harper and Row, 1978

Halberstam, David, *The Powers That Be,* New York: Knopf, 1979

Kendrick, Alexander, *Prime Time: The Life of Edward R. Murrow,* Boston: Little, Brown, 1969

Matusow, Barbara, *The Evening Stars,* New York: Ballantine, 1983

Murrow, Edward R., and Fred W. Friendly, editors, *See It Now,* New York: Simon and Schuster, 1955

O'Connor, John E., editor, *American History/American Television: Interpreting the Video Past,* New York: Frederick Ungar, 1983

Paley, William S., *As It Happened,* Garden City, New York: Doubleday, 1979

Persico, Joseph E., *Edward R. Murrow: An American Original,* New York: McGraw-Hill, 1988

Reeves, Thomas C., *The Life and Times of Joe McCarthy,* New York: Stein and Day, 1982

Smith, Sally Bedell, *In All His Glory,* New York: Simon and Schuster, 1990

Sperber, A.M., *Murrow: His Life and Times,* New York: Freundlich, 1986

Seeing Things

Canadian Drama Series

Seeing Things was one of the most popular series in Canadian television history. Throughout its run, the series had the same coproducers, David Barlow and its star, Louie Del Grande, and the same director, George McGowan, which is unheard of and impossible in the Hollywood model of television production. The three worked easily and well together and shared the same basic vision of the show. *Seeing Things* is basically a comedy/mystery. Louie Ciccone is handicapped by fragmentary psychic visions that, along with his conscience and a nose for news, compel him to solve the murders he glimpses in his visions. The tone of an episode often varied wildly. Yet no matter how improbable the plots, the consistent off-center vision that Barlow and Del Grande shared and McGowan's willingness to adapt his direction to the stylistic demands of the show, together with appropriately imaginative designers, gave it coherence.

Dashes of slapstick and farce pepper *Seeing Things,* which had remarkably little violence for a show centered on murder. In one episode, scrambling around chair legs and under tables in a nightclub, Louis escaped by biting his pursuer in the leg. Another distinctive feature of the series was its steady stream of ad-libbed one-liners. The timing was crisp and the delivery always throwaway and spontaneous. Running gags were found in most episodes. *Seeing Things* was very Canadian, with its sharp eye for the brief obsessions of American popular culture. These were sometimes deliberately subverted and sometimes mocked. Many of the jokes are topical, political, or social in their thrust. The series satirized the military, aging hippies, psychic fairs, beauty pageants, and hockey. There were also occasional complex takes on ethical questions, touching moments between characters, and solid cameo performances. The series provided self-reflexive moments, such as when Marge (played by Martha Gibson, Del Grande's wife), Louie's wife and partner in his adventures, wondered aloud why a murderer holding a gun on her was unburdening herself with a detailed confession. Although there were several writers, every script was distinctly flavored with the quirky sensibility shared by Barlow and Del Grande.

In *Seeing Things,* the protagonist, Louie Ciccone, was a reporter for a Toronto newspaper, living with his parents in the back room of their bakery. He was a very unwilling clairvoyant. He had to find the murderers using his own intelligence and his estranged wife as driver, goad, confidante, and occasional rescuer to fill in the missing pieces. Louie's klutzy, workaholic persona and domestic worries were threaded with allusive wit and literate one-liners, manic energy, and considerable acting skills.

Louie obsessed over finding the murderer glimpsed in his visions and on the possibility of getting back together with Marge. Often the two obsessions collided, so that his need to see murderers caught continually undercut his claim that Marge and his son, Jason, were more important to him than anything else. Nevertheless, eventually Marge and Louis did reunite in a gradual, psychologically credible narrative arc. His physical and social ineptitude was incurable, however, and an intrinsic and funny part of the character. He was also self-conscious, pushy, vain, indecisive, inventive, courageous, and compassionate, altogether a credible character rather than the formulaic hero of a typical police or mystery program.

Heather Redfern, the crown attorney, assisted Louie in many episodes. Blonde, single, and upper class, she was clearly intended to be a contrast to the Ciccones, creating moments of both sexual and class conflict in a series that had no recurring antagonist. Marge's new job as a real estate agent also provided new narrative possibilities. The setting of Toronto provided a very specific sense of place, which also anchored the series. Another strength of the series was the fact that most of Canada's best character actors appeared as guests on the show.

The series, like so many Canadian Broadcasting Corporation (CBC) series in the 1980s, subverted the message of authority. It offered ambiguity in the outcome of several episodes and presented irony with a wryness and whimsicality that connected it to another favorite series more than a decade later: *Due South.* The last season of *Seeing Things,* however, began to strain the format with ever more improbable plots, including the landing of a flying saucer. Although the main American networks were not interested in *Seeing Things,* which at 43 episodes over six seasons did not meet the necessary number of 60 episodes (for syndication) and which was made before specialty channels provided alternate outlets, the series did appear on the Public Broadcasting Service (PBS) and was very successfully sold in Europe, South Africa, and Australia.

MARY JANE MILLER

Cast

Louie Ciccone	Louie Del Grande
Martha Ciccone	Martha Gibson
Heather Redfern	Janet Laine
Albert Ciccone	Al Gordon
Anna Ciccone	Lynne Gordon
Jason Ciccone	Ivan Beaulieu
Max Perkins	Murray Westgate
Marlon Bede	Louis Negin
Robert Spenser	Cec Linder
Kenny Volker	Ratch Wallace
Detective Sergeant Brown	Frank Adamson

Producers

David Barlow and Louis Del Grande with George McGowan directing every episode

Programming History

CBC
1981–1987
43 episodes

Further Reading

Kentner, Peter, *TV North: Everything You Wanted to Know About Canadian Television,* Vancouver and Toronto: Whitecap, 2001

Miller, Mary Jane, "Copshows and Mysteries: Check Your Guns at the Border," in *Turn Up the Contrast 1952: CBC Television Drama Since 1952,* Vancouver: University of British Columbia Press, CBC Enterprises copublication, 1987

Miller, Mary Jane, *Rewind and Search: Conversations with Makers and Decision Makers of CBC Television Drama,* Montreal and Kingston: McGill-Queen's University Press, 1996

Seinfeld

U.S. Situation Comedy

Jerry Seinfeld, American stand-up comedian and author of the best-selling book *SeinLanguage* (1993), is now best known as the eponymous hero of *Seinfeld,* a sitcom that was a great success for the National Broadcasting Company (NBC) during nine seasons in the 1990s. However, for the show's fans in the United States and around the world, "hero" is not the right word to describe Jerry on *Seinfeld.* Nor would it describe the show's other main characters, Elaine, George, and (Cosmo) Kramer, all 30-something and leading the single life in New York. The program's distinctiveness lies in being a comedy made out of trivia and minutiae, a bricolage of casual incidents and situations of everyday metropolitan life, all of which belie any conventional notion of "heroism" or any notion, indeed, of distinction. Viewers saw Jerry in his apartment with bizarre neighbor Kramer constantly dropping in and Elaine and George visiting, in the café where they were all regular customers, or at Elaine's office, where she worked as a publisher until she lost her job. (She subsequently worked in a series of situations, usually as the assistant to eccentric, bizarre individuals.)

Seinfeld himself, in an interview, suggested that *Seinfeld* was adding something new to television comedy, some new representation of the quotidian that might be influencing other TV and film culture. He cited some of the coffee-shop conversation between the John Travolta and Samuel Jackson characters in Quentin Tarantino's *Pulp Fiction,* and Tarantino in turn has admitted to being a big fan of *Seinfeld.*

Seinfeld did not mix seemingly trivial conversation and incidents with sudden unnerving violence as did *Pulp Fiction,* whose main characters, gangsters, created a world of shattering absurdity. Jerry, Elaine, George, and Kramer instead led a life of quiet absurdity. They appeared always to be relentlessly superficial. Even to say they were friends would be too kind. If they did help each other, it was out of self-interest only. They created a comic world out of the banally cruel and amoral, of trivial lies, treachery, and betrayal. In their relations with each other, with anyone else they encountered, or with their families, they rarely found it in themselves to act out of altruism, kindness, generosity, support, courage, caring, sharing, concern, neighborliness, a sense of human community, or trust. Like comedy through the ages, they said the unsayable, did the undoable as they casually ignored sanctioned morality and established conventions. Watching someone being operated on, they passed callous remarks and accidentally popped a chocolate candy into the body.

George in particular was freely given to making trouble and then denying all responsibility; to boasting, deceiving, and lying. Viewers waited for him to do disgusting things, expecting, hoping, he would do them. He tried to get money out of a hospital when someone fell to his death from the hospital's window onto George's car. He made love on his parents' bed and left behind a used condom. He sold his father's beloved old clothes to a shop, saying his father had died and this was the deceased's dearest wish. He hoped an artist would die so his paintings would go up in value.

Jerry and a girlfriend, who could not make love in his apartment because his parents were visiting, entwined themselves in the flickering darkness when they went to see *Schindler's List* and consequently missed most of the film. Their behavior was reported to Jerry's Jewish parents by another acquaintance, the treacherous Newman. Much of *Seinfeld* involved similar comic humiliation and so recalled and reprised a long Jewish tradition of humor that flourished in the 20th century in vaudeville, radio, film, and television through the figure of the *schlemiel* (think of Woody Allen), who makes comedy out of failure, ineptitude, defeat, or minor disaster.

In *Seinfeld*, disasters multiplied for each character, except for the mysterious Kramer, a trickster figure, who (like trickster figures through the ages) always got out of daily work, was a renowned sexual reptile, generally out-tricked every adversary, and ignored the havoc he insisted on causing. In *Seinfeld*, Kramer functioned as pure sign of folly and misrule, turning the world upside down at every chance.

Elaine was Jerry's former girlfriend. With George she had a relationship of uneasiness, if not sharp mutual dislike. Elaine was sassy and spunky, but her spunkiness usually emerged as irritability and impatience (especially in restaurants or waiting to see a film). She picked arguments with almost everyone she encountered, including any boyfriend. In matters of romance, Elaine constantly self-destructed. So, too, did Jerry and George, usually quickly allowing a trivial difference or unfounded suspicion to end a relationship. Once Jerry insisted that he and Elaine make love again, but he could not perform, and here Elaine emerged as similar to the irrepressible female carnival figures of early modern Europe (as discussed by Natalie Zemon Davis in her famous essay "Women on Top"), overturning men's power and self-image.

Seinfeld also recalled a long comic tradition of farce that has descended from Elizabethan drama. In those plays and in the jigs that followed them, the audience was presented with a contestation of ideals and perspectives. Whatever moral order was realized in the play was placed in tension with its parody in the closing jig. There, the clown dominated as a festive Lord of Misrule, creating, for audiences to ponder, not a definite conclusion but an anarchy of values, a play of play and counterplay. Similarly, *Seinfeld* continuously presented an absurd mirror image of other television programs that, like Shakespeare's romances, hold out hope for relationships despite every obstacle that tries to rend lovers, friends, kin, or neighbors apart—obstacles that create amid the comedy sadness, pathos, and intensity.

The possible disadvantage of a genre such as absurdist farce is repetition and sameness, comic action turning into ritualized motion. Seinfeld himself commented that in *Seinfeld*, "you can't change the basic situation or the basic characters." Nevertheless, in the March 4, 1995, issue of *TV Week*, he rejected the suggestion that even the show's devotees thought the characters were becoming increasingly obnoxious and the jokes forced. While some contemporary satirical comedy, such as *Married... With Children*, may have fatally succumbed to this danger, *Seinfeld* remained one of the most innovative and inventive comedies in the history of American television until the program voluntarily ended its run in May 1998, when its final episode garnered enormous ratings (a 41.3 Nielsen rating and a 58 share) and inspired a media furor, with mixed critical reactions. The four primary characters were put on trial for "criminal indifference," for standing by while a carjacking occurred, thus affording past victims of their cruel indifference the chance to come forth and state their grievances—and forcing the TV audience to come to terms with the essentially soulless and selfish nature of Jerry and his friends.

JOHN DOCKER

See also **Comedy, Domestic Settings**

Cast

Jerry Seinfeld	Himself
Elaine Benes	Julia Louis-Dreyfus
George Costanza	Jason Alexander
Kramer	Michael Richards

Producers

Larry David, Jerry Seinfeld

Programming History

180 episodes
NBC

May 1990–July 1990	Thursday 9:30–10:00
January 1991–February 1991	Wednesday 9:30–10:00
April 1991–June 1991	Thursday 9:30–10:00
June 1991–December 1991	Wednesday 9:30–10:00
December 1991–January 1993	Wednesday 9:00–9:30
February 1993–August 1993	Thursday 9:30–10:00
August 1993–May 1998	Thursday 9:00–9:30

Further Reading

Davis, Natalie Zemon, *Society and Culture in Early Modern France*, Stanford, California: Stanford University Press, 1975

Docker, John, *Postmodernism and Popular Culture: A Cultural History*, Cambridge and New York: Cambridge University Press, 1994

Johnson, Carla, "Luckless in New York: The Schlemiel and the Schlimazel in Seinfeld," *Journal of Popular Film and Television* (Fall 1994)

Radway, Janice A., *Reading the Romance*, Chapel Hill: University of North Carolina Press, 1984

Rapping, Elayne, "The *Seinfeld* Syndrome," *The Progressive* (September 1995)

"Sein of the Times?" *TV Week* (March 4, 1995)

Wiles, David, *Shakespeare's Clown: Actor and Text in the Elizabethan Playhouse*, Cambridge: Cambridge University Press, 1987

Sellers, Peter (1925–1980)

British Comedian, Actor

While the late actor Peter Sellers is known primarily for his roles in film comedies such as the *Pink Panther* series, he first became a British celebrity as a member of the cast of *The Goon Show,* a satirical British Broadcasting Corporation (BBC) radio series. Originally aired in 1951, the show teamed Sellers with fellow comedians Spike Milligan and Harry Secombe. The program was a shocking departure for listeners accustomed to urbane humor from the BBC—the Goons combined a zany blend of odd characters in sketches that poked fun at every aspect of English society. Sellers used mimicry skills honed as a stand-up comedian in London striptease bars to create a number of distinctive characters with equally memorable names: Grytpype Thynne, Bluebottle, Willum Cobblers, and Major Bloodnok. The show acquired a cult following with BBC audiences around the world and helped launch Sellers's film career.

Goon Show influences can be traced to equally eccentric British television progeny, such as *Monty Python's Flying Circus* and *The Benny Hill Show.* The Goons, led by Sellers, created a distinctive media genre that combined Kafkaesque humor with hilariously stereotypical English characters. This new genre paved the way for the Pythons and others to follow in the 1960s and 1970s.

In 1979, Peter Sellers appeared in Hal Ashby's production of *Being There,* a film version of Jerzy Kosinski's satirical novel on the cultural influence of television. In the film, Sellers played Chauncey Gardiner, a none-too-bright gardener who is forcibly thrust into the outside world after the death of his benefactor. Sheltered in his employer's home, Chauncey's worldview is entirely shaped by the television shows he watches on sets scattered throughout the house. After being cast from this TV-defined Eden, Chauncey and his childlike innocence are challenged at every turn by the harsh realities of the outside world. In one memorable scene, he is menaced by members of an inner-city street gang as he urgently presses a TV remote control to make them "go away." In another scene, Sellers kisses a passionate female character played by Shirley MacLaine as he mimics a televised love scene that he is watching over her shoulder.

Being There reflected Kosinski's jaundiced view of the influence of television on modern culture and the tendency to confuse actual events with their symbolic media representations. In Kosinski's sardonic world, the innocent jabberings of a moronic child-man are mistaken as profound wisdom—at the end of the film Chauncey is feted as a presidential candidate.

This story resonated with Peter Sellers at first reading, and he pursued Kosinski for seven years for the film rights. During the making of the motion picture, Sellers became Chauncey Gardiner—so much so that friends were alarmed at his 24-hour-a-day transformation. The result was one of Sellers's funniest and most poignant screen roles. He was an innocent man cast adrift in a world full of duplicitous people and contrived mediated images. The film, like Kosinski's novel, is one of the most trenchant indictments of the role of television in society yet mounted in fictional form. The film was a fitting end to a career built on Sellers's own unique mimicry skills. He contrived a number of quirky illusory personas—a diverse world that included such memorable characters as Grytpype Thynne, Jacques Clouseau, and Chauncey Gardiner.

PETER B. SEEL

Peter (Richard Henry) Sellers. Born in Southsea, Hampshire, England, September 8, 1925. Attended St. Aloysius College, London. Married: 1) Anne Howe, 1951 (divorced, 1964); children: Michael and Sarah; 2): Britt Ekland, 1964 (divorced, 1969); child: Victoria; 3) Miranda Quarry, 1970 (divorced, 1974); 4) Lynne Frederick, 1977. Served in Royal Air Force, 1943–46. Began career in revue at the age of five; worked as drummer in dance band; entertainment director of holiday camp, 1946–47; vaudeville comedian, first at the Windmill Theatre, London, 1948, then on vaudeville circuit, 1949–56; made film debut, 1951; performer, *The Goon Show* and other radio programs, 1948–59; achieved international stardom in *Pink Panther* film series. Commander of the Order of the British Empire, 1966. Recipient: British Academy Best British Actor Award, 1959; San Francisco International Film Festival Golden Gate Award for Best Fiction Short, 1960; San Sebastian Award for Best British Actor, 1962; Teheran Film Festival Best Actor Award, 1973; *Evening News* Best Actor of the Year Award, 1975. Died in London, July 24, 1980.

Peter Sellers.
Courtesy of the Everett Collection

Television Series (selected)

1956	*The Idiot Weekly, Price 2d*
1956	*A Show Called Fred*
1956	*Son of Fred*
1957	*Yes, It's the Cathode Ray Tube Show*
1963	*The Best of Fred* (compilation)

Films

Penny Points to Paradise, 1951; *London Entertains*, 1951; *Let's Go Crazy*, 1951; *Down Among the Z Men*, 1952; *Super Secret Service*, 1953; *Orders Are Orders*, 1954; *John and Julie*, 1955; *The Lady-killers*, 1955; *The Case of the Mukkinese Battle-horn*, 1955; *The Man Who Never Was*, 1955; *The Smallest Show on Earth*, 1957; *Death of a Salesman*, 1957; *Cold Comfort*, 1957; *Insomnia Is Good for You*, 1957; *The Naked Truth*, 1958; *Up the Creek*, 1958; *Tom Thumb*, 1958; *Carlton-Browne of the F.O.*, 1958; *The Mouse That Roared*, 1959; *I'm All Right, Jack*, 1959; *Battle of the Sexes*, 1960; *Two-Way Stretch*, 1960; *The Running, Jumping and Standing Still Film* (also producer), 1960; *Never Let Go*, 1961; *The Millionairess*, 1961; *The Road to Hong Kong*, 1961; *Mister Topaze* (also director), 1961; *Only Two Can Play*, 1962; *Waltz of the Toreadors*, 1962; *Lolita*, 1962; *The Dock Brief*, 1963; *Heavens Above*, 1963; *The Wrong Arm of the Law*, 1963; *The Pink Panther*, 1963; *Dr. Strangelove; or, How I Learned to Stop Worrying and Love the Bomb*, 1964; *The World of Henry Orient*, 1964; *A Shot in the Dark*, 1964; *What's New Pussycat?*, 1965; *The Wrong Box*, 1966; *After the Fox*, 1966; *Casino Royale*, 1967; *The Bobo*, 1967; *Woman Times Seven*, 1967; *The Party*, 1968; *I Love You, Alice B. Toklas*, 1968; *The Magic Christian*, 1969; *Hoffman*, 1970; *There's a Girl in My Soup*, 1970; *A Day at the Beach*, 1970; *Simon, Simon*, 1970; *Where Does It Hurt?*, 1972; *Alice's Adventures in Wonderland*, 1972; *The Blockhouse*, 1973; *The Optimist*, 1973; *Soft Beds and Hard Battles*, 1973; *Ghost in the Noonday*, 1974; *The Great McGonagall*, 1974; *The Return of the Pink Panther*, 1974; *Murder by Death*, 1976; *The Pink Panther Strikes Again*, 1976; *Revenge of the Pink Panther*, 1978; *Being There*, 1979; *The Prisoner of Zenda*, 1979; *The Fiendish Plot of Dr. Fu Manchu*, 1980; *The Trail of the Pink Panther*, 1982.

Radio

Show Time, 1948; *Ray's a Laugh*, 1949; *The Goon Show*, 1951.

Recordings (selected)

I'm Walking Backwards for Christmas; The Ying Tong Song; Any Old Iron; A Hard Day's Night; Goodness Gracious Me; Bangers and Mash; The Best of Sellers; Songs for Swingin' Sellers.

Stage

Brouhaha, 1958.

Publication (selected)

The Book of the Goons, with Spike Milligan, 1974

Further Reading

Braun, Eric, "Authorized Sellers," *Films* (August 1982)

Evans, Peter, *Peter Sellers: The Mask Behind the Mask*, New York: New American Library, 1980

Lewis, Roger, *The Life and Death of Peter Sellers*, London: Century, 1994

McGillivray, D., "Peter Sellers," *Focus on Film* (Spring 1974)

McVay, D., "The Man Behind," *Films and Filming* (May 1963)

Miller, M., "Goonery and Guinness," *Films and Filming* (January 1983)

Peary, Gerald, "Peter Sellers," *American Film* (April 1990)

Sellers, Michael, with Sarah and Victoria Sellers, *P.S. I Love You: Peter Sellers, 1951–80*, New York: Dutton, 1981

Sinoux, J., "Bye Bye Birdie—Mun-Num," *Positif* (February 1981)

Sylvester, D., *Peter Sellers*, New York: Proteus, 1981

Thomson, D., "The Rest Is Sellers," *Film Comment* (September–October 1980)

Walker, A., *Peter Sellers: The Authorized Biography*, London: Weidenfeld and Nicholson, 1981

Selling of the Pentagon, The

U.S. Documentary

The Selling of the Pentagon was an important documentary aired in prime time on the Columbia Broadcasting System (CBS) on February 23, 1971. The aim of this film, produced by Peter Davis, was to examine the increasing utilization and cost to the taxpayers of public relations activities by the military-industrial complex in order to shape public opinion in favor of the military. The subject was not new, having already been greatly discussed in the press and debated in Congress. The junior senator from Arkansas, J. William Fulbright, had first raised the subject in a series of four widely publicized speeches in the Senate in December 1969. In November 1970, Fulbright published his book *The Pentagon Propaganda Machine,* and this text formed the core around which the network constructed its version of the senator's ideas. While the controversial nature of the subject matter was clearly understood by the producers and a strong reaction was anticipated, the virulence and direction of this reaction could not have been foreseen. In the end, the furor surrounding *The Selling of the Pentagon* would serve as a significant benchmark in evaluating the First Amendment rights of the broadcast media.

The documentary, narrated by Roger Mudd, concentrated on three areas of Pentagon activity to illustrate the theme of public manipulation: direct contacts with the public, Defense Department films, and the Pentagon's use of the commercial media—the press and television. From the opening sequence of "firepower display" at Armed Forces Day in Fort Jackson, South Carolina (culminating in the last "mad minute" when all the weapons on display were fired simultaneously), through the middle section, which showed clips of the anti-Communist film *Red Nightmare,* to the closing section, which detailed how the media are "managed" by the Pentagon, the documentary unveiled a massive and costly public relations effort to improve the public perception of the military. However, these facts, while open to some subjective interpretation, were not the real cause of the dispute.

The real issues of contention centered around how the producers had "reconstructed" several key interviews and speeches shown in the documentary. The first controversial sequence involved a lecture by Army Colonel John A. McNeil that began with Mudd's voice-over noting that "The Army has a regulation stating 'Personnel should not speak on the foreign policy implication of U.S. involvement in Vietnam.'" McNeil was then shown delivering what appeared to be a six-sentence passage from his talk, which made him seem to be contravening official military regulations. In fact, the sequence was reconstructed from several different passages over a wide range of pages, taken out of context in places.

The second of the controversial interview sequences was with Assistant Secretary of Defense Daniel Henkin on the reasons for the public displays of military equipment at state fairs and shopping centers. Again, many of Henkin's answers were taken out of context and juxtaposed, making him appear, in television critic Martin Mayer's words, "a weasler and a fool." Henkin, in keeping with government policy, had made his own tape recording of the interview, and he was therefore able to demonstrate how skillful editing had distorted what he had actually said.

The complaints about the show began only 14 minutes after it went on the air with phone calls to the network. The outcry in subsequent days was centered around two main sources: Representative F. Edward Hebert, chair of the House Armed Services Committee, and Representative Harley O. Staggers, chair of the House Committee on Interstate and Foreign Commerce and its Special Subcommittee on Investigations. On March 23, 1971, CBS ran the documentary again, and this time followed it with 20 minutes of critical remarks by Vice President Spiro T. Agnew, Representative Hebert, and Secretary of Defense Melvin Laird and a rebuttal by CBS News president Richard Salant. This presentation did not satisfy the politicians, and on April 7, Representative Staggers had subpoenas issued to CBS, demanding the record of the production of the documentary.

The next move was up to CBS, and on the afternoon of April 20, the network responded to the first executive session of the Special Subcommittee on Investigations through its deputy general counsel, John D. Appel. CBS disputed Representative Staggers's comment that "the American public has a right to know and understand the techniques and procedures which go into the production and presentation of the television news documentaries upon which they must rely for their knowledge of the great issues and controversies of the day." The network had voluntarily submitted the film and complete script of *The Selling of the Pentagon,* but it refused to supply the outtakes, draft notes, payments to persons appearing, and other material that had been subpoenaed.

The Federal Communications Commission (FCC) refused to become involved in the case, and the subcommittee held a series of hearings that included testimony from Assistant Secretary Henkin and Colonel John A. McNeil (who had in the interim filed a $6 million lawsuit against the network). On June 24, at the subcommittee's third meeting, the star witness was Frank Stanton, the president of CBS. Stanton claimed that he had "a duty to uphold the freedom of the broadcast press against congressional abridgment," and he pointed out the differences between print and broadcast journalism. He noted that these issues would not arise with the print media, but "because broadcasters need government licenses while other media do not, the First Amendment permits such an intrusion into the freedom of broadcast journalism, although it admittedly forbids the identical intrusion into other press media." There was a provocative exchange between Representative Springer over the definition of "the press," with the congressman trying to prove, with the aid of a 1956 edition of Webster's *New Collegiate Dictionary,* that broadcasting was not part of "the press." Stanton testified for more than four hours, and in the end he refused to submit to the subcommittee's subpoena.

In the midst of the furor concerning *The Selling of the Pentagon,* an even more important First Amendment issue was thrust on the public scene. On June 13, the *New York Times* published the first installment of the series of what became known as "The Pentagon Papers." This case moved rapidly through the courts, and on June 30, the U.S. Supreme Court, by a vote of six to three, allowed the unrestrained publication of the documents.

It was against this background that on June 28 the subcommittee voted unanimously to refer the entire case to its parent Committee on Interstate and Foreign Commerce. On July 1, the full committee voted 25 to 13 to report the matter to the House, with a recommendation that the network and Stanton be cited for contempt. Stanton could not help but notice the contrast between the two decisions: "This action is in disappointing contrast to the Supreme Court's ringing reaffirmation yesterday of the function of journalism in a free society."

On July 8, Staggers made his bid for House support with a floor speech and a letter to members of Congress. On July 13, in a surprisingly heated debate, the issue came to a head. In the end, one of the committee members, Representative Hastings Keith, introduced a motion to recommit the resolution to the committee, which was asked to report back to the floor with legislation that would more adequately express the intent of Congress and give authority to the FCC to move in a constitutional way that would require the networks to be as responsible for the fairness and honesty of their documentaries as they were for quiz shows and other programs. After a roll call vote, the resolution was approved 226 to 181, effectively negating the contempt citations. Staggers commented, "The networks now control this Congress." Stanton, as was to be expected, was extremely pleased by what he felt was "the decisive House vote."

What was the final outcome? Was the vote really that decisive? On July 15, Representative Keith followed through on his promise and introduced legislation that would have prohibited broadcasters from staging an event, or "juxtaposing or rearranging by editing," without indicating to the public that this had occurred. The proposed legislation never made it to the floor. The final outcome was a victory of sorts for CBS specifically and broadcast journalism in general, for never in modern history had the House failed to sustain the vote of one of its committees to cite for contempt.

The Selling of the Pentagon was a milestone in the development of the television documentary, not so much for what it contained but because it represented a clear statement that the networks could not be made to bend to government control in the technological era.

GARTH S. JOWETT

See also **Columbia Broadcasting System; Stanton, Frank; Vietnam on Television; Wallace, Mike**

Narrator
Roger Mudd

Producer
Peter Davis

Programming History
CBS
February 23, 1971

Further Reading

Fulbright, J. William, *The Pentagon Propaganda Machine,* New York: Liveright, 1970
Irvine, Reed J., "The Selling of *The Selling of the Pentagon,*" *National Review* (August 10, 1971)

Jowett, Garth S., "*The Selling of the Pentagon:* Television Confronts the First Amendment," in *American History/American Television: Interpreting the Video Past,* edited by John O'Connor, New York: Ungar, 1983

Mayer, Martin, *About Television,* New York: Harper and Row, 1972

Rogers, Jimmie N., and Theodore Clevenger, Jr., "*The Selling of the Pentagon:* Was CBS the Fulbright Propaganda Machine?," *Quarterly Journal of Speech* (October 1971)

Smith, F. Leslie, "*Selling of the Pentagon* and the First Amendment," *Journalism History* (Spring 1975)

September 11, 2001. *See* Terrorism

Serling, Rod (1924–1975)

U.S. Writer, Producer

Rod Serling was perhaps the most prolific writer in American television. It is estimated that during his career from the late 1940s to 1975, more than 200 of his teleplays were produced. This staggering body of work for television has ensured Serling's place in the history of the medium. His emphasis on character (psychology and motivation) and the expedient handling of incisive, direct, and forceful and painfully penetrating dialogue, alongside his moralizing subtext, placed him in a unique position to question humankind's prejudices and intolerance as he saw it.

Following army service, Serling entered Antioch College in Ohio as a student under the GI Bill, where he began writing radio and television scripts, selling a number while still an undergraduate. On leaving college, he went to work as a continuity writer for a Cincinnati, Ohio, television station, WLWT-TV, and then began writing a regular weekly series of live dramas for the anthology show *The Storm,* produced by Robert Huber for WKRC-TV in Cincinnati. Turning freelance in 1952, Serling sold scripts to such network anthologies as *Lux Video Theatre, Hallmark Hall of Fame, The Doctor, Studio One,* and *Kraft Television Theatre.* It was for the latter show that Serling wrote "Patterns" (American Broadcasting Company [ABC], January 12, 1955), a powerful drama about corporate politics and big-business power games. It was an instant success with both the viewers and the critics, winning him his first of six Emmy Awards (for Best

Original Teleplay Writing) as well as a Sylvania Award for Best Teleplay.

Serling followed this drama with, among others, an adaptation of Ring Lardner's "The Champion" (for *Climax,* 1955), "The Rack," (*U.S. Steel Hour,* 1955), "Incident in an Alley" (*U.S. Steel Hour,* 1955), "Noon on Doomsday" (*U.S. Steel Hour,* 1956), and "Forbidden Area" (*Playhouse 90,* 1956). "Forbidden Area" was his first script for *Playhouse 90* (an adaptation of a Pat Frank story) and was also that show's premiere episode. But it was *Playhouse 90*'s second presentation that brought him his greatest success: "Requiem for a Heavyweight" (Columbia Broadcasting System [CBS], October 11, 1956). This compelling yet overlong story of a boxer who knows that he is washed up but does not know anything else than the world of the ring projected Serling to the top ranks of the TV writing elite and brought him a gallery of awards, including another Emmy (for Best Teleplay Writing), a Harcourt-Brace Award, another Sylvania Award (for Best Teleplay Writing), a Television-Radio Writers' Annual Award, a Writers Guild of America Award, and the first ever George Foster Peabody Award for writing. *Playhouse 90* and CBS promptly signed him to a contract, and he became one of the show's chief writers (among such distinguished names as Horton Foote and Reginald Rose). Serling's next *Playhouse 90,* "The Comedian" (CBS, February 14, 1957), based on Ernest Lehman's story about an egomaniacal enter-

Rod Serling, *The Twilight Zone,* 1963.
Courtesy of the Everett Collection

tainer, gave him his third Emmy for Best Teleplay Writing.

But then, from 1958, his conflicts with networks and sponsors over censorship of his work became increasingly intense. "I can recall the blue-penciling of a script of mine called 'A Town Has Turned to Dust,'" he said in a 1962 *TV Guide* interview, "in which a reference to a 'mob of men in masks and sheets' was cut because of possible affront to Southern institutions." Eventually, these censorship battles led to Serling making a transition from live drama to filmed series television and his own *The Twilight Zone.*

Stemming from a Serling-scripted *Westinghouse–Desilu Playhouse* entry called "The Time Element" (November 1958), Serling created, executive-produced, hosted, and (for the most part) wrote the half-hour science-fantasy anthology *The Twilight Zone,* networked by CBS from 1959 to 1964. The series not only created a whole new programming genre for television but also offered Serling an opportunity to say things he could never get away with in more conventional dramatizations. The weekly tales remain memorable for allowing the viewer to enter "the middle ground between light and shadow, between science and superstition,"

which lay "between the pit of man's fears and the summit of his knowledge."

The Twilight Zone added two more Emmys (Outstanding Writing Achievement in Drama) to Serling's already impressive collection of tributes. His sixth and final Emmy came during *Twilight Zone*'s run, for the 1963 *Bob Hope Presents the Chrysler Theatre* segment "It's Mental Work" (also for Outstanding Writing Achievement in Drama, Adaptation). But it was with *The Twilight Zone* that Serling reached the peak of his success, for most of what followed after this period would be below Serling's personal standard.

In the fall of 1965, CBS premiered Serling's *The Loner,* a half-hour, post–Civil War western about a wandering, introspective cowboy in search of life's meaning, starring Lloyd Bridges. The story behind *The Loner* went back almost five years to the time when Serling believed that his *Twilight Zone* would not be renewed by CBS, and as an alternative he came up with a one-hour pilot script about a character he called the Loner, heading west after the Civil War. CBS turned it down. However, around the same time, *The Twilight Zone* was given the go-ahead for another season, so *The Loner* script was shelved. When in early 1965 CBS was looking for a half-hour western for their Saturday night schedules, independent producer William Dozier, remembering Serling's *The Loner* proposal from his CBS days, sold the package (now consisting of Serling as writer, Bridges as star, and Dozier as producer) to the network. The series of 26 episodes (14 of them by Serling) opened to poor ratings and lukewarm reviews. When CBS demanded more "action" (meaning less character and less motivation and more "running gun battles"), Serling refused to comply, causing a rift between the writer and the network. *The Loner* left the schedules in April 1966.

For the next few years, Serling occupied himself with various projects and programs. He served a two-year term as president of the National Academy of Television Arts and Sciences, hosted TV entertainment shows (*The Liar's Club,* 1969; *Rod Serling's Wonderful World of…,* 1970), and turned, once again, to screenplay work with adaptations of novels for *Planet of the Apes* (1968; based on the novel by Pierre Boulle) and *The Man* (1972; from the novel by Irving Wallace, which had actually started out as a telefilm). Not unlike other 1950s TV writers, Serling had based his earliest screenplays on his own television work: *Patterns* (United Artists, 1956), *The Rack* (MGM, 1956), *Incident in an Alley* (United Artists, 1962), and *Requiem for a Heavyweight* (Columbia, 1962).

In 1969, he was approached by producer Aaron Spelling to write a pilot for a series called *The New*

People (ABC, 1969–70), featuring an assorted group of young Americans stranded on a South Pacific atoll. Serling delivered his script but later commented on the *Lord of the Flies* theme that "it may work, but not for me." NBC's horror-fantasy anthology *Night Gallery* (1970–73) was to occupy his time during the early 1970s, following the pilot TV movie (NBC, 1969), adapted from his short-story collection (*The Season to Be Wary*), published in 1967. Based on the three stories (one directed by the young Steven Spielberg), the Mystery Writers of America presented him with their special Edgar Award for the suitably suspenseful scripts. Also known as *Rod Serling's Night Gallery* (he acted as host and sometime contributor), the series failed to come anywhere close to his *Twilight Zone* sense of "seriousness," as Serling had hoped, and the show quickly deteriorated, according to Tim Brooks and Earle Marsh, into "the supernatural equivalent of *Love, American Style*." There were, however, two Serling episodes that remain outstanding for their sense of compassion and morality: "They're Tearing Down Tim Riley's Bar" and "The Messiah on Mott Street"; both were nominated for Emmys.

After *Night Gallery* was canceled in 1973, Serling retreated to Ithaca College, in upstate New York, and taught writing. Teaching the art of writing sustained him more than anything else during the last few years of his life. *The Twilight Zone*, in constant reruns, remains a cultural milestone to Serling's art, craft, and practice.

TISE VAHIMAGI

See also **Anthology Drama; "Golden Age" of Television;** *Playhouse 90; Twilight Zone, The*

Rod Serling. Born Edward Rodman Serling in Syracuse, New York, December 25, 1924. Educated at Antioch College, Yellow Springs, Ohio, B.A. 1950. Married: Carolyn Kramer, 1948; two daughters. Served as paratrooper in U.S. Army during World War II. Worked as writer for WLW-Radio, Cincinnati, Ohio, 1946–48, WKRC-TV, Cincinnati, 1948–53; freelance writer, from 1953; producer, television series *The Twilight Zone*, 1959–64, and *Night Gallery*, from 1969; taught at Antioch College, 1950s, and Ithaca College, Ithaca, New York, 1970s. Honorary degrees: D.H.L., Emerson College, Boston, 1971, and Alfred University, New York, 1972; Litt.D., Ithaca College, 1972. President, National Academy of Television Arts and Sciences, 1965–66; member of the council, Writers Guild of America West, 1965–67. Recipient: six Emmy Awards; Sylvania Awards, 1955 and 1956; Christopher Awards, 1956 and 1971; Peabody Award, 1957; Hugo Awards, 1960, 1961, and 1962. Died in Rochester, New York, June 28, 1975.

Television Plays (selected)

1953	"Nightmare at Ground Zero," *Suspense*
1953	"Old MacDonald Had a Curve," *Kraft Television Theatre*
1954	"One for the Angels," *Danger*
1955	"Patterns," *Kraft Television Theatre*
1955–56	*U.S. Steel Hour*
1956	"Requiem for a Heavyweight," *Playhouse 90*
1956	"Forbidden Area," *Playhouse 90* (from Pat Frank's novel)
1957	"The Comedian," *Playhouse 90*
1959	"The Lonely," *Twilight Zone*
1959	"Time Enough at Last," *Twilight Zone*
1965–66	*The Loner*, 14 episodes
1966	*The Doomsday Flight*
1970	"A Storm in Summer," *Hallmark Hall of Fame*
1971	"Make Me Laugh," *Night Gallery*

Television Series (producer)

1959–64	*The Twilight Zone*
1970–73	*Night Gallery*

Films (writer)

Patterns, 1956; *Saddle the Wind* (with Thomas Thompson), 1958; *Requiem for a Heavyweight,* 1962; *The Yellow Canary,* 1963; *Seven Days in May,* 1963; *Assault on a Queen,* 1966; *Planet of the Apes* (with Michael Wilson), 1967; *The Man,* 1972.

Radio

The Zero Hour (host), 1973.

Stage

The Killing Season, 1968.

Publications

Stories from the Twilight Zone, 1960
More Stories from the Twilight Zone, 1961
New Stories from the Twilight Zone, 1962
Rod Serling's Triple W: Witches, Warlocks and Werewolves (introduction), 1963
From the Twilight Zone (short stories), 1962
Rod Serling's Twilight Zone Revisited (foreword), 1964

Chilling Stories from Rod Serling's The Twilight Zone (foreword), 1965
The Season To Be Wary, 1967
Rod Serling's Devils and Demons (introduction), 1967
Night Gallery (short stories), 1971
Night Gallery 2 (short stories), 1972
Rod Serling's Other Worlds, 1978

Further Reading

Efron, Edith, "Integrity and the TV Writer," *TV Guide* (April 21, 1962)

Engel, Joe, *Rod Serling: The Dreams and Nightmares of Life in the Twilight Zone,* Chicago: Contemporary Books, 1989
Sander, Gordon, *Serling: The Rise and Twilight of Television's Last Angry Man,* New York: Penguin, 1992
Wolfe, Peter, *In the Zone: The Twilight World of Rod Serling,* Bowling Green, Ohio: Bowling Green State University Popular Press, 1997

Sesame Street

Children's Educational Public Television Program

The brainchild of documentary film producer Joan Ganz Cooney, *Sesame Street*'s mission was to help prepare children for school, especially underprivileged inner-city children. Cooney and Carnegie Corporation Vice President Lloyd Morrisett held what might then have been considered a radical belief: that the much-maligned medium of television could be used to address a widespread educational need. They hoped to diminish the disparity in opportunity created by poverty and make a difference in the lives of children.

Eight million dollars in grants from foundations and the federal government were allocated for the research, planning, and production of one season of one-hour shows. Cooney headed the show's production unit, founding the Children's Television Workshop (CTW) in 1968. To the delight of its creators and funders, the show was an overnight success when it first aired on November 10, 1969. Over half the nation's 12 million preschoolers saw it during its first six-month run.

Sesame Street was designed as an experimental research project—a collaboration between television producers, educators, researchers, psychologists, sociologists, child development experts, artists, writers, and musicians. From the beginning, it was a curriculum-driven program emphasizing cognitive, social, emotional, and physical development. Every segment or song was designed to educate young viewers about a specific lesson, and every year the curriculum, created by psychologists and educators, has changed to remain current with the latest findings and suggestions of preschool experts. Young viewers explore letters and numbers as well as subtle but significant messages about love, life, family, and friendship.

Maintaining an intricate balance between education and entertainment was a constant challenge during the show's development. As material was produced, it was tested on target audiences for appeal and comprehension. The creators initially wanted a show with no fantasy and thus created the urban street setting. When the show was pilot tested in Philadelphia, however, it was poorly received. Researchers discovered that kids lost interest during the street segments and concluded that combining fantasy with reality was necessary.

Jim Henson's Muppets, built especially for TV, were used to entertain while fulfilling curriculum needs. Initially, the Muppets were not intended to be included in the street scenes but were to appear only in taped inserts between street segments, animations, and films. Researchers found, however, that children paid attention only when animation and Muppets appeared and concluded that Muppets were integral to the success of the program. Since the first nationally aired episode, Muppets have interacted with the humans as well as among themselves in their own segments.

Big Bird and Oscar were, respectively, the first Muppets to appear. Big Bird, operated since the first episode by Carroll Spinney, represents a six-year-old and, like most of the Muppets, acts as a surrogate child, asking questions that kids might ask adults in real life.

Other original Muppets included Ernie and Bert, Grover, Kermit the Frog, Cookie Monster, and Oscar the Grouch, the trash-can resident whose role is to help kids understand that negative feelings such as anger and irritability are natural. Elmo, representative of a three-and-a-half-year-old, joined the Muppet cast in 1979. In 1999, "Elmo's World" was added as a daily 15-minute segment that closes each hour. It broke new ground in electronic animation while helping children learn to explore their world.

Some of the early cast of human characters, including Bob (Bob McGrath) Susan (Loretta Long), Maria (Sonia Manzano), and Luis (Emilio Delgado), continue as cast members. Since 1971, Linda Bove has used sign language and provided a positive role model for hearing and nonhearing kids. Bove's is the longest-running role of any physically challenged person in a TV series. Among child performers, the show has always featured children from local elementary schools, mostly from disadvantaged neighborhoods.

Over the years, *Sesame Street* increasingly confronted some of life's serious problems. In 1982, the producers used the death of actor Will Lee (fix-it-shop proprietor Mr. Hooper) to address the questions that children inevitably ask when someone dies. In 2001, a series of episodes dealt with rebuilding after a disastrous hurricane. The show also acknowledged marriage, pregnancy, and parenthood with Maria and Luis, who married on the show.

Sesame Street has become the most widely watched TV series in the world. Taped at Kaufman Astoria Studios in Queens, New York, it appears several times daily on more than 300 Public Broadcasting Service (PBS) stations across the United States. It has been adapted into several international productions, reflecting local languages, customs, and educational needs, and is aired in more nearly 150 countries. Seventy percent of American preschool children watch *Sesame Street* at least once a week. Since the beginning, the show has also attracted an adult audience with its "Who's Who" of singers and actors and parodies of grown-up entertainment (e.g., "Monsterpiece Theater"). The show has hosted more than 250 celebrity guests.

Sesame Street also sets the record for being the most researched show in television history with more than 1,000 studies on record affirming the show's efficacy and impact. Several establish that educational television makes lasting, measurable contributions to learning. One study concluded that teens who watched *Sesame Street* when younger had better grades in school, read more books for pleasure, had higher levels of achievement motivation, and expressed less aggressive attitudes than those who watched TV rarely or not at all.

Sesame Street has won 76 Emmys, more than any show in history. It has also earned Grammys, Peabody Awards, Parent's Choice Awards, the Prix Jeunesse International, a Clio Award, and Action for Children's Television Special Achievement Awards. In its 33rd season in 2002, the show underwent format changes in order to compete with other shows that were aimed at two- to four-year-olds.

KATHLEEN COLLINS

See also **Children's Television; Cooney, Joan Ganz; Educational Television; Henson, Jim;** *Muppet Show, The;* **Sesame Workshop**

Selected Cast

Jim Henson	Kermit the Frog (1969–90)/ Ernie(1969–90)/Guy Smiley/ Papa Twiddlebug/ Captain Vegetable/ Sinister Sam/Additional Voices (1969–90) (voice)
Carroll Spinney	Big Bird/ Oscar the Grouch/ Bruno (voice)
Carlo Alban	Carlo (1997–present)
Paul Benedict	The Number-Painter (1969–74)
Linda Bove	Linda Bove (1971–)
Ruth Buzzi	Ruthie (1993–99)
Kevin Clash	Elmo/Baby Natasha/ Benny the Bunny/ Hoots the Owl/ Kingston Livingston III
Bruce Connelly	Barkley (1978–present) (voice)
Emilio Delgado	Luis Rodriguez (1971–)
Savion Glover	Savion (1990–95)
Alaina Reed Hall	Olivia (1976–88)
Richard Hunt	Don Music/Gladys the Cow/ Placido Flamingo/Sully/ Two-Headed Monster (II) (1969–92)/Forgetful Jones/ Sonny Friendly (voice)
Bill Irwin	Mr. Noodle (1998–2000)
Raul Julia	Rafael (1971–73)
Will Lee	Mr. Harold Hooper (1969–82)
Loretta Long	Susan Robinson (1969–)
Sonia Manzano	Maria Figeuroa Rodriguez (1974–)
Jim Martin	Oscar
Bob McGrath	Bob McGrath (1969–)
Hal Miller	Gordon (1971–73)
Alan Muraoka	Alan (1998–)
Jerry Nelson	Count von Count/ Herry Monster/Amazing Mumford/Two-Headed Monster (I)/Fat Blue/Simon

	Soundman/Sherlock Hemlock/Mr. Snuffleupagus (1971–77)/Herbert Birdsfoot/ Biff Hardhat/Fred the Wonderhorse/Brother Twiddlebug/Additional Voices (voice)
Roscoe Orman	Gordon Robinson (1973–)
Frank Oz	Bert/Grover/Cookie Monster/ Harvey Kneeslapper/Mama Twiddlebug/The Salesman/ Professor Hastings/Prince Charming/Additional Voices (voice)
Charlotte Rae	Molly the Mail Lady (1972–73)
Martin P. Robinson	Aloysius "Snuffy" Snuffleupagus/Telly Monster/ Slimey (voice)
Matt Robinson	Gordon (1969–71), Roosevelt Franklin (voice)
David Rudman	Baby Bear/Davey Monkey/ Cookie Monster (2001)/ Humphrey/Two-Headed Monster (1992–) (voice)
Buffy Sainte-Marie	Buffy (1976–91)
David Langston Smyrl	Mr. Handford (1992–present)
Steve Whitmire	Ernie (1990–)/Kermit the Frog (1990–) (voice)

Producers

Ann Burgund	Producer
Joan Ganz Cooney	Executive producer
Robert Cunniff	Producer
Shyrlee Dallard	Producer
Lynn Klugman	Supervising producer
M.M. Murphy	Producer
Dulcy Singer	Associate producer (executive producer 1984–94)
Jon Stone	Executive producer
Edith Zornow	Supervising film producer

Writers

Lou Berger (1998–2001)
Molly Boylan (1998–2001)
Sara Compton (1998–2001)
Annie Evans (1998–2001)
Chrissy Ferraro (1998–2001)
Judy Freudberg (1998–2001)
Tony Geiss (1998–2001)
Ian Ellis James (1998–2001)
Emily Perl Kingsley (1998–2001)
David Korr (1998–2001)
Sonia Manzano (1981–)
Joey Mazzarino (1998–2001)
Jeff Moss (1998–2000)
Cathi Rosenberg-Turow (1998–2001)
Adam Rudman (1998–2001)
Nancy Sans (1998–2001)
Luis Santeiro (1998–2001)
Josh Selig (1998–2001)
Norman Stiles (1982–92)
Belinda Ward (1998–2001)
John Weidman (1998–2001)
Mo Willems (1998–2001)

Programming History

PBS
November 1969–present

Further Reading

Borgenicht, David, *Sesame Street Unpaved: Scripts, Stories, Secrets and Songs,* New York: Hyperion, 1998

Cook, Thomas D., *"Sesame Street" Revisited,* New York: Russell Sage Foundation, 1975

Fisch, Shalom M., and Rosemarie T. Truglio, editors, *"G" is for Growing,* Mahwah, New Jersey: Lawrence Erlbaum Associates, 2001

Lesser, Gerald, *Children and Television: Lessons from Sesame Street,* New York: Random House, 1974

Polsky, Richard M., *Getting to Sesame Street: Origins of the Children's Television Workshop,* New York: Praeger, 1974

Sesame Workshop

U.S. Production Company

Sesame Workshop is a nonprofit organization created in 1967, as the Children's Television Workshop (CTW), for the purpose of producing the educational program *Sesame Street.* To emphasize that the organization's mission has moved beyond television production only, the workshop's name was changed to its present form in June 2000.

CTW was headed by Joan Ganz Cooney, a television producer who, with Lloyd Morrisett of the Markle Foundation, attracted funding from federal and private sources, including the U.S. Department of Health, Education, and Welfare; the National Institutes of Mental Health; the Carnegie and Ford foundations; and the Corporation for Public Broadcasting. *Sesame Street,* designed to promote the intellectual and cultural growth of preschoolers (particularly disadvantaged preschoolers), revolutionized children's educational television when it premiered in 1969 and established the CTW model for program development and research regarding children and television.

The "CTW model" refers to the unique process of educational program development at the workshop. The paradigm evolved under the direction of Cooney; Edward L. Palmer, director of research; and Gerald S. Lesser, chair of the CTW Board of Advisors. Each of the workshop's series begins with extensive initial planning sessions involving producers, researchers, content experts, and advisers. The concepts developed in these sessions are then translated into program segments and pretested with the target audience. Frequently, the testing extends for lengthy periods prior to actual production so that producers can see how the audience reacts to the educational messages embedded in the programs.

In preparing for *Sesame Street,* for example, the research and design focused on the demonstrable ability of the program's elements to attract attention, appeal to the audience, and be comprehensible. Researchers assessed the attention-holding power of material by presenting content in competition with potential distractions. The tactics that elicited the most interactivity among viewers were explored further. The research concluded with tests to assess what appropriate audiences recalled about the programming. As a result of these procedures, *Sesame Street* went on air with very specific attention-holding tactics, such as fast movement, humor, slapstick, and animation. It was packaged in a magazine format and presented a carefully planned curriculum that focused on teaching letters and number skills.

Program development at the workshop does not stop when programs are broadcast. In addition to the unusual attention to formative research, the CTW model also includes a strong commitment to summative research; as part of its summative research plan, the Educational Testing Service (ETS), was commissioned to evaluate *Sesame Street.* In a series of studies published by ETS in 1970 and 1972, researchers Ball and Bogatz found that viewing the program had a significant impact on test subjects and offered evidence of the development of a positive attitude toward school among those subjects. In a 1976 study, Cook and Connor discovered that parental encouragement was vital to learning and that advantaged families were more likely to watch *Sesame Street,* thus ironically arguing that the gap between that group and the disadvantaged was not narrowed by the availability of the program.

Broadcast continuously in the United States since 1969, *Sesame Street* is clearly the workshop's outstanding success. From its beginning as a weekday show designed to teach thinking skills and factual knowledge such as letters and number skills, *Sesame Street*'s curriculum has been broadened to include goals such as reasoning, bilingual skills, acceptance of special needs, ecology, and health. The program is viewed by almost half of all U.S. preschoolers on a weekly basis.

Versions of *Sesame Street* have been broadcast in more than 40 countries, with more than 20 showing the national editions of the program in 2002. The international productions share the U.S. programs' commitment to teaching learning skills and values, such as tolerance and kindness, but are specially tailored for the children in the nation or region in which they are broadcast. For example, the Egyptian show emphasizes the educational needs of girls, and, in the 2002–03 season, the South African version included a Muppet child living with AIDS. The Israeli–Palestinian coproduction begun in 1998 portrayed friendship and tolerance between Israeli and Palestinian Muppets and presented segments in both Hebrew and Arabic. However, by 2002, the coproduction (which now included Jordan as well) had eliminated stories about Arabs and Israelis interacting and changed its name to *Sesame Stories.* The changes reflected the producers' conclusion that the heightened conflict between Israel and the Palestinian Authority made too unrealistic the notion of a street where the two groups would meet as peaceful neighbors.

Following the success of *Sesame Street,* CTW went on to produce a number of other major educational programs, including *The Electric Company,* which premiered in 1971 and was in production for a decade. *The Electric Company* emphasized symbol and sound analysis and meaning in a half-hour program designed to help slower readers catch up and good readers reinforce their skills. *The Electric Company* used the CTW model, a magazine format, and a variety of entertaining and attention-grabbing production techniques. Formative research for the program included innovative eye-movement and eye-contact measures of appeal and attention. ETS evaluation found that *The Electric Company* fostered significant positive effects, particularly for the youngest target viewers. *Feeling Good,* a 24-episode experimental series, was programmed in 1974, designed to examine health issues and targeted particularly for young parents and low-income families. Funding difficulties and low ratings forced the program to be produced in stages with considerable format changes. Low public awareness of the program seemed to contribute to lack of demonstrable effects.

3-2-1 Contact, a 65-program series for 8- to 12-year-old children, premiered in 1980 and focused on science and technology. The goals were to promote scientific thinking, participation in science activities, and awareness of science as a career, particularly for women and minority children. It used a magazine format with continuing features such as a mystery/adventure dramatic component. Research by Mielke and Chen in 1980 and 1983 found *3-2-1 Contact* attractive to children, who responded particularly positively to the drama format used in the "Bloodhound Gang" segments.

Square One TV premiered in 1987 with the goal of increasing problem-solving ability and a positive attitude toward mathematics among 8- to 12-year-old children. Format features included Mathnet, game show parodies, and commercials. The program covered mathematical concepts from estimation through graphics, probabilities, and geometry. CTW research showed that viewers in the target age-group enjoyed improved problem-solving ability and more positive attitudes toward mathematics.

Ghostwriter, a series focusing on writing skills, premiered in 1992. The series' appeal was built around a computer that provided "ghostlike" clues that enabled a group of young people to solve problems. Of these workshop programs, only *Sesame Street* is still in production, but because there is always a new audience of children available, most of the programs can still be seen. These are only a sampling of the workshop's major projects. The workshop continues to produce many other television programs, including the recent animated series *Dragon Tales* and *Sagwa,* both intended for preschool viewers.

By the 1980s, many of the funds for CTW were generated from *Sesame Street* product sales, the Sesame Place Amusement Park, and *Sesame Street Live,* a touring theatrical production. CTW became an unhappy participant in the struggles over Public Broadcasting Service (PBS) funding in the mid-1990s, when the financial success of *Sesame Street* was used as an example of why public funding was not needed to support educational children's programming. Despite such difficulties, the workshop—and *Sesame Street* in particular—remain a hallmark of children's programming in the United States. In the early 21st century, Sesame Workshop continues to expand its efforts to educated and entertain children. Among other ventures, it presents an expansive website replete with interactive games for children, suggestions for crafts and other forms of creative play, advice for parents, features about members of the *Sesame Street* family and characters from other series, as well as information about the workshop, its mission, and its products. The workshop has also partnered with Nickelodeon to create a commercial-free, educational cable channel. Between 6:00 A.M. and 6:00 P.M., the channel is called Noggin and offers programming for preschool children; during the other 12 hours of the day, the channel is called The N and shows programs for older children and teens. Featuring new and classic programs produced by the workshop and by Nickelodeon, Noggin/The N reached 22 million households in 2001. Like Sesame Workshop, both Noggin and The N complement their TV offerings with interactive Internet sites.

ALISON ALEXANDER

See also **Children and Television; Cooney, Joan Ganz; Henson, Jim;** *Muppet Show, The*

Further Reading

Bryant, J., A. Alexander, and D. Brown, "Learning from Educational Television Programming," in *Learning from Television,* edited by M. Howe, London: Academic Press, 1983

"Children's Learning from Television: Research and Development at the Children's Television Workshop" (special issue), *Educational Technology Research and Development* (1990)

Clifford, B.R., B. Gunter, and J. McAleer, *Television and Children: Program Evaluation, Comprehension, and Impact,* Hillsdale, New Jersey: Lawrence Erlbaum Associates, 1995

Lesser, Gerald S., *Children and Television: Lessons from Sesame Street,* New York: Random House, 1974

Salamon, Julie, "Israeli-Palestinian Battles Intrude on *Sesame Street*," *New York Times* (July 30, 2002)

Sevareid, Eric (1912–1992)

U.S. Journalist

Eric Sevareid was one of the earliest of a group of intellectual, analytic, adventurous, and sometimes even controversial newspapermen handpicked by Edward R. Murrow as CBS Radio foreign correspondents. Later, Sevareid and others of this elite band of broadcast journalists, known as "Murrow's Boys," distinguished themselves in television. From 1964 until his retirement from the Columbia Broadcasting System (CBS) in 1977, Sevareid carried on the Murrow tradition of news analysis in his position as national correspondent for the *CBS Evening News.* There, his somber, eloquent commentaries were either praised as lucid and illuminating or criticized for sounding profound without ever reaching a conclusive point.

Sevareid's image as a scholarly commentator on the *CBS Evening News* was belied by an early career in which he was something of a swashbuckler. Sevareid was working at the *New York Herald Tribune*'s Paris office when his writing abilities caught the eye of Murrow, who offered him a job. Sevareid would later say of those early years, "We were like a young band of brothers in those early radio days with Murrow." In his final 1977 *CBS Evening News* commentary, Sevareid referred to Murrow as the man who "invented me."

As one of "Murrow's Boys" during World War II, Sevareid "scooped the world" with his broadcast of the news of the French surrender in 1940. He joined Murrow in covering the Battle of Britain, he was lost briefly after parachuting into the Burmese jungle when his plane developed engine trouble while covering the Burmese–China theater, he reported on Tito's partisans, and he landed with the first wave of U.S. troops in southern France, accompanying them all the way to Germany.

In 1946, after reporting on the founding of the United Nations, Sevareid wrote *Not So Wild a Dream,* which appeared in 11 printings and became a primary source on the lives of the generation of Americans who had lived through the Depression and World War II. For the 1976 edition of the book, he wrote, "It was a lucky stroke of timing to have been born and lived as an American in this last generation. It was good fortune to be a journalist in Washington, now the single news headquarters in the world since

Eric Sevareid.
Courtesy of the Everett Collection

ancient Rome. But we are not Rome; the world is too big, too varied."

Always considering himself a writer first, Sevareid felt uneasy behind a microphone and even less comfortable with television; nevertheless, he did such early Sunday "news-ghetto" programs as *Capitol Cloakroom* and *The American Week* and served as host and science reporter on the CBS series *Conquest*. As head of the CBS's Washington bureau from 1946 to 1959, Sevareid was an early critic of McCarthyism, and, in one of the few even mildly critical comments he ever made about his mentor, he observed that Murrow came to the issue rather late.

Serving as CBS's roving European correspondent from 1959 to 1961, Sevareid contributed stories to *CBS Reports* as well as serving as moderator of series such as *Town Meeting of the World, The Great Challenge, Where We Stand,* and *Years of Crisis.* In addition, he also contributed to the coverage of every presidential election from 1948 to 1976. However, one of Sevareid's scoops of those years, his 1965 exclusive interview with Adlai Stevenson shortly before Stevenson's death, for which Sevareid won a New York Newspaper Guild Page One Award, was not broadcast over CBS, appearing instead in *Look* magazine.

From 1963 until his retirement, Sevareid appeared on the *CBS Evening News with Walter Cronkite.* During that period, his Emmy and Peabody Award–winning two-minute commentaries, with their penchant to elucidate rather than advocate, inspired those who admired him to refer to him as the "Gray Eminence." On the other hand, those who were irked by his tendency to overemphasize the complexity of every issue nicknamed him "Eric Severalsides." Sevareid himself said that as he had grown older, his tendency was toward conservatism in foreign affairs and liberalism in domestic politics. Despite this perspective, he commented after a trip to South Vietnam in 1966 that prolonging the war was unwise and that a negotiated settlement was advisable. His commentary on the resignation speech of President Richard M. Nixon ("Few things in his presidency became him as much as his manner of leaving the presidency") was hardly as perceptive.

In addition to sustaining the Murrow tradition of news commentary at CBS, Sevareid, in keeping with another Murrow tradition, interviewed noted individuals such as West German Chancellor Willy Brandt, novelist Leo Rosten, and many others on the series *Conversations with Eric Sevareid.* In something of a spoof of this tradition, he also had a conversation with King George III (played by Peter Ustinov) titled *The Last King in America.*

After his retirement, Sevareid continued to be active as a CBS consultant and narrator of shows such as *Be-* *tween the Wars* (syndicated, 1978), a series on U.S. diplomacy between 1920 and 1941, *Enterprise* (Public Broadcasting Service [PBS], 1984), a series on American business, and *Eric Sevareid's Chronicle* (syndicated, 1982). His final appearance before his death in 1992 was on the 1991 CBS program *Remember Pearl Harbor.* Needless to say, Sevareid's presence at CBS was a link to the Murrow tradition, long after Murrow himself and many of his "Boys" left the network and after that tradition ceased to have significant practical relevance at CBS News.

ALBERT AUSTER

See also **Columbia Broadcasting System; Cronkite, Walter; Murrow, Edward R.; News, Network**

Eric Sevareid. Born in Velva, North Dakota, November 26, 1912. Educated at the University of Minnesota, B.A. in political science, 1935; studied at London School of Economics, and Alliance Française, Paris. Married: 1) Lois Finger, 1935 (divorced, 1962); two sons; 2) Belén Marshall, 1963; one daughter; 3) Suzanne St. Pierre. Worked as teenager as copyboy for the *Minneapolis Journal;* worked during college as freelancer for the *Minneapolis Star;* served on staff of the *Minneapolis Journal,* 1936–37; reporter, Paris edition of the *New York Herald Tribune,* 1938; recruited to join CBS Radio by Edward R. Murrow, 1939; traveled with French Army and Air Force for CBS, 1939–40, became first to report France's capitulation to Germany; assigned to CBS News Bureau in Washington, D.C., 1941–43; served as war correspondent in China, 1943–44, London, 1945; served as chief Washington correspondent for CBS, 1946–59; worked as European correspondent, 1959–61; moderator, numerous CBS News programs, 1961–64; served as commentator for the *CBS Evening News,* from 1963; national correspondent, CBS News, from 1964; hosted interview series, *Conversations with Eric Sevareid,* from 1977; consultant, CBS News, from 1977; reported on numerous presidential conventions. Received numerous honorary degrees. Recipient: Peabody Awards, 1950, 1964, and 1976; Emmy Awards, 1973, 1974, and 1977; two Overseas Press Club Awards; Harry S. Truman Award, 1981; numerous other awards. Died July 10, 1992.

Television

1957–58	*Conquest* (host and science reporter)
1963–77	*CBS Evening News* (commentator)
1964–77	*CBS Evening News* (national correspondent)
1977	*Conversations with Eric Sevareid*

Television Special

1959   *CBS Reports: Great Britain—*
            Blood, Sweat and Tears Plus Twenty
            Years

Publications

Canoeing with the Cree, 1935
Not So Wild a Dream, 1946
In One Ear, 1952
Small Sounds in the Night, 1956
Candidates 1960 (editor), 1959
This Is Eric Sevareid, 1964

Further Reading

Cloud, Stanley, and Lynne Olson, *The Murrow Boys: Pioneers on the Front Lines of Broadcast Journalism,* Boston, Massachusetts: Houghton Mifflin, 1996

Fensch, Thomas, editor, *Television News Anchors: An Anthology of Profiles of the Major Figures and Issues in United States Network Reporting,* Jefferson, North Carolina: McFarland, 1993

Gates, Gary Paul, *Air Time: The Inside Story of CBS News,* New York: Harper and Row, 1978

McCabe, Peter, *Bad News at Black Rock: The Sell-Out of CBS News,* New York: Arbor, 1987

Schoenbrun, David, *On and Off the Air: An Informal History of CBS News,* New York: Dutton, 1989

Schroth, Raymond A., *The American Journey of Eric Sevareid,* South Royalton, Vermont: Steerforth, 1995

Sex

Australian Lifestyle Show

Sex, also known as *Sex with Sophie Lee,* was a "lifestyle" show launched in Australia in 1992. Produced by Tim Clucas for the Nine Network, the show went to a second series in 1993 with a new presenter, the comedian Pamela Stevenson. *Sex* can be seen as the first show on Australian TV to try to modernize sexual attitudes and make sex a vital topic of mainstream public discussion in the HIV era, or it can be seen as an attempt by commercial television to consumerize sex itself, making sexual preference into a supermarket choice, and to use public education as an excuse for exploitative television.

The show was launched to phenomenally high ratings (a 32 share), largely on the lure of its presenter Sophie Lee's own reputation for sexiness. But the early episodes succeeded in mixing straightforward advice about common problems with some noteworthy firsts for prime-time television, especially by showing human reproductive organs, both male and female, on screen. Most notably, even though its own format comprised traditional magazine-style journalistic and "expert" segments, linked by a studio anchor in glamorous evening wear, *Sex* crossed one of television's most policed generic boundaries: characters (fiction) can have sex, while people (fact) can only talk about it. The presentation of ordinary people being sexual on screen and the screening of sexualized bodies (even if only in bizarre slow-motion "reconstruction" mode) was enough to give the show an unsettling, innovative feel and to ensure that *Sex* provoked widespread discussion in the press and popular magazines as well as rating highly. Not all reaction was positive; for instance, the president of General Motors Holden announced that the car company would not advertise during *Sex* because it wanted its products to be associated with "wholesome" topics.

Sophie Lee became progressively disenchanted with the lack of control she had over the items she was contracted to introduce, segments that began to interpret "sex" in terms of ratings potential rather than public utility. She left the show at the end of its first season, to be replaced by Pamela Stephenson, the Australian-born comedian best known for the 1970s British Broadcasting Corporation (BBC) series *Not the Nine O'clock News.* Stevenson recorded her links for *Sex* in a studio in Los Angeles, clearly regarding it as her brief to supply the "nudge, nudge, wink, wink" element. After the departure of Lee, without anyone on or behind the screen to argue for the show's importance in changing public attitudes to sex, the series slid from interesting experiment to unstylish exploitation and was canceled by the Nine Network after two seasons, to be replaced by safer lifestyle shows about money, home improvement, tourism, and gardening.

JOHN HARTLEY

See also **Lee, Sophie**

Hosts

Sophie Lee	1992
Pamela Stevenson	1993

Producer

Tim Clucas

Programming History

20 episodes
Nine Network

May 1992–July 1992	Thursday 8:30–9:00
February 1993–May 1993	Thursday 9:30–10:00

Sex and the City

U.S. Comedy Series

Sex and the City debuted on Home Box Office (HBO) in the summer of 1998. Its immediate success played a crucial role in the channel's development of original series by providing female-centered programming in contrast to the masculinity that defined programs such as *Oz* and *The Sopranos*. Though the series first drew attention for its risqué depiction of sex and nudity, critics and viewers quickly recognized significant emotional depth and complexity, qualities that gave its stories unmatchable resonance for some audiences. In some respects, *Sex and the City* continues the "new woman" comedy dating to early examples such as *That Girl* and *The Mary Tyler Moore Show.* But the series' unprecedented frank examination of the sexual desires and emotional needs of four distinct female characters helped it achieve the status of "watercooler" conversation for the small but specific demographic that subscribes to HBO.

Executive producer and writer Darren Star (*Beverly Hills, 90210,* and *Melrose Place*) adapted the series from a book of the same title written by Candace Bushnell that was based on her *New York Observer* newspaper column. Bushnell serves as the model for the character of Carrie Bradshaw, the actual "sexual anthropologist" who writes stories about sex and socializing in New York. The series reduces a much larger collection inhabitants in Bushnell's book to Carrie's three female friends: Charlotte, Miranda, and Samantha. Despite an offer from the American Broadcasting Company (ABC), Star chose to produce the series for HBO, recognizing that the premium cable channel could provide the opportunity for "elite" qualities in writing and production as well as provide a budget ($900,000 per episode) with which he could employ independent directors and writers. HBO also allows considerable freedom regarding content, allow-ing the series to derive humor from the sexual adventures of the four characters rather than from the double entendres and veiled discussion about sex typical of broadcast network sitcoms. Airing on commercial-free HBO also freed the show from a narrative structure dictated by commercial breaks and restricted to 23-minute episodes.

As the title suggests, issues of sex and dating provide the primary plots in *Sex and the City.* The series' quartet of main characters—all single, white women in their 30s—experience and discuss, quite explicitly, the singles' dating scene in New York City. Although the women are similar in many ways, each brings a distinct perspective to the series. Carrie, a newspaper columnist who writes about sex and dating, serves as the series narrator. In early episodes, this narration occurred as Carrie directly addressed the camera. In later episodes, her narration is provided through voice-over. Her friends often become subjects of her "research," and their dilemmas and situations inspire column topics. Samantha owns a public relations firm and is the most sexually carefree of the group. Often depicted as content to participate in endless one-night stands, she has no aspirations to marry or have children. Charlotte managed an art gallery until she married (then divorced, then remarried) and maintains a desire for a more conventional life of marriage and motherhood. Miranda, a corporate attorney, plays the realist and cynic to Samantha's excessively sexual identity and Charlotte's idealist fantasies. After an unexpected pregnancy, she embarks on single motherhood at the end of the series' fourth season, only to marry her child's father, Steve, in the sixth and final season.

With the exception of Carrie, the series rarely focuses on the characters' careers. The primary action takes place in the bars, restaurants, and clubs where the women meet for breakfast or lunch, have drinks, or spend their evenings. Although episodes often begin with the four meeting together, they commonly appear separately yet in stories with parallel themes, throughout the episode, with Carrie narrating transitions. The characters often walk and talk along the streets of Manhattan, enabling episodes to develop through dialogue more than action. The specific topics of Carrie's columns usually structure the episode. Each begins with a question: Can you be friends with an ex-boyfriend? How do you know if you are good in bed? Have New Yorkers evolved past relationships? Can you change a man? Why is there tension between married and single people? Why do men like to date models? Throughout the episode, each woman "answers" the question according to her personality and characterization.

The four remain the primary characters throughout the series, although a few boyfriends make repeat appearances, particularly in the later seasons in which the women explore long-term relationships. Charlotte meets, marries, and separates from Trey MacDougal during the third season; they later rekindle their relationship but ultimately divorce the next season. She falls in love with her divorce attorney, Harry Goldenblatt—a man who deviates significantly from her ideal beau—and converts to Judaism before marrying him in the final season. Her desire to have a family led to the divorce from Trey, and reproductive problems continue to ail her after marrying Harry. Miranda's balance of career and motherhood as a single parent becomes a primary storyline for her character as she and Steve Brady negotiate their relationship with each other and their roles as parents. Samantha eventually experiences a string of longer relationships, first with a woman, then with a male hotel tycoon, and finally with a much younger male model and actor. Throughout the relationships, she struggles with her desire to remain independent despite a simultaneous and contradictory desire for companionship. Carrie becomes engaged to Aidan Shaw, who briefly moves into her apartment. An affair with a recurring character, Mr. Big, leads to the end of the relationship with Aidan, but she and Big establish a friendship that survives his relocation to California. In the series' final season, Carrie meets Aleksandr Petrovsky, a significantly older Russian artist.

The first season of *Sex and the City* consisted of only 12 episodes, followed by 18 in each of the subsequent seasons. Once established, the series regularly drew an audience of approximately 6.4 million households, a strong performance for a cable network but significantly smaller than broadcast networks at the time. The series garnered Emmy Award nominations for Outstanding Comedy Series, writing, acting, directing, casting, and costumes and won the award for Outstanding Comedy Series in 2001.

AMANDA LOTZ

See also **HBO; Star, Darren**

Cast

Carrie Bradshaw	Sarah Jessica Parker
Samantha Jones	Kim Catrall
Charlotte York (MacDougal) Goldenblatt	Kristin Davis
Miranda Hobbs	Cynthia Nixon
Mr. Big	Chris Noth
Stanford Blatch	Willie Garson
Steve Brady	David Eigenberg
Aidan Shaw (2000–03)	John Corbett
Trey MacDougal (2000–02)	Kyle MacLachlan
Harry Goldenblatt (2002–04)	Evan Handler
Smith Jerrod (2003–04)	Jason Lewis
Aleksandr Petrovksy	Mikhail Baryshnikov

Producers

Darren Star, Michael Patrick King

Programming History

HBO

June 1998–August 1998	Sunday 9:00–9:30 12 episodes
June 1999–October 1999	Sunday 9:00–9:30 18 episodes
June 2000–October 2000	Sunday 9:00–9:30 18 episodes
June 2001–August 2001	Sunday 9:00–9:30 12 episodes
January 2002–February 2002	Sunday 9:00–9:30 6 episodes
July 2002–September 2002	Sunday 9:00–9:30 8 episodes
June 2003–September 2003	Sunday 9:00–9:30 12 episodes
January 2004–March 2004	Sunday 9:00–9:30 8 episodes

Further Reading

Arthurs, Jane, "*Sex and the City* and Consumer Culture: Remediating Postfeminist Drama," *Feminist Media Studies,* Vol. 3, No. 1 (March 2003)

Kim, L.S., "*Sex and the Single Girl* in Postfeminism: The F Word on Television," *Television & New Media,* Vol. 2 (November 2001)

Ross, Sharon Marie, "Talking Sex: Comparison Shopping Through Female Conversation in HBO's *Sex and the City*,"

in *American Viewed and Skewed: Television Situation Comedies,* edited by Mary M. Dalton and Laura R. Linder, Albany: State University of New York Press, forthcoming

Scarbrough, Marsha, "For a Good Time, Write *Sex and the City*," *Written By* (October 1999)

Sexual Orientation and Television

Once the freeze on television broadcast licenses was lifted by the Federal Communications Commission (FCC) in 1952, broadcast stations proliferated throughout the United States. Additionally, the FCC set the regulation standards for the mass production of television receivers, making them relatively inexpensive to produce and affordable for the middle-class American public. Having been a mostly East Coast, upper-class phenomenon before 1952, television broadcasting quickly became an economically profitable industry catering to perceived middle-class tastes.

Throughout the 1950s and 1960s, the television broadcast networks implicitly constructed the mainstream viewing public as replications of the idealized middle-class nuclear family, defined as monogamous, heterosexual couples with children. In response, the overwhelming trend was to provide programming targeted toward this consumer group. To a large degree, this construction stemmed from the larger context of American society, in which the ideals of heterosexuality and family dominated the overall hierarchy of sexual orientation.

However, this assumption was reinforced because the mode of distribution of programming and the measure of economic success were significantly different for television broadcasting than for most other forms of popular culture. For most other popular culture industries, consumers had to actively purchase a product (a movie ticket, a record, or a book). Economic success and popularity were determined by the number of sales of the cultural product. Within the American broadcasting context, however, the programming was distributed free of charge to anyone with a television receiver that could pick up the broadcast signal. The networks generated profits through advertising, selling the viewing audience as a potential target for commercial messages. In this mode of distribution, a network's success was determined by the number of viewers it attracted, not the number of programs sold. This interaction among the networks, advertisers, and the viewing audience developed into a very complex economic relationship.

Until the early 1970s and the introduction of demographic measurements, the networks quantified a mass audience as an index of a program's popularity to set commercial rates for advertisers. Since most television use by the American public has been and continues to be in a domestic environment, the networks and adver-

Soap, Billy Crystal, Richard Mulligan, 1977.
Courtesy of the Everett Collection

tisers easily assumed that the viewing audience in its values mirrored the idealized middle-class nuclear family of the 1950s. Given this institutional construction of the television viewer, the networks produced and broadcast a plethora of programs built around the values and concerns of the contemporary nuclear family. Series such as *I Love Lucy, Father Knows Best, Leave It to Beaver,* and *The Donna Reed Show* developed scripts explicitly exploring gender and sexual roles in the context of the 1950s. For example, *Father Knows Best* often defined appropriate and inappropriate gender behavior as Jim and Margaret Anderson negotiated their marital and implied (hetero)sexual relationship. Explicit discussion of sexual behavior was forbidden. In addition, the Anderson children were groomed for heterosexuality on a weekly basis as they entered into the adolescent dating arena. In the context of the series, same-sex romantic attraction was not offered as a viable or legitimate option for offspring Betty, Bud, and Kitten. Nor did episodes deal with many heterosexual options outside of conventional coupling, limited to traditional heterosexual norms.

Even series that were not located in the contemporary family milieu of the 1950s or 1960s reinforced a narrow range of heterosexual choices. In a series such as *Gunsmoke,* with its surrogate family, traditional heterosexual coupling was the status quo. What sexual tension existed in the series surfaced between Marshall Matt Dillon and saloon owner Miss Kitty, not between Matt and his deputy sidekick Chester. Even overt sexuality between Matt and Miss Kitty was seldom displayed in the series. After all, how was the wild expanse of the western prairie to be tamed if the product of sexuality was pleasure rather than population growth? Given the baby-boom mentality of the 1950s and 1960s, the sexual orientation of *Gunsmoke*'s characters and their sexuality replicated the dominant values of American society, at least as they were perceived by network programmers and advertisers.

This perception about sexuality began to shift slightly by the early 1970s as pleasure became more acceptable as the foundation for sexual activity. Even so, sexual orientation continued to be overwhelmingly defined as heterosexual, although an occasional gay or lesbian character began to make an appearance.

Several factors account for this cultural breakthrough. At this time, the Prime-Time Access Rule forced the networks out of the business of program production. As a result, the networks began to license programming from independent production companies, such as Norman Lear's Tandem Productions and MTM Enterprises. These independents were willing to address subject material, including explicit sexual

pleasure and homosexuality, that had previously been ignored by the networks.

Additionally, the networks and advertisers began to shift their conception used to market the viewing audience. In the ratings competition between the National Broadcasting Company (NBC) and the Columbia Broadcasting System (CBS) during this same period, undifferentiated mass numbers as the target of advertising and the basis for determining commercial rates gave way to the first wave of demographic marketing toward a younger, urban rather than older, rural audience. In conjunction with the moxie of independent program producers, sexuality, including explicitly gay characters, began to surface in programs because these young, urban viewers, at least in the perception of the networks and advertisers, were less inclined to take offense with potentially controversial topics.

Images of gay men and lesbians began to appear in fictional programming during the early 1970s for another reason as well. Culturally, gay men and lesbians became more visible in American society after the Stonewall riots in June 1969, a date now celebrated as a watershed moment of the modern gay rights movement. As gays and lesbians entered the struggle for social acceptance and legitimization within mainstream discourse, the emergence of gay characters became part and parcel of this burgeoning social consciousness. In response to a newfound possibility of representation, gay activist groups such as the National Gay Task Force (NGTF), formed in 1973, attacked any outright negative mainstream media images of gay men and lesbians.

Initially, single-episode gay characters, at best self-destructive and at worst evil, were used as narrative plot devices to create conflict among the regular characters of a prime-time series. This was not an acceptable representation for most gay activists. The first major conflict between gay activists and the networks occurred over just such a depiction in "The Other Martin Loring," an episode of *Marcus Welby, M.D.* during the 1973 broadcast season. The confrontation focused on the dilemma of a closeted gay man worried about the effect of his homosexuality on his family life. Welby's advice and the resolution to the narrative conflict finally rested on the repression of sexual desire. As Kathryn Montgomery (1989) points out, this initial conflict had little effect on preventing the broadcast of the episode. However, it did open the door for continued discussion between gay activists and the networks concerning subsequent representations.

Indeed, the networks began to solicit advice about gay representation before programming went into actual production. By 1978, the NGTF provided the networks a list of positive and negative images that it considered to be of greatest importance. From the negative perspective, the organization wanted to eliminate stereotypically effeminate gay men and butch lesbians as characters as well as inhibit the portrayals of gay characters as child molesters, mentally unbalanced, or promiscuous. In contrast, positive images would include gay characters within the mainstream of the television milieu. These images would reflect individuals performing their jobs well, who were personable and comfortable about their sexual orientation. Additionally, the NGTF asked to see more gay couples, more lesbian portrayals, and instances where gayness was incidental rather than the focus of a narrative controversy centered on sexual preference.

As one manner of achieving these positive goals, gay activists suggested that continuing regular gay or lesbian characters be used within a series format, expanding beyond the plot function of a "problem" that needed to be solved and eliminated. However, the inclusion of a recurring gay character created problems of its own. Story editors and scriptwriters had to maintain a delicate balance between creating gay characters who were too extreme in their behavior so as to be offensive to heterosexual mainstream viewers or were so innocuous that they become nearly indistinguishable in their gayness. Several series, beginning with *Soap* and *Dynasty* and more recently *Doctor, Doctor* and *Melrose Place,* have included regular gay characters as part of their narrative foundation, with varying degrees of success. Often within these series, the gay character is isolated from any connection to a larger gay community and lacks any presentation of overt sexuality. While it has certainly been acceptable for heterosexual individuals and couples to engage in displays of affection, it has been untenable, until recently, for gay characters to activate similar behavior.

Despite this glaring drawback, gay characters as series regulars have functioned differently in the narrative context than in a one-shot episodic appearance. For the most part, recurring gay characters have been comfortable with their sexual identity. The possible exception is Steven Carrington, oil heir apparent in *Dynasty,* who fluctuated in his sexual orientation from season to season. While a series regular's gayness could still initiate some problems in a series, his or her sexuality was no longer an outside problem. Rather, the series regular could provide a narrative position whereby sexual "otherness" could be used to discuss and critique the dominant representation of both homosexuality and heterosexuality. Contextually, adaptation to rather than the elimination of homosexuality became the narrative strategy.

Despite *Dynasty*'s wavering on the subject of homosexuality, early installments of the series illustrate this narrative shift. The gay subplots of this prime-time soap opera often performed a pivotal role in exposing the contradictions of heterosexual patriarchy. An excellent example is when Blake Carrington, the series' patriarchal figure, stood trial for the death of son Steven's gay lover. The courtroom setting of this particular subplot created an ideological arena for Steven to critique his father's homophobia, patriarchal dominance, and sense of socially constructed gender roles from an explicitly gay perspective. As can be seen by this example, a gay man or lesbian who appears as part of the regular constellation of a series' cast naturalizes gayness within the domain of mainstream broadcast narratives, thus allowing that sexual otherness a cultural voice of its own. In some instances of this process of naturalization, these fictional gay characters face many of the same problems that their heterosexual counterparts encounter. This has not necessarily meant that their sexual orientation has been ignored but rather that it has been woven together with other concerns to create multidimensional, sometimes contradictory characters that reflect some of the experience of gay men and lesbians in American society.

Since 1973, the broadcast networks, program producers, and gay activists have maintained an ongoing working relationship with each other. The Alliance for Gay and Lesbian Artists in the Entertainment Industry, an internal industry activist organization, has provided an important connection with outside gay activists. Often, gay men or lesbians within production companies have alerted activists about potential problems with plotlines or characters. Many producers and scriptwriters now elicit opinions from gay and lesbian activists in the preproduction process, thereby circumventing costly confrontations once a production is under way. In addition, network broadcast standards and practices departments have internalized many of the activist's concerns and criticisms, thus pressuring program producers to eliminate potential trouble spots from scripts. The activists have also learned to praise producers, directors, and scriptwriters creating appropriate gay-themed programming with positive reinforcement, such as yearly awards and congratulatory telegrams, letters, and e-mail messages. Because of this de facto system of checks and balances, antagonistic confrontations seldom arise between gay activists and the television broadcast industry.

The gay activists' success in dealing with the networks and program producers has also activated a strong response from religious and political conservatives since the mid-1970s. As Gitlin (1983) argues, these conservative social forces have regarded the social inroads made by gay men and lesbians as a threat to their own social power and deeply embedded patriarchal values, including traditional conceptions of the family, gender roles, and heterosexuality. Any positive representation of homosexuality (or even bisexuality) undermines the legitimacy of these traditional values. The conservative far right has been dominated by religious fundamentalist whites males such as Jerry Falwell and Donald Wildmon as well as white antifeminists such as Phyllis Schlafly. Indeed, Wildmon heads the American Family Association (AFA), a formidable advocacy organization that monitors the television broadcasting industry's presentation of sexuality with a Bible-thumping fervor.

In contrast to the gay activists who have been more than willing to confront the networks and program producers directly about the representation of sexual orientation, the AFA has employed an indirect approach. Providing members with postcards pre-addressed to advertisers, the AFA has often threatened a boycott of consumer products manufactured by companies placing commercials within the broadcast of objectionable programming. While the direct, preemptive approach of the gay activists appears so far to have been more successful with the commercial networks than the postbroadcast method used by the AFA, the latter organization's efforts have produced some effect. For one thing, advertisers who have come under fire from the AFA have begun to consider placement of a commercial in potentially objectionable programming less lucrative than they might have previously.

As a response to advertisers' reluctance to place commercials in programs that include a positive discussion of homosexuality, the networks' broadcast standards and practices departments have codified some of the AFA's concerns about sexual orientation as a means to counter any negative criticism from conservative advocacy groups. For one thing, the positive portrayal of any physically romantic or sexual interaction between gay or lesbian characters has been exorcised, generally, from programming content. In addition, any gay-themed script must include at least one character who presents a critique of homosexuality to provide a balanced discussion of the subject. As a side note, the Gay and Lesbian Alliance Against Defamation (GLAAD), formed in the mid-1980s, has appropriated AFA's practice of sending out pre-addressed postcards. GLAAD has also urged individuals to send them to advertisers, praising their bravery in placing commercials in gay-themed programming.

At times, program producers and the networks have ended up at the center of a cultural tug-of-war between gay activists and conservative religious fundamentalists. Perhaps the best illustration of this predicament occurred in the summer of 1977. The American Broadcasting Company (ABC) had scheduled *Soap* for the fall lineup. The series was created by Susan Harris as a satire on both the nuclear family and the overdrawn angst of daytime drama. One of the regular characters was Jody Dallas, a gay man. In addition, the heterosexual characters engaged in a number of extramarital affairs, hardly reinforcing traditional monogamy. ABC previewed the initial episodes of the series for local affiliates and gay activists. Some disgruntled station owners alerted the National Council of Churches, the forerunner of the AFA, about the risqué content of the show. In addition, the conservatives felt that the inclusion of Jody Dallas condoned homosexuality. As a result of the conservative backlash, some affiliates refused to carry *Soap*. Conservative forces picketed stations that did air the satire. Under threat of a product boycott, several potential sponsors backed out of buying time in the series. Gay activists were not pleased with the premise of the Dallas character either. He was too much the gay stereotype. In addition, Dallas was not particularly satisfied with his sexual orientation as he planned a sex change operation.

In an attempt to appease both sides, *Soap*'s producers adjusted the series after the first few episodes. Dallas's stereotypical elements were modified, nearly neutering the character in the process. In comparison to the other characters, his behavior became less explicitly sexual. Even so, he became more affirmative about his sexual orientation, dropping any desire to change his gender. Ironically, the more stable, less sexually outrageous Jody Dallas seemed to address conservative concerns about homosexuality as well. Without the overt presentation of Jody's sexual desire, apparently religious conservatives believed that the series did not condone homosexuality as strongly.

Throughout the 1980s and into the 1990s, opposing gay and conservative advocacy groups have continued to pressure the networks, program producers, and advertisers on the parameters of representation about sexual orientation. As in the case of *Soap*, gay and lesbian characters have usually appeared in a highly diluted form, nominally gay with perhaps a political stance but lacking sexuality. Only in a very few instances have these limits been successfully challenged, most notably in an episode of *Roseanne*, a domestic sitcom, and *Serving in Silence: The Margarethe Cammermeyer Story*, a made-for-television movie. In both instances, the cultural and economic clout of their respective production companies provided the impetus to include moments of intimacy and sexuality for lesbian characters. During the spring of 1994, Roseanne, as reigning prime-time diva and executive producer of her series, threatened to withhold an episode from ABC if it did not air with its lesbian kiss intact. The network initially balked but eventually broadcast the unedited episode rather than lose potential commercial profits from a top-ten series. The combined talents of Barbra Streisand, as executive producer, and Glenn Close, as additional executive producer and star, added production muscle to *Serving in Silence*. With their involvement, NBC gave the movie, dealing with both Cammermeyer's fight to be reinstated into the military as an open lesbian and her blossoming romantic relationship with her lover Diane, a green light. With Streisand's and Close's involvement providing an aura of quality and legitimacy, this production opened the cultural space for moments of physical intimacy as integral narrative elements. *Roseanne* and *Serving in Silence* have been hallmarks in the presentation of gay and lesbian experience in American television broadcasting.

A watershed of sorts was reached in the 1996–97 broadcast season. On *Ellen,* a series based around stand-up comedienne Ellen DeGeneres, a number of early episodes dropped thinly veiled innuendoes regarding main character Ellen Morgan's sexuality. For example, while shopping for a house, Morgan agrees with her real estate agent that a walk-in closet was as large as some apartments but that she would not want to live in it (which could be construed as a reference to being "in the closet," that is, hiding one's homosexuality). Writers peppered the series that season with double-entendre teasers, especially targeted for lesbian and gay viewers "in the know" about DeGeneres's own sexual predilections. By March 1997, rumors became public knowledge as DeGeneres confirmed both her own status as a lesbian and the production plans to bring her sitcom character out of the television closet. Though initially reluctant to give the go-ahead for such an episode, ABC set the air date for "The Puppy Episode" for April 30, 1997.

Despite aggressive attempts by the AFA and other conservative social groups to promote a boycott of Disney and ABC, the broadcast of "The Puppy Episode" was extremely successful, garnering the highest ratings for *Ellen* or any other regularly scheduled series on ABC for the 1996–97 broadcast season. At this historical juncture, ABC's promotional support, in conjunction with the overwhelming endorsement from other popular culture venues, did seem to promote the belief that "naming" oneself as gay was perfectly acceptable. "Behaving" gay became another issue altogether, as the conflicts between ABC and DeGeneres over program content and parental warnings in the fall of 1997 erupted into very public disagreements. When DeGeneres pushed for an on-screen romantic relationship that included a kiss, ABC balked. The very public conflict took its toll on comedienne DeGeneres as well as the overall tone of the series. By spring 1998, *Ellen*'s popularity had plummeted in the

Nielsen ratings, the only measure of success that really mattered to the networks. The series was canceled in flurry of public accusations and recriminations.

With this programming incident freshly embedded in both the networks' and the public's consciousness, NBC's inclusion of *Will & Grace,* another gay-centered sitcom, in its autumn 1998 Thursday night "must-see TV" lineup was somewhat surprising. Initially, *Will & Grace*'s narrative foundation was built on the enduring, and endearing, relationship between Will Truman, a gay man and successful lawyer, and Grace Adler, a heterosexual woman and his best friend since college. However, caustic secondary characters Jack McFarland, Will's outrageous and self-centered gay friend, and Karen Walker, Grace's wealthy, substance-using secretary, provide foils and broad contrasts to the title characters' relatively more levelheaded (read "mainstream") actions. Whether because of or in spite of the explicit "gayness" of the series, it has garnered audience favor, critical approval, and television industry esteem, with a number of Emmy wins. Indeed, that elusive on-screen gay kiss came to fruition during the series' second season. When Will and Jack are disappointed when a heavily promoted kiss between two men on a fictional NBC series fails to materialize, the two march to network headquarters to protest. Though brushed off by a closeted public relations denizen, they enact their protest—a lengthy kiss—in front Al Roker, *The Today Show* weatherman, as he broadcasts live in front of Rockefeller Center.

Even so, broadcast television has yet to include a gay kiss that encompasses either a romantic or a sexual punch. However, given *Will & Grace*'s continued success, the potential for such a momentous event looms on the horizon in broadcast television. In contrast, the American version of the British series *Queer as Folk* has moved far beyond the passionate same-sex kiss to include presentations of relatively frank depictions of sexual interactions. However, those depictions tend to be less frankly graphic than those presented on the original U.K. series. In addition, the 15-year-old sexually active gay teenager in the U.K. series appears as a 17-year-old in the U.S. version.

While gay men and lesbians inside and outside the television industry have applauded these cultural steps forward, the gains are by no means secure, especially outside the commercial networks, where gay activists have less social and economic power. In the American social context of the 1990s, the struggle between gay rights activists and anti–gay rights advocates has reached a crescendo. Both sides have confronted each other over the legitimacy of sexual orientation in the political and legislative arenas, with neither side winning any clear legal victories. However, a conservative shift has occurred in the political arena that could drastically impact gay and lesbian representation in noncommercial American public broadcasting. Because the federal government economically supports noncommercial broadcasting, funding for the Corporation for Public Broadcasting (CPB) can be reduced or eliminated altogether through the agendas of powerful political interests. Therefore, proactive intervention (techniques used by groups such as GLAAD with network representatives, program producers, and advertisers) has not worked as well in the noncommercial broadcast setting.

Once the bastion of liberal tolerance and a cultural podium for marginal social groups, the CPB has increasingly come under attack from conservative forces in Congress for precisely those reasons. Conservatives have threatened to eliminate funding and privatize CPB in response to the use of federal tax dollars to produce nontraditional programming, especially programming targeted to the gay community. Special programming such as Marlon Riggs's *Tongues Untied,* an exploration of gay African-American men's experiences with both homophobia and racism, and Masterpiece Theatre's production of Armistead Maupin's *Tales of the City,* a narrative set in the 1970s San Franciscan milieu of sexual experimentation, have been specific targets of conservatives. Both productions contained a fair amount of frank, adult language about sexuality and a modicum of nudity. Indeed, many Public Broadcasting Service (PBS) affiliates refused to air either program or, if they did broadcast the offerings, censored the material radically. *Tales of the City* generated enough controversy that conservative forces were able to pressure CPB to withdraw funding for the sequel, *More Tales of the City.*

As the social and political struggle over legitimization of gay rights accelerated in the mid-1990s, the inclusion and representation of gay men and lesbians in entertainment television programming continued to be a point of cultural conflict. Driven by the economic demands placed on network broadcasting as it competes with the relaxed standards on cable channels, programming broadened the parameters of acceptable content. Thus, the economic demands of commercial television may create an atmosphere for further presentation of alternatives to monogamous heterosexual orientation. In addition, the gay community has gained more interest from advertisers as a demographic social group with relatively more disposable income to spend. Indeed, some manufacturers of products, such as clothing, alcohol, and travel, have begun to produce print ads directly targeting gay men and lesbians. Similar advertising in television programming, specifically attracting a gay audience. is probably not far behind. In contrast, the strong shift to the conservative right in the political arena has already imposed government regulations on funding for the arts. The federal government has placed limits on the range of appropriate subject matter for grants from the National Endowment for the Arts, the National Endowment for the Humanities, and even the CPB. It is not outside the realm of possibility that conservative political forces will also attempt to regulate commercial television programming content.

With the proliferation of cable television distribution, however, such efforts might meet with limited success. The huge—and largely unexpected—2003 success of Bravo's *Queer Eye for the Straight Guy* indicates not only that there is an audience within the gay communities for material related to gay experience but also that a considerably larger audience will attend to gay-themed programming. This program, in which five gay men ("the Fab Five") engage in a "makeover" for a straight man, may have seemed a risky venture for the small network when it was acquired by NBC. Within weeks, however, word of mouth as well as mainstream press and electronic media publicity made the series sufficiently popular—and safe—for episodes to be presented on NBC's main schedule. By January 2004, Bravo announced that *Queer Eye* would go "on the road to Texas" for additional episodes, and the five cast members had negotiated for substantial raises.

As was the case with *Ellen* and *Will & Grace,* responses both within and outside the gay communities were mixed. But it seemed clear that such programs would no longer be taboo from first proposal. Given the larger context, issues about sexual orientation are hardly going to disappear in the near future. If anything, despite the success of a small number of programs, the number of confrontations over sexual orientation and the intensity of those conflicts will only increase.

RODNEY A. BUXTON

See also ***Ellen;*** **Gender and Television;** ***Queer as Folk; Soap***

Further Reading

Barnouw, Eric, *Tube of Plenty: The Evolution of American Television,* revised edition, Oxford: Oxford University Press, 1990

Brown, Les, *Television: The Business Behind the Box,* New York: Harvest Book/Harcourt Brace Jovanovich, 1971

Buxton, Rodney, "'After It Happened...': The Battle to Present AIDS in Television Drama, " in *Television: The Critical View,* 5th edition, edited by Horace Newcomb, New York and Oxford: Oxford University Press, 1994

Cowan, Geoffrey, *See No Evil: The Backstage Battle over Sex and Violence on Television,* New York: Simon and Schuster, 1980

Gitlin, Todd, *Inside Prime Time,* New York: Pantheon Books, 1983

Holtzman, Linda, *Media Messages: What Film, Television, and Popular Music Teach Us About Race, Class, Gender, and Sexual Orientation,* Armonk, New York: M.E. Sharpe, 2000

Montgomery, Kathryn, *Target: Prime Time,* New York and Oxford: Oxford University Press, 1989

Parish, James Robert, *Gays and Lesbians in Mainstream Cinema: Plots, Critiques, Casts and Credits for 272 Theatrical and Made-for-Television Hollywood Releases,* Jefferson, North Carolina: McFarland, 1993

Tropiano, Stephen, *The Prime Time Closet: A History of Gays and Lesbians on TV,* New York: Applause Books, 2002

Share

"Share" is an audience measurement term that identifies the percentage of television households with sets in use that are viewing a particular program during a given time period. If the total TV audience is represented by a pie, the audience for each program is a slice, or share, of that pie. The slices are not equal, however, since audience share varies widely according to the relative popularity of each program.

Share is a comparative tool. It allows station and network executives to determine how well their programs are doing when compared to competing programs on other broadcast or cable channels.

Share is closely associated with "rating," another measurement term. Both terms are derived from the same estimates of audience size, but the percentage quotient is calculated differently. Share measures the percentage of *active* TV viewers who are watching a particular program, while the rating for a program calculates the percentage of *all* television households—both those using TV and those not using TV.

For example, station WXXX airs *Jeopardy!* at 7:00 P.M. Sample data estimate that 10,000 of the city's 100,000 TV households (10 percent) are viewing that program. Some 40,000 households are viewing other programs, but another 50,000 are not using their TV sets. Since 10,000 of the 50,000 active viewers (20 percent) are watching *Jeopardy!,* that program has a share of 20, even though its rating (the percentage of TV households) is only 10.

Electronic media trade journals generally report both rating and share. Rating is expressed first and is given to the nearest tenth of a percent. Share follows and is rounded to the nearest whole percent. For example, an audience estimate for *60 Minutes* may report a 13.0/28, that is, 13 percent of the total TV households (the rating) and 28 percent of the viewing audience (the share).

If every television household were using TV during a given time period, the share and the rating would be equal. But since this never happens, the share for any program is always greater than its rating because different divisors are used to calculate the two equations.

The gap between share and rating is greatest during periods of very light viewing. An early morning newscast with a share of 30 and a rating of only 3 is competing very well against other programs in the same time block, even though the total number of viewers for all programs is small.

Share is useful as a comparative tool during virtually any portion of the day, however. When a program gains share, it usually does so at the expense of competing programs since the total audience for television during any given daypart is relatively stable.

Share can also be used to illustrate programming trends. One network may average its share of successive programs to illustrate its dominance on a particular weekday night. A new broadcast or cable network may average its share across an entire season to illustrate its increasingly competitive position over a previous season.

Share can be used to demonstrate industry trends. For example, the combined share of the American Broadcasting Company (ABC), the Columbia Broadcasting System (CBS), and the National Broadcasting Company (NBC) for the 1980–81 programming year was 90. This meant that 90 percent of the viewing audience was watching one of these three networks. The remaining 10 percent of the audience was distributed among independent stations, public television, and the few cable networks then in operation. By 1993–94, combined network share had dropped to 60, primarily because the cable networks collectively had captured one-third of the network viewers.

This erosion has continued, and during the 2001–02 season, combined network share for the four major U.S. networks (ABC, CBS, NBC, and FOX) fell below 50 for the first time. While the combined share for these four was 49, additional share for The WB and the

United Paramount Network (UPN) raised the total share for "over-the-air" networks to 57.

Some industry observers predict that network share will continue to decline; others assert that network share has "bottomed out" but may begin to show a slight gain in years to come. A study of network share measures the competition between traditional broadcasters and their new technology competitors.

Unless otherwise specified, share refers to the total universe of television households. Share can be used in demographics breakouts, however. A morning talk show may have a 2.2/20 for women 18 to 34 years of age. That would be the rating and share for this particular demographic grouping.

NORMAN FELSENTHAL

See also **A.C. Nielsen Company; Audience Research: Industry and Market Analysis; Cost-per-Thousand and Cost-per-Point; Demographics; Market; Programming; Ratings**

Further Reading

Beville, Hugh Malcolm, *Audience Ratings: Radio, Television, and Cable,* Hillsdale, New Jersey: Lawrence Erlbaum Associates, 1988

Rust, Roland T., and Naras V. Eechambadi, "Scheduling Network Television Programs: A Heuristic Audience Flow Approach to Maximizing Audience Share," *Journal of Advertising* (Spring 1989)

Webster, James C., and Lawrence W. Lichty, *Ratings Analysis: Theory and Practice,* Hillsdale, New Jersey: Lawrence Erlbaum Associates, 1992

Shatner, William (1931–)

U.S. Actor, Writer, Producer, Director

Dubbed the "theatrical wunderkind" in his native Canada for his performances in Shakespearean and classic dramas, William Shatner is perhaps best known for his roles in the popular series *Star Trek* and *T.J. Hooker.* But his body of work spans nearly 50 years in stage, film, and television and includes not only his work as an actor and company spokesperson but also that of writer, producer, and director.

In the 1950s, Shatner appeared in regional theatrical productions and toured with the Canadian National Repertory Theatre. In 1954, he was invited to join Tyrone Guthrie's Stratford Shakespeare Festival, where he played nearly 100 roles in 60 plays, including the title role of *Henry V* at age 22. Shatner traveled with the Stratford company when their production of *Tamburlaine the Great* opened on Broadway (1956), and although Shatner only had only a small role, he was noticed by a 20th Century-Fox studio representative. He rejected the offer of a lucrative seven-year contract in order to remain independent and retain the ability to choose his own roles. Shatner returned to Stratford for his third and final season.

A scholarship, plus a Tyrone Guthrie Award as the most promising actor, allowed him to return to New York. The myriad of anthology programs produced on the East Coast and Hollywood took advantage of the number of stage-trained actors available to them, and Shatner became one of the most sought-after performers in the live television productions. He found roles in anthologies such as *Good Year Playhouse, Studio One, Playhouse 90, Kaiser Aluminum Hour, Omnibus, U.S. Steel Hour,* and *Climax!* Shatner also worked in episodic television, including Rod Serling's *The Twilight Zone* (Columbia Broadcasting System [CBS]) and *The Man from U.N.C.L.E.* (National Broadcasting Company [NBC]) in an episode that also featured future *Star Trek* costar Leonard Nimoy. He had earlier turned down opportunities to star in television series for fear he would be typecast into a particular role. However, he overcame his apprehension to star in the short-lived *For the People* (CBS, 1965), playing determined New York Assistant District Attorney David Koster.

Shortly after the cancellation of that series, writer-producer Gene Roddenberry offered Shatner the opportunity to work in the second pilot for his fledgling science fiction series, replacing Jeffrey Hunter as captain of the USS *Enterprise. Star Trek* premiered on September 8, 1966, and William Shatner, as Captain James Tiberius Kirk, was on his way to becoming a cultural icon.

In an effort to avoid typecasting after *Star Trek* ended its three-year run, Shatner made numerous guest appearances on popular series, miniseries, and made-for-television films, including the critically acclaimed *The Andersonville Trial.* He returned to series television in the short-lived *Barbary Coast* playing Jeff Cable, an undercover agent in 1870s San Francisco.

Shatner continued working in guest roles, films, and stage work. He also toured in his one-man show *An Evening with William Shatner,* which combined dramatic readings with question-and-answer sessions with his audiences. Excerpts from this stage show were recorded and released as *William Shatner Live!* (1977).

Shatner once again returned to series television in 1982 as the star of Aaron Spelling's *T.J. Hooker,* playing a former Los Angeles detective who, after the shooting death of his partner, takes on the job of training new recruits at the LCPD police academy. The series was planned as an ensemble series with stories featuring the cadets. However, test audiences preferred Shatner's character, and the show was transformed into more of an action-adventure series, but, like *Star Trek,* it remained a character-driven show concentrating on the relationship of the characters over car chases and shoot-outs. Shatner made his directorial debut on the third-season episode "Gang War" (May 5, 1984). When the American Broadcasting Company (ABC) dropped the series in 1985, it was quickly picked up by CBS and became the first series geared directly for late night.

Shatner later hosted the reality-based *Rescue 911* (CBS, 1989–96). During its six seasons, the series credits over 300 lives saved by people who learned lifesaving techniques from the show. The series consistently won its Wednesday night time slot and won the 1990 People's Choice Award for Favorite New Dramatic Series.

A savvy businessman, Shatner is chief executive officer and minority partner of C.O.R.E. Digital Pictures, a Toronto special effects company. CORE (an acronym for "Company of Righteous Effects"), founded in 1994, has created effects for such films as *Fly Away Home* (1996), Disney's *Flubber* (1997), *X-Men* (2000), and *The Time Machine* (2002). In 1998, he signed on as spokesperson for the Internet company Priceline.com and starred in a series of radio and TV commercials that satirized his singing abilities.

An avid horseman, Shatner breeds horses on his Malibu ranch and each year hosts the Hollywood Charity Horse Show, which benefits Ahead with Horses, an organization that gives physically challenged children the experience of riding while boosting their confidence and self-esteem. He also raises and trains champion American saddlebreds on his Belle Rêve farm in Versailles, Kentucky.

Shatner has always maintained a good-natured attitude toward the roles with which he has been associated for the past 30 years. He even spoofed both his Kirk and his Hooker characters when hosting *Saturday Night Live* in 1986. He continues to satirize his characters and his reputation in films such as *Miss Congeniality* (2000) and *Showtime* (2002). His guest appearance as "The Big Giant Head" on *Third Rock from the Sun* garnered him his first Emmy Award in 1999. Shatner received his star on the Hollywood Walk of Fame in 1983.

SUSAN R. GIBBERMAN

*See also **Star Trek***

William Shatner. Born in Montreal, Quebec, Canada, March 22, 1931. Educated at McGill University. Married: 1) Gloria Rand, 1956 (divorced 1969); children: Leslie Carol, Lisabeth Mary, and Melanie Ann; 2) Marcy Lafferty, 1973 (divorced 1996); 3) Nerine Kidd, 1997 (died 1999); 4) Elizabeth Martin, 2001. Performer with the Stratford (Ontario) Shakespeare Festival, 1954–56; Broadway appearances: *Tamburlaine the Great* (debut), 1956; *The World of Suzie Wong,* 1958; *A Shot in the Dark,* 1961. Recipient: Tyrone Guthrie Award, 1956; Theatre World Award, 1958; Life Career Award from the Academy of Science Fiction, Fantasy and Horror Films, 1980; Saturn Award, 1983.

Television Series

1965	*For the People*
1966–69	*Star Trek*
1974–75	*Star Trek* (animated series)
1975–76	*Barbary Coast*
1982–87	*T.J. Hooker* (also director)
1989–96	*Rescue 911* (host, narrator)
1994	*TekWar* (also writer, producer, director)

Made-for-Television Movies and Miniseries

1970	*Sole Survivor* (CBS, January 9)
1970	*The Andersonville Trial* (PBS, May 17)
1971	*Vanished* (NBC, March 8–9)
1972	*The People* (ABC, January 22)
1971	*The Hound of the Baskervilles* (ABC, February 12)
1973	*Incident on a Dark Street* (NBC, January 13)
1973	*Go Ask Alice* (ABC, January 24)
1973	*The Horror at 37,000 Feet* (CBS, February 13)
1973	*Pioneer Woman* (ABC, December 19)
1974	*Indict and Convict* (ABC, January 6)
1974	*Pray for the Wildcats* (ABC, January 23)
1975	*The Barbary Coast* (ABC, May 4)
1976	*The Perilous Voyage* (NBC, July 29)

1977   *Testimony of Two Men* (syndicated, May 9, 16, and 23)

1978   *How the West Was Won* (ABC, episodes 4 and 5, March)

1978   *The Bastard (Kent Family Chronicles)* (syndicated, May 22–23)

1978   *Little Women* (NBC, October 2–3)

1978   *Crash* (ABC, October 29)

1979   *Disaster on the Coastliner* (ABC, October 29)

1980   *The Babysitter* (ABC, November 28)

1985   *North Beach and Rawhide* (CBS, November 12–13)

1994   *TekWar* (also writer, director) (USA Network, January 23)

1994   *TekLords* (also producer) (USA Network, February 20)

1994   *TekLab* (USA Network, February 27)

1994   *TekJustice* (USA Network, May 14)

Selected Television Guest Appearances

1956   *Goodyear Television Playhouse* ("All Summer Long," NBC, October 28)

1957   *Omnibus* ("Oedipus Rex," ABC, January 6)

1957   *Studio One* ("The Defender," February 25 and March 4)

1957   *Alfred Hitchcock Presents* ("The Glass Eye," CBS, October 6)

1958   *Kraft Television Theatre* ("The Velvet Trap," NBC, January 8)

1958   *United States Steel Hour* ("Walk with a Stranger," CBS, February 26)

1958   *Playhouse 90* ("A Town Has Turn to Dust," CBS, June 19)

1960   *Alfred Hitchcock Presents* ("Mother, May I Go Out to Swim," CBS, April 10)

1960   *The Twilight Zone* ("Nick of Time," CBS, November 18)

1960   *Alcoa Presents* ("The Promise," ABC, November 29)

1961   *Thriller* ("The Hungry Glass," NBC, January 3)

1961   *Dr. Kildare* ("Admitting Service," NBC, November 27)

1962   *Naked City* ("Portrait of a Painter," ABC, January 10)

1963   *The Twilight Zone* ("Nightmare at 20,000 Feet," CBS, October 11)

1964   *The Man from U.N.C.L.E.* ("The Project Stringas Affair," NBC, November 24)

1965   *The Fugitive* ("Stranger in the Mirror," ABC, December 7)

1966   *The Big Valley* ("A Time to Kill," ABC, January 19)

1966   *Gunsmoke* ("Quaker Girl," CBS, December 10)

1969   *The Virginian* ("Black Jade," NBC, December 31)

1970   *Ironside* ("Little Jerry Jessup," NBC, March 12)

1972   *Hawaii Five-O* ("You Don't Have to Kill to Get Rich, but It Helps," CBS, September 26)

1972   *Mission Impossible* ("Cocaine," CBS, October 21)

1972   *Marcus Welby* ("Heartbeat for Yesterday," ABC, December 12)

1973   *Barnaby Jones* ("To Catch a Dead Man," CBS, February 4)

1973   *Mannix* ("Search for a Whisper," CBS, February 18)

1974   *Kung Fu* ("A Small Beheading," ABC, September 21)

1974   *Police Story* ("Love, Mabel," NBC, November 26)

1976   *Columbo* ("Fade In to Murder," NBC, October 10)

1994   *Columbo* ("Butterfly in Shades of Grey," NBC, January 10)

1999   *Third Rock from the Sun* (playing "The Big Giant Head" in "Dick's Big Giant Headache," NBC, May 25)—Shatner was nominated for an Emmy Award for Outstanding Guest Actor in a Comedy Series

Selected Films

The Brothers Karamozov, 1958; *Judgment at Nuremberg,* 1961; *The Explosive Generation,* 1961; *The Intruder,* 1962; *The Outrage,* 1964; *Big Bad Mama,* 1974; *Star Trek: The Motion Picture,* 1979; *Visitng Hours,* 1981; *Star Trek II: The Wrath of Khan,* 1982; *Airplane II,* 1982; *Star Trek III: The Search for Spock,* 1984; *Star Trek IV: The Voyage Home,* 1986; *Star Trek V: The Final Frontier* (also screenplay, director), 1989; *Star Trek VI: The Undiscovered Country,* 1991; *Star Trek: Generations,* 1994; *Trekkies,* 1997; *Free Enterprise,* 1999; *Miss Congeniality,* 2000; *Falcon Down,* 2000; *Shoot or Be Shot,* 2000; *Groom Lake* (also writer, director), 2001; *Showtime,* 2002; *American Psycho II: All-American Girl,* 2002

Publications

Captain's Log: William Shatner's Personal Account of the Making of Star Trek V, The Final Frontier (as told by Lisabeth Shatner), 1989
I'm Working on That: A Trek from Science Fiction to Science Fact (and William Walters), 2002
Shatner: Where No Man…: The Authorized Biography of William Shatner (with Myrna Culbreath and Sandra Marshak), 1979
Star Trek Memories (with Chris Kreski), 1993
Star Trek Movie Memories (with Chris Kreski), 1994
Get a Life! (with Christ Kreski), 1999

Novels

Believe (with Michael Tobias), 1992

Benton Hawkes series:

The Law of War, 1998
Man O' War, 1996

Quest for Tomorrow series:

Delta Search, 1997
In Alien Hands, 1998
Step into Chaos, 1999
Beyond the Stars, 2000

Star Trek novels:

The Ashes of Eden (with Judith and Garfield Reeves-Stevens), 1995
The Return (with Judith and Garfield Reeves-Stevens), 1996
Avenger (with Judith and Garfield Reeves-Stevens), 1997
Spectre (with Judith and Garfield Reeves-Stevens), 1998
Dark Victory (with Judith and Garfield Reeves-Stevens), 1999
Preserver (with Judith and Garfield Reeves-Stevens), 2000
The Captain's Peril, 2002

"Tek" series:

TekWar, 1989
TekLords, 1991
TekLab, 1991
Tek Vengenace, 1992
Tek Secret, 1993
Tek Power, 1994
Tek Money, 1995
Tek Kill, 1996
Tek Net, 1997

Further Reading

"Bill Shatner: 27 Cents and a Bag Full of Dreams," *Chicago Tribune* (August 24, 1968)
Kiester, Edwin, Jr., "A Star's Trek: Spaceman to Lawman: In Fine Physical Shape, the Former Captain Kirk Is Now Playing a Rough-and-Tumble Cop—and Doing a Lot of His Own Stunts," *TV Guide* (August 14, 1982)
Maron, Linda, *Rescue 911: Extraordinary Stories* (with forward by William Shatner), New York: Berkley Books, 1995
Rensin, David, "William Shatner: A Farewell to Kirk," *TV Guide* (October 8, 1994)
Svetkey, Benjamin, "I'm Typing as Fast as I Can," *Entertainment Weekly* (January 15, 1993)
Wayne, George, "Starship Trooper," *Vanity Fair* (March 1999)
"William Shatner," *Current Biography,* New York: Bowker, 1987
Young, Stanley, "Beam Him Down," *People Weekly* (November 28, 1994)

Shaw, Bernard (1940–)

U.S. Broadcast Journalist

As principal Washington anchor for the Cable News Network (CNN), Bernard Shaw built a reputation for asking difficult questions and upholding unfaltering journalistic ethics. Shaw made a bold and courageous decision to join the all-news network at its beginning in 1980 despite wide skepticism that a 24-hour news network would attract viewer interest. Shaw was an important contributor to the network's eventual prominence as an international news leader.

His style and professionalism enabled him to secure impressive, exclusive interviews with important world leaders. His most visible, sensational—and some would say impressive—moment as a journalist came in 1991. In Baghdad, Iraq, to complete a follow-up interview with Iraqi President Saddam Hussein, Shaw was one of three CNN reporters who worked during a major attack by the Allied forces. With his colleagues, Shaw brought unprecedented live coverage of the Al-

Bernard Shaw, 1996.
Courtesy of the Everett Collection

lied forces' bombing. On January 16, 1991, more than a billion homes watched Shaw and his colleagues deliver around-the-clock coverage of Operation Desert Storm.

Shaw's coverage of the war earned him numerous national and international journalism prizes, including the Eduard Rhein Foundation's Cultural Journalistic Award, a George Foster Peabody Award, and a cable ACE Award for best newscaster of the year. Shaw's receipt of the Rhein Foundation Award was the first time this honor had been bestowed on a non-German.

Live coverage was not new for Shaw; he also presented live broadcasts of the events surrounding the student revolt in China's Tiananmen Square until CNN was forced by the Chinese government to discontinue coverage. His coverage of the uprising earned him and CNN considerable recognition. His awards for coverage of Tiananmen Square include a cable ACE for best news anchor and an Emmy for anchoring the single most outstanding news event. CNN won a Golden ACE, an Alfred I. duPont Columbia

University Silver Baton, and a Peabody for its coverage of China.

Shaw is best known for his political reporting at CNN. Through the 1990s, he was anchor of *The International Hour, The World Today,* and *Inside Politics.* He covered debates, primaries, conventions, and the hoopla of presidential campaigning.

In 1988, while moderating a presidential debate between George Bush and Michael Dukakis, Shaw asked Dukakis if he would change his mind about opposing the death penalty if his own wife were raped and killed. Political analysts credit Shaw's question and Dukakis's off-guard response with portraying Dukakis as unemotional. Dukakis's campaign never recovered from the backlash of his reaction to Shaw's question.

Refusing to call his departure from CNN a retirement, Shaw announced his "stepping back" from CNN during a live broadcast of *Inside Politics.* Shaw stepped back from the anchor chair on February 28, 2001, after dedicating 20 years to the network. Shaw also announced plans to work on an autobiography.

Shaw is a graduate of the University of Illinois, which established the Bernard Shaw Endowed Scholarship Fund to honor his career and assist promising young men and women who share his interests and integrity. Shaw is a major benefactor to that fund.

JOHN TEDESCO

See also **Anchor; Cable News Network**

Bernard Shaw. Born in Chicago, Illinois, May 22, 1940. Educated at the University of Illinois at Chicago, 1963–68. Married: Linda Allston, 1974; children: Amar Edgar, Anil Louise. Served in U.S. Marine Corps, Oahu, Hawaii, 1959–63. Reporter, WNUS, Chicago, 1963; news writer, WFLD, Chicago, 1965; reporter, WIND, 1966–68; White House reporter, Westinghouse Broadcasting Company, 1968–71; reporter, CBS News, 1971–74; correspondent, CBS News, 1974–77; Latin American bureau chief and correspondent, ABC, 1977–78; Capitol Hill correspondent, ABC, 1978–79; CNN News Anchor, 1980–2001. Honorary degrees: Marion College, 1985; University of Chicago, 1993; Northeastern University, 1994. Member: Society of Professional Journalists, National Press Club, Sigma Delta Chi. Recipient: International Platform Association's Lowell Thomas Electronic Journalist Award, 1988; Awards for Cable Excellence (ACE) from the National Academy of Cable Programming, 1988, 1990, 1993, 1994; Emmy Awards, 1989 and 1992; National Association of Black Journalists, Journalist of the Year Award, 1989; gold medal, International Film and TV Festival, 1989; Peabody Award, 1990; Congress of Racial Equality, Dr. Martin Luther King Jr. Award for Outstanding Achievement, 1993; University of Kansas, William Allen White Medallion for Distinguished Service, 1994; Distinguished Achievement Award in Broadcasting, University of Georgia Grady College of Journalism and Mass Communication.

Television

1980–2001   *CNN News*
1989   *The World Today*

Further Reading

Kellner, Douglas, *The Persian Gulf TV War*, Boulder, Colorado: Westview, 1992

Smith, Perry M., *How CNN Fought the War: A View from the Inside*, New York: Carol, 1991

Whittemore, Hank, *CNN, The Inside Story*, Boston, Massachusetts: Little, Brown, 1990

Wiener, Robert, *Live from Baghdad: Gathering News at Ground Zero*, New York: Doubleday, 1992

Sheen, Fulton J. (1895–1979)

U.S. Religious Broadcaster

Widely known by his Roman Catholic ecclesiastical title, Bishop Sheen established a very successful niche for religious programming in U.S. television's early days with his *Life Is Worth Living* program. Sheen's show originally aired on the Dumont network on Tuesday evenings in 1952 and then moved to the American Broadcasting Company (ABC), where it remained until Sheen withdrew it in 1957. The shows—really half-hour talks by Sheen—proved very popular and ultimately were carried on 123 ABC television stations and another 300 radio stations.

Life Is Worth Living followed a simple format. Sheen would choose a topic and, with only a blackboard for a prop and his church robes for costuming, would discuss the topic for his allotted 27 minutes. He spoke in a popular style, without notes but with a sprinkling of stories and jokes, having spent up to 30 hours preparing his presentation. Because the program was sponsored by the Admiral Corporation rather than the Catholic Church, Sheen avoided polemics and presented a kind of Christian humanism. In his autobiography, he noted that the show was not "a direct presentation of Christian doctrine but rather a reasoned approach to it beginning with something that was common to the audience." He covered topics as diverse as art, science, aviation, humor, Communism, and philosophy.

Like many others in television's early days, Sheen had moved into the medium from radio. As a professor at the Catholic University of America, he began commuting in 1928 from Washington, D.C., to broadcast on WLWL in New York. Two years later, he became the first regular speaker on *The Catholic Hour*, a sustaining time program on National Broadcasting Company (NBC) radio, sponsored by the National Council of Catholic Men. In 1940, he made his television debut presiding at New York City's first televised religious service.

After several years off, Sheen attempted to come back to television a number of times but without the success that had greeted *Life Is Worth Living*. He hosted a series on the life of Christ in the 1950s; in 1964, he worked on *Quo Vadis, America?;* and he revived the format of *Life Is Worth Living,* now called *The Bishop Sheen Program*. Television had changed, and his lecture style no longer commanded audience loyalty. He ended his long career in broadcasting with numerous guest appearances on television talk shows during the 1960s and 1970s.

Broadcasting was never Sheen's full-time occupation. He left the Catholic University of America in 1950 to become the national director of the Society for the Propagation of the Faith, a fund-raising office for missionaries, a position he held until Pope Paul VI named him bishop of Rochester, New York, in 1966.

Sheen's importance for television lies in two areas. First, he pioneered a nonsectarian style of religious programming and found commercial sponsors for his message. By doing this, he both adapted to and helped shape commercial broadcasting's attitudes toward religious shows. The need to develop audiences meant that only those programs with the widest possible appeal would find a place in mainstream or network programming. Second, Sheen provided a role model (if not an ideal) for the next generation of ministers interested in television—the televangelists. Many of the later stars of cable religious television have acknowledged that the widespread acceptance of Sheen's *Life*

Is Worth Living inspired their own forays into television. They too have hoped to escape the "Sunday morning ghetto" of religious programming for a place in the mainstream.

PAUL A. SOUKUP

See also **Religion on Television**

Fulton John Sheen. Born in El Paso, Illinois, May 8, 1895. Graduated from St. Viator College, Bourbonnais, Illinois, 1917, M.A. 1919; studied at St. Paul Seminary, Minnesota, ordained September 20, 1919; University of America, Washington, D.C., S.T.B and J.C.B. Catholic; University of Louvain, Belgium, Ph.D. 1923; Collegio Angelico, Rome, D.D. 1924; made *Agrege en Philosophie* at Louvain. Served in St. Patrick's parish, Peoria, Illinois, 1924–26; instructor in religion, Catholic University of America, 1926, remaining affiliated with university until 1950; preacher, WLWL Radio in New York, 1928; became regular preacher on NBC radio program *The Catholic Hour,* 1930; made papal chamberlain and given rank of monsignor, 1934; presided over New York's first televised religious service, 1940; director, U.S. activities for the Society for Propagation of the Faith, 1950–66; consecrated as auxiliary bishop of the New York archdiocese, June 11, 1951; began long-running television program *Life Is Worth Living,* 1952; bishop, Rochester, New York, 1966–69; made titular archbishop of Newport, Wales, 1969. Died in New York, December 10, 1979.

Television Series

1952–57	*Life Is Worth Living*
1955–57	*Mission to the World*
1961–68	*The Bishop Sheen Program*
1964	*Quo Vadis, America?*

Radio

The Catholic Hour, from 1930.

Publications (selected)

Peace of Soul, 1949
Three to Get Married, 1951
Life Is Worth Living, 1953
The Priest Is Not His Own, 1963
Missions and the World Crisis, 1964
That Tremendous Love, 1967
Treasure in Clay: The Autobiography of Fulton J. Sheen, 1980

Further Reading

Griffin, W., "Foreword," in *The Electronic Christian: 105 Readings from Fulton J. Sheen,* by Fulton J. Sheen, New York: Macmillan, 1979

Noonan, D.P., *The Passion of Fulton Sheen,* New York: Dodd, Mead, 1972

Sherlock Holmes

Mystery (Various National Productions)

Sherlock Holmes, the fictional character created by Sir Arthur Conan Doyle, may be the most popular literary character adapted to the performing arts. The adventures of Sherlock Holmes have been transformed for the dramatic stage (*Sherlock Holmes,* 1899; *The Crucifer of Blood,* 1978), the musical stage (*Baker Street,* 1965), ballet (*The Great Detective,* 1953), film, radio, and television. On television, the character has appeared in specials, series, parodies, animation, and made-for-television films and even in a recurring role-playing game by the android Data (Brent Spiner) on *Star Trek: The Next Generation.*

The actors who have undertaken the role for television include Ronald Howard (son of film actor Leslie Howard), Alan Napier, Peter Cushing, Christopher Lee, Frank Langella, Tom Baker (later the Doctor in *Doctor Who*), Edward Woodward, Charlton Heston, Roger Moore, Leonard Nimoy, Peter O'Toole (as the voice of the detective in the Australian animated *Sherlock Holmes and the Baskerville Case*), and Jeremy Brett. Even Basil Rathbone, who portrayed the character in 14 feature films and 8 years on the radio, played Holmes on the small screen. Comic actors such as Milton Berle, *Monty Python*'s John Cleese, Larry Hagman, and Peter Cook have all played the master sleuth in television parodies.

Sherlock Holmes was the first fictional character adapted for television. *The Three Garridebs,* a trial

Mystery: Sherlock Holmes, Jeremy Brett, 1984–94.
Courtesy of the Everett Collection

telecast, was broadcast on November 27, 1937, from the stage of New York City's Radio City Music Hall by the American Radio Relay League. The live presentation was augmented with filmed footage to link scenes together. Louis Hector played the detective, and William Podmore played his associate, Dr. Watson.

Until 1951, Holmes's appearances on television were limited to a variety of special broadcasts, including the hour-long parody *Sherlock Holmes in the Mystery of the Sen Sen Murder,* on the April 5, 1949, episode of the National Broadcasting Company's (NBC's) *Texaco Star Theatre.* The satire featured Milton Berle and Victor Moore as Holmes and Watson and a guest appearance by Basil Rathbone as Rathbone of Scotland Yard.

The first television series of Sherlock Holmes adventures was produced in the United Kingdom. Vandyke Pictures intended for its half-hour adaptation of *The Man with the Twisted Lip* to be the first of a six-episode series. However, the pilot, starring John Long-

den as Holmes and Campbell Singer as Watson, did not impress executives, and only the one episode was broadcast (in March 1951). Three months later, the British Broadcasting Corporation (BBC) aired its own pilot, an adaptation of *The Mazarin Stone,* with Andrew Osborn as Holmes and Philip King as Watson. In late 1951, the BBC produced the first television series of Sherlock Holmes adventures, but with a new producer and new actors (Alan Wheatley as Holmes and Raymond Francis as Watson). Six of Conan Doyle's stories were adapted to the 35-minute format by C.A. Lejeune, a film critic for *The Observer.*

Basil Rathbone, who for many years gave what was considered the definitive portrayal of Holmes, reprised his role as the detective in a half-hour live presentation for the May 26, 1953, episode of the Columbia Broadcasting System's (CBS's) *Suspense.* The episode, *The Adventures of the Black Baronet,* was adapted by Michael Dyne from an original story by crime novelist John Dickson Carr and Adrian Conan Doyle, son of the character's creator. The episode was intended as a pilot for a U.S. series, but it was not selected for programming by any network.

The first and only U.S. television series of Sherlock Holmes adventures finally aired in syndication in the fall of 1954. The 39 half-hour original stories were produced by Sheldon Reynolds and filmed in France by Guild Films. Ronald Howard starred as Holmes, and Howard Marion Crawford starred as Watson. The series' associate producer, Nicole Milinaire, is considered to be the first woman to attain a senior production role in a television series.

Since 1954, American adaptations of the Holmes stories have been limited to various made-for-television films (*The Return of the World's Greatest Detective* with Larry Hagman as Holmes, *Sherlock Holmes in New York* with Roger Moore as Holmes, and *The Hound of The Baskervilles*) or televised stage plays (Frank Langella's *Sherlock Holmes and The Crucifer of Blood* with Charlton Heston).

In addition to producing made-for-television Holmes films in Britain, the BBC continued to produce other series of Holmes adventures. A 1965 series of 12 adaptations was produced by David Goddard and featured Douglas Wilmer, who, *The Times* noted, bore an "uncanny resemblance" to the sleuth in the original book illustrations by Sydney Paget. A 1968 series starring Peter Cushing dispensed with many of the conventions invented by other actors for the character, such as the meerschaum pipe, the deer-stalker cap, and the phrase, "Elementary, my dear Watson." The series aspired to be true to the character as written in the novels. In an attempt to capitalize on Cushing's popular work in 1950s and 1960s horror films, the BBC series accentuated the elements of horror and violence in the original stories.

In 1984, Britain's Granada Television mounted the most popular series to date. Shown under various titles (*The Adventures of Sherlock Holmes, The Return of Sherlock Holmes,* and *The Casebook of Sherlock Holmes*) in Britain, the series was broadcast in the United States as part of the Public Broadcasting Service's (PBS's) *Mystery!* series. Critics have praised the high quality of the series' productions, including an authentic-looking Baker Street, and Jeremy Brett's performance as Holmes has been ranked as among the finest portrayals of the detective.

In 1998, BBC Radio became the first production company to complete dramatizations of all 60 Sherlock Holmes adventures, a project that began in 1989. These adaptations star Clive Merrison and Michael Williams as Holmes and Watson.

The appeal of the character has not been limited to English-speaking countries. An original teleplay, *Touha Sherlocka Holmes* (The Longing of Sherlock Holmes), in which Holmes is tempted to commit the perfect crime, was produced for Czechoslovakian television in 1972. In 1983, Russian television produced a series of five 80-minute adaptations of Conan Doyle's stories featuring leading Soviet actors Vassily Livanov and Vitaly Solomin as Holmes and Watson.

SUSAN R. GIBBERMAN

See also **British Programming; Detective Programs**

Further Reading

Bunson, Matthew E., *Encyclopedia Sherlockiana: An A-to-Z Guide to the World of the Great Detective,* New York: Macmillan, 1994

Collins, Max Allan, and John Javna, *The Best Crime and Detective TV: Perry Mason to Hill Street Blues, The Rockford Files to Murder, She Wrote,* New York: Harmony, 1988

deWall, Ronald Burt, *The World Bibliography of Sherlock Holmes and Dr. Watson: A Classified and Annotated List of Materials Relating to Their Lives and Adventures,* New York: Bramhall House, 1974

Eyles, Allen, *Sherlock Holmes: A Centenary Celebration,* New York: Harper and Row, 1986

Haining, Peter, *The Television Sherlock Holmes,* London: Virgin, 1994

"Holmes' 50-Year Journey on TV," *Variety* (January 20, 1988)

"Shadowing a Sleuth: Holmes Stalks the City by Television—Football Pictures Are Clear," *New York Times* (November 28, 1937)

"So Long, Sherlock...Remembering Jeremy Brett," *New Orleans Magazine* (December 1995)

Shore, Dinah (1917–1994)

U.S. Musical Performer, Talk Show Host

Dinah Shore ranks as one of the important on-air musical stars of the first two decades of television in the United States. Indeed, from 1956 through 1963, there were few TV personalities as well known as she was. More than any song she sang, Shore herself symbolized cheery optimism and southern charm, and she is most remembered for blowing a big kiss to viewers at the end of her 1950s variety show. As hostess, she sometimes danced and frequently participated in comedy skits, but she was best loved as a smooth vocalist reminiscent of a style associated with the 1940s.

Shore pioneered the prime-time color variety show when *The Dinah Shore Chevy Show* started in October 1956 on the National Broadcasting Company (NBC) and ran on Sunday nights until the end of the 1963 season. Sponsored by General Motors, then the largest corporation in the world, Shore helped make the low-priced Chevrolet automobile the most widely selling car up to that point in history.

Shore represented a rare woman able to achieve major success hosting a TV variety show. In the late 1950s, her enthusiasm and lack of pretension proved so popular that she was four times named to the list of the "most admired women in the world." Her desire to please showed in her singing style, which some purists dismissed as sentimental, but through her recording career she did earn nine gold records. Shore made listeners and later viewers feel good, and beginning with her first broadcasts on radio in the late 1930s and then on television, she was able to remain a constant presence in American broadcasting for more than 50 years.

When Fanny Rose Shore was old enough to go to school, in her hometown of Nashville, Tennessee, she found herself taunted for being Jewish in the decidedly

Dinah Shore.
Courtesy of the Everett Collection

non-Jewish world of a segregated Deep South. Undeterred, Shore logged experience on Nashville radio while in college, on her hometown's WSM-AM, best known as the home of the Grand Ole Opry. But Shore was no hillbilly singer, no typical southern belle. She took a degree in sociology at Vanderbilt University, putting herself through college with her radio earnings. Her show's theme song was the Ethel Waters blues-inspired "Dinah," and Shore changed her name accordingly. The success of her local radio show, *Our Little Cheerleader of Song,* enabled Shore to move to New York City to try to make it in Tin Pan Alley, then the center of the world of pop music.

Shore, by her own admission, did not have the vocal equipment of Ella Fitzgerald or Billie Holiday, and she never chose to reveal as much of herself in music as did her other idol, Peggy Lee. However, she was persistent. During the late 1930s, having auditioned unsuccessfully for such band leaders as Benny Goodman and Tommy and Jimmy Dorsey, Shore finally hooked up with the Xavier Cugat band. Through the 1940s, she sold a million copies of "Yes, My Darling Daughter," and that recording success was followed quickly by such hits as "Blues in the Night," "Shoo Fly Pie," "Buttons and Bows," "Dear Hearts and Gentle Peo-

ple," and "It's So Nice to Have a Man Around the House." During World War II, Shore sang these songs for the troops in Normandy and for shows at other Allied bases in Europe.

In 1950, Shore made a guest appearance on Bob Hope's first NBC television special. A year later, NBC assigned her a regular TV series that ran until 1956 on Tuesday and Thursday nights from 7:30 to 7:45 P.M. Eastern time, following 15 minutes of network news. This led, in time, to her Sunday night series. Radio Corporation of America (RCA) and NBC corporate chief David Sarnoff loved Shore's conservative vocal choices and middlebrow sensibilities. In retrospect, Shore's famed signature theme song, the catchy Chevrolet jingle, "See the USA in your Chevrolet," accompanied by her sweeping smooch to the audience, was so theatrically commercial it made Ed Sullivan seem subversive and Pat Boone look like a rock star. Shore did best when she played the safe 1950s nonthreatening "girl next door," with no blond (she was born a brunette) hair out of place, no joke offensive to anyone. The outcast of Nashville finally fit in.

The Dinah Shore Chevy Show rarely entered the top-20 ratings against the Columbia Broadcasting System's (CBS's) *General Electric Theater,* hosted by Ronald Reagan, which regularly won the time slot. Reagan had a better lead-in from Ed Sullivan. Still, Shore won Emmy Awards for Best Female Singer (1954–55), Best Female Personality (1956–57), and Best Actress in a Musical or Variety Series (1959).

After the *Chevy Show,* Shore went on to host three daytime television programs: the 90-minute talk show *Dinah!* (1970–74), *Dinah's Place* (1970–74), and *Dinah and Friends* (1979–84). Her TV career ended in 1991 on cable TV's Nashville Network with *A Conversation with Dinah.* By then, she was better known as Hollywood heartthrob Burt Reynolds's "older" girlfriend and as the sponsor of a major golf tournament for women.

DOUGLAS GOMERY

*See also **Dinah Shore Show, The (Various)***

Dinah Shore. Born Frances Rose Shore in Winchester, Tennessee, March 1, 1917. Educated at Vanderbilt University, Nashville, Tennessee, B.A. 1939. Married: 1) George Montgomery, 1943 (divorced, 1962); one daughter and one son; 2) Maurice Fabian Smith, 1963 (divorced, 1964). Singer, WNEW, New York, 1938; sustaining singer, NBC, 1938; signed contract with RCA-Victor, 1940; starred in *Chamber Music Society of Lower Basin Street,* NBC radio program, 1940; joined Eddie Cantor's radio program, 1941; starred in own radio program for General Foods, 1943; entertained U.S. troops in European theater of operations, 1944; hosted radio program for Procter and Gamble; starred in TV show for Chevrolet, 1956–63; hosted numerous variety and talk shows. Recipient: Emmy Awards, 1954, 1956, 1959, 1973, 1974, and 1976. Died in Beverly Hills, California, February 24, 1994.

Television Series

1951–57	*The Dinah Shore Show*
1956–63	*The Dinah Shore Chevy Show*
1970–74	*Dinah!*
1974–80	*Dinah's Place*
1976	*Dinah and Her New Best Friends*
1979–84	*Dinah and Friends*
1989–91	*A Conversation with Dinah*

Films

Thank Your Lucky Stars, 1943; *Up in Arms*, 1944; *Belle of the Yukon*, 1944; *Follow the Boys*, 1944; *Make Mine Music* (voice only), 1946; *Till the Clouds Roll By*, 1946; *Fun and Fancy Free* (voice only), 1947; *Aaron Slick from Punkin Crick*, 1952; *Oh, God!*, 1977; *Health*, 1979.

Publication

Someone's in the Kitchen with Dinah, 1971

Showtime Network

U.S. Cable Network

Showtime is a subscription-based network that broadcasts recently released and classic movies 24 hours per day via satellite without commercial interruption. In addition, it produces its own original programming and provides coverage of boxing events and occasionally live music. Next to the Home Box Office (HBO)/Cinemax cable block, Showtime is the second most popular subscription-based cable movie channel in the United States. Showtime was launched on July 1, 1976, by Viacom, Inc., in the wake of HBO's successful challenge of the Federal Communications Commission's (FCC's) satellite expansion rules. After making its start at a northern California cable company, Showtime went nationwide via satellite in 1978. In 1979, one of HBO's chief distributors, the Teleprompter Corporation, bought 50 percent of Showtime and subsequently dropped HBO from 250,000 households. Thus was born the market share competition between these two similar cable networks, a rivalry that would define the programming structure of Showtime throughout the 1980s and 1990s.

By the late 1980s, Showtime had fewer subscriptions than HBO but still aired very similar programs. Since 1994, however, when the current Showtime Networks chief executive officer, Matthew C. Blank, selected Jerry Ofsay to take charge the network's programming, the channel has aggressively pursued alternative original content and as a result has won awards for its daring and captured audiences that had fallen through the programming gaps of other cable channels. In 2003, Blank replaced Ofsay with a new chief of entertainment, Robert Greenblatt, previously the executive producer of HBO's popular series *Six Feet Under* in a drive to further improve Showtime's original programming and foster more contacts with Hollywood.

Touting its new "No Limits" logo, Showtime has recently sought to define itself as the edgier alternative to HBO. Although HBO has nearly twice the subscription rate and over twice Showtime's programming budget, Showtime has compensated and remained competitive in several ways. First, it has lowered its production costs by shooting much of its original programming in Canada; in addition, it produces all its original series in bulk. It has also been successful at luring Hollywood actors and directors to the network to make low-budget Showtime movies by encouraging them to produce their own pet projects without corporate interference. Showtime has pushed the envelope for nonmainstream content in its original shows, most notably in *Queer as*

Courtesy of the Everett Collection

Folk and *The L Word,* both of which have won acclaim for their candid representation of gay sexuality. The network makes a point of not censoring its writers. The result is a channel that has become a vital source of original cable programming in the early 2000s.

Following the multiplexing trend of other cable networks, Showtime has used its brand name to develop several specialized channels, such as Showtime Women, Showtime Family Zone, and Showtime Extreme, which are often prepackaged in cable and satellite subscriptions. In addition, the Showtime Network operates The Movie Channel and Flix; it also manages The Sundance Channel under the Showtime Network's corporate umbrella, although Robert Redford and Universal Studios are additional co-owners. Striving to be a technical pioneer, all the channels bearing the Showtime banner broadcast at least some of their daily content in high-definition format (HDTV) and broadcast all their programming in Dolby Digital 5.1 surround sound.

Showtime's parent company, Viacom, Inc., survived the media merger fervor of the 1980s and 1990s and has emerged as one of the most powerful conglomerates in the television industry. As a result, Showtime has been at least partially owned by several different companies in its history. In 1985, Viacom repurchased from Warner Amex the 50 percent of Showtime sold in 1979 to the Teleprompter Corporation. In June 1987, Sumner Redstone took over Viacom International, and soon afterward, in response to industry fears over the Time Warner merger in 1989, Viacom partially merged with TeleCommunications Inc., the largest cable operator in the country, which bought a 50 percent interest in Showtime. In 1992, Showtime announced the formation of the Showtime Entertainment Group, which was designed to make original motion pictures to premiere on Showtime, and then in 1994 the channel officially formed Showtime Networks, which included The Movie Channel and Flix. The Showtime Network added The Sundance Channel to its lineup in 1996.

Much of Showtime's programming history is entwined with HBO's, as the two have taken programming cues from one another. When Showtime and HBO first aired in the 1970s, both were used as uncensored outlets for recently released theatrical films before they premiered on the broadcast networks. However, as videocassette rentals claimed a growing portion of this second-run movie market, both channels began to create original content in the 1980s in an effort to retain their audiences. Utilizing the freedoms of cable TV, both simultaneously developed series that incorporated risqué content, such as nudity, sexuality, adult language, and drug use, making their programs unique to cable and removing any potential competition from the commercially funded broadcast channels. Two of Showtime's early series, *Brothers* and *It's Garry Shandling's Show,* were well received by cable audiences. *Brothers,* the first sitcom made specifically for cable TV, opened new social territory in 1984 because of its openly gay sexual content. *It's Garry Shandling's Show* was quickly purchased by the newly established FOX Network. Both shows unveiled a powerful American market for challenging prime-time content that could be accurately developed only outside the reign of the broadcast network censors. These viewing preferences were also reflected in the annual Academy of Television Arts and Sciences Awards (Emmys); by the late 1990s, both Showtime and HBO were receiving a substantial portion of the original programming nominations.

As Showtime and HBO continued to vie in the late 1990s for pay-TV market shares, the Showtime programmers took a different tack. They began to target specific underrepresented audiences. In 1999, they pursued African-American audiences with the drama series *Soul Food,* based on the popular movie of the same title. They also pursued the American Latino audience with *Resurrection Blvd.,* the first and only English-speaking television series with a predominantly Latino cast to air in the early 2000s. In 1999, they struck programming gold by adapting an openly gay British television series, *Queer as Folk,* which went on to become one of the network's highest-rated shows. These types of niche-focused programming decisions have allowed Showtime to continue to grow and innovate regardless of its share of the pay-TV movie channel market.

DANIEL ABRAM

Further Reading

Balio, Tino, editor, *Hollywood in the Age of Television,* Boston, Massachusetts: Unwin Hyman, 1990

Brown, Lester L., *Les Brown's Encyclopedia of Television,* 3rd ed., Washington, D.C.: Visible Ink, 1992

Case, Tony, "Spotlight on Showtime," *MediaWeek* (June 11, 2001)

Chunovic, Louis, "Showtime Faces Tough Choices," *Electronic Media* (November 12, 2001)

Frutkin, Alan James, "Delivering on Diversity," *MediaWeek* (July 26, 2000)

Goodridge, Mike, "Showtime for Greenblatt," *Advocate* (September 30, 2003)

Jankowski, Gene F., and David C. Fuchs, *Television Today and Tomorrow,* New York: Oxford University Press, 1995

Roman, James, *Love, Light, and a Dream: Television's Past, Present, and Future,* Westport, Connecticut: Praeger Publishers, 1996

Walker, James R., and Douglas A. Ferguson, *The Broadcast Television Industry,* Boston, Massachusetts: Allyn and Bacon, 1998

Tropiano, Stephen, *The Prime Time Closet: A History of Gays and Lesbians on TV,* New York: Applause Theater and Cinema, 2002

Silliphant, Stirling (1918–1996)

U.S. Writer

Stirling Silliphant was one of the most important and prolific writers of television drama in the 1960s, remembered particularly for his work on *Naked City* and *Route 66*. Although he had early success in the 1950s with a spate of feature films and went on to even greater big-screen achievements in the late 1960s and 1970s, Silliphant maintained a constant presence in television throughout his writing career and in the 1980s focused most of his attention on television movies, historical miniseries, and novels.

Silliphant's passage between big-screen and small-screen writing marked his work very early on. He began his association with the movies as a publicist, first for Disney and later 20th Century-Fox. Silliphant left that end of the business in 1953 to package an independent feature, *The Joe Louis Story* (honing his rewrite skills on the script). In 1955, he transformed a rejected screenplay into the novel *Maracaibo* (which was adapted by another writer and filmed three years later) and within the next three years saw five feature scripts produced, including Jacques Tourneur's *Nightfall* and Don Siegel's *The Lineup*. During the same period, he aimed his typewriter at television, generating dozens of scripts for such anthologies as *General Electric Theater*, *Alcoa-Goodyear Theatre*, *Suspicion*, *Schlitz Playhouse*, and *Alfred Hitchcock Presents* as well as two episodes of *Perry Mason*.

Silliphant was completing his sixth feature script (*Village of the Damned*) when independent producer Herbert B. Leonard (*Adventures of Rin Tin Tin* and *Circus Boy*) hired him to write the pilot for *Naked City*, a half-hour series based on the 1948 "semidocumentary" feature *The Naked City*. With a résumé composed almost exclusively of anthologies and features, Silliphant's proclivity for self-contained stories was consistent with Leonard's vision of the series as a character-oriented dramatic anthology with a police backdrop as opposed to a police procedural in the *Dragnet* mold. Silliphant wrote 31 of *Naked City*'s first 39 episodes, remembered today as taut, noirish 30-minute thrillers offering both character drama and gunplay. Canceled after one season in its original form, the series was resurrected as an hour-long show in 1960.

In the interim, Silliphant remained busy with scripts for such crime series as *Markham*, *Tightrope*, and *The Brothers Brannagan* as well as an unsold private eye

pilot, *Brock Callahan*. When *Naked City* was resurrected at a sponsor's behest for the 1960 season in the longer form, Silliphant was already collaborating with Leonard on another series–anthology hybrid, *Route 66*. (A third Leonard–Silliphant project for 1960 called *Three-Man Sub*—a sort of underwater Mediterranean variation on *Route 66*—did not sell.) Although he did write the pilot script and served as "executive story consultant" for the new version of *Naked City*, Silliphant would provide fewer scripts for the show because of his intense involvement with *Route 66*; still, the writing remained first-rate. The all–New York production offered a fascinating mix of action and Actor's Studio, yielding three seasons of compelling urban tragedy. The series was nominated for an Emmy in the Outstanding Drama category every year of its run.

Route 66 proved to be a critical and commercial hit despite early concerns from Screen Gems studio about its premise: two young drifters searching for meaning on the highways of America. Filmed on location across the United States, the wide-ranging backdrops and visual realism of *Route 66* and its mix of psychological drama, social commentary, romance, action, and big-name guest stars, all underlined by strong writing and supervision from Silliphant (and story editor Howard Rodman), paved the way for a four-year run. Spending much of this time writing and observing on the road, Silliphant would go on to write some three-fourths of *Route 66*'s 116 episodes. Silliphant calls those four years the most intensive period of writing in his career and the site of some of his best work.

Naked City was canceled in 1963 and *Route 66* a year later, but the "writing machine" (as one producer dubbed Silliphant in a *Time* magazine profile) did not pause. During the mid-1960s, Silliphant freelanced for *Bob Hope Presents the Chrysler Theater*, *Mr. Novak*, and *Rawhide*. In 1967, Silliphant made a triumphant return to features, winning an Academy Award for his adaptation *In the Heat of the Night*. Even with this big-screen success (followed up with such films as *Marlowe*, *Charly*, and *The New Centurions*), Silliphant did not abandon television. Despite a 1960 interview in which he eschewed the growing plague of "hyphenated billing"—alleging that the "miasma of memos and meetings" inevitably curtailed the insight and blunted the creativity of writer-producers—by 1971 Silliphant was one, serving as executive producer of the mystery series *Longstreet.* Notable as part of the 1970s-era cycle of "gimmick" detective series (*Cannon, Ironside,* and *McCloud*), *Longstreet*—the story of a blind insurance investigator—was otherwise unremarkable. A year later, the writer attempted to mount yet another picaresque series titled *Movin' On,* this time concerning a pair of itinerant stock-car racers (not to be confused with the 1974 series about truckers); the pilot aired as a TV movie, but the series did not sell. *Longstreet*'s cancellation after one season effectively ended Silliphant's involvement in the continuing-series form but not his television career.

Although he did pen several TV movies and his first miniseries, *Pearl* (based on his novel) during the 1970s, Silliphant concentrated most of his efforts in that decade on features. He produced *Shaft* in 1971 (and wrote the 1973 sequel *Shaft in Africa*); in 1972, he helped launch the popular cycle of disaster movies by scripting *The Poseidon Adventure,* followed by *The Towering Inferno* and *The Swarm;* and he turned out successful thrillers, such as *Telefon* and *The Enforcer* (Clint Eastwood's third "Dirty Harry" film). A few more features followed in the 1980s, but, for the most part, Silliphant settled back into television, scripting a succession of made-for-TV movies (and unsold pilots) and epic miniseries, such as *Mussolini: The Untold Story* and *Space.* True to form, the fertile author also found time during the decade to publish three adventure novels featuring roving adventurer John Locke.

Silliphant's writing career is remarkable not only for its sheer volume of output, its duration, and its spanning of television and feature work but also for the very fact that he kept an active hand in television after achieving big-screen success and that he considered television to be the medium most conducive to the writer's vision. Silliphant has charged that his *In the Heat of the Night* script was inferior to many of his *Naked City* teleplays. "As a matter of fact," he declared to writer William Froug, "I can think of at least twenty different television scripts I've written which I think are monumental in comparison." Truth be told, the bulk of Silliphant's features—most of which are adaptations—tended toward formula, while the passion for character and ideas comes through most strongly in the television work.

Silliphant repeatedly pronounced *Naked City* and *Route 66* as the best of his writing. It is difficult to disagree. These two series are surely Silliphant's finest achievements and rank among the most original and well-written dramas ever created for the medium. A *Variety* columnist observed in a 1962 review of *Route 66* that Silliphant "composes poetry which is often raw and tenuous, so it requires delicacy of treatment." As this suggests, Silliphant's "poetry" carried some risk. John Gregory Dunne cited Silliphant as a prime purveyor of television "pseudo-seriousness" in a 1965 article, and Silliphant himself admitted a proclivity for the overwrought phrase. But with the right director and actors, no writing for the screen has been more powerful. And if the intense demands of series writing—and writing on the road, at that—occasionally failed to limit a slight propensity for pretension that sometimes overwhelmed characterization or credibility, by and large Silliphant's scripts for *Naked City* and *Route 66* yielded moving renderings of troubled relationships and tortured psyches. Even his more purple moments speak to the ambitions he had for television as a dramatic form.

In 1968, *TV Guide* critic Dick Hobson lamented the exodus of writing talent from the medium, musing, "What became of writer Stirling Silliphant, whose *Naked City*'s and *Route 66*'s were once a repertory theater of contemporary life and times?" Ironically, when these programs aired in the early 1960s, they were largely overlooked by critics and government watchdogs preoccupied with indicting the "vast wasteland" and eulogizing the live drama. Meanwhile, Stirling Silliphant was on the road, clacking away at his typewriter, his "poetry" standing as living (broadcast) proof of television's capacity for brilliant writing and provocative drama. More than 30 years later, at the time of his death in 1996, the writing machine was still writing.

MARK ALVEY

*See also **Naked City;** **Police Programs;** **Route 66;** **Writer in Television***

Stirling Dale Silliphant. Born in Detroit, Michigan, January 16, 1918. Educated at the University of Southern California, B.A., magna cum laude, 1938. Married: Tiana Du Long, 1974; one daughter and two sons. Served as lieutenant, U.S. Navy, 1943–46. Publicity director, 20th Century-Fox, New York City, 1946–53; screenwriter, independent producer for various Hollywood studios, 1953–80s; moved to Thailand, where he continued to work on movie and TV projects, 1980s. Member: Writers Guild of America West, Mystery Writers Association, and Authors League. Recipient: Academy Award, Edgar Allen Poe Award, 1967; Golden Globe Awards, 1968 and 1969; Writer of the Year Award from the National Theater Owners, 1972; Image Award from the National Association for the Advancement of Colored People (NAACP), 1972; Writer of the Year Award from the National Theater Owners, 1974. Died, in Bangkok, April 26, 1996.

Television Series (principal writer)

1958–63	*Naked City* (also executive story consultant, 1960–63)
1960–64	*Route 66* (also co-creator)
1971–72	*Longstreet* (also executive producer)

Television Series (contributing writer; selected)

1953–62	*General Electric Theater*
1956–59	*Alfred Hitchcock Presents*
1957	*Perry Mason*
1957–60	*Alcoa-Goodyear Theater*
1958	*Suspicion*
1959	*Tightrope*
1960	*The Brothers Brannigan*
1964	*Mr. Novak*
1964	*Rawhide*
1964–66	*Bob Hope Presents the Chrysler Theater*

Made-for-Television Movies (writer)

1967	*Wings of Fire*
1971	*Longstreet* (also executive producer)
1972	*Movin' On*
1972	*The New Healers* (also producer)
1973	*A Time for Love* (also executive producer)
1975	*The First 36 Hours of Dr. Durant* (also executive producer)
1975	*Death Scream*
1979	*Salem's Lot* (executive producer only)
1981	*Fly Away Home* (also executive producer)
1981	*Golden Gate*
1981	*Hardcase*
1983	*Travis McGee*
1984	*Welcome to Paradise* (also executive producer)
1987	*The Three Kings* (also producer)
1993	*Sidney Sheldon's A Stranger in the Mirror*
1994	*Day of Reckoning*

Television Miniseries (writer)

| 1978 | *Pearl* (also executive producer) |
| 1985 | *Space* |

| 1985 | *Mussolini: The Untold Story* (also producer) |

Films (writer)

The Joe Louis Story (producer only), 1953; *Five Against the House,* 1955; *Nightfall,* 1956; *Huk!,* 1956; *Damn Citizen,* 1958; *The Lineup,* 1958; *Village of the Damned,* 1960; *The Slender Thread,* 1965; *In the Heat of the Night,* 1967; *Charly,* 1968; *Marlowe,* 1969; *The Liberation of L.B. Jones,* 1970; *A Walk in the Spring Rain* (also producer), 1970; *Murphy's War,* 1971; *Shaft* (producer only), 1971; *The Poseidon Adventure,* 1972; *The New Centurions,* 1972; *Shaft in Africa,* 1973; *The Towering Inferno,* 1974; *The Killer Elite,* 1975; *The Enforcer,* 1976; *Telefon,* 1977; *The Swarm,* 1978; *Circle of Iron,* 1978; *When Time Ran Out,* 1980; *Over the Top,* 1986; *Catch the Heat,* 1987; *The Grass Harp,* 1995.

Publications

Maracaibo (novel), 1953
"Lo, the Vanishing Writer," *Variety* (January 6, 1960)
The Slender Thread (novel), 1966
Pearl (novel), 1978
Steel Tiger (novel, John Locke Adventures), 1983
Bronze Bell (novel, John Locke Adventures), 1985
Silver Star (novel, John Locke Adventures), 1986

Further Reading

Dunne, John Gregory, "Take Back Your Kafka," *The New Republic* (September 4, 1965)
"The Fingers of God," *Time* (August 9, 1963)
Froug, William, *The Screenwriter Looks at the Screenwriter,* New York: Macmillan, 1972
Hobson, Dick, "TV's Disastrous Brain Drain," *TV Guide* (June 15, 1968)
"*Route 66,*" *Variety* (November 7, 1962)
"Silliphant Deplores That Bum Literary Rap Pinned on VidPix Writer," *Variety* (April 15, 1959)
"Steel Writer" (interview), *Writers' Digest* (March 1984)
Stempel, Tom, *Storytellers to the Nation: A History of American Television Writing,* New York: Continuum, 1992
"Stirling Silliphant" (interview), *American Film* (March 1988)

Silverman, Fred (1937–)

U.S. Media Executive, Producer

Fred Silverman devoted his life to programming television. He is the only person to have held key programming positions at all of the three traditional networks in the United States, and today he owns the Fred Silverman Company, which produces programs for those networks. What makes Silverman unique in the history of American network television is that he raced through network jobs while still in his 30s and that his career mysteriously waned after having waxed so splendidly for so long.

Silverman graduated with a master's degree from Ohio State University (his master's thesis analyzed programming practices at the American Broadcasting Company [ABC]) and went to work for WGN-TV in Chicago to oversee children's programs. Soon, however, he moved to the network level. He assumed responsibility for daytime programming at the Columbia Broadcasting System (CBS), where he later took charge of all of CBS Entertainment programming. During his tenure at CBS, Silverman remade the Saturday morning cartoon lineup and, in so doing, remade the ratings—from third to first. He also helped devise the programming strategy that brought *All in the Family, The Mary Tyler Moore Show,* and *The Waltons* to CBS. With the success of the CBS schedule assured, Silverman moved on. In 1975, he became head of ABC Entertainment.

From 1975 to 1978, Silverman took ABC from ratings parity with the other networks to ratings dominance over them. Among the shows and miniseries he was responsible for programming were *Rich Man, Poor Man, Roots, Charlie's Angels,* and *Starsky and Hutch.* Silverman made the "third" network a ratings power and, as some of these program selections suggest, is credited with creating what critics called "jiggle TV," the type of television that features beautiful, scantily clad, frolicking women. In short, he bore partial responsibility for programming both acclaimed and reviled. But he demonstrated at ABC the same touch he had at CBS—an almost unerring sense of what the public, in great numbers, would watch on television. In 1977, a *Time* magazine cover story referred to Silverman as the "man with the golden gut," ostensibly referring to his unfailing programming instincts. At the height of his power at ABC, Silverman left to take on the presidency of the National Broadcasting Company (NBC).

It was there, however, that whatever abilities brought him fame at the other two networks seemed to abandon Silverman. Some of his program selections were disastrous (*Supertrain* and *Hello, Larry,* an illconceived effort starring McLean Stevenson, formerly of *M*A*S*H*). In addition, without the success he had enjoyed earlier, his mercurial behavior was less tolerable. After three difficult years, he was replaced at NBC by Grant Tinker. Silverman's 18-year run with the networks was over.

Silverman left programming to make programs, but he did not enjoy immediate success. The first years for the Fred Silverman Company were difficult, particularly because the former program buyer was now

Fred Silverman.
Photo courtesy of The Fred Silverman Company

forced to try to sell programming to many of the persons he had alienated at the networks. But in 1985, Silverman and partner Dean Hargrove produced the first *Perry Mason* movie with Raymond Burr. It was wildly successful and established the formula that would drive Silverman's comeback in television. He took identifiable television stars from the recent past and recast them in formulaic dramas. Andy Griffith in *Matlock* and Carroll O'Connor in *In the Heat of the Night* are but two examples. Silverman also used his programming acumen to push for favorable time slots for his shows. Because Silverman has enjoyed great success with his production company, some industry observers have called him the Nixon of television.

Throughout his career in network television, Silverman was considered a hero in the industry because he could devise program schedules that delivered strong ratings. But during the latter stages of his network years, some industry observers saw a danger in so much television programming having the imprimatur of one individual. Moreover, his critics often looked beyond the bottom line and lamented the content of the programming used to build Silverman's various ratings empires. His work at ABC has been particularly criticized because of messages regarding sex and violence in the programs. Television programming has been criticized for appealing to the lowest common denominator in its quest for raw numbers of viewers, and more than once Silverman has been targeted as the chief instrument of that appeal. Indeed, columnist Richard Reeves observed in 1978 that Silverman had probably done more to lower the standards of the viewing audience than any other individual.

Of Silverman's comeback, this much can be said—he returned to his roots. His productions, using familiar faces and formulas that have enjoyed prior television success, can be seen as part of a larger pattern. It has been suggested that one current programming trend is to look back to a time when network television was at its peak. In the face of a complex and mercurial telecommunications landscape, those involved in broadcasting seek comfort from a time more stable. Many of the programs meeting this need are revivals, retrospectives, or old faces in new attire. One

need look no further than the "new" *Burke's Law, Columbo,* or Dick Van Dyke in *Diagnosis Murder.* Silverman has capitalized on this tendency and has very probably become its leading practitioner. In a time when the term "auteur," or author, is being applied to television producers, the career of Silverman suggests that an auteur could just as easily be the programmer as the program producer. For better or worse, few individuals have had as profound an impact on television programming for as long as Fred Silverman.

JOHN COOPER

See also **American Broadcasting Company;** *Charlie's Angels;* **Columbia Broadcasting System;** *Mary Tyler Moore Show;* **National Broadcasting Company;** *Perry Mason;* **Programming;** *Rich Man, Poor Man; Starsky and Hutch;* **Tartikoff, Brandon, Tinker, Grant; United States: Networks**

Fred Silverman. Born in New York City, 1937. Studied at Syracuse University, New York; Television and Theater Arts at Ohio State University, Athens, M.A. Worked for WGN-TV, Chicago, 1961–62; worked for WPIX-TV, New York City; director of daytime programs, then vice president of programs, CBS-TV, New York City, 1963–75; president, ABC Entertainment, New York City, 1975–78; president and chief executive officer, NBC, New York City, 1978–81; president, Fred Silverman Company, Los Angeles, from 1981.

Television Series (executive producer)

1985–94	*Perry Mason* (movies)
1986–95	*Matlock*
1987–93	*Jake and the Fatman*
1988–95	*In the Heat of the Night*
1989, 1990–91	*Father Dowling Mysteries*
1992–2001	*Diagnosis Murder*

Further Reading

Bedell, Sally, *Up the Tube: Prime-Time TV and the Silverman Years,* New York: Viking Press, 1981
Reeves, Richard, "The Dangers of Television in the Silverman Era," *Esquire* (April 25, 1978)

Silvers, Phil (1912–1985)

U.S. Actor, Comedian

Phil Silvers was one of the great stars for the Columbia Broadcasting System (CBS) during the late 1950s. Already a minor star on the vaudeville stage and in motion pictures, Silvers created, with writer-producer Nat Hiken, a pioneering television situation comedy, *You'll Never Get Rich.* In this satirical look at life in the U.S. Army, Silvers played Sergeant Ernest Bilko, the con man with a heart of gold.

You'll Never Get Rich premiered on CBS at the beginning of the 1955–56 TV season and soon became a hit. For three years, as CBS took command of the prime-time ratings race, *You'll Never Get Rich* was a fixture in the 8:00 P.M. Tuesday time slot. Between 1955 and 1958, the show was highly rated, and its success spelled the end of Milton Berle's Tuesday night reign on rival the National Broadcasting Company (NBC).

As played by Silvers, Bilko was an army lifer, a motor-pool master sergeant at isolated Fort Baxter, located near the fictional army small town of Roseville, Kansas. The show was a send-up of army life (or of any existence within any confined and rigid society) and loved by ex-GIs of World War II and the Korean conflict, a generation still close to its own military experiences and willing to laugh at them. With little to do in the U.S. Army of the Cold War era and stuck in the wide-open spaces of rural Kansas, Ernest "Ernie" Bilko spent most of his time planning and trying one elaborate scam after another. Always, predictably, they failed. Bilko was never able to make that one big score. But the comedy came in the trying.

His platoon, played by a cast of wonderful ex-burlesque comics and aspiring New York actors, reluctantly assisted him. His right-hand henchmen, the corporals Barbella and Henshaw, were ever by his side. The remainder of the group, following the pattern of numerous World War II films, seemed to have a man from every ethnic group: the brassy New Yorker, Private Fender; the Italian city boy, Private Paparelli; the high-strung country lad, Private Zimmerman; and the loveable slob, Private Doberman. Others who manned the platoon included black actors, making the program a rare, racially integrated TV situation comedy telecast in the 1950s.

If Silvers was the show's star, Nat Hiken, one of television's first writer-producers, was its creator-auteur. Hiken had first written for Fred Allen's hit radio show, then moved to television to help pen Milton Berle's *Texaco Star Theater.* His scripts provided a mine of comic gems for Bilko and company. Possibly the funniest is "The Case of Harry Speakup," in which a Bilko scheme backfires and he is forced to help induct a chimpanzee into the army. Only Bilko could run such a recruit past army doctors and psychiatrists, have him pass an IQ test and receive a uniform, be formally sworn in as a private, and then moments later be honorably discharged. No bureaucracy has ever been spoofed better than was the Cold War U.S. Army in this 26-minute comic masterpiece.

Nat Hiken did more than write wonderfully funny scripts. As a producer, he had an eye for talent. Guests on *You'll Never Get Rich* included a young Fred

Phil Silvers in the 1960s.
Courtesy of the Everett Collection

Gwynne in "The Eating Contest" (first telecast on November 15, 1955), a youthful Dick Van Dyke in "Bilko's Cousin" (first telecast on January 28, 1958), and Alan Alda in his first significant TV role in "Bilko, the Art Lover" (first telecast on March 7, 1958).

You'll Never Get Rich shot up in the ratings, and less than two months after the premiere, the program was renamed—not surprisingly—*The Phil Silvers Show,* with "You'll Never Get Rich" thereafter relegated to the subtitle. So popular was this show that in September 1957, as it started its second season, it inspired one of television's first paperback collections of published scripts.

Yet, as would be the case for many television programs since the 1950s, the Bilko magic fell out of prime-time favor almost as swiftly as it had seized the public's fascination. The end began in 1958, when CBS switched *The Phil Silvers Show* to Friday nights and moved Bilko and company to Camp Fremont in California. A year later, the show was off the schedule, although it has since functioned as a staple in syndication around the world. Phil Silvers had had his four-year run in television's spotlight.

He would find that spotlight again, briefly, in the 1963–64 television season, when CBS tried *The New Phil Silvers Show,* a knockoff of the earlier program. Here, Silvers played Harry Grafton, a plant foreman, trying (unsuccessfully) to get rich. It lasted but a single season, and thereafter Silvers filled out his career doing occasional TV specials.

But Silvers and Nat Hiken should always be remembered for their pioneering work with *You'll Never Get Rich.* This show hardly dates at all; its comic speed, invention, and ensemble performances rank it among television's greatest comic masterworks.

DOUGLAS GOMERY

See also **Comedy, Workplace;** *Phil Silvers Show, The;* **Workplace Programs**

Phil Silvers. Born Phillip Silversmith in Brooklyn, New York, May 11, 1912. Married: 1) Jo Carroll Dennison (divorced); 2) Evelyn Patrick (divorced); five daughters. Started career as vaudeville singer; became comedian in burlesque, then on Broadway; made screen debut in *The Hit Parade,* 1940; gained fame for television show *The Phil Silvers Show,* CBS, 1955–59. Recipient: Tony Awards, 1952 and 1972; Emmy Awards, 1955 and 1956. Died in Los Angeles, California, November 1, 1985.

Television Series

1955–59	*You'll Never Get Rich* (became *The Phil Silvers Show,* 1955)
1963–64	*The New Phil Silvers Show*

Made-for-Television Movies

1975	*The Deadly Tide*
1975	*All Trails Lead to Las Vegas*
1977	*The New Love Boat*
1978	*The Night They Took Miss Beautiful*
1979	*"Hey Abbott!"*
1979	*Goldie and the Boxer*

Films

The Hit Parade, 1940; *Strike Up the Band,* 1940; *Pride and Prejudice,* 1940; *Ball of Fire,* 1941; *The Penalty,* 1941; *The Wild Man of Borneo,* 1941; *Ice Capades,* 1941; *Tom, Dick and Harry,* 1941; *Lady Be Good,* 1941; *You're in the Army Now,* 1941; *Roxie Hart,* 1942; *All Through the Night,* 1942; *Tales of the Night,* 1942; *My Gal Sal,* 1942; *Footlight Serenade,* 1942; *Just Off Broadway,* 1942; *Coney Island,* 1943; *A Lady Takes a Chance,* 1943; *Cover Girl,* 1944; *Four Jills in a Jeep,* 1944; *Something for the Boys,* 1944; *Take It or Leave It,* 1944; *Billy Rose's Diamond Horseshoe,* 1945; *A Thousand and One Nights,* 1945; *If I'm Lucky,* 1946; *Summer Stock,* 1950; *Top Banana,* 1952; *Lucky Me,* 1956; *40 Pounds of Trouble,* 1962; *It's a Mad, Mad, Mad, Mad World,* 1963; *A Funny Thing Happened on the Way to the Forum,* 1966; *A Guide for the Married Man,* 1967; *Follow That Camel,* 1967; *Buona Sera, Mrs. Campbell,* 1968; *The Boatniks,* 1970; *The Strongest Man in the World,* 1975; *Won Ton Ton: The Dog Who Saved Hollywood,* 1975; *Murder by Death,* 1976; *The Chicken Chronicles,* 1976; *Racquet,* 1978; *There Goes the Bride,* 1979; *The Cheap Detective,* 1979; *The Happy Hooker Goes to Washington,* 1980; *Hollywood Blue,* 1980.

Stage (selected)

Yokel Boy, 1939; *High Button Shoes,* 1947; *Top Banana,* 1952; *Do Re Mi,* 1960, 1962; *How the Other Half Lives,* 1971; *A Funny Thing Happened on the Way to the Forum,* 1971–72.

Publication

This Laugh Is on Me: The Phil Silvers Story, with Robert Saffron, 1973

Further Reading

Everitt, David, "Kingmaker of Comedy," *Television Quarterly* (Summer 1990)

Everitt, David, "The Man Behind the Chutzpah of Master Sgt. Ernest Bilko," *New York Times* (April 14, 1996)

Hamamoto, Darrell Y., *Nervous Laughter: Television Situation Comedy and Liberal Democratic Ideology,* New York: Praeger, 1989

Javna, John, *The Best of TV Sitcoms: Burns and Allen to the Cosby Show, The Munsters to Mary Tyler Moore,* New York: Harmony Books, 1988

Marc, David, *Demographic Vistas: Television in American Culture,* Philadelphia: University of Pennsylvania Press, 1984; 2nd edition, 1996

Marc, David, *Comic Visions: Television Comedy and American Culture,* Boston, Massachusetts: Unwin Hyman, 1989; 2nd edition, Malden, Massachusetts: Blackwell Publishers, 1997

Simpsons, The

U.S. Animated Situation Comedy

The Simpsons, the longest-running cartoon on American prime-time network television and one of the longest-running television sitcoms ever, chronicles the animated adventures of Homer Simpson and his family. Debuting on the FOX network in 1989, critically acclaimed, culturally cynical, and economically very successful, *The Simpsons* helped define the satirical edge of prime-time television in the early 1990s and was the single most influential program in establishing FOX as a legitimate broadcast television network.

The Simpson household consists of five family members. The father, Homer, is a none-too-bright safety inspector for the local nuclear power plant in the show's fictional location, Springfield. A huge blue beehive hairdo characterizes his wife, Marge, often the moral center of the program. Their oldest child, Bart, a sassy ten-year-old and borderline juvenile delinquent, provided the early focus of the program. Lisa, the middle child, is a gifted, perceptive but sensitive saxophone player. Maggie is the voiceless toddler, observing all while constantly sucking on her pacifier. Besides the Simpson clan, other characters include Moe the bartender; Mr. Burns, the nasty owner of the Springfield Nuclear Power Plant; and Ned Flanders, the Simpsons' incredibly pious neighbor. These characters and others, and the world they inhabit, have taken on a dense, rich sense of familiarity. Audiences now recognize relationships and specific character traits that can predict developments and complications in any new plot.

The Simpsons is the creation of Matt Groening, a comic strip writer/artist who, until the debut of the program, was known mostly for his syndicated newspaper strip *Life in Hell.* Attracting the attention of influential writer-producer and Gracie Films executive James L. Brooks, Groening developed the cartoon family as a series of short vignettes featured on the FOX variety program *The Tracey Ullman Show* beginning in 1987.

A Christmas special followed in December 1989, and then *The Simpsons* became a regular series.

Despite its family sitcom format, *The Simpsons* draws its animated inspiration more from Bullwinkle J. Moose than Fred Flintstone. Like *The Bullwinkle Show,* two of the most striking characteristics of *The Simpsons* are its social criticism and its references to other cultural forms. John O'Connor, television critic for the *New York Times,* has labeled the program "the most radical show on prime time," and, indeed, *The Simpsons* often parodies the hypocrisy and contradictions found in social institutions such as the nuclear family (and nuclear power), the mass media, religion, and medicine. Homer tells his daughter Lisa that it is acceptable to steal things "from people you don't like." Reverend Lovejoy lies to Lisa about the contents of the Bible to win an argument. Krusty the Clown, the kid-vid program host, endorses dangerous products to make a quick buck. Homer comforts Marge about upcoming surgery with the observation that "America's health care system is second only to Japan's... Canada's... Sweden's... Great Britain's... well, all of Europe."

The critical nature of the program has been at times controversial, especially early in the show's run. Many elementary schools banned Bart Simpson T-shirts, singling out those with the slogan, "Underachiever, and Proud of It." U.S. President George Bush, Sr., and former U.S. Secretary of Education William Bennett publicly criticized the program for its subversive and antiauthority nature. After President Bush commented that families should be more like the Waltons and less like the Simpsons, Bart responded in one episode with, "Hey, we're just like the Waltons. We're praying for an end to the Depression, too."

In addition to its ironic lampoons, *The Simpsons* is also one of the most culturally literate entertainment programs on prime time. Viewers may note references to such cultural icons as *The Bridges of Madison County,* Ayn Rand, Susan Sontag, and the film *Barton Fink* in any given episode. These allusions extend far beyond explicit verbal notations. Cartoon technique allows free movement in *The Simpsons,* and manipulation of visual qualities—often mimicking comic strip perspectives and cinematic manipulation of space—creates an extraordinary sense of time, place, and movement. On occasion, *The Simpsons* has reproduced the actual camera movements of the films it models. At other times, the cartoonist's freedom and ability to visualize internal psychological states such as memory and dream have produced some of the program's most hilarious moments.

The unique nature of *The Simpsons* reveals much about the nature of the television industry. Specifically, the existence of the show illustrates the relationship of television's industrial context to its degree of content innovation. It was a program that came along at the right place and time, and it appealed to the right demographic groups. Groening has said that no other network besides FOX would have aired *The Simpsons,* and in fact conventional television producers had previously turned down Groening's programming ideas. The degree of competition in network television in the late 1980s helped open the door, however. Network television overall found itself in a more competitive environment in this period because of cable television and VCRs. The FOX network, specifically, was in an even more precarious economic position than the "big three: (American Broadcasting Company [ABC], Columbia Broadcasting System [CBS], and National Broadcasting Company [NBC]). Because FOX was the new, unestablished network, attempting to build audiences and attract advertisers, the normally restrictive nature of network television gatekeeping may have been loosened to allow the program on the air. In addition, the championing of *The Simpsons* by Brooks, an established producer with a strong track record, helped the program through the industrialized television filters that might have watered down the program's social criticism. Finally, the fact that the program draws young audiences especially attractive to advertisers also explains the network's willingness to air such an unconventional and risky program. The "tween" demographic, those between the ages of 12 and 17, is an especially key viewing group for *The Simpsons* as well as a primary consumer group targeted by advertisers.

The Simpsons was a watershed program in the establishment of the FOX network. The cartoon has been the FOX program most consistently praised by television critics. In the 1990s, *The Simpsons* won five Emmys for Outstanding Animated Programming (one

hour or less). In its December 31, 1999, "Person of the Century" issue, *Time* magazine chose *The Simpsons* as the best television program ever made. It was the first FOX program to reach the top ten in ratings despite the network's smaller number of affiliates compared to the big three. When FOX moved *The Simpsons* to Thursday night in 1990, it directly challenged the number one program of the network establishment at the time, *The Cosby Show.* Eventually, *The Simpsons* bested this powerful competitor in key male demographic groups. The schedule change and the subsequent success signaled FOX's staying power to the rest of the industry, and for viewers it was a powerful illustration of the innovative nature of FOX programming when compared to conventional television fare.

The Simpsons is also noteworthy for the enormous amount of merchandising it has sparked. *Simpsons* T-shirts, toys, buttons, golf balls, and other licensed materials were everywhere at the height of Simpsonsmania in the early 1990s. At one point, retailers were selling approximately 1 million *Simpsons* T-shirts per week. *The Simpsons* also inspired its own line of comic books, Bongo Comics.

The big three networks attempted to copy the success of the prime-time cartoon, but these efforts failed to duplicate *The Simpsons'* innovative nature and general appeal. Programs such as *Capital Critters, Fish Police,* and *Family Dog* were all short lived on the webs. However, FOX and cable networks have been able to find ratings success with such prime-time animation programs as *King of the Hill* (FOX) and *South Park* (Comedy Central). Groening was also a creative force behind *Futurama,* another FOX prime-time animated program that debuted in 1999. Such programs are one legacy of *The Simpsons.* Another is that with a two-year renewal provided by FOX in 2003, *The Simpsons* is positioned to become one of television's longest-running series in any genre, assuring its place in all future histories of the medium.

MATTHEW P. McALLISTER

See also **Brooks, James L.; Cartoons; Family on Television; FOX Broadcasting Company**

Cast (Voices)

Homer Simpson	Dan Castellaneta
Marge Simpson	Julie Kavner
Bartholomew J. "Bart" Simpson	Nancy Cartwright
Lisa Simpson	Yeardley Smith
Mrs. Krabappel	Marcia Wallace
Mr. Burns, Principal Skinner, Ned Flanders, Smithers, Otto the School Bus Driver (and others)	Harry Shearer

Moe, Apu, Chief Wiggins,
  Dr. Nick Riviera (and others)   Hank Azaria

Producers

Larina Adamson, Sherry Argaman, Joseph A.
  Boucher, James L. Brooks, David S. Cohen,
  Jonathan Collier, Gabor Csupo, Greg Daniels, Paul
  Germain, Matt Groening, Al Jean, Ken Keeler,
  Harold Kimmel, Jay Kogen, Colin A.B.V. Lewis,
  Jeff Martin, Ian Maxtone-Graham, J. Michael
  Mendel, George Meyer, David Mirkin, Frank Mula,
  Conan O'Brien, Bill Oakley, Margo Pipkin,
  Richard Raynis, Mike Reiss, David Richardson,
  Jace Richdale, Phil Roman, David Sachs, Richard
  Sakai, Bill Schultz, Mike Scully, David Silverman,
  Sam Simon, John Swartzwelder, Ken Tsumura, Jon
  Vitti, Josh Weinstein, Michael Wolf, Wallace Wolo-
  darsky

Programming History

FOX

December 1989–August 1990	Sunday 8:30–9:00
August 1990–May 1994	Thursday 8:00–8:30
September 1994–	Sunday 8:00–8:30

Further Reading

Berlant, Lauren, "The Theory of Infantile Citizenship," *Public Culture: Bulletin of the Society for Transnational Cultural Studies* (Spring 1993)

Coe, Steve, "Fox Hoping *Simpsons* Will Boost Slow Start," *Broadcasting* (October 8, 1990)

Corliss, Richard, "*Simpsons* Forever!" *Time* (May 2, 1994)

Elder, Sean, "Is TV the Coolest Invention Ever Invented? Subversive Cartoonist Matt Groening Goes Prime Time," *Mother Jones* (December 1989)

Freeman, Mike, "Fox Affils Deal for Radical Dude: *Simpsons* Pricing Appears to Remain Apace of Big-Ticket '80s Sitcoms," *Broadcasting & Cable* (March 1, 1993)

Henry, Matthew, "The Triumph of Popular Culture: Situation Comedy, Postmodernism and *The Simpsons*," *Studies in Popular Culture* (October 1994)

Irwin, William, Mark T. Conard, and Aeon J. Skoble, editors, *The Simpsons and Philosophy: The D'oh! of Homer*, Chicago: Open Court, 2001

Larson, Mary Strom, "Family Communication on Prime-Time Television," *Journal of Broadcasting and Electronic Media* (Summer 1993)

McConnell, Frank, "'Real' Cartoon Characters: *The Simpsons*," *Commonweal* (June 15, 1990)

Ozersky, Josh, "TV's Anti-Families: Married...with Malaise," *Tikkun* (January–February 1991)

Pinsky, Mark I., *The Gospel According to the Simpsons: The Spiritual Life of the World's Most Animated Family*, Louisville, Kentucky: Westminster John Knox Press, 2001

Rebeck, Victoria A., "Recognizing Ourselves in *The Simpsons*," *Christian Century* (June 27, 1990)

Stabile, Carol A., and Mark Harrison, editors, *Prime Time Animation: Television Animation and American Culture*, New York: Routledge, 2003

Waters, Harry F., "Family Feuds," *Newsweek* (April 23, 1990)

Zehme, Bill, "The Only Real People on TV," *Rolling Stone* (June 28, 1990)

Simulcasting

"Simulcasting" is a term used to describe the simultaneous transmission of a television and/or radio signal over two or more networks or two or more stations. In the United States, the most obvious example would be a major address by the president that might be carried simultaneously by three television networks (American Broadcasting Company [ABC], Columbia Broadcasting System [CBS], and National Broadcasting Company [NBC]), one or more cable networks (Cable News Network [CNN] and CNBC), and several radio networks.

The term has taken a different meaning during various periods in broadcasting. Initially, the term was applied to the simultaneous transmission of important events over two or more radio outlets. Later, it referred to the simultaneous transmission of programs on radio and television. This occurred during the 1960s, when some of the most popular radio programs became television programs but the audio portion was still simulcast on radio. This practice was short lived, however, as the number of homes with TV sets increased and radio shifted increasingly to music-based programming.

The very slow growth in FM radio during the 1950s and 1960s was due, in part, to the simulcasting of radio programming over co-owned AM and FM stations. In 1964, the Federal Communications Commission (FCC) acted to force the independence of FM stations by severely restricting the number of hours that AM and FM stations could simulcast during any given broadcast day, although protests by radio station owners delayed implementation of the rule until January 1, 1967. (Ironically, the FCC removed the restrictions on

AM/FM simulcasting a quarter of a century later so that struggling AM stations could simulcast the programming of their stronger FM sister stations.)

Simulcasting of musically oriented programs by television and FM stations occurred on an occasional basis during the 1970s and 1980s. Sometimes these programs included opera or other classical presentations; on other occasions, rock concerts were simulcast. The improved sound fidelity and stereo capability of newer television sets have diminished the need for such audio-enhancement simulcasting, although some TV/FM simulcasting still occurs.

The terrorist attacks on the World Trade Center in New York City and the Pentagon in Washington, D.C., on September 11, 2001, created a very different need for simulcasting. Immediately following these attacks, broadcast and cable networks simulcast their news coverage on co-owned cable networks that did not ordinarily carry news. ABC News was carried on the Entertainment and Sports Programming Network (ESPN); CBS covered the music networks Video Hits 1 (VH1) and, later in the day, Music Television (MTV); and CNN News was simulcast on both Turner Network Television (TNT) and the Turner Broadcasting System (TBS).

On a lighter note, simulcasting has even been used to carry two slightly different versions of the same program. When ESPN cablecast the film *Season on the Brink* (2002) about former Indiana University basketball coach Bobby Knight, the same movie was simulcast—but with the raw language and obscenities bleeped—on ESPN2.

Currently, the term "simulcasting" is most relevant to the development and adaptation of digital television. Both broadcasters and regulators recognize that newer, more advanced forms of television transmission will have to be phased in gradually since viewers with standard television receivers are not willing to accept the immediate obsolescence of their current TV sets.

As of 2002, many television stations in larger markets are simulcasting on two separate signals. A standard (NTSC analog) signal is broadcast over the television station's basic channel, while a second ATSC digital signal is transmitted over a separate channel allocated to that station specifically for this purpose by the FCC.

Initially, the FCC suggested that this simulcasting would continue until 2006, at which time 85 percent of U.S. households would be able to receive a digital signal. Simulcasting would then be discontinued, and the analog channels would be returned to the FCC for alternative use. As of 2002, that time frame seems very much in doubt, and observers speculate that analog/digital simulcasting will continue long past the 2006 date.

In addition to the simulcasting of analog and digital signals, the traditional simulcasting of major events by one or more television and/or cable outlets is a well-established practice and one not likely to end in the near term.

NORMAN FELSENTHAL

See also **Music on Television; Public Television**

Singing Detective, The

British Serial Drama

The Singing Detective (1986) is a six-part serial by one of British television's great experimental dramatists, Dennis Potter. Produced for the British Broadcasting Corporation (BBC) by Kenith Trodd and directed by Jon Amiel, it revolves around the personal entanglements—real, remembered, and imagined—of the thriller author Philip Marlow (played by Michael Gambon), who is suffering from acute psoriasis and from the side effects associated with its treatment. The result is a complex, multilayered text that weaves together, in heightened, antirealist form, the varied interests and themes of the detective thriller, the hospital drama, the musical, and the autobiography.

A first level of narrative centers on Marlow in his hospital bed. Set in the present, this narrative includes his fantasies and hallucinations. The second narrative is played out in Marlow's mind as he mentally rewrites his story *The Singing Detective*, with himself as hero, set in 1945. The third narrative, also set in 1945, consists of memories from his childhood as a nine-year-old boy in the Forest of Dean and in London, told through a series of flashbacks. The fourth area of narrative involves Marlow's fantasy about a conspiracy between his wife, Nicola, and a supposed lover, set in the present.

There are obvious parallels between the story and Potter's own personal history. Like Marlow, Potter was born and brought up in the Forest of Dean at about the same time that Marlow was a wartime evacuee, and like Marlow he stayed in Hammersmith with relations who had difficulty with his strong Gloucestershire accent. Two key incidents in *The Singing Detective* are based on real-life childhood incidents—Potter's mother, a pub pianist, being kissed by a man, and Potter's writing a four-letter word on the blackboard when his precocious facility as a young writer made him unpopular with other schoolchildren.

The serial is explicitly concerned with psychoanalysis: the spectator is constructed both as detective and as psychoanalyst in a drama that Potter described as "a detective story about how you find out about yourself." The text is rich in Freudian imagery and symbolism, and it deals with psychoanalytical technique as Dr. Gibbons attempts to involve a linguistically skeptical Marlow in the talking cure. Marlow's neurosis and paranoia are explicitly linked to his repression of painful childhood memories, notably his mother's adultery, her eventual suicide, and the mental breakdown of a fellow pupil after a beating by a teacher. At this level, for Potter the story was about "one man's paranoia and the ending of it."

However, *The Singing Detective* does not offer a straightforward case of autobiographical drama—Potter claimed the serial was "one of the least autobiographical pieces of work I've ever attempted"—nor does it lead to conventional psychological or psychoanalytical resolution. Potter translates basic concerns, instead, to a more complex level where the narrative and generic dimensions of the text endlessly merge and overlap, fusing past and present, fantasy and "reality," challenging the organic conventions of realist drama and mixing the stabilities of popular television with the textual instabilities of modernism and postmodernism.

The Singing Detective is thus not only the serial that the TV viewer is watching but also the fiction that Marlow is rewriting in his head. Although his name is not unfamiliar in the genre, Marlow is no conventional focus for identification: he is obstreperously unlikable and contradictory, and his illness has been hideously disfiguring. More important, he is sometimes not the major "focaliser" of the narrative at all, being repeatedly displaced by other themes and discourses in the process of a drama in which "character" itself rapidly becomes an unstable entity. The same character, for example, can appear in different narratives, played by

the same actor; characters from one narrative can appear in another; a character may lip-synch the lines of another character from a different narrative; or, in true Brechtian–Godardian style, characters may feel free to comment on their role or to speak directly to the camera.

Questions of time and its enigmas, past and present, are also rendered complex. In narrative 1, in the present, Marlow is reconstructing two pasts: the book he wrote a long time ago, which was itself set in the past, and a part of his childhood, also set in 1945. The main enigmas in his text are set in that year. In narrative 2, who killed the busker, Sonia, Amanda, Lili, and Mark Binney? And why? In narrative 3, who shat on the table? Why did Mrs. Marlow commit suicide? Although narratives 1 and 2 usually (but not always) follow story chronology, in narrative 3, it is not really clear what the actual chronology of the young Philip's life might be. In terms of narrative frequency, *The Singing Detective* is further marked by a high degree of repetition—of words, events, and visual images—as the same event, or part of it, is retold, reworked, or recontextualized.

The final shoot-out in the hospital thus merges narratives 1 and 2 by uniting past (1945) with the present time of its reconstruction (1986), that is, its reconstruction in Marlow's head rather than in his book itself. The "villain" who is killed is not just one of the characters but also the sick author himself, thus liberating the singing detective and ensuring an ending for narrative 2. Although it does not resolve any of the enigmas posed by this second narrative, the "dream" of the "sick" Marlow allows the Marlow who is "well" to get up and walk out of the hospital, concluding narrative 1. As he walks away down a long corridor on Nicola's arm, bird sounds from the Forest of Dean (narrative 3) are heard; past and present are again combined, even if, typically, they are not reconciled.

The Singing Detective thus refuses any simple reading, and it even contests the traditional definition of television "reading" altogether. It is witty, comic, and salacious yet also savage, bleak, and nihilistic. It is blunt and populist yet arcane and abstruse. Its key themes are language and communication; memory and representation; sexual and familial betrayal and guilt; the transition from childhood to adulthood; the relationships between religion, knowledge, and belief; and the processes of illness and of dying. While its themes are resonant, its most enduring claim on critical attention lies in its thoroughgoing engagement with the textual politics of modernism. Its swirl of meanings and enigmas render it British prime-time television's most sustained experiment with classic post-Brechtian strategies for antirealism, reflexivity, and textual deconstruction and for the encouragement of new reading practices on the part of the TV spectator.

PHILLIP DRUMMOND AND JANE REVELL

See also *Pennies from Heaven;* **Potter, Dennis; Trodd, Kenith**

Cast

Philip Marlow	Michael Gambon
Raymond Binney/	
Mark Binney/Finney	Patrick Malahide
Nurse Mills/Carlotta	Joanne Whalley
Dr. Gibbon	Bill Paterson
Philip Marlow (age ten)	Lyndon Davies
Nicola	Janet Suzman
Mrs. Marlow/Lili	Alison Steadman
Mr. Marlow	Jim Carter
Schoolteacher/Scarecrow	Janet Henfrey
Mark Binney (age ten)	William Speakman

Producers

John Harris, Kenith Trodd

Programming History

Six 60–80-minute episodes
BBC
November 16–December 21, 1986

Further Reading

Cook, John R., *Dennis Potter: A Life on Screen,* Manchester, United Kingdom, and New York: Manchester University Press, 1995

Corliss, Richard, "Notes from *The Singing Detective:* Dennis Potter Makes Beautiful Music from Painful Lives," *Time* (December 19, 1988)

Fuller, Graham, "Dennis Potter," *American Film* (March 1989)

Fuller, Graham, editor, *Potter on Potter,* London and Boston, Massachusetts: Faber and Faber, 1993

Gilbert, W. Stephen, *Fight and Kick and Bite: The Life and Work of Dennis Potter,* London: Hodder and Stoughton, 1995

Potter, Dennis, *An Interview with Dennis Potter: An Edited Transcript of Melvyn Bragg's Interview with Dennis Potter, Broadcast on the 5th of April, 1994,* London: Channel 4 Television, 1994

Potter, Dennis, *Seeing the Blossom: Two Interviews and a Lecture,* London and Boston, Massachusetts: Faber and Faber, 1994

Stead, Peter, *Dennis Potter,* Bridgend, United Kingdom: Seren, 1993

Wyver, John, "Arrows of Desire" (interview), *New Statesman and Society* (November 24, 1989)

Siskel and Ebert

U.S. Movie Review Program

Siskel and Ebert represented the first and most popular of the movie-review series genre that emerged on television in the mid-1970s. The lively series focused on the give-and-take interaction and opinions of its knowledgeable and often contentious cohosts, Gene Siskel, film critic of the *Chicago Tribune,* and Roger Ebert, film critic of the *Chicago Sun-Times.* Syndicated to approximately 200 markets across the United States, the spirited pair reached a potential 95 percent of the United States on a weekly basis.

Developed from an idea credited to producer Thea Flaum of Public Broadcasting Service (PBS) affiliate WTTW in Chicago, the original series, *Opening Soon at a Theater Near You,* was broadcast once a month to a local audience beginning in September 1975. Using brief clips of movies in current release, the rival critics debated the merits of the films, making simple "yes" or "no" decisions to signify positive and negative reviews. On those not-so-rare occasions when the two disagreed, sparks might fly, which delighted viewers. An additional element of interest featured Spot the Wonder Dog jumping onto a balcony seat and barking on cue to introduce the film designated "dog of the week."

After two seasons, the successful series was retitled *Sneak Previews* and appeared biweekly on the PBS network. By its fourth season, the show became a once-a-week feature on 180 to 190 outlets and achieved status as the highest-rated weekly entertainment series in the history of public broadcasting.

Based on the program's success, in 1980 WTTW made plans to remove the show from PBS and sell it commercially as a WTTW production. The two stars indicated that they were offered a take-it-or-leave-it contract that they declined. They left the series in 1981 to launch *At the Movies* for commercial television under the banner of Tribune Entertainment, a syndication arm of the *Chicago Tribune.* Basically utilizing the same format as *Sneak Previews,* the new series made some minor adjustments, including the replacement of the black-and-white Wonder Dog with Aroma the skunk, which ultimately was removed to make room for commercials. At WTTW, *Sneak Previews* replaced Siskel and Ebert with New York–based critics Jeffrey Lyons and Neal Gabler. In time, the PBS offering would settle on Lyons and Michael Medved as its hosts, and the show remained on air through the 1995–96 season.

Citing contractual problems with Tribune Entertainment, in 1986 Siskel and Ebert departed *At the Movies* for Buena Vista Television, a subsidiary of the Walt Disney Company, and created a new series titled *Siskel and Ebert at the Movies.* The order of the names was decided by the flip of a coin, and the show title was eventually shortened to *Siskel and Ebert.* Ebert also suggested the Romanesque thumbs-up/thumbs-down rating system, which became a distinctive Siskel–Ebert trademark. Their former show, *At the Movies,* acquired Rex Reed and Bill Harris as hosts and added news of show business to the format. Harris left the series in 1988 and was replaced by Dixie Whatley, former cohost on *Entertainment Tonight,* and the series continued into 1990.

Of all the different series and cohosts in this genre, the Siskel–Ebert partnership has remained the most celebrated. In 20 years of offering responsible commentary in an unedited spontaneous fashion, the two critics reviewed more than 4,000 films and compiled an impressive list of firsts and show milestones. In his defense of television film critics in the May/June 1990 issue of *Film Comment,* Ebert, the only film critic to have won a Pulitzer Prize for criticism, points out that *Siskel and Ebert* was the first national show to discuss the issue of film colorization, the benefits of letterbox video dubbing, and the technology of laser disks. *Siskel and Ebert* provided an outlet for the ongoing examination of minority and independent films, attacked the rating system of the Motion Picture Association of America as de facto censorship, and protested product placement (i.e., incidental advertising) within films. And in May 1989, extolling the virtues of black-and-white cinematography, they videotaped their show in monochrome—the first new syndicated program to do so in 25 years.

Siskel and Ebert's influence with audiences was also notable. Their thumbs-up reviews are credited with turning films such as *My Dinner with Andre* (1981), *One False Move* (1992), and *Hoop Dreams* (1994) into respectable box office hits. Thumbs-down reviews had the opposite effect: although many filmmakers contend that ultimately it is up to the public to choose which films they see, many directors and producers also have noted the benefits that exposure on *Siskel and Ebert* could provide. Notwithstanding, there were occasional disgruntled feelings. As reported in the *Los Angeles Times* (December 10, 1995), screenwriter Richard LaGravanese used "Siskel" as the name for one of the "bad guys" in his film *The Ref* after a negative review of his previous work *The Fisher King.*

Both Siskel and Ebert agreed that their animated dialogue was crucial to the show's success and more compelling than criticism from a solitary voice. They viewed their disagreements as those of two friends who had seen a movie and had a difference of opinion. But they had some intense moments, as evidenced in a pre-Oscar special broadcast in 1993 when an angry Ebert took exception to Siskel's revelation of the significant plot twist that concludes the film *The Crying Game.*

Through the years, the television industry recognized Siskel and Ebert with six national Emmy nominations and one local Emmy (1979). In 1984, the pair were among the first broadcasters initiated into the National Association of Television Programming Executives (NATPE) Hall of Fame. They also received NATPE's Iris Award for their achievement in nationally syndicated television. The Hollywood Radio and Television Society named them Men of the Year in 1993. As Richard Roeper wrote in the *Chicago Sun-Times* (October 15, 1995) on the occasion of their 20th anniversary, "Siskel and Ebert took serious film criticism and made it palatable to a mass audience—and in so doing, became celebrities themselves, as recognizable as most of the movie stars whose films they review."

In May 1998, the show weathered a potential setback when Siskel underwent brain surgery to remove a growth. Remarkably, he returned to the show and stayed with it until early February 1999, when he took another leave of absence for further rehabilitation and recuperation. On February 20, 1999, he passed away. In July 2000, the previously mentioned *Chicago Sun-Times* columnist Richard Roeper, one of 24 reviewers who guest hosted with Ebert over a 17-month period, was named Ebert's new permanent cohost. Roeper assumed Siskel's vacant seat in the balcony two months later, and the program was renamed *Ebert and Roeper and the Movies.* The show also brought in ZDTV's

Michaela Pereira with occasional reviews of online movies.

JOEL STERNBERG

See also **Movies on Television**

Hosts

Gene Siskel and Roger Ebert

Programming History

Syndicated   Various times

Further Reading

Arlidge, Ron, "'At the Movies' Rates Higher Than Improving 'Sneak,'" *Chicago Tribune* (November 11, 1982)
Anderson, John, "Why Is *Movies* So Successful? It's Simple," *Chicago Tribune TV Week* (September 1–7, 1985)

Bellafante, Ginia, "Pro Thumb Wrestling," *Time* (April 5, 1993)
Caro, Mark, "Gene Siskel, 1946–1999: A Man of Influence," *Chicago Tribune* (February 22, 1999)
Chipman, Ida, "'63 CMA Grad Gene Siskel Dies," *The Culver Citizen* (February 24, 1999)
Clark, Champ, "Tube: Spotlight on…Richard Roeper," *People Weekly* (September 25, 2000)
Ebert, Roger, "All Stars, or, Is There a Cure for Criticism of Film Criticism?," *Film Comment* (May/June 1990)
Ebert, Roger, "Gene Siskel, 1946–1999: Farewell, My Friend," *Chicago Sun-Times* (February 21, 1999)
Feder, Robert, "Seat Saved for Roeper," *Chicago Sun-Times* (July 11, 2000)
Feder, Robert, "It's Ebert and Roeper," *Chicago Sun-Times* (July 13, 2000)
Kogan, Rick, "Gene Siskel, 1946–1999: He Changed the Way We Look at Movies," *Chicago Tribune* (February 21, 1999)
Turan, Kenneth, "Rating TV's Movie Critics," *TV Guide* (March 18–24, 1989)
Zoglin, Richard, "'It Stinks!' 'You're Crazy!'" *Time* (May 25, 1987)

The Six Wives of Henry VIII

British Historical Drama Serial

The Six Wives of Henry VIII, first broadcast by the British Broadcasting Corporation (BBC) in 1970, became one of its most celebrated historical drama serials. The nine-hour, six-part series went on to be shown in some 70 countries and attracted no less than seven major awards, winning plaudits both for the quality of the performances and for its historical authenticity.

Towering over the series was the gargantuan figure of Henry himself, played by the hitherto unknown Australian actor Keith Michell, who earned an award for best television actor as a result of his efforts. Michell, who started out as an art teacher, owed the role to Laurence Olivier, who had been impressed by Michell while on tour in Australia and had brought him back to England in order to advance his career. The faith the BBC put in the young actor was more than amply rewarded; Michell went to extraordinary lengths to vitalize the larger-than-life character of the king.

The series was neatly split into six episodes, each one dealing with one of the six wives and tracing their varied experiences and sometimes bloody ends at the hands of one of England's most infamous rulers. The wives were played by Annette Crosbie, Dorothy Tutin, Anne Stallybrass, Elvi Hale, Angela Pleasance, and Rosalie Crutchley, all respected and proven stars of stage and screen. Annette Crosbie, playing Catherine of Aragon, collected an award for best actress for her performance.

Michell, though, was always the focus of attention. The task for the actor was to portray Henry at the different stages of his life, beginning with the athletic 18-year-old monarch and culminating in the oversize 56-year-old tyrant plagued by a variety of physical ailments. Playing the aging Henry in the later episodes proved the most demanding challenge. Michell, who boasted only half the girth of the real king, spent some four hours each day getting his makeup on and was then unable to take any sustenance except through a straw because of the padding tucked into his cheeks. The impersonation was entirely convincing, however, and critics hailed the attention to detail in costume and sets. No one, it seemed, twigged that Henry's mink robes were really made of rabbit fur or that the fabulous jewels studding his hats and coats were humble washers and screws sprayed with paint.

The lavishness of the costumes and settings and the brilliance of Michell and his costars ensured the success of the series, although some viewers expressed reservations. In particular, it was felt by some critics that the underlying theme of the lonely and essentially

The Six Wives of Henry VIII, Anne Stallybrass, Keith Michell, Dorothy Tutin, Annette Crosbie, 1971.
Courtesy of the Everett Collection

reasonable man beneath the outrageous outer persona was perhaps rather predictable and further that Michell—who admitted to admiring Henry's excesses—had a tendency to reduce Henry to caricature (a fault more clearly evident in the film *Henry VIII and His Six Wives,* which was spawned by the television series in 1972).

Whatever the criticisms, the success of *The Six Wives of Henry VIII* brought stardom to Michell and also did much to establish the BBC's cherished reputation for ambitious and historically authentic costume drama, consolidated a year later by the equally acclaimed series *Elizabeth R,* starring Glenda Jackson as Henry's daughter.

DAVID PICKERING

Cast

Henry VIII	Keith Michell
Catherine of Aragon	Annette Crosbie
Anne Boleyn	Dorothy Tutin
Jane Seymour	Anne Stallybrass
Anne of Cleves	Elvi Hale
Catherine Howard	Angela Pleasance
Catherine Parr	Rosalie Crutchley
Duke of Norfolk	Patrick Troughton
Lady Rochford	Sheila Burrell
Thomas Cranmer	Bernard Hepton
Thomas Cromwell	Wolfe Morris
Sir Thomas Seymour	John Ronane

Narrator

Anthony Quayle

Producers

Ronald Travers, Mark Shivas, Roderick Graham

Programming History

12 90-minute episodes
BBC 2
January 1–February 5, 1970

Further Reading

Trewin, J.C., editor, *The Six Wives of Henry VIII,* New York: Ungar, 1972

60 Minutes, 60 Minutes II

U.S. Newsmagazine Show

In 1967, Don Hewitt conceived of his new program, *60 Minutes*, as a strategy for addressing issues given insufficient time for analysis in two minutes of the *Evening News* but not deemed significant enough to justify an hour-long documentary. *60 Minutes* was born, then, in an environment of management tension and initial ambiguity regarding its form. Bill Leonard, vice president for news programming for the Columbia Broadcasting System (CBS), supported the new concept, but Richard Salant, president of the news division, argued that it countered that unit's commitment to the longer form and risked taking the hard edge off television journalism. In the end, Salant acquiesced.

Hewitt's direction remained flexible and uncertain, with design for the program possibly including any number of "pages" and "chapters," lasting 1 to 20 minutes and spanning breaking news, commentary, satire, interviews with politicians and celebrities, feature stories, and letters to the editor. CBS proclaimed the groundbreaking potential of this magazine form, announcing that no existing phrase could describe the series' configuration and that any attempt to gauge (or predict) the show's demographic appeal based on comparisons to traditional public affairs programming was a limited prospect. Yet by the time it had been on the air for a quarter of a century, the series' success was so established within the history of network programming that CBS and *60 Minutes* had competition from roughly half a dozen other prime-time magazine programs.

From September 1966 through December 1975, network management shifted the scheduling position of *60 Minutes* seven times. Its ratings were very low according to industry standards (although slightly higher than those of *CBS Reports* when aired in the same time slot), but critical response remained positive. In the 1970s, Hewitt, with a tone of self-aggrandizement, passionately publicized the methods that would make the series a success. Audiences must experience stories in the pit of their stomach, the narrative must take the viewer by the throat, and, noted Hewitt, when a segment is over, it is not significant what the audience has been told; what matters is "only what they remember of what you tell them." Hewitt predicted high ratings if *60 Minutes* packaged stories, not news items, as attrac-

tively as "Hollywood packages fiction." Such stories require drama, a simplified structure, a narrative maximizing conflict, a quick editing pace, and issues filtered through personalities. By acknowledging this marketing approach, Hewitt generated controversy in the television industry.

Several of *60 Minutes'* journalists had established their professional reputations before the series began, but with the program's growing success and significance, the correspondents reached international celebrity status, becoming crusaders, detectives, sensitive and introspective guides through social turmoil, and insightful investigators of the human psyche. A confrontational style of journalism, pioneered by Mike Wallace, grew and was embraced by a more confronta-

60 Minutes.
Courtesy of the Everett Collection

tional society. In the 1970s, certain correspondents seemed to speak for a public under siege by institutional greed and deceit.

Through it all, Hewitt remained sensitive to balancing the series through the use of varying casts. Wallace's role remained consistent as the crusading detective, played, as the series began, opposite Harry Reasoner's calm, analytical, and introspective persona. As correspondents were added (Morley Safer, Dan Rather, Ed Bradley, Diane Sawyer, Meredith Vieria, Steve Kroft, and Lesley Stahl), Hewitt developed complementary personas for each season's team. The correspondents became part of his "new form" of storytelling, allowing the audience to watch their intimate involvement in discovering information, tripping up an interviewee, or developing a narrative. As a result, the correspondents are often central to Hewitt's notion of stories as morality plays, the confrontation of vice and virtue.

The investigative segments of the series have made *60 Minutes* the focus of consistent examination by the press concerning such issues as journalism ethics and integrity. *60 Minutes* has been taken to task for having correspondents or representatives use false identities to generate stories, establishing sting operations for the camera, confronting the person under inquiry by surprise, and revealing new documents without prior notice to a cooperative interviewee in order to increase the shock value of the information. Despite widespread knowledge of these strong techniques, individuals still subject themselves to interviews, offering the audience an opportunity to anticipate who will win the battle. Indeed, companies frequently must weigh the benefits of voicing a corporate perspective on *60 Minutes* against the risk encountered by company representatives when facing the penetrating (aggressive) questioning and fact-finding by the correspondent. By raising these issues, the series has focused attention on emerging techniques of broadcast journalism.

In the late 1990s, the power of *60 Minutes* to confer unwarranted status on people appearing on the show crystallized with detrimental consequences to the series' credibility. Segments of the public vehemently objected to an hour-long interview with Timothy McVeigh, the individual convicted of bombing the federal building in Oklahoma City, and a repeat of the show with family members of the victims responding to McVeigh's statements. After Hewitt made the decision to air the assisted suicide performed by Jack Kervorkian (May 22, 1998), critics accused Hewitt of giving Kervorkian a vehicle to challenge the legal system and position himself as a martyr.

Critics, researchers, and the public continue to investigate the reasons behind the longevity of *60 Min-utes* as a popular culture phenomenon. The series' timeliness, its bold stand on topics, its access to powerful people, and its confrontations with institutions out of reach of the public all provide audiences with the pleasure of knowing that accountability does exist. For some, the program is compelling because of its crusades, such as its coverage of Lenell Geter, freed from life imprisonment after *60 Minutes* explored and analyzed his case. For others, the most appealing stories involve a subject's vigorous self-defense, as when Senator Alfonso D'Amato (Republican, New York) poured out his wrath in a 30-minute response to claims that he misused state funds. The series' perennial "light" moment, "A Few Minutes with Andy Rooney," confirms the value of personal opinion on otherwise mundane matters.

60 Minutes generates news about itself and thus keeps the series attractive by humanizing its trials and tribulations. Producers, correspondents, and Hewitt have played out issues in public. The announcement by CBS of a new magazine program, *West 57th,* geared to a younger audience, met with a bombardment of criticism and sarcasm from *60 Minutes'* personnel, creating well-publicized tension between both units working in the same building. Producer Marion Goldin twice quit *60 Minutes* after accusing the unit of sexism. Hewitt charged Rooney with hypocrisy for criticizing CBS owner Lawrence Tisch on air instead of quitting. Wallace has been reprimanded for using hidden cameras to tape a reporter who agreed to help him with a story. However, Wallace made an unprecedented "denouncement" on the air, without repercussions, of CBS management after they prevented testimony by Wigand against his former employer in the tobacco industry. Even when the series dropped to number 13 in the 1993–94 Nielsen ratings (after being first for two years), the drop became a "story." Hewitt and others blamed CBS, Inc., for losing affiliates in urban areas and for allowing the FOX network to win the bid for Sunday afternoon football, *60 Minutes'* longtime lead-in program.

When *Dateline NBC,* a similar newsmagazine, was programmed opposite *60 Minutes* in the spring of 1996, the press covered the move as a battle for the hearts and minds of the audience. However, for several months before the direct competition, Hewitt began to revamp *60 Minutes,* adding brief, hard news segments; announcing the production of new stories throughout the summer; adding a "commentary" section; and tracking down new and unfamiliar topics. Although the series has been criticized for sporadically following compelling stories broken by magazines such as *The Nation* instead of breaking news, the strategy meets Hewitt's mandate to impact a large audience. In its fourth decade, *60 Minutes* continues to shift strategy and change in form. With the arrival of *60 Minutes II* in January 1999, Hewitt faced the challenge of keeping the original series distinctive and maintaining its prominence among magazine programs.

When Leslie Moonves, president and chief executive officer of CBS Television, conceived of *60 Minutes II,* Hewitt and Wallace believed that he was motivated by profit making and trying to respond to the decisions of the American Broadcasting Company (ABC) and the National Broadcasting Company (NBC) to dedicate more programming time to other newsmagazines. For Hewitt, the new CBS program would lead to the "dumbing down" of the *60 Minutes* brand in order to attract the 18- to 49-year-olds absorbed by the soft-news and celebrity-oriented stories of the competition on other networks. The strong resistance of Hewitt and Wallace to *60 Minutes II* abated after Jeffrey Fager left his position as executive producer of the CBS *Evening News* to head the series, and Rather became a regular correspondent. Joining the series as correspondents were Bob Simon, Charlie Rose, and Vicki Mabrey, with Carol Marin as contributing correspondent, and Jeffrey Tingle, a Boston-based comic, as commentator. When Tingle's brand of humor failed, Charles Grodin came aboard in October 2000. Scott Pelley joined as the fifth correspondent late in 1999.

Fearing that the potential failure of *60 Minutes II* would permanently tarnish the original series, Hewitt and Fager took the further precaution of limiting the appearance on the new series of original *60 Minutes* correspondents to "classic" segments, updates of memorable stories from the original series. Since mid-2000, *60 Minutes II* has been the second-highest-rated newsmagazine behind *60 Minutes.* Hewitt, confident that the new series was "committed to the values" of *60 Minutes* as promised by CBS News President Andrew Heyward, permitted correspondents to contribute stories. Highlighting the tradition and strengths of *60 Minutes'* investigative reports, Bradley examined whether the massacre at Columbine High School could have been prevented, and Wallace revealed the practice of genetic discrimination.

In its first year, hoping to attract a younger audience, *60 Minutes II* offered profiles of Elton John, Madonna, Bonnie Raitt, Jody Foster, Pat Summit, and Oscar de la Hoya that transgressed timid celebrity gazing and storytelling. The series also featured in-depth reporting on such subjects as new research into the nature of the brain; a growing anarchist movement based in Seattle, Washington; a cover-up of a 1921 race riot in Tulsa, Oklahoma; and a variety of national and international conditions that fit the meticulous investigative format

established by the program's predecessor. *60 Minutes II* was not afraid to take risks in tracking down stories or to shy away from legal battles. Producers won a court challenge accusing them of infringing on patient confidentiality by airing footage from a microcamera attached to a hospital worker's eyeglasses, capturing patient mistreatment in one hospital administered be a corporation responsible for 91 hospitals. The series demonstrated that it could be an agent of change when a story on child labor in India resulted in U.S. Customs stopping cigarettes rolled by children from entering the country.

After the September 11, 2001, terrorist attacks on the United States, *60 Minutes II* secured a position as an invaluable and professional newsmagazine firmly anchored in the tradition and accomplishments of *60 Minutes. 60 Minutes* has built an extensive archive of film from stories on smallpox, the Middle East, international terrorism, Pakistan, the Taliban, Afghanistan, U.S. counterterrorism units, and biochemical warfare. The foresight and courage of *60 Minutes* to cover issues with minimal audience appeal and shunned by other newsmagazines was evident in the breadth and depth of its coverage of topics that gained fresh relevance in the United States' new war on terrorism. *60 Minutes II* employed the resources, film, and research reports of *60 Minutes* to live up to Don Hewitt's standard of broadcasting journalism.

RICHARD BARTONE

60 Minutes

Correspondents
Mike Wallace
Harry Reasoner (1968–70, 1978–91)
Morley Safer (1970–)
Dan Rather (1975–81)
Andrew Rooney (1978–)
Ed Bradley (1981–)
Diane Sawyer (1984–89)
Meredith Vieira (1989–91)
Steve Kroft (1989–)
Leslie Stahl (1991–)
Bob Simon (1997–)
Christiane Amanpour (1996–)
Carol Marin (2001–)

Producer
Don Hewitt

Programming History
CBS
September 1968–June 1971   Tuesday 10:00–11:00

January 1972–June 1972	Sunday 6:00–7:00
January 1973–June 1973	Sunday 6:00–7:00
June 1973–September 1973	Friday 8:00–9:00
January 1974–June 1974	Sunday 6:00–7:00
July 1974–September 1974	Sunday 9:30–10:30
September 1974–June 1975	Sunday 6:00–7:00
July 1975–September 1975	Sunday 9:30–10:00
December 1975–	Sunday 7:00–8:00

60 Minutes II

Correspondents
Dan Rather (1999–)
Bob Simon (1999–)
Charlie Rose (1999–)
Vicki Mabrey (1999–)
Scott Pelley (1999–)
Carol Marin (contributor, 1999–)
Jimmy Tingle (commentator, 1999–2000)
Charles Grodin (commentator, 2000–)

Producer
Jeffrey Fager (1999–)

Programming History

January 1999–June 1999	Wednesday 9:00–10:00
June 1999–July 2001	Tuesday 9:00–10:00
July 2001–January 2003	Wednesday 8:00–9:00
January 2003–	Wednesday 9:00–10:00

Executive Producer
Jeff Fager (1999–)

Senior Producers
Patti Hassler (1999–2000)
Michael R. Whitney (1999–2000)
Esther Kartiganer
Merri Lieberthal

Senior Broadcast Producer
Michael Whitney (2000)

Executive Editor
Patti Hassler (2000–)
Josh Howard (2003–)

Director
Arthur Bloom (1999–)

Reporters
Dan Rather (1999–)
Bob Simon (1999–)
Vicki Mabrey (1999–)
Charlie Rose (1999–)
Jimmy Tingle (commentator, 1999–2000)
Carol Marin (contributor, 1999–2002)
Gloria Borger (contributor, 1999–2002)
Scott Pelley (1999–)
Charles Grodin (commentator, 2000–03)
Lara Logan (contributor, 2002–)

Further Reading

Campbell, Richard, *"60 Minutes" and the News: A Mythology for Middle America,* Urbana: University of Illinois Press, 1991

Coffey, Frank, *"60 Minutes": 25 Years of Television's Finest Hour,* Los Angeles: General Publishing Group, 1993

Collins, Monica, "More than Ever, CBS' *60 Minutes* Proves to Be Timely, *Boston Herald* (October 23, 2001)

Fury, Kathleen, editor, *Dear 60 Minutes,* New York: Simon and Schuster, 1984

Gomery, Douglas, "The End of the Golden Age? While Their Ranks Continue to Swell, TV Newsmagazines' Ratings Are Sliding," *American Journalism Review* (March 1999)

Goodman, Walter, "A Televised Death: Prurient or Newsworthy, or Both," *New York Times* (November 25, 1998)

Grossman, Lawrence K., "CBS, *60 Minutes,* and the Unseen Interview," *Columbia Journalism Review* (January/February 1996)

Hewitt, Don, *Minute by Minute,* New York: Random House, 1985

Hewitt, Don, *Tell Me a Story: Fifty Years and 60 Minutes in Television,* New York: Public Affairs, 2001

Kirtley, Jane, "Skirmishing over Freedom of Speech," *American Journalism Review* (July/August 1999)

Madsen, Axel, *"60 Minutes": The Power and the Politics of America's Most Popular TV News Show,* New York: Dodd, Mead, 1984

"60 Minutes" Verbatim: Who Said What to Whom—The Complete Text of 114 Stories with Mike Wallace, Morley Safer, Dan Rather, and Andy Rooney, New York: Arno Press, 1980

Spragens, William C., *Electronic Magazines: Soft News Programs on Network Television,* Westport, Connecticut: Praeger, 1995

Wallace, Mike, and Gary Paul Gates, *Close Encounters,* New York: Morrow, 1984

$64,000 Question, The/The $64,000 Challenge

U.S. Quiz Shows

The premiere of *The $64,000 Question* as a summer replacement in 1955 marked the beginning of the big-money quiz shows. Following a U.S. Supreme Court ruling in 1954 that exempted "jackpot" quizzes from charges of illegal gambling, Louis G. Cowan, the creator and packager of the program; Revlon, its main sponsor; and the Columbia Broadcasting System (CBS) were able to bring this new type of quiz show on the air. Based on the popular 1940s radio quiz show *Take It or Leave It* with its famous $64 question, *The $64,000 Question* increased the prize money to an unprecedented, spectacular level. It also added public appeal with a security guard and a "trust officer" who monitored questions and prizes and its fairly elaborate set design, which included an "isolation booth" for the contestants. Intellectual "legitimacy" was further claimed through the employment of Professor Bergen Evans as "question supervisor." With its emphasis on high culture, academic knowledge, and its grave, ceremonious atmosphere, *The $64,000 Question* represented an attempt to gain more respectability for the relatively new and still despised television medium while at the same time appealing to a large audience.

Each contestant began his or her quest for fortune and fame by answering a question in an area of expertise for $64. Each subsequent correct answer doubled their prize money up to the $4,000 level. After this stage, contestants could advance only one level per week and were asked increasingly elaborate and difficult questions. They were allowed to quit the quiz at any level—and keep their winnings—but missing a question always eliminated the contestant. Nevertheless, contestants were guaranteed the $4,000 from the first round, and, if they missed a question after having reached the $8,000 level, they received an additional consolation prize—a new Cadillac. At this level, candidates were also moved from the studio floor to the "Revlon Isolation Booth," a shift designed to intensify the dramatic effects at the higher levels of the quiz.

Besides its use of such spectacular features, the appeal of *The $64,000 Question* was also strongly grounded in the audience's identification with returning contestants. Thus, many of the early competitors were transformed from "common people" into instant superstars. Policeman Redmond O'Hanlon, a Shakespeare expert, and shoemaker Gino Prato, an opera fan, are among the noted examples. The popularity of these and other contestants proved the viability of "the serialized contest," a concept that *The $64,000 Question* and many imitators (such as *Twenty-One* and *The Big Surprise*) followed.

Because of the immense success of *The $64,000 Question* (at one point in the 1955 season it had an 84.8 percent audience share), CBS and Cowan created a spin-off, *The $64,000 Challenge*. This program allowed those contestants from *The $64,000 Question* who had won at least $8,000 to continue their quiz show career. The format was changed into a more overt contest; two candidates competed against each other in a common area of expertise. As a minimum prize, contestants were guaranteed the amount at which they beat their opponents. Additionally, the $64,000 limit on winnings was removed, making the contests even longer and more spectacular.

The combination of these two shows allowed the most successful candidates to become virtual television regulars, as in the case of Teddy Nadler, who had accumulated $252,000 by the time *The $64,000 Challenge* was canceled. These programs held top rating spots until *Twenty-One* found a format and a contestant, Charles Van Doren, audiences found even more appealing.

The need for regular contestants to appear over long periods of time, one of the central factors in the popularity of the big-prize game shows, also proved to be a central factor in their downfall with the quiz show scandal of 1958. The sponsors of the programs implicitly expected and sometimes explicitly demanded that popular contestants be supplied with answers in advance, enabling them to defeat unpopular competitors and remain on the show for extended periods. Although no allegations against Entertainment Productions, Inc., and CBS were ever substantiated, Erik Barnouw (1970) points out that their production personnel claimed that Revlon had frequently tried to influence the outcome of the quizzes. Ultimately, both shows were canceled because of public indignation and waning ratings in the wake of the scandals.

One of the most significant results of the quiz show scandal and the involvement of sponsors in it was the shift in the power to program television. The scandal was used as an argument by the networks to eliminate completely sponsor-controlled programming in prime-time broadcasting and to take control of program production themselves.

OLAF HOERSCHELMANN

See also **Quiz and Game Shows**

The $64,000 Question

Emcee
Hal March

Assistant
Lynn Dollar

Authority
Bergen Evans

Programming History
CBS
June 1955–June 1958   Tuesday 10:00–10:30

September 1958–
  November 1958   Sunday 10:00–10:30

The $64,000 Challenge

Emcee
Sonny Fox (1956)
Ralph Story (1956–58)

Producers
Steve Carlin, Joe Cates

Programming History
CBS
April 1956–September 1958   Sunday 10:00–10:30

Further Reading

Barnouw, Erik, *A History of Broadcasting in the United States,* volume III, *The Image Empire, from 1953,* New York: Oxford University Press, 1970
Boddy, William, *Fifties Television: The Industry and Its Critics,* Urbana: University of Illinois Press, 1990
Schwartz, David, Steve Ryan, and Fred Wostbrock, *The Encyclopedia of Television Game Shows,* New York: Zoetrope, 1987; 3rd edition, New York: Facts on File, 1999

Skelton, Red (1913–1997)

U.S. Comedian

It was not until 1986, a full 15 years after his weekly television show had ended, that "one of America's clowns" received his overdue critical praise. Only then did the critics realize what the public had long known. Regardless of his passion for corny gags and slapstick comedy, Red Skelton was a gifted comedian. He was one of the few performers to succeed in four entertainment genres—vaudeville, radio, film, and television. To honor his lifetime achievements, Skelton received the Academy of Television Arts and Sciences Governor's Emmy Award in 1986 and the critical praise he deserved.

Skelton's youth was characterized by poverty and a fascination for vaudeville. It was the influence of vaudeville great Ed Wynn that led Skelton to perfect his own comedy routines. The basics of Skelton's vaudeville act consisted of pantomimes, pratfalls,

funny voices, crossed eyes, and numerous sight gags that would serve to identify him throughout his entertainment career. It was also during this period that Skelton began developing various comedy characters.

His radio show, which ran from 1941 to 1953, provided the opportunity to present his comedy to a mass audience. The limitations of the sound medium also made it necessary for him to develop further the characters he would later bring to television: Freddie the Freeloader; Clem Kadiddlehopper, the country bumpkin; Willy Lump Lump, the drunk; Cauliflower McPugg, the boxer; The Mean Widdle Kid; and San Fernando Red, the con man.

In conjunction with his radio show, Skelton also enjoyed film success, most notably in *Whistling in the Dark* (1941), *The Fuller Brush Man* (1948), *A Southern Yankee* (1948), and *The Yellow Cab Man* (1950).

Regardless of his vaudeville, radio, and film success, it would be television that would bring him his greatest fame and endear him to his largest audience.

The Red Skelton Show began in 1951 on the National Broadcasting Company (NBC) as a comedy-variety show. Skelton coproduced this initial show, which was a half-hour program on Sunday evenings. In its first year, the show finished fourth in the ratings and received the Emmy Award for Best Comedy Show. Unlike other radio comedians, Skelton's comedy act entailed more than his voice, and television provided the opportunity to display fully the showmanship talents he had begun to exhibit in vaudeville.

In 1953, the show moved to the Columbia Broadcasting System (CBS) on Tuesday nights, and in 1961 it received a second Emmy Award for Outstanding Writing Achievement in Comedy, expanding to an hour-long show the following year. In 1964, the show made the Nielsen Top 20, where it stayed until its end in 1970.

The show consisted of Skelton's opening monologue, performances by guest stars, and comedy sketches that included his various characters. Perhaps the most unique part of the show (and for all of television) was "The Silent Spot," a mime sketch that often featured Skelton's character Freddie the Freeloader. The only regulars on the show were Skelton and the David Rose Orchestra. *The Red Skelton Show* set the precedent for future comedy-variety shows, such as *The Carol Burnett Show.*

According to CBS, the show's 1970 cancellation was due to rising production costs and the network's desire to appeal to more upscale advertisers (the show finished seventh in its final season). The following year, Skelton returned to NBC with a half-hour comedy-variety show that included a cast of regulars. The show's premiere featured Vice President Spiro Agnew. This time, unfortunately, the uneven comedy failed to match Skelton's previous success. The show's cancellation marked the end of Skelton's television career, a run of 21 straight years that also included guest appearances on other television series and involvement with 13 television specials. The only television performer with a longer stay was Ed Sullivan (24 years as host of *The Ed Sullivan Show*).

Following his departure from television, Skelton maintained a low profile and performed at resorts, clubs, and casinos. In the early 1980s, a series of superb performances at Carnegie Hall received critical praise and briefly thrust him back into the public spotlight. The newfound interest in Skelton resulted in three comedy specials for Home Box Office (HBO).

Since his TV show was seldom rerun and is not syndicated, it is easy to forget Skelton's popularity. Based on longevity and audience size, *The Red Skelton Show* is the second-most popular show in TV history (*Gunsmoke* is first). As Groucho Marx once said, Red Skelton was "the most unacclaimed clown in show business." Marx noted that by using only a soft, battered hat as a prop, Skelton could entertain with a dozen characters. He died in 1997 at the age of 84.

ROBERT LEMIEUX

See also **The Red Skelton Show; Variety Programs**

Red Skelton. Born Richard Red Skelton in Vincennes, Indiana, July 18, 1913. Married: 1) Edna Marie Stilwell, 1930 (divorced, 1943); 2) Georgia Davis, 1945 (divorced, 1973); 3) Lothian Toland, 1976. Joined medicine show at age ten; later appeared in showboat stock, minstrel shows, vaudeville, burlesque, and circuses; began appearing on radio in 1936; starred in long-running *The Red Skelton Show* on television. Recipient: Emmy Awards, 1951, 1956, and 1960–61; ATAS Hall of Fame and Governor's Award, 1986. Died in Rancho Mirage, California, September 17, 1997.

Television Series
1951–53, 1953–70,
  1970–71   *The Red Skelton Show*

Made-for-Television Movie
1956   *The Big Slide*

Television Specials (selected)
1954   *The Red Skelton Revue*
1959   *The Red Skelton Chevy Special*
1960   *The Red Skelton Timex Special*
1966   *Clown Alley* (host, producer)
1982   *Red Skelton's Christmas Dinner*
1983   *Red Skelton's Funny Faces*
1984   *Red Skelton: A Royal Performance*

Films
Having Wonderful Time, 1938; *Seein' Red,* 1939; *Broadway Buckaroo,* 1939; *Flight Command,* 1940; *Lady Be Good,* 1941; *The People vs. Dr. Kildare,* 1941; *Dr. Kildare's Wedding Day,* 1941; *Whistling in the Dark,* 1941; *Whistling in Dixie,* 1942; *Ship Ahoy,* 1942; *Maisie Gets Her Man,* 1942; *Panama Hattie,* 1942; *DuBarry Was a Lady,* 1943; *Thousands Cheer,* 1943; *I Dood It,* 1943; *Whistling in Brooklyn,* 1943; *Bathing Beauty,* 1944; *Ziegfeld Follies,* 1944; *Radio Bugs* (voice only), 1944; *The Show-Off,* 1946; *Merton of the Movies,* 1947; *The*

Fuller Brush Man, 1948; *A Southern Yankee,* 1948; *Neptune's Daughter,* 1949; *The Yellow Cab Man,* 1950; *Three Little Words,* 1950; *The Fuller Brush Girl,* 1950; *Watch the Birdie,* 1951; *Duchess of Idaho,* 1950; *Excuse My Dust,* 1951; *Texas Carnival,* 1951; *Lovely to Look At,* 1952; *The Clown,* 1952; *Half a Hero,* 1953; *The Great Diamond Robbery,* 1953; *Susan Slept Here,* 1954; *Around the World in 80 Days,* 1956; *Public Pigeon No. 1,* 1957; *Ocean's Eleven,* 1960; *Those Magnificent Men in Their Flying Machines,* 1965.

Radio
The Red Skelton Show, 1941–53.

Publication

I Dood It, 1943

Further Reading

Adir, Karen, *The Great Clowns of American Television,* Jefferson, North Carolina: McFarland, 1988
Davidson, Bill, "I'm Nuts and I Know It," *Saturday Evening Post* (June 17, 1967)
Jennings, Dean, "Sad and Lonely Clown," *Saturday Evening Post* (June 2, 1962)
Marx, Arthur, *Red Skelton,* New York: Dutton, 1979
Rosten, Leo, "How to See RED—SKELTON—That Is," *Look* (October 23, 1951, and November 6, 1951)
Shearer, Lloyd, "Is He a Big Laugh!" *Collier's* (April 15, 1950)

Skippy

Australian Children's Program

Before the international sales success in the late 1980s and 1990s of Australian soap operas such as *Neighbours* and *Home and Away, Skippy* was the most successful series ever made in Australia. It had sales in more than 100 overseas markets and was syndicated on U.S. television. In addition, in a lucrative deal the series' central figure of Skippy, the bush kangaroo, was licensed to the U.S. breakfast food giant Kellogg's.

Skippy was produced by Fauna Productions, a partnership formed by film producer-director Lee Robinson and former film actor John McCallum, with a Sydney lawyer as the third partner. Robinson had had an extensive background in Australian documentary filmmaking and had created the position of Australian and Pacific film correspondent for the *High Adventure* series on U.S. television, hosted by newsman and explorer Lowell Thomas. Ever the internationalist, in the 1950s, Robinson had produced a series of feature films in Australia, in partnership with actor Chips Rafferty, that combined familiar Hollywood narrative structures. Drawing from such genres as the western, these films used exotic locations, flora, and fauna and were based in different parts of the Pacific.

McCallum, although born in Australia, had spent most of his professional life in Britain, where he had worked extensively on stage and in film. He returned to Australia to take a senior executive position with J.C. Williamson and Company, the largest theatrical group in Australia and New Zealand, where he became involved with the New Zealand comedy feature *They're a Weird Mob.* McCallum and Robinson, both of whom had been production managers on the film, briefly considered producing a spin-off television series. However, they followed the advice of the international distributor Global about what would sell well in the world market and finally decided on *Skippy.*

The genre that they settled on for *Skippy* was a family/children's series with a child and an animal at its center, in a familiar vein that stretched from *Lassie* to *Flipper.* The "difference" in the Australian series was the fact that it featured native flora and fauna. Skippy was a bush kangaroo (a universal symbol of Australia), and the series was set in a national park north of Sydney that featured bushland, waterways, and ocean shores. The series concerned ranger Matt Hammond (Ed Devereaux), his son Sonny (Garry Pankhurst), the latter's pet kangaroo, his brother (Ken James), and two other junior rangers played by Tony Bonner and Liza Goddard. All together, three different kangaroos played Skippy.

Airing between 1968 and 1970, *Skippy* resulted in 91 half-hour episodes together with one feature film, *Skippy and the Intruders.* The series was produced on film and in color, even though Australian television had not yet moved to a color transmission system, and was sold to the Packer-owned Nine Network, where it first aired in February 1968. With high production values, the program was costly to produce and an initial financial risk for the packaging company Fauna. However, Fauna soon achieved sufficient overseas sales to maintain their cash flow, and the series eventually achieved very high sales. In the meantime, Fauna had become bored producing *Skippy* and had embarked on a new series, *Barrier Reef*, which featured the reef off the northeastern coast of Australia, the largest coral formation in the world.

In the 1990s, *Skippy* has had to share international recognition with other Australian series, most especially *Neighbours*, but there is still strength in the former's format. In 1991, the Nine Network licensed the format from Fauna and produced a spin-off series, *The Adventures of Skippy*, which ran to 39 half-hour episodes and was again produced on film and in color. Although it was set in an animal sanctuary near the Gold Coast and featured a different group of children and adults, this second series did preserve both the theme song and the kangaroo character from the original.

ALBERT MORAN

Cast

Matt Hammond	Ed Devereaux
Sonny Hammond	Gary Pankhurst
Mark Hammond	Ken James
Clancy	Liza Goddard
Jerry King	Tony Bonner

Producers

John McCallum, Lee Robinson, Joy Cavill, Dennis Hill

Programming History

91 half-hour episodes
Nine Network

February 1968–November 1968	7:00–7:30
January 1969–November 1969	7:00–7:30
February 1970–May 1970	7:00–7:30

Slovakia. *See* Czech Republic

Smith, Howard K. (1914–2002)

U.S. Journalist

Howard K. Smith, an outspoken, often controversial television newsman, developed a career that spanned the decades from his sober analytic foreign news reporting at the Columbia Broadcasting System (CBS) as one of "Murrow's Boys" to years as co-anchor and commentator on *ABC Evening News*. Smith's career also saw his transformation from CBS's "resident radical" to his persona "Howard K. Agnew," a sobriquet granted by critics for his support of conservative Republican Vice President Spiro T. Agnew's bitter 1969 attack on TV news.

In 1940, Smith joined United Press as their correspondent in London and Copenhagen, and in 1941 he joined CBS news, where he replaced William L. Shirer as CBS's Berlin correspondent. The last American correspondent to leave Berlin after war was declared, Smith reached safety in Switzerland with a manuscript describing conditions in Germany, which became the basis for his best-selling book *Last Train from Berlin*.

During the war, Smith accompanied the Allied sweep through Belgium and the Netherlands and into Germany. He was on hand when the Germans surrendered to the Russians under Marshal Zhukov in 1945 and then covered the Nuremberg trials. In 1946, he succeeded Murrow as CBS's London correspondent and spent the next 11 years covering Europe and the Middle East.

Howard K. Smith.
Photo courtesy of Wisconsin Center for Film and Theater Research

In 1949, Smith published *The State of Europe,* advocating a planned economy and the welfare state for postwar Europe. Perhaps for this reason, and to some extent because of his radical past, he was named as a Communist supporter in *Red Channels,* a McCarthyite document purporting to uncover Communist conspiracy in the media industries. Smith hardly suffered from these accusations, however, since both Murrow and his overseas posting protected him. Indeed, in 1957, Smith returned to the United States and in 1960 was named chief of the CBS Washington Bureau, where he hosted programs such as *The Great Challenge, Face the Nation,* and the Emmy Award–winning *CBS Reports* documentary "The Population Explosion." He also served as the moderator of the first Kennedy–Nixon presidential debate.

As a southerner, Smith was more and more drawn to the battle over civil rights, and in 1961 he narrated a *CBS Reports* special, "Who Speaks for Birmingham?" His final commentary included a quote from Edmund Burke: "All that is necessary for the triumph of evil is for good men to do nothing." The quote was cut from the program. In a showdown with CBS Chairman William S. Paley, Smith resigned after Paley supported his executives over Smith and his alleged "editorializing."

Shortly thereafter, Smith signed with ABC News and began doing a weekly news show, *Howard K. Smith—News and Comment.* Smith's program made creative use of film, graphics, and animation and explored controversial topics such as illegitimacy, disar-

mament, physical fitness, the state of television, and the "goof-off Congress." The program won critical approval and generally high ratings. However, in 1962, Smith was again the center of controversy over his broadcast of a program titled "The Political Obituary of Richard Nixon."

This program followed Nixon's loss of the California governor's election in 1962. In his review of Nixon's career, Smith included an interview with Alger Hiss, whom Nixon, as a member of the House Un-American Activities Committee, had investigated for his alleged membership in and spying for the Communist Party and whose conviction for perjury in 1950 had helped launch Nixon's national political career. For balance, Smith also included Murray Chotiner, a Nixon supporter and campaign adviser. The result was an avalanche of telephone calls to the American Broadcasting Company (ABC) criticizing Smith for permitting a convicted perjurer and possible spy to appear on the program. Smith's sponsor quickly ended support of the show, and it was canceled. Some historians have contended that Smith's documentary enabled Nixon to regain some of the sympathy he had lost after the disastrous temper tantrum at his self-titled "last press conference."

Following the cancellation of his show, Smith covered news for ABC-TV's daily newscast and hosted the network's Sunday afternoon public affairs program *Issues and Answers.* In 1966, he became the host of the ABC documentary program *Scope.* Until then, *Scope* had been a general documentary show dealing with many topics. In 1966, the decision was made to devote all its programs to the Vietnam War. Between 1966 and its cancellation in 1968, the program dealt with seldom-touched issues of the war, such as the experience of African-American soldiers, North Vietnam, and the air war.

Unlike many other newsmen who became progressively disillusioned with the war, Smith became more and more hawkish as the war progressed. Among other things, he advocated bombing North Vietnam's dike system, bombing Haiphong, and invading Laos and Cambodia. Indeed, in one of his commentaries shortly after the Tet Offensive, Smith said, "There exists only one real alternative: that is to escalate, but this time on an overwhelming scale."

Smith's conservative drift on foreign affairs was also reflected in his domestic views. He was vociferous in his support of Vice President Agnew's 1969 "Des Moines speech," in which the vice president accused the TV networks' producers, newscasters, and commentators of a highly selective and often biased presentation of the news. Smith concurred and in salty language criticized network newsmen as, among other things, "conformist," for adhering to a liberal "party line," for "stupidity," and, at least in some cases, for lacking "the depth of a saucer."

In March 1969, Av Westin took over as head of ABC News and immediately installed Smith as the co-anchor of *ABC Evening News,* with Frank Reynolds. In 1971, Smith was teamed with the newly arrived former CBS newsman Harry Reasoner and given additional duties as commentator. Smith's support of the Vietnam War and Vice President Agnew's attacks on TV news stood him in good stead with President Nixon, who granted him the unique privilege of an hour-long solo interview in 1971 titled *White House Conversation: The President and Howard K. Smith.* Despite this, when evidence grew of Nixon's involvement in the Watergate scandal, Smith was the first major TV commentator to call for the president's resignation.

In 1975, Smith relinquished his co-anchor role on the *ABC Evening News* but stayed on as commentator. Following the 1977 arrival of Roone Arledge as head of ABC News, Smith found himself being used less and less. In 1979, he resigned from ABC, denouncing Arledge's evening newscast featuring Peter Jennings, Max Robinson, Frank Reynolds, and Barbara Walters as a "Punch and Judy Show." Following his retirement, Smith was inactive in television and radio. In 1996, he wrote an autobiography titled *Events Leading Up to My Death: The Life of a Twentieth-Century Reporter.* Smith was one of the last of TV newsmen who saw their role as not merely reporting the news but analyzing and commenting on it passionately. He died on February 15, 2002.

ALBERT AUSTER

See also **American Broadcasting Company; Arledge, Roone; Murrow, Edward R.; News, Network**

Howard K(ingsbury) Smith. Born in Ferriday, Louisiana, May 12, 1914. Educated at Tulane University, New Orleans, Louisiana, 1936; Heidelberg University, 1936; Rhodes Scholar, Merton College, Oxford, 1939. Married: Benedicte Traberg Smith, 1942; one daughter and one son. Worked as reporter for the *New Orleans Item-Tribune,* 1936–37; worked for United Press, Copenhagen, 1939, and Berlin, 1940; correspondent, CBS News radio, Berlin, 1941; European correspondent, CBS News, 1941–46; chief European correspondent, CBS News, 1946–57; correspondent, Washington, D.C., 1957; chief correspondent and general manager, CBS News, Washington, D.C., 1961; reporter and anchor, ABC television and radio networks, 1961–75; ABC news commentator, from 1975; host, *ABC News Closeup,* from 1979. Recipient: Peabody Award, 1960; Emmy Award, 1961; Paul White Memorial Award, 1961; duPont Commentator Award, 1962; Overseas Press Club Award, 1967; special congressional honoree for contribution to journalism; numerous other awards. Died in Bethesda, Maryland, February 15, 2002.

Television Series

1959	*Behind the News with Howard K. Smith*
1960–81	*Issues and Answers*
1960–63	*Face the Nation* (moderator)
1960–62	*Eyewitness to History* (narrator)
1961–62	*CBS Reports* (narrator)
1962–63	*Howard K. Smith—News and Comment*
1966–68	*ABC Scope*
1969–75	*ABC Evening News* (co-anchor)
1979	*ABC News Closeup*

Film

The Best Man (cameo), 1964.

Publications

Last Train from Berlin, 1942
The State of Europe, 1949
Washington, D.C.: The Story of Our Nation's Capital, 1967
Events Leading Up to My Death: The Life of a Twentieth-Century Reporter, 1996

Further Reading

Bliss, Edward, *Now the News: The Story of Broadcast Journalism,* New York: Columbia University Press, 1991
Fensch, Thomas, editor, *Television News Anchors: An Anthology of the Major Figures and Issues in United States Network Reporting,* Jefferson, North Carolina: McFarland, 1993
Gunther, Marc, *The House That Roone Built: The Inside Story of ABC News,* Boston, Massachusetts: Little, Brown, 1994

Smothers Brothers Comedy Hour, The

U.S. Comedy-Variety Program

The Smothers Brothers Comedy Hour, starring the folk-singing comedy duo Tom and Dick Smothers, premiered on the Columbia Broadcasting System (CBS) in February 1967. A variety show scheduled opposite the top-rated National Broadcasting Company (NBC) program *Bonanza,* the *Comedy Hour* attracted a younger, hipper, and more politically engaged audience than most other video offerings of the 1960s. The show's content featured irreverent digs at many dominant institutions, such as organized religion and the presidency. It also included sketches celebrating the hippie drug culture and material opposing the war in Vietnam. These elements made *The Smothers Brothers Comedy Hour* one of the most controversial television shows in the medium's history. Questions of taste and the Smothers's oppositional politics led to very public battles over censorship. As CBS attempted to dictate what was appropriate prime-time entertainment fare, the Smothers tried to push the boundaries of acceptable speech on the medium. The recurring skirmishes between the brothers and the network culminated on April 4, 1969, one week before the end of the season, when CBS summarily threw the show off the air. Network president Robert D. Wood charged that the Smotherses had not submitted a review tape of the upcoming show to the network in a timely manner. The Smotherses accused CBS of infringing on their First Amendment rights. It would be 20 years before the Smothers Brothers again appeared on CBS.

In their earliest days, however, the network and the brothers got along quite well. The Smotherses began their association with CBS in a failed situation comedy called *The Smothers Brothers Show,* which ran for one season in 1965–66. The show featured straight man Dick as a publishing executive and slow-witted, bumbling Tom as his deceased brother who had come back as an angel-in-training. The sitcom format did not prove to be appropriate for Tom and Dick's stand-up brand of comedy. CBS, feeling that the brothers still had potential, decided to give them another try in a different program format.

Considering how contentious *The Smothers Brothers Comedy Hour* became, it is worth noting that, in form and style, the show was quite traditional, avoiding the kinds of experiments associated with variety show rival, *Rowan and Martin's Laugh-In.* The brothers typically opened the show with a few minutes of stand-up song and banter. The show's final segment usually involved a big production number, often a costumed spoof, featuring dancing, singing, and comedy. Guest stars ran the gamut from countercultural icons such as the Jefferson Airplane and the Doors to older-generation, "establishment" favorites such as Kate Smith and Jimmy Durante. Nelson Riddle and his orchestra supplied musical accompaniment, and the show had its own resident dancers and singers who would have been as comfortable on *The Lawrence Welk Show* as on the Smothers's show.

The Smothers Brothers, Tom Smothers, Dick Smothers; c. 1965 around the time of their sitcom.
Courtesy of the Everett Collection

The show was noteworthy for some of the new, young talent it brought to the medium. Its corral of writers, many of whom were also performers, provided much of the energy and managed to offset some of the creakiness of the format and the older guest stars. Mason Williams, heading the writing staff, achieved fame not so much for his politically engaged writing but for his instant guitar classic "Classical Gas." Bob Einstein wrote for the show and also played the deadpan and very unamused cop, Officer Judy. He went on to greater fame as Super Dave. Finally, the then-unknown Steve Martin cut his comedic teeth as a staff writer for the show.

What also raised *The Smothers Brothers Comedy Hour* above the usual fare of comedy variety was the way the Smotherses and their writers dealt with some of their material. Dan Rowan of *Laugh-In* noted that while his show used politics as a platform for comedy, the Smotherses used comedy as a platform for politics. A recurring political sketch during the 1968 presidential year tracked regular cast member, the lugubrious Pat Paulsen, and his run for the nation's top office. Campaigners for Democratic contender Hubert Humphrey apparently worried that write-in votes for Paulsen would take needed votes away from their candidate.

Another *Comedy Hour* regular engaged in a different kind of subversive humor. Comedian Leigh French created the recurring hippie character Goldie O'Keefe, whose parody of afternoon advice shows for housewives, "Share a Little Tea with Goldie," was actually one long celebration of mind-altering drugs. "Tea" was a countercultural code word for marijuana, but the CBS censors seemed to be unaware of the connection. Goldie would open her sketches with salutations such as "Hi(gh)—and glad of it!"

While Goldie's comedy was occasionally censored for its prodrug messages, it never came in for the suppression focused on other material. One of the most famous instances was the censorship of folk singer Pete Seeger. Seeger had been invited to appear on the Smothers's second season premiere to sing his antiwar song "Waist Deep in the Big Muddy." The song—about a gung-ho military officer during World War II who attempts to force his men to ford a raging river only to be drowned in the muddy currents—was a thinly veiled metaphor for President Lyndon Johnson and his Vietnam policies. The censoring of Seeger created a public outcry, causing the network to relent and allow Seeger to reappear on the *Comedy Hour* later in the season to perform the song.

Other guests who wanted to perform material with an antiwar message also found themselves censored. Harry Belafonte was scheduled to do a calypso song called "Don't Stop the Carnival" with images from the riotous 1968 Chicago Democratic Convention chromakeyed behind him. Joan Baez wanted to dedicate a song to her draft-resisting husband, who was about to go to prison for his stance. In both cases, the network considered this material "political" and thus inappropriate for an "entertainment" format. Benjamin Spock, noted baby doctor and antiwar activist, was prevented from appearing as a guest of the show because, according to the network, he was a "convicted felon."

Other material that offended the network's notions of good taste also suffered the blue pencil. One regular guest performer, comedian David Steinberg, found his satirical sermonettes censored for being "sacrilegious." Even skits lampooning censorship, such as one in which Tom and guest Elaine May played motion picture censors trying to find a more palatable substitution for unacceptable dialogue, ended up being censored.

The significance of all this censorship and battles between the Smotherses and CBS is what Bert Spector has called a "clash of cultures." The political and taste values of two generations were colliding with each other over *The Smothers Brothers Comedy Hour*. The show, appearing at a pivotal moment of social and cultural change in the late 1960s, ended up embodying some of the turmoil and pitched conflict of the era. The Smotherses wanted to provide a space on prime-time television for the perspectives of a disaffected and rebellious youth movement deeply at odds with the dominant social order. CBS, with a viewership skewed to an older, more rural, more conservative demographic, could find the Smothers's embrace of antiestablishment politics and lifestyles only threatening.

In the aftermath of the show's cancellation, the Smotherses received a great deal of support in the popular press, including an editorial in the *New York Times* and a cover story in the slick magazine *Look*. Tom Smothers attempted to organize backing for a free-speech fight against the network among congressional and Federal Communications Commission members in Washington, D.C. While they were unsuccessful in forcing CBS to reinstate the show, the Smotherses did eventually win a suit against the network for breach of contract.

In the years following their banishment from CBS, the Smotherses attempted to re-create their variety show on the other two networks. In 1970, they did a summer show on the American Broadcasting Company (ABC) but were not picked up for the fall season. In 1975, they turned up on the National Broadcasting Company (NBC) with another variety show that disappeared at midseason. Then, finally, 20 years after being shown the door at CBS, the brothers were welcomed back for an anniversary special in February 1988. The success of the special, which reintroduced stalwarts Goldie O'Keefe (now a yuppie) and Pat Paulsen, led to another short-lived and uncontroversial run of *The Smothers Brothers Comedy Hour* on CBS. Most recently, in 1992, the Smotherses reedited episodes of the original *Comedy Hour* and ran them on the E! cable channel, providing introductions and interviews with the show's guests and writers to explain the show's controversies.

ANIKO BODROGHKOZY

See also **Columbia Broadcasting Company**

Regular Performers

Tom Smothers
Dick Smothers
Pat Paulsen
Leigh French
Bob Einstein
Mason Williams (1967–69)
Jennifer Warnes (1967–69)
John Hartford (1968–69)
Sally Struthers (1970)
Spencer Quinn (1970)
Betty Aberlin (1975)
Don Novello (1975)
Steve Martin (1975)
Nino Senporty (1975)

Dancers

The Louis Da Pron Dancers (1967–68)
The Ron Poindexter Dancers (1968–69)

Music

The Anita Kerr Singers (1967)
Nelson Riddle and His Orchestra (1967–69)
The Denny Vaughn Orchestra (1970)

Producers (1967–69)

Saul Ilson, Ernest Chambers, Chris Bearde, Allen Blye

Programming History

CBS
February 1967–June 1969   Sunday 9:00–10:00
ABC
July 1970–September 1970   Wednesday 10:00–11:00
NBC
January 1975–May 1975   Monday 8:00–9:00

Further Reading

Bodroghkozy, Aniko, "The Smothers Brothers Comedy Hour and the 1960s Youth Rebellion," in *The Revolution Wasn't Televised: Sixties Television and Social Conflict,* edited by Lynn Spigel and Michael Curtin, New York: Routledge, 1997

Carr, Steven Alan, "On the Edge of Tastelessness: CBS, the Smothers Brothers, and the Struggle for Control," *Cinema Journal* (Summer 1992)

Hendra, Tony, *Going Too Far,* New York: Doubleday, 1987

Kloman, William, "The Transmogrification of the Smothers Brothers," *Esquire* (October 1969)

Metz, Robert, *CBS: Reflections in a Bloodshot Eye,* Chicago: Playboy Press, 1975

Spector, Bert, "A Clash of Cultures: The Smothers Brothers vs. CBS Television," in *American History, American Television,* edited by John E. O'Connor, New York: Frederick Ungar, 1983

Soap

U.S. Serial Comedy

Soap was conceived by Susan Harris as a satire of the daytime soap operas. The show combined the serialized narrative of that genre with aspects of another U.S. television staple, the situation comedy, and was programmed in weekly, half-hour episodes. Harris, Paul Witt, and Tony Thomas had formed the Witt/Thomas/Harris company in 1976, and *Soap* was their first successful pitch to a network. They received a good response from Marcy Carsey and Tom Werner at the American Broadcasting Company (ABC), and Fred Silverman placed an order for the series. Casting began in November 1976, at which point director Jay Sandrich became involved. The producers and director created an ensemble of actors, several of whom had had considerable success on Broadway. They produced a one-hour pilot by combining two half-hour scripts and developed a "bible" for the show that outlined the continuing comical saga of two families, the Tates and the Campbells, through several potential years of their stories.

In the spring of 1977, *Newsweek* reviewed the new TV season and characterized *Soap* as a sex farce that would include, among other things, the seduction of a Catholic priest in a confessional. The writer of the piece had never seen the pilot, and his story was completely in error. However, that did not deter a massive protest by Roman Catholic and southern Baptist representatives condemning the show. Later, the National Council of Churches entered the campaign against *Soap*. Refusing to listen to reason, the religious lobby sought to generate a boycott of companies that sponsored *Soap*. In the summer, when the producers quite properly denied requests by church groups to have the pilot sent to them for viewing, the religious groups insisted they were denied opportunity to see an episode. That was simply not true. *Soap* was in production in late July in Hollywood, and each week any person walking through the lobby of the Sheraton-Universal Hotel could have secured tickets for the taping. The tapings were always open to the public, and any priest or preacher could have easily gone to the studio stage for that purpose.

This combination of irresponsible journalism and misguided moral outrage by persons of the cloth resulted in a dearth of sponsors. The campaign, led by ecclesiastical executives, sought to define and enforce a national morality by the use of prior censorship. It almost worked. Costs for advertising spots in the time slot for *Soap* were heavily discounted in order to achieve full sponsorship for the premiere on September 13, 1977. Only the commitment to the series by Silverman prevented its demise. Some ABC affiliates were picketed, and a few decided not to air the show. Other stations moved it from 9:30 P.M. to a late-night time slot. A United Press International story for September 14 reported a survey of persons who had watched the first episode of *Soap,* carried out by University of Richmond (Virginia) professors and their students. They discovered that 74 percent of viewers found *Soap* inoffensive, 26 percent were offended, and half of those offended said they were planning to watch it the next week. The day after the premiere, Sandrich, who had directed most of the *Mary Tyler Moore Show* episodes, stated, "If people will stay with us, they will find the show will grow." Still, producer Witt believes the show never fully recovered from the witch-hunting mentality that claimed banner headlines across the United States.

Despite these difficulties, all three of the producers recall the "joy of doing it." It was their first hit and arguably one of the most creative efforts by network television before or after. The scripts and acting were calculated to make audiences laugh—not snicker—at themselves. Indeed, in its own peculiar way, *Soap* addressed family values. In one of the more dramatic moments in the series, for example, Jessica Tate, with her entire family surrounding her, confronted the threat of evil, personified by an unseen demon, and commanded the menacing presence to be gone. She invoked the family as a solid unit of love and informed the demon, "You have come to the wrong house!"

Perhaps *Soap* was not quite the pace-setting show one might have hoped for since nothing quite like it has been seen since. In content, it had some characteristics of another pioneer effort, Norman Lear's *Mary Hartman, Mary Hartman.* However, the differences between the two were greater than the similarities, and each set a tone for what might be done with television, given freedom, imagination, and talent.

Soap was a ratings success on ABC and a hit in England and Japan. Despite the concerted attacks, it was the 13th most popular network program for the 1977–78 season. *Eight Is Enough* was rated 12th. *Soap* ended, however, under suspicion that resistance from ad agencies may have caused ABC to cancel at that point. The series may still be seen in syndication in various communities, and it is available on home video.

ROBERT S. ALLEY

See also **Harris, Susan; Sexual Orientation and Television; Silverman, Fred; Thomas, Tony; Witt, Paul Junger**

Cast

Chester Tate	Robert Mandan
Jessica Tate	Katherine Helmond
Corrine Tate (1977–80)	Diana Canova
Eunice Tate	Jennifer Salt
Billy Tate	Jimmy Baio
Benson (1977–79)	Robert Guillaume
The Major	Arthur Peterson
Mary Dallas Campbell	Cathryn Damon
Burt Campbell	Richard Mulligan
Jodie Dallas	Billy Crystal
Danny Dallas	Ted Wass
The Godfather (1977–78)	Richard Libertini
Claire (1977–78)	Kathryn Reynolds
Peter Campbell (1977)	Robert Urich
Chuck/Bob Campbell	Jay Johnson
Dennis Phillips (1978)	Bob Seagren
Father Timothy Flotsky (1978–79)	Sal Viscuso
Carol David (1978–81)	Rebecca Balding

Elaine Lefkowitz (1978–79)	Dinah Manoff	
Dutch (1978–81)	Donnelly Rhodes	
Sally (1978–79)	Caroline	
	McWilliams	
Detective Donahue (1978–80)	John Byner	
Alice (1979)	Randee Heller	
Mrs. David (1979–81)	Peggy Hope	
Millie (1979)	Candace Azzara	
Leslie Walker (1979–81)	Marla Pennington	
Polly Dawson (1979–81)	Lynne Moody	
Saunders (1980–81)	Roscoe Lee Brown	
Dr. Alan Posner (1980–81)	Allan Miller	
Attorney E. Ronald Mallu		
(1978–81)	Eugene Roche	
Carlos "El Puerco" Valdez		
(1980–81)	Gregory Sierra	
Maggie Chandler (1980–81)	Barbara Rhoades	
Gwen (1980–81)	Jesse Welles	

Producers

Paul Junger Witt, Tony Thomas, Susan Harris, J.D. Lobue, Dick Clair, Jenna McMahon

Programming History

83 30-minute episodes; 10 60-minute episodes
ABC

September 1977–March 1978	Tuesday 9:30–10:00
September 1978–March 1979	Thursday 9:30–10:00
September 1979–March 1980	Thursday 9:30–10:00
October 1980–January 1981	Wednesday 9:30–10:00
March 1981–April 1981	Monday 10:00–11:00

Soap Opera

The term "soap opera" was coined by the American press in the 1930s to denote the extraordinarily popular genre of serialized domestic radio dramas, which by 1940 represented some 90 percent of all commercially sponsored daytime broadcast hours. The "soap" in soap opera alluded to their sponsorship by manufacturers of household cleaning products, while "opera" suggested an ironic incongruity between the domestic narrative concerns of the daytime serial and the most elevated of dramatic forms. In the United States, the term continues to be applied primarily to the approximately 50 hours each week of daytime serial television drama broadcast by the American Broadcasting Company (ABC), the National Broadcasting Company, (NBC), and the Columbia Broadcasting System (CBS), but the meanings of the term, both in the United States and elsewhere, exceed this generic designation.

The defining quality of the soap opera form is its seriality. A serial narrative is a story told through a series of individual, narratively linked installments. Unlike episodic television programs, in which there is no narrative linkage between episodes and each episode tells a more or less self-contained story, the viewer's understanding of and pleasure in any given serial installment is predicated, to some degree, on his or her knowledge of what has happened in previous episodes. Further-

more, each serial episode always leaves narrative loose ends for the next episode to take up. The viewer's relationship with serial characters is also different from those in episodic television. In the latter, characters cannot undergo changes that transcend any given episode, and they seldom reference events from previous episodes. Serial characters do change across episodes (they age and even die), and they possess both histories and memories. Serial television is not merely narratively segmented; rather, its episodes are designed to be parceled out in regular installments so that both the telling of the serial story and its reception by viewers is institutionally regulated. (This generalization obviously does not anticipate the use of the viedotape recorder to "time shift" viewing).

Soap operas are of two basic narrative types: "open" soap operas, in which there is no end point toward which the action of the narrative moves, and "closed" soap operas, in which, no matter how attenuated the process, the narrative does eventually close. Examples of the open soap opera would include all U.S. daytime serials (*General Hospital, All My Children, The Guiding Light,* and so on); the wave of prime-time U.S. soaps in the 1980s (*Dallas, Dynasty,* and *Falcon Crest*); such British serials as *Coronation Street, EastEnders,* and *Brookside;* and most Australian serials (*Neighbours, Home and Away,* and *A Country Prac-*

Guiding Light.
Photo courtesy of Procter & Gamble

tice). The closed soap opera is more common in Latin America, where it dominates prime-time programming from Mexico to Chile. These *telenovelas* are broadcast nightly and may stretch over three or four months and hundreds of episodes. They are, however, designed eventually to end, and it is the anticipation of closure in both the design and the reception of the closed soap opera that makes it fundamentally different from the open form.

In the United States, at least, the term "soap opera" has never been value neutral. As noted previously, the term itself signals an aesthetic and cultural incongruity: the events of everyday life elevated to the subject matter of an operatic form. To call a film, novel, or play a "soap opera" is to label it as culturally and aesthetic inconsequential and unworthy. When in the early 1990s the fabric of domestic life among the British royal family began to unravel, the press around the world began to refer to the situation as a "royal soap opera," which immediately framed it as tawdry, sensational, and undignified.

Particularly in the United States, the connotation of "soap opera" as a degraded cultural and aesthetic form is inextricably bound to the gendered nature of its appeals and of its target audience. The soap opera always has been a "woman's" genre and, it has frequently been assumed (mainly by those who have never watched soap operas), of interest primarily or exclusively to uncultured working-class women with simple tastes and limited capacities. Thus, the soap opera has been the most easily parodied of all broadcasting genres and its presumed audience most easily stereotyped as the working-class "housewife" who allows the dishes to pile up and the children to run amok because of her "addiction" to soap operas. Despite the fact that the soap opera is demonstrably one of the most narratively complex genres of television drama whose enjoyment requires considerable knowledge by its viewers and despite the fact that its appeals for half a century have cut across social and demographic categories, the term continues to carry this sexist and classist baggage.

What most Americans have known as soap opera for more than half a century began as one of the hundreds of new programming forms tried out by commercial radio broadcasters in the late 1920s and early

General Hospital.
Photo courtesy of Procter & Gamble

1930s as both local stations and the newly formed networks attempted to marry the needs of advertisers with the listening interests of consumers. Specifically, broadcasters hoped to interest manufacturers of household cleaners, food products, and toiletries in the possibility of using daytime radio to reach their prime consumer market: women between the ages of 18 and 49.

In 1930, the manager of Chicago radio station WGN approached first a detergent company and then a margarine manufacturer with a proposal for a new type of program: a daily, 15-minute serialized drama set in the home of an Irish-American widow and her young unmarried daughter. Irna Phillips, who had recently left her job as a speech teacher to try her hand at radio, was assigned to write *Painted Dreams,* as the show was called, and play two of its three regular parts. The plots Phillips wrote revolved around morning conversations "Mother" Moynihan had with her daughter and their female boarder before the two young women went to their jobs at a hotel.

The antecedents of *Painted Dreams* and the dozens of other soap operas launched in the early 1930s are varied. The soap opera continued the tradition of women's domestic fiction of the 19th century, which had also been sustained in magazine stories of the 1920s and 1930s. It also drew on the conventions of the "woman's film" of the 1930s. The frequent homilies and admonitions offered by "Mother" Moynihan and her matriarchal counterparts on other early soap operas echoed those presented on the many advice programs commercial broadcasters presented in the early 1930s in response to the unprecedented social and economic dislocation experienced by American families as a result of the Great Depression. The serial narrative

format of the early soap opera was almost certainly inspired by the prime-time success of *Amos 'n' Andy,* the comic radio serial about "black" life on the South Side of Chicago (the show was written and performed by two white men), which by 1930 was the most popular radio show to that time.

In the absence of systematic audience measurement, it took several years for broadcasters and advertisers to realize the potential of the new soap opera genre. By 1937, however, the soap opera dominated the daytime commercial radio schedule and had become a crucial network programming strategy for attracting such large corporate sponsors as Procter and Gamble, Pillsbury, American Home Products, and General Foods. Most network soap operas were produced by advertising agencies, and some were owned by the sponsoring client.

Irna Phillips created and wrote some of the most successful radio soap operas in the 1930s and 1940s, including *Today's Children* (1932), *The Guiding Light* (1937), and *Woman in White* (1938). Her chief competition came from the husband–wife team of Frank and Anne Hummert, who were responsible for nearly half the soap operas introduced between 1932 and 1937, including *Ma Perkins* (1933) and *The Romance of Helen Trent* (1933).

On the eve of World War II, listeners could choose from among 64 daytime serials broadcast each week. During the war, so important had soap operas become in maintaining product recognition among consumers that Procter and Gamble continued to advertise Dreft detergent on its soap operas—despite the fact that the sale of it and other synthetic laundry detergents had been suspended for the duration. Soap operas continued to dominate daytime ratings and schedules in the immediate postwar period. In 1948, the ten highest-rated daytime programs were all soap operas, and of the top 30 daytime shows, all but five were soaps. The most popular nonserial daytime program, Arthur Godfrey, could manage only 12th place.

As television began to supplant radio as a national advertising medium in the late 1940s, the same companies that owned or sponsored radio soap operas looked to the new medium as a means of introducing new products and exploiting pent-up consumer demand. Procter and Gamble, which established its own radio soap opera production subsidiary in 1940, produced the first network television soap opera in 1950. *The First Hundred Years* ran for only two and demonstrated some of the problems of transplanting the radio genre to television. Everything that was left to the listener's imagination in the radio soap had to be given visual form on television. Production costs were two to three times that of a radio serial. Actors had to act and not merely read their lines. The complexity and uncertainty of producing 15 minutes of live television drama each weekday was vastly greater than was the case on radio. Furthermore, it was unclear in 1950 if the primary target audience for soap operas—women working in the home—could integrate the viewing of soaps into their daily routines. One could listen to a radio soap while doing other things, even in another room; television soaps required some degree of visual attention.

By the 1951–52 television season, broadcasters had demonstrated television's ability to attract daytime audiences, principally through the variety-talk format. CBS led the way in adapting the radio serial to television, introducing four daytime serials. The success of three of them—*Search for Tomorrow, Love of Life* (both produced by Roy Winsor), and *The Guiding Light*—established the soap opera as a regular part of network television daytime programming and CBS as the early leader in the genre. *The Guiding Light* was the first radio soap opera to make the transition to television and one of only two to do so successfully (The other was *The Brighter Day,* which ran for eight years). Between its television debut in 1952 and 1956, *The Guiding Light* was broadcast on both radio and television.

By the early 1960s, the radio soap opera—along with most aspects of network radio more generally—was a thing of the past, and "soap opera" in the United States now meant "television soap opera." The last network radio soap operas went off the air in November 1960. Still, television soap operas continued many of the conventions of their radio predecessors: live, week-daily episodes of 15 minutes; an unseen voice-over announcer to introduce and close each episode; organ music to provide a theme and punctuate the most dramatic moments; and each episode ending on an unresolved narrative moment with a "cliff-hanger" ending on Friday to draw the audience back on Monday.

The 30-minute soap opera was not introduced until 1956 with the debut of Irna Phillips's new soap for Procter and Gamble and CBS, *As the World Turns.* With an equivalent running time of two feature films each week, *As the World Turns* expanded the community of characters, slowed the narrative pace, emphasized the exploration of character, utilized multiple cameras to better capture facial expressions and reactions, and built its appeal less on individual action than on exploring the network of relationships among members of two extended families: the Lowells and the Hugheses. Although it took some months to catch on with audiences, *As the World Turns* demonstrated that viewers would watch a week-daily half-hour soap. Its ratings success, plus the enormous cost savings of

As the World Turns.
Photo courtesy of Procter & Gamble

producing one half-hour program rather than two 15-minute ones, persuaded producers that the 30-minute soap opera was the format of the future. The 15-minute soap was phased out, and all new soap operas introduced after 1956 were at least 30 minutes in length.

CBS's hegemony in soap operas was not challenged until 1963. None of the several half-hour soaps that NBC introduced in the wake of *As the World Turns'* popularity made the slightest dent in CBS's ratings. However, in April 1963, both NBC and ABC launched soaps with medical settings and themes: *The Doctors* and *General Hospital,* respectively. These were not the first medical television soaps, but they were the first to sustain audience interest over time and the first soaps produced by either network to achieve ratings even approaching those of the CBS serials. Their popularity also spawned the subgenre of the medical soap, in which the hospital replaces the home as the locus of action, plotlines center on the medical and emotional challenges patients present doctors and nurses, and the biological family is replaced or paralleled by the professional family as the structuring basis for the show's community of characters.

The therapeutic orientation of medical soaps also provided an excellent rationale for introducing a host of contemporary, sometimes controversial social issues that Irna Phillips and a few other writers believed soap audiences in the mid-1960s were prepared to accept as a part of the soap opera's moral universe. *Days of Our Lives* (co-created for NBC in 1965 by Irna Phillips and Ted Corday, the first director of *As the World Turns*) presented Dr. Tom Horton (played by film actor Macdonald Carey) and his colleagues at University Hospital with a host of medical, emotional, sexual, and psychiatric problems in the show's first years, including incest, impotence, amnesia, illegitimacy, and murder as a result of temporary insanity. This strategy made *Days of Our Lives* a breakthrough hit for NBC, and it anchored its daytime lineup through the late 1960s.

Medical soaps are particularly well suited to meet the unique narrative demands of the "never-ending" stories American soap operas tell. Their hospital settings provide opportunities for the intersection of professional and personal dramas. They also allow for the limitless introduction of new characters as hospital patients and personnel. The constant admission of new patients to the medical soap's hospitals facilitates the admission to the soap community of a succession of medical, personal, and social issues that can be attached to those patients. If audience response warrants, the patient can be "cured" and admitted to the central cohort of community members. If not, or if the social issue the patient represents proves to be too controversial, he or she can die or be discharged—both from the hospital and from the narrative. Such has been the appeal (to audiences and writers alike) of the medical soap that many nonmedical soaps have included doctors and nurses among their central characters and nurses' stations among their standing sets. Among them have been *As the World Turns, The Guiding Light, Search for Tomorrow,* and *Ryan's Hope.*

The latter half of the 1960s was a key period in the history of U.S. daytime soap operas. By 1965, both the popularity and the profitability of the television soap opera had been amply demonstrated. Soaps proved unrivaled in attracting female viewers aged between 18 and 49—the demographic group responsible for making most of the purchasing decisions for nondurable goods in the United States. Production costs were a fraction of those for prime-time drama, and once a new soap "found" its audience, broadcasters and advertisers knew that those viewers would be among television's most loyal. For the first time, CBS faced competition for the available daytime audience. With the success of *Another World* (another Irna Phillips vehicle launched in 1964), *Days of Our Lives,* and *The Doctors,* by 1966 NBC had a creditable lineup across the key afternoon time slots.

This competition sparked a period of unprecedented experimentation with the genre, as all three networks assumed that audiences would seek out a soap opera "with a difference." As the network with the most to gain (and the least to lose) by program innovation, ABC's new soaps represented the most radical departures from the genre's 35-year-old formula. Believing

that daytime audiences would also watch soaps during prime time, in September 1964 ABC introduced *Peyton Place,* a twice-weekly half-hour prime-time serial based on the best-selling 1957 novel by Grace Metalious and its successful film adaptation. Shot on film and starring film actress Dorothy Malone, *Peyton Place* was one of ABC's biggest prime-time hits of the 1964–65 television season and made stars of newcomers Mia Farrow and Ryan O'Neal. The show's ratings dropped after its first two seasons, however, and in terms of daytime soap longevity, its run was relatively brief: five years.

In 1966, ABC launched the most unusual daytime soap ever presented on American television. *Dark Shadows* was an over-the-top gothic serial, replete with a spooky mansion setting, young governess (lifted directly from Henry James's *The Turn of the Screw*), and a 200-year-old vampire. Broadcast in most markets in the late afternoon in order to catch high school students as well as adult women, *Dark Shadows* became something of a cult hit in its first season, and it did succeed in attracting to the soap opera form an audience of teenage viewers (male and female) and college students who were not addressed by more mainstream soaps. The show was too camp for most of those mainstream soap viewers, however, and it was canceled after five years.

ABC's most durable innovations in the soap opera genre during this period, however, took the form of two new mainstream soap operas, both created by Irna Phillips's protégé, Agnes Nixon. Nixon, who had apprenticed to Phillips for more than a decade as dialogue writer for most of her soaps and head writer of *The Guiding Light,* sold ABC on the idea of new soap that would foreground rather than suppress class and ethnic difference. *One Life to Live,* which debuted in 1968, centered initially on the family of wealthy WASP (white Anglo-Saxon Protestant) newspaper owner Victor Lord but established the Lords in relation to three working-class and ethnically "marked" families: the Irish-American Rileys, the Polish-American Woleks, and, after a year or two, the Jewish-American Siegels. Ethnic and class difference was played out primarily in terms of romantic entanglements.

Where most soap operas still avoided controversial social issues, Nixon exploited some of the social tensions then swirling through American society in the late 1960s. In 1969, *One Life to Live* introduced a black character who denied her racial identity (only to proudly proclaim it some months and dozens of episodes later). The following year when a teenage character is discovered to be a drug addict, she is sent to a "real-life" treatment center in New York, where the character interacts with actual patients.

Some of this sense of social "relevance" also found its way into Nixon's next venture for ABC, *All My Children,* which debuted in 1970. It was the first soap opera to write the Vietnam War into its stories, with one character drafted and (presumably) killed in action. Despite an antiwar speech delivered by his grieving mother, the political force of the plotline was blunted by the discovery that he was not really killed at all.

Even before *One Life to Live* broke new ground in its representation of class, race, and ethnicity, CBS gestured (rather tentatively, as it turns out) in the direction of social realism in response to the growing ratings success of NBC's and ABC's soaps. *Love Is a Many Splendored Thing* had been a successful 1955 film, with William Holden playing an American journalist working in Asia who falls in love with a young Eurasian woman, played by Jennifer Jones. Irna Phillips wrote the soap opera as a sequel to the film, in

which the couple's daughter moves to San Francisco and falls in love with a local doctor. *Love Is a Many Splendored Thing* debuted on September 18, 1967, its inaugural story (indeed, its very premise) concerning the social implications of this interracial romance. After only a few months, CBS, fearing protests from sponsors and audience groups, demanded that Phillips write her Eurasian heroine out of the show. She refused to do so and angrily resigned. Rather than cancel the show, however, CBS hired new writers who refocused it on three young, white characters (played by Donna Mills, David Birney, and Leslie Charleson).

What the replacement writers of *Love Is a Many Splendored Thing* did in a desperate attempt to save a wounded show Agnes Nixon did in a very premeditated fashion some 30 months later in *All My Children.* As its name suggests, *All My Children* was, like many radio and TV soaps before it, structured around a matriarch, the wealthy Phoebe Tyler (Ruth Warwick), but

All My Children.
Photo courtesy of Procter & Gamble

to a greater degree than its predecessors, it emphasized the romantic relationships among its "children." Nixon realized that after nearly two decades of television soaps, many in the viewing audience were aging out of the prime demographic group most sought by soap's sponsors and owners: women under the age of 50. *All My Children* used young adult characters and a regular injection of social controversy to appeal to viewers at the other end of the demographic spectrum. It was a tactic very much in tune with ABC's overall programming strategy in the 1960s, which also resulted in *The Flintstones* and *American Bandstand. All My Children* was the first soap opera whose organizational structure addressed what was to become the form's perennial demographic dilemma: how to keep the existing audience while adding younger recruits to it.

The problem of the "aging out" of a given soap opera's audience was particularly acute for CBS, whose leading soaps were by the early 1970s entering their second or third decade (*Search for Tomorrow, Love of Life, The Guiding Light, As the World Turns, Secret Storm,* and *The Edge of Night* were all launched between 1951 and 1957). Consequently, a troubling proportion of CBS's soap audience was aging out of the "quality" demographic range.

Thus, for the first time CBS found itself in the position of having to respond to the other networks' soap opera innovations. As its name rather baldly announces, *The Young and the Restless* was based on the premise that a soap opera about the sexual intrigues of attractive characters in their 20s would attract an audience of women also in their 20s. Devised for CBS by another of Irna Phillips's students, William Bell, and launched in 1973, *The Young and the Restless* is what might be called the first "Hollywood" soap. Not only was it shot in Hollywood (as some other soaps already were), but it also borrowed something of the "look" of a Hollywood film (particularly in its use of elaborate sets and high-key lighting), peopled Genoa City with soap opera's most conspicuously attractive citizens, dressed them in fashion-magazine wardrobes, and kept its plots focused on sex and its attendant problems and complications. The formula was almost immediately successful, and *The Young and the Restless* has remained one of the most popular soap operas for more than 20 years. It is also the stylistic progenitor of more recent "slick" soaps, such as *Santa Barbara* and *The Bold and the Beautiful.*

The early 1970s saw intense competition among the three networks for soap opera viewers. By this time, ABC, CBS, and NBC all had full slates of afternoon soap operas (at one point in this period, the three networks were airing ten hours of soaps every weekday), and the aggregate daily audience for soap operas had reached 20 million. With a fourfold difference in ad rates between low-rated and high-rated soaps and the latter having the potential of attracting $500,000 in ad revenue each week, soap operas became driven by the Nielsen ratings like never before.

The way in which these ratings pressures affected the writing of soap opera narratives speaks to the genre's unique mode of production. Since the days of radio soap operas, effective power over the creation and maintenance of each soap opera narrative world has been vested in the show's head writer. She (and to a greater degree than in any other form of television programming, the head writers of soap operas have been female) charts the narrative course for the soap opera over a six-month period and in doing so determines the immediate (and sometimes permanent) fates of each character, the nature of each intersecting plotline, and the speed with which each plotline moves toward some (however tentative) resolution. She then supervises the segmentation of this overall plot outline into weekly and then daily portions, usually assigning the actual writing of each episode to one of a team of scriptwriters ("dialoguers" as they are called in the business). The scripts then go back to the head writer for her approval before becoming the basis for each episode's actual production.

The long-term narrative trajectory of a soap opera is subject to adjustment as feedback is received from viewers by way of fan letters, market research, and, of course, the weekly Nielsen ratings figures, which in the 1970s were based on a national sample of some 1,200 television households. Looking over the head writer's shoulder, of course, is the network, whose profitability depends on advertising revenues, and the show's sponsor, who frequently was (and, in the case of four soaps today, still is) the show's owner.

By the early 1970s, head writers were under enormous pressure to attain the highest ratings possible, "win" the ratings race against the competition in the show's time slot, target the show's plots at the demographic group of most value to advertisers, take into account the production-budget implications of any plot developments (new sets or exterior shooting, for example), and maintain audience interest every week without pauses for summer hiatus or reruns. These pressures—and the financial stakes producing them—made soap opera head writers among the highest-paid writers in broadcasting (and the most highly paid women in the industry), but they also meant that, like the manager of a baseball team, she became the scapegoat if her "team" did not win.

If the mid- and late 1960s were periods of experimentation with the soap opera form itself, the early 1970s launched the era of incessant adjustments within the form—an era that has lasted to the present. Although individual soap operas attempted to establish defining differences from other soaps (in the early 1970s *As the World Turns* was centered on the extended Hughes family, *The Young and the Restless* was sexy and visually striking, *The Edge of Night* maintained elements of the police and courtroom drama, *General Hospital* foregrounded medical issues, and so on), to some degree all soap opera metanarratives over the past 25 years have drawn on common sets of tactical options, oscillating between opposed terms within each set: fantasy versus everyday life, a focus on individual character/actor "stars" versus the diffusion of interest across the larger soap opera community, social "relevance" versus more "traditional" soap opera narrative concerns of family and romance, an emphasis on one sensational plotline versus spreading the show's narrative energy across several plotlines at different stages of resolution, or attempting to attract younger viewers by concentrating on younger characters versus attempting to maintain the more adult viewer's interest through characters and plots presumably more to her liking.

At any given moment, the world of any given soap opera is in part the result of narrative decisions that have been made along all these parameters, mediated, of course, by the history of that particular soap opera's "world" and the personalities of the characters who inhabit it. Any head writer brought in to improve the flagging ratings of an ongoing soap is constrained in her exercise of these options by the fact that many of the show's viewers have a better sense of who the show's characters are and what is plausible to happen to them than she does. And being among the most vocal and devoted of all television viewers, soap opera fans are quick to respond when they feel a new head writer has driven the soap's narrative off course.

Despite the constant internal adjustments being made in any given soap opera, individual shows have demonstrated remarkable resilience, and, overall, soap operas exhibit infinitely greater stability than any prime-time genre. With the exception of several years in the late 1940s when Irna Phillips was in dispute with Procter and Gamble, *The Guiding Light* has been heard or seen every weekday since January 1937, making it the longest story ever told. Although long-running soap operas have been canceled (both *Love of Life* and *Search for Tomorrow* were canceled in the 1980s after 30-year runs) and others have come and gone, the incentive to keep an established soap going is considerable in light of the expense and risk of replacing it with a new soap opera, which can take a year or more to "find" its audience. Viewers who have invested years in watching a particular soap are not easily lured to a new one or, for that matter, to a competing soap on another network. In the mid-1970s, rather than replacing failing half-hour soaps with new ones, NBC began extending some of its existing soaps to a full hour (*Days of our Lives* and *Another World* were the first to be expanded in 1976).

In the 1980s, despite daytime soap operas' struggles to maintain audience in the face of declining overall viewership, the soap opera became more "visible" in the United States as a programming genre and cultural phenomenon than at any point in its history. Soap operas had always been "visible" to its large and loyal audience. By the 1980s, some 50 million persons in the United States "followed" one or more soap operas, including two-thirds of all women living in homes with televisions. As a cultural phenomenon, however, for 30 years the watching of soap operas had for the most part occurred undetected on the radar screen of public notice and comment. Ironically, soap opera viewing became the basis for a public fan culture in the late 1970s and early 1980s in part because more and more of the soap opera audience was unavailable during the day to watch. As increasing numbers of soap opera viewing women entered the paid workforce in the 1970s, they obviously found it difficult to "keep up" with the plots of their favorite soaps. A new genre of mass-market magazine emerged in response to this need. By 1982, ten new magazines had been launched that addressed the soap opera fan. For the occasional viewer, they contained plot synopses of all current soaps. For them and for more regular viewers, they also featured profiles of soap opera actors, "behind-the-scenes" articles on soap opera production, and letters-to-the-editor columns in which readers could respond to particular soap characters and plot developments. *Soap Opera Digest,* which began in 1975, had a circulation of 850,000 by 1990 and claimed a readership of four million. Soap opera magazines became an important focus of soap fan culture in the 1980s—a culture that was recognized (and exploited) by soap producers through their sponsorship or encouragement of public appearances by soap opera actors and more recently of soap opera "conventions."

Soaps and soap viewing also became more culturally "visible" in the 1980s as viewer demographics changed. By the beginning of the decade, fully 30 percent of the audience for soap operas was made up of groups outside the core demographic group of 18- to 49-year-old women, including substantial numbers of teenage boys and girls (up to 15 percent of the total audience for some soaps) and adult men (particularly those over 50). Underreported by the Nielsen ratings, soap opera viewing by some three million college students was confirmed by independent research in 1982.

The 1980s also was the decade in which the serial narrative form of the daytime soap opera became an important feature of prime-time programming as well. The program that sparked the prime-time soap boom of the 1980s was *Dallas*. Debuting in April 1978, *Dallas* was for its first year a one-hour episodic series concerning a wealthy but rough-edged Texas oil family. It was the enormous popularity of the "Who Shot J.R.?" cliff-hanger episode at the end of the second season (March 21, 1980) and the first episode the following season (November 21, 1980—the largest audience for any American television series to that time) that persuaded producers to transform the show into a full-blown serial.

Dallas borrowed not only the serial form from daytime soaps but also the structuring device of the extended family (the Ewings), complete with patriarch, matriarch, good son, bad son, and in-laws—all of whom lived in the same Texas-size house. The kinship and romance plots that could be generated around these core family members were, it was believed by the show's producers, the basis for attracting female viewers, while Ewing Oil's boardroom intrigues would draw adult males, accustomed to finding "masculine" genres (westerns, crime, and legal dramas) during *Dallas'* Sunday 10:00 P.M. time slot. By 1982, *Dallas* was one of the most popular programs in television history. It spawned direct imitators (most notably *Dynasty* and *Falcon Crest*) and a spin-off (*Knot's Landing*). Its success in adapting the daytime serial form to fit the requirements of the weekly one-hour format and the different demographics of the prime-time audience prompted the "serialization" of a host of prime-time dramas in the 1980s—the most successful among them *Hill Street Blues*, *St. Elsewhere*, and *L.A. Law*.

Dallas and *Dynasty* were also the first American serials (daytime or prime time) to be successfully marketed internationally. *Dallas* was broadcast in 57 countries, where it was seen by 300 million viewers. These two serials were particularly popular in western Europe, so much so that they provoked debates in a number of countries over American cultural imperialism and the appropriateness of state broadcasting systems spending public money to acquire American soap operas rather than to produce domestic drama. Producers in several European countries launched their own direct imitations of these slick American soaps, among them the German *Schwarzwaldklinik* and the French serial *Chateauvallon*.

But even as soap opera viewing came out of the closet in the 1980s and critics spoke (usually derisively) of the "soapoperafication" of prime time, daytime soaps struggled to deal with the compound blows struck by continuing changes in occupational patterns among women, the transformation of television technology (with the advent of the videotape recorder, satellite distribution of programming, and cable television), and the rise of competing and less expensive program forms. Between the early 1930s and the beginning of the 1970s, broadcasters and advertisers could count on a stable (and, throughout much of this period, expanding) audience for soap operas among what industry trade papers always referred to as "housewives": women working in the home, many of them caring for small children. But with the end of the postwar baby boom, American women joined the paid workforce in numbers unprecedented in peacetime. In 1977, the number of daytime households using television ("HUTs" in ratings terminology) began to decline and with it the aggregate audience for soap operas. Although daytime viewing figures have fluctuated somewhat since then, the trend over the past 20 years is clear: the audience for network programming in general and daytime programming specifically is shrinking.

In large measure, the overall drop in network viewing figures is attributable to changes in television technology, especially the extraordinarily rapid diffusion of the videotape recorder in the 1980s and, at the same time, an explosion in the number of viewing alternatives available on cable television. The penetration of the videotape recorder into the American household has had a paradoxical impact on the measurement of soap opera viewing. Although the soap opera is the genre most "time shifted" (recorded off the air for later viewing), soap opera viewing on videotape does not figure into audience ratings data, and even if it did, advertisers would discount such viewership, believing (accurately) that most viewers "zip" through commercials.

The wiring of most American cities for cable television in the 1970s and 1980s has meant the expansion of program alternatives in any given time period in many markets from three or four channels to more than 50. In the 1960s and 1970s, daytime television viewers were limited in the viewing choices in many time slots to two genres: the game show and the soap opera. By the 1990s, network soaps were competing not only against each other and against game shows but also against an array of cable alternatives, including one cable channel (Lifetime) targeted exclusively at the soap opera's core audience: women between the ages of 18 and 49.

For the three commercial networks, dispersed viewership across an increasingly fragmented market has meant lower ratings, reduced total advertising revenue, reduced advertising rates, and reduced profit margins. Although soap operas actually gained viewership in some audience segments in the 1980s—men and adolescents, in particular—these are not groups traditionally targeted by the companies whose advertising has sustained the genre for half a century. As they scrambled to staunch the outflow of audience to cable in the early 1990s, the networks and independent producers (who supply programming both to the networks and in syndication to local broadcasters) turned to daytime programming forms with minimal start-up costs and low production budgets, especially the talk show. In many markets, soap operas' strongest competition comes not from other soaps but from *Montel Williams, Ricki Lake, Jerry Springer,* or another of the dozens of talk shows that have been launched since 1990.

It is impossible here to set the history of serial drama in U.S. broadcasting in relation to the history of the form in the dozens of other countries where it has figured prominently—from China and India to Mexico and Brazil—except to say that the form has proven to be extraordinarily malleable and responsive to a wide variety of local institutional and social requirements. However, it may be instructive to contrast briefly the British experience with the serial drama with that surveyed here in the United States.

The tradition of broadcast serial drama in Britain goes back to 1940s radio and *The Archers,* a daily, 15-minute serial of country life broadcast by the British Broadcasting Corporation (BBC) initially as a means of educating farmers about better agricultural practices. The British television serial, on the other hand, grows out of the needs of commercial television in the late 1950s. Mandated to serve regional needs, the newly chartered "independent" (commercial) television services were eager to capture the growing audience of urban lower-middle-class and working-class television viewers. In December 1960, Manchester-based Granada Television introduced its viewers to *Coronation Street,* a serial set in a local working-class neighborhood. The following year, it was broadcast nationwide and has remained at or near the top of the prime-time television ratings nearly ever since.

Coronation Street's style, setting, and narrative concerns are informed by the gritty, urban, working-class plays, novels, and films of the 1950s—the so-called angry young man or kitchen sink movement. Where U.S. daytime serials were (and still are) usually disconnected from any particular locality, *Coronation Street* is unmistakably local. Where U.S. soaps usually downplay class as an axis of social division (except as a marker of wealth), *Coronation Street* began and has to some degree stayed a celebration of the institutions of working-class culture and community (especially the pub and the café)—even if that culture was by 1960 a historical memory and *Coronation Street's* representation of community a nostalgic fantasy.

In part because of the regionalism built into the commercial television system, all British soap operas since *Coronation Street* have been geographically and, to some degree, culturally specific in setting: *Crossroads* (1964–88) in the Midlands, *Emmerdale* (1972–) in the Yorkshire Dales, *Brookside* (1982–2004) in Liverpool, and the BBC's successful entry in the soap opera field *EastEnders* (1985–) in the East End of London. In addition, all these have been much more specific and explicit in their social and class settings than their American counterparts, and for this reason their fidelity to (and deviation from) some standard of social verisimilitude has been much more of an issue than has ever been the case with American soaps. *Coronation Street* has been criticized for its cozy, insulated, and outdated representation of the urban working-class community, which for decades seemed to have been bypassed by social change and strife.

Still, by American soap opera standards, British soaps are much more concerned with the material lives of their characters and the characters' positions within a larger social structure. *EastEnders,* when it was launched in 1985 the BBC's first venture into television serials in 20 years, was designed from the beginning to make contemporary material and social issues part of the fabric of its grubby East End community of pensioners, market traders, petty criminals, shopkeepers, the homeless, and the perennially unemployed.

Internationally, the most conspicuous and important development in the soap opera genre over the past 20 years has not involved the production, reception, or export of American soap operas (whether daytime or prime time) but rather the extraordinary popularity of domestic television serials in Latin America, India, Great Britain, Australia, and other countries and the international circulation of non-U.S. soaps to virtually every part of the world except the United States. With their *telenovelas* dominating prime-time schedules throughout the hemisphere, Latin American serial producers began seriously pursuing extraregional export possibilities in the mid-1970s. Brazil's TV Globo began exporting *telenovelas* to Europe in 1975. Within a decade, it was selling soap operas to nearly 100 countries around the world, its annual export revenues increasing fivefold between 1982 and 1987 alone. Mexico's Televisa exports serials to 59 countries, and its soap operas have topped the ratings in Korea, Russia, and Turkey. Venezuelan serials have attracted huge audiences in Spain, Italy, Greece, and Portugal. Latin American soap operas have penetrated the U.S. market but, thus far, only among its Spanish-speaking population: serials constitute a large share of the prime-time programming on Spanish-language cable and broadcast channels in the United States.

Although Australian serials had been shown in Britain for some years, they became a major force in British broadcasting with the huge success of Reg Grundy Productions' *Neighbours* in 1986. For most of the time since then, it has vied with either *EastEnders* or *Coronation Street* as Britain's most-viewed television program. *Neighbours* has been seen in more than 25 countries and has been called Australia's most successful cultural export.

The global circulation of non-U.S. serials since the 1970s is, in part, a function of the increased demand for television programming in general, caused by the growth of satellite and cable television around the world. It is also due, particularly in western and eastern Europe, to a shift in many countries away from a state-controlled public service television system to a "mixed" (public and commercial) or entirely commercial model. The low production cost of serials (in Latin America between $25,000 and $80,000 an episode) and their ability to recover these costs in their domestic markets mean that they can be offered on the international market at relatively low prices (as little as $3,000 per episode) in Europe. Given the large audiences they can attract and their low cost (particularly in relation to the cost of producing original drama), imported serials represent good value for satellite, cable, and broadcast services in many countries.

Ironically, American producers never seriously exploited the international market possibilities for daytime soap operas until the export success of Latin American serials in the 1980s and now find themselves following the lead of TV Globo and Venezuela's Radio Caracas. NBC's *The Bold and the Beautiful,* set in the fashion industry, is the first U.S. daytime soap to attract a substantial international following.

Derided by critics and disdained by social commentators from the 1930s to the 1990s, the soap opera is nevertheless the most effective and enduring broadcast advertising vehicle ever devised. It is also the most popular genre of television drama in the world today and probably in the history of world broadcasting: no other form of television fiction has attracted more viewers in more countries over a longer period of time.

ROBERT C. ALLEN

See also **Brookside; Coronation Street; Dallas; Dark Shadows; EastEnders; Genre; Nixon, Agnes; Peyton Place**

Further Reading

Allen, Robert C., *Speaking of Soap Operas,* Chapel Hill: University of North Carolina Press, 1985

Allen, Robert C., editor, *To Be Continued: Soap Operas Around the World,* London: Routledge, 1995

Ang, Ien, *Watching Dallas: Soap Opera and the Melodramatic Imagination,* London: Methuen, 1985

Buckingham, David, *Public Secrets: EastEnders and Its Audience,* London: British Film Institute, 1987

Cantor, Muriel G., and Suzanne Pingree, *The Soap Opera,* Beverly Hills, California: Sage, 1983

Cassata, Mary, and Thomas Skill, *Life on Daytime Television,* Norwood, New Jersey: Ablex, 1983

Dyer, Richard, with others, *Coronation Street,* London: British Film Institute, 1981

Geraghty, Christine, *Women and Soap Operas,* Cambridge: Polity Press, 1991

Hobson, Dorothy, *Crossroads: The Drama of a Soap Opera,* London: Methuen, 1982

Intintoli, Michael, *Taking Soaps Seriously: The World of Guiding Light,* New York: Praeger, 1984

Modleski, Tania, *Loving with a Vengeance: Mass-Produced Fantasies for Women,* Hamden, Connecticut: Archon Books, 1982

Nochimson, Martha, *No End to Her: Soap Opera and the Female Subject,* Berkeley: University of California Press, 1992

Silj, Alessandro, *East of Dallas: The European Challenge to American Television,* London: British Film Institute, 1988

Williams, Carol Traynor, *"It's Time for My Story": Soap Opera Sources, Structure, and Response,* Westport, Connecticut: Praeger, 1992

Social Class and Television

Social class has been a neglected factor in research on American television programs and audiences. Few studies have focused on the representation of class in television programming, although it has been a secondary topic in some studies, and more studies published in the 1990s give attention to class. Class was not often been considered in audience research, either, until media researchers from the cultural studies tradition directed more attention to this topic.

Television Representations of Social Class

Since the 1950s, researchers have surveyed television programming and compiled frequency counts of char-

Married . . . With Children, (rear) David Faustino, Christina Applegate, (front) Ed O'Neill, Katey Sagal, 1987–97.
©*20th Century Fox/Courtesy of the Everett Collection*

The Nanny, Daniel Davis, Fran Drescher, Lauren Lane, 1993–99; Season 5, #503 This Horse is Rockin'.
©*Columbia Pictures/Courtesy of the Everett Collection*

acters on network television, the most exhaustive being George Gerbner's cultural indicators project that conducted annual surveys over several years. Most such surveys concentrated on television drama and situation comedy, although some ventured to television news and other programming, A few included class as a category, but many more included occupation, from which class may be deduced. Combining these studies provides an indication of the relative frequency with which each class has been represented on television over several decades. The consistent pattern across the decades has been the near absence of working-class characters and an overabundance of upper-middle-class characters, an example of what Gerbner called "symbolic annihilation" of the working class, "erased" from the dominant cultural discourse established by television. A common working-class occupation depicted on television is uniformed police officers, and they appear typically as

background characters, often without names, in detective and crime series.

Studies of individual programs, typically very popular ones, are another common form of analysis. This method allows the researchers to examine the quality of representation, such as whether classes are portrayed more or less positively. For example, some studies of the American Broadcasting Company (ABC) sitcom *Roseanne* note its in-your-face challenge of middle-class respectability and its legitimation of working-class tastes and values, stances that are rare on television. Studies of the National Broadcasting Company (NBC) sitcom *The Cosby Show* analyze the family's upper-middle-class status and the mixed message this program presented for and about African Americans.

Other researchers have extended this method to examine an entire genre instead of a single show. Some book-length studies range over the spectrum of programming forms, with chapters on different genres that address issues of class. Situation comedies, and particularly domestic sitcoms, have been studied in this way. Studies of domestic sitcoms found strikingly persistent representations over five decades of prime-time television from the late 1940s through the 1990s: working-class men are invariably portrayed as incompetent and ineffectual buffoons, well-intentioned but dumb, lovable but not respected. Ralph Kramden, Fred Flintstone, Archie Bunker, and Homer Simpson are just the most famous examples. Heightening the contrast are wives and children who are often more intelligent, rational, and sensible than their husbands and fathers. Middle-class domestic situation comedies, by contrast, traditionally depict competent and mature husbands and fathers. Even in today's more cynical era, a middle-class male buffoon is a rarity. The persis-

Dynasty, Joan Collins, John Forsythe, Linda Evans, 1981–89.
Courtesy of the Everett Collection

tence of such negative images of the working class appear to arise from the demands of production and stereotypes incorporated into the work culture of the industry.

Some researchers report the prevalence of affluence and upward mobility on television and argue that these representations implicitly suggest that those who are not middle class or upwardly mobile have themselves to blame. Affluence is generally exaggerated: offices of lawyers, college professors, and other white-collar professionals are more plush than in real life. Whatever the profession, the characters typically are successes. Upward mobility is achieved through individual striving, reinforcing the idea that one's status is an indicator of one's ability, character, and moral worth. As if to temper desires of the audience, the economic benefits of upward mobility are frequently counterbalanced on television programs by the personal consequences of disrupted relations with family and friends. The rich are often depicted as unsympathetic and unsupportive of each other and as "bad" or unhappy people. These contrasts between classes convey the moral that money does not buy happiness.

Even the changed landscape of the television industry in the 1990s and early 2000s maintained many familiar representations of working-class men. In sitcoms with working-class settings and characters, such as *Dinosaurs, Roc, Grace Under Fire, King of Queens,* and *Grounded for Life,* the husband/father continues to be depicted as not too bright and not very competent. Series about the middle class, although more varied than in earlier decades, still include plenty of warmhearted and emotionally engaged families. Perhaps the most prominent of these is *8 Simple Rules for Dating My Daughter.* This series faced particular problems when star John Ritter, who portrayed a father who worked in his home as a sports writer, died unexpectedly. Rather than canceling the show, ABC wrote the father's death into the story, altering what had been a rather broad comedy into something more serious.

Some melodramas, however, did explore the difficulties confronted by middle-class families in times of economic constraint. The police procedural *N.Y.P.D. Blue* often turned to the private lives of hardworking detectives and acknowledged that their relatively low-paying positions made life in New York an ongoing struggle. This topic was particularly significant in the personal life of Andy Sipowicz, who for some time was presented as the single parent of a small child, then developed a relationship that led to marriage—to a colleague who was raising a niece and subsequently became pregnant with Sipowicz's baby. Discussions of money, apartment size, and future expenses were common in this sequence.

And perhaps the most noted depiction of class came with Home Box Office's (HBO's) *The Sopranos*. In this ongoing series, "middle-management mafia" types exhibit the trappings both of the newly wealthy and of their working-class New Jersey backgrounds. Class conflicts were particularly evident in the 2003 season-ending episode in which Tony Soprano promised to purchase a shorefront home for his wife, only to have the current owner renege on the deal. Tony's colleagues then bombard the snobbish resident with unceasing playback of Frank Sinatra recordings at ear-splitting levels.

These images are reinforced by the proliferation of talk shows that present real-life working-class people as exhibits in a "freak show," deviants who lack self-respect, moral values, or sexual control. Some researchers, however, have argued that these programs also give "voice" to individuals, groups, and classes previously excluded from television. They see the "freakish" behavior as a direct challenge to the approved decorum of televisual discourse.

Social Class and Television Audiences

Rarely has class been considered a variable in research on the effects of television viewing. This research tradition has concentrated on generalizations about psychological processes rather than on group differences. The few studies that have considered class conclude that there are no class differences in children's susceptibility to violence on television, in contrast to the usual stereotype of working-class children being more likely to be led into such behavior.

Studies of family television-use patterns have looked more broadly at how people interact with television sets. However, even in these studies, class is often peripheral. Books on television audiences seldom include social class as a topic in their indexes. One tradition of research has distinguished class differences in television use, contrasting working- and lower-class patterns of heavier and indiscriminate use (patterns that are widely disapproved of) with middle-class patterns of lighter, more selective use. More recent family communication research has continued to use these class distinctions.

Buried within the 1950s and 1960s sociological literature on working-class lifestyle are a few ethno-graphic observations on working-class uses of and responses to television. These have confirmed the tendency of working-class individuals to use the TV as filler and background to family interaction. They also reveal distinctive responses to program content: for example, working-class men prefer shows featuring characters sympathetic to working-class values, and these viewers identify with working-class types even when those types are written as peripheral characters or villains. Such findings contradict the notion of working-class viewers as passive and gullible.

Other studies have found significant differences in the orientations of working- and middle-class women to television shows. These latter studies draw on the British cultural studies tradition focusing on working-class viewers and their reactions to television. As with early U.S. community studies, British researchers found that working people construct their own alternative readings of television programs. In general, these studies find that, contrary to the stereotype offered in popular television criticism, working-class viewers are not the passive dupes with their eyes glued to the screen, nor are they the bumbling, ineffectual clowns often depicted in television comedies. Rather, working-class viewers use television to their advantage and interpret content to suit their own needs and interests.

RICHARD BUTSCH

See also **Family and Television; Gender and Television; Racism, Ethnicity, and Television**

Further Reading

Berk, Lynn, "The Great Middle American Dream Machine," *Journal of Communication* (Summer 1977)

Birmingham, Elizabeth, "Fearing the Freak," *Journal of Popular Film and Television,* Vol. 28 (Fall 2000)

Blum, Alan, "Lower-Class Negro Television Spectators," in *Blue Collar World,* edited by Arthur B. Shostak and William Gomberg, New York: Prentice Hall, 1964

Bryce, Jennifer, "Family Time and Television Use," in *Natural Audiences,* edited by Thomas Lindlof, Newbury Park, California: Sage, 1987

Buckingham, David, *Public Secrets: Eastenders and Its Audience,* London: BFI Publishing, 1987

Butsch, Richard, "Class and Gender in Four Decades of Television Situation Comedies," *Critical Studies in Mass Communication* (December 1992)

Butsch, Richard, "Industry and Image: Television and the Working-Class Buffoon," in *Gender, Race and Class in Media: A Text-Reader,* edited by Gail Dines and Jean Humez, Thousand Oaks, California: Sage, 1995; 2nd edition, Beverly Hills, California: Sage, 2002

Coleman, Robin Means, editor, *African American Audiences, Media, and Identity,* New York: Routledge, 2001

Freeman, Lewis, "Social Mobility in Television Comedies," *Critical Studies in Mass Communication* (December 1992)

Gans, Herbert, *The Urban Villagers,* New York: Free Press, 1962

Gauntlett, David, and Annette Hill, *TV Living: Television, Culture and Everyday Life,* London: Routledge, 1999

Gerbner, George, et al., "Cultural Indicators: Violence Profile No. 9," *Journal of Communication* (1978)

Glennon, Lynda, and Richard Butsch, "The Family As Portrayed on Television, 1946–1978," in *Television and Behavior: Technical Reviews,* vol. 2, edited by David Pearl et al., Washington, D.C.: U.S. Department of Health and Human Services, 1982

Glick, Ira, and Sidney Levy, *Living with Television,* Chicago: Aldine, 1962

Glynn, Kevin, *Tabloid Culture: Trash Taste, Popular Power, and the Transformation of American Television,* Durham, North Carolina: Duke University Press, 2000

Greenberg, Bradley, editor, *Life on Television: Content Analysis of U.S. TV Drama,* Norwood, New Jersey: Ablex, 1980

Himmelstein, Hal, *Television Myth and the American Mind,* New York: Praeger, 1984; 2nd edition, Westport, Connecticut: Praeger, 1994

Hobson, Dorothy, *Crossroads: The Drama of a Soap Opera,* London: Metheun, 1982

Holtzman, Linda, *Media Messages: What Film, Television, and Popular Music Teach Us About Race, Class, Gender, and Sexual Orientation,* Armonk, New York: M.E. Sharpe, 2000

Jhally, Sut, and Justin Lewis, *Enlightened Racism: The Cosby Show, Audiences, and the Myth of the American Dream,* Boulder, Colorado: Westview Press, 1992

Jordan, Amy, "Social Class, Temporal Orientation, and Mass Media Use Within the Family System," *Critical Studies in Mass Communication* (December 1992)

Lembo, Ron, *Thinking Through Television.* Cambridge: Cambridge University Press, 2000

Lipsitz, George, "The Meaning of Memory," *Cultural Anthropology* (1986)

Livingstone, Sonia, and Peter Lunt, *Talk on Television: Audience Participation and Public Debate,* London: Routledge, 1994

Marc, David, *Comic Visions: Television Comedy and American Culture,* Boston, Massachusetts: Unwin Hyman, 1989; 2nd edition, Malden, Massachusetts: Blackwell Publishers, 1997

McCarthy, Anna, *Ambient Television,* Durham, North Carolina: Duke University Press, 2001

Morley, David, *The Nationwide Audience: Structure and Decoding,* London: BFI Publishing, 1980

Press, Andrea L., *Women Watching Television: Gender, Class, and Generation in the American Television Experience,* Philadelphia: University of Pennsylvania Press, 1991

Press, Andrea L., and Elizabeth R. Cole, *Speaking of Abortion: Television and Authority in the Lives of Women,* Chicago: University of Chicago Press, 1999

Seiter, Ellen, et al., editors, *Remote Control: Television Audiences and Cultural Power,* London: Routledge, 1989

Sklar, Robert, "The Fonz, Laverne, Shirley, and the Great American Class Struggle," in his *Prime-Time America: Life on and Beyond the Television Screen,* New York and Oxford: Oxford University Press, 1980

Steeves, H.L., and M.C. Smith, "Class and Gender on Prime-Time Television Entertainment," *Journal of Communication Inquiry* (1987)

Taylor, Ella, *Prime-Time Families: Television Culture in Postwar America,* Berkeley: University of California Press, 1989

Thomas, Sari, and Brian Callahan, "Allocating Happiness: TV Families and Social Class," *Journal of Communication* (Summer 1982)

Turner, Graeme, "Audiences," in *British Cultural Studies: An Introduction,* London: Routledge, 1992

Society for Motion Picture and Television Engineers

While the history of motion pictures and television is typically linked to the rise of commercial mass entertainment, the extent of industry growth cannot be adequately explained without acknowledging the extensive benefits that came from technical standardization. Incorporated in July 1916, the Society for Motion Picture Engineers (SMPE) sought to act as a professional forum for its members and to publish technical findings "deemed worthy of permanent record." The impact of the society, however, extended far beyond the research reports published in SMPE's *Journal* and *Transactions.* With film pioneer Francis Jenkins installed as its charter president, the society took as its first task the development of a 35-millimeter format—the standard on which the motion picture and telefilm industries were built. Subsequent SMPE interventions codified two-color cinematography (November 1918), three-color Technicolor (August 1935), and optical sound-recording technologies (October 1930, September 1938). Although the organization began as a professional association for technical specialists, its public actions worked as an antidote to the high-risk economic and methodological instabilities that accompanied the introduction of each new film/television technology.

Research interests in television pre-dated by decades the formal addition of "Television" to the society's name in 1950 (SMPTE). Groundbreaking work was published on alternative delivery systems ("Radio Photographs, Radio Movies and Radio Vision" by C.F. Jenkins, May 1923), on vacuum-tube imaging devices ("Iconoscopes and Kinescopes" by V.K. Zworykin, May 1937), and on the Radio Corporation of America's (RCA's) field test of a comprehensive broadcasting system in New York (R.R. Beal, August 1937).

While this prewar flurry of engineering interest in television may suggest that society had a proactive and determining influence on the development of television technology, subsequent events demonstrate just how provisional SMPE's recommendations were. For example, although the *Journal* published standards for the Columbia Broadcasting System's (CBS's) new high-resolution color-television system in April 1942, other parties used coercion and economic clout to convince the U.S. government to opt for an inferior system in 1947. Disregarding the 1942 standards, the Federal Communications Commission (FCC) favored the less developed alternative of RCA/National Broadcasting Company (NBC), thereby forcing engineers to impose color information onto the limited black-and-white bandwidth of NTSC—a system that had itself been hastily (and some would say prematurely) adopted in 1941. Similarly, despite the open-ended, forward-thinking proposals put forth by Jenkins for theatrical television, pay-per-view TV, and set-licensing subsidies in 1923, the harsh regulatory realities of the FCC licensing freeze from 1948 to 1952 effectively deferred development of alternative delivery technologies for decades. A three-network oligopoly would dominate for almost 30 years as a result of the freeze, enabled by economic and regulatory collusion rather than engineering wisdom.

Although such actions demonstrate the limited influence of the society's recommendations on technology standards (SMPTE is not a government regulatory body like the FCC but an association of professionals representing a wide range of proprietary corporations), subsequent breakthroughs mark key points in the history of television technology. Standards for the eventual victor in the color-television race (NTSC) were finally published in April 1953. Engineers from Ampex disseminated information on the first commercially successful videotape recorder (VTR) in April 1957—an event that led to the precipitous death of the kinescope, initiated intense competition among VTR developers in the years that followed, and altered forever the way viewers see "liveness" (live-on-tape).

The international battle over high-definition television (HDTV) demonstrates the strategic role a standard-setting organization can take in the international arena. NHK in Japan had produced and begun marketing an HDTV system in the early 1980s, long before U.S. corporations entered the fray with working prototypes. Although the U.S. industry thus lagged behind foreign competitors in the race for viable "digital" video systems, SMPTE began to disseminate engineering standards for a spate of new digital television recording formats developed in Europe and Japan starting in December 1986. U.S. broadcasters initially resisted HDTV development because of the tremendous costs involved in changing over from current transmission systems. Eventually, however, the government intervened to dictate that the United States would ostensibly produce a single "consensus" *digital* HDTV system. The resulting "grand alliance" minimized the risk of losing an expensive research-and-development race, but foreign trade journalists complained that U.S. government muscle would lead unfairly to the privileging of U.S. HDTV standards in international markets despite the late entry of the United States into the high-definition arena. As this example shows, engineering standards can be political footballs used for economic leverage and technological nationalism.

What looked initially like an HDTV alliance, however, fell apart when competing interests (the computer, motion picture, and broadcast industries) took aim at the governmental regulators behind the initiative. Given the free-market ideology in play during the Clinton administration, the FCC proved unwilling to dictate a single technical standard for HDTV. The commission announced that it would allow "the market to decide" and then sanctioned 14 different technical standards (from 480p to 1080i) for what was now called "digital television" rather than HDTV. Four years of technical volatility and confusion followed despite FCC dictates that broadcasters had until 2003 to deliver new high-definition digital television. With ambivalent broadcasters mired in conflict with consumer electronics manufacturers and both at odds with the Hollywood establishment that has thrown its weight behind a competing system (24p), television's transition to digital has been stunted.

The volatility in this kind of pseudo–market environment demonstrates why such standards and engineering organizations as SMPTE have proved central participants in change. With regulators now essentially silent and with massive conglomeration defining the industry, SMPTE helps provide much-needed forms of rationality (scientific method) and a set of ground rules (benchmarks for those 14 competing digital formats) that keeps change intelligible and manageable.

SMPTE's future influence will depend on how well it comes to grips with several substantive changes. It must respond to the technological "convergence" blurring boundaries between film and electronic media, it must continue to demonstrate the value of common technical ground within the proprietary world of multinational corporations, and it must engage a membership that increasingly lies outside the confines of traditional film and television engineering. As studios are reduced to computerized desktops and practitioners with technical backgrounds cross over into creative capacities (and vice versa), technological discourses will become no less important or problematic. Given the capital-intensive and market-driven nature of electronic media, issues of standardization and technological "order" will be more crucial to the future of television than ever.

JOHN CALDWELL

See also **Standards; Television Technology**

Further Reading

Boddy, William, *Fifties Television: The Industry and Its Critics,* Urbana: University of Illinois Press, 1990

Bordwell, David, Kristin Thompson, and Janet Staiger, *Classical Hollywood Cinema,* New York: Columbia University Press, 1985
Caldwell, John, editor, *Electronic Media and Technoculture,* New Brunswick, New Jersey: Rutgers University Press, 2000
Gilder, George, *Life After Television,* New York: Norton, 1992
Hartwig, Robert L., *Basic TV Technology: Digital and Analogue,* London: Butterworth-Heinemann, 2000
Society for Motion Picture and Television Engineers, *Milestones in Motion Picture and Television Technology,* White Plains, New York: SMPTE, 1991
Watkinson, John, *Convergence in Broadcast and Communications Media,* London: Butterworth-Heinemann, 2001
Winston, Brian, *Misunderstanding Media,* Cambridge, Massachusetts: Harvard University Press, 1986
Winston, Brian, *Media, Technology and Society, A History: From the Telegraph to the Internet,* London: Routledge, 1998

Some Mothers Do 'Ave 'Em

British Comedy Series

Some Mothers Do 'Ave 'Em was a hugely popular British comedy series, broadcast by the British Broadcasting Corporation (BBC) in the 1970s. Initially considered unlikely to succeed, the series triumphed through the central performance of Michael Crawford as the hapless Frank Spencer and became one of the most popular comedy series of the decade, attracting a massive family audience.

Frank Spencer was the ultimate "loser," unemployable, unable to cope with even the simplest technology, and the victim of his surroundings. Every well-meaning attempt that he made to come to terms with the world ended in disaster, be it learning to drive, getting a job, or realizing some long-cherished dream. What saved him and kept the story comic was his innocence, his dogged persistence, and his outrage at the injustices he felt he had suffered.

The theme of the naive innocent comically struggling in an unforgiving world is an old one, but in this incarnation the most obvious antecedents for the slapstick Spencer character were such silent-movie clowns as Charlie Chaplin's tramp and, some three decades later, British cinema's Norman Wisdom. Writer Raymond Allen insisted, however, that he based the character on himself, quoting as his qualifications as the original Frank Spencer his outdated dress sense, complete lack of self-confidence, and overwhelming inability to do anything right. As proof of the character's origins, Allen recalled how he had bought himself a full-length raincoat to wear to the first rehearsals of the series in London—and was dismayed to see Crawford acquire one virtually the same as the perfect costume to play the role. The mac, together with the beret and the ill-fitting tanktop jumper, quickly became visual trademarks of the character.

It was Michael Crawford (really Michael Dumble Smith), complete with funny voice and bewildered expression, who turned Frank Spencer into a legend of British television comedy, employing the whole battery of his considerable comic skills. Disaster prone but defiant, the little man at odds with a society judging people solely by their competence and ability to fit in, he turned sets into battlefields as he fell foul of domestic appliances, motor vehicles, officials, in-laws, and just about anyone or anything else that had the misfortune to come into his vicinity.

Some Mothers Do 'Ave 'Em was essentially a one-joke escapade, with situations being set up chiefly to be exploited for the admittedly often inventive mayhem that could be contrived from them. What kept the series engaging, however, was the pathos that Crawford engendered in the character, making him human and, for all the silliness of many episodes, endearing. In this, Crawford was ably abetted by Michelle Dotrice, who played Frank Spencer's immensely long-suffering but steadfastly loyal (if occasionally despairing) girlfriend and, later, wife Betty.

In the tradition of the silent-movie stars, Crawford insisted on performing many of the hair-raising and life-threatening stunts himself, teetering in a car over lofty cliffs, dangling underneath a helicopter, and risking destruction under the wheels of a moving train in a way that would not have been tolerated by television companies and their insurers a few years later. The professionalism that he displayed in pulling off these stunts impressed even those who balked at the show's childish humor and overt sentimentalism. It is not so surprising that Crawford himself, after six years in the role, was able to escape the stereotype that threatened to obscure his talent and to establish himself as a leading West End and Broadway musical star.

DAVID PICKERING

Cast

Frank Spencer	Michael Crawford
Betty	Michele Dotrice

Producer

Michael Mills

Programming History

19 30-minute episodes; 3 50-minute specials
BBC

February 1973–March 1973	7 episodes
November 1973– December 1973	6 episodes
December 25, 1974	Christmas special
December 25, 1975	Christmas special
October 1978–December 1978	6 episodes
December 25, 1978	Christmas special

Sony Corporation

International Media Conglomerate

An innovative Japanese consumer-electronics company founded by Masaru Ibuka and Akio Morita in 1946, Sony started out manufacturing heating pads, rice cookers, and other small appliances but soon switched to high technology, bringing out Japan's first reel-to-reel magnetic tape recorder in 1950 and then its first FM transistor radio in 1955. Sony's later innovations in consumer electronics included the Trinitron color-television picture tube (1968), the Betamax videocassette recorder (1975), the Walkman personal stereo (1979), the compact disc player (1982), the 8-millimeter video camera (1985), and the Video Walkman (1988).

Sony's success in marketing its products worldwide rested on distinctive styling and "global localization," a practice that retained product development in Japan, while disbursing manufacturing among plants in Europe, the United States, and Asia. To maintain quality control, Sony dispatched large numbers of Japanese managers and engineers to supervise these plants.

Under the leadership of Norio Ohga, who joined the company 1959 and ran Sony's design center, Sony pursued the course of marrying Japanese consumer electronics with American entertainment software. After purchasing CBS Records for $2 billion in 1987, Sony initiated the Japanese invasion of Hollywood by acquiring Columbia Pictures Entertainment (CPE) from Coca-Cola for $3.4 billion in 1989. The following year, Sony's Japanese rival Matsushita Electric Industrial Company, the largest consumer-electronics company in the world, purchased MCA for $6.9 billion. The two takeovers led to charges that the Japanese were about to dominate American popular culture, but the controversy soon died out when it became apparent that Sony and Matsushita would have to stay aloof from production decisions if their studios were to compete effectively.

In 1989, the year Sony acquired CPE, Sony generated over $16 billion in revenues from the following categories: (1) video equipment other than TV—$4.3 billion, (2) audio equipment—$4.2 billion, (3) TV sets—$2.6 billion, (4) records—$2.6 billion, and (5) other products—$2.5 billion. The CPE acquisition, which included two major studios—Columbia Pictures and TriStar Pictures—home-video distribution, a theater chain, and an extensive film library, brought in an additional $1.6 billion in revenues.

By becoming vertically integrated, Sony hoped to create "synergies" in its operations, or, stated another way, Sony wanted to stimulate the sales of hardware by controlling the production and distribution of software. The company may have been reacting to the so-called format wars of the 1970s when Sony's Betamax lost out to Matsushita's VHS videotape recorder. Industry observers believed that the greater availability of VHS software in video stores naturally led consumers to choose VHS machines over Betamaxes. Sony would not make the same mistake again and found a way to protect itself as it contemplated introducing the 8-millimeter video and high-definition television systems it had in development.

To strengthen CPE as a producer of software, Sony spent an added $1 billion and perhaps more to acquire and refurbish new studios and to hire film producers Peter Guber and Jon Peters to run the company, which it renamed Sony Entertainment. Sony performed rea-sonably well under the new regime until 1993, but afterward, Columbia and TriStar struggled to fill their distribution pipelines. Virtually all of Sony's hits had been produced by independent producer affiliates, and when these deals lapsed, Sony lagged behind the other majors in motion picture production and market share. Some industry observers claimed Sony lacked "a clear strategy" for taking advantage of the rapid shifts in the entertainment business. After top production executives left Columbia and TriStar in 1994, Sony took a $3.2 billion loss on its motion picture business, reduced the book value of its studios by $2.7 billion, and announced that "it could never hope to recover its investment" in Hollywood.

TINO BALIO

See also **Betamax Case; Camcorder; Home Video; Time Shifting; Videocassette; Videotape**

Further Reading

Lardner, James, "Annals of Law; The Betamax Case, Part 1," *The New Yorker*(April 6, 1987)

Lardner, James, "Annals of Law; The Betamax Case, Part 2," *The New Yorker* (April 13, 1987)

Lyons, Nick, *The Sony Vision,* New York: Crown, 1976

Morita, Akio, *From a 500-Dollar Company to a Global Corporation: The Growth of Sony,* Pittsburgh, Pennsylvania: Carnegie-Mellon University Press, 1985

Morita, Akio, with Edwin M. Reingold and Mitsuko Shimomura, *Made in Japan: Akio Morita and Sony,* New York: Dutton, 1986

Sopranos, The

U.S. Drama

A defining program of the cable era, *The Sopranos* debuted on Home Box Office (HBO) in January 1999. The story of a New Jersey mafia boss and his nuclear and criminal families, it was the first cable series to achieve larger audience ratings than its broadcast competition. The series also received unprecedented critical acclaim. Even intellectuals who had previously disdained television hailed the show as a groundbreaking work of art.

A measure of the program's unique status as a cultural icon was the screening of the entire run of its first two seasons at the Museum of Modern Art in New York City, the featured item in a retrospective of gang-ster movies chosen by David Chase, *The Sopranos'* creator and executive producer.

The popularity of *The Sopranos* was particularly demoralizing for the broadcast networks, in decline through the 1980s and 1990s because of competition from cable and satellite subscriber networks. The show's success in the ratings against "free" network programs was decisive evidence that the mass audiences and consensus programming of the broadcast era were now historical artifacts. Although HBO's subscribers were only one-third of the total TV audience, the series reached an estimated 14 million viewers, 7.3 million TV homes, during its third and fourth seasons,

The Sopranos, Steven Van Zandt, James Gandolfini, Michael Imperioli, 4th season, 2002.
Courtesy of the Everett Collection

by far the largest continuing audience ever assembled by cable television. As one media business reporter put it, "HBO now has the first television megahit ever to be unavailable to the majority of viewers."

Probably the most complex narrative in the history of American television, *The Sopranos* marks a genuine watershed in popular culture. The series is a culmination—but also a deeply cynical and realistic revision—of the mythology of the gangster and the culture of the mafia as depicted in classic movies from the 1930s, in Mario Puzo's novels, and in the films of Francis Ford Coppola and Martin Scorsese.

Something of the show's revisionist, postheroic realism is captured in its brilliant title sequence. Quick images of the roof and wall tiles of the Lincoln Tunnel as photographed through the windshield of Tony Soprano's speeding car yield to the tunnel's exit ramp, the New York skyline briefly visible across the Hudson River through the passenger-side window (the twin towers of the World Trade Center were framed in a quick close shot of the car's side mirror during the first two seasons, but this image was removed after the events of September 11, 2001). Now images of New

Jersey's ugliest industrial sprawl (noxious Secaucus, polluted waterways, and smokestacks) rush past, followed by shots of highway exit signs, Tony steering, and the grimy downtowns of the dwindled cities in which Tony grew up and in which much of the series' action takes place. This quick tour of the terrain of *The Sopranos* concludes with shots of modest working-class, then middle-class, city homes and finally the forested road leading to the driveway of Tony's pretentious suburban brick palace. The sequence is a social history of his life and work, distilling essential elements of the saga of Tony Soprano (James Gandolfini), his dual identity as a suburban husband and father and as angst-ridden godfather in meaner streets than those of the mythic city across the river.

The movie gangsters are not merely implicit references in the series but also active presences. Tony's mob crew is fond of quoting *The Godfather* and other shaping ancestors, and such allusions often create complex ironies, suggesting how eagerly these "real" gangsters embrace the aggrandizing images of the movie culture. We see Tony tearfully watching *Public Enemy* (1931) on the day of his mother's funeral, and the famous Cagney melodrama about a gangster killer whose mother's love never wavers implicitly judges Tony's reptilian mother (Nancy Marchand in her last, great role) who terrorized him as a child and colluded with his Uncle Junior (Dominic Chianese) to have him killed because she blamed him for moving her to a nursing home.

The Sopranos takes full advantage of its freedom from the constraints of broadcast television. Even its female characters speak with the profane candor of real people; mayhem and murder are dramatized with pitiless, shocking directness; and there is considerable (but not full frontal) nudity. But this license in what is seen and heard is never gratuitous or sensational, and the many eruptions of crippling or murderous violence have disturbing authority in part because they take place in such mundanely realistic spaces and are committed or endured by unattractive, ordinary characters the audience has come to know. The series breaks with broadcast conventions in other ways as well, notably in its readiness to dramatize its characters' dreams and fantasies, some of which achieve a macabre, disorienting intensity.

But its sense of the ordinary, the quotidian, and the *not-mythic* is the real key to *The Sopranos*. Tony Soprano is a killer and mob boss, but he is also a middle-age father with a discontented spouse and a son and daughter no more deranged than most privileged teenagers in our high-tech, motorized, image-saturated suburbs. The juxtaposition—sometimes the intersection—of these alternate worlds generates complexities undreamt of in most movies or earlier forms of television. The program mobilizes a sustained, ongoing experience of moral ambiguity as Tony and some of his criminal cronies display a range of comic, sentimental, deeply ordinary traits in their dealings with aging parents, wives, children, and mistresses and then in other moments perform acts of sickening disloyalty, brutality, and murder.

This defining quality of the series emerged decisively in the fifth episode of the first season, in which Tony takes his daughter Meadow (Jamie-Lynn Sigler) on a tour of colleges in Maine and, in a stop at a gas station, recognizes an informer, once part of his crime family, now in hiding in the witness protection program. Scenes of intimate bonding between father and daughter are intercut with Tony's stalking of the informer, whom he ultimately attacks from behind and strangles with a wire. The murder is not quick, and the victim struggles hard before he dies. Moments before, this killer had been a doting father, communing with his daughter in a common American parenting ritual.

As this episode implies, *The Sopranos* does not, as many commentators have claimed, repudiate or totally transcend traditional television. For all its cable-licensed profanity, sex, and violence, the series embraces and deeply exploits TV's unique hospitality to serial narrative as well as the central subject of television drama of the broadcast era, its ideological core: the American family.

The show has a specific ancestry in *The Rockford Files* (1974–80, National Broadcasting Company [NBC]), whose staff David Chase joined in 1976 as writer and producer. That private-eye series starring James Garner was also a hybrid of comedy, crime, and (sometimes) family drama, and it used the format of the weekly series to explore the ongoing, changing relations among its recurring characters. Several episodes of *Rockford* clearly anticipate *The Sopranos*. In one of these, a two-part story first broadcast in 1977, George Loros, who plays the mob capo Raymond Curto in the HBO series, portrays a mafia hit man undone by his city boy's ignorance in the wilds of nature. This episode hints at the bleak murderous comedy of the memorable installment from the third season of *The Sopranos* in which Tony's henchmen Paulie Walnuts (Tony Sirico) and young Christopher Moltisanti (Michael Imperioli) are trapped together without food or transport in the wintry Pine Barrens of southern New Jersey.

The series format—traditional television's essential feature—is *The Sopranos*' fundamental resource as well, permitting the program to dramatize the unsteady maturation of Tony's children, for example, the ebb and flow of his cankered intimacy with his wife Carmella and the murderous shifting alliances and hostilities within his own crime family and among rival mobsters. As the series unfolded during its first four seasons, its account of the primary characters deepened; aspects of Tony's past emerged in fitful, accreting detail; and the experiences and inner lives of many secondary characters were explored more fully. At the start of its fifth season (as Chase signed a contract to supervise a sixth and final year of the show), the 52 hour-long chapters of *The Sopranos* had achieved a density and texture unique in American movies or television. The damaged, unstable family order of the show could be read as a compelling metaphor or distillation of the larger social order. In its enlarging power to explore personality as it evolves over time and in its stringent, ramifying stories of crime, injustice, greed, and ambition, the series had become a 21st-century equivalent of the great English and European novels of the 19th century.

DAVID THORBURN

See also **Chase, David;** *Rockford Files, The*

Further Reading

Chase, David Chase, *The Sopranos: Selected Scripts from Three Seasons,* New York: Warner Books, 2002

Holden, Stephen Holden, et al., *The New York Times on "The Sopranos,"* New York: The New York Times Books, 2000

James, Caryn, "'Sopranos': Blood, Bullets and Proust," *New York Times* (March 2, 2001)

Lavery, David, editor, *This Thing of Ours: Investigating The Sopranos,* New York: Columbia University Press, 2002

Remnick, David, "Is This the End of Rico?" *The New Yorker* (April 2, 2001)

Showalter, Elaine, "Mob Scene," *The American Prospect,* Vol. 11, No. 8 (February 28, 2000)

Warshow, Robert, "The Gangster as Tragic Hero," in *The Immediate Experience,* New York: Doubleday, 1962

Thanks to Micky DuPree for research assistance.

Soul Train

U.S. Music-Variety Show

Soul Train, the first black-oriented music variety show ever offered on American television, is one of the most successful weekly programs marketed in first-run syndication and one of the longest-running syndicated programs in American television history. The program first aired in syndication on October 2, 1971, and was an immediate success in a limited market of seven cities: Atlanta, Cleveland, Detroit, Houston, Los Angeles, Philadelphia, and San Francisco. Initially, syndicators had difficulty achieving their 25-city goal. However, *Soul Train*'s reputation as a "well produced" and "very entertaining" program gradually captured station directors' attention. By May 1972, the show was aired in 25 markets, many of them major cities.

The show's emergence and long-standing popularity marks a crucial moment in the history of African-American television production. Don Cornelius, the show's creator, began his career in radio broadcasting in Chicago in November 1966. At a time when African Americans were systematically denied media careers, Cornelius left his $250-a-week job selling insurance for Golden State Mutual Life to work in the news department at WVON radio for $50 a week. It was a bold move and clearly marked his committed optimism. By seizing a small opportunity to work in radio broadcasting, Cornelius was able to study broadcasting firsthand. His career advancement in radio included employment as a substitute disc jockey and host of talk shows. Radio broadcasting techniques informed Cornelius's vision of the television program *Soul Train.*

By February 1968, Cornelius was a sports anchorman on the black-oriented news program "A Black's View of the News" on WCIU-TV, Channel 26, a Chicago TV station specializing in ethnic programming. Cornelius pitched his idea for a black-oriented dance show to the management of WCIU-TV the following year. The station agreed to Cornelius's offer to produce the pilot at his own expense in exchange for studio space. The name *Soul Train* was taken from a local promotion Cornelius produced in 1969. To create publicity, he hired several Chicago entertainers to perform live shows at up to four high schools on the same day. The caravan performances from school to school reminded the producer of a train.

Cornelius screened his pilot to several sponsors. Initially, no advertising representatives were impressed by his idea for black-oriented television. The first support came from Sears, Roebuck and Company, which used *Soul Train* to advertise phonographs. This small agreement provided only a fraction of the actual cost of producing and airing the program. Yet, with this commitment, Cornelius persuaded WCIU-TV to allow the one-hour program to air five afternoons weekly on

Soul Train host Don Cornelius, circa mid 1970's.
Courtesy of the Everett Collection

a trial basis. The program premiered on WCIU-TV on August 17, 1970, and within a few days youth and young adult populations of Chicago were talking about this new local television breakthrough. The show also had the support of a plethora of Chicago-based entertainers. As an independent producer of the program, Cornelius acted as host, producer, and salesman five days a week. He worked without a salary until the local advertising community began to recognize the program as a legitimate advertising vehicle, and *Soul Train* began to pay for itself.

The *Soul Train* format includes guest musical performers, hosts, and performances by the *Soul Train* dancers. Set in a dance club environment, the show's hosts are black entertainers from the music, television, and film industries. The dancers are young women and men, fashionably dressed, who dance to the most popular songs on the rhythm-and-blues, soul, and rap charts. The show includes a game called "*The Soul Train* Scramble," in which the dancers compete for prizes. The program's focus on individual performers, in contrast to the ensemble dancing more common in televisual presentation, has been passed down to many music variety shows, such as *American Bandstand, Club MTV,* and *Solid Gold.*

The television show's success can be linked to the increasing importance of black-oriented radio programs taking advantage of FM stereo sound technology. With that support, soul and funk music exploded in popularity across the nation. Black record sales soared because of the increased radio airplay, and the opportunity to view popular performances without leaving home became the appeal of *Soul Train.*

The popularity of the show in Chicago prompted Cornelius to pursue national syndication of the program. One of the nation's largest black-owned companies, the Johnson Products Company, agreed to support the show in national syndication. Sears, Roebuck and Company increased its advertising support. In 1971, Cornelius moved the production of the *Soul*

Train to Hollywood. The show continued to showcase musical talent and to shine the spotlight on stand-up comedians. The program's presentation of vibrant black youth attracted viewers from different racial backgrounds and ethnicities to black entertainment. The show has been credited with bringing 1970s black popular culture into the American home.

In 1985, the Chicago-based Tribune Entertainment company became the exclusive distributor and syndicator of *Soul Train.* In 1987, the Tribune company helped launch the *Soul Train* Music Awards. This program is a live two-hour television special presented annually in prime-time syndication and reaches more than 90 percent of U.S. television households. The *Soul Train* Music Awards represent the ethos of the *Soul Train* program, which is to offer exposure for black recording artists on national television.

Don Cornelius stepped down as host in the late 1990s and was replaced by Mystro Clark, who, after three seasons, was replaced by Shemar Moore. Cornelius is now the executive producer for the show.

MARLA L. SHELTON

See also **Music on Television; Racism, Ethnicity, and Television**

Producer
Don Cornelius

Programming History
Syndicated (various times)
1971–

Further Reading

Meisler, Andy, "For *Soul Train*'s Conductor, Beat Goes On: A TV Show Sticks with Its Niche and a Time-Tested Formula," *New York Times* (August 7, 1995)
Reynolds, J.R., "Big Draw," *Billboard* (April 29, 1995)
Rule, Sheila, "Off the *Train*," *New York Times* (October 20, 1993)

South Africa

The South African television service, launched in 1976, is among the youngest in Africa but by far the most advanced on the continent. Propped by the country's large economy and high living standards among the minority populations, South Africa's television industry developed rapidly to become one of the first satellite-based broadcasting systems on the continent, with the most widely received national service.

The industry is dominated by a state organization, the South African Broadcasting Corporation (SABC), which was established in 1936 by an act of Parliament. The corporation, however, concentrated on radio broadcasting during its first 40 years of operation, as the racist National Party in power during most of this period opposed the introduction of television under the pretext of preserving cultural sovereignty. The launching of the communication satellite *Intelsat IV* in 1972 by Western countries ushered in new fears about the dangers of uncontrolled reception of international television via cheap satellite dishes. The South African government, fearing imperialism, swiftly resolved to introduce a national television service as an anti-imperial device.

Between 1976 and 1990, the SABC-TV service was state controlled and heavily censored and functioned as an arm of the government. SABC was banned from broadcasting pictures or voices of opposition figures, and its editorial policy was dictated through an institutional censoring structure.

The blackout on politically dissenting voices was discontinued in 1990 as the corporation purged itself of racial bias and shifted its focus to public service broadcasting. Since then, SABC-TV has balanced its programs to reflect the country's cultural and political diversity and embraced a policy of affirmative action in staff recruitment.

At inception, SABC-TV operated four national television channels: TV-1, TV-2, TV-3, and TV-4. This configuration was revised in a 1992 restructuring program; TV-1 retained its autonomy, and the rest were merged into a new multicultural channel called Contemporary Community Values Television (CCV-TV). The two national channels now compete for audiences and advertising with M-Net, a highly successful privately owned pay channel.

TV-1, the largest and most influential, was directed at the minority white population, with all programs broadcast in Afrikaans and English. Since mid-1986, the channel's 18-hour daily programming has been relayed through a transponder on an *Intelsat* satellite to 40 transmitting stations with an Effective Radiated Power (ERP) of 100 kilowatts and 42 stations with an ERP range of between 1 and 10 kilowatts. These transmissions are augmented by 63 gap fillers and an estimated 400 privately owned low-power transmitters, enabling the channel to be received by three-quarters of the country's population.

The CCTV channel broadcasts in nine local languages via 14 100-kilowatt terrestrial stations, nine 1- to 10-kilowatt stations, and 33 gap fillers. The channel's programming is received by 64 percent of the country's population.

SABC's domination of radio and television has enabled it to develop advanced products and services for its audience. The corporation offers simulcasting of dubbed material on television with the original soundtrack on radio Teledata, a teletext service initially established as a pilot project on spare TV-1 signal capacity, and has been expanded to a 24-hour service with over 180 pages of news, information, and educational material. Selected material from the Teledata database is also copied onto TV-1 outside program transmission to provide an auxiliary service that is available on all TV sets countrywide.

The Electronic Media Network, widely known by its acronym, M-Net, is South Africa's only private television channel. Founded by a consortium of newspaper publishers in October 1986 to counter the growing threat that the commercially driven SABC-TV posed to the newspaper industry, M-Net has grown into the most successful pay-TV station in the world outside the United States. Its nearly 850,000 subscribers (1995 estimate) received 120 hours a week of entertainment, documentaries, film, series, and miniseries. The large national audience is accessed through a number of leased or rented SABC terrestrial reception facilities.

The subscription service is offered on an internationally patented decoder originally developed from the American Oak Systems decoder technology. M-Net's subscriber management subsidiary, Multichoice Ltd, markets the programming services to individual subscribers across southern Africa. It also markets the Delta 9000 Plus decoders to pay-TV operations elsewhere; by 1994, it was marketing the technology to the Pelepiu pay-TV system in Italy. Another of its subsidiaries, M-Net International, has been actively seeking subscribers in tropical and northern Africa after successful operations in Namibia, Lesotho, and Swaziland. Through the use of two transponders on C-band satellites, the channel has a footprint covering the entire African continent and parts of the Middle East. During 1994, Multichoice Ltd signed an agreement with a private TV station in Tanzania to relay programming across the country via satellite. At the same time, M-Net International began broadcasting across Africa on a channel shared with British Broadcasting Corporation (BBC) World Service Television. Plans were also afoot to extend rebroadcast rights to sub-Saharan African countries and to expand satellite services and individual subscriptions.

Three small regional television stations are operated in the former homelands of Bophuthatswana, Transkei, and Ciskei. The Bophuthatswana television, Bop-TV, is a commercial operation that is aired via 18 small transmitters (all with ERP below 1 kilowatt) and relay stations in Johannesburg and Pretoria. The Transkei Broadcasting Corporation operates a television service that competes with the pay service of M-Net Transkei.

M-Net Transkei is a scrambled service except between 3:00 P.M. and 5:00 P.M., when its signal is unscrambled. The Rhena Church of South Africa runs two private TV stations in Ciskei and Transkei that broadcast in English via two small stations. Plans were under way in 1994 to install two 1-kilowatt transponders.

Since the early 1980s, South Africa has been considering venturing into satellite communications. The first involvement in satellite-aided broadcasting came in mid-1986, when a transponder was fitted on an *Intelsat* satellite to relay TV-1 to terrestrial transmitting stations. In early 1992, the C-band satellite service was upgraded from a hemispherical beam to a zonal beam to enhance the establishment of cellular transmitters in remote areas of the country. At the same time, the transmission standards were upgraded from B-MAC to PAL System 1. Together with the introduction of transmissions in the Ku-band range, these modifications are expected to provide television coverage to the entire country. The Ku-band satellite service is also expected to be utilized in telecommunication applications.

With over 150 production houses, South Africa has the largest broadcasting production industry on the continent. Local productions, from SABC teams and independent production houses, account for about 50 percent of airtime of SABC-TV and between 10 and 30 percent on M-Net. Both organizations have laid heavy emphasis on Afrikaans-language productions. However, independent producers, brought together by the Film and Television Foundation (FTF), have in the past lobbied for higher local content quotas. However, such proposals have been contested by M-Net on the grounds that pay-TV service is customer driven. The FTF suggests that where a broadcaster is unable to offer local content quotas, a levy should be introduced on the turnover to finance local productions.

NIXON K. KARIITHI

Further Reading

Bourgault, Louise Mahon, *Mass Media in Sub-Saharan Africa,* Bloomington: Indiana University Press, 1995

Hachten, William A., *Mass Communication in Africa: An Annotated Bibliography,* Madison: University of Wisconsin Press, 1971

Mytton, Graham, *Mass Communication in Africa,* London: Edward Arnold, 1983

Nixon, Rob, *Homelands, Harlem, and Hollywood: South African Culture and the World Beyond,* New York: Routledge, 1994

Prinsloo, Jeanne, and Costas Criticos, editors, *Media Matters in South Africa,* Durban, South Africa: Media Resource Centre, 1991

Wilcox, Dennis L., *Mass Media in Black Africa: Philosophy and Control,* New York: Praeger, 1975

South Korea

In the past half century, television broadcasting has been introduced in the majority of Western nations. In the 1950s, when television broadcasting evolved into the dominant electronic medium in the West, some Asian countries established their own television services. Korea, the fourth adopter in Asia, began television broadcasting on May 12, 1956, with the opening of HLKZ-TV, a commercially operated television station. HLKZ-TV was established by the RCA Distribution Company (KORCAD) in Seoul with 186 to 192 megahertz, 100-watt output, and 525 scanning lines.

Korean television celebrated its 40th birthday in 1996, and a great deal has changed in the past four decades. In 1956, there were only 300 television sets in Korea, but that number has climbed to an estimated 6.27 million by 1980, and television viewing has become the favorite form of entertainment or amusement for the mass audience. As of 1993, Koreans owned nearly 11.2 million television sets, a penetration rate of nearly 100 percent.

The early 1960s saw a phenomenal growth in television broadcasting. On December 31, 1961, the first full-scale television station, KEWS-TV, was established and began operation under the Ministry of Culture and Public Information. The second commercial television system, MBC-TV, following the first commercial television, TBC-TV, made its debut in 1969. The advent of MBC-TV brought significant development to the television industry in Korea, and after 1969 the television industry was characterized by furious competition among the three networks.

The 1970s were highlighted by government intervention into the media system in Korea. In 1972, President Park's government imposed censorship on media through the Martial Law Decree. The government revised the Broadcasting Law under the pretext of improving the quality of television programming. After the revision of the law, the government expanded its control of media content by requiring all television and radio stations to review programming before and after transmission. Although the government argued that its action was taken as a result of growing public criticism of broadcasting media practices, many accused the government of wanting to establish a monopoly over television broadcasting.

The 1980s were the golden years for Korea's television industry. Growth was phenomenal in every dimension: the number of programming hours per week rose from 56 in 1979 to nearly 88.5 in 1989, the number of television stations increased from 12 in 1979 to 78 by 1989, and the number of television sets grew from 4 million in 1979 to nearly 6 million in the same period. In 1981, another technological breakthrough happened: the introduction of color television. Color broadcasting, however, occasioned a renewal of strong competition among the networks.

As the decade progressed, more controversial entertainment programming appeared, prompting the government to establish a new broadcasting law. With the Broadcasting Law of 1987, the Korean Broadcasting Committee was established to oversee all broadcasting in the country. The most important feature of this law was that it guaranteed freedom of broadcasting. However, one of its main provisions required that television stations allocate at least 10 percent of their broadcasting hours to news programming, 40 percent to cultural/educational programming, and 20 percent to entertainment programming. At the time of the imposition of these new regulations, the three networks broke new ground by successfully broadcasting the 1988 Seoul Olympics. The coverage of the 24th Olympiad was the product of technological prowess and resourceful use of manpower by the Korean broadcasting industry.

Since the early 1980s, the structure of the Korean television industry has remained basically unchanged. The government ended the 27-year-long freeze on new commercial licenses by granting a license to SBS-TV in 1990. This breakthrough paved the way for competition between the public and the private networks.

Another technological breakthrough took place in the beginning of the 1990s with the introduction of cable television. In 1990, the government initiated an experimental multichannel and multipurpose cable television service. In addition, Korea launched its first broadcasting/communication satellite, *Mugungwha*, to 36,000 kilometers above the equator in 1995. The development of an integrated broadband network is expected to take the form of B-ISDN immediately after the turn of the century.

Regulation of Broadcasting

The aim of the latest Broadcasting Act, legislated on August 1, 1990, is to strive for the democratic formation of public opinion and improvement of national culture and to contribute to the promotion of broadcasting. The act consists of six chapters: (1) General Provisions, (2) Operations of the Broadcasting Stations and Broadcasting Corporations, (3) The Broadcasting Commission, (4) Payment and Collection of the Television Reception Fee, (5) Matters to Be Observed by the Broadcasting Stations, and (6) Remedy for Infringement.

In the article on the definition of terms, "broadcast" is defined as a transmission of wireless communication operated by a broadcast station for the purpose of propagating to the general public news, comments, and public opinion on politics, economy, society, culture, current events, education, music, entertainment, and so on. Accordingly, cable television is not subject to this act.

Article 3 of the act states that (1) the freedom of broadcast programming shall be guaranteed, and (2) no person shall regulate or interfere with the programming or operation of a broadcasting station without complying with the conditions as prescribed by this act or other acts.

Regarding the operation of broadcasting stations, it is prescribed that no person may hold stocks or quotas of the same broadcasting corporation, including stocks or quotas held by a person having a special relation, in excess of one-third of the total stocks or quotas.

No broadcasting corporation may concurrently operate any daily newspaper or communication enterprise under the control of the Registration of Periodicals. Inflow of foreign capital is also prohibited. That is, no broadcasting corporation shall receive any financial contribution on the pretext of donation, patronage, or other form of foreign government or organization, except a contribution from a foreign organization having an objective of education, physical training, religion, charity, or other international friendship that is approved by the Minister of Information.

Any person who has a television set in order to receive a television broadcast shall register the television set and pay the reception fee of 2,500 won (about U.S.$3) a month. Black-and-white television sets are not subject to the reception fee.

An Overview of Television Programming in Korea

Currently, the four networks (KBS-1TV, KBS-2TV, MBC-TV, and SBS-TV) offer four hours of daytime broadcasting beginning at 6:00 A.M., then resume broadcasting from 5:30 P.M. to midnight. There is no broadcasting between 10:00 A.M. and 5:30 P.M. on weekdays. However, the four networks operate an additional 7.5 hours on Saturday and Sunday.

A typical programming schedule for Korean television networks begins at 6:00 A.M. with either a "brief news report" or a "foreign-language lesson" (English or Japanese). Early morning programs offer daily news, information, and cultural/educational programs. Each network begins its evening schedule at 5:30 P.M. with an afternoon news brief, followed by a time slot reserved for network children's programming. After this, another news brief at 7:00 P.M. introduces prime time. The four networks fill the next three hours with programs ostensibly suitable for family viewing, including dramas, game shows, soap operas, variety shows, newsmagazines, situation comedies, occasional sports, and specials. Traditionally, networks also broadcast 40 to 50 minutes of "Nine O'clock News" during prime time. This news broadcast attracts many viewers and produces extremely high ratings. Over the course of the evening, each network also provides brief reports and sports news. Late-evening hours are usually devoted to imported programs, dramas, movies, and talk shows. Weekend programming is similar to weekday programming except that it is designed to attract specific types of viewers who are demographically desirable to advertisers.

In its early years, Korean television networks depended heavily on foreign imports, most from the United States, for their programming. Overall, imported programs averaged approximately one-third of the total programming hours in 1969. In 1983, 16 percent of programming originated outside the country. By 1987, imported programming had decreased to 10 percent, though in March 1987 the networks did still broadcast programs such as *Love Boat, Hawaii 5-0, Mission Impossible,* "Weekend American Movies," and cartoons.

In addition to watching imported television programs on Korean television networks, many Koreans also watch AFKN-TV, which is an affiliate of the American Forces Radio and Television Service, the second largest of five networks managed by the Army Broadcasting Service. AFKN has been broadcasting for 39 years as an information and entertainment medium for 60,000 U.S. military personnel, civilian employees, and dependents. AFKN-TV also plays a significant role for many young Koreans. No one is quite sure of the size of the Korean "shadow audience" for AFKN-TV. However, it is watched by so many ordinary people that all Korean newspapers and most television guides carry AFKN-TV along with Korean program schedules.

Research by Drs. Won-Yong Kim and Jong-keun Kang has mapped the "cultural outlook" of Korean television. Their sample includes all prime-time dramatic programming on three Korean television networks aired during 1990. It demonstrates that the world of Korean prime-time television significantly underrepresents children and adolescents. It grossly overrepresents adult groups, however—those who are between the ages of 20 and 39, who constitute one-third of the Korean population, make up 56.7 percent of the fictional population. In sum, age distribution in the world of Korean television is bell shaped as compared to the diagonal line of the Korean population.

Another significant difference between Korean prime-time drama and reality is that farmers and fishermen, who constitute 25 percent of the population, make up only 7.4 percent of television characters. Social class distribution among characters reveals that nearly half of all television characters appear in the "lower" part of a three-way classification.

With regard to violence, among 49 characters who are involved in violence, 44.9 percent commit violence, and 55.1 percent suffer it. Among them, mostly adult groups of both sexes are involved with violence. Children and adolescents of both sexes are never involved in violence, and young female adults are the most frequent victims in all age-groups.

Although these findings show somewhat different patterns between Korea and other countries, they are not strictly comparable with each other because of the differences among their media systems.

The Korean Television Audience

According to Media Service Korea, each household in Seoul has an average of 1.6 television sets. A poll conducted by KBS shows that Korean television viewers watch an average of a little over three hours on weekdays, 4.5 hours on Saturday, and about 5.5 hours on Sunday. When broken down by demographic information, men watch more television than women. On weekends, there were no differences in television viewing among age-groups.

In terms of ratings, the most popular time slot is between the hours of 9:00 P.M. and 10:00 P.M., and the highest-rated program is the 9:00 P.M. evening news. Approximately 70 percent of the adult audience watches the news program every night. The second-highest-rated time slot is between the hours of 7:00 A.M. and 8:00 A.M. The average ratings are 31 points on weekdays and 20 points on weekends.

Korean adults frequently watch news and comedy programs, while teenagers watch comedy programs more frequently, and people in the 30-to-50 age-group watch the news more. Men tend to watch more sports, but women tend to watch soap operas and movies.

In terms of information provided by audiences with reference to their stated uses and gratifications, the motive for watching television is most often described as intentions: "to get information" and "to understand other opinions and ways of life," "to get education and knowledge," and "to relax." Another study done by the KBS Broadcasting Culture Center indicates that many viewers considered watching television as a news-providing function. Others thought of it as a "craving for refreshment," a "social relation function," or "identification." The motives for watching television news are cited variously as a way to "get information from around the world," a practice done "out of habit" or with the intent "to listen to expert opinions and commentary." For soap operas, the stated reasons for viewing include "because they are interesting," "to kill time," and for some "they seem useful." People watch comedy "to alleviate stress" and "to have fun."

Television ratings and audience viewing information is studied by most broadcasting companies as well as research firms, and in Korea ratings have been measured by diary and people meter. Currently, a people meter is generally used for gathering ratings, and Media Service Korea is engaged in the business of providing the people meter ratings.

WON-YONG KIM

Further Reading

Chang, Won-Ho, *Mass Communication and Korea: Toward a Global Perspective for Research,* Seoul: Nanam Publishing House, 1990

Kang, Jong-Geun, "Cultural Indicators: The Korean Cultural Outlook Profile," Ph.D. diss., University of Massachusetts, 1988

Kang, Jong-Guen, and Michael Morgan, "Cultural Clash: U.S. Television Programs in Korea," *Journalism Quarterly* 65 (1988)

Kim, Kyu, Won-Yong Kim, and Jong-Geun Kang, *Broadcasting in Korea,* Seoul: Nanam Publishing House, 1994

Lee, Jae Won, "Korea," in *World Press Encyclopedia,* edited by M.B. Bank and J. Johnson, New York: Facts on File, 1982

South Park

U.S. Animated Program

Few television programs emerged from the margins of the television industry to mainstream impact as quickly and forcefully as *South Park.* From an animated college short film to cable's top-rated program and an award-winning feature film, Trey Parker and Matt Stone's aggressively vulgar and satirical cartoon helped establish Comedy Central's credibility and push the adult animation cycle of the 1990s forward. *South Park* took the critical tone of *The Simpsons* and *Beavis and Butt-Head* and made the satire more extreme, tackling issues from hate speech to euthanasia, as well as plumbing the depths of bad taste from anal probes to pornography, all in a cartoon about eight-year-olds in a "quiet little" Colorado town.

Parker and Stone met as film majors at the University of Colorado at Boulder, creating short films with a crude comedic sensibility. One of their shorts, "Jesus vs. Frosty," used rudimentary construction paper cutout animation techniques to introduce a quartet of eight-year-olds who profanely narrated a battle between holiday icons. Their films caught the eye of a FOX executive, Brian Graden, who paid the pair

$2,000 to create a video Christmas card with a similar sensibility. "The Spirit of Xmas," which featured a boorish battle for holiday supremacy between Jesus and Santa, eventually arbitrated by skater Brian Boitano, became a Hollywood sensation in 1995, circulating widely among producers and stars and eventually becoming one of the first videos to gain wide distribution on the Internet. Comedy Central capitalized on the underground popularity, contracting Stone and Parker to create an animated series based on the kids featured in both short films.

South Park debuted on Comedy Central in the summer of 1997 to much notoriety, cultural disdain, and instant popularity among the channel's young male audience. The series focused on the lives of nervous everyboy Stan, skeptical Jew Kyle, episodically killed Kenny, and the overweight, rude comedic centerpiece Cartman, with an ever-expanding host of supporting characters constituting the community of South Park, Colorado. While following the basic structure of a family sitcom, complete with episode-ending moral messages about what was learned each week, the show

South Park, Kenny, Cartman, Kyle, and Stan.
Courtesy of the Everett Collection

offered topical explorations into current events and social issues. Parker and Stone used computer techniques to imitate their construction paper aesthetic, embracing the flexibility of the technology to alter their animated sequences hours before airing programs, referring to their process as "virtually live animation." Viewers quickly made *South Park* Comedy Central's flagship program and the top-rated cable program of the late 1990s, recognizing that between the lowbrow references to "talking poo" and Chef's "salty chocolate balls" resided some of the most clever and sophisticated satire of its era.

Certainly *South Park* could have never come to air without the dual predecessors of *The Simpsons* and *Beavis and Butt-Head.* Like these two forebearers, *South Park*'s arrival provoked fears concerning its potential influences on children. Even though Comedy Central scheduled the show after 10:00 P.M. and prefaced every episode with a disclaimer stating, "The Following Program Contains Coarse Language and Due to Its Content It Should Not Be Viewed by Anyone," the assumption that all animation must be for kids led to condemnation from a host of critics. Additionally, the profane dialogue and cynicism coming out

of the mouths of elementary schoolers struck many as the nadir of televisual bad taste. This critique was intensified by the successful merchandizing of the characters, with T-shirts and toys that many felt were catering to children. Comedy Central realized that the negative publicity was drawing audiences to its taboo-busting program, especially among its core niche of young men, and thus supported and even highlighted the profane content and satire to maintain viewership.

Parker and Stone responded to anti–*South Park* critiques within the program itself, creating their own taboo media sensation, *The Terrance and Phillip Show.* The boys' favorite television program is a never-ending succession of poorly animated fart jokes, paralleling some critics' perspective on *South Park* itself. Adults within *South Park* condemn *Terrance and Phillip,* protesting the show's negative effects and profane sensibility to the fictitious Cartoon Channel. They extended this reflexivity to the feature film hit *South Park: Bigger, Longer and Uncut* in 1999; the highly profane film focused on the corrupting influence of *Terrance and Phillip*'s feature film, inspiring extreme vulgarity in the impressionable minds of South Park's youth, and resulting in a backlash that leads to U.S.

war with Canada and an attempted Armageddon led by Satan and his gay lover, Saddam Hussein. While certainly outrageous in every taboo-busting possibility, the film was hailed by many as one of the finest musicals and social satires in years.

South Park has declined in notoriety and ratings but remains a consistent presence, having reached 100 episodes in 2003 and rolled out deluxe DVD editions of early seasons. The show has cemented Comedy Central's brand identity as the destination spot for a mixture of crude and sophisticated humor aimed at young men, carried forward in varying degrees of success by programs such as *The Man Show, Crank Yankers, Insomniac with Dave Attell,* and *The Daily Show with Jon Stewart. South Park*'s role as the contemporary standard bearer for over-the-top social

satire on television was reinforced in 2003, when television pioneer Norman Lear joined the program as a creative consultant, endorsing Parker and Stone's brand of humor as the direct descendant of Lear's groundbreaking 1970s comedy.

JASON MITTELL

See also **Comedy Central**

Further Reading

Neuwirth, Allan, *Makin' Toons: Inside the Most Popular Animated TV Shows and Movies,* New York: Allworth Press, 2003
Stabile, Carol, and Mark Harrison, editors, *Prime Time Animation: Television Animation and American Culture,* London: Routledge, 2003

Southeast Asia

The precise geocultural borders of "Southeast" Asia may well be contestable. But in most accounts it includes the island-state of Singapore; the archipelagic nations of the Philippines and Indonesia; Brunei, which occupies a tiny corner of the island of Borneo (most of this island is part of Indonesia or Malaysia); and the mainland Asian countries of Burma (officially renamed Myanmar by its military rulers in 1989), Thailand, Malaysia, Laos, Cambodia, and Vietnam. Bordered by the India in the west and China in the northeast, this region was often portrayed by historians as a melting pot of Chinese and Indian cultural influences. Colonized by the British, the French, and the Spanish and later by Americans, the independent nations of Southeast Asia came into being through the middle of the 20th century.

In recent years, the Association of Southeast Asian Nations (which consists now of all the previously mentioned countries) has given a certain political currency to the idea of Southeast Asia. As with religion, and so with political and economic systems, Southeast Asia contains a great variety. Broadly speaking, the Philippines and Thailand could be described as unstable capitalist democracies, Singapore and Malaysia as authoritarian governments with open markets, Burma as a military dictatorship, Indonesia as beginning a transition to democracy after a long period of military rule, Laos and Vietnam as socialist states, and Cambodia as "democratizing" and Brunei,

the smallest state in Southeast Asia, as a constitutional monarchy.

Television was established in the region with technology and, often, funding from the United Kingdom, the United States, and Japan but has been implicated in the discourse of national identity of most of these nations. Beyond that, like their political histories, there is a great deal of diversity in the television industries of these nation-states.

History

Thailand and the Philippines were the first nations in Southeast Asia to introduce television in the early 1950s. In Thailand, as in the rest of Southeast Asia, television was initially state owned and closely connected with the older state-owned public broadcast radio. Modeled on U.S. television and like the privately owned radio stations, television in the Philippines was established with private capital. Burma was the last of the Southeast Asian nations to get television. Its first station, government owned and Japanese funded, opened in 1980.

In the Philippines, Santo Tomas University started experimental television broadcasts in 1950. In 1953, DZAQ-TV, established by the brother of then President Elpidio Quirino, started daily four-hour broadcasts. By the early 1960s (when Malaysia, Singapore, and Indonesia were just beginning television broadcast), there were six television stations in Manila, five of them owned by powerful political families that also had substantial interests in radio and print media. By the mid-1960s, there were 16 television stations and an estimated peak audience of over 1 million in and around Manila. The first regional stations started in 1968, in Cebu, Bacalod, and Dagupan, owned by the Chronicle Broadcasting Network (CBN), which already owned a television station in Manila and several major radio stations and newspapers.

No other Southeast Asian nation had privately owned television stations at this stage. In contrast to this flourishing industry, public broadcasting in the Philippines has a sad history. The Department of Public Information established the Public Broadcasting Service in 1962, but it lasted for only about a year before its facilities were handed over to a private operator.

In 1972, President Marcos declared martial law, and all media, including television, came under strict control of the government—thus, for the first time, bringing Philippines television in line with state-controlled television in the rest of the region. Marcos's rivals, such as the Lopez family, which through CBN has huge interests in the broadcast media, were forced to divest their interests in the industry. Five television stations operated during the Marcos era (1972–86) and were owned by Marcos cronies—a pattern not dissimilar to privatized television in Suharto's "New Order" regime in Indonesia in the late 1980s.

In Thailand, the establishment of television is even more directly caught up in the political conflict. Marshal Phibul Songkram became prime minister in 1948 after a military coup against the elected government. Both during his first period of rule (1938–44) and again in 1948–57, Phibul severely restricted the freedom of the press and used the radio quite deliberately to bolster his personal image. In the midst of political turbulence, the state-owned television was established in 1955 with the help of the United States. The Broadcast Law of 1955 authorized the state as the only lawful owner of radio and television broadcast facilities. The military started its own channel soon after and used it in part to destabilize the Phibul government. Both of these stations, though owned by sections of the government and deeply politicized in their content, were funded through advertising revenue.

By the end of the 1980s, there were five commercial channels whose ownership varied according to the role that the military was playing in politics at any particular time. After the military coup of 1991, all five were taken over by the military.

Television broadcast started in Indonesia in 1962 and in the following year in neighboring Malaysia and Singapore. In all three, television was fully government owned and controlled and remained so until the 1980s. Through most of that period, state television's agenda was overtly that of nation building and supporting the authoritarian governments of these countries.

In Indonesia, Televisi Republik Indonesia (TVRI) started broadcasting somewhat hastily in August 1962 in order to coincide with the start of the Asian Games in the capital, Jakarta. In 1965, the "Guided Democracy" of President Sukarno was overthrown by General Suharto, whose "New Order" remained in government until 1997.

It was not until the 1970s that television started to grow rapidly in terms of quantity of programming and audience reach. TVRI began to establish regional stations around the country whose main function was relaying programs from the organization's headquarters in Jakarta. In 1976, Indonesia became the first nation in Southeast Asia (and the fourth in the world) to launch its own satellite, *Palapa,* followed in 1983 by the much more powerful *Palapa Generation B.*

The television system that emerged in the shadow of the satellite was highly centralized, with very small amounts of regional programming in most areas. Even with the powerful satellite and with dozens of stations (some of these relay stations only), TVRI by its own estimates reached only about 35 percent of the far-flung archipelago and about 65 percent of the population. In 1986, in the hope of improving this reach, the government legalized the use of parabola antennae (whose spread it had in any case been unable to control). By the end of the 1980s, several foreign public and commercial broadcasters (including major global operators National Broadcasting Company [NBC], Star, and Cable News Network [CNN]) were also broadcasting via *Palapa* and therefore available through much of Indonesia via small and affordable parabola antennae. By some accounts, Indonesia had the fastest take-up of these antennae in Asia. By the mid-1980s, in Java and Sumatra, where the majority of the Indonesian population live, households connected to these (sometime several hundred households sharing one antennae) could pick up between 6 and 20 foreign broadcasts.

In 1963, while Malaysia and Singapore were still part of the Malaysian Federation, state-owned television was established, modeled in part on the British public service broadcaster. In neither case, however, would the national broadcaster gain the kind of autonomy from the government that the British Broadcasting Corporation (BBC) has had. In Indonesia, as in Malaysia and Singapore, television developed in the shadow of political turmoil (in Indonesia's case, a military coup and the massacre of hundreds of thousands of suspected Communists) and the anxiety of governments to protect themselves against opposition on the one hand and to protect the relatively new nation-states from fracturing along ethnic lines on the other.

In Malaysia, a second national network was started in 1969. In 1970, a satellite communication Earth Station was built, giving Malaysia vastly expanded capacity for live telecasts of international events. In Singapore, two channels were introduced at the same time, Channel 5 with Malay- and English-language programming and Channel 8 with Mandarin and Tamil programming.

While the Malaysian and Singapore broadcasts started about a year after the Indonesian one, television clearly grew much faster in these two countries than it did in Indonesia. However, through much of the 1970s, Indonesia was much less dependent on imported television programming than Malaysia or Singapore or indeed the much older television industries of the Philippines and Thailand. From around 1980, Singapore started producing more local programming, a trend that continued strongly into the 1990s.

While television in the countries discussed so far had varied degrees of state involvement, even state-owned television was from the very beginning dependent on advertising for its revenue, although Indonesia experimented briefly and unsuccessfully with fully state-funded television in the 1980s. Advertising revenue made state-monopoly television reasonably profitable in Indonesia, Malaysia, and especially Singapore, where television density quickly reached 100 percent of households. The economy grew rapidly, and every resident in the small island could be reached from a single station in the city-state.

The tiny nation-state of Brunei, between Malaysia and Indonesia, was the only nation in Southeast Asia that had television (1975) before it got independence from its colonial ruler, Great Britain, in 1984. The princely protectorate of Brunei started television with massive state funding in 1975. While one of the last nations in this part of Southeast Asia to have its own television, it used state-of-the-art color technology from the start, making it the first Southeast Asian national broadcaster to use full color. Set up with large-scale input from the BBC and generously funded by an oil-rich government, Brunei television has maintained it technological edge.

Citizens of Brunei had been tuning into Malaysian television since the late 1960s, and by 1973 there were already 3,000 television sets, a substantial number in a population of under half a million. It has been suggested that the reason for setting up national television was in part to counter what the government saw as the increasing influence of Malaysian television, particu-

larly significant in a nation that had no daily newspaper and that depended on broadcast for its political communication. While Malaysian television continues to saturate Brunei and while Brunei television content has been and remains dominated by imports, it also plays a highly significant role in government campaigns of various kinds and in the national political life of the country more generally.

Of the formerly British colonized countries of Southeast Asia, Burma was the last to get television. Controlled by a military regime since 1962, the nation became increasingly isolationist through the following decades. In 1980, the Burmese government, with Japanese aid, started television broadcasting in the capital, Rangoon, and surrounding areas. The reach of the broadcaster was expanded rapidly through a network of relay stations. Unlike other latecomers to television in the region, Brunei some years earlier, and Laos in 1983, Burma did not opt for color transmission and continues to broadcast in black and white. A second station, controlled by the Ministry of Defense, started in the 1990s. Both stations are dedicated to promoting government policy, though both carry popular music and traditional Burmese drama.

In the much more politically volatile parts of Southeast Asia, what in the colonial period was called French Indochina, Cambodia was the first to have television, which was established in 1966. There are similarities in the coming of television to Cambodia and Indonesia in that in both countries its establishment had much to do with the egos of authoritarian rulers: President Sukarno, the first president of independent Indonesia, and Norodom Sihanouk, the first king of independent Cambodia, who refused allow free elections or be bound by restrictions of a constitutional monarchy. Sihanouk was overthrown by Marshall Lon Nol in 1970 and was then replaced in 1975 by the mass-murdering Khmer Rouge regime of Pol Pot.

Cambodian state television broadcast for about four hours a day in its early years, and during the Lon Nol years this was made up largely of newsreels and documentaries donated by foreign missions. Pol Pot used radio for propaganda purposes, but infrastructure and human resources related to television were completely destroyed along with the educational, technological, and cultural infrastructure more generally.

In 1979, a Vietnamese-backed regime replaced the Khmer Rouge. While the new Cambodian government was in control of capital Phnom Penh, a civil war continued that formally ended only in 1991. Radio-Television Cambodia (RTC) was reestablished in 1983 and revived television broadcasts of a few hours a day three days a week. The broadcast hours were increased over the next few years, and by 1986 Cambodians in and around the capital could watch their national television every day, for about four to five hours. A few years later, Cambodia's first provincial station was opened. Both stations operated with minimal funding and old, low-quality production and broadcast technology.

In Vietnam, the establishment of television was part of the war effort for both the Americans and the North Vietnamese. The U.S. government committed itself to expanding radio and television into every remote corner of Vietnam in the conviction that this would be a decisive factor in nation building in South Vietnam. In February 1966, two channels were created, broadcasting from Saigon, one assigned to the government of South Vietnam (referred to in some documents as THVN) and the other to the American armed forces (AFVN). Like the radio stations, the television facilities became targets of repeated attack by the North Vietnamese forces.

In contemporary Vietnamese official history, the birth of television in Vietnam is associated with an experimental black-and-white television program on September 7, 1970, in Hanoi. A decision to establish a Television Film Studio under the General Information Department had been taken in 1968. In 1971, the studio was annexed to the Television Department as the backbone and a nucleus for the eventual development of national television. On both sides of divided Vietnam, television was established for political purposes by governments and in unified Vietnam remained under strict state control.

Laos, with a modern history almost as traumatic as Cambodia's, began its national television about the same time as RTC was being revived in the early 1980s. After decades of civil war, the U.S.-backed regime collapsed in 1975, and the Lao People's Democratic Republic was established under the Lao People's Revolutionary Party, committed to Socialism. In 1982, an earth satellite station was set up with Soviet aid for the purpose of receiving broadcasts from Moscow. The following year, again with the help of the Soviet bloc, Lao National Television started broadcasting from the capital, Vientiane. Like Brunei, Laos bypassed black-and-white television and went straight to color broadcasting. Unlike Brunei, however, Lao television was poorly resourced, and in a nation with mountainous terrain, high levels of poverty, and an undependable supply of electricity, it reached only a small section of the population in its early years and broadcast for only two or three hours a day.

Satellites, Global Television, and Privatization

As indicated previously, with the exception of the Philippines, television developed in much of Southeast Asia not only under the aegis of governments but also with a clear focus on nation building. By the mid-1980s, increasingly accessible new media technologies, particularly digitization and satellite broadcast, began to challenge the capacity of governments to police both the televisual national borders and individual citizens' consumption of audiovisual material. Videocassettes since the early 1980s and, later, VC-Ds and DVDs, easily smuggled in, broke the monopoly of governments over audiovisual entertainment. By the mid-1980s, communication satellites were broadcasting Western television programs across the world. In Southeast Asian cities and towns, increasingly cheaply available parabola antennae began to change the television landscape of most nations. The 1980s to mid-1990s was also a period of rapid economic growth, with the consequent rise in the number of television households throughout the region. Most of these nations have a variety of legal and illegal pay television, mostly under private ownership. However, viewers of pay television still constitute a very small part of the total audience in the region.

While the majority of governments in the region still ban the use of parabola antennae for private households to get global broadcasts, these are legal in Indonesia, the Philippines, and Thailand. However, the job of policing these bans is very difficult, and most of the governments, apart from Burma, have sought other ways of simultaneously accommodating and competing with overseas programming by diversifying their own program offerings and in some cases increasing the amount of imported material in their own broadcasts.

A new move toward privatization of television in the region started with the establishment of TV3 in Malaysia in 1983. However, TV3, as well as two newer private channels that started in 1995 and 1997, respectively, are all owned by companies with close links to senior members of the government. Singapore has also made some gestures toward loosening the grip of the state on television. But by most accounts, the corporatization of the state broadcaster has not made the system any more democratic or open. More than in any other part of Southeast Asia, the audience in Malaysia and Singapore appears to be segmented along ethnic lines, with particular stations concentrating on broadcasts in particular languages.

The most dramatic transformation to occur in the national television scene has been in Indonesia since the late 1980s. The first Indonesian private channel started in 1987. Four more started in the next five years, all with the capacity to broadcast nationally via the *Palapa* satellite. Four of the five private stations were owned by relatives and cronies of President

Suharto. Since the fall of the Suharto government, five more stations have started broadcasting. The private stations have decimated the audience of TVRI in the cities. At the turn of the century, political transformation generally and shifts in ownership of private stations in part as a consequence of the political change have made Indonesia, along with the Philippines, the most diverse and free television system in Southeast Asia.

In Thailand, all six of the terrestrial free-to-air networks remain state owned, though five are funded on a commercial basis, and the two most popular stations have been run by private companies since the early 1990s.

In the rest of Southeast Asia, television remains under government control, though all nations now have additional services for capital cities, and most have some regional stations capable of production and broadcasting. Burma is the only nation that has persisted with black-and-white television. It also broadcasts fewer imported programs than any of the other broadcasters and appears to be the most successful in limiting illegal parabolic antennae.

Vietnam had the most dramatic growth in television in the region in the last decade of the 20th century. It has three national networks, five regional networks, and one local station, which broadcasts in the Khmer language. All are state owned. According to VTV's own figures, television ownership is at 1 set per 11 persons. However, some 20 percent of the population lives in areas not reached by any television signal. The government is therefore planning to move toward digital television and satellite and cable delivery in a bid to further expand coverage.

Conclusion

Brunei (with 575 sets per 1,000) has the highest per capita television ownership in Southeast Asia and indeed one of the highest in the world; Burma (with 7.5 per 1,000) has the lowest in the region. In the region as a whole, however, television is the most significant medium of entertainment. While print and, more recently, the Internet are more important as news media in a region where illiteracy is a problem in a number of countries, television is likely to remain politically significant for some time to come.

While many of the nations in the region are persisting with some form of government control (however modified), states have effectively lost the monopoly they had up until the 1980s over the audiovisual consumption of their citizens. On the other hand, the nationalist panic over global television's colonization of Asia (exemplified by Star TV's aggressive move into China and India) has not come to fruition. Given the simultaneously globalizing and localizing capacity of television and digital technologies coming into the market, it is difficult to predict the direction of television in the region. As with the history of television in the region, its future, despite globalization of the media, is likely to be nationally specific.

KRISHNA SEN

Further Reading

Birch, D., *Singapore Media: Communication Strategies and Practices,* Melbourne: Longman Cheshire, 1993

Goonasekera, A., and D. Holaday, *Asian Communication Handbook,* Singapore: AMIC, 1998

Hukill, M., "Structures of Television in Singapore," in *Contemporary Television: Eastern Perspectives,* edited by D. French and N. Richards, London: Sage, 1996

Johnston, D., *Encyclopedia of International Media and Communications,* London: Academic Press, 2003

Kitley, P., *Television, Nation and Culture in Indonesia,* Athens: Ohio University Research in International Studies, 2002

Kokkeong, W., *Political Economy of Media and Culture in Peripheral Singapore: A Theory of Controlled Commodification.* Ann Arbor, Michigan: UMI Dissertation Services, 1991

Lent, J.A., *Broadcasting in Asia and the Pacific,* Hong Kong: Heinemann Asia, 1982

Loangdouangchanh, B., "Lao Mass Media in a Time of Reform," thesis, Curtin University, Perth, Australia, 2001

Marr, D., editor, *The Mass Media in Vietnam,* Canberra: Australian National University, 1998

McDaniel, D., *Broadcasting in the Malay World: Radio, Television, and Video in Brunei, Indonesia, Malaysia and Singapore,* Norwood, New Jersey: Ablex, 1994

Muntabhorn, V., *Mass Media Laws and Regulations in Thailand,* Singapore: AMIC, 1998

Sen, K., and D. Hill, *Media, Culture and Politics in Indonesia,* Melbourne: Oxford University Press, 2000

Styles, P., *Southeast Asian Television Study: Volume 6 Thailand,* North Sydney: Australian Film Commission, 1994

Styles, P., *Southeast Asian Television Study: Volume 7 Multi-Region,* North Sydney: Australian Film Commission, 1994

Venkateswaran, K.S., *Media Monitors in Asia,* Singapore: AMIC, 1996

Zahrom, N., "The Impact of the International Marketplace on the Organisation of Malaysian Television."

Space Program and Television

While the space program and the television industry contributed mightily to each other's growth, by the year 2000 their love affair had drawn to a close. In the 1960s, the first decade of space missions matched Hollywood productions for drama and suspense and pulled in some of the medium's largest audiences. America's first astronauts were among television's first celebrity heroes. Some television journalists, such as Walter Cronkite and the American Broadcasting Company's (ABC's) Jules Bergman (1930–87), became famous for chronicling the space program.

The Soviet Union's *Sputnik* satellite launch in 1957 was one of the earliest big stories for television news, then growing rapidly in popularity and influence. With the framing of the *Sputnik* story as an affront to American superiority and a military threat, the U.S. government justified a strong response: a program to beat the Soviets to space. Unfortunately, several of the earliest uncrewed U.S. test rockets crashed, further heightening the crisis atmosphere as each major attempt was anxiously reported on the 15-minute national evening newscasts.

Eventually, American satellites were launched successfully, and in 1959 seven military pilots were chosen for the astronaut corps. Television, egged on by the print press, elevated the astronauts to hero status, as celebrated as Hollywood's leading stars. Publicists from the National Aeronautics and Space Administration (NASA), the new civilian space agency, worked to fuel that perception. They schooled the seven in on-camera behavior and prohibited military uniforms, to the astronaut's discomfort but to the benefit of the program's all-civilian image.

Immediately after the flight of Alan Shepard in May 1961 (following the flight of Soviet cosmonaut Gagarin), Vice President Lyndon Johnson, with the heads of the NASA and the Defense Department, sent a report to President John F. Kennedy justifying the eventual $40 billion investment in a moon-landing program. From its inception, the crewed space program had at its core a propaganda objective: an American capture of the world's imagination. With Johnson's report as ammunition and the political goal of justifying massive government projects and fulfilling his vision of a "New Frontier," Kennedy went before Congress to challenge the nation to land a man on the moon before 1970.

The remaining five Mercury space flights (1961–63) and ten Gemini flights (1965–66) were covered virtually from launch to splashdown by adoring TV networks. Each mission promised new accomplishments, such as Ed White's first American spacewalk. For television news, it was a welcome reprieve from the 1960's morass of assassination, war, and inner-city unrest. However, by 1965 it was apparent to experts that the Soviets had no hope of putting someone on the moon, a fact that rarely entered the "space race" discourse, for this race was a boon to American industry.

The ideal marriage of space and television was not merely the result of political and ideological agendas or of technical and logistical circumstance but of more resonant connections between the program and American cultural mythology. The space program was a Puritan narrative, with its crew-cut NASA technocrats tirelessly striving toward the moon (ironically, many of these were recruits from defunct aerospace programs in Germany, Canada, and other nations), and a western narrative, with lone heroes conquering a formidable new frontier (from mostly western U.S. facilities). And as the parallel narrative to the Vietnam War, it offered an image of a reassuringly benign yet powerful government while simultaneously reinforcing Cold War fears in demonstrating the awesome power of rockets.

In 1967, three astronauts died in an early Apollo program test. The theme of astronaut as hero was tragically revived, and the public was reminded of the risks of conquering space. But the first of the Apollo flights (1968–72) were enormously successful, including the Christmas 1968 first lunar orbits by *Apollo 8*. The astronaut's reading from the Book of Genesis while in lunar orbit made for stirring television. In July 1969, the space-television narrative reached its climax, as the networks went on the air nearly full time to report the mission of *Apollo 11,* the first lunar landing; 528 million people around the world (but not in the Soviet Union) marveled at *Apollo 11* on television.

As with other Apollo missions providing TV coverage from the spacecraft, informal visits with the astronauts were highly scripted and made use of cue cards. Second moon walker Edwin Aldrin suggested that the United States Information Agency scripted *Apollo 8*'s Bible reading and Neil Armstrong's first words from the lunar surface. Whether Armstrong said "That's one small step for man" or whether he said "a man," as he intended (with the article "a" lost to static), has never been resolved. The blurry black-and-white images of

Armstrong jumping onto the lunar surface and the short surface explorations by Armstrong and Aldrin are widely regarded as television's first and perhaps greatest example of unifying a massive worldwide audience in common wonder and hope.

After the *Apollo 11* television spectacular, coverage of the following moon missions became increasingly brief and critical. Under considerable pressure to begin cutting back, NASA eliminated the last three planned Apollo missions, terminating the program with *Apollo 17* in 1972. NASA actually paid the networks to cover the last Apollo mission (NASA official Chris Kraft, Jr., quoted in Hurt, p. 282). Coverage was spectacular nonetheless, from the nail-biting return of the explosion-crippled *Apollo 13* spacecraft to the lengthy moonwalks and moon buggy rides of the last Apollos, covered live with color cameras. Such a part of American culture was NASA of the 1960s that it routinely provided technical assistance and advice to Hollywood, as with the many permutations of *Star Trek,* or provided entire series storylines, as with *I Dream of Jeanie.* Footage from NASA's massive film library appears in all manner of productions. British News company ITN (Independent Television News) operates the largest television news archive in the world and reports that *Apollo 11* moonwalk footage is the company's most-requested item.

Television coverage of the long-duration Skylab missions (1973–74) provided entertaining images of astronaut antics in weightlessness but was overshadowed by the Watergate hearings. Watergate signaled an end of the trust of government and hero worship characterizing the 1960s space program. NASA could no longer sell its heroes and expensive programs to the public. The heroism of ex-astronauts was often dismantled by the same media that had constructed it, as astronauts were exposed for shady business deals or personal dysfunction, criticized for making commercials, or doubted in new corporate and political roles.

Interest in space exploration was occasionally revived in the 1970s by spectacular accomplishments. In 1976, Americans watched live pictures of the Martian surface during the Viking landing, a visual thrill rivaling coverage of *Apollo 11.* In subsequent years, the Voyager and Pioneer spacecraft had close encounters with the outer planets of the solar system, sending back dazzling images, but at the time of this writing, *Voyager One* is leaving the solar system amid little fanfare. Television coverage of space outside of regular newscasts has become minimal.

Between the last Skylab mission and the first space shuttle orbital mission in 1981, the only crewed American space flight was Apollo-Soyuz in 1975, a public relations stunt intended as a tangible demonstration of

détente with the Soviet Union. The orbital linkup of three astronauts with two cosmonauts was entertaining if unimpressive by lunar mission. The mission was highly scripted and choreographed for a potential international television audience of a half billion. This was the first space mission broadcast live on television in the Soviet Union.

The first space shuttle test landings over California were covered live, with NASA providing remarkable pictures from chase planes as Enterprise (named after pressure from *Star Trek* fans) separated from its Boeing 747 mother plane and glided to Earth. Coverage of the long-delayed first shuttle space flight in 1981 was as abundant as in 1960s missions and occasionally reminiscent of 1960s coverage for its Cold War rhetoric—including the breathless reporting of a Soviet spy ship lurking off the coast as the shuttle Columbia returned from orbit.

Coverage of the space shuttle rapidly diminished, and live coverage of missions had ended long before the 25th shuttle mission on January 28, 1986. On that day, the shuttle *Challenger,* with a crew of seven including teacher and media darling Christine McAuliffe, exploded after liftoff. As President Ronald Reagan would speculate and the media would faithfully repeat, television became America's "electronic hearth," a common gathering place to seek understanding and solace. Television was unprepared for such a tragedy, with speechless anchors, an unfortunate tendency to repeat the videotape of the explosion constantly, and irresponsible speculation about the possibility of survivors. But as shared national tragedy, it was an event like none other.

Thanks in part to television, the history of the American space program and its role in American life has never been completely written. Television presented fleeting spectacles, devoid of analysis, perspective, and retrospective. Given that the United States has generally approached the space program as a television spectacle, there was initially little demand for a deeper analysis of space exploration. It has only been since the 1970s that writers and scholars have attempted to specify the place of the space program in American culture. While television may have obscured this issue, it presented such unforgettable images that few people who witnessed *Apollo 11, Viking,* or *Challenger* on television could forget it. In the new millennium, after over 100 shuttle mission and the full-time habitation of the International Space Station, the space program had become seemingly too ordinary for extensive television coverage.

In 2003, the second space shuttle tragedy proved as much. As the shuttle *Columbia* disintegrated over Texas, killing its crew of seven, initial television news coverage was intense. It quickly dropped off, however, and coverage of the investigation and aftermath of the accident was slight, as a new generation of Americans expressed little shock or interest. NASA now finds itself the victim of its own early success. Ambitious plans developed in the 1970s at the height of NASA's popularity have trapped it in expensive programs that now have little support from the scientific community or the public. In 2001, under the Bush administration, NASA developed plans to take tourists to space and sell advertising space on the sides of its rockets and spacecraft, as space exploration and exploitation increasingly shifts from the once invincible and highly visible NASA to the mostly secret efforts of the military and private industry.

CHRIS PATERSON

Further Reading

Aldrin, Edwin, and Wayne Warga, *Return to Earth,* New York: Random House, 1973

Atwill, William, *Fire and Power: The American Space Program as Postmodern Narrative,* Athens: University of Georgia Press, 1994

Axthelm, Pete, "Where Have All the Heroes Gone?" *Newsweek* (August 6, 1979)

Carpenter, M. Scott, et al., *We Seven,* New York: Simon and Schuster, 1962

Collins, Michael, *Carrying the Fire,* New York: Ballantine, 1974

Dunn, Marcia, "NASA Venturing into New Frontier: Space Commercials, Ads, Tourists, Too?," Associated Press via Lexis Nexis, 2001

Hurt, Harry, III, *For All Mankind,* New York: Atlantic Monthly Press, 1988

Vladimirov, Leonid, *The Russian Space Bluff,* London: Tom Stacey Ltd, 1971

Wolfe, Tom, *The Right Stuff,* New York: Farrar, Straus and Giroux, 1979

Spain

Five national channels serve 80 percent of Spain's 12 million TV households. Two of these, TVE-1 and TVE-2, are state owned, financed by subsidy and advertising. Antena-3 and Telecinco are private channels financed by advertising. Canal+, a terrestrial analog service, is private and financed by subscription.

Two digital satellite services, Vía Digital and Canal Satélite Digital (CSD), both private and financed by subscription, serve 16 percent of Spanish viewers. Four percent subscribe to cable services, although nearly 25 percent of all homes are capable of receiving cable. All the main national channels were obliged by law to broadcast digital signals by April 2002 in preparation for the complete analog switch-off of Spanish TV in 2012. In 2001, only 10 percent of viewers owned digital receivers.

Eight regional channels also contribute to the Spanish television environment: TV-3 and Canal 33 (financed by advertising and subsidy of the Catalan government), Canal Sur (financed by advertising and subsidy of the Andalusian government), Telemadrid (property of the Madrid regional government, financed by advertising and bank loans), Canal 9 (financed by advertising and subsidy of the Valencian government), TVG (financed by advertising and subsidy of the Galician government), and ETB-1 and ETB-2 (financed by advertising and subsidy of the Basque government). Projects for cable television in 2000 speculated that 3 million TV households will be connected, with 1 million subscribers. Residents in all 50 provinces also have access to dozens of additional low-power, local TV channels (often joined to websites), many of which are owned by local governments and financed in part by advertising. In Barcelona, there are 53 local TV channels; in Madrid, 25; and in Valencia, 30.

In 1908, the Spanish government enacted a law that gave the central state the right to establish and exploit "all systems and apparatuses related to the so-called Hertzian telegraph, ethereal telegraph, radiotelegraph, and other similar procedures already invented or that will be invented in the future." Scattered experiments in radio-wave communication evolved into regular radio broadcasts by 1921, with such events as Radio Castilla's program of concerts from the Royal Theater of Madrid. In 1924, the first official license for radio was granted, and all experimental stations were ordered to cease broadcasting and request state authorization. The first "legal," radio broadcast began in Barcelona, and, like most radio programs that preceded the Spanish Civil War (1936–39), it was launched by private investors to make a profit. The broadcasting law of 1934 defined radio as "an essential and exclusive function of the state," and the statute was amended in 1935 to confirm that all "sounds and images already in use or to be invented in the future" would be established and exploited by the state.

The government of the Second Republic (1931–39) kept centralized control over spectrum allocation and the diffusion of costly high-power transmitters while it encouraged independent operators to install low-power transmitters for local radio. Radio spread with investments in urban zones, and only one significant private chain, the Union Radio, showed signs of economic concentration. The conditions of the Spanish Civil War halted the growth of independent radio when broadcasters were transformed into voices of military propaganda on both sides of the conflict. The leader of the fascist insurgents, Francisco Franco, ordered the nationalization of all radio stations under the direction of the new state, and the existing collection of transmitters merged into a state-controlled network called Radio Nacional de España. Use of the distinct idioms of Basque, Catalan, and Galician was outlawed, and new laws aimed at the press gave the Ministry of the Interior full power to suppress communication that "directly, or indirectly, may tend to reduce the prestige of the Nation or Regime, to obstruct the work of the government of the new State, or sow pernicious ideas among the intellectually weak."

The first public demonstration of television took place in Barcelona in 1948 as part of a promotion by the multinational communications firm Philips. Experiments continued until October 1956, when the first official TV broadcast appeared on an estimated 600 television sets in Madrid. The initial program consisted of a Mass conducted by Franco's chaplain, a speech by the minister of information and tourism commemorating the 20-year regime, and a French-language documentary. Much of the early programming came from the U.S. Embassy, but there were also live transmissions of variety and children's shows, and a news program was started in 1957. By 1958, there were approximately 30,000 TV sets in Madrid. From the beginning, Television Española (TVE) was supported by advertising, although it also received subsidies derived from a luxury tax on television receivers. In 1959, TVE reached Barcelona via terrestrial lines, and a second studio was soon installed in that city. At the end of the decade, there were 50,000 sets in use. Through Eurovision, Spanish viewers joined European viewers in an audience of some 50 million, and one of the first images they shared was the historic meeting in Madrid between Franco and U.S. President Dwight Eisenhower. By 1962, TVE claimed that its sole VHF (very high frequency) channel covered 65 percent of the Spanish territory and was viewed regularly by 1 percent of the population.

Television was a strictly urban phenomenon at this time, and there were only two production centers, one in Madrid and one in Barcelona. Transmissions originated from Madrid and were relayed in one direction to the rest of the territory. In 1964, a modern studio and office building were erected in Madrid to commemorate the 28th anniversary of the regime, and a year later, a second channel (TVE-2, UHF [ultrahigh frequency]), with production studios located in Madrid and Barcelona, began testing. In 1965, the luxury tax on television sets was eliminated, making advertising the major resource for TVE-1 and TVE-2. Estimates put yearly advertising investment in Spanish television at $1 million by the early 1960s, while airtime increased from 28 to 70 hours a week between 1958 and 1964, rising to 110 hours in 1972. Advertising income for TVE multiplied 100 times between 1961 and 1973, reaching estimated totals of over $100 million.

In the early 1970s, new regional centers were constructed in Bilbao, Oviedo (Asturias), Santiago de Compostela (Galicia), Valencia, and Seville (Andalusia). The entire system was finally united with radio in 1973 and was placed under the management of one state-owned corporation, Radio Televisión Española (RTVE). The regional circuit was wired into a highly centralized network in which all regional broadcasts were obliged to pass through Madrid. The only centers with the capacity to produce programs of any length were those in Barcelona and the Canary Islands. Although the records of RTVE management during the Franco dictatorship are unreliable, one study for 1976 reported that the Barcelona center contributed 3 percent of the total broadcast hours, followed by the center at Las Palmas in the Canary Islands at 2.9 percent. The rest transmitted a negligible amount of 1.8 to 1.85 percent of the total. The one-way flow of broadcasting from the center to the regions was an effect of the Franco regime's centralism, which kept the regional centers (other than Barcelona and Las Palmas) from connecting with Madrid.

Television in Spain changed radically in the years following the death of Franco in 1975. In 1980, the government enacted a reform statute that established norms to ensure that a plurality of political parties would control RTVE. The law also stipulated that broadcasting should be treated as an essential public service and that it should defend open and free expression. The statute called for the upgrading of the regional circuit, with a view to this becoming the basis for a network of television stations operated by regional governments, whose recognition in the constitution of 1978 was part of the reorganization of Spain as a "state of the autonomies." The parliaments of the newly formed autonomous governments of the Basque country and Catalonia founded their own television systems: the Basques in May 1982, the Catalans a year later. These actions resulted in the most decisive change in the broadcast structure since radio was nationalized during the Spanish Civil War, as they contravened existing laws that gave the central state the right to control all technology using the electromagnetic spectrum. In response, the central government enacted the Third Channel Law in 1984 in order to regulate the establishment of any additional networks in the regions.

The Third Channel Law was designed to stabilize the process of decentralization of the television industry, and it was based in the principle of recognition for the cultures, languages, and communities within the Spanish territory, entities that had been suppressed during the 40-year Franco dictatorship. The law stipulated that regional networks remain under the state's control and within the RTVE infrastructure. Parliaments in Catalonia, the Basque country, and Galicia resisted control by the central state and set up technical structures that ran parallel to but separate from the national network. Despite ongoing legal battles between the central state and the regions over rights of access to regional airwaves and rights of ownership of the infrastructure, 11 autonomous broadcast companies have been founded, six of which were broadcasting regularly by 1995. In 1989, the directors of these systems agreed to merge into a national federation of autonomous broadcasters, known as the Federación de Organismos de Radio y Televisión Autonómicos (Federation of Autonomous Radio and Television Organizations [FORTA]).

Between 1975 and 1990, Spanish television emerged from a system of absolute state control to become a regulated system in which both privately and publicly owned channels compete for advertising sales within national and regional markets. This structure was completed with the development of the 1988 law and technical plan for private television. The law furnished three licenses for the bidding of private corporations, a three-phase framework for the extension of universal territorial coverage, and restrictions on legal ownership to promote multiple partnerships (rather than monopoly control) and to limit foreign ownership. The technical plan created an independent public company, Retevisión, to manage the network infrastructure, abolishing RTVE's economic and political control over the airwaves. As of 2002, all broadcasters must pay an access fee to use the public infrastructure. Regular transmissions from the private companies began in 1990.

A 1995 Cable Telecommunications Law limited licensed operators in each market to two, expanded the minimum market size to exclude small operators, and gave licensing power to a central authority. This law was modified in 1996 to return licensing power to local and regional authorities and make it easier for smaller towns to get cable. This legislation forced many of the smaller *videos comunitarios* to close, although at the turn of the 21st century nearly 500 remained in operation illegally throughout southern and southeastern Spain. Eventually, several large cable companies emerged, with one being operated by the national telephone monopoly, Telefónica, and another run by the national electric utility monopoly, Endesa.

Despite opportunities for growth in cable, the largest corporations put greater effort in launching new digital satellite services. Sogecable already ran Canal+ and had numerous channels of pay TV in the analog format ready to broadcast over France's *Astra* satellite. Telefónica's controlling interest in the Spanish *Hispasat* satellite gave them low-cost access to the DTH satellite market. Telefónica's satellite-TV service, Vía Digital, and Sogecable's Canal Satélite Digital (CSD) both began service in 1997. Since 1998, the two have discussed merging, but European Union (EU) regulators had blocked the deal through at least 2001. However, the merger was conditionally cleared by the Spanish government in November 2002. The clearance depends on conditions relating primarily to the merged company's acquisition and broadcasting rights to films and soccer matches. A third digital satellite system, Quiero, began operation in 2000. By 2002, CSD had 1.2 million subscribers, Vía Digital had 750,000, and a struggling Quiero had 220,000. Basic subscription packages include 35 to 42 channels, although more than 91 separate cable and satellite program channels are available.

On the regional scale, TV-3 and Canal 33 cover Catalonia with Catalan-language programs and have significant spillover into contiguous regions and parts of France, thereby reaching beyond their official audience of 5.8 million. Canal Sur covers the Andalusian audience of 6.7 million. Telemadrid, owned by the regional government of Madrid, reaches an official audience of 4.8 million. Valencia's Canal 9's 3.7 million viewers can watch programs in Valenciano, a language similar to Catalan. Signals of TVG in Galicia spill over into northern Portugal and parts of Asturias in Spain, bringing Galician-language programming to more than the region's 2.6 million viewers. ETB-1 and ETB-2 cover the Basque country and parts of surrounding provinces to reach beyond the official audience of 2 million; notably, ETB-1 broadcasts in the Basque language (Euskera), while ETB-2 does so in Spanish.

As of 2002, Telefónica Media owns around 47 percent of Antena 3; other companies that own part of Antena 3 are the banking group Banco Santander Central Hispano (BSCH), which owns over 10 percent directly as well as another 13 percent through its subsidiary,

Mecame; Bank of New York (12 percent); and Recoletos Cartera de Inversiones (10 percent). Other shareholders control less than 8 percent. Telecinco is owned by the Kirch Group of Munich (25 percent), Silvio Berlusconi's Mediaset of Italy (40 percent), and two Spanish firms, Grupo Planeta (10 percent) and the Grupo Correo de Comunicación (25 percent).

Via Digital is owned by Telefónica Media (approximately 49 percent); Strategic Management Company (19 percent); DTH Europa (10 percent); Galaxy Entertainment Latinamerica, a DirecTV subsidiary (7 percent); the Madrid-based publisher Grupo Recoletos, a subsidiary of the Pearson group, a British media conglomerate and publisher of *The Financial Times* (5 percent); Media Park (5 percent); and others (less than 6 percent). CSD is owned by Sogecable (approximately 83 percent), Warner Brothers (10 percent), Proarsa (4.5 percent), and the Telefónica subsidiary Antena 3 (2.5 percent). Sogecable's business of program production and packaging is vertically integrated with a film production company (Sogecine, also known as Sogetel), a film buyer (StudioCanal Spain), TV and film distribution outfits (Sogepac and Warner Sogefilms), and venues for both theatrical film exhibition (Warner Lusomundo Cines de España) and pay TV (Canal+). Major owners of Sogecable are Canal Plus France, a Vivendi-Universal property (21 percent); PRISA (21 percent); and major Spanish banks (30 percent). PRISA owns the largest-circulation newspaper in Spain, *El País,* and the top commercial radio station, Ser. The Quiero satellite company is owned by Auna (49 percent), Media Park (15 percent), Sofisclave (15 percent), Carlton Communications (7.5 percent), and smaller investors (13.5 percent).

Telefónica is the largest company in Spain, Europe's second-largest publicly listed multimedia company behind Vivendi-Universal and the largest single foreign investor in Latin America. It controls the third-largest Internet service in the world (Terra Lycos) and is the third-largest entertainment company in the Spanish-speaking world (after Argentina's Clarín and Mexico's Televisa). Between 1996 and 2000, Telefónica's market value grew fivefold to $135 billion, making it one of *Fortune*'s top-five global telecom firms. It operates the most extensive telephony network in Spain, with control over about 98 percent of the market. In 1997, while launching Vía Digital, Telefónica purchased Antena 3, one of Spain's commercial broadcasters; this acquisition, along with other acquisitions of Spanish film- and video-production companies, initiated a course of convergence to match those of AOL Time Warner and Vivendi-Universal. Telefónica also owns a leading European production house, Endemol, maker of such international hits as *Big Brother.* Telefónica's

Latin American media holdings include ATCO, a holding company that controls Televisión Federal, S.A.(Telefé), the leading commercial TV network in Argentina, which sells programming throughout Latin America, the United States, Europe, and Asia. ATCO also controls the AM and FM channels of Radio Continental, the third-largest radio system in Argentina. In addition, Telefónica Media owns Telearte, S.A (the third-ranked commercial TV channel, known as Canal Azul), as well as a radio network of 300 stations run by Telefónica's Uniprex S.A. (Onda Cero) and Cadena Voz de Radiodifusión S.A.

TVE-1, Telecinco, and Antena-3 attract over 75 percent of the Spanish television audience. Both channels of TVE typically share a third of the viewers, while the private broadcasters draw 40 to 45 percent of the viewers on average. The regional broadcasters together might bring in 15 to 18 percent of all viewers. Domestically produced programs, especially sports, usually top the ratings, with *telenovelas,* imported from or co-produced with Latin American suppliers, remaining very popular. Recently, domestic remakes of popular Latin American *telenovelas* have earned as high as a 31 percent share of the viewers. Additional improvements in domestic production have resulted from the EU policy obligating private TV firms to invest 5 percent of their revenues in European TV and film production. The bulk of imported programs, on average 20 to 30 percent of all programming on the national channels, comes from the United States. This is a change from 1990 figures, when imports took up 40 percent of the program schedule on TVE-1, 33 percent on Andalusia's Canal Sur, 34 percent on Catalonia's TV-3, 35 percent on Galicia's TVG, and 39 percent on the Basque ETB-1. In 1990, Telemadrid showed twice as many U.S. programs as it did Spanish ones, while a ratio of one to one could be seen on Valencia's Canal 9, the Basque ETB-2, and the two private channels.

Newer services such as Vía Digital and CSD initially depended on U.S. programs; together, Vía Digital and CSD spent more than $3 billion on imports in their first year of operation. Since then, Sogecable has enjoyed exclusive deals with all the major Hollywood studios except MGM, including multiyear deals with Paramount, Disney Channels, Universal, and AOL Time Warner; with the latter company, Sogecable has an exclusive contract to develop a Spanish version of the Cable News Network (CNN). Sogecable also acquired rights to televise 20th Century-Fox's recently released films in Spain, including exclusive pay-TV rights to the blockbuster *Titanic.* The company also benefited when Canal+'s parent firm, Vivendi, bought Universal. Vía Digital has held exclusive rights to MGM films and its libraries as well as Playboy TV,

BBC World, BBC Prime, and Eurosport. The service also works with national distributor Media Park and draws on its 33 percent stake in Spain's biggest film-production house, Lolafilms, for additional programming. Apart from movies, satellite TV programming consists mostly of sports and documentaries, staples of domestic production. Soccer dominates, but the celebrity-classic bullfight has also become an important new format, especially during festival seasons in Seville, Madrid, and Pamplona.

Language is a key characteristic of the Spanish TV culture. The regional firms in the Basque country, Galicia, Catalonia, and Valencia were founded with the objective of fomenting the regions' languages and cultures. In Galicia, 99 percent of the people understand Gallego, but only 14 percent actually prefer to watch TV in Gallego. Estimates are that 95 percent of the people in Catalonia understand Catalan, but only a third of the Catalans watch programs exclusively in the idiom. Up to 90 percent of the people in Valencia understand Valenciano, but 12 percent prefer TV only in that language. In the Basque region, as many as half the people claim to understand Euskera, but only one-fifth of the Basques show strong preferences for their TV in this language. These figures are dwarfed by the scale of the national population, where practically 100 percent of the people understand Spanish. Despite the linguistic, territorial, and financial limitations affecting the regional networks, they manage to retain a stable audience of viewers because of the political and cultural history of centralism in Spanish communication. For both the managers and the audiences of these systems, the presence of the local idiom alongside Spanish recalls the multilingual identity of the regions and helps sustain a sense of place as Spain positions itself within the European Union and opens its borders to globalized audiovisual production.

RICHARD MAXWELL

Further Reading

Bustamante, Enrique, "TV and Public Service in Spain: A Difficult Encounter," *Media, Culture and Society* (January 1989)

Jordan, Barry, and R. Morgan-Tamosunas, editors, *Contemporary Spanish Cultural Studies,* London: Arnold Publishers, 2000

Maxwell, Richard, *The Spectacle of Democracy: Spanish Television, Nationalism, and Political Transition,* Minneapolis: University of Minnesota Press, 1995

Report by the Think Tank on the Audiovisual Policy in the European Union, Luxembourg: Office for Official Publications of the European Communities, 1994

Villagrasa, J.M., "Spain: the Emergence of Commercial Television," in *The New Television in Europe,* edited by A. Silj, London: John Libbey, 1992

Spanish International Network

The Spanish International Network (SIN) was the first Spanish-language television network in the United States. From its inception in 1961, SIN was the U.S. subsidiary of Televisa, the Mexican entertainment conglomerate, which today holds a virtual monopoly on Mexican television and is the world's largest producer of Spanish-language television programming.

From the point of view of a U.S. entrepreneur in the early 1960s, the U.S. Spanish-speaking population was so small and so poor a community that it was not considered a viable advertising market. The 1960 Census counted 3.5 million U.S. residents with Spanish surnames. Mexican immigrants and Mexican Americans living in the United States constituted the vast majority of this population. (Large scale immigration from Puerto Rico, Cuba, and other Latin American countries had not yet begun.) Spanish-language advertising billed through the U.S. advertising industry amounted to $5 million annually, less than 0.1 percent of all advertising expenditures at that time. From the perspective of a Latin American entrepreneur, however, this U.S. Latino audience was one of the wealthiest Spanish-language markets in the world.

SIN was founded by Emilio Azcárraga, the "William Paley of Mexican broadcasting." An entrepreneurial visionary and the owner of theaters and recording companies, Azcárraga built first a radio, then a television empire in Mexico, before expanding it north of the border. SIN began with two television stations, KMEX, Los Angeles, and KWEX, San Antonio (Texas), and from the beginning had national ambitions. In fulfilling these aims, SIN pioneered the use of five communications technologies: the UHF (ultrahigh frequency) band, cable television, microwave and satellite interconnections, and repeater stations. All these applications contributed to rapid growth in the 1960s and 1970s, and by 1982 SIN could claim it was reaching 90 percent of the Spanish-speaking households in the United States through 16 owned-and-operated UHF stations, 100 repeater stations, and 200 cable outlets.

In these first decades, virtually every broadcast hour of each SIN affiliate was *Televisa* programming produced in Mexico: *telenovelas* (soap operas), movies, variety shows, and sports programming. The vertical integration of Azcárraga's transnational entertainment conglomerate gave tremendous economic advantages to early U.S. Spanish-language television. The performers under contract to Azcárraga's theaters and recording companies also worked for his television network. In other words, SIN programming had covered costs and produced a profit in Mexico before it was marketed in the United States.

After 1981 and the start of satellite distribution of its programming, SIN began producing programs in the United States. The network created a nightly national newscast, *Noticiero Univisión,* as well as national public service programming, such as voter registration drives. It also provided coverage of U.S. national events such as the Tournament of Roses Parade and Fourth of July celebrations. The larger network-owned stations also began airing two hours a day of locally produced news and public affairs programming. This programming represented a limited recognition by SIN that U.S. and Mexican television audiences had different needs and interests. Moreover, it was an attempt to modify the SIN audience profile from that of a "foreign" or "ethnic" group interested only in Mexican programming to that of a more "American" community participating in the same national rituals as the mainstream consumer market. Perhaps SIN's most enduring contribution to U.S. culture was its leading institutional role in the creation of a commercially viable, panethnic, national Hispanic market.

The entrepreneurial financial and marketing acumen displayed by Emilio Azcárraga (and from 1972 by his son and heir Emilio Azcárraga Milmo) in the creation and development of SIN were matched by his legal skills in maneuvering around U.S. communications law. The U.S. Communications Act of 1934 simply and explicitly bars "any alien or representative of any alien...or any corporation directly or indirectly controlled by...aliens" from owning U.S. broadcast station licenses. For Azcárraga and his SIN associates, perhaps the most salient part of this law is what it does *not* address. It does not prohibit the importation or distribution of foreign broadcast signals or programming. In other words, U.S. law does not limit foreign ownership of broadcast networks; it does bar foreign ownership of the principal means of dissemination of the programming, the broadcast station. On paper and in files of the Federal Communications Commission

(FCC), none of the SIN stations or affiliates was owned by Emilio Azcárraga or *Televisa.* Rather, the foreign-ownership prohibition was avoided by means of a time-honored business stratagem known, in Spanish, as the *presta nombre,* which translates literally to "lending a name" and can be rendered in colloquial English as a "front." SIN stations were owned by U.S. citizens with long-established professional and familial ties to Azcárraga and *Televisa,* with Azcárraga retaining a 25 percent interest (the limit permitted by law) in the SIN network.

Although long a subject of criticism by Latino community leaders and would-be U.S. Spanish-language television entrepreneurs, the foreign control of SIN was not successfully challenged until the mid-1980s, when a dissident shareholder filed a complaint with the FCC. In January 1986, the FCC ordered the sale of SIN. The FCC action was met with much excited anticipation by U.S. Latino groups who felt that for the first time since its creation 25 years earlier, there was a possibility that U.S. Spanish television would be controlled by U.S. Latino interests.

Several U.S. Latino investor groups were formed, but ultimately the bid (for $301.5 million) of Hallmark, Inc., of Kansas City, Missouri, the transnational greeting card company, received FCC approval. Hallmark changed the network's name to Univision, pledging to keep the network broadcasting in Spanish. Under the terms of the sale, *Televisa* was given, in addition to cash, a guaranteed U.S. customer (the new network, Univision, was given a right of first refusal for all *Televisa* programming), free advertising (for its records and tapes division) on Univision for two years, and 37.5 percent of the profits of its former stations for two years. After a quarter century, SIN ceased to exist as a corporate entity, leaving a significant cultural and economic legacy—a commercially viable U.S. Spanish-language television network and a new U.S. consumer group: the Hispanic market.

AMERICA RODRIGUEZ

See also **Univision**

Further Reading

All About the SIN Television Network, New York: SIN Television Network, 1984

Arrarte, Anne Moncreiff, "And Galavision Makes Three," *Advertising Age* (February 12, 1990)

Conference on Telecommunications and Latinos, Stanford, California: Stanford Center for Chicano Research, 1985

"Hispanic Broadcasting Comes of Age," *Broadcasting* (April 3, 1989)

Navarrete, Lisa, and Charles Kamasaki, *Out of the Picture: Hispanics in the Media: State of Hispanic America, 1994,*

Washington, D.C.: Policy Analysis Center, Office of Research Advocacy and Legislation: National Council of La Raza, 1994

Sobel, Robert, "Where's Spanish TV Going?," *Television-Radio Age* (November 23, 1987)

"Spanish Spending Power Growing Dramatically, but Consumers Retain Special Characteristics," *Television-Radio Age* (December 10, 1984)

Stilson, Janet, "New SIN Prexy Sets Sights Skyward: Aims to Double TV Web Revenue," *Variety* (September 24, 1986)

Special/Spectacular

The television special is, in many ways, as old as television itself. Television specials are (usually) one-time-only programs presented with great network fanfare and usually combining music, dance, and comedy routines (or "bits") presented in a variety format. When television was still new, specials were common, in part because weekly, ongoing shows were expensive to produce and were not yet proven as tools for securing long-term viewer loyalty. Hence, early television schedules did contain many one-time presentations, such as *The Damon Runyon Memorial Fund* (1950; TV's first telethon hosted by Milton Berle), the *Miss Television USA Contest* (1950; won by Edie Adams), *Amahl and the Night Visitors* (1951; the first *Hallmark Hall of Fame* program), and the *Ford 50th Anniversary Show* (1953; featuring duets between stage stars Mary Martin and Ethel Merman).

The TV special entered its greatest and most prolific phase in 1954, when genius programmer Sylvester "Pat" Weaver conceptualized what he called television "spectaculars." These one-of-a-kind, one-night broadcasts were Weaver's attempt to bring new and larger audiences and prestige to the television medium and to his network, the National Broadcasting Company (NBC). Breaking with the format of television at that time, the spectaculars regularly preempted the normal network program schedule of sponsored weekly shows. Weaver's move was a controversial gamble; in order to free up airtime for the presentation of his spectaculars (on every fourth Monday, Saturday, and Sunday), the network had to forgo sponsorship by single companies (basically money in the bank for the network) on the nights the sponsors' programs were preempted. Instead of relying on single sponsors, Weaver followed his trademark "magazine" formula for sponsorship, selling different segments of each spectacular to different sponsors and in the process laying the foundation for the future of multiple sponsorship and commercials on all of U.S. television.

In creating his spectaculars, Weaver drew on the talents of three producers: Fred Coe, Max Liebman, and Albert McCleery. Coe created his works for *Producer's Showcase* airing on Mondays, Liebman for his series *Max Liebman Presents* on Saturdays, and McCleery for *Hallmark Hall of Fame* on Sundays. Under Weaver and his team of producers, the spectacular could be a musical extravaganza (such as *Peter Pan,* with Mary Martin repeating her Broadway triumph), a play (such as Coe's *Our Town* with Paul Newman, Eva Marie Saint, and Frank Sinatra), or a dramatic film (such as Sir Laurence Olivier's *Richard III*).

In time, spectaculars became known by the less hyperbolic term "special," and generally they were shortened in length, with most lasting only one hour, as opposed to the 90 minutes to three hours sometimes taken by NBC. For the most part, specials took on a lighter tone, becoming variety oriented, with the emphasis on music, dance, and elaborate production numbers. This era of the special saw the presentation of such benchmark television offerings as *Astaire Time,* with Fred Astaire and Barrie Chase (1960); *Julie and Carol at Carnegie Hall,* with Julie Andrews and Carol Burnett (1962); *My Name Is Barbra,* starring Barbra Streisand (1964); and *Frank Sinatra: A Man and His Music* (1964).

These types of programs continued successfully into the late 1960s and 1970s, featuring such diverse talents as Carol Channing, Bill Cosby, Elvis Presley, Liza Minnelli, Lily Tomlin, Shirley MacLaine, Bette Midler, Ann-Margaret, Olivia Newton-John, Tom Jones, and Carol Burnett, who often paired herself with other performers, such as Beverly Sills, Dolly Parton, or Julie Andrews. Throughout this period, stars of contemporary television programs, such as Lynda Carter, Cheryl Ladd, and Ben Vereen, also headlined occasional hour-long specials, frequently with substantial ratings success.

As the weekly variety show all but disappeared from network television (*The Carol Burnett Show,* U.S. television's last successful variety show, ceased in 1978), the trend also signaled the beginning of the decline for the television music-dance special. As audiences began to select their musical entertainment from other media or in shorter forms, such as the music video, the hour-long, star-centered special began to appear dated. At the same time, the shows were proving too expensive to produce in relation to their ratings.

Currently, with the exception of such yearly traditions as award shows, Christmas specials, and pageants such as Miss USA, the television special/spectacular is now primarily the domain of channels other than the American Broadcasting Company (ABC), the Columbia Broadcasting System (CBS), FOX, or NBC. One still occasionally witnesses such programs. For example, on September 21, 2001, all four U.S. networks aired *America: A Tribute to Heroes,* a live two-hour special featuring musical performances and commentaries from celebrities to raise money for the relief effort aiding victims of the September 11 attacks on the World Trade Center and the Pentagon. However, such network specials are rare. In contrast, the Public Broadcasting Service (PBS) sometimes presents films of Broadway musicals, cable stations such as Home Box Office (HBO) air highly touted entertainment events, and pay-per-view has become an important purveyor of made-for-television extravaganzas. In a world of expanding numbers of television channels, it is difficult to know what future events might qualify as "special" and harder still to identify the truly "spectacular."

CARY O'DELL

See also **Coe, Fred;** *Peter Pan;* **Programming; Weaver, Sylvester (Pat)**

Further Reading

Bailey, Robert Lee, *An Examination of Prime Time Network Television Special Programs: 1948–1966,* New York: Arno, 1979

Terrace, Vincent, *Television Specials: 3,201 Entertainment Spectaculars, 1939–1993,* Jefferson, North Carolina: McFarland, 1995

Speight, Johnny (1920–1998)

British Writer, Producer

Johnny Speight was the creator of the British Broadcasting Corporation (BBC) series *Till Death Us Do Part,* on which the U.S. series *All in the Family* (Columbia Broadcasting System [CBS]) was based. As controversial in its time and place as was *All in the Family,* Speight's creation spawned a generation of relevant, hard-hitting sitcoms in both the United States and England.

A former factory worker and jazz musician, Speight began writing for television in 1956. In 1966, after serving as head writer for the *Arthur Haynes Show,* Speight launched *Till Death Us Do Part.* The series revolved around the different values and beliefs held by blue-collar bigot Alf Garnett and his liberal son-in-law Mike. Originally committed to shows about the family itself, Speight maneuvered *Till Death* to more relevant social issues. Norman Lear, who was working in feature films at the time, saw the series and, with partner Bud Yorkin, optioned the series for their company Tandem Productions. The resulting hit was *All in the Family,* which debuted on CBS in 1971.

Speight's more controversial episodes prompted the Conservative Central Office to ask for advance copies of the *Till Death* scripts. When Speight refused, the matter was soon dropped. In 1968, Speight produced a BBC movie version of the series, and in 1972 he penned a short-run revival of the series. During that run, the series reached 24 million viewers, making it the most popular show in Britain.

Speight wrote several plays, including *If There Weren't Any Blacks You'd Have to Invent Them,* which has been produced in at least 17 countries. He also won numerous awards, including numerous Screenwriters Guild Awards, and a Lifetime Achievement Award from the British Comedy Awards in 1996. He died of cancer in July 1998.

MICHAEL B. KASSEL

See also ***Till Death Us Do Part***

Johnny Speight. Born in Canning Town, London, England, June 2, 1920. Educated at St. Helen's Roman Catholic School, London. Married: Constance Beatrice Barrett, 1956; children: one daughter and two sons. Worked in a factory, then as a jazz drummer and insurance salesman; writer, BBC radio and television,

from 1956; created the sitcom *Till Death Us Do Part.*
Recipient: Screenwriters Guild Award, 1962, 1966,
1967, 1968; Prague Festival Award, 1969; *Evening
Standard* Award, 1977; Pye Award, for television writing, 1983; British Comedy Awards Lifetime Achievement Award, 1996. Died in Chorleywood,
Hertsfordshire, England, July 5, 1998.

Television Series (selected)

1960–66	*Arthur Haynes Show*
1966–75	*Till Death Us Do Part*
1969	*Curry and Chips*
1972	*Them*
1973	*Speight of Marty*
1979	*The Tea Ladies* (with Ray Galton)
1980	*Spooner's Patch* (with Ray Galton)
1982	*The Lady Is a Tramp*
1985	*In Sickness and in Health*
1989	*The 19th Hole*

Television Specials

1961	*The Compartment*
1962	*Playmates*
1963	*Shamrot*
1965	*If There Weren't Any Blacks You'd Have to Invent Them*
1967	*To Lucifer a Sun*
1970	*The Salesman*
1975	*For Richer…For Poorer*

Films (writer)

French Dressing, 1964; *Privilege,* 1967; *Till Death Us
Do Part,* 1968; *The Alf Garnett Saga,* 1972; *The Secret Policeman's Third Ball,* 1987.

Films (actor)

The Plank, 1967; *The Undertakers,* 1969; *Rhubarb,*
1970.

Radio (writer)

The Edmondo Ross Show, 1956–58; *The Morecambe
and Wise Show,* 1956–58; *The Frankie Howerd
Show,* 1956–58; *Early to Braden,* 1957–58; *The
Deadly Game of Chess,* 1958; *The April 8th Show
(Seven Days Early),* 1958; *The Eric Sykes Show,*
1960–61.

Stage (writer)

Mr. Venus, 1958; *The Art of Living* (with others),
1960; *The Compartment,* 1965; *The Knacker's
Yard,* 1962; *Playmates,* 1971; *If There Weren't Any
Blacks You'd Have to Invent Them,* 1965; *The Picture* (with others), 1967; *The Salesman,* 1970; *Till
Death Us Do Part,* 1973; *The Thoughts of Chairman Alf,* 1983.

Publications

It Stands to Reason: A Kind of Autobiography, 1973
*The Thoughts of Chairman Alf: Alf Garnett's Little
Blue Book; or, Where England Went Wrong: An
Open Letter to the People of Britain,* 1973
Pieces of Speight, 1974
*The Garnett Chronicles: The Life and Times of Alf
Garnett, Esq.,* 1986
For Richer, For Poorer: A Kind of Autobiography,
1992
Three Plays, 1998

Spelling, Aaron (1923–)

U.S. Producer

Aaron Spelling is one of television's most prolific and
successful producers of dramatic series and made-for-television films: by 2001, he had more than 182
television-production credits. Spelling began his career as a successful student playwright at Southern
Methodist University, where he won the Eugene
O'Neill Award for original one-act plays in 1947 and
1948. After graduating in 1950 and spending a few
years directing plays in the Dallas, Texas, area, and

then trying less than successfully to make his way on
Broadway, Spelling moved to Hollywood. There he
initially found work as an actor and later as a
scriptwriter for such anthology and episodic series as
*Dick Powell's Zane Grey Theater, Playhouse 90,
Wagon Train,* and *The Jane Wyman Theater.* Within a
few years, Spelling had become a producer at Four
Star Studio Productions, where he created *The Lloyd
Bridges Show* (1962–63), *Burke's Law* (1963–66), and

Aaron Spelling.
Photo courtesy of Spelling Television, Inc.

Honey West (1965–66) and helped develop *The Smothers Brothers Show* (1967–75).

Spelling's first really successful series, *The Mod Squad* (1968–73), was produced after he left Four Star and formed a partnership with Danny Thomas. During its five-year run, *Mod Squad* earned six Emmy Award nominations, including one for Outstanding Dramatic Series for the 1969–70 season. In 1972, Spelling formed a new partnership with Leonard Goldberg, which lasted until 1977 and produced such hits as *The Rookies* (1972–76), *Starsky and Hutch* (1972–76), and *Charlie's Angels* (1976–81). Spelling's string of series featuring both wealthy crime fighters and regular cops continued in the 1980s with *Hart to Hart* (1979–84), *Matt Houston* (1982–85), *Strike Force* (1981–82), *T.J. Hooker* (1982–87), and *McGruder and Loud* (1985).

Spelling also ventured into new genres with his innovative, hour-long comedy, *The Love Boat* (1977–86) and the prime-time serial *Dynasty* (1981–89). Reminiscent of the 1960s anthology comedy, *Love, American Style,* each episode of Spelling's *The Love Boat* turned the three separate comedy stories into three intertwined storylines. Intercutting three separate plots in short scenes that recapitulated and advanced each storyline plot was a brilliant strategy that enabled the series to appeal to different sets of viewers, each of whom might be attracted to a particular plotline, within a format that was admirably suited to the fragmented and distracted way that most people view television. Another Spelling innovation that first appeared in *The Love Boat* was the ritualized introductory sequence that formally presented the multiple plots in each week's episode as well as the series' main characters.

In 1980s television, Spelling was king. In 1984, Spelling's seven series on the American Broadcasting Company (ABC) accounted for one-third of the network's prime-time schedule, leading some critics to nickname ABC "Aaron's Broadcasting Company." Spelling's 18-year exclusive production deal with ABC ended in 1988, but his ability to create hit series did not. In the 1990s, he introduced the hit prime-time series *Beverly Hills 90210* (1990–2000) and *Melrose Place* (1992–99), for FOX, and his first daytime soap opera venture, *Sunset Beach* (1997–99), for the National Broadcasting Company (NBC).

Among the recurring thematic features that have characterized Spelling's productions over the years are socially relevant issues, such as the disaffected militant youth of the 1960s; institutional discrimination against women, racism, and homophobia; altruistic capitalism; conspicuous consumption and valorization of the wealthy; the optimistic, moralistic maxims that people can be both economically and morally successful; good ultimately triumphs over evil; the grass often looks greener but rarely is; and the affirmation of both the "caring company" work family (e.g., in *Hotel*) and the traditional kinship family. Stylistically, his productions have included high-key lighting, gratuitous displays of women's bodies, heavily orchestrated musical themes, lavish sets, and what Spelling himself thinks is the most important element in television: "style and attention to detail." Two Spelling series that stand out as anomalous among this auteur's prime-time and movie ventures are *Family* (ABC, 1976–80) and *7th Heaven* (The WB, 1996–). Spelling and Mike Nichols coproduced *Family,* a weekly hour-long drama, which many consider to be Spelling's best work. During the four years that this serious portrayal of an upper-middle-class suburban family was in first run, it won four Emmy Awards for the lead performers and was twice nominated for Outstanding Drama Series. *7th Heaven,* a wholesome drama about a Protestant minister, his wife, and their seven children living together in an American suburb, also has received numerous awards, including the Kids Choice Award, the Teen Choice Award, *TV Guide* Awards, the Entertainment Industry's Prism Award, the Media Project's Shine Award, and the Viewer's Choice Award.

"Innovator," "overachiever," "spin doctor," "angel," "king of pap," "ratings engineer," "TV's glitzmeister," "winner of six National Association for the Advancement of Colored People Image Awards": these are some of the labels Spelling's critics and admirers have used to describe this prolific, successful producer. One title that certainly describes the undeniable impact Spelling has left on four decades of television is that of television auteur.

LEAH R. VANDE BERG

See also Beverly Hills, 90210; Charlie's Angels; Dynasty; Melodrama; Starsky and Hutch

Aaron Spelling. Born in Dallas, Texas, April 22, 1923. Educated at the Sorbonne, Paris, 1945–46; Southern Methodist University, Dallas, Texas, B.A. 1950. Married: 1) Carolyn Jones, 1953 (divorced, 1964); 2) Carole Gene Marer, 1968; children: Tori and Randy. Served in U.S. Air Force, 1942–45, decorated with Bronze Star Medal, Purple Heart with oak leaf cluster. Actor, from 1953, appearing in 50 television shows and 12 films; began career as a writer after selling script to *Zane Grey Theater;* worked in production, Four Star, 1956–65; co-owner, with Danny Thomas, Thomas-Spelling Productions, 1968–72; copresident, Spelling-Goldberg Productions, 1972–77; president, Aaron Spelling Productions, Los Angeles, 1977–86, chair and chief executive officer, since 1986. Member: board of directors, American Film Institute; Writers Guild of America; Producers Guild of America; Caucus of Producers, Writers and Directors; Hollywood Radio and TV Society; Hollywood TV Academy of Arts and Sciences; Academy of Motion Picture Arts and Sciences. Recipient: Eugene O'Neill Awards, 1947 and 1948; six National Association for the Advancement of Colored People (NAACP) Image Awards; named Man of the Year by the Publicists Guild of America, 1971; named Man of the Year by Beverly Hills chapter of B'Nai B'rith, 1972, 1985; named Humanitarian of the Year, 1983; named Man of the Year by the Scopus Organization, 1993.

Television Series (selected; producer)

1956–62	*Dick Powell's Zane Grey Theater* (writer only)
1959–60	*Johnny Ringo*
1959–61	*The duPont Show with June Allyson*
1961–63	*The Dick Powell Show*
1963–65	*Burke's Law*
1964–70	*Daniel Boone*
1965–66	*Amos Burke—Secret Agent*
1967–69	*The Guns of Will Sonnett*
1968–73	*The Mod Squad*
1969–70	*The New People*
1974	*Firehouse*
1974	*Chopper One*
1975–76	*S.W.A.T.*
1975–79	*Starsky and Hutch*
1976–81	*Charlie's Angels*
1976–80	*Family*
1977–86	*The Love Boat*
1978–84	*Fantasy Island*
1979	*Friends*
1980	*B.A.D. Cats*
1981–89	*Dynasty*
1981–82	*Strike Force*
1983	*At Ease*
1983–88	*Hotel*
1984–85	*Glitter*
1984–85	*Finder of Lost Loves*
1985–87	*The Colbys*
1986	*Life with Lucy*
1989	*Nightingales*
1990–2000	*Beverly Hills, 90210*
1992	*2000 Malibu Road*
1992	*The Heights*
1992–99	*Melrose Place*
1994	*Winnetka Road*
1994–95	*Models, Inc.*
1995–96	*Savannah*
1995	*Malibu Shores*
1996–	*Seventh Heaven*
1997–99	*Sunset Beach*
1997	*Pacific Palisades*
1998	*The Love Boat: The Next Wave*
1998	*Buddy Faro*
1998–	*Charmed*
1999	*Rescue 77*
1999	*Safe Harbor*
2000	*Titans*
2001	*All Souls*

Made-for-Television Movies

1969	*The Over-the-Hill Gang*
1969	*Wake Me When the War Is Over*
1969	*The Monk*
1969	*The Pigeon*
1969	*The Ballad of Andy Crocker*
1969	*Carter's Army*
1970	*The Love War*
1970	*How Awful About Allan*
1970	*But I Don't Want to Get Married!*
1970	*The Old Man Who Cried Wolf*
1970	*Wild Women*
1970	*The House That Would Not Die*
1970	*The Over-the-Hill Gang Rides Again*
1970	*Crowhaven Farm*
1970	*Run Simon Run*

1970	*Yuma*
1970	*River of Gold*
1970	*Love Hate Love*
1971	*Congratulations, It's a Boy!*
1971	*Five Desperate Women*
1971	*The Last Child*
1971	*A Taste of Evil*
1971	*In Broad Daylight*
1971	*The Death of Me Yet*
1971	*The Reluctant Heroes*
1971	*If Tomorrow Comes*
1971	*The Trackers*
1971	*Two for the Money*
1972	*The Daughters of Joshua Cabe*
1972	*No Place to Run*
1972	*Say Goddbye, Maggie Cole*
1972	*Rolling Man*
1972	*The Bounty Man*
1972	*Home for the Holidays*
1972	*Every Man Needs One*
1972	*Chill Factor*
1973	*Snatched*
1973	*The Great American Beauty Contest*
1973	*The Letters*
1973	*The Bait*
1973	*Satan's School for Girls*
1973	*Hijack*
1973	*Letters from Three Lovers*
1973	*The Affair*
1974	*The Death Squad*
1974	*The Girl Who Came Gift-Wrapped*
1974	*Cry Panic*
1974	*Savages*
1974	*Death Sentence*
1974	*Hit Lady*
1974	*Death Cruise*
1974	*Only with Married Men*
1974	*California Split*
1975	*The Daughters of Joshua Cabe Return*
1975	*Murder on Flight 502*
1975	*The Legend of Valentino*
1976	*One of My Wives Is Missing*
1976	*The New Daughters of Joshua Cabe*
1976	*Death at Love House*
1976	*The Boy in the Plastic Bubble*
1976	*Baby Blue Marine*
1977	*Little Ladies of the Night*
1977	*The San Pedro Bums*
1978	*Cruise into Terror*
1978	*Wild and Wooly*
1978	*Kate Bliss and the Ticker Tape Kid*
1978	*The Users*
1979	*Beach Patrol*
1979	*The Power Within*
1980	*Casino*
1981	*The Best Little Girl in the World*
1982	*Massarait and the Brain*
1982	*The Wild Women of Chastity Gulch*
1983	*Shooting Stars*
1983	*The Making of a Male Model*
1984	*Velvet*
1985	*International Airport*
1986	*Dark Mansions*
1986	*T.J. Hooker: Blood Sport*
1987	*Cracked Up*
1988	*Divided We Stand*
1989	*Day One*
1990	*Rich Men, Single Women*
1991	*The Love Boat: A Valentine Voyage*
1991	*Jailbirds*
1992	*Back to the Streets of San Francisco*
1992	*Grass Roots*
1993	*And the Band Played On*
1993	*Sidney Sheldon's A Stranger in the Mirror*
1993	*Hart to Hart: Hart to Hart Returns*
1993	*Gulf City*
1994	*Jane's House*
1994	*Hart to Hart: Home Is Where the Hart Is*
1994	*Hart to Hart: Crimes of the Hart*
1994	*Hart to Hart: Old Friends Never Die*
1994	*Love on the Run*
1994	*Green Dolphin Beat*
1994	*Kindred: The Embraced*
1995	*Hart to Hart: Secrets of the Hart*
1995	*Hart to Hart: Two Harts in Three Quarters Time*
1996	*Hart to Hart: Till Death Do Us Hart*
1996	*Hart to Hart: Harts in High Season*
1996	*After Jimmy*
2000	*Satan's School for Girls* (remake)

Television Miniseries

1979	*The French Atlantic Affair*
1986	*Crossings*
1996	*A Season in Purgatory*

Films (selected)

Guns of the Timberland, 1959; *A Pair of Boots* (short), 1962; *My Daddy Can Lick Your Daddy* (short), 1962; *Mr. Mom*, 1983; *'night, Mother*, 1986; *Three O'Clock High*, 1987; *Surrender*, 1987; *Cross My Heart*, 1987; *Satisfaction*, 1988; *Loose Cannons*, 1990 *Soapdish*, 1991; *The Mod Squad*, 1999; *Charlie's Angels*, 2000.

Publication

Aaron Spelling: A Prime-Time Life, with Jefferson Graham, 1996

Further Reading

Bark, E., "Aaron Spelling," *Dallas Morning News* (March 12, 1989)

Budd, M., S. Craig, and C. Steinman, "*Fantasy Island:* Marketplace of Desire," *Journal of Communication* (1983)

Carson, T., "The King of Pap," *Village Voice* (April 12, 1994)

Coe, S., and D. Tobenkin, "Aaron Spelling: TV's Overachiever," *Broadcasting & Cable* (January 23, 1995)

Davis, I., "He's Baaaaaack! TV's King of Jiggle, Aaron Spelling," *Los Angeles Magazine* (April 1991)

Friedman, D., "Fox Sees Spelling As an Angel," *Variety* (January 6, 1988)

Goldenson, Leonard, *Beating the Odds,* New York: Scribners, 1991

Grover, Ronald, "Is Aaron Spelling Still in His Prime Time?," *BusinessWeek* (April 17, 1989)

Marc, David, "TV Auteurism," *American Film* (November 1981)

Marc, David, and Robert J. Thompson, *Prime Time, Prime Movers: From I Love Lucy to L.A. Law—America's Greatest TV Shows and the People Who Created Them,* Boston: Little, Brown, 1992

Pesman, Sandra, "Finding '90s on 'Winnetka Rd'" (interview), *Advertising Age* (April 11, 1994)

Quill, G., "Spin Doctor Spelling Aspires to the Heights of Hyperbole," *Toronto Star* (August 26, 1992)

Schwichtenberg, C., "A Patriarchal Voice in Heaven," *Jump Cut* (1984)

Seiter, E., "The Hegemony of Leisure: Aaron Spelling Presents *Hotel,*" in *Television in Transition,* edited by P. Drummond and R. Paterson, London: British Film Institute, 1985

Swartz, M., "Aaron Spelling: Entertainment's King of the Jiggle," *Texas Monthly* (September 1994)

Swartz, M., "Aaron Spelling: The Trash TV Titan," *Texas Monthly* (September 1994)

Thompson, H., "Messing with *Texas:* TV Glitzmeister Aaron Spelling Tries to Wake Up Michener's Epic Snooze," *Texas Monthly* (August 1994)

Thompson, R., "*Love Boat:* High Art on the High Seas," *Journal of American Culture* (1983)

Spin-Off

The spin-off is a television programming strategy that constructs new programs around characters appearing in programs already being broadcast or programs ending their current run. In some cases, the new venue is created for a familiar, regular character in the existing series (e.g., *Gomer Pyle, U.S.M.C.* from *The Andy Griffith Show*). In others, the existing series merely serves as an introduction to and promotion for a completely new program (*Mork and Mindy* from *Happy Days*).

Among the most famous examples of the spin-off are those from the work of producer Norman Lear and works by producers working at MTM Productions during the 1970s. A list of the originating programs with their spin-offs reads like a genealogy of popular television comedy. Thus, *All in the Family* begat *Maude,* which begat *Good Times,* and *The Jeffersons,* which begat *Checking In. All in the Family* also begat *Gloria,* which lasted only one season and begat nothing.

The Mary Tyler Moore Show begat *Phyllis, Rhoda,* and *Lou Grant,* and though none of these "offspring" engendered specific shows of their own, their producers went on to create numerous programs with the distinctive style of these earlier works.

Other prolific sources of spin-offs were *The Danny Thomas Show,* the source of *The Andy Griffith Show,* which led to *Gomer Pyle, U.S.M.C.* and *Mayberry, R.F.D.* From *Happy Days* the list includes *Laverne and Shirley, Joannie Loves Chachi, Mork and Mindy,* and *Out of the Blue.* As should be clear from these lists, a spin-off is no guarantee of success. For every *Wanted: Dead or Alive* (from *Trackdown*), there is a *Beverly Hill Buntz* (from *Hill Street Blues*).

The existence of spin-offs can lead to puzzling problems when one considers the relations among programs across the schedule. The long-running prime-time serial *Knots Landing,* for example, was a spin-off of *Dallas,* the most famous example of that genre. During the famous 1985–86 season of *Dallas,* the season that was "dreamt" by Pamela Ewing (Victoria Principal), various events on *Knots Landing* occurred in response to Bobby Ewing's (Patrick Duffy) "death." Yet no one on *Knots Landing* troubled to explain how the history of their own fictional world might be altered by the fact that a "year in the life of *Dallas*" never occurred.

In any instance, spin-offs attest to television's constant demand for new, if not always different, material. This demand often leads to mindless repetition and the

Different Strokes (Season 1), Todd Bridges, Charlotte Rae, Gary Coleman, Conrad Bain, Dana Plato, 1978–86.
Courtesy of the Everett Collection

The Facts of Life, Felice Schachter, Lisa Whelchel, Julie Anne Haddock, John Lawlor, Julie Piekarski, Molly Ringwald, Mindy Cohn, Charlotte Rae, Kim Fields, (1st Season), 1979–88.
Courtesy of the Everett Collection

most meager attempts to cash in on previous success. While spin-offs may lead to new sources of creativity in their own right, the result of applying this strategy is often no more than a program that temporarily fills a time slot.

Indeed, it should be noted that spin-offs often result from producers' financial arrangements or from deals made with actors portraying popular characters within an ensemble. Successful producers or popular actors frequently contract for future commitments from studios or networks. New shows constructed around proven, popular characters offer obvious advantages in these arrangements. One of the most successful U.S. television series in recent history, *Frasier,* was developed for performer Kelsey Grammer. The WB television network capitalized on the success of *Buffy the Vampire Slayer* by creating *Angel* for David Boreanaz. And as the final season of *Friends* began, word came that the National Broadcasting Company (NBC) would develop a series for Matt LeBlanc who portrayed the popular character, Joey. The example is interesting because NBC executives acknowledged that the Joey character was not intended to be the most prominent character when the series began. Yet no other actors were offered series developed around their

specific roles in *Friends.* In all these cases, the existence of a successful program offers the producer, the star, and the network a ready-made billboard for advertising new work.

A final version of the spin-off is related to variations on a program franchise or formula, variations that often cross national boundaries. It is important to remember that *All in the Family* and *Sanford and Son,* two of the most highly acclaimed shows produced by Norman Lear, were copies of British productions, *Till Death Us Do Part* and *Steptoe and Son,* respectively. Currently, the most prominent examples in the United States are the international versions of *Wheel of Fortune.* Licensed by the parent company Merv Griffin Productions to producers in other countries, some form of *Wheel* is popular from France to Taiwan, from Norway to Peru. In each country, small variations are created to express particular cultural expectations and attitudes. Because game shows are cheaply and easily produced, this type of the spin-off concept is likely to expand.

Similarly, producers and programmers take advantage of highly successful program "franchises," the total style and format of a production that can be copied or slightly modified to create new programs. The best example in recent U.S. television history is the *Law and Order* franchise. Though not initially a "hit," the first *Law and Order* series became staple viewing, a firmly "episodic" program in the midst of more serialized series. It satisfied viewers with its contained episodes, which also made it an outstanding and financially successful product for syndication. Producer Dick Wolf subsequently developed *Law and Order:*

SVU (Special Victims Unit), which dealt with sex crimes, and *Law and Order: CI* (Criminal Intent), which presented stories exploring the criminals' point of view. On occasion, characters from one or more of these series would "cross over" into action in another. These programs, like all other instances of spin-offs, attest to both television's unceasing demand for new content and narrative structures able to generate new stories.

HORACE NEWCOMB

Spitting Image

British Puppet/Satire Program

The premiere of *Spitting Image* opened with a puppet caricature of Israel's prime minister Menachem Begin wearing a magician's outfit. With a flourish, he produced a dove of peace from his top hat, then announced, "For my first trick...," only to then wring the bird's neck.

This was the first of many outrages perpetrated on the British public, who were either offended or delighted each week from 1984 to 1996. *Spitting Image* was roundly condemned for its lampooning of the royal family: the queen was portrayed as a harried housewife, beset by randy, dullard children and screaming grandkids. Britain's most cherished figure, the queen mother, was portrayed as a pleasant, if somewhat boozy, great-grandmother figure.

The Conservative leadership was a constant target. Margaret Thatcher's puppet was a needle-nosed Reagan groupie who consulted with Hitler on immigration policy and sold off England's infrastructure to baying packs of yuppies; her eventual successor, John Major, was portrayed as a dull, totally gray man who ate nothing but peas. The opposition Labour leaders, including Neil Kinnock as "Kinnochio," were pilloried for their inability to challenge decades of Tory rule.

In spite of its detractors, more than 12 million viewers (a quarter of England's adult population) watched *Spitting Image* on Central Independent Television, a subsidiary of ITV. The program's spin-off records, books, comics, and videos sold in the millions. It won an International Emmy for "Outstanding Popular Arts" program in the 1985–86 season, and a franchised edition appeared on Moscow television.

Spitting Image originated with Peter Fluck and Roger Law, who first met at Cambridge School of Art. They became involved in the liberal politics favored by art students, through which they met another stu-

Spitting Image: Down and Out at the White House, 1986, Ronald Reagan puppet.
©*NBC/Courtesy of the Everett Collection*

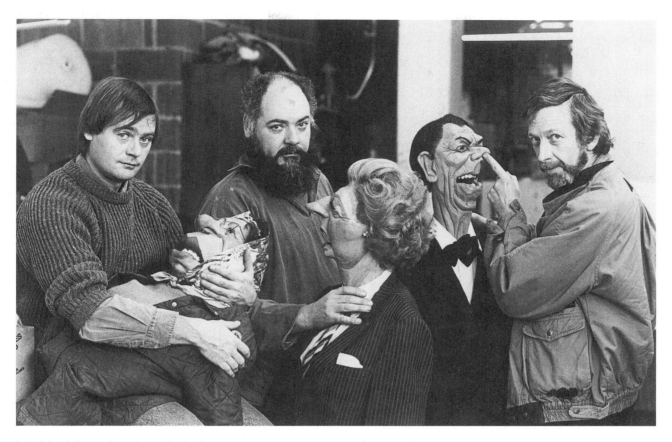

John Lloyd, Roger Law, Peter Fluck with their *Spitting Image* puppets of Queen Elizabeth, Margaret Thatcher, Ronald Reagan.
©*NBC/Courtesy of the Everett Collection*

dent, Peter Cook. In 1961, Cook fronted England's flowering of political satire by starring with Dudley Moore in the revue "Beyond the Fringe," which inspired the TV program *That Was the Week That Was.* Cook employed Law as an illustrator for his projects, such as the satire magazine *Private Eye* and a political comic strip in the *Observer* newspaper. Fluck and Law built separate careers in magazine illustration, and Law took two commissions in the music business that yielded classic album covers: The Jimi Hendrix Experience as Hindu deities for *Axis: Bold As Love* and *The Who Sell Out,* for which Roger Daltrey posed sitting in a bathtub filled with baked beans.

Fluck and Law each began working with sculpted caricatures, creating several images that appeared in London's *Sunday Times Magazine,* where Law had become an artistic director and reporter. In 1975 they formed a partnership, named Luck and Flaw, to turn out their three-dimensional portraits for such outlets as the *New York Times Magazine,* Germany's *Stern,* international editions of *Time,* and *National Lampoon.* The work proved barely profitable until 1981, when Martin Lambie-Nairn invited them to lunch.

Lambie-Nairn was a graphic designer at London Weekend Television. He thought that a political television program using puppets or animation might be a good investment, and he proposed to front Fluck and Law the capital for a pilot episode (thus the credit at the end of each episode, "From an original lunch by Martin Lambie-Nairn."). The pilot took two years to complete.

The pair quickly decided that the show should use puppets, which, like Jim Henson's Muppets, required two operators, for the face and one arm. (Henson, in fact, turned down an offer to collaborate on the puppet workshop.) The first puppet designs were bogged down by expensive, heavy electronics needed just to make their eyes move. After several months without any film being shot, Fluck cobbled together a simple mechanism using steel cable and air bulbs. The team also picked up Tony Hendra of *National Lampoon* (and later of *Spinal Tap*) as a writer and hired two producers: Jon Blair, a producer of current affairs programming, and John Lloyd of the *Not the Nine O'Clock News. Spitting Image,* the pilot's title, exhausted the resources of several backers, including

Spitting Image

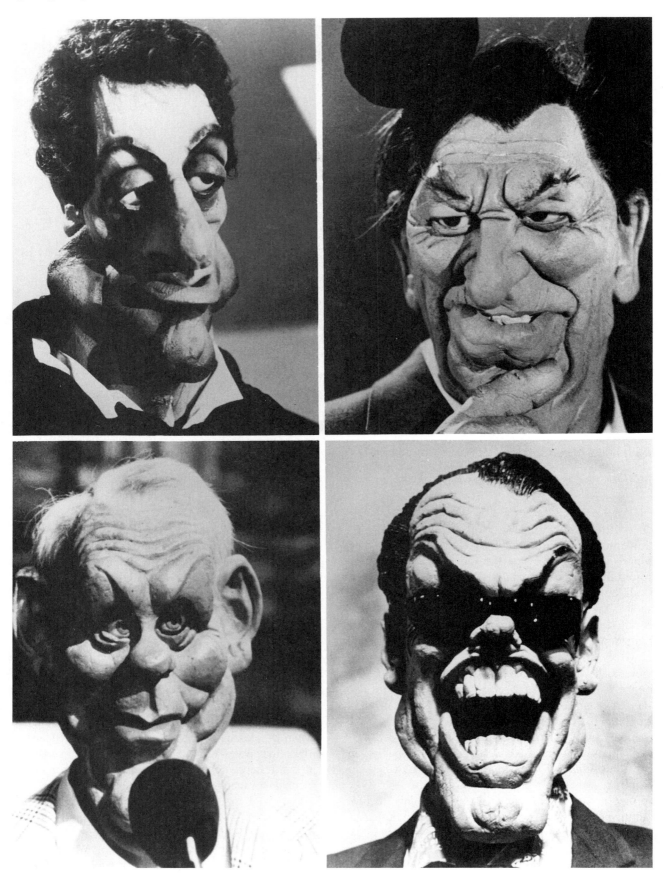

Spitting Image: Down and Out at the White House, 1986.
©NBC/Courtesy of the Everett Collection

2168

computer executive Clive Sinclair, before it was completed at a cost of £150,000, a record for a light-entertainment program.

In its first season, *Spitting Image* focused exclusively on politics and played to mediocre ratings. For the next round, Fluck and Law were obliged to caricature entertainment and sports figures as well, and the show's fortunes immediately improved. The partners worked out a schedule in which they spent the off-season stockpiling nontopical segments, such as music-video parodies (in one, Barry Manilow was all nose; another showed off Madonna's singing belly button). Each episode had a window of six minutes for fresh political commentary, written and taped the night before its broadcast.

The *Spitting Image* parodies reached a status not unlike that of *Mad* magazine in the early 1960s, as many of those whom the show caricatured took their skewering as a sign that they had "made it." While Thatcher has only commented, "I don't ever watch that program," members of the House of Commons had tapes of each show delivered to them the following Monday, and former Tory Defense Minister Michael Heseltine tried to purchase his puppet.

The commercial broadcaster Central Television gave *Spitting Image* few censorship problems. BBC radio, however, refused to play their first spin-off record, with a Prince Andrew imitator boasting, "I'm Just a Prince Who Can't Say No." "The Chicken Song," however, a single that parodied the sing-along ditties that infest pub jukeboxes and vacation discotheques every summer, reached number one on the charts.

The influence of U.S. politics on the British scene was apparent in frequent lampoons of Ronald Reagan. American news outlets excerpted a video with Ron and Nancy as "Leaders of the Pack," singing "Do Do Ron Ron." The befuddled Reagan also appeared in a serial thriller, "The President's Brain Is Missing," and was featured prominently in the Spitting Image–produced video for Genesis's song "Land of Confusion." In September 1986, the National Broadcasting Company (NBC) aired a two-part original *Spitting Image* special in which the secret arbiters of fame, including Bill Cosby and Ed McMahon, hatch a clandestine plot to have an overmuscled Sylvester Stallone elected president.

Spitting Image projects continued to appear on both sides of the Atlantic throughout the 1990s, and in 2000 many puppets from the program were auctioned off for charity. Numerous videos and musical recordings are available in Britain, where repeats of the program are shown on cable. American VCRs can play a compilation of *Spitting Image* music videos, a puppet production of "Peter and the Wolf," and a mock documentary, "Bumbledown: The Life and Times of Ronald Rea-

gan" (a double feature with the musical, "The Sound of Maggie!"). The group also collaborated with U.S. cable channel Comedy Central to illustrate a book by Glenn Eichler, *Bill and Hillary's 12-Step Recovery Guide*. The book was promoted through a series of commercial cutaways on the cable channel, featuring the puppet Clinton family.

MARK R. McDERMOTT

See also **British Programming**

Puppeteers
Peter Fluck
Roger Law

Voices
Chris Barrie
Steve Nallon
Enn Reitel
Harry Enfield
Pamela Stephenson
Jon Glover
Jan Ravens
Jessica Martin
Rory Bremner
Kate Robbins
Hugh Dennis

Producers
David Frost, Jon Blair, John Lloyd, Geoffrey Perkins, David Tyler, Bill Dare

Programming History
137 30-minute episodes; 4 45-minute episodes; 5 specials
ITV
February 26, 1984–June 17, 1984
January 6, 1985–March 24, 1985
January 5, 1986–February 9, 1986
March 30, 1986–May 4, 1986
September 14, 1986–November 2, 1986
November 1, 1987–December 6, 1987
April 17, 1988
October 29, 1988–December 11, 1988
May 6, 1989
June 11, 1989–July 16, 1989
November 12, 1989–December 17, 1989
May 13, 1990–June 24, 1990
November 11, 1990–December 6, 1990
November 10, 1991–December 15, 1991
April 8, 1992–May 17, 1992
October 4, 1992–November 8, 1992

Further Reading

Heller, Steven, "Spitting Images," *Print* (May–June 1986)

Iyer, Pico, and John Wright, "Stringing Along," *Time* (April 28, 1986)

Law, Roger, with Lewis Chester and Alex Evans, *A Nasty Piece of Work: The Art and Graft of Spitting Image,* London: Booth-Clibborn Editions, 1992

"Major Threat," *The Nation* (April 5, 1985)

O'Neil, Thomas, *The Emmys: Star Wars, Showdowns, and the Supreme Test of TV's Best,* New York: Penguin, 1992

Robinson, Andrew, "*Spitting Image:* Lampoon from Lime-house," *Sight and Sound* (Spring 1984)

Waters, Harry F., "Stringing Up the Celebrated," *Newsweek* (September 1, 1986)

Wolf, Matt, "Ace Puppeteers Pull No Punches with Clintons," *Chicago Tribune* (August 30, 1995)

Sponsor

Television in the United States is a profit-maximizing set of entities, an industry whose success is measured largely by its ability to deliver viewers to advertisers. The lure of television is its programs; commercial broadcasters seek shows of optimal value (be it in terms of ratings generated or demographics attracted) in order to maximize advertising revenue. The sponsor—the organization, corporation, institution, or other entity willing to pay the broadcaster revenue in exchange for the opportunity to advertise on television—stands at the center of program strategies. This situation requires recognition of the complex interrelationship between television networks and advertisers, two industries whose differing responsibilities and sometimes conflicting needs produce the programming that draws the audience to the advertisement. In U.S. television, the economic and industrial systems supporting these arrangements have their beginnings in radio broadcasting.

The emergence of radio in the early 1930s as an astonishingly effective means of delivering consumers to producers attracted an array of enthusiastic advertisers, and soon the radio schedule was dominated by shows named for their sponsors—the *Chase and Sanborn Hour,* the *Cliquot Club Eskimos,* and the *Maxwell House Concert,* for example. Produced for their clients by such advertising agencies as J. Walter Thompson and Young and Rubicam, the single-sponsored program was a staple of commercial broadcasting; it was an article of faith that if a listener identified a show with its sponsor, he or she was more likely to purchase the advertised product.

Although agency involvement in television was little more than tentative prior to 1948, advertisers soon embraced the new medium with great fervor; *Pabst Blue Ribbon Bouts, Camel Newsreel,* and the *Chesterfield Supper Club* were testimony to the steadfast belief in sponsor identification. However, as program costs soared in the early 1950s, it became increasingly difficult for agencies to assume the financial burdens of production, and even the concept of single sponsorship was subject to economic pressure.

By the 1952–53 season, television's spiraling costs (an average 500 percent rise in live-programming budgets from 1949 to 1952) threatened to drive many advertisers completely out of the market. Many sponsors turned to a nonnetwork syndication strategy, cobbling together enough local station buys across the country to approximate the kind of national coverage a network usually provided. Television executives—most notably Sylvester L. "Pat" Weaver at the National Broadcasting Company (NBC)—countered sponsor complaints by championing the idea of participation advertising, or the "magazine concept." Here, advertisers purchased discrete segments of shows (typically one- or two-minute blocks) rather than entire programs. Like magazines, which featured advertisements for a variety of products, the participation show might, depending on its length, carry commercials from up to four different sponsors. Similarly, just as a magazine's editorial practice was presumably divorced from its advertising content, the presence of multiple sponsors meant that no one advertiser could control the program.

Even as agencies relinquished responsibility for production, they still maintained some semblance of control over the content of the programs in which their clients advertised, a censorship role euphemistically referred to as "constructive influence." As one advertising executive noted, "If my client sells peanut butter and the script calls for a guy to be poisoned eating a peanut butter sandwich, you can bet we're going to switch that poison to a martini." Still, this type of input was mild compared to the actual melding of commer-

"Speedy" for Alka-Seltzer.
Photo courtesy of Bayer Corporation

cial and editorial content, a practice all but abandoned by the vast majority of agencies by 1953.

Despite Madison Avenue's initially hostile reaction, participation advertising ultimately became television's dominant paradigm for two reasons. One was purely cost; purchasing 30- to 60-minute blocks of prime time was prohibitively expensive to all but a few advertisers. More important, participation ads were the ideal promotional vehicle for packaged-goods companies manufacturing a cornucopia of brand names. While it is true that the magazine concept opened up television to an array of low-budget advertisers and thus expanded the medium's revenue base, it was companies such as Procter and Gamble that catalyzed the trend (ironically, given that Procter and Gamble today has operational control over two soap operas, *The Guiding Light* and *As the World Turns,* the last vestiges of single-sponsored shows on television). Further, back-to-back recessions in the mid-1950s provided an impetus for the producers

of recession-proof goods to scatter their spots throughout the schedule; their subsequent sales success solidified the advent of participation on the schedule. Without the economic rationale of single sponsorship, most advertisers chose to circulate their commercials through many different shows rather than rely on identification with a single program.

By 1960, sponsorship was no longer synonymous with control—it now merely meant the purchase of advertising time on somebody else's program. While sponsor identification remained important to such advertisers as Kraft and Revlon, most sponsors prized circulation over prestige; as a result, fewer agencies offered advertiser-licensed shows to the networks. The quiz scandals of 1958–59, often identified as the causative factor in network control of program procurement, were in actuality only a coda.

Ironically, it was the networks' assumption of programming control that resulted in a narrower and more conservative conception of program content, with a greater reliance on established genres and avoidance of technical or narrative experimentation. In an effort to provide shows that would offend no sponsor, network television's attempts to be all things to all advertisers drained the medium of its youthful vigor, plunging it into a premature middle age. By appealing to target audiences—at least in the early 1950s—advertisers were in many ways more responsive and innovative than the networks.

While the vestiges of single sponsorship remain in, of all places, public television—*ExxonMobil Masterpiece Theater,* for example—advertisers still wield enormous, if indirect, influence on program content. For example, in 1995 Procter and Gamble, the largest television advertiser in the United States, announced that it would no longer sponsor daytime talk shows whose content the company considered too salacious. Today's marketers believe that they can influence programs through selective breeding, bankrolling the content they support and pulling dollars from topics they do not.

MICHAEL MASHON

See also **Advertising; Advertising, Company Voice; Advertising Agency; "Golden Age" of Television; Programming; Sustaining Program**

Further Reading

Allen, Robert C., editor, *Channels of Discourse, Reassembled,* Chapel Hill: University of North Carolina Press, 1992

Barnouw, Erik, *The Sponsor: Notes on a Modern Potentate,* New York: Oxford University Press, 1978

Bellaire, Arthur, *TV Advertising: A Handbook of Modern Practice,* New York: Harper, 1959

Boddy, William, *Fifties Television: The Industry and Its Critics,* Urbana: University of Illinois Press, 1990

Cantor, Muriel B., *Prime-Time Television: Content and Control,* Beverly Hills, California: Sage, 1980

Ewen, Stuart, and Elizabeth Ewen, *Channels of Desire: Mass Images and the Shaping of American Consciousness,* New York: McGraw-Hill, 1982; 2nd edition, Minneapolis: University of Minnesota Press, 1992

Kepley, Vance, "The Weaver Years at NBC," *Wide Angle* (April 1990)

Sports and Television

The relationship between sports and television is now so firmly established that it is difficult to imagine their intersecting histories as anything other than a steady, synergistic march. While the sports–television nexus has developed substantially since the middle of the 20th century, this has been less a story of simple, linear progress than of difficult mutual accommodation and palpable tension. The widespread concern that television has taken over sports has, for the past two decades, been challenged by the proposition that it has become hostage to it. Closer integration of sports and television has been accompanied by wide swings in the degree of power held by each party. In the early 21st century, the pendulum seems to have swung back in favor of television, with the cost of sports broadcast rights falling in response to often disappointing commercial returns from their purchase. The end of the long economic boom in television sports, even if it is only a pause, provides an excellent opportunity to review the sports–television nexus over the past seven decades.

Sports are important to the development of television on many grounds. They have encouraged consumers to buy television sets and services in the first place; supply network, independent, satellite, and cable TV companies with vast quantities of content and loyal, sometimes spectacularly large audiences; and have helped place television at the center of contemporary society and culture. Correspondingly, television has been instrumental in the ascendancy of sports to its current position as one of the prime forms of popular culture, providing it with enormous audience outreach well beyond the field of play and vast injections of capital. Like many new technologies, television

Courtesy of ESPN

emerged first as a capability without a clear sense of purpose, and sports have helped provide television with a powerful justification for its existence.

The history of television sport is also characterized by competing ways of representing it. The two most influential of these can be described as the British and American modes of sports television that emerged within different national cultures and broadcast systems and as a result have provided contending reference points for debates about how sports are and should be displayed on television. Crudely, it might be argued that British sports television, through the publicly owned British Broadcasting Corporation (BBC), pioneered the sober representation of nation in and through sport, while in the United States, the first advances toward a commercial television sports market were made. These represent the anchor points for continuing debates about the quality of televised sporting events.

The Early Days of Sports on Television

When BBC Television was formed in 1936, sports was quickly placed on the program schedule. After successfully broadcasting radio sports in the 1920s, the BBC saw in great national sports events such as Wimbledon (tennis), the Derby (horseracing), and the FA Cup Final (soccer) ideal opportunities to meet its charter obligation of promoting national culture through "public service broadcasting." When the BBC lost its television monopoly in the United Kingdom in 1955 with the introduction of the commercial ITV service, it was reluctantly forced to compete for sports broadcasts and against ITV's livelier, more market-oriented, American-influenced way of representing sports. In this period, broadcast sports (along with great occasions of state, such as the 1953 coronation of Queen Elizabeth II) were an important factor in consumer decisions to purchase television sets (and to pay the compulsory TV license fee to support the BBC that exists to this day), with annual new TV set ownership increasing tenfold between 1946 and 1959.

In the United States, sports television commenced in 1939 with the broadcast of a baseball game between Columbia and Princeton universities, while in 1944 network sports broadcasting was inaugurated by the National Broadcasting Company's (NBC's) *Gillette Cavalcade of Sports* through its coverage of a boxing match. In the immediate post–World War II period, NBC offered sports fans the opportunity to watch, for the first time, broadcasts of baseball, football, and boxing in the comfort of their own homes. Just as subscription television in the late 20th century saw premium sports as a major "driver" for the take-up of cable and satellite services, television networks in the middle of that century saw sports as a major lure to purchase televisual technology. Sports, along with quiz shows and soap operas, played a major role in inducing the spectacular increase of over 700 percent in U.S. television ownership in the period 1948–50.

The Development of Sports

Sports, in the contemporary language of information technology, have emerged as a "killer application" for television. They have capitalized on the industrial development of sports whereby intermittent, chaotic game contests became organized into regular, rule-bound competitions in specialist venues with restricted access funded by paying customers. Sports can effortlessly discharge both news and entertainment functions. Their "nowness," and the physical presence of often scores of thousands of passionate citizens, means that they are newsworthy, while their vivid spectacle and unfolding drama make for enjoyable, even compelling viewing, especially for men (and increasingly for women). The rudimentary camera technology of the early phase of sports television was simply required to capture the event, programming that was much cheaper (though much less easily controlled) than studio-based genres. Roone Arledge, the producer of American Broadcasting Company (ABC) programs such as *Wide World of Sports* and *Monday Night Football,* is credited both with many technical innovations, such as replays and slow motion, and with openly treating sports as a form of show business. As long as sports organizations could be persuaded that television was generating interest in sports rather than siphoning potential consumers from the stadium to the home, television received from sports inexpensive, sponsored popular programming. Sports, though, came to realize their competitive economic value and began to play television corporations against one other in the quest to expand broadcast rights revenue in return for "rediffusion."

The position of sports in television schedules has varied considerably, sometimes heavily entrenched in prime time and at others confined mainly to less pivotal time slots. The amount of coverage of sports on television continued to expand into the late 1970s, its appeal to sponsors and advertisers undiminished. However, the cheapness of sports programming was eroded not so much by the rising cost of production (although multiple cameras and more sophisticated direction and commentary did increase broadcast budgets) as by the inflation of sports broadcast rights.

Both parties appreciated the elevated symbolic status of TV networks acquiring the rights to high-profile sports that, in turn, became even more conspicuous as a result of enhanced television coverage. Publicly funded broadcasters such as the BBC (which had first broadcast major sports events and sports magazine shows such as the long-running *Grandstand*) found themselves increasingly unable to compete with capital-rich commercial networks for sports broadcast rights, while, in the United States the coming of cable and, especially, dedicated sports channels such as the Entertainment and Sports Programming Network (ESPN) meant that sports television evolved into a seller's market in the 1970s and 1980s. For example, the ABC network paid U.S.$4.5 million to broadcast the 1968 Mexico City Olympics, while NBC paid U.S.$420 million for the 1992 Barcelona games. Such arrangements might have been sustainable as long as audience ratings and advertising revenues remained strong, but in the early 1980s audiences drifted away somewhat from sports television in response to greater provision of nonsports TV programming and of other, nonbroadcast leisure opportunities (ranging from videocassette recorders to video games).

The simultaneous erosion of the core sports TV audience (men ages 18–34) and of its appeal to advertisers (the "discovery" of female purchasing power) meant that advertisers were reluctant to pay television networks more money for smaller audiences to cover the cost of inflated broadcast rights. In the United States, the sports television market was artificially boosted in the 1990s by the inflationary tactics of the new FOX network, which outbid rival broadcasters of premium sports by a considerable measure in order to signal its arrival. For example, in 1994, its successful U.S.$350 million bid for the rights to football was three times that of the previous rights holder, the Columbia Broadcasting System (CBS).

Sports on television have developed a complex structural mix of public and commercial, free-to-air and pay broadcasting, and network and independent arrangements in regional, national, and global markets. In countries where national public broadcasters pioneered and dominated television, free-to-air commercial broadcasters such as ITV in the United Kingdom and Channel 9 in Australia have been successful in gaining much premium sports TV programming by exercising their economic power, only for both public and commercial free-to-air television to be challenged by "cashed-up" pay television operators. The most famous example of this development was the 1992 capture of the rights to English Premier League soccer by the Murdoch-led satellite broadcaster British Sky Broadcasting (BSkyB), a move that turned a loss-making company into a highly profitable one. This migration of sports to restricted, pay platforms has led to considerable dispute and, in many countries (including Australia and all the nations comprising the European Union), to the enactment of "antisiphoning" legislation to prevent the exclusive capture of major sports by pay television on the grounds that access to free-to-air broadcasts of sports events of major national significance is a right of "cultural citizenship."

Megamedia sports events, such as the Olympic Games and soccer's World Cup, have thus far resisted the temptation to award exclusivity to pay TV in return for vastly increased broadcast rights revenue on the grounds that such a move would restrict audience reach and the claims of such events to be global spectacles. Nonetheless, the 2002 KirchMedia debacle revealed that attempts by peak sports organizations to extract maximum revenues from free-to-air television can jeopardize even the greatest of media sports spectacles. In this case, the Fédération Internationale de Football Association (FIFA), soccer's governing body, sold its broadcast rights to a consortium made up of the Swiss sports marketing group ISL and the German KirchMedia for an unprecedented 2.3 billion euros. The consortium sought to on-sell those rights at greatly increased prices in order to recoup its investment. When the buyers resisted, ISL folded, and KirchMedia purchased the worldwide rights in full. Faced with opposition from sports telelvision–buying consortia such as the European Broadcasting Union (the previous rights holder), KirchMedia was forced to accept lower-than-anticipated broadcast rights fees and went into receivership, with some states (such as Germany, the host nation of the 2006 World Cup) required to underwrite televised coverage of the world's largest single sports event and most popular sport.

In the early 21st century, sports on television have inherited the problem of inflated broadcast rights and the dependency of sports on those rights. In 2002, for example, the United Kingdom's ITV Digital went into administration with debts of £178 million, leaving several soccer clubs without crucial, promised funds. ITV also paid an excessive amount (£183 million) for three-year, free-to-air Premier League soccer highlights, while in Italy the two foreign-owned pay-TV companies carrying premium soccer games, the French Telepiu and News Corporation's Stream, merged after both lost vast sums when competing against each other. In Australia, C7, the pay-TV sport channel specializing in Australian football coverage, also passed into history when its lost the football rights to a consortium led by Rupert Murdoch and Kerry Packer, thereby causing hardship for many clubs.

In 2002, annual reports, the value of American sports rights was written down by U.S.$3 billion, with the company most responsible for their inflation and for a third of the total write-down—Rupert Murdoch's News Corporation—admitting that it had overbid for them. It has been predicted that total 2002–06 major U.S. TV network losses on sports will be U.S.$1.3 billion. One way of overcoming the problem of recession in the broadcast sports industry is to be on both sides of the negotiating table—that is, to be simultaneously a buyer and a seller by having common ownership of TV companies and sports teams. For example, Disney owns the ABC network, most of ESPN, and the Mighty Ducks of Anaheim hockey team; News Corporation owns the Los Angeles Dodgers and has stakes in the Leeds United, Manchester City, and Sunderland soccer clubs; Granada TV has stakes in the Liverpool and Arsenal soccer clubs; and Silvio Berlusconi (the Italian prime minister) owns several television stations and leading Italian soccer club AC Milan. However, sports clubs can be a major drain on profits, and many of these holdings are currently on the market.

There is also some official resistance to such cozy arrangements, with the British government in 1998 blocking the £623 million takeover bid by BSkyB for Manchester United, one of the world's richest sport clubs, on the grounds that it was anticompetitive and against the public interest. Another coping strategy is the formation of new competitions, such as XFL, the disastrous 2001 American football tournament created by the World Wrestling Federation (WWF) and NBC that lost U.S.$70 million. In 2003, NBC, which had opted not to bid for the rights to the major sports leagues, adopted a more low-key strategy by televising, with modest success, the Arena Football League, a hybrid sport that provides a speedier television spectacle than that offered by the National Football League (NFL).

These problems and adjustments, however, do not prevent sports from continuing to be a key aspect of television programming. Sports can still be a highly marketable commodity and a compelling visual text. A 30-second advertisement during the Super Bowl broadcast currently costs U.S.$2.1 million, the cumulative audience of the 2002 Korea–Japan soccer World Cup was estimated to be 28.8 billion, and the International Olympic Committee (IOC) estimated that nine out of ten of people in the world with access to television watched at least some of the 2000 Sydney Olympic Games.

The Audience and Industry Attraction of Television Sports

Sports still retains considerable appeal for television companies and audiences alike. For television, sports consistently deliver large, loyal viewerships that are attractive to advertisers. While, as noted previously, there is a traditional bias toward young and middle-age men, sports has successfully sought female viewers (sometimes using the tactic of sexual objectification more frequently associated with the "male gaze" directed at females). Audiences for regular-season games (as opposed to playoff or championship matches) may be smaller than for many prime-time shows, but in production terms they are much cheaper to broadcast. Sports are especially good at filling the spaces in TV schedules. The live sports event is only one component of sports programming, with previews, postmatch appraisals, documentaries, retrospectives, quiz shows, replays, highlights, magazine programs, updates, and sports news reporting constituting a vast and flexible archive of sports content that is especially appealing to multichannel pay-television providers with extensive televisual space to fill. Pay-per-view sporting events, such as boxing matches, also represent one of few TV genres where customers are willing to pay for content on a one-off basis. Major sports television also has a highly valuable "spillover effect" whereby viewers are exposed to promotions for other shows in the hope that they will get into the habit of watching certain networks and channels. For "horizontally integrated" media and entertainment corporations with many different media functions, sports and sports merchandise can be easily cross-promoted across television channels, newspapers, magazines, radio, film, and the Internet. In countries such as Australia that impose regulatory quotas on local content and restrictions on material produced overseas, sports are also a readily available source of "indigenous" material.

The professional, industrial structure of sports is founded on the willingness of spectators to pay to watch, collectively, expert sportsmen and sportswomen in action. Television severs the physical, communal presence from spectatorship. In its live form, TV enables distant, dispersed, and domestic viewers to watch sports action in real time. At first, as noted previously, the technology was limited, with single, static black-and-white cameras offering a pleasing but much diminished version of the physical, in-stadium experience. However, the development of the technology and technique of sports television enhanced the viewing experience to such a degree that watching from home now rivals the pleasures of actually being at the site of the game. With the development of color television, multiple cameras inside and outside the stadium, close-ups, replays, slow motion, expert description and commentary, immediate postgame athlete interviews, and, by the end of the 20th century, interactive information services and even personalized program direction, televised sports have fashioned themselves into a strong sensory spectacle. So substantial have these developments in TV been that sports stadiums have been required to install large screens and to enable amplified athlete interviews in order to match elements of the home television viewing experience.

Spectators are drawn to sports by the aesthetic pleasure of gazing on athletic excellence, but most are also passionate supporters, identifying with athletes and teams on the basis of locality and nationality. Sports fans project onto athletes favorable and unfavorable qualities that, to a substantial degree, resemble the characterization of popular melodrama. Furthermore, sports contests (following Arledge) are fashioned by television into narratives, their "plots" unfolding under the gaze of commentators and viewers who interpret their significance through judgmental frameworks of virtue and dishonor. However, the sports script is never legally written in advance. The formal uncertainty of live sports contests (despite their frequently predictable outcomes) can create a strong sense that history is being made on screen. In the 2003 Rugby World Cup Final between England and Australia, for example, the final result was settled only by an England score 16 seconds from the end of a period of extra time before an estimated worldwide television audience of 300 million.

Just as modernity has produced societies that are increasingly fragmented and alienated, television both symbolically unites and splinters its audience by representing sports. In the early modern period of lesser social and spatial mobility, professional sportspeople tended to be embedded in the local communities in which they originated. Television then provided the capital to create a lucrative sports market that enabled elite sportspeople to travel far from home and so to become far more affluent than most of their fans. Paradoxically, therefore, at key sporting televisual moments, elite athletes are symbolically reintegrated into the communities that sports enabled them to leave behind. Modernity also heralded the rise of the dispersed, abstract entity of the nation-state, and there are few greater opportunities for a nation to feel unified than during major sports contests.

If sports television can be described as a genre, it has many variants arising from the different characteristics of specific sports in terms of their rhythms, tempos, rules, and spatial contexts. Individual contact

sports, for example, have a gladiatorial quality. Boxing has long been a key form of televised sports. The small, square ring is easy to capture on the small screen, with two men (and now some women) "slugging it out" in near proximity to a noisy crowd. The rounds in boxing are of a fixed duration, easily enabling the insertion of advertisements between rounds. A boxing match may last no more than a few seconds or minutes (requiring a good deal of spontaneous expert discussion), but the prescribed number of rounds ensures that a bout cannot overflow the program schedule. The televised buildup to the fight itself can engender considerable anticipation for casual viewers and boxing fans alike. Indeed, in the case of the "pseudosport" of wrestling as presented by WWF, the contest itself is a relatively small aspect of the total broadcast.

Indoor individual and team sports, including basketball, netball, ice hockey, and indoor tennis, have the advantage of a controlled environment akin to that of the television studio but at the cost of the visual richness of the outdoor broadcast. Sports such as football (both the American and the Australian versions), soccer, rugby, field hockey, tennis, baseball, and cricket generally take place on large, open, rectangular or oval fields. The pace of different sports range from the frenetic to the stately, thereby delivering highly variable viewing experiences. In the case of nonstadium sports, such as golf and marathon running, the landscape of rural and urban courses provides television sports with an almost tourist-like quality.

Television does more than merely represent sports. Its cultural and economic power is such that it has shaped many sports contests. Some sports may be deemed more telegenic than others and so prosper on television in a manner that is self-reproducing. It is mainly because of television that the five-day game of international cricket, with its capacity to end in a draw, spawned also a one-day game with a virtually guaranteed victor and loser. The rhythm of sports contests is dictated to varying degrees by "time-outs" for commercial breaks, penalty shoot-outs in soccer, and tie breakers in tennis in the interests of advertisements and program schedules. The time-zone convenience demands of major TV markets can result in boxing matches at midnight, Olympic marathons in the heat of the day, and baseball games played on early winter nights. Women's sports such as tennis, golf, netball, basketball, hockey, and soccer, furthermore, have all come under pressure to improve their televisual "salability" through more overt modes of sexual address.

Nonetheless, television alone cannot guarantee the success of sports. As noted previously, made-for-television contests using all the advantages of the medium but unsupported by a substantial fan base are rarely more than temporarily diverting novelties. Indeed, one of the characteristics of sports television is that it requires in-stadium spectators to perform for the cameras and microphones in order to supply the necessary atmosphere to turn the broadcast into a compelling spectacle. Without the atmospherics of large crowds on-screen, sports can appear unengaging, trivial, or absurd. For this reason, sparse crowds are hidden by tighter camera shots, and boom microphones are turned up to maximum volume. Sometimes—as in the case of a soccer match at Arsenal's Highbury stadium while under renovation—crowds have even been digitally faked for television.

Initially, it was believed that admitting television cameras into sporting events would lead to a reduced number of paying customers in the stadium. But television also made sports available to vastly greater numbers of viewers who could be "sold" to sponsors and advertisers than could possibly attend games, resulting not only in the astonishingly efficient promotion of sports but also in previously unimagined broadcast rights revenue. The cost to sports, of course, was a loss of autonomy. To return to the 2003 Rugby Union World Cup Final, the requirement of extra time disrupted the television schedule, resulting in medal presenters being instructed by television directors to speed things up. A dignified, symbolic moment of triumph thereby became an embarrassing, fast-forwarded farce. At such unfortunate moments, viewers can simultaneously apprehend both the pleasure and the pain of the submission of sports to the embrace of television.

DAVID ROWE

See also **Arledge, Roone; Grandstand; Hockey Night in Canada; Ohlmeyer, Don; Olympics and Television; Super Bowl**

Further Reading

Baker, A., and T. Boyd, editors, *Sports, Media, and the Politics of Identity,* Bloomington: Indiana University Press, 1999

Bernstein, A., and N. Blain, editors, *Sport, Media, Culture: Global and Local Dimensions,* London: Frank Cass, 2003

Birrell, S., and M.G. McDonald, editors, *Reading Sport: Critical Essays on Power and Representation,* Boston, Massachusetts: Northeastern University Press, 2000

Boyle, R., and R. Haynes, *Power Play: Sport, the Media & Popular Culture,* Harlow, United Kingdom: Pearson Education, 2000

Brookes, R., *Representing Sport,* London: Arnold, 2002

Chandler, J.M., *Television and National Sports: The United States and Britain,* Urbana: University of Illinois Press, 1988

Creedon, P.J., editor, *Women, Media and Sport: Challenging Gender Values,* Thousand Oaks, California: Sage, 1994

Goldlust, J., *Playing for Keeps: Sport, the Media and Society,* Melbourne: Longman Cheshire, 1987

Martin, R., and T. Miller, T. editors, *SportCult,* Minneapolis: University of Minnesota Press, 1999

Miller, T., *Sportsex,* Philadelphia, Pennsylvania: Temple University Press, 2001

Rader, B.G., *In Its Own Image: How Television Has Transformed Sports,* New York: Free Press, 1984

Roche, M., *Mega-Events and Modernity: Olympics and Expos in the Growth of Global Culture,* London and New York: Routledge, 2000

Rowe, D., *Sport, Culture and the Media: The Unruly Trinity,* 2nd edition, Maidenhead, United Kingdom, and Philadelphia, Pennsylvania: Open University Press, 2004

Wenner, L., editor, *MediaSport,* London: Routledge, 1998

Whannel, G., *Fields in Vision: Television Sport and Cultural Transformation,* London: Routledge, 1992

Sportscasters

The history of sportscasting, like almost everything else on television, had its roots in radio. Radio's first generation of great sportscasters—Graham McNamee, Ted Husing, and Grantland Rice, among others—transformed the airwaves into a "theater of the mind" in which hyperbole would become honored as an art. McNamee, a meat salesman before moving into sportscasting, is regarded as the first well-known play-by-play announcer, unapologetic about sacrificing accuracy for excitement. Perhaps unknowingly, McNamee was laying a foundation for the idea that the sportscaster could

be a personality, someone recognized not only for professional abilities but also for the knack of keeping an audience entertained. His emphasis on enthusiasm lives on today in the performances of men such as Dick Vitale and John Madden; their excitement for their favorite sport appears to be both genuine and the most important factor in identifying their popularity.

It would be incorrect to suggest that every sportscaster who followed McNamee adopted his strategy. It is important to note that some sportscasters frowned on the notion of becoming too dramatic or making themselves a part of the event they covered. They sought instead to "play it straight," to be less a fan and more a journalist. In doing so, they did not lose the respect of their peers or the public.

Unlike today, many of the early sportscasters regularly called the games not from the stadium but from a studio many miles away, where they read and "performed" details of the game as reported on a telegraph wire ticker. The announcers used sound effects and creative language to enhance the sense that they were present at the game. The system worked, provided that the ticker also worked. Perhaps the most notable "recreationist" landed his first job in the entertainment industry as a football announcer at an Iowa radio station. The year was 1932, and Ronald "Dutch" Reagan was paid $5 a game. Later, he would deliver similar re-created broadcasts of Chicago Cubs' games for another Iowa radio station (and much later, the so-called Great Communicator would be elected president of the United States).

Many of the next generation of distinguished radio sportscasters, such as Mel Allen, Red Barber, Lindsey Nelson, and Bill Stern, would later become prominent voices in television's first decades as a mass medium. Allen and Barber, famous for their play-by-play reporting for the Yankees and Dodgers, respectively, were the first broadcasters enshrined into the Baseball Hall of Fame. Barber eschewed the notion that a sportscaster should "root, root, root for the home team." Instead, he adopted an approach that might be called "objective" and let the action take center stage. Stern saw it differently. His fame developed partially from hosting a radio program filled with fictional stories about real athletes and people. Stern acknowledged that he developed a following because of these harmless diversions (as he called them). Indeed, he did. He was voted the nation's most popular sportscaster 13 times.

In the years immediately following World War II, television and sports used each other to expand their popularity with, and their ability to reach, a larger audience. Some scholars have suggested that during this period, sports teams and leagues had the advantage in the relationship because television networks desperately needed sports programming to fill the schedule. It was not uncommon for the networks to devote upward of 40 percent of their weeknight schedule to sports. Although roller derby and bowling played well on the small screen, boxing and professional wrestling were the sports best suited to the limitations of the first generation of television sets. Dennis James became the prototypical wrestling announcer. "I used to do whole wrestling matches in spontaneous poetry," he once said. His style showed that describing action in the

ring with eloquent elocution was entirely appropriate, even for a sport in which the stars often appeared to be more like actors than athletes. The prominent role that advertisers would play in the presentation of sports also developed in this period. For example, the Gillette company sponsored *Cavalcade of Sports,* which heavily promoted boxing and stayed on the air for 14 years.

Sportscasting in the 1950s followed the radio pattern of announcer enthusiasm. Many sportscasters and their employers conceived of their role as something akin to being ambassadors and fans of the game. This style was perhaps perfected in the Midwest, where baseball announcers became synonymous with the teams they covered on a daily basis. Harry Caray was the voice of the St. Louis Cardinals for 16 years before he was replaced by Jack Buck, a member of the baseball, football, and radio halls of fame. Buck remained with the team until his death in 2002. Caray eventually landed with the Chicago Cubs, for whom he worked from 1981 through 1998. He was appreciated far more for his passion for baseball and the Cubs than he was for his ability to broadcast a game. In short, he was a personality.

During the 1960s—the decade of the marriage of television and football—one of the more important revolutions in television sports was introduced, specifically on December 31, 1963, during an Army–Navy football game. Instant replay would figure prominently in the phenomenal rise in popularity of televised football during the 1960s and beyond. Moreover, Pete Rozelle, the commissioner of the National Football League (NFL), envisioned how his sport could play well on television, that it could mean more than simply seeing the two teams play. The television networks agreed, and in 1964, the Columbia Broadcasting System (CBS) paid an unprecedented $28 million dollars for television rights for NFL games and instantly recouped its investment with two $14 million sponsorship contracts, with Ford Motor Company and Philip Morris.

Soon networks were competing for the same fans in what was supposedly the most important football game of the season. The Super Bowl debuted in January 1967, and Rozelle allowed both CBS and the National Broadcasting Company (NBC) to televise it. A *Time* magazine report suggested the dual network idea was deliberate, as it forced both networks to promote the game and entice viewers to watch. The game itself did not attract a large in-person audience, but both networks brought out their primary football announcing teams. In pregame promotions, both emphasized the excellence of their sportscasters. CBS offered Ray Scott, Jack Whitaker, Frank Gifford, and Pat Summerall, while NBC featured Curt Gowdy and Paul Christman.

The American Broadcasting Company (ABC) remained in the shadows of CBS and NBC throughout the 1950s. Roone Arledge, a producer (and eventual president) at ABC, however, viewed spectator sports as involving more than a passive audience and brought ABC into a new light. He created what was destined to become the longest-running sports program in television, *Wide World of Sports,* and hired a young Baltimore announcer named James K. McManus to host the new show. McManus soon changed his name to Jim McKay and would go down in broadcast history as the man who first informed the world about the tragic terrorist attack that took the lives of 11 Israeli athletes at the 1972 Olympics in Munich, West Germany.

Arledge believed that a television network was not doing its job if it merely brought the game to the fans. Instead, he wanted to bring the fans to the game. He challenged his ABC crews to use all available production techniques to heighten the experience of the game. He wanted both men and women to feel like they were part of the in-stadium audience, even though they were sitting in their living rooms, at a bar, or some other location. In short, he wanted show business and sports to be linked.

Soon after he was named president of the network's sports division, Arledge brought professional football to ABC. *Monday Night Football* began in 1970. The three-man announcing team included Keith Jackson, Don Meredith, and Howard Cosell. Jackson lasted only one season and was replaced by Frank Gifford. The recipe for success had been created: the sexy Gifford, the easygoing Meredith, and the controversial Cosell remained together through 1973, when Meredith left. He returned in 1977, and the group (with Fran Tarkenton and O.J. Simpson intermittently joining the team) remained together through 1983.

Arledge was also guided by the notion that announcer-approval clauses, in which teams approved or disapproved announcers, were inappropriate. This policy made ABC the first network to allow—in fact, to welcome—critical commentary to accompany the play-by-play.

Cosell proved to be the beneficiary. He was not afraid to tackle issues he believed needed comment, and he developed a love–hate relationship with the audience. Cosell joined the elite ranks of Curt Gowdy, Chris Schenkel, McKay, Nelson, and Summerall when the National Academy of Television Arts and Sciences recognized his accomplishments with a Lifetime Achievement Award. He passed away one year later.

Cosell's star was shining brightest at a time when ABC's next superstar was beginning to make his mark. In 1980, Al Michaels was given what at the time seemed to be a rather mundane assignment: play-by-play announcer for the network's hockey coverage during the Winter Olympics. But the stunning gold medal victory by the U.S. hockey team and Michaels's cry of "Do you believe in miracles!" in the final seconds of the Americans' victory over the Soviet Union remain unforgettable more than two decades later.

One area in which Arledge did not serve as a pioneer was in the introduction of women as sportscasters. Former Miss America Phyllis George is generally credited with breaking sportscasting's gender barrier in 1975 when she joined *The NFL Today* on CBS, but at least one woman served as an analyst in the 1950s. Myrtle Power was signed by CBS after earning short-lived celebrity status as a baseball expert on the game show *The $64,000 Question.* While women have continued to make inroads into sportscasting (consider names such as Gayle Gardner and Lesley Visser), it has been a struggle. One of the lingering debates concerns whether female journalists should have access to male locker rooms. High-profile cases came to national prominence in the final decades of the 20th century. The most notable involved Lisa Olsen, a *Boston Herald* reporter who in 1990 accused several New England Patriot football players of exposing themselves and sexually harassing her while she interviewed other players.

The Entertainment and Sports Programming Network (ESPN) went on the air in 1979 and launched another new era of sportscasting. ESPN moved rapidly from covering quasi sports events such as tractor pulls to become a household phenomenon. It now reaches more than 80 million U.S. television households, making it the largest cable network. ESPN's tremendous success allowed it to expand on cable (ESPN2, ESPN Classic, ESPN News), radio (ESPN Radio), and into print (*ESPN The Magazine*). Moreover, it provides substantial live coverage of all four major professional sports leagues in the United States. Although ESPN does not own broadcast rights to any of the "March Madness" games, the annual men's college basketball tournament, it does have the analyst who perhaps can be called that sport's greatest ambassador, Dick Vitale. The ever-present, ever-high-octane, ever-positive Vitale, the quintessential personality, attracts rowdy basketball fans wherever he goes.

Chris Berman has been with ESPN from its infancy and remains one of its most popular announcers. A six-time National Sportscaster of the Year honoree, Berman is best known for the nicknames he has given various athletes (e.g., Roberto "Remember the" Alomar). His style, which might be described as "hey, you need to listen to me," not only fits well at ESPN but also is central in a period in which a sportscaster's personality seems to be as important as the knowledge he or she brings to the event being covered.

ESPN also should be recognized for hiring the first African-American woman in sports television. Robin Roberts joined ESPN in 1990 and wore many hats for the network before being named in 2002 the morning news host on ABC's *Good Morning America.*

ABC's run of success with *Monday Night Football* began to wane after Cosell's departure. The program regularly earned ratings in the high teens and lower 20s during the Gifford, Meredith, and Cosell years, but since 1986 the show has continued to lose audience share. Moreover, this was a period in which there seemed to be an ever-revolving door in the broadcast booth. Following the 2001 season, in which the average rating was 11.5 (the lowest ever), ABC announced it had hired John Madden, the most popular football analyst of this generation, at a reported $5 million per year. This was not the first time Madden's popularity was rewarded. In 1993, after FOX outbid CBS for the rights to broadcast National Football Conference (NFC) games, Madden negotiated a contract with Rupert Murdoch that earned him a reported $30 million over four years. With that deal, Madden became the highest-paid sportscaster of all time.

Madden says his "passion for the game" is what makes him tick. Perhaps surprisingly, his hiring did not generate immediate returns: ABC's ratings were no better in 2002 than in the previous year but were showing an increase in 2003.

ANTHONY MORETTI

See also **Arledge, Roone; McKay, Jim; Olympics and Television; Super Bowl**

The author wishes to recognize Jimmie Reeves, who wrote this section of the encyclopedia's first edition and who graciously allowed the author to contribute to the second edition.

Spriggs, Elizabeth (1929–)

British Actor

Elizabeth Spriggs is among Britain's most established and well-loved character actors. An associate artiste with the Royal Shakespeare Company, her illustrious work in the theater has run parallel with her lengthy and successful career in television. Work in the two media converged with her characterization of Sonia in Wesker's *Love Letters on Blue Paper,* a role she originally created for television and then transferred to the stage, winning her the West End Managers Award for 1978.

Her versatility is revealed by both her skill at adapting her style for television, resisting the tendency of many actors with a theatrical background to "play to the gallery," and her work in a diverse set of television genres. Listed among her credits are the particularly noteworthy roles of the long-suffering and self-sacrificing wife and mother, Connie Fox, in the drama series *Fox;* Harvey Moon's no-nonsense and strong-willed mother in the situation comedy series *Shine on Harvey Moon;* the God-fearing gossip, May, in the critically acclaimed and highly popular drama *Oranges Are Not the Only Fruit;* and the wayward and wonderfully funny nurse, Sairey Gamp, in the much-praised British Broadcasting Corporation (BBC) adaptation of *Martin Chuzzlewit.*

While to a great extent subject to the standard typecasting of older actresses, Spriggs takes the crones, gossips, and suffering matriarchs and transforms them with her engagingly strong and rooted presence. In doing so, she imbues the usual fare with additional weight and dimension.

Although there has been interest, particularly within feminist television criticism, in analyzing the representations of older female characters and the contributions of actresses to these characterizations, most of the attention has been paid to the soap opera genre. The wider terrain remains largely unexplored and unevaluated within television studies.

NICOLA STRANGE

Elizabeth Spriggs. Born in England, September 18, 1929. Educated at the Royal School of Music. Married: 1) Marshall Jones; 2) Murray Manson. Stage actor with the Bristol Old Vic and the Birmingham Repertory, 1958; joined the Royal Shakespeare Company, 1962; joined the National Theatre Company, 1976; numerous appearances on television and in motion pictures. Recipient: SWETM Best Supporting Actress Award, 1978.

Television Series

1982	*Shine On Harvey Moon*
1992–93	*The Young Indiana Jones Chronicles*
1998–	*Playing the Field*
2001–02	*Nice Guy Eddie*
2003	*Swiss Toni*

Television Play

1978	*Love Letters on Blue Paper*

Television Miniseries

1976	*The Glittering Prizes*
1980	*Fox*
1990	*Oranges Are Not the Only Fruit*
1994	*Middlemarch*
1994	*Takin' Over the Asylum*
1995	*Martin Chuzzlewit*
1999	*Wives and Daughters*

Made-for-Television Movies

1979	*Julius Caesar*
1982	*Merry Wives of Windsor*
1984	*The Cold Room*
1989	*Young Charlie Chaplin*
1992	*The Last Vampyre*
1999	*Alice in Wonderland*
1999	*A Christmas Carol*
2000	*The Sleeper*

2001	*Victoria and Albert*
2002	*Shackleton*

Films

Work Is a Four-Letter Word, 1967; *Three into Two Won't Go,* 1969; *An Unsuitable Job for a Woman,* 1981; *Richard's Things,* 1981; *Lady Chatterly's Lover,* 1981; *Going Undercover,* 1988; *Oranges Are Not the Only Fruit,* 1989; *Impromptu,* 1991; *Hour of the Pig,* 1993; *Sense and Sensibility,* 1995; *The Secret Agent,* 1996; *For My Baby; Paradise Road,* 1997; *Harry Potter and the Sorcerer's Stone,* 2001; *The Queen of Sheba's Pearls,* 2004.

Stage (selection)

Cleopatra, 1958; *The Cherry Orchard,* 1958; *The Beggar's Opera,* 1963; *The Representative,* 1963; *Victor,* 1964; *Marat/Sade,* 1965; *The Comedy of Errors,* 1965; *Timon of Athens,* 1965; *Hamlet,* 1965; *The Governor's Lady,* 1965–66; *The Government Inspector,* 1965–66; *Henry IV,* 1966; *Henry V,* 1966; *All's Well That Ends Well,* 1966; *Macbeth,* 1966; *Romeo and Juliet,* 1966; *Julius Caesar,* 1968; *The Merry Wives of Windsor,* 1968; *A Delicate Balance,* 1969; *Women Beware Women,* 1969; *Twelfth Night,* 1970; *London Assurance,* 1970; *The Winter's Tale,* 1970; *Twelfth Night,* 1970; *Major Barbara,* 1970; *Much Ado About Nothing,* 1972; *Blithe Spirit,* 1976; *The Country Wife,* 1977; *Volpone,* 1977; *Love Letters on Blue Paper,* 1978.

Spy Programs

Although individual series have enjoyed enormous popularity and cult followings, the spy genre overall has never been as successful or as ubiquitous in American television as westerns, medical dramas, and detective programs. Nevertheless, espionage-themed programs can boast a number of firsts, most notably the first African-American lead character in a regular dramatic series (*I Spy*), the first female action lead character in an hour-long American dramatic series (*The Girl from U.N.C.L.E.*), and the first Russian lead character in an American dramatic series (*The Man from U.N.C.L.E.*), the latter appearing less than three years after the Cuban missile crisis.

Except during the so-called spy-craze period of the mid-1960s, when it seemed that every action/adventure show borrowed elements from James Bond, spies as television action heroes have been far outnumbered by the more traditional figures of policemen and private investigators. Even when they do appear, television spies (or "secret agents") are often presented as international crime fighters rather than as true undercover operators, with the emphasis on justice and law enforcement rather than on clandestine activities. As a result, there are few "pure" spy programs and most of the long-running ones can be classed in other genre categories, including westerns (*The Wild, Wild West*),

The Man from U.N.C.L.E., David McCallum, Robert Vaughn, Leo G. Carroll, 1964–68.
Courtesy of the Everett Collection

situation comedy (*Get Smart*), and science fiction (*The Avengers* and *The Prisoner*).

The boundaries between the spy and other television genres is extremely fluid, and the elements of the typical spy program are variable and not easily defined. On television, spies and detectives have a great deal in common. Both are tough, sometimes world-weary individuals who live and work on the edges of normal society. Their antagonists are rich, powerful, clever, and often apparently "respectable." In both genres, because of the wealth and resources of the villain, the heroes must use extralegal means in order to triumph. Before they do, they must progress through various narrative situations, including the assignment of the case/mission; investigation of the crime; abduction by the villain; interrogation and/or torture; at least one long, complicated chase; and a final shoot-out or brawl.

The average secret agent tends to be more cerebral and sophisticated than the average detective and, if not wealthy himself, at least comfortable with the trappings of wealth. Money is not an important incentive, however. The secret agent's motives are personal and philosophical, a dedication to certain moral or political ideals, or simply a taste for the game of espionage it-self. In its focus on the "game"—the hero's intellectual ability to decipher clues, solve complex mysteries, and outmaneuver the bad guys—the television spy plot may resemble the classical detective story. Indeed, the chess metaphor appears often in each.

Nevertheless, there are several subtle differences that distinguish the television secret agent from the detective, and these can be seen in the transformation of Amos Burke, the title character of the popular series *Burke's Law*. For the first two years of the series' run, Burke (played by Gene Barry) was a Los Angeles chief of detectives who also happened to be a millionaire. In solving his homicide cases, Burke was chauffeured around in a silver Rolls Royce. His cases were typical whodunits involving the rich and glamorous portrayed by large casts of guest stars.

Then in 1965, in order to cash in on the spy craze, Captain Amos Burke, detective, became Amos Burke, secret agent. Since he was already suave, sophisticated, witty, and charming, no character tinkering was needed. However, several important changes were made. Burke left the Los Angeles Police Department to work for a U.S. government intelligence agency, his only contact being a mysterious character called simply "The Man" (played by Carl Benton Reid). Burke's operating milieu subsequently expanded from the confines of the Los Angeles area to include the entire world. No longer a local millionaire sleuth, Burke became a continent-hopping agent, and his quarry changed from small-time murderers to international criminals whose schemes and machinations had global consequences.

These changes, then, define the essential elements of the television spy series: (1) The active presence of a government or quasi government agency in the life of the protagonist. The agency is shown to be involved in clandestine and/or espionage activities. (2) Villains who are often foreign, usually eccentric, and whose crimes have larger political consequences. Most commonly, these villains desire either to take over the world or to destroy it. (3) An expansion of the plot setting beyond local and even national boundaries to include a variety of countries and exotic locales.

Since James Bond appeared on the literary and, later, cinematic scene, spy stories have also incorporated a number of stylistic motifs of his creator, Ian Fleming. These include ironic humor; the use martial arts techniques for self-defense; a preoccupation with expensive clothes, cars, food, accommodations, and leisure pursuits; the presence of beautiful women either as agents, antagonists, or innocent bystanders caught up in the plot; and a fascination with weaponry and high technology.

The importance of these motifs should not be underestimated. For example, *Honey West* was essentially a series about a female detective similar to the later *Remington Steele.* Yet critics have always categorized it as a spy program simply because of its stylistic trappings, most notably, Honey West's pet ocelot and the one-piece black jumpsuit worn by the star, Anne Francis, so reminiscent of the wardrobe of *The Avengers'* Emma Peel (Diana Rigg). On the other hand, series such as *Tightrope* and the later *Wiseguy,* both of which feature lead characters working undercover, are not considered spy programs because the international reach of the enemy crime syndicates is not emphasized and because the heroes appear and function as police officers.

The primary reason why spy shows are so few and far between on television is that the genre does not adapt well to the production and aesthetic needs of the medium. In their book *The Spy Story* (1987), John G. Cawelti and Bruce A. Rosenberg delineate two subcategories of spy fiction, both of which can be applied to spy stories on television.

The first, originating with James Buchan (*The Thirty-Nine Steps*) and other "clubmen" writers and reinvented by Ian Fleming, consists of colorful, imaginative adventures with roving, honorable heroes, dastardly villains, and exotic settings. By comparison, the second subcategory, identified with Eric Ambler, Grahame Green, and more recently John Le Carré, contains tales of espionage more realistically presented. Concerned with corruption, betrayal, and conspiracy, these stories feature a grayer mood, more circumscribed settings, and ordinary protagonists who seem, at first glance, not much different than the people they oppose. The plotting is complicated and subtle, and the endings are often downbeat, leaving the agent sadly disillusioned or dead. The chief difference between the two subcategories is the moral base of the narrative. In the first group, good and evil is rendered in stark black and white. In the second, the morality is ambiguous.

As with their literary equivalents, television spy stories may be similarly divided into the romantic and the realistic, although, as one might expect, there is considerable overlap. Both types present problems in adapting to the television medium.

The romantic spy adventure, while meeting the aesthetic needs of the medium for simplicity in storytelling, escapist interest, and fast-paced excitement, requires foreign locations, numerous props, expensive wardrobes, and other production details that can severely strain a limited television budget. On the other hand, although the realistic espionage story is likely to be less expensive to produce, the difficult themes, depressive mood, and often unattractive characters do not lend themselves to the medium, particularly to the demands of a weekly network series.

As a result, to be produced for television, both types of spy stories must be "domesticated," both literally and figuratively. For the romantic spy program, elements of the so-called Bond formula of "sex, snobbery, and sadism" must be toned down to small-screen standards. The intensity of torture sequences may be tempered by the use of outlandishly humorous devices and Perils of Pauline–style narrow escapes. Weapons may fire sleep-inducing darts (*The Man from U.N.C.L.E.*), or the hero may not carry a gun at all (as in the quasi-espionage series *MacGyver*).

Location shoots must also be kept to a minimum. Both *The Man from U.N.C.L.E.* and *The Girl from U.N.C.L.E.,* filmed on the MGM backlot, used an ingenious swish-pan technique to get from one location to another. *I Spy* traveled overseas but filmed a number of episodes in each country it visited. *The Prisoner* was shot at an actual resort village at the Hotel Portmeiron in North Wales.

Adderly was fortunate enough to find Canadian locations that could mimic the landscape of the Soviet Union and other European countries. More recently, series such as *The Scarecrow and Mrs. King* confine themselves to U.S. settings, saving stories set in foreign locales for season finales and sweeps weeks.

Several realistic, even dyspeptic, espionage series, such as *Danger Man, Callan,* and *Sandbaggers,* enjoyed healthy runs in the United Kingdom, but only one of these, *Danger Man,* ever crossed the Atlantic to be seen in the States. To make the plotlines and characters of realistic spy programs more appealing to American audiences, television producers have employed a number of different strategies. For example, *Danger Man* was retitled *Secret Agent,* and a snazzy Johnny Rivers song was added to the opening and closing credits. Both *I Led Three Lives* in the 1950s and *The Equalizer* in the 1980s exploited anxieties that were close to home for the audience, mining Red Scare paranoia in the case of the earlier show and fears of urban crime in the latter.

Another strategy used by creators of realistic spy programs is to make the central character morally certain. Although he was often surrounded by double-crossing colleagues and double agents in *Secret Agent,* John Drake's (Patrick McGoohan's) own loyalty was never in question. In *The Equalizer,* Edward Woodward, who earlier played a lonely, cold-blooded assassin in *Callan,* returned as Robert McCall, a retired CIA operative. McCall clearly had a past career similar to Callan's but now deeply regretted it. To expiate his past sins, McCall became the self-styled Equalizer of the title, dedicating his life and skills to protecting the weak and innocent free of charge. McCall was also given a family—an estranged son, a dead wife, and a daughter whose existence he discovered during the run of the series.

Surrounding the usually isolated secret agent with family, colleagues, and friends is yet another television strategy for domesticating both strains of the genre. Humor and a fraternity-boy camaraderie between Kelly Robinson (Robert Culp) and Alexander Scott (Bill Cosby) leavened *I Spy*'s sometimes bleak Cold War ideology, while the developing romance between the two lead characters (Bruce Boxleitner and Kate Jackson) kept interest high between chases in *The Scarecrow and Mrs. King*. In *Under Cover*, an intensely realistic series that featured plotlines drawn directly from recent world events, the husband and wife agents (Anthony John Denison and Linda Purl) were forced to juggle the dangerous demands of their profession with the everyday problems of home and family life. Finally, those spy stories that, for whatever reason, could not be domesticated, such as adaptations of best-selling spy thrillers, generally ended up on cable or the Public Broadcasting Service (PBS) or on network television as TV movies and miniseries.

The history of the spy on television reflects this continuing tension between the genre and the medium and between romantic and realistic tendencies. Whenever public interest in foreign affairs is on the rise, spy programs of both types proliferate, with fictional villains reflecting the country's current political enemies.

The first regular spy series appeared on U.S. television in the early 1950s. A handful, including an early series also called *I Spy* (hosted by Raymond Massey) and *Behind Closed Doors* (hosted by Bruce Gordon), were anthologies. Others, such as *Biff Baker* (Alan Hale, Jr.) and *Hunter* (the first of four series called *Hunter*, this one starring Barry Nelson), featured gentlemen amateurs caught up in foreign intrigue through chance or patriotism. The rest, which usually had the word "danger" in their titles (*Doorway to Danger*, *Dangerous Assignment*, and *Passport to Danger*), were undistinguished half-hour series about professional agents battling Communists. These series lasted, with only three exceptions, a year or less.

Those exceptions were *I Led Three Lives*, *Foreign Intrigue*, and *Five Fingers*. *I Led Three Lives* was an enormously popular hit series based on the real-life story of FBI undercover agent Herbert Philbrick who infiltrated the American Communist Party. A favorite of J. Edgar Hoover (who considered it a public service), the show reportedly was taken so seriously by some viewers that they wrote the producers to report suspected Communists in their neighborhood. *Foreign Intrigue*, a syndicated series, boasted colorful European locations but replaceable stars (five in four years played four various wire-service correspondents and a

hotel owner) who stumble across international criminals. Only the last, *Five Fingers*, starring David Hedison as double agent Victor Sebastian, even hinted at the cool, hip style that was to be the hallmark of spy shows in the 1960s.

An interesting oddity during this period was an adaptation of Ian Fleming's *Casino Royale* for the anthology series *Climax*, in which the British James Bond is transformed into an American agent, "Jimmy" Bond (Barry Nelson), confronting a French Communist villain named Le Sheef (originally Le Chiffre). After a tense game of baccarat, Le Sheef (played by a sleepwalking Peter Lorre) captures Bond, confines him in a hotel bathtub, and rather bizarrely tortures him by twisting his bare toes with pliers.

There is no doubt that the mid-1960s was the high-water mark for the spy genre. Spies were everywhere—in books, on records, and on the big and little screens—and their images were emblazoned on countless mass-produced articles from toys to toiletries. Most were hour-long color shows that featured pairs or teams of professional agents of various races, genders, and cultural backgrounds. The pace was fast and the style cool, with lots of outrageous villains, sexual innuendo, technical gadgetry, and tongue-in-cheek humor. A third subcategory of the genre, the spy "spoof," developed during this time (*Get Smart*, created by Mel Brooks and Buck Henry, is the quintessential example), but there was so much humor in the "serious" shows that it was often difficult to distinguish spoofs from the real thing.

By 1968, the high spirits had soured, and the spy craze came to a fitting end with the unsettlingly paranoiac series *The Prisoner*, created and produced by its star, ex–secret agent Patrick McGoohan. Still, many of the shows of this period, including *The Man from U.N.C.L.E.*, *The Avengers*, *I Spy*, *The Wild, Wild West*, *Mission: Impossible*, and even *The Prisoner*, have enjoyed continued life in periodic film and television revivals and in cult fan followings throughout the world.

The decade of the 1970s saw a few sporadic attempts to breathe new life into a moribund genre. All the spy series introduced during this period featured gimmicky characters who worked for organizations identified by acronyms. Among the gimmicks were an agent with a photographic memory (*The Delphi Bureau*), agents fitted with electronic devices connected to a computer (*Search*), an agent accompanied by a giant assistant with a steel hand filled with gadgets (*A Man Called Sloane*), and a superhuman cyborg (*The Six Million Dollar Man*). With the exception of the last, which appealed primarily to children, all were quickly canceled.

The beginning of the next decade saw several "return" movies of 1960s favorites such as *Get Smart, The Wild, Wild West,* and *The Man from U.N.C.L.E.* as well as quality television adaptations of John Le Carré's *Tinker, Tailor, Soldier, Spy* and *Smiley's People* by the British Broadcasting Corporation (BBC; shown on PBS in the United States). This eventually led to a minirevival in spy programs in the mid-1980s that included serious, gritty series such as *The Equalizer* and adaptations of best-selling spy novels, including Le Carre's *A Perfect Spy,* Len Deighton's *Game Set Match,* Ken Follett's *Key to Rebecca,* and Robert Ludlum's *The Bourne Identity.* As with Amos Burke in the 1960s, action series such as *The A-Team* began to boost their ratings by injecting espionage elements into their formulas.

However, unlike their predecessors of 20 years previous, the spies of the 1980s were less fantastic and more pragmatic, with believable technology and a postmodern sensibility. Even romantic adventure series such as *Airwolf* and *Scarecrow and Mrs. King* were given a realistic edge. Indeed, this trend toward intense realism reached its culmination in *Under Cover,* a series so realistic that it was canceled by a nervous American Broadcasting Company (ABC) af-

ter less than a month on the air. In January 1991, a two-part episode of *Under Cover,* in which Iraq planned to fire a virus-carrying missile at Israel, was pulled from the schedule when the war in Kuwait broke out.

For the 1994–95 season, the fledgling FOX network offered two spy series, *Fortune Hunter,* a James Bond clone, and a revival of *Get Smart* starring an aging Don Adams and Barbara Feldon. Both series were canceled after extremely abbreviated runs.

CYNTHIA W. WALKER

*See also **Avengers; Get Smart; I Spy; Man from U.N.C.L.E./The Girl from U.N.C.L.E.; Mission: Impossible; Prisoner; Tinker, Tailor, Soldier, Spy***

Further Reading

Cawleti, John G., and Bruce A. Rosenberg, *The Spy Story,* Chicago, Illinois: University of Chicago Press, 1987

Harper, Ralph, *The World of the Thriller,* Cleveland, Ohio: Press of Case Western Reserve University, 1969

McCormick, Donald, and Kathy Fletcher, *Spy Fiction: A Connoisseur's Guide,* New York: Facts on File, 1990

Meyers, Richard, *TV Detectives,* San Diego, California: A.S. Barnes, 1981

Snelling, O.F., *007 James Bond: A Report,* New York: New American Library, 1964

Standards

Recorded video signals are rather complex and tightly structured. The standard unit of video is a frame. Similar to film, motion video is created by displaying progressive frames at a rate fast enough for the human eye and brain to perceive continuous motion. The basic means by which video images are recorded and displayed is a scanning process. When a video image is recorded by most cameras, a beam of electrons sweeps across the recording surface in a progressive series of lines. This basic technology is simple enough, widely understood, and, after a certain point, easily manufactured. The concept can be applied and the effect of a video image can be achieved, however, in various ways, with varying rates of electronic activity. Line frequencies and scanning rates are flexible, determined in part by a level of user (producer and viewer) satisfaction and in part by concerns of equipment manufacturers and broadcasters. Consequently, not all video or television systems are alike. The variations among them are defined in terms of "standards."

In the United States, industry-wide agreement on engineering standards for television did not come until 1941, when the Federal Communications Commission (FCC) decided to adopt a black-and-white standard (postponing the issue of color). The FCC accepted the National Television System Committee (also referred to as the National Television Standards Committee [NTSC]) recommendations and set line frequency at 525 per frame scanned at a rate of approximately 30 frames per second (29.97 to be exact). In 1953, corporate interests (the Columbia Broadcasting System [CBS] and the Radio Corporation of America [RCA]/National Broadcasting Company [NBC]) agreed to another proposal that allowed the NTSC to establish color television standards; these standards were compatible with those already set for black-and-white transmission.

These standards are not, however, uniformly accepted elsewhere. There are presently three world standards for transmitting a color video signal. The

NTSC recommendations accepted by the FCC as a national standard for the United States in 1953 are used in several other countries, including Canada, Chile, Costa Rica, Cuba, El Salvador, Guatemala, Honduras, Japan, Mexico, Panama, the Philippines, Puerto Rico, South Korea, and Taiwan.

PAL (phase alternating line) and SECAM (sequential couleur a memoire) are the two other major worldwide television standards. PAL is a modified form of NTSC and specifies a different means of encoding and transmitting color video designed to eliminate some NTSC problems, specifically a shift in chroma phase (hue). PAL uses 625 lines per frame (versus NTSC's 525) scanned at a rate of 25 frames per second (versus NTSC's 29.97) and operates at a 50-Hertz frequency (versus NTSC's 60-Hertz frequency). The PAL system is standard in more countries than NTSC or SECAM, including Argentina, Australia, Belgium, Brazil, China, Denmark, Finland, Great Britain, India, Indonesia, Ireland, Italy, Norway, New Zealand, the Netherlands, Portugal, Spain, Sweden, Switzerland, and Turkey.

SECAM is a video color system developed by the French; though it differs from PAL, it too uses 625 lines per frame, scanned at a rate of 25 frames per second, and operates at a 50-Hertz frequency. SECAM is used in France as well as several other countries, including Egypt, Germany, Greece, Haiti, Iran, Iraq, North Korea, Poland, and parts of the former Soviet Union.

There are enough differences between these three standards so that a videotape recorded using PAL will not play on a VCR set up for NTSC or SECAM and vice versa. NTSC, PAL, and SECAM are thus incompatible with each other. Standards converters can convert video from one standard to another, but the resultant image is often poor. Digital standards converters can provide better-quality converted video. Productions intended to be broadcast or released in different video standards are often shot on film, which can be converted to any video standard with reasonably good quality.

Recent developments in high-definition television (HDTV) have closed the gap between the technical quality of broadcast television and motion pictures. HDTV doubles the current broadcast NTSC number of scanning lines per frame—from 525 to 1,050 or 1,125, depending on the specific system—with a fourfold improvement in resolution (and a change to a widescreen format).

ERIC FREEDMAN

See also **Society for Motion Picture and Television Engineers**

Further Reading

Browne, Steven E., *Video Editing: A Postproduction Primer,* Boston, Massachusetts: Focal, 1989; 2nd edition, 1993

Caruso, James R., and Mavis E. Arthur, *Video Editing and Post Production,* Englewood Cliffs, New Jersey: Prentice Hall, 1992

Inglis, Andrew F. *Video Engineering.* New York: McGraw-Hill, 1993.

Lenk, John D., *Lenk's Video Handbook: Operations and Troubleshooting,* New York: McGraw-Hill, 1991.

Zettl, Herbert, *Television Production Handbook,* London: Pitman, 1961; 5th edition, Belmont, California: Wadsworth, 1992

Standards and Practices

"Standards and practices" is the term most American networks use for what many, especially in the creative community, refer to as the "network censors." Standards and practices departments (known as program practices at the Columbia Broadcasting System [CBS]) are maintained at each of the broadcast and many of the cable networks. The concept came about as a direct outgrowth of the trusteeship model: broadcasters were said to have a responsibility to the public interest as a result of their having access to a scarce resource. Another factor was the fear of propaganda, deemed to have been so effective in World War I. The most important consideration, however, was the unprecedented reality that radio—and later television—content came into the home, unforeseen, often unbidden, and sometimes unwelcome. Historically, therefore, lest an offended audience demand government intervention, the charge of standards and practice has been to review all nonnews broadcast matter, including entertainment, sports, and commercials, for compliance with legal, policy, factual, and community standards.

The broadcasters' insistence on setting and maintaining their own standards goes back to 1921, when engineers were instructed to use an emergency switch in the event that a performer or guest used language or brought up topics that were held to be unsuitable. During radio's first decade, taboos included any mention of price or even the location of a sponsoring store. Later, the networks would have an organist at the ready in a standby studio. A noted incident is said to have occurred in 1932, when a major administration spokesman was reporting on the government's progress in dealing with the Great Depression. He allegedly used the word "damn," a light went on in the standby studio, and the nation heard organ arpeggios.

By the late 1930s, the networks had established so-called continuity acceptance procedures to ensure that their advertising policies and federal law were adhered to. Later, as the role of radio in American life became more clearly understood, a body of written policy was articulated, generally on a case-by-case basis, to guide not only advertisers and their agencies but also programmers and producers in entertainment and other programming.

More than 67 percent of all television stations subscribed to the National Association of Broadcasters (NAB) Code adopted in 1950 (a similar radio code had been in operation since 1935). In addition to provisions that addressed historic concerns respecting the "advancement of education and culture," responsibility toward children, community responsibility, and general program standards, the NAB Code also included advertising standards and time limits for non-program material defined as "billboards, commercials, promotional announcements and all credits in excess of 30 seconds per program." In 1982, in settlement of an antitrust suit brought by the U.S. Department of Justice, the NAB and the federal government entered into a consent decree abolishing the time standards and the industry-wide limitations on the number and length of commercials they provided. The Code program standards had been suspended in 1976 after a federal judge in Los Angeles ruled that the "family hour" violated the First Amendment. After the demise of the Code, the networks, which had already developed their own written standards, took over the entire burden.

Standards—and the broadcasters' efforts to implement them—come to the fore whenever an apparent breach of the implicit obligation to respect the public trust occurs. Notable examples of perceived abuse that resulted in expanding the duties and enlarging standards and practices operations include the celebrated 1938 broadcast by Orson Welles's Mercury Theater of "The War of the Worlds," which simulated a radio broadcast interrupted by news reports describing the landing of Martians; the quiz show scandals of the 1950s; congressional hearings into violence; and concern over the possible blurring of fact and fiction in early docudrama. By 1985, a traditional network's department had no fewer than 80 people on its staff. Each episode of every series was reviewed in script form and as it was recorded.

With the changes in ownership of the traditional networks, the emergence of the cable networks, and the deregulatory climate, there has been considerable relaxation of the process—not every episode is reviewed once a series is established—but the essential responsibilities of the editors remain the same. These include, in addition to compliance with the law, serving as surrogates for the network's affiliates who are licensed to be responsive to their local communities; reflecting the concerns of advertisers and ensuring that the programming is acceptable to the bulk of the mass audience. This involves serving as guardians of taste with respect to language, sexual, and other materials inappropriate for children and the suitability of advertising, especially of personal products.

Commercial clearance involves the close screening of more than 50,000 announcements a year, falling into about 70 different product categories. The Federal Trade Commission's statements in the early 1970s that not only permitted but virtually mandated comparative advertising resulted in the establishment of courtlike procedures to adjudicate between advertisers making conflicting claims. By the mid-1980s, at least 25 percent of all commercials contained comparisons to named competitor's products or services.

Critics contend, with some justification, that standards and practices is anachronistic paternalism at best and most often a form of censorship; the networks claim the publisher's right to exercise their judgment as to what is appropriate for broadcast to the American public. The affiliated stations sometimes complain but are generally, though not always, satisfied that the networks are sufficiently vigilant as their surrogates. Network and sales executives worry that the very process of vetting leads to pettifoggery and rigidity. Advertisers rail at the scrupulous insistence that all claims be substantiated, as the law requires. By far the most frequent complaints, however, are heard from the creative community, which argues that the networks are too accommodating of the most conservative members of the audience and that only by "pushing the envelope" with respect to sex, violence, or language can the medium advance.

By the beginning of the new millenium, these conflicts reached new intensity. Cable networks such as Home Box Office (HBO) used their status as "subscriber" services to support production of material far too "extreme" for broadcast television or basic cable services. Although HBO could make the claim that it was "not TV, it's HBO," the development of ongoing series such as *OZ, The Sopranos, Sex and the City,* and *The Wire* made the channel seem to some like television without standards and to others television with the freedom to create in a manner equal to that of literature or film. These series took full advantage of the opportunity to use strong language and to depict sexual activities and violence in ways unseen in the period of network television dominance. Showtime, another subscriber-supported cable service, adapted *Queer as Folk,* a British series, for American audiences. In this case, some aspects of the British version were "toned down," suggesting that a form of "standards and practices judgment" was still in place. The success of these and other original for-cable-television programs encouraged both the programmers and the creative community to use the opportunities for more and more "daring" content.

Recognizing the relative acceptance of these programs and the critical successes accompanying their presentation, other cable outlets began to offer more material that would have been rejected by conventional networks. FX offered *The Shield,* focused on the complicated character of a corrupt police officer, and *Nip/Tuck* an exploration of the moral quandaries of cosmetic surgeons. The former contained language, violence, and ethical positions that challenged standard notions of cultural acceptance, while the latter not only depicted sexual activity but also used graphic visual depictions of surgical procedures to define its "realism." Network television followed suit in some ways with relaxation of regulations on language and more daring depictions of sexual activity—often in programs containing "warnings" to viewers that some aspects of the program might be unacceptable. This practice, it seems, throws the decision to "censor" or approve of more "creative," "realistic," or "honest" depictions to the viewer rather than reserve the power of those choices at the industrial level.

The primary purpose of standards and practices has always been to maintain the networks' most precious asset, its audience-in-being—the delivery of a significant share of television households, hour after hour, to the advertising community. Secondary purposes, historically, have included protecting the networks' images as responsible and responsive institutions, as sources of reliable information and satisfying entertainment for the entire family, and even as precious national resources. In the final analysis, if the concern for not giving offense has contributed to blandness, it must also be credited for making a commercially supported national system possible. To the degree that this arrangement has changed, it is a mark of alterations in both society and the media industries.

GEORGE DESSART

See also **Censorship**

Further Reading

Adler, Keith, *Advertising Resource Handbook,* East Lansing, Michigan: Advertising Resources, Inc., 1989

Barnouw, Erik, *A Tower in Babel: A History of Broadcasting,* volume 1, New York: Oxford University Press, 1970

Broadcast Self-Regulation, 2nd edition, Washington, D.C.: NAB Code Authority, 1977

Dessart, George, "Of Tastes and Times: Some Challenging Reflections on Television's Elastic Standards and Astounding Practices," *Television Quarterly,* (1992)

Henderson, Alice M., and Helaine Doktori, "How the Networks Monitor Program Content," in *Television as a Social Issue: The Eighth Applied Social Psychology Annual,* edited by Stuart Oskam, Newbury Park, California: Sage Publications, 1988

Legal Guide to FCC Rules, Regulations and Policies, Washington, D.C.: National Association of Broadcasters, 1977

Pember, Don R., *Mass Media Law,* Dubuque, Iowa: Brown Publishers, 1977; 5th edition, 1990

"Program Standards for the CBS Television Network," in *Television as a Social Issue: The Eighth Applied Social Psychology Annual,* edited by Stuart Oskam, Newbury Park, California: Sage Publications, 1988

Sensitive Theme Programming and the New American Mainstream, New York: Social Research Unit, Marketing and Research Services, ABC, n.d.

The Television Code, 22nd edition, Washington, D.C.: Code Authority, National Association of Broadcasters, 1981

Stanton, Frank (1908–)

U.S. Media Executive

Frank Stanton is a distinguished broadcast executive known for the leadership he brought to the Columbia Broadcasting System (CBS), Inc., during his 25-year presidency (1946–71). His guidance gave CBS crucial stability during the company's critical growth period. More than just a corporate president, however, Stanton acquired a reputation as the unofficial spokesperson for the broadcasting industry. His opinions were routinely sought, his speeches repeatedly quoted, and his testimony before Congress recognized as a major part of any debate in the broadcasting field.

Stanton was fascinated with radio from his days in graduate school at Ohio State University, chiefly by the question of why people reacted positively to certain radio shows but negatively to others. He used his doctoral research in the psychology department to answer this question, examining why and how people perceive various stimuli. He analyzed the audio and visual effectiveness of information transmission and established test procedures for making rough measurements of their effectiveness. His dissertation, "A Critique of Present Methods and a New Plan for Studying Radio Listening Behavior," caught the attention of CBS and launched his career in the audience research department in 1935.

In 1937, Stanton began a collaboration with Dr. Paul Lazarsfeld of Columbia University. They devised a program analysis system nicknamed "Little Annie." While Stanton tends to downplay the importance of the machine, others have credited it with being the first qualitative measurement device. "Little Annie" determines the probability of a program's appeal by suggesting how large an audience that program would be likely to attract. The system was devised for radio but continues to be used for television, reporting an accuracy rate of 85 percent.

Stanton was promoted to vice president of CBS in 1942 and in 1946, at the age of 38, to the presidency. In this position, he guided CBS through a period of diversification and expansion. He reorganized the company in 1951, creating separate administrations for radio, TV, and CBS Laboratories, a plan that served as a model for other broadcast companies. He helped CBS expand its operations by decentralizing its administration and creating autonomous divisions with a range of new investments, including the purchase of the New York Yankees in 1964. CBS also bought the book publisher Holt, Rinehart and Winston and Creative Playthings, manufacturer of high-quality educational toys. Diversification paid off for CBS; the company earned $1 billion in annual sales in 1969.

As president of CBS, Stanton concentrated on organizational and policy questions, leaving the entertainment programming and the discovering and nurturing of talent to the chair, William S. Paley. Stanton was also responsible for the political issues growing out of the network's news department. He was instrumental in bringing about the 1960 Kennedy–Nixon televised presidential debate and is known for his efforts to repeal section 315 of the Federal Communications Act, which requires networks to grant equal time to all po-

Frank Stanton.
Photo courtesy of Frank Stanton

litical candidates. A staunch proponent of broadcast journalism and defender of broadcasting's First Amendment rights, he led campaigns before Congress and in the courts on behalf of the broadcast industry for access and protection equal to that of the printed press.

Stanton's greatest battle with the government occurred in 1971 and focused on just this parallel to print-press rights. The controversy surrounded *The Selling of the Pentagon,* a CBS News documentary that exposed the huge expenditure of public funds, partly illegal, to promote militarism. The confrontation raised the issue of whether television news programming deserved protection under the First Amendment. Against threat of jail, Stanton refused the subpoena from the House Commerce Committee ordering him to provide copies of the outtakes and scripts from the documentary. He claimed that such materials are protected by the freedom of the press guaranteed by the First Amendment. Stanton observed that if such subpoena actions were allowed, there would be a "chilling effect" on broadcast journalism.

But long before this particular case and long before Watergate or Vietnam, CBS was the first broadcasting network to seriously examine the negative side of Washington politics on television. One of the earliest of these explorations occurred on the news program *See It Now,* in which host Edward R. Murrow confronted U.S. Senator Joseph McCarthy. The program was constructed using film clips of McCarthy's accusatory speeches and Murrow refuting his charges. McCarthy demanded, and was granted, time for a response, and in that blustery performance many observers see the downfall of McCarthyism. In retrospect, the two programs were among the most important in the history of television.

Documentaries, even of this immediate sort, however, had a more difficult time attracting sponsors than did entertainment programs, and for this reason *See It Now* was canceled following the 1958 season. Appalled by what the broadcasting industry had become, Murrow spoke before the Television News Directors Association and delivered what was to become known as one of the most famous public tongue lashings in media history, aimed directly at Stanton and Paley. The relationship between Stanton and Murrow soured into accusations and name-calling and was widely reported in the press.

Stanton received the title of vice chair in 1972, one year before the mandatory retirement age of 65. On retiring, Stanton still held $13 million worth of CBS stock, and he remained a director of CBS and consultant to the corporation under a contract that lasted until

1987. From 1976 to 1995, he was a director of Interpublic Group, which now owns Foote Cone & Belding/True North Communications and the MWW Group.

GARTH JOWETT AND LAURA ASHLEY

See also **Audience Research, Industry and Marketing Perspective; Columbia Broadcasting System; Murrow, Edward R.; Paley, William S.;** *See It Now; Selling of the Pentagon*

Frank Stanton. Born in Muskegon, Michigan, March 20, 1908. Educated at Ohio Wesleyan University, Delaware, Ohio, B.A. 1930; Ohio State University, Ph.D. 1935; diplomate from American Board of Professional Psychology. Worked in CBS research department (later CBS-TV), New York City, 1935–45, vice president, 1942, president, CBS Inc., 1946–71 (was cited by three committees of the House of Representatives for contempt of Congress for refusal to grant access to CBS News' "outtakes" in connection with the CBS broadcast of *The Selling of the Pentagon,* 1971), vice chair, 1972–73, president emeritus, since 1973; chair, Rand Corporation, Santa Monica, California, 1961–67, trustee, 1957–78; U.S. Advanced Communications Info., Washington, D.C., 1964–73; chair, ARC, Washington, D.C., 1973–79, vice chair, League of Red Cross Societies, Geneva, Switzerland, 1973–80; chair, visiting committee, Kennedy School of Government, 1979–85; chair (now retired), Broadcast International, Inc.; director, Capital Income Builder, Inc., Capital World Growth and Income Fund, Inc., Sony Music Entertainment, Inc. Member: founding member and chair, Center for Advanced Study in Behavioral Sciences, Stanford, California, 1953–60, trustee, 1953–71; Business Council, Washington, D.C., since 1956 (honorary); National Portrait Gallery Commission, Washington, D.C., since 1973; board of overseers, Harvard College, 1978–84; President's Committee on Arts and Humanities, Washington, 1983–90; honorary director and trustee, William Benton Foundation, Bryant Park Restoration Corporation, Educational Broadcasting Corporation; emeritus trustee and director, Lincoln Center for the Performing Arts, Rockefeller Foundation, Carnegie Institution Washington, D.C.. Recipient: Paul White Memorial Awards, Radio and TV News Directors Association, 1957 and 1971; Peabody Awards, 1959, 1960, 1961, 1964, and 1972; Trustees Awards, National Academy of Television Arts and Sciences, 1959 and 1972; Special Honor Award, AIA, 1967; International Directorate Award, National Academy of Television Arts and Sciences, 1980; named to TV Academy Hall of Fame, 1986, Market Research Council of New York, 1988.

Films

Some Physiological Reactions to Emotional Stimuli, 1932; *Factors in Visual Depth Perception,* 1936.

Publications

Radio Research, 1941, 1941 (editor, with Paul Lazarsfeld)

Radio Research, 1942–43, 1943 (editor, with Paul Lazarsfeld)
Communications Research, 1948–49, 1949 (editor, with Paul Lazarsfeld)

Further Reading

Smith, Sally Bedell, *In All His Glory: The Life of William S. Paley, the Legendary Tycoon and His Brilliant Circle,* New York: Simon and Schuster, 1990

Star, Darren

U.S. Writer-Producer

As a young teen living in Potomac, Maryland, Darren Star used money given to him for his bar mitzvah to subscribe to the Hollywood trade publication *Variety.* Such an early interest in the entertainment industry served him well, as Star created his first series before he turned 30. Although Star's television career has been brief in comparison with other writers and producers, in just a decade he established a solid reputation for building successful series that tapped the pulse of the post–baby boom generation of viewers. Star's contributions span melodrama and comedy as well as a variety of network contexts, including FOX's upstart days and premium cable service Home Box Office (HBO).

Star's high-profile television career began by writing the pilot script for *Beverly Hills, 90210,* a series that paired him with iconic sexagenarian Aaron Spelling. The series, over which Star and Spelling shared creative control, became the FOX network's breakout hit drama. FOX nearly canceled it repeatedly during its first season, but a relaunch during the repeat-heavy summer time period established the series, its stars, and consequently the network. Star approached the series as a "*thirtysomething* for teens" and emphasized teen social issues such as drinking, pregnancy, and rape amidst the series' melodramatic personal relationships. FOX requested Star for the series pilot because a screenplay he sold at age 24, the story of a teenager who thinks he is an alien (*Doin' Time on Planet Earth,* 1988), indicated Star's talent for writing from a teen's point of view.

Star then moved to *Melrose Place,* a pseudo-spin-off from *Beverly Hills, 90210,* designed as a scheduling match for the series in terms of genre but with a focus on a group of characters a few years older than the *Beverly Hills* teens. *Melrose Place* provided further association with Spelling, but Star reportedly balked at the shift to campy, over-the-top play with the soap genre that began with addition of Heather Locklear to the cast, although the adjustments to the series likely account for much of its subsequent success.

While Star vacationed during the summer of 1994, his agent pitched a new series to the Columbia Broadcasting System (CBS), and the network returned with an offer for 13 episodes. CBS's exceptional offer to cover all production costs (rather than just the licensing fee that usually required producers to take a loss in the range of $300,000 to half a million dollars per episode) provided an opportunity Star could not turn down, but his departure from *Melrose Place* created some animosity with Spelling, who forced him out of a continuing consulting role. The new series returned Star to the East Coast for a serial drama about the personal and professional manipulations of those associated with a glossy New York magazine.

CBS positioned the new series, *Central Park West,* as the showpiece in its attempt to shift away from its audience base of older adults. The series sought to recreate the opulence and character antagonisms of *Dallas* and *Dynasty* but did not last long enough to establish characters or story. Despite heavy promotion and reliance on many of the narrative and visual features that had proven successful in *Beverly Hills, 90210* and *Melrose Place, Central Park West* failed to find an audience. The network ordered radical retooling and then cancellation. CBS reduced its attempted brand shift after the sale of the network to Westinghouse and the departure of its top programming executive.

The following summer, Star met with HBO to propose a series inspired by Candace Bushnell's *New York Observer* sex column. The lack of content restrictions afforded by the subscriber-based cable network allowed exceptionally frank examination of the sexual acts and emotional relationships of four single women living in Manhattan. *Sex and the City* reinvigorated the television comedy form with its film style, direct camera address, and sophisticated stories. Star left the show after its third season, returning to broadcast network series that were potentially more lucrative although also restricted by network control that Star likened to "being in an Eastern bloc country." *Sex and the City* was a critical and popular success and appeared on HBO for a total of six seasons.

Star created two series in 2000: *Grosse Pointe* on The WB and *The $treet* for FOX. With *Grosse Pointe*, he parodied his start with the series' show-within-a-show comedy about the production of a teen soap opera. Built on the premise that the drama behind the scenes of television series trumps what is on air, the series provided a funny and pointed critique of the industry, the melodrama genre, and its stars. *Grosse Pointe* required last-minute adjustments and garnered publicity after Spelling complained about a character who apparently referenced his daughter Tori, who played a central role in *Beverly Hills, 90210*. The series had difficulty finding an audience in part to because of The WB's lack of an appropriate half-hour series with which to schedule it. The network shifted *Grosse Pointe's* time slot throughout the season, but the series failed to find an audience and was not renewed.

The $treet sent Star back to New York for a short-lived look at the mostly male world of Wall Street and finance. A lavish cost of $2.3 million per episode led to the series' exceptionally distinct promotions for the show and announced the entry of the also short-lived Artists Television Group (ATG) production studio onto the Hollywood production scene. Promotions, however, were all that most viewers saw of *The $treet*. FOX canceled the program after little more than a month on the air. The series had the misfortune of appearing just as the U.S. economy began sputtering and on the heels of *Bull*, a similar series with more complexly drawn characters, presented on Turner Network Television (TNT) on cable.

Explaining the failure of *Grosse Pointe* and *The $treet* in an interview with National Public Radio's Terri Gross, Star reflected that none of his series had succeeded in their first season but found audiences and their distinction in their second year. Despite the lack of opportunity to refine *Central Park West*, *Grosse Pointe*, and *The $treet*, Star had already achieved rapid success in the Hollywood creative community, capitalizing on the culture and style of the second generation of television viewers. In 2003, Star acted as executive producer on a new series for the National Broadcasting Company (NBC), *Miss Match*, about a young divorce lawyer who moonlights as a matchmaker.

AMANDA LOTZ

See also **Beverly Hills, 90210; FOX Broadcasting Company;** *Sex and the City;* **Spelling, Aaron**

Television Series

1992–95	*Beverly Hills, 90210* (creator; coproducer 1990; supervising producer 1991–92; executive producer 1992–95; writer 1990–92; director)
1992–95	*Melrose Place* (executive producer 1992; writer 1992–95)
1995	*Central Park West* (creator; producer)
1998–2000	*Sex and the City* (creator; executive producer; director)
2000	*Grosse Pointe* (creator; executive producer; writer; director)
2000	*The $treet* (co-creator; executive producer)
2003	*Miss Match* (co-creator; executive producer)

Films

Doin' Time on Planet Earth (1988); *If Looks Could Kill* (1991)

Further Reading

DeVries, Hilary, "Hit Man," *Los Angeles Magazine* (November 2000)

Frutkin, Alan James, "Rising Star," *MEDIAWEEK* (October 2, 2000)

Rose, Frank, "Soap Gets in Their Eye," *Esquire* (May 1996)

Star Trek

U.S. Science Fiction Program

With the premiere of *Star Trek* on the National Broadcasting Company (NBC) in September 1966, few could have imagined that this ambitious yet often uneven science fiction series would go on to become one of the most actively celebrated and financially lucrative narrative franchises in television history. Although the original series enjoyed only a modest run of three seasons and 79 episodes, the story world created by that series eventually led to a library of popular novelizations and comic books, a cycle of motion pictures, an international fan community, and a number of spin-off series that have made the *Star Trek* universe a bedrock property for Paramount Studios from the 1980s on.

Star Trek followed the adventures of the USS *Enterprise,* a flagship in a 23rd-century interplanetary alliance known as "the Federation." The ship's five-year mission was "to seek out new life and new civilizations, to boldly go where no man has gone before," a mandate that series creator and philosophical wellspring Gene Roddenberry described as "*Wagon Train* in space." Each episode brought the crew of the *Enterprise* in contact with new alien races or baffling wonders of the universe. When not exploring the galaxy, the crew of the *Enterprise* often scrapped with the two main threats to the Federation's benevolent democratization of space, the Hun-like Klingons and the more cerebral yet equally menacing Romulans.

The program's main protagonists, Captain James T. Kirk (William Shatner), Mr. Spock (Leonard Nimoy), and Dr. Leonard McCoy (DeForest Kelly), remain three of the most familiar (and most parodied) characters in television memory. As commander of the *Enterprise,* the hypermasculine Kirk engaged in equal amounts of fisticuffs and intergalactic romance and was known for his nerves of steel in negotiating the difficulties and dangers presented by the ship's mission. McCoy was the ship's cantankerous chief medical officer who, when not saving patients, gave the other two leads frequent personal and professional advice. Perhaps most complex and popular of the characters was Spock. Half human and half Vulcan, Spock struggled to maintain the absolute emotional control demanded by his Vulcan heritage and yet occasionally

fell prey to the foibles of a more human existence. In addition to the three leads, *Star Trek* featured a stable of secondary characters who also became central to the show's identity. These included the ship's chief engineer, Scotty (James Doohan), and an ethnically diverse supporting cast featuring Uhura (Nichelle Nichols), Chekov (Walter Koening), Sulu (George Takei), Yeoman Rand (Grace Lee Whitney), and Nurse Chapel (Majel Barrett).

Scripts for the original series varied greatly in quality, ranging from the literate time-travel tragedy of Harlan Ellison's "City on the Edge of Forever" and the Sophoclean conflict of Theodore Sturgeon's "Amok Time" to less inspired stock adventure plots, such as Kirk's battle to the death with a giant lizard creature in "Arena." With varying degrees of success, many episodes addressed the social and political climate of late 1960s America, including the Vietnam allegory "A Private Little War," a rather heavy-handed treatment of racism in "Let That Be Your Last Battlefield," and even an encounter with space hippies in "The Way to Eden."

NBC threatened to cancel *Star Trek* after its second season, but, persuaded to some degree by a large letter-writing campaign by fans to save the show, the network picked up the series for a third and final year. Canceled in 1969, *Star Trek* went on to a new life in syndication, where it found an even larger audience and quickly became a major phenomenon within popular culture. Beginning with a network of memorabilia collectors, fans of the show became increasingly organized, gathering at *Star Trek* conventions to trade merchandise, meet stars from the show, and watch old episodes. Such fans came to be known as "Trekkies" and were noted (and often ridiculed) for their extreme devotion to the show and their encyclopedic knowledge of every episode. Through this explosion of interest, many elements of the *Star Trek* universe made their way into the larger lexicon of popular culture, including the often-heard line, "Beam me up, Scotty" (a reference to the ship's teleportation device) as well as Spock's signature commentary on the "illogic" of human culture. Along with Spock's distinctively pointed ears, other aspects of Vulcan culture also became widely popularized as televi-

Star Trek, James Doohan, DeForest Kelley, Walter Koenig, Majel Barrett, William Shatner, Nichelle Nichols, Leonard Nimoy, George Takei, 1966–69.
©*Paramount/Courtesy of the Everett Collection*

sion lore, including the Vulcan "mind-meld" and the Vulcan salute, "live long and prosper."

As Trekkie culture continued to grow around the show during the 1970s, a central topic of conversation among fans concerned rumors that the series might one day return to the airwaves. There was talk that the series might return with the original cast, with a new cast, or in a new sequel format. Such rumors were often fueled by a general sense among fans that the show had been unjustly canceled in the first place and thus deserved a second run. Initially, Paramount did not seem convinced of the commercial potential of resurrecting the story world in any form, but by the late 1970s the studio announced that a motion picture version of the series featuring the original cast was under development. *Star Trek: The Motion Picture* premiered in 1979, and though it was a very clumsy translation of the series into the language of big-budget, big-screen science fiction, it proved to be such a hit that Paramount developed a chain of sequels, including *Star Trek II: The Wrath of Khan* (1982), *Star Trek III: The Search for Spock* (1984), and *Star Trek IV: The Voyage Home* (1986).

By the mid-1980s, the *Star Trek* mythos had proven so commercially viable that Paramount announced plans for a new *Star Trek* series for television. Once again supervised by Roddenberry, *Star Trek: The Next Generation* debuted in first-run syndication in 1987 and went on to become one of the highest-rated syndicated shows in history. Set in the 24th century, this series followed the adventures of a new crew on a new *Enterprise* (earlier versions of the ship having been destroyed in the movie series). The series was extremely successful at establishing a new story world that still maintained a continuity with the premise, spirit, and history of the original series. On the new *Enterprise,* the command functions were divided between a more cultured captain, Jean-Luc Picard (Patrick Stewart), and his younger, more headstrong "Number One," Commander William Riker (Jonathan Frakes). Spock's character functions were distributed across a number of new crew members, including ship's counselor and Betazoid telepath, Deanna Troi (Marina Sirtis); the highly advanced android, Lt. Commander Data (Brent Spiner), who provided the show with "logical" com-

Star Trek: The Next Generation, Year 4, 1990–91, (Front), LeVar Burton, Patrick Stewart, Jonathan Frakes, Brent Spiner, (Back), Whoopi Goldberg, Gates McFadden, Michael Dorn, Marina Sirtis, Wil Wheaton.
©Paramount/Courtesy of the Everett Collection

mentary as ironic counterpoint to the peculiarities of human culture; and, finally, Lieutenant Worf (Michael Dorn), a Klingon raised by a human family who struggled to reconcile his warrior heritage with the demands of the Federation. Other important characters included Lt. Geordi La Forge (LeVar Burton), the ship's blind engineer whose "vision" was processed by a high-tech visor; Dr. Beverly Crusher (Gates McFadden), the ship's medical officer and implicit romantic foil for Picard; and Wesley Crusher (Wil Wheaton), the doctor's precocious son.

Running for 178 episodes, *Star Trek: The Next Generation* was able to develop its characters and storylines in much more detail than the original series. As with many other hour-long dramas of its era, the series abandoned a wholly episodic format in favor of more serialized narratives that better showcased the expanded ensemble cast. Continuing over the run of the series were recurring encounters with Q, a seemingly omnipotent yet extremely petulant entity; the Borg, a menacing race of mechanized beings; and Lor, Data's "evil" android brother. Other continuing stories included intrigue and civil war in the Klingon empire, Data's ongoing quest to become more fully human, and often-volatile political difficulties with the Romulans. This change in the narrative structure of the series from wholly episodic to a more serialized form can be attributed in some part to the activities of the original series' enormous fan following. A central part of fan culture in the 1970s and 1980s involved fans writing their own *Star Trek*–based stories, often filling in blanks left by the original series and elaborating incidents only briefly mentioned in a given episode. *Star Trek: The Next Generation* greatly expanded the potential for such creative elaboration by presenting a more complex story world, one that actively encouraged the audience to think of the series as a foundation for imagining a larger textual universe.

Despite the show's continuing success, Paramount canceled *Star Trek: The Next Generation* after seven seasons to turn the series into a film property and make room for new television spin-offs, thus beginning a careful orchestration of the studio's *Star Trek* interests in both film and television. The cast of the original series returned to the theater for *Star Trek 5* and *Star Trek 6*, leading finally to *Star Trek: Generations*, in which the original cast turned over the cinematic baton to the crew of *Next Generation.*

Star Trek: Deep Space Nine premiered in January 1993 as the eventual replacement for *Next Generation* on television. In contrast to the usually optimistic and highly mobile structure of the first two series, *Deep Space Nine* was a much more claustrophobic reading of the *Star Trek* universe. Set aboard an aging space station in orbit around a recently liberated planet, Bajor, the series generated its storylines from the aftermath of the war over Bajor and from a nearby "wormhole" that brought diverse travelers to the station from across the galaxy. The series ended with the 1997–98 season.

Hoping to compete with FOX and Warner Brothers in creating new broadcast networks, Paramount developed a fourth *Star Trek* series as the anchor for their United Paramount Network (UPN). *Star Trek: Voyager* inaugurated UPN in January 1995, serving as the network's first broadcast. Responding perhaps to the stage-bound qualities and tepid reception of *Deep Space Nine*, *Voyager* opted for a premise that maximized the crew's ability to travel and encounter new adventures. Stranded in a distant part of the galaxy after a freak plasma storm, the USS *Voyager* found itself 75 years away from Earth and faced with the arduous mission of returning home. Like all television programs, *Voyager* required some fine-tuning to help with the ratings. Most successful was the addition of Jeri Ryan as the sexy Borg crew member, 7 of 9.

Both *Deep Space Nine* and *Voyager* attracted the core fans of *Star Trek*, as expected, but neither series was as popular with the public at large as the programs they were designed to replace. With *Voyager*'s mission coming to an end in 2001, Paramount debated the future direction of the franchise. In particular, producers were concerned over the "aging" of the franchise (and its core audience). The result was *Enterprise*, premiering in the fall of 2001. In an attempt to attract a new generation of Trekkies, *Enterprise* moved the franchise from the 24th century to Earth's more immediate future. A prequel to all other installments in the Trek universe, the series features former *Quantum Leap* star Scott Bakula as the captain of the very first *Enterprise* on its very first mission to interstellar space (under Vulcan supervision). Gone is creator Roddenberry's signature utopian humanism, replaced by darker stories and a more sinister production design. The bid for a younger demographic even includes replacing the trademark bombast of the opening credit score with a more teen-friendly pop theme. Early ratings have indicated that the strategy is working, suggesting that Paramount has once again found a way to revitalize and extend its most famous and long-lived property. Expected to run seven seasons, *Enterprise* will likely solidify *Star Trek*'s position as the most elaborately developed narrative world in the history of television.

JEFFREY SCONCE

See also **Roddenberry, Gene; Science Fiction Programs; Shatner, William**

Cast

Captain James T. Kirk	William Shatner
Mr. Spock	Leonard Nimoy
Dr. Leonard McCoy	DeForest Kelley
Yeoman Janice Rand	
(1966–67)	Grace Lee Whitney
Sulu	George Takei
Uhura	Nichelle Nichols
Engineer Montgomery Scott	James Doohan
Nurse Christine Chapel	Majel Barrett
Ensign Pavel Chekov	
(1967–69)	Walter Koenig

Producers

Gene Roddenberry, John Meredyth Lucas, Gene L. Coon, Fred Freiberger

Programming History

79 episodes
NBC

September 1966–August 1967	Thursday 8:30–9:30
September 1967–August 1968	Friday 8:30–9:30
September 1968–April 1969	Friday 10:00–11:00
June 1969–September 1969	Tuesday 7:30–8:30

Further Reading

Alexander, David, and Ray Bradbury, *Star Trek Creator: The Authorized Biography of Gene Roddenberry,* New York: Roc, 1994

Asherman, Allan, *The Star Trek Compendium,* New York: Pocket Books, 1989

Dillard, J.M., and Susan Sackett, *Star Trek, Where No One Has Gone Before: A History in Pictures,* New York: Pocket Books, 1994

Gerrold, David, *The World of Star Trek,* New York, Ballantine, 1974

Gibberman, Susan R., *Star Trek: An Annotated Guide to Resources on the Development, the Phenomenon, the People, the Television Series, the Films, the Novels, and the Recordings,* Jefferson, North Carolina: McFarland, 1991

Jenkins, Henry, *Textual Poachers: Television Fans and Participatory Culture,* New York: Routledge, 1992

Nemecek, Larry, *The Star Trek: The Next Generation Companion,* New York: Pocket Books, 1992

Okuda, Michael, Denise Okuda, Debbie Mirek, and Doug Drexler, *The Star Trek Encyclopedia: A Reference Guide to the Future,* New York: Pocket Books, 1994

Shatner, William, with Chris Kreski, *Star Trek Memories,* New York: HarperCollins, 1993

Trimble, Bjo, *The Star Trek Concordance,* New York: Ballantine, 1976

Tulloch, John, and Henry Jenkins, *Science Fiction Audiences: Watching Doctor Who and Star Trek,* London and New York: Routledge, 1995

Van Hise, James, and Hal Schuster, *Trek: The Unauthorized Story of the Movies,* Las Vegas, Nevada: Pioneer Books, 1995

Whitfield, Stephen E., and Gene Roddenberry, *The Making of Star Trek,* New York, Ballantine, 1968

STAR-TV. *See* Satellite

Starowicz, Mark (1946–)

Canadian Broadcast Journalist, Producer

During his 30 years in radio and television with the Canadian Broadcasting Corporation (CBC), Mark Starowicz has produced a number of the more influential current affairs and documentary programs in Canadian broadcast history.

After beginning his career in newspaper journalism, Starowicz assumed the role of producer within the current affairs division of CBC Radio at the age of 24. During the 1970s, Starowicz produced a total of five CBC Radio programs, including *Radio Free Friday, Five Nights,* and *Commentary.* He received particular critical acclaim for his reworking of *As It Happens* (1973–76) and the creation of *Sunday Morning* (1976–80), a three-hour weekend review.

CBC News programming chief Peter Herrndorf provided Starowicz's entry into television in 1979 by appointing him chair of a committee examining the corporation's news programming strategies. This resulted in the controversial move of *The National* news broadcast to 10:00 P.M. from its 11:00 P.M. slot and the creation of *The Journal,* a current affairs and documentary program with Starowicz as executive producer. These decisions sought to take advantage of the larger audience numbers available at 10:00 (10 million viewers) than at 11:00 (4.5 million) and were part of the CBC's strategy in the 1980s to invest its decreasing resources in its traditionally strong area of news and current affairs.

Despite Starowicz's lack of experience in television journalism, *The Journal* was a great success, both critically and in terms of viewership, and served to establish him as Canadian television journalism's new star. *The Journal* achieved an average 1.6 million viewers in its first year and comparable numbers during its ten-year run. Rather than decreasing the audience shares of its competitors, the hour-long combination of *The National* (22 minutes) and *The Journal* (38 minutes) actually increased the number of total viewers during the 10:00 P.M. time slot.

To deliver *The Journal,* Starowicz compiled a young staff, many of whom, like Starowicz, had previously worked only in radio. Hosts during the broadcast's life included Barbara Frum (formerly of *As It*

Mark Starowicz.
Photo courtesy of Mark Starowicz

Happens), Mary Lou Finlay, Peter Kent, and Bill Cameron. Under Starowicz's leadership, *The Journal* produced a total of 2,772 broadcasts between 1982 and 1992, consisting of 5,150 interviews and an amazing 2,200 documentaries. *The Journal* was notable for the depth with which it would develop stories, dedicating an entire broadcast to a single documentary if the subject required. For the interview segment of the show, Starowicz successfully reinvented the "double-ender" technique (originally employed during the 1960s on the Columbia Broadcasting System's [CBS's] *See It Now),* wherein the anchor would interview guests who appeared to the viewing audience to be projected on an in-studio screen. The high quality and volume of material were made possible by factors such as a staff of more than 100, a budget of approximately $8 million per year (1980 Canadian dollars), and producer-reporter teams with as much as one month of lead time for story preparation.

On the cancellation of *The Journal* in 1992, Starowicz accepted the position of executive producer of documentaries at the CBC. Since 1990, Starowicz has overseen the weekly documentary prime-time series *Witness,* and he has served as senior producer for *Life and Times.* The one-hour *Witness* consists of acquired, coproduced, and in-house documentaries dealing with a diverse array of often socially and politically charged issues. Although Starowicz's role as executive producer emphasizes his capacity to orchestrate talent, he also has produced and directed his own documentaries, including *The Third Angel* (1991) and *Red Capitalism* (1993). He sees his role at CBC Documentaries as an opportunity to continue the strong documentary tradition in Canada, started in the 1940s by John Grierson and the National Film Board. Significantly, Starowicz was able to get the CBC management to agree to the broadcasting of "point-of-view" documentaries, breaking free of the somewhat mythological pursuit of journalist "objectivity."

Starowicz regularly writes and lectures on issues of Canadian identity, history, and culture. He cites the absence of Canadian content in its own mass media and the dangers posed by U.S. cultural industries as key threats to Canada, and he has proposed countermeasures, such as the introduction of a tax on U.S. media imports, continued public support for the CBC, the development of a second public national network, and the extended financing of independent film and television production. However, some might argue that his greatest contribution to the health of Canadian identity has been the highly successful documentary series *Canada: A People's History,* which he created and executive produced for the CBC. This 17-part, award-winning exploration of Canadian history, first broadcast in 2001, provided audiences with an intimate and lyrical reading of the forces and individuals that shaped Canadian society. The success of this series led the CBC to appoint Starowicz in 2002 to serve as executive producer of a new production unit, CineNorth, dedicated to creating high-quality documentaries for domestic broadcast, video, and international sales.

KEITH CHRISTOPHER HAMPSON

See also **Canada: A People's History; Canadian Programming in English;** *National/The Journal*

Mark Starowicz. Born in Worksop, England, September 8, 1946. Educated at Loyola College High School, 1964; University of Grenoble, 1964; McGill University, B.A. 1968. Married: Anne, 1982; children: Caitlin-Elizabeth and Madeline Anne. Reporter, *Montreal Gazette,* 1964–68; editor, *McGill Daily,* 1968–69; reporter, *Toronto Star,* 1969–70; cofounder and writer, *The Last Post* magazine, 1969–73; producer, CBC Radio series, 1970–79; chair, Task Force to Reform CBC TV News and Current Affairs, 1979; executive producer, television program *The Journal,* 1982–92; executive documentary producer, CBC, since 1992. Member: Association of Toronto Producers and Directors. Recipient: Canadian Broadcasting League's Cybil Award, 1973; Ohio State Documentary Award, 1973; Anik Award, 1987; Gemini Award, 1987 and 2001.

Television Series

| 1982–92 | *The Journal* |
| 1990– | *Witness* |

Television Documentaries (selected)

1991	*The Third Angel*
1993	*Red Capitalism*
1994	*Romeo and Juliet in Sarajevo* (coproducer)
1994	*Escaping from History* (coproducer)
1994	*The Gods of Our Fathers* (coproducer)
1994	*The Tribal Mind* (coproducer)
1994	*The Bomb Under the World* (coproducer)
1994	*The Body Parts Business* (coproducer)
1996	*The Dawn of the Eye*
2001	*Canada: A People's History*
2002	*Asteroid!*
2002	*Dominion of the Air*

Radio

Five Nights, 1970–73; *Radio Free Friday,* 1970–73; *Commentary,* 1970–73; *As It Happens,* 1973–76; *Sunday Morning,* 1976–80.

Further Reading

"CBC Producer Promoted," *Winnipeg Free Press* (November 28, 1992)

"CBC Resignation Means There's Room at the Top for Starowicz," *Montreal Gazette* (June 25, 1994)

Clark, Penney, "Engaging the Field: A Conversation with Mark Starowicz," *Canadian Social Studies,* Vol. 36 (Winter 2002)

"Starowicz Stays with CBC-TV as the New Boss of Documentaries," *Toronto Star* (November 26, 1992)

"Turning Your TV to the Final Nation State?" *Globe and Mail* (April 10, 1993)

Underwood, Nora, "Twenty Years After," *Maclean's* (March 21, 1988)

Starsky and Hutch

U.S. Police Drama

At first glance, *Starsky and Hutch* (1975–79, American Broadcasting Company [ABC]) seems of a piece with *Baretta, The Streets of San Francisco,* or even producer Aaron Spelling's own *Charlie's Angels*—one more post-1960s police series with street smarts and social cognizance, one that expresses at least a passing familiarity with youth culture. Yet on closer inspection, swarthy Dave Starsky (Paul Michael Glaser) and sensitive surfer Ken Hutchinson (David Soul), confirmed bachelors and disco-era pretty boys, seem to have taken the cop show maxim "Always watch your partner's back" well past their own private Rubicon.

The series was originally part of a logical progression by Spelling (with and without partner Leonard Goldberg) that traced the thread of the detective drama through the fraying social fabric at the end of the 1960s. Beginning with *The Mod Squad* (cops as hippies), this thread took him in logical sequence to *The Rookies* (cops as hippie commune), *S.W.A.T.* (cops as hippie commune turned collectivist cell/paramilitary cadre), and finally *Charlie's Angels* (ex-cops as burgeoning feminists/Manson Family pinups). This was before Spelling jettisoned the cop show altogether and simply leached the raw hedonism out of 1960s liberalism—with *The Love Boat, Fantasy Island, Family*

(sautéed in hubris), and, ultimately, the neo-Sirkian *Beverly Hills, 90210* and *Melrose Place.*

In this context, the freewheeling duo of Starsky and Hutch might seem the perfect bisecting point on a straight line between *Adam-12*'s Reed and Malloy and *Miami Vice*'s Crockett and Tubbs. *Butch Cassidy and the Sundance Kid* (1969) had ushered in the "buddy film" cycle, just then reaching its culmination with *All the President's Men,* and, in fact, the pair physically resemble no one so much as the high-gloss Redford and Hoffman assaying the golden boys of broadsheet exposé, Woodward and Bernstein.

Yet viewed in retrospect, the bond between Starsky and Hutch seems at very least a curious one. Putting aside the ubiquitous costumes and leather or Starsky's Coca-Cola–striped Ford Torino and Hutch's immense .357 Magnum handgun, which Marshall McLuhan or Sigmund Freud might well have had a field day with, the drama always seems built around the specific gravity of their friendship. There is much of what can only be termed flirting—compliments, mutual admiration, sly winks, sidelong glances, knowing smiles. They are constantly touching each other or indulging in excruciating cheek and banter—or else going "undercover" in various fey disguises. All the women who pass be-

Starsky and Hutch, Paul Michael Glaser, David Soul, 1975–79,
Courtesy of the Everett Collection

tween them—and their number is considerable, including significant ones from their past—are revealed by the final commercial break as liars or users or criminals or fatal attractions. And should one wind up alone with a woman, the other invariably retreats to a bar and drowns his sorrows. Following the inevitable betrayal, it is not uncommon for the boys to collapse sobbing into each other's arms.

This apparent secret agenda is perhaps best demonstrated in the opening credits themselves. Initially, these merely comprised interchangeable action sequences—Hutch on the prowl, Starsky flashing his badge. But by the second season, the action footage had been collapsed into a few quick images, followed by split screen for the titles. To the left are three vertically stacked images: Hutch in a cowboy hat, both in construction outfits, and Starsky as Charlie Chaplin and Hutch in whiteface. Meanwhile, to the right, Starsky takes Hutch down in a full romantic clinch, the looks on their faces notably pained.

Next follows a series of quick clips: Starsky waits patiently while Hutch stops to ogle a bikini-clad dancer and finally gets his attention only by blowing lightly on his cheek. Both gamble in a casino, decked out in pinstripe Gatsby suits and fedoras, à la *The Sting.* Starsky, in an apron, fastidiously combs out a woman's wig, while Hutch sits dejectedly, shoulders squared, a dress pattern pinned around him. Hutch watches straight faced while Starsky attempts the samba, festooned in thick bangles, flowing robes, and a Carmen Miranda headpiece. Each is then introduced individually—Soul shouting into the camera in freeze-frame, his mouth swollen in an enormous yawning oval, and Glaser as he ties a scarf foppishly to one side, frozen randily in midtwinkle. Finally, a boiler-room explosion blows Starsky into Hutch's arms.

The entire sequence takes exactly one minute, with no single image longer than five seconds. And each scene is entirely explained away in context. Yet in the space of 60 seconds, these two gentlemen are depicted in at least four cases of literal or figurative transvestism, four cases of masculine hyperbole (encompassing at least two of the Village People), several prominent homosexual clichés (hairdresser, Carnival bacchanalian), a send-up of one of filmdom's most famous all-male couples, a wealth of Freudian imagery (including the pointed metaphor of fruit), two full-body embraces, two freeze-frames defining them in both homoerotic deed and dress, and one clear-cut instance where the oral stimulation of a man prevails over the visual stimulation of a woman. This would seem to indicate a preoccupation on the part of someone with something. (And this does not even begin to address their dubiously named informant Huggy Bear—a flamboyant and markedly androgynous pimp.)

The tone of all this is uniformly playful, almost a parlor game for those in the know (not unlike *Dirty Harry,* whose most famous sequence—the bank robbery—is bookended on one side by Clint Eastwood biting into a hot dog and on the other by a fire hydrant ejaculating over the attendant carnage). Meanwhile, the rather generic storylines consistently play fast and loose with gender.

Altogether, *Starsky and Hutch* is a fascinating digression for episodic television—especially considering that it was apparently conducted entirely beneath the pervasive radar of network censors.

PAUL CULLUM

See also **Police Programs; Spelling, Aaron**

Cast

Detective Dave Starsky	Paul Michael Glaser
Detective Ken Hutchinson (Hutch)	David Soul
Captain Harold Dobey	Bernie Hamilton
Huggy Bear	Antonio Fargas

Producers
Aaron Spelling, Leonard Goldberg, Joseph T. Naar

Programming History
92 episodes
ABC

September 1975–September 1976	Wednesday 10:00–11:00
September 1976–January 1978	Saturday 9:00–10:00
January 1978–August 1978	Wednesday 10:00–11:00

September 1978–May 1979   Tuesday
    10:00–11:00

August 1979   Tuesday
    10:00–11:00

Further Reading

Collins, Max Allen, *The Best of Crime and Detective TV: Perry Mason to Hill Street Blues, The Rockford Files to Murder, She Wrote,* New York: Harmony Books, 1989

Crew, B. Keith, "Acting Like Cops: The Social Reality of Crime and Law on TV Police Dramas," in *Marginal Conventions: Popular Culture, Mass Media and Social Deviance,* edited by Clinton R. Sanders, Bowling Green, Ohio: Popular Culture Press, 1990

Grant, Judith, "Prime-Time Crime: Television Portrayals of Law Enforcement," *Journal of American Culture* (Spring 1992)

Hurd, Geoffrey, "The Television Presentation of the Police," in *Popular Television and Film,* edited by Tony Bennett, Susan Boyd-Bowman, Colin Mercer, and Janet Woollacott, London: British Film Institute, 1981

Inciardi, James A., and Juliet L. Dee, "From the Keystone Cops to *Miami Vice:* Images of Policing in American Popular Culture," *Journal of Popular Culture* (Fall 1987)

Kaminsky, Stuart, and Jeffrey H. Mahan, editors, *American Television Genres,* Chicago: Nelson-Hall, 1985

Marc, David, *Demographic Vistas: Television in American Culture,* Philadelphia: University of Pennsylvania Press, 1984; 2nd edition, 1996

Station and Station Group

A television station is an organization that broadcasts one video and audio signal on a specified frequency, or channel. A station can produce or originate its own programming, purchase individual programs from a program producer or syndicator, or affiliate with a "network" that provides a partial or complete schedule of programming. The term "station" is usually used to designate a local broadcast facility that includes origination and/or playback equipment and a transmitter, with the station being the last link between program producers and the viewer. As the number of television channels available is limited, permission to operate a television station must usually be obtained from a governmental agency (in the United States, television stations are licensed by the Federal Communications Commission [FCC]) and must operate within technical limitations to avoid interfering with signals from other television stations.

Television stations can be classified as "commercial" or "public," depending on whether their source of funding is advertising revenue or government subsidy (although some stations rely on both). Most television stations are divided into departments according to the primary functions of the station. The programming department is responsible for procuring and/or producing programming for the station and scheduling the individual programs into a program schedule. The engineering department is responsible for the technical upkeep of station equipment, including transmitters, video recorders, switching equipment, and production equipment. The production department is responsible for producing local programs, commercial announcements, and other materials needed for broadcast. Most

stations also have a news department that specializes in the production of news broadcasts. Commercial stations have a sales department responsible for selling commercial advertisements; many noncommercial stations have a similar "underwriting" department responsible for soliciting funds for the station. The promotions department is responsible for informing the audience about the program schedule using announcements on the station and in other media, such as newspapers and radio. Finally, many stations also have a business department responsible for collecting and distributing the revenues of the station. These departments are usually supervised by a station manager, general manager, or both.

An organization that owns or operates more than one station is known as a "station group." There is a great deal of diversity in the manner in which groups operate individual stations. Some groups operate all the stations as a single unit, buying and scheduling programming for the station group as a unit in order to take advantage of economies of scale in negotiating the purchase price of programming or equipment. Other groups operate each station autonomously, with minimal group control over the daily operation of each station.

In the United States, the size of a station group is limited by federal regulations. As a result, the concentration of ownership of local television stations is extremely low, with 1,333 commercial television stations in the United States being operated by more than 100 station groups as of early 2003. There are a number of methods of determining the top station group, with the companies holding those rankings constantly changing as new ownership rules allow an increase in the number of stations a company may own. The FCC, in computing the maximum, legal reach of a station group, weights UHF (ultrahigh frequency) stations (channels 14–69) as having only half the reach of VHF (very high frequency) stations (channels 2–13). This "UHF handicap" allows some companies to own stations covering a greater percentage of the United States than the legal maximum.

As of April 2003, *Broadcasting & Cable* magazine ranked Viacom as the top station group in the United States, owning 39 television stations covering 39 percent of the U.S. population. Paxson Communications Corporation controlled more commercial television stations than any other group, owning 61 (mostly UHF) stations that provide an FCC-weighted coverage of 31 percent of the United States.

Changes in broadcast ownership restrictions in the United States are expected to lead to larger station groups and increasing cross-ownership of television stations and other media, especially newspapers. Most television stations and stations groups are owned by companies with interests in other media, ranging from radio stations and newspapers to cable television networks, movie studios, and websites.

AUGUST GRANT

For more information, see:
www.fcc.gov
www.broadcastingandcable.com

Steadicam

More than any other device, Steadicam liberated the film/video image from the rigid constraints of tripods and pedestal supports and enabled a fluidity of style that has become a prominent motif in contemporary production. The Steadicam was not commercially marketed by Cinema Products (CP) until 1976, but cinematographer Garett Brown's early experiments in 1969 and 1970 led to the first prototype of the device, termed "Brown's Stabilizer," in 1973. Adoption of the device was slow in the 1970s, in part because of the difficulty of training capable operators; then, prominent use of Steadicam in films such as Stanley Kubrick's *The Shining* (1980) popularized the look and increased demand and usage of the device. Eventually, thousands of feature films and television programs worldwide employed Steadicam, and the Academy of Motion Picture Arts and Sciences (AMPAS) awarded it an Oscar for technical achievement.

Steadicam is a counterbalanced device that works by shifting the center of gravity outside the camera body and onto the operator's body via a movable arm and a patented three-axis gimble. The operator's vertical and horizontal movements are isolated from the camera by a spring and hinged arm attached to a special vest. As cinematographer Eric Fletcher notes, "This arrangement of springs is much like a drafting table lamp designed to provide a calibrated amount of lift to make the camera and sled float in space." Most striking is the nearly unrestricted mobility and movement of the camera, which allows for 360 degrees of tilt and 270 degrees of pan, at heights from 4 inches to 6 feet above the ground. The ability to operate the camera without pressing one's eyes to the camera's viewfinder makes this possible. The operator can instead move and orient the camera's image away for his or her eyes by monitoring a DC-powered, onboard "video assist" screen. With fingertip control of the camera's tilts and pans, Steadicam relies on the operator's physical skills to move nimbly through sets. Operators liken the task to the demands of ballet or long-distance running.

Steadicam has offered television directors and cinematographers benefits that are both logistical (speed of use and streamlined labor) and aesthetic (a film look that has been deemed dynamic and high tech). The cinematic fluidity that has become Steadicam's trademark is not limited to feature films. The device helped make exhibitionist cinematography a defining property of music videos after Music Television (MTV) emerged in 1981. Indeed, it became an almost obligatory piece of rental equipment for shoots in this genre. Most music videos, like prime-time television, were shot on film, and the Steadicam became a regular production component in both arenas. *Miami Vice*'s much-celebrated hybridization of music video and the cop genre (1984–89) made use of Steadicam flourishes even as the series inserted music-video-like segments within individual episodes. Elements that critics of the show termed "overproduction" (stylized design, "excessively lensed" photography, and overmixed sound-

A stedicam and its operator.
Photo courtesy of Jens Bogehegn

lengthy moves that previously could consume inordinate amounts of program time. Thus, Steadicam provided not just a stylistic edge; it also offered concrete production economies.

The popularity of Steadicam was also affected by the growth of electronic field production. By the late 1980s, CP had begun marketing its "EFP" version, a smaller variant better suited for 20- to 25-pound camcorder packages such as the Betacam and for the syndicated, industrial, and off-prime programming that embraced camcorders. At nearly 90 pounds loaded and at a cost of $40,000, the original Steadicam still represented a major investment. Steadicam EFP, by contrast, allowed tabloid and reality shows to move "show-time glitz" quickly into and out of their fragmentary exposés and "re-creations." As channel competition heated up and production of syndicated programming increased, Steadicam was but one stylistic tactic used to push a show above the "clutter" of look-alike programming. By the early 1990s, CP also marketed a "JR" version intended for the home market and "event videographers." It weighed just 2 pounds and cost $600, and with it CP hoped to tap into the discriminating "prosumer" market, a niche that used 8-millimeter video and 3-pound cameras. However, video equipment makers were now building digital motion-reduction systems directly into camcorders, and JR remained a special-interest resource.

While the miniaturization of cameras might imply a limited future for Steadicam, several trends suggest otherwise. High-definition television (HDTV) cameras remain heavy armfuls, and Steadicam frequently becomes merely a component in more complicated camera-control configurations. As a fluid but secure way of mounting a camera, Steadicam is now commonly used at the end of cranes, cars, trucks, and helicopters—in extensions that synthesize its patented flourish into hybrid forms of presentational power.

While CP argued that the device made viewers "active participants" in a scene rather than "passive observers," it would be wrong to anthropomorphize the effect only in terms of human subjectivity. The Steadicam flourish is more like an out-of-body experience. A shot that races 6 inches above the ground over vast distances is less a personal point of view than it is quadripedal or cybernetic sensation, more like a "smart bomb" than an ontological form of realism. A stylistic aggression over space results, in part, because Steadicam works to disengage the film/video camera from the operator's eyes, dissociating the camera from the controlling distance of classic eye-level perspective. In the 1970s and 1980s, video-assist monitors, linked to the camera's viewfinder by fiber-optic connections, made this optical "disembodiment" tech-

tracks) were well suited for CP's pitch that Steadicam was "the best way to put production value on the screen." Postmodern stylization such as that of *Miami Vice* defined American television in the 1980s, and Steadicam became a recognizable tool in prime time's menu of embellishment and "house looks," the signature visual qualities of individual production companies. The Academy of Television Arts and Sciences (ATAS), following AMPAS's lead, acknowledged Steadicam's impact on television with an Emmy.

Although Steadicam has a distinct stylistic function, many practitioners in the early 1980s embraced the technology for more pragmatic reasons: Steadicam is a cost-effective substitute for dolly or crane shots. Not only can the device preempt costly crane and dolly rentals and the time needed to lay track across a set or location, but it also cut to the heart of the stratified labor equation that producers imported to prime time from Hollywood. On scenes employing Steadicam, the director of photography, the "A" camera operator, the focus puller, and one or more assistants can merely stand aside as a single Steadicam operator executes nically possible on the Steadicam and other motion-control devices, liberating cameras to sweep and traverse diegetic worlds. Because running through obstruction-filled sets with a 90-pound apparatus myopically pressed to one's cornea can only spell disaster, operators quickly grasped the physical wisdom of using a flat LCD (liquid crystal display) video-assist monitor to frame shots. Yet the true impact of Steadicam, video assist, and motion control has less to do with how operators frame images than with how film and television after 1980 turned the autonomous vision of the technologically disengaged eye into a stylistic index of cinematic and televisual authority.

In the 1994–95 season, 75 percent of the scenes in *ER,* the National Broadcasting Company's (NBC's) influential and top-rated series, were shot using the Steadicam, a previously unheard-of level of Steadicam usage. Many of these scenes were included in the spectacular and complicated "one-E.R." sequences that defined the show: complicated flowing actions shot in one take with multiple moves and no cutaways. Citing these astonishing visual moments, trade-magazine recognition confirmed that Steadicam's autonomous techno-eye now also provided a acknowledged programming edge.

Several recent trends outside feature film and prime-time television have begun to challenge Steadicam's dominant place in the production repertoire. The widespread use of extremely lightweight DVCAM and mini-DV cameras has stimulated the development of a range of smaller and alternative "counterbalanced" vest- and handheld camera supports by competitors. The ratings successes of "reality television" (*Survivor, Temptation Island,* and so on) in the early 21st century led to widespread acceptance of the handheld "shaky cam" in prime-time U.S. programming. The box office success of *The Blair Witch Project* and the third "law" of "Dogme" filmmakers Lars von Trier and Thomas Vinterberg ("The camera must be handheld") further legitimized the jerky (Steadicam-less) handheld camera in big-screen filmmaking. Directors who still need to put high-production value on the screen (with heavy cameras), however, will continue to rely on Steadicam and its permutations.

JOHN THORNTON CALDWELL

See also **Miami Vice; Reality Television**

Further Reading

Caldwell, John, *Televisuality: Style, Crisis, and Authority in American Television,* New Brunswick, New Jersey: Rutgers University Press, 1995

Comer, Brook, "Steadicam Hits Its Stride," *American Cinematographer,* Vol. 74, No. 2 (February 1993)

Geuens, Jean-Pierre, "Visuality and Power: The Work of the Steadicam," *Film Quarterly,* Vol. 47, No. 2 (Winter 1993)

Oppenheimer, Jean, "Lights, Camera: Eye-Popping Cinematography, Along with Sound and Editing, Are Breaking New Ground in Hour Dramas," *The Hollywood Reporter* (June 6, 1995)

Steptoe and Son

British Situation Comedy

Steptoe and Son was the most popular situation comedy in British television history and one of the most successful. At the height of its fame in the early 1960s, it regularly topped the ratings and commanded audiences in excess of 20 million. In 1966, Labour Prime Minister Harold Wilson asked the British Broadcasting Corporation (BBC) to delay the transmission of a repeat episode on election day until after the polls closed because he was worried that many of his party's supporters would stay in to watch it rather than going out to vote.

Its creators, Ray Galton and Alan Simpson, were already well known and highly successful as the scriptwriters for Tony Hancock. Indeed, it was Hancock's decision, the most disastrous of his career, to sever his links with Galton and Simpson that brought about the birth of *Steptoe and Son.* The BBC offered them a series of ten separate half-hour comedies, to be cast and produced according to their wishes, which they grabbed with alacrity, keen to produce more diverse material after such a long time working with the same star.

The most successful of these comedies, transmitted in January 1962 under the banner title of *Comedy Playhouse,* was "The Offer," featuring a father-and-son firm of "totters," or rag-and-bone men. As soon as he saw it, the head of Light Entertainment, Tom

Steptoe and Son, Harry H. Corbett, Wilfrid Brambell, 1972.
Courtesy of the Everett Collection

Sloane, knew it was a natural for a whole series. Galton and Simpson resisted at first, reluctant to commit themselves to another long-term venture, but they were worn down by Sloane's persistence and the fact that he was clearly right.

The first series of *Steptoe and Son* was transmitted in June and July 1962 and consisted of five episodes. A further three series, of seven episodes each, followed in the next three years. The producer of all four series was Duncan Wood.

The basic plotline of *Steptoe and Son* is very simple, and most episodes are in some way a variation on it. Albert Steptoe is an old-time rag-and-bone man, a veteran of World War I who inherited the family business of the title from his father. He is a widower and lives with his son, Harold, and together they continue the business, with Harold doing most of the work. Albert is settled in his life and his lowly position in society, but Harold has dreams of betterment. He wants to be sophisticated and to enjoy the "swinging sixties." Above all, he wants to escape from his father and make

a life of his own, something that Albert is prepared to go to any lengths to prevent. The comedy thus comes from the conflict of the generation gap and the interdependency of the characters. However hard he tries, we know that Harold will never get away. So, in his heart, does he, and that is his tragedy. Apart from anything else, his father is by far the smarter of the two.

The success of this formula was partly the result of the universality of the theme and partly the casting of the two leads. Galton and Simpson believed that they should cast straight actors rather than comedians and so signed up Wilfrid Brambell to play Albert and Harry H. Corbett as Harold. Between them, the writers and actors created two immortal characters and some extremely poignant drama as well as the hilarious comedy. The television correspondent of *The Times* wrote in 1962, "*Steptoe and Son* virtually obliterates the division between drama and comedy."

A typical episode would see Albert ruining Harold's plans, whether it be in love, business, or cultural pursuits. In "The Bird," Harold brings home a girl, only to find his father taking a bath in the main room. In "Sunday for Seven Days," Albert ruins Harold's choice of Fellini's *8 1/2* for an evening at the cinema. His father's generally uncouth behavior frequently provokes Harold to utter the only catchphrase of the series: an exasperated "You dirty old man!"

In 1965, Galton and Simpson decided to stop writing the show while it was still an enormous success, although radio versions were produced in the following two years, and the format was introduced to U.S. television as *Sanford and Son*. However, with the arrival of color television in Britain in 1967 and increased competition in comedy from the commercial network, the BBC decided in the early 1970s to bring back some of its top comedy successes of the mid-1960s. *Steptoe and Son* returned in 1970 for a further four series, a total of 30 episodes, between then and 1974.

The effectiveness of the show was in no way diminished. Indeed, the familiarity of the characters allowed the show to carry on where it had left off and achieve the same quality as before. Two feature films were also made of *Steptoe and Son*, though without the success of the television shows.

No more shows were made after 1974, but there is a footnote to the *Steptoe* story. Many programs made on videotape were wiped by the BBC for purposes of economy in the early 1970s, including virtually all of the fifth and sixth series of *Steptoe and Son*. However, Ray Galton had made copies from the masters on the very first domestic video format, and these became the only surviving copies. In 1990, he handed them to the National Film and Television Archive, which restored them to a viewable form and publicized the find with a theatrical showing. Although the technical quality was poor and they played only in black and white, the BBC transmitted a few of them to enormous success. The rest of the restored episodes were then transmitted, followed by all the black-and-white episodes from the 1960s, breaking the BBC's usual resistance to repeating black-and-white programs.

Alas, the two leads were not around to witness the revival. Brambell died in 1985, following his screen son Corbett, who had died in 1983.

STEVE BRYANT

Cast

Albert Steptoe	Wilfrid Brambell
Harold Steptoe	Harry H. Corbett

Producers

Duncan Wood, John Howard Davies, David Craft, Graeme Muir, Douglas Argent

Programming History

55 30-minute episodes; 2 45-minute specials
BBC

June 1962–July 1962	6 episodes
January 1963–February 1963	7 episodes
January 1964–February 1964	7 episodes
October 1965–November 1965	7 episodes
March 1970–April 1970	7 episodes
November 1970–December 1970	8 episodes
February 1972–April 1972	7 episodes
December 1973	Christmas special
September 1974–October 1974	6 episodes
December 1974	Christmas special

Further Reading

Burke, Michael, "You Dirty Old Man!" *The People* (January 9, 1994)
"How We Met: Ray Galton and Alan Simpson," *The Independent* (June 11, 1995)

Steve Allen Show, The (various)

U.S. Comedy-Variety Program

One of the most famous ratings wars in television history began on June 24, 1956. That night, the National Broadcasting Company (NBC) debuted *The Steve Allen Show* opposite the eighth-anniversary program of what had become a television institution, *The Ed Sullivan Show*, on the Columbia Broadcasting System (CBS). The two hosts were markedly different. Sullivan was a rigorous master of ceremonies, known for enforcing strict conformity for both his guests and the members of his audience. In contrast, Allen was inno-

The Steve Allen Show, 1956–61, Elvis Presley, Steve Allen; among Elvis' first TV appearances singing "Hound Dog," 1956. *Courtesy of the Everett Collection*

vative, funny, and whimsical. Whereas Allen liked to improvise and ad-lib on his program, creating material and responding to guests and the audience on the spot, *The Ed Sullivan Show* followed a much more constrained format.

The appearances of Elvis Presley on the two programs serve to illustrate the differences between them. When Presley appeared on *The Ed Sullivan Show,* Sullivan instructed the camera operators to shoot the picture only from the waist up. On *The Steve Allen Show,* Presley appeared in a tuxedo and serenaded a basset hound with his hit "You Ain't Nothing but a Hound Dog." Both strategies appeased nervous network censors, but each is emblematic of the show it served.

Relations between the two prominent hosts were not cordial and reached a low point in October 1956. For his October 21 program, Allen scheduled a tribute to the late actor James Dean. When he learned that Sullivan planned to air his own tribute to Dean a week earlier, Allen charged that Sullivan had stolen his idea. Sullivan denied the charges and accused Allen of lying. Allen moved his segment to October 14, when both programs paid tribute to the actor and showed clips from his last movie, *Giant.*

Much of Allen's work on *The Steve Allen Show* (actually the second program produced under this title) resembled previous performances by him on *The Tonight Show,* which he had hosted since 1954 (after several months of hosting both series, Allen left *The Tonight Show* at the end of 1956). He often opened the program casually, seated at the piano. He would chat with the audience, participate in skits, and introduce guests. Television critic Jack Gould considered the new program merely an expanded version of *The Tonight Show* and characterized it as "mostly routine stuff." Gould did concede that "more imagination could take the program far." *The Steve Allen Show* offered Allen a natural setting for what Gould termed his "conditioned social gift" of "creating spontaneous comedy in front of an audience in a given situation."

Allen also continued something else he had begun on *The Tonight Show,* discovering new talent. Andy Williams, Eydie Gorme, and Steve Lawrence got their starts on *The Tonight Show.* On the new show, Allen's man-in-the-street interview segments launched the careers of comedians Bill Dana, Pat Harrington, Jr., Louis Nye, Tom Poston, and Don Knotts. Dana played the timid Hispanic José Jiminez, and Harrington appeared as the suave Italian golfer Guido Panzino. Characters created by Nye, Poston, and Knotts were the best known of the group. Nye portrayed the effete and cosmopolitan Gordon Hathaway, whose cry "Hi Ho Steverino" became a trademark of the program. Poston was the sympathetic and innocent guy who would candidly answer any question but who could never remember his name. Probably the best-remembered character was the nervous Mr. Morrison portrayed by Knotts. Often Morrison's initials were related to his occupation. On one segment, he was introduced as K.B. Morrison, whose job in a munitions factory was to place the pins in hand grenades. When asked what the initials stood for, Knotts replied, "Kaa Boom!" Invariably, Allen would ask Knotts if he were nervous and always got the quick one-word reply, "No!!!" Allen characterized the cast as the "happiest, most relaxed professional family in television."

Allen became known for the outrageous. He conducted a geography lesson using a map of the world in the shape of a cube. He opened a program by having the camera shoot from underneath a transparent stage. Looking down at the camera, Allen remarked, "What if a drunk suddenly staggered into your living room and saw this shot?"

Although Allen won some of the ratings battles with Sullivan, he ultimately lost the war. In 1959, NBC moved *The Steve Allen Show* to Monday nights. The following year, it went to the American Broadcasting Company (ABC) for a 14-week run. In 1961, Allen renamed the program *The Steve Allen Playhouse* and took it into syndication, where it ran for three years.

LINDSY E. PACK

See also **Allen, Steve;** *Tonight Show, The*

Steve Allen Show, The (various)

The Steve Allen Show

Regular Performer
Steve Allen

Programming History
CBS

December 1950–March 1951	Monday–Friday	7:00–7:30
July 1952–September 1952	Thursday	8:30–9:00

The Steve Allen Show

Regular Performers
Steve Allen
Louis Nye
Gene Rayburn (1956–59)
Skitch Henderson (1956–59)
Marilyn Jacobs (1956–57)
Tom Poston (1956–59, 1961)
Gabe Dell (1956–57, 1958–61)
Don Knotts (1956–60)
Dayton Allen (1958–61)
Pat Harrington, Jr. (1958–61)
Cal Howard (1959–60)
Bill Dana (1959–60)
Joey Forman (1961)
Buck Henry (1961)
Jayne Meadows (1961)
John Cameron Swayze (1957–58)
The Smothers Brothers (1961)
Tim Conway (1961)
Don Penny (1961)

Music
Les Brown and His Band (1959–61)

Programming History
NBC

June 1956–June 1958	Sunday	8:00–9:00
September 1958–March 1959	Sunday	8:00–9:00
March 1959	Sunday	7:30–9:00
April 1959–June 1959	Sunday	7:30–8:30
September 1959–June 1960	Monday	10:00–11:00

ABC		
September 1961–December 1961	Wednesday	7:30–8:30

The Steve Allen Comedy Hour

Regular Performers
Steve Allen
Jayne Meadows
Louis Nye
Ruth Buzzi
John Byner

Dancers
The David Winters Dancers

Music
The Terry Gibbs Band

Programming History
CBS

June 1967–August 1967	Wednesday	10:00–11:00

The Steve Allen Comedy Hour

Regular Performers
Steve Allen
Joe Baker
Joey Forman
Tom Leopold
Bill Saluga
Bob Shaw
Helen Brooks
Carol Donelly
Fred Smoot
Nancy Steen
Catherine O'Hara
Kaye Ballard
Doris Hess
Tim Lund
Tim Gibbon

Music
Terry Gibbs and His Band

Programming History
NBC

October 1980	Saturday	10:00–11:00

December 1980

January 1981

Tuesday
10:00–11:00
Saturday
10:00–11:00

Further Reading

Allen, Steve, *Mark It and Strike It: An Autobiography,* New York: Holt, 1960

Allen, Steve, *Hi Ho Steverino! My Adventures in the Wonderful Wacky World of Television,* Fort Lee, New Jersey: Barricade, 1992

Gould, Jack, "To Meet Steve Allen," *New York Times* (June 24, 1956)

Gould, Jack, "Tribute to Actor Starts TV War," *New York Times* (October 4, 1956)

Shanley, J.P., "Trio of Thriving TV Bananas," *New York Times* (November 10, 1956)

"Steve Allen," *Current Biography Yearbook,* New York: H.W. Wilson, 1982

Strangers. *See XYY Man*

Streaming Video

It is not TV on the web—yet. But streaming media technology is making it possible to inexpensively send audio and video content to any computer connected to the Internet.

Prior to the introduction of streaming media, a media file would have to be completely downloaded to a user's machine before it could be played. Using "downloadable" media meant that the user would have to wait to hear or see the material they requested. Depending on the speed of the user's connection and the length of the audio or video clip, this wait could be as long as an hour. MP3 music files are examples of downloadable media.

With the introduction of RealAudio in 1995, RealNetworks pioneered a new approach to significantly reduce the wait time required to begin playing media files. Streaming media allows the simultaneously download and playback of audio and video. When a user requests a streaming media file (usually by clicking on a link on a web page), several things happen. First, the user's computer launches a streaming media player. The two leading streaming media players are RealOnePlayer by RealNetworks and Windows Media Player by Microsoft. Basic versions of both players are free downloads. In the next stage, the streaming media player begins downloading the media file. When a certain amount of the file (usually 30 seconds) has been downloaded, the media player begins to play back the file. As long as the media file downloads faster than it plays, the user experiences uninterrupted audio and video.

In order to deliver video and audio via the Internet, streaming media has had to address two challenges: file size and variable bandwidth. Compared to the text and graphics that comprised the majority of early Internet content, audio and video files are huge. To distribute audio and video, file sizes must be significantly reduced. Streaming media uses three approaches to reduce the size of media files: compression, frame rate reduction, and image size reduction.

Compression techniques reduce redundant and marginally valuable information from media files to reduce their size. One of the most common compression techniques used by streaming media is frame differencing. In compressing streaming media files, the video material is analyzed to determine which visual elements (or pixels) change from one frame to the next. In transmitting the streaming file, only those elements that change are transmitted. In this way, the amount of information that has to be downloaded is significantly reduced.

The physical dimensions of video are reduced to reduce file size. Whereas the typical computer screen displays at 640 by 480 pixels, streaming media video sizes are usually 240 by 180 pixels. This smaller video image translates into a smaller file sizes for streaming media content.

Video streaming on the Museum of Broadcast Communications' website (www.museum.tv).
Courtesy of Museum of Broadcast Communications (MBC) & Alphazeta Inc.

The final way in which the file size for streaming media video files is reduced is by reducing the number of video frames displayed per second. Typical television video is displayed at 30 frames per second to achieve the perception of motion. Streaming video files reduce the frame rate to around 15 frames per second. This reduced frame rate still produces fluid motion but with much-reduced file sizes.

The second challenge facing streaming media is variable bandwidth. Network congestion causes the speed at which data is transmitted via the Internet (throughput) to vary widely. For the user to experience uninterrupted audio and video, there must be a method to level out the peaks and valleys in transmission speeds. Streaming media uses a "buffer" to guarantee consistent playback. The streaming media player downloads a reserve of audio and video information into the buffer before it begins to play. Then the player releases a steady flow of data from the

buffer for playback. The buffer absorbs the fluctuations in transmission speeds to guarantee constant and interrupted playback. Should the buffer "drain" during playback, the video will stop to allow the buffer to be refilled. This "rebuffering" is common with slower connection speeds and in times of heavy network traffic.

At present, streaming media does not threaten the dominance of broadcast television. The amount of processing power required on the receiving end necessitates that streaming media be played on a computer, and few viewers are willing to replace their television set with a computer. But streaming media does hold promise in certain niche markets. Sports have been an important application for streaming media because it allows fans living out of a given television market to follow their favorite teams. Streaming media also plays an important role in distance education by offering audio and video of lectures. Streaming media has been prevalent in the online distribution of adult entertainment/pornography materials. High levels of viewer motivation encourage users to tolerate the special limitations of streaming media to experience content that is important to them.

In its early days, most streaming media was available for free. However, new business models have evolved, and subscription is playing an increasing role in online media. Major League Baseball (MLB), the National Basketball Association (NBA), and the National Association for Stock Car Auto Racing (NASCAR) have all developed "pay for play" offerings that allow viewers to pay a single monthly subscription to access all events. And MLB has even developed a new product called "Custom Cuts," which offers edited games that can be viewed in much less time.

Increasingly, streaming media is being used to complement existing television programming. Networks are using streaming media to distribute portions of their programming such as promos and highlights. However, video producers are discovering that the special nature of streaming media requires different production approaches. The small screen size in streaming media presentations favors close-ups. Reduced frame rates affect screen transitions, such as dissolves. And compression techniques can significantly impact the playback of pans and handheld shots. Video producers are now becoming more adept at selecting only certain types of scenes to be distributed via streaming video or are shooting special video for streaming distribution.

Currently, there is a large and growing number of streaming media users. RealNetworks reports that it currently has over 300 million unique users of its streaming media players. As broadband connectivity proliferates, there is every reason to believe that streaming media will continue to grow.

SCOTT SHAMP

Street Legal

Canadian Drama

When *Street Legal* completed its eighth and final season, one TV journalist called it "unblushingly sentimental, unblinkingly campy, unabashedly Canadian and completely addictive." The one-hour Canadian Broadcasting Corporation (CBC) drama series about a group of Toronto lawyers stands as a landmark event in Canadian broadcasting history. After taking two years to find its niche, it became extremely popular. In its last six seasons, it regularly drew about 1 million viewers, the benchmark of a Canadian hit.

The series debuted in 1987 with Maryke McEwen as executive producer. It experienced a rocky start, with good story ideas but weak execution, lacking style in directing and consequently suffering low ratings. The theme music, however, was immediately identifiable—a distinctive, raunchy, rollicking saxophone piece by Mickey Erbe and Maribeth Solomon. At that time, the show revolved around just three lawyers: Carrie Barr (played by Sonja Smits), Leon Robinovitch (Eric Peterson), and Chuck Tchobanian (C. David Johnson). Carrie and Leon were the committed, left-wing social activists, while Chuck was a motorcycle-riding, reckless, aggressive, 1980s lawyer.

From the third through the seventh seasons, Brenda Greenberg was first senior producer and then executive producer, with Nada Harcourt taking over for the final season. As CBC's director of programming in 1987, Ivan Fecan hired a Canadian script doctor at the Columbia Broadcasting System (CBS), Carla Singer, to work with the producer on improving the show. It was after this that *Street Legal* began to find its niche, introducing aggressive, sultry, high-heeled, risk-taking Olivia Novak (played by Cynthia Dale) to contrast the niceness of the Carrie Barr character. Olivia became the most memorable and best-known character, but other characters were also added. Alana (Julie Khaner) was a confident and compassionate judge, married to Leon, who confidently battled sexism in the workplace. Rob Diamond (Albert Schultz) handled the business affairs of the firm. In the fourth season, the first African-Canadian continuing character was introduced—crown prosecutor Dillon (Anthony Sherwood). He had love affairs with Carrie and then with Mercedes (Alison Sealy-Smith), the no-nonsense black Caribbean secretary, and later joined the firm. New lawyer Laura (Maria Del Mar) clashed with Olivia and romanced

Street Legal.
Photo courtesy of CBC Television

Olivia's ex-husband and partner, Chuck. Ron Lea played a nasty crown prosecutor called Brian Maloney, an in-joke to Canadians, who immediately connected him to the Conservative prime minister, lawyer Brian Mulroney. The enlarged ensemble cast allowed for more storylines and increased conflict.

The usual prime-time soap opera shenanigans ensued, with ex-husbands and ex-wives reappearing, romances beginning and ending, children being born and adopted, promotions and firings, hirings and resignations, all against the backdrop of the Canadian legal system and the Toronto scene. The lawyers all wore gowns and addressed the court in Canadian legal terms, giving a different feeling from its U.S. counterpart, *L.A. Law,* although the two shows were coincidentally developed and aired at the same time.

The issues addressed were also definably Canadian as well as international. Leon fought an employment equity case for a candidate for the Royal Canadian Mounted Police as well as representing an African-Canadian nurse in front of the Human Rights Commission. Olivia became a producer of a Canadian movie. Chuck defended a wealthy native cigarette smuggler charged with conspiracy to commit murder. Leon represented the survivors of a mine disaster and then ran for mayor of Toronto. Leon and Alana became involved with a Mexican refugee, eight months pregnant, who got in trouble with CSIS, the Canadian intelligence agency. Human-interest stories intertwined with the political issues and the characters' personal lives.

Street Legal represented a very important step in the Canadian television industry. Along with the CTV series *E.N.G.,* set in a Toronto television newsroom, the series established Canadian dramatic television stars. Cynthia Dale, who played vixen Olivia, became nationally famous and went on to star in another series, as a Niagara Falls private eye in *Taking the Falls.* She said that she received letters from young girls who want to grow up to be just like Olivia. In one episode, when ogled and harassed by a construction worker as she passed his job site, Olivia knocked him off his sawhorse with her hefty briefcase. The scene was then inscribed into the new credit sequence.

The rest of the cast members also went on to other work, but the problem of a Canadian star system remains. There are few series produced, even among all the networks, and often their stars will return to theater or radio or to auditioning again for TV parts. One reason *Street Legal* ended was that CBC could not afford to have two dramatic series on air at the same time, and the older program was supplanted by *Side Effects,* a medical drama. In the spring of 1994, the show wrapped up with a two-hour movie, which drew a whopping 1.6 million viewers.

JANICE KAYE

Cast

Charles Tchobanian	C. David Johnson
Olivia Novak	Cynthia Dale
Dillon Beck	Anthony Sherwood
Alana Robinovitch	Julie Khaner
Rob Diamond	Albert Schultz
Laura Crosby	Maria Del Mar
Brian Maloney	Ron Lea
Leon Robinovitch	Eric Peterson
Mercedes	Alison Sealoy-Smith
Carrington Barr	Sonja Smits
Steve	Mark Saunders
Nick Del Gado	David James Elliott

Producers

Maryke McEwen, Brenda Greenberg, Nada Harcourt

Programming History

126 episodes
CBC

January 1987–March 1988	Tuesday 8:00–9:00
November 1988–March 1991	Friday 8:00–9:00
November 1991–March 1993	Friday 9:00–10:00
November 1993–March 1994	Tuesday 9:00–10:00

Further Reading

Miller, Mary Jane, "Inflecting the Formula: The First Seasons of *Street Legal* and *L.A. Law*," in *The Beaver Bites Back?: American Popular Culture in Canada,* edited by David H. Flatery and Frank E. Manning, Montreal: McGill-Queen's University Press, 1993

Street-Porter, Janet (1946–)

Television Presenter, Executive

Janet Street-Porter's career in television has been in two roles; one in front of the camera, as a magazine and talk show presenter, and the other behind the camera, as a producer and television executive. With her punk appearance and streetwise approach, her work as a presenter was focused on young audiences where she gained a reputation as a trend spotter. Behind the camera, her career evolved from innovative youth and music program making to innovative programming.

Leaving midway through a course at the Architectural Association, Street-Porter took up work in journalism with *Petticoat* magazine and the *Daily Mail* newspaper. She followed this with radio presentations on London radio station LBC before being approached by John Birt at London Weekend Television (LWT) to work as a television presenter. During her time at LWT, she worked on various magazine programs, such as *The London Weekend Show* and *The Six O'Clock Show,* and worked alongside television veterans Clive James and Russell Harty on *Saturday Night People* and with Auberon Waugh on *Around Midnight.*

By the early 1980s, Street-Porter had gained celebrity status not only for her directness and skill as a presenter but also for her colorful appearance (especially her brightly colored glasses and hair) and her London accent (referred to as a "strangled" or "exaggerated" cockney accent). She became a regular target for the tabloids. On one occasion, shortly after her appointment to the British Broadcasting Corporation (BBC), *The Sun* published a picture of her on the front page opposite the head of a horse. Much caricatured, she also became easy target for impersonators, featuring regularly on the popular satirical shows *Not the Nine O'clock News* and *Spitting Image.*

In 1980, Street-Porter moved behind the camera into production. As a producer, she continued in her specialty of music, style, and fashion programs aimed at young audiences. Programs included: *20th Century Box,* a topical show for and about young Londoners; *The C(h)at Show,* an all-female talk show; *Bliss,* a music, fashion, and style program; *Paintbox,* a ten-minute experimental music series; and *Get Fresh!,* a Saturday morning entertainment show.

In 1987, along with former LWT colleague Jane Hewland, Street-Porter created *Network 7* for Channel 4. A two-hour program for Sunday lunchtime, describing itself as "TV's first electronic tabloid," again aimed at young audiences, *Network 7* offered news, gossip fashion, and celebrity interviews. *Network 7* had a high-tech look, using music video techniques: a combination of varied camera angles; strong graphics; young, good-looking presenters; and "infobars" (a stream of information running along the bottom of the screen). Winner of a BAFTA Award for Originality in 1988, *Network 7* proved to be a prototype for many youth programs to follow.

Her success led to her appointment as head of youth programs and entertainment features at the BBC in 1988. With her reputation as a trend spotter, Street-Porter was brought in to address the problem of the BBC's lack of policy toward the much-coveted youth audience. After six months, Street-Porter launched *DEF II* (described as a channel within a channel) on BBC 2 from 6:00 P.M. to 7:30 P.M. Mondays and Wednesdays ("Def" was supposedly a slang term for "happening" or "cool"). The *DEF II* slots would usually include nostalgic cult programs (e.g., *Mission Impossible* and *Battlestar Galactica*) and commissioning innovative youth programs, such as *The Rough Guides, Reportage, Behind the Beat,* and *Rapido.*

In 1991, Street-Porter's role was extended to include commissioning entertainment shows as head of youth programs and entertainment features. This period included success as a producer with Ruby Wax in *The Full Wax* and the award-winning *The Vampyr: A Soap Opera.* (*The Vampyr,* a modern version of Heinrich Maschner's 19th-century romantic opera, won the Prix Italia in 1993.) In 1994, Street-Porter moved to a new post as head of independent productions for BBC's entertainment group. This would not prove as successful, and she decided to leave the BBC for a new project.

In September 1994, Street-Porter was appointed managing director of L!ve TV, the Mirror Newspaper Group's venture into cable television. Based in London's Canary Wharf, L!ve TV was to be Britain's first live, 24-hour cable channel. Street-Porter's vision for the channel was high tech, colorful, fast, and trendy. L!ve TV launched in June 1995 amid press reports of differences of opinion on the channel's content. A BBC team captured the behind-the-scenes tensions in a fly-on-the-wall documentary, *Nightmare on Canary Wharf* (shown on BBC in December 1995). Three months after the launch, Street-Porter left L!ve TV.

In August 1995, Street-Porter was invited to deliver the MacTaggart Memorial Lecture, the opening speech of the Edinburgh International Television Festival. She was only the third woman in the festival's 20-year history to do so (the others were Christine Ockrent in 1988 and Verity Lambert in 1990). She chose the occasion to launch an attack on what she saw as the domination of the television industry by what she described as the "four Ms" (male, middle class, middle aged, and mediocre) and the lack of investment in talent. The speech was widely reported in the press.

After her earlier departure from presentation, Street-Porter has made occasional appearances in front of the camera, in discussion programs, as a cultural commentator, and presenting shows involving one of her favorite pastimes, walking. (She was president of the Ramblers' Association from 1994 to 1997.) In 1998, *Coast to Coast,* a seven-part series following Street-Porter on a 516-mile walk from Dungeness, Kent, to North Wales to discover the state of Britain, was aired. In 1999, *As the Crow Flies* was a seven-part series tracking her attempt to walk the 350-mile journey from Edinburgh to London in a straight line.

In 1999, Street-Porter returned to journalism as editor of *The Independent on Sunday.* Although she left the post in 2001, she still writes features and articles for both *The Independent on Sunday* and its sister paper, *The Independent.*

KATHLEEN LUCKEY

Janet Street-Porter. Born Janet Bull in London, England, December 17, 1946. Married: 1) Tim Street-Porter (divorced 1975); 2) Tony Elliott (divorced 1978); 3) Frank Cvitanovich (divorced 1988); 4) David Sorkin 1996 (divorced). Established reputation as a presenter of youth program and talk shows before moving to television production; achieved success for innovative programming before becoming head of youth programs and entertainment features at BBC; managing director, L!ve TV, 24-hour live cable channel. Recipient: British Academy of Film and Television Arts Award, 1988; Prix Italia, 1993; Fellowship of Royal Television Society, 1994.

Television

As Presenter

1975–79   *The London Weekend Show*
1978–80   *Saturday Night People*

1982–3	*The 6 O'Clock Show*
1983	*After Midnight*
1983	*Women Talking*
1994	*The Longest Walk*
1995	*Street-Porter's Men*
1997	*Travels with Pevsner*
1998	*Coast to Coast*
1999	*As the Crow Flies*
2000	*Cathedral Calls*

As Producer

1980–81	*20th Century Box*
1982	*The C(h)at Show* (and presenter)
1985	*Paintbox*
1985	*Bliss*
1986	*Get Fresh*
1987	*Network 7*
1988	*Reportage*
1989	*A–Z of Belief*
1990	*Style Trial*
1990	*283 Useful Ideas from Japan*
1991–92	*The Full Wax*

1991	*Paramount City*
1992	*The Vampyr: A Soap Opera*

Publications

Coast to Coast, 1998
As the Crow Flies, 1999

Further Reading

Barber, Lynn, "Eternal Yoof," *Observer Life Magazine* (February 15, 1998)

Dougary, Ginny, "Janet Street Porter: Madam Youth," in *Executive Tart and Other Myths: Media Women Talk Back,* London: Virago, 1994

Horrie, Chris, and Adam Nathan, *Live TV: Tellybrats and Topless Darts, The Uncut Story of Tabloid Television,* London: Simon and Schuster UK Ltd, 1988

Lury, Karen, "Network 7: Youth Becomes 'Yoof,'" in *British Youth Television: Cynicism and Enchantment,* New York: Oxford Television Series, Clarendon Press, 2001; Oxford: Oxford University Press, 2001

Street-Porter, Janet, "It's Managers vs Talent on TV Tonight," *The Independent* (August 26, 1995)

Toynbee, Polly, "A Dangerous Talent, As Seen on TV," *The Independent* (September 16, 1995)

Studio

Studios are an integral part of independent television production, providing television programming created either by independent producers or, at times, by the studio itself. Studios have a long history with television. In 1944, three years before the Federal Communications Commission (FCC) approved commercial broadcasting in the United States, RKO Studios announced plans to package theatrical releases and programming for television. Five years later, Paramount explored the profit potential of the new medium. By the early 1950s, Columbia and Universal-International had also started television subsidiaries. However, these early efforts were merely false starts. Low ad revenues and overall industry instability resulting from the 1948 antitrust action against studio-owned theater chains made it difficult for studios to earn profits from television.

However, by the mid-1950s, the U.S. networks had successfully wrestled programming control away from commercial sponsors, and studios came to provide the link between programming and a new breed of independent producers and syndicators. The most significant of these early studios—which began as an independent production company—was Desilu, founded in 1951 by Lucille Ball and Desi Arnaz. On the strength of its hit sitcom *I Love Lucy,* Desilu became a production empire that, by the late 1950s, rivaled the size and output of the largest motion picture studios. The company also solidified the position of the telefilm and independent producer's role in the medium. Under the leadership of Arnaz, Desilu hosted numerous successful independent producers, including Danny Thomas and Quinn Martin.

By this time, other studios were getting into the act, with Universal providing studio services for Jack Webb's Mark VII productions and MCA's Revue Studios filming such series as *Alfred Hitchcock Presents* and *Leave It to Beaver;* although the Revue programs were quite diverse, they shared many studio qualities, including the same catalog of incidental and transitional music.

With its string of hit westerns, including *Cheyenne, Sugarfoot,* and *Bronco Lane,* Warner Brothers studio became central to the rise of the action-oriented telefilm. These shows were paired with a group of slick, contemporary detective shows, such as *77 Sunset Strip* and *Hawaiian Eye.* In many ways, Warner Brothers was instrumental in discovering the techniques, narrative strategies, and modes of production needed for a large film studio to shift into the production of series television.

Another prolific 1960s independent producer/studio was Filmways, which began as a commercial production company. The studio's fortune grew when it joined with independent producer Paul Henning, creator and producer of such hits as *The Beverly Hillbillies, Green Acres,* and *Petticoat Junction.*

As the corn-pone silliness of such rural sitcoms gave way to the 1970s new age of relevance, Filmways was eclipsed by another major studio that also began as an independent: MTM Enterprises. Fueled by the fame of actress Mary Tyler Moore and the business sense of her then-husband Grant Tinker, MTM became a major television studio that provided everything from writers and producers to stages and cameras. At the same time, the television divisions of 20th Century-Fox and Paramount Pictures were turning out such hits as *M*A*S*H* and *Happy Days.*

Producer/studios such as Desilu and MTM have since faded, with most major television production provided by independents working in contractual relations with major studios such as 20th Century-Fox, Paramount, MCA-Universal, and Warner Communication. For example, *The Simpsons,* which is independently produced by James L. Brooks's Gracie Films, is filmed by 20th Century-Fox (which, in the case of *The Simpsons,* farms out much of its animation to overseas production houses). In the sea of production logos

flooding the end credits of most contemporary series, the final credit is often that of a major film studio.

Increasingly, however, mergers and acquisitions in the media industries have led to a system of vertical integration in which U.S. television networks own studios and rely on them to provide content for prime-time programming. Disney's purchase of the American Broadcasting Company (ABC), Viacom's purchase of the Columbia Broadcasting System (CBS), and, in 2003–04, the National Broadcasting Company's (NBC's) purchase of Vivendi-Universal sealed these relationships and provided the "big three" networks with in-house program suppliers. FOX was created when News Corporation's chief executive officer, Rupert Murdoch, and media mogul Barry Diller achieved a conglomerate comprising television stations and a studio. Add to this Viacom's ownership of United Paramount Network (UPN) and Time Warner's major stake in The WB, and it is clear that most television content can now be provided by production entities owned by the distributors. The days of "independent producers" and smaller studios seem be numbered.

MICHAEL B. KASSEL

Further Reading

Anderson, Christopher, *Hollywood TV: The Studio System in the Fifties,* Austin: University of Texas Press, 1994
Boddy, William, *Fifties Television: The Industry and Its Critics,* Urbana: University of Illinois Press, 1990
Eastman, Susan Tyler, Sydney Head, and Lewis Klein, *Broadcast/Cable Programming Strategies and Practices,* Belmont, California: Wadsworth, 1981; 3rd edition, 1989

Studio One

U.S. Anthology Drama

Studio One was one of the most significant U.S. anthology drama series during the 1950s. Like other anthology series of the time (*Robert Montgomery Presents, Philco Television Playhouse/Goodyear Playhouse,* and *Kraft Television Theatre*), the format was organized around the weekly presentation of a one-hour, live-television play. Several hours of live drama were provided by the networks per week, each play

different; such risk and diversity is hard to come by today.

Writing about television, Stanley Cavell has argued that "what is memorable, treasurable, criticizable, is not primarily the individual work, but the program, the format, not this or that day of *I Love Lucy,* but the program as such." While this admonition might admirably apply to the telefilm series that came later, the 1950s

Studio One: "Wuthering Heights."
Photo courtesy of Wisconsin Center for Film and Theater Research

drama anthologies were premised on the fact that they were different every week. However, the drama anthologies shared at least one thing in common—the one-hour live format—and because of that very fact, they had to distinguish themselves from each other. The producers for each series worked to develop a "house style," a distinctive reputation for a certain kind of difference and diversity, whether based on quality writing, attention to character over theme, or, more typically, technical and artistic innovation that developed the form. A full assessment would necessarily consider each distinctive anthology series (and assess its "distinctiveness" from the others) as a whole and the failures and achievements of individual productions.

Studio One was the longest-running drama anthology series, lasting ten years from 1948 to 1958, from the "big freeze" through the "golden age" to the made-in-Hollywood 90-minute film format: in all, over 500 plays were produced. From the beginning, *Studio One*'s "house style" was foregrounded not only by the quality of its writers but also by its production innova-

tions, professionalism, and experimentation within the limits of live production.

Studio One began as a CBS Radio drama anthology show in the mid-1940s. Then, in 1948, Columbia Broadcasting System (CBS) drama supervisor Worthington Miner translated the series to television. Its first TV production was an adaptation by Miner of "The Storm" (November 7, 1948). In Miner's hands, the series emphasized certain "quality" characteristics: adaptation (usually of classical works, such as the 1948 production of *Julius Caesar*) and innovation ("Battleship Bismarck," 1949). *Studio One* adopted a serious tone under Miner but also a pioneering spirit. For example, "Battleship Bismarck" made advanced use of telecine inserts and three-camera live editing within a confined and waterlogged set. Miner left to join the National Broadcasting Company (NBC) in 1952, but the show regained an even clearer sense of identity and purpose when Felix Jackson became the producer in 1953. Jackson used two directors, Paul Nickell and Franklin Schaffner, each with his own technical staff, who would alternate according to the material. Nickell was given the more "sensitive" scripts, Schaffner the epics, the action. Both directors were committed to pushing the live studio drama to the limits. Nickell in particular stands as one of the greatest—and most unsung—television directors: he never made the mistake of thinking a good TV drama has to look like a film.

By the mid-1950s, dramatic anthologies typically became less focused on adaptation, and more emphasis was placed on new works written for television, often giving attention to contemporary issues. *Studio One* followed this trend. In many cases, the same writers, such as Reginald Rose, who had adapted for *Studio One,* now wrote original teleplays. Rose worked as an adapter until 1954, the year he wrote "12 Angry Men" and the controversial "Thunder on Sycamore Street." The latter story, about racial hatred, was modified to satisfy southern television station owners, replacing a black protagonist with a convict. By 1955, *Studio One* was receiving more than 500 unsolicited manuscripts per week.

However, it was *Studio One*'s technical innovation, rather than its coterie of writers, that made the series distinctive. Its chief rival in the ratings, Fred Coe's *Philco Television Playhouse/Goodyear Playhouse,* had a superior stable of writers (Paddy Chayefsky, Rod Serling, Horton Foote, Robert Alan Aurthur, and Tad Mosel—most of whom later worked for *Studio One*), but it could not match *Studio One*'s technical daring. *Philco/Goodyear* developed a reputation for plays that explored the psychological realism of character, using many close-ups, but this was influenced by other factors. As Mosel recalled, "I think that began because the sets were so cheap; if you pulled back you'd photograph those awful sets. Directors began moving in to faces so you wouldn't see the sets. *Studio One* had much more lavish productions, they had more money."

After 1955, *Studio One* joined the general decline of the other New York–based dramas. Network programmers began to favor anthologies that fit 90-minute slots (such as CBS *Playhouse 90*) and drama shot on film, often in Hollywood. Eventually, *Studio One* joined the drift to Hollywood and film. By 1957, the anthology was renamed *Studio One in Hollywood*—and the sponsor, Westinghouse, withdrew from the series.

Studio One's achievements have to be measured in terms of technical and stylistic superiority over rival anthologies. With plays such as "Dry Run" and "Shakedown Cruise" (both set on a flooded submarine, built in the studio) and "Twelve Angry Men," *Studio One* was the first to use four-walled sets, hiding the cameras behind flying walls or using portholes to conceal cameras between shots. The freedom to innovate was in part due to CBS's policy of giving directors relative autonomy from network interference and the stability of the Schaffner–Nickell partnership, but it is also a pioneering quality that can be traced back to Worthington Miner and the late 1940s. Miner was quite clear that he wanted *Studio One* to advance the medium via its experimental storytelling techniques: "I was fascinated by the new medium and convinced that television was somewhere between drama and film...a live performance staged for multiple cameras."

However, with the mature *Studio One* productions of the early and mid-1950s, one has the sense that the movements of the cameras were *not* subordinate to the requirements of the performance—quite the opposite. For example, "The Hospital" was an adaptation produced during the 1952 season and directed by Schaffner. This play seemed to achieve the impossible: it literally denied the existence of live studio time. Flashbacks and other interruptions could be achieved with some narrative jigging to allow for costume and scene changes. Still, unlike film, live studio time was real time, and the ineluctable rule of live drama was that the length of a performance was as long as it took to see it. But Schaffner had a reputation for thinking that nothing was impossible for live television. Most other anthologies of the period used a static three-camera live-studio setup, where two cameras were used for close-ups and the other for the two-shots. In such an arrangement, the television camera acted as a simple, efficient, relay. Schaffner favored instead a mobile mise-en-scène; his cameras were constantly on the move, with actors and props positioned and choreographed for the cameras.

This play concerned the drama of a local hospital, following the various staff and patients through typical medical crises. Although the transmitted play lasted 50 minutes, the story time took up only 18 minutes. Some scenes were therefore repeated during the three acts, using a different viewpoint and requiring the actors to restage precisely their initial scenes. As some scenes were lengthened or modified in the light of what viewers saw previously, the audience gained a greater understanding of the events from each character's viewpoint. Although this would be relatively simple to achieve on film, for live drama it involved complex methods of panning and camera movement to capture and expand the chronicity of events and repeat them exactly as it had gone before. Schaffner achieved this by using several cranes to snake through the various sets as the scenes were played and repeated, often in a different order. Doing what seemed technically impossible was therefore foregrounded in this drama, and the complexity of this achievement was emphasized by the ironic commentary of one of the hospital patients who, with head bandaged, was able to explain at the end, as the sponsors shouted for their advertisements, "Time? There is no time. Time is only an illusion." And *Studio One* could prove it.

JASON J. JACOBS

See also **Anthology Drama; "Golden Age" of Television; Miner, Worthington; Schaffner, Franklin**

Spokesperson (1949–58)
Betty Furness

Producers
Herbert Brodkin, Worthington Miner, Fletcher
  Markle, Felix Jackson, Norman Felton, Gordon
  Duff, William Brown, Paul Nickell, Franklin
  Schaffner, Charles H. Schultz

Programming History
466 episodes
CBS
November 1948–March 1949   Sunday
                                                            7:30–8:30
March 1949–May 1949   Sunday
                                                            7:00–8:00
May 1949–September 1949   Wednesday
                                                            10:00–11:00
September 1949–September 1958   Monday
                                                            10:00–11:00

Further Reading

Averson, Richard, and David Manning White, editors, *Electronic Drama: Television Plays of the Sixties,* Boston: Beacon, 1971
Brooks, Tim, and Earle Marsh, editors, *The Complete Directory of Prime Time Network TV Shows: 1946–Present,* New York: Ballantine, 1992
Gianakos, Larry James, *Television Drama Series Programming: A Comprehensive Chronicle, 1947–1959,* Metuchen, New Jersey: Scarecrow, 1980
Hawes, William, *The American Television Drama: The Experimental Years,* University: University of Alabama Press, 1986
Kindem, Gorham, editor, *The Live Television Generation of Hollywood Film Directors: Interviews with Seven Directors,* Jefferson, North Carolina: McFarland, 1994
MacDonald, J. Fred, *One Nation Under Television: The Rise and Decline of Network TV,* New York: Pantheon, 1990
Miner, Worthington, *Worthington Miner, Interviewed by Franklin Schaffner,* Metuchen, New Jersey: Scarecrow, 1985
Skutch, Ira, *Ira Skutch: I Remember Television: A Memoir,* Metuchen, New Jersey: Scarecrow Press, 1989
Stempel, Tom, *Storytellers to the Nation: A History of American Television Writing,* New York: Continuum, 1992
Sturcken, Frank, *Live Television: The Golden Age of 1946–1958 in New York,* Jefferson, North Carolina: McFarland, 1990
Wicking, Christopher, and Tise Vahimagi, *The American Vein: Directors and Directions in Television,* New York: Dutton, 1979
Wilk, Max, *The Golden Age of Television: Notes from the Survivors,* New York: Delacorte Press, 1976

Subtitling

Subtitling is the written translation of the spoken language (source language) of a television program or film into the language of the viewing audience (the target language); the translated text usually appears in two lines at the foot of the screen at the same time that the dialogue or narration in the source language is heard.

This simultaneous provision of meaning in two different languages, one in oral and the other in written text, is thus a new form of language transfer created by film and further developed by television. It combines the two ancient forms of interlingual communication: "interpretation," involving speaking only, and "translation," involving writing only. The concept is sometimes used synonymously with "captioning." In terms of technical production and display on the screen, there is no difference between the two, although it is useful to reserve the term "caption" for the screen display of writing in the same language as the oral text.

Subtitling is, together with dubbing, the main form of translation or "language transfer" in television, which is increasingly developing into a global medium in a world fragmented by about 5,000 languages. The scope of language-transfer activity depends on the relative power of the television market of each country; its cultural, linguistic, and communication environment; and audience preferences. For example, compared to North America, the countries of the European Union have a larger population, more TV viewers, more TV households, and more program production. However, linguistic fragmentation has undermined these countries' ability to perform effectively in the global market or compete with the powerful, monolingual audiovisual economy of the United States. As a step toward the building of a "European single market," the Council of European Communities took measures in 1990 to overcome the "language barrier" by, among other means, promoting dubbing, subtitling, and multilingual broadcasting. The deregulated market of eastern Europe, too, is linguistically fragmented and heavily dependent on imports, with the annual total of foreign programs broadcast in eastern Europe estimated to be 19,000 hours in 1992. English has emerged as the largest source language in the world. Many countries prefer to import programs from the Anglophone audiovisual market in part because it is more economical to conduct language transfer from a single source language.

The ideal in subtitling is to translate each utterance in full and display it synchronically with the spoken words on the screen. However, the medium imposes serious constraints on full-text translation. One major obstacle involves the limitations of the screen space. Each line, recorded on videotape, consists of approximately 40 characters or typographic spaces (letters, punctuation marks, numbers, and word spaces) in the Roman alphabet, although proportional spacing (e.g., more space for "M" and less for "l") allows more room for words, which average five letters in English. Another constraint is the duration of a subtitle, which depends on the quantity and complexity of the text, the speed of the dialogue, the average viewer's reading speed (150–180 words per minute), and the necessary intervals between subtitles. Taking into account various factors, the optimum display time has been estimated to be four seconds for one line and six to eight seconds for two lines. As a result, the subtitler often presents the source-language dialogue or narration in condensed form. Loss or change of meaning also happens because the written text cannot transfer all the nuances of the spoken language. Other problems relate to the reception process. Unlike the printed page, the changing screen does not allow the viewer to reread a line, which disappears in a few seconds. Audiences have to divide the viewing time between two different activities, reading the subtitles and watching the moving picture, and constantly interrelating the two kinds of text. Thus, subtitling has created not only a new form of translation but also new reading processes and reading audiences. This type of reading demands different literacy skills, which are individually and, often, effectively acquired in the process of viewing.

Despite the limitations of subtitling, selectively outlined here, some broadcasters and viewers prefer it to dubbing insofar as it does not interfere with the source language. Although viewers of subtitled programs are not usually familiar with the source language, it is argued that they derive more authentic meaning by hearing the original speech. Preference for one or the other form of language transfer depends on the cultural, political, linguistic, and viewing traditions of each country as well as economic considerations, such as audiovisual market size, import policies, and the relative cost of each transfer method. It is known, for example, that Europe is divided into "subtitling countries" (e.g., Belgium, Cyprus, Finland, Greece, the Netherlands, Portugal, and Scandinavia) and "dubbing countries" (France, Germany, Italy, and Spain). Dubbing is usually more expensive, more complex, and more time consuming than subtitling or voice-over. Still, some of the economically troubled countries of eastern Europe (Bulgaria, the Czech Republic, Hungary, and Slovakia) dubbed the majority of their imported programs in 1992. In these countries, as in others, the professional community of actors supports the dubbing process as a source of employment.

Language transfer involves more than facilitating the viewer's comprehension of unfamiliar language. For example, the European Commission has recommended subtitling as a means of improving knowledge of foreign languages within the European Union. Technological innovations are rapidly changing the production, delivery, and reception of subtitles. Some satellite broadcasters provide multilingual subtitling by using a teletext-based system, which allows the simultaneous transmission of up to seven sets of subtitles in different languages. The viewer can choose any language by dialing the assigned teletext page. Subtitling has usually been a postproduction activity, but real-time subtitling for live broadcasting is available. An interpreter watches a live broadcast and provides simultaneous translation (interpretation) by speaking into a microphone connected to the headphone of a high-speed "audio typist." The interpreted text appears on the screen while it is keyed on the adapted keyboard of a computer programmed for formatting and boxing subtitles. This kind of heavily mediated subtitling will no doubt be simplified when technological advance in voice recognition allows the direct transcription of the interpreted text. By the early 2000s, the demand for subtitling was growing, especially in Europe, Asia, and Africa; digital broadcasting is expected to revolutionize audiovisual translation by, among other things, facilitating live subtitling; at the same time, a variety of software systems already allows more efficient production of subtitles.

AMIR HASSANPOUR

See also **Closed Captioning; Dubbing; Language and Television; Voice-Over**

Further Reading

Dries, Josephine, "Breaking Language Barriers Behind the Broken Wall," *Intermedia* (December/January 1994)

Kilborn, Richard, "'Speak My Language': Current Attitudes to Television Subtitling and Dubbing," *Media, Culture and Society* (1993)

Luyken, Georg-Michael, *Overcoming Language Barriers in Television: Dubbing and Subtitling for the European Audience,* Manchester, United Kingdom: European Institute for the Media, 1991

Sullivan, Ed (1902–1974)

U.S. Variety Show Host

Anyone who watched television in the United States between 1948 and 1971 saw Ed Sullivan. Even if viewers did not watch his Sunday night variety show regularly, chances are they tuned in occasionally to see a favorite singer or comedian. Milton Berle may have been Mr. Television in the early years of TV, but for almost a quarter of a century, Sullivan was Mr. Sunday Night. Considered by many to be the embodiment of banal, middlebrow taste, Sullivan exposed a generation of Americans to virtually everything the culture had to offer in the field of art and entertainment.

Sullivan began as a journalist. It was his column in the *New York Daily News* that launched him as an emcee of vaudeville revues and charity events. This led to a role in a regular televised variety show in 1948. Known as the *Toast of the Town* until 1955, it became *The Ed Sullivan Show* in September of that year. According to Columbia Broadcasting System (CBS) president William S. Paley, Sullivan was chosen to host the network's Sunday night program because CBS could not hold anyone comparable to Berle. Ironically, Sullivan outlasted Berle in large measure because of his (Sullivan's) lack of personality. Berle came to be identified with a particular brand of comedy that was fading from popularity. On the other hand, Sullivan simply introduced acts, then stepped into the wings.

Ed Sullivan's stiff physical appearance, evident discomfort before the camera, and awkward vocal mannerisms (including the oft-imitated description of his program as a "reeeeeelly big shoe") made him an unlikely candidate to become a television star and national institution. But what Sullivan lacked in screen presence and personal charisma he made up for with a canny ability to locate and showcase talent. More than anything else, his show was an extension of vaudeville tradition. In an era before networks attempted to gear a program's appeal to a narrow demographic group, Sullivan was obliged to attract the widest possible audience. He did so by booking acts from every spectrum of entertainment: performers of the classics such as Itzhak Perlman, Margot Fonteyn, and Rudolf Nureyev; comedians such as Buster Keaton, Bob Hope, Henny Youngman, Joan Rivers, and George Carlin; and

Ed Sullivan.
Courtesy of the Everett Collection

singers such as Elvis Presley, Mahalia Jackson, Kate Smith, the Beatles, James Brown, and Sister Sourire, the Singing Nun. Sports stars appeared on the same stage as Shakespearean actors. Poets and artists shared the spotlight with dancing bears and trained dogs. And then there were the ubiquitous "specialty acts," such as Topo Gigio, the marionette mouse with the thick Italian accent enlisted to "humanize" Sullivan, and Señor Wences, the ventriloquist who appeared more than 20 times, talking to his lipstick-smeared hand and a wooden head in a box. Sullivan's program was a variety show in the fullest sense of the term. While he was not so notable for "firsts," Sullivan did seem to convey a kind of approval on emerging acts. Elvis Presley and many other performers had appeared on network television before ever showing up on the Sullivan program, but taking his stage once during prime time on Sunday night meant more than a dozen appearances on any other show.

Although Sullivan relented to the blacklist in 1950, apologizing for booking tap dancer and alleged Communist sympathizer Paul Draper, he was noted for his support of civil rights. At a time when virtually all sponsors balked at permitting black performers to take the stage, Sullivan embraced Pearl Bailey over the objections of his sponsors. He also showcased black entertainers as diverse as Nat "King" Cole, Leontyne Price, Louis Armstrong, George Kirby, Richard Pryor, Duke Ellington, Richie Havens, and the Supremes.

Sullivan attempted to keep up with the times, booking rock bands and young comedians, but by the time his show was canceled in 1971, he had been eclipsed in the ratings by "hipper" variety programs, such as *Rowan and Martin's Laugh-In* and *The Flip Wilson Show.* Sullivan became victim to his own age and CBS's desire to appeal to a younger demographic, regardless of his show's health in the ratings. He died in 1974.

Since *The Ed Sullivan Show* ended in 1971, no other program on American television has approached the diversity and depth of Sullivan's weekly variety show. Periodic specials drawing from the hundreds of hours of Sullivan shows, as well as the venue of the *Late Show with David Letterman* (taped in the same theater used for *The Ed Sullivan Show*), continue to serve as a tribute to Sullivan's unique place in broadcasting. Ed Sullivan remains an important figure in American broadcasting because of his talents as a producer and his willingness to chip away at the entrenched racism that existed in television's first decades.

ERIC SCHAEFER

See also **Ed Sullivan Show, The**

Ed(ward Vincent) Sullivan. Born in New York City, September 28, 1902. Married: Sylvia Weinstein, 1930; one daughter. Covered high school sports as a reporter, *Port Chester Daily Item;* joined *Hartford Post,* 1919; reporter and columnist, *New York Evening Mail,* 1920–24; writer, *New York World,* 1924–25, and *Morning Telegraph,* 1925–27; sportswriter, *New York Evening Graphic,* 1927–29, Broadway columnist, 1929–32; columnist, *New York Daily News,* from 1932; launched radio program over Columbia Station WCBS (then WABC), showcasing new talent, 1932; staged benefit revues during World War II; host, CBS radio program *Ed Sullivan Entertains,* from 1942; host, CBS television variety program *Toast of the Town* (later *The Ed Sullivan Show*), 1948–71. Died in New York, October 13, 1974.

Television Series

1948–71   *Toast of the Town* (became *The Ed
                Sullivan Show,* 1955)

Films (writer)

There Goes My Heart (original story), 1938; *Big Town Czar* (also actor), 1939; *Ma, He's Makin' Eyes at Me,* 1940.

Radio

Ed Sullivan Show, 1932; *Ed Sullivan Entertains,* 1942.

Further Reading

Astor, David, "Ed Sullivan Was Also a Syndicated Writer," *Editor and Publisher* (December 7, 1991)

Barnouw, Erik, *Tube of Plenty: The Evolution of American Television,* New York: Oxford University Press, 1975; 2nd revised edition, 1990

Bowles, Jerry, *A Thousand Sundays: The Story of the Ed Sullivan Show,* New York: Putnam's, 1980

Falkenburg, Claudia, and Andrew Solt, editors, *A Really Big Show: A Visual History of the Ed Sullivan Show,* New York: Viking, 1992

Harris, Michael David, *Always on Sunday/Ed Sullivan: An Inside View,* New York: Signet, 1968

Wertheim, Arthur Frank, "The Rise and Fall of Milton Berle," in *American History/American Television: Interpreting the Video Past,* edited by John E. O'Connor, New York: Unger, 1983

Super Bowl

The Super Bowl is the premier annual television event in the United States. Early in its history, it became the most-watched television show of the year and the most expensive advertising time in American television. It is the championship game between the winning teams in the American Football Conference (AFC) and the National Football Conference (NFC) to determine the championship of the National Football League (NFL).

First played in 1967 with the official title "The First AFL-NFL World Championship Game," the Super Bowl was given its current name two years later when a high-bouncing consumer toy, the "superball," inspired Lamar Hunt to suggest it to Pete Rozelle, then commissioner of the NFL. In addition, in 1969, the New York Jets of the upstart younger and less respected of the two leagues became the first AFC team to win the Super Bowl, signaling a new parity between the leagues. The first two Championship Games had been won easily by the Green Bay Packers under legendary coach Vince Lombardi. When AFC teams won Super Bowls III and IV (NFL marketing also settled early on the monumental-looking Roman numerals for each year's game), the status of the Super Bowl as football's pinnacle was irrevocably established. Sports had been a staple of television programming since the first telecast of a Columbia University baseball game on May 17, 1939, by the National Broadcasting Company's (NBC's) experimental station W2XBS. A professional football game was telecast later that year in which the Brooklyn Dodgers beat the Philadelphia Eagles 23 to 14, and football in ensuing decades established itself as an ideal sport for the particular framing, presentation, and pace of television.

Super Bowl audience size and advertising costs became the highest of any television programming in the early 1970s. All the 10 top-rated television programs of all time are Super Bowls. Annual viewership in the United States has exceeded 130 million for recent Super Bowls, and ratings have usually exceeded 40.0 with a 60 share. To reach the Super Bowl audience, advertising costs were under $100,000 for a 30-second spot for the first half dozen games, but three decades later 30 seconds of airtime cost more than $2 million. A segment of the audience watches primarily to view the expensively produced advertisements being rolled out for the first time in the Super Bowl telecast, and the new ads are instantly evaluated and discussed in newspapers, talk shows, and elsewhere. Among the most famous of the one-time-only Super Bowl ads is the 1984 Macintosh "Brave New World" ad, in which a lone dissenter charges forward to smash a huge television screen transmitting Big Brother dictates to the docile masses. The advertisement was kept under wraps prior to the game and never aired again commercially despite its storied success. Advertisers consider the Super Bowl audience ideal because of its size, inclusive demographics, and event atmosphere.

Pregame and halftime entertainment at the Super Bowl have grown from standard football fare to major extravaganzas. The first Super Bowls featured university marching bands playing the "Star Spangled Banner" to open the game and performing numbers on the field between halves. As the prominence of the Super Bowl became more massive, the anthem was given over to celebrities; past performers have included Mariah Carey, the Dixie Chicks, Jewel, Cher, Billy Joel, Aaron Neville, and Whitney Houston. The halftime ceremony also grew into a massively expensive and complex entertainment extravaganza featuring the biggest names in American popular music, including No Doubt, Shania Twain, Backstreet Boys, Aerosmith, N'Sync, U2, and Britney Spears. The game is packaged with extravagant features: breathless analysis during the preceding week, pregame specials, grandiose player introductions, the massively produced national anthem with jet flyovers and fireworks, a blimp hovering overhead like a holy spirit, aerial pictures of the stadium, tightly edited fast-paced openings and bridges, verbal hyperbole by the announcers, and an overall pageantry and spectacle traditionally reserved for the most important and sacred of public occasions. The network that has bought rights to the game employs several dozen cameras and nearly as many videotape machines to capture the action. Network program promotions crowd in next to the pricey commercials, and the whole package is transmitted overseas to American troops who are, in turn, shown watching the game at a preselected post in Afghanistan, Iraq, or another far-flung American military location.

The game is not played at either team's home site but rather in a neutral, usually fair-weather city, most commonly New Orleans, Miami, Los Angeles. The first 35 televised Super Bowls occurred in January, shifting over the years from mid- to late January, but the league now leans toward an early February date. This is a prime television period because of winter weather in many parts of the country and the absence of competing events. The date also allows the NFL to complete a 16-game regular season, with a bye week for each team, and four rounds of playoff games. The winning team is awarded the Lombardi Trophy, made by Tiffany & Co. of New York and valued at $12,000; each winning team member receives a Super Bowl ring valued at $5,000 and a payment larger than the median annual income for Americans. The winners become heroes to millions and later pay a visit to the White House to meet the president.

Critics have noted that America's number one media event features a male-only game, although the television coverage incorporates women and the NFL markets itself strategically to women. The game is also physically violent compared to most sports. African-American athletes are very overrepresented on NFL rosters compared to their proportion in the total population, but they are underrepresented among team owners. The Super Bowl attracts interest outside North America largely as a curiosity. Despite NFL marketing overseas and sponsorship of NFL Europe, few people outside the United States and Canada understand American football or care. The international equivalent to the Super Bowl is the soccer World Cup Final, which attracts an audience several times larger than the Super Bowl.

The Super Bowl is primarily a television event, but in the days preceding the game, it also generates television specials, newspaper pullout sections, magazine cover stories, special meal recipes, commercial product tie-ins, celebrity features, and every other accoutrement that accompanies extreme public attention. Rising above politics, religion, or other partisan loyalties, it has become virtually mandatory viewing, an occasion for major celebrations with family and friends, and the most prominent secular high holiday in American culture.

MICHAEL R. REAL

See also **Sports and Television**

Further Reading

Oriard, Michael, *Reading Football: How the Popular Press Created an American Spectacle,* Chapel Hill, University of North Carolina Press, 1993

Rader, Benjamin G., *In Its Own Image: How Television Has Transformed Sport,* New York: Free Press, 1984

Weibusch, John, editor, *The NFL Super Bowl Companion: Personal Memories of America's Biggest Game,* Chicago: Triumph Books, 2002

Weiss, Don, *The Making of the Super Bowl,* New York: McGraw-Hill, 2003

Wenner, Lawrence, editor, *MediaSport,* New York: Routledge, 1989

Wenner, Lawrence, editor, *Media, Sports, & Society,* Newbury Park, California: Sage Publications, 1989

Superstation

A superstation is an independent broadcast station whose signal is picked up and redistributed by satellite to local cable television systems. Within its originating market, the station can be received off the air using a home antenna. Once uplinked to a satellite, however, the station functions as a cable program service or cable "network."

The origins of modern superstations can be traced back to the start of distant signal importation by early cable (CATV) systems using microwave relays. At first, the relays simply brought signals to communities too remote to receive them using rooftop or community antennas, but as cable systems began to penetrate television markets with one or more local stations, operators often would import the signals of popular, well-financed stations from major metropolitan areas to make their service more appealing to potential subscribers. In effect, the distant signals were combined with local signals to create a distinct cable programming package. All of today's superstations were carried by microwave at one time; however, the actual term "superstation" was not used until the late 1970s, shortly after Ted Turner's Atlanta, Georgia, station, WTBS, became the first independent station to be carried by satellite.

Not only was Turner's station the first satellite-delivered independent station (and the second satellite-delivered cable program service overall), it was an

SuperStation WTBS

Courtesy of the Everett Collection

innovator in the type of programming that would be most successful on cable. As with many cable-only program services, the popularity of superstations stems largely from their numerous movie screenings and extensive sports coverage—program types available in much smaller quantities from the broadcast networks and their affiliates. Superstation status also gives an independent station an economic advantage when competing with other stations for the broadcast rights to popular syndicated series. The evolution of WTBS's successful program schedule represents an aggressive effort to acquire these sorts of programs.

The existence of WTBS dates back to 1968, when Turner purchased a failing UHF (ultrahigh frequency) station. He quickly changed the fortunes of his new station (which he called WTCG during its early years) by using old movies and syndicated television series to counterprogram network affiliate stations, going after such audience segments as children and people not watching the news. By the early 1970s, Turner's station also offered local sports programming: first professional wrestling and later baseball, basketball, and hockey. By 1972, WTCG had become popular enough in the Atlanta metropolitan area that its signal had begun to be carried by microwave to cable systems throughout Georgia and northern Florida. In 1976, when Turner uplinked his signal to a communications satellite, WTCG's potential coverage was extended to locations as distant as Canada and Alaska. The station was renamed WTBS (for Turner Broadcasting System) in the late 1970s to reflect the scope of its new operations.

Within the next few years, the signals of other major-market independent stations also began to be carried on satellite. However, the stations that followed WTBS to satellite carriage represent a different category of superstation. WTBS is considered to be an "active" superstation because it pursues superstation status as part of day-to-day operations: programming targets a nationwide market more than a local market, and national advertising is sought. WTBS currently is the only active superstation.

"Passive" superstations, by contrast, traditionally have done little or nothing to acknowledge themselves as superstations. Satellite common carriers such as United Video, Inc., and EMI Communications Corp. retransmit the stations' signals without any formal consent, sometimes against the stations' wishes. Despite their potential to be viewed thousands of miles away, passive superstations have continued to direct the greater portion of their programming and advertising toward local or regional markets. As with any cable program service, cable operators pay per-subscriber fees for the use of passive superstations' signals. However, the fees are paid to the common carriers, not to the stations.

As cable's popularity continues, passive superstations are giving more recognition to their own superstation status, often having an employee who functions as a liaison to the satellite carrier and possibly to the cable systems taking the service. Nonetheless, most continue to feel that their priorities remain with their local markets.

The five "passive" superstations currently in operation are: WOR and WPIX, New York; WSBK, Boston; WGN, Chicago; KTLA, Los Angeles; and KTVT, Dallas, Texas. It is worth noting that this group includes some of the country's most long-standing broadcast stations. Like WTBS, these stations have been extremely successful in counterprogramming other stations. All carry local sports, for example. WOR features Mets baseball, WPIX the Yankees, WSBK the Red Sox, WGN the Cubs, KTLA the Dodgers, and KTVT the Rangers. All these stations also carry other sports teams. Most also feature regularly scheduled movie programs, often with well-known hosts. Since the late 1990s, several of the passive superstations have opted to affiliate with the new broadcast "mininetworks" (United Paramount Network [UPN] and The WB), enhancing their own programming schedules as well as providing additional viewership for the new networks. For example, Chicago's WGN is affiliated with The WB network.

The popularity of independent stations as cable program services has surprised many, particularly those who have touted cable's potential to provide programming substantially different from that of broadcast television. This popularity indicates quite a lot about the economics of satellite-served cable, a new vehicle for television programming that has had to compete with the established and resource-laden broadcast networks. In many instances, the formula for success has been found in program schedules that are familiar to television audiences but that nonetheless differ from those of the "big three" networks (American Broadcasting Company [ABC], National Broadcasting Company [NBC], and Columbia Broadcasting System

[CBS])—a formula that independent stations have been following for decades.

MEGAN MULLEN

See also **Cable Networks; Geography and Television; Turner Broadcasting Systems; Turner, Ted; United States: Cable Television; UPN Television Network; WB Television Network**

Further Reading

Bibb, Porter, *It Ain't As Easy As It Looks: Ted Turner's Amazing Story,* New York: Crown, 1993

Garay, Ronald, *Cable Television: A Reference Guide to Information,* New York: Greenwood, 1988

Golbert, Robert, and Gerald Jay Goldberg, *Citizen Turner: The Wild Rise of an American Tycoon,* New York: Harcourt Brace, 1995

Mair, George, *Inside HBO: The Billion Dollar War Between HBO, Hollywood, and the Home Video Revolution,* New York: Dodd, Mead, 1988

Moshavi, Sharon D., "Turner Superstation: Where Does It Go from Here?" *Broadcasting* (October 29, 1990)

Sherman, Barry L., *Telecommunications Management: The Broadcast and Cable Industries,* New York: McGraw-Hill, 1987

Williams, Christian, *Lead, Follow, or Get Out of the Way: The Story of Ted Turner,* New York: Times Books, 1981

Survivor

U.K./U.S. Reality Show

For 13 consecutive weeks during the summer of 2000, the Columbia Broadcasting System's (CBS's) *Survivor* ruled U.S. television by attracting audiences from all demographics (especially from the coveted key advertiser demographic of adults 18–49) who kept tuning in to find out the whereabouts of the adventure game's contestants. Adapted from a British series, *Survivor* is a reality-based show that strands 16 castaways for 39 days in a remote location (the first installment was set on the island of Pulau Tiga, 20 miles off the coast of Borneo), with the show's host, Jeff Probst, as their sole contact with the outside world. Equipped only with essential clothing and one "luxury" item, contestants had both to help and to compete with each other in order to "survive"—that is, be the last person standing on the island. The last "survivor" would win $1 million. *Survivor* became a cultural phenomenon with ratings that proved the viability of scheduling original TV programming during the summer. Furthermore, it ushered in (with a short decline after the events of September 11, 2001) network television's foray into reality-based shows as a financial alternative to more expensive scripted programming. In response to the subsequent explosion of "reality TV" heralded by *Survivor,* the Academy of Television Arts and Sciences created two prime-time categories in its Emmy Awards competition. In August 2001, *Survivor* won two awards: Outstanding Non-Fiction Program with a game show element and Outstanding Sound Mixing for a Non-Fiction Program.

Even if unscripted, *Survivor* provided a rather stable narrative structure. Right before arriving to the island, the 16 contestants were divided into two groups (named after two Pulau Tiga beaches): the Tagi Tribe and the Pagong Tribe. Every few days, the tribes will compete against each other in two different types of challenges: the first one provided specific material prizes (maps, food, beer, matches, and the use of cell phones), and the second one excused the winning tribe from going to Tribal Council (the place for voting contestants off the game and the only traditional shooting stage on the island). Consequently, winning the second challenge meant not having to eliminate a member of the tribe. When the number of contestants went down to ten, the two tribes were merged into the Rattana tribe. Its members were, in the order that they were voted off ending with the winner, Gervase, Gretchen, Greg, Jenna, Colleen, Sean, Susan, Rudy, Kelly, and Richard. At this point, the structure of the two challenges remained in place; however, prizes went to single contestants, and the second challenge provided individual immunity against being voted off during Tribal Council.

The importance both of winning challenges and of remaining on the island, along with the physical and psychological demands of the whole experience, created a dramatic intensity among the contestants that lent itself to very crude and emotional interpersonal encounters. As Executive Producer Mark Burnett explains, *Survivor* is about both "Machiavellian politics at their most primal" and "how [someone] can manipulate complicated team dynamics under pressure." Since contestants were taped 24 hours of the day (by cameramen or recording devices hidden all over the island), viewers had access to these high-strung, spontaneous responses, which became the core of the show's spectacle. The ubiquitous state of surveillance under which the castaways lived, along with particular acts of "self-preservation" (e.g., creating alliances and backstabbing other contestants), and excessive sensationalism (e.g., eating bugs and rats and killing a wild boar) made the popular press call *Survivor* both "voyeur TV" and an "extreme reality show."

These two rubrics point toward the show's broader genre ("reality TV"), which was further layered with an eclectic construction design to appeal to diverse audiences. As Burnett explains, he envisioned *Survivor* as "something akin to *Gilligan's Island* meets *Lord of the Flies* meets *Ten Little Indians* meets *The Real World*." Burnett's allusion to literary texts and contemporary media phenomena exemplifies the show's attempt to cater to CBS's older and more traditional core audience while bringing younger viewers to the network. The show succeeded in all ratings fronts. As Rick Kissell explained, helped by its final episode's exceptional ratings, *Survivor* ranked as "the most-watched series of the 1999–2000 season, with its 13-episode average of 28.25 million viewers." The two-hour finale averaged 51.69 million viewers, more than any program during the season, except the Super Bowl. The final episode "topped a 50 share in all key demo breakdowns, including a 54 in adults 18–49 and an incredible 60 share in adults 18–34." In addition, *Survivor*'s 28.6 rating and 45 share in homes "makes it the highest-rated summer broadcast since such marks were first kept beginning in 1987."

Survivor's ratings success was even more impressive since it aired during the summer, a period when TV viewership dwindles considerably. *Survivor* further accomplished a very desirable feat for any TV series: its ratings, both overall and in all key demographics, increased with each successive episode (with the exception of the fifth installment that posted slight dips). As Josef Adalian and Michael Schneider reported, CBS capitalized on the series' popularity by asking "as much as $600,000 for 30-second spots during the skein's Aug. 23 finale—a rate on par with what NBC usually gets for ads on *ER*." At this point, the network's ad revenues were considerably substantial since CBS "had pre-sold the show to eight sponsors in order to hedge [its] gamble." Furthermore, as Josef Adalian indicated, "*Survivor* served as a successful first test of the new age of corporate synergy within

the newly merged Viacom/CBS behemoth," with ads for the reality show appearing frequently in "younger-friendly Viacom outlets such as MTV [Music Television] and VH1 [Video Hits 1]" as well as "three separate Infinity radio stations." After its summer success, CBS moved the *Survivor* franchise to Thursday nights during TV's regular season. Six more installments have already aired (*Survivor: The Australian Outback, Survivor: Africa, Survivor: Marquesas, Survivor: Thailand, Survivor: The Amazon,* and *Survivor: Panama*). *Survivor* has helped CBS regain competitiveness in the ratings battle by shaking up its "elderly-oriented" image and bringing younger audiences to the network. In addition, the franchise's voyeuristic and sensationalist elements triggered debates about the strategies that *Survivor* as well as other reality-TV shows were employing to attract audiences.

GILBERTO M. BLASINI

See also **Reality Television**

Host
Jeff Probst

Original Contestants
Tagi Tribe: Dirk Been, Rudy Boesch, Sonja Christopher, Richard Hatch, Susan Hawk, Sean Kenniff, Stacey Stillman, Kelley Wiglesworth

Pagong Tribe: B.B. Andersen, Greg Buis, Gretchen Cordy, Ramona Gray, Colleen Haskell, Joel Klug, Jenna Lewis, Gervase Peterson

Producers
Maria Baltazzi, Jay Bienstock, John Feist

Programming History (U.S.)
CBS	Thursday 8:00–9:00
Season 1:	May 31, 2000–August 23, 2000
Special:	*Survivor: The Reunion,* August 23, 2000
Season 2:	January 28, 2001–May 3, 2001
Special:	*Survivor: The Outback Reunion,* May 3, 2001
Special:	*Back from the Outback,* May 10, 2001
Special:	*Survivor: Countdown to Africa,* October 4, 2001
Season 3:	October 11, 2001–January 10, 2002
Special:	*Survivor: Africa—The Reunion,* January 10, 2002
Special:	*Survivor: Back from Africa.* January 17, 2002

Further Reading

Adalian, Josef, "*Survivor* Finds Young Aud," *Variety* (June 2, 2000)

Adalian, Josef, and Michael Schneider, "Eye to Keep Reality in Check, Prexy Sez," *Variety* (July 24, 2000)

Burnett, Mark, with Martin Dugard, *Survivor, The Ultimate Game: The Official Companion Book to the CBS Television Show,* New York: TV Books, 2000

"Eye in Shipshape for Start of *Survivor,*" *Variety* (June 1, 2000)

Kissell, Rick, "An Eye-land Paradise," *Variety* (August 24, 2000)

Schneider, Michael, and Josef Adalian, "Peek-a-boo Boom." *Variety* (June 21, 2000)

Suspense

U.S. Anthology Series

Suspense, an anthology drama featuring stories of mystery and the macabre, was broadcast live from New York on Tuesday evenings from 9:30 to 10:00 P.M. over the Columbia Broadcasting System (CBS). The original series began on March 1, 1949, and continued for four seasons until August 1954. It was revived briefly between March and September 1964.

Suspense was based on the famous radio program of the same name and was one of many early television shows that had its origin in the older medium. The radio program began in 1942 and was broadcast weekly from Hollywood. Scripts were generally of high quality and featured at least one well-known stage or film performer. The famous broadcast of 1948 titled "Sorry Wrong Number" starred Agnes Moorehead in a thrilling tale of an invalid woman who accidentally overhears a telephone conversation in which arrangements for her own murder are being discussed. For the rest of the program, she tries frantically to telephone someone for help. A stunning concept for the aural medium, the episode was later made into a film. In addition to such fine writing, the radio *Suspense* featured outstanding music by Bernard Herrmann and excellent production values. The program attracted a loyal following of listeners until September 1962. When it left the air, *Suspense* was the only remaining regularly scheduled drama on commercial network radio.

The television version of this popular show attempted to create the atmosphere of its radio predecessor by using the same opening announcement—"And now, a tale well calculated to keep you in…SUSPENSE!"—accompanied by the Bernard Herrmann theme played on a Hammond organ rather than by an orchestra. The television version, however, was not able to attain the generally high quality of the radio program. Part of the problem was the program's length. Thirty minutes hardly allowed sufficient time to develop characters of any subtlety. In addition, the fact that the program was broadcast live from a New York studio severely restricted the mobility of its actions. It seemed too that writers sometimes offended the public by presenting subjects considered to be too violent for the conservative tastes of the early 1950s.

The first broadcast, titled "Revenge," was given a very negative review by *New York Times* radio and television columnist Jack Gould. He candidly stated that the program had more "corn than chill" and that the drab story about a man who stabs his wife while she is posing for a photograph gave actors "little opportunity for anything more than the most stereotyped portrayals." Gould noted that the most interesting thing about the program was its interspersing of live studio material with film to show exterior actions. Despite the interesting technique, Gould asserted that the exteriors could have been dispensed with entirely without doing harm to the story.

He also complained of the excessive verbal explanation and dialogue that was too simplified. He contended that the presence of pictures should free the dialogue from exposition and allow it to be more elo-

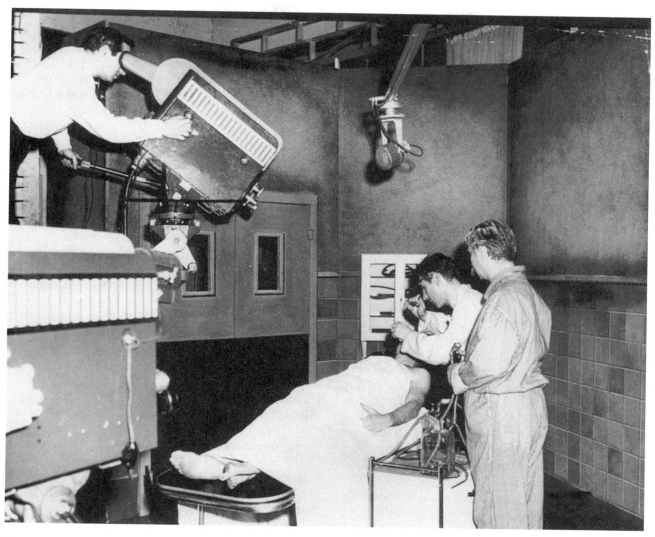

Suspense.
Photo courtesy of Wisconsin Center for Film and Theater Research

quent. As he put it, "With the pictures saying so much, the dialogue can afford to have more substance and be more subtle." His review concluded with a telling observation on the new medium: "The lesson of the first installment of *Suspense* is that among all the mass media, television promises to demand a very high degree of compact and knowing craftsmanship for a mystery to be truly successful."

Gould continued to attend to the series, however, and became incensed about another episode, titled "Breakdown." Written by Francis Cockrell and Louis Polloch, the episode starred Ellen Violett and Don Briggs. The story focuses on a cruel and tyrannical office boss who breaks his neck in a plane crash and is taken for dead until just before his body is cremated.

Gould did not object so much to the story as to its mode of presentation. He was particularly upset by

what he called "the unrelieved vividness of the details of death which no war correspondent would think of mentioning even in a dispatch from a battlefield." In closing, Gould stated, "Both the sponsor, an auto accessories concern, and CBS should be thoroughly ashamed of themselves for their behavior last night. Mystery, murders, and suspense certainly have their place in any dramatic form. But a sustained and neurotic preoccupation with physical suffering for its own sake has nothing whatever to do with good theater. It is time for everyone concerned with *Suspense* to grow up."

Most *Suspense* episodes were more conventional than "Breakdown." The program titled "F.O.B. Vienna" of April 28, 1953, was fairly typical. It starred Walter Matthau and Jayne Meadows in the story of an American businessman who has accompanied a shipment of lathes to Austria and is trying to keep them out of the hands of Communists. The shipment ends up in Hamburg, and Matthau tracks it there with the help of Meadows, who plays a newspaper reporter. At the last minute, he is able to destroy the shipment as the police arrive to round up the Communists. The ordinary script was not, in fact, very suspenseful, and much of it cried for action impossible to depict within the confines of the studio.

A more successful broadcast was "All Hallows Eve" of October 28, 1952. Based on the story "Markheim" by Robert Louis Stevenson, this is the account of a man who murders his pawnbroker and is then visited by the devil, who urges him to kill the man's housekeeper in order to cover up his crime. In an attempt to atone for his utterly delinquent life, the man draws back at the last moment and tells the housekeeper to call the police because he has just murdered her master. Thwarted in his efforts to gain another soul, the devil disappears. Produced by Martin Manulis, this episode made excellent use of the pawnshop set. With its peculiar artifacts and many mirrors that reflect the face of the murderer as he thinks guiltily about his deed, the sense of confined space becomes central to the tale. Franchot Tone gave an outstanding performance as the main character. *Suspense* broadcast a number of other adaptations during its four years on the air. The program drew heavily on classic mystery and suspense offerings, including "The Suicide Club" and "Dr. Jekyll and Mr. Hyde" by Stevenson, "The Mystery of Edwin Drood" and "The Signal Man" by Charles Dickens, and "The Cask of Amontillado" by Edgar Allen Poe.

On May 26, 1953, *Suspense* broadcast its only Sherlock Holmes story. "The Adventure of the Black Baronet" was written by Sir Arthur Conan Doyle and John Dickson as an extension of the original Sherlock Holmes stories. The television adaptation was by Michael Dyne and starred Basil Rathbone as Holmes and Martyn Green as Dr. Watson. Jack Gould gave the program an unfavorable review, saying that much subtlety and brilliance of the Holmes character had been sacrificed by the compression of the story into 30 minutes. He added that Rathbone seemed unhappy with his part and that Martyn Greene was not as effective as Nigel Bruce, who had played Dr. Watson to Rathbone's Holmes on the radio. The production was only one of many instances in which the television version of *Suspense* paled in comparison to its radio counterpart.

Henry B. Aldridge

See also **Anthology Drama**

Narrator
Paul Frees

Producers
Robert Stevens, David Herlwell, Martin Manulis

Programming History
CBS

March 1949–June 1950	Tuesday 9:30–10:00
August 1950–August 1954	Tuesday 9:30–10:00
March 1964–September 1964	Wednesday 8:30–10:00

Susskind, David (1920–1987)

U.S. Producer, Talk Show Host

David Susskind was a key "mover and shaker" in the television industry during the medium's "golden age" and continued to take a high profile as a media personality long after the gold turned to waste through some kind of reverse alchemy. In the process of leaving his mark on the histories of both live drama and television talk, Susskind would be honored with a Peabody Award, a Christopher Award, and 47 Emmy Awards.

As Jack Gould observed in 1960, there were "virtually two Susskinds." One was a behind-the-scenes figure who was a major force, perhaps the major force, in the East Coast branch of the television industry in the 1950s; the other Susskind was the public man who would first achieve celebrityhood as the moderator-interviewer of *Open End,* a Sunday night discussion series aired by WNTA-TV in New York City. Some might say that his achievements were surpassed only by his arrogance. Described by his critics as "combative," "controversial," "blunt," and "endearingly narcissistic," Susskind once aspired to be "the Cecil B.

David Susskind, 1965.
Courtesy of the Everett Collection

DeMille of television." As a self-styled "iconoclast" and "rebel," Susskind cultivated a reputation as a television insider who was an outspoken critic of the medium and its mediocrity. According to Susskind, "Ninety-five percent of the stuff shown on it [TV] is trash."

Susskind's ability to get things done, his genius as a logistician, was honed in the U.S. Navy during World War II. Serving as a communications officer aboard an attack transport, Susskind saw action at Iwo Jima and Okinawa. By the time he was discharged in 1946, he had given up his old ambition of landing a "job at Harvard as a teacher" and set his sights on show business. He actually went looking for his first job in his Navy uniform and quickly found a position as a press agent for Warner Brothers studios.

It was as an agent, that most despised, parasitic, and necessary of show business professionals, that the behind-the-scenes Susskind would first encounter success. After a brief stint as a talent scout for Century Artists, Susskind worked his way into the Music Corporation of America's television program department, where he managed such personalities as Jerry Lewis and Dinah Shore. In the early 1950s, he came to New York and joined Alfred Levy to form Talent Associates, Ltd, an agency that would represent creative personnel rather than actors and specialize in packaging programs for the infant television industry. The new firm's first package sale was the *Philco Television Playhouse,* a live, one-hour drama series on which Susskind would later find his first job as producer, filling in for one of his clients, Fred Coe. After this heady experience, Susskind reinvented himself as a producer whose horizons extended far beyond the small screen, producing more than a dozen movies and more than half a dozen stage plays in his 40-year career. As to television, in addition to serving as a producer on *The Kaiser Aluminum Hour, The duPont Show of the Week,* and *Kraft Television Theatre* (among others), he was also the executive producer of *Armstrong Circle Theater.* During this period, Talent Associates, Ltd, also thrived. In 1959, Susskind's company contracted for $9 million in live shows, more than the combined efforts of the three major television networks.

From the 1960s to the 1980s, Susskind would come into his own. *Open End,* a forum that sometimes lasted for hours, went on the air in 1958. Called "Open Mouth" by Susskind's detractors, the show originally started at 11:00 P.M. and ran until the topics—or the participants—were exhausted. In 1961, the show was cut to two hours and went into syndication; in 1967, the title was changed to *The David Susskind Show.* Susskind's most significant interview by far was with Soviet Premier Nikita S. Khrushchev. Broadcast in October 1960, during the chilliest days of the Cold War, the interview dominated the headlines across the United States. Although station breaks featured a spot for Radio Free Europe depicting an ax-wielding Communist soldier smashing a radio set, most observers scored the event as a propaganda coup for the impish Krushchev. As Jack Gould put it, "The televised tête-à-tête terminated in an atmosphere of Russian glee and Western chagrin."

In his 29 years as a talk show host and moderator, the abrasive Susskind would often rub a guest the wrong way, resulting in what he termed "awkward moments." Tony Curtis even threatened to punch him "right on his big nose" after Susskind characterized Curtis as "a passionate amoeba." Susskind courted controversy by addressing such hot-button subjects as civil rights, abortion, terrorism, drugs, and a number of exotic or alternative lifestyles. His guests were as wide ranging as his discussion topics. The roster of people who accepted invitations to appear on his show includes Harry S. Truman, Richard M. Nixon, Robert F. Kennedy, Vietnam veterans, and even a ski-masked professional killer.

Susskind continued to be intermittently involved as a producer of prestige programming, including *Hedda Gabler* (1961), *The Price* (1971), *The Glass*

Menagerie (1973), and *Eleanor and Franklin* (1976). It is ironic, yet somehow fitting, that the grand impresario who introduced millions of television viewers to Willy Loman would himself suffer the death of a traveling salesman. Susskind died of a heart attack at the age of 66 in 1987.

JIMMIE L. REEVES

See also **"Golden Age" of Television; Talk Show**

David Susskind. Born in New York City, December 19, 1920. Educated at University of Wisconsin; Harvard University, graduated with honors 1942. Married: 1) Phyllis Briskin, 1939 (divorced); 2) Joyce Davidson, 1966 (divorced, 1986); three daughters and one son. Served in U.S. Navy, 1943–46. Began career as a press agent; founder with Alfred Levy, Talent Associates Ltd; hired by Music Corporation of America to produce *Philco Television Playhouse;* produced other early television programs; hosted own talk show for nearly 30 years; expanded production activities to Broadway and films; company purchased by Norton Simon, Inc., renamed Talent Associates-Norton Simon, for theatrical as well as film production, 1970; company sold to Time-Life Films, 1977. Recipient: Peabody Award, Christopher Award, and numerous Emmy Awards. Died in New York City, February 22, 1987.

Television Series (selected)

1947–58	*Kraft Television Theatre*
1948–55	*Philco Television Playhouse*
1950–63	*Armstrong Circle Theater*
1952–55	*Mr. Peepers*
1956–57	*Kaiser Aluminum Hour*
1954–56	*Justice*
1958–67	*Open End* (host)
1958–87	*The David Susskind Show* (formerly *Open End;* host)
1960–61	*Witness*
1962	*Festival of Performing Arts*
1963–64	*East Side/West Side*
1965–67	*Supermarket Sweep*
1965–70	*Get Smart*
1967–70	*He and She*
1967	*Good Company*

Made-for-Television Movies (selected)

1960	*The Moon and Sixpence*
1967	*The Ages of Man*
1967	*Death of a Salesman*
1972	*Look Homeward, Angel*
1973	*The Bridge of San Luis Rey*
1973	*The Glass Menagerie*
1976	*Caesar and Cleopatra*
1976	*Truman at Potsdam*
1976	*Eleanor and Franklin: The White House Years*

Films (selected)

Edge of the City, 1957; *Raisin in the Sun,* 1961; *Requiem for a Heavyweight,* 1961; *All the Way Home,* 1963; *Lovers and Other Strangers,* 1969; *Alice Doesn't Live Here Anymore,* 1974; *Loving Couples,* 1980; *Fort Apache, The Bronx,* 1981.

Stage (selected)

A Very Special Baby, 1959; *Rashomon,* 1959; *Kelly,* 1965; *All in Good Time,* 1965; *Brief Lives,* 1967.

Further Reading

Asinof, Eliot, *Bleeding Between the Lines,* New York: Holt, Rinehart and Winston, 1979

Sustaining Program

U.S. Programming Policy

In the U.S. broadcasting industry, a program that does not receive commercial sponsorship or advertising support is known as a sustaining program. When the term was first used, sustaining programming included a wide variety of noncommercial programming offered by radio stations and networks to attract audiences to the new medium. Currently, most sustaining programming on commercial television is confined to public affairs, religious, and special news programs that are not sponsored.

Howdy Doody, Howdy Doody, Buffalo Bob Smith, 1947–60; 1948 episode.
Courtesy of the Everett Collection

At its inception, radio programming was envisioned by many, including industry leaders (such as David Sarnoff, a guiding force behind the development of the Radio Corporation of America [RCA] and the National Broadcasting Company [NBC]) and government officials (such as then–Secretary of Commerce Herbert Hoover) as sustaining, that is, provided by stations or networks as a public service. Since programming was needed in order to sell radio transmitters and receivers, it was expected that the stations and networks established by manufacturers such as RCA would provide this programming and finance it from the profits on the sale of equipment. Programming provided by stations not associated with manufacturers was expected to be supported through endowments or municipal financing.

The vision of a commercial-free, public service medium was short lived, as American Telephone and Telegraph (AT&T) began exploiting the commercial potential of radio in 1922. However, the public service responsibility of stations licensed to operate on scarce, public broadcast frequencies was affirmed in the Radio Act of 1927 and reaffirmed in the Communications Act of 1934 (section 303), which states that the Federal Communications Commission (FCC) shall regulate the industry as required by "public convenience, interest, or necessity." The "public interest" standard was further delineated by the FCC in a 1946 document titled *Public Service Responsibility of Broadcast Licensees,* commonly known as the "Blue Book." It states that devoting a reasonable percentage of broadcast time to sustaining programs is one criterion for operating in the public interest. Sustaining programming was deemed to be important because it helped the station maintain a balance in program content and provided time for programs not appropriate for sponsorship, programs serving minority interests or tastes, and nonprofit and experimental programs. All licensees were expected to broadcast sustaining programs throughout the program schedule at times when the audience was expected to be awake. Thus, the importance of sustaining programming was firmly established before television began operation, and these standards were applied to the new medium.

Sustaining programming also became important in network affiliate contracts. In the early days of radio, NBC charged its affiliates for the sustaining programs they accepted and paid affiliates a small flat fee for broadcast of sponsored programs. In the early 1930s, William Paley, president of the Columbia Broadcasting System (CBS), used sustaining programs to secure greater carriage of sponsored programs, offering the sustaining schedule free in return for an exclusive option on any part of the affiliate's schedule for sponsored programs. Thus, sustaining programming became a bargaining point in network affiliate contracts.

When experimental television was launched in the late 1930s, only sustaining programming was authorized by the FCC. The NBC schedule in 1939 included films supplied by outside sources; in-studio performances, including interviews, musical performances, humorous skits, and educational demonstrations; and remote broadcasts, mostly of sporting events. Although NBC did not receive compensation to air these programs and shouldered much of the live and remote production costs, advertisers still had an influence on sustaining programming. In the January 1941 issue of *The Annals of the American Academy,* David Sarnoff, then president of RCA and chairman of the board of NBC, wrote that "invitations have been extended to members of the advertising industry to work with us in creating programs having advertising value, at no cost to the sponsors during this experimental period." When commercial operation was authorized in July 1941, NBC was prepared to convert many of its sustaining programs to commercially sponsored programs; however, World War II curtailed the development of television and of commercial and sustaining programming.

As television regrouped after the war, sustaining programming became an important part of the industry's push to sell television receivers and transmitters. Since the financial strategy of many organizations was to use radio profits to provide funds for the fledgling television medium, a side effect of increased sustaining programming on television was the decrease in sustaining programming on radio as programs were dropped in favor of sponsored programming. Sustaining programming on television was varied, including dramatic series, educational programs, political events, and public affairs programs. However, many programs (such as *The Howdy Doody Show*) that began as sustaining quickly found sponsors once they became popular. As a result, the amount of sustaining programming on commercial television quickly diminished.

Further, after the freeze on the allocation of station licenses was lifted in 1950, channel space was allotted for educational stations. Industry leaders began to argue that much of the public service responsibility of broadcasting was being shouldered by these stations.

One of the more remarkable recent sustaining programs on commercial television was *Cartoon All-Stars to the Rescue* (an animated antidrug program), which was aired without advertisements in 1990 simultaneously on the American Broadcasting Company (ABC), CBS, NBC, FOX, Telemundo, Univision, the Canadian Broadcasting Corporation, CTV, Global Television (Canada), Televisa (Mexico), and Armed Forces Television; several hundred independent stations; plus the Black Entertainment Network, Disney Channel, Nickelodeon, the Turner Broadcasting System, and the USA Network on cable. However, this program is the exception.

With the deregulatory push of the 1980s and the argument that nonprofit, experimental, and minority programming is being provided by educational and public television, little regulatory attention is given to sustaining programming on commercial television. Currently, many programs that fulfill the FCC requirement for "public service" programming are sponsored and are, therefore, not sustaining.

SUZANNE WILLIAMS-RAUTIOLLA

See also **Advertising; Advertising, Company Voice; Programming; Public Interest, Convenience, and Necessity; Sponsor; United States: Networks**

Further Reading

Banning, William P., *Commercial Broadcasting Pioneer: The WEAF Experiment, 1922–1926,* Cambridge, Massachusetts: Harvard University Press, 1946

Barnouw, Erik, *The Golden Web: A History of Broadcasting in the United States, Volume II—1933–1953,* New York: Oxford University Press, 1968

"Cartoon Characters Enlisted in Anti-Drug War," *Broadcasting* (April 23, 1990)

Federal Communications Commission, *Public Service Responsibility of Broadcast Licensees,* Washington, D.C.: U.S. Government Printing Office, March 7, 1946

Lichty, Lawrence W., and Malachi C. Topping, *American Broadcasting,* New York: Hastings House, 1975

Sarnoff, David, "Possible Social Effects of Television," *The Annals of the American Academy* (January 1941)

Sarnoff, David, *Looking Ahead: The Papers of David Sarnoff,* New York: McGraw-Hill, 1968

United States Congress, *Radio Act of 1927,* 69th Congress, 2nd Session, H. Res. 9971, Washington, D.C.: U.S. Government Printing Office, 1927

United States Congress, *Communications Act of 1934,* 73rd Congress, 2nd Session, S. Res. 3285, Washington, D.C.: U.S. Government Printing Office, 1934

Suzuki, David (1936–)

Canadian Scientist, Television Personality, Host

A household name in English-speaking Canada, David Suzuki has almost single-handedly popularized some of the most complex scientific issues of our times, largely through the medium of television. While students, teachers, and heads of state continually laud his attempts to demystify contemporary science and nature, some in Canada's science community argue that Suzuki's work on environmental issues in particular is politically biased. Politics aside, Suzuki's awards of recognition clearly attest to his accomplishments: Canada's most prestigious award, the Order of Canada; UNESCO's Kalinga Prize; and the United Nations Environmental Program Medal are among the honors he has been granted.

David Suzuki.
Photo courtesy of CBC Television

Growing up as a third-generation Japanese Canadian, Suzuki, along with his sisters and his mother, was placed in internment camps in 1942 by the Canadian government. After the war, Suzuki and his family were forbidden by law to return to their Vancouver home, so they relocated to London, Ontario.

As a young academic on the faculty at the University of Alberta, Edmonton, Suzuki began his illustrious television career by teaching science on campus TV. Some ten years later, this experience, coupled with his scientific expertise, landed Suzuki (now on the faculty of the University of British Columbia) a host position on the weekly television program *Suzuki on Science*, broadcast by the Canadian Broadcasting Corporation (CBC; 1971–72). Suzuki would later extend his skills to radio, where in 1974 he launched the CBC science affairs program *Quirks and Quarks*.

Although Suzuki continued on radio, his greatest impact clearly remains in the sphere of Canadian public television. In 1974, he embarked on his most successful broadcasting position, first as host of the CBC's television series *Science Magazine*. More important, five years later he became host of the well-established series *The Nature of Things*. The longest-running science and nature television series in North America, *The Nature of Things* is the CBC's top-

selling international program. Established in 1960, the program has been seen by viewers in more than 90 countries, including on the Discovery Channel in the United States. The program's mandate is to cover a broad range of topics, including natural history and the environment, medicine, science, and technology.

The Nature of Things, like Suzuki's work in general, surveys the scientific landscape though a critical, humanistic lens. Such an approach has increasingly lent itself to investigations of controversial contemporary issues of social importance. Suzuki's outspoken views on the clear-cutting of old-growth forests on Canada's west coast, for example, has gained him many friends (and enemies) in logging and environmentalist circles. Whatever one's opinion of his views, however, it would be safe to say that Suzuki remains the voice of popular science on the Canadian airwaves.

GREG ELMER

See also **Nature of Things, The; Science Programs**

David Suzuki. Born in Vancouver, British Columbia, Canada, March 24, 1936. Educated at Amherst College, Massachusetts, B.A. 1958; University of Chicago, Ph.D. 1961; postdoctoral research, the Rocky Mountain Biological Laboratory. Married: 1) Setsuko Joane Sunahara, 1958 (divorced, 1965); children: Tamiko, Laura, Troy; 2) Tara Elizabeth Cullis, 1972; children: Severn Cullis-Suzuki and Sarika Cullis-Suzuki. Held positions as research and teaching assistant, 1957–59; research associate, Oak Ridge National Laboratory, Tennessee, 1961; assistant professor, University of Alberta, 1962–63; assistant professor, 1963–69, and professor, 1969–2001; professor emeritus since 2001, University of British Columbia, Vancouver; television and radio host, various science programs; syndicated newspaper columnist, since 1989; author of numerous books and scientific articles; president, 1991–94, and chair, since 1994, David Suzuki Foundation. Recipient: E.W.R. Steacie Memorial Fellowship, 1969–71; Outstanding Japanese-Canadian of the Year Award, 1972; Order of Canada, 1976; Science Council of British Columbia Gold Medal, 1981; United Nations Environment Program (UNEP) Medal, 1985; Biological Council of Canada Gold Medal, 1986; UNESCO's Kalinga Award, 1986; Global 500 Roll of Honor, UNEP, 1989; Canadian Booksellers Association's Author of the Year, 1990; Environmental Achievement Award, Environment Canada, 1990; Gemini Award, 1992, 1994, and 1997.

Television Series

1971–72	*Suzuki on Science*
1974–74	*Interface: Science and Society*

1974–79	*Science Magazine*
1979–	*The Nature of Things*
1979	*Chickadee*
1980	*Just Ask, Inc.*
1984	*Night Video*
1984	*Futurescan*
1985	*A Planet for the Taking*
1993	*The Secret of Life* (Public Broadcasting Service [PBS] title; on BBC as *Cracking the Code*)
1995	*The Brain: Our Universe Within*

Television Specials

1972	*Men, Money and Microscopes*
1975	*Earthwatch*
1977	*The Hottest Show on Earth* (also co-writer)
1977	*Trouble in the Forest*
1978	*Tankerbomb*
1979	*Why Should I Care?*
1979	*How Will We Keep Warm* (Part 1 of *The Remarkable Society* series)
1986	*Fragile Harvest* (narrator)
1989	*Alaska Turns 30*
1989	*The Nature Connection*
1991	*Voices in the Forest*
1991	*James Bay: The Wind That Keeps on Blowing*
1991	*Dealing with Drugs*
1992	*A Climate for Change*
1992	*Sea of Slaughter*
1993	*Trading Futures: Living in a Global Economy*

1994	*Water: To the Last Drop*
1995	*Cyberspace*
1995	*The Damned*

Radio

Quirks and Quarks, 1974–79; *Earthwatch,* 1980; *Discover with David Suzuki,* 1981; *Expanding Horizons in Medicine,* 1982; *David Suzuki's Discovery,* 1983–96; *U.B.C. Perspectives,* 1986–89; *It's a Matter of Survival,* 1989; *From Naked Ape to Superspecies,* 1999.

Publications (selected)

An Introduction to Genetic Analysis, with A.J.F. Griffiths, 1976

Metamorphosis: Stages in a Life, 1987

David Suzuki Talks about AIDS, 1987; second edition, 1989

Genethics: The Ethics of Engineering Life, with Peter Knudtson, 1989; fifth edition, 1993

Inventing the Future, 1989

It's a Matter of Survival, 1990

Wisdom of the Elders, with Peter Knudtson, 1992

The Secret of Life: Redesigning the Living World, with Joseph Levine, 1993

Time to Change: Essays, 1994

The Japan We Never Knew: A Journey of Discovery, with Keibo Oiwa, 1996

Earth Time: Essays, 1998

The Sacred Balance: Rediscovering Our Place in Nature, with Amanda McConnell, 1998

Swallow, Norman (1921–2000)

British Producer, Media Executive

Norman Swallow's career in British broadcasting, from his joining the British Broadcasting Corporation (BBC) in 1946 through to his continuing involvement in independent production, was that of a major pioneer of the British television documentary and, more broadly, a significant contributor to public service television.

Swallow went to school in Manchester, England, and studied history at Oxford before entering wartime military service. His first work for the BBC was in radio "drama-documentary," where he tackled a number of historical and social themes as a writer and producer. After moving to television, Swallow was a producer of the general-election broadcast of 1951, which marked a decisive shift in television's treatment of elections, to a distinctive form of extended national coverage and commentary. One year later, he became the series director of *Special Enquiry,* a BBC documentary series that concerned itself primarily with investigation into contemporary social issues. The series ran from 1952 to 1957 and was undoubtedly one of the most important innovations in television journalism of the period, acting as an influence on a whole range of later work. In devising the series with his colleagues, Swallow was influenced both by the work of the 1930s British documentary film movement (as represented in films such as *Housing Problems* [1935]) and by the kind of feature journalism, making extensive use of location interviews, developed within BBC Radio.

Special Enquiry started with a program investigating life in the slum tenements of Glasgow. Following this program, newspapers expressed widespread and positive appreciation of the new series. *Special Enquiry* went on to engage with a variety of issues to do with housing, poverty, health, aging, and education, among other topics. As quoted in *Popular Television in Britain,* Swallow described the response the first program received: "We had many phone calls, even letters, from people who, because they know nothing about it, hadn't seen that sort of thing before, wouldn't believe it. They thought we were lying. That it was somehow fiction. So this was a television breakthrough."

One of the most controversial programs in the series, "Has Britain a Colour Bar?," investigated racial prejudice against immigrants, taking the city of Birmingham as an example. Like all the programs in the series, it consisted of a filmed report by an on-location investigative reporter (here Rene Cutforth), together with interview sequences. Following a convention of the period, interviews in *Special Enquiry* were often presented as direct-to-camera testimony, giving the series something of the feel of an "access program" and linking it back to the precedent of direct address by ordinary people in the 1930s "classic" *Housing Problems.* The "Colour Bar" edition caused extensive public discussion, not least for the frankness with which racial prejudice was revealed in the speech of some of the participants, including trade union officials. There was also a powerful, partly dramatized scene in which a newly arrived immigrant looked for lodgings, to be repeatedly turned away by landladies, sometimes with the reason made perfectly clear. The *Daily Express* thought the program to be "one of the most outspoken...ever screened."

At the time, Swallow was also the series producer of *The World Is Ours,* made in cooperation with the United Nations and produced within the BBC's new documentary department, headed by the distinguished filmmaker Paul Rotha. In 1960, Swallow became assistant editor of *Panorama* at a time when this series

was establishing itself as the leading current affairs program on British television. Three years later, he resigned to set up an independent company with Denis Mitchell, one the most brilliantly original documentary directors ever to work for British television. Together, the two did a series for Granada called *This England,* which further extended television's exploration of working-class life through a relaxed approach that kept commentary to a minimum. During this period, Swallow made *A Wedding on Saturday,* a film about a wedding in a northern mining village, which won the Prix Italia in 1965.

Going back to the BBC in 1968, after a period of work that included the first Anglo-Soviet coproduction, *Ten Days That Shook the World* (on the Russian Revolution) for Granada, Swallow became series editor of the arts program *Omnibus.* During his first year, editions of this series included Ken Russell's much-admired biographical film on Delius and Tony Palmer's pathbreaking program on popular music, *All My Loving.* Swallow went on to become the BBC's head of arts features before shifting northward again, to rejoin Granada, where, among other things, he worked on the 1985 series *Television,* an ambitious attempt at tracing the history and significance of the medium across the world.

Swallow wrote extensively on the medium for newspapers and journals, and his widely cited book *Factual Television* remains one of the most thoughtful and sustained reflections on its subject by a practitioner. He was television adviser for the planning of the British Film Institute's Museum of the Moving Image, established in London's South Bank arts complex.

The career of Swallow was both distinctive and representative. It was distinctive in his contribution (particularly in the shaping and supportive role of series editor) both to the investigative documentary and to arts programming, where his interests, enthusiasm, and creative empathy extended well beyond the confines of southern middle-class England. It was representative insofar as his ability to be both popular and serious, intellectually engaged yet fully aware of the need to address a general audience, displayed the best qualities of British public service television. Swallow died in 2000.

JOHN CORNER

See also **British Programming;** *Panorama;* **Producer in Television**

Norman Swallow. Born in Manchester, Lancashire, England, February 17, 1921. Attended Manchester Grammar School; Keble College, Oxford. Served in

British Army, 1941–46. Began career as writer-producer of documentaries, BBC, 1948; producer of documentaries, from 1950; coproduced television coverage of the general election, 1951; produced monthly BBC program *Special Inquiry,* 1952–57; study tour of Middle East, India, Pakistan, and Ceylon (now Sri Lanka), 1956–57; assisted head of films for the BBC, 1957; writer-producer for *On Target,* 1959; appointed chief assistant, BBC Television, 1960; assistant editor, *Panorama,* 1961; joined Denis Mitchell Films, 1963; head of arts features, BBC Television, 1972–74; executive producer, Granada Television, from 1974; freelance producer-director, since 1985. Recipient: Desmond Davis Award, 1977; Emmy Award, 1982. Died in London, December 5, 2000.

Television Series

1952–57	*Special Inquiry* (producer)
1953	*Panorama* (assistant editor)
1954–56	*The World Is Ours* (producer)
1959	*On Target* (producer and writer)
1968–72	*Omnibus* (producer)

Television Specials

1964	*A Wedding on Saturday* (producer and writer)
1977	*The Christians* (producer)
1978	*Clouds of Glory* (producer)
1979	*I Look Like This* (producer)
1980	*This England* (coproducer)
1982	*A Lot of Happiness* (producer)
1986	*The Last Day* (producer and director)
1989	*Johnny and Alf Go Home* (producer)

Publications (selected)

"Documentary TV Journalism," in *Television in the Making,* edited by Paul Rotha, 1956
Factual Television, 1966
"Denis Mitchell," *The Listener* (April 24, 1975)
Eisenstein: A Documentary Portrait, 1976

Further Reading

Corner, John, "Documentary Voices," in *Popular Television in Britain: Studies in Cultural History,* London: British Film Institute, 1991

Sweden

For 67 years, broadcasting in Sweden was entrusted to a publicly owned and regulated company financed on a totally noncommercial basis. Only in 1992 were privately owned commercial radio and television services allowed.

Radio broadcasting started in 1925. The single network was patterned after the British Broadcasting Corporation (BBC), with a strong commitment to public service ideology, while the chaotic situation in the United States at the time was a model to be avoided. Three lodestars for Swedish broadcasting policy had emerged as guiding principles for broadcasting: accountability by parliamentary control, popular education as a primary purpose, and equal service to all. All services developed within these goals were to be financed by a license fee paid on radio receivers.

Television services started in 1957. The decision to entrust them to the same public service company as radio was controversial. Television in Sweden was long synonymous with Sveriges Radio and, after 1978, the separate but affiliated company Sveriges Television (SVT). Public service television had a monopoly on Swedish viewers from the start in September 1957 until New Year's Eve 1987, when the first satellite channel started transmitting to Swedish households from the United Kingdom. In the monopoly era, radio and television were characterized by a kind of cultural paternalism; as defined by the early planners for radio, the media should enlighten and teach. The cultural elite remained highly skeptical of commercialism in broadcasting.

Television took Sweden by storm. Households were quick to purchase TV sets despite their relatively high price. Living rooms throughout the land were rearranged around the new medium. Paternalistic or not, whatever the single channel had to offer got nationwide attention.

Television soon became, and still is, the dominant medium during election campaigns, and the parties anxiously monitor every newscast and debate. The World Cup Soccer tournament of 1958 was a technical triumph for the fledgling company, and with it SVT entered into international collaboration. News reporting evolved into a daily evening newscast (Aktuellt) in 1962.

Theatrical productions, documentaries, and other nonfiction dominated programming, while feature films, serial fiction, and entertainment occupied a smaller share of airtime. Original dramatic productions have been important for SVT from the start. The legendary film director Alf Sjöberg directed *Hamlet* for live trial transmission as early as 1955. Ingmar Bergman made his television debut in 1957 and continued to produce widely acclaimed productions for SVT, including *Scenes from a Marriage, The Magic Flute,* and *Fanny and Alexander.*

A special fee for television (in addition to the radio license fee) generated revenue that enabled the company to extend distribution and expand production capacity. However, Parliament, which controlled the purse strings, was not particularly keen for the company to lengthen program schedules. The general sentiment there was that people should not spend too much time watching television.

In spite of this view, 12 years after the first channel came on the air, Swedish viewers gained access to a second channel, also produced by Sveriges Television and financed by receiver license revenue. The control of television by the nonprofit monopoly came under fire again in the 1960s, but in 1966, Olof Palme, then minister of cultural affairs (later prime minister), emphatically rejected the idea of a privately owned, commercial rival. The profit motive, he argued, was a threat to program quality.

In the wake of the wave of radicalism that swept through Europe in the late 1960s, Sveriges Television experienced some hard times. Some programs had been highly critical of the Social Democrats and their allies, the trade unions. These programs were analyzed in detail after complaints were filed with the Broadcasting Commission, the regulatory organ that supervises public service broadcasters' fulfillment of the Broadcasting Act and their contractual agreements with the government. The Board of Governors, which at that time included representatives of central institutions of Swedish society, were also asked to keep a tighter rein on the company's staff. Some believe that the government's irritation lay behind a program of budget reductions that was imposed on the company in the 1970s. By that time, virtually all Swedish households had TV sets, ending the possibility of increases in funds derived from licensing more and more sets; any increase in SVT's budget would instead require raising the amount of the annual fee.

In 1986, the two channels were given new, contrasting missions. TV1 remained an all-round channel with all in-house production located in Stockholm. TV2, however, was to produce all its programs from ten district offices that the Riksdag had instructed SVT to

establish. At least half of all first-run productions (excluding news and live sports) were to originate in TV2. The aim was to ensure that more of the country would be represented in programming and to create a wider market for independent producers. (In the current contractual agreement, for 2002–06, the quota for programming originating through this strategy has been raised to 55 percent.)

In addition to original material created by TV1 and TV2, both channels filled out their schedules with a selection of foreign programs. Programs from the BBC and ITV have always been a priority. Despite an ambition to mirror many different cultures outside Sweden, a good share of program imports comes from the United Kingdom and the United States.

What finally brought the Riksdag to dissolve SVT's monopoly in 1991 was the advent of foreign-based satellite channels that addressed the Swedish audience directly as well as via carriage on cable networks. It became apparent that further resistance was futile. Unless a domestic commercial channel were allowed, advertising revenue that might be used for domestic production would flow abroad. Therefore, in 1992 a concession to transmit over the terrestrial network was granted to TV4, a private channel. The terms of the concession contained assumptions similar to those supporting public service broadcasting: TV4 must be accessible throughout Sweden, offer good news coverage of the entire country, and carry a specified volume of Swedish-produced programming for children and youth. In return, the channel would have a monopoly on TV advertising over the terrestrial network, albeit the rules for advertising were less liberal than the European Union (EU) regulation applying to satellite channels based in other EU countries.

TV4 had started as a satellite/cable channel. When it began transmitting via the terrestrial network, it was an immediate success in terms of both economic returns and ratings. Within a few years, TV4 had become the single most popular channel in Sweden and the prime commercial contender. Today, Bonnier, Sweden's largest media group, controls the largest share of the channel. TV4's principal rivals in the competition for advertising revenue are TV3 and U.S.-owned Kanal5. That TV4 is accessible to all households and can sell local advertising gives the channel a competitive advantage.

Two companies now dominate viewers' consumption: SVT (42 percent), whose two channels are exclusively license financed, and TV4 (28 percent). Other Swedish commercial channels together have about 20 percent of the market, while the remaining 10 percent is shared by a number of pay-TV channels and foreign satellite channels. Digital distribution got under way in

1999 and is slowly growing. Still, it will be some years before a multitude of digital channels fragments the audience because the size of the Swedish market will limit the number of viable channels.

The Swedish market is small, about 4 million households, which means that potential payers of license fees, targets for TV commercials and subscribers to pay-TV channels are few. They can support only a limited number of costly productions or upscale program acquisitions. The occasions when mass audiences do gather around their sets (major sports events and very popular entertainment programs) suggest, however, that television might attract more viewers more of the time were greater resources put into programs.

The public service channels continue to be predominantly informational, although they do offer some very popular serial fiction, entertainment, and special events that reach a good share of the population. The Olympic Games and World Cup Soccer Championships are examples, as is *Robinson,* the Swedish version of the British format best known by its American title, *Survivor.* Commercially financed channels are steered by demographics and relatively small budgets. In recent years, several Swedish program concepts have been exported to other European countries. So far, the growing pay-TV market has invested little in commissioned Swedish production except for soccer and ice hockey matches. Even though SVT's share of total television revenue is less than half, the public service broadcaster still puts more money into Swedish productions than all the commercial channels together.

For the public service channels, the public's willingness to pay the receiver license fee (currently SEK 1,740 p.a., of which 60 percent goes to SVT, 35 percent to public service radio, and 5 percent to educational broadcasting) is crucial. Yearly polls show that most people feel they are getting value for money. A majority of Swedes want the SVT channels to remain free of commercials, and the share voicing that view has increased over the past decade. Irritation over advertising messages on the commercial channels is growing. In many countries, pay TV has proven a strong competitor, but Swedish households remain lukewarm. In fact, one viewer in three is content with only the three nationally distributed terrestrial channels: SVT1, SVT2, and TV4.

TV4 is the largest channel thanks to a combination of news, family entertainment, and commissioned serial fiction. In the late 1990s, TV4 altered its program mix to include more fiction and entertainment after having lost some of its market share to satellite channels. Competition for young viewers tops the agenda for all channels operating on the Swedish market today. In their attempts to capture young viewers, all the

channels are offering more Swedish and Anglophone entertainment: serial drama, reality soaps, and magazines.

Swedish programs do attract viewers. In 2000, they represented 70 to 80 percent of total airtime on the SVT channels. The commercial channels carry less: 50 percent of the programs on TV4 are Swedish productions and roughly 15 percent on the principal Swedish satellite channels. SVT produces most of its Swedish output in house, with the exception of some entertainment and programs for youth. The other companies commission programs mainly from independent producers, which has stimulated growth in this business sector.

SVT has a strong position among children and older viewers and dominates in news production and Swedish drama. Teenagers and young adults prefer the private channels, which offer more fiction and series. But SVT's fiction production is highly valued both by Swedish viewers and on the international program market. The company's capacity enables it to take part in coproductions and makes it one of the leading film producers in northern Europe. SVT has been recognized with a number of International Emmy Awards: for the original drama, *The Tattooed Widow,* in 1998; for photographer Lennart Nilsson's remarkable medical series, *The Miracle of Life,* in 1996; and for the ballet performance, *Rök,* also in 1996.

Despite the proliferation of channels, viewing time has not increased notably since the days before satellite and cable. Sweden has among the lowest viewing figures in Europe, with an average 2.5 hours per day and person. In the monopoly era, the low figures were generally attributed to the seriousness of SVT's output. More important factors are probably the high rate of employment outside the home among women and leisure activities outside the home. Then there is the "midnight sun factor": viewing plummets during the summer months.

Digital Television

Conversion to digital mode has been discussed in Sweden since the mid-1990s. In 1996, the Riksdag moved to allocate a number of digital frequencies in the terrestrial network that might accommodate 35 to 40 channels (compared to three analog channels today). Satellite channels are almost totally digital, and cable is partially converted. The role of the public sector in this development is controversial; critics find it an inappropriate use of public funds. Most viewers (two out of three) receive television via cable or satellite dish and have no use for the terrestrial network. Judgments differ as to whether the terrestrial network, with its fewer channels and higher cost of distribution, will be competitive with other digital platforms. All things considered, it would appear that multiple distribution systems will continue to operate alongside one another in the digital age.

Digital television poses many challenges. For SVT, the challenge is how to finance a more segmented output without either commercial revenue or commercial incentives. The public service broadcaster's presence in a variety of technical platforms is accorded value per se. SVT plans at least four digital channels: the present all-around channels plus niche channels for news and special events and young viewers. The commercial channels have a similar strategy in mind: a broad channel to enhance brand-name awareness, complemented by specialized channels and interactive services for pay. For them, the challenge is to retain their commercial revenue in an increasingly international media environment.

OLOF HULTÉN

Further Reading

Carlsson, Ulla, and Harrie, Eva, editors, *Media Trends 2001 in Denmark, Finland, Iceland, Norway and Sweden,* Göteborg: Nordicom, Göteborg University, 2001

Edin, Anna, "The Well-Organized Competition: On the Development of Internal Competititon in Swedish Television Monopoly," *Nordicom Review,* No. 1 (1998)

Ewertsson, Lena, *The Triumph of Technology over Politics. Reconstructing Television Systems: The Example of Sweden.* Linköping: Linköping University, Department of Technology and Social Change, 2001

Hultén, Olof, *Mass Media and State Support in Sweden,* 2nd edition, Stockholm: Swedish Institute, 1984

Hultén, Olof, Sweden: "Broadcasting and the Social Project," in *Public Broadcasting for the 21st Century,* edited by Marc Raboy, Acamedia Monograph 17, Luton: University of Luton Press, John Libbey Media, Luton, 1995

Hultén, Olof, "Diversity or Conformity? Television Programming in Competitive Situations," *Nordicom Review,* No. 1 (1995)

Kleberg, Madeleine, "The History of Swedish Television— Three Stages," in *Television in Scandinavia: History, Politics and Aestethics,* edited by Ib Bondebjerg and Francesco Bono, Luton: John Libbey Media, 1996

Noam, Eli, Sweden, in *Television in Europe,* New York: Oxford University Press, 1991

Nowak, Kjell, "Television in Sweden 1986: Position and Prospects," Stockholm University, Center for Mass Communication Research, 1987.

Ortmark, Åke, "Freedom's Boundaries," in *Television and Political Life: Studies in Six European Countries,* edited by Anthony Smith, London: Macmillan, 1979

Weibull, Lennart, "Sweden," in *Television and the Viewer Interest: Explorations in the Responsiveness of European Broadcasters,* edited by Jeremy Mitchell and Jay G. Blumler, London: John Libbey, 1994

Sweeney, The

British Police Drama

The Sweeney was the top-rated British police series of the 1970s, bringing a new level of toughness and action to the genre and displaying police officers bending the rules to beat crime. The series was created by Ian Kennedy-Martin and produced by Ted Childs for Euston Films (a Thames Television subsidiary) and went out midweek in prime time on ITV, the main commercial channel. In all, 54 episodes were made, and the program ran for four seasons.

The Sweeney focused on the exploits of Jack Regan, a maverick detective inspector (D.I.) attached to the Flying Squad, the metropolitan police's elite armed-robbery unit, and featured John Thaw in the leading role. The program, which derived its title from "Sweeney Todd," the Cockney rhyming slang for "Flying Squad," was a spin-off from the successful 1974 TV film *Regan,* which had first introduced the protago-nist and established his professional relationships with his assistant, Detective Sargeant (D.S.) George Carter (played by Dennis Waterman) and his "governor," Detective Chief Inspector (D.C.I.) Haskins (played by Garfield Morgan). Each episode in the series adopted the same basic narrative format—a three-act structure (with acts separated by advertisements) preceded by a prologue that triggered the crime narrative. The first two acts were devoted to obtaining intelligence about a forthcoming robbery, often through tip-offs from informers or surveillance; the third involved the capture of the robbery gang, characteristically involving adrenalin-pumping action with car chases, screaming tires, spectacular smashes, and hand-to-hand fighting. The narrative was often further complicated through the addition of an antiauthority thread in which Regan challenged Haskins's "rule-book" approach or through the introduction of casual sex relationships in which one of the detectives became involved with an available woman.

The program's realism was considerable, and few other crime series have achieved so authentic an impression of the policing of London's underworld. To an extent, this was achieved by adopting the same visual style, fast action, and cynical outlook as contemporary rogue-cop films, such as *Dirty Harry* and *The French Connection.* Equally, though, the program relied on detailed inside knowledge of the actual circumstances in which the Flying Squad operated and the sometimes rather dubious means used to secure prosecutions. The series' storylines frequently blurred the sharp distinctions that are normally drawn between good and evil characters in crime melodrama. Regan and Carter were shown inhabiting the same sleazy world as the criminals, mixing with low-lifes to obtain their leads, and adopting the same vernacular. Both law enforcers and lawbreakers indulged in womanizing and heavy drinking and used physical violence to achieve their objectives. The extent to which Regan was prepared to bend and break the rules to "nick villains" was well established in the pilot film, when he threatened a suspect with a longer sentence if he did not cooperate: "My sergeant is going to hit me, but I am going to say it's you." Throughout the series, however, the viewer's sense of Regan's integrity remained secure. Even though he might need to beat up suspects, strike deals with criminals, or, on one occasion, burglarize the office of the D.C.I. to read his own personal file, such actions were legitimized in the narrative as the only means available to the serious crime fighter to keep on top and to cut through the dead weight of bureaucracy that continually threatened to impede the cause of justice.

Unsurprisingly, the series provoked fierce controversy, chiefly because of its potential to influence the public image of the police at a time of considerable social upheaval. However, the dark (if not confused) moral world that the series represented was difficult to fault on purely realistic grounds since, at the time of transmission, a prominent officer in the Squad was under investigation and was eventually imprisoned for corruption. Considered in wider cultural terms, the program has been viewed as part of the general ideological shift to the right that occurred in the 1970s in Britain, as the postwar social-democratic consensus broke down. James Donald, notably, has argued that *The Sweeney* was fueled by popular anxieties about law and order stimulated by the press campaign on mugging and that episodes provided a "mapping fantasy" for the acting out of unconscious authoritarian urges.

The Sweeney had sold to 51 countries by 1985 and inspired two successful feature films. It also established Dennis Waterman and John Thaw as household names with the British public. The series secured the reputation of Euston Films as a leading production company, and it created an influential model in Britain not just for crime series on ITV but for the production of cost-effective, high-quality drama in general. The lean and efficient production operation that Euston pioneered in *The Sweeney,* relying on short-term contracts and shooting entirely with 16-millimeter film, has been generally adopted across the industry; with the exception of soap operas, the great majority of drama projects today are manned by freelance crews and produced on film.

BOB MILLINGTON

See also **Thaw, John; Waterman, Dennis**

Cast

D.I. Jack Regan	John Thaw
D.S. George Carter	Dennis Waterman
D.C.I. Frank Haskins	Garfield Morgan

Producer

Ted Childs

Programming History

53 50-minute episodes; 1 77-minute episode
ITV

January 1975–March 1975	14 episodes
September 1975–November 1975	13 episodes
September 1976–December 1976	13 episodes
September 1978–December 1978	14 episodes

Further Reading

Alvarado, Manuel, and John Stewart, *Made for Television: Euston Films Ltd.,* London: British Film Institute/Methuen, 1985

Clarke, Alan, "This Is Not the Boy Scouts," in *Popular Culture and Social Relations,* edited by Tony Bennett, Colin Mercer, and Janet Woollacott, Milton Keynes, England, and Philadelphia, Pennsylvania: Open University Press, 1986

Donald, James, "Anxious Moments in *The Sweeney,*" in *Made for Television: Euston Films Ltd.,* by Manuel Alvarado and John Stewart, London: British Film Institute/Methuen, 1985

Hurd, Geoffrey, "The Television Presentation of the Police," in *Popular Television and Film: A Reader,* edited by Tony Bennett et al., London: British Film Institute/Open University Press, 1981

Switzerland

Switzerland, surrounded by Germany, Italy, France, Austria, and the small country of Liechtenstein, is a multilingual and multicultural society. Because of its unique topography—a total of 41,293 square miles, most of it unpopulated mountain ranges—Switzerland is highly segmented. Nearly 7 million inhabitants speak different languages and live in completely different surroundings. From industrialized cities such as Basel or Zurich to remote locations in closed-off valleys, they share a somewhat vague notion about what it means to be "Swiss." Still, commonalities have succeeded in overcoming the ever-present language barriers. So far, they have proven strong enough to keep Switzerland one of the few countries in western Europe out of the European Union.

Television in Switzerland began in 1949 with an official delegation of Swiss technicians (and some staff members of General Electric) watching an experimental program, broadcast from Torino in Italy about 90 miles away. The first programs produced in Switzerland, in 1953, were received in Zurich only. By 1955, there were 8,600 television sets in Switzerland, 2,300 of them in public rooms and 6,300 in private households. In 1994, there were 2.6 million television license fee holders in Switzerland.

Television, as developed in the 1950s and 1960s, was meant to be a tool of public communication and education. The technical objective was reception in all Swiss households (a goal still not attained because of topography), but television broadcast had a political and social mission as well. "Audiovision," as it was termed, was supposed to play an important part in the national integration of different languages, regions, religions, generations, and ways of living. Since there was, until 1992, only one network officially assigned with the mission to broadcast television programs, politicians of all parties kept an eye on content and on those responsible for developing and managing the broadcasting system.

The date July 20, 1953, marked the official beginning of Swiss broadcasting. Programming that night consisted of a demonstration of traditional Swiss woodcrafts and the recitation of a poem, "The Blind." Older Swiss citizens often remember broadcasts of live sports events that were viewed in crowded restaurants rather than at home. At the time, television was a social event.

Early viewers were especially interested in nature programs. And though educational programs rarely dealt with social problems, news and documentaries were something else. "Objectivity" was the key word during the 1970s, and some television programmers, labeled as left-wing radicals by more conservative parties, were constantly accused of undermining Swiss democracy.

When the French- and Italian-speaking communities received their own television programs, news was still produced in one place, with different crews using the same facilities and sharing a single set until 1982. Heidi Abel began announcing programs in 1954 and went on to present many different kinds of programs. She finally found her place as a talk show host covering the most sensitive topics with wit and courage.

Fiction programs, expensive to produce, did not develop for some time. Early production included Swiss plays, mostly comedies, that were adapted for the stage and televised rather than being true television productions. All other types of fiction required coproduction with wealthier neighbors. Some miniseries and series have been developed, including *Die Sechs Kummerbuben, Heidi,* and *Die Direktorin.* The animated children's series *Pingu* achieved worldwide fame.

In the 1990s, family sitcoms based on American examples have become popular in all regions. In the German-speaking region, the popular program is *Fascht e Familie,* while in the French region, the favorite is *La petit Famille.* It is worth noting that some of the local stations have begun to produce experimental fiction. *The Eden Family,* for example, is a "dark" family sitcom, a parody of *The Addams Family* in which the characters live in a gay community.

The Swiss Broadcasting Company (SBC) is still organized as a private nonprofit association, not as a state institution. It is supported with license fees paid every month. Advertising on television was introduced in 1965 and proved to be a most important additional source of income.

The system appears as complex as its political structure and its somewhat fragmented cultural identity. Radio and television stations are commercially or noncommercially organized. Yet the public broadcaster SBC (radio and television) is still by far the biggest distributor of programs, beating other (foreign) stations in ratings. The SBC provides programs for a mainly German-speaking audience (64 percent) as well as the considerably smaller French-speaking (19 percent) and Italian-speaking (8 percent) communities. There is also a tiny Romansh-speaking audience in the east of the country (0.6 percent in 1990) counting on at least one weekly nnewsmagazine being broadcast. There are four SBC television channels and nearly a dozen SBC radio channels all together, all of them distributed terrestrially. Seventy-six percent of all Swiss television and radio households are cabled.

A considerable number of small, local television stations and/or text services were registered by 1995, most of them experimental and with very limited frequency ranges each. This domestic competition has been less influential than that caused by international developments such as the ongoing deregulation process in the European television market. More and more commercial television stations have emerged through-

out Switzerland since the 1980s, changing viewing habits and taking a toll on the ratings. When legislation changed in 1992, allowing private television broadcasters to find (or at least search for) their specific segments in a more open market, those broadcasters were waiting in the wings, thus urging the public broadcaster SRG to develop market-oriented strategies as well.

URSULA GANZ-BLAETTLER

Further Reading

Bonfadelli, Heinz, and Walter Hättenschwiler, "Switzerland: A Multilingual Culture Tries to Keep Its Identity," in *Audience Responses to Media Diversification: Coping with Plenty,* edited by L. Becker and K. Schönbach, Hillsdale, New Jersey: Lawrence Erlbaum Associates, 1989

Meier, Werner A., and Ulrich Saxer, "Switzerland," in *The Media in Western Europe: The Euromedia Handbook,* London and Newbury Park, California: Sage, 1992

Sykes, Eric (1923–)

British Comedy Actor

Eric Sykes, who cultivated his talent for comedy while serving in the army in World War II, worked as a writer on radio and a writer-performer on television through the 1950s before having his greatest success, the long-running British Broadcasting Corporation (BBC) sitcom *Sykes Versus TV,* which debuted in 1960. The services had proved to be fertile ground for aspiring entertainers, and many of Britain's favorite stars of the 1950s had discovered their performing skills while on wartime duty. Following the end of hostilities, these talents found themselves taking their acts on stage before getting the chance to do radio or television. Sykes was one such talent. He wrote comedy scripts as well as performing and eventually scripting one of radio's most popular comedies, *Educating Archie,* which was a prolific breeding ground for comic talent. His many appearances on TV were usually comedy-variety specials, and he developed a format for such one-offs featuring himself as a harassed producer struggling to put on a show and meeting with various obstacles.

But it was in 1960 that Sykes enjoyed his most enduring success, with his *Sykes and a ...* Comedy writer Johnny Speight collaborated with Sykes on the idea of a sitcom based loosely on Sykes existing stage persona.

In the idea, Sykes would live in suburbia with his wife, getting involved in simple plots centering on everyday problems. However, Sykes soon realized that by making his partner his sister rather than his wife, he would have more scope in storylines, with either or both of them able to get romantically entangled with other people. Comedy actor Hattie Jacques, who had worked with Sykes on the radio, was chosen as the sister, and the first series, written by Speight, proved to be a success. The second series, written by Sykes and other writers from storylines suggested by Speight, consolidated that success. Subsequent series were all written by Sykes alone. The TV character Sykes was a proud, rather work-shy individual with somewhat childish habits, as if part of him had not grown up. His sister Hattie was formidable in stature but timid by nature and was easily inveigled into her brother's schemes. It was a departure for a big woman to be portrayed on TV in this way, but it was probably Hattie Jacques's radio career that had allowed her to formulate such characters, as her gentle voice belied her size, allowing her to portray, on radio, small, timorous women.

The format was simple but enduring. Each week a single idea would be taken, and every possible comedic situation of the theme would be exploited. For example, in one episode ("Sykes and a Bath"), Sykes gets his toe stuck in the tap while having a bath, and the entire program revolves around efforts to free him; in another highly memorable segment, Sykes and his sister accidentally get handcuffed together and spend the whole episode trying to do cope with ordinary domestic situations while remaining connected. By concentrating on this technique, Sykes was able to come up with seemingly endless storylines in which to place his characters.

The series was called simply *Sykes and a...*, with that week's theme filling the blank word (e.g., "Sykes and a Telephone" and "Sykes and a Holiday). It became the longest-running sitcom of its time, continuing, with one notable seven-year break between 1965 and 1972, for 127 episodes, until Hattie Jacques's death in 1980. (On its return in 1972, the program was retitled *Sykes*.)

During the run of the sitcom, Sykes also made a series of short, dialogue-free films for the cinema, utilizing the same structure as the TV show: one idea exploited to the limit, comedically. The most famous of these was called *The Plank* (1967) and focused just on the mishaps caused by a man carrying a large plank around—incidentally, one of the *Sykes* episodes also used this concept. Later he remade two of these short films, *The Plank* and *Rhubarb* (1969), for television: *The Plank* (Thames, 1979) and *Rhubarb, Rhubarb* (Thames, 1980). Subsequently, Sykes, now a huge comedy star because of the success of the famous sitcom, appeared in specials and the odd series but never managed to re-create the popularity of *Sykes*. His long-lasting top-flight career is even more remarkable considering that he has been dogged by hearing problems since 1952 and later from sight problems as well. Despite such challenges, he has continued working apace, appearing in the 2001 horror film *The Others* and on the London stage (also in 2001) in Ray Cooney's farce *Caught in the Net*.

DICK FIDDY

Eric Sykes. Born in Oldham, England, May 4, 1923. Served in British Army, World War II. Married: Edith. Began career as performer in military service; radio and television writer, 1950s; star of comedy series, *Sykes and a...*; star of short films based on television character. Recipient: O.B.E., 1986.

Television Series (selected)

1952	*The Howerd Crowd* (writer)	
1958–65	*Sykes and a...*	
1969	*Curry and Chips*	
1972–80	*Sykes*	
1989	*The Nineteenth Hole*	

Television Specials (selected)

1955	*Pantomania* (writer, director, performer)
1955	*Skyes Directs a Dress Rehearsal*
1959	*Gala Opening*
1971	*Sykes and a Big, Big Show*
1978	*Sykes and a Big, Big Show*
1979	*The Plank*
1980	*Rhubarb, Rhubarb*

Films (selected)

Watch Your Stern, 1960; *Invasion Quartet,* 1962; *Kill or Cure,* 1962; *Heaven's Above,* 1963; *One Way Pendulum,* 1965; *Those Magnificent Men in Their Flying Machines,* 1965; *Rotten to the Core,* 1965; *The Liquidator,* 1966; *The Spy with the Cold Nose,* 1966; *The Plank,* 1967; *Shalako,* 1968; *Monte Carlo or Bust,* 1969; *Rhubarb,* 1970; *The Alf Garnett Saga,* 1972; *Theatre of Blood,* 1973; *Splitting Heirs,* 1993; *The Others,* 2001.

Radio (selected)

Educating Archie; Variety Bandbox.

Stage (selected)

Big Bad Mouse; The Nineteenth Hole, 1992; *Caught in the Net,* 2001.

Sylvania Waters

Australian Documentary

Sylvania Waters, a documentary television series that followed the lives of an Australian family, premiered on Australian television in 1992. A 12-part coproduction by the Australian Broadcasting Commission (ABC) and the British Broadcasting Corporation (BBC), the controversial program chronicled the existence of a couple, Noeline Baker and Laurie Donaher, and their largely adult offspring. The series took its name from the wealthy harborside suburb in southern Sydney where Noeline and Laurie reside.

Billed as a "real life" soap opera, *Sylvania Waters* was shot over a six-month period by a camera crew who lived with the Donaher-Bakers. According to an agreement struck with the family, the crew was allowed to film "anywhere, at any time—except when family members were using the bathroom or making love." While ABC publicity for the documentary series emphasized the couple's newfound wealth and luxurious lifestyle, the tightly edited result ruthlessly scrutinized the entrenched interpersonal conflicts that lay beneath the surface of the blended family's easygoing facade.

Like its 1978 British prototype, *The Family,* which brought instant infamy to the Wilkins family of Reading, and the 1973 U.S. program *An American Family,* which chronicled the lives of the Loud family in Santa Barbara, California, *Sylvania Waters* focused a national microscope on the values and behavior of the Donaher-Baker family. Noeline and Laurie's unwed status, Noeline's drinking problem, Laurie's racism, their materialism, and the family's routine domestic disputes all became issues discussed widely in the Australian media.

A particularly passionate public debate erupted over the question of whether executive producer of *Sylvania Waters,* Paul Watson, who also produced *The Family* for the BBC, had chosen an Australian family that pandered to a British stereotype. Writing in the *Sydney Morning Herald,* popular cultural critic Richard Glover summed up these concerns when he wrote that the family was "hardly a surprising British choice: in Noeline and Laurie, every British preconception about the Aussies comes alive.... Meet Australia's new ambassadors: a family whose members are variously materialistic, argumentative, uncultured, heavy drinking, and acquisitive."

The debate intensified when the series screened in Britain and became the subject of widespread commentary in the press there. The tabloid newspaper *The Sun* headlined a story on the series "Meet Noeline: By Tonight You'll Hate Her Too," while *The Guardian* criticized "Noeline's bigotry and gruesome materialism." Critics of *Sylvania Waters* argued that this adverse publicity was proof that the producers of the series had effectively "set up" the Donaher-Baker family to feed British prejudices about Australians.

During the screening of the series, Noeline Baker, Laurie Donaher, and their extended family also became the subject of intense media interest. While a number of family members claimed that the series had caused a family rift, they continued to give numerous press, radio, and television interviews and guest hosted radio and television programs, both in Australia and in the United Kingdom.

On the level of genre, *Sylvania Waters* was also widely understood as representing a new trend dubbed "reality" television. This ambiguous term—generally identified by the use of unembellished documentary-style footage of ordinary people for entertainment purposes—has been used to describe a number of programs that debuted in Australia in the early 1990s, including *Cops,* which showed footage of police arresting suspects, and *Hard Copy,* a current affairs program that made frequent use of amateur video material.

CATHARINE LUMBY

Executive Producers
Paul Watson, Pamela Wilson

Programming History
12 half-hour episodes
ABC
July 1992–October 1992   Tuesday 9:30–10:00

Further Reading

Cunningham, Stuart, *Contemporary Australian Television,* Sydney: University of New South Wales Press, 1994

Syndication

Syndication is the practice of selling rights to the presentation of television programs, especially to more than one customer, such as a television station, a cable channel, or a programming service such as a national broadcasting system. The syndication of television programs is a fundamental financial component of television industries. Long a crucial factor in the economics of the U.S. industry, syndication is now a worldwide activity involving the sales of programming produced in many countries.

A syndicator is a firm that acquires the rights to programs for purposes of marketing them to additional customers. In fact, the syndication marketplace provides the bulk of programming seen by the public. For the internal U.S. market, for example, syndication is the source of the reruns often seen on broadcast television and of much material seen on cable networks. Internationally, large amounts of American television programming are sold through syndication for programming alongside material produced locally. Material not available in syndication includes current network prime-time programs, live news programs, and live coverage of sporting and other special events. Even current U.S. programs, however, may be syndicated in international markets, and U.S. viewers may sometimes see imported programs, usually from England or Latin America, currently programmed in other countries.

The price for a syndicated television series is determined by its success with audiences and the number and type of "run" in which the program appears. A *national run* is the presentation of a film or program one time to a national audience. This notion of national run has been borrowed from the history of distributing theatrical films. Any number of theaters or communities may be included in the first run of a production, but as soon as any location receives a second presentation, the second national run has begun. Generally, the cost of rights to present a television series declines as it is presented in later and later runs, although, as indicated here, that rule does not always hold in the international market.

Repeated sales of television programs, both within the United States and throughout the world, have long been central to the profitability of the U.S. television industry. Soon after U.S. television production shifted from live performance to film in the late 1950s, shrewd sales personnel realized that television products had additional life. Audiences would watch the same program a second time and perhaps return for repeated viewing. Moreover, many countries found it far more economical to purchase the syndicated rights to U.S. television programs than to produce their own, opening a vast market for American products.

The cost of U.S. television programming in the international marketplace is generally based on whatever those markets will bear. Programs often cost more in European markets than in Africa or Latin America. No matter how small the syndication fee, however, the sales of programming produce additional income for their original production companies. In abstract economic terms, this is an example of "public good theory," in which new profits are gained at no additional costs or at the marginal costs incurred in the marketing process.

Historically, syndication, whether domestic or international, served to underwrite the risky process of producing for U.S. network television. From the late 1960s through the mid-1990s, special regulations (the "Financial Interest and Syndication" rules) governed relations between television networks and independent production companies. Under these rules, ownership of the rights to the programs reverted to the producer/production company after a specified number of network runs. Profits from any other sales, including syndication, generally benefited the production community. For this reason, many production companies were willing to produce original programs at a loss, betting on the enormous income that might rise from successful syndication. Many "failed" programs could be created with the profits from one or two successfully syndicated shows.

One way of classifying television programs in the syndication marketplace is by the first national run of the program. If the first run of a program was as part of a national network schedule, then as the program is marketed for subsequent runs to other programmers, it is referred to as "off-network syndication." Thus, a cable programmer who buys the rights to presentation of a situation comedy presented by the National Broadcasting Company (NBC) is buying off-network syndication. *Dallas,* presented in first run on the Columbia Broadcasting System (CBS) in the 1978 season, was (and still is) heavily programmed throughout the world through off-network syndication.

If a program is initially made to be sold to programmers other than the major networks, however, then the program is known as "first-run syndication." An example would be the weekly program *Star Search with Ed McMahon,* produced by Television Program Executives (TPE) and Bob Banner Associates. Similarly, Paramount Television's *Star Trek: The Next Generation* was produced for first-run syndication. On occasion, a television program originally developed for network programming will be shifted into the first-run syndication mode. This is the case with *Baywatch.* A program that failed to attract a sufficient audience when programmed by NBC in 1989, this series was canceled after a single season, but it then went into production as a first-run syndicated product and became enormously successful in international markets.

First-run syndication is often the origin of programs presented as programming "strips," that is, at the same time Monday through Friday. This is the case with *Entertainment Tonight,* another Paramount production, and also with numerous programs in the "tabloid TV," game show, and cartoon genres.

Barter syndication is a financial arrangement that supports a growing segment of the syndication marketplace. In barter syndication, an advertiser purchases in advance all or some part of the advertising opportunities (commercial spots) in a syndicated program, no matter where the production is to be seen in any run. The advertiser benefits from the barter arrangement by ensuring a friendly program environment for ads. The programmer—an independent station or a cable programmer—benefits because advertising slots are presold, ensuring that the cost to acquire the program will be at least partially covered. While this practice may reduce opportunities for the programmer to sell advertising time, the trade-off is considered a favorable one. The producer of the program also benefits because the prior purchase of advertising opportunities provides funds that may represent an important part of the production budget.

Increasingly, syndication is part of the worldwide television marketplace, and the producers are not always part of the U.S. industry. Brazilian, Venezuelan, and Mexican *telenovelas* are programmed throughout the Spanish-speaking world and even in less predictable contexts such as India and Russia. British programming is seen in North America and Australia, throughout Europe, and across the rest of the world. In these cases and many others, syndication is seen as an economic benefit. As in the U.S. context, the profits generated by syndication can be used to produce other material on a speculative basis and to bolster the production of the first-run production process. As television-distribution channels proliferate throughout the world and the demand for product to fill those channels grows, it is likely that more and more producers in more and more contexts will create materials for sale to the syndication market.

JAMES E. FLETCHER

See also **Cable Networks; Financial Interest and Syndication Rules; International Television Program Markets; National Association of Television Programming Executives; Prime-Time Access Rule; Programming; Superstation; Reruns/Repeats; Turner Broadcasting System**

Further Reading

Blumler, Jay G., "Prospects for Creativity in the New Television Marketplace: Evidence from Program Makers," *Journal of Communication* (Autumn 1990)

Covington, William G., Jr., "The Financial Interest and Syndication Rules in Retrospect: History and Analysis," *Communications and the Law* (June 1994)

Fletcher, James E., "The Syndication Marketplace," in *Media Economics: Theory and Practice,* edited by Allison Alexander, James Owers, and Rod Carveth, Hillsdale, New Jersey: Lawrence Erlbaum Associates, 1993

"Glossary of Syndication Terms," *Advertising Age* (April 16, 1990)

Kaplar, Richard T., *The Financial Interest and Syndication Rules: Prime Time for Repeal,* Washington, D.C.: Media Institute, 1990

Lazarus, P.N., "Distribution: A Disorderly Dissertation," in *The Movie Business Book,* edited by J.E. Squires, Englewood Cliffs, New Jersey: Prentice Hall, 1983

"Syndication in the 1990s," *Advertising Age* (April 10, 1995)

"What Is Syndication," *Advertising Age* (May 16, 1994)

Wildman, Steven S., and Stephen E. Siwek, *International Trade in Films and Television Programs,* Cambridge, Massachusetts: Ballinger, 1988.

T

Tabloid Television in the United States

"Tabloid television" is the name often used to describe a group of journalistic program formats that achieved high visibility and great popularity during the mid- to late 1980s and early 1990s. Generally used with a derisive intonation, the label designates a loosely delineated collection of related genres rather than a singular cohesive one. It has typically been taken to include three primary types of popular journalism. The first is so-called "reality TV," which inserts minicams into a variety of ordinary scenarios such as urban law enforcement, and extraordinary ones such as spectacular accidents and rescues. Examples include *COPS, American Detective,* and *Rescue 911.* In "reality TV," however, post-hoc reenactments may substitute for "actual footage," and "actual footage" might itself be carefully orchestrated and edited in a variety of ways to match social expectations regarding the characteristics of cops and criminals, for example, and the conventions of television narrative. Tabloid television's second primary type includes unconventional newscasts and documentary programs such as *A Current Affair, Sightings,* and *Unsolved Mysteries.* Each of these shows simultaneously embodies and violates television's established journalistic conventions.

A Current Affair, for instance, copies the structure of the evening newscast, at times apparently only to parody it by transgressing norms of realistic representation or substituting mockery and laughter for high seriousness and reverentially solemn tones. The third primary type of tabloid television is the issue-oriented talk show, including *Donahue, Oprah* and *The Ricki Lake Show.* Like the other kinds of tabloid TV programs, these differ from "serious journalism" both in form and content. They typically value confrontation over "impartiality" and "objectivity," and include a multiplicity of contesting voices that challenges the traditional central role of the journalistic commentator or anchor. Additionally, they often deal with issues considered too "offensive" or "trivial" for serious journalism (such as marginalized sexual practices or the politics of romance and family life).

In the United States, tabloid television's explosion was abetted by a number of significant changes in broadcasting that occurred during the 1980s. Among the most important of these were the expansion of cable television, a threefold increase in the number of independent broadcasting stations operating in the United States, and the appearance of the FOX Network, owned by tabloid newspaper mogul Rupert Murdoch. One consequence of these industrial changes was an unprecedented level of demand for new programs designed specifically for syndication. Because of their relatively low production costs compared to fictional television, tabloid shows began to look increasingly attractive to producers of syndicated programming. Moreover, a long writers' strike in 1988, by reducing the production of drama on U.S. television, enhanced the value of "reality TV" and was directly responsible for tabloid-style FOX Network shows such as *COPS* and *America's Most Wanted*. These shows, produced with a minimum of narration or dialogue, were considered "writer proof," unaffected by unplanned production interruptions such as strikes.

The forms of tabloid television that emerged and became popular in the 1980s were not merely products of industrial dynamics and economics, though. They were also inevitably linked to the social context of the period, much of which in the United States was defined by Reaganism. As social historian Paul Boyer puts it, "Reaganism was a matter of mood and symbolism as much as of specific [government] programs." Assuming that the media do not "reflect" social history so much as they increasingly become an arena within which it is struggled over and played out, it is possible to find both consonance and dissonance between tabloid television and Reaganism.

Among the significant currents of meaning that Reaganism brought to the surface of American culture during the 1980s were those swirling around collective anxieties over crime, drugs and, ultimately, race. For example, Reaganism helped popularize both a "war on drugs" and a politically successful "victims' rights" movement. The "war on drugs" saturated the electronic media with images of an urban battleground steeped in violent criminality that all too often struck at "innocent victims." Tabloid television played a significant role in both the circulation of images associated with the "drug war" and in the articulation of a populist sense of "victimhood." FOX's *America's Most Wanted*, for example, specialized in cinematically sophisticated reenactments of "actual crimes" followed by an open call for audience members to phone in whatever tips they might be able to provide the police that would help track down missing suspects or escaped fugitives. This premise implies not only a supportive stance towards police departments and crime victims, but also suggests that, in and of themselves, official institutions are incapable of ensuring social order. This was a premise that was extended in local as well as network broadcasting.

Thus, questions about the politics of these programs, which are quite contradictory and therefore difficult to assess, are unavoidable. On the one hand, the popularity of the shows indicates a level of popular distrust toward social institutions from which many people feel alienated. This distrust is often articulated as a class antagonism directed against "the system." Much crime-fighter tabloidism therefore appeals to the populist perception that only the people are capable of looking after their own interests, for "the system" is too often concerned with the narrow interests of the socially privileged. Thus, programs such as *COPS*,

where minicams follow "the men and women of law enforcement" into dangerous situations, aren't interested in the upper echelons of police management and administration, but rather focus on the rank and file. In their emphasis upon the working conditions of "ordinary" cops, such programs resonate powerfully with a working-class awareness that blue-collar folks inevitably labor under treacherous and difficult conditions and are poorly rewarded for it. As well, they appeal to a very real sense of vulnerability produced by a society in which the socially weak are far more likely to be criminally victimized than the powerful and the privileged.

On the other hand, these programs are part of a contemporary form of white racism that substitutes coded words and issues such as "crime" and "drugs" for explicit ways of talking about race. As John Fiske has argued, this facilitates the exertion of racial power while enabling its agents to deny that race is involved at all. So, even though the individual criminals and suspects represented in these programs may often be white (albeit lower-class "white trash"), an emphasis on rampant urban disorder appeals to deeply rooted anxieties in the white imagination regarding people of color presumed to be "out of control" and therefore in need of stepped-up policing. One of the primary responses to these white anxieties in contemporary America has been a massive expansion of urban surveillance systems. Such systems have the two-fold aim of "visibilizing" non-white populations in particular—and therefore making them available for social discipline—and of encouraging people to police themselves with greater circumspection and vigor. There is much justification for the view that reality-based "tabloid TV" is partly an extension of such surveillance practices. The case of Stephen Randall Dye, a fugitive who turned himself over to police after agonizing for two weeks over a story about him on *America's Most Wanted*, provides anecdotal evidence in support of this position (Bartley, 1990).

Tabloidism's partial and populist distrust toward institutions of law and order is extended to the judicial system in the programs *Final Appeal* and *Trial and Error*. Like *America's Most Wanted*, these shows produce reenactments of crimes, but these are supplemented by further reenactments of the trials of the people accused and convicted of those crimes. Rather than supporting these convictions, *Final Appeal* and *Trial and Error* reexamine and question the validity of those criminal verdicts that have resulted in actual incarcerations. The voice-over narration from *Trial and Error's* opening segment encapsulates the logic these programs follow:

"Beyond a reasonable doubt." This is the guardian phrase that empowers juries to protect the innocent in

America.... The most conservative estimates say that we wrongfully convict and imprison between six and seven thousand people every year. Two half-brothers were within sixteen hours of being executed when it was discovered that the prosecution's star witness was actually nowhere near the crime scene, and she'd only seen it in a dream. A couple in Southern California was convicted of a murder that never even occurred. The alleged victim was found alive and well and living in San Francisco years later.... Witnesses sometimes lie, confessions are sometimes coerced, lawyers are sometimes incompetent, and sometimes juries make mistakes.

Final Appeal and *Trial and Error* ultimately question whether our courts ever operate "beyond a reasonable doubt." In doing this, they appeal to a form of popular skepticism that, at particular times and in particular contexts, turns against the judicial system and rejects its discursive power to produce authoritative truths. The first trial of the police officers accused of assaulting Rodney King and the urban uprisings that answered its "not-guilty" verdict (despite the beating having been captured on video) provide the most obvious examples of this sort of popular skepticism erupting explosively, and demonstrate that faith in American criminal justice is largely a consequence of one's position in American society. In turn, programs such as *Final Appeal* and *Trial and Error* demonstrate one of the ways in which tabloid television is capable of tapping into widespread suspicions of officialdom shared by many people who occupy positions of social subordination.

The view that tabloid television circulates beliefs that appeal to a popular skepticism toward official truths receives anecdotal support from California's Attorney General Dan Lungren. Lungren has coined the term "Oprahization" to describe changes in American juries that many prosecutors feel have increased the difficulty of securing criminal convictions. Says Lungren, "people have become so set on the *Oprah* view, they bring that into the jury box with them" (Gregory, 1994). According to a professional jury consultant, "talk-show watchers...are considered more likely" than others "to distrust the official version" of events produced by prosecuting attorneys in courtrooms across the land (Gregory, 1994). Los Angeles District Attorney Gil Garcetti has gone so far as to pronounce that the criminal justice system is "on the verge of a crisis of credibility" due to these changes in the sensibilities of jurors (Gregory, 1994).

Talk shows, then, also appeal to a popular skepticism toward official truths. And like the other tabloid programs, their emergence and success bears no small relationship to Reaganism. In Elayne Rapping's words, "the people on these shows are an emotional vanguard, blowing the lid off the idea that America is anything like the place Ronald Reagan pretended to live in." It's

no coincidence that tabloid talk shows achieved their highest visibility and popularity in the wake of Reagan, for Reaganism's widening of gaps between rich and poor, men and women, and whites and blacks, brought social differences into clear definition and sharpened the conflicts around them (Fiske, 1994). If Reaganism entailed a widespread cultural repression of voices and identities representing social difference, Reaganism's repressed others returned with a vengeance on TV's tabloid talk shows, which invite the participation of people whose voices are often excluded from American commercial media discourse, such as African Americans, Latinos and Latinas, sex-industry workers, "ordinary" women, blue- and "pink-" collar laborers, the homeless, the HIV-positive, people living with AIDS, youths, gay men, lesbians, cross-dressers, transsexuals, convicted criminals, prison inmates, and other socially marginalized groups. This is not to say that tabloid talk shows have a political agenda of anti-racism, anti-sexism, anti-classism, or anti-homophobia, but rather that in opening themselves to the participation of a very broad range of voices, they necessarily encourage potentially progressive conflicts over cultural, racial, and sexual politics. In particular, these shows often emphasize what we might call "the politics of normality." A number of prominent commentators such as Erving Goffman and Michel Foucault have examined the role of norms as instruments of power that facilitate the efficient identification of deviance, which is typically punished or subjected to "treatment" and social discipline. But tabloid talk shows are marked by a level of indiscipline that often disrupts the enforcement of norms and allows people who are disadvantaged by those norms to talk back against them.

The last genre of tabloid television includes unconventional newscasts and documentary programs such as *A Current Affair* and *Sightings*. It is difficult to generalize about these programs, though often they utilize approaches to storytelling that violate the norms of mainstream journalistic practice in a number of ways. One is to disavow the seriousness of conventional journalism. For example, *A Current Affair*, one of the early definers of American television's tabloid style, was originally anchored by Maury Povich, a refugee from "serious" news whose style was playfully irreverent. This gave much offense to conventional journalists such as Philip Weiss, who writes of Povich that "the rubber-faced lewdness his role calls for, the alacrity with which he moves through a half-dozen expressions and voices (from very soft to wired and mean) is a motility reminiscent of the veteran porn star." In his autobiography, Povich writes that his own scorn for the pretensions of the quality press shaped the agenda at *A Current Affair*, which he describes as a "daily fix of silliness, irony, and tub-thumping anger" infused with "an odor of disrespect for authority." He explains that "somehow the notion had come about that news was church business and had to be uttered with ponderous and humorless reverence; instead news was a circus delivered by clowns and dancing bears and should be taken with a lot of serious skepticism."

The significance of *A Current Affair*'s frequent disavowal of the seriousness of more traditional or "respectable" journalistic forms is suggested in Allon White's observation that "seriousness always has more to do with power than with content. The authority to designate what is to be taken seriously (and the authority to enforce reverential solemnity in certain contexts) is a way of creating and maintaining power." Official definitions of "serious journalism," such as those taught in university courses and circulated by the "respectable press," seemed to reinforce an established vision of "that information which the people *need*," often as prescribed by a community of experts whose lives are quite removed from those of ordinary people. Consequently, analysts such as Fiske argue that tabloid television's negotiated refusal of mainstream journalistic seriousness embodies an irreverent, laughing popular skepticism toward official definitions of truth that serve the interests of the socially powerful despite their constant appeals to "objectivity."

Besides mocking the seriousness of mainstream news, some tabloid programs, such as *Sightings* and *Unsolved Mysteries,* confer seriousness upon issues that would likely be treated with laughing dismissal, if at all, in traditional newscasts. Thus, *Sightings* featured stories about house hauntings, werewolves in the British countryside, and psychic detectives, while *Unsolved Mysteries* has delved into the paranormal terrain of UFO sightings and alien abductions. Popular interest and "belief" in such issues persists despite, or perhaps because of, official denials of their "truth" and "seriousness," and this antagonism between popular belief and official truth is part of the more general antagonism between the social interests of ordinary people and those of the powerful. *Sightings* opened each broadcast with a refreshing disclaimer that nicely encapsulates the difference between its attitude toward the process of informing and that which guides more conventional journalistic enterprises: "The following program deals with controversial subjects. The theories expressed are not the only possible interpretation. The viewer is invited to make a judgment based on all available information."

By transgressing certain norms of conventional journalism, tabloid television has drawn the scorn of a great many critics who feel that journalistic TV should address "loftier" issues in more "tasteful" and serious ways. And it has shown that television can be quite adept at speaking to a variety of forms of the popular skepticism with which some of our social institutions, and the versions of truth they pronounce, are viewed.

KEVIN GLYNN

See also **America's Most Wanted; COPS**

Further Reading

Bartley, Diane, "John Walsh: Fighting Back," *Saturday Evening Post* (April 1990)

Bird, S. Elizabeth, *For Inquiring Minds: A Cultural Study of Supermarket Tabloids,* Knoxville: University of Tennessee Press, 1992

Boyer, Paul, "Introduction: Reaganism: Reflections on an Era," in *Reagan as President,* edited by Paul Boyer, Chicago: Ivan R. Dee, 1990

Campbell, Richard, "Word vs. Image: Elitism, Popularity and TV News," *Television Quarterly* (1991)

Dahlgren, Peter, and Colin Sparks, editors, *Journalism and Popular Culture,* London: Sage, 1992

Fiske, John, *Understanding Popular Culture,* Boston: Unwin Hyman, 1989

Fiske, John, "Popularity and the Politics of Information," in *Journalism and Popular Culture,* edited by Peter Dahlgren and Colin Sparks, London: Sage, 1992

Fiske, John, *MediaMatters: Everyday Culture and Political Change,* Minneapolis: University of Minnesota Press, 1994

Fiske, John, and Kevin Glynn, "Trials of the Postmodern," *Cultural Studies* (October 1995)

Glynn, Kevin, "Tabloid Television's Transgressive Aesthetic: *A Current Affair* and the Shows that Taste Forgot," *Wide Angle* (April 1990)

Glynn, Kevin, "Reading Supermarket Tabloids as Menippean Satire," *Communication Studies* (Spring 1993)

Goffman, Erving, *Stigma: Notes on the Management of Spoiled Identity,* Englewood Cliffs, New Jersey: Prentice-Hall, 1963

Gregory, Sophfronia Scott, "Oprah! Oprah in the Court!" *Time* (June 1994)

Katz, Jon, "Covering the Cops: A TV Show Moves in where Journalists Fear to Tread," *Columbia Journalism Review* (February 1993)

Mellencamp, Patricia, *High Anxiety: Catastrophe, Scandal, Age, and Comedy,* Bloomington: Indiana University Press, 1992

Morse, Margaret, "The Television News Personality and Credibility: Reflections on the News in Transition," in *Studies in Entertainment: Critical Approaches to Mass Culture,* edited by Tania Modleski, Bloomington: Indiana University Press, 1986

Pauly, John J. "Rupert Murdoch and the Demonology of Professional Journalism," in *Media, Myths, and Narratives: Television and the Press,* edited by James Carey, Newbury Park, California: Sage, 1988

Povich, Maury, with Ken Gross, *Current Affairs: A Life on the Edge,* New York: Berkeley, 1991

Rapping, Elayne, "Daytime Inquiries," *The Progressive* (October 1991)

Rose, Frank, "Celebrity Victims: Crime Casualties Are Turning into Stars on Tabloid TV," *New York* (July 1989)

Seagal, Debra, "Tales from the Cutting-room Floor," *Harper's* (November 1993)

Weiss, Philip, "Bad Rap for TV Tabs," *Columbia Journalism Review* (May 1989)

Taiwan

The birth of the television era in Taiwan began when the China Broadcasting Corporation (CBC) brought Chiang Kai-shek's third Presidential Inauguration live to 50 television screens in May 1960. This event also marked the beginning of the extensive political influence of the three terrestrial broadcasting systems on all facets of life in the country. Taiwan Television Enterprise (TTV), the first network, was established in 1962 with a significant transfer of Japanese expertise and an initial 40 percent investment by the four leading Japanese electronic firms. China Television Company (CTV) was launched with exclusively domestic financing in 1969, and Chinese Television System (CTS) was transformed from an educational to a general broadcasting service in 1971. More than three decades later, these three networks remain dominated by their stockholders which are, respectively, the Taiwan Provincial Government, the political party Kuomintang, and the Ministries of Defense and Education. Ideological control—exercised by these major underwriters—remains apparent in both news and entertainment programming. In order to claim its political legitimacy over local Taiwanese politics, for example, the KMT government pronounced Mandarin as the official language in Taiwan and restricted the use of Fukienese to only 20 percent of television programming, despite the fact that it was used by the vast majority of the population in the 1960s.

Since the development of a political movement by opposition parties, principally the Democratic Progressive Party (DPP), in the early 1980s, the KMT government has been under pressure to begin relaxation of its media monopoly. Opposition leaders fought for alternative voices with a massive wave of print-media publications, followed by the creation of numerous underground radio broadcasting stations. Government crackdown on these activities proved ineffective when many opposition-party members were voted into the legislature, and the movement was backed by a significant number of intellectuals. In 1995, the Taipei city government, headed by a renowned DPP leader, fought for a 30 percent share of TTV by threatening to block a signal license renewal. Ultimately, the attempt was dropped in exchange for a goodwill promise on the part of TTV to tone down its political partisanship. Furthermore, the legislature passed a regulation in 1996 that raised every terrestrial station's annual license fee from TWD\$60,000 (approximately US\$2,000) to TWD\$10 million (approximately US\$330,000), effective immediately.

These developments signal a passing of a television monarchy controlled by the three networks, which coincides with the emergence of the Fourth Channel, a catch-all name for all underground cable systems and channels. This Fourth Channel surfaced as a powerful media alternative in 1994 with the official launch of TVBS and its landmark call-in program, *2100 All Citizens Talk*. A fourth official national television network is also in development, its license granted to People's Broadcasting Corporation, which consists largely of supporters of the opposition party, DPP. It is scheduled to be on air in February 1997, one year earlier than originally planned.

When the fourth channel begins programming, like the other broadcasters, it will turn to one of three types of sources for content: internal production by the networks, contracted domestic production by independent production companies, and foreign imports. The government ruled that foreign imports should not exceed 30 percent of the total daily programming hours, and all foreign programs are required to use either Mandarin voice-over or Mandarin subtitles. CTS is particularly known for its effort in localizing its entertainment programming; the network wrote television history in 1994 when it first mixed Mandarin with Fukienese in its 8:00 P.M. prime-time drama series, *When Brothers Meet*. Instead of the never-ending Romeo and Juliet-style of love-and-hate romance, this program established a dramatic genre new to Taiwanese television, in which real-life conflicts were recreated in the context of real-life societal events. *When Brothers Meet* not only took the lead in the television prime-time ratings, it also began a continuing success in television drama for CTS.

With the exception of news, all television programs are subject to review by the Government Information Office (GIO). Even in newsrooms, however, self-censorship is practiced. Commercial air time (advertising) is limited to ten minutes per hour on terrestrial systems. Cable systems are limited to six minutes per hour, and coalition efforts are underway for some regional satellite broadcasters to unite in protesting the government's preferential treatment of the free-to-air terrestrials. In other areas, however, cable has its own advantages. Cigarette and liquor commercials are barred from free-to-air stations, yet in 1996 commercials for liquor were allowed on cable after 9:00 P.M.

Such regulations are truly significant in economic terms. While 99.9 percent of the country receives broadcast television and 67 percent of homes own at least two television sets, cable has penetrated 76 percent of the 5.6 million television households, according to Nielsen-SRT's second quarterly Media Index Report, released in July 1996. It is receivable in over 4.4 million homes and, since 1994, the channel share of all cable stations has surpassed the combined share of the three terrestrial systems. As of June 1996, cable homes or cable individuals spent two-thirds of their viewing time with cable. Certainly, the phenomenal cable growth in Taiwan from 18 percent of market penetration in 1991 to 50 percent in 1993 and the 76 percent of 1996 coincides with the economic well-being of the country.

Not surprisingly, the cable industry has been considered a highly lucrative market by both domestic and foreign investors. The Cable Law, however, passed in August 1993, explicitly outlawed foreign shareholding. Cross-media ownership is disallowed between newspaper owners, free-to-air broadcasters, and cable operators and programmers. Further regulations restrict any shareholder to no more than 10 percent of the total assets value.

Other regulations focus more precisely on cable systems. In the area of programming, for example, domestically produced programs must represent at least 20 percent of the total programming hours. Nevertheless, in light of the fact that the Cable Law is designed exclusively to bring the system operators under control, cable programmers have often tested the limit of the law and frequently go their own way. The constant power struggles between system operators and cable-program suppliers have left the GIO powerless most of the time.

In one area, however, the cable industry finally came under restriction in the fall of 1994 after severe protests by U.S. copyright organizations. Cable operators engaged in extreme violations of copyright laws, airing everything from movies to sitcoms and variety shows without payment, which resulted in substantial revenue loss to the program copyright owners. Under threat from the U.S. government, authorities in Taiwan finally began an all-out effort to crack down on the illegal cable operators. The resulting rising costs for program purchases drove some operators out of business and contributed to a significant consolidation of cable systems in recent years.

Financial concerns also affect the terrestrial systems. Despite the fact that all three are financially dominated by the various government offices, they are essentially commercial rather than public stations. In 1995, they garnered 5 percent of the total TWD$29.6 billion (US$985 million) advertising revenues, with TTV slightly edging ahead of CTS by 3 percent and CTV by 6 percent. In the same year, television advertising revenues accounted for approximately 40 percent of total advertising expenditures, topping newspapers by nearly 10 percent. With significant cable growth, 90 percent of the top 300 advertisers replied in a 1995 survey that they were prepared to invest 15–20 percent of their advertising budget in cable.

Essentially, the TV-advertising market has changed from a sellers' market to a buyers' market. The three terrestrial networks are predicted to lose a quarter of net television advertising to other channels in 1997 and, by 2005, less than half the net total is expected go to the terrestrial systems. On the other hand, TV advertising is predicted to nearly double between 1995 and 2000 to US$1.8 billion, and will almost triple to US$2.7 billion in 2005. International advertisers dominate the top-20 list of largest advertisers in Taiwan. Ford leads the category with total annual billings of some TWD$1.592 billion (US$53 million), followed by Procter and Gamble with TWD$1.103 billion (US$37 million), Toyota with TWD$1.005 billion (US$33.5 million), and Mavibel, Kao, Matsushita, Hong Kong Shanghai Bank, AC Johnson, and Nestlé among the biggest spenders.

These advertisers present their products in one of the most complex, multicultural media environments in the world. In a country with a population of more than 22 million, more than 180 satellite channels and 130 cable operators compete for audiences. A typical cable household receives 70 channels, all as part of the basic tier. In the movie category alone, more than 12 channels show movies originating from the United States, Spain, France, Italy, the United Kingdom, Russia, Japan, China, Hong Kong, and other countries.

In the face of this 70-channel environment, all regional satellite channels have made "channel localization" an integral part of their programming effort. They have created specific channel "identities" related to specific Asian countries and regions. Such localization has gone beyond the use of specific languages and has led regional broadcasters to produce "locally correct" cable content by teaming up with the local production entities or houses in the various Asian countries. The Discovery Channel, HBO, ESPN, MTV, and Disney are all prime examples of entities competing against these local cable channels and their localized content. Much of the programming effort by these "global" suppliers was, in fact, launched as an attempt to use the Taiwan market as a testbed for eventual programming in China.

The influx of new local and international cable channels is far from over. For every type of channel already in place, another is in formation. The Scholars' Corporation announced the launch of a five-channel package in May 1996; a very popular local channel, SanLi, was preparing for the release of its third channel; the Videoland Group was getting ready for its fourth channel; and the general-interest Super Channel, which came on the scene in October 1995, added another channel devoted to sports.

The cable attraction has resulted in a large decline of viewership on the three terrestrial networks. Even the 7:00–8:00 P.M. news hour on the networks, dominant for almost three decades, is losing audience share to cable. Individual program ratings among viewers aged four and above have generally declined among all program genres.

On the other hand, almost every regional satellite channel and cable station has steadily gained viewership and momentum. Cable's niche-programming orientation has led to the creation of many channels with clearly definable audience profiles. When analyzed within target audiences, some cable channel ratings even surpass those of the three networks. The current television climate may be summarized as follows: (1) A typical viewer spends an average of 2.2 hours daily watching television. Individuals with cable spend more time watching television than their non-cable counterparts. (2) "Program loyalty" has replaced "channel loyalty" in describing the viewer's logic of television choice. Viewers select specific types of programs and move among channels to do so. (3) Related to this development, a cable channel is often recognized because it carries a few popular programs. It is programs that define the character of any channel, not the channel itself, even for the 24-hour news channel. (4) Prime time on cable is virtually 23 hours a day; the only hour excluded is the 8:00–9:00 P.M. slot for the daily drama series. (5) The new television ecology has gradually given rise to new sales and marketing concepts. Program suppliers can no longer simply emphasize "how many" viewers are watching; instead, it is the determination of "who" is watching that helps deliver the audience to the advertisers, who have been obliged to follow the same trend as program-makers in tailoring their advertisements to ever-more carefully targeted niche audiences.

Behind this multi-channel, multicultural viewing environment is a series of questions baffling the policy-makers. The seemingly vast program choices conceal the reality that programming homogeneity still outweighs its heterogeneity. Not only are schedules for the three terrestrial networks similar across all parts of the day, but the same high level of repetition is also frequently observed within and among the cable channels. The 130 cable operators have spent a great deal of money buying channels only to find that such operations are virtually the opposite of the principle of a "natural monopoly" normally used to describe the cable industry. The government, for its part, is busy making cable laws only to find that participants in the industry have invented new games that defy the regulations. While new channels continue to be rolled out on a monthly basis, new communications technologies such as the Internet are aggressively pursued and applied by many programmers to add to their marketing effort and competitive edge. The television market in Taiwan is far from saturated. It is instead loaded—with selection, repetition, excitement, energy, and challenges.

ZOE TAN

Further Reading

Baum, Julian, "We Intercept This Broadcast: Taiwan Moves to Rein in Cable-TV Operators," *Far Eastern Economic Review* (July 29, 1993)

Baum, Julian, "Untangling the Wires," *Far Eastern Economic Review* (October 27, 1993)

"Boxing Clever," *The Economist* (September 16, 1995)

Nielsen SRG, *Asia Pacific Television Channels,* Shrub Oak, New York: Baskerville Communications, 1996

Nielsen SRG, *Asia Pacific Television Revenues,* Shrub Oak, New York: Baskerville Communications, 1996

"Taiwan's Covert Cablers," *The Economist* (November 20, 1993)

"Tying Up Cable Television: Taiwan," *The Economist* (September 18, 1993)

Talk Shows in the United States

Like the soap opera, the talk show is an invention of 20th-century broadcasting. It takes a very old form of communication—conversation—and transforms it into a low-cost but highly popular form of information and entertainment through the institutions, practices, and technologies of television. The talk show developed out of 40 years of television practice and antecedent talk traditions from radio, vaudeville, and popular theater.

A talk show is quite clearly and self-consciously built around its talk. To remain on the air in commercial television, a talk show must adhere to strict time and money constraints—allowing time, for instance, for the advertising spots that must appear throughout the show. The talk show must begin and end within these rigid time limits and, playing to an audience of millions, be highly tuned to topics that will interest that mass audience. For its business managers, the television talk show is one product among many, and these managers are usually not amenable to anything that will interfere with profits and ratings. Finally, this kind of show is almost always anchored by a host or team of hosts.

Host/Forms

Talk shows are often identified by the host's name in the title, an indication of the importance of the host in the history of the television talk show. A good example of the importance of the host to the form a talk show takes would be *The Tonight Show*. *The Tonight Show* premiered on NBC in 1954 with Steve Allen as its first host. While it maintained a distinctive format and style throughout its first four decades on the air, *The Tonight Show* changed significantly with each successive host. Steve Allen, Ernie Kovacs, Jack Paar, and Johnny Carson each took *The Tonight Show* in a significant new direction, as has its current host, Jay Leno. Each of these hosts imprinted the show with distinctive personalities and management styles.

Although many talk shows run for only weeks or months before being taken off the air, once established, talk shows and talk-show hosts tend to have long runs. The average number of years on television for the 35 major American talk-show hosts listed at the end of this essay was 18 years. Successful talk show hosts such as Mike Wallace, Johnny Carson, and Barbara Walters bridge generations of viewers. The longevity of these "superstars" increases their impact on the forms and formats of television talk with which they are associated.

Television talk shows originally emerged out of two central traditions: news and entertainment. Over time, hybrid forms developed that mixed news, public affairs, and entertainment. These hybrid forms occupy a middle-ground position between news and entertainment, although their hosts (Phil Donahue, Oprah Winfrey, and Geraldo Rivera, for example) often got their training in journalism. Approximately one-third of the major talk-show hosts listed at the end of the essay

came out of news. The other two-thirds came from entertainment (comedy in particular).

Within the journalistic tradition, the names Edward R. Murrow, Mike Wallace, Ted Koppel, and Bill Moyers stand out. News-talk hosts such as Murrow, Koppel, and Moyers do not have bands, sidekicks, or a studio audience. Their roles as talk-show hosts are extensions of their roles as reporters and news commentators. Their shows appear in the evening, when more middle-aged and older-aged viewers are watching. The morning host teams that mix "happy talk" and information also often come from a news background. This format was pioneered by NBC's Sylvester "Pat" Weaver and host Dave Garroway with the *Today* show in the early 1950s. Hosts who started out on early-morning news-talk shows and went on to anchor the evening news or prime-time interview shows include Walter Cronkite, John Chancellor, Barbara Walters, Tom Brokaw, and Jane Pauley. Each developed a distinctive style within the more conversational format of her or his morning show.

Coming from a journalism background but engaging in a wider arena of cultural topics are hosts such as Donahue, Winfrey, and Rivera. Mixing news, entertainment, and public affairs, Donahue established "talk television," an extension of the "hot topic" live radio call-in shows of the 1960s. Donahue himself ran a radio show in Dayton, Ohio, before premiering his daytime television talk show there. Donahue's Dayton show, later syndicated nationally, featured audience members talking about the social issues that affected their lives.

Within the field of entertainment/variety talk, it was the late-night talk show that assumed special importance. Late-night talk picked up steam when it garnered national attention during the talk-show "wars" of the late 1960s and early 1970s. During this time, Carson defended his ratings throne on *The Tonight Show* against challengers Joey Bishop, David Frost, Dick Cavett, and Merv Griffin. Late-night talk-show wars again received front-page headlines when Carson's successors, Leno, David Letterman, Chevy Chase, Arsenio Hall, Dennis Miller, and others engaged in fierce ratings battles after Carson's retirement. Within the United States these talk-show wars assumed epic proportions in the press, and the impact that late-night entertainment talk-show hosts had over their audiences seemed, at times, to assume that of political leaders or leaders of state. In an age in which political theorists had become increasingly pessimistic about the possibilities of democracy within the public sphere, late-night talk-show hosts became sanctioned court jesters who appeared free to mock and question basic American values and political ideas through hu-

Dick Cavett.
Courtesy of the Everett Collection

mor. Throughout the 1960s, 1970s, and 1980s, Carson's monologue on *The Tonight Show* was considered a litmus test of public opinion, a form of commentary on the news. Leno and Letterman's comic commentary continued the tradition.

At times of crisis, the limitation of the court jester's role within commercial television sometimes becomes more evident. This happened when Bill Maher made a joke on ABC's late-night talk show *Politically Incorrect* after the terrorist attacks on the World Trade Center and Pentagon on September 11, 2001. His joke was in the form of a question that asked how much courage it took to bomb radical Islamic guerrilla fighters hiding in caves from a strategic fighter jet thousands of feet in the air. The joke brought down a firestorm of outrage on Maher, including threats from advertisers to cancel their commercials and refusals by local stations to air the show, although there were some who defended the host's right to make the joke, and even an email campaign in his support. After the events of September 11, at least from the point of view of commercial broadcasting, the freedom to make jokes only extended so far, and many comedy writers and talk-show hosts curtailed their jokes about President George W. Bush and his administration during this time.

The ratings battle between Leno and Letterman in the early 1990s echoed the earlier battles between Carson, Cavett, and Griffin. But it is not just comic ability that has been demanded of the late-night hosts. They must possess a lively, quick-paced interview technique, a persistent curiosity arising directly from their comic worldviews, lively conversational skills, and an ability to listen to and elicit information from a wide range of showbusiness and "civilian" guests. It is no wonder that a relatively small number of 1990s hosts survived more than a few years on the air to become stars. Indeed, in all categories of the television talk show over four decades on the air, fewer than three dozen news and entertainment talk show hosts in the United States have achieved the status of stars.

Talk Formats

While talk-show hosts represent a potpourri of styles and approaches, the number of talk-show formats is actually quite limited. For example, a general-interest hard-news or public-affairs show can be built around an expert panel (such as *Washington Week in Review*), a panel and news figure *(Meet the Press)*, a magazine format for a single topic *(Nightline)*, a magazine format that deals with multiple topics *(60 Minutes)*, or a one-on-one host–guest interview (Moyers's *World of Ideas*). These are the standard formats for the discussion of hard-news topics. Similarly, a general-interest soft-news talk show that mixes entertainment, news, and public affairs can also be built around a single topic (such as *Donahue, Oprah,* or *Geraldo*), a magazine multiple-topic format *(Today, Good Morning America)*, or a one-on-one host–guest interview (Barbara Walters's interview specials). There are also special-interest news/information formats that focus on such subjects as economics *(Wall Street Week)*, sports *(Sports Club)*, homemaking/fashion *(Ern Westmore Show)*, personal psychology *(Dr. Ruth)*, home repair *(This Old House)*, literature *(Author Meets the Critic)*, and cooking (Julia Child's programs).

Entertainment talk shows are represented by a similarly limited number of formats. By far the most prevalent is the informal, celebrity-guest/host talk show, which takes on different characteristics depending on when in the day it is broadcast. The late-night entertainment talk show, with the publicity it received through the "talk-show wars," grew rapidly in popularity among viewers during its first four decades on the air. There have also been morning versions of the informal, host–guest entertainment variety show (such as the *Will Rodgers Jr. Show*), daytime versions *(The Robert Q. Lewis Show)*, and special topic versions *(American Bandstand)*. Some entertainment talk

Mike Douglas Show, Mike Douglas, Ralph Nader, 1961–82; 1973 episode. *Courtesy of the Everett Collection*

shows have featured comedy through satirical takes on talk shows *(Fernwood Tonight, The Larry Sanders Show),* monologues *(The Henry Morgan Show),* or comedy dialogue *(Dave and Charley).* Some game shows have been built sufficiently around their talk so that they are arguably talk shows in disguise (Groucho Marx's *You Bet Your Life,* for instance). There are also a whole range of shows that are not conventionally known as "talk shows" but feature "fresh" talk and are built primarily around that talk. These shows center on social encounters or events adapted to television, such as a religious service *(Life Is Worth Living),* an academic seminar *(Seminar),* a talent contest *(Talent Scouts),* a practical joke *(Candid Camera),* mating rituals *(The Dating Game),* a forensic event *(People's Court),* or a mixed social event *(House Party).* The line between "television talk" and what formally constitutes a talk show is often not easy to draw and shifts over time as new forms of television talk emerge.

Cycles of Talk: The History of the Television Talk Show

Although new hosts and talk shows in the United States often appear in rapid succession, usually following expansion cycles in the industry, significant changes in television talk occur more slowly. These changes have traditionally come about at the hands of a relatively small number of influential talk-show hosts and programmers, and have occurred within distinct periods of television history.

The term "talk show" was a relatively late invention, coming into use in the mid-1960s, but shows based on various forms of more-or-less spontaneous talk were a staple of broadcasting from its earliest days. Radio talk shows of one kind or another made

up 24 percent of all radio programming from 1927 to 1956, with general-variety talk, audience-participation, human interest, and panel shows comprising as much as 40 to 60 percent of the daytime schedule. Network television from 1949 to 1973 filled over half its daytime program hours with talk programming, devoting 15 to 20 percent of its evening schedule to talk shows of one kind or another. As the networks went into decline, their viewership dropping from 90 percent to 65 percent of the audience between the 1980s and the 1990s, talk shows were one form of programming that continued to expand on the networks and in syndication. By the summer of 1993, the television page of *USA Today* listed 17 talk shows and local papers as many as 27. In all, from 1948 to 1993, more than 200 talk shows appeared on the air. These shows can be broken down into four cycles of television talk-show history, which correspond to four major periods of television history itself.

The first cycle took place from 1948 to 1962 and featured such hosts as Godfrey, Garroway, Murrow, Arlene Francis, and Paar. These hosts had extensive radio experience before coming to television, and they were the founders of television talk. During this time, the talk show's basic forms—coming largely out of previous radio and stage traditions—took shape.

The second cycle covers the period from 1962 to 1972, when the networks took over from sponsors and advertising agencies as the dominant forces in talk programming. A small but vigorous syndicated talk industry grew during this period as well. In the 1960s and early 1970s, three figures established themselves on the U.S. networks as talk hosts with staying power: Carson, Walters, and Wallace. Each was associated with a program that became an established profit center for its network, and each used that position to negotiate a sustained status with the network that propelled her or him into the 1970s and 1980s as a star of television talk.

The third cycle of television talk lasted from 1970 to 1980. During this decade, challenges to network domination arose from a number of quarters. While the networks themselves were initiating few new talk shows by 1969, syndicated talk programming exploded. Twenty new talk shows went on the air in 1969 (until then, the average number of new shows rarely exceeded five per year). It was a boom period for television talk—and the time of the first nationally publicized "talk-show wars." New technologies of production (cheaper television studios and production costs), new methods of distribution (satellite transmission and cable), and key regulatory decisions by the U.S. Federal Communications Commission (FCC) made nationally syndicated talk increasingly profitable and attractive to investors.

Live with Regis and Kathie Lee, Kathie Lee Gifford, Regis Philbin. *Courtesy of the Everett Collection*

Talk show hosts such as Donahue took advantage of the situation. Expanding his program from 40 markets in 1974 to a national audience of 167 markets in 1979, Donahue became the number one syndicated talk-show host in the United States by the late 1970s. Other new talk-show hosts entered the field as well. *Bill Moyers' Journal* went on the Public Broadcasting Service (PBS) in 1970, and William Buckley's *Firing Line,* which had appeared previously in syndication, launched on PBS a year later. Both Moyers and Buckley—representing liberal and conservative viewpoints, respectively—were to remain significant figures on public broadcasting for the next two decades. During this time, independent stations and station groups, first-run syndication, cable, and VCRs all began to weaken the networks' once invincible hold over national audiences.

The fourth cycle of television talk took place in the period from 1980 to 1992, a period that has been commonly referred to as the "post-network" era. Donahue's success in syndication was emulated by others, most notably Winfrey, whose Donahue-style audience-participation show went into national syndication in 1986. Winfrey set a new record for syndication earnings, grossing over $100 million per year from the start of her show's syndication. She became, financially, the most successful talk show host on television.

But since the early 1980s the networks had been vigorously fighting back. CBS's *Late Night with David Letterman* and Koppel's *Nightline* on ABC were two network attempts to win back audiences. Both shows gained steady ratings over time and established Koppel and Letterman as stars of television talk.

A fifth cycle of talk was represented by the rise of a series of new talk-show hosts who gained large followings. By the mid-1990s, "trash talk" had become increasingly popular, and Ricki Lake, one of the first

The Ricki Lake Show, Ricki Lake. *Courtesy of the Everett Collection*

syndicated talk-show hosts to capitalize on this form, had been outdistanced by Jerry Springer, who took this carnivalesque form of TV talk, supported by a clever multimedia merchandising strategy, to new levels of grotesquerie. Also in the 1990s, Rosie O'Donnell reestablished the warm, "family" tradition of the daytime talk show pioneered by the comfortable daytime syndicated talk-show hosts of the 1970s (Dinah Shore, Griffin, and Mike Douglas). Garry Shandling took the self-reflexive traditions of TV talk developed by Letterman to a new level in *The Larry Sanders Show,* mixing fictional and improvisational forms of TV talk. And Maher took his successful Comedy Central fusion of news talk and comedy, *Politically Incorrect,* to a regular berth on ABC after Koppel's *Nightline.* The audiences were treated to other mixtures and experiments: shows such as *The Man Show,* which satirized male gender roles (or celebrated them, depending on your point of view), or *The View,* featuring veteran talk star Walters but representing a successful experiment of five women hosting a show collectively. The 1990s, as the above examples indicate, were a time in which new forms, blends, mixtures, and experiments made an appearance among the tried-and-true formulas of television talk.

Paradigm Shifts in Late-Night Entertainment: Carson to Letterman

Johnny Carson, for 30 years the "King of Late Night," and his successor, David Letterman, are in many ways alike. Their rise to fame could be described by the same basic story. A young man from the American heartland comes to the city, making his way through its absurdities and frustrations with feckless humor. This exemplary middle American is "square" and at the same time sophisticated; innocent, though also ironic and irreverent. Straddling the worlds of common sense and showbusiness, the young man becomes a national jester—and is so anointed by the press.

The "type" Carson and Letterman represent can be traced to earlier archetypes: the "Yankee" character in early American theater and the "Toby" character of 19th-century tent repertory. Carson brought his version of this character to television at the end of the Eisenhower and beginning of the Kennedy era, poking fun at American consumerism and politics in the late 1950s and 1960s.

Letterman brought his own version of this sharp-eyed American character to the television screen two decades later, at the beginning of the Reagan era. By this time the youth revolts of the 1960s and 1970s were already on the wane, and Letterman replaced the politics of confrontation represented by the satire of such shows as *Saturday Night Live* and *SCTV* with a politics of accommodation, removal, and irony. His ironic stance was increasingly acknowledged as capturing the "voice" of his generation and, whether as cause or effect, Letterman became a generational symbol.

The shift from Carson to Letterman represented not only a cultural change but a new way of looking at television as a medium. Carson's camera was rooted in the neutral gaze of the proscenium-arch tradition; Letterman's camera, by contrast, roamed wildly and flamboyantly through the studio. Carson acknowledged the camera with sly asides; Letterman's constant, neurotic intimacy with the camera, characterized by his habit of moving right up to the lens and speaking directly into it, represented a new level of self-consciousness about the medium. He extended the "self-referentiality" that Carson himself had promoted over the years on his talk show. Indeed, Letterman represented a movement from what has been called a *transparent* form of television—the viewer taking for granted, and looking through, the forms of television (camera, lighting, switching, and so on)—to an *opaque* form, in which the technology and practices of the medium itself become a focus of the show. Letterman changed late-night talk forever with his postmodern irreverence and mocking play with the forms of television talk.

Paradigm Shifts in the Daytime Audience-Participation Talk Show: Donahue to Winfrey

When Oprah Winfrey rose to national syndication success in 1986 by challenging Phil Donahue in major markets across the United States and winning ratings victories in many of these markets, she did not change the format of the audience-participation talk show. That remained essentially as Donahue had established it 20 years before. What changed was the cultural dynamics of this kind of show, and that shift was in turn a direct reflection of the person who hosted it.

The ratings battle that ensued in 1986 was between, on the one hand, a black woman raised by a religious grandmother and strict father within the fold of a black church in the South, and on the one, and a white, male, liberal, Catholic Midwesterner who had gone to the University of Notre Dame and been permanently influenced by the women's movement. Just as Jackie Robinson had broken professional baseball's color barrier four decades earlier, Winfrey broke the color line for national television talk show hosts in 1986. Like the hero of a children's story by Horatio Alger, she became one of the great rags-to-riches successes of the 1980s (by the early 1990s, *People Weekly* was proclaiming her "the richest woman in show business," with an estimated worth of $200 million), and as Arsenio Hall and Bob Costas ended their six- and seven-year runs on talk television in the early 1990s, it became clear that Oprah Winfrey had staying power. She remained one of the few prominent talk show hosts of the 1980s to survive within the cluttered talk-show landscape of the mid-1990s, and now into the 21st century.

Several factors contributed to this success. For one thing, Winfrey had a smart management team and a full-press, national marketing campaign to catapult her into competition with Donahue. The national syndication deal had been worked out by Winfrey's representative, attorney-manager Jeffrey Jacobs, and thanks to management at her show's distributor, King World, her marketing plan was a classic one. Executives at King World believed the media would pounce on "a war with Donahue," so they created one. The first step was to send tapes of Winfrey's shows to "focus groups" in several localities to see how they responded. The results were positive. The next step was to show tapes to selected station groups—small network alliances of a half-dozen or more stations under a single owner. These groups would be offered exclusive broadcast rights. As the reactions began to come in, King World adjusted its tactics. Rather than making blanket offers, they decided to open separate negotiations in each city and market. The gamble paid off. Winfrey's track record proved her a hot-enough commodity to win better deals through individual station negotiation.

To launch Winfrey on the air, King World kicked off a major advertising campaign. Media publications trumpeted *The Oprah Winfrey Show*'s ratings victories over *Donahue* in Baltimore and Chicago. The "*Donahue*-buster" strategy was tempered by Winfrey herself, who worked hard not to appear too arrogant or conceited. When asked about head-on competition with Donahue, she replied that in a majority of markets she did not compete with him directly, and that while Donahue would certainly remain "the king," she just wanted to be "a part of the monarchy." By the time *The Oprah Winfrey Show* went national in September 1986, it had been picked up by more than 180 stations—approaching *Donahue*'s 200-plus.

In addition to refined marketing and advertising techniques, cultural issues also featured prominently in Winfrey's campaign. Winfrey's role as talk-show host was inseparable from her identity as an African-American woman. Her African-American heritage and roots surfaced frequently in press accounts. One critic described her in a 1986 *Spy* magazine article as "capaciously built, black, and extremely noisy." These and other comments on her "black" style were not lost on Winfrey. She confronted the issue of race constantly and was very conscious of her image as an African-American role model.

When a *USA Today* reporter queried Winfrey bluntly about the issue of race in August 1986, asking her, "as someone who is not pencil-thin, white, nor blond," how she was "transcending barriers that have hindered many in television," Winfrey replied as follows:

> I've been able to do it because my race and gender have never been an issue for me. I've been blessed in knowing who I am, and I am a part of a great legacy. I've crossed over on the backs of Sojourner Truth, and Harriet Tubman, and Fannie Lou Hamer, and Madam C.J. Walker. Because of them I can now soar. Because of them I can now live the dream.

Winfrey's remarks represent the "double-voiced" identity of many successful African-American public figures. Such figures, according to Henry Louis Gates, demonstrate their "own membership in the human community and then…resistance to that community." In the mid-1980s, then, the image of Winfrey as national talk-show host played against both white and black systems of values and aesthetics. It was her vitality as a double sign, not simply her role as an Horatio Alger figure, that made her compelling to a national audience in the United States.

In the late 1990s and into the new century, a number of new talk-show hosts emerged. Two hosts who began their careers on the cable channel Comedy Central, Bill Maher and Jon Stewart, gained increasing national visibility around this time. As noted previously, Maher moved his *Politically Incorrect* show to a late-night time slot on ABC. As host of *The Daily Show* on Comedy Central, Stewart has received many accolades, including a "talk show host of the year" award from *Time* magazine and a Peabody Award for his comedy news coverage of the 2000 elections. In daytime talk, Rosie O'Donnell's entry into the increasingly crowded daytime talk market employed a national syndication marketing campaign that was reminiscent of Winfrey's, and probably learned from it. O'Donnell created a strong following immediately after appearance on the air in 1996 and maintained it through the 1990s. In 2002 news that O'Donnell was gay, and openly so, did not seem to damage her show or her relationship with her national audience, but O'Donnell nevertheless chose to make that year her last on as a talk-show host. In news talk, Katie Couric, who had been co-anchor of the *Today* show since the early 1990s, signed a multiyear, multimillion-dollar contract in 2002 that put her in the superstar category. Couric's life off-camera (the death of her husband, her single-mother status, and her high-profile relationship with producer Tom Werner) helped stimulate interest in her career from fans and network executives. The personal lives of female hosts—Winfrey, O'Donnell, and Couric, for example—all seemed to receive more attention than those of their male peers.

Conclusion

Talk shows have become increasingly important on U.S. television and their hosts increasingly influential. They speak to cultural ideas and ideals as forcefully as politicians or educators. National talk-show hosts become surrogates for the citizen. Interrogators on the news or clown princes and jesters on entertainment talk shows, major television hosts have a license to question and mock—as long as they play within the rules. An investigation of the American television talk show must, finally, delineate and examine those rules.

The first governing principle of the television talk show is that everything that occurs on the show is framed by the host, who characteristically has a high degree of control over both the show and the production team. From a production point of view, the host is the managing editor; from a marketing point of view, the host is the label that sells the product; from a power and organizational point of view, the host's star value is the fulcrum of power in contract negotiations with advertisers, network executives, and syndicators. Without a "brand-name" host, a show may continue, but it will not be the same.

A second principle of the television talk show is that it is experienced in the present tense. This is true whether the show is live or taped in front of a studio audience and shown as if live a few hours later. Live, taped, or shown in "reruns," talk shows are conducted, and viewers participate in them, as if host, guest, and viewer occupy the same moment.

As social texts, television talk shows are highly sensitive to the topics of their social and cultural moment. These topics may concern passing fashions or connect to deeper preoccupations. References to the O.J. Simpson trial on television talk shows in the mid-1990s, for example, reflected a preoccupation in the United States with domestic violence and issues of gender, race, and class. Talk shows are, in this sense, social histories of their times.

While it is host-centered, occurring in a real or imagined present tense, sensitive to the historical moment, and based on a form of public/private intimacy, the television talk show is also a commodity. Talk shows traditionally have been cheap to produce. In 1992 a talk show cost less than $100,000 (compared to up to $1 million or more for a prime-time drama of the same length). By the early 1990s developments in video technology made talk shows even more economical to produce and touched off a wave of new talk shows on the air. Still, the rule of the marketplace prevailed. A joke on Carson's final episode of *The Tonight Show* that contained 75 words and ran 30 seconds was worth approximately $150,000—the cost to advertisers of a 30-second "spot" on that show. Each word of the joke cost approximately $2,000. Although the rates of Carson's last show were particularly high, commercial time on television is always expensive, and an industry of network and station "reps," time buyers and sellers work constantly to negotiate and manage the cost of talk commodities on the television market. If a talk show makes money over time, its contract will likely be renewed. If it does not, no matter how valuable or critically acclaimed it may be, it will be pulled from the air. A commodity so valuable must be carefully managed and planned. It must fit the commercial imperatives and time limits of for-profit television. Although it can be entertaining, even "outrageous," it must never seriously alienate advertisers or viewers.

As we can see from the examples above, talk shows are shaped by many hands and guided by a clear set of principles. These rules are so well known that hosts, guests, and viewers rarely stop to think about them. What appears to be one of television's most unfettered and spontaneous forms turns out to be, on closer inves-

tigation, one of its most complex and, occasionally, artful creations.

BERNARD M. TIMBERG

See also **Allen, Steve;** *Arsenio Hall Show, The;* **Carson, Johnny; Couric, Katie; Donahue, Phil; Emerson, Faye;** *Ernie Kovacs Show, The (Various);* **Frost, David; Griffin, Merv; King, Larry; Kovacs, Ernie;** *Late Show with David Letterman (Late Night with David Letterman);* **Letterman, David; Murrow, Edward R.;** *Parkinson;* **Pauley, Jane; Philbin, Regis; Rivera, Geraldo; Shore, Dinah; Susskind, David; Wallace, Mike; Walters, Barbara; Winfrey, Oprah**

Major U.S. Talk Show Hosts, 1948–2002

Faye Emerson (1949–60), Arthur Godfrey (1948–61), Arlene Francis (1949–75), Dave Garroway (1949–61, 1969), Garry Moore (1951–77), Art Linkletter (1950–70), Steve Allen (1950–84), Ernie Kovacs (1951–61), Mike Wallace (1951–), Merv Griffin (1951–86), Edward R. Murrow (1952–59), Dinah Shore (1951–63, 1970–84, 1987–91), Jack Paar (1952–65, 1975), Mike Douglas (1953–82), Johnny Carson (1951–92), David Susskind (1958–87), Barbara Walters (1961–), Regis Philbin (1963–), David Frost (1964–65, 1969–73, 1977–), William Buckley (1966–), Dick Cavett (1968–72, 1975, 1977–82, 1986, 1992–), Joan Rivers (1969, 1983–), Phil Donahue (1969–96, 2002), Bill Moyers (1971–), Tom Snyder (1973–82, 1994–), Geraldo Rivera (1974–), Jane Pauley (1976–), Jay Leno (1977, 1987–),Ted Koppel (1979–), David Letterman (1980–), John Mclaughlin (1982–), Arsenio Hall (1983–), Larry King (1983–), Oprah Winfrey (1986–), Sally Jesse Raphaël (1986–), Katie Couric (1990–), Jerry Springer (1991–), Jon Stewart (1991–), Rosie O'Donnell (1996–2002), Bill Maher (1998–2002).

COMPILED BY ROBERT ERLER AND BERNARD TIMBERG

Further Reading

Carter, Bill, *The Late Shift: Letterman, Leno, and the Network Battle for the Night,* New York: Hyperion, 1994

Corliss, Richard, "The Talk of Our Town," *Film Comment* (January–February 1981)

Donahue, Phil, *Donahue: My Own Story,* New York: Simon and Schuster, 1979

Downs, Hugh, *On Camera: My 10,000 Hours on Television,* New York: Putnam, 1986

Heaton, Jeanne Albronda, and Nona Leigh, *Tuning in Trouble: Talk TV's Destructive Impact on Mental Health,* San Francisco: Josey-Bass, 1995

Himmelstein, Hal, *Television Myth and the American Mind,* New York: Praeger, 1995

Hirsch, Alan, *Talking Heads: Political Talk Shows and Their*

Star Pundits, New York: St. Martin's Press, 1991

Latham, Caroline, *The David Letterman Story: An Unauthorized Biography,* New York: Franklin Watts, 1987

Livingstone, Sonia, and Peter Lunt, *Talk on Television: Audience Participation and Public Debate,* London: Routledge, 1994

Munson, Wayne, *All Talk: The Talkshow in Media Culture,* Philadelphia, Pennsylvania: Temple University Press, 1993

Priest, Patricia Joyner, *Public Intimacies: Talk Show Partici-*

pants and Tell-All TV, Creskill, New Jersey: Hampton, 1995

Timberg, Bernard, "The Unspoken Rules of Television Talk," in *Television: The Critical View,* edited by Horace Newcomb, New York: Oxford University Press, 1976; 6th edition, 2000

Timberg, Bernard, and Robert Erler, *Television Talk: A History of the Talk Show,* Austin: University of Texas Press, 2002

Tynan, Kenneth, *Show People,* New York: Simon and Schuster, 1979

Talking Heads

U.K. Series

Talking Heads was a series of six critically acclaimed dramatic monologues penned for television by the renowned writer Alan Bennett. Eschewing visual dynamism in favor of strong writing and intimate solo performances, the series featured different characters relating, direct to camera, compelling tales of mundane personal drama and private unhappiness. First transmitted in Britain in 1988, it was followed up ten years later by another series of six programs under the banner *Talking Heads 2.*

Known for his stage plays (such as *Forty Years On,* 1968) and feature films (such as *The Madness of King George,* 1995), as well as his writing for television, Bennett wrote the first series after experimenting with the format in the 1982 television and radio play *A Woman of No Importance.* In interview with Albert Hunt, Bennett claimed that the simple format and economy of production of *A Woman of No Importance* was partly inspired by his own original desire to direct, something he had never done before on stage or television. Yet Bennett may have recognized the dramatic possibilities of the form while delivering satirical monologues on stage as part of *Beyond the Fringe* at the Edinburgh Festival in 1960. In the event, Bennett did *not* direct *A Woman of No Importance,* but he was able to go on and direct one of the dramas in the first series of *Talking Heads,* "Bed Among the Lentils," and act in another, "A Chip in the Sugar."

Crucially, the monologue format, with an almost static camera, pared-down visuals, and direct address, allowed Bennett to demonstrate his finely tuned sense of observation which explored the warm humor of the everyday, while also drawing on some of the darker themes of his larger oeuvre. The themes of *Talking Heads* are distinctly adult, not in the sense that there

are explicit sexual references or bad language, but because they are predominantly about, and performed by, people in middle age or older, particularly women.

With scripts written with particular performers in mind (recurring names being Patricia Routledge, Julie Walters, and Thora Hird) colloquialisms or turns of phrase powerfully evoke a specific class, region, or generation. Bennett's scripts depict ordinary people trapped by frustration or loneliness, people marginalized, often by the most mundane circumstances, and out of touch with mainstream cosmopolitan and popular culture. Most of the stories, running between 30 and 50 minutes, are set in a drab suburban or provincial milieu—often signified by dull domestic settings such as living rooms or kitchens.

Yet what is also significant about Bennett's *Talking Heads* scripts is what is often *not* said, or only vaguely hinted at—with implicit references to mental illness, repressed homosexuality, or sexual abuse. As each drama unfolds over a series of sequences—with the told events predominantly taking a downward trajectory—the viewer gains more insight into the character and what motivates them, sometimes with surprising consequences. In "A Woman of Letters," for example, Patricia Routledge plays Miss Ruddock, a lonely woman who obsessively writes letters of complaint. At first appearing to be a public-spirited busybody, it soon becomes apparent that she has caused upset with accusations of child abuse and neglect, and has been before the courts on charges of harassment. The program concludes with Miss Ruddock in jail, yet a more fulfilled and less lonely woman.

Significantly, the program format not only emphasizes the strength of writing, but also of theatrical performance, and this has two closely related dramatic effects. First, the mid- to close-up shots of actors speaking directly to camera demands carefully nuanced and intimate performances, with actors unable to hide in the long shot, or among other characters. Furthermore, long takes (some lasting as long as eleven minutes) add an extra layer of tension to the performance. Second, as Albert Hunt argues, the direct address to camera establishes a theatrical relationship between actor and audience, unlike the action between characters viewed by an audience separated by a fourth wall.

This direct address, alienating and adding to the "staginess" of the drama on the one hand, fuses profoundly with the subject matter, on the other, as the narration of what Hunt describes as "gossip" treats the viewer as a confidante or friend. This has much in common with what the psychologists Donald Horton and R. Richard Wohl describe as a "para-social interaction," where direct address to camera emulates the basic form of human face-to-face interaction, establishing a form of "intimacy at a distance." As such, the viewer comes to sympathize with the character's experience or dilemma, and perhaps even feel complicit in and accepting of the action being related. Yet "para-social interaction" is a one-way process where the viewer is free from reciprocal obligations and therefore does not have to befriend the character or do anything to alleviate their situation. Reading between the lines, picking up on what is not said, the viewer can even take a patronizing, omnipotent position—seeing or knowing more than the main character themselves.

This raises the question of whether *Talking Heads* is an enhancing or pessimistic view of the human condition. On the one hand, John Pym has argued that *Talking Heads* is characterized by "unrelieved melancholy," and that most of the characters in the first series are self-deluders. Indeed, it could be argued that this is never more cruelly demonstrated than by Julie Walter's character in "Her Big Chance," a relentlessly dimwitted actress trying to take herself seriously in a cheap, schlock video. These stories might therefore depict persons felled by hubris, or suggest that people are necessarily blind to what they cannot see, that no-one can live outside of their own context or "think outside the box."

On the other hand, Bennett's accounts are often described as warm, wry, or affectionate, and Albert Hunt suggests that the behavior of the alcoholic protagonist in "Bed Among the Lentils" provides a "blueprint for survival." So too it could be argued that all the characters in these tales are trying to make do in a difficult world, and that survival is, ultimately, honorable. In any event, Bennett's rich and multi-layered scripts,

and his actors' compelling performances, provide nothing less than mature, sophisticated and often moving drama.

ROB TURNOCK

See also **Bennett, Alan**

Cast

Graham ("A Chip in the Sugar," series one)	Alan Bennett
Miss Ruddock ("A Lady of Letters," series one)	Patricia Routledge
Susan ("Bed Among the Lentils," series one)	Maggie Smith
Muriel ("Soldiering On," series one)	Stephanie Cole
Leslie ("Her Big Chance," series one)	Julie Walters
Doris ("A Cream Cracker Under the Settee," series one)	Thora Hird
Miss Fozzard ("Miss Fozzard Finds Her Feet," series two)	Patricia Routledge
Celia ("The Hand of God," series two)	Eileen Atkins
Wilfred ("Playing Sandwiches," series two)	David Haig
Marjory ("The Outside Dog," series two)	Julie Walters
Rosemary ("Nights in the Gardens of Spain," series two)	Penelope Wilton
Violet ("Waiting for the Telegram," series two)	Thora Hird

Producers

Innes Lloyd (series one), Mark Shivas (series two)

Programming History

12 Episodes
BBC 2

April–May 1988	Sunday 9:30–10:00/10:20
October–November 1998	Tuesday 9:50–10:20/10:30

Further Reading

Horton, Donald, and R. Richard Wohl, "Mass Communication and Para-Social Interaction: Observation on Intimacy at a Distance," in *Psychiatry* 19/3 (1956)

Hunt, Albert, *Talking Heads: 'Bed Among the Lentils'*," in *British Television Drama in the 1980s*, edited by George. W. Brandt, Cambridge: Cambridge University Press, 1993

Pym, John, "Older Women: *Talking Heads*," in *Sight and Sound* 57/3 (1988)

Tarses, Jay (1939–)

U.S. Writer, Producer

Jay Tarses, a self-proclaimed outsider from the mainstream Hollywood television industry, achieved a reputation in the 1970s and 1980s as a "maverick" writer and producer. Tarses has been critically praised for introducing a bold new form of half-hour comedy series, often called character comedy or "dramedy," which achieved a radical stylistic break from the traditional sitcom formula. Tarses has had an ambivalent relationship with the three major U.S. networks (ABC, CBS, and NBC), which have often criticized, and frequently canceled, his shows for being too dark, inaccessible, and not "funny" enough for traditional sitcom audience expectations.

Beginning as a writer and actor with a Pittsburgh, Pennsylvania, theater company, Tarses reportedly worked as a New York City truck driver for the *Candid Camera* series before beginning a career in advertising. In the late 1960s he teamed with Tom Patchett as a stand-up comedy duo performing dry, semi-satirical material on the coffeehouse circuit. The Patchett-Tarses team turned to television writing, gaining credits on musical variety shows and assorted sitcoms prior to working on the writing staff of *The Carol Burnett Show,* for which they won an Emmy in 1972. The two went on to become collaborative executive producers for MTM Enterprises, where they achieved their first major impact on television history, as writers and producers for the original *Bob Newhart Show* (CBS, 1972–78), in which Newhart played an introverted psychologist surrounded by a circle of interesting and quirkily eccentric characters.

Building upon their success with *The Bob Newhart Show,* Tarses and Patchett developed *The Tony Randall Show* (ABC/CBS, 1976–78), another MTM series, starring Randall as a widowed Philadelphia judge surrounded by his children, housekeeper, secretary, friends, and legal associates. Apparently, this sitcom was the site of great tension between the producers and the networks over the nature and style of the type of innovative "character comedy" that Tarses and Patchett were trying to introduce. During this period, they also produced several other short-lived and often-controversial series, including *We've Got Each Other* (CBS, 1977–78), a domestic sitcom about the personal and professional lives of a professional couple, their colleagues, and neighbors, and *Mary* (CBS, 1978), a comedy/variety hour attempting to revive the televisual charisma of Mary Tyler Moore. However, *Mary* was a ratings disaster of such magnitude that it was canceled after three episodes, and its embarrassing failure "drummed us out of the TV business for a while," according to Tarses. During a hiatus from television following this experience, the Patchett-Tarses team turned to writing screenplays, including two Muppet movies. The writing/producing team returned to television with the poorly received *Open All Night* (ABC, 1981–82), a sitcom about a convenience store with an ensemble of eccentric customers, and the notable *Buffalo Bill* (NBC, 1983–84), about an unlikable, egomaniacal talk show host, Bill Bittinger (played by Dabney Coleman), and his ensemble of television station coworkers.

During this period, Tarses split from Patchett and developed *The Faculty* (ABC, 1985). Canceled after one episode, this program about embattled high-school teachers was characterized by its black humor and mock documentary interviews. The ABC network reportedly asked Tarses to reshoot the pilot because they felt it was too dark and they wanted more emphasis on the students rather than the faculty; when he refused, the series was dropped.

Tarses achieved a critical comeback as producer and occasional writer and director of the controversial "dramedy" *The Days and Nights of Molly Dodd* (NBC/Lifetime, 1987–91). Originally produced for NBC, this series starred Blair Brown as a divorced woman living alone on New York City's Upper West Side, surrounded by an ensemble of quirky and likable characters representing her family, friends, and lovers. After it was canceled by NBC, the series was picked up by the Lifetime cable network, which continued production of the series, reshaped to be aimed strategically at a female audience of a certain age, class, and income level. The same year that *Molly Dodd* debuted, Tarses also introduced *The "Slap" Maxwell Story* (ABC, 1987–88), another critically acclaimed "dramedy" about the professional and personal tribulations of an arrogant, provocative sportswriter, played by Dabney Coleman. In the 1990s, Tarses was far less active as a television producer; his most notable production in this

Tarses, Jay

decade was *Public Morals,* which he cocreated with Steven Bochco. On CBS's schedule for the fall of 1996, this ensemble cop sitcom became the target of a protest campaign by the American Family Association and other conservative watchdogs because its dialogue was peppered with profanity and sexual references. Twelve episodes of the series were shot, but only one made it to air before CBS canceled the program.

In addition to writing and producing, Tarses has occasionally played cameo roles in his series (for example, as a neighborhood cop in *Open All Night* and a garbage collector in *Molly Dodd*) as well as playing a writer for a cartoon studio in a 1984 MTM sitcom, *The Duck Factory,* and appearing in episodes of a number of other programs and in one film (*Teen Wolf,* 1985).

The dramatic/character comedies written and produced by Tarses have operated in what has been considered "uncharted territory" in the U.S. television industry. In terms of production style, they have generally not been shot as traditional sitcoms (four cameras, on videotape, in a studio before a live audience, with an added laugh track). Tarses has generally worked independently of the studio system, shooting in a cinematic style in warehouses or on location, and using a single 35mm film camera. He has characterized his work as low budget, preferring to put his money into writing and actors rather than sets. Tarses's characters are distinguished as not always sympathetic or charismatic (an example is Bill Bittinger on *Buffalo Bill*). His dialogue is markedly low key and "quirky," with a humor best described as biting and often darkly satirical, sometimes surreal, and written in a subtle comedic rhythm that eschews punch lines. Unlike traditional episodic sitcoms, which attempt to solve problems in one episode, the narrative elements of Tarses's dramedies are serial, continuing from episode to episode.

Perhaps Tarses's two greatest contributions to the U.S. television industry have been his creativity in constantly pushing the limits of television style—both visually and narratively, and his willingness (often eagerness) to do battle with the networks to champion the broadcasting of innovative and nonformulaic forms of narrative television at the expense of audience ratings. Tarses has increasingly refused to play the Hollywood programming "game," yet he produced what were some of the freshest and most daring television series of the 1970s and 1980s.

PAMELA WILSON

See also **Dramedy**

Jay Tarses. Born in Baltimore, Maryland, July 3, 1939. Educated at Williams College, Williamstown,

Massachusetts; Ithaca College, Ithaca, New York, B.F.A. Married Rachel Newdell, 1963; three children, including Jamie Tarses, the first woman to become president of a U.S. network (ABC). Production assistant in New York for *Candid Camera,* 1963; worked in advertising and promotion, Armstrong Cork Company, Lancaster, Pennsylvania; joined Tom Patchett in stand-up comedy team, playing the coffeehouse and college circuit, late 1960s; with Patchett, television writer, staff of *The Carol Burnett Show, The Bob Newhart Show,* and others; independent television producer since 1981. Recipient: Emmy Award, 1972; Writers Guild of America Award, 1987.

Television Series

1967–79	*The Carol Burnett Show* (with Tom Patchett; writer)
1970–71	*Make Your Own Kind of Music* (performer, writer)
1972–78	*The Bob Newhart Show* (with Tom Patchett; executive producer, writer)
1976–78	*The Tony Randall Show* (with Tom Patchett; creator, executive producer, writer)
1977–78	*We've Got Each Other* (with Tom Patchett; creator, executive producer, writer)
1978	*Mary* (with Tom Patchett; creator, producer, writer)
1981–82	*Open All Night* (with Tom Patchett; actor, creator, producer, writer)
1983–84	*Buffalo Bill* (with Tom Patchett; creator, executive producer, writer)
1984	*The Duck Factory* (actor)
1987–88, 1989–91	*The Days and Nights of Molly Dodd* (creator, producer, writer, director, actor)
1987–88	*The "Slap" Maxwell Story* (creator, producer, writer, director)
1992	*Smoldering Lust* (creator, producer, writer, director)
1996	*Public Morals* (with Steven Bochco; creator, producer)

Television Pilots

1977	*The Chopped Liver Brothers* (executive producer, actor; with Tom Patchett)
1985	*The Faculty* (executive producer, director, writer)
1990	*Baltimore*
1994	*Harvey Berger, Salesman*
1995	*Jackass Junior High*
1997	*Veronica's Video*

Films

Up the Academy (writer, with Tom Patchett), 1977; *The Great Muppet Caper* (writer, with Tom Patchett), 1981; *The Muppets Take Manhattan* (writer, with Tom Patchett), 1984; *Teen Wolf* (actor), 1985.

Further Reading

Christensen, Mark, "Even Career Girls Get the Blues: Is Prime Time Ready for *The Days and Nights of Molly Dodd?*" *Rolling Stone* (May 21, 1987)

Christensen, Mark, "Jay Tarses" (interview), *Rolling Stone* (December 17, 1987)

"The Humorous Days and Nights of Jay Tarses," *Broadcasting* (February 6, 1989)

Kaufman, Peter, "The Quixotic Days and Nights of Jay Tarses" (interview), *New York Times* (June 6, 1993)

Mathewes-Green, Frederica, "While TV Moguls Dither, Parents' Guide Deliver," *Policy Review* (March/April 1997)

Meisler, Andy, "Jay Tarses: 'I Don't Do Sitcoms'," *New York Times* (August 2, 1987)

Ross, Chuck, "What in the World Is Molly Dodd?" *Television-Radio Age* (August 17, 1987)

Schneider, Michael, "The MTM 'College'," *Electronic Media* 17 (March 9, 1998)

Wilson, Pam, "Upscale Feminine Angst: Molly Dodd, The Lifetime Cable Network and Gender Marketing," *Camera Obscura* (1995)

Tartikoff, Brandon (1949–1997)

U.S. Media Executive, Producer

An independent producer and former president of Paramount Pictures, Brandon Tartikoff served from 1980 to 1991 as the youngest and most accomplished president of NBC's entertainment division. During his tenure at NBC, Tartikoff developed a blockbuster Thursday-night lineup that helped the ailing network rank number-one in primetime for the first time in 30 years.

Tartikoff, an admitted "child of television," confessed that he once dreamed of being the next Ed Sullivan, but his television career began at the local level. After undergraduate work in broadcasting at Yale, Tartikoff broke into the business at WTNH in New Haven, Connecticut. Driven to make it to the big leagues, he soon landed a job at the ABC-owned-and-operated WLS in Chicago, the third-largest market in the country. He worked under the tutelage of Lew Erlicht, his eventual rival.

In the mid-1970s, ABC President Fred Silverman was impressed by Tartikoff's high-camp promo for a series of "monkey-movies" dubbed "Gorilla My Dreams." Silverman recruited Tartikoff for manager of dramatic development at ABC. Three years later, the up-and-coming 30-year-old "boy wonder" of television was snatched up by third-place NBC, where Silverman had become president in 1978. Tartikoff was named head of the entertainment division, where he stayed for the next 12 years, the longest any individual has held that position.

NBC's ratings breakthrough came in 1984, when Tartikoff happened to see Bill Cosby doing a monologue on *The Tonight Show.* Convinced Cosby's family-based banter would make for an excellent sitcom, Tartikoff recruited the comedian and producers Tom Werner and Marcy Carsey. The resulting *Cosby Show* not only helped resurrect the failing sitcom format, but became the building block for a Thursday-night schedule that included *Family Ties, Cheers,* and *Night Court.*

Tartikoff was at the helm for the development of *Hill Street Blues,* produced by MTM Entertainment, which exploded in popularity among its fiercely loyal audience in its second season after receiving critical acclaim and an armload of Emmy awards in its first. He shepherded *An Early Frost,* the first made-for-television movie about AIDS, through production. *Miami Vice* was also conceived under Tartikoff; according to executive producer Michael Mann, the head of entertainment presented him with a short memo which read: "MTV. Cops."

By 1991, when Tartikoff left NBC to head Paramount Pictures, the network had been ranked first in the ratings for six consecutive years. Tartikoff was replaced by Warren Littlefield. A series of organiza-

Brandon Tartikoff.
Courtesy of the Everett Collection

Brandon Tartikoff. Born on Long Island, New York, January 13, 1949. Educated at Yale University, New Haven, Connecticut, B.A. with honors 1970. Married: Lily Samuels, 1982; one daughter. Director of advertising and promotion, WTNH-TV, New Haven, 1971–73; programming executive for dramatic programming, WLS, Chicago, 1973–76; manager, dramatic development, ABC, New York City, 1976–77; writer, producer, Graffiti; director of comedy programs, NBC entertainment, Burbank, California, 1977–78, vice president of programs, 1978–80, president, 1980–90; chair, NBC Entertainment Group, until 1991; chair, Paramount Pictures, 1991–92; independent producer, from 1992. Recipient: Tree of Life Award, Jewish National Foundation, 1986; Broadcaster of the Year, Television, Radio and Advertising Club of Philadelphia, 1986. Died August 27, 1997.

Publications

The Last Great Ride, with Charles Leehrsen. New York: Turtle Bay Books, 1992.

Further Reading

"Brandon Tartikoff" (interview), *Mediaweek* (January 23, 1995)
Carter, Bill, "The Man who Owns Prime Time," *New York Times Magazine* (March 4, 1990)
Carter, Bill, "Tartikoff's 11 Years at NBC: One for the Record Books," *New York Times* (May 6, 1991)
Christensen, Mark, and Cameron Stauth, *The Sweeps: Behind the Scenes in Network TV,* New York: Morrow, 1984
Coe, Steve, "Tartikoff Urges Networks to Take Risks," *Broadcasting* (May 20, 1991)
Hammer, Joshua, "A TV King's Rough Passage," *Newsweek* (December 9, 1991)
Mandese, Joe, "Tartikoff Is Still One of TV's Idea Men" (interview), *Advertising Age* (July 5, 1993)
McClellan, Steve, "Grabbing the Grazers in a Crowded Field," *Broadcasting* (February 1, 1993)
"Tartikoff Talks" (interview), *Broadcasting* (June 4, 1990)
Zoglin, Richard, "Return of the Slugger," *Time* (January 24, 1994)

tional changes at Paramount and a near-fatal auto accident later led Tartikoff out of the studio arena and into the realm of independent production. Tartikoff passed away due to Hodgkins disease on August 27, 1997.

MICHAEL B. KASSEL

See also **Cosby Show, The; Early Frost, An; Hill Street Blues; Miami Vice; National Broadcasting Company**

Taxi

U.S. Situation Comedy

Taxi's television history is filled with contradictions. Produced by some of U.S. television comedy's most well-regarded talent, the show was canceled by two different networks. Despite winning 14 Emmy Awards in only five seasons, the program's ratings were rock bottom for its final seasons. Although it thrives in syn-

Taxi.
Photo courtesy of David Davis

dication and is still well loved by many viewers, *Taxi* will be best remembered as the ancestral bridge between two of the most successful sitcoms in U.S. television history: *The Mary Tyler Moore Show* and *Cheers.*

In the mid-1970s, MTM Productions had achieved both critical and popular success with a range of programming. So it was an unexpected move when four of the company's finest writers and producers, James L. Brooks, Stan Daniels, David Davis, and Ed Weinberger, jumped off the stable ship of MTM in 1978 to form their own production company, John Charles Walters Company. To launch their new venture, they looked back to an idea that Brooks and Davis had previously considered with MTM: the daily life of a New York City taxi company. From MTM head Grant Tinker, they purchased the rights to the newspaper article that had initiated the concept and began producing this new show at Paramount for ABC. They brought a few other MTM veterans along for the ride, including director James Burrows and writer/producers Glen and Les Charles.

Although *Taxi* certainly bore many of the trademark signs of "quality television" as exemplified by MTM, other changes in style and focus distinguished this program from an MTM product. After working on the middle-class, female-centered worlds of *The Mary Tyler Moore Show, Rhoda,* and *Phyllis* for years, the group at John Charles Walters wanted to create a program focusing on blue-collar male experience. MTM programs all had clearly defined settings, but *Taxi*'s creators wanted a show that was firmly rooted in a city's identity—*Taxi*'s situations and mood were distinctly New York. Despite MTM Productions' innovations in creating ensemble character comedy, there was always one central star around which the ensemble revolved. In *Taxi,* Judd Hirsch's Alex Rieger was a main character, but his importance seemed secondary to the centrality of the ensemble and the Sunshine Cab Company itself. While *The Mary Tyler Moore Show* proudly proclaimed that "you're going to make it on your own," the destitute drivers of *Taxi* were doomed to perpetual failure; the closest any of them came to happiness was Rieger's content acceptance of his lot in life.

Taxi debuted on September 12, 1978, amid a strong ABC Tuesday-night lineup. It followed *Three's Company,* a wildly successful example of the type of show against which MTM "quality" sitcoms reacted. *Taxi* used this strong position to end the season ninth in the ratings and garner its first of three straight Emmys for Outstanding Comedy Series. The show's success was due to its excellent writing, Burrows's award-winning directing (using his innovative four-camera tech-

nique), and the largely unknown but talented cast. Danny DeVito's Louie DePalma soon became one of the most despised men on television, possibly the most unredeemable and worthless character ever to reside on the small screen. Andy Kaufman's foreign mechanic Latka Gravas provided over-the-top comedy within an ensemble emphasizing subtle character humor. But Kaufman sometimes also brought a demonic edge to the character, an echo of his infamous appearances on *Saturday Night Live* as a macho wrestler of women and Mighty Mouse lip-syncher. In the second season Christopher Lloyd's Reverend Jim Ignatowski was added to the group as television's first drugged-out, 1960s-generation burn-out character. But Lloyd's Emmy-winning performance created in Jim more than just a storehouse of fried brain cells; he established a deep, complex humanity that moved far beyond mere caricature. The program launched successful movie careers for DeVito and Lloyd, as well as the fairly notable television careers of Tony Danza and Marilu Henner; Kaufman's controversial career would certainly have continued had he not died of cancer in 1984.

In its third season, ABC moved *Taxi* from beneath *Three's Company*'s protective wing to a more competitive Wednesday night slot; the ratings plummeted, and *Taxi* finished the next two years in 53rd place. ABC canceled the show in early 1982 as part of a larger network push away from "quality" and toward the Aaron Spelling-produced popular fare of *Dynasty* and *The Love Boat.* HBO bid for the show, looking for it to become the first ongoing sitcom for the pay channel, but it lost out to NBC, which scheduled the series for the 1982–83 season. Ironically, this reunited the show's executive producers with their former boss Tinker, who had taken over NBC. Tinker's reign at NBC was focused, not surprisingly, on "quality" programming, which he hoped would attract viewers to the perennially last-place network. *Taxi* was partnered with a very compatible show on Thursday night, *Cheers,* created by *Taxi* veterans Charles, Burrows, and Charles. Although this lineup featured some notably distinctive and successful programs (the comedies were sandwiched between the dramas *Fame* and *Hill Street Blues*) the ratings were dreadful, and *Taxi* finished the season in 73rd place. NBC was willing to give the low-rated *Cheers* another chance, but the network felt *Taxi* had run its course and canceled it at the end of the season. Had *Taxi* been given another year or two in the same slot, it would have been part of one of the most successful nights on television, featuring *The Cosby Show* (co-created by *Taxi* creator Weinberger), *Family Ties, Hill Street Blues, L.A. Law,* and eventual powerhouse *Cheers.*

Taxi lives on in syndication, and was recreated with original cast members in the 1999 Andy Kaufman biopic, *Man on the Moon,* but its most significant place in U.S. television history is as the middle generation between *The Mary Tyler Moore Show* and *Cheers.* It served as a transition between the star-driven, middle-class character comedy of MTM programs and the location-centered, ensemble comedy inhabited by the losers of *Cheers.* Considered one of the great U.S. sitcoms of its era, *Taxi* stands as a prime example of the constant tension in television programming between standards of quality and reliance on high ratings to determine success.

JASON MITTELL

See also **Brooks, James L.; Burrows, James; Charles, Glen and Les;** *Cheers;* **Comedy, Workplace Settings;** *Mary Tyler Moore Show, The;* **Weinberger, Ed**

Cast

Alex Rieger	Judd Hirsch
Bobby Wheeler (1978–81)	Jeff Conaway
Louie DePalma	Danny DeVito
Elaine Nardo	Marilu Henner
Tony Banta	Tony Danza
John Burns (1978–79)	Randall Carver
Latka Gravas	Andy Kaufman
Reverend Jim Ignatowski (1979–83)	
	Christopher Lloyd
Simka Gravas (1981–83)	Carol Kane

Producers

James L. Brooks, Stan Daniels, Ed Weinberger, David Davis, Glen Charles, Les Charles, Ian Praiser, Richard Sakai, Howard Gewirtz

Programming History

111 episodes

ABC

September 1978–October 1980	Tuesday 9:30–10:00
November 1980–January 1981	Wednesday 9:00–9:30
February 1981–June 1982	Thursday 9:30–10:00
NBC	
September 1982–December 1982	Thursday 9:30–10:00
January 1983–February 1983	Saturday 9:30–10:00
March 1983–May 1983	Wednesday 9:30–10:00
June 1983–July 1983	Wednesday 10:30–11:00

Further Reading

Feuer, Jane, Paul Kerr, and Tise Vahimagi, editors, *MTM: "Quality Television,"* London: British Film Institute, 1984

Sorensen, Jeff, *The Taxi Book,* New York: St. Martin's Press, 1987

Waldron, Vince, *Classic Sitcoms: A Celebration of the Best of Prime-Time Comedy,* New York: Macmillan, 1987

Teaser

A teaser is a television strategy for attracting the audience's attention and holding it over a span of time. Typically, a teaser consists of auditory or visual information, or both, providing the viewer a glimpse of what he or she can expect as programming continues. Teasers are used in several types of programming.

In news broadcasts, for example, a newscaster may address viewers in a fashion such as: "The state legislature gets ready for a showdown on taxes. Details when we return." The audience is being teased with information, and the purpose is to keep a viewer tuned to the station during a commercial. Similarly, teasers can also be used to keep a viewer tuned to a newscast. An anchor may begin a newscast with a tease for an upcoming story, like the state legislature story above, then shift the focus: "But first, we bring you our top story…"

According to David Keith Cohler, there are two types of news teasers. The first is best described as a headline, which contains the essential information about a story. In sports the headline may be: "Angels shut-out Pirates. Highlights when we return." The second type of teaser is more vague and leaves the reader wondering what exactly the news is about to report, as in the "showdown on taxes" example mentioned above.

For Richard D. Yoakam and Charles F. Cremer, there is little difference between "teasers" and "bumpers," since both are designed to promote upcoming stories. Thus, a simple, "We'll return in a moment" would qualify as a teaser as well as a bumper. So would a short video clip of a dramatic moment or a humorous exchange of words taken from the segment coming up after some commercials. Thus, anything designed to get the attention of viewers and hold their attention through some span of time may be referred to as a teaser.

This is clearly the case in other types of programming. Daytime talk shows, for example, often open with provocative summaries of their content, then cut to commercials. The teaser is designed to titillate the audience and entice it into returning.

Teasers for dramatic programming are similar. Short clips from the upcoming program can be used to highlight the most powerful or humorous moments. Bits of tense dialogue, jokes, or tender moments can all be excerpted for use as an immediate promotion of the program at hand.

A related programming strategy uses the precommercial sequence to remind the audience of past events at the same time it pulls them into the current program. These summaries are often introduced with a voice-over announcement: for example, "Previously on *Hill Street Blues.*" In many cases (*Dallas* is a good example), the summary-teaser also serves as a prologue, indicating which stories, from the ever-growing collection of interrelated narratives, will be explored in the upcoming episode.

In the age of the remote-control device, a number of programs have abandoned teasers, plunging directly into the dramatic action of the narrative, sometimes without even an intervening commercial between the end of one program and the start of the next. However, in some cases it is still a prologue or a teaser, selected from the most powerful moments of previous and new material, that is presented to the fickle audience. This strategy, it is hoped, prevents viewers from instantly changing the channel to "surf" between programs.

RAUL D. TOVARES

Further Reading

Cohler, David Keith, *Broadcast Journalism: A Guide for the Presentation of Radio and Television News,* Englewood Cliffs, New Jersey: Prentice Hall, 1985

Yoakam, Richard D., and Charles F. Cremer, *ENG: Television News and the New Technology,* Carbondale: Southern Illinois University Press, 1985

Technology, Television

Although television seems a thoroughly modern invention, widely available only since the mid-20th century, the concept of recreating moving images electrically was developed much earlier than is generally thought. It can be traced at least to 1884 when Paul G. Nipkow created the rotating scanning disk, which provided a way of sending a representation of a moving image over a wire using varying electrical signals created by mechanically scanning that moving image.

Mechanical scanning of an image involved a spinning disk, with a spiral grouping of holes, located at both the sending and receiving ends. At the sending end, a photocell-like device varied the strength of an electrical signal at a rate proportional to the amount of light hitting the cell through the holes in the disk. At the receiving end, a source of light correspondingly varied in intensity at the rate of the electrical signal it received and could be seen through the holes in the rotating disk, thereby recreating a crude copy of the image scanned at the sending end. Today, moving images are scanned electronically as described below and the varying electronic signal representing the scanned images can be transmitted or sent through wire to be recreated at the receiver or monitor.

The earliest practical mechanical scanning and transmitting of moving images occurred in the mid-1920s, and by the early 1930s electronic scanning had generally replaced the mechanical scanning methods. At first, the images were crude—little more than shadow-pictures—but as the potential for television as a profit-making medium became apparent, more money and effort went into television experimentation, and improvements continued through the 1930s; regular transmissions by the BBC began in Britain in 1936, using a 405-line, electronic system developed by EMI.

By 1941 technical standards for the scanning and transmission of television images in the United States had been agreed upon, and these standards have, in general, been maintained ever since. The U.S. standard, known as National Television System Committee (NTSC), utilizes 525-line, 60-field, 30-frame, interlaced scanning. This means that images are scanned in the television camera and reproduced in the television receiver or monitor 30 times each second. Each full image, or frame, is scanned by dividing the image into 525 horizontal lines and then sequentially scanning first all the even lines (every other line) from top to bottom, creating one field, and then scanning the odd-numbered lines in the same manner, creating a second field. The two fields, when combined (interlaced), create one frame. Therefore, 30 complete images or frames, each made up of two fields, are created each second. Because it is not possible to perceive individual changes in light and image happening so quickly, the 30-times-per-second scanned images are perceived as continuous movement, a trait known as "persistence of vision," similar to motion-picture viewing (which operates at 24 frames per second). The NTSC standard is used in Canada, parts of Asia, including Japan, and much of Latin America, as well as in the United States. There are two other "standards" in common use today. The PAL systems, a 25-frame-per-second standard with a number of variants, are used throughout most of western Europe and India, as well as other areas. The SECAM 25-frame-per-second standard is used in many parts of the world, including France, Russia, and most of eastern Europe. Both PAL and SECAM use a 625-line picture, giving a sharper image resolution than NTSC. Countries that use 60-hertz (cycles per second; Hz) AC (alternating current) power have adopted a 30-frame-per-second television system. Countries that utilize a 50-Hz power system have a 25-frame-per-second television system. In all these television systems, therefore the frame-per-second rate is equal to half the AC power frequency.

The aspect ratio of the television screen—the ratio of the horizontal dimension to the vertical dimension—is 4:3. For instance, if a TV receiver screen is 16-inches wide, the screen will be 12-inches high. (TV picture tubes are defined by their diagonal measurement, so in this example the screen would be described as a 20-inch TV.) Often, motion pictures are shown on television in a "letter-box" format. Because motion pictures are usually shot in an aspect ratio greater than 4:3, it is necessary to leave a black space at the top and bottom of the television screen so that the film can be viewed in a form resembling its theatrical dimensions, without cutting off the sides. High-definition television (HDTV) also utilizes a greater aspect ratio, generally 16:9.

The television camera consists of a lens to focus an image onto the front surface of one or more pick-up-devices, and—within the camera housing—the pick-up-device(s) and the electronics to make the camera work. A viewfinder to monitor the camera's images is normally mounted in or on the camera. The pick-up-device, either a camera tube or charge-coupled device (CCD), reads the focused visual image and converts the image into a varying electronic signal that represents the image. On high-quality cameras, three pick-up-devices are often utilized; one to pick up each of the three additive primary colors (blue, green, and red) that make up the color image.

The face of the camera tube has a photoemissive material that gives off electrical energy when exposed to light. The stronger the light at any given point, the more energy is emitted by the tube. By reading the amount of energy on the surface of the camera tube at each point, an electronic representation of the visual image can be created. The camera tube "reads" the amount of energy that the focused image creates on its surface by scanning the image, both horizontally and vertically, with a moving electron beam. The scanning functions by means of precise magnetic deflection of the beam.

The CCD replaces the camera tube in most modern cameras, commonly called "chip cameras." This solid-state device measures the energy at each one of a grid of discrete points on its surface, known as pixels; converts this information into a numeric equivalent and stores this figure as binary information; and then sends out this varying electronic signal, which represents the image. CCD image pick-up devices are becoming more popular due to their small size, long life, greater sensitivity and light tolerance, minimal power requirements, less image distortion, and ruggedness.

In the receiver's, or monitor's, picture tube, the camera tube process is essentially reversed. The face of the picture tube is coated with a phosphor-like material that glows when struck by a beam of electrons. The glow lasts long enough to make the scanned image visible to the viewer. An electron gun shoots the thin beam of electrons at the face of the screen from within the picture tube. The beam's direction is varied in a precise manner by magnetic deflection in a way that matches or synchronizes with the original image scanned by the television camera. Color picture tubes can have one electron gun (such as in the Trinitron), or three guns, one for each primary color. One major difference between a receiver and a monitor should be mentioned here. A receiver (such as a domestic TV set) is able to tune in a television station frequency and show the images being transmitted. A monitor (such as those used to display CCTV pictures in a security control room) does not have a tuning component and can receive video signals by wire only.

At a television station, the electronic signal from a television camera can be combined or mixed with video signals from other devices—such as video tape players, computers, film chains or telecines (motion-picture and slide-projector units whose outputs have been converted to video signals)—using what is known as a switcher. The switcher is also used to create various special visual effects electronically. The video output from the switcher can then be recorded, sent to another studio or master control room, or sent directly to a transmitter.

The complete video signal sent to a transmitter or through wire to a monitor consists of signals representing the picture (luminance), color (chrominance), and synchronization. Synchronizing signals force the receiver to lock onto (sync-up) and reproduce the original image correctly. Otherwise, for example, the receiver might begin to scan an image that starts halfway down the screen.

Television stations are assigned a specific transmitting frequency and operating power. In the United States, VHF (very-high frequency) television, channels 2 through 13, occupies a portion of the electromagnetic spectrum between 54 and 216 MHz (million Hertz, or 1 million cycles-per-second). Channels 2–6 are located between 54 and 88 MHz. The FM radio band, 88–108 MHz, is located between television channels 6 and 7. Channels 7 through 13 are located between 174 and 216 MHz. UHF (ultra-high frequency) television, originally channels 14 to 83, was assigned the frequency range from 470 to 890 MHz. In 1966 the Federal Communications Commission (FCC) discontinued issuing licenses for UHF television stations above channel 69. In 1970 the FCC took away the frequency range from 807 to 890 MHz for other communication uses, and so the UHF band now consists of channels 14–69, from 470 to 806 MHz. The upper end of this current range, channels 52 through 69, is being coveted for other frequency spectrum uses, and it appears that the number of channels in the UHF band available for use by television will continue to decrease. Each television channel has a frequency bandwidth of 6 MHz. So, for instance, channel 2 occupies the spectrum between 54 MHz and 60 MHz. Within its assigned band, each station transmits the video signal as described earlier, an audio signal, and specialized signals such as closed-captioning information.

In the television transmitter, a carrier wave is created at an assigned frequency. This carrier wave travels at the speed of light through space with specific transmission or propagation characteristics determined by the individual frequency. The video signal is piggy-backed onto the much higher-frequency carrier wave using a process known as "modulation." Modulation, in the simplest terms, means that the carrier wave is modulated, or varied slightly, at the rate of the signal being piggy-backed. In a television transmission, the video signal varies the amplitude or strength of the carrier wave at the rate of the video signal. This is known as "amplitude modulation" (AM) and is similar to the method used to transmit the audio of an AM radio station. However, the television station audio signal is piggy-backed onto the carrier wave using frequency modulation (FM). With television audio, the carrier wave's frequency (instead of its amplitude) is varied slightly at the rate of the audio signal.

The modulated carrier wave is sent from the transmitter to an antenna. The antenna then radiates the signal out into space in a pattern determined by the physical design of the transmitting antenna. Traditionally, the transmitter and antenna were terrestrially located, but now television signals can be radiated or delivered by transmitters and antennas located on satellites in orbit around Earth. In this case, the television signal is transmitted to the satellite at one frequency and then retransmitted at a different frequency by the satellite's transmitter back to Earth.

Besides delivery by carrier-wave transmission, television is often sent through cable directly to homes and businesses. These signals are delivered by satellite, over-the-air from terrestrial antennas, and sometimes directly from video players to the distribution equipment of cable television (CATV) service providers for feeding directly into homes. The signals are sent at specific carrier-wave frequencies (sometimes called "radio frequencies" [RF]) as chosen by the cable service provider.

A television receiver picks up the transmitted television signals sent over the air or by cable or satellite, selects the necessary video and audio signals that have been piggy-backed on the carrier wave, discards the carrier wave, and amplifies and converts the video and audio signals into picture and sound. A television monitor accepts direct video signals to provide pictures and, sometimes, audio signals to provide sound. As mentioned above, a monitor cannot receive carrier waves.

As computer and digital technologies are merged with traditional television, significant and positive changes are being witnessed in a number of areas. The utilization of digital storage equipment and methods is providing ever-more effective means of accessing, duplicating, archiving, and transferring traditional program materials. When such materials are stored on computer-like servers, the need for moving-part recording and playback equipment can sometimes be eliminated, thereby improving reliability. In addition, digital storage saves significant physical space. The FCC has mandated that all U.S. television stations must transmit digitally by 2006. By early 2002, 229 stations in 80 markets, representing 74 percent of U.S. TV households, were transmitting a digital signal. With a conversion cost of $2 million to $10 million per station (a not-insignificant expense), two results are being seen. First, a strong market is being created for companies offering digital transmitters and other digital equipment. Second, a large number of stations have begun requesting extensions from the FCC, putting into question the viability of the 2006 deadline. An additional factor is that consumers seem to have little interest in digital television. As of 2003, it remained to be seen whether or not the FCC will require that all future television sets be able to receive digital signals in order to strengthen the market for digital television. In the United Kingdom, where the government has announced that analogue transmissions will be turned off in a rolling program between 2006 and 2010, both the BBC and commercial broadcasters have created several new channels that are free-to-air but only available digitally, as a way of encouraging and accelerating the take-up of new digital TV sets.

High-definition television (HDTV) advances have been slow, owing to a continuing reluctance to agree standards, limited program material, and an accompanying lack of consumer confidence and a viable market. As more television stations and networks show letterbox-formatted programming, there should be increasing acceptance, and eventual consumer demand for HDTV. In the meantime, however, high-definition, as well as digital, technology is being used more and more in the production of programming material.

As television technology continues to evolve, equipment quality is becoming more refined, weight and size are decreasing, and costs are becoming lower. An important example of this can be seen in videophone technology for television. First used commercially by CNN in April 2001 while covering the incident of a U.S. spy plane forced to land by the Chinese, within six months this technology had been integrated into the standard equipment of international news correspondents. The videophone gear, slightly larger than a laptop computer, allows field reporters in remote locations to send television camera images via satellite to their bureaus across the world. As coalition military forces became engaged in Afghanistan in late 2001 and 2002, this equipment emerged as the standard way for correspondents to report from the field.

From primitive experimentation in the 1920s and 1930s through the advent of commercial television in the late 1940s to the establishment of color television as the standard by the mid-1960s, television has grown quickly to become perhaps the most important single influence on society today. From a source of information and entertainment to what some have dubbed the real "soma" of Aldous Huxley's *Brave New World,* television has become the present era's most influential medium. While the medium continues to evolve and change, its importance, influence, and pervasiveness appear to continue unabated. How will new technology change the face of television? Once the realm of science fiction, we are now seeing new delivery systems, on-call access, a greater number of available channels, two-way interaction, and the coupling of television and the computer. We are in the process of experiencing better technical quality, including improved resolution, HDTV, the convenience of flatter and lighter television receivers, and digital processing and transmission. And yet, the basic standard for television broadcast technology in the United States has been with us, with only minor changes and improvements, for well over 50 years.

STEVE RUNYON

See also **High-Definition Television**

Further Reading

Brice, Richard, *Newnes Guide to Digital Television,* Woburn, Massachusetts: Butterworth-Heinemann, 2000

Ciciora, Walter, James Farmer, and David Large, *Modern Cable Television Technology: Video, Voice, and Data Communications,* San Francisco: Morgan Kaufman Publishers, 1998

Hartwig, Robert L., *Basic TV Technology: Digital and Analog (Media Manuals),* 3rd edition, Woburn, Massachusetts: Butterworth-Heinemann, 2000

Luther, Arch C., and Andrew F. Inglis, *Video Engineering,* 3rd edition, New York: McGraw-Hill, 1999

Shrader, Robert L., *Electronic Communication,* New York: McGraw-Hill, 1959; 6th edition, 1990

Whitaker, Jerry C., and K. Blair Benson, *Standard Handbook of Television and Video Engineering,* 3rd edition, New York: McGraw-Hill, 2000

Whitaker, Jerry C., *DTV Handbook: The Revolution in Digital Video,* 3rd edition, New York: McGraw-Hill, 2001

Teenagers and Television in the United States

Emerging somewhat concurrently in American popular consciousness during the 1930s and 1940s, television and teenagers (that is, the awareness of teenage years as a phase of life distinct from childhood and adulthood) have a lengthy, albeit uneven, relationship, particularly with regard to representation. Indeed, programming schedules from the early years of telecasting to the present reveal significant fluctuations in TV's depiction of teenagers. The two periods in which teenagers received the most attention from the television industry in the United States are approximately 1946–66 and 1980–2000, periods marked by substantial upswings in the American economy and teen population, as well as experimentation with TV programming strategies. In contrast, the years between 1966 and 1980, which were marked by economic recession and a decline in the teen population, witnessed the least amount of teen-oriented programming.

With a few notable exceptions, teen programming has focused primarily on white, heterosexual, middle-class teenagers, who compose one of the most lucrative consumer markets, given their propensity to shop often and indiscriminately, as well as their willingness to spend money on new and non-essential products. While TV reviews and programming schedules from the initial period of network television suggest that teenagers were the targeted demographic for early teen programming, as discussed in more detail below, contemporary TV ratings and marketing research suggest that today's teen programming is directed less to teenagers than to an audience comprised of viewers between 12 and 34 who share a youthful sensibility.

Teen Programming, Late 1940s to Mid-1960s

The development of teen-specific television programming must be considered within the larger context of the history of the teen consumer market. Due to the decrease in available jobs and the rise of progressive education initiatives during the Depression, adolescents were increasingly separated from adult work environments and encouraged to enroll in school over the course of the 1930s. This phenomenon led to a popular understanding of youth in their "teen" years (13 to 19) as forming a unique demographic group. With the rise of U.S. involvement in World War II, many adolescents left school and earned considerable income through their participation in the war economy. Because of an increase in their spending habits and purchasing power, these war-time youth laborers formed the first teenage consumer market. Media industries were quick to cash in on this new niche market, and teen-specific texts appeared in virtually every medium possible across the entertainment landscape of the 1940s, including novels, theatrical plays, motion pictures, comic books, and radio programs.

With its development curtailed during World War II, television was the last form of media to direct its attention to teenagers. Yet, given TV's emergence within the broadcasting industry, which was already catering to teenage consumers via radio, it took but moments for television to join in the feeding frenzy over the burgeoning teen market. Indeed, although families were appealed to as the primary audience during television's initial phase, reviews and programming schedules demonstrate that the early TV industry attempted to attract the lucrative teenage consumer market through a broad assortment of teen-oriented programs.

The first teen series to appear on television was *Teen Canteen,* which debuted in 1946. Broadcasting youth talent from a variety of teen canteens in New York state, the show remained on the air for two years, moving from its original home on WRGB in Schenectady to WPIX in New York City. Several other teen-oriented variety shows, such as *Teen Time Tunes* (Dumont 1949), were introduced during TV's initial experimental period, as were teenage quiz shows such as *Junior High School Quiz* (CBS 1946), talent shows such as *Paul Whiteman's TV Teen Club* (ABC 1949–54), and sports programs such as *High School Football* (WNBW-Washington, D.C. 1950). As was the case for much early TV programming content, several music shows popular with teenagers migrated from radio to television during this period also, including *Coke Time with Eddie Fisher* (NBC 1953–57). Perhaps the most successful programs with teenage viewers were those shows that combined popular music and dance, such as *Teen Twirl* (WNBK-Cleveland 1955), *Teen Club Party* (WGN-Chicago 1957), and the enormously popular *American Bandstand* (WFIL-Philadelphia 1952–57; ABC 1957–87), the longest-running music/dance show on U.S. television to date.

A variety of educational shows were also produced for teenagers during the late 1940s and early 1950s.

For example, several teenage discussion programs, such as *Teenage Book Club* (ABC 1948) and *Today's Teens* (WENR-Chicago 1951), appeared during this initial phase of telecasting. Several teen news magazines debuted during this period also, including *Youth Wants to Know* (NBC 1951–58), *The New York Times Youth Forum* (Dumont 1952–55), and *Junior Press Conference* (WFIL-Philadelphia 1952; ABC 1953–60). The first (if not the only) juvenile court series, *Youth Court* (KTLA-Los Angeles 1958), was introduced during television's first decade also.

While real teenagers were featured in many of TV's first news, music, and talent programs, teen characters made their television debut via several early prime-time domestic comedies that migrated from radio, such as *The Aldrich Family* (NBC 1949–53), *The Goldbergs* (CBS/NBC/Dumont 1949–54), and *The Life of Riley* (NBC 1949–50, 1953–58). As the TV and advertising industries began to focus more specifically on middle-class suburban consumers during the 1950s, a slew of situation comedies featuring white, middle-class families dominated the prime-time programming schedule, including *The Adventures of Ozzie and Harriet* (ABC 1952–66), *Make Room for Daddy* (ABC/CBS 1953–64), *Father Knows Best* (CBS/NBC 1954–62), *Leave It to Beaver* (CBS 1957–58; ABC 1958–63), and *The Donna Reed Show* (ABC 1958–66). Interestingly, each of these suburban family sitcoms featured teenage characters who, over the course of the 1950s, moved further into the spotlight on such shows, perhaps due to marketers' discovery that teenagers had considerable power in establishing consumer trends among both younger and older viewers.

More significant to the development of teen TV programming, however, was the introduction of several school comedies during the 1950s, such as *Mr. Peepers* (NBC 1952–55) and *Our Miss Brooks* (CBS 1952–56). Unlike family programs, these school shows placed teenagers in non-domestic contexts, and thus called attention to the different social activities, spaces, and relationships that separated teens from adults and produced a distinct teen culture. By depicting teenagers in educational settings rather than family homes, these shows set the stage for later teen-oriented series, such as *The Many Loves of Dobie Gillis* (CBS 1959–63). Although *A Date with Judy* (ABC 1951, 1952–53) and *Meet Corliss Archer* (CBS 1951–52; syndicated 1954–55) were the first TV shows whose titles featured a teen character's name, *The Many Loves of Dobie Gillis* was the first prime-time series to consistently privilege teenage characters, activities, and spaces over those associated with family shows.

Following the success of *The Many Loves of Dobie Gillis*, particularly with young female viewers, a number of girl-centered sitcoms emerged in the late 1950s and early 1960s, including *Too Young to Go Steady* (NBC 1959), *Peck's Bad Girl* (CBS 1959–60), *Margie* (ABC 1961–62), *Fair Exchange* (CBS 1962–63), *The Patty Duke Show* (ABC 1963–66), *Karen* (NBC 1964–65), *Tammy* (ABC 1965–66), and *Gidget* (ABC 1965–66). Together with *The Many Loves of Dobie Gillis,* these girl sitcoms helped to solidify many of the conventions of teen-oriented TV programming: the foregrounding of teen characters over adults, the privileging of schools over family homes as settings for action, and a focus on various stereotypical coming-of-age issues, especially dating, earning spending money, and negotiating intergenerational conflict. In turn, all of these sitcoms reproduced the white, middle-class, heterosexual milieu associated with earlier family and school comedies.

In light of the increasing popularity of rock music among teenagers during the late 1950s and early 1960s (particularly after Elvis Presley's successful appearance on several variety shows), TV executives further integrated this new music into programming in order to attract the teen demographic. For example, ABC brought several music programs to a national audience in the late 1950s and early 1960s, including the enormously successful *American Bandstand* and *Shindig* (1964–66). Interestingly, it was because of these shows' focus on rock, a form of popular music derived in part from African-American music, that the first black teenagers appeared on television.

Although teenagers appeared in a wide assortment of television shows and thus across the daily broadcasting schedule during TV's initial experimental period, teen programming became increasingly confined to two genres—the music/dance show and the situation comedy—as well as two timeslots—late afternoons and early prime-time—over the course of the late 1950s and early 1960s. This trend would continue until the early 1990s.

The considerable attention paid to teenagers in programming during television's first two decades is best explained by several developments in the TV industry's programming patterns. First, the early years of telecasting were quite experimental, and a wide assortment of programming content was tested in both local and national markets, including shows directed to teenagers. Second, since the advertising industry was extremely interested in the teen demographic during this period, numerous teen-centered shows were programmed in an attempt to reach that market. Third, the large amount of teen programming during the first two decades of television is related to the development of ABC as a TV network. Often constructed in postwar broadcasting discourse as the "new kid on the block" because of its late emergence, ABC struggled far behind CBS and NBC during the networks' transition into television. In an effort to build its audience and gain more advertising revenue, ABC exploited its reputation as the youthful TV network by programming shows appealing to young families with children.

ABC's reputation as the youth-oriented network was further enhanced in the mid-1950s through a partnership with Walt Disney Studios that resulted in the network's broadcasting of *Disneyland* (1954–61). ABC's ties to youthfulness did not begin or end with Disney, however, as is evidenced by the network's ongoing appeal to teenagers throughout the 1950s and 1960s via such programs as *A Date with Judy, Junior Press Conference, American Bandstand,* and *Gidget.* In fact, ABC was also the first network to feature a teenager in a cartoon series, Judy in *The Jetsons* (1962–63). Furthermore, the network's placement of *Shindig* and *The Patty Duke Show* back-to-back during the 1964–65 season created the first block of teen programming on prime-time television. Thus, to a much greater degree than the other two TV networks, ABC helped to integrate teenagers and television during the medium's first two decades in the United States.

Teen Programming, Mid-1960s to Late 1970s

In comparison to the early years of network television, the period between the mid 1960s and the late 1970s saw far less attention paid to teenagers by the TV industry and advertisers. Indeed, despite the popularity of teen-centered sitcoms in the late 1950s and early 1960s, all of those series had ceased production by the summer of 1966. The decline of the teen sitcom during this period is partly the result of teen and media marketing research that demonstrated teenagers' minimal television viewing due to their involvement in various activities outside the family home. Beholden to advertisers for revenue, the TV networks were hesitant to program content for demographic groups that did not often watch television, and therefore commercials.

This rapid decrease in teen representation on television is related also to other transformations happening within the United States during this period. Most significantly, American youth culture changed dramatically over the course of the 1960s and 1970s. For instance, in the mid 1960s the teenage population as a proportion of the total U.S. population began to decline rapidly, a phenomenon that would continue throughout the 1970s as a result of a substantial decrease in the U.S. birth rate. Moreover, by the mid 1960s, the first teenagers exposed to television had aged into young adults, and many were attending college and becoming involved in political and social activism. Often postponing marriage, children, and full-time labor as they pursued further education and alternative lifestyles, these young adults required new forms of entertainment that appealed to their increased knowledge and mature experiences. As a result of these various phenomena, the television industry of the 1960s and early 1970s redirected its attention away from teenagers and teen sitcoms, and toward young adults and more mature fare, producing such programs as *The Mod Squad* (ABC 1968–73), and *Hank* (NBC 1965–66)—the first prime-time show centering on college life.

Although teenagers received little representation in the form of teen sitcoms during the late 1960s and 1970s, teen characters were featured in several animated cartoon series from this period, including *The Archie Show* (CBS 1968–76; NBC 1977–78), *Sabrina, the Teenage Witch* (CBS 1969–74; NBC 1977–78), *Scooby-Doo* (CBS 1969–71, 1978–79), and *Josie and the Pussycats* (CBS 1970–74; NBC 1975–76). In addition, teenagers appeared in several family sit-coms, including *The Brady Bunch* (ABC 1969–74) and *The Partridge Family* (ABC 1970–74). Not surprisingly, these cartoons and family shows featured the same type of characters as their targeted audience members: white, middle-class heterosexuals.

While cartoon series and family sitcoms from the late 1960s and early 1970s rarely addressed topical social issues, such as the Vietnam War or the civil rights movement, other programs from this period did attempt to draw attention to some of these contemporary concerns. For example, *Room 222* (ABC 1969–74), the first dramatic school series, focused on a racially integrated high school in Los Angeles. One of the few teen-centered shows of this period, *Room 222* was highly regarded for its foregrounding of contemporary teenage problems, such as drug use and dropping out of school.

In addition to *Room 222,* several sitcoms were introduced during this period that also drew attention to the experiences of African Americans, including *Good Times* (CBS 1974–79), a family comedy which focused on working-class, urban struggle, and *What's Happening!!* (ABC 1976–79), a teen-oriented sitcom about three male adolescents. *Soul Train* (WCIU-Chicago 1970; syndicated 1971–present), a music/dance program that modeled itself after *American Bandstand,* but featured African-American music, performers, and fans, was introduced during this period also. As the presence of these African-American-themed series suggests, 1970s' television programming demonstrated far more recognition of racial diversity than that of earlier periods. Moreover, such programming revealed an increase in the amount of attention paid to the African-

American consumer market by TV executives and advertisers.

Although the introduction of African-American shows during the 1970s signaled transformations in not only the TV industry but U.S. society at large, there was a considerable segment of the white, middle-class television audience that longed for the allegedly more wholesome times of the 1950s, when issues such as race and class oppression were not explicitly addressed on TV. In addition, several influential interest groups were lobbying the FCC during this period for less sex and violence on television. In response to such concerns, TV executives programmed a variety of nostalgia shows, such as *Little House on the Prairie* (NBC 1974–83) and *The Waltons* (CBS 1972–81), which focused on rural white families during earlier periods of American history.

In an effort to compete with such "quality" nostalgia programming, ABC introduced two domestic series that merged traditional values with contemporary social issues, *Eight is Enough* (ABC 1977–81), which focused on a middle-class white family with eight children, and *Family* (1976–80), which centered on a middle-class white working couple and their children. Both of these series featured teenage characters and often raised contemporary teen issues, such as substance abuse and homosexuality. (Interestingly, despite the television industry's relative lack of attention to teenagers during this period, Kristy McNichol became the first teenage actor to earn an Emmy. In fact, she received two awards for her performance as the teenage daughter on *Family*.)

As a result of a gradual upswing in the teen population and the American economy during the mid-to-late 1970s, teen-specific shows slowly returned to television. The most popular of these shows was *Happy Days* (ABC 1974–84), a sit-com that focused on white, middle-class teenage life in the 1950s. ABC executives attempted to tap further into teen interest and adult nostalgia by adapting two book series continuously popular with different generations of young readers, *The Hardy Boys* and *The Nancy Drew Mysteries* (ABC 1977–79). In addition to *What's Happening!!*, *Welcome Back, Kotter* (ABC 1975–79), which focused on delinquent white, male youth in a Brooklyn school, was one of the few teen programs of the 1970s to focus on contemporary teenagers.

Teen Programming, Early 1980s to Early 2000s

Although teen characters appeared in several family sit-coms of the 1980s, including *Family Ties* (NBC 1982–89), *The Cosby Show* (NBC 1984–92), *Married...with Children* (FOX 1987–97), and *Roseanne* (ABC 1988–97), teenagers gained far more representational space during this period via shows that featured them outside the family home. In fact, the majority of 1980s' teen series focused specifically on high-school experiences. For example, *The Facts of Life* (NBC 1979–88) featured the predominantly teen female milieu of a girls' boarding school. (Though audiences had been introduced to contemporary teen girl issues via the family sitcom *One Day at a Time* [CBS 1975–84], *The Facts of Life* was the first girl-centered sitcom broadcast since 1966, and thus marked a shift away from the male-dominated teen programming of the 1970s.)

Several other school-oriented shows were introduced in the 1980s also, including *Fame* (NBC 1982–83), a dramatic series based on a film about the racially and class-integrated High School of Performing Arts in New York City; *Head of the Class* (ABC 1986–91), which focused on students "gifted" with superior intelligence; and *Saved by the Bell* (NBC 1989–93), which began airing during afternoons and moved later into prime-time. Although not strictly located within the educational milieu, *The Wonder Years* (ABC 1988–93) often made use of school sitcom conventions in its depiction of a teenage boy growing up in the 1960s. *Doogie Howser, M.D.* (ABC 1989–93) attempted to merge the different spheres of high school and higher education by focusing on a gifted teen in medical school. Meanwhile, *A Different World* (NBC 1987–93), a spin-off of *The Cosby Show*, featured the first African-American college youth on TV.

Perhaps the most significant teen-specific television phenomenon of the 1980s was the introduction of Music Television (MTV). Debuting in 1981, MTV began as a cable network devoted to the broadcasting of promotional videos for popular music. Taking many of its cues from earlier teen-oriented music shows, like *American Bandstand*, MTV has consistently promoted itself as a youth-oriented medium. Continuously ranked as the network most watched by teenagers, MTV has appealed primarily to white, upper-middle-class, male adolescent viewers (specifically those with cable or satellite subscriptions), a niche market that prior to the 1980s showed little interest in watching television.

As MTV expanded its appeal to teenagers throughout the 1990s and afterwards, particularly by internationalizing its operations and moving beyond its original music-oriented programming, other TV networks also increased their attention to teens. Indeed, teenagers had more prime-time representation between 1990 and 2000 than during the previous two decades combined. The large amount of teen-specific programming during this period was no doubt the result of tremendous booms in both the American economy and the teen population. In turn, this rise in teen programming is related to various transformations in the TV industry, especially the increased amount of media-industry conglomeration and the introduction of cable and satellite delivery systems.

One of the more significant aspects of this period was the TV and advertising industries' specific appeal to female youth as television viewers. Given the considerable amount of recent marketing research demonstrating that girls tend to watch TV more than boys (due in part to female youth having less independence from parents and homes), girls, who also tend to shop more than boys, became the most appealing niche market for those advertisers interested in attracting the large 1990s' teen demographic.

Not surprisingly, the teen sitcom was one of the primary genres to feature teenagers in the 1990s. Several popular teen comedies from the 1980s continued into the next decade, while a considerable number of new shows were introduced also, including *Hull High* (NBC 1990), *Fresh Prince of Bel Air* (NBC 1990–96), *Blossom* (NBC 1991–95), *Phenom* (ABC 1993–94), *Boy Meets World* (ABC 1993–2000), *Sister, Sister* (WB 1994–99), *Moesha* (UPN 1995–2001), *Clueless* (ABC 1996–97; UPN 1997–99), *Sabrina, the Teenage Witch* (ABC 1996–2001; WB 2001–present), and *That '70s Show* (FOX 1998–present). Attesting to the considerable popularity of *Saved by the Bell,* when the series ended in 1993, a new show based on the original was introduced, *Saved by the Bell: The New Class* (NBC 1993–2000).

Although teenage representation in 1990s' television was largely associated with the teen sitcom, teenage characters also appeared in animated cartoons, such as *Beavis and Butt-head* (MTV 1993–97) and *Daria* (MTV 1997–2001). One of the most significant programming phenomena of this period, however, was the emergence of the teen-centered dramatic serial, which merged conventions of soap operas, teen sitcoms, and other genres that have traditionally featured adult characters, such as horror and science fiction. Some of the more popular teen serials introduced in the 1990s include *Beverly Hills, 90210* (FOX 1990–2000), *Party of Five* (FOX 1994–2000), *Buffy the Vampire Slayer* (WB 1997–2001; UPN 2001–2003), *Dawson's Creek* (WB 1998–2002), and *Roswell* (WB 1999–2002).

Many of these teen serials relied on the coming-of-age tropes already associated with the teen sitcom; however, due to their adherence to melodramatic conventions, these serials also included issues of concern to contemporary teenagers, such as sexual experimentation, gang membership, and teen pregnancy. While the majority of 1990s' teen programs focused on white, middle-class teenagers, a considerable number

of series included various types of youth marginalized by the TV industry in earlier periods. For example, several teen sitcoms focused specifically on African-American youth, including *Hull High, Fresh Prince of Bel Air, Moesha,* and *Sister, Sister,* while many other teen shows featured mixed-race casts. In turn, several teen serials from this period included forms of youth identity traditionally excluded from TV programming. For instance, *My So-Called Life* (ABC 1994–95) was the first prime-time series to include a bisexual teenager; *The Mystery Files of Shelby Woo* (Nickelodeon 1996–99) was the first prime-time program to feature an Asian-American teen; and *Dangerous Minds* (ABC 1996–97) was the first prime-time show to focus on Latino youth.

Teenage TV Viewing and the "Teen" Demographic

While the broadcasting of teen programming is clearly related to marketers' attempts to attract a specific group of consumers, research on TV viewing habits conducted at various points during the past five decades demonstrates that teenagers use this medium far less than any other demographic group except infants. Because of their interest in non-domestic activities that involve the privileging of peer, rather than familial, relationships, many teenagers do not rely on television as their primary leisure activity. Although television has always competed for teen consumers with other forms of entertainment and leisure, the increasing penetration of personal computers, the Internet, and the World Wide Web into American homes over the course of the late-20th and early-21st centuries has led to an even greater decline in teen TV viewing.

The fifty-odd-year tradition of teenagers' minimal television use calls into question the assumed relationship between teen programming and teenage viewers. Indeed, ratings for many recent teen-centered series suggest that those individuals perhaps most invested in teen programming today are not teenagers (who typically steer clear of products marketed as "teen"), but rather those viewers who look to teenagers as role models, especially pre-teens and young adults. Thus, while the teen audience originally constructed by early TV executives and advertisers may have been restricted to actual teenagers, today's "teen" demographic now encompasses viewers between the ages of 12 and 34.

The recent expansion of TV's "teen" demographic is due to transformations in both the television industry and generational identities over the last few decades. For instance, better nutrition is causing children to mature physically at an earlier age than ever before, and advertisers are encouraging them to adopt aspirational behaviors at younger ages than members of previous generations. These children often look up to teenagers as their primary role models. At the same time, an increasing number of young adults, particularly those of the middle class, are prolonging adolescence via their enrollment in college, as well as graduate and professional schools. Moreover, a considerable number of these young adults are postponing or rejecting the traditional rituals of adulthood, particularly marriage and children, and continue to be drawn to various aspects of youth culture.

As a result of these various social phenomena, adolescence is no longer a life stage associated with only those in their teenage years, and has become instead an identity that describes a much broader group of individuals. This expansion of adolescent identity works well in relation to the marketplace, since youthfulness is an attitude and lifestyle that is particularly exploitable in American society. Thus manufacturers, retailers, and advertisers use youthfulness to cash in on not just teenagers, but also pre-teens, who are encouraged by the market to buy commodities produced for older consumers, as well as many adults, who, despite their age, are encouraged by the market to think, act, look, and, most importantly, shop as if they were young.

These changes in generational identity are interestingly related to recent transformations in the television industry. For instance, over the last two decades, the traditional mass audience has been increasingly fragmented due to the greater amount of programming made possible via cable and satellite delivery systems. Thus, networks are no longer able to rely on earlier programming strategies to attract a large audience, such as broadcasting programs targeting families with children. As a result, in the 1980s and early 1990s networks began to turn to other programming strategies, especially narrowcasting, which appeals to smaller, lucrative demographic segments, such as middle-class women. Nevertheless, since narrowcasting cannot attract a large enough number of viewers to maintain the high ratings needed to satisfy advertisers, new networks struggling to get a foothold in the industry have built their audiences by attracting a coalition of viewers who do not share a similar demographic identity, but have a similar sensibility or aspire to a similar lifestyle. (This strategy of targeting viewers with particular interests is now far easier as the result of new digital TV technologies, such as TiVo, that record data on individual viewers' programming interests, which is then made available to advertisers.)

Given that the "teen" demographic is now seen as one of the most lucrative markets, young networks such as FOX and WB have targeted upscale viewers aged 12 to 34 who share a youthful sensibility to build their coalition audiences. To attract such viewers, these networks have relied considerably on teen programming. Moreover, in an attempt to reach the most lucrative segment of this demographic—those who own a personal computer and subscribe to an Internet service provider—these networks have developed websites, like www.buffy.com, that supplement their teen series. By visiting such a website, viewers can join a show's official fan club, purchase products related to the series or its network, and obtain information about the show's history, stars, and upcoming episodes. In addition, several websites associated with teen series include chat rooms where fans communicate with other viewers and, at times, a show's production staff.

The development of such TV-associated websites, the transformation of the teen demographic, the inclusion of teenagers in traditionally adult-oriented genres, and the debut of teen-oriented cable networks are all evidence of the profoundly different nature of the contemporary television industry and teen programming. Given that the teenage population in the United States is predicted to increase until 2010, and marketers' reliance on discourses of youthfulness shows no evidence of abating anytime soon, we can reasonably expect that teenagers will continue to have a strong presence in TV programming during the remainder of the 21st century's first decade.

MARY CELESTE KEARNEY

*See also **American Bandstand; Beavis and Butthead; Beverly Hills, 90210; Buffy the Vampire Slayer; Different World, A; Happy Days; Monkees, The;** MTV; **Room 222; Wonder Years, The***

Further Reading

Gilbert, Eugene, *Advertising and Marketing to Young People,* New York: Printers' Ink Books, 1957

Kearney, Mary Celeste, "The Changing Face of Teen Television, or Why We All Love *Buffy,*" in *Red Noise: Critical Writings on* Buffy the Vampire Slayer, edited by Elana Levine and Lisa Parks, Durham, North Carolina: Duke University Press, 2002

Leibman, Nina C., *Living Room Lectures: The Fifties Family in Film and Television,* Austin: University of Texas Press, 1995

Luckett, Moya, "Girl Watchers: Patty Duke and Teen TV," *The Revolution Wasn't Televised: Sixties Television and Social Conflict,* edited by Lynn Spigel and Michael Curtin, New York: Routledge, 1997

Palladino, Grace, *Teenagers: An American History,* New York: Basic Books, 1996

Spigel, Lynn, *Make Room for TV: Television and the Family Ideal in Postwar America,* Chicago: University of Chicago Press, 1992

Taylor, Ella, *Prime-Time Families: Television Culture in Postwar America,* Berkeley: University of California Press, 1989

Zollo, Peter, *Wise Up to Teens: Insights into Marketing and Advertising to Teenagers,* New York: New Strategist Publications, 1995; 2nd edition, 1999

Telcos

Telephone companies (telcos) have always figured in the history of U.S. television, though in most other countries they have been minor players until the convergence of telephony, computer, and broadcasting technologies in the 1990s. The earliest involvement of telephone companies in broadcasting dates to AT&T's interest in radio. Before World War I, AT&T was one among several companies actively experimenting with radio waves in order to control what seemed to be an imminent wireless communication era. AT&T's ownership stake in the government-formed Radio Corporation of America (RCA) in the early 1920s seemed to guarantee the phone company a role in radio broadcasting, specifically with respect to developing the international market, selling transmitters, and providing telephony. However, AT&T's definition of telephony broadened in 1922 when it offered a special toll broadcasting service allowing people to use its "radio telephony" channels to send out their own programs—for a fee. At that time, AT&T eschewed any interest in controlling content. It used its long-distance lines to broadcast sports events, music, and other entertainment, avowing that it desired only its rightful opportunity to transmit. Nevertheless, by 1924 the phone company had a regular radio programming schedule.

Its early control over broadcasting was broken up, however, by the Federal Trade Commission's objections to the apparent growing monopoly power in radio. In 1926 a new structure was created to answer monopoly charges against AT&T, relegating the phone company to a role in transmission only while other companies involved in radio (General Electric, Westinghouse, and RCA) formed the National Broadcasting Company and developed programming and an audience-oriented service.

AT&T, then the United States' regulated, dominant national telephone carrier, operated as the transmission system for networked broadcasting for several decades, conveying first radio and later television signals across the country, thereby enabling the formation of national networks through its long-distance links. The carriage fees it accumulated from broadcasters were enormous, and as the sanctioned, monopoly inter-state common carrier, AT&T had the business to itself even though that monopoly role was at times contested. The company's first serious setbacks in the form of competition from other carriers did not occur until the mid-1970s.

In the 1970s regulatory liberalization in two realms undermined AT&T's control of transmission services essential to television. First, communication satellites, an outgrowth of the U.S. space program, provided new, efficient and economical ways to transmit messages or signals over long distances. Although AT&T retained a major role for itself in international satellite communication through provisions in the 1962 Communication Satellite Act (it was a partner in the public corporation Comsat, designated to operate U.S. satellite communications within the international satellite network Intelsat), that Act set the stage for other companies to enter into domestic satellite services. The so-called "open skies" policy adopted in 1972 by the Federal Trade Commission's successor in the real of broadcasting, the Federal Communications Commission (FCC), allowed financially qualified carriers to provide domestic satellite communications, opening a new market and method for interstate transmissions. Ultimately, this development provided crucial alternatives to television's (and cable television's) continued reliance on AT&T for transmission. In particular, telephone companies were unable to control domestic satellite services, which became the preferred and cost-effective method for broadcast and cable television networks to deliver their signals, thus ending their dependence on AT&T for interconnection. The successful launch of HBO nationwide on RCA's Satcom satellite in 1975 bypassed AT&T and illustrated a future for cable television independent of the telcos. The Public Broadcasting Service moved to satellite distribution of its signal in 1978, followed by the major television networks' migration from AT&T to satellites controlled by other carriers in the mid-1980s.

The second realm concerned the cable industry. Skirmishes between telcos and the young cable television industry prompted the FCC and Congress to limit telcos' ability to own and operate cable television systems. Because early cable systems relied on retransmitted broadcast fare, it seemed logical for a carrier such as AT&T to establish cable systems using its lines to transmit content from broadcasters to subscribers. However, the FCC ruled in 1970 that telcos could operate systems only in small, rural populations. As well, in 1978, affirming that AT&T had abused its power in overcharging companies that wished to use its poles to establish cable television service, Congress enacted the Pole Attachment Act authorizing the FCC to "regulate the rates and conditions for pole attachments," effectively removing the telcos' control over a key access and right-of-way issue and allowing cable television to expand under more favorable terms. It was clear that the FCC intended to restrain the telcos' ability to enter into or otherwise control this new television medium. The cable television industry's insistence on this restraint is in part reflected in a section of the later 1984 Cable Communications Act that reiterated the 1970 telco–cable cross-ownership ban and explicitly forbade telephone companies from offering cable television services.

However, telephone companies' interest in video services never died. If the aforementioned two new communication technologies ultimately underscored telcos' limited hold on an expanding set of services, they also can be counted among the causes of a massive restructuring of the U.S. telephone system under the 1982 Modification of Final Judgment (MFJ), a federal court ruling that broke up AT&T's monopoly telephone service in the United States. The result of a long-standing inquiry into AT&T's vertical integration and possible abuse of power under antitrust laws, the MFJ separated long-distance (interexchange) service from local telephone service, determining that the former would be a new competitive marketplace while the latter would be relegated to continuing monopoly service. AT&T restructured, spinning off the "Baby Bells" (regional companies that were restricted to the provision of a local telephone service) and moving into the newly competitive long-distance service market. Both sets of companies, AT&T and other long-distance service providers (interexchange carriers), as well as the local service providers, again eyed the provision of video services as one among a number of future competitive possibilities.

The MFJ put several restrictions on AT&T, the most notable being a seven-year restriction on entering into "electronic publishing." Nevertheless, by the late 1980s and 1990s AT&T, as well as several other telcos, had constructed a number of strategic liaisons with cable television, computer, software, and even movie companies in order to position themselves for new video and multimedia services. Such liaisons built on the telephone companies' longstanding interest in new media as well as their abortive history of attempting to provide teletext or videotext services in conjunction with publishers.

In the 1980s and 1990s, notions of media competition were shifting, and many industries, analysts and policymakers foresaw a future in which various media platforms could provide services that cut across traditional industry definitions. Amid the deregulatory fever of the 1980s initiated by the AT&T divestiture, the FCC recommended lifting the cable–telco cross-ownership ban in 1988, but the requisite Congressional action was not forthcoming. Nevertheless, continued restructuring of telecommunications industries proceeded, ultimately facilitating the convergence of what had been conceived originally as quite separate video, voice, and data services.

Moving toward the landmark 1996 Telecommunications Act, in 1992 the FCC issued its "Video Dialtone" order allowing telcos (such as the "Baby Bells" or other local exchange companies) to provide the technological platforms for video services to subscribers. Essentially this also allowed them to enter the video services business, albeit without permitting them directly to own programming. One year later, in response to separate suits brought by telcos, several district courts began lifting the cable–telco cross-ownership ban. The first such suit was brought in 1993 (*Chesapeake and Potomac Telephone Co. of Virginia v. U.S., 830 F. Supp. 909*) by Bell Atlantic, a telco that, in the same year, proposed a merger with the largest cable company in the United States, TCI, a deal which later collapsed. Additionally, in the mid-1990s several telcos announced plans to provide video services as cable companies which would allow them to own programming rather than as telephone companies operating a video dialtone platform. Full-scale telco competition with cable companies and their broad entry into the video programming marketplace seemed imminent.

The desire of telephone companies to enter new markets, especially those providing video programming, was one major impetus behind the 1996 legislation that restructured American media industries. The 1996 Telecommunications Act authorized telephone and cable companies to enter each other's businesses, and also allowed then-monopoly local-exchange phone companies, the Baby Bells, to compete with long-distance companies (and vice versa), and to move into various other businesses as well. The act prompted major new initiatives and restructuring across the telecommunications industries. However, in spite of Congress's anticipation of the emergence of a far more competitive framework for delivering video programming, the cable–telco struggle did not materialize. Instead, wholesale mergers and acquisitions ensued in numerous communications industries, resulting in a new corporate and organizational profile for radio, broadcasting, cable, and telephony providers, and the newer service of providing Internet access. Because the Act coincided with a burst of services dependent on fast, packet-switched networks and growing computer penetration in homes and businesses, organizational restructuring was accompanied by the emergence of new services that once again depended heavily on existing transmission providers and the networks operated by telephone companies.

The raft of mergers among telephone companies accompanied new service opportunities. The industry shrank to many fewer companies within a few years of the 1996 act. For example, by 2001 the seven Baby Bells had become four: Southwestern Bell purchased PacTel (serving the west coast) and Ameritech (serving the Midwest), and later renamed itself SBC; Bell Atlantic (eastern seaboard) merged with NYNEX (New York region), and later merged again with the large independent phone company GTE to become Verizon; US West, serving 14 western states, was bought by long-distance carrier Qwest. Only Bell South made no major, comparable acquisition. However, even as their numbers shrank, the companies themselves took on more extensive services, including providing both dial-up and broadband Internet connections, wireless telephony, backbone Internet transmission (Qwest and Sprint in particular) and local and long-distance voice communications.

On the long-distance company front, AT&T's old competitor MCI was purchased by upstart long-distance company Worldcom in 1997, only for that company to be distressed under accounting scandals (filing for bankruptcy in 2002). AT&T was split into several different companies since its divestiture, and the 1996 act catalyzed its merger with the large cable Multiple System Operators MediaOne, and later TCI, in March 1999, making AT&T the largest cable company in the country. As part of that merger it acquired the substantial programming resources of Liberty Media, a holding company controlling numerous cable programming networks that AT&T spun off in August 2001. AT&T Broadband later merged with Comcast, yet another large cable operator.

What was common to all the telecommunications companies was the recognition that the networks—particularly new, digital, fiber-based networks—were, in the emerging age of the Internet, of renewed importance. Some, such as Sprint and Qwest, invested large sums of money in constructing digital nationwide packet-switched networks in order to be ready for an environment dependent on Internet protocol modes. Qwest also began to offer video programming over its telephone lines in a handful of markets using fiber-based, very high-speed digital subscriber lines (DSLs). The Baby Bells, which experienced relatively little erosion of their customer base to competition within the first five years after the 1996 Act, focused more on achieving the ability to offer long-distance telephone services within their territories and on readying their networks in metropolitan regions for offering broadband ISP connections. Such services, based on digital subscriber-line technology that conventionally utilizes the already in-place copper wires, accelerated among the telcos when cable companies offered broadband cable modem services. The telcos' DSL services had the advantage of using already existing connections to homes to support phone and Internet access services simultaneously. At the same time, cable systems upgraded their regional infrastructure to hybrid fiber-coaxial cable physical plant to enable digital programming delivery as well as fast Internet access using cable modems. The cable companies were finally competing with the telephone companies, but in the unanticipated service area of providing high-speed Internet connectivity.

A significant development barely glimpsed at the time of the 1996 Telecommunications Act—the growing significance of the Internet and its future role in providing audio and video content—has reshaped the business plans of telephone companies alongside those of all other media businesses. Competition between cable operators and telephone companies primarily has focused on Internet services in the first years of the new century, each industry using its own enhanced infrastructure rather than building entirely new networks. However, the telephone companies are poised to make that investment in new plant, as packet-switched networks become mandatory for services dependent on Internet protocols. For example, Voice over Internet Protocol or VoIP is one such service that enables inexpensive long-distance calling using packet-switched networks. Additionally, some telephone companies are offering cable-style television services over their broadband networks. Enabling high-speed connections to subscribers and cost-efficient connections to the national Internet backbones are far higher priorities in the early 21st century than could have been anticipated in 1996, and entirely new services are probably not far behind.

With new emphasis on creating an information infrastructure providing multiple services, the role of telephone companies, in providing digital video programming and Internet-based audio and video media, seems certain. Deregulating telcos and other communications industries has set the stage for creating a new generation of digital services as well as an entirely new set of corporate powers. A new tier of services will join voice and data transmission as key elements in the telephone business, and television is likely to be one of them.

SHARON STROVER

See also **U.S. Policy: Telecommunications Act of 1996**

Further Reading

Barnouw, E., *Tube of Plenty: The Evolution of American Television,* New York: Oxford University Press, 1975

Horwitz, R., *The Irony of Regulatory Reform: The Deregulation of American Telecommunications,* New York: Oxford University Press, 1989

Negroponte, N., *Being Digital,* New York: Knopf, and London: Hodder and Stoughton, 1995

Oxley, Michael G., "The Cable–Telco Cross-Ownership Prohibition: First Amendment Infringement Through Obsolescence," *Federal Communications Law Journal* (December 1993)

Parsons, P., and Robert M. Frieden, *The Cable and Satellite Television Industries,* Boston: Allyn and Bacon, 1998

Telecommunications Act of 1996

U.S. Communications Policy Legislation

The Telecommunications Act of 1996, which passed on February 1 of that year, became the first successful attempt to rewrite the 70-year old Communications Act of 1934. The 1996 law, which took nearly four years of legislative work, refocused federal communications policymaking after years of confused, intergovernmental attempts to regulate the rapidly evolving telecommunications industry. The act provided for increased competition among different technologies and greatly lessened ownership and regulatory burdens in various telecommunications sections, while preserving Congress's leadership role as the dominant policymaker.

While portions of the act became effective immediately after President Bill Clinton signed the legislation, much of the implementation needed to wait for the Federal Communications Commission (FCC) to promulgate new or revised rules and regulations. Noting the historic nature of the bill, President Clinton claimed that the legislation would "provide open access for all citizens to the Information Superhighway." However, many public-interest groups expressed concern that the effect of the act would be to undermine public-interest values of access.

At the time of passage, the act included several highly controversial provisions that were seen as restricting speech and violating constitutional protections. Within hours of the president's signing, a number of civil liberties groups, led by the American Civil Liberties Union (ACLU), sought an injunction against indecency provisions included in the legislation.

The Telecommunications Act of 1996 is a complex reform of U.S. communication policymaking, which attempts to provide similar ground rules and a level playing field in virtually all sectors of the communications industries. The act's provisions fall into five general areas: radio and television broadcasting; cable television; telephone services; Internet and online computer services; and telecommunications equipment manufacturing.

The Telecommunications Act fundamentally changed U.S. communication policy by abolishing many of the cross-market barriers that prohibited dominant players from one communications-industry sector, such as telecommunications, from providing services in another industry sector, such as cable television. Since 1996 new mergers and acquisitions, consolidations, and integration of services previously barred under FCC rules and antitrust provisions of federal law have occurred.

Radio and Television Broadcasting

The act incorporated numerous changes to the rules dealing with radio and television ownership under the Communications Act of 1934. Notably, broadcasters received substantial regulatory relief from federal restrictions on station-ownership requirements. The basic structure of the broadcast industry was fundamentally altered, abolishing 60 years of restrictions upheld since the Communications Act of 1934. Ownership limits on television stations were lifted, with group owners now able to purchase television stations with a maximum service-area cap of 35 percent of the U.S. population. Limits on the number of radio stations that may be commonly owned were completely lifted, although the legislation prescribes limits on the number of licenses that may be owned within specific markets or geographical areas.

Terms of license for both radio and television were increased to eight years, and previous rules allowing competing applications for license renewals were dramatically altered in favor of incumbent licensees. New provisions under the act prevent the filing of a competing application at license-renewal time unless the FCC first finds that a station has *not* served the public interest or has committed other serious violations of agency or federal rules. This provision has made it very difficult for citizens' groups to mount a license challenge against a broadcast station. The language in the 1996 bill gives the FCC no guidance as to how to interpret the "public-interest" standard in light of the legislated mandates embedded in the act. According to public-interest groups opposed to the relaxation of ownership provisions, the combined effect of the new rules has been to accelerate increased ownership of most major media outlets by a few communications conglomerates. Within five years of the act's passage, substantial consolidation within the broadcasting industry and telecommunications sectors had occurred.

The Telecommunications Act of 1996 also made significant changes in FCC rules regarding station affiliations and cross-ownership restrictions. Stations may choose affiliation with more than one network. Although broadcasting networks are barred from merging or buying-out other networks, they have been freed to started new program services. For the first time, broadcasters can own cable television systems, and some television licensees have been granted waivers to operate newspapers in the same market. The legislation also affirmed the continuation of local marketing agreements (LMAs) and waived previous restrictions on common control of radio and television stations in the top fifty markets, the one-to-a-market rule.

Perhaps the biggest concession to the broadcast industry centered around provisions for allowing the FCC to allocate extra spectrum for the creation of advanced television (ATV) and ancillary services. Eligibility for advanced television licenses was limited to existing television licensees, ensuring current broadcasters a future in providing digital and enhanced television services. Subsequent actions by the FCC authorized an additional 6-MHz spectrum for a digital television service. The commission has developed a timetable and plan for migration to digital television. However, although the FCC has established a transition deadline, set for 2006, it seems unlikely that broadcasters will have digital television services in place by that time.

Not all portions of the Telecommunications Act were welcomed by broadcasters. The use of the V-chip was opposed by many in the broadcast industry. The law mandates use of new technology to allow parents to exercise control over channels viewed, and section 551 requires the development of a system to identify and rate video programming that contains sexual, violent, or indecent material. Congress also included language within the act to mandate the manufacture of televisions with V-chip technology, and the FCC has implemented rules.

Generally, however, the Telecommunication Act of 1996 provides for new possibilities for broadcasters and calls for the FCC to eliminate unnecessary oversight rules. Under the mandate, the FCC is required to revisit its regulatory requirements biennially to determine whether the rules are in the public interest. This review process has allowed the commission to restate its policy interpretations as leadership in the commission has changed.

Common Carriers and Telecommunication Services

While the Telecommunications Act set out to create a deregulated environment to promote competition in telephony and speed the introduction of advanced communication services by opening all telecommunications markets to competition, there is debate within the policy community as to the effectiveness of the legislation. Within the area of long-distance telephony, major players have seen a sharp increase in competition from smaller service providers, but consolidation in the industry has resulted in a sharp decline of the number of regional Bell operating companies (RBOCs) providing local telephony service. Language within title 2 of the bill, meant to encourage competition within local telephony markets, has failed to generate meaningful competition in most areas of the United States.

The Telecommunications Act also provides for cable television and other public utilities to be able to provide telecommunications services in competition with telephone companies. High-speed broadband services using cable modems and Internet telephony are two examples of services allowed as a result of the legislation, although the introduction and consumer acceptance of such services has been relatively slow. Common carriers were allowed to provide video services through telecommunications networks on a nondiscriminatory basis. To make competition among common carriers more viable, telephone-number portability was mandated in the act, as was access to local network connections.

The law preserved the longstanding notion of providing "universal service" (affordable telecommunications services to all users), and language within the act called for making enhanced telecommunications services available to rural as well as urban users. The act also provided for the interconnection of all schools to advanced telecommunication services, paid through access fees assessed to long-distance telephone calls. Hospitals and libraries benefited from universal access provisions of the act.

Perhaps the most controversial portion of the Telecommunications Act of 1996 was subsection title 5, the Communications Decency Act (CDA). The CDA made it a criminal offense for Internet Service Providers (ISPs) to knowingly disseminate indecent material to minors. Prior to passage of the bill, language in the CDA was roundly criticized by civil rights and First Amendment groups alike, and Congress, fearing a constitutional challenge to the entire legislative package, provided for fast-track judicial review of title 5. In June 1997, in *Reno* v. *ACLU,* the U.S. Supreme Court declared the Communications Decency Act to be unconstitutional, although it continued to affirm the FCC's right to enforce an indecency standard on broadcasters.

States and local entities are restricted under the act from imposing local zoning regulations to prohibit the placement and growth of the wireless telecommunication services within the local community.

Cable Television Services

The Telecommunications Act lifted the cable/telephony company (telco) cross-ownership and service restrictions that had been imposed by the Cable Act of 1984. A wide range of cross-ownership barriers between broadcast, cable, and telecommunications were lifted in the hope of spurring competition. As a result, AT&T, the largest long-distance carrier in the United States, became the largest cable operator when it purchased TeleCommunications Incorporated (TCI), to provide enhanced telecommunications services via cable. The act also deregulated upper-tier rates for cable services and allowed cable operators to aggregate their equipment costs in more traditional accounting methods in hopes of providing incentives for new programming and services.

Cable operators were eligible to purchase broadcasting facilities and to provide telecommunication services that could compete with telephony companies. Broadband services, such as high-speed cable modems, and IP telephony are examples of advanced services that Congress hoped would provide competition to common carriers. Five years after the passage of the act, however, only 6 percent of Americans were receiving advanced services through cable operators.

The Telecommunications Act's Impact

The overall impact of the Telecommunications Act of 1996 on consumers has been hard to gauge. Generally, the law's passage coincided with a buoyant economy and a broad expansion of telecommunication investment and growth of Internet services. Investment in telecommunications grew at an unprecedented 25 percent per year rate until 2001, when there was a marked slowdown in each of the these areas. However, an overextension in installing new telecommunication infrastructure and shaky accounting practices caused the demise of many small and large telecommunications companies. As a result, since 2001 there has been a general retrenchment of telecommunications revenues and deflating of investment in the industrial sector. In the five years after the law passed, telecommunications services did not see the expected increase in competition or lowering of costs associated with moving toward a market economy. By 2002, traditional local telephone companies still controlled 92 percent of all local traffic, and long-distance telephone services look virtually unchanged from 1996. Growth in wireless telephony has been significant, but the major players are giant telecommunications conglomerates.

Competition within industry segments has failed to materialize. Cable television has seen some growth in competition from direct broadcast satellite services, but the number of players in the broadcasting field has generally diminished, marginalizing smaller broadcasters in favor of larger group owners. Competition between service sections has failed to materialize too, as both cable- and satellite-service companies continue to consolidate. The hoped-for competition between cable- and telecommunications-service providers has also not occurred. Few telecommunications companies appear interested in providing video-service options, and growth in IP telephony has failed to meet industry expectations. In broadcasting, most television stations missed the deadline for meeting FCC requirements in the transition to digital television, and consumer acceptance of digital sets has been slowed by standardization problems between broadcasters and cable operators for set-top boxes and digital must-carry requirements.

Critics of the legislation point to the continued convergence of telecommunications services among several large media conglomerates as an indication that the act has failed in its intent to establish new and low-cost alternatives to traditional telecommunication services. Consumer groups point to rising cable and local telephone rates as indicators of failed attempts to stimulate cross-industry competition. While growth in telecommunications is seen as essential, the overall effect of the Telecommunications Act of 1996 in the first five years since its passage was disappointing.

FRITZ MESSERE

See also **Allocation; Cable Networks; Cable Television: United States; Communications Act of 1934; License; Ownership; Telcos**

Further Reading

Andrews, E.L., "Congress Votes to Reshape Communications Industry Ending a 4-Year Struggle," *New York Times* (February 2, 1996)

Andrews, E.L., "What the Bill Already Did," *New York Times* (February 2, 1996)

Andrews, E.L., "President Signs Telecommunications Bill," *New York Times* (February 9, 1996)

Hinden, S., "The Greatest Telecommunications Show in Years: The 1996 Legislation Leaves Fund Managers Wondering: Which Company's Act Is a Winner?" *Washington Post* (March 24, 1996)

Lewis, P.H., "Internet Courtroom Battle Gets Cyberspace," *New York Times* (March 20, 1996)

Nichols, John, and Robert W. McChesney, "Turning the Tide: It's Time to Fight the Enronization of the Media," *In These Times* (April 15, 2002)

Raysman, R., and P. Brown, "Liability of Internet Access Provider under Decency Act," *New York Law Journal* (March 12, 1996)

Rosenbush, Steve, "Broadband Policy: Did Somebody say Oligopoly?" *Business Week* (March 18, 2002)

Rosenbush, Steve, and Peter Elstrom, "Eight Lessons from the Telecom Mess," *Business Week* (August 13, 2001)

Roycroft, Trevor R., "The Telecom Act: Law of Unintended Consequences?" *Public Utilities Fortnightly* (February 1, 2000)

Telecommunications Industry Association, "The Telecom Act from A to Z," *www.tiaonline.org/policy/telecom_act/a-to-z.cfm*

Telefilm Canada

Canadian Television and Film Development Corporation

Telefilm Canada is a Crown Corporation of the Canadian federal government. Its mandate is to support the development and promotion of television programs and feature films by the Canadian private sector. Telefilm is neither a producer nor a distributor, and it is not equipped with a production studio; instead, it acts primarily as a banker and deals principally with independent Canadian producers. To this end, Telefilm invests over $175 million annually through a variety of funds and programs that encompass production, distribution, and marketing, scriptwriting, dubbing and subtitling, festivals, and professional development. In 2000–2001, Telefilm funded the development or production of nearly 800 projects. Telefilm Canada also administers the official coproduction treaties that exist between Canada and 57 countries, including France, Great Britain, Germany, Australia, and New Zealand.

Until 1984 Telefilm Canada was known as the Canadian Film Development Corporation (CFDC). The CFDC began operations in 1968 with a budget of $10 million and a mandate to foster and promote the development of a feature-film industry in Canada through the provision of loans, grants, and awards to Canadian producers and filmmakers. Unlike the National Film Board of Canada (NFB), or the Canadian Broadcasting Corporation (CBC), the CFDC was expected to be-

come a self-financing agency, interested as much (if not more) in the profitability of the films it supported as in their contribution to Canada's cultural life.

By 1971 the CFDC had exhausted its original budget and recouped barely $600,000, or roughly 9 percent, of its investments in 64 projects. In keeping with its commercial orientation, the CFDC contributed to a number of films, such as *Love is a 4 Letter World* (1970), that came to be referred to as "maple-syrup porn." At the same time, the CFDC invested in a number of films such as *Goin' Down the Road* (1970) that have come to be regarded as Canadian classics.

The federal government approved a second allotment of $10 million in 1971, and for the next six years the CFDC and industry representatives struggled to establish a clear set of corporate objectives. One option, which would have transformed the CFDC into something of an arts council for feature films and brought it closer in line with the mandate of the NFB, was to rechannel CFDC money into a system of grants that would provide for the production of a small number of Canadian films a year. The other option was to rechannel the CFDC's priorities toward the production of feature films with strong box-office potential, in particular films that would be attractive to the Hollywood majors.

This second option became viable after changes in

tax regulations were accompanied by a change in the CFDC's financial practices. In 1974 the capital cost allowance for Canadian feature films was extended from 30 percent to 100 percent. In 1978 the CFDC shifted its focus from the provision of equity financing for low- and medium-budget Canadian films to the provision of bridge financing for projects that were designed to take advantage of the tax shelter. Both the number of productions and average budgets soared. Measured in terms of employment and total dollars spent, the tax-shelter boom was a success. However, many of the films produced during this period were never distributed, and many of the ones that did receive distribution were second-rate attempts at films that mimicked Hollywood's standard fare (notable examples include *Meatballs* and *Running*). By 1980 there was growing criticism of the direction taken by the CFDC, particularly from French-Canadian producers and filmmakers who benefited far less than their English-Canadian counterparts from the CFDC's shift in investment priorities. The tax-shelter boom came to a crashing halt in 1980.

The establishment of the Canadian Broadcast Program Development Fund in July 1983 dramatically shifted the CFDC's priorities from feature films to television programming. To reflect this shift in investment priorities, the CFDC was renamed Telefilm Canada in February 1984. The Broadcast Fund has four overall objectives: to stimulate production of high-quality, culturally relevant Canadian television programs in targeted categories (drama, children's, documentary, and variety programming); to reach the broadest possible audience with those programs through scheduling during prime-time viewing hours; to stimulate the development of the independent production industry; and to maintain an appropriate regional, linguistic, and private/public broadcaster balance in the distribution of public funds. The fund had an initial budget of $254 million spread over five years. Since 1988 Telefilm has invested more than $60 million annually in television programming. On average its participation represents 33 percent of the total production budget.

The Broadcast Fund has been enormously successful in achieving its original objectives. Between 1986 and 1990, for example, the fund helped finance close to $800 million in total production volume in 2,275 hours of original television programming, of which more than 1,000 hours consisted of dramatic programming exhibited during peak viewing hours. Among these programs were *Anne of Green Gables*, the various *Degrassi* series, *E.N.G.*, *Danger Bay*, *Love and War*, *Due South*, and *The Boys of St. Vincent*. In terms of audience reach, viewing of Canadian programs in peak time has increased substantially. The Broadcast Fund has also played a crucial role in providing independent Canadian producers with the leverage to expand into export markets.

In April 2001 Telefilm undertook the administration of a new Canadian Feature Film Fund (CFFF). With an annual budget of $100 million, the CFFF has four objectives: to develop and retain talented creators in Canada; to encourage quality and diversity of Canadian feature films; to build larger audiences through improved marketing and distribution; and to preserve and disseminate a collection of Canadian films.

As a lender, Telefilm Canada is still a failure in the sense that it recoups only a small percentage of its annual investments. As a cultural agency and a support structure for Canada's independent producers, Telefilm has been remarkably successful, especially in terms of television programming. It is still the case that Canadians view far more foreign than domestic programming, but without Telefilm's presence there would be virtually no production of Canadian dramatic programming.

TED MAGDER

See also **Anne of Green Gables; Boys of St. Vincent, The; Canadian Programming in English; Canadian Programming in French; Danger Bay; Degrassi; E.N.G.**

Further Reading

Ayscough, Suzan, "Canadian Film Funder Tightens Purse Strings," *Variety* (March 30, 1992)

Ayscough, Suzan, "The Experiment That Spawned an Industry," *Variety* (November 16, 1992)

Ayscough, Suzan, "Factions Fracture Pic Funds," *Variety* (November 16, 1992)

Kelly, Brendan, "Canada Funder Feels Sting of Budget Cuts," *Variety* (December 14, 1992)

Kelly, Brendan, "Canadian Film Plan Rekindles Old Uproar," *Variety* (April 19, 1993)

Kelly, Brendan, "More Homegrown Up There," *Variety* (April 24, 1995)

Magder, Ted, *Canada's Hollywood: The Canadian State and Feature Films*, Toronto: University of Toronto Press, 1993

Magder, Ted, "Film and Video Production," in *The Cultural Industries in Canada*, edited by Michael Dorland, Toronto: Lorimer, 1996

Pendakur, Manjunath, *Canadian Dreams and American Control: The Political Economy of the Canadian Film Industry*, Detroit, Michigan: Wayne State University Press, 1990

Posner, Michael, *Canadian Dreams: The Making and Marketing of Independent Films*, Vancouver: Douglas and McIntyre, 1993

Wallace, Bruce, Joseph Treen, and Robert Enright, "A Campaign in Support of Entertainment," *Maclean's* (March 17, 1986)

Winikoff, Kenneth, "They Always Get Their Film: The Canadian Government Has Sired a National Cinema, but Can a Film Industry Thrive when Every Taxpayer Is a Producer?" *American Film* (July 1990)

Telemundo

U.S. Network

Telemundo is the second-largest Spanish-language television network in the United States, reaching 90 percent of Hispanic households in 100 U.S. markets. As of 2002, Telemundo owns and operates 10 full-power UHF stations and 8 low-power stations, has 40 broadcast affiliates, and is offered on 310 cable and wireless systems. While the network has grown steadily since its inception in 1986, it has also consistently run a distant second behind Spanish-language broadcasting giant Univision. As a result of its second-place status, Telemundo has undergone a number of key transformations in terms of programming strategies, management, and ownership. At the heart of these changes are competing definitions of the Hispanic audience and its importance in the U.S. media economy. Charting the ebb and flow of Telemundo's fortunes sheds light not only the growing importance of Spanish-language broadcasting in U.S. television, but also the relationship between media and identity in a multi-cultural environment.

Telemundo's history is marked by an initial period of expansion followed by instability, changing ownership, and increasing diversification. Telemundo Group, Inc. first emerged on the television radar in 1986 under the control of investors Saul Steinberg and Henry Silverman of Reliance Capital Group. Steinberg and Silverman were enticed by the growth potential of the Hispanic market and initially invested in a number of television stations directly serving that market. The first two stations acquired by the investors, and used as the foundation for Telemundo, were WSCU in Miami and KWAQ in San Juan, Puerto Rico. Following these initial purchases, the company quickly expanded by taking over WNJU in Linden, New Jersey, as well as KTMD in the important Texas market of Houston/Galveston. It also established affiliations with Chicago station WSNS, and KVDA in San Antonio. According to Patricia Constantakis-Valdés, in the period between 1988 and 1991, Telemundo expanded even further, with stations and affiliates in Dallas/Ft. Worth, Lubbock, Albuquerque, Tucson, Phoenix, and Yakima in Washington.

The network's programming during this period stayed fairly close to the format established by Univision: news, sports, variety shows, talk shows, and tabloid news shows. The network also scheduled *telenovelas*—the staple of Spanish-language programming—mostly imported from Mexico, Venezuela, and Brazil. One particularly important *telenovela,* however, was *Angelica Mi Vida,* produced in Puerto Rico and based on the lives of Hispanic Americans. Additionally, the nightly news segment, *Noteciero Telemundo,* was produced in Hialeah, Florida (the location of the network's corporate headquarters). This emphasis on shows produced in the U.S. and targeting a specifically Hispanic identity has continued to sit at the tumultuous center of Telemundo's programming strategies.

Following the initial period of growth, Joaquin F. Blaya, who had previously served as president and CEO of Univision, took over the same post at Telemundo. With Blaya at the helm, Telemundo continued to expand its holdings and increase its emphasis on young Hispanic viewers. During this time, Telemundo, Univision, and Nielson Media Research developed a ratings system specifically designed to chart the viewing habits of the Hispanic community in the U.S. Continuous expansion and investment without the benefit of comparably increasing advertising revenue, however, led to a financial collapse in July 1993, and the network filed for bankruptcy.

As detailed by Alex Avila, Telemundo was resuscitated in 1994 when Leon Black and his company, Apollo Advisors L.P., purchased the network for $83 million. Shortly thereafter, Joaquin Blaya resigned his position and Roland Hernandez took over as President and CEO. Under Hernandez, Telemundo arranged for access to *telenovelas* from TV Azteca, the largest independent network in Mexico—a move that would ease the burden of costly U.S.-based production. This move also allowed the network new competitive leverage with Univision, whose exclusive deals with production and export giants Televisa (Mexico) and Venvision (Venezuela) had previously crippled Telemundo's access to relatively inexpensive Spanish-language programming sources outside the U.S. As a result, Telemundo's programming continued to look like that of Univision, despite continued efforts to differentiate itself and pursue younger viewers. Patricia Constantakis-Valdés indicates that, as of 1995, Telemundo's programming consisted mostly of movies and *telenovelas,* but still included game shows, talk shows, variety shows, sports, and news. As with Univision, approximately half of this programming was being produced in the U.S. By 1996, Telemundo's advertising revenues had increased by over 20 percent from the previous year.

But competing with Univision proved no simple task, and access to TV Azteca's programs was no cure for deeper problems at the network. Univision's dominance was, in large part, a matter of habit and familiarity for a large number of older viewers, and no injection of like-minded programming was going to undo a more than two-decade head start. Furthermore, the Mexico-produced *telenovelas* from TV Azteca failed to connect with younger viewers who found them increasingly irrelevant to their own experience. Despite the increased ad revenues, Telemundo's share of the Hispanic audience continued to drop, from 37 percent in 1993 to 18 percent in 1996. As ratings failed to rise, advertisers began to abandon the network, and by 1997, Telemundo was in dire straits again. In an effort to stem the tide of advertiser attrition and to give the ratings a boost, Telemundo decided to change direction and counter-program against Univision, removing *telenovelas* and replacing them with nightly feature films, and moving their news an hour earlier to avoid direct competition. At the same time, the network began actively to seek out potential investors and programming partners. Interested groups included syndication giant King World Productions, Rupert Murdoch's News Corporation, and Sony Pictures Entertainment.

In November 1997, Sony teamed up with Liberty Media, Apollo Management, and Bastion Capital Fund to purchase Telemundo for $539 million. Apollo retained 50 percent ownership while Sony and Liberty, because of regulatory restrictions, each held a 25 percent share. The deal received FCC approval in July 1998. The immediate effects of this transition were the removal of Roland Hernandez as president and CEO, a programming overhaul that included radical counter-programming strategies, and a growing fear that the network would be assimilated into the mold of one of the U.S. networks.

Hernandez was replaced by Peter Tortorici in August 1998. Tortorici was a veteran of U.S. television with experience at the network level, having served as an executive in CBS's entertainment division. The programming overhaul also betrayed a move toward the U.S. network model. Under the direction of a new president of entertainment, Nely Galan, Telemundo mounted a campaign designed to court the younger, bilingual Hispanic audience. As Galan herself stated in November 1998: "Our projection is all about Latinos in the U.S. It's not about Latin Americans." The result of this strategy was a greater emphasis on U.S.-produced programs and a focus on the genres that drive English-language television: sitcoms, action-adventure series, reality shows, talk shows, and game shows. Emphasizing the bi-cultural slant of this strategy, the network's motto during this period was "The Best of Two Worlds."

For the 1998–99 season, Tortorici and Galan oversaw the scheduling of a number of series that were essentially Spanish-language re-makes of once-popular U.S. hits, the licenses for which were, not coincidentally, owned by Sony. These shows included: *Angeles (Charlie's Angels), Solo En América (One Day at a Time), Reyes y Rey (Starsky and Hutch or Miami Vice), Una Familia con Angel (Who's The Boss?), Los Recien Casados (The Newlywed Game),* and *Buscando Pareja (The Dating Game).* Additionally, the network experimented with English subtitles and programs in "Spanglish."

These counter-programming moves initially helped boost the ratings, but only for a short period. As soon as the novelty of the effort wore away, network affiliates began to report precipitous drops in their audience share. In July 1999, Tortorici was replaced by James McNamara (born and raised in Panama), and Telemundo unceremoniously dropped most of the re-makes from the schedule. McNamara returned televnovelas to the center of the network's programming strategy, taking advantage of a new production deal with TV Azteca (negotiated by Tortorici before his departure). The network also purchased CBS/TeleNoticias, a Spanish and Portuguese news network. As McNamara stated: "We feel there are a few fundamental building blocks or pillars to building our business; novelas, news, sports, and variety/comedy shows." He also insisted on a return to strictly Spanish-language programming. Nely Galan also left the network in 1999.

Despite the network's movement back toward more traditional and proven programming, Telemundo has continued to move forward as well, diversifying its holdings and growing as a media corporation under McNamara. The network controls Telemundo Cable, which owns two cable networks: Telemundo International, and Mun2. In keeping with long-held desires to capture the youth market, Mun2 targets 18–34 year old viewers with a steady diet of music videos, entertainment shows, young dramas, comedies, movies, and game shows. Telemundo Cable also distributes Videorola, a Mexico-based music video channel.

But the network's growth, as the Sony purchase indicated, is in turn part of other diversification strategies as well. In 2000, NBC purchased Telemundo from Sony for nearly $2 billion. The once autonomous Spanish-language network has now been folded into

NBC's own growth strategy as it eyes the increasingly lucrative Latino market. That market currently accounts for almost 13 percent of the entire U.S. population and is expected to continue to be the fastest-growing population group in the United States for many years to come.

One of the major fears in the Hispanic media market following Sony's purchase of the network was that the relationship between Spanish-language television networks and the Hispanic communities they served would be irrevocably altered: that conglomeration would adversely affect the identity of the Spanish-language networks themselves and thus reduce their effectiveness in serving the Hispanic community. And while Telemundo seems to have regained a solid footing in the Hispanic media market thanks to its own diversification strategies, the future of its programming under NBC's guiding hand remains to be seen.

JONATHAN NICHOLS-PETHICK

See also **Telenovela; Univision**

Further Reading

Avila, Alex, "Trading Punches," *Hispanic* (January/February 1997)

Consoli, John, "Telemundo Shifts Direction," *MediaWeek* (June 22, 1998)

Constantakis-Valdés, Patricia, "Telemundo," *The Encyclopedia of Television,* 1st edition, edited by Horace Newcomb, 3 vols, Chicago and London: Fitzroy Dearborn Publishers, 1996

Dallas, Joe, "U.S. Hispanic: The Hispanic Nation," *Television Latin America* (January 1, 2002)

Davila, Arlene, "Mapping Latinidad: Language and Culture in the Spanish TV Battlefront," *Television and New Media* 1.1 (2000)

Donohue, Steve, "New Look Boosts Telemundo's Ratings," *Electronic Media* (November 9, 1998)

Esparza, Elia, "The Telemundo Takeover," *Hispanic* (January/February 1998)

Murphy, Jeremy, "NBC Eyes Telemundo Fit," *MediaWeek* (October 15, 2001)

Whitefield, Mimi, "Strictly Español," *The San Diego Union-Tribune* (April 4, 2000)

Telenovela

The *telenovela* is a form of melodramatic serialized fiction produced and aired in most Latin-American countries. These programs have traditionally been compared to English-language soap operas. However, even though the two genres share some characteristics and similar roots, the *telenovela* has evolved in the last three decades into a genre with its own unique characteristics. For example, *telenovelas* in most Latin-American countries are aired in prime-time six days a week, attract a broad audience across age and gender lines, and command the highest advertising rates. They last about six months and come to a climactic close.

Telenovelas generally vary from 180 to 200 episodes, but sometimes specific *telenovelas* might be extended for a longer period due to successful ratings. The first *telenovelas* produced in Latin America in the 1950s were shorter, lasting between 15 and 20 episodes, and were shown a few times a week. As they became more popular and more technically sophisticated, they were expanded, becoming the leading genre in the daily prime-time schedule.

Unlike U.S. soap operas that tend to rely on the family as a central unit of the narrative, Latin American *telenovelas* focus on the relationship between a romantic couple as the main motivator for plot development. During the early phases of their evolution in Latin America, until the mid-1960s, most *telenovelas* relied on conventional melodramatic narratives in which the romantic couple confronted opposition to their staying together. As the genre progressed in different nations at different rhythms, it became more attuned to local culture. The Peruvian *Simplemente Maria,* for example, a version of the Cinderella story, dealt with the problems of urban migration. The Brazilian *Beto Rockfeller* presented the story of an antihero who worked as a shoe-shop employee and pretended to be a millionaire; he became simultaneously involved with two women, one rich and one poor. An immediate hit in 1968, this *telenovela* appears to have led to the most dramatic changes in that nation's version of the genre: it introduced the use of colloquial dialogue, presented social satire, and offered new stylistic elements, such as the use of historical events in the plot, more natural acting, and improvisation.

The Globo network, Brazil's largest, which was only beginning to produce *telenovelas* in the late 1960s, soon took the lead and imposed these new trends upon the *telenovela* market. Indeed, Globo owes its international recognition and economic powerhouse status to the *telenovela.* In the 1970s Globo invested heavily in the quality of its *telenovelas,* using external locations traditionally avoided because of production costs. Globo's export success forced other producers in the region to implement changes in production values and modernize their narratives to remain competitive. Mexico, for example, after dominating the international market for several years, had to adapt its *telenovelas* according to the influences of its main competitors, especially Argentina, Brazil, and Venezuela.

There are important national distinctions within the genre in the areas of topic selection, structure, and production values, and there are also clear distinctions between the *telenovelas* produced in the 1960s and those made in the 1990s, in terms of both content and production values. As Patricia Aufderheide has pointed out, recent *telenovelas* in Brazil "dealt with bureaucratic corruption, single motherhood, and the environment; class differences are foregrounded in Mexican *novelas* and Cuba's *novelas* are bitingly topical as well as ideologically correct." In Colombia recent *telenovelas* have dealt with the social violence of viewers' daily lives, but melodramatic plots that avoid topical issues are becoming more popular. In Brazil, the treatment of racism is surfacing in *telenovelas* after being considered a taboo subject for several years.

The roots of the Latin American *telenovelas* go back to the radio soap operas produced in the United States, but they were also influenced by the serialized novels published in the local press. The origins of the melodramatic serialized romance date back to the sentimental novel in 18th-century England, as well as 19th-century French serialized novels, the *feuilletons.* In the late-19th and early-20th centuries, several Latin American countries also published local writers' novels in a serialized form. However, the proliferation of *radionovelas* that would later provide personnel as well as expertise to *telenovela* producers started in Cuba in the late 1930s. According to Katz and Wedell, the Colgate and Sydney Ross companies were responsible for the proliferation of *radionovelas* in pre-Castro Cuba. In the beginning stages of *telenovelas* in Latin America, in the 1950s, Cuba was an important exporter of the genre to the region, providing actors, producers, and screenplays. U.S. multinational corporations and advertising agencies were also instrumental in disseminating the new genre in the region. Corporations such as Unilever were interested in expanding their market to housewives by promoting *telenovelas* that contained their own product tie-ins. Direct influence of the United States on the growth and development of *telenovelas* in the region subsided af-

ter the mid-1960s, and the genre slowly evolved in different directions in different countries. In the 1950s and early 1960s, *telenovelas* were primarily adaptations of novels and other literary forms, and only a few Latin-American scriptwriters constructed original narratives. By the late 1960s, local markets started producing their own stories, bringing in local influences, and shaping the narratives to particular audiences.

Today, the leading *telenovela* producers in the region are Televisa, Venevision, and Globo, the leading networks in Mexico, Venezuela, and Brazil, respectively. These networks not only produce *telenovelas* for the local market but also export to other Latin American nations and to the rest of the world. Televisa, for instance, is the leading supplier of *telenovelas* to the Spanish-speaking market in the United States. Since the mid-1990s, however, the supremacy of Televisa and Globo has been challenged. In Mexico, the upstart TV Azteca produced more contemporary *telenovelas* dealing with social and political issues as a way of challenging Televisa's hold on the audience. In Brazil, SBT, the second-largest network in the country, attempted to increase its own production as well as coproductions with an Argentinean network, but high costs and low ratings for those productions pushed the network to rely on Mexican melodramas, which proved a challenge to Globo's supremacy. *Marimar,* produced by Televisa and broadcast in Brazil in late 1996, helped to solidify SBT as a serious player during prime time.

However, the decade's success story was *Betty La Fea,* a Colombian *telenovela.* A success in Latin America, it became a hit in the United States, boosting Telemundo's ratings. *Betty La Fea* was the story of the antiheroine, and the actress in the title role had to undergo hours of makeup to become *La Fea,* the ugly one. In this *telenovela,* the "ugly woman" becomes a successful businesswoman and gains the love of the hero without compromising her integrity. The story seemed to strike a chord among viewers in the region, and *Betty La Fea* became, like *Simplemente Maria* and *Escrava Isaura,* a landmark in the history of the genre.

ANTONIO C. LA PASTINA

See also **Brazil; Mexico; Soap Opera; Téléroman**

Further Reading

Allen, R., editor, *To Be Continued...: Soap Operas and Global Media Culture,* New York: Routledge, 1995

Aufderheide, Patricia, "Latin American Grassroots Video: Beyond Television," *Public Culture* (1993)

Hernandez, O., and Emile G. McAnany, "Cultural Industries in the Free Trade Era: A Look at Mexican Telenovelas," in *Representing Mexico: Transnationalism and the Politics of Culture since the Revolution,* Washington, D.C.: Woodrow Wilson Center, 1997

Katz, Elihu, and George Wedell, *Broadcasting in the Third World: Promise and Performance,* Cambridge, Massachusetts: Harvard University Press, 1977

La Pastina, Antonio, "Product Placement in Brazilian Prime-time Television: The Case of the Reception of a *Telenovela,*" *Journal of Broadcasting and Electronic Media* 45/4 (2001)

Lopez, A., "The Melodrama in Latin America," in *Imitations of Life: A Reader on Film and Television Melodrama,* edited by Marcia Landy, Detroit, Michigan: Wayne State University Press, 1991

Mattelart, Michèle, and Armand Mattelart, *The Carnival of Images: Brazilian Television Fiction,* translated by David Buxton, New York: Bergin and Garvey, 1990

Melo, J.M., *The Presence of the Brazilian Telenovelas in the International Market: Case Study of Globo Network,* São Paulo: University of São Paulo, 1991

Rogers, E., and L. Antola, "Telenovelas: A Latin American Success Story," *Journal of Communication* (1985)

Singhal, A., "Harnessing the Potential of Entertainment-Education *Telenovelas,*" *Gazette* (January 1993)

Sinclair, John, "Mexico, Brazil, and the Latin World," in *New Patterns in Global Television: Peripheral Vision,* edited by John Sinclair, Elizabeth Jacka, and Stuart Cunningham, Oxford and New York: Oxford University Press, 1996

Sinclair, John, *Latin American Television: A Global View,* Oxford and New York: Oxford University Press, 1999

Straubhaar, Joseph, "The Development of the *Telenovela* as the Pre-eminent Form of Brazilian Popular Culture," *Studies in Latin American Popular Culture* (1982)

Tufte, Thomas, *Living with the Rubbish Queen: Telenovelas, Culture and Modernity in Brazil,* Luton, England: University of Luton Press, 2000

Vink, Nico, *The Telenovela and Emancipation: A Study of Television and Social Change in Brazil,* Amsterdam: Royal Tropical Institute, 1988

Téléroman

As a television genre, the weekly, prime-time *téléroman* can be defined as a television drama in a realist style, comprising a series of continuous episodes, broadcast at the same time each week and characterized by a sequentiality that is either episodic, overlapping, or both.

The genre is generally recognized, both at home and abroad, as being specific to the French-language television industry in Canada, located in the province of Quebec and intimately associated with Quebec society and its dominant Francophone culture (French speakers make up 82 percent of the province's nearly 7 million inhabitants).

The term literally means "television novel," which strongly suggests its direct lineage with the modern, especially the 19th-century, popular novel. The serial character of the *téléroman* makes it a descendant of Charles Dickens, Alexandre Dumas, and Eugene Sue, whose works were published as series, one chapter or episode at a time, in the popular daily penny-press, weekly journals, or monthly magazines of their time; only after the serialization had finished would a novel be published in book form. The purpose was, of course, to build customer loyalty for the papers and magazines, a function not unlike that of the *téléroman* for the visual medium of television.

This new literature of the 19th century testified to the technologies of modern mass communications in a liberal, urban, industrial, capitalist society. Because of its proximity to the United States, Quebec has benefited and profited from these new technologies and even produced a cottage industry of popular serial novels, both within the pages of the popular press and between the covers of chapbooks.

With the advent of radio, both public and private, the serial novel became a permanent fixture of programming with such favorite *radioromans* (radio novels) as *La Pension Velder, Jeunesse dorée, La famille Plouffe,* and the granddaddy of them all, *Un homme et son péché.* These serials developed, of course, under the far-reaching shadow of the U.S. radio soap opera. While importing many of that genre's basic characteristics, the Quebec *radioroman* showed the imprint of local cultural moorings, particularly in its reference to the history of this French-speaking population on the North American continent dating back to the establishment of the colony in 1604, its nationalistic fervor, its agrarian heritage, and its forced adaptation to accelerated industrialization, urbanization, and modernization.

There were no in-house writers for these radio plays; one could not earn a decent living writing *radioromans* or, for that matter, any type of novel. Still, many of the first *telenovelists* were *radionovelists,* who were also established literary novelists. A literary profession of successful, independent novelists and *telenovelists* has only emerged since the mid-1980s.

With the advent of television, classical and modern theater (also prominent on Canadian radio, as in the United States) moved onto the small screen along with

The Plouffe Family.
Photo courtesy of National Archives of Canada/CBC Collection

the *radioroman*. As elsewhere, theater was short-lived on TV while the *radioroman* went on to become the *téléroman*. Building on the loyal following of the *radioroman* by "bringing to life" the main characters of two of the best-loved and most enduring radio productions, *Un homme et son péché* and *La famille Plouffe,* the *téléroman* was able to experiment with new themes and new styles of writing. It thus adapted the century-old popular novel to this modern medium without sacrificing tradition and its most endearing qualities.

As an indication not only of the rapid growth of the *téléroman* but also of the centrality of the position it holds within both the television industry and the public discourse on television itself, one can cite the following figures. A recent repertoire lists nearly 600 titles of original works of fiction, including *téléromans,* pro-

duced by Quebecois screenwriters to the delight of tens of millions of television viewers from 1952 to 1992. A comparable feat is not to be found in any other French-language television industry, including France's. Nor is the popularity of locally produced television fiction in Quebec to be equaled anywhere else, particularly in terms of the loyalty that the *téléroman* commands. For example, in the early 1980s the "Who Killed J.R.?" episode of *Dallas* set a new standard in U.S. television market research with its 54-point market share, and it has rarely been challenged since. In contrast, in Quebec a 50-point market share is considered the basic standard of a successful show, with the yearly bestsellers reaching the high 70s and low 80s.

Not surprisingly, the *téléroman* has spawned some small but vibrant secondary commercial ventures and represents some notable investments by other communications industries. For example, a glossy magazine, *Téléroman,* is published four times a year with a readership of some 50,000. The well-established television guides, such as *TV Hebdo* (with nearly 1 million readers), often feature well-known faces of actors or characters of popular *téléromans* on its cover. Each year, moreover, *TV Hebdo* devotes a special edition to the current lineup of best- and least-known *téléromans.* Every major daily newspaper publishes the weekly schedule of television programming and has a television critic whose main subject is the *téléroman:* its costs, production, writers, actors, characters, intrigues, and audience rates. Talk shows quite regularly invite authors, actors, and TV characters to meet live studio audiences. Even "serious" public affairs television shows, magazines, and newspapers give thoughtful attention to the phenomenon. Of course, the *téléroman,* with its well-known and beloved characters, is a bonanza for advertising agencies selling everything from sundries to soft drinks to automobiles; *téléroman* actors are the spokespersons for industries; they appear on public announcements and telethons for the sick and the needy.

Most importantly, these well-known and well-loved actors and characters have contributed to the birth and growth of a thriving, creative, French-language Quebec-based advertising industry. Not too many years ago, this industry's main revenue came from translating English language, Toronto- or New York-conceived television commercials. Today, French-language advertisements for national Canadian and American brand names are conceived and produced in Quebec. This industry has become a remarkable success story in its own right, creating ads for Pepsi, Bell Canada, General Motors, and others.

Another commercial spin-off, besides the inevitable merchandizing of images of *téléroman* characters as dolls, on lunch boxes, and on posters, is the phenomenon of "living museums." Here the sets—whether original or reconstructed—of *téléromans* such as *Un homme et son péché, Le temps d'une paix, Les filles de Caleb,* or *Cormoran* are rebuilt in their "natural" outdoor surroundings. These *téléromans* are historically grounded, either in a specific timeframe such as the 1930s or 1940s, or in the lives of past public and semipublic figures. The actual historical site on which these sets are built, the authentic dwellings upon which they are grafted, even the now-permanent presence of actual descendants of the romanticized characters in these reconstructed settings, all lend a "museum-like" and educational quality to these commercial enterprises. The *téléroman* is thus much more than a television genre, it is also an industry in itself and a generator of economic activities in industrially related sectors.

One of the recurring themes in the *téléroman* is the city, and this city is Montreal, the largest French-language city in North America. It is a character in its own right in the same manner as the London of Dickens, the Paris of Honoré de Balzac and Émile Zola, or New York and Los Angeles for the modern U.S. television series. The *téléroman* often looks and sounds like an indictment of the city with its wealth of social problems—anonymous violence, corruption, abused children, battered women, drug abuse, solitude, poverty, homelessness. However, it is also an ode to the city's magnetism—riches, arts, adventure, beauty, fulfillment, empowerment, enlightenment, and, above all, the chance for true love. The *téléroman* exudes both a sense of *déjà vu* and "elsewhereism."

The *téléroman* focuses on the ordinary, even on the antihero who is allowed to fail, sometimes disastrously. It reaches into the banality of everyday life to gather the stuff out of which characters of flesh and blood appear on the television screen, live and evolve, cry and laugh, cheat and repent, love and hate, and sometimes disappear. The fact that ordinariness can be both enticing and serialized yet still command loyalty from seasoned viewers of a half-century of television drama, is the greatest homage that can be paid to these writers, producers, and actors. The popularity, for example, of *Chambres en ville,* an exploration of the pains and joys of growing up as a teenager in Montreal, attests to the skill of these professionals.

Another remarkable feature of the Quebecois *téléroman* lies in its distinctive mixture of gendered worldviews. This particular mixture can be traced to the presence and influence of the women working in the *téléroman*'s creative communities. *Telenovelists* include women such as former journalist Fabienne Larouche, former journalist and Quebec cabinet minister Lise Payette, and her daughter Sylvie. Renowned female actors of both theater and screen play lead roles in the *téléroman,* and women novelists whose best-selling novels have been adapted to the television genre, such as Arlette Cousture (*Les filles de Caleb*) and Francine Ouellet (*Au nom du père*), often contribute to the creative process.

The last few years have seen three unrelated but significant shifts, whose impact on the *téléroman* is yet to be measured. First, the weekly episodes of a regular series are decreasing in number. Second, the traditionally weak export market may have found its niche: the selling of franchised concepts rather than dubbing rights for televised series. Finally, the arrival of a new technology combining television with the Internet means, for example, that while one is watching a dramatic series, one may chat interactively on the Internet about the show, with both the program and the chat window appearing simultaneously on the TV screen.

The *téléroman,* like other works of fiction in many other societies, is a testimony to the creative use of technology, in this case a technology to transmit at a distance and in real time, images and sounds. Through the efforts and talents of many artists, professionals, and technicians, a world of fiction is created. It is a world in which reality takes on certain meanings for a geographically, socially, historically, and culturally designated community. That the *téléroman* succeeds in achieving this sort of world is not unique; what is unique is the fashion in which it does so. The *téléroman* thus contributes a small but original viewpoint, or narrative, to the accumulated human legacy of past efforts to give meaning to the lives of ordinary people.

ROGER DE LA GARDE AND GISÈLE TCHOUNGUI

See also **Canadian Programming in French;** *Famille Plouffe, La;* **Soap Opera; Telenovela**

Teletext

Telextext is a system of transmitting text and graphics as part of a television signal. The teletext information is contained in the vertical blanking interval, the portion of the television signal in which the electron beam is turned off between frames. Another service that uses the vertical blanking interval is closed captioning.

Teletext systems transmit news and information to subscribers, either superimposed over the television picture or on separate, full-screen pages. To receive teletext information, the receiving television requires either a built-in or add-on decoder. The viewer typically accesses the information via a remote-control keypad. Teletext is distinguished from videotex in that it is essentially a one-way system, while videotex offers greater interactivity.

By modern computer standards, teletext is a low-resolution medium. A broadcast signal can transmit up to 200 user-selectable pages. When a user selects a page, it can take up to 20 seconds to load. Each page is limited to seven colors, plus black and white, and can hold up to 24 rows of 40 characters. This means that a one-screen news story is limited to about 80 words.

In the 1970s and early 1980s there was substantial development in creating teletext technology and programming. In the United Kingdom, the British Broadcasting Corporation (BBC) began its CEEFAX service in 1974. The IBA instituted its ORACLE system in 1975. While teletext achieved high levels of awareness in the U.K., it reached small audiences compared to the television viewing audience; its most common (and still continuing) use there is to provide subtitles for the hearing-impaired.

Canada's TELIDON system featured a vector-based graphic system that permitted more advanced graphics to be loaded in the low-bandwidth medium. This technology became part of the NABTS protocol that became most popular in the United States, where the Federal Communications Commission (FCC) authorized teletext service in 1983. The FCC declined to set a technical standard for teletext, opening the door for many incompatible systems. In the US there were also many different business models for teletext. An early version, KEYFAX, was transmitted via satellite on superstation WTBS beginning in 1982, and cost $19.90 per month, including rental of the decoder. This system survived for two years, when it was abandoned for a videotex service. Other systems required the viewer to purchase a decoder for up to $300. Some were created to be advertiser-supported or were designed to appeal to narrow audiences, such as classified ads or financial information.

By 1985, teletext was in decline in the United States. It was hampered by availability and price of decoders, lack of technical standards, increased interest in videotex, poor-quality graphics, limited information, and no clear business model. Videotex systems that followed also struggled, until the Internet gained the necessary critical mass to deliver the kinds of services the pioneers of teletext systems had dreamed of and hoped to provide.

DAVID KAMERER

See also **Closed Captioning; Videotex and Online Services**

Further Reading

Aumente, Jerome, *New Electronic Pathways: Videotex, Teletext, and Online Databases.* Newbury Park, California: Sage, 1987

Graziplene, Leonard R., *Teletext: its Promise and Demise,* Cranbury, New Jersey: Associated University Presses, 2000

Telethon

A telethon is a live program devised to raise money for national or local charities, or for nonprofit organizations. Their unusual length (often taking up most of a day's programming, or running through the night) led them to be described colloquially as "television marathons," and thus eventually "telethons." Numerous examples of the form all over the world have raised billions of dollars for various causes. For American viewers, the Jerry Lewis Muscular Dystrophy Association (MDA) effort is perhaps the quintessential telethon. Hosted by Lewis since 1966, it is broadcast internationally, free of charge, by local U.S. stations signing on as part of the annual Labor Day "Love Network." The event, along with Lewis's off-key, emotional rendition of the song "Walk On," have become synonymous with Labor Day itself.

The first telethon, a 16-hour event broadcast by NBC and hosted by Milton Berle in 1949, raised $1.1 million for the Damon Runyan Memorial Cancer Fund. Berle's pioneering effort set the tone for years to follow: a big-name star at the fore; a battery of telephone operators to collect pledges; and stage, film, and TV personalities appearing among impassioned pleas for donations. Jerry Lewis was one of the personalities to appear with Berle during the first telethon.

Telethons began showing their age in the early 1990s, as various groups representing the disabled argued that telethons, with their accent on cures, paint a helpless and pathetic picture of people with disabilities. Lewis, a fervent campaigner for finding a cure for muscular dystrophy, has dismissed such complaints and continues his traditional approach. The MDA telethon has raised over $1.5 billion for muscular dystrophy, receiving $56.8 million in pledges in 2001.

In addition to the MDA event, other annual telethons in the United States include those for Easter Seals, the Arthritis Foundation, United Cerebral Palsy, and the United Negro College Fund. On the local level, U.S. public television stations have borrowed from the form to raise money during their viewer pledge drives.

On September 21, 2001, a telethon became the focal point for an unprecedented instance of cooperation in the television industry. That evening, ABC, CBS, FOX, NBC, PBS, and two dozen U.S. cable channels all simulcast the two-hour, commercial-free telethon *America: A Tribute to Heroes,* which raised millions of dollars for a United Way–administered relief effort for the victims of the September 11 terrorist attacks on the United States. The telethon was also broadcast live in 150 other nations, with an estimated audience of 60 million viewers, and it has been released on video, CD, and DVD.

In the United Kingdom, the two most durable telethons have been the annual Children in Need Appeal (since 1980), and the more irregular Comic Relief

Jerry Lewis with poster child at the Labor Day MDA Telethon.
Courtesy of the Everett Collection

Jerry Lewis hosts the Labor Day weekend telethon for Muscular Dystrophy, 1980s.
Courtesy of the Everett Collection

ridiculous, such as people getting their friends to sponsor them to sit in a bath of custard). These spots are interspersed in the program with appearances by celebrities, who generally perform rather than make direct appeals for money themselves. Comic Relief is fronted by comedians, who often produce elaborate original material for broadcast during the event. The third element in the programming are short films showing the people around the world on whom the money is spent, always carefully emphasizing their dignity and resilience in the face of adversity rather than portraying them as helpless. Children in Need raised £26 million ($47 million) in 2002, while the Comic Relief event in March 2003 raised more than £61 million ($110 million).

Perhaps the most spectacular one-off telethon was Live Aid, broadcast on July 13, 1985, comprising two overlapping concerts, one from Wembley Stadium in London, the other from JFK Stadium in Philadelphia, which together formed a continuous 16-hour event featuring many of the world's most famous bands of the time. Worldwide viewing figures were estimated at 1.5 billion, and pledges received during and after the concert totaled about $100 million.

MICHAEL B. KASSEL

See also **Special/Spectacular**

Further Reading

"Charity Balls," *New Statesman and Society* (June 1, 1990)
Dempsey, John, "TV Stations Line Up for 'Flood Aid,'" *Variety* (August 2, 1993)
"Jerry Lewis Criticized over Telethon's Approach," *New York Times* (September 6, 1992)
Johnson, Mary, "Jerry's Kids," *The Nation* (September 14, 1992)
Karpf, Anne, "'Give Us a Break, not a Begging Bowl,'" *New Statesman* (May 27, 1988)
Kruger, Barbara, "Barbara Kruger on Television," *Artforum* (November 1989)
Shapiro, Joseph P., "Disabling 'Jerry's Kids,'" *U.S. News and World Report* (September 14, 1992)

Day (since 1988), both broadcast on the BBC. Rather than appealing for individual causes, both these events raise money for a large coalition of charities—Children in Need for medical, educational, and social-program charities working with children, and Comic Relief splitting its funds between agricultural and sanitation projects in the developing world and disability and poverty-alleviation work in the United Kingdom.

Both telethons show events from around the country that have been locally organized to raise money by individual sponsorship (often with an element of the

---

Television Studies

"Television studies" is the relatively recent name given to the academic study of television. Modeled by analogy with longer-established fields of study such as "film studies," the name suggests that there is an object, "television," which, in courses named, for example, "Introduction to Television Studies," is the self-evident object of study using accepted methodologies. This may be increasingly the case, but it is important to grasp that most of the formative academic research on television was first developed for other fields and contexts. The "television" of television studies is a relatively new phenomenon, just as many of the key television scholars are employed in departments of sociology, politics, communication arts, speech, theater, media, and film studies. If it is now possible to speak of this field of study in the English-speaking world in a way in which it was not in, say, 1970, its distinctive characteristics include disciplinary hybridity and a continuing debate about how to conceptualize the object of study, "television." These debates, which are and have been both political and methodological, are further complicated in an international frame by the historical peculiarities of national broadcasting systems. Thus, for example, the television studies that developed in Britain or Scandinavia, while often addressing individual U.S. television programs, did so within the taken-for-granted dominance of public-service models. In contrast, the U.S. system is distinguished by the normality of advertising spots and breaks. In the first instance then, television studies signifies the contested, often nationally inflected, academic address to television as the primary object of study—rather than, for example, television as part of international media economies or television as the site of drama in performance. (Significantly, as advertiser-supported commercial television has spread throughout the world, often altering the reach, role, and function of public-service television, those who study either system have found it necessary to reconfigure some of their motivating questions and methods.)

There have been two prerequisites for the development of television studies in the West—and it is primarily a Western phenomenon, which is not to imply that there is not, for example, a substantial literature on Indian television (cf. Krishnan and Dighe, 1990). The first was that television as such be regarded as worthy of study. This apparently obvious point is significant in relation to a medium that has historically attracted distrust, fear, and contempt. These responses, which often involve the invocation of television as both origin and symptom of social ills, have, as many scholars have pointed out, homologies with responses to earlier popular genres and forms such as the novel and the cinema. The second prerequisite was that television be granted, conceptually, some autonomy and specificity as a medium. Thus television had to be regarded as more than simply a transmitter of world, civic, or artistic events, and as distinguishable from other of the "mass media." Indeed, much of the literature of television studies could be characterized as attempting to formulate accounts of the specificity of television, often using comparison with, on the one hand, radio

(broadcast, liveness, civic address) and on the other, cinema (moving pictures, fantasy), with particular attention, as discussed below, to debate about the nature of the television text and the television audience. Increasingly significant also are the emergent histories of television, whether it be the autobiographical accounts of insiders, such as Grace Wyndham Goldie's history of her years at the BBC, *Facing the Nation,* or the painstaking archival research of historians such as William Boddy with his history of the quiz scandals in 1950s U.S. television or Lynn Spigel with her pioneering study of the way in which television was "installed" in the U.S. living room in the 1950s, *Make Room for TV.*

Television studies emerges in the 1970s and 1980s from three major bodies of commentary on television: journalism, literary/dramatic criticism, and the social sciences. The first, and most familiar, was daily and weekly journalism. This has generally taken the form of guides to viewing and reviews of recent programs. Television reviewing has, historically, been strongly personally voiced, with this authorial voice rendering continuity to the diverse topics and programs addressed. Some of this writing has offered formulations of great insight in its address to television form—for example the work of James Thurber, Raymond Williams, Philip Purser, or Nancy Banks-Smith—which is only now being recognized as one of the origins of the discipline of television studies. The second body of commentary is also organized through ideas of authorship, but here it is the writer or dramatist who forms the legitimation for the attention to television. Critical method here is extrapolated from traditional literary and dramatic criticism, and the television attracts serious critical attention as a "home theater." Representative texts here would be the early collection edited by Howard Thomas, *Armchair Theatre* (1959) or the later, more academic volume edited by George Brandt, *British Television Drama* (1981). Until the 1980s, the address of this type of work was almost exclusively to "high culture": plays and occasionally series by known playwrights, often featuring theatrical actors. Only with an understanding of this context is it possible to see how exceptional is Raymond Williams's defense of television soap opera in *Drama in Performance* (1968), or Horace Newcomb's validation of popular genres in *TV: The Most Popular Art* (1974).

Both of these bodies of commentary are mainly concerned to address what was shown on the screen, and thus conceive of television mainly as a text within the arts and humanities academic traditions. Other early attention to television draws, in different ways, on the social sciences, addressing the production, circulation, and function of television in contemporary society.

Here, research has tended not to address the television text as such, but instead to conceptualize television either through notions of its social function and effects, or within a governing question of *cui bono?* (whose good is served?). Thus television, along with other of the mass media, is conceptualized within frameworks principally concerned with the maintenance of social order: the reproduction of the status quo, the relationship between the state, media ownership, and citizenship, and the constitution of the public sphere. With these concerns, privileged areas of inquiry have tended to be non-textual: patterns of international cross-media ownership; national and international regulation of media production and distribution; professional ideologies; public opinion; media audiences. Methodologies here have been greatly contested, particularly in the extent to which Marxist frameworks, or those associated with the critical sociology of the Frankfurt School, have been employed. These debates have been given further impetus in recent years by research undertaken under the loose definition of cultural studies. In this case the privileged texts—if attention has been directed at texts—have been news and current affairs, and particularly special events such as elections, industrial disputes, and wars. It is this body of work that is least represented in "television studies," which, as an emergent discipline, tends toward the textualization of its object of study. The British journal *Media, Culture and Society* provides an exemplary instance of media research—in which television plays some part—in the traditions of critical sociology and political economy.

Much innovatory work in television studies has been focused on the definition of the television text. Indeed, this debate could be seen as one of the constituting frameworks of the field. The common-sense view points to the individual program as a unit, and this view has firm grounding in the way television is produced. Television is, for the most part, made as programs or runs of programs: series, serials, and miniseries. However, this is not necessarily how television is watched, despite the considerable currency of the view that it is somehow better for the viewer to choose to watch particular programs rather that just having the television on. Indeed, BBC television in the 1950s featured "interludes" between programs—most famously "The Potter's Wheel," a short film showing a pair of hands making a clay pot on a wheel—to demarcate programs clearly and ensure that viewers did not just drift from one to the next. It is precisely this possible "drifting" through an evening's viewing that has come to seem, to many commentators, one of the unique features of television watching, and hence something that must be attended to in any account of the television text.

The inaugural formulation is Raymond Williams's argument, in his 1974 book, *Television: Technology and Cultural Form,* that "the defining feature of broadcasting" is "planned flow." Williams developed these ideas through reflecting on four years of reviewing television for the BBC's weekly periodical *The Listener,* when he suggests that the separating of the television text into recognizable generic program units, which makes the reviewer's job much easier, somehow misses "the central television experience: the fact of flow" (1974). Williams's own discussion of flow draws on analysis of both British and U.S. television, and he is careful to insist on the national variation of broadcasting systems and types and management of flow, but his attempt to describe what is specific to the watching of television has been internationally generative, particularly in combination with some of the more recent empirical studies of how people do (or do not) watch television.

If Williams's idea of flow has been principally understood to focus attention on television viewing as involving more viewing and less choosing than a critical focus on individual programs would suggest, other critics have picked up the micro-narratives of which so much television is composed. Thus John Ellis approached the television text using a model ultimately derived from film studies, although he is precisely concerned, in his book *Visible Fictions,* to differentiate cinema and television. Ellis suggests that the key unit of the television text is the "segment," which he defines as "small, sequential unities of images and sounds whose maximum duration seems to be about five minutes" (1982). Broadcast television, Ellis argues, is composed of different types of combinations of segment: sometimes sequential, as in drama series, sometimes cumulative, as in news broadcasts and commercials. As with Williams's "flow," the radical element in Ellis's "segment" is the way in which it transgresses common-sense boundaries such as "program," "documentary," or "fiction" to bring to the analyst's attention common and defining features of broadcast television as a medium.

However, it has also been argued that the television text cannot be conceptualized without attention to the structure of national broadcasting institutions and the financing of program production. In this context, Nick Browne has argued that the U.S. television system is best approached through a notion of the "super-text." Browne is concerned to address the specificities of the U.S. commercial television system in contrast to the public-service models—particularly the British one—which have been so generative a context for such thinkers as Raymond Williams and Stuart Hall. Browne defines the "super-text" as, initially, a television program plus all of the introductory and interstitial material (trailers, commercials, voice-overs and so on) encountered during that program's slot in the schedule. He is thus insisting on an "impure" idea of the text, arguing that the program as broadcast at a particular time in the working week, interrupted by advertisements and announcements, condenses the political economy of television. Advertising, in Browne's schema, is the central mediating institution in U.S. television, linking program schedules to the wider world of production and consumption.

The final concept to be considered in discussing the television text is Newcomb and Hirsch's idea of the "viewing strip" (1987). This concept suggests a mediation between broadcast provision and individual choice, attempting to grasp the way in which each individual negotiates his or her way through the "flow" on offer, putting together a sequence of viewing of their own selection. Thus different individuals might produce very different "texts"—viewing strips—from the same night's viewing. Implicit within the notion of the viewing strip—although not a prerequisite—is the remote-control device, allowing easy channel changing and surfing. And it is this tool of audience agency, embodied in the remote control, that points us to the second substantial area of innovatory scholarship in television studies, the address to the audience.

The hybrid disciplinary origins of television studies are particularly evident in the approach to the television audience. Here, particularly in the 1980s, we find the convergence of potentially antagonistic paradigms. Very simply, on the one hand, research traditions in the social sciences focus on the empirical investigation of the already existing audience. Research design here tends to seek representative samples of particular populations presumed to correlate with viewers of a particular type of programming (adolescent boys and violence; women and soap opera, and so on). Research on the television audience has historically been dominated, particularly in the United States, by large-scale quantitative surveys, often designed using a model of the "effects" of the media, of which television is not necessarily a differentiated element. Within the social sciences, this "effects" model has been challenged by what is known as the "uses and gratifications" model. In James Halloran's famous formulation, "we should ask not what the media does to people, but what people do to the media" (Halloran, 1970). Herta Herzog's 1944 research on the listeners to radio daytime serials was an inaugural project within this "uses and gratifications" tradition, which in the late 1980s produced the project on the international decoding of the U.S. prime-time serial, *Dallas* (Liebes and Katz, 1990).

On the other hand, this social-science history of empirical audience investigation has been confronted by ideas of a textually constituted "reader"—a concept originating in literary and film studies. This produces a very different conceptualization of the audience, drawing on literary, semiotic, and psychoanalytic theory to suggest—in different and disputed ways—that the text constructs a "subject position" from which it is intelligible. In this body of work, the context of consumption and the social origins of audience members are irrelevant to the making of meaning, which originates in the text. However—and it is thus that we see the potential convergence with social-science "uses and gratifications" models—literary theorists such as Umberto Eco have questioned the extent to which the reader should be seen as active in meaning-making (1979). It is, in this context, difficult to separate the development of television studies, as such, from that of cultural studies, for it is within cultural studies that we begin to find the most sophisticated theorizations and empirical investigations of the complex, contextual interplay of text and "reader" in the making of meaning.

The first discussions of television in the field of cultural studies are those of Stuart Hall in essays such as his 1974 paper "Encoding and Decoding in Television Discourse" (Hall, 1997) and David Morley's audience research (1980). However, this television-specific work cannot theoretically be completely separated from other cultural studies work conducted at Birmingham University in the 1970s, such as that of Dick Hebdige and Angela McRobbie, which stressed the often oppositional agency of individuals in response to contemporary culture. British cultural studies has proved a successful export, its theoretical paradigms meeting and sometimes clashing with those used internationally in the more generalized academic reorientation toward the study of popular culture and entertainment in the 1970s and 1980s. Influential scholars working within, or closely related to, cultural-studies paradigms include Ien Ang and John Fiske. Ang's work on the television audience ranges from a study of *Dallas* fans in the Netherlands to the interrogation of existing ideas of audience in a postmodern, global context. John Fiske's work has been particularly successful in introducing British cultural studies to a U.S. audience, and his 1987 book *Television Culture* was one of the first books about television to take seriously the feminist agenda that has been so important to the recent development of the field. For if television studies is understood as a barely established institutional space, carved out by scholars of television from, on the one hand, mass communications and traditional Marxist political economy, and on the other, cinema, drama, and literary studies, then the significance of feminist research to the establishment of this connotationally feminized field cannot be underestimated, even if it is not always recognized. E. Ann Kaplan's collection, *Regarding Television,* gives some indication of formulations in this area from the early 1980s.

The interest of new social movements in issues of representation, which has been fruitful for film and literary studies as well as for television studies, has produced sustained interventions by a range of scholars, approaching mainly "texts" with questions about the representation of particular social groups and the interpretation of programs such as *thirtysomething, Cagney and Lacey, The Cosby Show,* or various soap operas. Feminist scholars have, since the mid-1970s, tended to focus particularly on programs "for" women and those that have key female protagonists. Key work here includes Julie D'Acci's study of *Cagney and Lacey* and the now substantial literature on soap opera (Seiter *et al.,* 1989). Research by Sut Jhally and Justin Lewis has addressed the complex meanings about class and "race" produced by viewers of *The Cosby Show,* but most audience research in this "representational" paradigm has been with white audiences. Jacqueline Bobo and Ellen Seiter argue that this is partly a consequence of the "whiteness" of the academy, which makes research about viewing in the domestic environment potentially a further extension of surveillance for those ethnicized by the dominant culture.

Television studies in the 1990s, was characterized by work in four main areas. The most formative for the emergent discipline have been the work on the definition and interpretation of the television text and the new media ethnographies of viewing, which emphasize both the contexts and the social relations of viewing. However, there is a considerable history of "production studies," which trace the complex interplay of factors involved in getting programs on screen. Examples here might include Tom Burns's study of the professional culture of the BBC (1977), Philip Schlesinger's study of "The News" (1978), the study of MTM co-edited by Jane Feuer, Paul Kerr, and Tise Vahimagi (1984), or Todd Gitlin's *Inside Prime Time* (1983, 2000). The fourth area, television history, has also been increasingly significant. Not only does the historical endeavor frequently necessitate working with vanished sources—such as the programs—but it has also involved the use of material of contested evidentiary status (for example, advertisements in women's magazines, as opposed to producer statements). This history of television is a rapidly expanding field, creating a retrospective history for the discipline, but also documenting the period of nationally regulated terrestrial broadcasting—the "television" of "television studies"—which was coming to an end.

The changes in the television industries occurring from the mid-1980s to the present led to still other questions, some of them variations on old themes, others developed in response to shifts in technology, policy, programming strategies, or alterations in social contexts. Studies of television texts continued to explore form and history, as in Aniko Bodroghkozy's *Groove Tube,* an exploration of television programs as they related to, represented, and appealed to young people. The popularity and socio-cultural significance—and financial success—of so-called "reality television" and "tabloid" television were explored in James Friedman's *Reality Squared: Televisual Discourse and the Real* (2002) and Kevin Glynn's *Tabloid Culture* (2000). These works not only worked toward definitions of these forms, but related them to earlier versions and examined responses from a range of sources. Other studies recognized that definitions of television studies tightly bound to prime-time fictional programming, or to news, or soap opera—and focused primarily on the experience of these forms in the home—were limited from the outset. Anna McCarthy's *Ambient Television* (2001), for example, explored the uses of television in taverns, department stores, installations, and other locations outside the home, thus calling into question conventional notions about the medium, its "viewers and audiences," and their practices.

Other studies were focused on technological changes that altered practices in the television industries, the experience of television users, or both. John Thornton Caldwell's *Televisuality* (1995) argued for a powerful redefinition of the medium based on the rise of digital production technologies and the expansion of distribution systems. Ellen Seiter's *Television and New Media Audiences* (1998) extended approaches developed in the analysis of popular television to users of new media such as the internet. Significantly, the first academic journal to use the term "television studies" was *Television and New Media Studies,* first published in 2000. Article titles ranged over all the topics mentioned here, from textual definition and theory, to analysis of specific programs, to essays on television history, and, as the journal title indicates, to exploration of new "screen" media. In these ways, television studies has kept pace with alterations in the varied experiences of the medium—industrial, individual, social, and cultural.

CHARLOTTE BRUNSDON

See also **Audience Research; Criticism, Television (Journalistic)**

Further Reading

Ang, Ien, *Watching Dallas,* London: Methuen, 1985

Ang, Ien, *Desperately Seeking the Audience,* London: Routledge, 1993

Ang, Ien, *Living Room Wars,* London: Routledge, 1995

Bobo, Jacqueline, and Seiter, Ellen, "Black Feminism and Media Criticism: The Women of Brewster Place," *Screen* (London), 1991; reprinted in *Feminist Television Criticism: A Reader,* edited by Charlotte Brunsdon, Julie D'Acci, and Lynn Spigel, Oxford: Clarendon Press, and New York: Oxford University Press, 1997

Boddy, William, *Fifties Television: The Industry and its Critics,* Urbana: University of Illinois Press, 1990

Bodroghkozy, Aniko, *Groove Tube: Sixties Television and the Youth Rebellion,* Durham, North Carolina: Duke University Press, 2001

Brandt, George, *British Television Drama,* Cambridge: Cambridge University Press, 1981

Browne, Nick, "The Political Economy of the Television (Super) Text," *Quarterly Review of Film Studies* (1984)

Burns, Tom, *The BBC: Public Institution, Private World,* London: Macmillan, 1977

Caldwell, John Thornton, *Televisuality: Style, Crisis, and Authority in American Television,* New Brunswick, New Jersey: Rutgers University Press, 1995

D'Acci, Julie, *Defining Women: Television and the Case of Cagney and Lacey,* Chapel Hill: University of North Carolina Press, 1994

Eco, Umberto, *The Role of the Reader,* Bloomington: University of Indiana Press, 1979

Ellis, John, *Visible Fictions,* London: Routledge and Kegan Paul, 1982

Feuer, Jane, Paul Kerr, and Tise Vahimagi, *MTM: "Quality Television,"* London: British Film Institute, 1984

Fiske, John, *Television Culture,* London: Methuen, 1987

Fiske, John, and John Hartley, *Reading Television,* London: Methuen, 1978

Friedman, James, ed., *Reality Squared: Televisual Discourse on the Real,* New Brunswick, New Jersey: Rutgers University Press, 2002

Goldie, Grace Wyndham, *Facing the Nation: Television and Politics, 1936–1976,* London: Bodley Head, 1978

Glynn, Kevin, *Tabloid Culture: Trash Taste, Popular Power, and the Transformation of American Television,* Durham, North Carolina: Duke University Press, 2000

Hall, Stuart, *et al.,* editors, *Culture, Media, Language,* London: Hutchinson and the Centre for Contemporary Cultural Studies, 1980

Hall, Stuart, *Early Writings on Television,* London: Routledge, 1997

Halloran, James, *The Effects of Television,* London: Panther, 1970

Hebdige, Dick, *Subculture and the Meaning of Style,* London: Methuen, 1978

Herzog, Herta, "What Do We really Know about Daytime Serial Listeners," in *Radio Research 1942–43,* edited by Paul Lazersfeld and Frank Stanton, New York: Duell, Sloan and Pearce, 1944

Jhally, Sut, and Justin Lewis, *Enlightened Racism: The Cosby Show and the Myth of the American Dream,* Boulder, Colorado: Westview Press, 1992

Kaplan, E. Ann, *Regarding Television,* Los Angeles: American Film Institute, 1983

Krishnan, Prabha, and Anita Dighe, *Affirmation and Denial: Construction of Femininity on Indian Television,* New Delhi: Sage, 1990

Liebes, Tamar, and Elihu Katz, *The Export of Meaning: Cross-cultural Readings of* Dallas, New York: Oxford University Press, 1990

McCarthy, Anna, *Ambient Television,* Durham, North Carolina: Duke University Press, 2001

McRobbie, Angela, *Feminism and Youth Culture,* Basingstoke, England: Macmillan, 1991

Morley, David, *The Nationwide Audience,* London: British Film Institute, 1980

Morley, David, *Television, Audiences and Cultural Power,* London: Routledge, 1992

Newcomb, Horace, *TV: The Most Popular Art,* New York: Doubleday, 1974

Newcomb, Horace, and Paul Hirsch, "Television as a Cultural Forum: Implications for Research," in, *Television: The Critical View,* edited by Horace Newcomb, New York: Oxford University Press, 1994

O'Connor, Alan, editor, *Raymond Williams on Television,* London: Routledge, 1989

Purser, Philip, *Done Viewing,* London: Quartet, 1992

Schlesinger, Philip, *Putting "Reality" Together,* London: Constable, 1978

Seiter, Ellen, *et al., Remote Control,* London: Routledge, 1989

Seiter, Ellen, *Television and New Media Audiences,* Oxford: Clarendon Press, 1999

Spigel, Lynn, *Make Room for TV,* Chicago: University of Chicago Press, 1993

Television and New Media, quarterly journal (2000–)

Thomas, Howard, editor, *The Armchair Theatre,* London: Weidenfeld and Nicolson, 1959

Thurber, James, *The Beast in Me and other Animals,* New York: Harcourt Brace, 1948

Williams, Raymond, *Drama in Performance,* London: C.A. Watts, 1968

Williams, Raymond, *Television, Technology and Cultural Form,* London: Fontana, 1974

Terrorism

"Terrorism" is a term that cannot be given a stable definition; to do so forestalls any attempt to examine the major feature of its relation to television in the contemporary world. As the central public arena for organizing ways of picturing and talking about social and political life, TV plays a pivotal role in the contest between competing definitions, accounts, and explanations of terrorism.

Politicians frequently try to limit the terms of this competition by asserting the primacy of their preferred versions. Jeanne Kirkpatrick, former U.S. representative to the United Nations, for example, had no difficulty recognizing "terrorism" when she saw it, arguing that "what the terrorist does is kill, maim, kidnap, torture. His victims may be schoolchildren.... industrialists returning home from work, political leaders or diplomats". Television journalists, in contrast, prefer to work with less elastic definitions. The BBC's *News Guide,* for example, advises reporters that "the best general rule" is to use the term "terrorist" when civilians are attacked and "guerrillas" when the targets are members of the official security forces.

Which term is used in any particular context is inextricably tied to judgments about the legitimacy of the action in question and of the political system against which it is directed. Terms like "guerrilla," "partisan," or "freedom fighter" carry positive connotations of varying degrees, suggesting a perhaps justified struggle against an occupying power or an oppressive state; to label an action as "terrorist" is, by the same token, to consign it to illegitimacy.

For most of the television age, from the end of World War II to the collapse of the Soviet Union, the deployment of positive and negative political labels was an integral part of Cold War politics and its dualistic view of the world. In the West, the term "terrorism" was used extensively to characterize enemies of the United States and its allies, as in President Reagan's assertion in 1985 that Libya, Cuba, Nicaragua, and North Korea constituted a "confederation of terrorist states" intent on undermining American attempts "to bring stable and democratic government" to the developing world. Conversely, friendly states, such as Argentina, could wage a full scale internal war against "terrorism," using a definition elastic enough to embrace almost anyone who criticized the regime or held unacceptable opinions, and attract comparatively little censure from Western governments despite the fact that this wholesale use of state terror killed and maimed many more civilians than the more publicized incidents of "retail" (in distinction to "wholesale") terror—targeted assassinations, kidnappings and bombings.

The relations between internal terrorism and the state raise particularly difficult questions for liberal democracies. By undermining the state's claim to a legitimate monopoly of force within its borders, acts of "retail" terror pose a clear threat to internal security. And, in the case of subnational and separatist movements that refuse to recognize the integrity of those borders, they directly challenge its political legitimacy.

The seige of the Munich Olympic Village, 1972: The apartment of the Israeli Olympic team in Munich after the Arab guerrilla terrorist attack, 1972.
Courtesy of the Everett Collection/CSU Archives

Faced with these challenges, liberal democracies have two choices. Either they can abide by their own declared principles, permit open political debate on the underlying causes and claims of terrorist movements, uphold the rule of law, and respond to insurgent violence through the procedures of due process. Or they can curtail public debate and civil liberties in the name of effective security. The British state's response to the conflict in Northern Ireland, and to British television's attempts to cover it, illustrate this tension particularly well.

Television journalism in Britain has faced a particular problem in reporting "the Irish Question" since the Republican movement has adopted a dual strategy using both the ballot box and the bullet, pursuing its claim for the ultimate reunification of Ireland electorally, through the legal political party, Sinn Féin, and militarily, through the campaign waged by the illegal Irish Republican Army. Added to which, the British state's response has been ambiguous. Ostensibly, as Prime Minister Thatcher argued in 1990, although "they are at war with us.... we can only fight them with the civil law." Then Home Secretary Douglas Hurd admitted in 1989 that, in his view "with the Provisional IRA...it is nothing to do with a political cause any more. They are professional killers.... No political solution will cope with that. They just have to be extirpated." Television journalists' attempts to explore these contradictions produced two of the bitterest peacetime confrontations between British broadcasters and the British state.

Soon after British troops were first sent to Northern Ireland in the early 1970s, there were suspicions that the due process of arrest and trial was being breached by a covert but officially sanctioned shoot-to-kill policy directed against suspected members of Republican paramilitary groups. In 1988, three members of an IRA active service unit were shot dead by members of an elite British counter-terrorist unit in Gibraltar. Contrary to the initial official statements, they were later found to be unarmed and not in the process of planting a car bomb as first claimed. One of the leading commercial television companies, Thames Television, produced a documentary entitled *Death on the Rock,* raising questions about the incident. It was greeted with a barrage of hostile criticism from leading Conservative politicians, including Prime Minister Thatcher. The tone of official condemnation was perfectly caught in an editorial headline in the country's best-selling daily paper *The Sun,* claiming that the program was "just IRA propaganda."

The representation of the Provisional IRA was at the heart of an earlier major conflict, over a 1985 BBC documentary entitled *At the Edge of the Union.* This featured an extended profile of Martin McGuinness of Sinn Féin, widely thought to be a leading IRA executive responsible for planning bombings. The program gave him space to explain his views and showed him in his local community and at home with his family. The then Home Secretary Leon Brittan (who had not seen the film) wrote to the chairman of the BBC's Board of Governors urging them not to show it, arguing that "Even if [it] and any surrounding material were, as a whole, to present terrorist organizations in a wholly unfavorable light, I would still ask you not to permit it to be broadcast." The governors convened an emergency meeting and decided to cancel the scheduled screening. This very public vote of no confidence in the judgment of the corporation's senior editors and managers was unprecedented and was met with an equally unprecedented response from BBC journalists. They staged a one-day strike protesting against government interference with the Corporation's independence.

In his letter, Brittan had claimed that it was "damaging to security and therefore to the public interest to provide a boost to the morale of the terrorists and their apologists in this way." Refusing this conflation of "security" with the "public interest" is at the heart of television journalism's struggle to provide an adequate information base for a mature democracy. As the BBC's assistant director general put it in 1988, "it is necessary for the maintenance of democracy that unpopular, even dangerous, views are heard and thoroughly understood. The argument about the 'national interest' demanding censorship of such voices is glib and intrinsically dangerous. Who determines the 'national interest?' How far does the 'national interest' ex-

tend?" His argument was soundly rejected by the government. In the autumn of 1988, they instructed broadcasters not to transmit direct speech from members of eleven Irish organizations, including Sinn Féin, leading to the ludicrous situation in which actors dubbed the words of proscribed interviewees over film of them speaking. This ban was lifted in 1994, but its imposition illustrates the permanent potential for conflict between official conceptions of security and the national interest and broadcasters' desire to provide full information, rational debate, and relevant contextualization on areas of political controversy and dispute. As the BBC's former director general, Ian Trethowan, pointed out, the basic dilemma posed by television's treatment of terrorism is absolutely "central to the ordering of a civilized society: how to avoid encouraging terrorism and violence while keeping a free and democratic people properly informed."

Television's ability to strike this balance is not just a question for news, current affairs, and documentary production, however. The images and accounts of terrorism offered by television drama and entertainment are also important in orchestrating the continual contest between the discourse of government and the state, the discourses of legitimated opposition groups, and the discourses of insurgent movements. This struggle is not simply for visibility—to be seen and heard. It is also for credibility—to have one's views discussed seriously and one's case examined with care. The communicative weapons in this battle are, however, unevenly distributed.

As the saturation coverage that the U.S. news media gave to the Shi'ite hijacking of a TWA passenger jet at Beirut in 1985 demonstrated very clearly, spectacular acts of retail terror can command a high degree of visibility. But the power to contextualize and to grant or withhold legitimacy lies with the array of official spokespeople who comment on the event and help construct its public meaning. As the American political scientist David Paletz has noted, because television news "generally ignores the motivations, objectives and long-term goals of violent organizations," it effectively prevents "their causes from gaining legitimacy with the public." This has led some commentators to speculate that exclusion from the general process of meaning-making is likely to generate ever more spectacular acts designed to capitalize on the access provided by the highly visible propaganda of the deed.

Bernard Lewis, one of America's leading experts on the Arab world, noted in his comments on the hijacking of the TWA airliner that those who plotted the incident "knew that they could count on the American press and television to provide them with unlimited publicity and perhaps even some form of advocacy," but because the coverage ignored the political roots of the action in the complex power struggles within Shi'ite Islam, it did little to explain its causes or to foster informed debate on appropriate responses. As the television critic of the *Financial Times* of London put it; "There is a criticism to be made of the coverage of these events, but it is not that television aided and abetted terrorists. On the contrary, it is that television failed to convey, or even to consider, the reasons for what President Reagan called 'ugly, vicious, evil terrorism.'"

News is a relatively closed form of television programming. It privileges the views of spokespeople for governments and state agencies and generally organizes stories to converge around officially sanctioned resolutions. Other program forms—documentaries, for example—are potentially at least more open. They may allow a broader spectrum of perspectives into play, including those that voice alternative or oppositional viewpoints. They may stage debates and pose awkward questions rather than offer familiar answers.

Both these strategies became brutally apparent following the attacks on the World Trade Center in New York on September 11, 2001. News coverage was the dominant form, beginning with live coverage of the actions. Many viewers were tuned to ongoing reports of the first plane's strike when they saw the second strike on their television screens. News reports of the attack on the Pentagon were interspersed with speculation regarding still other planes headed toward Washington. The crash of the fourth plane in Pennsylvania was described cautiously at first as "potentially" involved in the coordinated attacks, then, with information from telephone messages from passengers, confirmed as part of the plan.

News coverage continued for days, providing information on events, rescue efforts, background, responses, and other related factors. But it also included interviews with the families of victims, often drawing heavily on emotional moments. Viewers could easily relate to these more personal accounts, given that the entire country was caught up in its first-ever experience of something so immediate and, to rely on the term, terrifying.

Some of these news accounts were quickly edited with other information into network "examinations" of the events, programs approaching conventional documentaries in length and style—file footage, talking-head interviews, background information, speculation as to motive, intent, technique, and long-term implications.

In the following months, numerous documentaries have explored specific aspects of the events of September 11. Many of these have attempted varying types of "explanation," from computerized analyses of how and why the buildings were vulnerable to such attacks, to explorations of individual lives. A few have challenged conventional accounts of events to take a more critical look at alternative explanations of the political events and personalities, the strategies of the attackers, and the role of the U.S. government, the responses of various agencies involved, and the implications for future international relations. Still other documentaries have explored Islamic culture, international attitudes toward U.S. policies and culture, and such specific topics as responses of children, religious understanding of the problem of evil, and plans to build memorials at "Ground Zero."

In the aftermath of the attacks, in the ongoing "War on Terror" conducted by the Bush administration, a war that has led to engagement in Afghanistan, the defeat of the Baathist regime in Iraq, and the capture of Saddam Hussein, television's reliance on notions of "terror" and "terrorism" has come to occupy an almost regular spot on the schedules. It is unlikely that, for many years to come, September 11th will pass in the United States without news and documentaries that return in some way to that day in 2001 and to the topic.

Television in a democratic society requires the greatest possible diversity of open program forms if it is to address the issues raised by terrorism in the complexity they merit. Whether the emerging forces of technological change in production and reception, channel proliferation, increased competition for audiences, and transnational distribution will advance or block this ideal is a question well worth examining.

GRAHAM MURDOCK

See also **Death on the Rock**

Further Reading

Alali, A. Odasu, and Gary W. Byrd, *Terrorism and the News Media: A Selected, Annotated Bibliography,* Jefferson, North Carolina: McFarland, 1994

Alali, A. Odasu, and Kenoye Kelvin Eke, editors, *Media Coverage of Terrorism: Methods of Diffusion,* Newbury Park, California: Sage, 1991

Alexander, Yonah, and Robert G. Picard, editors, *In the Camera's Eye: News Coverage of Terrorist Events,* Washington, D.C.: Brassey's, 1991

Dobkin, Bethami A., *Tales of Terror: Television News and the Construction of the Terrorist Threat,* New York: Praeger, 1992

Livingston, Steven, *The Terrorism Spectacle,* Boulder, Colorado: Westview, 1994

Miller, Abraham, editor, *Terrorism, the Media, and the Law,* Dobbs Ferry, New York: Transnational, 1982

Nacos, Brigitte Lebens, *Terrorism and the Media: From the Iran Hostage Crisis to the World Trade Center Bombing,* New York: Columbia University Press, 1994

O'Neill, Michael J., *Terrorist Spectaculars: Should TV Coverage Be Curbed?,* New York: Priority Press, 1986

Paletz, David L., and Alex Peter Schmid, editors, *Terrorism and the Media,* Newbury Park, California: Sage, 1991

Picard, Robert G., *Media Portrayals of Terrorism: Functions and Meanings of News Coverage,* Ames: Iowa State University Press, 1993

Schaffert, Richard W., *Media Coverage and Political Terrorists: A Quantitative Analysis,* New York: Praeger, 1992

Signorielli, Nancy, and George Gerbner, *Violence and Terror in the Mass Media: An Annotated Bibliography,* New York: Greenwood Press, 1988

Weimann, Gabriel, and Conrad Winn, *The Theater of Terror: Mass Media and International Terrorists,* New York: Longman, 1994

That Girl

U.S. Situation Comedy

That Girl was one of the first television shows in the United States to focus on the single working woman, preceding CBS's *Mary Tyler Moore Show* by four years. This situation comedy followed heroine Ann Marie's adventures as she struggled to establish herself on the New York stage while supporting herself with a variety of temporary jobs.

That Girl was reputedly inspired by the life of its star, Marlo Thomas. The daughter of famous television comedian Danny Thomas wanted success on her own merits, so she moved to Britain, where her father was unknown. After five years struggling, she won acclaim in Mike Nichol's 1965 London production of *Barefoot in the Park.* Returning home, she starred in an ABC pilot, *Two's Company,* about a model married to a photographer. Although it was not picked up, ABC head Ed Sherick offered Thomas other roles, including the lead in *My Mother, the Car.* She rejected these parts and instead approached the network with an idea for a show called *Miss Independence,* centered on the life of a young, single career woman. ABC was interested but wanted some kind of chaperone as a regular character.

Like *The Patty Duke Show, Peyton Place,* and *Gidget, That Girl* was one of many shows ABC targeted at the young female audience during the mid- to late 1960s. The network had successfully turned to this up-and-coming demographic as early as 1963, capitalizing on the nascent women's movement and youth revolution. Like most of these shows, *That Girl* followed an already established trend, offering a diluted and sanitized version of the glamorized single-woman lifestyle popularized by the likes of Helen Gurley Brown, Mary McCarthy, and Jacqueline Susann. Un-

like those writers' heroines, however, Ann Marie remained, at the behest of network standards and practices offices, chaste. The executives even wanted her to marry steady boyfriend, magazine executive Don Hollinger (whom she met in the first episode), but Thomas resisted, consenting only to a September 1970 engagement.

While it focused on a self-supporting woman, *That Girl* did not center on the workplace (unlike *The Mary Tyler Moore Show*), largely because Ann's employment was essentially itinerant. Instead, her efforts to succeed revealed a merging of public and private life. The erratic nature of her employment undermined everyday routines of working life, positioning her independence as highly precarious—particularly when contrasted to the steady rituals of Don's career. Ann's temporary jobs presented comedic opportunities as she struggled to retain her dignity in the face of often demeaning circumstances while foregrounding her continued reliance on her parents and Don. Female independence was thus presented as a site of struggle, both against the restrictions of the male-dominated workplace and the social and familial pressures for marriage. Meanwhile, Ann's very choice of profession—the stage—undermined her desire for success, casting it in terms of fantasy. This lack of realism was evident from the start. Even Thomas noted that her struggling actress heroine never changed or developed. This refusal of change ultimately led to the show's 1971 cancellation: despite good ratings, Thomas announced that she could not face playing the same character for eternity.

MOYA LUCKETT

See also Mary Tyler Moore Show, The

That Girl, Marlo Thomas, 1966–71; 1969 episode.
Courtesy of the Everett Collection

Cast

Ann Marie	Marlo Thomas
Don Hollinger	Ted Bessell
Lou Marie	Lew Parker
Helen Marie (1966–70)	Rosemary DeCamp
Judy Bessemer (1966–67)	Bonnie Scott
Dr. Leon Bessemer (1966–67)	Dabney Coleman
Jules Benedict	Billie De Wolfe
Jerry Bauman	Bernie Kopell
Ruth Bauman (1967–69)	Carolyn Daniels
Ruth Bauman (1969–71)	Alice Borden
Harvey Peck (1966–67)	Ronnie Schell
George Lester (1966–67)	George Carlin
Seymour Schwimmer (1967–68)	Don Penny
Margie "Pete" Peterson (1967–68)	
Mary	Ruth Buzzi
Gloria	Reva Rose
Jonathan Adams	Bobo Lewis
Bert Hollinger	Forest Compton
Mildred Hollinger	Frank Faylen
Sandi Hollinger	Mabel Albertson
Nino	Cloris Leachman
Mr. Brantano	Gino Conforti
Mrs. Brantano	Frank Puglia
Sandy Stone	Renata Vanni
	Morty Gunty

Producers

Bill Persky, Sam Denoff, Bernie Orenstein, Saul Turteltaub, Jerry Davis

Programming History

136 episodes
ABC

September 1966–April 1967	Thursday 9:30–10:00
April 1967–January 1969	Thursday 9:00–9:30
February 1969–September 1970	Thursday 8:00–8:30
September 1970–September 1971	Friday 9:00–9:30

Further Reading

Cole, Stephen, *That Book about That Girl: The Unofficial Companion,* Los Angeles: Renaissance Books, 1999

Douglas, Susan J., *Where the Girls Are: Growing Up Female with the Mass Media,* New York: Times Books, 1994

That Was the Week That Was

British Satirical Review

The idea for *That Was the Week That Was* (which familiarly became known as *TW3*) came partly from the then director general of the BBC, Hugh Greene, who wanted to "prick the pomposity of public figures." However, it was the team of Ned Sherrin, Alasdair Milne, and Donald Baverstock that was responsible for developing the program's successful format. The trio had previously worked on the BBC's daily early-evening news magazine show *Tonight* (1957–65; revived and revamped version, 1975–79) and the lighthearted style and wide-ranging brief of that show often allowed certain items to be covered in a tongue-in-cheek, irreverent, or even satirical way. *TW3,* in its late-night Saturday slot, moved those elements a stage further and, taking a lead from the increased liberalism of theater and cinema in Britain, was able to discuss and dissect the week's news and newsmakers using startlingly direct language and illustration. Whereas *Tonight* was gentle, *TW3* was savage, unflinching in its devotion to highlighting cant and hypocrisy and seemingly fearless in its near-libelous accusations and innuendos. It became an influential, controversial, and groundbreaking satire series, which pushed back the barriers of what was acceptable comment on television. Complaints poured in, but so did congratulations and, despite enormous political pressure, Hugh Greene—determined in his quest to see a modern, harder BBC through the 1960s—stood by his brainchild.

Stylistically, the show broke many rules. Although it was commonplace on "live" shows of the 1950s (such as the rock 'n' roll show *6–5 Special*) to see the cumbersome cameras being pushed from one set to the next, *TW3* went beyond that. A camera mounted high up in the studio would offer a bird's-eye view of the entire proceedings, showing the complete studio set-up with the flimsy sketch sets, the musicians, backroom personnel, the audience, other cameras, and so on. It seemed to indicate that the viewing audience was to be treated as equals, and that both creator and viewer knew it was a studio, knew the sketches were not really set in a doctor's waiting-room but in a three-walled mock-up, knew that make-up girls would wait in the wings with powder and paint—so why hide it? The format of the show was simple, rigid enough to keep it all together, flexible enough to let items lengthen or shorten or disappear altogether, depending on time. Millicent Martin (the only permanent female member of the team) would sing the title song (music by Ron Grainer, with Caryl Brahms providing a new set of lyrics each week relating to the news of the past few days), then David Frost, as host, would introduce the proceedings and act as link man between the items, often appearing himself in sketches or giving monologues. (Originally, John Bird was to be host, but declined; Sherrin saw Frost at a club, doing an act where he gave a press conference as Prime Minister Harold MacMillan, and offered him the role of cohost with Brian Redhead, who dropped out after doing the untransmitted pilot.) Bernard Levin interviewed people in the news or with strongly held views, and his acid wit added an edge that occasionally produced flare-ups both verbal and physical. (A member of the studio au-

dience once punched Levin during the program, rather ineffectually, following a scathing review he had written.) Lance Percival acted in sketches and sang topical calypsos (a device used on *Tonight*), many of which were ad-libbed. David Kernan was a resident singer whose strength was his ability to parody other singers and styles; Timothy Birdsall drew cartoons, Al Mancini pulled faces, and the engine room was provided by Willie Rushton, Kenneth Cope, and Roy Kinnear who fleshed out the sketches and comic chatter. The show occasionally featured guest artists—most famously, comedian Frankie Howerd, whose popularity had waned somewhat. His one appearance on *TW3* managed to dramatically resurrect his career, as his humor seemed to work for both traditionalists and this new, younger, harder generation.

The writing credits for the show read like a *Who's Who* of the sharp young talent of the time: John Albery, John Antrobus, Christopher Booker, Malcolm Bradbury, John Braine, Quentin Crewe, Brian Glanville, Gerald Kaufman, Herbert Kretzmer, David Nathan and Dennis Potter, David Nobbs, Peter Shaffer, Kenneth Tynan, Stephen Vinaver, Keith Waterhouse, and Willis Hall—plus contributions from the show's creative staff: Sherrin, Frost, and Levin.

Memorable moments from the series include Gerald Kaufman's list of silent MPs, highlighting politicians who had not spoken in the House of Commons in ten or fifteen years. The sketch caused a furor when it was read out by the team, despite the fact that the information was readily available. Kenneth Cope's "confession" monologue (written by John Braine) featured a figure, hidden in shadows, who confessed to being heterosexual and related the misery this identity can cause. Frost's scathing profile of Home Secretary Henry Brooke insinuated, among other things, that his intractability in an immigration case had led to the murder of the subject. Millicent Martin sang with black-faced minstrels about racism in the southern United States. And most memorable of all was the truly serious edition immediately following President John Kennedy's assassination. The whole show was given over to the subject, tackling the shock felt and the implications of the shooting with rare solemnity and dignity. (That episode was lodged at the Smithsonian Institution.)

A U.S. version of the series (also featuring Frost) debuted 10 January 1964 on NBC and ran until May 1965. Singer Nancy Ames took the Millicent Martin role and Buck Henry, Pat Englund, and Alan Alda were among the regulars. The show proved equally groundbreaking in the United States and, like the British version, was no stranger to controversy.

DICK FIDDY

See also **Frost, David**

Cast
David Frost
Millicent Martin
Bernard Levin
Lance Percival
Roy Kinnear
William Rushton
Timothy Birdsall
John Wells
Kenneth Cope
David Kernan
Al Mancini
John Bird
Eleanor Bron
Roy Hudd

Producer
Ned Sherrin

Programming History
36 50-minute episodes; 1 150-minute special; 1 100-minute special
BBC

September 29, 1962	150-minute special
November 24, 1962–April 27, 1963	23 episodes
September 28, 1963–December 21, 1963	13 episodes
December 28, 1963	100-minute special

Further Reading

Campey, George, J.T. Archer, and Ian Coates, *The BBC Book of That Was the Week That Was,* London: British Broadcasting Corporation, 1963

Frost, David, *That Was the Week That Was,* London: W.H. Allen, 1963

Thaw, John (1942–2002)

British Actor

A versatile and successful British actor, John Thaw worked in television, theater, and cinema. But the small screen guaranteed him almost continual employment throughout his exceptional career.

After training at the Royal Academy of Dramatic Art, at a 1960 stage debut he was "discovered" and promoted by Granada TV. His first TV outing was in 1961; after that he took the lead role in an impressive array of series. He had parts ranging from *The Avengers* to *Z Cars,* and the lead in the series *Redcap* before his big break in *The Sweeney* (1974–78), a landmark in the police-action genre. Thaw played rough-mannered detective Jack Regan of the Flying Squad. *The Sweeney* was described as a U.S.-influenced imitation of West Coast shows, and was prominent in debates about the levels of violence and bad language on television, being criticized for glamorizing guns and car chases. Its superiority over standard violent fare, however, owed much to Thaw's performance, along with the growing rapport between his and Dennis Waterman's characters and the show's constant originality.

For years after *The Sweeney,* Thaw found it difficult to throw off the Jack Regan image, but in 1987 he began another long-running detective series for which he is perhaps best known. *Inspector Morse* was remarkably popular with critics and audiences internationally. Its ITV ratings in Britain were second only to those of *Coronation Street.* Again, the show owed much of its success to Thaw's central performance, for which he twice won a British Academy of Film and Television Award (BAFTA). He held together Morse's eccentricities, as the irascible, world-weary, and introspective crossword and classical-music lover. Julian Mitchell, writer of several episodes of *Morse,* saw Thaw as the consummate TV actor: "His technique is perfect, and by seeming to do very little he conveys so much." In this way he suggested hidden depths to Morse, and conveyed his troubled morality. The tranquility and gentle English manner associated with *Morse* were a far cry from *The Sweeney,* and it gained fans as an antidote to violent American television.

Audiences were accustomed to Thaw's downbeat manner in gloomy roles, but he claimed to prefer do-

John Thaw, in the *Inspector Morse* TV series; episode "The Wolvercote Tongue," December 1988.
Courtesy of the Everett Collection

ing comedy. He played the lead in the sitcom *Home to Roost,* appeared with *Sweeney* partner Waterman in the 1976 *Morecambe and Wise Christmas Show,* and starred in the widely derided *A Year in Provence,* which lost a record 10 million viewers during one series.

Despite this, Thaw remained a very bankable star. *Kavanagh QC,* a part written especially for him after *Provence,* was another big hit. He was back on familiar territory as a barrister reconciling principle and his working-class roots with a lucrative law practice.

Thaw saw himself as a "jobbing actor, no different from a plumber." Part of his success may have been a result of his ability to play everyman roles that people could relate to easily. Despite a distinctly unclassical repertoire, he continued to act on stage whenever his busy TV career allowed, latterly in "special guest star" roles. He also appeared in several feature films, including two *Sweeney* films, and Richard Attenborough's *Cry Freedom* (1987). John Thaw died on February 21, 2002.

GUY JOWETT

See also **Sweeney, The**

John Thaw. Born in Manchester, Lancashire, England, January 3, 1942. Attended Dulcie Technical High School, Manchester; Royal Academy of Dramatic Art (Vanbrugh Award, Liverpool Playhouse Award). Married: 1) Sally Alexander (divorced); child: Abigail; 2) Sheila Hancock, 1973; children: Joanna and stepdaughter Melanie. Stage debut, Liverpool Playhouse, 1960; London debut, Royal Court Theatre, 1961; became widely familiar to television audiences in *The Sweeney* and subsequently as star of the *Inspector Morse* series. Commander of the Order of the British Empire, 1993. Recipient: British Academy of Film and Television Arts Award for Best Television Actor, 1990 and 1993. Died February 21, 2002, due to cancer of the esophagus.

Television Series and Miniseries

1965–66	*Redcap*
1974	*Thick As Thieves*
1974–78	*The Sweeney*
1983	*Mitch*
1985–89	*Home to Roost*
1987–2000	*Inspector Morse*
1991	*Stanley and the Women*
1992	*A Year in Provence*
1995–2001	*Kavanagh QC*
1999	*Plastic Man*
1999	*The Second World War in Color* (voice only)
1999	*The Waiting Time*
2000	*Britain at War in Color* (voice only)
2001	*The Glass*

Made-for-Television Movies

1981	*Drake's Venture*
1997	*Into the Blue*
1998	*Goodnight Mr. Tom*
2001	*Buried Treasure*

Television Specials

1974	*Regan*
1984	*The Life and Death of King John*
1992	*Bomber Harris*
1993	*The Mystery of Morse*
1994	*The Absence of War*

Films

Nil Carborundum, 1962; *The Loneliness of the Long Distance Runner,* 1962; *Five to One,* 1963; *Dead Man's Chest,* 1965; *The Bofors Gun,* 1968; *Praise Marx and Pass the Ammunition,* 1970; *The Last Grenade,* 1970; *The Abominable Dr. Phibes,* 1971;

Dr. Phibes Rises Again, 1972; *The Sensible Action of Lieutenant Holst,* 1976; *The Sweeney,* 1977; *The Sweeney II,* 1978; *Dinner at the Sporting Club,* 1978; *The Grass is Singing,* 1981; *Asking for Trouble,* 1987; *Business As Usual,* 1987; *Cry Freedom,* 1987; *Charlie,* 1992; *Monsignor Renard,* 1999.

Stage
A Shred of Evidence, 1960; *The Fire Raisers,* 1961; *Women Beware Women,* 1962; *Semi-Detached,*

1962; *So What About Love?,* 1969; *Random Happenings in the Hebrides,* 1970; *The Lady from the Sea,* 1971; *Collaborators,* 1973; *Absurd Person Singular,* 1976; *Night and Day,* 1978; *Sergeant Musgrave's Dance,* 1982; *Twelfth Night,* 1983; *The Time of Your Life,* 1983; *Henry VIII,* 1983; *Pygmalion,* 1984; *All My Sons,* 1988; *The Absence of War,* 1993.

Theme Songs

Theme songs are perhaps television's most underrated aesthetic component. While scholarly attention has long been lavished on issues of representation, narrative, and (to a somewhat lesser extent) visual style, television music has been only rarely considered, and theme songs even less so. However, theme songs are one of the most iconic aspects of a series, branding it with an aural identity that is ritually repeated in every episode (and subsequent rerun), and firmly lodged in the collective brain of popular culture. Just a few notes from a popular theme song such as *The Twilight Zone* or *Scooby-Doo* can quickly convey an entire sensibility. Theme songs come in several varieties: instrumentals, songs with lyrics, and previously existing compositions adapted to a particular series.

Instrumental themes have long been effective in anchoring programs to particular aesthetic and cultural sensibilities. For example, Henry Mancini's smoky, driving *Peter Gunn* theme is still an evocative take on the postwar private eye. Similarly, a few years later, Laurie Johnson's jaunty theme for *The Avengers* effectively captured that series' signature cocktail of sex, wit, and derring-do, while Lalo Schifrin's blazingly minimalist *Mission: Impossible* theme became one of the most recognizable themes of all time. Other hailed instrumentals include the themes to *The Twilight Zone* and *The X-Files,* which eerily suggest the fear of the unknown; the themes to *Doctor Kildare* and *St. Elsewhere,* which calmly indicate melodrama and care; and the themes to *The Andy Griffith Show* and *Northern Exposure,* which convey a laid-back, rural sensibility.

Instrumental themes also mark significant changes in genre. The themes of 1950s police series such as *Dragnet* and *Highway Patrol* emphasized a martial,

no-nonsense "law and order" mood. However, police series of the 1970s, such as *Hawaii Five-O* or *S.W.A.T.,* generally featured hard, brassy themes that promised gritty urban action, while recent themes have been more brooding than ballistic, reflecting their series' contemplative moods (for instance, *Homicide: Life On The Streets* and *NYPD Blue*). Instrumental sitcom themes have ranged over an even greater terrain, taking in bouncy and childlike *(Leave It To Beaver)*; suburban and swinging *(The Dick Van Dyke Show)*; urban and funky *(Sanford And Son)*; sensitive and melancholic *(Taxi)*; easygoing and jazzy *(The Cosby Show)*; bluesy and working class *(Roseanne)*; and ironic and chaotic *(The Simpsons),* among many other moods.

Theme songs with lyrics convey a more intimate expression of a series' context, as their explicit declarations match their protagonists' depicted social and emotional aspirations. Accordingly, such themes are often heard in post-1970 sitcoms, which generally focus on their characters' quests for community and emotional security, such as *Alice, All In The Family, Diff'rent Strokes, Friends, The Golden Girls, Good Times, Laverne & Shirley, Malcolm In The Middle, The Mary Tyler Moore Show, One Day At A Time, Scrubs, Welcome Back, Kotter,* and *WKRP In Cincinnati.* In the case of *All In The Family,* the theme was even performed on camera by two of its main characters (Archie and Edith Bunker) in every episode, vividly depicting their perspectives.

Occasionally, sitcom lyrics even provide a detailed exposition of a program's basic situation. This trend was heard most famously in the themes to 1960s and 1970s series such as *The Beverly Hillbillies, The Brady Bunch, F Troop, Gilligan's Island, Green Acres,* and

The Patty Duke Show. Such themes were archly resurrected in a few 1990s sitcoms (such as *Fresh Prince of Bel-Air, Herman's Head,* and *The Nanny,* which managed to rhyme "crushing scenes" with "Flushing, Queens").

Existing compositions have also often become popular television theme songs. Charles Gounod's "Funeral March of the Marionettes" is probably better known as the theme to *Alfred Hitchcock Presents,* while John Philip Sousa's "Liberty Bell March" now has a similar connotation thanks to its use on *Monty Python's Flying Circus.* Seventeenth century composer Jean-Joseph Mouret's Rondeau from *Symphonies and Fanfares for the King's Supper* still serves as the fanfare to *Masterpiece Theatre.* The original hit recording of "Rock Around The Clock" (performed by Bill Haley and the Comets) appropriately opened each episode of *Happy Days* during its first two seasons (complete with a jukebox motif, with the song starting as the needle hit the record), before being replaced with an original, eponymous song. A languid instrumental of "Georgia On My Mind" was used as the theme for the Atlanta-set *Designing Women* until its last season, when Ray Charles appeared in the credits (with the cast draping his piano), to sing the song. More recent uses of existing songs include: Carole King's "If You Leave I Will Follow" (from her popular 1970 album *Tapestry*), which was re-recorded as a duet between King and her daughter Louise Goffin to evoke the mother–daughter sentiments of *Gilmore Girls;* The Who's "Who Are You?," which graces *CSI: Crime Scene Investigation* for its

rock ethos, familiarity with the target audience, and lyrical confluence with the series' subject matter; and Diane Warren's soft-rock ballad "Where My Heart Will Take Me," which bombastically connects the spacefarers of *Star Trek: Enterprise* to sentimental longing.

Although well-conceived television theme songs become popular and recognizable with viewers, they have only rarely become full-fledged pop hits with listeners, in terms of radio airplay and sales. Jan Hammer's *Miami Vice* theme, released as a single in 1985, is still the all-time best-selling television theme song; other notable hits include the themes from *The Greatest American Hero, S.W.A.T.,* and *Welcome Back, Kotter.* Beyond the theme song, entire soundtrack albums have been released featuring music heard in (or "inspired by") particular series. This practice began in the 1950s with the likes of Mancini's *Mr. Lucky* and *Peter Gunn* albums, but continues to this day. Some soundtrack releases are collections of incidental music (e.g. *Star Trek, The Twilight Zone, Xena: Warrior Princess*), while others are compilations of pop songs that are featured in their respective programs (e.g. *Beverly Hills 90210, Friends, The Heights, Smallville*).

DEREK KOMPARE

Further Reading and Listening

Burlingame, Jon, *TV's Biggest Hits: The Story of Television Themes from "Dragnet" to "Friends,"* Lexington, Massachusetts: Museum of our National Heritage, 1996
Television's Greatest Hits Volumes 1–7, Recordings, TVT Records, 1986–96

thirtysomething

U.S. Drama

Winner of an Emmy Award for Best Dramatic Series in 1988, *thirtysomething* (ABC, 1987–91) represented a new kind of hour-long drama, a series that focused on the domestic and professional lives of a group of young urban professionals ("yuppies"), a socio-economic category of increasing interest to the television industry. The series attracted a cult audience of viewers who strongly identified with one or more of its eight central characters, a circle of friends living in Philadelphia, Pennsylvania. Its stylistic and storyline innovations led critics to respect it for being "as close

to the level of an art form as weekly television ever gets," as the *New York Times* put it. When the series was canceled due to poor ratings, a *Newsweek* eulogy reflected the sense on the part of "baby boomers" of losing a rendezvous with their mirrored lifestyle: "the value of the Tuesday night meetings was that art, even on the small screen, reflected our lives back at us to be considered as new." Hostile critics, on the other hand, were relieved that the self-indulgent whines of "yuppiedom" had finally been banished from the schedules.

The show *thirtysomething* spearheaded ABC's drive

to reach a demographically younger and culturally more capital-rich audience. Cover stories in *Rolling Stone* and *Entertainment Weekly* explored the parallels between the actors' and characters' lives, as well as the rapport the program generated with its audience, who were seen as sharing the characters' inner conflicts. Michael Steadman, an advertising copywriter struggling with the claims of his liberal Jewish background, and his wife Hope, a part-time journalist and activist and a full-time mother, were the "settled" couple. The Steadmans were contrasted with Elliot, a not-really-grown-up graphic artist who was Michael's best friend at the University of Pennsylvania, and Elliot's long-suffering wife Nancy, an illustrator who separated from him and developed ovarian cancer in subsequent seasons. Three unmarried friends also dating back from college days complete the roster of characters: Ellyn, a career executive in city government; Gary, English teacher at a liberal arts college; and Melissa, a freelance photographer and Michael's cousin. While the two couples wrestled with their marriages and raising their children, the three others had a series of love affairs with outsiders to the circle. For Gary, after a quasi-incestuous relation with Melissa, fate held a child out of wedlock with a temperamental feminist named Susanna; failure to win tenure at the college; life as a househusband; and, finally, in one of the series' most publicized episodes, sudden death in an automobile accident.

The title, referring to the age of the characters, was written as one word (to represent "togetherness") and in lower case (to evoke e.e. cummings and the refusal of authority). "Real life is an acquired taste" was the network promo for the series, as its makers explored the boundaries between soap operatics and verisimilitude, between melodrama and realism. Co-creators Edward Zwick and Marshall Herskovitz (who had met at the American Film Institute) claimed a "mandate of small moments examined closely," dealing with "worlds of incremental change" loosely modeled on their own lives and those of their friends. Central to Zwick and Herskovitz's sense of this fictional world was a high degree of self-consciousness and media awareness. "Very *Big Chill*," as one character put it, referring to Lawrence Kasdan's 1983 film. That movie was often seen as a progenitor of the series, defining a generation through its nostalgia for its fancy-free days before adulthood. *The Big Chill* focus on a "reunion of friends" in turn refers to the small-budget film *Return of the Secaucus Seven* made by John Sayles in 1980. Yet another touchstone for the cinematically literate makers of *thirtysomething* was Frank Capra's film *It's a Wonderful Life* (1946), the perennial favorite of American moviegoers, to which homage was paid in

thirtysomething, Ken Olin and Mel Harris, 1987–91.
Courtesy of the Everett Collection

the production company's "Bedford Falls" logo. Capra's political liberalism emerged in the series in the distaste for patriarchal and capitalist power (with that power embodied in Miles, the ruthless CEO of the advertising company where Michael and Elliot worked), while a film aesthetic carried over into the series' cinematography, intertextual references, and ambitious storylines, which occasionally incorporated flashback, daydream, and fantasy sequences. This complex mixture of cinematic and cultural antecedents can be summed up by suggesting that in many ways *thirtysomething*'s four seasons brought the sophistication of Woody Allen's films to the small screen.

Although in the vanguard for centering on "new" (postfeminist) men, for privileging "female truth," and for dealing with touchy issues within sexual relations as well as with disease and death, the series never really challenged gender roles. It is true that the problem of the domestication of men, of defining them within a familial role without lessening their desirability and their sense of self-fulfillment, was one of the series' key preoccupations, but *thirtysomething* ultimately endorsed the traditional sexual division of labor. Although it was the first series to show a homosexual couple in bed together, the series posed any alternative to the heterosexual couple very gingerly. Nevertheless, the prominence of a therapeutic discourse, and the negotiation of identity in the postmodern era, won *thirtysomething* accolades from professional psychologists.

The series was occasionally criticized, too, for its social and political insularity, for not dealing with problems outside the affluent lifestyle and 1960s values of its characters. Zwick and Herskovitz described it as "a show about creating your own family. All these people live apart from where they grew up, and so they're trying to fashion a new sense of home—one made up of friends, where holidays, job triumphs, illnesses, and gossip all take on a kind of bittersweet significance."

The series' influence was evident long after it moved to syndication on the Lifetime cable network and its creators moved on to feature-film careers and other television series. That influence can be noted in the look and sound of certain TV advertisements, in other series with feminine sensibilities and preoccupations with the transition from childhood to maturity *(Sisters),* and in situation comedies about groups of friends who talk all the time *(Seinfeld). My So-Called Life* (ABC, 1994), a later and less successful series produced by many of the same personnel, extended the subjectivity principle to a teenage girl caught between her family and school friends. That series was perhaps an indication of a new shift in the targeting of "generational audiences," the new focus now on "twentysomethings," as television searched for a way to reach the offspring of the baby boomers.

SUSAN EMMANUEL

See also **Zwick, Edward and Marshall Herskovitz**

Cast

Michael Steadman	Ken Olin
Hope Murdoch Steadman	Mel Harris
Janey Steadman	Brittany and Lacey Craven
Elliot Weston	Timothy Busfield
Nancy Weston	Patricia Wettig
Ethan Weston	Luke Rossi
Brittany Weston	Jordana "Bink" Shapiro
Melissa Steadman	Melanie Mayron
Ellyn Warren	Polly Draper
Professor Gary Shepherd	Peter Horton
Miles Drentell (1989–91)	David Clennon
Susannah Hart (1989–91)	Patricia Kalember

Producers

Edward Zwick, Marshall Herskovitz, Scott Winant

Programming History

85 episodes
ABC

September 1987–September 1988	Tuesday 10:00–11:00
December 1988–May 1991	Tuesday 10:00–11:00
July 1991–September 1991	Tuesday 10:00–11:00

Further Reading

Heide, Margaret J., "Mothering Ambivalence: The Treatment of Women's Gender Role Conflicts over Work and Family on *thirtysomething," Women's Studies: An Interdisciplinary Journal* (1992)

Heide, Margaret J., *Television Culture and Women's Lives: Thirtysomething and the Contradictions of Gender,* Philadelphia: University of Pennsylvania Press, 1995

Joyrich, Lynne, "All That Heaven Allows: TV Melodrama, Postmodernism, and Consumer Culture," *Camera Obscura* (January 1988)

"*thirtysomething*: A Chronicle of Everyday Life," *New York Times* (24 February 1988)

Torres, Sasha, "Melodrama, Masculinity, and the Family: *thirtysomething* As Therapy," in *Male Trouble,* edited by Constance Penley and Sharon Willis, Minneapolis: University of Minnesota Press, 1993

This Hour Has Seven Days

Canadian Public Affairs Series

This Hour Has Seven Days has repeatedly been cited as the most exciting and innovative public affairs television series in the history of Canadian broadcasting. It was certainly the most popular, drawing more than 3 million viewers at the time of its controversial cancellation by CBC management, which was unable to withstand the cries of outrage from offended guardians of public morality and the growing insurgence of the *Seven Days* production team. The creation of two young producers, Patrick Watson and Douglas Leiterman, the series debuted on October 4, 1964 and came to its well-publicized end after 50 episodes on May 8, 1966.

Watson and Leiterman had worked together as co-producers on two previous public affairs series, *Close-Up* and *Inquiry*. Given the go-ahead to create a new public-affairs series, they envisioned a show that would be stimulating and exciting for the Canadian public, and that would develop a wider and more informed audience than previous public-affairs shows. Both producers were deeply committed to the importance of public-service broadcasting and to the importance of pushing the boundaries of television journalism to reflect the techniques of investigation and advocacy more prevalent in print journalism. Leiterman in particular argued against the prevailing ideology of CBC journalistic practice that called for adhering to the strict tenets of objectivity and "studious neutrality." Watson brought a more intellectual approach to the show, having studied English literature and linguistics in undergraduate and graduate school.

The show was launched by the CBC with great fanfare in the fall of 1964 with a relatively large budget of over $30,000 per show, about twice the average of other public-affairs programs. The first year's shows were cohosted by John Drainie, Laurier LaPierre, an academic historian turned TV talent, and Carole Simpson, soon replaced by Dinah Christie. The role of the women was limited primarily to songs or satire. Upon Drainie's illness at the start of the second year, Watson was persuaded to abandon his producer role to join the on-air team, a move that CBC management thought would reduce the controversial style of the program. A very talented and energetic young team of producers, reporters, interviewers, and filmmakers was recruited. They included some of the prime future talent in Canadian documentary film and television, such as Beryl Fox, Donald Brittain, Allan King, Daryl Duke, Peter Pearson, Alexander Ross, and Larry Zolf.

Clearly inspired by the earlier British satirical review of the news, *That Was the Week That Was, Seven Days* employed a one-hour, magazine format that combined satirical songs and skits with aggressive bear-pit-style interviews, investigative reports, and mini-documentaries. On an irregular basis, the entire show would be devoted to an in-depth documentary film under the title "Document." Several important award-winning films were produced and shown. One of the most noted was Beryl Fox's "Mills of the Gods," a moving examination of life for U.S. soldiers and Vietnam peasants during the Vietnam War. A distinct

point of view, which was new to public-affairs TV, was often clearly present in these productions.

A concrete example of one show's lineup might best illustrate the basic elements of the magazine format and explain why the series made CBC executives nervous, while upsetting the more traditional journalists and members of the public. The episode for 24 October 1965 opened with a satirical and irreverent song by Christie about the Ku Klux Klan, followed by preview cuts of later show segments, credits, and a welcome of the live studio audience by LaPierre. (Live audiences were a staple of the program, contributing to its actuality impact.) The first story was a filmed report on the funeral for a Sudbury, Ontario, policeman, including an interview with his family and a colleague. It underscored the important role of unrecognized policemen across Canada. The second story focused on the current federal election, featuring sometimes irreverent street interviews from Toronto and Vancouver and finishing with a shot of an empty chair and the question of whether the party leaders will show up to be questioned. The next segment was a satirical sketch portraying Harold Wilson, then prime minister of the United Kingdom, in conversation with Lester Pearson, then prime minister of Canada and running for reelection. The fourth story was a short feature on *Penthouse* magazine with pictures, interviews with the publisher and two British clergy, and commentary about the objectification of women. The fifth story was an on-location interview of Orson Welles by Watson. The sixth story was a filmed, almost lyrical, portrait of the Canadian boxer George Chuvalo. Running almost 23 minutes was the final story on the Ku Klux Klan (KKK). After an introduction by Christie, a satire of the Ku Klux Klan appearance before the U.S. House Un-American Activities Committee, and a short film on the civil rights struggle in the United States, two members of the Klan were invited into the "hot seat" to be interviewed in full costume. About halfway through the interview and after a question as to whether the Klansmen would shake hands with a black man, a black civil rights leader from the United States was invited to join the interview. There was some exchange of views, then the interviewer tried to get the KKK members to shake hands with the black leader, at which time they stood up and left the set. The show closed with a request for feedback and a reprise of the Christie song.

The fast pace, the topicality of many of the segments, the portrayal and incitement of conflict, the irreverence of songs and skits, and the occasional emotionalism of the on-air team members, all added to the popularity and the controversy that built around *Seven Days*. LaPierre was once shown wiping away a tear after a filmed interview—a gesture that the CBC President

Ouimet remembered angrily years later as one more affront to appropriate journalistic practice. The production team was proud of its nontraditional approaches to portraying the news, selecting guests, and even the way it gathered material for the show. At different times, "regular" journalists accused *Seven Days* reporters of stealing material or of poaching on their territory. One of the final straws for the program was going behind the scenes of a "Miss Canada Pageant" to film and interview contestants in their hotel rooms and bedclothes, despite the fact that the rival CTV network had an exclusive coverage contract with the pageant. This and other journalistic "improprieties" led to a memo from Bud Walker, vice president of the CBC, that foreshadowed the demise of the series.

The cancellation of *Seven Days* and the firing of Watson and LaPierre in the spring of 1966 (Leiterman was later forced out also) was met with a large public outcry, probably the largest in Canadian history for any TV program, and certainly for any public affairs program. Partly orchestrated by Watson, Leiterman, and LaPierre, there were public demonstrations, thousands of letters and phone calls, indignant editorials, threats to resign by CBC staff, and calls for Parliamentary inquiries. As a result, a Parliamentary committee hearing that favorably featured the *Seven Days* team stretched over several weeks. Prime Minister Pearson appointed a special investigator, which kept the program in the news for several more weeks. The final reports seemed to chastise both sides in the dispute but was harshest with the CBC for its heavy-handedness and bureaucratic timidity. Watson, Leiterman, and LaPierre were public heroes for a time. Several members of management resigned, at least two in protest at the handling of the show and its principals. Vice president Walker lost his job, ostensibly for the way he handled the dispute but also as a demonstration to politicians that the CBC had gotten the message.

Despite its nontraditional approaches, *Seven Days* usually dealt with mainstream concerns and issues, taking a slightly left-leaning perspective on social issues. It might have challenged members of the Canadian elite, but it rarely went outside the frame of dominant beliefs. It was often creative in the way that it visualized stories originating in studio, considering the available technology; further, it imaginatively took advantage of the recent breakthroughs in hand-held cameras and portable sound recording in its filmed stories and documentaries. Watson, Leiterman, and the *Seven Days* team often seemed to achieve the goal of involving the viewer in the emotion and actuality of television, while innovating on and stretching the conventions of TV journalism. It is also clear that the team was often seduced by the power of television to embarrass guests or sensationalize issues through manipulative set-ups, such as the KKK interview. The series often entertained, perhaps more than it informed, foreshadowing the current concern and debate over the line between news and entertainment. While the program demonstrated ways to attract, provoke, and stimulate a mass audience for current affairs, the conflict and ultimate sanction that resulted made it difficult for television journalists to experiment or take on controversial issues for several years afterward. In the years since *Seven Days* aired, it has taken on the mythic mantle of "that was the way it was in the good old days" of Canadian TV journalism. While much of that reputation is deserved, the series also needs to be appreciated with a critical eye and ear.

WILLIAM O. GILSDORF

See also **Watson, Patrick**

Hosts

Laurier LaPierre, John Drainie, Patrick Watson, Dinah Christie, Carole Simpson, and others

Producers

Patrick Watson, Douglas Leiterman, Bill Hogg, Reeves Haggan, Hugh Gauntlett, Robert Hoyt, Ken Lefolii

Director

David Rushkin

Programming History

CBC
October 4, 1964–May 8, 1966   Sunday 10:00–11:00

Further Reading

Koch, Eric, *Inside Seven Days: The Show That Shook the Nation,* Scarborough, Ontario: Prentice-Hall, 1986

Nash, Knowlton, *The Microphone Wars: A History of Triumph and Betrayal at the CBC,* Toronto: McClelland and Stewart, 1994

Peers, Frank W., *The Public Eye: Television and the Politics of Canadian Broadcasting, 1952–1968,* Toronto: University of Toronto Press, 1979

Rutherford, Paul, *Prime Time Canada,* Toronto: University of Toronto Press, 1990

Stewart, Sandy, *Here's Looking at Us,* Toronto: CBC Enterprises, 1986

This Is Your Life

U.S. Biography Program

This Is Your Life, which was broadcast from 1952 to 1961, is one of the best-remembered television series from the 1950s. The format of *This Is Your Life* was based on a rather simple principle—guests were surprised with a presentation of their past life in the form of a narrative read by host Ralph Edwards and reminiscences by relatives and friends. But the format was also quite shrewd in its exploitation of television's capacity for forging intimacy with viewers through live transmission and on-air displays of sentimentality.

This Is Your Life was the creation of Edwards, who was also the host of radio's popular *Truth or Consequences.* In a 1946 radio broadcast of the latter program, Edwards presented a capsule narrative of the past life of a disabled World War II veteran who was having difficulties adjusting to postwar life. Edwards received such positive feedback from this show that he developed the formula for a separate radio program called *This Is Your Life.* It began airing on radio in 1948 and became a live television program in 1952, running on the NBC network until 1961, and reappearing in syndicated versions briefly in the early 1970s and 1980s (during this last period, it was hosted by actor Joseph Campanella). The British version of the program had a longer lifespan. Beginning on the BBC in 1955 and hosted by Eamonn Andrews, it ran first until 1964, then (still with Andrews) transferred to Thames Television in 1969, where it ran continuously until 1993, with Michael Aspel succeeding Andrews as host in 1988. It then transferred back to the BBC, still fronted by Aspel, for a final nine-year run from 1994 until its final cancellation in 2003.

In its network television years, the U.S. *This Is Your Life* alternated in presenting the life stories of entertainment personalities and those of "ordinary" people who had contributed in some way to their communities. Edwards always insisted that the theme of "Love thy neighbor" was clear no matter who was the subject of a particular program. The host was often quoted as saying that the lives under examination must represent something "constructive," must have been "given a lift 'above and beyond the call of duty' and...in turn, he or she has passed on the help to another." For that reason, the emotion expressed by the guest, who having first been surprised by Edwards with the on-air announcement, "This is your life!," and then with the appearance of people from his or her past, was justified as a source of audience inspiration rather than voyeurism.

Entertainment personalities who were subjects of the program ranged from broadcast journalist Lowell Thomas (who displayed obvious anger and embarrassment over the "surprise") to singer Nat "King" Cole, from the famous silent film star Gloria Swanson to contemporary movie favorite Debbie Reynolds. While Edwards claimed that there were few "leaks" to the subjects about the show (if there were leaks, that subject was immediately dropped), there were several notable occasions when guests were informed in advance of their tributes—for example, Eddie Cantor was told because his heart trouble worried producers regarding the show's "surprise factor," and singer-actress Lillian Roth and actress Frances Farmer were told because their well-known troubled pasts were considered subjects too delicate (and perhaps unpredictable) for the program's usual spectacle of surprise.

When *This Is Your Life* reviewed the lives of "ordinary people," Edwards and the show staff relied on help from the individual's community. In some ways the program's coverage of individuals whose accomplishments were achieved despite handicaps was ahead of its time when indicating how the subject had surmounted societal bigotry. However, even as the series displayed some of the contradictions so prevalent in the 1950s, it also shared with its time a Cold War fervor for conformity and patriotism that worked against its more liberal impulses. For example, in a 1958 program featuring a Japanese-American druggist who had been sent to an internment camp during World War II, the life narrative recounts his struggle to establish a pharmacy practice in a bigoted community. But Edwards praises the subject's behavior in the internment camp when he squelched a camp uprising protesting forced labor. At the end of the show, members from his most recent community embrace him and Edwards announces that Richard Nixon (then vice president of the United States) has donated an American flag, and Ivory soap has donated money for a flagpole for the town, in recognition of its overcoming racial prejudice.

In the late 1980s Edwards and his production company made many of the episodes featuring Hollywood celebrities that are now available for rebroadcast. American Movie Classics (AMC) cable network channel aired these for several years to accompany screenings of movies from studio-era Hollywood.

MARY DESJARDINS

Host
Ralph Edwards

Announcer
Bob Warren

Producers
Axel Greenberg, Al Pascholl, Richard Gottlieb, Bill Carruthers, Jim Washburn

Programming History
NBC

October 1952–June 1953	Wednesday 10:00–10:30
June 1953–August 1953	Tuesday 9:30–10:00
July 1953–June 1958	Wednesday 9:30–10:00
September 1958–September 1960	Wednesday 10:00–10:30
September 1960–September 1961	Sunday 10:30–11:00

Further Reading

Balling, Fredda, "The World Is His Neighbor," *TV-Radio Mirror* (June 1959)
Hall, Gladys, "Four Magic Words," *TV-Radio Mirror* (1954)

Thomas, Danny (1914–1991)

U.S. Comedian, Actor

Danny Thomas was one of television's most beloved and enduring entertainers. His comedic talents were surpassed only by his shrewd production activities and his well-known philanthropy. Thomas began his career as the stand-up comic Amos Jacobs, developing his storytelling shtick into a familiar routine of lengthy narratives peppered with a blend of Irish, Yiddish, Lebanese, and Italian witticisms. Quite often these routines tended toward sentimentality, only to be rescued in the end by what Thomas called the "treacle cutter," a one-liner designed to elevate the maudlin bathos into irony.

Like many early television comics, Thomas developed his routines touring in a variety of clubs. Restricted mostly to his home environs of the Midwest, he secured a three-year deal at Chicago's 5100 Club, where he was spotted by the powerful head of the William Morris Agency. "Uncle" Abe Lastfogel was to become Danny's mentor, overseeing his New York nightclub appearances, arranging a USO tour for him with Marlene Dietrich, and landing him a part on Fanny Brice's radio show. By 1945 Thomas was declared "best newcomer in radio" by the trade papers, and Joe Pasternak cast him in his film, *The Unfinished Dance*. Refusing the advice of three different studio heads to surgically alter his trademark nose, Thomas's film career was short-lived, but fairly respectable. In the early 1950s he left the film industry to good reviews for his costarring role in the Doris Day vehicle *I'll See You in My Dreams* (1951), and for his title role appearance in the 1953 Warner Brothers remake of *The Jazz Singer.*

Meanwhile, tired of the nightclub circuit, Thomas was anxiously pursuing a television series. His first television appearance was on NBC's *Four Star Revue,* where he costarred with Jimmy Durante, Jack Carson, and Ed Wynn. The variety-show format, with its fast-paced, three-minute sketches, was ill-suited to Danny's comedic style, which depended upon expository monologues and lengthy narratives. For the series' second season, the network ordered a format change wherein the four rotating hosts were replaced by a procession of headliners. With all the hosts except Ed Wynn departing, the program became the *All Star Revue.*

Thomas obtained his own program when agent Abe Lastfogel pressured fledgling network ABC into accepting Thomas as part of their terms for acquiring the much-coveted Ray Bolger. ABC, familiar with Thomas's previously ill-received television performances, insisted upon a sitcom. It was during a prolonged brainstorming session with producer Lou Edleman and writer Mel Shavelson that Thomas inadvertently came up with the autobiographical premise that was to become *Make Room for Daddy*. As the three worked futilely into the night, Thomas grew impatient and pleaded that he simply wanted a series so that he could stay put with his family for awhile. The result was *Make Room for Daddy*, a show that revolved around the absentee-father dilemmas of traveling singer-comic "Danny Williams." The title was suggested by Thomas' real-life wife, Rose Marie, who during Danny's frequent tours allowed their children to sleep with her. Upon her husband's return, the children would have to empty dresser drawers and leave the master bed to, quite literally, "make room for Daddy."

Incorporating Thomas's singing and story-telling talents, the program was a blend of domestic comedy and variety program (during Danny's fictionalized "nightclub engagements"). It became one of television's most successful comedies, winning numerous awards, including best new show for the 1952–53 season. Despite its success, the program underwent a number of transformations, most notably when Jean Hagen, who played the part of wife Margaret, left the series to attend to her film and stage careers. For the fourth season, Danny played a widower, and a succession of guest stars appeared as potential replacement wives. In the 1956 season finale, Danny proposed to guest star Marjorie Lord, who, along with child star Angela Cartwright, joined the Williams family for the program's remaining seven years. The start of the 1957 television season also saw the program on a new network (CBS), after ABC president (and Hagen ally) Robert Kintner lost interest in the series. The newly titled *Danny Thomas Show* slid into the spot formally occupied by CBS's mega-hit *I Love Lucy*, where it remained in the top ten until voluntarily leaving the network when the performers sought new avenues of creative expression.

While starring in *Make Room for Daddy*, Thomas met Sheldon Leonard, a former gangster-type actor with aspirations to directing. Leonard took over as director of the program midway into its first season, eventually becoming executive producer. Together, Thomas and Leonard established Thomas-Leonard Productions, a powerhouse production company based on the Desilu lot; their company was responsible for a multitude of successful series, including *The Real McCoys, The Andy Griffith Show, The Joey*

Marlo and Danny Thomas, father and daughter, during the 1980s.
Courtesy of the Everett Collection

Bishop Show, The Bill Dana Show, and *The Dick Van Dyke Show*. In 1965, when Leonard left to develop *I Spy*, Thomas continued independently, producing *The Danny Thomas Hour*, an anthology series for NBC, and joining with Aaron Spelling to create and produce *The Mod Squad* and other programs. While a 1967 attempt to buy Desilu from Lucille Ball was unsuccessful, Thomas continued to create and produce programs under the banner of Danny Thomas Productions.

Thomas had an enormous and positive impact upon the growing medium. The off-camera stand-up routines he performed for the in-studio audience just prior to filming each episode of *Make Room for Daddy* were imitated on other programs and institutionalized as the now commonplace "warm-up." *The Andy Griffith Show* was the first real spin-off for network television, originating in a 1960 episode of *The Danny Thomas Show*. As a producer, Thomas read scripts and supervised a plethora of top-rated programs, and he was personally responsible for casting Mary Tyler Moore as Laura Petrie in *The Dick Van Dyke Show*. His influence as producer continued not only in his own projects but through the work of his children, notably daughter Marlo, who is a renowned actress, producer, and director, and his son Tony, who with partners Susan Harris and Paul Junger Witt is responsible for a veritable catalogue of 1970s and 1980s hit programs, including *Soap* and *The Golden Girls.*

Danny Thomas's personal integrity was as well known as his acting and producing talents. In the 1950s he successfully protected two blacklisted writers who continued to write for his television series under assumed names. In 1983 he was awarded the Congressional Medal of Honor for his work in establishing the St. Jude's Children's Research Hospital, a cause he continued to promote and support until his death in 1991.

Nina C. Leibman

See also **Andy Griffith Show, The; Dick Van Dyke Show, The**

Danny Thomas. Born Muzyad Yakhoob in Deerfield, Michigan, January 6, 1914. Married: Rose Marie Cassaniti, 1936; two daughters and one son. Began career in radio, Detroit, Michigan, 1934; worked as master of ceremonies in nightclub, 1938–40; appeared on Chicago radio, 1940; worked as master of ceremonies, 5100 Club, Chicago, 1940–43; developed own radio and television programs, performed in clubs and theaters worldwide throughout 1940s; performed overseas during World War II with Marlene Dietrich and company, and solo; performed with Fanny Brice on radio, 1944; made motion picture debut in *The Unfinished Dance,* 1946; starred in long-running television series, *Make Room for Daddy;* produced successful television series such as *The Dick Van Dyke Show.* Founder, St. Jude's Children's Research Hospital, 1962, Memphis, Tennessee. Recipient: Emmy Award, 1954; Layman's Award from the American Medical Association; Better World Award from the Veterans of Foreign Wars, 1972; Michelangelo Award from Boys Town of Italy, 1973; Humanitarian Award from Lions International, 1975; Father Flanagan–Boys Town Award, 1981; Murray-Green-Meany Award, AFL-CIO, 1981; Hubert H. Humphrey Award, Touchdown Club, 1981; American Education Award, 1984; Humanitarian Award, Variety Clubs International, 1984; Congressional Medal of Honor, 1984; Sword of Loyola Award, Loyola University, Chicago, 1985; decorated Knight of Malta; knight commander with star, Knights of the

Holy Sepulchre, Pope Paul VI. Died in Los Angeles, California, February 6, 1991.

Television Series

1950–52	*All Star Revue*
1953–57	*Make Room for Daddy*
1957–64	*The Danny Thomas Show*
1964–68	*Danny Thomas Specials*
1967–68	*The Danny Thomas Hour*
1970	*Make Room for Granddaddy*
1976–77	*The Practice*
1980–81	*I'm a Big Girl Now*
1986	*One Big Family*

Made-for-Television Movie

1988	*Side By Side*

Films

The Unfinished Dance, 1946; *The Big City,* 1947; *Call Me Mister,* 1948; *I'll See You in My Dreams,* 1951; *The Jazz Singer,* 1953

Publication

Make Room for Danny (with Bill Davidson), 1991

Further Reading

Gelbart, Larry, "The Man Could Make a Short Story Long," *New York Times* (17 February 1991)

Grote, David, *The End of Comedy: The Sit-com and the Comedic Tradition,* Hamden, Connecticut: Archon Books, 1983

Hamamoto, Darrell Y., *Nervous Laughter: Television Situation Comedy and Liberal Democratic Ideology,* New York: Praeger, 1989

Javna, John, *The Best of TV Sitcoms: Burns and Allen to The Cosby Show, The Munsters to Mary Tyler Moore,* New York: Harmony Books, 1988

Jones, Gerard, *Honey, I'm Home!: Sitcoms, Selling the American Dream,* New York: Grove Weidenfeld, 1992

Leibman, Nina C., *Living Room Lectures: The Fifties Family in Film and Television,* Austin: University of Texas Press, 1995

Marc, David, *Comic Visions: Television Comedy and American Culture,* Boston : Unwin Hyman, 1989; 2nd edition, Malden, Massachusetts: Blackwell, 1997

Mitz, Rick, *The Great TV Sitcom Book,* New York: R. Marek, 1980

Waldron, Vince, *Classic Sitcoms: A Celebration of the Best of Prime-Time Comedy,* New York: Macmillan, 1987

Thomas, Tony (1948–)

U.S. Producer

Tony Thomas, a native of California and member of one of U.S. television's leading families (his father was Danny Thomas), began his own TV career as an associate producer at Screen Gems, moving from that position to become a producer at Spelling/Goldberg Productions. These associations brought Thomas into early contact with his future partner, Paul Junger Witt, who also started his career at Screen Gems. Indeed, their first significant venture together was the award-winning made-for-television movie *Brian's Song,* which Witt produced. The Academy of Television Arts and Sciences recognized *Brian's Song* with five Emmys, including one for Outstanding Single Program.

In 1975, Thomas and Witt formed their own company, Witt/Thomas Productions, and a year later the two men joined with the talented writer Susan Harris to form a second entity, Witt/Thomas/Harris. The three launched their first series in 1977, the highly acclaimed *Soap.* Brutally attacked by a reviewer for *Newsweek,* who had not even seen the show, *Soap* quickly drew fire from uninformed conservative religious leaders who threatened to boycott the ABC comedy. As Thomas recalls, it was very close to the time of the first broadcast before a full complement of sponsors was assembled. Sponsorship of the series was a continuing difficulty for the network. The producers credit Fred Silverman of ABC for standing firmly behind their creation in spite of the attacks.

There followed a string of successes, including *Empty Nest, Benson,* and *The Golden Girls,* for which Thomas, along with Witt and Harris, received Emmys in 1985–86 and 1986–87. Other series from the production company have included *Blossom* (1991–95), *The John Larroquette Show* (1993–96), *Pearl* (1996), *Common Law* (1996), and *The Secret Lives of Men* (1998).

Through the company, Thomas also began producing feature films with Witt. Working with Touchstone Pictures, they produced the Oscar-winning film *Dead Poets' Society* (1989). Their feature work also includes the 1992 release *Final Analysis,* and the 2002 film *Insomnia* starring Al Pacino and Robin Williams, coproduced by Steven Soderbergh and George Clooney.

Tony Thomas is active in fundraising efforts on behalf of St. Jude's Hospital, founded by his father in 1961. It is the world's largest childhood cancer research center.

ROBERT S. ALLEY

See also **Benson; Golden Girls; Harris, Susan; Soap; Witt Paul Junger**

Tony (Anthony C.) Thomas. Born in Los Angeles, California, December 7, 1948. Educated at the University of San Diego. Assistant to the producer, *Young Rebels,* 1970; associate producer, *Getting Together,* 1971; associate producer, *Brian's Song,* 1972: associate producer and producer for numerous other television series; with Paul Junger Witt formed Witt/Thomas production company, 1975; later, with Susan Harris, formed Witt/Thomas/Harris production company, 1976. Recipient: two Emmy Awards.

Television Series (selected)

1970–71	*Young Rebels* (assistant to the producer)
1971–72	*Getting Together* (associate producer)
1976–77	*The Practice*
1977	*Loves Me, Loves Me Not*
1977–81	*Soap*
1979–86	*Benson*
1982–83	*It Takes Two*
1983	*Just Married*
1985–92	*The Golden Girls*
1987–90	*Beauty and the Beast*
1988–95	*Empty Nest*
1991–93	*Nurses*
1991	*Good and Evil*
1991–95	*Blossom*
1991–93	*Herman's Head*
1991–93	*Nurses*
1993	*Whoops*
1993–96	*The John Larroquette Show*
1995	*Brotherly Love*
1995	*Muscle*
1996	*Local Heroes*
1996	*Pearl*
1996	*Common Law*
1996	*Radiant Heroes*

| 1998 | *The Secret Lives of Men* |
| 1999 | *Everything's Relative* |

Films

Firstborn, 1984; *Dead Poets' Society,* 1988; *Final Analysis,* 1992; *Mixed Nuts,* 1994; *Insomnia,* 2002.

Made-for-Television Movies (selected)

| 1972 | *Brian's Song* (associate producer) |
| 1973 | *Blood Sport* |

Thorn Birds, The

U.S. Miniseries

The miniseries *The Thorn Birds,* based on Colleen Mc-Cullough's 1977 best-selling novel, was broadcast on ABC for 10 hours between March 27 and 30, 1983. Set primarily on Drogheda, a fictional sheep station in the Australian outback, the melodrama focused on the multigenerational Cleary family and spanned the years from 1920 to 1962.

At the outset, the family—patriarch Paddy Cleary (Richard Kiley), his wife, Fiona (Jean Simmons), and children—moved from New Zealand to Australia to help run Drogheda, owned by Paddy's wealthy sister, Mary Carson (Barbara Stanwyck). Over the years, numerous deaths and disasters (fire, a drowning, a goring by a wild boar) were to befall the family.

While the saga recounted the story of the entire Cleary clan, it focused primarily on the lone Cleary daughter, Meggie (Rachel Ward) and her relationship with Father Ralph de Bricassart (Richard Chamberlain). Although they met when she was just a child, Meggie grew up and fell in love with the handsome young Catholic priest who had been banished to the outback for a previous disobedience. Father Ralph was torn between his own love for Meggie, his love for God, and his ambition to rise in the Catholic hierarchy. Spurred on by the spiteful Mary Carson, who was herself attracted to the priest, Father Ralph was forced to choose between his own advancement in the Church and his love for Meggie. He chose the former and soon found himself at the Vatican. As Father Ralph rose quickly through the hierarchy of the Catholic Church (eventually becoming a cardinal), Meggie married a sheep shearer named Luke O'Neill (Bryan Brown), bore a daughter (played as an adult by Mare Winningham), and ended up working as a maid in Queensland.

Years later, de Bricassart returned to Australia and to Meggie, who eventually left her husband. In the controversial third episode, the two consummated their relationship in what *Newsweek*'s Harry F. Waters called "the most erotic love scene ever to ignite the home screen," but de Bricassart still was unable to give up the Church. Unbeknownst to him, Meggie gave birth to his son (played as an adult by Philip Anglim), who in an ironic twist of fate himself became a priest before dying in a drowning accident. As in McCullough's novel, the key underlying message of this miniseries was that each generation is doomed to repeat the missteps and failures of the previous generation.

While winning the 1983 Golden Globe Award for Best Miniseries, *The Thorn Birds* was not without controversy. The subject matter of a priest breaking his vow of celibacy was contestable enough, but the fact that ABC chose to broadcast the program beginning on Palm Sunday and running through Holy Week raised the ire of the United States Catholic Conference. In response, McDonald's Corporation initially requested that its franchisees not advertise during the broadcasts. In the end, however, the company simply advised its franchisees to advertise only before Father Ralph and Meggie had consummated their relationship.

Despite its controversial subject matter (or perhaps because of it), *The Thorn Birds* garnered an average 41 rating and 59 share over the course of its four-night run, making it then the second-highest-rated miniseries ever, after *Roots* (1977). Its controversial third episode, in which Meggie and Father Ralph consummated their relationship, was at the time the fourth-highest-rated network entertainment show of all time (preceded only by the final episode of *M*A*S*H,* the "Who Shot J.R.?" episode of *Dallas,* and the eighth episode of *Roots*). In the end, an estimated 110–140

The Thorn Birds, Christopher Plummer, Richard Chamberlain, 1983.
Courtesy of the Everett Collection

The Thorn Birds, Rachel Ward, Richard Chamberlain, 1983.
Courtesy of the Everett Collection

million viewers saw all or some of the miniseries. *TV Guide,* in fact, has listed *The Thorn Birds* as one of the top 20 programs of the 1980s.

Produced for an estimated $21 million, *The Thorn Birds* appeared during the heyday of the network television miniseries, from the late 1970s to the mid-1980s, when the form was seen as "the salvation of commercial television." In this context, *The Thorn Birds* stood out for both its controversial qualities and its success. Like *Roots* and *The Winds of War* before it, *The Thorn Birds* exemplified the miniseries genre—family sagas spanning multiple generations, featuring large, big-name casts, and laden with tales of love, sex, tragedy, and transcendence that kept the audience coming back night after night. In 1996 ABC broadcast a sequel to *The Thorn Birds,* in which Father Ralph and Meggie are again separated and again struggle with their passion and their consciences. Though widely promoted, the program received far less attention from both critics and audiences.

SHARON R. MAZZARELLA

Cast

Father Ralph de Bricassart	Richard Chamberlain
Meggie Cleary (as a girl)	Sydney Penny
Meggie Cleary (adult)	Rachel Ward
Mary Carson	Barbara Stanwyck
Fiona Cleary	Jean Simmons
Archbishop Contini-Verchese	Christopher Plummer
Rainer Hartheim	Ken Howard
Justine O'Neill	Mare Winningham
Anne Mueller	Piper Laurie
Paddy Cleary	Richard Kiley
Luddie Mueller	Earl Holliman
Luke O'Neill	Bryan Brown
Sarah MacQueen	Antoinette Bower
Stuart Cleary	Dwier Brown
Alastair MacQueen	John de Lancie
Angus MacQueen	Bill Morey
Stuart Cleary (as a boy)	Vidal Peterson
Miss Carmichael	Holly Palance
Judy	Stephanie Faracy
Dane O'Neill	Philip Anglim
Frank Cleary	John Friedrich
Mrs. Smith	Allyn Ann McLerie
Harry Gough	Richard Venture
Pete	Barry Corbin
Jack Cleary	Stephen Burns

Bob Cleary	Brett Cullen	
Annie	Meg Wylie	
Sister Agatha	Nan Martin	
Barker at the fair	Wally Dalton	
Arne Swenson	Chard Hayward	
Doc Wilson	Rance Howard	
Martha	Lucinda Dooling	
Phaedre	Aspa Nakopolou	

Producers
David Wolper, Edward Lewis, Stan Margulies

Programming History
4 episodes
ABC
March 27–30, 1983

Further Reading

Bawer, Bruce, "Grand Allusions Sacred and Profane," *Emmy Magazine* (March/April 1982)
Morris, Gwen, "An Australian Ingredient in American Soaps: *The Thorn Birds* by Colleen McCullough," *Journal of Popular Culture* (Spring 1991)
Waters, Harry F., "Sex and Sin in the Outback," *Newsweek* (28 March 1983)

Three's Company

U.S. Situation Comedy

Three's Company, an enormously popular yet critically despised sitcom farce about a young man living platonically with two young women, aired on ABC from 1977 to 1984. After a spring try-out of six episodes beginning Thursday March 15, 1977, *Three's Company* ranked number 11 among all U.S. TV shows for the entire 1976–77 season—at that time, an unheard-of feat for a new show. The next year, *Three's Company* moved to Tuesdays behind ABC powerhouses *Happy Days* and *Laverne and Shirley,* which it also followed that year as number three in the ratings. In 1978–79 *Three's Company* nudged out *Happy Days* for the number-two spot, and late in that season moved its caustic landlords onto their own short-lived spin-off, *The Ropers* (which ranked number eight among all network shows after a spring tryout of six episodes, but was canceled in 1980 after a dismal second season). In 1979–80 *Three's Company* shot past both of its lead-ins to become the highest-rated TV comedy in the United States. That summer ABC ran back-to-back reruns of the show in its daytime lineup, foreshadowing huge success in syndication, which the series entered in 1982, two years before its network demise.

Three's Company entered the television scene in the midst of TV's "jiggle era," which began in 1976 with ABC's *Charlie's Angels* and was the medium's response to the sexual revolution and the swinging single. *Three's Company,* though otherwise apolitical in content, was the first sitcom to address the sexual implications and frustrations of unmarried and unrelated men and women living together, which in 1977 was still somewhat taboo. In the minds of many, male-female cohabitation was anything but innocent and, apparently, would lead only to the evils of premarital sex. *Three's Company* toyed with this dilemma in its premise, an Americanized version of the 1973–76 British TV comedy *Man about the House.*

Set in Santa Monica, California, the series chronicled the innuendo-laden, slapstick-prone misadventures of the affably klutzy bachelor Jack Tripper (played by John Ritter) and two single, attractive women, one a cute, down-to-earth brunette named Janet Wood (Joyce DeWitt), the other a sexy, dim-witted blonde named Christmas "Chrissy" Snow (Suzanne Somers). The three shared an apartment in order to beat the high cost of living, but Jack was also present to provide "manly protection." Though he never broke his vow of keeping a "strictly platonic" relationship with his roommates (the three were really best friends who always looked after each other), the series was rife with double entendres. Antagonists in this domestic farce were the trio's downstairs landlords, first the prudish Stanley Roper, an Archie Bunker-type played by Norman Fell, and later the comically swaggering "ladies man" Ralph Furley, played by Don Knotts. The landlords were so suspicious of the "threesome" arrangement that they would not permit it until after Jack told them he was gay, a "lifestyle" against which, ironically, neither discriminated by refusing housing. Though Jack was a heterosexual with many girlfriends, he masqueraded as an effeminate "man's man" around the near-sighted Roper, who called him "one of the girls," and Furley, who often tried to "convert" him; this comic device played heavily at first but was toned down considerably by the show's fourth season. When out of Roper's and Furley's reach, Jack and his upstairs buddy, Larry Dallas (Richard Kline), leered at and lusted after every female in sight, including, in early episodes, Janet and Chrissy. Chrissy, especially, was prone to bouncing around the apartment, braless, in tight sweaters, when she was not clad in a towel, nightie, short-shorts, or bathing suit. The irony here was that even though sex was so ingrained in the *Three's Company* consciousness, nobody on the show ever seemed to be actually engaging in intercourse, not even the show's only married characters, the sex-starved Helen Roper (Audra Lindley) and her impotent handyman husband, Stanley, the butt of numerous faulty plumbing jokes.

Three's Company's sexiness and libidinal preoccupation helped gain the show tremendous ratings and media exposure. A February 1978 *Newsweek* cover story on "Sex and TV" featured the trio in a sexy, staged shot. *Sixty Minutes* presented an interview with Somers, who, in the tradition of *Charlie's Angels'* Farrah Fawcett, became a sex symbol and magazine cover-girl with top-selling posters, dolls, and other merchandise. TV critics and other intellectuals rallied against the show, calling its humor sophomoric, if not insulting. Feminists objected to what they called exploitative portrayals of women (primarily in the Chrissy character) as bubble-brained "sexpots." And while *Three's Company* was not as harshly condemned among conservative educators and religious organizations as its ABC counterpart *Soap* (a more satirical comedy with a shock value so high that ABC almost delayed its premiere in the fall of 1977), it received low marks from the Parent-Teacher Association and was targeted in a list of shows whose sponsors were to be boycotted, produced by Reverend Donald Wildmon's National Federation for Decency.

Although *Three's Company* would become notorious as titillation television, its origins are that of British bedroom farce and "socially relevant" American sitcoms. In 1976, *M*A*S*H* writer and producer Larry Gelbart penned an initial *Three's Company* pilot script, borrowing scenario and characterizations from Thames Television's *Man about the House*. However, that pilot, with Ritter, Fell, Lindley, and two other actresses, did not sell. Fred Silverman, programming chief at ABC, requested a revamped pilot for a show he believed would be a breakthrough in sexiness the

Three's Company, Joyce DeWitt, John Ritter, Suzanne Somers, 1977–84; first season.
Courtesy of the Everett Collection

same way that CBS's *All in the Family* was in bigotry. Therefore, show owners Ted Bergman and Don Taffner commissioned *All in the Family* Emmy-winning head writers and *Jeffersons* producers Don Nicholl, Michael Ross, and Bernie West to rewrite the pilot. The roommates, in Gelbart's script an aspiring filmmaker and two actresses, took on more bourgeois jobs in the new pilot—Jack became a gourmet cooking student, Janet a florist, and Chrissy an office secretary. The female leads were recast (DeWitt was added for the second pilot, and Somers for the third), the chemistry clicked, and ABC bought the series.

Most critics called *Three's Company* an illegitimate attempt to use the TV sitcom's new openness for its own cheap laughs. However, Gerard Jones, author of *Honey, I'm Home! Sitcoms, Selling the American Dream,* notes that the minds behind *Three's Company* intelligently responded to the times. He suggests that producers Nicholl, Ross, and West recognized that even the highly praised work of producer Norman Lear "had always been simple titillation." The producers simply went a step further. They "took advantage of TV's new hipness" to present even more titillation "in completely undemanding form," thus creating "an ingenious trivialization that the public was waiting for."

Although *Three's Company* jiggled beneath the thin clothing of titillation, the show was basically innocent and harmless, a contradiction that annoyed some critics. Its comedy, framed in the contemporary trapping of sexual innuendo, was basically broad farce in the tradition of *I Love Lucy,* very physical and filled with misunderstandings. (Lucille Ball loved *Three's Company* and Ritter's pratfalls so much she hosted the show's 1982 retrospective special.) As fast-paced, pie-in-your-face farce, *Three's Company* spent little time on characterization, but underlying themes of care and concern among the roommates often fueled the comedy and occasionally led to a tender resolve by episode's end.

Behind the scenes, three was company until the fall of 1980, when Somers and her husband/manager, Alan Hamel, asked for a raise for her from $30,000 per episode to $150,000 per episode plus 10 percent of the show's profits. Costars Ritter and DeWitt, confused and angry, refused to work with Somers, whose role was reduced to a phone-call from a separate soundstage at the end of each episode (Chrissy had been sent to take care of her ailing mother in Fresno, California). For the remainder of the 1980–81 season, Jenilee Harrison performed as a "temporary" roommate, Chrissy's clumsy cousin Cindy Snow. By the fall of 1981, Somers was officially fired, and Priscilla Barnes was cast as a permanent replacement, playing nurse Terri Alden, a more sophisticated blonde (Harrison's character moved out to attend a university but occasionally visited through the spring of 1982). Viewership dropped when Somers left, but *Three's Company* remained very popular, focusing more on Ritter's physical abilities and his character's transition from cooking student to owner of Jack's Bistro, a French cuisine restaurant.

Three's Company, weathering key cast changes and Americans' waning interest in sitcoms, remained a top-ten hit through the 1982–83 season. In 1984, however, after 174 episodes, a final People's Choice Award as Favorite Comedy Series, and an eighth, embattled season in which it dropped out of the top 30 in the face of competition from NBC's *The A-Team, Three's Company* changed its format. A final one-hour episode saw Janet get married, Terri move to Hawaii, and Jack fall in love and move in with his new girlfriend. Ritter, who won an Emmy for Outstanding Male Lead in a Comedy in 1984, was the only *Three's Company* cast member to remain when production resumed in the fall with a new cast and new title. Recycling much of its parent show's comic formula, *Three's a Crowd* focused on Jack Tripper's relationship with his live-in girlfriend (Mary Cadorette), whose disapproving father (*Soap*'s Robert Mandan) became their landlord. This incarnation lasted one season.

Three's Company might seem tame television by more recent standards, but it pushed the proverbial envelope in the late 1970s, opening the door for sexier, if not sillier, comedies offering audiences both titillation and mindless escape.

Chris Mann

See also **Comedy, Domestic Settings**

Cast

Jack Tripper	John Ritter
Janet Wood	Joyce DeWitt
Chrissy Snow (1977–81)	Suzanne Somers
Helen Roper (1977–79)	Audra Lindley
Stanley Roper ((1977–79)	Norman Fell
Larry Dallas (1978–84)	Richard Kline
Ralph Furley (1979–84)	Don Knotts
Lana Shields (1979–80)	Ann Wedgeworth
Cindy Snow (1980–82)	Jenilee Harrison
Terri Alden (1981–84)	Priscilla Barnes
Mike, the Bartender (1981–84)	Brad Blaisdell

Producers

Don Nicholl, Michael Ross, Bernie West, Budd Gossman, Bill Richmond, Gene Perret, George Burdit, George Sunga, Joseph Staretski

Programming History

164 episodes
ABC

March 1977–April 1977	Thursday 9:30–10:00
August 1977–September 1977	Thursday 9:30–10:00
September 1977–May 1984	Tuesday 9:00–9:30
May 1984–September 1984	Tuesday 8:30–9:00

Further Reading

Hamamoto, Darrell Y., *Nervous Laughter: Television Situation Comedy and Liberal Democratic Ideology,* New York: Praeger, 1989

Javna, John, *The Best of TV Sitcoms: Burns and Allen to the Cosby Show, The Munsters to Mary Tyler Moore,* New York: Harmony, 1988

Jones, Gerard, *Honey, I'm Home! Sitcoms, Selling the American Dream,* New York: Grove Weidenfeld, 1992

Waldron, Vince, *Classic Sitcoms: A Celebration of the Best of Prime-Time Comedy,* New York: Macmillan, 1987

Thunderbirds

British Children's Program

Thunderbirds, an action-packed, science fiction puppet drama that portrayed the heroic adventures of the members of the secret International Rescue organization, was first broadcast in 1965. At a moment's notice, the IR would mobilize its high-tech rescue craft to disasters on land, underground, underwater and in outer space. The program became a worldwide success and still remains on television today.

AP Films (Anderson Provis Films) had a successful track record in the production of puppet series for children with *The Adventures of Twizzle, Torchy the Battery Boy,* and *Four Feather Falls.* Under the patronage of Lew Grade at ATV (Associated Television) they had achieved international success with *Supercar, Fireball XL5,* and *Stingray.* In 1964, when Lew Grade asked Gerry Anderson for a new series, AP Films produced "Trapped in the Sky," a 25-minute pilot for *Thunderbirds.* Lew Grade asked that the programs be lengthened to an hour at a cost of nearly £40,000 an episode. (AP Films' first three series with ATV had earned over £3 million in the United States alone.)

Gerry Anderson and his team—his wife Sylvia, Reg Hill, John Read, Derek Meddings and Barry Gray—had built up a wealth of experience creating their new form of puppet program. Great care was taken to disguise the jerky movements of the puppets; the tungsten strings were sprayed with color powder, shots of the puppets walking were minimal (they were often shot from the waist up) and real hands were often used for close-ups. Departing from traditional puppet show techniques in which puppets were dangled in front of flat backdrops, the puppets were placed into three-dimensional action scenes. This was achieved by use of detailed scenery and model-making, developing the puppets electronically enabling them to lip-sync the pre-recorded dialogue, creating realistic special effects in miniature, and use of specialized sound effects. The company dubbed this new type of production "Supermarionation."

Shot in color (like *Stingray*), *Thunderbirds* was made for adults as well as children. For this reason it was given an early evening slot of 6:35 P.M. when first broadcast on Saturday, October 2, 1965. Set in 2063, *Thunderbirds* revolved around the lives and adven-

tures of the Tracy family, the principal members of the International Rescue organization, based on a remote Tracy Island in the Pacific. The head of the family was Jeff Tracy, a millionaire ex-astronaut with five sons; Scott, Virgil, Alan, Gordon, and John (named after five of the seven original Mercury astronauts). The five sons manned the five specialized rescue craft, the Thunderbirds. Thunderbird 1, piloted by Scott, was usually the first on the scene and would co-ordinate rescue operations. Thunderbird 2, piloted by Virgil, was a heavy transport craft that carried specialized rescue equipment in a detachable "pod." Thunderbird 3, piloted by Alan, was a spacecraft. Thunderbird 4, piloted by Gordon, was an underwater rescue craft, usually transported via Thunderbird 2. Thunderbird 5, manned by John, was a permanent space station monitoring communications for rescue calls. The Tracy family was joined on the island by scientific genius "Brains," faithful servant Kyrano and his daughter Tin Tin (Alan's love interest) with an occasional appearance from Grandma. Two other members of the International Rescue team were based in the UK—the glamorous London agent, Lady Penelope Creighton-Ward, and her cockney chauffeur Parker. Parker drove Lady Penelope's heavily armed pink Rolls Royce, registration plate FAB 1. Lady Penelope also owned a yacht, FAB2. (The letters F.A.B. were also used in communications between the Tracy brothers and base—usually to confirm instructions.) In his biography Gerry Anderson comments that "part of the success of *Thunderbirds* was due to the fact that it ran for an hour an episode. That enabled the character development we couldn't feature in previous shows."

The program always started with a dramatic countdown, illustrated with the five aircraft, accompanied by "5, 4, 3, 2, 1 . . . Thunderbirds are go!" Then came a montage of highlights of the following program. The launches of Thunderbirds 1, 2, and 3 were particularly memorable sequences. Thunderbird 1 would launch from its underground silo through the retractable swimming pool. Thunderbird 2 would emerge from behind an artificial cliff-face and crawl between two lines of palm trees that bent to the ground to allow its wings to pass. Thunderbird 3 would blast off through the center of the circular house. These unconventional take offs were all a part of the emphasis on the secrecy of International Rescue and its base. Photography and tracking of the aircraft was prohibited. The greatest IR adversary was a villain called The Hood who possessed strange mind-altering powers, especially effective on his half-brother Kyrano. The Hood made frequent appearances at the scenes of disasters (usually in disguise) hoping to photograph the Thunderbirds and their crew in action.

Storylines mainly revolved around rescue operations. The disasters were a mixture of man-made (machinery going haywire, sabotage), and natural (floods and landslides). In his biography Anderson says the decision to avoid politics and make the causes of the disasters natural disasters or sabotage was deliberate. Tension was built up to a dramatic finale with a well-paced story, underscored by Barry Gray's incidental music.

First shown on the Independent Television network at different times across the UK, it was not until 1991 that *Thunderbirds* was first networked, attracting an audience of 5 million viewers when re-run on BBC 2. A digitally remastered *Thunderbirds* was broadcast on BBC 2 in 2000. Two feature films were also made. *Thunderbirds Are Go!* was released in 1966 and *Thunderbird Six* in 1968. In January 1993 the long-running children's program *Blue Peter* was overwhelmed with requests for fact-sheets on how to make a model of Tracy Island, which had been demonstrated on the program. After 90,000 requests the BBC decided to repeat the program instead. *Thunderbirds* characters have continually remained in the spotlight; in advertising campaigns; when Parker was featured in Dire Straits's "Elvis Calling" video, and in Lady Penelope's "guest appearance" in an episode of *Absolutely Fabulous*.

The program has been spoofed on many occasions. One of the best known was Peter Cook and Dudley Moore's "Superthunderstingcar" performed in the first series of *Not Only... But Also*. A stage show, *Thunderbirds FAB*, mimicked the actions of the Thunderbirds and Captain Scarlet puppets to the accompaniment of Barry Gray's music. The show appeared on London's West End stage in 1991 and returned in 1993 and 2000.

KATHLEEN LUCKEY

Broadcast History
32 50 minute episodes
ATV
October 2, 1965–April 2, 1966
October 2–30, 1966 and December 25, 1966.

Principal credits
AP Films in Association with ATV and ITC Worldwide Distrubtion
Created by Gerry and Sylvia Anderson
Executive Producer: Gerry Anderson
Producer: Reg Hill
Director of Photography: John Read
Music: Barry Gray
Art Director: Bob Bell
Special Effects Supervisor: Derek Meddings
Puppetry Supervision: Mary Turner
Character visualization: Sylvia Anderson
Directors: Brian Burgess, David Elliott, David Lane, Alan Pattillo and Desmond Saunders.
Scripts: Gerry and Sylvia Anderson, Tony Barwick, Martin Clump, Alan Fennell, Alan Pattillo, Donald Robertson and Dennis Spooner.

Voices
Jeff Tracy	Peter Dyneley
Scott Tracy	Shane Rimmer
Virgil Tracy	David Holliday, Jeremy Wilkin
Alan Tracy	Matt Zimmerman
Gordon Tracy	David Graham
John Tracy	Ray Barrett
Brains	David Graham
Parker	David Graham
Kyrano	David Graham
Tin Tin	Christine Finn
Lady Penelope	Sylvia Anderson
The Hood	Ray Barrett

Further Reading
Archer, Simon, and Stan Nicholls, *Gerry Anderson—The Authorized Biography,* London: Legend, 1996

Home, Anna, *Into the Box of Delights: A History of Children's Television,* London: BBC Books, 1993

Lister, David, "'Supermarionation' proves its indestructible audience appeal," *The Independent* (January 18, 1992)

Payne, Stephen, and Paul Mount, "Gerry Anderson Interview," *Starburst* 102 (February 1987)

Tiananmen Square

Tiananmen Square will forever be remembered as a political rally that turned into a bloody massacre viewed on live television. The square in Beijing, China, was the site of a pro-democracy student demonstration in the spring of 1989, a demonstration violently crushed by the Chinese military. News organizations from all over the world had previously stationed prime-time news anchors and camera crews in Beijing to provide live broadcasts of Soviet President Mikhail Gorbachev's visit to the city. Consequently, scenes of the brutal crackdown were broadcast throughout the world. These images embittered the international public toward the Chinese government and had a profound impact on subsequent foreign-policy decisions.

Thousands of students from China's pro-democracy movement planned to use the state visit and the obligatory media coverage for their purposes. They had assembled and camped in Tiananmen Square for two weeks in late May and early June. Among their demands were the rights to free speech and a free press, and they erected a statue—modeled on the Statue of Liberty though with both arms supporting the torch—that they named the "Goddess of Democracy." Their cause and the images they employed thus resonated with audiences around the world.

However, this hopeful demonstration came to a sudden and horrifying end. On the night of June 3 and into the early morning hours of June 4, the army launched an assault on the unarmed civilians in the square. The military stormed the area with tanks and machine guns, firing into the crowd at random. Hundreds of young students were killed and thousands wounded in the attack. Scenes of brutality and chaos were broadcast from Tiananmen Square, and there were reports of students and civilians being imprisoned in other parts of China.

The fear inspired by the government's crackdown was so powerful that, almost immediately, students and demonstration organizers stopped talking to the media. The excitement and generous spirit with which interviews had been granted just two days before had eerily disappeared. An official news blackout was imposed, and in addition to sources drying up, reporters and crews themselves were being threatened and interrogated. In a tragic distortion of intentions, the televised interviews and pictures were also used by Chinese officials to identify and incarcerate many of the students involved. The Chinese citizens outside Beijing never really saw or heard the true horror of what happened. They received "official" versions from the state-run news organization. These broadcasts described scenes of violent student protesters and angry dissidents attacking innocent government authorities.

The Western media was not so easily manipulated. Even though human-rights violations were thought to be commonplace under Communist Party rule, the topics had received little consistent or significant mention in the mainstream media. Tiananmen Square, however, received continuous coverage during the first day of the massacre, representing one of the earliest efforts by U.S. news media to devote non-stop air-time to a breaking international news event. Seldom before had live television so graphically exposed the abuse of individual rights and disregard for human life. In one of the most dramatic moments of the event, audiences were able to watch a Chinese government official physically unplug the satellite transmitter carrying CBS's broadcast. As *CBS Evening News* anchor Dan Rather stood by, registering his protest, television screens suddenly carried nothing but blurred static until New York transmission opened its own feed to network affiliate stations.

China experienced nearly three years of economic sanctions and scorn from the international community after the massacre, yet the Chinese government continued its hard-line policies toward all civilian dissent. On subsequent anniversaries of the military attack, Beijing has maintained an official position of denial and repression. Each year on June 4, a heavy police presence stifles the city and international news broadcasts commemorating the event are interrupted and blocked. Hotels have all been instructed to unplug their satellite connections to CNN.

Despite the government's attempts at censorship, the images broadcast from Tiananmen Square cannot be erased from public memory. However, the anger of the international community seems to have dissipated over the years, as evidenced by Beijing's successful bid to host the 2008 Olympics. When that announcement was made in 2001, hundreds of thousands of people once again flocked to the square—this time to celebrate before the television cameras. Nevertheless, few who watched the coverage will ever forget the sight of a

The student uprising in Tiananmen Square.
Courtesy of AP/Wide World Photos

lone student standing defiantly against a column of army tanks, or of soldiers clubbing demonstrators until they were bloody and lifeless, or the panic-stricken faces of the people in the square. Although the Chinese government would like to strike Tiananmen Square from the record books, television has ensured that its lessons will be taught for many years to come.

JENNIFER HOLT

See also **News, National; Satellite**

Further Reading

Calhoun, Craig J., *Neither Gods nor Emperors: Students and the Struggle for Democracy in China,* Berkeley: University of California Press, 1994

"China: The Weeks of Living Dangerously," *Broadcasting* (June 12, 1989)

Li, Peter, Steven Mark, and Marjorie H. Li, editors, *Culture and Politics in China: The Anatomy of Tiananmen Square,* New Brunswick, New Jersey: Transaction Books, 1991

Salisbury, Harrison Evans, *Tiananmen Diary: Thirteen Days in June,* Boston: Little, Brown, 1989

Tonetto, Walter, editor, *Earth against Heaven: A Tiananmen Square Anthology,* Wollongong, Australia: Five Islands Press, 1990

Watson, Trevor, *Tremble and Obey: An ABC Correspondent's Account of the Bloody Beijing Uprising,* Crows Nest, Australia: ABC Enterprises for the Australian Broadcasting Corporation, 1990

Yang, L.Y., and Marshall L. Wagner, editors, *Tiananmen: China's Struggle for Democracy—Its Prelude, Development, Aftermath, and Impact,* Baltimore: University of Maryland Press, 1990

Till Death Us Do Part

British Situation Comedy

One of the first British shows to take a serious and sustained interest in race themes was *Till Death Us Do Part,* originally broadcast in the mid-1960s on BBC1. Five weeks into the first series, the show had already toppled its immediate competitor, *Coronation Street,* in the ratings war. Although the idea for the series had been in the mind of its creator, Johnny Speight, for several years, it was not until Frank Muir took over comedy at the BBC that production began, initially as a pilot but subsequently as a fully fledged series. The comedy centered on the Garnett family, with the main "star" of the show in the person of the patriarch, Alf, sometimes known as Chairman Alf for his willingness to engage in scurrilous diatribes against the Labour party. The other significant target of his rantings were black people, and it is for the extreme views expressed by Alf on issues of race that the program is most remembered (and denounced).

Although Alf's creator argued at the time of the original broadcasts (and since) that his intention was to expose racist bigotry through the exaggerated utterances of Alf, many commentators contend that this intention backfired. The enormous popularity of the show signified that there was something about it that appealed to a significant proportion of the viewing public. Wherever the series has been shown—in Great Britain or in the United States or Germany (the last two in local adaptations)—the effects have by no means always been what the author intended. Alf's rhetoric was not always seen as the voice of the ignorant bigot, but often as the stifled cry of the authentic (white) working class. While the Garnett family, and Alf in particular, were clearly represented as disgraceful and abject characters, extreme even as caricatures, many critiques of the show suggest that part of its fascination for the audience was the "kernel of truth" buried in the lunatic wailings. Thus, the crucial difference between Alf's grotesque soliloquies and the viewers' beliefs was that Alf was simply too stupid to understand that racist sentiment must be concealed beneath a sheen of respectability: the persuasive and polished performance of Alessandra Mussolini, granddaughter of the dictator, in her Italian political career is more credible than Alf's degenerate ramblings, but contains much the same message.

The inflammatory and controversial subject matter of the show and its U.S. counterpart, *All in the Family,* ensured that both programs became the focus of academic inquiry. Research findings were mixed, some suggesting that such shows had a neutral effect on viewers while others claimed that viewers identified heavily with the xenophobic ravings of Alf/Archie. It is likely that many British viewers, worried by the alleged "immigrant avalanche" constantly reported in the media during the 1960s, and fueled by Irish Protestant leader Enoch Powell's rabid jingoism, found a certain resonance in the racist bigotry espoused by Alf. Although Alf was challenged in his more ludicrous diatribes by his daughter Rita and son-in-law Mike, with the odd wry observation from his long-suffering wife, "Old Moo," Warren Mitchell's powerful performance as Alf relegated the rest to mere bit players, as deserving butts of his wild wit.

Through Alf, a cascade of fear and prejudice was given unique prime-time exposure and articulated with such passion that during its transmission, 12 million viewers (then half the adult British population) tuned in to watch. It is highly unlikely that all these viewers were laughing at—rather than with—Alf, that they were all making wholly satirical readings of Alf's obscene racism and applauding Speight's clever exposition as they cackled at the "jokes." Looking again at the show from today's perspective, the virulent racism stands out as extraordinary, and its nature and extent have never been repeated on British television. *Till Death Us Do Part* may have been written as brave social commentary, but decades later, it looks seriously flawed and gives the lie to the notion that what the writer intends is always "correctly" interpreted and understood by her/his audience.

There is little evidence to support the claim of program producers and writers that mixing humor with bigotry will automatically underline the stupidity of the latter through the clever device of the former. If bigots do not perceive such programs as satire, and much of the research conducted so far seems to indicate that a satirical reading is by no means universal, then they are unlikely to become less prejudiced as a result of watching these shows. At the end of the 1980s, an Alf Garnett exhibition was staged at London's Museum of the

Moving Image, where visitors pressed buttons representing particular social problems and Alf appeared on video to opine on the selected subject. It is a strange idea and exemplifies the ease with which TV characters can make the transition from one medium to another, in this instance mutating from demon to sage in one easy movement. If it is a little too glib, from the smug security of a contemporary standpoint, to label *Till Death Us Do Part* as a straightforwardly racist text, it is nonetheless instructive to consider the limits of acceptability that prevail in any given decade and to continue the campaign for equality and respect while at the same time supporting the radical take.

More than three decades since it first aired, repeats of *Till Death Us Do Part* continue to be broadcast. The program continues to be a subject for comment and criticism.

KAREN ROSS

*See also **All in the Family; Speight, Johnny***

Cast

Alf Garnett	Warren Mitchell
Else Garnett	Dandy Nichols
Rita	Una Stubbs
Mike	Anthony Booth

Producers

Dennis Main Wilson, David Croft, Graeme Muir

Programming History

52 half-hour episodes; 1 45-minute special
BBC

July 1965	Comedy Playhouse (pilot)
June 1966–August 1966	7 episodes
December 1966–February 1967	10 episodes
January 1968–February 1968	7 episodes
September 1972–October 1972	6 episodes
December 1972	Christmas special
January 1974–February 1974	7 episodes
December 1974–February 1975	7 episodes
November 1975–December 1975	6 episodes

Further Reading

Cantor, Muriel G., *Prime-Time Television: Content and Control,* Beverly Hills, California, and London: Sage, 1980; 2nd edition, with Joel Cantor, 1992

Daniels, Therese, and Jane Gerson, *The Colour Black: Black Images in British Television,* London: British Film Institute, 1989

Ross, Karen, *Black and White Media: Black Images in Popular Film and Television,* Cambridge: Polity Press, 1995

Vidmar, Neil, and Milton Rokeach, "Archie Bunker's Bigotry," *Journal of Communication* (1974)

Tillstrom, Burr (1917–1985)

U.S. Puppeteer

Burr Tillstrom, the creative talent behind the extraordinarily successful *Kukla, Fran and Ollie* programs, was one of television's earliest pioneers and a principal participant in a number of television "firsts." In the late 1930s Tillstrom joined the RCA Victor television demonstration show for a tour throughout the midwestern United States. At the completion of the tour, he was invited to present his Kuklapolitan Players at the 1939 New York World's Fair, where he demonstrated the new medium at the RCA Victor exhibit. In the spring of 1940, RCA sent Tillstrom to Bermuda to do the first ship-to-shore telecasts. The Kuklapolitans were also featured on the 1941 premiere broadcast of the Balaban and Katz station WBKB in Chicago. By drawing large audiences for television puppetry, Tillstrom opened the door for future puppeteers and their puppets, such as Paul Winchell and Jerry Mahoney, Shari Lewis and Lamb Chop, and Jim Henson and the Muppets.

Tillstrom demonstrated his improvisational talents at an early age when he entertained neighborhood children using teddy bears, dolls, and any other objects that he could animate to mimic performances and film stories. Following one year of college during the mid-

1930s, he joined the Chicago Park District's puppet theater, created under the auspices of the Works Progress Administration (WPA), and developed his own puppets and characters after work. Kukla, the puppet who was the first member of the Kuklapolitan Players, was actually designed and constructed by Tillstrom for a friend in 1936, but Tillstrom found he could not part with his creation. The character remained nameless until a chance meeting with Russian ballerina Tamara Toumanova, who, upon seeing the puppet, called him "kukla" (Russian for "doll" and a term of endearment).

The format for *Kukla, Fran and Ollie* had its roots in Tillstrom's work at the 1939 World's Fair. His puppets, who served as an entr'acte for another marionette group, made comments to the audience and interacted with actresses and models (exhibit spokespersons) invited onto the stage. Tillstrom performed more than 2,000 shows at the fair, each performance different because he disliked repetition.

Tillstrom continued to hone his craft by performing with other marionette troupes and managing the puppet theater at Marshall Field's department store in Chicago. He performed benefits for the United Service Organization (USO) during World War II and at local hospitals for the Red Cross. During a 1941 bond-selling rally in Chicago, Tillstrom met a young radio singer and personality, Fran Allison, who later joined his troupe for a trial 13-week local program, a trial that lasted for many years and attracted millions of fans.

Tillstrom created each puppet on *Kukla, Fran and Ollie* by hand and was the sole manipulator and voice for 15 characters. He shifted easily—usually with only a momentary pause—among characters, and created unique personalities and voices for each "kid" (as he referred to his creations), ranging from the sweet voice of Kukla, the baritone singing voice of Ollie, and the flirtatious Buelah Witch, to the indistinguishable gibberish of Cecil Bill. Standing behind the small stage, Tillstrom could observe the onstage action through the use of a small monitor, a technique that was later adopted and expanded by Jim Henson for *The Muppet Show*.

Although he is most closely identified with *Kukla, Fran and Ollie*, Tillstrom was featured on the U.S. version of *That Was the Week That Was* (TW3) in 1964 without the Kuklapolitans. He won a special Emmy Award for a hand-ballet symbolizing the emotional conflicts caused by the Berlin Wall crisis. His work on TW3 was cited by the George Foster Peabody committee, which in 1965 decided to recognize distinguished individual achievements rather than general program categories after chiding the radio and television indus-

Kukla, Fran and Ollie, Kukla, Burr Tillstrom, Oliver J. Dragon, 1952–62.
Courtesy of the Everett Collection

try for "a dreary sameness and steady conformity" in its programming.

Following his success on television in various reincarnations and syndicated specials of *Kukla, Fran and Ollie,* including a Broadway production, annual holiday productions at Chicago's Goodman Theatre, and a sound recording (for which he was nominated for a Best Recording for Children Grammy Award in 1972), Tillstrom brought his characters to the printed page in his 1984 work *The Dragon Who Lived Downstairs*. A generous spirit who enjoyed sharing his knowledge and experience with future performers, Tillstrom served as an artist-in-residence at Hope College in Holland, Michigan. At the time of his death in December 1985, he was working on a musical adaptation of his life story for television. On March 23, 1986 Tillstrom was inducted posthumously into the Hall of Fame of the Academy of Television Arts and Sciences for his significant contributions to the art of television. Fran Allison accepted the award on his behalf.

SUSAN R. GIBBERMAN

See also **Allison, Fran; Chicago School of Television; Children and Television, Henson, Jim;** *Kukla, Fran, and Ollie*

Burr Tillstrom. Born in Chicago, Illinois, October 13, 1917. Attended the University of Chicago, 1935. Puppeteer from the early 1930s; created the puppet Kukla, 1936; manager of the puppet exhibits and marionette theater, Marshall Field and Company, Chicago, 1938; joined the RCA Victor television demonstration show, 1939; produced television show on Chicago television station WBKB with his "Kuklapolitans," 1947; program picked up by NBC, 1948–52; show moved to ABC, 1954–57; revived for PBS, 1969; staged a Broadway production with the Kuklapolitans, 1960; host, CBS Children's Film Festival, 1970s; appeared on NBC series *That Was the Week that Was,* 1964–65. Recipient: More than 50 entertainment awards, including five Emmys. Died in Palm Springs, California, December 6, 1985.

Television Series

1948–52, 1954–57, 1961–62, 1969–71, 1975–76	*Kukla, Fran and Ollie*
1964–65	*That Was the Week That Was*

Television Specials (selected)

1953	*The Ford 50th Anniversary Show*
1953	*St. George and the Dragon*
1954	*The Kukla, Fran and Ollie Mikado*
1954	*Many Moons* (adaptation)
1955	*The Kuklapolitan Easter Show*
1955	*Alice in Wonderland* (Cheshire Cat)
1968	*The Reluctant Dragon*

Publication

The Kuklapolitan Players Present the Dragon Who Lived Downstairs, 1984

Further Reading

Adams, Rosemary K., "Here We Are Again: *Kukla, Fran and Ollie,*" *Chicago History* (Fall 1997)

Brown, Joe, "Burr Tillstrom's Intimate World," *Washington Post* (December 22, 1982)

"Burr Tillstrom Dies at 68; Creator of 'Kukla, Fran, Ollie,'" *Variety* (December 11, 1985)

Christiansen, Richard, "Burr Tillstrom: An Innovator Who Had his Hand in Here-and-Now Projects," *Chicago Tribune* (December 15, 1985)

Corren, Donald, "Kukla, Me, and Ollie: Remembering Chicago's Legendary Puppeteer, Burr Tillstrom," *Chicago Magazine* (July 1986)

Crimmins, Jerry, "Burr Tillstrom, 68, Originated 'Kukla,'" *Chicago Tribune* (December 7, 1985)

Mitchard, Jacquelyn, "Kukla, Fran, Ollie, and Me," *TV Guide* (November 16, 1996)

Nix, Crystal, "Burr Tillstrom, Puppeteer, Dies," *New York Times* (December 8, 1985)

Shales, Tom, "A Troupe's Worth of Talent Died with Burr Tillstrom," *Chicago Tribune* (December 18, 1985)

Stover, Carol, "*Kukla, Fran and Ollie:* A Show for All Time," *Antiques and Collecting Magazine* (May 1997)

Terkel, Studs, "Burr Tillstrom, 1966 and 1978," in Terkel's *The Spectator: Talk about Movies and Plays with the People Who Make Them,* New York: New Press, 1999

Time Shifting

The practice of recording a television program onto videotape with a video cassette recorder (VCR) or onto a computer hard drive in a digital video recorder (DVR, also known as the personal video recorder, PVR) for the purpose of playing the program back later at a more convenient time for the viewer, is known as "time shifting." By law, with few exceptions, a person is not permitted to make an unauthorized copy of a copyrighted work like a television show. One exception to this is the concept of "fair use." Fair use allows for the copying and use of copyrighted material for certain nonprofit, educational, and/or entertainment purposes.

The VCR was introduced into the home television market in the United States during the mid-1970s. As the sale of VCRs increased in the early 1980s, more and more viewers began taping programs off the air. Program producers and other copyright owners went

to court to stop what they believed to be infringement of their copyrights. Universal Studios sued Sony Corporation, the inventor and patent holder of the Betamax VCR, in hopes of either stopping home taping of television programs or charging royalties for such copying. A U.S. Court of Appeals ruled in Universal's favor, but the matter went to the U.S. Supreme Court, which issued its famous "Betamax" decision in 1984. In that decision, the justices granted permission for home television viewers to record television shows for purposes of viewing them later at a more convenient time (i.e., time shifting). The high court ruled that such copying constituted fair use and would not hurt the market value of the programming itself to program producers. The court's decision was vague on the issue of "warehousing" tape copies. For example, if a viewer is a fan of a soap opera such as *As The World Turns* and makes copies of each and every episode with the intention of building a library of the entire program series for repeated playback in the future, that would be warehousing. The court may have left this matter deliberately vague, however, because it would be virtually impossible to enforce a ban on such warehousing without violating a person's right to privacy. The unauthorized copying issue is raised again each time a new electronic media technology is introduced to the public. The courts are likely to continue to support the concept of time shifting and other, similar personal uses of these technologies in the future. Programming schedules have begun to reflect this practice. In the United Kingdom, for example, educational programs for both schools and the Open University are shown through the night on the assumption that teachers and other users will record them for use during the day.

The introduction of the DVR in the late 1990s made copying and storing programs still easier for viewers. The digital technology required no bulky tapes to purchase, no clock to set for timed recording, and no storage and searching for tapes when playback is desired. Instead, the television set is connected to a digital hard drive comparable to that in a computer. By subscribing to a commercial service, viewers are able to select programs weeks in advance and, with the touch of a button, command the machine to record and store the program. The user may even program the machine to collect every episode of a television series, or to search for similar programs. The digital recorder also allows viewer control of "live television," pausing the recording, delaying initial viewing, and fast-forward through commercials.

The TiVo was the first digital recorder on the market, soon followed by Replay. The first Replay machines automatically skipped commercials in recorded material. The technology also allowed for digital "file swapping." Faced with lawsuits, Replay removed these capabilities from the machines, though it is still possible to fast-forward through the interruptions.

One other form of time-shifting also developed at the end of the decade. "Re-purposing" became a programming strategy in which television distributors provided the same program in different venues, often within very short time periods. Re-purposing meant that a program appearing on network television might appear on a cable network later in the same week. While the practice was frustrating for traditional broadcasters who realized viewers might forego their network programming for other preferences when the content would be available at a later time, it was financially attractive to the owners of multiple distribution outlets. To date the practice is not widely used.

ROBERT G. FINNEY

See also **Betamax Case; Copyright Law and Television; Home Video; Sony Corporation; Videocassette; Videotape**

Further Reading

Levy, Mark R., editor, *The VCR Age: Home Video and Mass Communication,* Newbury Park, California: Sage, 1989
Levy, Mark R., and Barrie Gunter, *Home Video and the Changing Nature of the Television Audience,* London: Libbey, 1988

Time Warner

U.S. Media Conglomerate

Time Warner, known as AOL Time Warner from 2001 to 2003, has evolved from its origins in film and publishing into one of the world's largest media conglomerates. Time Warner's television interests encompass both cable and broadcasting, and both distribution and programming. Time Warner Cable is one of the largest multiple system cable operators in the U.S. Time Warner's broadcast network, the WB, founded in 1995, has carried hit series such as *Buffy the Vampire Slayer, Dawson's Creek,* and *Seventh Heaven.*

Warner's film and television production subsidiaries have produced programming shown on a variety of broadcast and cable networks, including *Friends, ER, Gilmore Girls, The West Wing, Everybody Loves Raymond, The Drew Carey Show, Six Feet Under,* and *Smallville.* Time Warner's cable networks include premium pay cable channels such as Cinemax and Home Box Office. The Turner networks (Turner Network Television, Turner Broadcasting System, Turner Classic Movies, Cartoon, and Cable News Network) are among the top-rated cable networks for both general and niche audiences.

Time Warner's other subsidiaries include film production and distribution (Warner Brothers, Castle Rock, New Line), home video (Warner Home Video), and theatrical film exhibition (over 1,000 screens internationally). The Time/Life magazine publishing division, founded by Henry Luce in 1922, includes *Time, People, Sports Illustrated,* and *In Style,* and accounts for nearly a fifth of all magazine advertising revenues. Time Warner's book-publishing division includes Warner Books and Little, Brown and Company. Time Warner has stakes in various online media, including the Netscape browser, Compuserve, MovieFone, Instant Messenger, and America Online, the largest single internet service provider.

Although Warner Brothers had diversified its film business into the recording industry in the 1920s with the advent of sound movies, it only became a full-fledged diversified media conglomerate when Steve Ross's Kinney Corporation acquired it in 1969. Ross renamed it Warner Communications, Inc., and expanded into cable, publishing, and video games (for the Atari computer). Ross's management strategy was to foster competition and creative autonomy among divisions in order to attract and retain creative and managerial talent. WCI was known for its fractious internal politics, usually smoothed over by favors from Ross, a polymath with a taste for sweeping gestures and private jets. In 1989, looking to merge with a partner with complementary media holdings, Ross won a protracted legal battle with Paramount over Time Inc., publishers of *Time* magazine. However, the resulting merged company, Time Warner, went heavily into debt to finance the merger. When Ross died from cancer a few years later, bitter internal debates among Time Warner's film, music, and publishing divisions over "synergy" resulted in a protracted power struggle.

By 1993 Gerald Levin emerged the winner. Levin, a lawyer by training, had joined Time in 1972 when it acquired a small cable company in Manhattan known as Home Box Office. In 1976 Levin convinced Time to put HBO on a satellite feed (rather than microwave or landline) to deliver exclusive sports and film programming to local cable-operating systems. This innovation galvanized the growth of national cable networks and the subsequent increase of cable penetration into the majority of U.S. homes. Levin had paired an old distribution system (cable wires) with a new one (satellite feeds); he would attempt to replicate this early success throughout his tenure at Time Warner.

However, tensions over "synergy" simmered throughout the 1990s. For example, the film division refused to sell pay-cable rights for its films to HBO for less than what it thought it could receive from other pay-cable services. Warner Music was reluctant to license its artists' work to the film division. Conflicts among the divisions reflected concerns that each would suffer reduced divisional profits if forced to sell their products at a discount to buyers within the conglomerate. Thus, despite occasional successes such as the franchise of *Batman* feature films, the concept of "synergy" fell from favor. In 1996 Levin reversed his course toward streamlining the conglomerate and instead oversaw the purchase of cable magnate Ted Turner's company (TBS, TNT, CNN). The absorption of Turner's cable networks solidified Time Warner's market power in television: its combination of cable-operating systems in top markets with Turner's highly rated cable networks gave Time Warner strong negotiating leverage with competitors. Time Warner also developed an interactive television service, the Full Service Network. Unlike one-way cable service, this was a two-way distribution platform that could provide video-on-demand, retail sales, games, and communication services. However, the technology and implementation costs remained too high in the mid-1990s; Time Warner was forced to take large losses on its investment.

By the late 1990s, Internet networking and the World Wide Web threatened to replace or converge with television as the next mass-distribution platform. Levin oversaw a number of online initiatives at Time Warner, including Pathfinder, an attempt to link Time Warner's companies through the Web. In 1999, concerned that Time Warner would lose its competitive edge because of its dependence on "old media" businesses such as magazines and film, Levin reached an agreement with Steve Case, then head of America Online, to merge the two companies.

America Online had evolved from a small online game company to the largest single Internet service provider (ISP) in the world, peaking at over 20 million subscribers in 2000. Case's clever marketing strategies for AOL were rooted in his own experience as a frustrated online user in the 1980s. Case realized that if the online experience could be easy to use, fun, and affordable, it could reach a mass market. Instead of trying to sell its software to consumers wary of computers, AOL freely distributed millions of copies of its software through mass mailings. Having had a free introduction to the service, users then paid AOL based on time spent online. By 1992, AOL had overtaken competing ISPs, redesigned itself to provide its subscribers access to the rest of the Internet from within AOL, and changed its pricing to a flat monthly fee. Noting that most subscribers preferred user-generated content such as chat rooms, AOL also reversed its relationships with professional content providers, such as *Newsweek* magazine. Rather than paying to display repurposed content, AOL asked the providers to pay for access to AOL users' screens. This not only reduced overhead but generated a new form of revenue for AOL, as content providers accepted AOL's terms in order to maintain access to millions of potential customers.

However, AOL's rapid success and subsequently overvalued stock exposed the company to hostile takeover attempts (from powerful companies such as Microsoft). Case also knew that the dial-up Internet access market would begin to shrink once broadband Internet access became more available. Broadband, whether over DSL phone lines or cable lines, offered the possibility of larger markets for online content and services. Case's selection of Time Warner as a merger partner was thus predicated in part on Time Warner's control of cable-operating systems in top markets. After having had little success in convincing other cable operators to offer AOL broadband services over their wires, Case and Levin theorized that the combination of AOL's online services brand with Time Warner's cable pipes would give AOL Time Warner a competitive advantage.

The merger of AOL and Time Warner, announced in January 2000 just before the collapse of the dot-com boom in April 2000, was completed in January 2001. In order to gain regulators' approval for their merger, AOL Time Warner had to contend with claims by competitors that its online and cable market dominance would create "bottlenecks," which would allow AOL Time Warner to discriminate against unaffiliated content providers. AOL Time Warner had to guarantee competitors' access to its cable lines. Confident that they could aggregate the conglomerate's 100 million subscribers, Case and Levin argued that the conglomerate's cross-promotion of AOL online services (both dial-up and broadband), *Time* magazine subscriptions, Time Warner cable subscriptions, as well as HBO subscriptions, would provide a stable source of revenue as well as fuel for rapid growth. AOL Time Warner would be positioned to become the market leader in entertainment technology services such as video-on-demand, interactive television, and broadband.

However, by 2003, as Time Warner's stock price suffered severe decline, the merger was heavily criticized by investors for pursuing the aim of media convergence at the cost of its core businesses. Broadband penetration lagged behind optimistic estimates, and the feasibility of interactive television was unclear. Conflicts between Time Warner executives and AOL executives broke out into the open. The number of AOL's dial-up subscribers flattened out, and its advertising revenues dropped drastically after the collapse of many of its dot-com advertisers. AOL, rather than being the "crown jewel" of the new, merged company, threatened to pull down the value of the entire conglomerate. A series of executive resignations followed, including Levin and Case, who continued to insist that their vision that "convergence is the wave of the future" was accurate despite the market's slowness in accepting it.

Renamed Time Warner in 2003, CEO Richard Parsons reduced the conglomerate's debt by selling less profitable divisions, such as Warner Music Group, and its interest in the cable network Comedy Central. Although the AOL Time Warner merger did not immediately result in a "fundamental transformation of the media and communications industries," as Case had claimed in 2001, Time Warner's focus on amalgamation as its key strategy for managing risk and reducing competition continues to shape the structure of the television industry, as well as the media and entertainment industry at large.

CYNTHIA B. MEYERS

See also **Case, Steve; Levin, Gerald; Media Conglomerates**

Further Reading

Auletta, Ken, "Leviathan: How Much Bigger Can AOL Time Warner Get?" *New Yorker* (October 29, 2001)

Bruck, Connie, *Master of the Game: Steve Ross and the Creation of Time Warner,* New York: Simon and Schuster, 1994

Klein, Alec, *Steve Case, Jerry Levin, and the Collapse of AOL Time Warner,* New York: Simon and Schuster, 2003

Swisher, Kara, *AOL.com,* New York: Random House, 1999

Swisher, Kara, *There Must Be a Pony in Here Somewhere: The AOL Time Warner Debacle and the Quest for a Digital Future,* New York: Crown, 2003

Tinker, Grant (1926–)

U.S. Producer and Media Executive

Although Grant Tinker's career in television spanned more than 30 years and a number of positions in network programming and production, he is best known for his work in the 1970s and 1980s as founder and president of MTM Enterprises, and as "the man who saved NBC" when he served as the network's chair and chief executive officer from 1981 to 1986. Throughout his career, he has been associated with literate, sophisticated programming usually referred to as "quality television."

His stint as chair and chief executive officer was not Tinker's first experience with NBC. In 1949, after graduation from Dartmouth College, he became the network's original executive trainee, learning about each of its departments before settling into a job in the station's night operations. He left the network in 1951 for employment in a series of production and programming jobs in radio, television, and advertising. He served as director of program development at McCann Erickson in the early 1950s, when advertisers were responsible for producing much of the networks' schedules, and at Warwick and Legler, where he rehabilitated Revlon's corporate image after it had been tarnished in the quiz-show scandals. He also served as Benton and Bowles's vice president in charge of programs, where he was involved in developing Procter and Gamble's *The Dick Van Dyke Show,* and where he met his second wife, Mary Tyler Moore.

Tinker returned to NBC in the early 1960s as west-coast head of programs, with responsibility for program development of a number of popular series, including *Bonanza, I Spy, Dr. Kildare,* and *The Man from U.N.C.L.E.* After returning to New York to serve as the network's vice president in charge of programs, he left NBC to work as a production executive at Universal (where he was instrumental in birthing *It Takes a Thief* and *Marcus Welby, M.D.,* as well as *The ABC Movie of the Week*) and Twentieth Century-FOX.

When Mary Tyler Moore was offered a 13-episode series commitment from CBS in 1970, the couple formed MTM Enterprises to produce *The Mary Tyler Moore Show.* Tinker put into practice his philosophy of hiring the best creative people and letting them work without interference from executives at the networks or at MTM. He built MTM into a "writers' company"

that produced some of the most successful and award-winning series of the 1970s and 1980s. Beginning with the writer-producer team of James Brooks and Allan Burns, who created *The Mary Tyler Moore Show,* Tinker and MTM nurtured the talents of a host of top writers and producers whose work would go on to dominate U.S. network television schedules and the Emmy Awards through the 1990s. The staff included Gary David Goldberg, Steven Bochco, Bruce Paltrow, Mark Tinker, Hugh Wilson, Joshua Brand, and John Falsey. MTM's early hits were primarily sitcoms in the *Mary Tyler Moore* mold (including spin-offs *Rhoda* and *Phyllis*) as well as *The Bob Newhart Show* and *WKRP in Cincinnati.* Beginning in the late 1970s and 1980s, however, MTM produced a number of network television's most successful and innovative dramas, including *Lou Grant, The White Shadow, Remington Steele, Hill Street Blues,* and *St. Elsewhere,* shows that benefited from Tinker's combination of benign neglect in creative matters and tenacious support in dealing with the networks.

In 1981 Tinker left MTM to become chair and chief executive officer of NBC, the perennial last-place network. With no shows in the Nielsen top ten, and only two in the top twenty, NBC had suffered through a season of dismal profits (one-sixth the level of ABC's or CBS's) and affiliate defections. Based on the belief that good-quality programming makes a strong network, Tinker worked with programming chief Brandon Tartikoff to revitalize NBC's prime-time schedule. They allowed low-rated but promising series to remain on the schedule until those programs built an audience, and they courted the best producers to supply the network with programs. Under this philosophy, NBC recovered the upscale urban audience prized by advertisers, earned industry approval with more Emmy Awards than CBS and ABC combined, and finally rose to first place in the ratings with such blockbusters as the famed Thursday night lineup—*Cosby, Family Ties, Cheers, Night Court,* and *Hill Street Blues*—billed as "the best night of television on television." That his programming strategy relied heavily on work from MTM (*Hill Street Blues, St. Elsewhere,* and *Remington Steele*) and MTM alumni (Goldberg's *Family Ties,* Charles Burrows and Glen and Les Charles's *Cheers*)

Grant Tinker with wife Mary Tyler Moore.
Courtesy of the Everett Collection

for good taste on television. Tinker joined Connecticut Senator Joe Lieberman in calling for more responsible programming during Congressional hearings in 1998, and was an outspoken critic of the genre of "reality programming" in 2000 and 2001. Tinker has earned a variety of awards celebrating his career in television, including the Producers Guild's Lifetime Achievement Award in television (1991) and induction into the Academy of Television Arts and Sciences' Television Hall of Fame (1997).

SUSAN McLELAND

See also **Dick Van Dyke Show, The; Mary Tyler Moore Show, The; Moore, Mary Tyler; National Broadcasting Company**

Grant Tinker. Born in Stamford, Connecticut, January 11, 1926. Educated at Dartmouth College. Married: 1) Ruth Byerly (divorced); one daughter and three sons; 2) Mary Tyler Moore, 1963 (divorced, 1981). Worked in radio program department, NBC, 1949–51; TV department, McCann-Erickson Advertising Agency, 1954–58; Benton and Bowles Advertising Agency, 1958–61; vice president of programs, west coast, NBC, 1961–66; vice president in charge of programming, west coast, NBC, New York City, 1966–67; vice president, Universal TV, 1968–69; vice president, Twentieth Century-FOX, 1969–70; president, Mary Tyler Moore (MTM) Enterprises, Inc., 1970–81; chair of the board and chief executive officer, NBC, Burbank, California, 1981–86; independent producer, Burbank, since 1986; president, GTG Entertainment, Culver City, California, 1986–90. Recipient: Producers Guild's Lifetime Achievement Award in television, 1991; inducted into Academy of Television Arts and Sciences' Television Hall of Fame, 1997.

Publications

Tinker in Television: From General Sarnoff to General Electric, with Bud Rukeyser, 1994

Further Reading

Auletta, Ken, *Three Blind Mice: How the TV Networks Lost Their Way,* New York: Random House, 1991
Coe, Steve, "Tinker Writes the Book on Television: Former NBC Chairman Looks at 40 Years inside the Magic Box," *Broadcasting and Cable* (September 5, 1994)
"NBC's Tortoise Overtakes the Hares," *Broadcasting* (November 5, 1984)
"With NBC Still Rated No. 3, Grant Tinker Ponders His Own Decisions—And the Audience's" (interview), *People Weekly* (May 14, 1984)

eventually cost Tinker his share of MTM, when NBC's parent company RCA ordered him to sell in the early 1980s. In any case, NBC's turnaround helped shore up the network system in an era when new programming alternatives such as cable and VCRs had begun eroding the once-monolithic network audience. Tinker left NBC in 1986, shortly after it was acquired by General Electric.

Tinker next tried to repeat the success of MTM Enterprises by forming GTG (Grant Tinker-Gannett) Entertainment with the communications giant Gannett, producer of the syndicated news-magazine *USA Today on TV* and the dramatic program *WIOU,* which aired for a short time on CBS. The partnership was dissolved in 1990. Since then, Tinker has written an autobiography, served on the boards of a variety of charitable organizations, and maintained his position as watchdog

Tinker, Tailor, Soldier, Spy

British Thriller/Miniseries

When first broadcast in September 1979, *Tinker, Tailor, Soldier, Spy* was variously regarded as "turgid, obscure, and pretentious," or as "a great success." It is in keeping with the ambiguous nature of John Le Carré's narratives that one can simultaneously agree with both formulations without contradiction. As one character in the story, Roy Bland, paraphrasing F. Scott Fitzgerald, observes: "An artist is a bloke who can hold two fundamentally opposing views and still function." The tension is a consequence of the themes of deception and duplicity at the center of the narrative: To those who, like former BBC Director General Sir Hugh Greene, prefer the moral certainties of novelist John Buchan's version of British Intelligence, Le Carré's world will not only be difficult to follow but morally perplexing. On the other hand, the success of the serial was not only demonstrated by good audience ratings but also by general critical acclaim for the acting, a judgment ratified by subsequent BAFTA awards for best actor (Alec Guinness), and for the camerawork of Tony Pierce-Roberts. An ambivalent reception also greeted *Tinker, Tailor, Soldier, Spy* in the United States, where the serial failed to be picked up for broadcast by the networks but won critical acclaim when shown on PBS.

Le Carré published his first novel, *Call For the Dead,* in 1961, and his first major novelistic success, *The Spy Who Came in from the Cold* (1963), was turned into a film in 1966, but *Tinker, Tailor, Soldier, Spy,* which also began as a novel, published in 1974, was his first venture into television. He rejected the project of turning it into a film because the plot would have to be compressed in order to fit a feature-length movie, but he thought that the space afforded by TV serialization would do justice to his narrative. He was also impressed with the skill of Arthur Hopcraft's teleplay, which extensively reordered the structure of the novel in order to clarify the narrative for a television audience without violating its essential character (for example, Hopcraft began the narrative with the debacle in Czechoslovakia, which the novel does not treat until chapter 27). Le Carré was even more taken by the interpretation of protagonist George Smiley provided by Alec Guinness. Indeed, as he was writing *Smiley's People* (1980), Le Carré found himself visualizing Guinness in the role and incorporated some of the insights afforded by the actor in the final part of the trilogy (the second part, *The Honourable Schoolboy,* 1977, has not been dramatized). A trivial example will stand for many. During the production of *Tinker, Tailor,* Guinness complained that the characterizing idiosyncrasy of Smiley, polishing his glasses with the fat end of his tie, cannot be done naturally because in London's cold weather, Smiley would wear a three-piece suit, thus a handkerchief must be substituted for the tie. At the end of *Smiley's People,* Le Carré includes a teasingly oblique rejoinder: "From long habit, Smiley had taken off his spectacles and was absently polishing them on the fat end of his tie, *even though he had to delve for it among the folds of his tweed coat*" (emphasis added). *Smiley's People* was itself dramatized by the BBC, with Alec Guinness reprising the title role to great acclaim, in 1982.

The story of *Tinker, Tailor* has an archetypal simplicity reminiscent of the *Odyssey:* the scorned outsider investigates the running of the kingdom, testing the loyalty of his subjects and kin by means of plausible stories before disposing of the usurpers and restoring righteous rule. In Le Carré's modern story, the elements are transposed onto the landscape of conflicted modern Europe in the throes of the Cold War.

A botched espionage operation in Czechoslovakia ensures that Control (Head of British Intelligence) and his associates are discredited. Shortly after this debacle, Control dies; his able lieutenant Smiley is retired; and the two are succeeded by four operatives they have trained whose codenames are Tinker, Tailor, Soldier, and Spy: Percy Alleline, Bill Haydon, Roy Bland, and Toby Esterhaze. Six months later, Riki Tarr, a maverick Far Eastern agent, turns up in London with a story suggesting there is a mole (a deeply concealed double agent) in the Circus (intelligence headquarters, located at Cambridge Circus). Lacon of the Cabinet Office entices Smiley out of retirement to investigate the story. Smiley gradually pieces together the story by analyzing files, interrogating witnesses, and trawling through his own memory and those of other retired Circus personnel, notably Connie Sachs (a brilliant cameo role played by Beryl Reid), until he finally unmasks the mole "Gerald" at the heart of the Circus.

The mood of the story, however, is far from simple. Duplicity and betrayal, personal as well as public (Smiley's upper-class wife is sexually promiscuous, betraying him with "Gerald"), informs every aspect of the scene. While the traitor is eventually unmasked, the corrupt nature of the intelligence service serves as a microcosm of contemporary England: secretive, manipulative, class-ridden, materialistic, and emotionally sterile. Thus, if the Augean stables have been cleaned, they will soon be soiled again. This downbeat tone accounts for the serial not being taken up by the U.S. networks and marks it off from the charismatic spy adventures of James Bond, but it also accounts for its particular appeal to British middle-brow audiences.

The spy genre is virtually a British invention: although other countries produce spy writers, the centrality of the genre to British culture is long-standing and inescapable: John Buchan, Somerset Maugham, Graham Greene, Ian Fleming, Frederick Forsyth, and Len Deighton, as well as Le Carré, have all achieved international success for their spy stories—not to mention the achievements in television drama by Dennis Potter (*The Blade on the Feather*) and Alan Bennett (*An Englishman Abroad* and *A Question of Attribution*). To account for this obsession with spies, we only have to consider the political circumstances of Britain in the 20th and 21st centuries: a declining imperial power, whose overseas possessions must be ruled and defended more by information than by outright physical force; an offshore island of a divided Europe, seeing itself threatened in the 20th century by German, then Soviet, military ambitions. Perhaps even more significant than these external threats are those from within. Holding a disproportionate share of positions of power in the cabinet, Whitehall, the BBC, and government institutions, the ruling class comprises an elite educated in public schools and at Oxbridge, and such a class, which maintains its grip on power by exclusion, is liable to marginalize or demonize those who openly challenge its assumptions. The result is liable to be subversion from within—a tactic fostered by the duplicitous jockeying for power of rival gangs in the enclosed masculine world of the public schools. The symbolic and emotional link between the world of the public school and that of the Circus is established in *Tinker, Tailor* by the character of Jim Prideaux. This injured and betrayed agent teaches at a prep school after his failed Czech mission and enlists the aid of a hero-worshipping pupil as his watcher. Thus,

the fictions that Le Carré invented have their counterpart in the real world and tap familiar English fears and obsessions. In the same year, 1979, that saw the serialization of *Tinker, Tailor*, the BBC also produced two documentary series, *Public School* and *Spy*, that reinforced the connections between real events and Le Carré's work. An episode in the latter series, "The Climate of Treason," concerned itself with speculating about the identity of the "Fourth Man" (a fourth double agent within MI5, after Burgess, MacLean, and Philby). On November 15, 1979, Margaret Thatcher publicly identified the art historian Sir Anthony Blunt, Surveyor of the Queen's Pictures (curator of the royal collection), as the Fourth Man, recruited by the Russians in the 1930s while at Cambridge. Le Carré's novel was read as a fictionalized version of these events.

The success of *Tinker, Tailor* lies in its realism, which is portrayed not only in the characters (and Guinness's Smiley is as definitive a performance as Sir Laurence Olivier's Richard in *Richard III* or Edith Evans as Lady Bracknell) but also in the serial's depiction of the way intelligence institutions work. However, the claim for realism must not be pressed too far; Le Carré has admitted that he invented much of the vocabulary used in the novel—babysitters, lamplighters, the Circus, the nursery, moles—though he was also amused to discover that real agents appropriated some of his terms once the stories were published. Moreover, much intelligence work is bureaucratic and boring: Smiley's reflections turn the drudgery of reading files into a fascinating intellectual puzzle that, unlike the real experience, always produces significant information.

At the symbolic level, however, the portrayal of the workings of bureaucracy *is* authentic: bureaucracies serve those who govern by gathering, processing, and controlling access to information. In a world increasingly governed by means of information, those who control it have power and wealth, so that the resonance of Le Carré's story will carry beyond the Cold War setting that is its point of departure.

BRENDAN KENNY

Cast (selected)

George Smiley	Alec Guinness
Annie Smiley	Siân Phillips
Tinker (Percy Alleline)	Michael Aldridge
Soldier (Roy Bland)	Terence Rigby
Poor Man (Toby Esterhaze)	Bernard Hepton
Peter Guillam	Michael Jayston
Lacon	Anthony Bate
Control	Alexander Knox

Producer
Jonathan Powell

Programming History
7 50-minute episodes
BBC
September 10, 1979–October 22, 1979

Further Reading

Bloom, Harold, *John Le Carré,* New York: Chelsea, 1987
Bold, Alan Norman, *The Quest for Le Carré,* New York: St. Martin's Press, 1988
Lewis, Peter, *John le Carré,* New York: Ungar, 1985
Monaghan, David John, "Le Carré and England: A Spy's-Eye View," *Modern Fiction Studies* (Autumn 1983)

Tisch, Laurence (1923–2003)

U.S. Media Mogul

In 1986, Laurence Tisch, a fabled Wall Street investor, took control of CBS, often considered the crown jewel of American broadcasting. Tisch ran the CBS network, its owned and operated television stations, and other corporate properties until 1995. Throughout the decade he was in charge, he manipulated and modified CBS, looking to cash in with an eventual sale of the property. In 1995 the deal came through. Westinghouse offered $5 billion for CBS; Tisch personally made an estimated $2 billion.

In the view of many television critics and media industry observers, Tisch badly mismanaged the former "Tiffany network" with policies that caused ratings to drop, earnings to fall, and affiliates to defect. In a stunning pair of 1994 deals, fellow mogul Rupert Murdoch contracted broadcasting rights for the National Football League (NFL) and tempted a number of CBS affiliates to switch to the FOX Broadcasting Company. CBS was further embarrassed when Tisch demoted Connie Chung from her position as co-anchor with Dan Rather of the *CBS Evening News.* Media pundits lambasted Tisch for CBS's decision to offer golf coverage on a Sunday afternoon in May 1995, while ABC and NBC carried President Bill Clinton's address to the mourners of the Oklahoma City bombing. CBS opted to stay with the golf tournament to save $1 million in advertising.

Andy Rooney, long a fixture on CBS's highest-rated show, *60 Minutes,* stated openly what many in the industry felt about Tisch's negative impact on CBS's long-fabled news division. On rival network ABC's *Primetime Live,* Rooney castigated Tisch for allowing CBS to slip: "We need a hero in the business. I don't see why someone like Larry Tisch…doesn't say, 'I've got all this money, why don't I just make the best news division in the world.'"

Tisch's relations with CBS had not begun on such a rancorous note. During the mid-1980s, when Ted Turner tried to make a make a hostile bid for CBS, longtime CBS chief William S. Paley looked for a "white knight" to save his beloved company. In October 1985 Paley and his hand-chosen corporate directors asked Tisch to join the CBS board and thwart Turner. Before his takeover, Tisch had simply been another anonymous New York City multimillionaire, making money in tobacco, insurance, and hotels. His rescue of CBS made him a media celebrity.

After serving in the U.S. Army's intelligence office during World War II, Tisch joined forces with his younger brother, Bob, and began his rise to corporate power and profit with the 1949 purchase of Laurel-in-the-Pines, a New Jersey hotel. For the next decade, the brothers bought and sold hotels, particularly in Miami Beach, Florida, and Atlantic City, New Jersey. In 1959 the Tisch brothers bought the Loews theater chain from Metro-Goldwyn-Mayer and changed the name of their company to Loews Corporation.

From this base they continued to expand their investment efforts and by the mid-1980s, Loews Corporation ranked as a multibillion-dollar conglomerate success story. Loews was built by acquiring other companies through tender offers, beginning with the takeover of Lorillard, a tobacco products company, in 1968. In early 1974 Loews announced it had acquired just over 5 percent of an insurance subsidiary, CNA Financial, then an independent company. Before the end of that year, Loews had successfully completed a hostile tender offer for the company's stock, and CNA be-

Laurence Tisch, 1999.
©Sean Roberts/Everett Collection

came the principal source of Loews' income. In the case of both Lorillard and CNA, the Tisch brothers reversed the fortunes of ailing companies and made millions in the process.

Privately, Laurence Tisch then began to undertake philanthropic causes. He managed the investments of the Metropolitan Museum of Art, provided endowment and buildings for New York University, and led fundraising for the United Jewish Appeal.

In 1986, Paley stepped aside and Tisch became not only CBS's major stockholder but also its chief executive officer. To no-one's surprise, Tisch restructured the company into a "lean and mean" operation. Within months he had launched the biggest single staff and budget reduction in network TV history. When the dust had settled, hundreds had lost their long-secure jobs, news bureaus had been shuttered, and CBS was a shell of its former self.

On a larger corporate scale, Tisch systematically began to sell every CBS property not connected to televi-

sion. First sold was CBS's educational and professional publishing, which included Holt, Rinehart and Winston, one of the United States' leading publishers of textbooks; and W.B. Saunders, a major publisher of medical books. CBS picked up $500 million in the deal.

That sum proved to be small change when compared to the $2 billion paid by Sony Corporation of Japan for the CBS Music Group. One of the world's dominant record and compact disc companies, CBS Music boasted a stable of stars that then included Bruce Springsteen, Michael Jackson, the Rolling Stones, Billy Joel, Cindy Lauper, Paul McCartney, and James Taylor. This single 1987 sale enabled the new CBS to earn a substantial profit that year.

With the layoffs, budget cuts, and sales of CBS properties completed, Tisch faced the need to improve TV programming. This proved difficult, and speculation began about precisely when Tisch would cash in his CBS stock. Potential buyers for the network included MCA/Universal Pictures, Disney, Viacom, and QVC, a television home-shopping company. Throughout the early 1990s, Tisch quietly engineered stock repurchases by CBS, and, by selling much of his own stock back to the corporation, he covered his original investment. Whatever he would receive for his remaining 18 percent of the company would be pure profit. Thus, the 1995 Westinghouse deal moved Tisch from the status of a multimillionaire to a multibillionaire. In television history, however, Laurence Tisch will be remembered for first rescuing, and then decimating, the once-dominant television network.

DOUGLAS GOMERY

See also **Columbia Broadcasting System; Paley, William S.**

Laurence Alan Tisch. Born in New York City, March 15, 1923. Educated at New York University, B.S., 1942; University of Pennsylvania, M.A. in industrial engineering, 1943; studied at Harvard Law School, 1946. Married: Wilma Stein, 1948; four sons. Served in U.S. Army, Office of Strategic Services, during World War II. President, Tisch Hotels, Inc., New York City, 1946–74; chair of the board and chief executive officer, Loews Corp., New York City, from 1960, cochief executive officer, from 1988; president, chief executive officer, CBS Inc., New York City, from 1986, chair, president, chief executive officer, board of directors, from 1990. Chair and member of board of directors, CNA Finance Corporation, Chicago. Board of directors: Bulove Corporation, New York City; ADP Corporation; Petrie Stores Corporation; R.H. Macy and Company; United Jewish Appeal Federation;

chair, board of trustees, New York University. Trustee: Metropolitan Museum of Art, New York City; New York Public Library; Carnegie Corporation. Died November 15, 2003.

Further Reading

Auletta, Ken, *Three Blind Mice: How the TV Networks Lost Their Way,* New York: Random House, 1991

Auletta, Ken, "Network for Sale?" *New Yorker* (July 25, 1994)

Diamond, Edwin, "The Tisching of CBS: The New Chief Takes Control—But Where Is He Going?" *New York Times* (May 16, 1988)

Klein, Edward, "Eye of the Storm," *New York Times* (April 15, 1991)

"Larry Tisch and the New Realism at CBS" (interview), *Broadcasting* (October 27, 1986)

Loftus, Jack, "Tisch Is Keeping it Simple: Bets the Farm on CBS-TV" (interview), *Television-Radio Age* (September 28, 1987)

McCabe, Peter, *Bad News at Black Rock: The Sell-Out of CBS News,* New York: Arbor House, 1987

Peretz, Martin, "Media Moguls," *New Republic* (September 4, 1995)

"The Perils of Networking," *Economist* (December 10, 1994)

Tiswas

U.K. Children's Series

Tiswas (an acronym for "Today Is Saturday, Watch And Smile") initially aired on January 5, 1974, not networked but broadcast on ITV in the Midlands area only, the area of Britain where the commercial television franchise was held by ATV (Associated TeleVision). A freewheeling, loosely scripted, and unpredictable mishmash of jokes, sketches, cartoons, pop clips, celebrity guests, and spoof features, the show quickly became essential watching for pre-teens fascinated by its irreverent approach and scatological style, which frequently involved guests getting soaked or immersed in "gunge." Each week an audience of lucky youngsters would cram in the studio to watch the riotous action take place, and occasionally get involved in the mayhem. The main presenter in those early days was John Asher, aided and abetted by Trevor East and Chris Tarrant (later to become producer of the series), who would make the largest initial on-screen splash and who, much later, would reach even greater heights as the host of *Who Wants To Be A Millionaire?* Tarrant seemed totally at ease among the chaos and cheerfully kept going as the madness unfolded around him. By the second series the show was even crazier, and was beginning to attract an older audience in addition to the targeted pre-teens.

In 1976 the BBC started its own live marathon-length Saturday morning children's show, *The Multi Coloured Swap Shop* and, seemingly to counteract the impact of this move, some other ITV regions (Anglia serving east England, Granada serving Lancashire, HTV serving Wales and the west, Southern TV, and Scottish Television serving Central Scotland) also started carrying *Tiswas*. By this time John Asher had left the team and Sally James had joined. This last move served to attract even more older audience members, especially adolescent boys and their fathers, who took a shine to James and her "rock chick" appeal. The presenters continued to deal out doses of slime and buckets of water, but the slop value of the show was increased considerably the following year (1977) with the introduction of the Phantom Flan Flinger, a masked custard-pie throwing and water-slinging mystery man who would be responsible for drenching many of the celebrity guests who appeared on the show.

The series went from strength to strength and further consolidated in 1979, when it was also transmitted in the Grampian (North East Scotland), LWT (London), Westward (South West England), and Yorkshire Television regions, virtually covering the land. This was to be the show's most popular period, with a winning team of varying personnel including, alongside Tarrant and James, larger-than-life impressionist Lenny Henry; comedian (later *Dr. Who* star) Sylvester McCoy; former pop singer John Gorman; veteran Irish comic Frank Carson, and the dry-witted Bob Carolgees whose puppet, punk dog Spit, became a firm favorite with audience members and home viewers. By this time celebrities were lining up to be on the show.

Victims included Paul McCartney, Genesis, Cliff Richard, Kate Bush, The Clash, and senior newscaster Trevor McDonald—mercilessly soaked while reading a spoof news item. Other recurring favorite moments of the show were: The Cage, in which adult audience members were imprisoned and regularly soaked by having buckets of water thrown over them; Compost Corner, a pastiche gardening segment also ending up with someone getting wet; the Dying Fly, in which the audience members were encouraged to lie on their back and wiggle their legs and arms in the air; the pop interview, which would start normally enough but was prone to end in chaos; and the small children talent slot, during which young audience members were given the chance to show off their (often excruciating) party pieces.

By the end of the 1979 season the show had become so popular that the central team (Tarrant, James, Gorman and Carolgees) had toured as The Four Bucketeers, soaking audiences up and down the country and releasing a minor hit single ("The Bucket of Water Song"). The adult appeal of *Tiswas* had grown considerably; this was reflected occasionally by the (often unintentionally) risqué nature of some of the items. It proved impossible to resist this older appeal and Tarrant, Gorman and Carolgees left in 1981 to produce and present *OTT* (Over The Top) from 1982, a late-night adult version of *Tiswas*. However, the intentionally rude and crude nature of the new show failed to spark interest or engender the sort of cult appeal that had turned *Tiswas* into a phenomenon. *Tiswas* itself continued unabashed at first, but soon after showed signs of wear and tear, and ended in April 1982. The series had revolutionized U.K. children's broadcasting, paving the way for a saucier, livelier approach to the field and demonstrating to no little extent the appeal of slapstick comedy, pop music, and silliness to both the young and the young at heart.

DICK FIDDY

See also **Children and Television**

Cast (Presenters/Performers)
John Asher (1974)
Chris Tarrant (1974–81)
Trevor East (1975–78)
Sally James (1977–82)
John Gorman (1977–81)
Lenny Henry (1977–81)
Bob Carolgees (1979–81)
Frank Carson
Jim Davidson
Sylvester McCoy (1977–79)
Clive Webb (1980–82)
Gordon Astley (1981–82)
Dan Hegarty (1980–82)
David Rappaport (1981–82)
Emil Wolk
Terry Coates
Trevor James

Producer
Chris Tarrant

Program Compiler
Peter Matthews

Production Company
ATV
1974–1982   Saturday morning

TiVo™. *See* Convergence

Todman, Bill. *See* Goodson, Mark, and Bill Todman

Tommy Hunter Show, The

Canadian Country Music Program

Known as "Canada's Country Gentleman," Tommy Hunter was for many years one of Canada's most popular and best-known television personalities. He became a fixture on Canadian television as the host of *The Tommy Hunter Show,* one of North America's longest-running variety shows, and is also one of the few figures in Canadian popular music to have established his reputation through television rather than through recording and radio airplay. He has received numerous awards for his role in television, in country music, and in Canadian cultural life.

The Ontario native's career in television started when he was 19 years old on *Country Hoedown,* a weekly country-music program produced by and aired on the Canadian Broadcasting Corporation (CBC), where Hunter would spend the rest of his television career. The show was an on-stage revue with a house band and featured various musical guests from both Canada and the United States. Starting out as a rhythm guitarist, Hunter soon became a featured performer on the show, which led to his own daily noontime CBC radio program, *The Tommy Hunter Show;* it became a television series in 1965.

Much of *Country Hoedown*'s format and tone were carried over into *The Tommy Hunter Show.* Over its 27-year run on CBC (1965–92)—rerun three times a week on the Nashville Network between 1983 and 1991—the show was noted for nurturing Canadian country music, which it showcased alongside big-name American country stars. Hunter wanted to break with the hokey, country-hick feel that characterized such shows as *Hee Haw,* however, and tried to present country music as "respectable." The result was a program that some labeled a country version of *The Lawrence Welk Show.* Inspired by television variety-show hosts such as Johnny Carson and Perry Como, Hunter felt that the host should have a relaxed, comfortable style, establishing a certain rapport with the audience. By sticking to his country-purist approach, he was able to establish such a rapport, building up an intensely loyal fan base that planned its Saturday evenings around *The Tommy Hunter Show.* Over the years, Hunter sustained an ongoing battle with CBC producers who wanted to rely on demographics and make the show more slick. He maintained that targeted programming precluded estab-

lishing a real relationship with the audience. His show relied upon the on-stage revue format, which mixed various musical sequences with dance and other country entertainment. Despite attempts to alter the program by incorporating other styles and sensibilities, Hunter persevered in maintaining the show's traditional country tone. It was this purist approach that would ultimately sound the show's death knell, however, and a lack of younger viewers and slipping audience ratings led to its cancellation in 1992.

As a long-running music television program, *The Tommy Hunter Show* demonstrates that television's imbrication with popular music dates back long before the rise of MTV and the music video. Hence, while it provided country music fans with entertainment each week, Hunter's program also helped to rearticulate a brand of country music that many associated with Nashville as a Canadian popular-music genre, in a period that saw the rise of a Canadian cultural nationalism that sought to define itself principally by contrast with American culture. Indeed, through the program's year-in, year-out presence on the CBC, the state-owned broadcaster and self-styled "national network," the country music of *The Tommy Hunter Show* became a national symbol for many Canadians, and Tommy Hunter a figure of "Canadianness." This ability of television to reach around the generic division of popular music into record or radio formats, then, helped shape a "Canadian country music" genre, which would combine the traditional music of Canadian folk performers with the country music of artists like Tommy Hunter.

As much as *The Tommy Hunter Show* displayed how television intervenes into other areas of popular culture such as popular music, it also threw into relief the tensions that arise between them. Behind-the-scenes conflict between CBC television workers and Tommy Hunter, a country musician, derived from their emergence from two separate cultural formations: on the one hand, the world of television production, with its own sensibilities and priorities; and on the other hand, the world of country music, with its distinctive internal organization and logic. CBC personnel wanted to target specific demographic ranges in their audience by "updating" the show with natty set designs and a wider variety of musical styles. But Hunter's desire for austere

Tommy Hunter.
Courtesy of Country Music Hall of Fame and Museum

sets and traditional country music, and his concern for providing family entertainment for a country audience, derived from the emphases on "sincerity" and "authenticity" that underpin country music's self-image as a genre and define fundamental aspects of the country music world. Indeed, the conflicts behind *The Tommy Hunter Show* foreshadowed a later reticence toward music videos on the part of the country music industry as a whole, wary of the video-clip format's "slickness" as being antithetical to country music's "authenticity."

The privileged role played by authenticity in country music, with its accompanying stress on "ordinary people," was central to *The Tommy Hunter Show*. Although based in Toronto, the show went on the road frequently, playing to sold-out audiences across Canada. Hunter's insistence that the set in each city reflect the locale of the taping illustrated his constant striving to reinsert a local feel into the globalizing pull of television. A harsh critic of the television industry even as a television star, Hunter felt that TV programmers had little understanding of country-music audiences; for Hunter, the institutional imperatives of a mass-mediated country music compromised his audience's position. These views carried over to his recording career. Hunter preferred to record albums independently rather than with major record labels, reasoning that this would allow him to aim at pleasing country audiences, rather than radio stations. And in 1992, following cancellation of *The Tommy Hunter Show,* he toured Canada with a stage version of the show, playing to sold-out audiences, meeting his fans from the other side of the television screen.

The only program to survive a wave of rural, family-oriented CBC programming in the 1950s and 1960s that included such shows as *Don Messer's Jubilee, The Tommy Hunter Show* was a country show produced in an urban environment. It was a family-oriented show in an age of splintering demographics. It made a country singer into a television star. And in the process it had a profound impact on the Canadian popular-music landscape. By the end of the show's run, Hunter had won three Juno Awards as Canada's best male country singer (1967–69) and become the fifth Canadian to be inducted into the Country Music Hall of Fame's Walkway of Stars (1990) for his music; he received an award from the Broadcast Executive Society as well as a Gemini Award for best Canadian variety show (1991); and he was named to the Order of Canada for his part in Canadian cultural life.

BRAM ABRAMSON

Regular Performer
Tommy Hunter

Producers
Dave Thomas, Bill Lynn, David Koyle, Les Pouliot, Maurice Abraham, Joan Toson, and others

Programming History
CBC
1965–70	Half-hour weekly during fall/winter season
1970–92	One-hour weekly

Further Reading

Conrad, Charles, "Work Songs, Hegemony, and Illusions of Self," *Critical Studies in Mass Communication* (Spring 1988)

Fenster, Mark, "Country Music Video," *Popular Music* (1988)

Hunter, Tommy, with Liane Heller, *My Story,* Agincourt, Ontario: Methuen, 1985

Lacey, Liam, "Canada's Country Gentleman," *Globe and Mail* (October 24, 1987)

Marquis, Greg, "Country Music: The Folk Music of Canada," *Queen's Quarterly* (Summer 1988)

Tonight

British Magazine Program

Tonight was a 40-minute topical magazine program broadcast every weekday evening between 6:00 P.M. and 7:00 P.M., and was first broadcast by the BBC in February 1957. The program was produced under the aegis of the BBC's Talks Department by Alasdair Milne (who became director-general of the BBC in the 1980s) and edited by Donald Baverstock (who became head of programmes for BBC television in the 1960s). It was presented by Cliff Michelmore, who had already collaborated with Baverstock and Milne on *Highlight,* a shorter, less ambitious version of *Tonight.* With *Tonight,* Michelmore quickly acquired status as a broadcaster, picking up an award for artistic achievement, and twice named Television Personality of the Year. Indeed, *Tonight* was significant for its ability to attract and cultivate new broadcasting talent, and over its eight-year run managed to launch a number of notable careers, including those of Alan Whicker, Ned Sherrin, Julian Pettifer, and Trevor Philpott.

The program was conceived by the BBC as their way to fill the space created by the then-recent relaxation of the rule of the "toddlers' truce," when television had previously closed down for an hour to allow parents to see their children off to bed. As such, *Tonight* went out to a new and untried audience, an audience who, at this time of the evening, would be quite active rather than settled, who would be busy preparing food, putting children to bed, or getting ready to go out. *Tonight* was designed around the needs of this audience, and its style reflected this: the tone was brisk and informal, mixing the light with the serious, and items were kept short, allowing audiences to "dip in" at their convenience. This emphasis on the needs of the audience was something of a departure for the BBC, which had tended to adopt a paternalistic tone with its viewers, giving them not what they wanted but what they *should* want. *Tonight* was going to be different. It was not to talk down to the viewer, but would, as the *Radio Times* put it, "be a reflection of what you and your family talk about at the end of the day." In Baverstock's words, *Tonight* would "celebrate communication with the audience," and, indeed, the program came across not as the institutional voice of the BBC but as the voice of the people.

Tonight was recognized by many to be evidence of the BBC's fight back against the new Independent Television (ITV) companies that were quickly gaining ground and by 1957 had overtaken the BBC (which was still broadcasting only one TV channel), with a 72 percent share of the audience. But if *Tonight* was largely a result of competition and the breaking of the monopoly, which in effect forced the BBC to adopt a more populist programming philosophy, the style and content of the program also reflected broader social and cultural changes. *Tonight* seemed to capture an emerging attitude of disrespect and popular skepticism toward institutions and those in authority. Furthermore, the adjectives that were often used to describe the program at the time, such as "irreverent," "modern," and "informal," could have easily described the mood that was beginning to inform other areas of the arts and popular culture in Britain at that time.

Tonight introduced a number of innovations to British television. It was one of the first programs to editorialize and adopt a point of view, flaunting the public-service demands of balance and impartiality. The program also introduced a new (some might say aggressive) style of interviewing, where guests would be pushed and harassed if it was thought they were being evasive or dishonest. *Tonight* eschewed the carefully prepared question-and-answer format that had prevailed in current affairs programming until then. Furthermore, broadcasters had tended to fetishize the production process, concealing the means of communication and carefully guarding against mistakes and technical breakdowns that threatened to demystify the production. *Tonight,* however, kept in view such things as monitors and telephones. Its interviews were kept unscripted and any technical faults or mistakes were skillfully incorporated into the program flow, giving *Tonight* an air of spontaneity and immediacy.

Tonight was meant to be a temporary response to the ending of the "toddlers' truce," and was initially given a three-month run. It quickly proved popular, however, and within a year was drawing audiences of over 8 million. In addition, the program won critical acclaim, receiving the Guild of Television Producers Award for best factual program in 1957 and 1958. The program generated other material as well, including feature-length documentaries, and was the inspiration behind *That Was the Week That Was,* a show that stepped up

Tonight's irreverent, hard-hitting approach for a late-night adult audience.

Baverstock left *Tonight* in 1961 to become assistant controller of programs, and his place was taken by Alasdair Milne. Milne proved to be a capable editor and indeed oversaw a number of innovations, including the feature-length documentaries.

However, the program would not be the same without Baverstock, whose leadership and vision had made *Tonight* something of an individual success. By 1962 it was argued that the program had become rigid and stale. As is the case with many innovative and ground-breaking enterprises, the program could not sustain the pace of its initial inventiveness. The final edition went out in June 1965. Nevertheless, in its eight-year run, *Tonight* had established a format for current-affairs programming that mixed the light with the serious, which blurred distinctions between education and entertainment, and which managed in the process to soften the image of the BBC, transforming it, as Watkins has noted, from an "enormous over-sober responsible corporation," to something that looked "more like a man and a brother."

PETER MCLUSKIE

Anchor
Cliff Michelmore

Field Reporters
Derek Hart
Geoffrey Johnson Smith

Alan Whicker
Fyfe Robertson
Trevor Philpott
Macdonald Hastings
Julian Pettifer
Kenneth Allsop
Brian Redhead
Magnus Magnusson

Producer
Donald Baverstock

Director
Alasdair Milne

Programming History
BBC
1957–65   Weeknights 6:00–7:00

Further Reading

Briggs, Asa, *The History of Broadcasting in the United Kingdom,* volume 5: *Competition,* Oxford: Oxford University Press, 1995

Corner, John, editor, *Popular Television in Britain,* London: British Film Institute, 1991

Goldie, Grace Wyndham, *Facing the Nation: Broadcasting and Politics, 1936–76,* London: Bodley Head, 1977

Watkins, G., editor, *Tonight* (BFI Dossier 15), London: British Film Institute, 1982

Tonight Show, The

U.S. Talk/Variety Show

A long-running late-night program, *The Tonight Show* was the first, and for decades the most-watched, network talk program on U.S. television. Since 1954 NBC has aired a number of versions of the show, which has seen four principal hosts and consistently used one format, except for a brief diversion in the series' early days, when what started out as a music, comedy, and talk program hosted by Steve Allen became, for a time, a magazine-type program, broadcasting news and entertainment segments from various correspondents located in different cities nationally; that short-lived format, however, lacked the appeal of a comedy-interview show revolving around one dynamic host. From mid-1957 until the time of writing, Jack Paar, Johnny Carson, and Jay Leno have each followed Allen's lead and hosted a show of celebrity interviews, humor, and music, although each host has led the show with his own signature style.

Late night talk in the first three decades of U.S. television was dominated by *The Tonight Show* and, for

The Tonight Show with Jay Leno.
Courtesy of the Everett Collection

the majority of that time, by Johnny Carson. However, during the 1980s and early 1990s, the late-night landscape began to change as more talk shows took to the air. Change was accelerated by the appeal of David Letterman and a combination of other factors, including the relative inexpensiveness of producing such shows, audience interest in celebrity and entertainment gossip, and an overall increased reliance in U.S. culture on the talk show as a forum for information and debate about the important, as well as unimportant, issues of the day. The late-night talk genre expanded as network competitors and comrades sought the kind of success that was originally the province of *The Tonight Show.*

Each of *The Tonight Show*'s principal hosts has brought his own unique talent and title to the program. All of the shows have featured an opening monologue, a sidekick or cohost, in-house musicians, and cadre of guest hosts. Steve Allen's *Tonight!* featured his musical talents and penchant for a distinctive brand of comedy. He was well known for performing his own musical numbers on the piano and for humorous antics such as on-the-street improvisations and bantering with the audience, both of which were forerunners to the kinds of comedy stunts that became a staple much later on *Late Night with David Letterman,* also on NBC. In 1957 Allen left *Tonight!* to concentrate on another variety show he hosted on Sunday evenings.

Allen's version of the show was immediately followed by the unsuccessful magazine format, *Tonight:* *America After Dark,* which lasted only a few weeks. That show was led by Jack Lescoulie, but he was never the central figure Allen had been. Essentially, Lescoulie introduced the segments and correspondents around the nation.

In July 1957 Jack Paar took over as new host of *The Jack Paar Show.* Paar brought the show back to its instudio interview format. More a conversationalist than comedian, Paar drew audiences to his show by bringing on interesting guests, from entertainers to politicians. Audiences also watched for the controversy that occasionally erupted on the show. Paar did not shy away from politics or confrontation and often became emotionally involved with his subject matter and guests. He had a few stormy run-ins, both on camera and off, and finally left the show following controversy surrounding his broadcast from the Berlin Wall in 1962.

With another change in hosts came a complete change in tone and style. In October 1962 Johnny Carson took over as host of *The Tonight Show Starring Johnny Carson.* Carson was more emotionally detached and less political than Paar; like Allen, he was a comic. Named the "king of late night," Carson hosted the show for 30 years, from 1962 to 1992. During that time, the show moved from New York City to Burbank, California. Carson was known for his glib sense of humor and his middle-American appeal, and quickly recognized his increasing popularity as well as the strain of doing comedy and talk five nights a week. He threatened to leave the show, but he was lured back with a generous offer that included a huge salary increase and more time off. Guest hosts during Carson's tenure included comedians Joan Rivers, Jay Leno, and David Letterman.

When Carson retired, Leno was appointed the next principal host of the series, now named *The Tonight Show with Jay Leno.* A well-known stand-up comedian, Leno brought to the show his own writers and comic style, showcasing the latter in his opening monologues, banter with guests, and unique comic bits.

Changes in Leno's show have reflected major changes in television since the medium's earlier days. For example, by the late 1980s, shows hosted by Joan Rivers and Arsenio Hall helped late-night talk to become slightly less dominated by white males, while on Leno's program the studio band has been led by two black musicians: the first leader was accomplished jazz musician Branford Marsalis; he has been followed by Kevin Eubanks.

Another big change for *The Tonight Show* during Leno's tenure has been the program's first serious competition. Starting in the mid- to late 1980s, television talk shows, both daytime and late-night, multi-

The Tonight Show, Ed McMahon, Johnny Carson, 1962–92.
Courtesy of the Everett Collection

plied in number. The in-studio talk program was inexpensive to produce, and audiences were increasingly drawn to the sensationalism and celebrity showcased each day and night on television. Some late-night talk shows—including those hosted by Joan Rivers, Chevy Chase, and Pat Sajak on the FOX network—came and went quickly. Popular comedian Arsenio Hall's late-night talk show was on the air for several years before cancellation; for a time *The Arsenio Hall Show* had a wide following, attracting mostly a young black audience, a segment previously ignored in late-night talk. Especially successful in late night was the up-and-coming David Letterman. *Late Night with David Letterman* started out on NBC, airing immediately after *The Tonight Show* from 1982 until 1993. Passed over for the host position on *The Tonight Show* when Leno

was chosen for the post, Letterman moved to CBS where his new show, *The Late Show with David Letterman,* has run in direct competition with Leno.

Since the debut of *The Late Show, The Tonight Show* has for the first time had to share the late-night spotlight. The competing host/comedians, Leno and Letterman, are polished performers with large audiences. They have become, as Carson had been, the gauge by which mainstream entertainment and politics are measured. On both programs comedy is delivered—and guests and issues of the day are treated—in the same way, as gossip and light entertainment. The growing influence of both programs can also be measured by the influential guests each has featured. Political figures such as Bill Clinton, Al Gore, George W. Bush, and New York City Mayor Rudolph Giuliani have all

Kinescope of Jack Paar quitting as host of *The Tonight Show* (1957–60) after NBC censored his "water closet" joke, 1960. *Courtesy of the Everett Collection*

made appearances on the late-night programs to reach large audiences, thus enhancing the shows' cultural influence. After more than four decades, *The Tonight Show* still outlines and defines, even when it is not at the forefront of, the essence of contemporary televised culture in the United States.

KATHERINE FRY

See also **Allen, Steve;** *Arsenio Hall Show, The;* **Carson, Johnny; Downs, Hugh; Leno, Jay; Letterman, David; Talk Show**

The Tonight Show
September 1954–January 1957

Hosts
Steve Allen
Ernie Kovacs (1956–57)

Regular Performers
Gene Rayburn
Steve Lawrence
Eydie Gorme
Pat Marshall (1954–55)
Pat Kirby (1955–57)
Hy Averback (1955)
Skitch Henderson and His Orchestra
Peter Handley (1956–57)

The Tonight Show with Steve Allen, 1954–57.
Courtesy of the Everett Collection

Maureen Arthur (1956–57)
Bill Wendell (1956–57)
Barbara Loden (1956–57)
LeRoy Holmes and Orchestra (1956–57)

Tonight! America after Dark
January 28, 1957–July 26, 1957

Hosts
Jack Lescoulie (January 1957–June 1957)
Al "Jazzbo" Collins (June–July 1957)

The Jack Paar Show
July 1957–March 1962

Host
Jack Paar

Regular Performers
Hugh Downs
Jose Melis and Orchestra
Tedi Thurman (1957)
Dody Goodman (1957–58)

The Tonight Show
April 2, 1962–September 28, 1962

Announcers
Hugh Downs
John Haskell
Ed Herlihy

Regular Performers
Skitch Henderson and His Orchestra

The Tonight Show Starring Johnny Carson
October 1962–May 1992

Host
Johnny Carson

Regular Performers
Ed McMahon
Skitch Henderson (1962–66)
Milton Delugg (1966–67)
Doc Severinsen (1967–92)
Tommy Newsom (1968–92)

The Tonight Show with Jay Leno
May 1992–

Host
Jay Leno

Regular Performers
Branford Marsalis (1992–95)
Kevin Eubanks (1995–)

Programming History (all versions)
NBC

September 1954–October 1956	Monday-Friday 11:30 P.M.–1:00 A.M.
October 1956–January 1957	Monday-Friday 11:30 P.M.–12:30 A.M.
January 1957–December 1966	Monday-Friday 11:15 P.M.–1:00 A.M.
January 1965–September 1966	Saturday or Sunday 11:15 P.M.–1:00 A.M.
September 1966–September 1975	Saturday or Sunday 11:30 P.M.–1:00 A.M.
January 1967–September 1980	Monday-Friday 11:30 P.M.–1:00 A.M.
September 1980–August 1991	Monday-Friday 11:30 P.M.–12:30 A.M.
September 1991–	Monday-Friday 11:35 P.M.–12:35 A.M.

Further Reading

Carter, Bill, *The Late Shift: Letterman, Leno, and the Network Battle for the Night,* New York: Hyperion, 1994

Cox, Stephen, *Here's Johnny!: Thirty Years of America's Favorite Late-Night Entertainment,* New York: Harmony, 1992

De Cordova, Frederick, *Johnny Came Lately: An Autobiography,* New York: Simon and Schuster, 1988

Metz, Robert, *The Tonight Show,* New York: Playboy, 1980

Munson, Wayne, *All Talk: The Talkshow in Media Culture,* Philadelphia, Pennsylvania: Temple University Press, 1993

Smith, Ronald L., *Johnny Carson: An Unauthorized Biography,* New York: St. Martin's Press, 1987

Tynan, Kenneth, *Show People,* New York: Simon and Schuster, 1979

Top of the Pops

British Music Program

Top of the Pops is Britain's longest-running pop-music program. It was first broadcast in January 1964 and since then has occupied a prime-time slot on BBC television. Its primary value has been in introducing generations of youngsters to the pleasures and excitement of pop music, while for older people the show has become a reassuringly familiar item in the television schedules.

The key to the show's initial success lay in its revolutionary new format. Before 1964 (and to a large extent after), pop shows tended to respond to emerging trends and fashions. Earlier shows such as *The Twist* and *The Trad Fad* were a response to current dance and music styles, while the highly popular *Ready, Steady, Go!* was largely a mod program and tended to showcase mod lifestyles and tastes. The problem with such shows was that their life cycle was bound to the fashion or style that it reflected: when the trend passed, so did the show. The *Top of the Pops* format was unique because it was based upon the top-20 music chart (expanding to the top 40 in 1984). This has meant that the show has not been associated with any particular fashion or trend; it has no angle on pop music but merely responds objectively to whatever is popular at a given moment. In this way, *Top of the Pops* is always going to be current, and at the cutting edge of pop music.

The format of the chart "countdown," coupled with the policy of only featuring records moving up the charts, has provided the show with a certain structure and dynamism. Unlike many other pop shows, *Top of the Pops* contains the narrative ingredients of development, anticipation, and closure: with each episode, as the countdown commences, the audience is kept in suspense by the big question: "Who will be top of the pops this week?"

In many respects, the *Top of the Pops* format has been informed by radio, which traditionally had been closer to the pulse of teen tastes and pop trends than TV. The top-20 format was already an established feature of radio, and *Top of the Pops* presenters were nearly always radio DJs. To this end, early episodes of the program tended to show a DJ putting the disc on the turntable with a fade to the performer miming to the song. The program was about records and hits, and even when the performer was unavailable for the show, the record would still go on, a policy that sometimes meant using improvised, and often innovative, visual effects to cover the absence of the performer.

Another factor contributing to the show's continuing popularity is its accessibility: while ostensibly aimed at a fairly narrow age-range of teenagers, *Top of the Pops* has nevertheless always thought of itself as a family show. Indeed, audience research carried out in the 1980s found that the majority of the viewing constituency was over 25 years old. This appeal to a wider family audience has no doubt contributed to the show's continuing success and buoyant ratings. However, it has also left the show open to charges of conservatism and policing standards in musical taste; the show's infamous banning of the Sex Pistols and Frankie Goes to Hollywood is often cited as proof of this conservatism.

Top of the Pops has been an important actor in the music business, with immense ability to make or break a performer. An appearance on the show can almost guarantee an immediate leap up the charts. Similarly, pop-music retailers have found that their sales often peak the day after the show is broadcast. There is no doubt therefore that *Top of the Pops* has functioned as a powerful gatekeeper to the industry, and performers and promoters continue to clamor for a spot on the show.

Although the basic format of the chart countdown has remained constant over the years, the show has introduced many changes to keep itself up to date. Innovations such as the video chart, the "breakers" spot,

Top of the Pops.
Copyright © BBC Photo Librrary

Europarade, and the introduction of live broadcasts, have all functioned to keep *Top of the Pops* in step with new audiences and a changing music scene.

The program's high point was the mid-1970s, when audience figures regularly reached 16 million. This popularity undoubtedly reflected trends in the music industry that saw record sales peak at roughly the same time. However, the acts that were appearing on the show were peculiarly televisual and complemented perfectly the medium's newly acquired color: the dominance of television-inspired novelty acts such as the Goodies and the Wombles, as well as the emergence of glam rock with its theatricality and glitz, seemed to return pop music to the values of showbiz and entertainment.

The number of viewers steadily declined after the mid-1970s. At first, some blamed the initial shock of punk music, which lacked the kind of "razzmatazz" on which *Top of the Pops* thrived. Punk reintroduced notions of authenticity, and its anticommercial stance sat uneasily with the show's emphasis on glamour and entertainment. But even though the 1980s saw the return of flamboyant pop performers, led by New Romanticism and the New Pop, the loss of viewership nevertheless continued. This loss was partly related to a decline in the singles market and an increase in television channels dedicated to the music scene. It also reflected the general competitiveness of the television industry in the 1980s. Some feared the series would soon be cancelled.

However, by the mid-1990s the series began to make a return. This revival has been largely attributed to the vision of the producer Chris Cowey, who introduced a number of innovations—including a format less dependent on the charts; the banning of music videos, which meant artists had to appear in person; and the banning of miming, which meant that artists had to actually perform. The success of the format abroad has also meant the series has come to play an important role in the BBC's commercial fortunes: by 2000 estimates suggested that the format is broadcast in 87 countries and that revenue generated by this li-

censing has amounted to more than £10 million a year. As a result, the series will likely continue to make a regular appearance in the BBC schedules.

PETER McLUSKIE

See also **Music on Television**

Producers
Johnny Stewart, Robin Nash, Chris Cowey

Programming History
BBC
January 1964–

Further Reading

Blacknell, S., *The Story of Top of the Pops,* London: Patrick Stephens, 1985
Cubitt, S., "*Top of the Pops:* The Politics of the Living Room," in *Television Mythologies,* edited L. Masterman, London: Comedia, 1986

Touched by an Angel

U.S. Drama Series

Touched by an Angel was not the first television program to address religious topics in prime time, but it has been widely hailed as both the most successful and the most influential program to do so. The program began airing on CBS in 1994, and although many critics initially scorned the show for its sentimentality, it became one of that network's strongest shows in its second year. During its peak seasons between 1996 and 1999, *Touched by an Angel* was consistently rated one of the top three most-watched television dramas, according to Nielsen audience measurement surveys. Although its ratings had dipped by the 2000–2001 season, it was the first dramatic program CBS chose to air after news coverage of the September 11, 2001, events had ceased. Following that event, the feel-good program surged to some of the best Nielsen numbers in its history.

The program held significance for several reasons. The initial and surprising success of *Touched by an Angel* rescued CBS from its financially beleaguered position and moved it out of its third-place position in

mid-1990s audience ratings. More significantly for the long-term, however, the program demonstrated that dramatic television could address religious topics and find a sizeable audience in doing so. In an era often characterized by programs featuring a cynical viewpoint, such as *Seinfeld,* this came as a surprise and led to several other experiments with religion on television. The 1997 season alone heralded seven series that made some reference to religion or spirituality in the wake of the popularity of *Touched by an Angel.* The trend continued into 2003, when the series *Joan of Arcadia,* about a young woman who receives visitations from God in the guise of ordinary people, had its debut.

The show was originally created in response to the television audience's reported interest in seeing more prime-time programming about religion. Before the pilot aired, however, CBS president Peter Tortorici replaced the program's creator, John Masius (also of *St. Elsewhere*), with Martha Williamson, who was brought in to brighten the story. Williamson, a longtime producer and "show doctor," wanted to create an uplifting story with a spiritual feel. With her guidance, the program approached religious faith earnestly yet gingerly, referencing familiar Christian scriptures, prayer, and of course angelic messengers, yet rarely mentioning particular religious traditions or organizations. The angels, Tess (Della Reese), Monica (Roma Downey), and Andrew (John Dye) talked people out of crime and suicide, rescued children from fires, guided people through illnesses and death, and led people to participate in ethical behavior and even advocacy efforts, in each episode telling the suffering, "God loves you." *Touched by an Angel* tackled AIDS, spouse abuse, autism, and mental illness, but also (and more controversially) civil rights in China, slavery in the Sudan, global warming, and cloning. While the program's core audience was older women, it was frequently heralded as one of few shows that parents could watch with their children in the early prime-time hours.

Special guest stars to the series have included Bill Cosby, Kirk Douglas, Debbie Reynolds, Phylicia Rashad, Hank Aaron, John Heard, Charlotte Church, Kirk Cameron, Stephanie Zimbalist, Margot Kidder, Chad Lowe, the Mormon Tabernacle Choir, and many others.

Touched by an Angel tapped into the widespread changes that are altering the religious landscape of America at the beginning of the millennium. In addition to a rising number of people who affirm their belief in angels, more Americans now identify themselves as "spiritual" and view spirituality as a personal practice that may be distinct from more formal practices of religion. *Touched by an Angel* succeeded in acquainting Hollywood decision-makers with the potential for viable religious programming in this new religious environment.

LYNN SCHOFIELD CLARK

See also **Religion on Television**

Cast (selected)

Tess	Della Reese
Monica	Roma Downey
Andrew	John Dye
Gloria (2001–03)	Valerie Bertinelli

CBS Productions in association with Moon Water Productions

Executive Producer
Martha Williamson

Co-Executive Producer
Brian Bird

Creator
John Masius

Programming History
CBS

1994–1995	Wednesday 9:00–10:00
1995–1996	Saturday 9:00–10:00
1996–2001	Sunday 8:00–9:00
2001–2003	Saturday 8:00–9:00

Tour of the White House with Mrs. John F. Kennedy, A

U.S. Documentary

On the night of February 14, 1962, three out of four American television viewers tuned to CBS or NBC to watch *A Tour of the White House with Mrs. John F. Kennedy.* Four nights later, ABC rebroadcast the program to a sizable national audience before it then moved on to syndication in more than 50 countries around the globe. In all, it was estimated that hundreds of millions of people saw the program, making it the most widely viewed documentary during the genre's so-called "golden age." The White House tour is also notable because it marked a shift in network news strategies, since it was the first prime-time documentary to court explicitly a female audience.

Between 1960 and 1962, most network documen-

Jacqueline Kennedy.
Courtesy of the Everett Collection

taries focused on major public issues such as foreign policy, civil rights, and national politics. These domains were overwhelmingly dominated by men, and the programs were exclusively hosted by male journalists. Yet historians of the period have shown that many American women were beginning to express dissatisfaction with their domestic roles and their limited access to public life. Not only did women's magazines of this period discuss such concerns, but readers seemed fascinated by feature articles about women who played prominent roles in public life. Jacqueline Kennedy was an especially intriguing figure as she accompanied her husband on diplomatic expeditions and was seen chatting with French President De Gaulle, toasting with Khrushchev, and delivering speeches in Spanish to enthusiastic crowds in Latin America. She even jetted off to India on her own for a quasi-official goodwill visit. She quickly became a significant public figure in the popular media, her every move closely followed by millions of American women.

Consequently, Jacqueline Kennedy's campaign to redecorate the White House with authentic furnishings and period pieces drew extensive coverage. Taking the lead in fund-raising and planning, she achieved her goals in a little over a year, and, as the project neared completion, she acceded to requests from the networks for a televised tour of the residence. It was agreed that CBS producer Perry Wolff, Hollywood feature-film director Franklin Schaffner, and CBS correspondent Charles Collingwood would play leading roles in organizing the program, but that the three networks would share the costs and each would be allowed to broadcast the finished documentary. The weekend before the videotaping, nine tons of equipment were put in place by 54 technicians, and cut-away segments were taped in advance. The segments featuring Jacqueline Kennedy were recorded during an eight-hour session on the following Monday.

The final product, though awkward in some regards, effectively represents changing attitudes about the public and private roles of American women. On the one hand, here was Jacqueline Kennedy fulfilling her domestic duty by providing visitors with a tour of her home. On the other hand, she also was performing a public duty as the authoritative voice of the documentary: providing details on her renovation efforts, informing the audience about the historical significance of various furnishings, and even assuming the position of voice-over narrator during extended passages of the program. In fact, this was the first prime-time documentary from the period in which a woman narrated large segments of the text. Her authoritative status is further accentuated by her position at the center of the screen. This framing is striking in retrospect because correspondent Charles Collingwood, who "escorts" Mrs. Kennedy from room to room, repeatedly walks out of the frame, leaving her alone to deliver descriptions of White House decor and its national significance. Only at the very end of the program, when President Kennedy "drops in" for a brief interview, is Jacqueline repositioned in a subordinate role as wife and mother. Sitting quietly as the two men talk, she listens attentively while her husband hails her restoration efforts as a significant contribution to public awareness of the nation's heritage.

The ambiguities at work in this program seem to be linked to widespread ambivalence about the social status of the American woman at the time of this broadcast. Jacqueline Kennedy takes a national audience on a tour of her home, which is at once a private and public space. It is her family's dwelling, but also a representation of the nation's home. Furthermore, she is presented both as a mother—indeed, the national symbol of motherhood—and as a modern woman: a patron of the arts, a historical preservationist, and a key figure in producing the nation's collective memory. In these respects, she might be seen as symbolic of female aspirations to enter the public sphere, and this may help to explain the documentary's popularity with female viewers.

The White House tour was soon joined by a number of similar productions, each of which drew prime-time audiences as large as those for fictional entertainment. For example, *The World of Sophia Loren* and *The World of Jacqueline Kennedy* each drew a third of the nightly audience, while *Elizabeth Taylor's London* drew close to half. In general, elite television critics reviewed these programs skeptically, noting that entertainment values were privileged at the expense of a more critical assessment of their subject matter. Yet the appeal of these programs may have had less to do with the dichotomy between entertainment and information *per se* than with the way in which they tapped into women's fantasies about living a more public life while largely maintaining their conventional feminine attributes. As numerous feminist scholars have argued, one of the fundamental appeals of television programming is the opportunity it affords for the viewer to fantasize about situations and identities that are not part of one's everyday existence. In the early 1960s, such fantasies may have been important not only for women who chafed at the constraints of domesticity, but also for women who were imagining new possibilities.

MICHAEL CURTIN

See also **Documentary; Secondari, John**

Further Reading

Curtin, Michael, *Redeeming the Wasteland: Television Documentary and Cold War Politics,* New Brunswick, New Jersey: Rutgers University Press, 1995
Watson, Mary Ann, *The Expanding Vista: American Television in the Kennedy Years,* New York: Oxford University Press, 1990

Trade Magazines

The television industry is analyzed and reported on by a variety of trade magazines reflecting the perspectives of programmers, producers, advertisers, media buyers, networks, syndicators, and station owners, as well as those in emerging technology sectors. The general television trade press is complemented by coverage of television in the advertising and entertainment industry trade press. Additional specialty magazines cover cable television, satellites, newsgathering, religious programming, and public broadcasting. The advent of satellite distribution and the expansion of transnational media corporations have led to a growing internationalization of television-industry press coverage.

Broadcasting and Cable covers top stories of general industry interest, including regulatory issues, ratings, company and personnel changes, advertising and marketing strategies, and programming trends. Aimed at broadcast executives, *Broadcasting and Cable*'s concise journalistic coverage has been recognized as an authoritative source for industry news. Originating as a radio trade paper named *Broadcasting* in 1931, the weekly eventually expanded its coverage into the media of television and cable. Along the way, it was also known as *Broadcasting-Telecasting* (1945–57), and absorbed other important trade publications such as *Broadcast Advertising* (in 1936) and *Television* (in 1968). Currently, *Broadcasting and Cable* consists of sections that cover the top weekly stories, broadcasting, cable, and technology. Additional columns treat federal lawmaking, personnel moves, and station sales. Recently, *Broadcasting and Cable* has expanded coverage of new media technologies; its "Telemedia Week" section covers the World Wide Web, interactive media, CD-ROMs, and Internet developments.

Television Week, formerly known as *Electronic Media* (1982–), a tabloid-size weekly, covers American visual electronic media (television, cable, and video). Aimed at managerial executives, *Television Week* reports on production and distribution, emerging and interactive technologies, network and affiliate news, regulatory developments, and programming. *Television Week* often draws on perspectives from throughout the industry when it covers such debates as the conversion to digital television. With its regular features such as "The Insider," "Viewpoint," and "Converging Media," and sections on deals, ratings, Hollywood, Washington, career moves, and special reports on a variety of topics, *Television Week* is an excellent source for tracking current events in the television industry.

Since the majority of U.S. television viewers subscribe to cable, there are several important trade publications devoted to the cable industry. Since 1980, the tabloid-size weekly *Multichannel News* has sought to provide breaking news to managers and suppliers of cable operating systems, including stories on programming, marketing, regulatory issues, and industry dealmaking. Features such as "Broadband Week" and "Pay-per-View" highlight how changing technologies are affecting the cable-operating business. *Cable FAX's CableWORLD,* a biweekly since 1989, is aimed at the cable executive with little spare time and provides concise news sections on cable operations, technology, financing, advertising, and programming, as well as broadband services.

Satellite transmission, while crucial to distributing network and cable programming, has developed into a key competitor to cable with the advent of direct broadcast satellite services (DBS). The monthly *Satellite Broadband* covers the latest technology trends affecting both broadcasting and broadband services. *Via Satellite* (1986–) covers the applications of satellite technology to international broadcasting. In addition to satellite company and personnel news, articles in *Via Satellite* address the financial and technological issues of satellite broadcasting, the changing policy and regulatory environments worldwide, and potential future applications of satellite broadcasting. Likewise, *Satellite Week* (1979–) reports on the satellite broadcasting industry, its changing international markets and regulatory environments.

Advertising industry trades *Advertising Age* (1930–) and *Adweek* (1960–) cover television from the perspective of media buyers. Advertising agencies buy time on television for their clients' commercials and thus seek up-to-date and accurate information on ratings, programming strategies, schedule shifts, regulatory changes, and personnel moves. Pertinent articles in both weeklies concern specific commercial campaigns, sponsorship issues, demographic research, effectiveness of network versus cable television advertising, advertising agency activities, production company news, and ratings information. Since media buyers are customers of station managers and network executives, the editorial opinions of *Advertising Age* and *Adweek* sometimes differ from those of *Broadcasting and Cable* and *Television Week.*

The long-lived show business trade periodicals *Variety* (weekly), *Daily Variety,* and *The Hollywood Reporter* also report on the television industry. The tabloid-size weekly *Variety* has covered entertainment industries such as vaudeville, film, television, radio, music, and theater since 1905. In addition to extensive hard-news coverage of show-business and insider "buzz," *Variety* is renowned for its often jocular headline style (for example, "Vid Biz in Rewind," and "Greenlights Turn Red"). *Variety*'s television section includes news about programs, talent deals, production companies, broadcast and cable networks, regulatory issues, syndication deals, and regular Nielsen ratings reports. *Variety*'s "World News" section also includes articles on international broadcasting. Additionally, in-depth television program reviews provide production information, analysis of production values, and predictions of a program's potential success or failure. *Daily Variety,* the daily counterpart to the weekly *Variety,* provides daily updates in two editions, one from Hollywood, the other from New York ("Gotham").

The Hollywood Reporter has been a daily news magazine for the entertainment industry since 1930. It also publishes an International Weekly edition, as well as Special Editions on various topics. Its television coverage includes ratings, business and financial news, studio and talent deals for new programs, distribution, stock prices, personalities, and entertainment industry events. *The Hollywood Reporter*'s television program reviews include behind-the-scenes production information. Its regular section "Convergence" addresses how digital technologies are affecting entertainment industries.

Other trade publications address specific television fields. For information on the broadcast news business, *Communicator* (1988–), published monthly by the Radio-Television News Directors' Association, offers coverage of television news production, personnel moves, network–station relations, and local news markets. For religious broadcasters, *NRB Magazine* (1969–) is published by the National Religious Broadcasters group. *NRB Magazine* covers religious programming strategies, personnel training, international religious broadcasting, and news analysis. The biweekly newsletter, *Public Broadcasting Report,* serves noncommercial broadcasters such as CPB, PBS, and NPR, covering topics such as regulation, programming, funding, career moves, and new technologies.

For historical research purposes, several now-defunct trade publications offer much information on the earlier decades of the television industry. In addition to *Broadcasting-Telecasting* mentioned above, *Sponsor* (1946–68) and *Television* (1944–68) are excellent sources for articles on evolving programming strategies, regulatory issues, financing, advertising techniques, and intra-industry competition. Early issues of *Television* include many "how to" articles, often designed for the advertising agencies then in charge of much program production. Likewise, early issues of *Sponsor,* which was subtitled *Buyers of Broadcast Advertising,* trace the attitudes of advertisers and sponsors toward the decline of national network radio and the rise of network television, reflecting shifts in programming strategies and increased network control of television programming.

The biweekly *Television/Radio Age,* which originated as *Television Age* in 1953, provided analytic coverage of television-industry issues until 1989. Arguing that few other industries had grown as rapidly or faced as many problems as television, the magazine's editors sought to provide in-depth analysis with which to address the television industry's regulatory, financial, and programming concerns. In addition to publishing articles written by major broadcasting executives, many *Television/Radio Age* articles closely examine specific advertising campaigns, ratings trends and techniques, network programming strategies, and Wall Street financing.

The discontinued *Channels* (1981–90) is also a

good source for analytic articles on the television industry of the 1980s. Originally subtitled *of Communications,* and edited by well-known television journalist Les Brown, *Channels* was later subtitled *The Business of Communications,* and sought to analyze the expanding role of television in society while reporting on the regulatory environment, production deals, programming strategies, and media markets.

Trade publications in Canada, Australia, and Great Britain not only cover national television industries but also report on the international aspects of the television industry. The Canadian monthly *Broadcaster* (1942–) often addresses issues such as how to develop and sustain Canadian-produced programming that can be competitive with well-financed and well-distributed programming from the United States. Aimed at broadcast managers, *Broadcaster* reports on developments in technology, financing, advertising, and programming, in addition to news about the state-owned Canadian Broadcasting Corporation. *Canadian Communication Reports* monitors Canada's broadcasting, cable, and pay-TV distribution industries. Information about the Canadian cable television industry can be found in *Cablecaster* (1989–), which covers the management, technology, regulation, and programming of Canadian cable television. A more technical perspective on Canadian broadcasting is provided by *Broadcast Technology* (1975–), also known as *Broadcast 1 Technology.* Although originally designed for technicians, *Broadcast Technology* has expanded into business reporting and includes articles on programming, marketing, and personnel changes.

The Australian television industry is covered by *Encore,* which reports on all audiovisual production industries in Australia. *Encore* emphasizes production news, including stories on new program series and financing arrangements, but it also covers new technology developments and regulatory issues. *B and T* (1950–), formerly known as *Broadcasting and Television,* covers Australian media markets, ratings, new productions, network strategies, and media personnel moves, as does the more advertising-trade oriented *AdNews.*

British television trade press maintains a strong international slant and is a useful source for news about European television industries. The weekly *Broadcast* (1973–), formerly known as *Television Mail,* covers British television and cable programming, regulation, financing, technology, and ratings, in addition to articles on the international scope of trends in programming and technology. *Screen Digest* (1971–) provides summaries of world news of the film, television, video, satellite, and consumer electronics industries. *Screen Digest* covers industry events and conventions, publications, and market research data for "screen media worldwide." *TBI* (or *Television Business International,* 1988–) covers international broadcast, cable, and satellite markets for the broadcast executive, including articles in English, German, and Japanese. *TV World* (1977–), subtitled *Award Winning International Magazine for the Television Industry,* focuses on programming, usually profiling the trends in a particular country for a section of each issue, in addition to reviewing specific productions and festivals. Designed for executives in broadcast production and distribution, both commercial and public-service, *TV World* also covers the technological developments in satellite and cable delivery systems, the shifting alliances among transnational media companies, and international conventions such as NATPE and VIDCOM. *TV World*'s truly international scope makes it an excellent source for information on the television industry worldwide.

The diversity of these trade magazines reflects the multifaceted nature of today's television industry. Since its beginnings, the television industry has been closely tied to the film and advertising industries. Now television has expanded beyond broadcasting into cable, satellites, and interactive technologies. An examination of trade publications reflecting these different perspectives should provide the reader with insights into the history and future of the rapidly changing international television industry.

CYNTHIA MEYERS

Further Reading

Advertising Age
Crain Communications
711 Third Avenue
New York, NY 10017
USA
www.adage.com

AdNews
www.adnews.com.au
Adweek
770 Broadway
New York, NY 10003
USA
www.adweek.com

B and T Weekly
Locked Bag 2999
Chatswood DC
NSW Australia 2067
www.bandt.com.au

Broadcast
Emap Media Ltd.
33–39 Bowling Green Lane
London EC1R 0DA
United Kingdom
www.broadcastnow.co.uk

Trade Magazines

Broadcaster
Southam Business Communications
1450 Don Mills Rd.
Toronto, Ontario M3B 2X7
Canada
www.broadcastermagazine.com

Broadcasting and Cable
360 Park Avenue South
New York, NY 10010
USA
www.broadcastingcable.com

Cable FAX's CableWORLD
PBI Media
1201 Seven Locks Road, Suite 300
Potomac, MD 20854
USA
www.cableworld.com

Cablecaster
1450 Don Mills Rd.
Toronto, Ontario M3B 2X7
Canada
www.cablecastermagazine.com

Canadian Communications Reports
1800–160 Elgin Street
Ottawa, Ontario K2P 2C4
Canada
www.decima.ca/publishing

Communicator
Radio-Television News Directors Association
1600 K Street NW, Suite 700
Washington, DC 20006
USA
www.rtnda.org/communicator/current.shtml

Daily Variety
5700 Wilshire Boulevard, Suite 120
Los Angeles, CA 90036
USA
www.variety.com

Encore (address unconfirmed)
Reed Business Information
www.encoremagazine.com.au

The Hollywood Reporter
5055 Wilshire Boulevard
Los Angeles, CA 90036
USA
www.hollywoodreporter.com

Multichannel News
Reed Business Information
360 Park Avenue South
New York, NY 10010
USA
www.multichannelnews.com

NRB Magazine
National Religious Broadcasters
9510 Technology Drive
Manassas, VA 20110
USA
www.nrb.org/nrbmagazine

Public Broadcasting Report
Warren Communications News
2115 Ward Court, NW
Washington, DC 20037
USA
www.warren-news.com

Satellite Broadband
Primedia, Inc.
745 Fifth Avenue
New York, NY 10151
USA

Satellite Week
Warren Communications News
2115 Ward Ct., NW
Washington, DC 20037
USA
www.warren-news.com

Screen Digest
Lymehouse Studios
38 Georgiana Street
London NW1 0EB
United Kingdom
www.screendigest.com

Television Business International
Informa Telecoms and Media Group
Mortimer House
37–41 Mortimer Street
London W1T 3JH
UK
www.informamedia.com

Television Week
6500 Wilshire Boulevard, Suite 2300
Los Angeles, CA 90048
www.tvweek.com

Variety
Reed Business Information
5700 Wilshire Boulevard, Suite 120
Los Angeles, CA 90036
USA
www.variety.com

Via Satellite
PBI Media
1201 Seven Locks Road, Suite 300
Potomac, MD 20854
USA
www.telecomweb.com

Translators and Boosters

Television translators are broadcast devices that receive a transmitted signal from over the air, automatically convert the frequency, and re-transmit the signal on a separate channel. Closely related are TV boosters, which amplify the incoming channel and re-transmit it, but without translating from one frequency to another.

In the United States, television stations originally were assigned to specific channels and communities, in a pattern designed to distribute service as widely as possible to all communities. The distribution plan adopted by the Federal Communications Commission in 1952 utilized a highly simplified model of physical terrain, and predicted desired coverage in a fairly smooth radius outward from the transmitter location. In reality, an obstacle such as a 9,000-foot mountain would completely block any reception.

TV boosters began as a practical self-help solution to this problem wherever the terrain was mountainous, but especially in the inter-mountain West between the Front Range of the Rockies and the Cascades (in the northern United States) through the Sierra and Coastal ranges of California in the south. Typically, a local TV repairman or appliance salesman offering the latest in console TV sets would install a sensitive receiver on the other side of the ridge, bring the signal to the near side, and boost the signal on channel from high above the community into the valley floor.

The first booster probably was built by Ed Parsons in 1948, to extend the reach of his cable system in Astoria, Oregon. Other boosters in the Pacific Northwest soon followed. In 1954, an FCC inspector went out to Bridgeport, Washington, and ordered the local booster shut down, because it was operating without a license. It soon was returned to extra-legal operation, under the auspices of the Bridgeport Junior Chamber of Commerce. The FCC issued a cease-and-desist order, but on appeal, the Circuit Court of Appeals for the D.C. Circuit refused to enforce the order, holding that the FCC had a statutory duty to make provision for the use of broadcast channels, and had been remiss in not devising a means for boosters to be licensed (*C. J. Community Services* v. *FCC*. D.C. Cir., 1957).

In Colorado, Governor Ed Johnson began issuing state "licenses," appointing the local operators to his communication "staff," and ordering them to continue their efforts to boost television signals on channel. By 1956, there already were some 800 unlicensed boost-ers and translators known to be in operation. The first stirrings of cable television, or community antenna television, as it was then known, were in the same interval after 1948. As an alternative delivery mechanism, cable was the natural competitor to boosters and translators. Where cable gained initial inroads, as in Pennsylvania, it had the advantage that each home user was connected and could be charged a monthly fee. The boosters were typically supported by donations, and were a broadcast service with no toll-keeper. As cable took its initial steps as a fledgling industry, it sought protection from the FCC, urging that translators and boosters be restricted or outlawed.

Because of this early rivalry, and especially because the FCC was wedded to its pre-conceived plan for the orderly development of television in accord with the assignments it issued, the FCC refused to approve boosters and authorized translators in 1956, except for the virgin territory of UHF (channels 10–83). Power was limited to 10 watts. The rural residents essentially ignored this action, and continued to offer VHF service on channels 2 through 13, increasingly moving away from the primitive booster, in favor of cleaner translator technology.

In 1958 the FCC announced that it was stepping up enforcement efforts, intending to get the extra-legals off the air in 90 days. Congress was deluged with protests of this action, and the Senate Committee on Interstate and Foreign Commerce conducted field hearings during 1959 in Montana, Idaho, Colorado, Utah, and Wyoming. In July 1960 Congress amended the Communications Act to waive operator requirements and otherwise authorize booster and translator operations, including those already on the air. Three weeks later, the FCC authorized VHF translators for the first time.

Translators continue to be an important component of rural TV delivery, especially in the West. As of December 31, 1995 the FCC reported 4,844 licensed translators, slightly over one-half operating on UHF. All of these re-broadcast a primary TV station. In 1982, the FCC made provision for them to originate their own programs, as low-power television stations broadcasting to a restricted local radius, and an additional 1,787 LPTVs have been licensed.

MICHAEL COUZENS

See also **Low Power Television; United States: Cable Television**

2365

Further Reading

Cox, Kenneth A., "The Problem of Television Service for Smaller Communities," *Staff Report to the Senate Committee on Interstate and Foreign Commerce,* Washington, D.C.: December 26, 1958

Federal Communications Commission, *Report and Recommendations in the Low Power Television Inquiry* (BC Docket No. 78–153), September 9, 1980

U.S. Senate, Committee on Interstate and Foreign Commerce, *Report to Accompany Senate 1886,* 86th Congress, 1st Session, Washington, D.C., September 4, 1959

Tribune Broadcasting

U.S. Broadcaster

Tribune Broadcasting, a division of the Chicago Tribune Company, is the fourth-largest broadcaster in the United States, and the country's largest television group not owned by a network. It currently owns and operates 23 television stations, with ten in the 12 largest markets and sixteen in the top 30 markets. Combined with cable and satellite coverage from its national superstation, WGN-TV, in the early part of the new millennium Tribune Broadcasting reaches more than 80 percent of television households in the United States.

A preeminent model of growth and diversity, Tribune Broadcasting's influence and impact is also enhanced by ownership of 50,000-watt Chicago-based WGN-AM, plus minority investments totaling approximately 25 percent ownership in the WB television network, 31 percent in the TV Food Network, 9 percent in the Golf Channel, and 25 percent in the iBlast Networks, the latter a company utilizing the digital television spectrum for distributing broadband content and data services to consumers. According to the Tribune Company's *Annual Report* for 2000, "iBlast has aggregated part of the spectrum from local television stations in 246 markets covering 93 percent of the United States."

Historically, the Tribune Company's roots trace back to publication of its parent-company newspaper, the *Chicago Tribune,* beginning in 1847. In 1924, it began broadcasting on its AM pioneer, WGN (World's Greatest Newspaper), and in 1948, jumped on the television bandwagon with WGN-TV and New York-based WPIX-TV. In 1981, Tribune Broadcasting was formed and James C. Dowdle was hired as its first president and chief executive officer. A year later, the Tribune Entertainment Company was created as a Tribune Broadcasting subsidiary and quickly became a leading developer and supplier of television programming to domestic and international markets via syndication, cable, and broadcast networks.

In May 1985, Tribune Broadcasting increased its television holdings to six stations when it acquired Los Angeles-based KTLA-TV for a record-setting $510 million. Anticipating revenues of approximately $100 million and expanding the Tribune's reach to 19.6 percent of all U.S. television households, as *Business Week* reported on June 13, 1985, the KTLA purchase enhanced Dowdle's plan to utilize viewership of Tribune Broadcasting outlets "as a captive customer base" for Tribune programming.

Early Tribune programming efforts are numerous and offer a variety of formats including movies, cartoon and action series, miniseries, specials, late night entertainment, and targeted programming for minority audiences. In sports, national broadcasts of the Chicago Cubs baseball team, a Tribune Company acquisition in 1981, realized daily audiences of nearly 30 million households via WGN-TV. In 1987, Tribune Broadcasting gave the controversial talk-show host Geraldo Rivera a home, and his across-the-board show aired successfully for 11 years. Then, in 1990, a joint venture with Ted Turner's Cable News Network brought CNN affiliate status to Tribune stations. Under terms of the initial 10-year contract, the two companies would also co-produce documentaries, miniseries, and news specials.

Continuing its expansion, in 1991, Tribune Broadcasting launched its first regional television programming service, ChicagoLand Television (CLTV), under the auspices of its new subsidiary, Tribune Regional Programming, Inc. Dedicated to Chicago-area news, sports, and information, CLTV capitalized on the multimedia resources of the *Chicago Tribune,* WGN radio, WGN television and the Chicago Cubs with the bulk of its programming to be produced by its own staff in its own studios. Within two years, Tribune Regional Programming combined with Tele-Communications, Inc. (TCI) to provide CLTV 24 hours a day to TCI's 300,000 metropolitan-Chicago cable customers.

In 1993, Tribune Broadcasting combined with Warner Brothers for the creation of a new prime-time television network, the WB, slated to begin operations in the fall of 1994. Tribune stations in New York, Los Angeles, Philadelphia, Atlanta, Denver, and New Orleans were initially slotted as affiliates, and the network, reaching out to 18–49-year-olds in prime time evening slots, instantly covered 85 percent of American households. As of 2000, 16 of Tribune Broadcasting's 23 stations were network affiliates and network programs included such popular notables as *Seventh Heaven, Felicity, Angel, Dawson's Creek* and *Gilmore Girls.*

On August 1, 1994, in an organizational restructuring, Dowdle was promoted to executive vice president of Tribune Media Operations and Dennis J. Fitz-Simons, former Tribune television-group president, was elevated to Tribune Broadcasting executive vice president. Reporting to Dowdle, FitzSimons would direct operations of the unit's then-eight television stations, the Tribune News Network, Tribune Entertainment, the six station radio group, Tribune Radio Networks and the recently acquired Farm Journal Inc. In 2000, when Dowdle retired, FitzSimons was promoted to executive vice president of the Tribune Company, retaining his Tribune Broadcasting presidency and assuming responsibility for publishing, entertainment, and the Chicago Cubs.

By 2001, the Los Angeles-based Tribune Entertainment subsidiary was distributing nine series representing approximately 15 hours of first-run and off-network programming per week, including four of the season's top-ten weekly syndicated hours: *Mutant X, Gene Roddenberry's Andromeda, BeastMaster,* and *Gene Roddenberry's Final Conflict.* In addition, Tribune Entertainment distributed the weekly *Soul Train*—at 30 seasons, the nation's longest-running music and variety program, and *U.S. Farm Report,* the longest-running series in syndication history at more than 36 years. Tribune Entertainment continued its distribution of television movies to domestic stations, and its distribution of specials, such as *Live from the Academy Awards,* the *Prism Awards,* and the *Soul Train Music Awards.* It was also handling barter arrangements for programs from numerous television production companies including, among others, NBC Enterprises' *Weakest Link* and FremantleMedia North America's *Family Feud.*

Maintaining an edge in state-of-the-art facilities, Tribune Entertainment announced in February 2001 the formation of Tribune Studios—renovation and conversion of 70,000 square feet of soundstage space on the former ten-acre KTLA-TV Hollywood studio lot. Phased for completion over a two-year period, Tribune Studios would represent the first all-digital studio lot in the United States.

As Dowdle pointed out in his profile in *Channels* magazine of August 13, 1990, Tribune Broadcasting has been successful by capitalizing on those things under its control: effective management, production, acquisition, and marketing. Through aggressive movement, confident development in multiple directions, and the strong leadership of Dowdle and FitzSimons, the company has grown and diversified, resulting in the creation of a competitive Tribune Broadcasting footprint that is influential in both the domestic and international marketplace.

JOEL STERNBERG

See also **WB Television Network**

Tribune Broadcast Holdings

Television Stations
WPIX-TV, New York
KTLA-TV, Los Angeles
WGN-TV, Chicago
WPHL-TV, Philadelphia
WLVI-TV, Boston
KDAF-TV, Dallas
WBDC-TV, Washington
WATL-TV, Atlanta
KHWB-TV, Houston
KCPO-TV, Seattle
KTWB-TV, Seattle
WBZL-TV, Miami/Ft. Lauderdale
KWGN-TV, Denver
KTXL-TV, Sacramento
KSWB-TV, San Diego
WXIN-TV, Indianapolis
WTIC-TV, Hartford/New Haven
WTXX-TV, Waterbury CT
WXMI-TV, Grand Rapids
WGNO-TV, New Orleans
WNOL-TV, New Orleans
WPMT-TV, Harrisburg-Lancaster-Lebanon-York
WEWB-TV, Albany

Cable Holdings
CLTV News, Chicago
Central Florida News 13 (joint venture with Time
    Warner Communications), Orlando
TV Food Network (31 percent)
WB Network (25 percent)
The Golf Channel (9 percent)

Tribune Broadcasting

Radio Stations
WGN-AM, Chicago (and others)

Sports Franchises
Chicago Cubs

Digital Networks
iBlast Networks (25 percent)

Further Reading

Grego, Melissa, "All-Digital Revamp for Trib Lot," *Daily Variety* vol. 382 (February 26, 2001)

Grossman, Ron, and Charles Leroux, "Chicago and the Tribune Ride Waves of Change Together," *Chicago Tribune* (March 18, 2001)

Hoover's Handbook of American Business, Austin, Texas: Hoover's Business Press, 1999

Kaufman, Debra, "Hollywood Hot for Digital," *Broadcasting & Cable* 131 (April 25, 2001)

"McCormick Co.: Much is Ventured But Nothing Gains This Year," *Crain's Chicago Business* (April 1, 2002)

McCormick, Brian, "Trib Must Resume Media Hunt Or Be Hunted; Unfettered AOL Time Warner Considered Logical Suitor," *Crain's Chicago Business* (February 25, 2002)

Merrion, Paul, "Trib Superstation's New Chief Eyeing Broadened Horizons," *Crain's Chicago Business* (February 25, 2002)

Satzman, Darrell, "Hollywood Heritage," *Style: Los Angeles Business Journal* (August 27, 2001)

Sweeney, Patrick, "Tribune Broadcasting Sells Three Denver Radio Stations," *Denver Business Journal* (March 1, 2002)

Wendt, Lloyd, *Chicago Tribune: The Rise of a Great American Newspaper,* Chicago: Rand McNally, 1979

Trodd, Kenith

British Producer

Few television producers ever gain name recognition beyond their industry, but Kenith Trodd is arguably one who has. Described as the most successful of all British television drama producers, he is the winner of countless awards for the many one-off plays and films he has shepherded to the screen, and a figure seen as indispensable to the health of the drama department of the BBC, in which he has worked almost continuously for more than 30 years. Trodd's career is also unusual in that it has spanned the history of British television drama—from its golden age of experimentation in the 1960s to today's more hard-nosed era of cost-efficiency and ratings imperatives.

Trodd is perhaps best known for his work with the doyen of television playwrights, Dennis Potter. Both came from similar working-class and Christian fundamentalist backgrounds (the son of a crane driver, Trodd was brought up as a member of the Plymouth Brethren). Both did National Service as Russian-language clerks at Whitehall, where, during the height of the Cold War, they became firm friends with shared left-wing convictions. It was only at Oxford, from 1956 to 1959, that they found a convenient outlet for their political views, rising to become stars of a radical network of working-class students that gained national media coverage and taught them about the value of courting public controversy.

Originally, Trodd had intended to become an academic, and it was only after returning from a stint of teaching in Africa in 1964 that he received an offer from another ex-Oxford friend, Roger Smith, that would change his life. Smith had been appointed story editor of the innovative *Wednesday Play* slot and desperately needed two assistants to help him recruit as many new writers to television as possible. Along with Tony Garnett, Trodd joined the BBC just at the time the single television play was entering a radical phase of experimentation and permissiveness, as a new generation of talent began to make its presence felt. Working as a story editor on *The Wednesday Play* and *Thirty Minute Theatre* (a shorter experimental play slot), Trodd became central to this wave of innovation in the 1960s, nurturing writers such as Potter, Jim Allen, and Simon Gray.

In 1968 Trodd gained his chance to become a drama producer when, along with Garnett, he was lured to the rival commercial company London Weekend Television (LWT), on the promise of forming an autonomous unit within the organization. Notable as the first independent drama production company in British TV, Kestrel scored some successes during its two-year association with LWT, but the arrangement ended in acrimony, with Trodd eventually decamping back to the BBC, where he became producer of the *Play for Today* slot throughout the 1970s.

Never any stranger to trouble, he returned to a drama department in political turmoil, as managers cracked down on the freedoms program-makers had enjoyed during the 1960s. While producing some of Potter's most controversial work, Trodd often had to make a public fuss to defend the writer's freedom, most notably in 1976 when BBC management decided not to broadcast *Brimstone and Treacle.* He also found himself held at arm's length by BBC management as a suspected communist sympathizer for his support of a range of radical left-wing practitioners.

Though these difficulties were eventually resolved, Trodd continued to campaign for greater independence within the BBC, particularly after the success of his Potter serial *Pennies from Heaven* in 1978. In marked contrast to Potter, he became a passionate advocate for TV drama filmed on location rather than recorded in the studio (the dominant practice up to that time). This drive for change came to a head in 1979, when he again left the BBC for LWT, as part of a deal involving the formation of an independent production company with Potter. Once more, the arrangement ended in acrimony. Trodd returned to the BBC, but this time on the eve of the foundation of Channel 4 (1982), the network that would do so much to legitimize the concept of the independent producer in British television.

In the early 1980s, Trodd became chair of the Association of Independent Producers as one of the new breed of "independents," although he continued to work within the very heart of institutional television at the BBC. Under his influence, however, things were changing there, too. He had finally achieved his goal of remaining within the corporation while being able to produce independent projects as well. This ideal soon became accepted practice, as did his campaign for shooting on film.

In 1984 Trodd formed part of a BBC working party convened to examine how the corporation should respond to the feature filmmaking for TV and theatrical release that Channel 4 had pioneered. The outcome was the abandonment of the old concept of the studio *Play for Today* and the introduction of new BBC film slots, *Screen One* and *Screen Two,* with Trodd helping to oversee the first batch of films in 1985.

Despite the success of his campaigning, Trodd's career after that point raises uncomfortable questions about whether he has made himself somewhat redundant by the changes he helped bring about in the 1980s. The decline in the annual number of single-drama slots due to the increased costs of filmmaking, plus the corresponding decline in writers and directors required to fill these slots, indicates a much tougher and more competitive environment than the one that allowed him to experiment with new ideas and untried

talent in the 1960s. Nor, despite the success of a few of his BBC "single films," such as *After Pilkington* (1987) and *She's Been Away* (1989), has there been anything like the constant stream of outstanding material that secured his reputation in the 1970s. A rift with Potter in the late 1980s also did not help matters in this respect; however, the two reconciled before the playwright's death in 1994, and Trodd produced Potter's last two works for television, *Karaoke* and its sequel *Cold Lazarus,* both in 1996. Despite these projects, it remains true that Trodd's function has changed from the days when, as a BBC tyro, he filled his many play slots with a motley crew of young writers and directors—the question is whether it has changed for the best.

JOHN COOK

See also **British Programming; Channel 4;** *Film on Four;* **Garnett, Tony; Loach, Ken;** *Pennies from Heaven;* **Potter, Dennis;** *Wednesday Play*

Kenith Trodd. Born in Southampton, Hampshire, England. Educated at Oxford. Began television career as story-editor, *The Wednesday Play,* 1964; producer, London Weekend Television, 1968–70; producer, BBC Drama Department, 1970–79; producer, London Weekend Television, and partner with playwright Dennis Potter, 1979; BBC Drama Department and independent film producer, from 1980. Recipient: Royal Television Society Silver Medal, 1986–87; British Academy of Film and Television Arts Alan Clarke Award, 1993.

Television Plays (selected)

1969	*Faith and Henry*
1969	*Moonlight on the Highway*
1971	*Roll on Four O'Clock*
1971	*Paper Roses*
1975	*The Whip Hand*
1976	*Double Dare*
1976	*Brimstone and Treacle*
1976	*Your Man from the Six Counties*
1978	*Pennies from Heaven*
1978	*Dinner at the Sporting Club*
1979	*Blue Remembered Hills*
1979	*Coming Out*
1980	*Billy*
1980	*Shadows on Our Skin*
1980	*Caught on a Train*
1980	*Blade on the Feather*
1980	*Rain in the Roof*
1980	*Cream in My Coffee*
1981	*A United Kingdom*
1982	*The Ballroom of Romance*

1983	*Videostars*		1990	*Old Flames*
1985	*Four Days in July*		1991	*They Never Slept*
1985	*Unfair Exchanges*		1992	*Femme Fatale*
1986	*The Singing Detective*		1994	*Bambino Mio*
1986	*Past Caring*		1995	*It Might Be You*
1987	*After Pilkington*		1996	*Karaoke*
1987	*Brimstone and Treacle*		1996	*Cold Lazarus*
1987	*Visitors*		1997	*The Fix*
1988	*Christabel*			
1989	*Here Is the News*			
1989	*She's Been Away*			
1990	*He's Asking for Me*			

Film
Circle of Friends, 1994

Troughton, Patrick (1920–1987)

British Actor

Patrick Troughton was the second actor to take on the mantle of British television's Doctor Who in the long-running science-fiction series of the same name, playing the role for three years, from 1966 to 1969. This was by no means the only part he played on television, and he also had a full and varied career as an actor in the theater and in the cinema. However, it is for his flamboyant and quixotic portrayal of BBC's celebrated Time Lord that he is usually remembered.

Troughton followed William Hartnell as Doctor Who after his predecessor, suffering from multiple sclerosis and disillusioned with the changing character of the program (which had originally been intended to have a strong educational content), withdrew from the series. Troughton determined at once that his Doctor would be in marked contrast to the white-haired dotty professor-type depicted by Hartnell, and in his hands the Doctor became a colorfully whimsical and capricious penny-whistle-playing eccentric who could be testy, courageous, and downright enigmatic as the mood took him. Such a radical change in character was made possible within the confines of the program through the introduction of the concept that the Doctor underwent a mysterious regenerative metamorphosis at various stages of his centuries-long existence.

Troughton settled quickly into the role, and children throughout Britain cowered behind the sofa as his Doctor did weekly battle with such fearsome alien foes as the Daleks and the Cybermen. After three years, he finally passed the responsibility for playing television's famous Time Lord on to Jon Pertwee.

By the time he was selected to play Doctor Who, Troughton had long established his reputation as a performer in a wide range of roles and productions, being particularly well regarded as a Shakespearean actor. Among the most acclaimed of his previous appearances had been his performance as Adolph Hitler in the play *Eva Braun* at Edinburgh's Gateway Theatre in 1950, and supporting roles in Laurence Olivier's Shakespearean films *Hamlet* and *Richard III.* On television he had made appearances in such enduringly popular series as *Coronation Street,* in which he was George Barton, and *Doctor Finlay's Casebook.* Notable among his later credits on the small screen were the series *The Six Wives of Henry VIII,* in which he was cast as the Duke of Norfolk, the World War II prison-camp drama *Colditz,* and the sitcom *The Two of Us,* in which he gave his usual good value as Nicholas Lyndhurst's grandfather Perce (after Troughton's death, Tenniel Evans took over the role). Always a jobbing actor who was ready to turn his hand to a variety of roles of contrasting sizes, his familiar face would pop up in all manner of series, and he guest starred on *Special Branch, The Protectors, The Goodies, Churchill's People, Minder,* and *Inspector Morse,* to name but a few.

But it was with *Doctor Who* that Troughton's name was destined to remain indelibly linked in the last

Patrick Troughton as Doctor Who.
Courtesy of the Everett Collection

Television Series

1962–63	*Man of the World*
1966–69	*Doctor Who*
1970–71	*The Six Wives of Henry VIII*
1972–74	*Colditz*
1982–84	*Foxy Lady*
1986–87	*The Two of Us*

Television Specials

1950	*Toad of Toad Hall*
1953	*Robin Hood*
1955	*The Scarlet Pimpernel*
1960	*The Splendid Spur*
1987	*Knights of God*

Films

Hamlet, 1948; *Escape,* 1948; *Cardboard Cavalier,* 1949; *Badger's Green,* 1949; *Waterfront,* 1950; *Treasure Island,* 1950; *Chance of a Lifetime,* 1950; *The Woman with No Name,* 1950; *White Corridors,* 1951; *The Franchise Affair,* 1951; *The Black Knight,* 1954; *Richard III,* 1955; *The Curse of Frankenstein,* 1957; *The Moonraker,* 1958; *Misalliance,* 1959; *Phantom of the Opera,* 1962; *Jason and the Argonauts,* 1963; *The Gorgon,* 1964; *Frankenstein and the Monster from Hell,* 1973; *The Omen,* 1976; *Sinbad and the Eye of the Tiger,* 1977.

Stage (selected)

Eva Braun, 1950

Further Reading

Haining, Peter, *Doctor Who, The Key to Time: A Year-by-Year Record,* London: W.H. Allen, 1984
Peel, John, and Terry Nation, *The Official Doctor Who and the Daleks Book,* New York: St. Martin's Press, 1988
Tulloch, John, and Manuel Alvarado, *Doctor Who: The Unfolding Text,* New York: St. Martin's Press, 1983
Tulloch, John, and Henry Jenkins, *Science Fiction Audiences: Watching Doctor Who and Star Trek,* London and New York: Routledge, 1995

years of his life. His death occurred while he was actually attending a *Doctor Who* convention in the United States.

DAVID PICKERING

See also **Doctor Who**

Patrick George Troughton. Born in London, March 25, 1920. Attended schools in London; Embassy School of Acting, London; Leighton Rollin's Studio for Actors, Long Island, New York. Married three times; children: Joanna, Jane, Jill (stepdaughter), David, Michael, Peter, Mark, and Graham (stepson). Served in Royal Navy during World War II. Joined Bristol Old Vic, concentrating on Shakespeare productions, 1946; made film and television debuts, 1948; achieved fame as central character in television's *Doctor Who,* 1966. Died March 28, 1987.

Turkey

The case of Turkey, where the deregulation of the broadcasting industry followed the penetration of technology, offers an interesting and illuminating example of the relationship between technological change, globalization, and national identity. Until 1990, when the first commercial channel began broadcasting from abroad (illegally, via satellite), TV and radio broadcasts were tightly controlled by the government. While popular programming on state television was dominated by American imports, educational and informational programs were indicative of high governmental influence. This was due to a turbulent political landscape shaped, from the republic's inception on, by Kemalist ideologies (such as secularism and Western modernism), state and military intervention in every aspect of life, and a culturalist approach to all things "national." Like radio, television, in this landscape, was seen as a handy but highly risky tool. While total control over state broadcasts meant power to shape public opinion for the government, allowing broadcasters other than the state was a risky road not to be taken until the 1990s.

From its inception in the 1930s, the broadcasting service in Turkey was set up as a centralized and state-controlled entity, similar to the telegraph and telephone services that preceded it. Although radio broadcasting in Turkey began at around the same time as in other countries, television broadcasting came very late. The primary reason for the delay was economic. By the 1950s, Turkey had left behind the early republican era in favor of multiparty politics, popular elections, and more liberal economics. Despite these changes, Turkey would see a series of economic crises and breakdowns of democracy in following decades. Although it was resolved that television broadcasting would contribute to the fast-changing social structure of Turkey, it was thought to be an unnecessarily expensive investment to make. Thus, regular broadcasting had to wait until the late 1960s.

The preparations for providing a laboratory environment that would allow experimentation with TV broadcasting began in 1948, and the first such broadcast was made from a transmission station at the Department of Electrical Engineering at Istanbul Technical University (ITU) on July 9, 1952. The two-hour broadcasts continued once a week on Saturdays, and included domestic and foreign films, entertainment, and discussion programs, but were received by a very limited number of viewers in Istanbul. Since the system was experimental, there was no broadcasting policy, directorial board, or administrative unit in charge of programming. By 1957, there were 160–170 receivers in Istanbul.

The 1960s marked Turkish political and social life with many significant incidents, including the beginning of state television broadcasts. Following the technical aid agreement signed between the German Federal Republic and Turkey in 1963, a television training center was built in Ankara. After the 1960 military coup, the 1961 constitution, in order to prevent abuse of the airwaves by the ruling party, redefined the broadcast institution's status as an autonomous state organization. Thus, on January 31, 1968, the Turkish Radio and Television Corporation (TRT), successor to the earlier radio broadcasting institution, broadcast its first program, *The History of the Turkish Revolution,* to its Ankara audiences. Broadcasting to Istanbul and Izmir was made possible in 1971 when a radio-link line was finished by the PTT (Post Telephone and Telegraph). TV sets, at first considered luxury items, soon became commonplace. Even the poorest neighborhoods with no running water or phone lines were soon to meet *Bonanza* and *Dennis the Menace.*

The late 1960s witnessed constant tension between the government and the now-autonomous TRT. Within two years of the 1960 coup, Süleyman Demirel and his Justice Party (JP) came to power. The new government had little sympathy for the liberal reforms instigated by the military. This created a series of conflicts. Because the new government was unsuccessful in its attempts to strip the TRT of its autonomy, it then attempted to exert pressure on it by, for example, freezing the license fee to restrict budgets and by increasing intervention in programming content. On February 16, 1969, for example, a labor march took place in Istanbul that ended with fights between marchers and police. The TRT, which included the march in its evening news hour with footage of the incident, was immediately prohibited from broadcasting the program by Demirel. In short, the first years of television broadcasting in Turkey, up until 1970, were marked by the TRT administration's struggle against the government to maintain its autonomy.

Meanwhile, the regular ITU broadcasts had continued, and went on until March 6, 1970, when they were halted due to the student movements that preceded the military coup of the following year. In 1971, all broadcasting facilities and transmitters of ITU were transferred to the TRT when the military declared martial law, accusing Demirel of abusing the state institutions and of wrongdoing, and forcing him to resign. The newly amended constitution, issued following the coup, had an authoritarian bent, which also affected broadcasting. Control of TRT was given to a general, and broadcasting once again became state-dominated. Although the 1972 constitution affirmed the TRT's independence from party politics, instead of speaking of the TRT as autonomous, it was now described as "impartial," which in practice meant that the TRT remained a medium of the governing party throughout this era.

Until the end of the 1970s, directors-general of the

TRT came and went, each being subject to criticism either from the right or the left. Television broadcasting in this era, far from introducing a more pluralistic media scene, merely represented the state of institutional politics. It was during this era that politics and politicians became mediatized in Turkey. Addresses to the nation and election campaign speeches were regular fare on the TRT's broadcasts, along with sports programs and popular American series.

Domestic right–left clashes, which claimed hundreds of lives up until 1980, led to a new military coup, and an army general once again took over the TRT as its new director general. As after the previous coup, the 1982 constitution and the 1983 broadcasting legislation that emerged from it paid lip service to reducing governmental control over the TRT and maintaining its impartiality. As part of the legislation that went into force on January 1, 1984, a High Authority Commission for radio and television was established with members appointed largely by the president of the republic. That body in turn appointed the administrative council and the director general of the TRT. The High Authority Commission established program policy guidelines for broadcasting, but could control programs only after their airing. The Commission also made recommendations on the establishment of new broadcast stations, and granted licenses for non-public and cable television, which came in 1988. Although all members of the Commission were required to hold university degrees, and eight of the twelve members were selected from noted personalities in broadcasting, in practice the presidents of the republic tended to sympathize with the government, and thus the commission had a substantial partisan tilt despite all of its educational credentials.

In terms of programming content, the 1983 legislation provided for indigenous programs to be given priority over foreign ones (which were seen as having corrupting effects, to some degree), so as to help stimulate necessary social changes. However, imported programs continued to constitute a substantial amount of airtime. The government also had the right to present its own monthly half-hour programs, and could ban programs or news items for security reasons. Programs were required to operate in accordance with the principles of the constitution, which gave the TRT the task of promoting values such as patriotism and Kemalism. Television programs at this time were seen as an important element in the creation of a sense of national unity, through use of an homogenized official Turkish language, programming national folkloric music, and presenting a collective understanding of national history. Another very important issue that led to

further tightening of governmental control over the TRT in the mid-1980s was the clash between the Turkish state and the separatist movement started by Kurdish Workers' Party (PKK). As a result of the growing conflict, programs about "anarchy and terror" were required to be broadcast on a regular basis. The TRT was supposed to assume a standpoint supporting the state regarding the Kurdish problem and terrorism. During the mid-1980s, the TRT was also seeking means to bring broadcasts to more people in remote areas, especially in the southeast, to counter propaganda from the PKK. Second and third channels, TRT 2 (1986) and TRT 3 (1989), together with GAP TV (targeting audiences in southeast Turkey), were attempts to satisfy this need for diversity in programming by the TRT. TRT 2 was of cultural nature, broadcasting quality programs like classic films, documentaries, and news hours in English for foreign diplomats and visitors, while the TRT3 was mainly targeted at young audiences, for educational and entertainment purposes.

The TRT broadcasts went color in 1984, and weekly broadcasting was increased from 113 to 130 hours in 1988. Despite the technical progress it achieved, TRT programming in the 1980s was extremely ideology-laden, aimed at shaping public opinion on issues ranging from economic measures to state security policies. In short, throughout the 1980s the TRT remained a highly bureaucratic and politicized body, and "impartiality" remained a thing of legislative rhetoric rather than of deed. However, there was not much that could be done by the TRT itself, which was restrained by the TRT law.

In 1990, TRT 4 started experimental broadcasts of an educational nature, and the same year day-time programs were also initiated, targeted primarily to a female audience. The TRT, at this time, was also seeking opportunities to become a major player in the Turkish geolinguistic market. Outcomes of this endeavor included TRT-INT, beamed via satellite in 1990 primarily to Turkish citizens living abroad (mainly in Germany but including all of Europe and North Africa), and TRT-AVRASYA, beaming programs via satellite to the Turkic republics of Central Asia and Azerbaijan in 1992. But the most important development of the early 1990s was the first private channel's pirate broadcasts in 1990, which changed the whole electronic-media scene in Turkey.

Although many private satellite dishes were already installed to receive European channels and CNN, the Swiss-based station, Star 1 (owned by Magic Box), broadcasting from Germany via EUTELSAT F-10 East, hit the medium as the first private channel to reach Turkey in 1990. The very legality of Star 1 was, of course, the major issue at stake. However, there was very little political debate at the beginning, and the station had the president's blessing. One of the partners of Magic Box was Ahmet Özal, the elder son of the president of the time, Turgut Özal, an absolute free marketeer and aggressive advocate of the free circulation of goods and ideas. Özal told reporters that even though it was unconstitutional to set up private television channels on Turkish soil, there was nothing illegal about broadcasting into Turkey from abroad, as did CNN. Private broadcasts went on, but the policy changes would not catch up until the mid-1990s.

Other channels followed rapidly in Star 1's wake. By the end of 1992, Show TV, Kanal 6, Flash TV, HBB, and the second Magic Box station, Teleon, were also broadcasting into Turkey from abroad. At the beginning, viewers had to have satellite dishes. Soon, municipalities bought dishes and transmitters and re-broadcast the satellite channels locally, an easy way to win popular support.

The TRT suffered heavy audience-share losses in a matter of few years following the emergence of the private TV channels. But private broadcasting was immediately welcomed as a part of Turkey's media scene by the audience *and* by certain agencies of the state, even though the stations were of "illegal" status. For instance, the Turkish Football Federation, a unit of the Ministry of Youth and Sports, signed agreements with Magic Box to sell the right to broadcast Turkish soccer league games to Star 1, with devastating consequences for TRT's ratings. The TRT, in this process, began to imitate the global channels, modifying its formerly elitist and culturalist agenda. While some circles criticized the TRT for damaging its position as a public institution by engaging in commercial competition and promoting consumerism, some saw it as a positive change.

The private channels' popularity was also due to their policy of giving significant airtime to newsworthy topics, and to the presentation of their version of national news, which often conflicted with that of the TRT. In one incident, for example, stringers covering a May Day parade filmed police beating marchers and even a member of Parliament, while the TRT's version of the event was one of "disturbances caused by fringe radicals." Social and political issues such as sexuality, homosexuality, and Kurdish and Islamic identities also became everyday topics of the news hours and TV forums. Thus, formerly restricted topics such as military

personas and coups immediately became regular fare on comedy programs. Nevertheless, while a few programs, such as *Siyaset Meydani* (Political Forum), dealt with the issues in a serious light, most others made it part of their sensational discourse. Responses were mixed. Academic and intellectual circles both praised the private channels for challenging the TRT and heavily criticized them for their extremely commercialized program content. Conservatives, on the other hand, were enraged with morally "loose" programming, and "family" channels came into existence. This played a role in the rapid rise of political Islam in the 1990s. All in all, through the commercial channels, ethnic/cultural differences and political identities that had been excluded from the TRT's rhetoric of "homogenous nationhood" became part of a collective consciousness for Turkish audiences throughout the 1990s.

In line with its turbulent history, Turkish television in the early 2000s remains in flux. Today, in addition to the TRT channels, 16 national, 14 regional, and 294 local TV channels are in operation. The High Commission is still responsible for monitoring all the broadcasting for any "indiscreet," "indecent," or "unauthorized" programming, although promising amendments that will give further freedoms to media outlets seem to be on the way. Although many have come to regard the TRT as a public enterprise, "real" public-service television is still missing from the Turkish media scene. Filling that gap would be the next positive development for Turkish audiences.

MIYASE CHRISTENSEN

Further Reading

Aksoy, A. and Sahin, H., "Global Media and Cultural Identity in Turkey," *Journal of Communication* 43/2 (1993)

Oncu, A., "Cultural Politics on the Landscape of Turkish Commercial Television," *Public Culture* 8 (1995)

Schlesinger, P., "On National Identity: Some Conceptions and Misconceptions Criticized," *Social Science Information* 26/2 (1987)

Turam, E., *Medyanın Siyasi Hayata Etkileri* [Impacts of the Media on Political Life], Istanbul: İrfan Yayıncılık, 1994

Turam, E., *2000'li Yıllara Doğru Türkiye'de TV* [TV in Turkey toward the 21st Century], Istanbul: Altın Kitaplar Yayınevi, 1996

Yengin, H., *Ekranın Büyüsü: Batıda Değişen Televizyon Yayıncılığının Boyutları ve Türkiye'de Özel Televizyonlar* [The Lure of the Screen: Dimensions of the Changing Television Broadcasting in the West and Private TVs in Turkey], Istanbul: Der Yayinevi, 1994

Turner Broadcasting System

U.S. Media Conglomerate

Over the course of four decades, Turner Broadcasting System (TBS) has grown from a regional outdoor advertising firm into one of the world's largest and most successful media conglomerates. Beginning in the late 1960s, Ted Turner changed his father's company, Turner Advertising, first into Turner Communications Company and then into Turner Broadcasting System. Each name-change represented a stage in the building of an empire that would come to encompass broadcast television and radio, cable program services, movie and television production companies, home video, and sports teams.

TBS began with Turner's purchase in 1968 of failing UHF station WJRJ in Atlanta, Georgia. He immediately renamed the station WTCG (for Turner Communications Group) and began to look for programming. What Turner found were old movies and syndicated television series, many of which he purchased outright with a view toward unrestricted future showings. He used these to counterprogram the network affiliates, going after such audience segments as children and people who did not watch the news. By the early 1970s, WTCG also offered local sports programming—first professional wrestling and then Atlanta Braves baseball, Atlanta Hawks basketball, and Atlanta Flames hockey. In 1976 Turner purchased the Braves, securing long-term access to his single most critical source of programming.

The combination of old movies and TV programs and the sports coverage proved to be a formula for success. By 1972 WTCG boasted a 15 percent share of the Atlanta audience, and the station's signal had begun to be carried by microwave to cable systems in the Atlanta region. When Turner heard about Home Box Office's groundbreaking satellite debut in 1975, he quickly began preparations to use the same technology to extend WTCG's signal. Through a series of adroit negotiations, Turner set up (as a business separate from Turner Communications) a company called Southern Satellite Systems, Inc., to uplink WTCG's signal to an RCA communications satellite. In 1976 WTCG became the second satellite-delivered cable program service and the first satellite superstation.

The superstation was renamed WTBS in the late 1970s. In 1980 Cable News Network (CNN), the first of Turner Broadcasting System's cable-only program services, was launched. Throughout the following decade, CNN branched into specialized news services, including CNN Radio, CNN International, CNN Headline News, and CNN Airport Network.

During the 1980s, strategic programming acquisitions led to more new cable ventures for Turner Broadcasting. In 1986 Turner added the entire MGM film library to his existing stock of old movies. Two years later, Turner Network Television (TNT), a general-interest cable program service that features many movies, was launched. The Turner film library also supplies Turner Classic Movies, launched in 1994. Turner's 1991 acquisition of Hanna-Barbera Cartoons (both the production studio and the syndication library), ensured a continuous supply of programming for both the TBS superstation and the Cartoon Network, launched in 1992. Several foreign-language versions of the Cartoon Network now exist or are being developed. Finally, in addition to the TBS superstation's established market position as a sports programming outlet, Turner Broadcasting also owns Sportsouth, a regional sports programming service.

Other Turner holdings include New Line Cinema, Castle Rock Entertainment, Turner Entertainment Company, Turner Pictures Worldwide, Turner Home Entertainment, Turner Publishing, Turner Educational Services, Turner Interactive, and the Atlanta Hawks.

From the earliest efforts to revamp WTCG, much of Ted Turner's television success has been based on his ability, and that of his employees, to acquire innovative and inexpensive sources of programming and to make that programming available through as many outlets as possible. Thus, Turner Broadcasting System's current holdings represent both program material—in the form of film and television libraries, production houses, and sports teams—and the means of distributing that programming.

In 1995 TBS entered into an agreement to become part of the Time Warner media conglomerate. The merger was approved, and in 2001 the corporation merged yet again with America Online, the nation's largest Internet service provider. Those companies originally launched as part of the Turner Broadcasting empire continue to grow and play a major role as content producers for AOL Time Warner, now the world's largest media conglomerate. In March 2001 veteran television executive Jamie Kellner (former chairman of the WB network) was brought in to head the Turner Broadcasting division of AOL Time Warner (now Time Warner).

MEGAN MULLEN

See also **Cable Networks; Cable News Network; Superstation; Turner, Ted; United States: Cable**

Further Reading

Amdur, Meredith, "The Boundless Ted Turner: Road to Globalization," *Broadcasting and Cable* (April 11, 1994)

Bibb, Porter, *It Ain't As Easy As it Looks: Ted Turner's Amazing Story,* New York: Crown, 1993

Carter, Bill, "Ted Turner Is Not Afraid to Turn His Personal Vision into a Multimillion-Dollar Project for His Company," *New York Times* (November 22, 1993)

Carter, Bill, "Ted Turner's Time of Discontent" (interview), *New York Times* (June 6, 1993)

Corliss, Richard, "Time Warner's Head Turner," *Time* (September 11, 1995)

"Europe Plan by Turner," *New York Times* (March 9, 1993)

Fabrikant, Geraldine, "Government Review of Turner-Time Warner Deal," *New York Times* (October 10, 1995)

Goldberg, Robert, and Gerald Jay Goldberg, *Citizen Turner: The Wild Rise of an American Tycoon,* New York: Harcourt Brace, 1995

Lander, Mark, "Time Warner and Turner Seal Merger: After 5 Weeks, a $7.5 Billion Stock Deal," *New York Times* (September 23, 1995)

Roberts, Johnnie L., "An Urge to Merge: Foxes in the Chicken Coop," *Newsweek* (September 11, 1995)

Roberts, Johnnie L., "Time's Uneasy Pieces," *Newsweek* (October 2, 1995)

Taub, James, "Reaching for Conquest," *Channels of Communication* (July–August 1983)

Turner, Ted (1938–)

U.S. Media Executive

Ted Turner is one of the entrepreneurs responsible for rethinking the way we use television, especially cable television, from the 1970s onward. However, Turner is known, loved, or hated as much for his unique personal style as for any particular accomplishment. He is a flamboyant Southern businessman in industries normally run from New York and Los Angeles. Turner's penchant for wringing every possible use from his corporations enabled him to establish a corporate empire that touched virtually every area of the entertainment industry. In 1995, in what could be the most significant personal and financial deal of his career, he agreed to merge his holdings with those of international media conglomerate Time Warner, an unusually powerful managing partner. His wealth and personal influence grew as a result, until Internet service provider America Online (AOL) purchased Time Warner-Turner in 2000, and he was shifted out of the conglomerate's power center. Marginalized as AOL Time Warner's figurehead vice president, Turner watched as the corporation's chief executive, Gerald Levin, took over control of Turner's former media holdings. Turner has since decried the increasing conglomeration of the cable marketplace.

Turner's career in broadcasting began in 1970, when Turner Communications, a family billboard company, merged with Rice Broadcasting and gained control of WTCG, Channel 17, in Atlanta, Georgia. WTCG succeeded under Turner's ownership; where it was losing $900,000 before the merger in 1970, it earned $1.8 million in revenue in 1973. Turner made WTCG cable's first "superstation," broadcast by satellite to cable households throughout the United States. Renamed WTBS (for Turner Broadcasting System) in 1979, the station remained one of the most popular basic-cable options as the number of cable households grew in the 1980s. The program schedule featured a mixture of movies and series produced by Turner subsidiaries, reruns from Turner's vast entertainment libraries, broadcasts of Turner-owned Atlanta Braves' and Hawks' games, and shows related to Turner's interest in the environment, such as explorer *Jacques Cousteau's Undersea Adventures* and Audubon Society specials.

Turner's second great innovation in cable, the Cable News Network (CNN), was launched in 1980. Turner's personal involvement in CNN appeared to handicap the network from the start, since WTBS's joke-filled late-night news program and CNN's

Ted Turner.
Courtesy of the Everett Collection

shoestring budget suggested that Turner would not commit to serious journalism. But CNN's 24-hour news programming gained viewer loyalty and industry respect as it challenged—and often surpassed—the major networks' authority in reporting breaking events, most notably the Persian Gulf War in 1991, which first brought CNN to widespread international attention. Turner, as well, refashioned himself as a global newsman as CNN expanded into new markets (by 1995, it reached 156 million subscribers in 140 countries around the world); for example, he banned the word "foreign" from CNN newscasts in favor of "international." Following Turner's philosophy of finding as many outlets for his products as possible, the CNN franchise has grown to include CNN International, CNN Headline News, CNN Radio, and CNN Airport Network, as well as a variety of computer on-line services.

Turner's holdings were not limited to cable networks, although he also owned Turner Network Television (TNT), Turner Classic Movies, Sportsouth, and the Cartoon Network. His Turner Entertainment Company managed one of the world's largest film libraries, including the MGM library, with licensing rights for Hollywood classics such as *Gone with the Wind, The Wizard of Oz,* and *Citizen Kane.* Production companies included New Line Cinema, Castle Rock Entertainment (which produced *Seinfeld*), Hanna-Barbera Cartoons, and Turner Pictures Worldwide; all provided programming sources for his cable and broadcast outlets. His Turner Home Entertainment managed the video release of titles from the Turner library, as well as overseeing a publishing house, educational services company, and a division devoted to exploring ways to bring Turner titles online. Throughout his career, Turner also endeavored to purchase one of the three major networks, targeting each for takeover as it became financially vulnerable.

Turner's possessions cannot begin to capture the essence of the personality that has made him one of the entertainment industry's most recognizable figures. He earned the nickname "Captain Outrageous" during his yachting days (winning the America's Cup in the *Courageous* in 1977, but losing the sail-off to defend it for the United States in 1980), but his reputation for eccentric behavior has not been limited to the sporting arena. When his efforts to "colorize" films from his extensive black-and-white movie library—thereby broadening the films' appeal to audiences who prefer color—raised the hackles of film lovers and prompted congressional hearings on the authorship and ownership of cinematic texts, Turner threatened to add color to *Citizen Kane,* the 1941 Orson Welles classic that has been lauded as the greatest film ever made (he did not follow through on that threat).

Turner has actively sought publicity both for himself and for a number of causes he supports, such as the environmental movement and world peace. Most spectacularly, he earned front-page headlines in 1997 for donating $1 billion of his then approximately $3 billion fortune to the United Nations for peacekeeping, health, and children's issues. Other causes earned support through their association with Turner's media or sports holdings. Two examples are WTBS's *Captain Planet* environmental cartoon and the Goodwill Games between U.S. and Soviet athletes (then internationally, between 1986 and 2001), to which Turner had broadcasting rights. With his third wife, the former actress, fitness guru, political activist, and multimedia mogul Jane Fonda, Turner added support for Native American causes (including a series of original films on TNT) to atone for his earlier "racist" promotions of the Atlanta Braves. Long accustomed to his role as "captain of his own fate," Turner suffered a series of personal and professional losses in 2000 and 2001, from the dissolution of his marriage to Fonda to the erosion of his power base in the corporate United States. Still, Turner remains one of the world's richest men, managing his charitable foundation, promoting the benefits of bison meat from his Montana ranch, and producing historical films in lieu of a more traditional retirement.

SUSAN MCLELAND

See also **Cable Networks; Cable News Network; Colorization; Superstation; Time Warner; Turner Broadcasting System; United States: Cable**

Ted (Robert Edward) Turner. Born in Cincinnati, Ohio, November 19, 1938. Educated at Brown University. Married: 1) Judy Nye, 1960 (divorced); one daughter and one son; 2) Jane Shirley Smith, 1965 (divorced, 1988); one daughter and two sons; 3) Jane Fonda, 1991 (divorced, 2001). Account executive, Turner Advertising Company, Atlanta, Georgia, 1961–63, president and chief operating officer, 1963–70; president and chair of the board, Turner Broadcasting System, Inc., Atlanta, from 1970; chair of the board, Better World Society, Washington, 1985–90. Honorary degrees: D.Sc. in Commerce, Drexel University, 1982; LL.D., Samford University (Birmingham, Alabama), 1982, Atlanta University, 1984; D. Entrepreneurial Sciences, Central New England College of Technology, 1983; D. in Public Administration, Massachusetts Maritime Academy, 1984; D. in Business Administration, University of Charleston, 1985. Board of directors: Martin Luther King Center, Atlanta. Recipient: America's Cup in his yacht *Courageous,* 1977; named yachtsman of the year four times; outstanding Entrepreneur of the Year Award, *Sales Marketing and Management Magazine,* 1979; National Cable Television Association President's Award, 1979 and 1989; National News Media Award, Veterans of Foreign Wars (VFW), 1981; Special Award, Edinburgh International Television Festival, Scotland, 1982; Media Awareness Award, United Vietnam Veterans' Organization, 1983; Special Olympics Award, Special Olympics Committee, 1983; World Telecommunications Pioneer Award, New York State Broadcasters' Association, 1984; Golden Plate Award, American Academy of Achievement, 1984; Silver Satellite Award, American Women in Radio and Television; Lifetime Achievement Award, New York International Film and Television Festival, 1984; Tree of Life Award, Jewish National Fund, 1985; Golden Ace Award, National Cable Television Academy, 1987; Sol Taishoff Award, National Press Foundation, 1988; Chairman's Award, Cable Advertising Bureau, 1988; Directorate Award NATAS, 1989; Paul White Award, Radio and Television News Directors' Association Award, 1989; *Time* Man of the Year, 1991; numerous other awards.

Further Reading

Adler, Jerry, "Jane and Ted's Excellent Adventure," *Esquire* (February 1991)

Bibb, Porter, *It Ain't As Easy As It Looks: Ted Turner's Amazing Story,* New York: Crown, 1993

Bruck, Connie, "Jerry's Deal," *New Yorker* (February 19, 1996)

Carter, Bill, "Ted Turner's Time of Discontent" (interview), *New York Times* (June 6, 1993)

Chakravarty, Subrata N., "What New Worlds to Conquer?" *Forbes* (January 4, 1993)

Dawson, Greg, "Ted Turner: Let Others Tinker with the Message: He Transforms the Medium Itself" (interview), *American Film* (January–February 1989)

Fabrikant, Geraldine, "Government Review of Turner-Time Warner Deal," *New York Times* (October 10, 1995)

Fahey, Alison, "'They're Not So Big': Turner Pleased with Battle against the Networks," *Advertising Age* (October 28, 1991)

Goldberg, Robert, and Gerald Jay Goldberg, *Citizen Turner: The Wild Rise of an American Tycoon,* New York: Harcourt Brace, 1995

Greenwald, John, and John Moody, "Hands across the Cable: The Inside Story of How Media Titans Overcame Competitors and Egos to Create a $20 Billion Giant," *Time* (October 2, 1995)

"Hear, O Israel," *Economist* (November 4, 1989)

Henry, William A., III, "History As It Happens," *Time* (January 6, 1992)

Lanham, Julie, "The Greening of Ted Turner," *Humanist* (November–December 1989)

Painton, Priscilla, "The Taming of Ted Turner," *Time* (January 6, 1992)

Scully, Sean, "Turner Backs Violence Guidelines," *Broadcasting and Cable* (June 28, 1993)

Stern, Christopher, "FTC Puts TW/Turner under Microscope," *Broadcasting and Cable* (April 29, 1996)

Stutz, Bruce, "Ted Turner Turns It On" (interview), *Audubon* (November–December 1991)

Vaughan, Roger, *The Grand Gesture: Ted Turner, Mariner, and the America's Cup,* Boston: Little, Brown, 1975

Whittemore, Hank, *CNN, The Inside Story,* Boston: Little, Brown, 1990

Williams, Christian, *Lead, Follow or Get out of the Way: The Story of Ted Turner,* New York: Times Books, 1981

Zoglin, Richard, "The Greening of Ted Turner: As His Once Shaky Ventures Thrive, He Turns into a Liberal Activist," *Time* (January 22, 1990)

20th Century, The

U.S. Historical Documentary Program

From the one-hour premiere episode "Churchill, Man of the Century" (October 20, 1957) to its last episode, *The 20th Century* unit produced 112 half-hour historical compilation films and 107 half-hour "originally photographed documentaries" or contemporary documentaries. Narrated by Walter Cronkite, the series achieved critical praise, a substantial audience, and a dedicated sponsor, the Prudential Insurance Company of America, primarily with its historical compilation films. The compilation documentaries combined film footage from disparate archival sources—national and international, public and private—with testimony from eyewitnesses, to represent history. Programs averaged 13 million viewers a week but periodically reached 20 million for the action-oriented installments. The series foreshadowed the production and marketing strategies of weekly compilation and documentary series that populate cable television today.

Irving Gitlin, CBS vice president of public affairs programming, originally conceived the series as broad topic compilations based on Mark Sullivan's writings, *Our Times*. Burton Benjamin, whose career at CBS news began as the series' producer and progressed to executive producer, radically revised the concept. He stressed compilations focused on one man's impact on his times, or an event (such as "Patton and the Third Army" or "Woodrow Wilson: The Fight for Peace"). These were to be interspersed with more traditional biographical sketches of individual lives (such as "Mussolini," "Gandhi," and "Admiral Byrd"). Benjamin also added a mix of "back of the book" stories, or historical episodes receiving scant attention in English-language history texts and unfamiliar to the general public in the United States. These "essays" dealt with individuals, such as Mustafa Kemal Atatürk ("The Incredible Turk"), and topics, such as the Kiska campaign ("The Frozen War"), and the Danish resistance movement ("Sabotage"), both lesser-known fronts of World War II. The series' researchers, both literary and film, were instructed to pursue detailed factual information that would add the unknown to the familiar. Information such as the $8.50 price levied on those who wished to watch Goering's wedding parade or the details of Rommel's visit to his family on D-Day surrounded primary story elements. With the assistance of associate producer Isaac Kleinerman, editor and film researcher for *Victory at Sea* (NBC, 1952–53) and *Project XX* (NBC, 1954–73), the series established a successful formula by stressing pivotal dramatic incidents in battles, conflicts, political uprisings, and the repercussions of actions by great (though always male) leaders. Accounting for the many battle-oriented programs, Benjamin admitted that the series was "as much a show biz show as any dramatic half-hour." But when the availability of dramatic and unusual footage of personalities existed for an historical period or event, such as "Paris in the Twenties" and "The Olympics," the unit produced broad-canvas compilation films. On a weekly basis, audiences stayed with the series, expecting the unique and unfamiliar even in recognizable topics.

When the series started to look familiar, Benjamin revised. In the third season the series shifted to the individual in history and more contemporary topics. The biographical form slowly expanded to contemporary persons in the arts and sciences, law, and politics while giving "eyewitnesses" a more complex role in the compilation films. The striking contribution by German Captain Willi Bratgi to the episode "The Remagen Bridge," dramatically describing how a U.S. shell changed history's course by accidentally severing a detonation cable and thus preventing the destruction of the allies' last crossing-point over the Rhine in March 1945, led the production team to search out other such figures with strong emotional and informational ties to the past. From 1961 through the series' end, the most innovative compilations used central, compelling personalities to weave a dramatic structure. These included Countess Nina Von Stauffenberg and Captain Axel Von Dem Bussche in "The Plots against Hitler," and Mine Okubo, author of *Citizen 13360* in "The Nisei: The Pride and the Shame." But as the series progressed, contemporary documentaries gradually outnumbered compilation films. Contemporary documentaries depicted the enduring value of democracy's struggle against communism, the modernization of the United States, and the pioneering human spirit facing adversity.

Although accepted by the public, a group of 28 of the contemporary documentaries shown over the 9

The 20th Century.
Photo courtesy of Wisconsin Center for Film and Theater Research

years were greeted with criticism. These depicted U.S. military defense systems and hardware and functioned as publicity releases for the Department of Defense, and were criticized for their simple equation of liberty with technology. A dozen of these documentaries dealt with aviation, space exploration, or plane and rocket development because of Cronkite's interest in these topics. By filming documentaries such as "Vertijet" and "SAC: Aloft and Below," the producers received extraordinary military assistance in declassifying footage in government archives for the compilation films. Still, Benjamin strove for journalistic integrity in a politicized atmosphere, even canceling biographies on General MacArthur and Curtis LeMay when the military requested final script approval.

Social and political change overseas dominated the list of contemporary subjects. Although evident in the compilation films, the series' anticommunist ideology and commitment to democratic modernization was blatant in programs such as "Poland on a Tightrope" and "Sweden: Trouble in Paradise." Periodically, the producers sought new approaches to the contemporary documentary, in response to waning critical reception and audience desire for the dramatic. When the NFL football player Sam Huff was outfitted with a microphone and transmitter, in "The Violent World of Sam Huff," the landscape of television documentary shifted. Other experiments in quasi-cinema-verité documentaries, such as "Rhodes Scholar" and "Duke Ellington Swings through Japan," illustrated new approaches for television. But strong diversions from the series' dominant form and content, such as the grim Appalachian conditions depicted in "Depressed Area, U.S.A.," were rare and usually came from freelance film directors such as Willard Van Dyke and Leo Seltzer.

CBS executives admired the series' meticulous production process. The producers allocated 24 weeks for a program's production, with each stage such as literary research, film research, location shooting, editing, script writing, and music allocated a specific time parameter on a flow chart. By the sixth season, the series ran itself, allowing Benjamin to work simultaneously on other CBS news projects. Into this production mechanism, Benjamin periodically added the attraction of established journalists and historians, including John Toland, Robert Shaplen, Sidney Hertzberg, and Hanson Baldwin. Although Alfredo Antonini composed music for 50 percent of the programs, Franz Waxman, Glen Paxton, George Kleinsinger, George Antheil, and others contributed original scores, working with Antonini and the CBS Orchestra within strict time limitations. This would be the last time a documentary series turned consistently to talent outside a network.

The sponsor, Prudential, supported the series' use of these film, literary, and musical figures, but became a restraint on the series' creative potential. The company approved and prioritized each year's topics, submitted by Benjamin and Kleinerman, and admitted not wanting controversial programs on social and religious topics. The sponsor—and the Department of Defense—also expected a conservative and uncritical representation of military activity, past and present.

Certain subjects, such as gambling, the labor movement, and U.S. relations with Canada, were rejected by Prudential. Even though Benjamin was aware of the corporate perspective, he fought several years for the approval to air biographies of Lenin, Trotsky and the American socialist Norman Thomas. Prudential directly limited the boundaries of subjects and investigation of any issue they deemed potentially upsetting to a large audience. Prudential withdrew sponsorship after the ninth season, when sports programming reduced the number of available time slots to 18, and the production unit's value to new directions in news and documentary could not assure Prudential the recognizable and dramatic compilation film and documentary subjects deemed suitable for its audience.

RICHARD BARTONE

See also **Columbia Broadcasting System; Cronkite, Walter**

Narrator
Walter Cronkite

Programming History
219 episodes
CBS

October 1957–May 1958	Sunday 6:30–7:00
September 1958–August 1961	Sunday 6:30–7:00
September 1961–August 1966	Sunday 6:00–6:30
January 1968–October 1968	Sunday 6:00–6:30
January 1969–September 1969	Sunday 6:00–6:30
January 1970	Sunday 6:00–6:30

Further Reading

Bartone, Richard C., "The Twentieth Century (CBS, 1957–1966) Television Series: A History and Analysis," Ph.D. diss., New York University, 1985

Benjamin, Burton, "From Bustles to Bikinis—And All That Drama," *Variety* (July 27, 1960)

Benjamin, Burton, "TV Documentarian's Dream in Challenging World," *Variety* (January 4, 1961)

Benjamin, Burton, "The Documentary Heritage," *Television Quarterly* (February 1962)

Benjamin, Burton, *The Documentary: An Endangered Species* (paper no. 6, Gannett Center for Media Studies), New York: Columbia University, October 1987

Bluem, William A., *Documentary in American Television: Form, Function, Method,* New York: Hastings House, 1977

Burns, Bret, "The Changing Techniques for TV Documentaries," *National Observer* (December 17, 1962)

Cronkite, Walter, "Television and the News," in *The Eighth Art,* edited by Robert Lewis Shayon, New York: Holt, Rinehart and Winston, 1962

Crosby, John, "The Right Kind of Documentary," *New York Herald Tribune* (November 4, 1957)

Gates, Gary Paul, *Air Time: The Inside Story of CBS News,* New York: Harper and Row, 1978

Higgins, Robert, "First Eight Years of *The Twentieth Century,*" *TV Guide* (June 5–11, 1964)

"History Is Terribly Dramatic," *Christian Science Monitor* (October 17, 1959)

Kleiner, Dick, "Bud and Ike—CBS Film Detectives," *New York World Telegram* (March 14, 1959)

Kleinerman, Isaac, "Shooting and Searching behind the Iron Curtain," *Variety* (January 6, 1960)

Krisher, Bernard, "They Find the World in Different Shape," *New York Telegram* (January 28, 1961)

Leyda, Jay, *Films Beget Films,* New York: Hill and Wang, 1964

Patureau, Alan, "The Man Behind *20th Century* Success," *Newsday* (August 22, 1963)

Reed, Dena, "Isaac Kleinerman: Recorder of World Facts," *American Red Cross Journal* (January 1961)

Sapinsley, Barbara, "We Get Letters," *Television Quarterly* (Winter 1964)

Shanley, John P., "Japanese Agent Returns to Naval Base for *Twentieth Century* Telecast," *New York Times* (November 26, 1961)

United States Congress, House Committee on Interstate and Foreign Commerce, *Television Network Program Procurement* (testimony by Henry M. Kennedy, second vice president, Public Relations and Advertising, Prudential), 88th Congress, 1st session, 1963

20/20

U.S. News Magazine Program

20/20's premiere on July 6, 1978 elicited such brutal reviews that Roone Arledge, president of ABC News and ABC Sports, took control of the series' production from Robert Shanks, the executive producer. Arledge supported Shanks's choices of co-anchors Robert Hughes, art critic for *Time* (and later famous for his classic 1981 series on modern art for the BBC, *The Shock of the New*), and Harold Hayes, previously the editor of *Esquire,* hoping print journalists would improve television news standards at ABC. But Hughes's Australian and Hayes's southern U.S. accents were almost incomprehensible to Arledge. The first episode, with a haphazard structure that ended with embarrassing animated segments of Jimmy Carter singing "Georgia on my Mind," and Walter Cronkite parodying himself, was disappointing. Hughes and Hayes were fired and Arledge appointed Hugh Downs anchor for the second show amid criticism of what some considered Downs's bland on-camera persona.

The series shifted from a monthly to weekly schedule in fall 1979 with Av Westin as Executive Producer. By early 1984, *20/20* delivered health reports, the popular consumer alert segment "Give Me a Break" by John Stossel, crime stories, segments on popular-culture trends, investigative reports, and interviews by Barbara Walters. Although Westin trusted his producers' skills and judgments in pursuing unorthodox stories, he defined their audience as having "zero knowledge and zero tolerance." Consequently, a story needed to immediately inform within an emotional and compelling narrative. Westin frequently scruti-

nized demographics, noting story topics receiving high ratings and redirecting upcoming stories for that demographic profile.

In September 1984 Barbara Walters became co-anchor, bringing a reputation for high-profile exclusive interviews. Downs expressed concern that Walters's interviews evaded the newsworthy, that she opted instead to probe the personal lives of people in entertainment, sports, politics, and current headlines. Still, Walters's interviews sparked powerful emotional moments and discovered painful vulnerabilities in order to display empathy toward her subjects, and in some cases Americans heard significant national and international political leaders for the first time when being interviewed by her. Some interviews did remain troubling when ABC News promoted them as covering a wide range of pressing issues, only for Walters to focus on personal matters. And in 1998 Downs would not be associated with what he termed "tabloid journalism," and refused to co-anchor when Walters' interviewed ex-sports commentator Marv Albert, whose guilty plea for assault led to an exposé of a sordid sexual lifestyle.

From the series' inception, Arledge believed the passionate reporting of another contributor, Geraldo Rivera (credited as "Special Correspondent"), was one key to success. A moral imperative informed Rivera's investigative reports, protecting the public from social injustice, institutional corruption, and government oppression. Rivera completed some of the earliest news magazine stories on AIDS, HIV in the nation's blood supply, and Agent Orange, approaching each story as a battle between the disenfranchised and a powerful, uncaring government. Combative and often angry, Rivera did what was necessary to get a story. But he was accused of unethical journalistic practices often enough for Arledge to create a groundbreaking television series, *Viewpoint,* where television journalists interrogated their techniques and the public interrogated broadcast journalists. Embroiled in controversy, Rivera's "resignation" finally came in October 1985 after publicly condemning Arledge for killing a colleague's story on the relationship between Marilyn Monroe and Robert F. and John F. Kennedy.

The production history of *20/20* reveals much about the relationship between ABC's Entertainment and News Divisions as well as about tense dynamics within the ABC News Division. In February 1987, to the production unit's dismay, Av Westin was fired after circulating within ABC News a document critical of Arledge's management. Within a few months, the Entertainment Division announced they would take over *20/20*'s Thursday time slot in fall 1988 to revive a dramatic series, shifting *20/20* to Friday at 10 P.M. Since Friday evening had a smaller potential audience and a different demographic profile, the move seemed to indicate that *20/20* was being set up for imminent failure. Arledge fought the change but had no influence on the Entertainment Division's attitude toward *20/20*'s contribution to the network. The production unit was demoralized and felt "betrayed" by ABC.

But the low production costs of *20/20* made it a profitable venture and ABC News began adding editions, airing between two and four weekly editions from fall 1997 through summer 2002. Two editions of *20/20,* on Thursday and Friday, aired in fall 1997. But in the same period a slow-simmering tension between *20/20* and the ABC news magazine series *Primetime Live* finally erupted. Co-anchored by Diane Sawyer and Sam Donaldson, *Primetime Live* had appeared since 1991 on Wednesday evening. The press reported intense battles of egos, deceptions, and backstabbing between Sawyer and Walters to secure the "must-get" interview. ABC tried to squelch media coverage, and reduce time-consuming competition by changing the title of *Primetime Live* to *20/20 Wednesday* in fall 1998. Sawyer and Walters were teamed on a fall 1998 edition of *20/20 Sunday* to demonstrate no hard feelings existed between the celebrity reporters. This Sunday collaboration did not last beyond spring 1999.

In October 1999, ABC News premiered *20/20 Downtown* on Thursday designed, according to Victor Neufeld, to capture a younger audience with "ultra fascinating" stories and "very compelling and intense" narratives for an "edgier," non-traditional viewer. ABC News had declared *20/20* a franchise, positioned to build a brand image, but the attempt proved short-lived.

20/20 did air four editions a week during part of the 1998–99 season, but ABC News never developed the different *20/20* editions so that three or four ran concurrently for a substantial period of time. Confusion reigned as anchors and correspondents moved from one edition to another. Certain editions were cancelled after one season or went on hiatus for weeks or months. Program titles changed several times for most of the editions. *20/20* became *20/20 Monday,* and *20/20 Thursday* became *20/20 Downtown.*

Various editions became defined by the egos, personalities, and journalistic styles within each production unit. Amid a flurry of change, ABC announced in May 2000 that *Primetime Thursday,* anchored by Diane Sawyer, would begin in the fall. With *Who Wants to Be a Millionaire?* as a lead-in, *Primetime Thursday* received excellent ratings. Thus, *20/20* lost a strong Thursday position and Walters publicly expressed dismay at ABC for failing to support *20/20 Friday* with a strong lead-in show, an issue that would be raised at her contract renewal.

20/20 did develop strength on Friday, however, with Neufeld as executive producer, but ABC Entertainment "bounced" *20/20* to Wednesday evenings from September 1, 2000 to January 11, 2001, using Friday to revive another dramatic series. The shift to Wednesday lasted seven weeks and the series then went on hiatus until December. The series ran the risk of losing its audience. Infuriated, Barbara Walters told the press a clause in her contract permitted departure from the series, and criticized ABC executives on her afternoon talk show, *The View,* for mistreating her and for their disregard for the series.

During the 1999–2000 season reservations about the news judgment of Victor Neufeld, executive producer of all editions from 1987 through spring 2000, became pronounced inside ABC. Neufeld, it was suggested, took no risks, claiming *20/20* viewers were "conservative" and occupied a "traditional household" (one reason ABC News developed *20/20 Downtown*). Neufeld insisted that *20/20*'s success came from the "high impact, high emotion story" about the human condition. Producers working to maintain new editions of *20/20* took this to mean more "tabloid journalism." For the PBS on-line edition of *The News Hour with Jim Lehrer* on January 13, 1999, correspondent Terrence Smith discussed limitations in the types of stories being aired, and an absence of news qualities on all magazine shows. Asked why foreign stories rarely, if ever, appeared on *20/20,* Neufeld replied he "hadn't found that many interesting foreign stories." He also told researchers conducting a study on television news magazines for the "Project for Excellence in Journalism" that: "Our obligation is not to deliver the news. Our obligation is to do good programming." In the summer of 2000 Neufeld was "moved up" to senior executive producer of *20/20*. Different executive producers were appointed for the remaining editions.

As the reformulation of *20/20* editions played out, Hugh Downs retired in September 1999 from what became the flagship Friday evening edition of *20/20*. Walters remained sole anchor until January 2002 when John Miller, a reporter at ABC News since 1997, became co-anchor. Miller resigned in December 2002 to pursue a different career and John Stossell was quickly named co-anchor in May 2003. The end result of the flurry of competitive activity at ABC News, and Barbara Walters's perseverance in fighting for important stories and "must-get" interviews, is one remaining edition of *20/20*, scheduled, as of fall 2003, for Fridays at 10 P.M.

RICHARD BARTONE

See also **American Broadcasting Company; Arledge, Roone; Downs, Hugh; News, Network; Walters, Barbara**

Hosts/Anchors

Premiere episode	Harold Hayes
Premiere Episode	Robert Hughes
1978–1999	Hugh Downs
1984–	Barbara Walters
1998–2002	Connie Chung
1998–2000	Charles Gibson
1998–2000	Diane Sawyer
1999–2002	Jack Ford
2002–2003	John Miller
2003–	John Stossel

Producers

Bob Shanks (1978–1979); Av Westin (1979–1987); Victor Neufeld (1988–2000)

Executive Producer

Victor Neufeld (2000–2003)

Senior Executive Producer

David Sloan (2000–)

Reporters/Correspondents

1978–	Timothy Johnson
1978–1984	Thomas Hoving
1978–1981	Dave Marash
1978–1986; 1998–2001	Sylvia Chase
1978–1985	Geraldo Rivera
1978–1980	Dr. Carl Sagan
1977–1991	Sandy Vanocur
1979–	Tom Jarriel
1980–	Bob Brown
1981–	Joel Siegel
1981–2002	John Stossel
1981–1984	Barbara Walters
1986–1991	Stone Philips
1986–	Lynn Sherr
1989–	Jay Schadler
1993–1995	Catherine Crier
1994–	Brian Ross
1995–	Arnold Diaz
1995–	Deborah Roberts
1997–2001	John Miller
1997–	Bill Ritter
1998–	John Quinones
1998–	Chris Wallace
1999–	Christopher Cuomo
1999–	Cynthia McFadden
1999–2002	Nancy Snyderman
1999–	Elizabeth Vargas
2000–	Jamie Floyd
2001–	Juju Chang

Broadcast History

June 6, 1978 Premiere	Thursday 10:00–11:00
June 1978–August 1978	Tuesday 10:00–11:00
September 1978–April 1979	(sporadically broadcast, time and day varied)
May 1979–August 1987	Thursday 10:00–11:00
September 1987–September 2001	Friday 10:00–11:00
September 1997–December 1997	Thursday 10:00–11:00
June 1998–August 1998	Monday 9:00–10:00
September 1998–August 2000	Wednesday 10:00–11:00
November 1998–March 1999	Sunday 9:00–10:00
October 1998–August 2000	Thursday 10:00–11:00
February 1999–January 2000	Monday 8:00–9:00
September 2000–December 2000	Monday 8:00–9:00
June 2001–July 2001	Monday 8:00–9:00
September 2001–November 2001	Wednesday 10:00–11:00
January 2002–April 2002	Wednesday 10:00–11:00 P.M.
January 2002–	Friday 10:00–11:00

Further Reading

Arledge, Roone, *Roone: A Memoir,* New York: HarperCollins, 2003

Carter, Bill, "*20/20* Gives *60 Minutes* a Run for its Ratings," *New York Times* (April 21, 1991)

Gerard, Jeremy, "*20/20* Staff Reported Seething Over Change," *New York Times* (July 21, 1988)

Goodman, Walter, "Just Plain Folks, White House Style," *New York Times* (September 24, 1996)

Grossman, Lawrence K., "TV News: The Great Celebrity Chase," *Columbia Journalism Review* (July–August 1998)

Lafayette, Jon, "*20/20 Downtown:* No Jacket Required," *Electronic Media* (October 25, 1999)

Rutenberg, Jim, "Move against Barbara Walters Touches a Nerve," *New York Times* (May 21, 2001)

Rutenberg, Jim, "Working to Unite Stars and Factions at ABC News," *New York Times* (February 11, 2002)

Westin, Av, *Newswatch: How TV Decides the News,* New York: Simon and Schuster, 1982

24-Hour News

Today, cable television subscribers can watch news at any time of the day or night. Continuous live news coverage from around the world (made possible, in large part, by satellite technology) is available 24 hours a day, seven days a week. Three major U.S. cable news networks—CNN, MSNBC, and FOX News—present live news as well as talk, opinion, debate, and punditry, while sister networks focus on specific areas such as top stories (CNN Headline News) and financial news (CNBC). C-SPAN (Cable Satellite Public Affairs Network) and C-SPAN 2 offer live, unedited coverage of the proceedings of the U.S. House of Representatives and Senate, respectively, in combination with coverage of political conventions, news conferences, and national campaigns. Local 24-hour news channels—NY1 in New York City and BayTV in San Francisco, to name just two—have proliferated across the United States. In addition, news programming is available 24 hours a day on such international networks as BBC World.

Before the 1980s, the three national broadcast networks—ABC, CBS, and NBC—were the gatekeepers of news on television in the United States. At 6:30 P.M. Eastern Time, Monday through Friday, each of the three majors presented 22 minutes of news (plus commercials) to the nation from their headquarters in New York. When, in 1980, Atlanta-based cable entrepreneur Ted Turner launched CNN (Cable News Network), a round-the-clock, all-news network reaching 1.7 million cable television households, skeptics said he would never come up with enough news to fill 24 hours of programming. CNN was widely maligned as "Chicken Noodle News." But over the next two decades, CNN came to redefine what qualified as news, what news viewers demanded, and what sort of news programming both cable and broadcast networks provided, in the United States and around the world.

Although CNN failed to turn a profit in its first five years, it continued to expand and diversify, with the launch of CNN Headline News in 1981 and CNN International in 1985. A few news events proved to be major milestones for CNN, and for the public's understanding and growing viewership of "news on demand." In 1986, when the space shuttle *Challenger* exploded shortly after takeoff, CNN was the only network airing live coverage of the launch—and, therefore, of the crisis. By 1989, CNN reached 50 million U.S. television households. But the network truly came of age in 1991, when it was the only network to report live from the Iraqi capital on the opening night of the Persian Gulf War, and a worldwide audience of one billion people—one of the largest in television history for a non-sporting event—tuned in. Later that year, *Time* magazine recognized Turner, CNN's founder, as its "Man of the Year." By 1996, CNN had been acquired by media giant Time Warner, and it was more profitable than the three major networks' news divisions combined (though its ratings have, over the years, remained at a fraction of the overall ratings of ABC, CBS, NBC, and Australian media tycoon Rupert Murdoch's relative newcomer FOX network).

CNN has garnered praise for its focus on international news, maintaining many more overseas bureaus than its U.S. competitors. It has also been cited as emblematic of an era in which information has proliferated but knowledge is ever more scarce—and television news standards have degenerated. In the 1990s, the network drew many viewers, but also much criticism, for its in-depth coverage of events that never would have gained such attention from the broadcast networks—its live cablecast of the 1992 press conference in which Gennifer Flowers revealed her affair with presidential candidate Bill Clinton, for instance, or its gavel-to-gavel coverage of the criminal trial of celebrity sports figure O.J. Simpson. CNN's ratings soared during such high-profile events, but diminished considerably once the events had played out.

Still, by the mid-1990s, major media outlets were scrambling to reinvent themselves in light of CNN's ascendancy. The U.S. broadcast networks could not compete with CNN in terms of immediacy or range of coverage, so their national news broadcasts began to focus on fewer stories with more analysis, as well as on "soft" news relating to health and lifestyle trends.

In 1995–96, ABC, NBC, and FOX each announced plans to launch their own 24-hour news networks. ABC's project died on the drawing board. But FOX News Channel and MSNBC, a collaboration between NBC and high-tech corporation Microsoft, remain CNN competitors to this day. Both of these newer networks defined themselves in contrast to CNN's style and content. While CNN's viewers tend to be close to or older than the legal retirement age, MSNBC went for the coveted 25-to-54 demographic with slick sets and a more youthful focus. From the outset, MSNBC emphasized the synergy between its television channel and website, with an eye toward the future of 24-hour news on the Internet. FOX's Murdoch has long complained about the "liberal bias" of the news media (and of CNN in particular), and his FOX News Channel, while promising "fair and balanced" coverage, tends to reflect its owner's conservative politics, most notably in the popular opinion program *The O'Reilly Factor,* with vitriolic host Bill O'Reilly. By early 2002, FOX News boasted a daily viewership of 654,000; CNN, 595,000; and MSNBC, 295,000. FOX's edge was particularly significant because that channel was available in 9 million fewer homes than CNN's total of 86.2 million.

Following a different trajectory from the other cable news networks, non-profit C-SPAN was founded in 1979 as a public service by a group of cable industry executives. It began 24-hour-a-day programming in 1982, and C-SPAN 2, launched in 1986, went to 24 hours in 1987. The channels' position in the cable landscape began to look uncertain after the 1992 cable act's "must-carry" provision led some cable operators to drop C-SPAN to make room for broadcast stations they were now required to carry, and again in 1996, when Rupert Murdoch offered the country's largest cable company, TCI (TeleCommunications, Inc.), the unheard-of price of $11 per subscriber to carry his FOX News Channel. But after an impassioned letter-writing campaign among C-SPAN fans, an op-ed onslaught by C-SPAN head Brian Lamb, and a change of leadership at TCI, C-SPAN ended the 1990s in a more

secure position. In 2002, C-SPAN reached 86.5 million subscribers.

Local all-news cable channels—some owned by cable companies, others owned or operated by major daily newspapers, and still others independent ventures—began to enter the fray as early as the late 1980s, and continue to grow in number. At the other end of the spectrum are international 24-hour news channels like BBC World and EuroNews, launched by a consortium of European public service broadcasters, competing in the global market with CNN International and maintaining a non-U.S.-centric perspective on world news. In mid-2003, BBC World (launched in 1995) was available in more than 250 million homes in over 200 countries; its success is attributed to a combination of its ability to use the full resources of BBC News—the largest broadcast news-gathering organization in the world—and the careful localization of its non-news programming to reflect the varying interests of its regional markets.

Many commentators point to the fact that the advent of 24-hour news has shaped more than how viewers understand their world. The term "CNN effect" is used in two ways. One sense refers to a drop in consumer spending when people stay home to watch the news during a crisis. The sense in which the "CNN effect" (or "CNN factor" or "CNN curve") is more commonly employed, however, refers to the diplomatic repercussions of widely available news on demand. To what degree does instant news or continuous coverage of an event affect foreign-policy decisions? Are officials more likely to intervene in far-off conflicts—and possibly make over-hasty choices—if the events are immediately visible on TV? In this view, 24-hour news marks an important chapter not only in media history, but in world history.

BETH KRACKLAUER

See also **Cable News Network (CNN); FOX Broadcasting Company; MSNBC; Murdoch, Rupert K.; Turner, Ted**

Further Reading

Aufderheide, Pat, "C-SPAN's Fight for Respect," *Columbia Journalism Review* 36/2 (July/August 1997)

Auletta, Ken, "The Lost Tycoon," *New Yorker* (April 23, 2001)

Barkin, Steve M., *American Television News: The Media Marketplace and the Public Interest,* Armonk, New York: M.E. Sharpe, 2003

Fallows, James, "The Age of Murdoch," *Atlantic Monthly* (September 2003)

Goldberg, Robert and Gerald Jay Goldberg, *Citizen Turner: The Wild Rise of an American Tycoon,* New York: Harcourt Brace, 1995

Kavanagh, Michael, "BBC Launches News Channel," *Electronic Media* 16/47 (November 17, 1997).

Robinson, Piers, *The CNN Effect: The Myth of News, Foreign Policy and Intervention,* London: Routledge, 2002

Seib, Philip, *Going Live: Getting the News Right in a Real-Time, Online World.* Lanham, Maryland: Rowman and Littlefield, 2001

Siklos, Richard, and Amy Cortese, "This Little Peacock is Showing Some Pluck," *Business Week* 3591 (August 17, 1998).

Silvia, Tony, editor, *Global News: Perspectives on the Information Age,* Ames: Iowa State University Press, 2001

Smillie, Dirk, "'Mini CNNs' Fill a Niche on Local Cable Channels," *Christian Science Monitor* (January 17, 1997)

Zelizer, Barbie, "CNN, the Gulf War, and Journalistic Practice," *Journal of Communication* 42/1 (Winter 1992)

Twilight Zone, The

U.S. Science-Fantasy Anthology

The Twilight Zone is generally considered to be the first "adult" science-fantasy anthology series to appear on American television, introducing the late 1950s TV audience to an entertaining, and at the same time thought-provoking, collection of human-condition stories wrapped within fantastic themes. Although the series is usually labeled a science fiction program, its true sphere was fantasy, embracing elements of the supernatural, the psychological, and "the almost-but-not-quite; the unbelievable told in terms that can be believed" (Rod Serling).

During the show's five-year, 155-episode run on CBS (1959–64), it received three Emmy Awards (Rod Serling, twice, for Outstanding Writing Achievement in Drama, and George Clemens for Outstanding Achievement in Cinematography), three World Science Fiction Convention Hugo Awards (for Dramatic Presentation: 1960, 1961, 1962), a Directors Guild Award (John Brahm), a Producers Guild Award (Buck Houghton for Best Produced Series), and the 1961 Unit Award for Outstanding Contributions to Better Race Relations, among numerous other awards and presentations.

The brainchild of one of the most successful young playwrights of his time (with such "Golden Age" TV successes as *Patterns* and *Requiem for a Heavyweight*), Serling's *The Twilight Zone* began life as a story called "The Time Element," which Serling had submitted to CBS, where it was produced as part of the *Westinghouse-Desilu Playhouse* anthology. Although it was little more than a simple time-warp tale, starring William Bendix as a man who believes he goes back in time to the attack on Pearl Harbor, the TV presentation received an extraordinary amount of complimentary mail and prompted CBS to commission a *Twilight Zone* pilot for a possible series. With his "Time Ele-

ment" script already used, Serling prepared another story that would be the pilot episode for the series. "Where Is Everybody?" opened *The Twilight Zone* on October 2, 1959 and featured a riveting one-man performance by Earl Holliman as a psychologically stressed Air Force man who hallucinates that he is completely alone in a deserted but spookily "lived in" town (he is actually undergoing an isolation experiment). It was this hallucinatory human stress situation placed in a could-be science-fantasy landscape, complete with an O. Henry-type "snapper ending," that was to become the standard structure of *The Twilight Zone*. "Here's what *The Twilight Zone* is," explained Serling to *TV Guide* in November 1959. "It's an anthology series, half hour in length, that delves into the odd, the bizarre, the unexpected. It probes into the dimension of imagination but with a concern for taste and for an adult audience too long considered to have IQs in negative figures."

Serling's contract with the network stipulated that he would write 80 percent of the first season's scripts, which would be produced under Serling's own Cayuga Productions banner. In fact, the prolific Serling ended up writing well over 50 percent of the show's teleplays during its entire five-year run. This enormous output was for the most part supported by two other writers of distinction in the science-fantasy genre: Richard Matheson and Charles Beaumont. Matheson's literary and screenplay work before and during the series ran parallel to that of Beaumont—not surprisingly, since they were personal friends and often script-writing collaborators during their early days in television. Matheson's early writing had included the short story collection *Born of Man and Woman* and a novel, *I Am Legend* (both published 1954), and later the screenplays for *The Incredible Shrinking Man* (1957; from his own

The Twilight Zone, Jonathan Winters, Jack Klugman, 1959–64; "A Game of Pool."
Courtesy of the Everett Collection

The Twilight Zone, Anne Francis, James Milhollin, 1959–64; "The After Hours."
Courtesy of the Everett Collection

novel), and the Poe adaptations *House of Usher* (1960), and *The Pit and the Pendulum* (1961). Beaumont's work included similar science fiction and horror-fantasy writings, with the short-story collections *Shadow Play* (published 1957) and *Yonder* (1958), as well as screenplays for *Premature Burial* (1962) and *The Haunted Palace* (1963), alongside others in a similar vein. Their individual scripts for *The Twilight Zone* were perhaps the nearest in style and story flavor to Serling's own work.

George Clayton Johnson was another young writer who, emerging from Beaumont's circle of writer friends, produced some outstanding scripts for the series, including the crackling life-or-death bet story "A Game of Pool," featuring excellent performances from Jack Klugman and Jonathan Winters. Earl Hamner, Jr., later to be creator and narrator of the long-running *The Waltons,* supplied eight scripts to the series, most of which featured good-natured rural folk and duplicitous city slickers. The renowned science fiction author Ray Bradbury was asked by Serling to contribute to the series before the show had even started, but due to the richness of Bradbury's written work, he contributed

only one script, "I Sing the Body Electric," based on his own short story.

As an anthology focusing on the "dimension of imagination" and using parable and suggestion as basic techniques, *The Twilight Zone* favored only a dozen or so story themes. For instance, the most recurring theme involved time warps and accidental journeys through time: a World War I flier lands at a modern jet air base (Matheson's "The Last Flight"); a man finds himself back in 1865 and tries to prevent the assassination of President Lincoln (Serling's "Back There"); three soldiers on National Guard maneuvers in Montana find themselves back in 1876 at Little Big Horn (Serling's "The 7th Is Made up of Phantoms"). Another theme explored the confrontation with death/the dead: a girl keeps seeing the same hitchhiker on the road ahead, beckoning her toward a fatal accident (Serling's "The Hitchhiker," from Lucille Fletcher's radio play); an aged recluse, fearing a meeting with Death, reluctantly helps a wounded policeman on her doorstep and cares for him overnight before she realizes that he is Death, coming to claim her (Johnson's "Nothing in the Dark"). Expected science fiction motifs regarding aliens and alien contact, both benevolent and hostile, provide another story arena: a timid little fellow accustomed to being used as a doormat by his

The Twilight Zone, Burgess Meredith, 1959–64; "Time Enough at Last."
Courtesy of the Everett Collection

The Twilight Zone, Art Carney, 1959–64; "Night of the Meek."
Courtesy of the Everett Collection

fellow man is endowed with superhuman strength by a visiting scientist from Mars (Serling's "Mr. Dingle, the Strong"); visiting aliens promise to show the people of Earth how to end the misery of war, pestilence, and famine until a code clerk finally deciphers their master manual for Earth and discovers a cookbook (Serling's "To Serve Man," from a Damon Knight story). Other themes common to the series were robots, with Matheson's excellent "Steel" a standout; the devil (Beaumont's "The Howling Man"); nostalgia (Serling's "Walking Distance" and "A Stop at Willoughby"); machines (Serling's "The Fever"); angels (Serling's poetic "A Passage for Trumpet"); and premonitions, dreams, and sleep (Beaumont's "Perchance to Dream"). The general tone of many *Twilight Zone* stories was cautionary, that humans can never be too sure of anything that appears real or otherwise.

In 1983 Warner Brothers, Steven Spielberg, and John Landis produced *Twilight Zone: The Movie,* a four-segment tribute to the original series. The film presents pieces directed by Landis (also written by Landis), Spielberg (written by George Clayton Johnson, Richard Matheson, Josh Rogan, based on the original 1962 episode "Kick the Can"), Joe Dante (written

by Matheson, based on the original 1961 episode "It's a Good Life"), and George Miller (written by Matheson from his own story and original 1963 episode "Nightmare at 20,000 Feet").

From 1985 onward, CBS Entertainment produced a new series of *The Twilight Zone.* Honored science fiction scribe Harlan Ellison acted as creative consultant under executive producer Philip DeGuere; the series is particularly noted for the prominent participating directors, such as Wes Craven, William Friedkin, and Joe Dante. In more recent times, *Twilight Zone: Rod Serling's Lost Classics* presented a two-hour TV movie based on two unproduced works discovered by the late writer's widow and literary executor, Carol Serling. Robert Markowitz directed both "The Theater" (scripted by Matheson from Serling's original story) and "Where the Dead Are" (from a completed Serling script).

With its subtext of escape from reality, a nostalgia for simpler times, and a hunger for otherworldly adventures, it seems appropriate that the original *Twilight Zone* series appeared at about the right time to take viewers away (albeit briefly) from the contemporary real-life fears of the Cold War, the Berlin Wall, the Cuban Missile Crisis, and John Kennedy's assassination. *The Twilight Zone* directly or indirectly inspired such later fantasy and science fiction anthologies as *Thriller* (1960–62), with its dark Val Lewtonesque atmosphere, and the superb *Outer Limits* (1963–64), a tribute to 1950s science fiction cinema when it was at its most imaginative. Such programs testify to both Rod Serling's and *The Twilight Zone*'s spirit of poetry and principle.

TISE VAHIMAGI

See also **Science Fiction Programs; Sterling, Rod**

Host/Creator
Rod Serling (1959–65)

Narrators
Charles Aidman (1985–87)
Robin Ward (1988–89)

Producers
Buck Houghton (1959–62), Herbert Hirschman (1963), Brad Granet (1963–64), William Froug (1963–64), Harvey Frand (1985–86)

Programming History

1959–64:	137 30-minute episodes; 18 1-hour episodes
1985–87:	24 1-hour episodes; 19 30-minute episodes
1988–89:	30 30-minute episodes
CBS	
October 1959–September 1962	Friday 10:00–10:30
September 1961–September 1964	Friday 9:30–10:00
January 1963–September 1963	Thursday 9:00–10:00
May 1965–September 1965	Sunday 9:00–10:00
September 1985–April 1986	Friday 8:00–9:00
June 1986–September 1986	Friday 8:00–9:00
September 1986–October 1986	Saturday 10:00–11:00
December 1986	Thursday 8:00–8:30
July 1987	Friday 10:00–11:00
1987–88	First-run syndication

Further Reading

Boddy, William, "Entering the *Twilight Zone*," *Screen* (July–October 1984)

Javna, John, *The Best of Science Fiction TV: The Critics' Choice: From Captain Video to Star Trek, from The Jetsons to Robotech,* New York: Harmony, 1987

Lentz, Harris M., *Science Fiction, Horror, and Fantasy Film and Television Credits: Over 10,000 Actors, Actresses, Directors,* Jefferson, North Carolina: McFarland, 1983

Lentz, Harris M., *Science Fiction, Horror, and Fantasy Film and Television Credits, Supplement 2, through 1993,* Jefferson, North Carolina: McFarland, 1994

Presnell, Don, and Marty McGee, *A Critical History of Television's The Twilight Zone, 1959–1964,* Jefferson, North Carolina: McFarland, 1998

Rothenberg, Randall, "Synergy of Surrealism and *The Twilight Zone*," *New York Times* (April 2, 1991)

Sander, Gordon F., *Serling: The Rise and Twilight of Television's Last Angry Man,* New York: Dutton, 1992

Schumer, Arlen, *Visions from the Twilight Zone,* San Francisco: Chronicle, 1990

Serling, Rod, "Ideas behind The Twilight Zone," *TV Guide* (November 7, 1959)

Wolfe, Peter, *In the Zone: The Twilight World of Rod Serling,* Bowling Green, Ohio: Bowling Green State University Popular Press, 1997

Zicree, Marc Scott, *The Twilight Zone Companion,* Toronto and New York: Bantam, 1982

Ziegler, Robert E., "Moving Out of Sight: Fantastic Vision in *The Twilight Zone*," *Lamar Journal of the Humanities* (Fall 1987)

Twin Peaks

U.S. Serial Drama

Scheduled to appear as a limited-run, midseason replacement series on ABC, *Twin Peaks* attracted considerable critical attention even before its premiere in the spring of 1990. Both the network and national critics aggressively publicized the show as an unprecedented form of television drama, one that promised to defy the established conventions of television narrative while also exploring a tone considerably more sinister than previously seen in the medium. In short, critics promoted the series as a rare example of television "art," a program that publicists predicted would attract a more upscale, sophisticated, and demographically desirable audience to television. Upon its premiere, the series generated even more critical admiration in the press, placed higher than expected in the ratings, and in speculating on the question "Who killed Laura Palmer?" gave Americans the most talked-about television enigma since "Who Shot J.R.?"

The "artistic" status of *Twin Peaks* stemmed from the unique pedigrees of the series' co-creators, writer-producer Mark Frost and writer-director David Lynch. Frost was most known for his work as a writer and story editor for the highly acclaimed *Hill Street Blues,* where he had mastered the techniques of orchestrating a large ensemble drama in a serial format. Lynch, meanwhile, had fashioned one of Hollywood's more eccentric cinematic careers as the director of the cult favorite *Eraserhead* (1978), the Academy Award–winning *The Elephant Man* (1980), the epic box-office flop *Dune* (1984), and the perverse art-house hit *Blue Velvet* (1986). A prominent American auteur, Lynch was already well known for his oblique narrative strategies, macabre mise-en-scènes, and obsessive thematic concerns.

Twin Peaks combined the strengths of both Frost and Lynch, featuring an extended cast of characters occupying a world not far removed from the sinister small town Lynch had explored in *Blue Velvet.* Ostensibly a murder mystery, the series centers on FBI agent Dale Cooper and his investigation of a murder in the northwestern town of Twin Peaks, a few miles from the Canadian border. The victim, high-school prom queen Laura Palmer, is found wrapped in plastic and floating in a lake. Cooper gradually uncovers an ever-more baroque network of secrets and mysteries surrounding Laura's death, all of which seem to suggest an unspeakable evil presence in the town. Quickly integrating himself into the melodramatic intrigues of the community, Cooper's search for Laura's murderer eventually leads him to track "Killer Bob," a malleable and apparently supernatural entity inhabiting the deep woods of the Pacific Northwest.

Although the enigma of Laura's killer was pivotal to the series' popularity—so much so that *TV Guide* featured a forum of popular novelists offering their own solutions to the murder mystery—*Twin Peaks* as an avowedly "artistic" text was in many ways more about style, tone, and detail than narrative. Many viewers were attracted to the series' calculated sense of

Twin Peaks, Joan Chen, Michael Ontkean, Kyle MacLachlan, Piper Laurie, 1990–91.
Courtesy of the Everett Collection

strangeness, a quality that led *Time* to dub Lynch as "the czar of bizarre." As in Lynch's other work, *Twin Peaks* deftly balanced parody, pathos, and disturbing expressionism, often mocking the conventions of television melodrama while defamiliarizing and intensifying them. The entire first hour of the premiere episode, for example, covered only a single plot point, showing the protracted emotional responses of Laura's family and friends as they learned of her death. This slow yet highly overwrought storyline was apparently considered so disruptive by ABC that the network briefly discussed airing the first hour without commercial interruption (although this could have been a strategy designed to promote the program as "art"). Throughout the run of the series, the storyline accommodated many such directorial set-pieces, stylistic tours-de-force that allowed the "Lynchian" sensibility to make its artistic presence felt most acutely. The brooding synthesizer score and dreamy jazz interludes provided by composer Angelo Badalamenti, who had worked previously with Lynch, also greatly enhanced the eerie, bizarre, and melancholy atmosphere.

As the series progressed, its proliferation of sinister enigmas led the viewer deeper into ambiguity and continually frustrated any hope of definitive closure. Appropriately, the first season ended with a cliff-hanger that left many of the major characters imperiled, and still provided no clear solution to Laura Palmer's murder. Perhaps because of the series' obstinate refusal to move toward a traditional resolution, coupled with its escalating sense of the bizarre, the initially high ratings dropped over the course of the series' run. Despite such difficulties, and in the face of a perhaps inevitable critical backlash against the series, ABC renewed the show for a second season, moving it to the Saturday schedule in an effort to attract the program's quality demographics to a night usually abandoned by such audiences. After providing a relatively "definitive" solution to the mystery of Laura's killer early in the second season, the series attempted to introduce new characters and enigmas to reinvigorate the storyline, but the transition from what had essentially been an eight-episode miniseries in the first season to an open-ended serial in the second had a significant, and many would say negative, impact on the show. The series attempted to maintain its sense of mystery and pervasive dread, but having already escalated its narrative stakes into supernatural and extraterrestrial plotlines, individual episodes increasingly had to resort to either absurdist comedy or self-reflexive commentary to sustain an increasingly convoluted world. After juggling the troubled series across its schedule for several months, ABC finally canceled the series after just 30 episodes in total, packaging the second season's concluding two episodes together as a grand finale.

Exported in slightly different versions, *Twin Peaks* proved to be a major hit internationally, especially in Japan. In the United States, the brief but dramatic success of *Twin Peaks* inspired a cycle of shows that attempted to capitalize on the American public's previously untested affinity for the strange and bizarre. Series as diverse as *Northern Exposure* (CBS), *Picket Fences* (CBS), *The X-Files* (FOX), and *American Gothic* (CBS) have all been described in journalistic criticism as bearing the influence of *Twin Peaks*. The series also spawned a devoted and appropriately obsessed fan culture. In keeping with the program's artistic status, fan activity around the show concentrated on providing ever-closer textual readings of the individual episodes, looking for hidden clues that would help clarify the series' rather obtuse narrative logic. This core audience was the primary target of a cinematic prequel to the series released in 1993, *Twin Peaks: Fire Walk with Me*. Again directed by Lynch, *Fire Walk with Me* chronicled Laura Palmer's activities in the days just before her death. Freed from some of the constraints of network standards and practices, Lynch's cinematic treatment of *Twin Peaks* was an even more violent, disturbing, and obsessive reading of the mythical community, and it provided an interesting commentary and counterpoint to the series as a whole.

Lynch once again attempted to bring his neo-noir surrealism to network television with *Mulholland Drive,* a pilot that was ultimately rejected by a cautious ABC. Lynch had the last laugh, however, at least artistically. Taking the core footage of the pilot, Lynch rescripted and reshaped the project into a feature-length film. *Mulholland Drive* went on to be one of the most critically acclaimed films of 2001.

JEFFREY SCONCE

See also **Movie Professionals and Television**

Cast

Dale Cooper	Kyle MacLachlan
Sheriff Harry S. Truman	Michael Ontkean
Shelly Johnson	Madchen Amick
Bobby Briggs	Dana Ashbrook
Benjamin Horne	Richard Beymer
Donna Marie Hayward	Lara Flynn Boyle
Audrey Horne	Sherilyn Fenn
Dr. William Hayward	Warren Frost
Norma Jennings	Peggy Lipton
James Hurley	James Marshall
"Big Ed" Hurley	Everett McGill
Pete Martell	Jack Nance
Leland Palmer	Ray Wise
Catherine Packard Martell	Piper Laurie
Montana	Rick Giolito
Midge Loomer	Adele Gilbert
Male Parole Board Officer	James Craven
Female Parole Board Member #2	Mary Chalon
Emory Battis	Don Amendolia
The Dwarf	Michael J. Anderson
Jeffrey Marsh	John Apicella
Ronette Pulaski	Phoebe Augustine
Johnny Horne	Robert Bauer
Mrs. Tremond	Frances Bay
Ernie Niles	James Booth
Mayor Dwyane Milford	John Boylan
Richard Tremayne	Ian Buchanan
Blackie O'Reilly	Victoria Catlin
Josie Packard	Joan Chen
The Log Lady/Margaret	Catherine E. Coulson
Herself	Julee Cruise
Sylvia Horne	Jan D'Arcy
Leo Johnson	Eric DaRe
Maj. Garland Briggs	Don S. Davis
Eileen Hayward	Mary Jo Deschanel
DEA Agent Dennis/Denise Bryson	David Duchovny
Agent Albert Rosenfield	Miguel Ferrer
Deputy Andy Brennan	Harry Goaz
Nancy O'Reilly	Galyn Gorg
Annie Blackburn	Heather Graham
Vivian Smythe	Jane Greer
Nicolas "Little Nicky" Needleman	Joshua Harris
Mike Nelson	Gary Hershberger
Deputy Tommy "Hawk" Hill	Michael Horse

Jerry Horne
Madeleine Ferguson/Laura
  Palmer
Lana Budding
Malcolm Sloan
Pierre Tremond
Agent Gordon Cole
Diane, Cooper's secretary
Caroline Powell Earle
Evelyn Marsh
Hank Jennings
Andrew Packard
Jones
RCMP Officer Preston King
Jacques Renault
The Giant
Jonathan Kumagai
Jean Renault
Lucy Moran
Janek Pulaski
Doctor Lawrence Jacoby
Nadine Hurley
Bob
Suburbis Pulaski
Elizabeth Briggs
Harold Smith
Trudy
Philip Michael Gerard/
  Mike/The One-Armed Man
Harriet Hayward
Bartender
Thomas Eckhardt
Swabbie
Windom Earle
Joey Paulson
Bernard Renault
Emerald/Jade
Roger Hardy
Chet
Mrs. Tremond
Jared
The Room-Service Waiter
Tojamura
Sarah Palmer
John Justice Wheeler
Gwen Morton
Female Parole Board
  Member #1
Einar Thorson
Heba
Theodora Ridgely
Jenny
Decker
Tim Pinkle

David Patrick Kelly

Sheryl Lee
Robyn Lively
Nicholas Love
Austin Jack Lynch
David Lynch
Carol Lynley
Brenda E. Mathers
Annette McCarthy
Chris Mulkey
Dan O'Herlihy
Brenda Strong
Gavan O'Herlihy
Walter Olkewicz
Carel Struycken
Mak Takano
Michael Parks
Kimmy Robertson
Alan Ogle
Russ Tamblyn
Wendy Robie
Frank Silva
Michelle Milantoni
Charlotte Stewart
Lenny Von Dohlen
Jill Rogosheske

Al Strobel
Jessica Wallenfells
Kim Lentz
David Warner
Charlie Spradling
Kenneth Welsh
Brett Vadset
Clay Wilcox
Erika Anderson
Clarence Williams III
Lance Davis
Mae Williams
Peter Michael Goetz
Hank Worden
Fumio Yamaguchi
Grace Zabriskie
Billy Zane
Kathleen Wilhoite

Mary Bond Davis
Brian Straub
Mary Stavin
Eve Brent
Lisa Ann Cabasa
Charles Hoyes
David L. Lander

Gersten Hayward
Mr. Neff
Eolani Jacoby

Alicia Witt
Mark Lowenthal
Jennifer Aquino

Producers

David Lynch, Mark Frost, Gregg Fienberg, David J.
  Latt, Harley Peyton

Programming History

30 episodes
ABC

April 8, 1990	Sunday 9:00–11:00
April 1990–May 1990	Thursday 9:00–10:00
August 1990–February 1991	Saturday 10:00–11:00
March 1991–April 1991	Thursday 9:00–10:00
June 10, 1991	Monday 9:00–11:00

Further Reading

Carrion, Maria M., "*Twin Peaks* and the Circular Ruins of Fiction: Figuring (Out) the Acts of Reading," *Literature/Film Quarterly* (1993)

Carroll, Michael, "Agent Cooper's Errand in the Wilderness: *Twin Peaks* and American Mythology," *Literature/Film Quarterly* (1993)

Davenport, Randi, "The Knowing Spectator of *Twin Peaks*: Culture, Feminism, and Family Violence," *Literature/Film Quarterly* (1993)

Deutsch, Helen, "'Is It Easier to Believe?' Narrative Innocence from *Clarissa* to *Twin Peaks*," *Arizona Quarterly: A Journal of American Literature, Culture, and Theory* (1993)

Giffone, Tony, "*Twin Peaks* as Post-Modernist Parody: David Lynch's Subversion of the British Detective Narrative," *The Mid-Atlantic Almanac: The Journal of the Mid-Atlantic Popular/American Culture Association* (1992)

Horne, Philip, "Henry Hill and Laura Palmer," *London Review of Books* (December 20, 1990)

Huskey, Melynda, "*Twin Peaks*: Rewriting the Sensation Novel," *Literature/Film Quarterly* (1993)

Kimball, Samuel, "'Into the Light, Leland, into the Light': Emerson, Oedipus, and the Blindness of Male Desire in David Lynch's *Twin Peaks*," *Genders* (1993)

Lavery, David, editor, "Peaked Out," special issue of *Literature/Film Quarterly* (1993)

Ledwon, Lenora, "*Twin Peaks* and the Television Gothic," *Literature/Film Quarterly* (1993)

Nickerson, Catherine, "Serial Detection and Serial Killers in *Twin Peaks*," *Literature/Film Quarterly* (1993)

Nochimson, Martha, "Desire under the Douglas Firs: Entering the Body of Reality in *Twin Peaks*," *Film Quarterly* (1992)

Pollard, Scott, "Cooper, Details, and the Patriotic Mission of *Twin Peaks*," *Literature/Film Quarterly* (1993)

Shoos, Diane, Diana George, and Joseph Comprone, "*Twin Peaks* and the Look of Television: Visual Literacy in the Writing Classroom," *Journal of Advanced Composition* (Fall 1993)

Stevenson, Diane, "Family Romance, Family Violence: David Lynch's *Twin Peaks*," *Boulevard* (Spring 1993)

Zaniello, Tom, "Hitched or Lynched: Who Directed *Twin Peaks*?" *Studies in Popular Culture* (October 1994)

2000 Presidential Election Coverage

Although network television projections had prematurely awarded New Mexico to Democratic candidate Al Gore, the epicenter of controversy surrounding electronic media coverage on the night of November 7, 2000 consisted of two consecutive pronouncements—both of them wrong—awarding Florida, and ultimately the presidency, first to Gore, and then to George W. Bush. In one of the tightest presidential elections in American history, NBC declared Gore the victor at 7:49 P.M. EST based on Voter News Service (VNS) tabulations of exit polls and early precinct totals in Florida. Within minutes, CBS, CNN, FOX, ABC, and VNS itself followed suit, and declared Gore the winner. At 9:38 P.M., however, VNS retracted its projection for Florida after CNN discovered a tabulation error that mistakenly gave Gore a 96 percent margin of victory in the state's historically conservative Duval County. CNN withdrew its call for Gore at 9:45 P.M., and within minutes, CBS, FOX, and ABC followed suit. Then, at 2:16 A.M., under the leadership of Bush's first cousin John Ellis, the election coverage team for the Fox News Network declared Bush the winner. Within minutes, ABC, CBS, CNN, and NBC followed suit.

Ending weeks of litigating, political maneuvering, and heated public denunciations of so-called liberal media bias, the U.S. Supreme Court ultimately intervened in the election on December 12, 2000, voting 5–4 to bar a recount of the Florida vote and thus effectively anointing Bush president. Despite losing the popular vote to Gore by more than half a million votes, Bush received 271 electoral college votes to Gore's 267, the narrowest margin since 1876, when Rutherford B. Hayes, after disputed recounts in four states, beat Samuel J. Tilden by a single electoral vote.

The evening topped off a campaign that might otherwise have been more memorable for the satirical impersonations of Will Ferrell as Bush and Darrell Hammond as Gore on the popular late-night comedy-variety show *Saturday Night Live*. Despite early tempests involving allegedly subliminal Republican campaign ads ("RATS" briefly appeared in one television advertisement for Bush as part of an animated special effect flying the word "DEMOCRATS" into the shot) and an instance when Bush was caught on tape calling *New York Times* reporter Adam Clymer an obscene term, the election seemed primarily notable for the lackadaisical voter response it generated.

After November 7, a new iconography for the presidential campaign emerged on television. Dan Rather infamously boasted early in the evening to CBS viewers "if we say somebody's carried the state, you can take that to the bank. Book it!" After the predictions seemed less invincible, NBC political analyst Tim Russert made the low-tech combination of personal whiteboard and red dry erase marker a household image. The cable channel C-SPAN, normally broadcasting hearings and Congressional votes to fulfill its public affairs programming mandate, featured reruns of the *Saturday Night Live* sketches. The image of wide-eyed Judge Robert Rosenberg inspecting questionable Broward County ballots behind a magnifying glass became a lightning rod for all that was wrong with the voting and recount process in Florida.

Rather than pursue disturbing, historic, and ongoing irregularities in the voting process, such as the deliberate purging of black voters from Florida's voter rolls, subsequent Congressional hearings focused on television coverage of election night. Billy Tauzin (R-LA), chair of the House Energy and Commerce Committee, set the tone of the investigation in the months leading up to the February 14, 2001, hearings when he accused the networks of harboring "probable bias" in painting "a very disturbing picture," in which television executives wanted the country to believe "that Al Gore was sweeping the country." Hauling the executives of FOX, CBS, CNN, NBC, and the Voter News Service before Congress, Tauzin proceeded to soften his charges of network bias. Network executives, in turn, proceeded to blame Voter News Service as the culprit, and pledged both to take a more active role in VNS's affairs by sitting on its Board of Directors, as well as to overhaul the consortium's data-gathering procedures to better reflect changes in the electorate, such as accounting for a rise in absentee ballots.

While the 2000 Presidential Election was in large part marked by how its aftermath played out on television, it also was marked by what was not seen: an encroaching privatization of the public interest, and increasingly sophisticated forms of virtual gerrymandering (or dividing an area into voting districts so as to give an advantage to one party). For example, VNS was symptomatic of the massive downsizing of network news operations beginning in the 1980s. Rather than conduct their own research competitively, ABC,

CBS, CNN, NBC, and the Associated Press formed the consortium after the 1992 election to create a monolithic election-day newsgathering entity. In February 2000, VNS threatened to sue both the online *Slate* magazine and *National Review Online* after their websites published VNS exit poll data. Given that VNS was the sole source for election news, this oligopolistic behavior seemed somewhat at odds with the commitment to the First Amendment normally found among media organizations. After the November 2000 elections, VNS contracted the Battelle Memorial Institute, a defense and CIA contractor, to develop an entirely new computerized system to tabulate election results. However, the $8 million overhaul of VNS's data analysis became overloaded and crashed early during coverage of the Congressional elections on November 5, 2002. By January 2003, the major cable operators and networks had decided to disband their consortium, but not before valuable demographic data of that election had been lost forever.

Meanwhile, the story of how Florida Governor Jeb Bush, Secretary of State Katherine Harris, and Florida Director of Elections Clayton Roberts paid $4 million to DBT, a private company that ended up purging electoral rolls of 22,000 black Democratic voters, has yet to be covered by a single mainstream newsmedia outlet in the United States. The story instead aired in Great Britain as part of the BBC television newsmagazine show *Newsnight* on February 16, 2001.

STEVEN CARR

See also **Political Processes and Television; U.S. Presidency and Television**

Further Reading

Frankovic, Kathleen A., "News Organizations' Responses to the Mistakes of Election 2000: Why They Will Continue to Project Elections," *Public Opinion Quarterly* 67 (Spring 2003)

Kellner, Douglas, *Grand Theft 2000: Media Spectacle and a Stolen Election.* Lanham, Maryland: Rowman and Littlefield, 2001

Palast, Greg, "What Really Happened in Florida?" *Newsnight,* London, BBC (February 16, 2001); transcript available at *http://news.bbc.co.uk/1/hi/events/newsnight/1174115.stm*

United States Congress, House Energy and Commerce Committee, *Hearings on Election Night Coverage by the Networks.* 107th Congress, 1st session. Washington, D.C.: GPO, 2001; transcript available at *http://frwebgate.access.gpo.gov/cgi-bin/getdoc.cgi?dbname=107_house_hearings&docid=f:71490.pdf*

227

U.S. Domestic Comedy

The show *227*, initially aired in September 1985, was broadcast for five seasons on NBC before its final episode in July 1990. Based on a play of the same name, this situation comedy was set primarily around an apartment building (number 227) located in a racially mixed neighborhood of Washington, D.C. Featuring an ensemble cast that included such noted African-American television personalities as Marla Gibbs, Hal Williams, Alaina Reed Hall, and Jackee (Harry), *227* succeeded in becoming a top-rated television program. Surviving criticisms and early comparisons to other television programs with predominantly African-American principals, *227* proved a successful comedy, humorously portraying the everyday lives of apartment building 227.

The original play, *227,* had been written by Christine Houston of Chicago and performed by Marla Gibbs's own Cross Roads Academy, a local community theater troupe in Los Angeles. After its successful theatrical debut, *227* was soon adapted and produced for television by Lorimar. In its earliest episodes, *227* was criticized as being too much like *The Cosby Show,* another highly successful, predominantly African-American sitcom broadcast on NBC in the 1980s. However, even in its first year, *227* proved successful in its own right, earning top ratings that opening season. While *The Cosby Show* portrayed an image of upper-middle-class success, *227* supporters argued, *227* depicted a more working-class image of the same strong community and family values.

With most episodes taking place within and around the apartment building, from the front steps to the laundry room to the individual apartments, *227* invited the viewer within the most mundane and personal aspects of its characters' lives. The Jenkins, Mary and Lester, were one of the families struggling day by day to survive their various duties and commitments. Mary, played by Marla Gibbs (whose 11 seasons as the feisty, verbally aggressive maid Florence on *The Jeffersons* no doubt prepared her for this similarly outspoken character), was a mother of one, juggling the numerous responsibilities of household, family, and personal life with invariably humorous results. Lester, played by Hal Williams, was a father and small-time contractor struggling to stay on top of his own family and job responsibilities. Together, Mary and Lester had their hands full with daughter Brenda (Regina King), a studious, talented, and mostly well-behaved girl just beginning adolescence.

Other important characters included Rose Holloway, Mary's confidante in gossip, portrayed by Alaina Reed. Rose, the landlady of building 227, often sat with Mary on the front steps as they laughed and gossiped about various other residents. In particular, Rose and Mary enjoyed discussing and berating sexually outspoken tenant Sandra Clark, the building's resident vamp. Played by Jackee, the one-named wonder who made Sandra, and herself, famous, Sandra's whining voice and wiggling, tight-dressed body became staple features of *227*. Her many men friends and sexually oriented antics a source of constant humor, Sandra sauntered through episode after episode, occasionally eliciting help from Mary for some dilemma she was experiencing. Another frequent front-porch gossip was Pearl Shay (Helen Martin), an older woman who often leaned out her front window to comment on Rose and Mary's discussions. The grandmother of young Calvin Dobbs (Curtis Baldwin), the burgeoning love interest of Brenda Jenkins, Pearl's time was frequently spent scolding and disciplining this gangly adolescent grandson.

Successful in depicting the everyday aspects of its many characters' lives, *227* offered an interesting working-class version of African-American values and images. The program brought the viewer within its characters' lives, providing a personal look within this entertaining apartment complex.

BRENT MALIN

See also **Comedy, Domestic Settings; Racism, Ethnicity, and Television**

Cast

Mary Jenkins	Marla Gibbs
Lester Jenkins	Hal Williams
Rose Lee Holloway	Alaina Reed-Hall
Sandra Clark	Jackee (Harry)
Brenda Jenkins	Regina King
Tiffany Holloway (1985–86)	Kia Goodwin
Pearl Shay	Helen Martin
Calvin Dobbs	Curtis Baldwin
Alexandria DeWitt (1988–89)	Countess Vaughn
Eva Rawley (1989–90)	Toukie A. Smith
Julian C. Barlow (1989–90)	Paul Winfield
Dylan McMillan (1989–90)	Barry Sobel
Travis Filmore (1989–90)	Stoney Jackson
Warren Merriwether (1989–90)	Kevin Peter Hall

Producers

Bill Boulware, Bob Myer, Bob Young

Programming History

116 episodes
NBC

September 1985–March 1986	Saturday 9:30–10:00
April 1986–June 1986	Saturday 9:30–10:00
June 1986–May 1987	Saturday 8:30–9:00
June 1987–July 1987	Saturday 8:00–8:30
July 1987–September 1988	Saturday 8:30–9:00
October 1988–July 1989	Saturday 8:00–8:30
September 1989–February 1990	Saturday 8:30–9:00
April 1990–May 1990	Sunday 8:30–9:00
June 1990–July 1990	Saturday 8:00–8:30

Further Reading

Collier, Aldore, "Jackee Harry: How her TV Role Is Ruining her Love Life," *Ebony* (June 1987)

Dates, Jannette, and William Barlow, editors, *Split Images: African Americans in the Mass Media,* Washington, D.C.: Howard University Press, 1990

Randolph, Laura B., "Who Is Toukie Smith and Why Are People Talking about Her?," *Ebony* (May 1990)

Sanders, Richard, "After Mopping up as the Maid on *The Jeffersons*, Marla Gibbs Polishes her Image as the Star of *227*," *People Weekly* (November 25, 1985)

"Thurston Sees *227* Sales Growth with Affiliates Staying with Sitcoms," *Television-Radio Age* (July 24, 1989)

Whitaker, Charles, "Brassy, Sassy Jackee Is on a Roll," *Ebony* (January 1988)

U

Uncounted Enemy: A Vietnam Deception, The

U.S. Documentary

The *CBS Reports* documentary "The Uncounted Enemy: A Vietnam Deception," which aired on January 23, 1982, engendered one of the most bitter controversies in television history. The 90-minute program spawned a three-year ordeal for CBS, including disclosures by *TV Guide* that the report violated CBS News standards, an internal investigation by Burton (Bud) Benjamin, and an unprecedented $120 million libel suit by retired U.S. Army General William C. Westmoreland.

Westmoreland sued producer George Crile III, correspondent Mike Wallace, and others for alleging that Westmoreland participated in a conspiracy to defraud the American public about progress in the Vietnam War. The suit was dropped, however, before reaching the jury, with CBS merely issuing a statement saying the network never meant to impugn the general's patriotism.

CBS subsequently lost its libel insurance. The controversy also had implications for the debate over repeal of the financial interest and syndication rules. CBS chair Tom Wyman twice admonished his news division in 1984 for hindering broadcast deregulation. In part as a result of the controversies, fewer CBS documentaries were produced than ever before.

The lawsuit generated an abundance of literature, as well as soul-searching among broadcast journalists regarding ethics, First Amendment protection, libel law, and the politicization of TV news. Unlike the case for a similar, but lesser, controversy over *The Selling of the Pentagon*, "The Uncounted Enemy" failed to uplift TV news and instead contributed to the documentary's decline.

The program states that the 1968 Tet Offensive stunned Americans because U.S. military leaders in South Vietnam arbitrarily discounted the size of the enemy that was reflected in Central Intelligence Agency (CIA) reports. Former intelligence officers testify that field command reports withheld information from Washington and the press, ostensibly under orders from higher military command, and that a 300,000-troop ceiling was imposed on official reports to reflect favorable progress in the war. This manipulation of information was characterized as a "conspiracy" in print ads and at the top of the broadcast.

The first part of the documentary chronicles the CIA-MACV (Military Assistance Command, Vietnam) dispute over intelligence estimates. Part 2 reports that prior to Tet, infiltration down the Ho Chi Minh Trail exceeded 20,000 North Vietnamese per month. Again, the report alleges, these figures were discounted. The last segment charges that intelligence officers purged government databases to hide the deception.

The most provocative scene features correspondent Mike Wallace interviewing Westmoreland. An extreme close-up captures the general trying to wet his dry mouth as Wallace fires questions. The visual image in conjunction with other program material suggests that Westmoreland engineered a conspiracy, and, as viewers can see, he appears guilty. Westmoreland publicly rebuked these claims and demanded 45 minutes of open airtime to reject "The Uncounted Enemy" assertions. CBS refused the request.

In the spring of 1982, a CBS News employee disclosed to *TV Guide* that producer George Crile had violated network standards in making the program. The May 24 story by Sally Bedell and Don Kowet, "Anatomy of a Smear: How CBS News Broke the Rules and 'Got' Gen. Westmoreland," stipulated how the production strayed from accepted practices. Significantly, *TV Guide* never disputed the premise of the program. The writers attacked the journalistic process, pointing out, for instance, that Crile screened interviews of other participants for one witness and then shot a second interview, that he avoided interviewing witnesses who would counter his thesis, and that answers to various questions were edited into a single response.

CBS News president Van Gordon Sauter, who was new to his position, appointed veteran documentary producer Burton Benjamin to investigate. His analysis, known as the "Benjamin Report," corroborated *TV Guide*'s claims.

According to a report in *The American Lawyer*, several conservative organizations, such as the Richard Mellon Scaife Foundation, the Olin Foundation, and the Smith Richardson Foundation, financed Westmoreland's suit in September 1982. One goal of the Smith Richardson Foundation was to kill *CBS Reports*. Another was to turn back the 1964 *New York Times v. Sullivan* rule, which required that public officials prove "actual malice" to win a libel judgment. The *Westmoreland* case went to trial two years later and was discontinued in February 1985.

One of the significant by-products of the controversy is the "Benjamin Report." Benjamin's effort remains widely respected within the journalistic community for revealing unfair aspects of the program's production. Some observers, however, have criticized the report for having a "prosecutorial tone," for failing to come to terms with the producer's purpose, and for measuring fairness and balance by a mathematical scale. In his conclusion, Benjamin acknowledges the enduring value of the documentary: "To get a group of high-ranking military men and former Central Intelligence Agents to say that this is what happened was an achievement of no small dimension." The production flaws, however, overshadowed the program's positive attributes.

While the legal controversy raged in the press, there was much debate about whether the libel suit and the internal investigation by CBS News would have a chilling effect on journalism and lead to self-censorship. Most journalists believed that reporting would continue unabated and that the self-scrutiny and review of procedures caused by the event were good for the profession. At corporate-executive levels, however, the impact of the Westmoreland lawsuit was profound.

In 1993 the General Motors Corporation sued NBC over a report on *Dateline*, in which a GM truck was rigged to burst into flames upon impact in a demonstration crash. NBC corporate management fired the news director and producer and issued a public apology in exchange for GM dropping the suit. In 1995 Philip Morris sued Capital Cities/ABC for an unprecedented $10 billion over a report on the newsmagazine *Day One* that alleged that the tobacco company manipulated cigarette nicotine levels. The case was settled without trial. And later in 1995, the Brown and Williamson tobacco company threatened to sue CBS if they aired an interview on *60 Minutes* in which a former Brown and Williamson employee testified that it was widely known in the industry that cigarettes were a delivery device for nicotine and that smoking was addictive. CBS pulled the segment rather than risk a lawsuit. Eventually, the information became public, which contributed to the landmark settlement between the tobacco industry and various governments. Even though CBS had a scoop that proved to be factual, the network censored itself to avoid a lawsuit. The controversy that enveloped "The Uncounted Enemy" demonstrated that wealthy corporations, political foundations, or individuals can use the threat or action of litigation to chill the press and prevent a full airing of matters of public interest.

"The Uncounted Enemy" helps explain an aspect of Tet and gives voice to intelligence officers who were silenced during the war. But the program tries unsuccessfully to resolve a complex subject in 90 minutes, and it fails to convey the context of national self-delusion presented in lengthier treatments, such as the 13-hour PBS series, *Vietnam: A Television History* (1983) or Neil Sheehan's book *A Bright Shining Lie: John Paul Vann and America in Vietnam* (1988). CIA analyst George Allen, who was interviewed in "The Uncounted Enemy," explained in a letter to Burton Benjamin in June 1982 his belief that the intelligence dispute was "a symptom of a larger and more fundamental problem, i.e., the tendency of every American administration from Eisenhower through Nixon toward self-delusion with respect to Indochina." Allen reasserted his support for "The Uncounted Enemy" as a valid illustration of the larger issue and subsequently used the program as a case study in politicized intelligence.

Although many works disprove the conspiracy charge, General Westmoreland did subsequently acknowledge the potential significance of a public disclosure of intelligence information prior to Tet. Appearing on the NBC *Today* show in May 1993, Westmoreland explained: "It was the surprise element, I think, that did the damage. And if I had to do it over again, I would have called a press conference and made known to the media the intelligence we had."

Many of the individuals who appeared in or produced the documentary have subsequently died: Col. Gains Hawkins (1987), Sam Adams (1988), Burton Benjamin (1988), Roger Colloff (1992), George Carver Jr. (1994), Lt. Gen. Daniel Graham (1996). George Crile III continues to produce stories for CBS News, including the premiere segment of *60 Minutes II*.

TOM MASCARO

See also **Columbia Broadcasting System; Documentary; Stanton, Frank; Wallace, Mike**

Correspondent
Mike Wallace

Producer
George Crile III

Programming History
CBS
January 23, 1982

Further Reading

Bedell, Sally, and Dan Kowet, "Anatomy of a Smear: How CBS News Broke the Rules and 'Got' Gen. Westmoreland," *TV Guide* (May 24, 1982)
Benjamin, Burton, *Fair Play,* New York: Harper and Row, 1988
The CBS Benjamin Report, Washington, D.C.: Media Institute, 1984
Loftus, Jack, "Goldwater Points a Loaded Gun at CBS," *Variety* (August 25, 1982)
Schneir, Walter, and Miriam Schneir, "The Right's Attack on the Press," *The Nation* (March 30, 1985)
Vietnam: A Documentary Collection—Westmoreland v. CBS (microfiche), New York: Clearwater, 1985.

Undercurrents

British Video Magazine

Undercurrents is a British video magazine specializing in alternative news stories that mainstream television news programs tend to ignore, marginalize, or cover in a one-sided fashion. *Undercurrents* emerged as an outlet for material being filmed by Thomas Harding and colleagues at Small World Productions, a nonprofit media production company specializing in environmental and campaigning videos shot on minimal budgets using camcorders. Frustrated with trying to produce material acceptable to mainstream television, Harding and colleague Jamie Hartzell invested in a VHS edit suite and set about editing material from more than 100 videotapes shot by themselves and other video activists, covering a variety of environmental and social justice protests.

The first issue of *Undercurrents,* published in April 1994, featured "ninety minutes of high energy, passionate, in-yer-face action. Not what you see on television." (Harding, 1997). Each issue of *Undercurrents* contained a range of items, on different topics and of varied duration. A summary of the items in the first issue gives a good idea of the nature of the material:

"Street Stories" was a ten-minute round-up of stories not covered on mainstream television; "Totally Out of Order" a 16-minute, four-part film on the new Criminal Justice Act and its likely effect on the activities of protesters, ravers, travelers, and squatters; "The Drainer" was a three-minute film about an unemployed man who supplements his benefit by retrieving coins from gutters; "When Seals Take Control" presented a light-hearted look at media coverage of direct action, lasting six minutes; "Bash the Baddy" was a seven-minute film of an Oxford Councillor being interrogated by an environmental activist on the subject of traffic in Oxford city center; and the longest item was "You've Got To Be Choking," a two-part award-winning film, lasting 35 minutes, charting the progress of the campaign to stop the building of a link road to the M11 motorway in northeast London.

The variety and eclecticism of the contents of each video was intentional, a deliberate departure from the formulaic predictability of mainstream news and current affairs where the agenda is predetermined and where stories are dealt with in a conventional manner.

Undercurrents.
Photo courtesy of CBC Television

Paul O'Connor, a video activist involved with *Undercurrents* from the beginning, was responsible for editing issue 6 in 1996, a process lasting five months that he describes in Thomas Harding's *The Video Activist Handbook* (1997). After deciding on a list of possible issues to be covered and recruiting activists to film and edit them (a process that lasted from July to October) O'Connor started putting all the material together for the finished video: "I start seeing the advantage of having a wide diversity of videos. They complement each other—the rough with the smooth, the long with the short, the humorous with the serious—and I can see that people are making a change in all walks of life, in many different ways" (Harding, 1997). By the end of November, 500 copies of issue 6 had been duplicated, to be sent out to subscribers, the majority of copies of *Undercurrents* being sold by mail order rather than through retail outlets, resulting in a higher percentage of the takings going to the producers. While only 1,000 copies of each issue were duplicated, Harding estimates the total audience to be over 40,000, including group screenings and tapes being passed on to friends.

Undercurrents is not only a video magazine but an organization responsible for training activists from all over Britain in the use of camcorders in their campaigns. It has also helped to set up two other video magazines in the Netherlands and in Australia. Along with other oppositional groups, *Undercurrents* has clearly benefited from the "camcorder revolution" of the 1990s, with the inexpensive, lightweight domestic camcorder being adopted for a range of alternative, political purposes. Given the conservatism of the mainstream news media, organizations like *Undercurrents* have exploited the opportunity to provide an alternative viewpoint on contemporary social issues, especially the environment and global capitalism. While the broadcasting corporations have a stranglehold over most news reporting, the video magazine offers an alternative form of news distribution, providing an opportunity to bypass the conventional news media and make available alternative and oppositional views on important topics.

Issue 10 of *Undercurrents* was published in April 1999 and included an item on the new Labour government's arms sales to repressive regimes, showing that *Undercurrents* was not restricted to targeting the Conservative government whose policies had encouraged the growth of video activism. Since issue 10, publication of the video magazine has been discontinued, but *Undercurrents* continues its alternative news activities via its website. The rise of demonstrations against global capitalism has shown that there is still a need for an alternative news organization, and in December 2001 *Undercurrents* released a video on "Globalization and the Media," exploring mainstream reporting of "the increasing Corporate control of the world" (*Undercurrents* website press release, December 6, 2001). The video featured activist footage from the G8 protests in Genoa, links between Britain's main commercial broadcaster and Shell Oil, and the ways in which media activists are using the Internet to bypass mainstream media. Indeed the Internet may prove to be the main outlet for *Undercurrents* as an alternative news agency in the 21st century.

LEZ COOKE

See also **Activist Television; Camcorder**

Further Reading

Harding, Thomas, *The Video Activist,* London and Chicago: Pluto Press, 1997
Hattenstone, Simon, "Candid Camcorder," *The Guardian* (December 5, 1994)
Moreton, Cole, "'Resistance Culture' Sets Up News Network," *Independent on Sunday* (February 5, 1995)
O'Connor, Paul, "Undercurrents or 'The News You Don't See on the News,'" *Filmwaves* 13 (autumn 2000)

Unions/Guilds

The television industry is one of the more highly organized, or, unionized, in the United States. Qualified candidates are numerous for a few available jobs. Producing and airing programs lend themselves to odd working hours, location shoots, holidays, weekends, long working days, and often short-term temporary employment. Such conditions would normally permit management to exploit employees by offering low wages, few fringe benefits, and no job security to employees. Historically, unionization in U.S. industry began to eliminate such exploitation, and the television industry is no exception.

Although some of the unions in television and film today grew out of earlier creative guilds like Actors' Equity and the Dramatists' Guild, the primary reference point for effective unionization of the industry was passage of the National Labor Relations Act in 1935. Known as the Wagner Act, in honor of its congressional sponsor, it was a major piece of "New Deal" legislation passed during the Franklin D. Roosevelt administration. The NLRA made it legal for workers to form unions. It set up the National Labor Relations Board as an arm of government to enforce it. Unions could bargain for wages and working conditions.

Today, unions and guilds representing employees in television and film bargain with networks and production companies for minimum wage scales, pension funds, and other fringe benefits. A major bargaining issue in recent years between producers and creative guilds has been residuals—royalties paid to actors, directors, and writers for airing programs originally and in subsequent replays and reruns and for cassette sales and rentals.

The degree of unionization in television today varies considerably by geographic region. Television stations and cable systems in most of the larger media markets, like New York City, Los Angeles, and Chicago, are almost totally unionized. Local television stations and cable systems in small markets, however, may not be unionized. Networks and major production companies are all unionized, whereas small independent producers tend not to be.

The term "union" in the television industry describes labor organizations that represent technical personnel and are referred to as "below-the-line" unions. The term "guild" describes labor organizations that represent creative personnel, and are referred to as "above-the-line" unions. These designations result from their actual position on the pages of production budgets in which "creative" and "technical" costs are divided by a line. In a typical television show production budget, below-the-line costs are fixed, whereas above-the-line costs are flexible. For example, the budget for a one-hour drama enters a camera operator's wages below the line because there is a standard wage scale in the union contract with management for camera operators shooting a one-hour drama. The salary for the show's leading actor is entered above the line because there is considerable disparity between a relatively unknown actor's salary and the salary of a major TV star.

Four very large unions represent most below-the-line technical personnel in television and cable today: the National Association of Broadcast Employees and Technicians (NABET), the International Brotherhood of Electrical Workers (IBEW), the International Alliance of Theatrical and Stage Employees (IATSE), and the Communication Workers of America (CWA).

NABET began as a union of engineers at NBC in 1933. It is the only union among the four devoted exclusively to representing workers employed in broadcasting, film, recording, and allied industries. Today it is the exclusive bargaining agent for below-the-line personnel at the ABC, NBC, FOX, and PBS networks, as well as at many local independent television stations in large cities.

IBEW is one of the largest unions in the United States and represents workers in construction, manufacturing, and utilities, in addition to below-the-line personnel at CBS, Disney, independent TV stations, and some cable companies.

IATSE was founded in New York City in 1893 as the National Alliance of Theatrical StageEmployees. Today, it is organized primarily along craft lines with over 800 local chapters, each representing specialized occupations within the union's overall national membership of more than 70,000 workers. In the Los Angeles area alone, some of the occupations represented by separate local chapters are: set designers-model makers, illustrators-matte artists, costumers, makeup artists-hair stylists, film editors, film cartoonists, script supervisors, film set painters, studio electricians, stagehands, and story analysts. IATSE represents almost every below-the-line occupation at the major production studios and many independent production companies that produce shows on film for theaters, television, and cable.

CWA, historically, has represented workers in the telephone industry and other common carrier fields. In recent years, it has increased its membership and influence in the cable television industry, and represents below-the-line personnel in cable multiple system operators, cable networks, and local cable companies.

There are many above-the-line guilds representing creative workers in television. The major guilds with the most influence are: the American Federation of Television and Radio Artists (AFTRA), the Screen Actors Guild (SAG), the Directors Guild of America (DGA), the Writers Guild of America (East and West; known as WGAE and WGAW), and the American Federation of Musicians (AFM). Most members of these unions do not work full time or regularly, and those who do almost never work for minimum wage scale.

AFTRA grew out of the American Federation of Radio Artists, founded in 1937. It added television performers and "television" to its name in 1952. Today, AFTRA represents over 70,000 performers nationally who appear on television or cable programs that are produced on videotape or broadcast live. In addition to actors, this number includes many performers such as announcers, dancers, newspersons, sportscasters, game show emcees, talk show hosts, stunt people, and sound effects artists. AFTRA has about 30,000 members in its Los Angeles area alone, a small percentage of whom earn their living primarily from performing on radio, cable, or television. Most television performers work other jobs to support themselves while seeking occasional temporary employment as a television, cable, film, or radio performer.

SAG represents performers who appear on television or cable programs produced on film. These include feature films produced for theatrical release and later aired on television in addition to film programs produced expressly for television exhibition. Related to SAG is the Screen Extras Guild (SEG), which represents bit performers who appear in programs produced on film. Most celebrities and successful performers belong to both AFTRA and SAG, so they are not limited from performing in all three production modes of live, tape, or film.

The DGA was organized originally in 1936 as the Screen Directors Guild by a group of famous film directors, including King Vidor and Howard Hawks. Television directors were admitted in 1950, and the name Directors Guild of America was adopted in 1960. Today, it has a West chapter in Hollywood and an East chapter in New York City. It represents directors, associate directors, unit production managers, stage managers, and production assistants in television, and directors, assistant directors, and stage managers in film. Both chapters work cooperatively to represent their members regardless of the location of a production or shoot. The East chapter, for example, represents most play directors, and the West chapter represents most film directors.

The WGAE (East) and the WGAW (West) are incorporated separately because of differing laws of incorporation in New York and California. WGAE is located in New York City, and WGAW is located in Los Angeles. Though incorporated separately, they function as a single organization that represents the interests of over 8,000 members nationally, although the WGAE has only half the membership of the WGAW, and has a significant number of playwrights among its membership, whereas WGAW is dominated by screenwriters. In 1962 WGA also joined with sister guilds in Great Britain, Canada, Australia, and New Zealand to form an international union alliance among these English-speaking nations.

The AFM began in 1896 and represents musicians, including vocalists and instrumentalists who perform live or on film, tape, record, or disk. It has local chapters throughout the United States that bargain with local television stations and cable systems in geographic regions they cover.

With computers, satellites, and digital technology globalizing electronic communication, unions and guilds will continue to add new occupational groups to their membership and become increasingly more international in scope. These new technologies have also led to a wide range of new issues for the groups. Rights and ownership have been complicated by the ease of digital copying. Payment for new forms of distribution, such as DVD collections of television series, is central to negotiations by writers and directors. Original programs developed for cable television are sometimes compensated at rates that differ from network broadcast, and in other situations programs written and produced for broadcast are moved by owners to cable outlets in the strategy of "repurposing." All these developments have made the work of guild leaders and representatives more complicated in their efforts to protect the interests of members. In a democratic society like the United States, viable unions remain necessary to provide oversight of big business and management policies and practices toward their employees, and these tasks will undoubtedly become even more complex in the future.

ROBERT G. FINNEY

Further Reading

Bielby, William T., and Denise D. Bielby, *The 1989 Hollywood Writers' Report: Unequal Access, Unequal Pay,* West Hollywood, California: Writers Guild of America, West, 1989

Block, Alex Ben, "Hollywood's Labor Pains; Lower Revenues and Rising Costs Are Spawning a Tough New Attitude to Unions by TV Networks and Producers," *Channels: The Business of Communications* (July–August 1988)

Directors Guild of America, *Constitution and Bylaws,* Hollywood, California, 1991

The Journal, Los Angeles, California: Writers Guild of America, 1982

The Journal of the Producers Guild of America, Beverly Hills, California, 1982–

Prindle, David F., *The Politics of Glamour: Ideology and Democracy in the Screen Actors Guild,* Madison: University of Wisconsin Press, 1988

Schwartz, Nancy Lynn, *The Hollywood Writers' Wars,* New York: Knopf, 1982

The Story of the Screen Actors Guild, Hollywood, California: Screen Actors Guild, 1966

United Kingdom. *See* British Television; Ireland; Scotland; Wales

---

United States Congress and Television

The first effort to link the U.S. Congress and broadcasting occurred in 1922, when Representative Vincent M. Brennan introduced a bill to allow radio coverage of U.S. House of Representatives proceedings. The bill failed, and not until the late 1940s was the idea revived. Television, having arrived as a mass medium by then, was allowed in 1948 to cover hearings of the Senate Armed Services Committee. Since few Americans had television receivers in 1948, it was not until the early 1950s that televised congressional hearings generated any viewer interest.

Two televised Senate hearings during the 1950s caused a sensation. Hearings conducted by the Senate Special Committee to Investigate Organized Crime in Interstate Commerce brought the faces and words of notorious mobsters into millions of U.S. homes via coast-to-coast network television. A short time later, Americans once more were drawn to their television screens to watch the hearings of a Senate Committee on Government Operations subcommittee investigating alleged communist infiltration of the U.S. Armed Forces. The hearings were better known as the Army-McCarthy Hearings, identified closely with subcommittee chairperson, Senator Joseph McCarthy.

Two decades later, in 1973, the Senate Select Committee on Presidential Campaign Activities conducted what became known as the Watergate Hearings. Evidence of misdeeds by President Richard Nixon led the next year to House Judiciary Committee hearings on articles of presidential impeachment. Nearly all public deliberations of both of these committees were televised gavel-to-gavel.

Serious attention to allowing television coverage of actual congressional floor proceedings arose once more with the 1973 formation of the Joint Committee on Congressional Operations. The committee's charge was to examine means by which Congress could better communicate with the American public. The committee's subsequent recommendation that television be allowed in the U.S. House and Senate chambers met with resistance in the latter body, but House members seemed more receptive. As a result, House Speaker Thomas (Tip) O'Neill Jr. ordered testing of a House television system to begin in March 1977. Remote-controlled cameras placed at strategic locations in the House chamber were to be used so as not to disrupt House decorum. The television test proved a success. However, full implementation of House television

Live television coverage of the 104th U.S. Congress.
Photo courtesy of C-SPAN

coverage awaited a decision from the House Rules Committee on who would finally control the television cameras—the House itself or television networks, who would remain independent of House authority. The Rules Committee decision that the House would best be served by retaining such control was approved by a vote of 235-to-150 in June 1978. Nine months later, on March 19, 1979, the House television system was fully in place, and live telecasts of House floor deliberations began.

Television from the U.S. Senate chambers would have to wait still longer. Although a number of senators supported the idea of Senate television, a powerful block opposed it. Senate television opponents saw cameras as disruptive to Senate decorum and incapable of presenting a favorable image of Senate debate to the American public. Senate television proponents nonetheless prevailed, and the Senate Rules Commit-

tee recommendation to allow testing of a Senate chamber television system was approved by a vote of 67-to-21 on February 27, 1986. The tests were satisfactory enough to convince members of the Senate to vote on July 29, 1986, to allow gavel-to-gavel coverage of Senate floor proceedings.

Both the U.S. Senate and House include rules for television coverage among their general procedural rules for committee and chamber conduct. Concern over protecting witness privacy and due-process rights led the Senate to allow individual committee chairpersons to adopt television rules most appropriate for their particular committee. Such rules generally require that television coverage be prohibited at the request of a committee witness; that television cameras, lights, and microphones be unobtrusive; that television personnel conduct themselves in an orderly fashion inside the hearing room; and that no commercial sponsorship of committee hearings be allowed. House rules are similar to Senate rules regarding the conduct of televised hearings. However, House rules require that television be allowed to cover House committee hearings only upon a majority vote of the committee members.

The manner by which House floor proceedings are televised is entirely under the authority of the speaker of the House. The speaker decides when and if proceedings will be televised and who will be authorized to distribute the television signals to the public. House rules originally required that television cameras focus only on House members as they spoke from lecterns or in the well of the House. Cameras were not to pan the House chamber to show what oftentimes was a sea of empty chairs. Rules prohibiting such panning were abolished by the speaker in 1984.

Senate rules for televising chamber proceedings fall under the authority of the Senate Rules and Administration Committee. Most rules are similar to those in the House, save for the prohibition on panning the chamber that remains in effect (except during roll-call votes) for the Senate chamber.

When television coverage of their respective chambers was under discussion, few if any members of Congress anticipated the role television might play in presidential impeachment. Nonetheless, from late 1998, when the U.S. House voted to impeach President Bill Clinton, until early 1999, when the U.S. Senate tried the president, television provided unprecedented, nearly gavel-to-gavel coverage of these momentous events. Some precedent had been set in 1974, when U.S. House and Senate leadership had prepared ground rules for television's presence during possible impeachment proceedings against President Nixon. At that time, rules for how television would cover events as they unfolded in both the House and Senate chambers without disturbing decorum or damaging the president's due process rights had been determined. Congressional leaders had only to update slightly these rules for their application to President Clinton's impeachment and trial. Congressional participants joined with millions of worldwide viewers at the trial's conclusion in near-universal praise of the manner by which television had fulfilled its crucial role during such a historic occasion.

Whether television has improved public debate in either the House or Senate is uncertain. Some observers argue that television has led to more grandstanding and contentious rhetoric on the House floor, whereas Senate debate appears more disciplined and more substantive. However, there is general agreement that persons who view televised House and Senate proceedings are introduced to a vast array of issues and debates unimagined before television arrived.

RON GARAY

See also **Parliament and Television; Political Processes and Television; U.S. Presidency and Television; Watergate**

Further Reading

Blanchard, Robert, editor, *Congress and the News Media,* New York: Hastings House, 1974

Congressional Research Service, *Congress and Mass Communications: An Institutional Perspective,* prepared for the Joint Committee on Congressional Operations, 93rd Congress, Second Session, 1974

Crain, W. Mark, and Brian Goff, *Televised Legislatures: Political Information Technology and Public Choice,* Boston: Kluwer Academic Publishers, 1988

Garay, Ronald, *Congressional Television: A Legislative History,* Westport, Connecticut: Greenwood, 1984

Garay, Ronald, "Televising Presidential Impeachment: The U.S. Congress Sets the Stage," *Historical Journal of Film, Radio, and Television* (March 1999)

Graber, Doris, *Mass Media and American Politics,* 5th edition, Washington, D.C.: CQ Press, 1997

Hess, Stephen, *Live from Capitol Hill! Studies of Congress and the Media,* Washington, D.C.: Brookings Institution, 1991

Krasno, Jonathan S., and Daniel E. Seltz, *Buying Time: Television Advertising and the 1998 Congressional Elections,* New York: Brennan Center for Justice, 2000

Schlesinger, Arthur M., and Roger Bruns, editors, *Congress Investigates: A Documented History, 1792–1974,* New York: Chelsea House, 1975

Shuman, Samuel I., *Broadcasting and Telecasting of Judicial and Legislative Proceedings,* Ann Arbor: University of Michigan Legislative Research Center, 1956

Straight, Michael, *Trial by Television,* Boston: Beacon Press, 1954

Summers, Robert E., "The Role of Congressional Broadcasting in a Democratic Society," Ph.D. diss., Ohio State University, 1955

Twentieth Century Fund Task Force on Broadcasting and the Legislature, *Openly Arrived At,* New York: Twentieth Century Fund, 1974

U.S. Congress, Joint Committee on Congressional Operations, *A Clear Message to the People,* 94th Congress, First Session, 1975

U.S. Congress, Joint Committee on Congressional Operations, *Broadcasting House and Senate Proceedings,* 93rd Congress, Second Session, 1974

U.S. Congress, Joint Committee on Congressional Operations, *Congress and Mass Communications,* 93rd Congress, Second Session, 1974

U.S. House of Representatives, House Committee on Rules, *Broadcasting the Proceedings of the House,* 95th Congress, Second Session, 1978

United States Presidency and Television (Historical Overview)

Ten dates, some momentous, some merely curious, tell the story of presidential television. In its own way, each date sheds light on the complex relationship between the U.S. presidency and the American television industry. Over the years, that relationship has grown complex and tempestuous (virtually every president from Harry Truman through Bill Clinton has become disaffected with the nation's press). More than anything else, however, this relationship has been symbiotic—the president and the press now depend upon one another for sustenance. Ten dates explain why.

September 23, 1952: Vice Presidential Candidate Richard Nixon's "Checkers" Speech

Oddly, it was Richard Nixon, who was pilloried by the press throughout his career, who discovered the political power of the new medium of television. Imaginatively, aggressively, in the "Checkers" speech, vice presidential candidate Nixon used television in a way it had never been used before, in order to lay out his personal finances and his cultural virtues and, hence, to save his place on the Republican national team (and, ultimately, his place in the American political pantheon). That same year, 1952, also witnessed the first televised coverage of a national party convention and the first TV advertisements. However, it was Nixon's famous speech that transformed the political environment from party-based to candidate-controlled. By using television as he did—personally, candidly, visually (his wife Pat sat demurely next to him during the broadcast)—Nixon single-handedly created a new political style.

January 19, 1955: President Dwight Eisenhower's Press Conference

When he agreed to let the television cameras into the White House for the first time in U.S. history, Dwight Eisenhower changed the presidency in fundamental ways. Until that point, the White House press corps had been a cozy outfit but very much on the president's leash or, at least, the lesser partner in a complex politi-cal arrangement. Television changed that. The hue and cry let out by the deans of U.S. print journalism proved it, as did television's growing popularity among the American people. More proof awaited. It was not long after Eisenhower opened the doors to television that U.S. presidents found themselves arranging their workdays around network schedules. To have a political announcement receive top billing on the nightly news, that announcement had to be made by 2:00 P.M. Eastern Standard Time. If the news to be shared was bad news, the White House would choose the slowest news days, Saturday and Sunday, to make the announcement. These may seem like small expediencies, but they presaged a fundamental shift of power in Washington, D.C. After Eisenhower, television was no longer a novelty but a central premise in all political logic.

January 25, 1961: President John F. Kennedy's Press Conference

Before Ronald Reagan and Bill Clinton, there was John F. Kennedy. No U.S. president has better understood television than these three. By holding the first live press conference in the nation's history, Kennedy showed that boldness and amiability may trump all suits in an age of television. In his short time in office, Kennedy also showed that all communication, even presidential communication, must be relational; that the substance of one's remarks is irrelevant if one cannot say it effortlessly; and that being "online" and "in real time" bring a special energy to politics. Prescient as he was, Kennedy would therefore not have been surprised to learn that 50 percent of the American people now find television news more believable and more attractive than print news (which attracts a mere quarter of the populace). Kennedy would also not be surprised at the advent of CNN, the all-news, all-day channel, nor would he be surprised to learn that C-SPAN (Congress's cable channel) has also become popular in certain quarters. Being the innovator he was, Kennedy fundamentally changed the temporal dimensions of U.S. politics. Forever more, his successors would be required to perform the presidency during each moment of each day they held office.

February 27, 1968: CBS Anchorman Walter Cronkite's Evaluation of the Vietnam War

President Lyndon Johnson, we are told, knew he had lost the Vietnam War when, during an evening documentary, CBS news anchor Walter Cronkite declared the conflict a "quagmire." To be sure, Cronkite's hard-hitting special was nuanced and respectful of the presidency, but it also brought proof to the nation's living rooms that the president's resolve had been misplaced. Cronkite's broadcast was therefore an important step in altering the power balance between the White House and the networks. CBS's Dan Rather continued that trend, facing-down Nixon during one cantankerous press conference and, later, George H.W. Bush during an interview about the Iran-Contra scandal. Sam Donaldson and Ted Koppel of ABC News also took special delight in deflating political egos, as did CNN's Peter Arnett who frustrated George Bush Sr.'s efforts during the Gulf War by continuing to broadcast from the Baghdad Hilton even as U.S. bombs were falling on that city. Some attribute the press's new aggressiveness to their somnolence during the Watergate affair, but it could also be credited to the replacement of politics' old barter system, which featured material costs and rewards, by an entertainment-based celebrity system featuring personal achievements and rivalries. In this latter system, it is every person for him- or herself, the president included.

November 25, 1968: The Inauguration of the White House's Office of Communication

One of Nixon's first acts as president was to appoint Herb Klein to oversee a newly enlarged unit in the White House that would coordinate all out-going communications. This act, perhaps more than any other, signaled that the new president would be an active player in the persuasion game and that he would deal with the mass media in increasingly innovative ways. Perhaps Nixon sensed the trends scholars would later unearth: (1) that citizens who see a political speech in person react far more favorably than those who see it through television reporters' eyes; (2) that the average presidential "sound bite" has been reduced to 9.8 seconds in the average nightly news story; and (3) that negative news stories about the president have increased over time. This is the bad news for presidents in the age of television. The good news is that 97 percent of CBS's nightly newscasts feature the president (usually as the lead story), and 20 percent of a typical broadcast will be devoted to comings and goings in the White House. In other words, the president is the fulcrum around which television reportage pivots; hence, he is well advised to monitor carefully the information he releases (or refuses to release).

September 17, 1976: President Gerald Ford's Pasadena Speech

Neither President Gerald Ford's address nor the occasion was memorable. His was a standard stump speech, this time at the annual reception of the Pasadena Golden Circle. However, the speech's sheer banality signaled its importance; Ford spoke to the group not because he needed to convince them of something but because their predictable, on-camera applause would certify his broader worthiness to the American people. Ford gave some 200 speeches of this sort during the 1976 campaign. Unlike President Truman, who spoke to all-comers on the village green during the 1948 election, Ford addressed such "closed" audiences almost exclusively during his re-election run. In addition, Ford and his successors spoke in ritualistic settings 40 percent of the time, since bunting, too, photographs well. The constant need for media coverage has thereby turned the modern president into a continual campaigner and the White House into a kind of national booking agency. It is little wonder, then, that the traditional press conference, with its contentiousness and unpredictability, has become rare.

January 20, 1981: The Inauguration of President Ronald Reagan

Ronald Reagan grew up with television, and television with him. By the time he became president, both had matured. Reagan brought to the camera what the camera most prized: a strong visual presence and a vaunted affability. He was the rare kind of politician who even liked his detractors, and television made those feelings obvious. Reagan also had the ability to concretize the most abstract of issues—deficits, territorial jurisdictions, nuclear stalemates. By finding the essential narrative in these matters, and then by humanizing those narratives, he produced his own unique style. Television favors that style, since TV is, after all, the most intimate of the mass media, with its ability to *show* emotion and to do so in tight-focus. Thus, it is not surprising that political advertising has now become Reaganesque: visual, touching, elliptical, never noisy or brash. Like Reagan, modern political advertising never extends its stay; typically, it says in 30 seconds all that needs to be said and then it says no more.

January 16, 1991: President George Bush Sr.'s Declaration of the Gulf War

From the beginning, President George H.W. Bush was determined not to turn the Gulf War into another Vietnam. His military commanders shared that determination. But what, exactly, are the lessons of Vietnam? From the standpoint of television they are these: (1) make the conflict an air war, not a ground war, because ground soldiers can be interviewed on camera; (2) make it a short war, not a long war, because television has a short attention span; and (3) make it a technical war, not a political war, because Americans love the technocratic and fall out with one another over ends and means. Blessedly, the Gulf War was short, and, via a complex network of satellite feeds, it entertained the American people with its visuals: SCUD missiles exploding, oil-slicks spreading, yellow ribbons flying. Iraq's Saddam Hussein fought back, on television, in avuncular poses with captured innocents and by staying tuned to CNN from his bunker. The Gulf War therefore marked an almost postmodern turn in the history of warfare.

October 25, 1992: The Richmond, Virginia, Presidential Candidates' Debate

Several trends converged to produce the second presidential debate of 1992. In the capital of the Old South, President George Bush Sr., Democratic Party candidate Clinton, and Reform Party candidate Ross Perot squared off with one another in the presence of 200 "average Americans," who questioned them for some 90 minutes. The debate's format, not its content, became its headline; the working press had been cut out of the proceedings, and few seemed to mourn their passing. The president of the United States face-to-face with the populace; here, surely, was democracy recaptured. The 1992 campaign expanded upon this theme, with the candidates repairing to the cozy studio (and cozy questions) of talk show host Larry King. Thereafter, they made the rounds of the morning talk-over-coffee shows. The decision to seek out these friendly climes followed from the advice politicians had been receiving for years: choose your own audience and occasion, forsake the press, emphasize your humanity. Coupled with fax machines, e-mail, cable specials, direct-mail videos, and the like, these "alternative media formats" completed a cycle whereby the president became a rhetorical entrepreneur and the nation's press an afterthought.

April 20, 1993: President Bill Clinton's MTV Appearance

Not a historic date, perhaps, but a suggestive one. It was on this date that President Clinton discussed his underwear preferences with the American people (briefs, not boxers, as it turned out). In television's increasingly postmodern world, all texts, whether serious or sophomoric, swirl together in the same discontinuous field of experience. To be sure, Clinton made his disclosure because he had been asked to do so by a member of the MTV generation, not because he felt a sudden need to purge himself. In doing so, however, Clinton exposed several rules connected to the new phenomenology of politics: (1) because of television's celebrity system, presidents are losing their distinctiveness as social actors and hence are often judged by standards formerly used to assess rock singers and movie stars; (2) because of television's sense of intimacy, the American people feel they know their presidents as persons and hence no longer feel the need for party guidance; (3) because of the medium's archly cynical worldview, those who watch politics on television are increasingly turning away from the policy sphere, years of hyperfamiliarity having finally bred contempt for politics itself.

For good and ill, then, presidential television grew apace between 1952 and the present. It began as a little-used, somewhat feared, medium of exchange and transformed itself into a central aspect of American political culture. In doing so, television changed almost everything about life in the White House. It changed what presidents do and how they do it. It changed network programming routines, launched an entire subset of the U.S. advertising industry, affected military strategy and military deployment, and affected how and why voters vote and for whom they cast their ballots. In 1992 presidential hopeful Perot tested the practical limits of this technology by buying sufficient airtime to make himself an instant candidate as well as an instantly serious candidate. History records that he failed to achieve his goal. However, if another independent candidate has sufficient money and has sufficient skill to harness television's capacity to mold public opinion, that candidate may succeed at some later time. This would add yet another important date to the history of presidential television.

RODERICK P. HART AND MARY TRIECE

See also **Clinton Impeachment Trial; Political Processes and Television; 2000 Presidential Election Coverage**

Further Reading

Allen, Craig, "'Robert Montgomery Presents': Hollywood Debut in the Eisenhower White House," *Journal of Broadcasting and Electronic Media* (fall 1991)

Benjamin, Louise M., "Broadcast Campaign Precedents from the 1924 Presidential Election," *Journal of Broadcasting and Electronic Media* (fall 1987)

Brody, Richard A., *Assessing the President: The Media, Elite Opinion, and Public Support,* Stanford, California: Stanford University Press, 1991

Devlin, L. Patrick, "Contrasts in Presidential Campaign Commercials of 1992," *American Behavioral Scientist* (November–December 1993)

Grossman, Michael B., and Martha J. Kumar, *Portraying the President: The White House and the News Media,* Baltimore, Maryland: Johns Hopkins University Press, 1981

Hart, Roderick P., *The Sound of Leadership: Presidential Communication in the Modern Age,* Chicago: University of Chicago Press, 1987

Hart, Roderick P., *Seducing America: How Television Charms the Modern Voter,* New York: Oxford University Press, 1994

Hinckley, Barbara, *The Symbolic Presidency: How Presidents Portray Themselves,* New York: Routledge, 1990

Iyengar, Shanto, and Donald Kinder, *News That Matters: Television and American Opinion,* Chicago: University of Chicago Press, 1987

Jamieson, Kathleen H., *Eloquence in an Electronic Age: The Transformation of Political Speechmaking,* New York: Oxford University Press, 1988

Jamieson, Kathleen H., and David S. Birdsell, *Presidential Debates: The Challenge of Creating an Informed Electorate,* New York: Oxford University Press, 1988

Kaid, Lynda Lee, "Political Argumentation and Violations of Audience Expectations: An Analysis of the Bush-Rather Encounter," *Journal of Broadcasting and Electronic Media* (winter 1990)

Kaid, Lynda Lee, "Television News and Presidential Campaigns: The Legitimization of Televised Political Advertising," *Social Science Quarterly* (June 1993)

Lemert, James B., "Do Televised Presidential Debates Help Inform Voters?" *Journal of Broadcasting and Electronic Media* (winter 1993)

Lowry, Dennis T., "Effects of TV 'Instant Analysis and Querulous Criticism': Following the Bush-Dukakis Debate," *Journalism Quarterly* (winter 1990)

MacNeil, Robert, "Taking Back the System," *Television Quarterly* (spring 1992)

Maltese, John A., *Spin Control: The White House Office of Communications and the Management of Presidential News,* Chapel Hill: University of North Carolina Press, 1992

Meyrowitz, Joshua, *No Sense of Place: The Impact of Electronic Media on Social Behavior,* New York: Oxford University Press, 1985

Mickelson, Sig, *From Whistle Stop to Sound Bite: Four Decades of Politics and Television,* New York: Praeger, 1989

Miller, Arthur H., and Bruce E. Gronbeck, editors, *Presidential Campaigns and American Self Images,* Boulder, Colorado: Westview Press, 1994

Morreale, Joanne, *The Presidential Campaign Film: A Critical History,* Westport, Connecticut: Praeger, 1993

Patterson, Thomas E., *Out of Order,* New York: Alfred A. Knopf, 1993

Ranney, Austin, *Channels of Power: The Impact of Television on American Politics,* New York: Basic Books, 1983

Rosenstiel, Tom, *Strange Bedfellows: How Television and the Presidential Candidates Changed American Politics,* New York: Hyperion, 1993

Sabato, Larry, *Feeding Frenzy: How Attack Journalism Has Transformed American Politics,* New York: Free Press, 1991

Smith, Carolyn D., *Presidential Press Conferences: A Critical Approach,* New York: Praeger, 1990

Smith, Craig Allen, and Kathy B. Smith, *The White House Speaks: Presidential Leadership as Persuasion,* Westport, Connecticut: Praeger, 1994

Stone, David M., *Nixon and the Politics of Public Television,* New York: Garland, 1985

Tulis, Jeffrey K., *The Rhetorical Presidency,* Princeton, New Jersey: Princeton University Press, 1987

Watson, Mary Ann, "How Kennedy Invented Political Television," *Television Quarterly* (spring 1991)

West, Darrell M., *Air Wars: Television Advertising in Election Campaigns, 1952–1992,* Washington D.C.: Congressional Quarterly, 1993; second edition as *Air Wars: Television Advertising in Election Campaigns, 1952–1996,* 1997

Universal (NBC-Universal, Vivendi Universal)

International Media Conglomerate

In 2000 the flamboyant French executive Jean-Marie Messier proudly announced the takeover of the North American beverages giant Seagram by the Paris-based conglomerate Vivendi. Through this deal, Vivendi engulfed Seagram's interests in the global media and cultural industry. The former French waterworks firm Vivendi suddenly became one of the major multimedia conglomerates in the world and a significant power in the film, television, music, publishing, advertising, telecoms, and other entertainment sectors. The most prestigious jewel in Vivendi's media crown was Universal (including film and television production and distribution, theme parks, cable television, music and book publishing activities), establishing the French (European) dream to counter the American hegemony in the film entertainment industry. Three years later, however, the dream was over and, after an intense period of controversy and rivalry, Vivendi Universal (VU) sold its major U.S. entertainment assets to General Electric, the owner of NBC.

In order to understand this turbulent and strange episode in the history of American-European media business relations, it is best to go back to the roots of Vivendi and its predecessor CGE. Founded in 1853, the Compagnie Générale des Eaux (CGE) began as a civil engineering and utilities (water) company. In the 19th and 20th centuries, CGE grew into a stable multinational player with an impressive workforce all over Europe and with interests in energy, transport, construction, and communications. In the 1980s and 1990s, CGE increased its interests in the media and communication sector with new major activities in the fields of television (mainly through the establishment in 1983 of the Canal 1 pay TV group), telecom (e.g., in Poland and Cegetel, the second largest operator in France), publishing, and advertising. In the meantime it also developed a similar acquisition policy in various other fields, such as transportation (e.g., Scandinavia, New Zealand). When in 1998 CGE finally controlled Havas, the powerful French conglomerate with major activities in the world of publishing, advertising, and news services, the group became known as Vivendi.

By 2000, when Vivendi's chief executive Jean-Marie Messier turned his attention to Seagram, Vivendi had become an ambitious and (for some observers) voracious player in various businesses, with an increased interest in the media and communications sectors. Similar to CGE/Vivendi, Seagram had moved from its original core business (beverages) into a wider area with increasing media-oriented activities. Especially since the mid-1990s, the Bronfman family (major stakeholders in Seagram) had increased its interests in several communications sectors, mainly through acquisitions in the publishing (e.g., Putnam Berkley in 1996), television, music, and film industries. A historical deal occurred in 1995, when Seagram bought MCA from Matsushita for $5.7 billion, renaming it Universal. This deal was considered at the time as a major loss for the Japanese corporation and manufacturer of audiovisual hardware brands such as Panasonic and JVC, because it had acquired MCA/Universal only

five years earlier for a record bid of $6.9 billion. Another important transaction, putting Seagram in the forefront of the global cultural industry, dealt with the $10.4 billion acquisition of Philips' software arm Polygram in 1998.

From this perspective, the 2000 deal to buy Seagram for $34 billion fully illustrated Messier's aggressive policy and megalomaniac vision. At the time of Seagram's acquisition, French and Western European news media wholeheartedly welcomed the creation of the new group, named Vivendi Universal (VU) and headquartered in Paris. Through this merger, the corporation became the world's leading music company, while it possessed the second largest film library and controlled an impressive network of theme parks. VU also increased its control in the audiovisual (film and television) production and distribution field, as well as in the publishing, advertising, Internet, and telecom sectors. At the same time, Messier decided to concentrate more fully on these communications and media activities, gradually selling off Vivendi's other (new) interests, such as those in the beverages business.

However, Messier's position ran into conflicts with major stakeholders such as Edgar Bronfman Jr., the former chairman of Seagram, while its breakneck expansion strategy soon proved to be financially disastrous. In two years time, VU had an overall debt of 19 billion euro. The Messier saga ended in the summer of 2002, when he was fired and replaced by Jean-René Fourtou. The new chief executive immediately announced that he would focus on diminishing the company's debt and remove those departments within the corporation currently losing revenue.

First, Fourtou decided to sell a major part of Vivendi Environnement, the older engineering and services arm, reducing Vivendi's part in it from 63 to 40.8 percent. Second, Vivendi Publishing, one of the major publishing corporations in the world, was put up for sale, and acquired by the French publisher Lagardère. Other publishing companies, such as Houghton Mifflin, were sold to a consortium of U.S. investors. Many other parts of the VU empire were displayed for sale, including several European cable channels such as the Italian Telepiu.

In the midst of this intense selling campaign, VU urgently needed more investment to retain its majority stake of 70 percent in Cegetel, which had grown into one of the world's leading mobile phone companies. While Fourtou first claimed that VU's American media and communications branch (Vivendi Universal Entertainment) was not for sale, he decided by April 2003 to dismantle VU's activities in the United States. After a turbulent summer of bidding and exchanges, VU entered exclusive talks with General Electric's NBC over the formation of a new company, to be called NBC Universal. The new company, with an estimated value of $43 billion, is now owned 80 percent by GE and 20 percent by VU.

This merger, which illustrates once more the intensity of globalization and concentration tendencies in today's communications sector, creates another world leader with many assets, to sit alongside Time-Warner, Viacom, Disney, and News Corp. For Fourtou, who claimed that VU might soon change its name, the deal with GE constituted an important step in consolidating VU's media and communications interests and in making it a profitable company again. For NBC, the merger created a link to one of the major film studios and its impressive library.

DANIEL BILTEREYST

See also **Media Conglomerates; Mergers and Acquisitions; National Broadcasting Company**

Further Reading

Deans, Jason, "Bronfman Readies Bid To Buy Back Universal," *The Guardian* (May 21, 2003)
Johnson, Jo, and Martine Orange, *The Man Who Tried To Buy the World. Jean-Marie Messier & Vivendi Universal,* London: Viking, 2003
Wasserstein, Bruce, *Big Deal,* New York: Warner, 1998

University Challenge

U.K. Quiz Show

University Challenge was first broadcast on Britain's ITV network in 1962. Originally made for a 13-week run, it came off the air in 1987 and was Britain's longest running television quiz show. Resurrected by its makers Granada Television for BBC 2 in 1994, it has celebrated its 40th anniversary and is still going strong.

University Challenge was conceived during the early years of U.K. commercial television. Granada had only started broadcasting in 1956, but three years later it was mired in Britain's quiz show scandal. Granada's *Twenty One* quiz paid out the largest amount of cash ever by a British TV show. Shortly thereafter, a runner-up contestant went public with the fact that he received help with his answers. In 1960 Granada submitted evidence to the Pilkington Committee on commercial television, stating "It is a mistake to think of programs as 'highbrow' or 'lowbrow' ... [these] are snob words ... never underestimate the public's intelligence—always underestimate their knowledge." Granada and ITV were ripe for an intellectual quiz, where kudos were the greatest prize.

Based on the Emmy award-winning American program *College Bowl,* the format was simple. Two teams of four university students each competed. The questions were noted for their difficulty and went from the classics and applied sciences to general knowledge. Individuals would buzz in for an initial question, the "starter for ten" (points). A successful answer would give the team a chance to answer three more themed questions, each worth five points. For these the team could confer, but must always answer through the captain, who sits third from the left. Incorrect interruptions of the starter would cost the team five points, and the starter (and chance for the bonuses) would be thrown over to the other team. Incorrect answers to the bonus questions would not be passed across. The quiz rules only varied slightly through the years. In the first series any contestant could be asked to speak on any subject for 45 seconds. The show always included two picture rounds and one music round. Originally teams would attempt to win three matches in a row to qualify for an end-of-series knockout. When the show moved to the BBC this was replaced by a straight knockout format.

The affable Bamber Gascoigne fronted the new program. A Cambridge graduate, he brought with him the scholarly humor of the university common room. His ease with the complexity of the questions (sometimes up to 50 or so words long) and background knowledge helped each episode maintain its momentum. The quiz indeed felt like a varsity race, with the questions being delivered with greater and greater speed until the final gong. Gascoigne was always ready to say "have to hurry you," which, with "starter for ten" became recognizable catchphrases. The program's iconography also included a split screen effect. Both teams were seated at long desks in the studio, but on screen one team was positioned directly above the other. During one season the two tier desks were built in the studio, but this was later abandoned. Partisan studio audiences and the range of team mascots helped to enliven the program. Students would introduce themselves at the beginning, and after their name would always give the subject that they were "reading" (studying or majoring in). Competitors were addressed by their surnames throughout, and on buzzing in the announcer would quickly give the college name and the surname of the student before the answer was given.

Despite its 10:45 P.M. slot, the program succeeded in the ratings. Within two years it moved to a networked prime-time 7:00 p.m. slot, immediately preceding the ITV hit *Coronation Street,* also made by Granada. Ratings reached up to 12 million. As the ratings fell the program was bounced around the schedules, later becoming a regular staple of Sunday afternoons. Regional scheduling then denied the program a networked slot.

Eventually the show seemed to lose its appeal and was dropped by the London weekend franchisee LWT in 1983. With Thames, the London weekday broadcaster, refusing to dislodge any other program to show *University Challenge,* the end was in sight. In 1987, after an attempt to strip the show across the weekday daytime schedule, the plug was pulled. *University Challenge* went off the air 25 years after the first match between Leeds and Reading universities. Gascoigne had never missed a recording.

In 1992 a celebrity special was made as part of a BBC 2 theme night tribute to Granada. Gascoigne, the split screen, mascots, and "starters for ten" were back. This one-off proved popular, and BBC 2 commissioned the show. Gascoigne, however, was not to return. After much media speculation, the host's position was given to Jeremy Paxman, a journalist and already a familiar figure in the United Kingdom. The regular front man of the BBC 2 flagship current affairs program *Newsnight,* Paxman was known for his acerbic wit and aggressive interviewing style. Where Gascoigne had affability, Paxman brought authority, and although ready to congratulate or chat with the contestants, he carried with him a ready putdown and a hint of menace. The set was updated and mascots were banned. Gascoigne made a special appearance to present the trophy to the first season's winners.

In 2002, the program's 40th anniversary, a series of *University Challenge Reunited* was aired, bringing together past team members to compete against other teams from seasons past. Past competitors had made it into the elite of British politics, journalism, and enter-

tainment. These included politicians David Mellor and Malcolm Rifkind, journalists John Simpson, Andrew Morton, and Clive James, and actor Stephen Fry.

University Challenge reflected huge changes in British society and higher education. It showed the new reach of higher education, and always featured the Twentieth Century "Redbrick" universities as well as the traditional Oxford and Cambridge [Oxbridge] colleges. In the 1990s, most U.K. polytechnics became universities and, along with the Open University, often appear. The 1997 Open University team won the series and included the shows oldest ever player, Ida Staples (73 years old). Notable failures by teams were traditionally picked over by the press, always ready for an excuse to rail against the state of Britain's education system.

NIGEL SPICER

See also **Quiz and Game Shows; Quiz Show Scandals**

Presenters
Bamber Gascoigne (1962–87)
Jeremy Paxman (1994–)

Creator
Don Reid

Producers
Barrie Heads, Patricia Owtram, Douglas Terry, Peter Mullings, Kieran Roberts, Peter Gwyn

Programming History
ITV
1962–87   Scheduling varied according to ITV region
BBC 2
1992–   Wednesday 8.00–8.30 or 8.30–9.00
 2002   University Challenge Reunited: Monday 8.30–9.00

Further Reading

Buscombe, Edward, editor, *Granada; The First 25 Years,* BFI Dossier Series, no. 9, London: British Film Institute, 1981
Gilbert, W. Stephen, "Off Air," *Broadcast* (July 27, 1981)
Paxman, Jeremy, "The Brainy Bunch," *The Guardian* (November 7, 1998)

Univision

U.S. Network

Univision (in Spanish, *Univisión*), the largest Spanish-language television network in the United States with more than 600 affiliates, has historical roots in Mexican broadcasting. Since 1992, Univision has been owned by a consortium headed by Jerry Perenchino, an entertainment financier who once owned a New Jersey Spanish language television station. Twenty-five percent of the network is owned by Venevision, a Venezuelan media company, another 25 percent by the Mexican entertainment conglomerate, Televisa, the largest producer of Spanish-language television programming in the world.

This structural configuration is often viewed as but a marginal variation in Televisa's long-standing domination of U.S. Spanish-language television. The majority of Univision programming is produced in Mexico, by Televisa, as it has been since the first Spanish-language television stations were established in the United States in 1961. The network was then called SIN, the Spanish International Network. In 1986, the Federal Communications Commission (FCC) found SIN to be in violation of the U.S. law that prohibits foreign ownership of U.S. broadcast stations. Televisa was ordered to divest itself of its U.S. subsidiary, and SIN was sold to Hallmark Cards of Kansas City, Missouri, and renamed Univision.

Under Hallmark ownership, about half of Univision programming was Televisa rebroadcasts (*telenovelas* or soap operas, sports, movies, and variety programming), and half was produced in the United States. The U.S.-produced programming, which included a *telenovela*, a situation comedy, and greatly expanded national U.S. news and public affairs programming, proved popular with U.S. Latino audiences. Nonetheless, between 1986 and 1992, Hallmark, which had financed its purchase of the Spanish-language network with junk bonds, was unable to recover its initial investment in Univision. In 1992 Hallmark sold the network to the Perenchino group, which prominently featured Televisa. Among the new owners' first moves was the firing of about a third of the network's Miami-based staff. This resulted in the cancellation of most of the U.S.-produced programs, and the re-creation of a broadcast day largely comprised of Televisa programs.

Univision has been at the forefront of the creation of a national "Hispanic market," the notion that U.S. Latinos are an attractive, commercially viable market segment, and so an audience that advertisers should attempt to reach. Prior to the mid-1980s, the Hispanic population was configured as three markets: Puerto Rican in the eastern United States, Cuban in south Florida, and Mexican in the southwest. Advertising agencies, accordingly, produced three separate Spanish-language advertising campaigns. Univision's extensive market and audience research persuaded Madison Avenue that these three audiences should be considered one national audience. This effort was given a major boost by the Hispanic Nielsen Survey, a

Courtesy of Univision

specially designed methodology for measuring U.S. Spanish-language television audiences, commissioned by Univision and Telemundo, and implemented by the A.C. Nielsen Company in the early 1990s. This new audience measurement system found a U.S. Spanish-language television audience 30 to 40 percent larger than had previously been identified.

Network research conducted by Univision shows that most of its audience are recent Latin American immigrants. Another group is made up of those who have lived in the United States for years, who, because of a myriad of factors, prefer to view television in the Spanish language. Most of these immigrant audience members are from Mexico, though an increasing proportion are Central American. A smaller portion of the Univision audience is more acculturated, bilingual U.S. Latinos, a generally wealthier group much sought after by network planners. Overall, Univision research shows that about 70 percent of the Univision audience is Mexican or Mexican American, 10 percent each Puerto Rican and Cuban American, with the remainder from other Latin American countries.

The most watched Univision programs are Televisa *telenovelas,* serialized melodramas which, in contrast to U.S. soap operas, usually end after two or three months. Also, notably present in the Univision top is the nightly U.S. national newscast, the *Noticiero Univisión.* Apparently the Univision immigrant audience, while maintaining its links to "the old country" through the traditional *telenovelas,* is also seeking out knowledge of its adopted U.S. home. Each year the U.S. Spanish-speaking audience has more television programs among which to choose. Telemundo, another

U.S. Spanish-language television network founded in 1986, has grown to several hundred affiliates. Galavision and Showtime en Español, two premium cable channels, as well as several regional Spanish-language cable networks, including Spanish-language ESPN and MTV, are challenging Univision's previously uncontested hold on U.S. Spanish-language television.

America Rodriguez

See also **Spanish International Network; Telemundo; Telenovela**

Further Reading

Aguirre, Adalberto, Jr., "Critical Notes Regarding the Dislocation of Chicanos by the Spanish-Language Television Industry in the United States," *Ethnic and Racial Studies* (January 1993)

Andrews, Edmund L., "FCC Clears Hallmark Sale of Univision TV Network," *New York Times* (October 1, 1992)

Foisie, Geoffrey, "Nielsen Expands Hispanic TV Ratings," *Broadcasting and Cable* (August 8, 1994)

Fisher, Christy, "Ratings Worth $40 Million? Networks Have No Doubts," *Advertising Age* (January 24, 1994)

"Hispanic Networks Building Up Steam; Ad Rates Seen Rising," *Television-Radio Age* (November 27, 1989)

Mendoza, Rick, "The Year Belongs to Univision," *Hispanic Business* (December 1994)

Rodriguez, America, *Made in the USA: The Constructions of Univision News,* Ph.D. diss., University of California, San Diego, 1993

Ruprecht, Gustavo, "Tuning in to Cultural Diversity," *Americas* (July–August 1990)

Silva, Samuel, "The Latin Superchannels," *World Press Review* (November 1991)

Waters, Harry F., "The New Voice of America," *Newsweek* (June 12, 1989)

Untouchables, The

U.S. Crime Series

Based on the 1947 novel by Eliot Ness and Oscar Fraley, *The Untouchables* was the first dramatic series created at Desilu Productions, the studio owned by Desi Arnaz and Lucille Ball, which became famous for providing situation comedies to U.S. television. Airing on ABC from 1959 to 1963, the series was panned for what critics at the time deemed "excessive and senseless violence." However, it was enormously popular

with audiences and made names for producer Quinn Martin and actor Robert Stack.

The series centered on a greatly embellished version of the real-life Eliot Ness, played by Stack, and his incorruptible treasury agents whom Chicago newspapers had dubbed "the Untouchables." Their battles against organized crime served as the source material for the television series. While the fictional Ness and his Un-

The Untouchables, 1959–63, Robert Stack.
Courtesy of the Everett Collection

touchables were somewhat lifeless characters, the back-stories and motivations established for the series' criminals were incredibly well defined. This was due, in large part, to the talented guest actors—including Robert Redford, William Bendix, Lloyd Nolan, J. Carroll Naish, and Peter Falk—who played the series' criminal kingpins. This led to one of the basic problems of the series: the criminals appeared more human than the heroes.

The series began as a two-hour made-for-television movie documenting Ness's fight against Chicago mob leader Al Capone. The movie, and its episodic counterpart, maintained an earthy grittiness through the use of stark sets and dark, studio back-lot exterior sequences. A realistic mood was added by narrator Walter Winchell (who had, incidentally, a few years before, broken the real-life scandal of Lucille Ball's alleged communist ties during the McCarthy-era blacklisting period). Winchell's staccato delivery of introductory background material set the stage for each week's episode.

ABC justified the series' violence on grounds of historical accuracy, yet the network often violated the same rule by having their fictional Ness responsible for nabbing mob leaders such as George "Bugsy" Moran and Ma Barker, figures with whom he had no actual dealings. Indeed, a number of FBI agents complained about their real-life victories being credited to the fictionalized Ness. Such pressure eventually forced ABC to create additional FBI characters to portray more accurately the people involved in the show's historically based cases.

The Untouchables also drew controversy for its stereotyped ethnic characters. The Italian-American community protested the series' use of Italian names for criminal characters. The Capone family also brought a $1 million lawsuit against producer Arnaz for using the Capone likeness for profit. This was particularly upsetting for Arnaz, a classmate and friend of Capone's son.

The show was tremendously successful in its second season, but its popularity rapidly declined when NBC countered with the musical variety program *Sing Along with Mitch*. Producer Martin converted his *Untouchables* success into an impressive string of cop-based dramatic hits, including *The FBI* (1965) and *The Streets of San Francisco* (1972). Stack became a popular TV actor and starred in other successful dramas in which he played similar crime fighters and adventurers. Since 1987, he has hosted *Unsolved Mysteries*, a popular "reality" program. *The Untouchables* inspired two revivals: a 1980s movie version, as well as a 1990s syndicated series.

MICHAEL B. KASSEL

See also **Arnaz, Desi; Martin, Quinn; Police Programs;** *Westinghouse-Desilu Playhouse*

Narrator
Walter Winchell

Cast

Eliot Ness	Robert Stack
Agent Martin Flaherty (1959–60)	Jerry Paris
Agent William Youngfellow	Able Fernandez
Agent Enrico Rossi	Nick Georgiade
Agent Cam Allison (1960)	Anthony George
Agent Lee Hobson (1960–63)	Paul Picerni
Agent Jack Rossman (1960–63)	Steve London
Frank Nitti	Bruce Gordon
Al Capone	Neville Brand
"Bugs" Moran	Lloyd Nolan
Dutch Schultz	Lawrence Dobkin
"Mad Dog" Coll	Clu Gulager

Producers
Quinn Martin, Jerry Thorpe, Leonard Freeman, Howard Hoffman, Alan A. Armer, Alvin Cooperman, Lloyd Richards, Fred Freiberger, Charles Russell

Programming History
114 episodes
ABC
October 1959–October
  1961   Thursday 9:30–10:30
October 1961–September
  1962   Thursday 10:00–11:00
September 1962–September
  1963   Tuesday 9:30–10:30

Further Reading

Arnaz, Desi, *A Book,* New York: Warner, 1976
Boddy, William, *Fifties Television: The Industry and Its Critics,* Urbana: University of Illinois Press, 1990
Powers, Richard Gid, *G-Men: Hoover's F.B.I. in American Popular Culture,* Carbondale: Southern Illinois University Press, 1983

UPN Television Network

U.S. Network

In January of 2002, when CBS President and CEO Les Moonves added the United Paramount Network (UPN) to his Viacom-rooted media dynasty, he steadfastly maintained that UPN would retain its own "identity." Ironically, the acquisition of a clear brand identity has been fairly elusive for UPN. The fledgling network or "netlet's" trek toward fifth network status, in terms of its programming strategies and its internal and external corporate frameworks, has been both arduous and precarious. Since its launch in January of 1995, UPN has been a netlet desperately seeking a safe, secure, and lucrative niche.

While *Star Trek Voyager* was considered the mainstay of the netlet's first season of programming, by the fall of its second season, UPN (like its netlet brethren, the WB) turned to narrowcasting to build an "urban" audience base—adopting the "black block" programming strategy first utilized by FOX in the early 1990s. By 1996 UPN's primetime lineup (*In the House, Malcolm and Eddie, Goode Behavior,* and *Sparks*) mirrored the counter-programming strategy used by FOX through the mid-1990s with the multicultural Thursday night lineup of *Martin, Living Single,* and *New York Undercover.* UPN President and CEO Dean Valentine (1997–2002) acknowledged that the netlet's early strategy had been "to jumpstart and gain an audience by targeting African Americans." This strategy, introduced by his predecessor, Lucy Salhany (1995–97), had brought a large number of African-American viewers into the UPN fold—and, as Valentine noted, "we are happy to have them." By 2000 UPN's Monday night black comedy block boasted the positivist teen sitcom, *Moesha* (1996–2001), the second highest rated UPN series behind *Voyager;* the "movin' on up" domestic comedy and transplant from ABC, *The Hughleys* (1998–2002); and the decidedly broader mother-daughter *Moesha* spin-off, *The Parkers* (1999–), which has been the highest rated series among the African-American audiences since its premiere.

UPN, along with the WB, avoided condemnation when Kwesi Mfume, the National Association for the Advancement of Colored People president, blasted the networks for offering a 1999–2000 fall lineup that was "a virtual whitewash of programming," and threatened a boycott of network programming, However, the netlet's niche product has not been unproblematic. As "The African American Television Report," aptly states, over half of the African-American characters seen on network television as series regulars are in sitcoms, with a majority on the upstart netlets, UPN and the WB. Unfortunately, on UPN, those comedies included such short-lived series like the ill-conceived *Homeboys from Outer Space,* which took minstrelsy into the future, and the Civil War sitcom, *The Secret Diary of Desmond Pfeiffer,* which was taken off the air in response to widespread public outcry. Furthermore, even series developed in the post-1999 era of "new" racial consciousness, like *Girlfriends* and *The Parkers* (members of UPN's sitcom class of 1999 and 2000, respectively), seem to lapse into stereotypical representations of hyper-sexualized black women and broad, boisterous comedy.

Until the 1999–2000 season, UPN's ratings fate was tied to maintaining the viewership for its black situation comedies. For the most part, with the exception of a respectable trekker following for *Voyager* (and a small but dedicated fan base for the supernaturally tinged cop series, *The Sentinel*), no other type of programming had established an audience. Thus the netlet's "urban" niche constructed a de facto brand identity—at least temporarily. Since 1996, two of the netlet's programming hours had been dedicated to a brand of niche programming that caters to the black audience, a population not being adequately served by the major networks. However, as UPN's programming schedule expanded from three nights (six hours) to five nights (ten hours), the amount of programming time dedicated to black-oriented shows remained unchanged. Valentine maintained that the broadening of the audience was necessary because "any network following a narrowcast is ultimately doomed to failure." Valentine's assertion—that broadcasters have a "social responsibility to court a wider audience" and thus "bring America together and unite it"—justified a shift in the netlet's programming paradigm. The implementation of this new, and more expansive approach proved correct the prediction made by A.J. Jacobs in his 1996 article, "Black to the Future": "the bigger UPN and the WB get, the whiter they become."

Fiscal solvency had proven to be as elusive for UPN as creating a brand identity and finding an audience. UPN had lost over $500 million by the time Viacom activated a buy-sell clause in its contract in April of 2000, forcing partner Chris-Craft to sell its half-interest. When Viacom placed UPN under the umbrella of CBS with Moonves at the helm, there was the expectation that, by combining the networks' management and operations, both the network and the netlet would benefit. Despite the less than amicable departures of UPN president and CEO Dean Valentine, and Paramount Television Group's chairman Kerry Mc-Cluggage, who had overseen UPN programming since its 1995 inception, both Moonves and Viacom President Mel Karmarzin repeatedly mentioned the retention of each media outlet's distinct identity on the air.

Under Moonves's tutelage, CBS had gone from the "blue-haired" programming of *Murder She Wrote* and solid numbers with the over-35 crowd to the pinnacle of "cool" reality programming with the *Survivor* franchise, dramatic hipness with *CSI: Crime Scene Investigation,* and a decade high rating with the lucrative 18–49 demographic. While Moonves tried to assuage fears that UPN would become CBS2 by assuring that the netlet would retain its own identity, UPN remained

Courtesy of the Everett Collection

a netlet without a unified programming profile with black-oriented sitcom staples in the same lineup as the testosterone-tinged shows.

Since adding the World Wrestling Federation's *WWF Smackdown* as the centerpiece of the Thursday night lineup in 1999 and by airing other new and ongoing male-oriented programs—including science fiction-influenced series like netlet mainstay, *Voyager,* its prequel successor, *Enterprise,* and the time travel thriller, *Seven Days*—UPN continues to offer an alternative to netlet rival the WB's teen-centered programming (*Dawson's Creek, Felicit,y* and a swath of less successful adolescent dramedies). Despite the fact that the *Smackdown* deal gave both the fiscal and programming advantage to WWF's Vince McMahon, the initial acquisition expanded the UPN audience base by adding the "boy block" to the "black block." While the WWF-inspired viewer surge bode well for UPN as their overall numbers moved closer to those of the network Big Four, it clearly illustrated how viewer allegiances were usually tied to only one of the five nights of programming—each of which seemed constructed for a different niche.

In the new millennium, the netlet continues to broaden its audience base—this time narrowcasting for the female demographic. In 2001 UPN was able to woo Joss Whedon's teen occult dramedy, *Buffy the Vampire Slayer* away from the WB by paying more than twice the previous per episode cost (from $1 million per episode to $2.3 million per episode) and by granting the series' creative team greater artistic freedom. *Buffy*'s presence (airing Tuesday) and the addition of *Enterprise* (airing Wednesday) in the netlet's prime-time lineup undoubtedly contributed to its double-digit jump (25 percent) in the highly coveted 18–34 demographic, and 27 percent with females 18–34.

As a part of this audience expansion strategy, Moonves's choice of former Lifetime Channel senior programming executive, Dawn Tarnofsky-Ostroff, speaks to the netlet's desire to broaden a cross-gender viewer base and bring some sense of consistency to

UPN's rather eclectic brand identity. In the spring of 2002, UPN's pursuit of branding was further problematized when Moonves and Tarnofsky-Ostroff allocated or "repurposed" time slots from the netlet's prime-time schedule for airing short-lived CBS-developed projects (like the occult drama *Wolf Lake*, and the reality show *The Amazing Race*). Despite the less than enthusiastic audience response to recycled CBS shows, the CBS-UPN marriage, which does little to brand UPN, continues to provide myriad opportunities for network-netlet programming synergy.

While the fate of any netlet is relatively uncertain, UPN, as a new adoptee in the vast Viacom fold, under the "protection" of CBS, its network big brother, this netlet without a niche, may end up rounding out the "Big Five."

BAMBI L. HAGGINS

See also **Moonves, Leslie R.; WB Television Network**

Further Reading

Bogle, Donald, *Prime Time Blues: African Americans on Network Television,* New York: Farrar, Straus and Giroux, 2001

Braxton, Greg, "UPN Will Try To Widen Its Appeal; Television: Network's New Leader Denies Abandoning African Americans in Favor of White Viewers; Rather, He Plans An 'All Inclusive' Approach," *Los Angeles Times* (December 10, 1997)

Freeman, Michael, "NBC Will Win Sweeps But UPN Sees Big Gains," *Electronic Media* (February 25, 2002)

Freeman, Michael, "A New Dawn-ing for UPN; Netlet Pins Its Programming Hopes on Lifetime TV Veteran Tarnofsky-Ostroff," *Electronic Media* (January 28, 2002)

Greppi, Michele, "Valentine vs. UPN in Legal Smackdown," *Electronic Media* (September 10, 2001)

Jacobs, A.J., "Black to the Future," *BIZ* (June 14, 1996)

Lowry, Brian, "For Rival UPN and WB: The Future Is a Matter of Focus," *Los Angeles Times* (July 27, 1998)

MacDonald, J. Fred, *Blacks and White TV: Afro-Americans in Television Since 1948,* Chicago: Nelson Hall, 1992

Schlosser, Joe, "Eye to Eye with Moonves," *Broadcasting and Cable* (January 21, 2002)

Upstairs, Downstairs

British Serial Drama

Upstairs, Downstairs, originally produced in England by Sagitta Productions for London Weekend Television (LWT), became one of the most popular programs in the history of *Masterpiece Theatre* on the U.S. Public Broadcasting Service (PBS) and is beloved throughout much of the world. The series presents the narrative of the upper-class Bellamy family and their servants during the turbulent first third of the 20th century in Britain. Their stories, focused individually but always illustrative of complex and intertwined relationships, unfold chronologically, highlighting members of both the upstairs biological family and the downstairs "work family" of servants.

The series accurately represented and mirrored the societal milieu of its time and has been greatly acclaimed for the producers' and authors' meticulous attention to accurate period detail. Historical events served as the context for the characters' situations and actions in a narrative that carried them from 1903 Edwardian England, through World War I and the political upheavals of the 1920s, to a conclusion set soon after the stock market crash in the summer of 1930. *Upstairs, Downstairs* captured and held a rapt televi-

sion audience through 68 episodes in Britain and 55 in the United States. It was the most extensive series on *Masterpiece Theatre* and brought a new and refreshing image of British television to many Americans whose only perception of British programming, not necessarily correct, was of ponderous adaptations of dated British literature. In so doing, the series brought a great many new viewers to PBS and *Masterpiece Theatre*.

According to long-time *Masterpiece Theatre* host Alistair Cooke, quoted in Terrence O'Flaherty's *Masterpiece Theatre,* "I loved *Upstairs, Downstairs*. When I first saw it, my reaction was, 'I'll be amazed if this thing doesn't really hit the headlines. It's marvelous. It allows you to identify with the downstairs people while vicariously enjoying the life of the upstairs people.'" Followed closely episode by episode, the upstairs and downstairs families became a part of "our" family. The audience genuinely cared about the characters, came to know them intimately, and developed a strong empathy for them.

The Bellamys and their staff of domestic servants resided in a five-story townhouse at 165 Eaton Place, Belgravia, in London, an address well known to the se-

Upstairs, Downstairs.
Photo courtesy of Frank Goodman Associates

ries' many fans. The upstairs family includes Lord Richard Bellamy (David Langton); his first wife, Lady Marjorie (Rachel Gurney), who dies tragically on the Titanic; their two children, James (Simon Williams) and Elizabeth (Nicola Pagett); Richard's second wife, Virginia (Hannah Gordon); James's wife, Hazel (Meg Wynn Owen), who dies in a flu epidemic; and Georgina Worsley (Lesley-Anne Down), cousin to James and Elizabeth. Among the most memorable of the downstairs staff are Hudson the butler (Gordon Jackson), Mrs. Bridges the cook (Angela Baddeley), Rose (Jean Marsh), Ruby (Jenny Tomasin), Edward (Christopher Beeny), and Daisy (Jacqueline Tong). Among the many other characters who appeared in a number of episodes, perhaps Sarah (Pauline Collins), Watkins (John Alderton), Sir Geoffrey the family solicitor (Raymond Huntley), and Lady Pru (Joan Benham) are the most fondly remembered by viewers. The large cast, only partially noted here, is considered to include some of the best actors from British stage, film, and television. The series earned the respect of professional peers as well as that of the audience. Its cast won numerous awards, both in Britain and the United States, including eight Emmys, Writers Guild of Great Britain Awards, American Drama Critics Circle Awards, Golden Globe Awards, and a Peabody Award. Angela Baddeley received the Commander of the British Empire, awarded in the Queen's 1975 New Year's Honours List. According to Queen Elizabeth II, *Upstairs, Downstairs* was her favorite program in 1975, and Baddeley's Mrs. Bridges was her favorite character. In addition, Gordon Jackson received the coveted Queen's Order of the British Empire Award.

The idea for the series came from actresses Jean Marsh (who played the role of house-parlor maid Rose) and Eileen Atkins. The series was developed by John Hawkesworth, whose long and distinguished career in film and television extends from art director on the film *The Third Man* to producer of the well-regarded Sherlock Holmes series featuring Jeremy Brett. *Upstairs, Downstairs* was the first program from LWT to be purchased for *Masterpiece Theatre* and only the second non-BBC program to be scheduled. *Upstairs, Downstairs* was one of the first series of its type to be produced on videotape rather than film (though certain scenes, mainly exteriors and location shots, were shot on film). It was one of the first series on *Masterpiece Theatre* that was not biographical or based on a written work. It was created purely for television. As originally produced for British television, each episode in the series was written in three acts. On *Masterpiece Theatre,* each episode was shown without interruption.

Significant confusion was created when the series was shown on U.S. television because 13 of the first 26 episodes produced for British television were not shown. This created a rather bizarre lack of continuity. Six of the first original British episodes had been taped in black and white due to a strike. *Masterpiece Theatre* only wanted episodes in color and so the first episode ("On Trial") was revised and reshot in color for American television. Of the first 26 original episodes shot for British TV, episodes 2 through 9, 11 and 12, 16, 19, and 20 were not shown on U.S. television. These "lost" episodes were not made available for American viewing until 1989. The original black-and-white version of episode 1 has never been made available to American television.

Upstairs, Downstairs was first shown on British television in 1971 and continued through four series of 13 episodes each (two Edwardian series, a later prewar series, and a World War I series) and a fifth series of 16 episodes (postwar), making a total of 68 episodes produced and broadcast. A spin-off from the original series, *Thomas and Sarah,* featured the continued story of Sarah the parlor maid (Pauline Collins) and Thomas Watkins the chauffeur (John Alderton) together after leaving service at 165 Eaton Place. A total of 13 one-hour episodes were produced by LWT for original broadcast in 1979.

On *Masterpiece Theatre,* the original 26 Edwardian period episodes, pared down to 13, were first shown January 6 to March 31, 1974. From November 3, 1974, to January 26, 1975, the post-Edwardian, prewar series of 13 episodes was broadcast. The 13 World War I episodes were shown January 1 to March 28, 1976. The final series of 16 postwar episodes was broadcast January 16 to May 1, 1977 making, in all, 55 episodes shown on *Masterpiece Theatre.* The 55 episodes were later repeated on *Masterpiece Theatre,* and selected episodes were shown as a part of a "10th Anniversary Season Festival of Favorites" and as a part of the "Twentieth Anniversary Favorites" series early in 1991. *Upstairs, Downstairs* was the inspiration for the short-lived CBS television series *Beacon Hill,* which concerned a well-to-do Boston family and their domestic staff during the 1920s (broadcast fall 1975).

Upstairs, Downstairs is one of the highest rated programs in the history of PBS. The series has been syndicated to both commercial and noncommercial stations in the United States and is one of the most successful and watched dramatic series in television history. It is estimated that approximately 1 billion people in more than 40 countries have enjoyed *Upstairs, Downstairs,* and the series is still in active syndication. The entire series has been released on videotape and DVD.

STEVE RUNYON

See also **British Programming; Jackson, Gordon; Miniseries**

Cast

Lady Marjorie Bellamy	Rachel Gurney
Richard Bellamy	David Langton
James	Simon Williams
Elizabeth	Nicola Pagett
Hudson	Gordon Jackson
Mrs. Bridges	Angela Baddeley
Rose	Jean Marsh
Sarah	Pauline Collins
Emily	Evin Crowley
Alfred	George Innes

Roberts	Patsy Smart
Pearce	Brian Osborne
Edward	Christopher Beeny
Laurence	Ian Ogilvy
Ruby	Jenny Tomasin
Watkins	John Alderton
Hazel	Meg Wynn Owen
Daisy	Jacqueline Tong
Georgina Worsley	Lesley-Anne Down
Virginia	Hannah Gordon
Alice	Anne Yarker
William	Jonathan Seely
Frederick	Gareth Hunt
Lily	Karen Dotrice

Producers

Rex Firkin, John Hawkesworth

Programming History

68 50-minute episodes
ITV
October 1971–March 1972
October 1972–January 1973
October 1973–January 1974
September 1974–December 1974

Further Reading

Cooke, Alistair, *Masterpieces: A Decade of Masterpiece Theatre,* New York: VNU Books International-Alfred A. Knopf, 1981

Floyd, Patty Lou, *Backstairs with Upstairs, Downstairs,* New York: St. Martin's Press, 1988

Hardwick, Mollie, *The World of Upstairs, Downstairs,* New York: Holt, Rinehart and Winston, 1976

O'Flaherty, Terrence, *Masterpiece Theatre: A Celebration of 25 Years of Outstanding Television,* San Francisco, California: KQED Books, 1996

V

Valour and the Horror, The

Canadian Documentary

Aired on the publicly owned Canadian Broadcasting Corporation (CBC), *The Valour and the Horror* is a Canadian-made documentary about three controversial aspects of Canada's participation in World War II. This three-part series caused a controversy almost unprecedented in the history of Canadian television. Canadian veterans, outraged by what they considered an inaccurate and highly biased account of the war, sued Brian and Terence McKenna, the series directors, for libel. An account of the controversy surrounding *The Valour and the Horror,* with statements by the directors and the CBC ombudsman as well as an examination of the series by various historians can be found in David J. Bercuson and S.F. Wise's *The Valour and the Horror Revisited.*

The Valour and the Horror consists of three separate two-hour segments, which aired on consecutive Sunday evenings in 1992. In the first, "Savage Christmas Hong Kong 1941," the McKennas explore the ill-preparedness of the Canadian troops stationed in Hong Kong, the loss of the city to the Japanese, and the barbarous treatment of Canadian troops interned in slave-labor camps for the duration of the war. Arguably the most moving of the three episodes, "Savage Christmas" was the least controversial. The eyewitness testimony of two surviving veterans, combined with archival photographs and reenactments of letters written by prisoners of war, testifies to the strength of emotion that can be generated by television documentary.

The second episode, "Death by Moonlight: Bomber Command," proved to be the most controversial of the three episodes. It details the blanket bombing of German cities carried out by Canadian Lancaster bombers, including the firestorm caused by the bombings of Dresden and Munich. The McKennas claim that the blanket bombing, which caused enormous casualties among both German civilians and Canadian air crews, did nothing to hasten the end of the war and was merely an act of great brutality with little military significance. In particular, British commander Sir Arthur "Bomber" Harris is cited for his bloodthirstiness.

"In Desperate Battle: Normandy 1944," the third episode, deals primarily with the massive loss of Canadian troops at Verrieres Ridge during the assault on Normandy, citing the incompetence and inexperience of Canadian military leadership as the cause for the high casualty rate. This episode also accuses the Canadian forces of war crimes against German soldiers—war crimes that were never prosecuted after the war.

All three episodes combine black-and-white archival footage of the war with present-day interviews with both allied and enemy veterans and civilians. Each episode has a voice-over narration by Brian McKenna and is accompanied by music taken from Gabriel Faure's Requiem of 1893. The sections taken from the Requiem are those sung primarily by young boys. The accompaniment was perhaps chosen because, throughout each episode, the McKennas em-

The Valour and the Horror.
Photo courtesy of Galafilm, Inc.

phasize the youth of the combatants and the terrible but preventable waste of both Canada's young men and innocent German civilians, including babies ripped from their mothers' arms by the wind during the firestorms that followed the bombing.

The youthfulness of the soldiers is also emphasized in some very controversial reenactments in which actors speak lines taken from the letters and diaries of Canadian and British military personnel. Although these reenactments are well marked as such, veterans have claimed that they are misleading and extremely selective about what they include. Reenactments, which are more characteristic of "reality" TV programs such as *America's Most Wanted* and *Rescue 911,* are problematic in conventional documentary practice. As Bill Nichols argues in *Representing Reality,* "documentaries run some risks of credibility in reenacting an event: the special indexical bond between image and historical event is ruptured." Certainly, reenactments are more conventional in television than in cinematic documentary.

The battle that ensued over *The Valour and the Hor-*ror was a battle over the interpretation of history and the responsibilities of publicly funded television. The McKennas have argued that, in the tradition of investigative journalism, they wished to set aside the official account of the war and examine events from the point of view of the participants. They have also argued that the real story has never been told and that their own research has shown gross incompetence, mismanagement, and cover-ups on the part of the Canadian government. Historians and veterans have argued that *The Valour and the Horror* is a revisionist history that is both historically inaccurate and poorly researched.

The major complaints against *The Valour and the Horror* by historians are its lack of context, poor research, and bias that led to misinterpretation and inaccuracy. The McKennas, in defending themselves, have to a degree been their own worst enemies. By claiming that their series is fact, and contains no fiction, and also by claiming that their research is "bullet proof," they have set themselves up for all kinds of attacks—attacks that have also affected the status of publicly funded television in Canada. Publicly funded institutions are particularly vulnerable to attacks by powerful lobbies, whose animosity can and does jeopardize the institutions' financial stability. *The Valour and the Horror* can be seen as a particularly acrimonious chapter in the continuing battle between a publicly funded institution and the taxpayers who support it. In this, it is not unlike the battle waged in the United States between veterans and the Smithsonian Institute over the representation of the bombing of Hiroshima and Nagasaki.

JEANNETTE SLONIOWSKI

Producers
Arnie Gelbart, André Lamy, Adam Symansky (National Film Board of Canada producer), Darce Fardy (Canadian Broadcasting Corporation producer)

Directors
Brian McKenna, Terence McKenna

Writers
Brian McKenna, Terence McKenna

Programming History
January 1992   three parts

Further Reading

Bercuson, David J., and S.F. Wise, *The Valour and the Horror Revisited,* Montreal: McGill-Queen's University Press, 1994

Findlay, Timothy, "*The Valour and the Horror,*" *Journal of Canadian Studies,* 27 (winter 1992–93)

Nichols, Bill, *Representing Reality,* Bloomington: Indiana University Press, 1991

Nichols, Bill, *Blurred Boundaries,* Bloomington: Indiana University Press, 1994

Taras, David, "The Struggle over *The Valour and the Horror:* Media Power and the

Portrayal of War," *Canadian Journal of Political Science,* 28 (December 1995)

Van Dyke, Dick (1925–)

U.S. Actor

Dick Van Dyke's entertainment career began during World War II, when he participated in variety shows and worked as an announcer while serving in the U.S. military. That career has continued into the present, with more than five decades of work as an actor on network and local television, on stage, and in motion pictures. Van Dyke began working in television as host of variety programs in Atlanta, Georgia, and his first foray into network television came in 1956, as the emcee of CBS Television's *Cartoon Theatre.*

It was Van Dyke's role as Rob Petrie on the classic CBS situation comedy *The Dick Van Dyke Show* that ensured his place in television history. He was cast by series creator Carl Reiner and series producer Sheldon Leonard in the role of a television comedy writer (Reiner himself played this role in the series pilot, *Head of the Family*). Selected over another television pioneer, Johnny Carson, and plucked from a starring role on the Broadway stage in *Bye Bye Birdie,* Van Dyke used his unique talent for physical comedy, coupled with his ability to sing and dance, to play Robert Simpson Petrie, the head writer of the *Alan Brady Show.* Complementing Van Dyke was a veteran cast of talented comedic actors including Rose Marie, Morey Amsterdam, Jerry Paris, Carl Reiner (as Alan Brady),

as well as a newcomer to television, Mary Tyler Moore, who played Rob's wife Laura Petrie.

In many ways, *The Dick Van Dyke Show* broke new ground in network television. The series created quite a stir when, in the early 1960s, husband and wife, although still depicted sleeping in separate beds, were shown to have a physical relationship. Moore was also allowed to wear capri pants, a style unseen on TV at the time. However, the quintessential example of the innovations offered by *The Dick Van Dyke Show* are seen in the episode "That's My Boy??" The network initially rejected the script for this episode, and only an appeal from Leonard himself secured permission to film it. In this episode, Rob is convinced that the baby he and Laura brought home from the hospital is not theirs, but a baby belonging to another couple, the Peters. Constant mix-ups with flowers and candy at the hospital, caused by the similarity in names (Petrie and Peters), leads Rob to believe that the babies were somehow switched, and he decides to confront the Peters family. Only when the Peters show up at Rob and Laura's house does Rob learn that the Peters are African American. Some have speculated that the overwhelming positive reaction by audiences to this episode inspired Leonard to cast

Dick Van Dyke.
Photo courtesy of Dick Van Dyke

another future television megastar, Bill Cosby, in *I Spy*.

Van Dyke won three Emmy Awards for his role in *The Dick Van Dyke Show*, and the series received four Emmy Awards for outstanding comedy series. The series, which began in 1961, ended its network television run in 1966, although audiences have continued to enjoy the program through its extended life in syndication.

Van Dyke went on to star in such feature films as *Chitty Chitty Bang Bang, Mary Poppins*, and *The Comic*, while also continuing to be a staple on network television in *The New Dick Van Dyke Show, Van Dyke and Company* (for which he received his fourth Emmy), and a critically acclaimed and Emmy-nominated dramatic performance in the made-for-television movie *The Morning After*. In the 1990s, he starred in the prime-time series *Diagnosis Murder* for CBS, which costarred his son Barry Van Dyke.

THOMAS A. BIRK

See also **Comedy, Domestic Settings; Comedy, Workplace; Dick Van Dyke Show, The; Moore, Mary Tyler; Reiner, Carl**

Dick Van Dyke. Born in West Plains, Missouri, December 13, 1925. Married: Marjorie Willett, 1948 (divorced, 1984); children: Barry, Carrie-Beth, Christian, and Stacy. Served in U.S. Army Air Corps during World War II. Founded advertising agency with Wayne Williams, Danville, Illinois, 1946; appeared with Phillip Erickson in pantomime act The Merry Mutes, Eric and Van, 1947–53; television master of ceremonies, *The Music Shop*, Atlanta, Georgia; hosted television variety show, *The Dick Van Dyke Show*, New Orleans, Louisiana; master of ceremonies, *The Morning Show*, CBS, 1955, and *Cartoon Theatre*, 1956; hosted weekly television show *Flair*, ABC, 1960; performed on Broadway in *Bye Bye Birdie*, 1960–61; starred in weekly television sitcom *The Dick Van Dyke Show*, CBS, 1961–66; performed in such films as *Mary Poppins*, 1965, and *Chitty Chitty Bang Bang*, 1968; returned to television series format with *Diagnosis Murder*, 1993; chair, Nick at Nite, from 1992. Recipient: Theater World Award, 1960; Antoinette Perry Award, 1961; four Emmy Awards.

Television Series (selected)

1955–56	*The Morning Show* (master of ceremonies)
1956	*Cartoon Theatre* (host)
1958–59	*Mother's Day* (host)
1959	*Laugh Line* (host)
1960	*Flair* (host)
1961–66	*The Dick Van Dyke Show*
1971–74	*The New Dick Van Dyke Show*
1976	*Van Dyke and Company*
1988	*The Van Dyke Show*
1993–2001	*Diagnosis Murder*
2003	*The Alan Brady Show* (voice)

Made-for-Television Movies

1974	*The Morning After*
1977	*Tubby the Tuba* (voice only)
1982	*Drop-Out Father*
1982	*The Country Girl*
1983	*Found Money*
1985	*Breakfast with Les and Bess*
1986	*Strong Medicine*
1987	*Ghost of a Chance*
1991	*Daughters of Privilege*
2002	*A Town Without Pity*
2002	*Without Warning*
2003	*The Gin Game*

Films

Bye Bye Birdie, 1963; *What a Way To Go*, 1964; *Lt. Robin Crusoe, USN*, 1965; *Mary Poppins*, 1965;

Divorce American Style, 1967; *Never a Dull Moment,* 1967; *Chitty Chitty Bang Bang,* 1968; *The Comic,* 1969; *Some Kind of Nut,* 1969; *Cold Turkey,* 1971; *The Runner Stumbles,* 1979; *Drop-Out Father,* 1982; *Dick Tracy,* 1990; *Freddie Goes to Washington* (voice only), 1992.

Stage

The Girls Against the Boys, 1959; *Bye Bye Birdie,* 1960–61.

Publication

Faith, Hope, and Hilarity, 1970

Further Reading

Grote, David, *The End of Comedy: The Sit-com and the Comedic Tradition,* Hamden, Connecticut: Archon Books, 1983

Hamamoto, Darrell Y., *Nervous Laughter: Television Situation Comedy and Liberal Democratic Ideology,* New York: Praeger, 1989

Javna, John, *The Best of TV Sitcoms: Burns and Allen to The Cosby Show, The Munsters to Mary Tyler Moore.* New York: Harmony Books, 1988.

Jones, Gerard, *Honey, I'm Home!: Sitcoms, Selling the American Dream,* New York: Grove Weidenfeld, 1992

Karlen, Neal, "A Familiar Face Introduces Himself to a New Generation" (interview), *New York Times* (October 21, 1992)

Leibman, Nina, *Living Room Lectures: The Fifties Family in Film and Television,* Austin: University of Texas Press, 1995

Marc, David, *Comic Visions: Television Comedy and American Culture,* Boston: Unwin Hyman, 1989

Mitz, Rick, *The Great TV Sitcom Book,* New York: R. Marek, 1980

Waldron, Vince, *Classic Sitcoms: A Celebration of the Best of Prime-time Comedy,* New York: Macmillan, 1987

Waldron, Vince, *The Official Dick Van Dyke Show Book: The Definitive History and Ultimate Viewer's Guide to Television's Most Enduring Comedy,* New York: Hyperion, 1994

Weissman, G., and C.S. Sanders, *The Dick Van Dyke Show: Anatomy of a Classic,* New York: St. Martin's Press, 1983

Variety Programs

Variety programs were among the most popular prime-time shows in the early years of American television. *Texaco Star Theater* starring Milton Berle was so popular for its first two or three years in the late 1940s and early 1950s that restaurants closed the night it was on, water usage plummeted during its hour, and, in 1949, almost 75 percent of the television audience watched it every week. Whether emphasizing musical performance or comedy, or equal portions of each, the variety genre provided early television with the spectacular entertainment values that television and advertising executives believed were important to its growth as a popular medium.

Variety shows almost always featured musical (instrumental, vocal, and dance) performances and comedy sketches, and sometimes acrobatics, animal or magic tricks, and dramatic recitations. Some had musical or comedy stars as hosts, often already known from radio or the recording industry, who displayed their talents solo or with guest performers. Others featured personalities, such as Ted Mack or Ed Sullivan, who acted as emcees and provided continuity for what was basically a series of unrelated acts. This genre was produced by both networks and local television stations. Some of the most popular musical variety programs, such as *The Lawrence Welk Show* and *The Liberace Show,* began as local productions for Los Angeles stations. The form has its heritage in 19th-century American entertainment—minstrel, vaudeville, and burlesque shows—and the 20th-century nightclub and Catskills resorts revues (where such talents as Sid Caesar, Imogene Coca, and Carl Reiner were found).

These forms of entertainment emphasized presentational or performative aspects—immediacy, spontaneity, and spectacle—over story line and character development. Performers might develop a "persona," but this character mask would usually represent a well-known stereotype or exhibit a particular vocal or dance talent, rather than embody a fleshed-out character growing within the context of dramatic situations. The vaudeville show, which had achieved a middle-class following by the 20th century, presented a series of unrelated acts, featured stars or "headliners," in addition to supporting acts. Many of the form's most important stars made the transition to radio or films in the 1920s and 1930s, and some of these, such as Ed Wynn, were also among the stars of television's first variety shows. Two of the most significant "headliners" of vaudeville and stars of radio, Jack Benny and Burns and Allen made a successful transition to television, but while

The Sonny and Cher Comedy Hour, Sonny and Cher, portrait
for the debut episode, August 1, 1971.
Courtesy of the Everett Collection

their shows retained aspects of vaudeville and variety
(especially Benny's program with movie star guests
and the regularly featured singer Dennis Day), they
also combined those elements with the narrative features of situation comedy. A less-successful radio comedian, Milton Berle, brought vaudeville back in a
much bigger way (his and other television variety-
vaudeville shows were called "vaudeo") because his
performances emphasized the visual spectacle of the
live stage impossible on radio.

The spontaneous, rowdy antics and adult humor of
Milton Berle, or of Sid Caesar and company on *Your
Show of Shows,* were most popular on the east coast,
where they could be aired live (before the coaxial cable was laid across the country), and where an urban
population might be familiar with these performance
styles from nightclubs and resorts. As demographics
and ratings from other parts of the country became
more important to advertisers and networks, as telefilm
programming (usually sitcoms and western dramas)
became more successful, and as moral watchdog
groups and cultural pundits criticized the genre for its

"blue" jokes, some comedy-variety shows fell out of
favor. The gentle, childlike humor of Red Skelton became more popular than the cross-dressing of Berle,
just as the various comic "personas" of Jackie Gleason
(such as the Poor Soul, Joe the Bartender, and Ralph
Kramden) proved more acceptable to wide audiences
than the foreign-movie spoofs performed by Caesar
and company. While Berle and Caesar stayed on the air
for most of the 1950s, it was these other comics and
their variety hours that made the transitions into the
1960s.

Variety shows emphasizing music, such as *The Dinah Shore Show, The Perry Como Show, The Tennessee Ernie Ford Show, The Lawrence Welk Show,
Your Hit Parade, The Bell Telephone Hour,* and *The
Voice of Firestone* (the latter two emphasizing classical
music performance), had long runs and little controversy. Nat "King" Cole, the first major black performer
to have a network variety series, had a great difficulty
securing sponsors for his show when it debuted in
1956, and most of the important black musical stars of
the time (and many of the white ones as well) appeared
for reduced fees to help save the show. NBC canceled
it a little over a year after its debut.

Besides several of the above mentioned shows,
*The Smothers Brothers Show, The Carol Burnett
Show,* and *The Ed Sullivan Show* (which would leave
the air in 1971 after 23 years) found success in the
1960s, even as the prime-time schedule became
more and more filled with dramatic programs and
situation comedies. *The Smothers Brothers Show*
caused some controversy with its anti-Vietnam War
jokes, and the brothers tangled with CBS over Pete
Seeger's singing of "Waist Deep in the Big Muddy."
Ed Sullivan stayed popular by booking rock acts,
such as the Beatles and the Rolling Stones, and Carol
Burnett continued the delicious spoofing of films that
Your Show of Shows had started. For the most part,
however, the cultural changes in the late 1960s and
1970s overtook the relevance of the variety form.
*The Glen Campbell Goodtime Hour, The Sonny and
Cher Comedy Hour, Tony Orlando and Dawn*—all
shows featuring popular music stars with a youth
culture following—achieved some popularity in the
1970s. *Rowan and Martin's Laugh-In,* a different
type of variety program, prefigured the faster, more
culturally literate and irreverent style that would survive, in limited form, into the 1990s. Clearly more
oriented toward satire and sketch comedy than to the
music-variety form of other programs, *Laugh-In* in
its way recalled the inventiveness of *Your Show of
Shows.*

Only one show from the 1970s, with the focus on
the youth demographic, has lasted into the 21st cen-

tury: NBC's *Saturday Night Live.* This program, mainly emphasizing satirical comedy and featuring a different host and musical guest or group every week, has captured the teen, college, and young adult crowd with a late-night airing (11:30 P.M. Eastern and Pacific time). Although critics periodically call for its demise as the quality of writing waxes and wanes, the show has created film and television stars out of many of its regular performers. In the late 1990s, FOX Television started airing *MAD TV,* its own entry into Saturday late-night variety programming. *MAD TV,* based on the irreverent satire magazine of the same name published since the 1950s, is actually structured much like its NBC competitor, but it features celebrity or musical guests less frequently. Although these network variety shows have remained popular and a reunion special of *The Carol Burnett Show* in late 2001 received surprisingly high ratings, the general lack of the genre on television despite the proliferation of new channels, may suggest its permanent eclipse, as the viewer with a remote control can now create his or her own variety show, switching from stand-up comedy on A&E or Comedy Central to ballet and opera on PBS or Bravo, from rock and roll on MTV to country music on TNN.

MARY DESJARDINS

See also **Burnett, Carol;** *Carol Burnett Show, The; Ed Sullivan Show, The; Original Amateur Hour, The; Saturday Night Live;* **Sullivan, Ed; Special/Spectacular**

Further Reading

Krolik, Richard, "Here's to the Musical Variety Show!" *Television Quarterly* (spring 1992)

Marc, David, *Comic Visions: Television Comedy and American Culture,* Boston : Unwin Hyman, 1989; 2nd edition, Malden, Massachusetts: Blackwell Publishers, 1997

Marc, David, "Carol Burnett: The Last of the Big-time Comedy-Variety Stars," *Quarterly Review of Film and Video* (July 1992)

Shulman, Arthur, and Roger Youman, *How Sweet It Was,* New York: Bonanza, 1966

Spector, Bert, "A Clash of Cultures: The Smothers Brothers vs. CBS Television," in *American History/American Television: Interpreting the Video Past,* edited by John E. O'Connor, New York: Ungar, 1987

Spigel, Lynn, *Make Room for TV: Television and the Family Ideal in Postwar America,* Chicago: University of Chicago Press, 1992

Wertheim, Arthur Frank, "The Rise and Fall of Milton Berle," in *American History/American Television: Interpreting the Video Past,* edited by John E. O'Connor, New York: Ungar, 1987

Wilk, Max, *The Golden Age of Television: Notes from the Survivors,* New York: Delacorte Press, 1976

Very British Coup, A

U.K. Drama Series

A Very British Coup was a high-minded political drama serial that posited a simple question: how would the establishment and the United States respond to the popular election of a far-left government in the United Kingdom? A well-acted and compelling drama, first transmitted in the summer of 1988, it reflected growing public concerns and anxieties about the right-wing politics of the Reagan-Thatcher era and the burgeoning industrial military complex.

The series was based on the 1982 same-titled novel written by Labour Party supporter, and later member of Parliament, Chris Mullin. It was adapted by the respected scriptwriter Alan Plater, who had a list of credits to his name, including episodes of the police series *Z Cars,* and adaptations of major literary works such as *The Barchester Chronicles* (1983), based on books by Anthony Trollope.

The drama surrounded the election of a far-left Labour government in the "near future" led by third-generation steelworker and socialist Harry Perkins. Played by Ray McAnally, Perkins sported a Stalin-like moustache, displayed Machiavellian cunning, but retained an avuncular manner and a passion for equality and decency. With a radical agenda to re-nationalize major industries, increase spending on welfare provision, introduce "open government," curb press monopoly, oust the American military from U.K. soil, and unilaterally disarm Britain's nuclear capability, Perkins and his government made many enemies in the political, economic, media, and military establishment.

The first episode followed Perkins from election through to an economic crisis, with the International Monetary Fund only offering to bail out the British economy with a loan conditional on a policy U-turn.

The episode ended on a triumphant note instead, when the foreign secretary secured a more preferable loan from the Moscow State Bank after a secret visit to Sweden. The second episode saw the honeymoon over, and secret service and press colluding to make the foreign secretary resign. The country started to sink to its knees after a debilitating power-workers strike, and, for many British viewers, this was a strong reminder of the power strikes during the "winter of discontent" 1978–79. The strike was only broken, however, when the union leader in charge was exposed as a CIA agent provocateur.

In the final episode, Perkins horrified the U.S. government and British military after showing the decommissioning of a nuclear missile live on television. In an attempt to stop Perkins from going any further, the "behind-the-scenes powers-that-be" conspired to force him to resign in favor of a more moderate candidate. Yet in the climactic resignation address to the nation, Perkins melodramatically turned the tables, exposing those who had sought to topple him, and called for a general election to canvass the will of the people. As Perkins made his speech live on television, the drama cut to a reaction shot of the head of the secret service, surrounded by senior military officers, repeating Henry II's infamous plea to the knights who murdered Thomas Becket at Canterbury Cathedral: "Who will free me from this turbulent priest?"

In the final scene, the ending was, in one sense, ambiguous, but the implication was clear. Perkins stood in front of his mirror in his Sheffield Council flat, shaving in anticipation of polling day (returning almost full circle to where the drama began). As the screen faded to black, the sound of helicopters grew louder.

Out of context, the drama of A Very British Coup seems overly paranoid and melodramatic, yet at the time of transmission it reflected a real world of disquiet and anxiety. In Britain, the 1980s was a period of rapid social change. On the one hand it could be characterized by the yuppie boom, the growth in communications technologies and white collar employment, and the birth of the "me" generation. On the other hand it also saw rising unemployment and the suppression of the union movement, the (temporary) collapse of the Labour Party, the concentration of media power in the hands of a partisan minority, and the fear of increased government surveillance. The return to an aggressive anti-communist coldwar rhetoric concerned many, as did the stationing of U.S. nuclear weaponry on British soil. Many genuinely feared the possibility of a nuclear holocaust.

On transmission, Plater's adaptation also seemed to have a louder ring of truth as it closely followed allegations that senior British secret service officers at M15 had plotted to overthrow the Labour Prime Minister Harold Wilson in the early 1970s. These potentially spurious allegations were given an additional fillip when the British government banned publication of these claims in the United Kingdom.

Tapping into this unease, the aesthetic style of A Very British Coup often overlaps dialogue with images of people talking on telephones, computer screens scrolling through banks of data, and shots of undercover officers sitting in cars or on motorbikes observing the action. This suggests an overwhelming sense of surveillance. In a subtle post-Watergate twist, the drama also suggests that the calls of the prime minister are not bugged by MI5, but by U.S. intelligence, and then passed to the British secret service.

Notably, in A Very British Coup, the political realm is marked out as a profane place. Several scenes with Perkins take place in toilets, or while he is shaving (the first episode begins with a shot of urine splashing into a toilet bowl). This has the double effect of humanizing Perkins and his cause, whilst also showing that all power has a visceral and vulnerable side.

Ray McAnally was surrounded by an excellent cast: Keith Allen as a rough diamond investigative journalist turned spin doctor; Alan MacNaughtan as the intransigent secret service chief; and Tim McInnerny, playing against type, as a humorless secret service henchman. It was directed by Mick Jackson, whose career began in documentary before making the shocking drama-documentary Threads (1984), about a nuclear attack on Britain. He later moved to Hollywood to work on LA Story (1991) and The Bodyguard (1992). The program won numerous awards, including an Emmy for best television drama.

ROB TURNOCK

Cast

Harry Perkins	Ray McAnally
Sir Percy Browne	Alan MacNaughtan
Thompson	Keith Allen
Liz	Christine Kavanagh
Wainwright	Geoffrey Beevers
Fiennes	Tim McInnerny
Newsome	Jim Carter
Fison	Philip Madoc

Producers

Sally Hibbin, Ann Skinner

Programming History

Channel 4
June 19, June 26, and
July 3, 1988   Sunday 9:15–10:15

Victory at Sea

U.S. Compilation Documentary

Victory at Sea, a 26-episode series on World War II, represented one of the most ambitious documentary undertakings of early network television. The venture paid off handsomely for NBC and its parent company, RCA, in that it generated considerable residual income through syndication and several spin-off properties. It also helped establish compilation documentaries, programs composed of existing archival footage, as a sturdy television genre.

The series premiered on the last Sunday of October 1952, and subsequent episodes played each Sunday afternoon through May 1953. Each half-hour installment dealt with some aspect of World War II naval warfare and highlighted each of the sea war's major campaigns: the Battle of the North Atlantic, the attack on Pearl Harbor, the Battle of Midway, antisubmarine patrol in the South Atlantic, the Leyte Gulf campaign, and others. Each episode was composed of archival footage originally accumulated by the U.S., British, Japanese, or German navies. The footage was carefully edited and organized to bring out the drama of each campaign. That drama was enhanced by the program's sententious voice-over narration and by Richard Rodgers's stirring musical score.

Victory at Sea won instant praise and loyal viewers. Television critics greeted it as breakthrough for the young television industry: an entertaining documentary series that still provided a vivid record of recent history. The *New York Times* praised the series for its "rare power"; *The New Yorker* pronounced the combat footage "beyond compare"; and *Harper's* proclaimed that *"Victory at Sea* [has] created a new art form." The program eventually garnered 13 industry awards, including a Peabody and a special Emmy.

The project resulted from the determination of its producer, Henry Salomon, and from the fact that NBC was in a position to develop and exploit a project in compilation filmmaking. Salomon had served in the U.S. Navy during the war and was assigned to help historian Samuel Eliot Morison write the Navy's official history of its combat operations. In that capacity, Salomon learned of the vast amounts film footage the various warring navies had accumulated. He left military service in 1948, convinced that the footage could

be organized into a comprehensive historical account of the conflict. He eventually broached the idea to his old Harvard classmate Robert Sarnoff, who happened to be the son of RCA Chairman David Sarnoff and a rising executive in NBC's television network. The younger Sarnoff was about to take over the network's new film division as NBC anticipated shifting more of its schedule from live to filmed programming. A full documentary series drawn entirely from extant film footage fit perfectly with plans for the company's film division.

Production began in 1951 with Salomon assigned to oversee the enterprise. NBC committed the then-substantial sum of $500,000 to the project. Salomon put together a staff of newsreel veterans to assemble and edit the footage. The research took them to archives in North America, Europe, and Asia through 1951 and early 1952. Meanwhile Salomon received the full cooperation of the U.S. Navy, which expected to receive beneficial publicity from the series. The crew eventually assembled 60 million feet of film, roughly 11,000 miles. This was eventually edited down to 61,000 feet. Salomon scored a coup when musical celebrity Richard Rodgers agreed to compose the program's music. Rodgers was fresh from several Broadway successes, and his name added prestige to the entire project. More important, it offered the opportunity for NBC's parent company, RCA, to market the score through its record division.

When the finished series was first broadcast, it did not yet have sponsorship. NBC placed it in the lineup of cultural programs on Sunday afternoon. The company promoted it as a high-prestige program, an example of history brought to life in the living room through the new medium of television. In so doing, the company was actually preparing to exploit the program in lucrative residual markets. As a film (rather than live) production, it could be rebroadcast indefinitely. Furthermore, the fact that *Victory at Sea* dealt with a historical subject meant that its information value would not depreciate as would a current-affairs documentary.

Victory at Sea went into syndication in May 1953 and enjoyed a decade of resounding success. It played on 206 local stations over the course of ten years. It

Victory at Sea, 1952–53.
Courtesy of the Everett Collection

had as many as 20 reruns in some markets. This interest continued through the mid-1960s, when one year's syndication income equaled the program's entire production cost. NBC also aggressively marketed the program overseas. By 1964 *Victory at Sea* had played in 40 foreign markets. Meanwhile, NBC recut the material into a 90-minute feature. United Artists distributed the film theatrically in 1954, and it was subsequently broadcast in NBC's prime-time schedule in 1960 and 1963. The Richard Rodgers score was sold in several record versions through RCA-Victor. By 1963 the album version had grossed $4 million, and one tune from the collection, "No Other Love," earned an additional $500,000 as a single.

The combination of prestige and residual income persuaded NBC to make a long-term commitment to the compilation documentary as a genre. NBC retained the *Victory at Sea* production crew as Project XX, a permanent production unit specializing in prime-time documentary specials on historical subjects. The unit continued its work through the early 1970s, producing some 22 feature-length documentaries for the network.

Victory at Sea demonstrated the commercial possibilities of compilation documentaries to other networks as well. Such programs as *Air Power* and *Winston Churchill: The Valiant Years* directly imitated the *Victory at Sea* model, and the success of CBS's long-running historical series *The 20th Century* owed much to the example set by Salomon and his NBC colleagues. The fact that such programs still continue to play in syndication in the expanded cable market demonstrates the staying power of the compilation genre.

VANCE KEPLEY JR.

See also **War on Television**

Narrator
Leonard Graves

Producer
Henry Salomon

Music Composer
Richard Rodgers

Programming History
26 episodes
NBC
October 1952–May 1953   Sunday nonprime time

Victory at Sea, 1952–53.
Courtesy of the Everett Collection

Further Reading

Bluem, William, *Documentary in American Television,* New York: Hastings, 1965

Kepley, Vance, Jr., "The Origins of NBC's Project XX in Compilation Documentaries," *Journalism Quarterly* (1984)

Leyda, Jay, *Films Beget Film,* New York: Hill and Wang, 1964

Video Editing

Television historians have had little to say about post-production, despite the central role that video-editing practices and technologies have played in the changing look and sound of television. Video editing developed through three historical phases: physical film/tape cutting, electronic linear editing, and digital nonlinear editing. Even before the development of a successful videotape recording format in 1956 (the Ampex VR-

1000), time zone requirements for national broadcasting required a means of recording and transporting programs. Kinescopes, filmed recordings of live video shows for delayed airing in other time zones, were used for this practice. Minimal film editing of these kinescopes was an obligatory part of network television.

Once videotape found widespread use, the term "stop-and-go recording" was used to designate those "live" shows that would be shot in pieces then later edited together. Physically splicing the two-inch quad videotape proved cumbersome and unforgiving, however, and NBC/Burbank developed a system in 1957 that used 16mm kinescopes, not for broadcasting, but as "work-prints" to rough-cut a show before physically handling the videotape. Audible cues on the film's optical soundtrack allowed tape editors to match-back frame-for-frame each cut. Essentially, this was the first "offline" system for video. Known as ESG, this system of rough-cutting film and conforming on tape (a reversal of what would become standard industry practice in the 1990s) reached its zenith in 1968 with *Rowan and Martin's Laugh-In*. That show required 350 to 400 tape-splices and 60 hours of physical splicing to build up each episode's edit master.

A cleaner way to manipulate prerecorded video elements had, however, been introduced in 1963 with Ampex's all electronic Editec. With VTRs (videotape recorders) now controlled by computers, and in- and out-points marked by audible tones, the era of electronic "transfer editing" had begun. Original source recordings were left unaltered, and discrete video shots and sounds were re-recorded in a new sequence on a second-generation edit master. In 1967 other technologies added options now commonplace in video-editing studios. Ampex introduced the HS-100 videodisc recorder (a prototype for now requisite slow-motion and freeze-frame effects) that was used extensively by ABC in the 1968 Olympics. Helical-scan VTRs (which threaded and recorded tape in a spiral pattern around a rotating head) appeared at the same time and ushered in a decade in which technological formats were increasingly miniaturized (enabled in part by the shift to fully transistorized VTRs, like the RCA TR-22, in 1961). New users and markets opened up with the shift to helical: educational, community activist, and cable cooperatives all began producing on the half-inch EIAJ format that followed; producers of commercials and industrial video made the three-quarter-inch U-matic format pioneered by Sony in 1973 its workhorse platform for nearly two decades; newsrooms jettisoned 16mm news film (along with its labs and unions) for the same videocassette-based format in the late 1970s;

even networks and affiliates replaced venerable two-inch quad machines with one-inch helical starting in 1977.

The standardization of "time-code" editing, more than any other development, made this proliferating use viable. Developed by EECO in 1967, time-code was awarded an Emmy in 1971 and standardized by SMPTE shortly thereafter. The process assigned each video frame a digital "audio address," allowed editors to manage lists of hundreds of shots, and made frame accuracy and rapidly cut sequences a norm. The explosive growth of nonnetwork video in the 1970s was directly tied to these and other refinements in electronic editing.

Nonlinear digital editing, a third phase, began in the late 1980s both as a response to the shortcomings of electronic transfer editing, and as a result of economic and institutional changes (the influence of music video, and the merging of film and television). To creative personnel trained in film, state-of-the-art online video suites had become little more than engineering monoliths that prevented cutting-edge directors from working intuitively. In linear time-code editing, for example, changes made at minute 12 of a program meant that the entire program after that point had to be re-edited to accommodate the change in program duration. Time-code editing, which made this possible, also essentially quantified the process, so that the art of editing meant merely managing frame in/out numbers for shots on extensive edit decision lists (EDLs). With more than 80 percent of prime-time television still shot on film by the end of the 1980s, the complicated abstractions and obsolescence that characterized these linear video formats also meant that many Hollywood television producers simply preferred to deliver programs to the networks from film prints—cut on flatbeds and conformed from negatives. The capital-intensive nature of video postproduction also segregated labor in the suites. Directors were clients who delegated edit rendering tasks to house technicians and DVE artists. Online linear editing was neither spontaneous nor user-friendly.

Nonlinear procedures minimized the use of videotape entirely and attacked the linear straightjacket on several fronts. Beginning in 1983, systems were developed to download or digitize (rather than record) film/video footage onto videodiscs (LaserEdit, LucasArts' EditDroid, CMX 6000) or computer hard-drive arrays (Lightworks, the Cube). This created the possibility of random-access retrieval as an "edited" sequence. Yet nonlinear marked an aesthetic and methodological shift as much as a technological breakthrough. Nonlinear technologies desegregated the editing crafts; synthesized postproduction down to the desktop level, the personal-computer scale; allowed users to intervene, rework, and revise edited sequences without re-creating entire programs; and enabled editors to render and recall for clients at will numerous stylistic variations of the same show. Directors and producers now commonly did their own editing, in their own offices. When Avid launched its Composer in 1989, the trade journals marveled at its "32 levels of undo," and its ability to eliminate changes and restore previously edited sequences. Nothing was locked in stone.

This openness allowed for a kind of experimentation and formal volatility perfectly suited for the stylistic excesses that characterized contemporary television in the late 1980s and 1990s. When systems like the Avid and the Media 100 were upgraded to on-line mastering systems in the 1990s—complete with on-command digital video effects—the anything-can-go-anywhere premise made televisual embellishment an obligatory user challenge. The geometric growth of hard-disc memory storage, the pervasive paradigm of desktop publishing, and the pressure to make editing less an engineering accomplishment than a film artist's intuitive statement sold nonlinear procedures and technologies to the industry.

Video editing faces a trajectory far less predictable than that of the 1950s, when an industrial-corporate triumvirate of Ampex/RCA/NBC controlled technology and use. The future is open largely because editing applications have proliferated far beyond those developed for network oligopoly. Video is everywhere. Nonlinear established its beachhead in the production of commercials and music videos, not in network television. Still, by 1993, the mainstream Academy of Television Arts and Sciences had lauded Avid's nonlinear system with an Emmy. By 1995 traditional television equipment manufacturers such as Sony, Panasonic, and Grass Valley were covering their bets by selling user-friendly, nonlinear Avid-clones even as they continued slugging it out over digital tape-based electronic editing systems.

Although prime-time producing factories like Universal/MCA Television continued using a range of film, linear, and nonlinear systems through the mid-1990s, in a few short years digital technology would dominate postproduction. Even as Avid's Composer and Symphony systems were standard in high-resolution online work, a range of new technologies and standards undercut Avid's market share. While marketed initially as "industrial" and "nonbroadcast" technologies, Sony's DVCAM format and Apple's firewire protocol (both with 4:1:1 compression), pro-

vide cost-effective alternatives for image processing and data storage, and edit systems utilizing these formats rapidly spread in popularity. Sensing corporate decline, Avid rebuffed the very partner (Apple) that had made Avid synonymous with nonlinear work, by announcing that it would discontinue Macintosh support and make systems only for NT platforms in 1997–98. Apple got the last laugh, however, with its launch of Final Cut Pro (FCP) in 1999, an inexpensive editing program for Macintoshes that was built internally around the new DV compression and firewire.

Today, FCP makes filmmaking available to any consumer, even as it is widely utilized in postproduction, providing a system that even online editors can use outside of the online suites. Initially denigrated by high-end editors, FCP systems now are available with uncompressed and high-definition boards manufactured by Pinnacle and others; a development that further complicates the institutional appetite for segregating prime-time/high-definition work from industrial/consumer applications. Many of the new prime-time reality shows of the early 2000s, such as *Temptation Island,* for example, employed FCP, since the thousands of "unplanned" hours of DV-CAM footage now had to be waded through by gangs of low-paid production assistants before they could ever be assembled as a show by editors. In some ways, this was a throwback to the old Hollywood studio system, which utilized many assistants, and a retreat from the new status nonlinear had achieved by combining the entire editing process into single multitasked workstation. In this way, aesthetic and generic changes in television affect changes and uses of technologies.

The need for ever-higher resolutions (and therefore faster processing and increased data storage) continues to challenge editors and manufacturers. Rather than forever increase the storage, speed, and cost of each nonlinear work station, companies such as Quantel have developed common, large "servers" that can be accessed by scores of editors working simultaneously at remote workstations. These "wide area networks" represent but one way that postproduction executives and manufacturers juggle the inflationary costs of higher-resolution quality with the economies of data storage. At the same time, audiences at home now edit their own programming flows with personal video recorders such as TiVo and Video Replay that utilize the very storage and processing technologies that standardized nonlinear editing in the industry.

JOHN THORNTON CALDWELL

See also **Videotape**

Further Reading

Anderson, Gary H., *Video Editing and Postproduction,* White Plains, New York: Knowledge Industry Publications, 1988

Browne, Stephen E., *Videotape Editing: A Postproduction Primer,* Boston: Focal, 1989

Caldwell, John Thornton, *Televisuality: Style, Crisis, and Au-thority in American Television,* New Brunswick, New Jersey: Rutgers University Press, 1995

Dancyger, Ken, *The Technique of Film and Video Editing,* Boston: Focal, 1993

Scheieder, Arthur, *Electronic Post-Production and Videotape Editing,* Boston: Focal, 1989

Zettl, Herb, *Television Production Handbook,* Belmont, California: Wadsworth, 1992

Video-on-Demand. *See* **Pay-per-View/Video-on-Demand**

Videocassette

In 1956 the Ampex company announced that it had developed a new device: the videotape machine. This large reel-to-reel tape machine used four record heads (and was for this reason given the name "quad") and two-inch wide tape. The invention was quickly embraced by the broadcasting community, and on November 30, 1956, CBS broadcast the first program using videotape. Videotape is very similar in composition to audiotape. Most videotape consists of a Mylar backing, a strong, flexible plastic material that provides a base for a thin layer of ferrous oxide. This oxide is easily magnetized and is the substance that stores the video and audio information.

In 1969 Sony introduced its EIAJ-standard three-quarter-inch U-Matic series videocassette system. Although there were earlier attempts to establish a standard cassette or cartridge system, the U-Matic format was the first to become solidly accepted by educational and industrial users. Similar in construction and function to the audiocassette, the videocassette is a plastic container in which a videotape moves from supply reel to take-up reel, recording and playing back short program segments through a videocassette recorder. This form of construction emerged as a distinct improvement on earlier, reel-to-reel videotape recording and playback systems. The cassette systems, especially after they were integrated with camera and sound systems, enabled ease of movement and flexible shooting arrangements. The new devices helped create a wave of video field production ranging from what is now known as "electronic news gathering" to the use of video by political activist groups, educators, and home enthusiasts.

This last group was always perceived by video hardware manufacturers as a vast opportunity for further sales. After several abortive attempts to establish a consumer market with a home cartridge or cassette system, Sony finally succeeded with its Betamax format. Sony's success with Betamax was followed closely by other manufacturers with VHS (the "video home system"), a consumer-quality half-inch videocassette system introduced by JVC. Although the VHS format still dominates the home entertainment field, several competing formats are vying for both the consumer market and the professional field. The greatly improved Super-VHS (S-VHS) format has technical specifications that equal broadcast and cable TV quality. The S-VHS system is in turn being challenged by two 8mm cassette formats—Video 8 (a consumer-grade video format developed by Sony that uses eight-millimeter-wide tape) and Hi8 (an improvement on Sony's Video-8 format that uses metal particle tape and a higher luminance bandwidth). Other formats that are competing for the professional market include the half-inch Betacam and Betacam SP systems, the half-inch M-formats (M and M-II), three-quarter-inch U-matic SP, and the even more recent digital formats (D-1 and D-2).

It is safe to say that the development of videocassette systems has transformed many aspects of televisual industries and more general experience with television. The innovations within news services, the rapid expansion of home video systems that transformed the financial base of the film industry, and the acceptance of "video" as an everyday aspect of contemporary experience all rely to a great extent on the videocassette.

ERIC FREEDMAN

See also **Ancillary Markets; Betamax Case; Camcorder; Home Video; Sony Corporation; Videotape**

Further Reading

Browne, Steven E., *Video Editing: A Postproduction Primer,* Boston: Focal, 1989; second edition, 1993

Burrows, Thomas D., Donald N. Wood, and Lynne Schafer Gross, *Television Production: Disciplines and Techniques,* Dubuque, Iowa: Brown, 1978; fifth edition, 1992

Zettl, Herbert, *Television Production Handbook,* London: Pitman, 1961; fifth edition, Belmont, California: Wadsworth, 1992

Videodisc

Videodiscs are a storage medium for video programming. While some early mechanical television systems, such as John Logie Baird's, used spinning discs as part of the apparatus, modern videodiscs were developed and marketed in the 1970s as an alternative to videotape for the developing home video industry.

TelDec, a partnership between Telefunken and Decca, introduced an early disc system in 1975 in Germany. Called TeD (for Television Disc) it resembled a conventional phonograph system, with a needle reading grooves in the discs. The disc ran at 1,500 revolutions per minute (rpm) and played about ten minutes per disc. The system failed due its short playing time, lack of a software market, and many technical problems due to its fairly primitive hardware base, which couldn't deliver the bandwidth necessary for quality video playback.

Subsequent development of videodisc systems was divided into two distinct technical approaches. Capacitance systems resembled traditional phonograph systems, although the grooves' function is simply to guide the stylus over the disc surface, where pits on the disc would be read as an electrical signal and decoded into audio and video. Optical systems used a laser beam to read pits on a disc.

Both RCA in the United States and JVC in Japan developed capacitance systems in the 1970s. JVC's format was called VHD and utilized a ten-inch disc spinning at 900 rpm, yielding two video frames per rotation. VHD was sold only in Japan, and was eventually withdrawn after optical videodiscs came to dominate the Japanese market in the early 1990s.

In March 1981, RCA introduced its SelectaVision videodisc system after a substantial research program and a massive advertising campaign. This system featured a 12-inch vinyl disc that spun at speeds of up to 450 revolutions per minute, with four frames read in each rotation. When not playing, the disc was protected by a plastic caddy. The RCA system was a contact system, with an electrode at the end of a stylus reading variations in capacitance on the grooved disc.

RCA supported its rollout of SelectaVision by marketing discs of recent films, classic films, documentaries and how-to programs. They were sold at RCA dealers and were priced between $14.95 and $24.95. At launch, there were 100 titles available.

Philips and MCA developed similar optical videodisc systems that used a laser to read pits on a disc in 1972. Their systems were conformed in 1976, and players using this standard were first available in 1978. This system used a disc rotation of 1,800 rpm, and held 54,000 frames per side of disc, for a continuous playing time of 30 minutes. This method of encoding, called CAV (constant angular velocity) put each frame in its own track, with the adjacent tracks in concentric circles from the inside to the outside. Since each frame had its own unique address, CAV discs excelled at displaying still frames, short motion sequences, slow motion, and random access to individual frames or sequences.

These special features made it possible to use video, and video players, in entirely new ways. Educators embraced the discs as powerful teaching tools, and corporations adopted videodisc for industrial training and sales kiosks. Interactivity was boosted, first, by the creation of bar codes that could be bound into a book or lesson plan, making short motion sequences or still frames available on demand with the simple swipe of a light pen. Educational technologists called this "level 1 interactivity." Later, sophisticated videodisc machines with microprocessors provided built-in interactivity (level 2), and, finally, external microcomputers were linked to videodisc players. In this setup (level 3 interactivity) the student would follow a text on a computer screen, occasionally clicking a button that would trigger a motion sequence on an adjacent video screen.

Later, in order to fit an entire feature film on one disc, the CLV subformat was developed. This system could hold up to 60 minutes of video per side by varying the rotational speed of the disc from 600 to 1,800 rpm and by arraying the tracks in a long spiral, similar to a record album. While this system was more efficient than CAV, ordinary players could not access the special features available on CAV discs.

Videodiscs appeared after consumer videotape formats such as Betamax and VHS were introduced, and struggled to reach success in the marketplace. While videodisc players offered high-quality audio and video playback, consumers regarded videocassette recorders, which could record off the air as well as play prerecorded movies, as being more flexible.

As the home video industry evolved, tape became the most common rental medium, further limiting the sales of videodisc hardware and software. Competing formats also hurt the videodisc industry, in comparison to the video rental industry, which settled on VHS tape. As home videocassette recorders became a mass medium, their prices dropped significantly, while videodisc players, as a niche medium, remained expensive.

RCA bowed out of the home videodisc market in April 1984, after selling only about 550,000 players and losing $580 million in the venture. MCA's optical system, initially called DiscoVision, and later, LaserDisc, got a renewed lease on life by becoming the de facto disc system. As home video became more popular, connoisseurs would purchase videodiscs as the best signal source for their large-screen televisions and surround sound systems. As the audio compact disc diffused into the marketplace, videodisc players were developed that could play audio CDs, as well as new digital soundtracks on conventional videodiscs. These "combi-players" helped keep the format alive into the 1990s.

As the audio compact disc gained in popularity in the 1990s, researchers set out to develop a videodisc with the same appealing form factor. An early attempt was Philips's CD-I, or compact disk-interactive format. The CD-I players required a hardware add-on cartridge to handle MPEG decoding, and the discs faced the same limitation of laserdiscs: they could only hold about an hour of video. Since feature films typically run up to two hours, this meant that movies on CD-I had to be distributed on two discs.

It was not until the development of DVD that the right combination of technology, price, software support, and consumer acceptance converged to deliver a successful, mass market videodisc format.

DAVID KAMERER

Further Reading

Graham, Margaret, *RCA and the VideoDisc: The Business of Research,* Cambridge: Cambridge University Press, 1986
Sigel, Efrem, *Video Discs,* White Plains, New York: Knowledge Industry Publications, 1980

Videotape

As the 21st century began, videotape was probably familiar to most of the world's television viewers. The videocassette recorder was widely used in the home, in industry, and in education. Despite these widespread and common uses, however, videotape is of relatively recent origin. Its immediate antecedent is, of course, audiotape. Its immediate successor may be the digitally formatted disk (DVD), with even newer storage media under development.

The processes of recording audiotape and videotape work on the same principle. An audio or video recording head is a small electromagnet containing two coils of wires separated by a gap. An electrical current passing through the wires causes a magnetic charge to cross the gap. When tape coated with metal particles passes through the gap, patterns are set on the material. On audiotape, each syllable, musical note, or sneeze sets down its own distinct pattern. For videotape, which carries several hundred times as much information as audiotape, each image has its own pattern.

In the late 1940s and early 1950s, the explosive growth of television created an enormous demand for a way to record programs. Until links could be established through television lines or microwave broadcast relay, a blurry kinescope was the only means by which a network program could be recorded and replayed on different local television stations. As a result, television programs were unstable, ephemeral events. Once transmitted electronically, they were, for the most part, lost in time and space, unavailable for repeated use as either aesthetic, informational, or economic artifacts.

In 1951 engineers at Bing Crosby Enterprises demonstrated a black-and-white videotape recorder that used one-inch tape (tape size refers to tape width) running at 100 inches per second. At that rate, a reel of tape three feet in diameter held about 15 minutes of video. Crosby continued to fund the research, driven not only by a sense of commercial possibilities for videotape, but reportedly also by his wish to record television programs so that he could play golf without being restricted to live performances. Two years later, RCA engineers developed a recorder that reproduced not only black-and-white but color pictures. However, tape ran past the heads at a blinding 360 inches per second, which is 20 miles per hour. Neither machine produced pictures of adequate quality for broadcast. It simply was not possible to produce a stable picture at such a high tape speed.

During this same period, Ampex, a small electronics firm in California, was building a machine on a different principle, spinning the recording head. They succeeded in 1956 with a recorder the size of two washing machines. Four video heads rotated at 14,400 revolutions per minute, each head recording one part of a tape that was two inches wide. One of the engineers on the project, Ray M. Dolby, later became famous for his tape noise reduction process and his multisource theater sound system.

The quality of Ampex recordings was such an improvement over fuzzy kinescope images that broadcasters who saw the first demonstration, presented at a national convention, actually jumped to their feet to cheer and applaud. The television industry responded so enthusiastically that Ampex could not produce machines fast enough. It was the true beginning of the video age.

West Coast television stations could now, without sacrificing picture quality, delay live East Coast news and entertainment broadcasts for three hours until evening prime time, when most viewers reached their homes after work. By 1958 the networks were recording video in color, and by 1960 a recorder was synchronized with television studio electronics for the familiar film-editing techniques of the "dissolve" and "wipe."

Large two-inch reel-to-reel Ampex machines survived for a generation before they were replaced by more compact and efficient one-inch reel-to-reel machines and three-quarter-inch cassette machines. By 1990 most of the bigger recorders had been retired.

While U.S. companies were manufacturing two-inch, four-head, quadruplex scan machines, Japanese engineers were building the prototype of a helical scan machine that employed a single spinning head. Toshiba introduced the first helical scan VTR machine in 1959. JVC soon followed. The picture quality produced by these machines would remain inferior to "quad" machines for another ten years, unsuitable for the broadcast industry. But the smaller, more user-friendly helical scan machines, costing a fraction of the price of larger machines, quickly dominated the industrial and educational markets.

In 1972 Sony introduced the Port-a-pak black-and-white video recorder, weighing less than ten pounds. The tape had to be threaded by hand, but the Port-a-Pak was an important step on the way to electronic news gathering, known in the television industry as ENG. The next big step, Sony's U-matic three-quarter-inch tape machine, which played tape cassettes, eliminated physical handling of tape. CBS-TV News sent a camera team equipped with an Ikegami video camera and a U-Matic tape recorder to cover President Richard Nixon's trip to Moscow. News stories were soon being microwaved back to stations for taping or live feeds. Prior to these developments, the visual portion of news broadcasts had been produced on film. Videotape was the far superior medium for news. It needed no developing time, was reusable, and was more suited to the television's sense of immediacy. With the coming of videotape, television news editors replaced razor blades with electronic editing devices.

With broadcasting, educational, and industrial markets in hand, Japanese video companies turned their attention to the potentially vast home market. Hobbyists had already shown the way. With slightly modified portable reel-to-reel machines, they were taping television programs at home to play again later.

Sony, whose research was led by Nobutoshi Kihara, had considered the home market from the start. Recognizing that not only television stations but viewers ought to be able to time-shift programs, Sony president Akio Morita said, "People do not have to read a book when it's delivered. Why should they have to see a TV program when it's delivered?" Sony introduced its half-inch Betamax machine in 1975. A year later, rival Japanese companies, led by JVC, brought out VHS machines, a format incompatible with Betamax. VHS gradually captured the home market. People at home could simply and inexpensively record television programs and could buy or rent tapes. At last it was possible to go to the movies without leaving home.

Tape renting began when businessman Andre Blay made a deal to buy cassette production rights to 50 Twentieth Century Fox movies. Blay discovered that few customers wanted to buy his tapes, but everyone wanted to rent them.

The motion picture industry considered the videodisc a better way to bring a movie into the home, pointing out its sharper picture image, stereo sound, lower cost, and copy protection. However, the public wanted recording capability, not so much to copy rented films illegally as to record movies and television programs off the air for later playback. Videodisc players could not match the flexibility of videocassette recorders for time-shifting. In the battle over competing disc and tape formats, VHS tapes emerged the clear winner—at least in the first round.

In the first decade of the 21st century, a little more than 100 years after motion pictures were invented, millions of users could make movies, aided by nonlinear editing machines and computer programs that became better and cheaper year by year. Video cameras found their way into schools as learning tools. The high school library is now often referred to as "the media center," and the video yearbook has joined the printed version. Even in elementary schools, curious fingers are pushing camera buttons.

Videotape has also introduced specific changes at a very different level, expanding the production community in the professional arena. It is possible to produce a motion picture of technically acceptable quality at modest cost. For example, two young men barely out of college used videotape and nonlinear editing to make the feature film *The Blair Witch Project;* costing around $35,000 to produce, that movie has reportedly earned upward of $150 million. The phrase "desktop video" has become part of our language, often in relation to desktop publishing.

Videotape has had wide impact everywhere on Earth, including remote villages, where inexpensive tapes bring information and entertainment. A truck carrying a videotape player, a television set, and a portable generator is not an uncommon sight in many parts of the world. People living as far from urban centers as the Kayapo of the Brazil rainforest and the Inuit of northern Canada have been introduced to video and have themselves produced tapes to argue for political justice and to record their cultural heritage.

Several Third World governments have actively promoted videotape programs for adult education. For example, the Village Video Network in several countries provides an exchange for tapes on such subjects as farming, nutrition, and population control. International groups have given some villages video cameras and training to produce their own films, which are later shown to other villages.

Another result of video diffusion has been a widening of video journalism capability. The taping of Rodney King being beaten by members of the Los Angeles Police Department is just one example of how ordinary citizens are making a difference not only in news coverage but in the course of events. The potential for a video vigilantism by "visualantes" has not gone unnoticed, with its effects reaching not only journalism but law enforcement itself.

Far less significant uses of videotape technology have also developed. Replacing the traditional matchmaker, for example, is the video dating club. Participants tell a video camera of their interests, their virtues, and the type of person they would like to meet. They look at other videotapes and their videotape is shown to prospects.

Serious social and legal problems are also directly related to the easy use of this technology. Video piracy is rampant. A vast underground network feeds millions of illegal copies of videotaped movies throughout the world. The national film industries of a number of countries have been battered both by the pirating of their own films and by the influx of cheap illegal copies of Western films.

Some of these issues may be resolved with the development of still newer technologies. For both the video and computer industries, the future of information storage and retrieval may lie not with tape but with such optical media as CD-ROM and DVD, which offer the advantages of high density, random access, and no physical contact between the storage medium and the pickup device. As with the earlier videotape "revolution," the television and film industries are now shifting their investments and altering their industrial practices to deal with the newer, digitally based devices. The results of these changes for consumers, educators, and journalists are not easily predicted, yet there is no question that all these groups will experience alteration in media use akin to that caused by the introduction of videotape.

IRVING FANG

See also **Betamax Case; Home Video; Reruns/ Repeats; Sony Corporation**

Further Reading

Dobrow, Julia R., editor, *Social and Cultural Aspects of VCR Use,* Hillsdale, New Jersey: Lawrence Erlbaum, 1990

Videotex and Online Services

Videotex is the umbrella term used to describe interactive services built on computing and telecommunications technologies. Intended for personal use by a mass market, videotex systems electronically deliver text, graphics, audio, and video content via telephone lines or coaxial cable for display on a television set, video terminal, or personal computer. Users communicate with the service provider's computer and access through computer links called gateways content from outside information providers. All online systems, including the Internet, fall under this definition.

In the United States, videotex systems developed erratically as first newspaper publishers, then database operators, explored its technical and commercial potential. Early European videotex systems, such as the highly successful French Teletel service, became better established thanks to direct government support. Ultimately, the confluence of advancing personal computing technology, graphical user interface software, and the development of the World Wide Web portion of the Internet created a global standard for interactivity, displacing earlier videotex models.

Great Britain is credited with developing the first videotex system. Created by the British Post Office, Viewdata, later renamed Prestel, was demonstrated in 1974 and launched commercially in 1979. It operated until 1994. Other nations such as Germany, Japan, Finland, and the Netherlands introduced videotex services in the early 1980s, but France was the most successful.

France's Teletel, a simple text and graphics system commonly known as Minitel, was publicly demonstrated in 1980 and tested using 270,000 Minitel terminals. Equipped with a small screen and fold-down keyboard, the Minitel terminals were supplied free by state-owned France Telecom and installed in 2.5 million homes and offices by 1986. In addition to government support, another key to Minitel's national acceptance was the creation of a "trigger application" that would encourage repeat usage. Fast access to a national telephone directory provided this incentive, and consumer use of thousands of services, especially train schedules and reservations, dating services, and chat rooms grew rapidly.

According to the Organization for Economic Cooperation and Development, by the end of 1990 there were 6.8 million videotex users outside the United States. Germany's Bildschirmtext had over 250,000

users, and Great Britain's Prestel had 160,000. France's Minitel was the leader, and by November 1994, 14 million people were accessing services from 26,000 providers. Minitel use grew further in the mid-1990s thanks to access-enabling modem cards for personal computers. However, Minitel usage declined with the growth of the more sophisticated Internet. In 2000 Minitel use in total minutes dropped 11 percent after declining 7 percent in 1999. Although still useful in noncomputer households, Minitel's eventual demise is generally accepted.

The U.S. introduction of videotex dates to trials and commercial launches by newspaper publishers in the 1980s. Concerned with declining readership, publishers saw videotex as their electronic future and partnered with leading technology and telecommunication companies to offer text-and-graphics capable videotex systems. Their arrival was trumpeted by forecasts of extraordinary consumer market potential.

Knight-Ridder and AT&T partnered to form Viewtron, launched a trial in 1980, and started commercial operation in October 1983. The Miami area service required a dedicated AT&T Sceptre terminal, which retailed for about $600. To attract more subscribers, Viewtron later experimented with terminal rental, reduced monthly fees, and personal computer compatibility. The system folded in March 1986 with losses estimated at $50 million.

Gateway, a joint venture between Times Mirror and Infomart, a Canadian software firm, introduced its system in Orange County, California, in October 1984. Service was provided through decoder boxes attached to television sets. By mid-1985, the television-based service was discontinued, and personal computer owners were targeted. Nevertheless, Gateway closed in March 1986 after reportedly losing $30 million.

The *Chicago Sun-Times,* Centel Communications, and Honeywell began operating KeyCom in Chicago in January 1985. KeyCom also targeted the growing personal computer market but attracted few paying customers and closed after just six months.

The pioneering videotex services failed to realize commercial success for a number of reasons: system interfaces were complex; many followed a newspaper model, providing news and information already available less expensively in other media; some required the simultaneous use of the television and telephone by one person in the household, limiting the activities of others; and consumers felt the connect time and equipment charges were too high.

During this time, interest in online, text-only database and bulletin board services was growing among computer hobbyists. In 1978 CompuServe, which began as a mainframe time-sharing service, started offering to PC users access to a bulletin board with connect time paid for in one-minute increments. By 1980 CompuServe had attracted several thousand subscribers, and *The Columbus Dispatch* became the first newspaper to offer an electronic edition on the service. Within two years, 11 U.S. newspapers were on CompuServe, which, by the end of 1983, had 63,000 subscribers. Other database services included Delphi, founded by General Videotex Corporation in 1982 as an online encyclopedia, and General Electric's Genie, which entered the market in October 1985 with stock purchasing and financial advice services.

These database systems were joined by two text-and-graphics services designed for personal computer owners. IBM, Sears, and CBS (which dropped out in 1986) formed Trintex, later renamed Prodigy, in 1984. Test marketing began in mid-1988 followed by a national rollout of the service in September 1990. Quantum Computer Services, founded in 1985 and later renamed America Online, Inc., launched its Applelink and PC-link videotex services in 1988.

In the early 1990s, these online services worked to develop their user interfaces and create the most compelling package of content and services, pricing, and promotion. They all offered a bundle of proprietary content and services, including electronic mail, sports, weather, news from full-text magazines and newspapers, stock quotes, brokerage services, games, interest group forums and bulletin boards, and travel booking. Subscribers typically paid for a basic level of service plus surcharges for additional time and access to so-called enhanced or professional services.

By January 1991, IBM and Sears had spent approximately $650 million on Prodigy. A year later the service claimed 1.25 million subscribers, displacing CompuServe as the largest U.S. online service. But strategic missteps made Prodigy a lightening-rod for criticism. High electronic mail volume led Prodigy to levy a surcharge on heavy users. Subscribers were angered and thousands left the service. Prodigy also raised contentious First Amendment issues by censoring its online bulletin board postings for sexual content, going so far as to shut down its sexually explicit "frank discussion" forum.

In 1992, as competition intensified, Prodigy and CompuServe revised their price and content packages to attract new members. To address consumer concerns

of accumulating excessive charges, Prodigy introduced basic and enhanced service packages for flat monthly fees. CompuServe, relatively unknown outside the computer industry, rolled out new advertising intended to boost its brand awareness. Meanwhile, AOL's membership was increasing rapidly, and the service developed a Windows version that became available in January 1993.

The mid-1990s was a time of extraordinarily rapid change for online services. Subscribership grew as consumers who bought computers sought to maximize their utility. Graphical interfaces were created to facilitate online service use. Mosaic, the first graphical browser for the World Wide Web, was released by the University of Illinois, soon to be followed by Netscape's first navigator.

Prodigy defined online services for mainstream America with its 1993 national television advertising telling consumers "You gotta get this thing!" In April 1993, AOL revised its pricing plan to provide more hours for a set monthly fee, while, in July, Prodigy again angered its customer base by abandoning its just-introduced flat rate pricing in favor of standard, monthly fee plus hourly use packages.

Subscriber growth accelerated in 1994 with AOL, which reported 600,000 members in February reaching 1 million users by July. Prodigy reported over 2 million subscribers in May. Not to be left behind on the Internet front, AOL set to work on its own Web browser and Prodigy was offering Web browsing by the year's end.

Chaos continued to reign in 1995 as the online services expanded their content, upgraded their interfaces, introduced audio and video content, and waged price wars. Overall subscribership increased 64 percent, reaching 8.5 million users. A mass market was being created amidst the cutthroat competition.

Aggressive marketing enabled AOL, whose proprietary content offered novices a well-outfitted first stop on the Web, to exceed 4 million subscribers at the close of 1995. CompuServe held second place with 3.9 million users, and Prodigy, the first family-oriented service, saw its growth stalled at 2 million subscribers. The Microsoft Network (MSN) debuted in the summer, quickly attracting 600,000 subscribers. Losers in the competition were industry also-rans Delphi and GEnie.

Looking for additional avenues of growth, the online services were exploring service delivery to America's televisions. WebTV Networks, Inc., founded in 1995, blazed the trail, but the service failed to gain a significant following. Microsoft purchased WebTV in August 1997, renaming it MSN TV in July 2001. With fewer than 1 million subscribers and no recent growth, MSN TV appears to be fading.

In 1996 the online services were aligning with the World Wide Web to grow subscribership and revenues with updated Web-based content and electronic commerce. AOL and Prodigy enhanced their Internet access, but for Prodigy the effort came too late. Once the leading online service, by May Prodigy lost nearly half of its 2 million subscribers due to lagging technology, underdeveloped content, and difficulty of use. After investing over $1 billion, IBM and Sears sold the service to International Wireless. General Electric also sold GEnie after its user base declined from over 200,000 to 20,000.

AOL's tremendous growth overwhelmed its system, which crashed for almost the entire day on August 7, 1996, earning it the nickname "America Offline." Nevertheless, just weeks later, AOL acted to gain even more subscribers by adopting flat-rate pricing of $19.95 per month for unlimited access, breaking with the industry's traditional pricing model. Competitors had little choice but to follow suit.

By the late 1990s, online services had evolved into Internet service providers (ISPs), aggregating content and serving as portals for exploring the Internet. AOL continued to experience service reliability problems and agreed to refunds for millions of its members. In early 1997, CompuServe and Prodigy created ads ridiculing those service lapses. Still, it was clear AOL's marketing strategies were working.

By the turn of the century, there were over 4,500 ISPs in the United States. The online service business had matured with communications functions—e-mail, chat, instant messaging—and the Internet among its main attractions. Videotex had arrived. Telecommunications Reports International reported a third quarter 2001 total of 67.9 million U.S. subscribers to online services. AOL, which had acquired CompuServe and Netscape, remained the dominant player with over 25 million members, followed distantly by MSN, Prodigy, CompuServe, and others.

The migration of dial-up ISP subscribers to higher capacity broadband cable and digital subscriber line (DSL) services is the industry's most recent trend. Of the available methods of Internet access, only cable modem and DSL are showing sizable growth. This will undoubtedly create more change in this dynamic medium.

RANDY JACOBS

Further Reading

Conniff, Michael, "Video Text Is a Terminal Case," *Editor & Publisher* (December 19, 1992)

Hawkins, Donald, "Lessons from the 'Videotex School of Hard Knocks,'" *Online* (January 1991)

Kelley, Tina, "A World of Choices to Plug in to the Net," *New York Times* (May 20, 1999)

Kornbluth, Jesse, "Who Needs America Online?" *New York Times* (December 24, 1995)

O'Leary, Mick, "Consumer Services Prosper in Frantic '95," *Database* (December 1995)

Rading, Alan, "CompuServe Chases Prodigy with Rates, Ads," *Advertising Age* (February 24, 1992)

Tagliabue, John, "Online Cohabitation: Internet and Minitel," *New York Times* (June 2, 2001)

Thomas, Kim, "Keyed Up and Ready for Battle: Minitel Is Trying to Fight Off the Challenge of Its More Glamorous Rival, the Internet," *Financial Times* (August 20, 1996)

Truell, Peter, "Follow the French," *Wall Street Journal* (November 14, 1991)

Vietnam: A Television History

U.S. Compilation Documentary

When it aired in 1983, *Vietnam: A Television History* was the most successful documentary produced by public television. Nearly 9 percent of all U.S. households tuned in to watch the first episode, and an average of 9.7 million Americans watched each of the 13 episodes. A second showing of the documentary in the summer of 1984 garnered roughly a 4 percent share in the five largest television markets.

Before it aired in the United States, more than 200 high schools and universities nationwide paid for the license to record and show the documentary in the classroom as a television course on the Vietnam War. In conjunction with this educational effort, the Asian Society's periodical, *Focus on Asian Studies,* published a special issue titled "Vietnam: A Teacher's Guide" to aid teachers in the use of this documentary in the classroom.

The roots of the documentary reach back to 1977,

Vietnam: A Television History, Vietnamese families fleeing village, carrying belongings.
Photo courtesy of Wisconsin Center for Film and Theater Research

Vietnam: A Television History, U.S. soldiers marching in front of airplane.
Photo courtesy of Wisconsin Center for Film and Theater Research

when filmmaker Richard Ellison and foreign correspondent Stanley Karnow first discussed the project. Karnow had been a journalist in Paris during the 1950s and a correspondent in French Indochina since 1959. Karnow and Ellison then signed on Lawrence Lichty, then professor at the University of Wisconsin, as director of media research to help gather, organize, and edit media material ranging from audio- and videotapes and film coverage to still photographs and testimonials. As a result, *Vietnam: A Television History* became a "compilation" documentary, relying heavily on a combination of fixed moments (photographs, written text) as well as fluid moments (moving video and film).

The final cost of the project totaled approximately $4.5 million. At the time of its broadcast in 1983, it

Vietnam: A Television History, Henry Kissinger and Nguyen Van Thieu shaking hands.
Photo courtesy of Wisconsin Center for Film and Theater Research

was one of the most expensive ventures ever undertaken by public television. While the initial funding came from WGBH-TV Boston and the National Endowment for the Humanities, the Corporation for Public Broadcasting refused financial support. Ellison and Karnow sought additional backing abroad, gaining support from Britain's Associated Television (later to become Central Independent Television). Coproduction with French Television (Antenne-2) enabled the documentarians to gain access to important archives from the French occupation of the region. Antenne-2 produced the earliest episodes of the documentary, and Associated Television partially produced the fifth episode.

Karnow and Ellison saw the documentary as an opportunity to present both sides of the Vietnam War story, the U.S. perspective and the Vietnamese perspective. Throughout the 1960s and 1970s, documentaries and films on the Vietnam War tended to look solely at U.S. involvement and its consequences both at home and in the war-torn region. Karnow and Ellison sought to produce a more comprehensive historical account that traced the history of foreign invasion and subsequent Vietnamese cultural development over several hundred years. Both producers believed that by providing a more comprehensive view of Vietnam, the documentary could become a vehicle for reconciliation as well as reflection.

The series aired first in Great Britain to good reviews, although it did not receive the high ratings it achieved in the United States. At the time of its broadcast in the United States in the fall of 1983, the documentary received very positive reviews from the *New York Times,* the *Washington Post,* and *Variety.* Furthermore, both *Time* and *Newsweek* hailed the series as fair, brilliant, and objective.

However, other critics of the documentary were less complimentary and viewed it as overly generous to the North Vietnamese. The organization Accuracy in Media (AIM) produced and aired a response to the documentary seeking to "correct" the inaccurate depiction of Vietnam in the series. PBS's decision to air the two-hour show, titled *Television's Vietnam: The Real Story,* was seen by many liberal critics as bowing to overt political pressure. In fact, PBS's concession to air AIM's response to the documentary (its own production) was rare, perhaps unprecedented, in television history.

The controversy surrounding *Vietnam: A Television History* and the response to it, *Television's Vietnam: The Real Story,* raise the important question of bias in documentary production. Bias in the interpretation of historical events has fueled, and continues to fuel, rigorous debates among historians, politicians, and citizens. The experience Karnow and Ellison had in creating this documentary underscores the sense that the more "producers" involved in a project, the more difficult the task of controlling for bias becomes. The episodes prepared by the British and French teams were noticeably more anti-American in tone.

Despite the controversy, *Vietnam: A Television History* remains one of the most popular history documentaries used in educational forums. It inspired Stanley Karnow's best-selling book *Vietnam: A History,* which was billed as a "companion" to the PBS series. Both in the United States and around the world, the book remains a popular history text for college courses concerning the war and the controversy surrounding that conflict.

HANNAH GOURGEY

See also **Documentary: War on Television**

Further Reading

Banerian, James, editor, *Losers Are Pirates: A Close Look at the PBS Series "Vietnam: A Television History,"* Phoenix, Arizona: Sphinx, 1985

Bluem, A. William, *Documentary in American Television: Form, Function, and Method,* New York: Hastings House, 1965

Karnow, Stanley, *Vietnam: A History,* New York: Viking, and Middlesex, England: Penguin Books, 1983; second edition, New York: Penguin Books, 1997

Lichty, Lawrence, "*Vietnam: A Television History:* Media Research and Some Comments," in *New Challenges for Documentary,* edited by Alan Rosenthal, Berkeley: University of California Press, 1988

Maurer, Marvin, "Screening Nuclear War and Vietnam," *Society* (November–December 1985)

McGrory, Mary, "The Strategy of Stubbornness and the Policy All Too Familiar," *Washington Post* (December 22, 1983)

O'Connor, John E., *Teaching with Film and Television,* Washington, D.C.: American Historical Association, 1987

Renov, Michael, editor, *Theorizing Documentary,* New York and London: Routledge, 1993

Rhodes, Susan, editor, "Vietnam: A Teacher's Guide," *Focus on Asian Studies* (fall 1983)

Springer, Claudia, "*Vietnam: A Television History* and the Equivocal Nature of Objectivity," *Wide Angle* (1985)

Toplin, Robert Brent, "The Filmmaker as Historian," *American Historical Review* (December 1988)

Walkowitz, Daniel, "Visual History: The Craft of the Historian Filmmaker," *Public Historian* (winter 1985)

Vietnam on Television

Vietnam was the first "television war." The medium was in its infancy during the Korean conflict, its audience and technology still too limited to play a major role. The first "living-room war," as Michael Arlen called Vietnam, began in mid-1965, when President Lyndon Johnson dispatched large numbers of U.S. combat troops, beginning what is still surely the biggest story television news has ever covered. The Saigon bureau was for years the third largest the networks maintained, after New York and Washington, D.C., with five camera crews on duty most of the time.

What was the effect of television on the development and outcome of the war? The conventional wisdom has generally been that, for better or for worse, the medium was an antiwar influence. It brought the horror of war night after night into people's living rooms and eventually inspired revulsion and exhaustion. The argument has often been made that any war reported in an unrestricted way by television would eventually lose public support. Researchers, however, have quite consistently told another story.

There were, to be sure, occasions when television did deliver images of violence and suffering. In August 1965, after a series of high-level discussions that illustrate the unprecedented character of the story, CBS aired a report by Morley Safer that showed U.S. Marines lighting the thatched roofs of the village of Cam Ne with Zippo lighters and included critical commentary on the treatment of the villagers. This story could never have passed the censorship of World War II or Korea, and it generated an angry reaction from President Johnson. In 1968, during the Tet offensive, viewers of NBC news saw Col. Nguyen Ngoc Loan blow out the brains of his captive in a Saigon street. And in 1972, during the North Vietnamese spring offensive, the audience witnessed the aftermath of an errant napalm strike, in which South Vietnamese planes mistook their own fleeing civilians for North Vietnamese troops.

These incidents were dramatic, but far from typical of Vietnam coverage. Blood and gore were rarely shown. Just under a quarter of film reports from Vietnam showed images of the dead or wounded, most of these fleeting and not particularly graphic. Network concerns about audience sensibilities combined with the inaccessibility of much of the worst suffering to keep a good deal of the horror of war off the screen. The violence in news reports often involved little more than puffs of smoke in the distance, as aircraft bombed the unseen enemy. Only during the 1968 Tet and 1972 spring offensives, when the war came into urban areas, did its suffering and destruction appear with any regularity on TV.

For the first few years of the "living room war," most of the coverage was upbeat. It typically began with a battlefield round-up, written from wire reports based on the daily press briefing in Saigon (the "Five O'clock Follies," as journalists called it) read by the anchor and illustrated with a battle map. These reports had a World War II feel to them—journalists no less than generals are prone to "fighting the last war"—with fronts and "big victories" and a strong sense of progress and energy.

The battlefield round-up would normally be followed by a policy story from Washington, and then a film report from the field—typically about five days old, since film had to be flown to the United States for processing. As with most television news, the emphasis was on the visual and above all the personal: "American boys in action" was the story, and reports emphasized their bravery and their skill in handling the technology of war. A number of reports directly countered Morley Safer's Cam Ne story; they showed the burning of huts, which was a routine part of many search-and-destroy operations, but emphasized that it was necessary because these were Communist villages. On Thursdays, the weekly casualty figures released in Saigon would be reported, appearing next to the flags of the combatants, and, of course, always showing a good "score" for the United States.

Television crews quickly learned that what New York wanted was "bang-bang" footage, and this, along with the emphasis on the U.S. soldier, meant that coverage of Vietnamese politics and of the Vietnamese generally was quite limited. The search for action footage also meant it was a dangerous assignment: nine network personnel died in Indochina, and many more were wounded.

Later in the war, after Tet and the beginning of U.S. troop withdrawals in 1969, television coverage began to change. The focus was still on "American boys," to be sure, and the troops were still presented in a sympathetic light. But journalists grew skeptical of claims of progress, and the course of the war was presented more as an eternal recurrence than a string of decisive victories. There was more emphasis on the human

costs of the war, though generally without graphic visuals. On Thanksgiving Day 1970, for example, Ed Rabel of CBS reported on the death of one soldier killed by a mine, interviewing his buddies, who told their feelings about his death and about a war they considered senseless. An important part of the dynamic of the change in TV news was that the "up-close and personal" style of television began to cut the other way: in the early years, when morale was strong, television reflected the upbeat tone of the troops. But as withdrawals continued and morale declined, the tone of field reporting changed. This shift was paralleled by developments on the home front. Here, divisions over the war received increasing air time, and the antiwar movement, which had been vilified as Communist-inspired in the early years, was more often accepted as a legitimate political movement.

Some accounts of television's role in this war assign a key role to a special broadcast by Walter Cronkite wrapping up his reporting on the Tet Offensive. On February 27, 1968, Cronkite closed his special broadcast titled *Report from Vietnam: Who, What, When, Where, Why?* by expressing his view that the war was unwinnable, and that the United States would have to find a way out. Some of Lyndon Johnson's aides have recalled that the president watched the broadcast and declared that he knew at that moment he would have to change course. A month later, Johnson declined to run for reelection and announced that he was seeking a way out of the war; David Halberstam has written that "it was the first time in American history a war had been declared over by an anchorman" (see Singal, 1987).

Cronkite's change of views certainly dramatized the collapse of consensus on the war. But it did not create that collapse, and there were enough strong factors pushing toward a change in policy that it is hard to know how much impact Cronkite had. By the fall of 1967, polls were already showing a majority of Americans expressing the opinion that it had been a "mistake" to get involved in Vietnam; and by the time of Cronkite's broadcast, two successive secretaries of defense had concluded that the war could not be won at reasonable cost. Indeed, with the major changes in television's portrayal of the war still to come, television was probably more a follower than a leader in the nation's change of course in Vietnam.

Vietnam has not been a favorite subject for television fiction, unlike World War II, which was the subject of shows ranging from action-adventure series like *Combat* to such sitcoms as *Hogan's Heroes*. During the Vietnam War itself, it was virtually never touched in television fiction—except, of course, in disguised form on *M*A*S*H*. After Hollywood scored commercially with *The Deer Hunter* (1978), a number of scripts were commissioned, and NBC put one pilot, *6:00 Follies,* on the air. All fell victim to bad previews and ratings, and to political bickering and discomfort in the networks and studios. Todd Gitlin quotes one network executive as saying, "I don't think people want to hear about Vietnam. I think it was destined for failure simply because I don't think it's a funny war." World War II, of course, was not any funnier. The real difference is probably that Vietnam could not plausibly be portrayed either as heroic or as consensual, and commercially successful television fiction needs both heroes and a sense of "family" among the major characters.

An important change did take place in 1980, just as shows set in Vietnam were being rejected. *Magnum, P.I.* premiered that year, beginning a trend toward portrayals of Vietnam veterans as central characters in television fiction. Before 1980, vets normally appeared in minor roles, often portrayed as unstable and socially marginal. With *Magnum, P.I.* and later *The A-Team, Riptide, Airwolf,* and others, the veteran emerged as a hero, and in this sense the war experience, stripped of the contentious backdrop of the war itself, became suitable for television. These characters drew strength from their Vietnam experience, including a preserved wartime camaraderie that enabled them to act as a team. They also tended to stand apart from dominant social institutions, reflecting the loss of confidence in these institutions produced by Vietnam, without requiring extensive discussion of the politics of the war.

Not until *Tour of Duty* in 1987 and *China Beach* in 1988 did series set in Vietnam find a place on the schedule. Both were moderate ratings successes; they stand as the only major Vietnam series to date. The most distinguished, *China Beach,* often showed war from a perspective rarely seen in post–World War II popular culture: that of the women whose job it was to patch up shattered bodies and souls. It also included plenty of the more traditional elements of male war stories, and over the years it drifted away from the war, in the direction of the traditional concern of melodrama with personal relationships. But it does represent a significant Vietnam-inspired change in television's representation of war.

DANIEL C. HALLIN

See also ***China Beach;*** **Documentary;** *Selling of the Pentagon, The; 60 Minutes; Uncounted Enemy, The;* **Wallace, Mike; War on Television**

Further Reading

Anderegg, Michael A., *Inventing Vietnam: The War in Film and Television,* Philadelphia, Pennsylvania: Temple University Press, 1991

Berg, Rick, "Losing Vietnam: Covering the War in an Age of Technology," in *The Vietnam War and American Culture,* edited by John Carlos Rowe and Rick Berg, New York: Columbia University Press, 1991

Braestrup, Peter, *Big Story: How the American Press and Television Reported and Interpreted the Crisis of Tet 1968 in Vietnam and Washington,* Boulder, Colorado: Westview Press, 1977

Gibson, James William, "American Paramilitary Culture and the Reconstruction of the Vietnam War," in *Vietnam Images: War and Representation,* edited by Jeffrey Walsh and James Aulich, New York: St. Martin's Press, 1989

Gitlin, Todd, *Inside Prime Time,* New York: Pantheon, 1983

Hallin, Daniel C., *The "Uncensored War": The Media and Vietnam,* New York: Oxford University Press, 1986

Hammond, William M., *Public Affairs: The Military and the Media, 1962–1968,* Washington, D.C.: Center of Military History, U.S. Army, 1988

Heilbronn, Lisa M., "Coming Home a Hero: The Changing Image of the Vietnam Vet on Prime-Time Television," *Journal of Popular Film and Television* (spring 1985)

Martin, Andrew, "Vietnam and Melodramatic Representation," *East-West Film Journal* (June 1990)

Rollins, Peter C., "Historical Interpretation or Ambush Journalism? CBS vs. Westmoreland in *The Uncounted Enemy: A Vietnam Deception,*" *War, Literature, and the Arts* (1990)

Rollins, Peter C., "The Vietnam War: Perceptions Through Literature, Film, and Television," *American Quarterly* (1984)

Rowe, John Carlos, "From Documentary to Docudrama: Vietnam on Television in the 1980s," *Genre* (Winter 1988)

Rowe, John Carlos, "'Bringing It All Back Home': American Recyclings of the Vietnam War," in *The Violence of Representation: Literature and the History of Violence,* edited by Nancy Armstrong and Leonard Tennenhouse, London: Routledge, 1989

Rowe, John Carlos, and Rick Berg, editors, *The Vietnam War and American Culture,* New York: Columbia University Press, 1991

Singal, Daniel J., *The Making of a Quagmire: America and Vietnam During the Kennedy Era,* New York: Knopf, 1987

Springer, Claudia, "*Vietnam: A Television History* and the Equivocal Nature of Objectivity," *Wide Angle* (1985)

Trotta, Liz, *Fighting for Air: In the Trenches with Television News,* New York: Simon and Schuster, 1991

Turner, Kathleen J., *Lyndon Johnson's Dual War: Vietnam and the Press,* Chicago: University of Chicago Press, 1985

Violence and Television

Underlying concern for the level of violence in society has lead authorities in several countries to set up investigative bodies to examine the portrayal of violence on television. In 1969 the U.S. Surgeon General was given the task of exploring evidence of a link between television and subsequent aggression. The research that was a product of this inquiry attempted to find a "scientific" answer to the issue of whether television violence causes aggressive behavior, in much the way an earlier investigation had examined the link between cigarettes and lung cancer. The conclusions of the report were equivocal, and while some saw this as reflecting vested interests in the membership of the committee, research over the following years has not silenced the debate. While in 1985 the American Psychological Association stated that the overwhelming weight of evidence supports a causal relation, there is not unanimity even among American psychologists for this position. Not only the specific conclusions but the whole "scientific" framework of what has become known as "effects research" has been challenged. Reports by the British Broadcasting Standards Council and the Australian Broadcasting Tribunal investigation into TV violence in Australia, in the late 1980s and early 1990s, reflect a very different set of questions and perspectives.

The traditional question of whether viewing violence can make audiences more aggressive has been investigated by a variety of techniques. As social science, and psychology in particular, attempted to emulate the rigorous methods of the physical sciences, the question of television and violence was transferred to careful laboratory experiments. Inevitably, the nature of the issue placed practical and ethical constraints on scientific inquiry. A range of studies found evidence that subjects exposed to violent filmed models were subsequently more aggressive (see Bandura). Questions have been raised, however, as to what extent these findings can be generalized to natural viewing situations. What did participants understand about the task they were given? What did they think was expected of them? Can the measures of aggression used in such studies, such as hitting dolls or supposedly inflicting harm by pushing buttons be compared to violent behavior in real-world settings? Are these effects too short-term to be of practical concern?

One strategy to overcome some of these problems was to conduct studies in natural settings such as preschools or reform homes. Children watched violent or nonviolent television over a period of several weeks and the changes in their behavior were monitored. Such studies resemble more closely the context in which children normally watch television and measure the kinds of aggressive behavior that create concern. Results, however, have been varied, and the practical difficulties of controlling natural environments over a period of time mean that critics have been quick to point to flaws in specific studies.

From time to time, researchers have been able to capitalize on naturally occurring changes, gathering data over the period when television is first introduced to a community. A Canadian study compared children in two communities already receiving television to those in a community where television was introduced during the course of the study. Increases in children's aggressive behavior over time were found to accompany the introduction of television. A similar conclusion was drawn from a major study into the effects of the introduction of television in South Africa.

An alternative to manipulating or monitoring group changes in exposure to violence is simply to measure the amount of television violence children view and relate it to their level of aggressive behavior. While many studies have found a clear association between higher levels of violent viewing and more aggressive behavior, proving that television caused the aggression is a more complex issue. It is quite possible that aggressive children choose to watch more violent programs, or that features of their home, socioeconomic, or school background explain both their viewing habits and their aggression. Attempts to test these alternative models have involved complex statistical techniques and, perhaps most powerfully, studies of children over extended periods of time, in some cases over many years. Studies by Huesmann and his colleagues have followed children in a variety of different countries. They argue that the results of their research demonstrate that the extent of TV viewing in young children is an independent source of later aggression. They also suggest that aggressive children choose to watch more violent programs, which in turn stimulates further aggression. The research group gathered data from a range of countries, and these data indicate that the relationship can be found even in countries where

The Lawman, John Russell, Peter Brown, 1958–62.
Courtesy of the Everett Collection

screen violence is much lower than in the United States. A comparison of Finland to the United States found, however, no relationship between violent viewing and aggressive behavior in Finnish girls. This suggests that the impact of television has to be understood in a cultural context and involves social expectations about appropriate gender roles.

Critics of these attempts to relate viewing and aggression have questioned both the accuracy of the methods by which reports of television habits and preferences were gained, either from parents or by retrospective recall, and the measures used to demonstrate aggression. In reviewing debates on research findings, it becomes clear that any study can be perceived as flawed by those taking an opposing position. However, supporters of the effects tradition point to the cumulative weight of research with different methodological characteristics; a meta-analysis by Paik and Comstock of more than 200 studies found a moderate effect of screen violence on aggressive behavior.

Even among researchers who are convinced of a causal link between television and violence, explanations of when and why such a link is forged are varied. One of the simplest ideas is that children imitate the violence they see on television. Items associated with violence through television viewing can serve as cues to trigger aggressive behavior in natural settings. The marketing of toys linked to violent programs taps into these processes. Children are more likely to reenact the violence they have seen on television when they have available products that they have seen being used in violent scenarios. The challenge for social-learning theorists has been to identify under what conditions modeling occurs. Does it depend on viewers' emotional state (for instance, a high level of frustration) or on a permissive social environment? Is it important whether the violence is seen to be socially rewarded or punished? It has also been claimed that high levels of exposure to violent programs desensitize children, making them more tolerant of and less distressed by violence. Thus, children who had been watching a violent program were less willing to intervene and less physiologically aroused when younger children whom they had been asked to monitor via a television screen were seen fighting than those children who had watched a nonviolent program. Alternatively, high arousal itself has been suggested as an instigator of violence. The significance of such an explanation is that it does not focus on violence as such; other high-action, faster-cutting programs may also stimulate aggression. It is evident that once focus shifts from proving causation to identifying processes, the characteristics of particular violent programs become important, because programs vary in many ways besides being classifiable as violent or nonviolent.

The traditional violence-effects approach has been criticized as employing a hypodermic model, where the link between television violence and viewer aggression is seen as automatic. Such an approach not only ignored the complexity of television programs but also how responses to television are mediated by characteristics of viewers, by their thoughts and values. As psychology has become more concerned with human thinking, there has been greater interest in how viewers, particularly children, interpret the television they watch. Research has shown that children's judgments of violent actions relate to their understanding of the plot. This understanding in turn may be influenced by such issues as plot complexity, the presence and placement of commercial breaks, the age of the child, and so on. Rather than seeing violence as a behavior pattern that children internalize and reproduce on cue, children are seen to develop schematic understandings of violence. The values they attach to such behavior may depend on more complex issues, such as the extent to which they identify with a violent character, the apparent justifiability of their actions, and the rewards or punishments perceived for acting aggressively.

It has often been feared that children are particularly

The Untouchables, Robert Stack, 1959–63.
Courtesy of the Everett Collection

Buck Rogers in the 25th Century, Gil Gerard, 1979–81.
Courtesy of the Everett Collection

vulnerable to violence on television because their immature cognitive development does not enable them to discriminate between real and fictional violence. In a detailed study of children's responses to television and cartoons in particular, Hodge and Tripp found that children could make what they termed "modality judgments" as young as six years old. They were well aware that the cartoon was not real. What developed at a later stage was an understanding of certain programs as realistic, building the links between television and life experience. Such research demonstrates a coming together of psychological and cultural approaches to television. Researchers interested in the structure of program meanings and in children's psychological processes can collaborate to increase our knowledge of how children actively interpret a violent cartoon.

Another dimension of the television violence debate has been a concern that frequent viewing of violence on television makes people unrealistically fearful of violence in their own environment. Gerbner's "enculturation" thesis appeared supported by evidence that heavier viewers of television believed the world to be more violent than those who watched television less. Alternative explanations have been offered for these findings, with reference to both social class (heavy viewers may actually live in more dangerous areas) and personality variables. It has also been suggested that those fearful of violence may choose to watch violent programs such as crime dramas, where offenders

are caught and punished. Again, viewers are seen as actively responding to violence on television, rather than simply being conditioned by it. Gerbner presents a valuable description of the violent content on television, differentiating between those who are portrayed as attackers and those who are the victims in our television world. Yet, Greenberg has argued against a cumulative drip-drip-drip view of how television affects viewers' perceptions of the world. Instead, he poses a "drench" hypothesis that single critical images can have powerful effects, presumably for good or ill.

Traditional television-violence-effects research employed simple objective criteria for determining the extent of violence in a program. A feature of this approach has been the development of objective definitions of violence that have enabled researchers to quantify the extent of violence on our screens (80 percent of prime-time American television contains at least one incident of physical violence). From this perspective, cartoons are just as violent as news footage, and a comic cartoon like *Tom and Jerry* is among the most violent on television. Such judgments do not accord with public perceptions, and in recent years there has been an interest in discovering what the public consider violent. A carefully controlled study of audience perceptions of violence was conducted in Britain by Barrie Gunter. He found that viewers rated an action as more violent if the program were closer to their life experience than if the same sort of action appeared

Hunter, Stepfanie Kramer, Fred Dryer, 1984.
Courtesy of the Everett Collection

on a cartoon, western, or science fiction drama. He also found that ratings of violence were linked in complex ways to characteristics of the attacker, victim, and setting, and to the personality of the rater. This focus on what audiences found violent and disturbing and what they believed would disturb children has provided a rather different framework for considering issues of violence on television.

Research for the Australian investigation of violence on television, in contrast to the U.S. Surgeon General's report, was not concerned with establishing causal links but on finding how audience groups reacted to specific programs. The aim was to improve the quality of guidelines to programmers and the information provided for prospective audiences. The research concluded that the most important dimension for viewers in responding to violence was whether the subject matter was about real life. The interest in public perceptions of violence of television has stimulated new research techniques. British researchers have asked

their subjects to make editing decisions as to what cuts are appropriate before material is put to air. Docherty has argued that certain material, both fiction and nonfiction, can elicit strong emotional reactions, which he has termed "deep play." Individuals' reactions to a horror movie such as *Nightmare on Elm Street* appeared largely a question of taste. In contrast, a docudrama about soccer (football) hooliganism provoked polarized and intense reactions. Some viewers thought the violent material was important and should not be cut; others reacted with great hostility to a portrayal of violence that challenged their sense of social order.

The issue of the appropriate level of televised violence arises not just with fictional violence but also with the televising of news footage. When terrorists attacked the United States on September 11, 2001, some of the televised images—particularly the crashing of the second airplane into the World Trade Center and the subsequent collapse of the two towers—resembled scenes from the disaster-movie genre, but this violence clearly generated an intense emotional reaction based on its reality, immediacy, and national threat. For a time, the significance of the story and the saturation media coverage overwhelmed concerns about the impact of the footage on the young and vulnerable. Generally, however, television stations attempt a balance between reporting what is occurring in the world and making the violence they cover palatable for the living room. Reporters have put themselves at risk attempting to film savage violence in a way that can tell their story but not overwhelm the viewers. The violence of the Vietnam War played out nightly in American living rooms, and this coverage has been seen as a major factor in generating the antiwar movement. Coverage of the Gulf War and the "war on terrorism," however, indicates how use of the media, especially television, has become part of policymakers' wartime strategy. Research on the role of the media in the Gulf War suggests that viewers were often happy to be spared the details of the war as long as their side was winning. It is perhaps unsurprising that, despite concern expressed about the impact of such a violent crisis on impressionable children, the news image that evoked most anger and sadness in British children was on the plight of sea birds covered in oil.

The televised portrayal of the war—the sanitized images of high technology, the frequently employed analogy of the video game, the absence of blood and gore—is thus relevant to the discussion of violence and television. The fact that the political debates about violence on television have focused so strongly on the potential harm to children may act to divert attention away from the way certain violence is censored in the interests of the state. An excessive focus on screen violence can deflect attention from the complex issues of state and interpersonal violence that exist in our world.

Until recently, the potential of television to challenge viewers to think about issues of violence has been largely ignored. A study by Tulloch and Tulloch of children's responses to violence in a series of programs has found young people more disturbed by a narrative about a husband's violent assault on his wife than the objectively more serious violence of a Vietnam War series. Their research has demonstrated clearly that the meanings children attach to violence on television is a function of their age, gender, and social class. Not only does this confirm other findings that relate the perception of violence to personal significance, it points to the potential educative effects of violence on television. Once the portrayal of violence is not seen as necessarily increasing violence, the ways programs can work toward the promotion of nonviolence can be investigated.

However, despite attempts to broaden the debate about violence and television, the dominance within the United States of the media-effects tradition was again illustrated in responses to a series of headline-grabbing incidents of violence in American schools, particularly the deadly shootings in April 1999 at Columbine High School in Littleton, Colorado. At this time, new-media forms, video games, and the Internet were identified alongside television and film as causes of young people's aggression. The debates that followed the shootings, including testimony given to Congress, illustrated the gap between causal and cultural models. Grossman, a military psychologist, extended the desensitization approach to television violence to claim that video games are training children to be killers by helping to erode a natural reluctance to take human life. Taking a media studies perspective, Henry Jenkins argued that it was important to look at what young people did with the media, not what the media did to them. Young people are active media consumers, taking from media their own meanings. Some of these meanings are destructive of themselves and others, while some are a basis for creativity and positive social interaction. From this perspective, if we wish to engage with concerns about media violence, we need to foster young people's critical consumption of a diversity of media forms and content.

MARIAN TULLOCH AND JOHN TULLOCH

See also **Audience Research: Effects Analysis; Audience Research: Industry and Market Analysis; Broadcasting Standards Commission; Children and Television; Detective Programs; Police Programs; Standards and Practices; Terrorism; War on Television; Western**

Further Reading

Australian Broadcasting Tribunal, *TV Violence in Australia*, Sydney: Commonwealth of Australia, 1990

Bandura, A., *Aggression: A Social Learning Analysis*, Englewood Cliffs, New Jersey: Prentice-Hall, 1973

Cumberbatch, D., and D. Howitt, *A Measure of Uncertainty: The Effects of the Mass Media*, London: John Libbey, 1989

Friedlich-Cofer, L., and A.C. Huston, "Television Violence and Aggression: The Debate Continues," *Psychological Bulletin* (1986)

Friedman, J.L., "Television Violence and Aggression: A Rejoinder," *Psychological Bulletin* (1986)

Greenberg, B.S., and W. Gantz, editors, *Desert Storm and the Mass Media*, Cresskill, New Jersey: Hampton Press, 1993

Gunter, B., *Dimensions of Television Violence*, Aldershot, England: Gower Press, 1985

Gunter, B., and J. McAleer, *Children and Television: The One Eyed Monster?* London: Routledge, 1990

Hodge, R., and D. Tripp, *Children and Television: A Semiotic Approach*, Cambridge: Polity, 1986

Huesman, L.R., and L.D. Eron, editors, *Television and the Aggressive Child: A Cross National Comparison,* Hillsdale, New Jersey: Erlbaum, 1986

Jenkins, H., "The Uses and Abuses of Popular Culture: Raising Children in the Digital Age," *College Board Review* 189/190 (2000)

Oskamp, S., editor, "Television as a Social Issue," *Applied Social Psychology Annual 8,* Newbury Park, California: Sage, 1988

Paik, H., and G. Comstock, "The Effects of Television Violence on Anti-social Behavior: A Meta-analysis," *Communication Research,* 21 (1994)

Tulloch, J.C., and M.I. Tulloch, "Discourses About Violence: Critical Theory and the 'TV Violence' Debate," *Text* (1992)

Wober M., and B. Gunter, *Television and Social Control,* Aldershot, England: Gower Press, 1988

Vivendi. *See* Universal

Voice of Firestone, The

U.S. Music Program

One of network television's preeminent cultural offerings, *The Voice of Firestone* was broadcast live for approximately 12 seasons between 1949 and 1963. With its 46-piece orchestra under the direction of Howard Barlow, this prestigious, award-winning series offered viewers weekly classical and semiclassical concerts featuring celebrated vocalists and musicians. This series was also highly representative of the debate that still rages over the importance of ratings and mass-audience appeals as opposed to cultural-intellectual appeals targeted to comparatively small audiences in the development of network television schedules.

Sponsored throughout its history by the Firestone Tire and Rubber Company, *The Voice of Firestone* began as a radio offering in December 1928 and transferred to television as an NBC simulcast on September 5, 1949. Long on musical value but often short on television production value, the show was faulted occasionally for its somewhat stilted visual style, its pretentious nature, and its garish costume choices. In time, however, the series drew critical praise and a consistent audience of 2 million to 3 million people per broadcast.

Notwithstanding its "small" viewership, the Firestone series vigorously maintained its classical/semi-classical format, adding only an occasional popular music broadcast with stars from Broadway, night clubs, or the recording industry, as well as an occasional theme show developed around various topics of interest, such as 4-H clubs, highway safety, or the United Nations. The program attracted the great performers of the day for nominal fees, with Rise Stevens setting the record for most program appearances at 47. In his *Los Angeles Times* feature of November 1, 1992, Walter Price observed that the Metropolitan Opera star "had the face, figure, and uncanny sense of the camera to tower above the others in effect."

In 1954 *The Voice of Firestone*'s audience size became a major issue. Citing low ratings and the negative effect of those ratings on other programs scheduled around it, NBC demanded a time change. Historically, the show had been broadcast in a Monday, 8:30–9:00 P.M., prime-time period. As an alternative, NBC officials suggested leaving the Monday evening radio program in its established time but moving the television version to Sunday at 5:30 P.M., or to an earlier or later slot on Monday. Firestone officials, considering the millions of dollars their company had spent for air time and talent fees over the previous 26 years, refused to budge.

Determined to lure viewers away from *Arthur God-*

frey's *Talent Scouts,* CBS's highly rated competition for the time period, NBC exercised control of its schedule and canceled both the radio and television versions of *The Voice of Firestone,* effective June 7, 1954. The following week, the simulcast reappeared on ABC in its traditional day and time, where it remained until June 1957. In that month, the radio portion was dropped, but after a summer hiatus the television show returned on Monday evenings at 9:00 P.M. In June 1959, despite more popular music in its format, poor ratings again forced the show's cancellation, it being replaced by the short-lived detective series *Bourbon Street Beat.*

Amid numerous critical outbursts, threats of Federal Communications Commission action, and a joint resolution by the National Education Association and National Congress of Parents and Teachers lamenting its cancellation, all three networks offered *Voice of Firestone* fringe time slots, which the Firestone Company rejected. ABC officials indicated that the series was simply the victim of the greater attention paid to television ratings. In radio, critics pointed out, audience delivery to program adjacencies was never considered as important as it was in television, and concert music programs in prime time were regarded as too weak to hold ratings through the evening schedule. Condemning the loss of the Firestone program, Norman Cousins wrote in his May 9, 1959, *Saturday Review* editorial that stations were now pursuing a policy designed to eliminate high-quality programs "even if sponsors are willing to pay for them." Cousins decried the fact that station managers measured program weakness through ratings, and a "'weak spot' in the evening programming . . . must not be allowed to affect the big winners."

The Voice of Firestone was brought back to ABC on Sunday evenings, 10:00–10:30 P.M., in September 1962. However, despite numerous commendations, positive critical reviews, and a star-studded rotation of musical conductors and performers, the audience remained at 2.5 million people. *The Voice of Firestone* left the air for its third and final time in June 1963. With its passing, the American public lost an alterna-

tive form of entertainment whose long heritage was one of quality, good taste, and integrity.

JOEL STERNBERG

See also **Advertising, Company Voice; Music on Television**

Narrator
John Daly (1958–59)

Regular Performers
Howard Barlow and the Firestone Concert Orchestra

Programming History

NBC	
September 1949–June 1954	Monday 8:30–9:00
ABC	
June 1954–June 1957	Monday 8:30–9:00
September 1957–June 1959	Monday 9:00–9:30
September 1962–June 1963	Sunday 10:00–10:30

Further Reading

Adams, Val, "Firestone Show to End on June 1," *New York Times* (April 15, 1959)

Brooks, Tim, and Earle Marsh, *The Complete Directory to Prime Time Network TV Shows 1946–Present,* New York: Ballantine, 1979; fifth edition, 1992

Cousins, Norman, "The Public Still Owns the Air," *Saturday Review* (May 9, 1959)

"Firestone at 8:30," *Newsweek* (June 21, 1954)

"Firestone Loses Its Voice," *Business Week* (May 22, 1954)

"Firestone's Voice Silenced by NBC," *New York Times* (May 15, 1954)

Gould, Jack, "Radio-TV in Review," *New York Times* (May 26, 1954)

"Old Opera House Now Big TV Show," *New York Times* (June 15, 1954)

Price, Walter, "Before MTV, There Was Opera," *Los Angeles Times* (November 1, 1992)

Spalding, John Wendell, "An Historical and Descriptive Analysis of 'The Voice of Firestone' Radio and Television Program, 1928–1959," Ph.D. diss., University of Michigan, 1961

Voice-over

Voice-over is the speaking of a person or presenter (announcer, reporter, anchor, commentator, etc.) who is not seen on the screen while her or his voice is heard. Occasionally, a narrator may be seen in a shot but not be speaking the words heard in the voice-over.

Voice-over has diverse uses in a variety of television genres. Like other forms of television talk, it aims at being informal, simple, and conversational. However, except for on-the-spot reporting such as sports events, voice-over is often less spontaneous than the language of talk shows; it is heavily scripted, especially in genres such as the documentary. Voice-over is not simply descriptive; it also contextualizes, analyses, and interprets images and events. Commentaries have the power to reverse the significance of a particular visual content. Voice-over is, therefore, an active intervention or mediation in the process of generating and transmitting meaning. However, viewers are rarely aware or critical of the scope of mediation in part because the visual image itself confers credibility and authenticity on the voice-over. But voice is at times more credible than vision; it is an integral part of a person's identity. This was experienced in the 1988 British government ban on broadcast interviews with representatives of 11 Irish organizations, including Sinn Fein, the political wing of the Irish Republican Army. Broadcasters were allowed, however, to voice-over or caption a banned representative's words.

Voice-over is used as a form of language transfer or translation. Viewers of news programs are familiar with the use of voice-over translation of statements or responses of interviewees who do not speak in the language of the viewing audience. Inherited from radio, this form of language transfer allows the first and last few words in the original language to be heard, and then fades them down for revoicing a full translation. The voice-over should be synchronous with the speaker's talk, except when a still picture is used to replace footage or live broadcast. Usually gender parity between the original and revoiced speakers is maintained.

As a form of language transfer, voice-over is not limited to the translation of brief monologues; sometimes it is used to cover whole programs such as parliamentary debates, conferences, or discussions. Its production is usually less expensive than dubbing and subtitling. Some countries, such as Poland and the Balkan states, use voice-over as the main method of revoicing imported television programs. Usually, the revoicing is done without much performance or acting, even when it involves drama genres.

AMIR HASSANPOUR

See also **Dubbing; Language and Television; Subtitling**

Further Reading

Blu, Susan, and Molly Ann Mullin, *Word of Mouth: A Guide to Commercial Voice-Over Excellence,* second edition, Pomegranate Press, 1999

Collins, Richard, "Seeing Is Believing: The Ideology of Naturalism," in *Documentary and the Mass Media,* edited by John Corner, London: Edward Arnold, 1986

Dries, Josephine, "Breaking Language Barriers Behind the Broken Wall," *Intermedia* (December/January 1994)

Karamitroglou, Fotios, *Towards a Methodology for the Investigation of Norms in Audiovisual Translation: The Choice Between Subtitling and Revoicing in Greece,* Amsterdam and Atlanta, Georgia: Radopi, 2000

Murdock, Graham, "Patrolling the Border: British Broadcasting and the Irish Question in the 1980s," *Journal of Communication* (1991)

Wilson, Tony, *Watching Television: Hermeneutics, Reception and Popular Culture,* Cambridge: Polity Press, 1993

W (formerly Women's Television Network)

Canadian Cable Network

The development of cable television as a feasible distribution system gave rise to increased opportunities and demand for channels delivering distinctive content. In many contexts "women's networks" of various types have provided one popular form of distinction. These networks advertise themselves as serving female viewers, often scheduling programming conventionally associated with female viewing pleasures, such as talk shows, versions of soap opera, or melodrama. Given the size of the female audience, the volume of women's household goods purchases, and their presumably identifiable viewing habits, the strategy of targeting a sex-specific audience developed as one of the more feasible and successful experiments involving "niche audiences."

In June 1994, the Canadian Radio-television and Telecommunications Commission (CRTC) granted a license for the Women's Television Network (WTN), which became one of seven "specialty" channels added to Canadian cable offerings in January 1995. Supporters argued the need for such a niche network for business reasons, citing the quantity of female viewership (the impetus behind the U.S. cable network Lifetime). But the license was also granted in recognition of the limited access women had to creative, production, and executive positions in Canadian television.

Yet WTN was mired in controversy from its inception. The issue was not its programs but the manner in which cable providers introduced the seven specialty channels in 1995. Initially, cable subscribers were forced to accept a rate hike with the addition of most of the channels. Later, however, they were given an option not to accept those channels requiring an increase in monthly fees. WTN was fortunate to be included among channels offered within the standard package, requiring no additional fee for its service. This was a key to ensuring the network had ample time to develop its identity and audience.

Moffat Communications controlled a 68 percent interest in WTN at its launch. Other stakeholders included a group of women investors, The Barde Group (8.42 percent), Ron Rhodes (12 percent), and Michael Ihnat (10 percent), all of whom had lobbied for a women's network until they found a corporation large enough to make a cable license possible. Moffat was a moderate-sized cable and broadcast entity at the time that also owned CKY-TV, the CTV affiliate in Winnipeg, and various other cable interests. Moffat's ownership also based the network in Winnipeg, rather than the more common media center, Toronto. Although it purchased some high-profile programming from other sources, WTN mandated that 70 percent of its schedule be Canadian and spent $9 million on Canadian productions in 1996. The network featured some U.S. exports, including *The Mary Tyler Moore Show* and *Rhoda,* as well as, in its early years, British drama and comedies such as *French and Saunders.* It also programmed documentaries and biography series focused on women and their lives and featured regular film blocks in prime time. For example, on Fridays WTN offered *Through Her Eyes,* a series of films directed by women from around the world.

The network achieved limited success in its first few months (an estimated audience of 23,000 in February 1995). The network was initially unavailable in Montreal, preventing it from reaching that city's sizable market. At the end of six months it was the least watched of the new specialty channels. As a result, executives responded to criticism that the initial programming was too serious and feminist by reconfiguring the network's profile. One television critic cited the replacement of the hard-hitting public affairs talk show *POV: Women* with *Take 3* (a lifestyle series) as illustrative of the shift introduced by the fall of 1995.

The program alterations proved successful, garnering many positive reviews of the network, and by August 2000 WTN's viewership ranked in the upper half of specialty channels. After establishing itself the network was able to reincorporate some of the more serious public affairs programming. *Open for Discussion,* for example, featured a regular call-in show scheduled to follow issue-oriented movies exploring topics such as domestic abuse or rape. WTN also made a significant public service investment through its WTN Foundation, which sponsored projects such as a girls' television camp in Ottawa and other outreach programs, many aimed at helping women enter the television industry. Other projects benefited women in a more general sense—inmates from a women's correctional facility, for example, staffed *Open for Discussion,* earning money for their families.

By 2000 Moffat was the sole owner of WTN, and in March 2001 sold the network to Corus Entertainment Inc. for $205 million (Canadian). Corus, a spin-off of Shaw Communication, is one of Canada's leading entertainment conglomerates, with holdings including 52 radio stations as well as specialty, pay, conventional, and digital television services. Corus quickly drew criticism by closing the Winnipeg office and firing all but three of nearly 80 WTN employees. The network was moved to the Corus facility in Toronto, where it expected to employ no more than 25.

Corus relaunched WTN as W in April 2002, adding U.S. exports *Ally McBeal, The Huntress,* and *Chicago Hope* to the schedule, while eliminating the *Herstory* biography series, *Hot Topics,* and the weekly screening of international films. Pubic relations staff described the network's new focus as featuring more movies and music specials and less "femme-related" programming. The network also added a dual feed for western Canada.

W airs programs also available on U.S. women's networks Lifetime and Oxygen Media, including *Strong Medicine, The Division,* and *Beyond Chance,* all produced for Lifetime. Oxygen airs *The Sunday Night Sex Show* and *Debbie Travis' Painted House,* both originally produced for WTN. Before the relaunch as W, the Canadian network bore more similarity to Oxygen, with its more explicitly feminist address. The adjustment in programming and the brand shift have made it more comparable to the generally "feminine" address of Lifetime.

AMANDA LOTZ

*See also **Gender and Television; Lifetime***

Further Reading

Atherton, Tony, "WTN Savours Sweet Success," *Ottawa Citizen* (August 12, 2000)

Atherton, Tony, "Women's Channel to be More Entertaining as W," *Ottawa Citizen* (April 15, 2002)

MacDonald, Fiona, "WTN Provides a Different Viewpoint," *Playback* (June 11, 2001)

Portman, Jamie, "New Women's Network About Marketing, Not Gender," *Ottawa Citizen* (January 29, 1995)

Wagon Train

U.S. Western

Wagon Train, a fusion of the popular western genre and the weekly star vehicle, premiered on Wednesday nights, 7:30–8:30 P.M., in September 1957 on NBC. The show took its initial inspiration from John Ford's 1950 film *The Wagonmaster.* NBC and Revue productions, an MCA unit for producing telefilms, conceived of the program as a unique entry into the growing stable of western genre telefilm, combining quality writing and direction with weekly guest stars known for their work in other media, primarily motion pictures.

Wagon Train, Robert Horton, Ward Bond, 1957–65.
Courtesy of the Everett Collection

Each week, a star such as Ernest Borgnine (who appeared in the first episode, "The Willie Moran Story"), Shelly Winters, Lou Costello, or Jane Wyman would appear along with series regulars Ward Bond and Robert Horton. The show, filmed on location in California's San Fernando Valley, had an impressive budget of $100,000 per episode, at a time when competing hour-long westerns, such as ABC's *Sugarfoot,* cost approximately $70,000 per episode.

Star presence enticed viewers; powerful writing and directing made the show a success. With experience in other westerns, such as *Gunsmoke* and *Tales of Wells Fargo,* writers including western novelist Borden Chase and future director Sam Peckinpah developed scripts that eventually became episodes. Directors familiar with the western telefilm contributed experience, as did personnel who had been involved with *GE Theatre,* a program influential in the conception of *Wagon Train*'s use of stars. Promotional materials suggested that motion picture directors John Ford, Leo McCarey, and Frank Capra had expressed interest in directing future episodes; whether wishful thinking or real possibility, *Wagon Train*'s producers envisioned their western as television on a par with motion pictures.

Each episode revolved around characters and personalities who were traveling by wagon train caravan from St. Joseph, Missouri, to California. Series regulars conducted the train through perils and adventures associated with the landscapes and inhabitants of the American West. The star vehicle format worked in tandem with the episodic nature of series television, giving audiences a glimpse into the concerns of different pioneers and adventurers from week to week. Returning cast members gave the show stability: audiences expected complaints and comedy from Charlie Wooster, the train's cook, and clashes of experience with exuberance in the relationship between the wagonmaster and his dashing frontier scouts. The recurring cast's interrelationships, problems, and camaraderie contributed greatly to the sense of "family" that bound disparate elements of the series together.

Wagon Train lasted eight seasons, moving from NBC to ABC in September 1962. Its format expanded to 90 minutes in 1963 but returned to hour length for its final run from 1964 to 1965. It survived several cast changes: Ward Bond (Major Adams), the original wagonmaster, died during filming in 1960 and was replaced by John McIntyre (Chris Hale); Robert Horton (Flint McCullogh) left the series in 1962 and was replaced as frontier scout by Robert Fuller (Cooper Smith). Only two characters survived the eight-year run in their original positions: Frank McGrath, as comical cook Charlie Wooster, and Terry Wilson's assistant wagonmaster Bill Hawks.

The show's ability to survive a network switch and periodic cast changes during its eight-year run attests to its popularity. In the fall of 1959, two years after its inception, the show was number one in Great Britain; of seven westerns in the Nielsen top ten in the United States, *Wagon Train* competed constantly with *Gunsmoke* for supremacy. By 1959 the show was firmly ensconced in the top 25 programs in the United States; it bounced as high as number one in the spring of 1960 and maintained its number one position over *Gunsmoke* throughout the 1961–62 season. In a field awash with westerns, *Wagon Train* established a unique style reminiscent of the anthology drama but indelibly entrenched in western traditions.

KATHRYN C. D'ALESSANDRO

See also **Cheyenne; Gunsmoke; Have Gun—Will Travel; Warner Brothers Presents; Western**

Cast

Major Seth Adams (1957–61)	Ward Bond
Flint McCullough (1957–62)	Robert Horton
Bill Hawks	Terry Wilson
Charlie Wooster	Frank McGrath
Duke Shannon (1961–64)	Scott Miller

Chris Hale (1961–65)	John McIntire	September 1963–September	
Barnaby West (1963–65)	Michael Burns	1964	Monday 8:30–9:30
Cooper Smith (1963–65)	Robert Fuller	September 1964–September	
		1965	Sunday 7:30–8:30

Producers
Howard Christie, Richard Lewis

Programming History
442 episodes
NBC
September 1957–September
1962   Wednesday 7:30–8:30
ABC
September 1962–September
1963   Wednesday 7:30–8:30

Further Reading

Brauer, Ralph, *The Horse, the Gun, and the Piece of Property: Changing Images of the TV Western,* Bowling Green, Ohio: Popular Press, 1975

Cawelti, John, *The Six-Gun Mystique,* Bowling Green, Ohio: Popular Press, 1984

MacDonald, J. Fred, *Who Shot the Sheriff?: The Rise and Fall of the Television Western,* New York: Praeger, 1987

West, Richard, *Television Westerns: Major and Minor Series, 1946–1978,* Jefferson, North Carolina: McFarland, 1987

Yoggy, Gary A., *Riding the Video Range: The Rise and Fall of the Western on Television,* Jefferson, North Carolina: McFarland, 1995

Wales

As a small but culturally and linguistically distinct nation within the United Kingdom, Wales offers an enlightening case study of the role of television in constructing cultural identity. Broadcasting in Wales has played a crucial role in ensuring the survival of the Welsh language, one of the oldest languages spoken on a daily basis in Europe. Coupled with recent educational policies, which include Welsh-language instruction as either a core or secondary subject in all Welsh schools, and Europe-wide recognition of the cultural and linguistic rights of indigenous speakers, the nation has seen a slight increase in the percentage of Welsh speakers. Welsh television currently comprises BBC 1 Wales and BBC 2 Wales; the independent television (ITV) commercial-franchise holder, Harlech Television (HTV Wales); and Sianel Pedwar Cymru (Channel 4 Wales [S4C]), the Welsh equivalent of Britain's commercial Channel 4. BBC 1 Wales, BBC 2 Wales, and HTV Wales broadcast entirely in English, whereas S4C's schedules contain a mix of locally produced Welsh-language and English-language Channel 4 U.K. programs. Welsh-language television is the progeny of battles over the national and cultural rights of a linguistic minority who, from the outset of television in Britain, lobbied hard for Welsh-language programming. Of the 2.7 million population of Wales, 20 percent (500,000) speak Welsh, and since November 1,

1982, the bilingual minority have been able to view Welsh-language programs on S4C during the lunch and prime-time periods, seven days a week.

From the outset of television in Wales, the mountainous topography of the country presented broadcasters with transmission problems; despite the construction of new and more powerful transmitters, gaps in service persisted as late as the 1980s. At the time of the opening of the first transmitter in Wales, 36,236 households had a combined radio and television license, a number that more than doubled to 82,324 by September 1953, in anticipation of the televising of the coronation of Queen Elizabeth II. By 1959, 50 percent of Welsh households had a television set (450,720 licenses); 70 percent of those viewers received their broadcasts from the Welsh transmitter (Wenvoe), which also reached an identical viewing base in southwest England. However, 10 percent of the Welsh population could still not receive television, and 20 percent received their programs from transmitters located in England.

A key player in early Welsh-language television was Alun Oldfield-Davies (senior regional BBC controller from 1957 to 1967), who persuaded the BBC in 1952 to allow Welsh-language programs to be occasionally transmitted from the Welsh transmitter outside network hours. Oldfield-Davies went on to become an inveterate campaigner for Welsh-language television and stepped up his lobbying with the introduction of commercial television in Wales in 1956. The first television program broadcast entirely in Welsh was transmitted on St. David's Day (Wales's patron saint's day), March 1, 1953, and featured a religious service from Cardiff's Tabernacle Baptist Chapel. The first Welsh-language feature program was a portrait of the Welsh bibliophile Bob Owen; despite replacing only the test card, the program antagonized English viewers, who complained about the incomprehensible language. This reaction was to intensify in later years, when English programs were substituted by Welsh-language productions.

The Broadcast Council for Wales (BCW) was established as an advisory body in 1955, although its presence had little impact on the tardy appearance of full production facilities in Cardiff, the last regional center in the United Kingdom to be adequately equipped for production in 1959. (The BBC expanded the Broadway Methodist Chapel in Cardiff, a site that had functioned as a drive-in studio since 1954.) The first program filmed before a live audience in Wales took place in 1953, while the first televised rugby match and Welsh-language play, *Cap Wil Tomos* (Wil Tomos's Cap) were both transmitted in January 1955. (The first televised English-language play produced in Wales, *Wind of Heaven,* was broadcast in June 1956.) However, despite these important breakthroughs in Welsh television, the number of programs locally produced for both bilingual and English-speaking audiences remained small; for example, in 1954, only 2 hours and 40 minutes of English programming and 1 hour and 25 minutes of Welsh-language programming were broadcast each week. The first regular Welsh-language program, *Cefndir* (Background), aired in February 1957; introduced by Wyn Roberts, the show adopted a magazine format featuring topical items.

The BBC's monopoly in British broadcasting was broken with the launch of ITV, which could first be received by the inhabitants of northeast Wales (and many in northwest Wales) in 1956, following the launch of Granada television in Manchester, England. South Wales did not receive ITV until Television Wales West (TWW) was awarded a franchise in 1958 and opened a transmitter in the south, which also served the southwest of England. More than a little complacent that the commercial imperatives of ITV would preclude Welsh-language ITV broadcasts, the BBC was stunned when the ITV Granada studios in Manchester launched a series of twice-weekly, 60-minute Welsh-language programs, greatly overshadowing the BBC's weekly provision of one half-hour. As a result, the political stakes involved in addressing

the interests of Welsh-language viewers were raised, although both the BBC and ITV recognized the low ratings generated by such programs, given the minority status of Welsh-language speakers. Gwynfor Evans, who went on to play a pivotal role in the emergence of S4C in the early 1980s, joined the BCW in 1957 and, along with Plaid Cymru (the Welsh Nationalist Party), vigorously lobbied for an increase in Welsh-language broadcasting. The issue of Welsh-language programming for children also assumed a greater urgency in the late 1950s. The broadcasting demands of the campaigners were given institutional recognition in 1960 with the publication of the findings of the Pilkington Committee (the first broadcasting inquiry mainly concerned with television), which argued that "the language and culture of Wales would suffer irreparable harm" if Welsh-language production were not increased.

A second ITV franchise, Television Wales West and North (TWWN, known in Wales as Teledu Cymru [Welsh Television]), began broadcasting in Wales in September 1962. Initially transmitting 11 hours a week of Welsh-language and Welsh-interest programming, TWWN obtained half of its programs from TWW. However, TWWN's future as a broadcaster was short-lived; facing bankruptcy, it was taken over by TWW in September 1963. At this time, the BBC and ITV reached an agreement over the scheduling of Welsh-language programs, requiring that each broadcaster's schedule be exchanged so as to avoid a clash of Welsh-language programs (which would leave non-Welsh speakers no alternative broadcast during this time slot). By and large, the policy worked, although some overlapping did occur.

In 1963 the BBC in Wales broadcast three hours of programming for Welsh viewers per week and occasionally produced programs exclusively for the network. *Heddiw* (Today), a long-running Welsh-language weekday news bulletin, was broadcast outside network hours from 1:00 to 1:25 P.M., while its English-language equivalent, *Wales Today,* occupied an early-evening slot between 6:10 and 6:25 P.M. TWW also had its own Welsh-language magazine program called *Y Dydd* (The Day).

BBC Wales was launched in February 1964, when it received its own wavelength for television broadcasting (Channel 13). Oldfield-Davies was central in orchestrating the move and oversaw its implementation (television sets had to be converted in order to receive Channel 13). Up to this point, most Welsh-language programs had been transmitted during nonnetwork hours; the introduction of BBC Wales meant that Wales would opt out of the national service for a prescribed number of hours per week (8.9 hours per week in 1964) in order to transmit locally produced English- and Welsh-language programs. However, the arrival of BBC Wales meant that non-Welsh-speaking viewers whose aerials received BBC Wales from Welsh transmitters had no way of opting out of this system, unless they could also pick up the national BBC service by pointing their aerials toward English transmitters. The inclusion of a small number of Welsh-language programs on the television schedules at this time thus incensed some English-speaking Welsh viewers, who claimed that they were more poorly served by the BBC than other English-speaking national minorities, such as the Scots, and resented losing programs to Welsh-language productions. By the fall of 1984, 68 percent of Welsh people received programs from transmitters offering BBC Wales, a number that increased to 75 percent by June 1970. BBC 2, the first BBC service transmitted on UHF, was launched in southeast England in 1962, reaching south Wales and southwest England in 1965. By the early 1970s, it was available to 90 percent of Welsh television homes. The first color program produced by BBC Wales was transmitted on July 9, 1970, and consisted of coverage of the Llangollen Eisteddfod.

As pressure for more Welsh-language programs increased, TWW's franchise was successfully challenged in 1968 by John Morgan and Lord Harlech. Commencing in March 1958, HTV pledged to address the "particular needs and wishes of Wales," and a ten-member committee was established to consider a range of topics affecting broadcasting in Wales. These issues were addressed more forcefully in a 1969 booklet published by Cymdeithas yr Iaith Gymraeg (the Welsh Language Society) titled *Broadcasting in Wales: To Enrich or Destroy Our National Life?* Facing a wall of silence from BBC Wales following publication of the document, three members of the society embarked on a campaign of civil disobedience and in May 1970 interrupted a program broadcast from Bangor in north Wales. The following year, a small group of men unlawfully gained entry to the Granada television studios in Manchester and caused limited damage to television equipment; television masts were also climbed; Parliament was interrupted; and roads were blocked. In addition to these high-profile disturbances, hundreds of people were prosecuted for not paying their television license fees. In the fall of 1970, the society submitted a document to the Welsh Broadcasting Authority (WBA) containing the first proposal for a fourth Welsh channel; an interim scheme proposed by the society suggested that the unallotted fourth UHF channel in Wales should transmit 25 hours of Welsh-language programming a week and should be jointly administered by a BBC Wales and HTV committee.

Soon after, ITV made a formal submission requesting that the fourth channel be used as a second ITV service broadcasting all HTV's current Welsh-language programming and making HTV Wales an all-English channel. The battle for a Welsh fourth channel had begun in earnest.

Against a backdrop of ongoing campaigns by the Welsh Language Society in the early and mid-1970s, the Crawford Committee on Broadcast Coverage examined patterns of rural reception in Wales and explored the possibility of using the fourth channel for Welsh-language programming. Those in favor of retaining the current system of integration argued that a separate Welsh-language channel would "ghettoize" the language and culture (a view supported by the 1977 Annan Report commissioned by the Labour government); they also drew attention to the fact that English-speaking viewers would still be deprived of English programs broadcast on the U.K. fourth channel and questioned whether there was a solid enough economic and cultural base in Wales to maintain a fourth channel. An average of 12 hours a week of Welsh- and English-language programs (seven and five hours, respectively) were broadcast on BBC Wales between 1964 and 1974, with almost half the time taken up with news and current-affairs programs such as *Heddiw, Cywain* (Gathering), *Wales Today,* and *Week In Week Out.*

Welsh-language television up to this point had gained a reputation of being quite highbrow, often consisting of nonfiction programs examining major Welsh institutions and traditions. However, sports, especially the national game of rugby, were enormously popular and always guaranteed representation and high ratings on the schedules. Moreover, the 1974 launch of the hugely successful Welsh-language soap opera *Pobol y Cwm* (People of the Valley) did even more to shift the balance toward popular programming. *Pobol y Cwm*'s 20-minute episodes are currently broadcast five days a week; the continuing serial is the highest-rated program on S4C, attracting an average viewership of 180,000. English subtitles are available on teletext on daily episodes, and the five episodes are repeated on Sunday afternoon with open subtitles.

Welsh-speaking comedic stars also made their mark in light entertainment during the 1970s; performers included Ryan Davies, who enjoyed widespread fame with his partner Ronnie Williams in the 1971 show *Ryan a Ronnie,* and in the first Welsh sitcom, *Fo a Fe* (Him and Him; the title derived from north and south Walean dialects for "him"), written by Rhydderch Jones. Stand-up comedian Max Boyce also became a household name with his own 1978 one-man series. Religious programming was still popular with audiences (as it had been on radio), and a BBC Sunday half-hour hymn-singing program titled *Dechrau Canu, Dechrau Canmol* (Begin Singing, Begin Praising) drew large audiences. Two successful English-language programs made for the BBC network in the mid-1970s included a seven-hour miniseries on the life of Welsh politician David Lloyd George (1977) and an animated children's cartoon titled *Ivor the Engine* (1976). One of the most successful English-language dramas of the 1970s, a program regularly repeated on Welsh television, was *Grand Slam* (1975), which hilariously documented the exploits of a group of Welsh rugby fans traveling to Paris for an international match.

Meanwhile, political lobbying for a fourth Welsh-language channel intensified as the Welsh Language Society organized walking tours, petitions, leaflet distribution, and the public burning of BBC television licenses. Published in November 1975, the government-sponsored Siberry Report recommended that the Welsh fourth channel should broadcast 25 hours a week of Welsh-language programs, with the BBC and HTV each responsible for three and a half days a week. Welsh members of Parliament also argued that the seven hours of programming on BBC Wales opened up by the transfer of Welsh-language programs to a fourth channel should be filled with BBC Wales programs in English, rather than BBC network material. In their 1979 general election manifestos, both Labour and Conservative parties pledged support for a fourth Welsh channel; however, facing resistance to the plan from the independent broadcasting authority (IBA) and HTV, Conservative Party Home Secretary William Whitelaw repudiated the Welsh fourth channel in a speech given at Cambridge University in September 1979. Welsh reaction was swift; at Plaid Cymru's annual conference in October, a fund was established into which supporters opposed to Whitelaw's decision could deposit their television license fee (2,000 protesters pledged support and a number received prison sentences the following spring). Noted political and academic figures in Wales also joined the campaign and were arrested for civil disobedience. It was, however, the intervention of Plaid Cymru member of Parliament Gwynfor Evans that had the most profound effect on public and political opinion. In May 1980, Evans announced that he would go on a hunger strike on October 5 and continue with the protest until the government restored its earlier promise of giving Wales a fourth Welsh-language channel. In the wake of public demonstrations during visits to Wales by Prime Minister Margaret Thatcher and Welsh Secretary Nicholas Edwards, Cledwyn Evans (Labour's former foreign secretary) led a depu-

tation to Whitelaw's office in London demanding that the decision be reversed. The government finally backed down on September 17, stating that a Welsh Fourth Channel Authority would be formed (provisions were incorporated into the 1980 Broadcasting Bill through a House of Lords amendment). The BBC would be responsible for providing ten hours per week, and HTV and independent companies eight hours per week. S4C had finally arrived.

Funded by an annual budget from the Treasury, which is based on a rate of 3.2 percent of the net advertising revenue of all terrestrial television in the United Kingdom, S4C is a commissioning broadcaster (rather than a program producer), with program announcements and promotions the only material produced in-house. By the mid-1990s, S4C was annually transmitting approximately 1,753 locally produced hours of programming in Welsh, and 5,041 hours in English; the English-language broadcasts were rescheduled U.K. C4's output. These figures translate into roughly 30 hours of programming per week in Welsh and 93 hours per week in English. S4C reaches a target share of approximately 20 percent of Welsh-speaking viewers, although its remit also includes targeting both Welsh learners and English speakers through the use of teletext services that enable participating viewers to call up English subtitles for most Welsh programs. Some 75 percent of all local advertisers produce campaigns in both Welsh and English on S4C, while a number of multinational companies, such as McDonald's and Volvo, have also advertised in Welsh.

Of the 30 hours of Welsh-language programming shown on S4C each week, ten hours come from BBC Wales; the remaining 20 come from HTV Wales and independent producers. BBC Wales also produces ten hours of English-language programming for viewers living in Wales, which is broadcast on BBC 1 and BBC 2. The BBC's Royal Charter charges the BBC to provide services reflecting "the cultures, tastes, interests, and languages of that country," and via the BCW, the service is regularly reviewed to ensure that programs meet the requirements set down in the Royal Charter. HTV Wales produced 588 hours of English-language programs for Wales during 1995, a figure that amounted to approximately 25 hours per week.

Since January 1, 1993, S4C has been responsible for selling its own advertising (previously overseen by HTV); this has meant that revenues can now be plowed directly back into program production. S4C provides a wide range of program genres, including news and current affairs, drama, games, and quizzes, and youth and children's programming. The main S4C news service, *Newyddion* (News), is provided by BBC

Wales; S4C also has two investigative news shows, *Taro Naw* (Strike Now) and *Yr Byd ar Bedwar* (The World on Four), as well as documentaries exploring the diverse lives of Welsh men and women: *Hel Straeon* (Gather Stories), *Cefn Gwlad* (Countryside), and *Filltir Sgwar* (Square Mile). Recent comedy series have included *Nosan Llawen* (Folk Evening of Entertainment), *Licyris Olsorts* (Licorice Allsorts), and the satirical show *Pelydr X* (X-Ray). Series examining contemporary issues through the lens of popular drama have included *Hafren*, a hospital drama; *Halen yn y Gwaed* (Salt in the Blood), which followed the lives of a ferry crew sailing between Wales and Ireland; *A55*, a hard-hitting series about juvenile crime; and *Pris y Farchnad* (Market Price), which examined the lives of a family of auctioneers. Children and teenage viewers are catered to via *Sali Mali; Rownd a Rownd* (Round and Round), which looks at the exploits of a paper round; and *Rap*, a magazine program for Welsh learners.

Non-Welsh-speaking viewers receive their local news from BBC Wales's *Wales Today* and HTV Wales's *Wales This Week*. Other recent nonfiction programs have included *Grass Roots, The Really Helpful Show, The Once and Future Valleys*, and *The Infirmary*, from HTV Wales; and *Between Ourselves, All Our Lives*, and *Homeland*, produced by BBC Wales.

Thanks to S4C, Wales now has a thriving independent production sector centered in Cardiff (where 46 percent of the Welsh media industry is located) and Caernarfon. Welsh television's success in the field of children's animation has continued, with *Wil Cwac Cwac* and *SuperTed* making their first appearance in 1982 (both have appeared on the Disney Channel in the United States), followed by *Fireman Sam* and *Toucan Tecs*. By the early 1990s, Cardiff boasted five animation houses, 45 independent production companies, and a pool of approximately 150 professional animators. Animation coproductions from the mid-1990s included *Shakespeare: The Animated Tales, Operavox: The Animated Operas, Testament: The Bible in Animation, The Little Engine That Could*, and *The Legend of Lochnagar*. More than 90 of S4C's programs have been exported to almost 100 countries worldwide, and coproductions have been negotiated with production companies in France, Italy, Germany, Australia, and the United States.

It is important to note that the political advocacy that secured the rights of Welsh speakers within a broadcasting system for Wales ultimately benefited both Welsh and English speakers, since the language campaign fostered the production of more English-language programs for Wales as a whole. The current system of Welsh broadcasting would certainly never

have existed had it not been doggedly pursued by Welsh-language activists. Recent audience research into the penetration levels of S4C indicates that in the mid-1990s, between 80 and 85 percent of Welsh speakers watched S4C at some point each week, and between 65 and 70 percent of all viewers (English- and Welsh-speaking) tuned in to S4C some time each week. The S4C model in Wales has been emulated by several other European linguistic minorities, including the Basque channel Euskal Telebista 1 in Spain (launched in 1982) and a Catalan channel started in 1983.

Digital television, which was being received in 30 percent of Welsh homes by the end of 2000, has doubtless had an impact on the terrestrial channels serving Wales. If the obvious benefits of digital television—greater channel choice, Internet access, and interactive services—far outweigh the disadvantages, S4C, BBC Wales, and HTV Wales are nevertheless concerned that they will lose viewers to digital television. S4C in west and southwest Wales saw an increase in its share of Welsh-speaking viewers in peak time, but the number of Welsh-speaking viewers in north Wales diminished. Digital television is therefore something of a mixed blessing for S4C, since it is now committed to providing programming for its digital service (expanding Welsh-language programming to morning and late-night television) while also ensuring quality programming on its analog service. S4C therefore continues to deal with the challenge of catering to widely varying tastes in its commissioning of programs, attempting to reflect the social, cultural, and geographical diversity of Wales on one channel. One criticism has focused on the incursions of English and "low-quality" Welsh expressions into programming, although S4C executives argue that the desire to maintain high linguistic standards on S4C is tempered by the need to inject realism into the representation of Welsh-language use.

The two-and-one-half-year-old BBC channel Choice Wales, which featured new talent and experimental approaches to programming, was replaced in March 2001 by BBC 2 Wales digital service. There is great optimism about this service for Wales; it is generally hoped that it will lead to innovative programming and a larger share for Welsh-speaking audiences. BBC 2 Wales digital also means that Welsh expatriates will be able to receive the service via satellite throughout the United Kingdom. Drama and major documentary series, while costly (the average cost for all-Welsh-language programs is £27,093 [approximately $40,000]), are still considered good value for money, with their high production costs offset by an increase in repeated programs and acquired programming that can be broadcast on digital platforms. Network exposure for programming from Wales has struggled to attract audiences, with the much anticipated drama series *Border Café* coming under heavy criticism for its poor audience ratings. Many viewers in Wales continue to take issue with the crass stereotypes of Welsh people and Welsh culture on network programs, and some have lobbied BBC Wales for more programs made in Wales about Wales for the British network audience. With more programming hours to fill in both Welsh and English, terrestrial and digital broadcasters face exciting new challenges as they battle for audiences in an increasingly competitive and splintered marketplace.

ALISON GRIFFITHS

See also **Ireland; Language and Television; Scotland**

Further Reading

BBC Wales Annual Review 1994/95, Cardiff, Wales: BBC Wales, 1995

Bevan, David, "The Mobilization of Cultural Minorities," *Media, Culture, and Society* (1984)

Blanchard, Simon, and David Morley, editors, *What's This Channel Four?* London: Comedia, 1982

Browne, Donald R., *Electronic Media and Indigenous Peoples: A Voice of Our Own?* Ames: Iowa University Press, 1996

Cooke, Philip, and Carmel Gahan, "The Television Industry in Wales," *Regional Industrial Research/Igam Ogam Research: S4C, BBC Wales, and WDA* (1988)

Curtis, Tony, editor, *Wales: The Imagined Nation: Essays in Cultural and in National Identity,* Bridgend: Poetry Wales Press, 1986

Davies, John, *Broadcasting and the BBC Wales in Wales,* Cardiff: University of Wales Press, 1994

Griffiths, Alison, "National and Cultural Identity in a Welsh Language Soap Opera," in *To Be Continued: Soap Operas Around the World,* edited by Robert C. Allen, London: Routledge, 1995

Howell, W.J., Jr., "Bilingual Broadcasting and the Survival of Authentic Culture in Wales and Ireland," *Journal of Communication* (autumn 1982)

Howell, W.J., Jr., "Britain's Fourth Channel and the Welsh-Language Controversy," *Journal of Broadcasting* (spring 1981)

HTV Annual Report and Accounts, 1995, Cardiff: Westdale Press, 1996

National Broadcasting Council for Wales Annual Reports

S4C Annual Report and Accounts, Cardiff: S4C, 1995

Williams, Eyrun Ogwen, "The BBC and the Regional Question in Wales," in *The Regions, the Nations, and the BBC,* edited by Sylvia Harvey and Kevin Robbins, London: British Film Institute, 1993

Walking with Dinosaurs

British Natural History/Science Series

Television natural history programming remains a staple of the medium and has been responsible for a vast body of spectacular and fascinating material. By the end of the 1990s, however, though its popularity seemed as great as ever and several dedicated cable and satellite channels endlessly recycled its output, the feeling was taking hold that, despite the continuous search for gimmicky new techniques, there was virtually no scope for innovation in the genre. Then along came *Walking with Dinosaurs,* which took as its starting point the presentation of the life of extinct creatures in much the same way as living creatures were presented in conventional natural history programs.

The obvious inspiration was the Steven Spielberg movie *Jurassic Park,* which not only had demonstrated the technical ability to present credible moving images of dinosaurs, but had created intense public interest in the subject. The same Soft Image software as had been used in the movie was employed for the television series, with the images created at the Framestore facility in London, and similarly large-scale animatronic heads were also used for close-ups on location. Academic experts on dinosaurs were consulted throughout the process in order that the lives of these creatures be portrayed as accurately as possible, although some things, like their color, remain unknown and had to be guessed.

Unlike *Jurassic Park,* however, the dinosaurs had to be placed in locations that contained the correct ancient species of trees and other habitat. These were found in Chile, New Zealand, and New Caledonia, amongst others. The animators then had to place the dinosaurs into the locations in such a way that the lighting of both images was consistent and the dinosaurs looked as though they were interacting with the location.

To increase the sense of a traditional natural history program, the producers decided to present it as though individual living dinosaurs were being filmed by a camera team and the narrative built around the footage captured. Series producer Tim Haines, interviewed in *Radio Times* (October 2–8, 1999), said, "We followed all the rules the paleontologists gave us, then directed the action like it was a real natural history programme. We had to be utterly convinced it was all real, even though we were making educated guesses. It's the conviction that what you see is real that drags you into accepting it."

The six parts of *Walking with Dinosaurs* covered such topics as the growth of a long-necked sauropod from birth to adulthood, dinosaur life in the waters and the skies, and the reasons dinosaurs became extinct. Though originated in Britain, it was a major international coproduction, the BBC's partners being the Discovery Channel (United States), TV Asahi (Japan), Proseiben (Germany), and France 3. As with other natural history coproductions, this enabled easy versioning for different countries and helped ensure worldwide success. The British version was narrated by actor Kenneth Branagh.

In Britain, *Walking with Dinosaurs* came at a time when educational documentary programming in the public service tradition was considered under threat from "infotainment" and the ubiquitous "docusoaps." Following its success, it was cited as proof that well-made educational programming was capable of capturing significant audiences, and it prompted an overdue policy shift in the commissioning of factual programming.

Naturally, it also instigated a series of follow-up programs from the same production team. As well as the inevitable "making of" documentary, a Christmas special, *The Ballad of Big Al,* and accompanying documentary *Big Al Uncovered* (BBC, 2000) explored the life of an allosaur. The next full series was *Walking with Beasts* (BBC, 2002), which used the same techniques to present a natural history of the now-extinct giant mammals that lived in the period between the disappearance of the dinosaurs and the coming of man. A further innovation associated with this series was the presentation of background detail on an interactive television service.

STEVE BRYANT

Narrator
Kenneth Branagh

Producers
John Lynch, Tim Haines, Jasper James

Program History
Six episodes, plus "making of" documentary and series special
BBC/Discovery Channel/TV Asahi/Prosieben Media/France 3
October 4, 1999–November 8, 1999
Walking with Dinosaurs Special: The Ballad of Big Al
  December 25, 2000

Wallace, Mike (1918–)

U.S. Broadcast Journalist

Although he spent many years in broadcasting before turning to journalism, Mike Wallace became one of the United States' most enduring and prominent television news personalities. Primarily known for his work on the long-running CBS magazine series *60 Minutes,* he developed a reputation as an inquisitorial interviewer, authoritative documentary narrator, and powerful investigative reporter. While his journalistic credentials and tactics have been questioned at times, his longevity, celebrity, and ability to land big interviews have made him one of the most important news figures in the history of television.

Wallace's early career differed from those of his well-known peers at CBS News. Edward R. Murrow, Walter Cronkite, Eric Sevareid, Andy Rooney, and others worked as wartime radio and print correspondents before moving to television. Wallace, however, studied broadcasting at the University of Michigan and began an acting and announcing career in 1939. Throughout the 1940s, he performed in a variety of radio genres—quiz shows, talk shows, serials, commercials, and news readings. After service in the Navy, the baritone-voiced radio raconteur landed a string of early television jobs in Chicago. As early as 1949, "Myron"

Wallace acted in the police drama *Stand by for Crime,* and he later appeared on the CBS anthology programs *Suspense* and *Studio One.* He emceed local and network TV quiz and panel shows while also working in radio news for CBS from 1951 to 1955. Wallace's move into interviewing at the network level came in the form of two husband-and-wife talk shows, *All Around the Town* and *Mike and Buff,* which CBS adapted from a successful Chicago radio program. With his wife, Buff Cobb, Wallace visited New York locations and conducted live interviews with celebrities and passers-by. After a three-season run on CBS, Wallace had a brief stint in 1954 as a Broadway actor before returning to television.

In 1955 Wallace began anchoring nightly newscasts for the DuMont network's New York affiliate. The following year his producer, Ted Yates, created the vehicle that brought Wallace to prominence. *Night Beat* was a live, late-night hour of interviews in which Wallace grilled a pair of celebrity guests every weeknight. Armed with solid research and provocative questions, the seasoned announcer with a flair for the dramatic turned into a hard-hitting investigative journalist and probing personality reporter. With the nervy Wallace as its anchor, *Night Beat* developed a hard edge lacking in most television talk. Using only a black backdrop and smoke from his cigarette for atmosphere, Wallace asked pointed, even mischievous questions that made guests squirm. Most were framed in tight close-up, revealing the sweat elicited by Wallace's barbs and the show's harsh klieg lights.

After a successful first season, during which Wallace interviewed such celebrities as Norman Mailer, Salvador Dali, Thurgood Marshall, Ayn Rand, Hugh Hefner, William Buckley, and prominent politicians, the program moved to ABC as a half-hour prime-time show called *The Mike Wallace Interview.* Promoted as "Mike Malice" and "the Terrible Torquemada of the TV Inquisition," Wallace continued to talk to prominent personalities about controversial issues. However, ABC executives, particularly after brushes with libel suits, proved wary of Wallace's brinkmanship. The show lasted only through 1958, turning more cerebral in its final weeks when the Ford Foundation became its sponsor. Intellectuals such as Reinhold Niebuhr, Aldous Huxley, and William O. Douglas replaced the Klansmen, ex-mobsters, movie stars, and more sensational interviewees seen before.

For the next five years, Wallace continued to parlay his celebrity into odd jobs on New York and network TV as quizmaster, pitchman for cigarettes, chat show host (*PM East,* 1961–62), and newsreader, but he began to sharpen his focus on mainstream journalism as well. He anchored *Newsbeat* (1959–61), one of the first half-hour nightly news programs, for an indepen-

Mike Wallace.
Photo courtesy of Mike Wallace

dent New York station and also began working as host for David L. Wolper's TV documentary series *Biography,* narrating 65 episodes of the syndicated program. (His distinctive voice continues to be heard in many such educational productions, including *The 20th Century with Mike Wallace,* which CBS produces as a cable series for A&E and the History Channel. Increasingly, he became a field correspondent. After a chain of Westinghouse-owned stations hired Wallace to cover the 1960 political conventions, he started traveling extensively, supplying the stations with daily radio and TV reports from across the country (*Closeup U.S.A.,* 1960) and abroad (*Around the World in 40 Days,* 1962).

At this point in his life, as he described in his 1984 autobiography, Wallace decided to "go straight," giving up higher-paying entertainment jobs for a career exclusively devoted to news. In 1963 (a year in which the networks expanded their news divisions), the *CBS Morning News with Mike Wallace* premiered. Wallace remained on the show for three years before resuming full-time reporter's duties. Although seen frequently on other CBS News assignments (Vietnam, the Middle East), Wallace's beat was the Richard Nixon comeback campaign. A confessed Nixon apologist, he nevertheless rejected an offer in 1968 to be the candidate's press secretary.

Instead, that fall Wallace began regular duties for *60 Minutes,* the prime-time news magazine for which he and Harry Reasoner had done a pilot in February 1968. To contrast with the mild-mannered Reasoner, producer Don Hewitt cast Wallace in his usual role as the abrasive, tough-guy reporter. While he could be charming when doing softer features and celebrity profiles, Wallace maintained his reputation as a bruising inquisitor who gave his subjects "Mike fright." With his personal contacts in the Nixon (and later Reagan) circles, he proved an adept reporter on national politics, particularly during Watergate. Throughout his run on *60 Minutes,* he consistently landed timely and exclusive interviews with important newsmakers.

As *60 Minutes* was becoming a mainstay of TV news, Wallace developed its most familiar modus operandi: the ambush interview. Sometimes using hidden cameras and one-way mirrors, Wallace would confront scam artists and other wrongdoers caught in the act. Field producers did most of the investigative work, but Wallace added the theatrical panache as he performed his on-camera muckraking. His tactics have been both praised and criticized. While he has won numerous awards as a sort of national ombudsman, a reporter with the resources and ability to expose corruption, some critics have judged his methods too sensational, unfair, and even unethical.

Twice Wallace was entangled in landmark libel cases. His *60 Minutes* report "The Selling of Colonel Herbert" (1973) questioned a whistleblower's veracity about war crimes. Herbert sued Wallace's producer. Although the news team was exonerated, the U.S. Supreme Court ruled in *Herbert v. Lando* (1979) that the plaintiff had the right to examine the materials produced during the editorial process. A far bigger case followed when Wallace interviewed General William Westmoreland for the *CBS Reports* documentary "The Uncounted Enemy: A Vietnam Deception" (1982). When *TV Guide* and CBS's own in-house investigation charged that the producers had violated standards of fairness, Westmoreland sued the network. The charges Wallace aired—conspiracy to cover up the actual number of Viet Cong troops—were substantiated by trial evidence, but CBS's editorial tactics proved suspect. Early in 1985, just before Wallace was to testify, CBS issued an apology and Westmoreland dropped the suit.

Despite such occasional setbacks, Wallace continued his globetrotting reports and "make-'em-sweat" interviews into the next century. A CBS News special, *Mike Wallace, Then and Now* (1990), offered a retrospective of his first 50 years in broadcasting. In the de-

cade that followed, he offered another televised memoir, *Mike Wallace Remembers* (1997), and hundreds more hours of news programming. Considerable notoriety surrounded his 1995 interview with Dr. Jeffrey Wigand, a former tobacco executive turned whistleblower. CBS lawyers suspended the broadcast, until leaked transcripts appeared in print. Wallace criticized his network in a 1996 exposé coproduced by PBS and CBC. The story of Wigand, Wallace, and Wallace's producer was dramatized in the Hollywood film *The Insider* (1999). Amid it all, the senior correspondent of U.S. television journalism continued his *60 Minutes* work unabated, surpassing 1,500 episodes in 2001. In April 2002, however, Wallace announced his intent to cut back considerably on his television work and, beginning with the 2002–03 season, to appear less frequently on *60 Minutes.*

DAN STREIBLE

See also **60 Minutes; Talk Show;** *Uncounted Enemy, The*

Mike (Myron Leon) Wallace. Born in Brookline, Massachusetts, May 9, 1918. Educated at the University of Michigan, B.A., 1939. Married: 1) Norma Kaphan, 1940 (divorced, 1948); 2) Buff Cobb, 1949 (divorced, 1955); 3) Lorraine Perigord, 1955 (divorced); 4) Mary Yates; children: Peter (deceased), Christopher, and Pauline. Served in U.S. Navy, 1943–46. Newscaster, announcer, and continuity writer, radio station WOOD WASH, Grand Rapids, Michigan, 1939–40; newscaster, narrator, announcer, WXYZ Radio, Detroit, Michigan, 1940–41, on such shows as *The Lone Ranger* and *The Green Hornet;* freelance radio worker, Chicago, announcer for the soap opera *Road of Life,* 1941–42, *Ma Perkins,* and *The Guiding Light;* acted in *The Crime Files of Flamon;* news radio announcer, *Chicago Sun's Air Edition,* 1941–43, 1946–48; announced radio programs such as *Curtain Time, Fact or Fiction,* and *Sky King;* host, *Mike and Buff,* with his wife, New York City, 1950–53; host, various television and radio shows and narrator, various documentaries, 1951–59; star, Broadway comedy *Reclining Figure,* 1954; organized news department for DuMont's WABD-TV, 1955; anchor in newscasts and host for various interview shows, 1956–63; CBS News staff correspondent, since 1963; co-editor and cohost of *60 Minutes,* since 1968. Member: American Federation of Television and Radio Artists; Academy of Television Arts and Sciences (executive vice president, 1960–61). Recipient: 20 Emmy Awards; Peabody Awards, 1963, 1971, and 1993; duPont-Columbia Journalism Awards, 1971 and 1983;

Golden Globe, 1958; Robert F. Kennedy Journalism Award, 1996.

Television Series (selected)

1951–53	*Mike and Buff*
1951–52	*All Around Town*
1953–54	*I'll Buy That*
1956–57	*The Big Surprise*
1956–57	*Night Beat*
1957–58	*The Mike Wallace Interview*
1961–62	*PM East*
1963–66	*CBS Morning News with Mike Wallace*
1968–	*60 Minutes*
1995–	*20th Century with Mike Wallace*

Stage

Reclining Figure (actor), 1954.

Publications

Mike Wallace Asks: Highlights from 46 Controversial Interviews, 1958

A Mike Wallace Interview with William O. Douglas, 1958

"Interview with Martin Luther King," *New York Post* (July 11, 1958)

Close Encounters, with Gary Paul Gates, 1984

"The Roles of Edie Davis," *Washington Post* (October 30, 1987)

"*60 Minutes* into the 21st century!" *Television Quarterly* (Winter 1990)

"5 Badfellas: In a Lifetime of Interviewing, It's Not the Heads of State You Remember but the Guys Named 'Lunchy,' " *Forbes* (October 23, 1995)

"The Press Needs a National Monitor," *Wall Street Journal* (December 18, 1996)

"You Don't Need Technology to Tell the Truth," *Inc.* (May 2000)

"Role Models [Edward Murrow]," *Columbia Journalism Review* (May–June 2001)

"Mind and Body," *New York Times* (December 11, 2001)

Further Reading

Adler, Renata, *Reckless Disregard: Westmoreland v. CBS et al., Sharon v. Time,* New York: Knopf, 1986

Bar-Illan, David, "*60 Minutes* and the Temple Mount," *Commentary* (February 1991)

Barron, James, "Wallace Is Rebuked for Taping Interview on Hidden Camera," *New York Times* (November 17, 1994)

Benjamin, Burton, *Fair Play: CBS, General Westmoreland, and How a Television Documentary Went Wrong,* New York: Harper and Row, 1988

Brewin, Bob, and Sydney Shaw, *Vietnam on Trial: Westmoreland vs. CBS,* New York: Atheneum, 1987

CBS News, "*60 Minutes*" *Verbatim,* New York: Arno Press/CBS News, 1980

Clark, Kenneth R., "Getting Good Being Bad: Chicago's Salute Brings Mike Wallace Back to His Roots," *Chicago Tribune* (September 20, 1989)

Colford, Paul D., "The Very Demanding Mr. Wallace," *Newsday* (October 13, 1988)

Darrach, Brad, "Mike Wallace: The Grand in at 75," *Life* (June 1993)

Gay, Verne, "Mike Wallace Brings Back a Distinguished Series," *Newsday* (September 14, 1994)

Goodman, Walter, "Covering Tobacco: A Cautionary Tale," *New York Times* (April 2, 1996)

Griffith, Thomas, "Water-Torture Journalism," *Time* (May 23, 1983)

Hall, Jane, "The Frustrations of Tough Guy Mike Wallace," *Los Angeles Times* (September 26, 1990)

Johnson, Peter, "He Makes Time Stand Still," *USA Today* (May 8, 2000)

Kaplan, Peter W., "For Mike Wallace: A Welcome Pause from Trial," *New York Times* (December 21, 1984)

King, Susan, "Q and A: Mike Wallace: 40 Years of Asking," *Los Angeles Times* (September 23, 1990)

Lardner, James, "Up Against the Wallace," *Washington Post* (September 18, 1977)

Moore, Mike, "Divided Loyalties: Peter Jennings and Mike Wallace in No-Man's-Land," *The Quill* (February 1989)

"Myron Leon Wallace: Fifth Estater," *Broadcasting* (March 9, 1992)

Rosenthal, Donna, "Mike Without Malice," *San Francisco Chronicle* (September 23, 1990)

Shales, Tom, "Mike Wallace's Unforgettable Minutes," *Washington Post* (September 11, 1997)

"*60 Minutes:* A Candid Conversation About Hard News, Muckraking, and Showbiz with the Creator and Correspondents of America's Most Trusted Television Show," *Playboy* (March 1985)

Vietnam: A Documentary Collection—Westmoreland v. CBS, New York: Clearwater, 1985

Walsh, Mary (1952–)

Canadian Performer

Mary Walsh can be credited with single-handedly bringing Newfoundland culture to the rest of Canada through the medium of television. As the creator and costar of *This Hour Has 22 Minutes,* Walsh has won 11 Gemini Awards, Canada's television honors. The bitingly satirical show has become a favorite, skewering politics in general, Toronto in particular, and anything else that strikes Walsh's fancy. No topic is taboo. The show takes its title from the outrageously controversial newsmagazine show *This Hour Has Seven Days,* which ran on CBC from 1964 to 1966.

A Canadian precursor to Britain's Tracey Ullman, Walsh has introduced Canadian audiences over the years to a range of wacky Newfoundland archetypes, including the sharp-tongued, purple-housecoated know-it-all, Marg Delahunty, and the slovenly rooming-house owner, Mrs. Budgell. Her costars, fellow Newfoundlanders Cathy Jones, Greg Thomey, and Rick Mercer, all write their own characters as well.

Walsh's off-the-wall but pointed humor results in part from her unusual upbringing in St. John's, the capital of Newfoundland. One of eight siblings, at the age of eight months she contracted pneumonia and was dispatched next door to live with a still-beloved maiden aunt. She thus grew up away from her own troubled and hard-drinking family, feeling abandoned. She was also influenced by the strict rules of a convent education in the overwhelmingly Roman Catholic province of Newfoundland.

After taking acting classes at Ryerson Polytechnical Institute in Toronto and working a summer job at CBC radio in St. John's, Walsh began acting at Theatre Passe Muraille in Toronto. It was there that she met Cathy Jones, Dyan Olsen, Greg Malone, and Tommy Sexton; together they would become the comedy troupe Codco, named after the fish that has, until recently, supported the Newfoundland culture and economy for hundreds of years. Their first production, *Cod on a Stick* (1973), was a play based on the experiences of Newfoundlanders in Toronto. It was a time of "Newfie jokes," Canada's equivalent of the racist "Polack jokes." But Codco turned the tables on Torontonians, forcing them to laugh at themselves.

After touring the play successfully throughout Newfoundland, Codco stayed in their home province and continued to develop wickedly satirical sketches and characters, which they soon parlayed into the CBC television series *Codco.* The half-hour show lasted seven seasons, from 1987 to 1993, reaching a nationwide audience.

Politicians are a particular target of the left-wing Walsh's wrathful humor: referring to Preston Manning, the conservative leader of the Reform Party, she put these words in the mouth of Marg Delahunty: "I've always enjoyed Mr. Manning's speeches. And I'm sure they're even more edifying in the original German." About a right-wing media figure, she has this to say: "That's typical of those people: they want everything—all the power and the money, and the right to call themselves victims too." Of the ongoing one-way rivalry between Newfoundland and Toronto, she has said: "I forgive Toronto and all the people in it. Toronto was the first large city I ever went to and I thought every large city was like that—cold and icy, like being in Eaton's [department store] all the time. But then I realized...it's very much a part of being specifically Toronto. It is just its outward style." She also jabs at the United States, describing her short stay in Colorado after high school and her exasperation at some Americans' misguided belief that they defeated Canada in the War of 1812.

Walsh, who is actively involved in social issues through her work in the theater, won the Best Supporting Actress Award at the Atlantic Film Festival in 1992 for her performance in *Secret Nation* and has guest-starred on the children's show *The Adventures of Dudley the Dragon.* She also starred as Molly Bloom at Ottawa's National Arts Centre, as well as in Eugene O'Neill's *A Moon for the Misbegotten,* in London, Ontario. In 1992, she directed Ann-Marie MacDonald's *Goodnight Desdemona, Good Morning Juliet* at Montreal's Centaur Theatre.

Walsh also hosts her own series on CBC, *Mary Walsh: Open Book,* which is a literary talk show, and continues to appear in films.

JANICE KAYE

See also **Canadian Broadcasting in English;** *Codco*

Mary Walsh. Born in St. John's, Newfoundland, Canada, 1952. Studied at Ryerson Polytechnical Institute, Toronto. Began career at CBC radio, St. John's, Newfoundland; began acting career at Theatre Passe Muraille, Toronto; cofounder, Codco performance group, 1973; toured Canada with Codco, 1970s–80s; with *Codco* television program, 1987–93; in film, from 1991. Recipient: Best Supporting Actress, Atlantic Film Festival, 1992; numerous Gemini Awards.

Television Series
1987–93   *Codco*
1993–   *This Hour Has 22 Minutes*

Television Miniseries
1993   *Boys of St. Vincent*
2002   *Random Passage*

Made-for-Television Movies
1997   *Major Crime*
2002   *Bleacher Burns*
2002   *Behind the Red Door*

Films
Secret Nation, 1991; *Buried on Sunday*, 1993; *Extraordinary Visitor*, 1998; *The Divine Ryans*, 1999; *New Waterford Girl*, 1999; *Violet*, 2000; *Mambo Italiano*, 2003.

Stage
A Moon for the Misbegotten; Goodnight Desdemona, Good Morning Juliet (director).

Walt Disney Programs (Various Titles)

U.S. Cartoons, Films, and Children's Programming

Walt Disney was not only one of the most important producers in motion picture history but one of the most important producers in American television history as well. He pioneered a relationship between the motion picture industry and the fledgling television industry, helped ensure the success of a third television network, promoted the transition from live broadcasts to film, and championed the conversion to color television in the mid-1960s.

Although Disney was quoted in the 1930s as having no interest in television, that opinion had changed by the early 1950s, when television burst onto the American social scene. On Christmas Day in 1950 for NBC, and again in 1951 for CBS, Disney produced hour-long specials that employed a number of clips from various Disney films and short subjects. Both specials achieved excellent ratings, and soon all three networks were wooing Disney to create an entire series for them.

Disney's interest in television was stimulated by his attempts to construct the Disneyland theme park in Anaheim, California. Encountering difficulty in financing the project, Walt offered network executives a television series in return for the network making a substantial investment in the park. ABC, trailing substantially behind NBC and CBS, had just merged with United Paramount Theatres in 1953 and used this new influx of cash to fulfill Disney's request. The resultant anthology series, appropriately named *Disneyland*, premiered in late 1954, quickly becoming the first ABC program to crack the Nielsen top 20.

Disney's relationship with ABC contradicted the strategy espoused by the rest of the film industry. During this period, Hollywood studios viewed television as a competitor to motion pictures and attempted to crush the medium. Walt Disney, however, quickly saw TV's potential as a promotional tool. The first two specials combined old footage with promotions for upcoming theatrical releases such as *Alice in Wonderland* (1951). Disney's first Emmy Award would be awarded for an hour-long *Disneyland* episode about the filming of *20,000 Leagues Under the Sea* (1954), which was titled "Operation Undersea" but humorously known in the industry as "The Long, Long Trailer." The series also worked to advertise the park, with individual episodes devoted specifically to its construction.

Other studios soon attempted to duplicate Disney's success. Series such as *The MGM Parade* and *Warner Brothers Presents* quickly appeared, promoting the studios' latest releases. These programs disappeared almost as quickly, mainly because Disney and his studio had constructed a unique image for themselves as producers of family entertainment. With a backlog of animated features and shorts, Disney came to television already known for entertaining children around the world (knowing the value of this backlog, Disney held onto the television rights to all of his films, at a time when all the other studios were raising revenue by selling off the permanent television rights to their entire pre-1948 film catalogs). From years of marketing toward children, Disney understood how children could influence their parents to buy products. After *Disneyland*'s "Davy Crockett" episodes created a merchandising phenomenon, Disney introduced *The Mickey Mouse Club,* a daily afternoon series. With this show, one of the first attempts to target television programming at children, advertisers now conceived of children as a marketable group and initiated a tradition of weekday-afternoon programming oriented toward younger audiences.

The studio's background in film production led to the decision to film the *Mickey Mouse Club* episodes, allowing for higher production values, rather than performing them live. The high-quality look of the series (and the subsequent involvement of other film studios in television production) helped shift television programming from live broadcasts to filmed entertainment. Long before color television technology became regulated and promoted, *Disneyland* episodes were filmed in color. Disney would promote the conversion to color when the anthology series, renamed *Walt Disney's Wonderful World of Color,* moved in 1961 to NBC, which was beginning color broadcasts.

Disney's importance to television as a producer of programming is incalculable. His success had an enormous effect on decisions by motion picture studios to enter into television production, thus guaranteeing programming for the fledgling medium. Yet Disney is important as a television icon as well. Working as host for the anthology series bearing the Disney name until the end of his life in 1966, Walt Disney quickly became identified by most children as "Uncle Walt." With an easy-going manner and a warm smile, he spoke to viewers in a Midwestern twang, enthusiastically demonstrating how certain special effects were created for his films, explaining the latest advances in space technology, or narrating a beloved fairy tale accompanied by scenes from his animated features. Usually filmed in a set that looked like his studio office, Disney gave the impression that he would drop all business to spend some time with his audience or engage in banter with cartoon characters Mickey Mouse and Donald Duck (who "magically" interacted with him as if they actually existed in the same space). More than in any other way, Disney's presence and persona helped represent his company as promoter of American family values and television itself as a "family medium." Even after his death, the company's television produc-

tions and subsequent cable channel have reinforced that image of wholesome family entertainment.

SEAN GRIFFIN

See also **Cartoons; Disney, Walt; Eisner, Michael**

Disneyland

Executive Producer/Host
Walt Disney

Programming History
ABC
October 1954–September 1958   Wednesday 7:30–8:30

Walt Disney Presents

Executive Producer/Host
Walt Disney

Programming History
ABC

September 1958–September 1959	Friday 8:00–9:00
September 1959–September 1960	Friday 7:30–8:30
September 1960–September 1961	Sunday 6:30–7:30

Walt Disney's Wonderful World of Color (title changed to *The Wonderful World of Disney,* 1969–79; as *Disney's Wonderful World,* 1979–81)

Executive Producer/Host
Walt Disney (1961–66)

Narrator
Dick Wesson (from 1966)

Programming History
NBC

September 1961–August 1975	Sunday 7:30–8:30
September 1975–September 1981	Sunday 7:00–8:00

Walt Disney

Programming History
CBS

September 1981–January 1983	Saturday 8:00–9:00
January 1983–February 1983	Tuesday 8:00–9:00
July 1983–September 1983	Saturday 8:00–9:00

The Disney Sunday Movie

Executive Producer/Host
Michael Eisner

Programming History
ABC

February 1986–September 1987	Sunday 7:00–9:00
September 1987–September 1988	Sunday 7:00–8:00

The Magical World of Disney

Executive Producer/Host
Michael Eisner

Programming History
NBC

October 1988–July 1989	Sunday 7:00–8:00
July 1989	Sunday 8:00–9:00
August 1989–May 1990	Sunday 7:00–8:00
May 1990–July 1990	Sunday 7:00–9:00
July 1990–August 1990	Sunday 8:00–9:00
August 1990–September 1990	Sunday 7:00–8:00

The Wonderful World of Disney

Executive Producer/Host
Michael Eisner

Programming History
ABC

September 1997–	Sunday 7:00–9:00

Further Reading

Anderson, Christopher, *Hollywood TV: The Studio System in the Fifties,* Austin: University of Texas Press, 1994

Flower, Joe, *Prince of the Magic Kingdom: Michael Eisner and the Re-Making of Disney,* New York: Wiley, 1991

Greene, Katherine, and Richard Greene, *The Man Behind the Magic: The Story of Walt Disney,* New York: Viking, 1991

Holliss, Richard, and Brian Sibley, *The Disney Studio Story,* New York: Crown, 1988

Schickel, Richard, *The Disney Version,* New York: Simon and Schuster, 1968

Smoodin, Eric, editor, *Disney Discourse: Producing the Magic Kingdom,* New York: Routledge, 1994

Walters, Barbara (1931–)

U.S. Broadcast Journalist

Although Barbara Walters would later downplay her relationship with the feminist movement, her early career is marked by a number of moves that were partially responsible for breaking down the all-male facade of U.S. network news. A *Today* show regular for 15 years, including two years as the first official female cohost, she was originally a visible presence in the program's feature segments and then went on to cover hard news—including President Richard Nixon's historic visit to the People's Republic of China in 1972, when she was part of the NBC News team. Her most controversial breakthrough involved her decision in 1976 to leave *Today* to coanchor the *ABC Evening News* with Harry Reasoner, the first time a woman was allowed the privileged position of network evening anchor, for a record-breaking seven-figure salary. Public reaction to both her salary and approach to the news—which critics claimed led to the creeping infotainment mentality that threatens traditional (male) reporting—undercut ABC News ratings, and she was quickly bumped from the anchor desk.

After that public relations disaster, Walters undertook a comeback on ABC with *The Barbara Walters Special,* an occasional series of interviews with heads of state, newsmakers, sports figures, and Hollywood celebrities that have consistently topped the ratings and made news in themselves. In 1977 she arranged the first joint interview with Egyptian president Anwar Sadat and Israeli prime minister Menachem Begin; she has interviewed every U.S. president and first lady since the Nixon administration, as well as political figures as diverse as British prime minister Margaret Thatcher, U.S. presidential contender Ross Perot, and Russian president Boris Yeltsin. Walters had numerous

Barbara Walters.
Photo courtesy of Barbara Walters/Capital Cities/ABC, Inc.

comebacks and triumphs. Returned to ABC's anchor desk in 1984 as cohost (with Hugh Downs) of the newsmagazine *20/20,* she became sole anchor in 1999. Her pre-Oscar and "Ten Most Fascinating People of the Year" broadcasts have become annual television events. In 1997 she returned to daytime with *The View,* a popular and celebrated news/issues/talk show featuring Walters and a team of "real women" commentators who discuss, kvetch, interview, and opine about current events.

Despite her status as both national celebrity and the recipient of numerous awards from journalists, television broadcasters, and women's groups, public reaction to Walters has remained ambivalent, perhaps as a result of changing notions of the nature of "news" in the television era. Walters's interviews have not been limited to figures embroiled in the matters covered by hard-news subjects such as politics and war; many of her more popular specials (and *20/20* segments) have been celebrity interviews and chats with more tawdry news figures. Her 1999 interview with Monica Lewinsky, the intern whose affair with President Bill Clinton led to his impeachment, was the highest-rated "news" program ever broadcast by a single network. Other memorable moments (such as the time she asked actress Katherine Hepburn what kind of tree she would

like to be) have worked to undercut her image as a serious journalist. The late Gilda Radner's classic parody of Walters's distinctive style as "Baba Wawa" on *Saturday Night Live* remains popular as a timeless critique of the cult of personality in television journalism.

Walters began her career in broadcast journalism as a writer for CBS News. She also served as the youngest producer with NBC's New York station, WNBC-TV, before joining *Today.* After less than a year as a writer for *Today,* she was promoted to reporter-at-large (or, as then-host Hugh Downs described her, "the new '*Today* girl' "), although gender politics at the time severely constrained her role. According to Walters, she was not allowed to write for the male correspondents or to ask questions in "male-dominated" areas such as economics or politics, and she was forbidden to interview guests on-camera until all of the men on *Today* had finished asking their questions. Thanks in part to Walters's contributions, these commandments no longer apply.

SUSAN MCLELAND

See also **Anchor; Gender and Television; News, Network**

Barbara Walters. Born in Boston, Massachusetts, September 25, 1931. Educated at Sarah Lawrence College, Bronxville, New York, B.A. in English, 1953. Married: 1) Robert Katz (annulled); child: Jacqueline Dena; 2) Lee Guber, 1963 (divorced, 1976); 3) Merv Adelson, 1986 (divorced, 1992). Worked as a secretary at an advertising agency; assistant to the publicity director, NBC's WRCA-TV, New York; producer and writer, WRCA; writer and producer, WPIX Radio and CBS-TV; worked for a theatrical public relations firm; hired for NBC's *Today* show, 1961, regular panel member, 1964–74, cohost, 1974–76; moderator of the syndicated program *Not for Women Only,* 1974–76; newscaster, ABC Evening News, 1976–78; host, *The Barbara Walters Special,* since 1976; cohost, ABC-TV news show *20/20* since 1984 and ABC-TV talk show *The View* since 1997. L.H.D.: Ohio State University, 1971, Marymount College, 1975, and Wheaton College, 1983. Recipient: National Association of Television Program Executives Award, 1975; International Radio and Television Society's Broadcaster of the Year, 1975; Emmy Awards, 1975, 1980, 1982, and 1983; Lowell Thomas Award, 1990; International Women's Media Foundation Lifetime Achievement Award, 1992; Academy of Television Arts and Sciences Hall of Fame, 1990.

Television

1961–76	*Today* (cohost, 1974–76)
1974–76	*Not for Women Only*

1976–78	*ABC Evening News* (coanchor)
1976–	*The Barbara Walters Special*
1984–	*20/20* (anchor)
1997–	*The View* (producer, cohost)
2001	*Iyanla* (executive producer)

Radio

Emphasis, early 1970s; *Moderator,* early 1970s.

Publication

How to Talk to Practically Anybody About Practically Anything, 1970

Further Reading

Carter, Bill, "Tender Trap," *New York Times Magazine* (August 23, 1992)
Gelfman, Judith S., *Women in Television News,* New York: Columbia University Press, 1976
Gottlieb, Martin, "Dangerous Liaisons: Journalists and Their Sources," *Columbia Journalism Review* (July–August 1989)
Miller, Mark Crispin, "Barbara Walters's Theater of Revenge," *Harper's Magazine* (November 1989)
Oppenheimer, Jerry, "The Barbara: 20/20 Vision Reveals Ms. Walters as Queen B," *Washington Journalism Review* (May 1990)
Paisner, Daniel, *The Imperfect Mirror: Inside Stories of Television Newswomen,* New York: Morrow, 1989
Reed, Julia, "Woman in the News," *Vogue* (February 1992)
Sanders, Marlene, and Marcia Rock, *Waiting for Prime Time: The Women of Television News,* Urbana: University of Illinois Press, 1988
Wulf, Steve, "Barb's Wired," *Time* (November 6, 1995)

Waltons, The

U.S. Drama

The Waltons was a highly successful family drama series of the 1970s that portrayed a sense of family in sharp contrast to the problem-ridden urban families of such "socially relevant" sitcoms as *All in the Family, Maude,* or *Sanford and Son,* which vied with it for top billing in the Nielsen ratings. Set in the fictitious rural community of Walton's Mountain, Virginia, during the 1930s, the episodic narrative focused on a large and dignified, "salt-of-the-earth" rural white family consisting of grandparents, parents, and seven children. Based on the semiautobiographical writings of Earl Hamner Jr., much of the early narrative was enunciated from the perspective of the oldest son, John Boy, an aspiring writer. The series was based on Hamner's novel *Spencer's Mountain,* which had been made into a feature film of the same name and subsequently adapted as a CBS-TV holiday special, *The Homecoming,* in 1971. The initial public reaction to the special was so overwhelming that executives Lee Rich and Bob Jacks of the newly formed Lorimar Productions convinced CBS to continue it as a series, with Hamner as co–executive producer and story editor.

Lorimar executives constructed the series to emphasize both the locale (the Blue Ridge Mountains) and the historical period (the Great Depression), hoping to evoke a nostalgia for the recent past. They proposed to walk that fine line between "excessive sentimentality and believable human warmth" and took care not to caricature the mountain culture of the family, desiring to portray them as descendants of pioneer stock rather than stereotypical "hillbillies." Production notes in the Hamner papers emphasize the respect to be afforded the family and its culture: "That the Waltons are poor should be obvious, but there should be no hint of squalor or debased living conditions usually associated with poverty." Producers also stressed that *The Waltons* would not be like earlier wholesome family series *Father Knows Best* or *I Remember Mama* transplanted to the Blue Ridge Mountains of Virginia, but instead would be "the continuing story of a seventeen-year-old boy who wants to be a writer, growing up during the Depression in a large and loving family."

Premiering in the fall of 1972, the hour-long dramatic series was scheduled in what was considered a "suicidal" time slot against two popular Thursday-night shows, ABC's *The Mod Squad* and NBC's top-rated *The Flip Wilson Show.* By its second season, *The Waltons* achieved the valedictory rank in the overall ratings and stayed in the top 20 shows for the next several years. During its first season, the series garnered

The Waltons, Michael Learned, Richard Thomas, Ralph Waite, Jon Walmsley, Ellen Corby, Will Geer, Kami Cotler, David W. Harper, Judy Norton-Taylor, Eric Scott, Mary Beth McDonough, 1972–81.
Courtesy of the Everett Collection

Emmy Awards for Outstanding Drama Series, Best Dramatic Actor (Richard Thomas) and Actress (Michael Learned), Best Supporting Actress (Ellen Corby), and Best Dramatic Writing (John McGreevey), and it continued to receive Emmys for acting and/or writing for the next half a decade. The series endured until 1981, with the extended family maturing and changing, surviving the loss of some characters, the addition of new supporting characters, and the sociohistorical changes as the community weathered the Depression era and entered that of World War II. The cast has reunited for a number of holiday and wedding specials in the nearly 15 years since the series ended, and the Walton family has endured in the United States' mythic imagination as well as in ratings popularity.

The Walton family was portrayed as a cohesive and nearly self-sufficient social world. The family members operated as a team, full of collective wisdom and insight, yet always finding narrative (and physical) space for their individuality. In addition to the continuing narrative development of each regular character and of the family dynamics over the course of the series, each episode frequently dealt with a conflict or tension introduced by an outsider who happened into the community (Robert E. Ziegler described these characters as "foreigners, drifters, fugitives, orphans, and others just passing through"), bringing their own problems, which were potentially disruptive influences on the harmony and equilibrium of the Walton's Mountain community. The narrative of each episode worked through the resolution of these tensions within the household, as well as the healing or spiritual uplift achieved by the outsider characters as they assimilated the values of the family and learned their lessons of love and morality.

The series was critically praised as being bittersweet, "wholesome," emotion-laden viewing. Reviewers noted that the series conveyed a vivid authenticity of both historical time and cultural place, as well as an emotional verisimilitude regarding the portrayal of a certain type of family life rooted in that time and place. Devoted viewers besieged the network, producers, and cast members with fan letters praising the show and expressing their degree of emotional identification with many aspects of the series. Many considered the series to be the epitome of television's capacity for romantic, effective, and moving storytelling in its evocation of childhood and its ability to tap into a deep desire for a mythicized community and family intimacy.

Yet the series also had its detractors, who complained that *The Waltons* was too sweet, sappily sentimental, and exploitative of viewers' emotions. Hal Crowther remarked that its "homey wisdom and Sunday school platitudes have been known to make me gag"; others labeled it an "obviously corny, totally unreal family" with characters too good to be true. Many recognized in the show an "intolerable wistfulness" for a romanticized past constructed through the creation of false memory and hopeless longing. Some critics noted that such a romanticized image of the era could make viewers forget the real nature of rural poverty. "The Depression was not a time for the making of strong souls" or healthy, well-nourished bodies, according to Anne Roiphe, who criticized the series for associating poverty with elevated moral values and neutralizing the social, economic, and political upheavals of the 1930s "behind a wall of tradition, goodness and good fortune." Roiphe noted how skillfully the media producers were able to design and articulate myths of American happiness and innocence during the historical period the series portrayed; however, the viewers who admired the series also eagerly participated in that construction of a mythical past. Other critics have noted that despite its embrace of liberal humanitarian values (against racism, etc.), *The Waltons'* inherent conservatism has made it ripe for appropriation by right-wing "family values" religious groups. Indeed, it became a benchmark series for the Family Channel, the media outlet for Pat Robertson's Christian Coalition, which held exclusive syndication rights for the series in the early 1990s. In the intervening years, conservative politicians have often cited *The Waltons* as the archetypal family embodying wholesome American "family values." In the American collective imagination, then, Hamner's family has become more than just a television series; it is a signifier that elicits the mythos of an era of prewar innocence and of a particular structure of intergenerational family and community relationships.

PAMELA WILSON

See also **Family on Television; Melodrama**

Narrator
Earl Hamner Jr.

Cast

John Walton	Ralph Waite
Olivia Walton (1972–80)	Michael Learned
Zeb (Grandpa) Walton (1972–78)	Will Geer
Esther (Grandma) Walton (1972–79)	Ellen Corby
John Boy Walton (1972–77)	Richard Thomas
John Boy Walton (1979–81)	Robert Wightman
Mary Ellen Walton Willard	Judy Norton-Taylor
Jim-Bob Walton	David W. Harper
Elizabeth Walton	Kami Cotler
Jason Walton	Jon Walmsley
Erin Walton Donough	Mary Elizabeth Mc-
Ben Walton	Eric Scott
Ike Godsey	Joe Conley
Corabeth Godsey (1974–81)	Ronnie Claire Edwards
Sheriff Ep Bridges	John Crawford
Mamie Baldwin	Helen Kleeb
Emily Baldwin	Mary Jackson
Verdie Foster	Lynn Hamilton
Rev. Matthew Fordwick (1972–77)	John Ritter
Rosemary Hunter Fordwick (1973–77)	Mariclare Costello
Yancy Tucker (1972–79)	Robert Donner
Flossie Brimmer (1972–77)	Nora Marlowe
Maude Gormsley (1973–79)	Merie Earle
Dr. Curtis Willard (1976–78)	Tom Bower
Rev. Hank Buchanan (1977–78)	Peter Fax
J.D. Pickett (1978–81)	Lewis Arquette
John Curtis Willard (1978–81)	Marshall Reed and
Michael Reed	
Cindy Brunson Walton (1979–81)	Leslie Winston
Rose Burton (1979–81)	Peggy Rea
Serena Burton (1979–80)	Martha Nix
Jeffrey Burton (1979–80)	Keith Mitchell
Toni Hazleton (1981)	Lisa Harrison
Arlington Wescott Jones (Jonesy) (1981)	Richard Gilliland

Producers
Lee Rich, Earl Hamner Jr., Robert L. Jacks, Andy White, Rod Peterson

Programming History
178 episodes
CBS
September 1972–August 1981   Thursday 8:00–9:00

Further Reading

Crowther, Hal, "Boxed In," *The Humanist* (July–August 1976)
Roiphe, Anne, "The Waltons," *New York Times Magazine* (November 18, 1973)
"Wholesome Sentiment in the Blue Ridge," *Life* (October 13, 1972)
Ziegler, Robert E., "Memory-Spaces: Themes of the House and the Mountain in *The Waltons*," *Journal of Popular Culture* (1981)

War Game, The

British Drama

More than three decades after its production, *The War Game* remains the most controversial and, perhaps, the most telling television film on nuclear war. Directed by the young Peter Watkins for the BBC, its depiction of the impact of Soviet nuclear attack on Britain caused turmoil at the corporation and in government. Although it went on to win an Oscar for Best Documentary Feature in 1966, it was denied transmission in Britain until 1985. Announcing the decision to hold back *The War Game* in 1965, the BBC explained that the film was too horrifying for the medium of broadcasting, expressing a particular concern for "children, the very old, or the unbalanced."

However, both BBC internal documents and declassified Cabinet papers of the period reflect the high degree of political anxiety generated by the film and suggest that although the BBC was keen to assert its independence and its liberalism, *The War Game* was indeed the victim of high-level censorship. The popular press of the day, for their part, largely approved the ban, often reading the film as propaganda for the youthful Campaign for Nuclear Disarmament.

The film imagines a period of some four months, beginning with the days leading up to nuclear attack. In a show of solidarity with the Chinese invasion of South Vietnam, the Russian and East German authorities have sealed off all access to Berlin and have threatened to invade the western sector of the city unless the United States withdraws its threat to use tactical nuclear weapons against the invading Chinese. When two North Atlantic Treaty Organization (NATO) divisions attempt to reach Berlin, they are overrun by communist forces, triggering the U.S. president's release of nuclear warheads to NATO. The Soviet Union calls NATO's bluff, leading to a preemptive strike by the allies and, in a self-protective measure, the Soviet launch against Britain.

Shot in newsreel-style black and white, and running just over three-quarters of an hour, *The War Game* works on a number of levels. The main discourse is that of the documentary exposition itself, chronicling and dramatizing the main stages and the key features of the countdown to attack and the immediate consequences of the bombing. A second discourse, also playing on the relationship between documentary and drama, takes the form of two types of *vox pop* interviews, which punctuate the text: interviews that illustrate the contemporary public's consciousness of the issues, exposing widespread ignorance; and clearly fictional interviews with (imaginary) key figures as the attack scenario itself develops and extends.

Further elements go some way to suggesting contexts for the public's failure to perceive the realities of nuclear war. One strand of the film highlights the pathetically inadequate information purveyed by the official civil defense self-help manual (cover price: nine old pence). A fourth level of comment, provided by intertitles, exposes the bankruptcy of statements on the nuclear threat emerging from religious sources such as Vatican Council II of the Roman Catholic Church.

The film concentrates on southeast England and, in particular, the town of Rochester in Kent. It bleakly illustrates the social chaos of the period before attack, focusing on the personal and ideological conflicts likely to arise from the enforced evacuation of large numbers of the urban population and on the impracticality of building viable domestic shelters capable of withstanding the power of the nuclear bomb—as the price of basics such as planks and sandbags escalates nonetheless. The film depicts the immediate horrors of a nuclear explosion by invoking memories of the firestorms of Dresden and Hiroshima, the earthquakes and the blinding light, 30 times more powerful than the midday sun, which is capable of melting upturned eyeballs from many miles away.

The remainder of the film concentrates on the rapid disintegration of the social fabric in the aftermath of the attack, as civilization disappears. In images of chilling and provocative power, policemen are depicted as executioners of the terminally ill and of minor criminals. The effects of radiation sickness are explained and illustrated, along with the psychological devastation that would befall survivors and the dying in a mute and apathetic world. There is a good chance of all this happening, the film suggests, by 1980.

The film's enduring power thus derives from a variety of sources. These include its cool articulation of momentary images—a child's eyes burned by a distant nuclear airburst as the film itself goes into negative; a bucketful of wedding rings collected as a register of the dead; a derelict building that has become an impromptu furnace for the incineration of bodies too nu-

The War Game, 1965.
Courtesy of the Everett Collection

merous to bury; "Stille Nacht" playing on a gramophone, which, in the absence of electricity, must be turned by hand.

At a structural level, the film achieves its overall rhetorical power through both its mixture and its separation of documentary and dramatic modes. It does not, for example, offer the purely "dramatic" spectacle of later TV nuclear dramas such as the U.S. *The Day After* (1983) or the British *Threads* (1984), with their more traditional identifications around character and plot. Nor does it simply document the drama in the manner of Watkins's previous *Culloden* (1965), in which the television camera revisits the battlefield of 1746 and interviews participants, or of *Cathy Come Home* (1966), Ken Loach's similar merging of the domains of documentary and drama to survey the rising problem of homelessness in 1960s Britain.

The War Game, on the contrary, confuses and yet demarcates the two modes, documentary and drama. The "dramatic" sequences, with their highly "documentary" look, are retained as fragmentary and discontinuous illustrations of an ongoing documentary narrative, which itself disorientingly moves back and forth between, on the one hand, statements and assumptions that this is "really happening" before our eyes and, on the other hand, other signals and warnings that this is how it "could be" and "might look."

The British television audience was deprived of *The War Game* for two decades, until a moment in history that was ironically close to the events in Eastern Europe that canceled the particular cold war scenario underpinning the film. The banning of it, however, made the film a cause célèbre, and its notoriety grew in the troubled later 1960s, as the film reached significant audiences in art-house cinemas and through the antinuclear movement. Introducing the 1985 broadcast, Ludovic Kennedy estimated that, by then, the film had already reached as many as 6 million viewers.

PHILLIP DRUMMOND

See also **Watkins, Peter**

War Game, The

Producer
Peter Watkins

Programming History
BBC 1
July 31, 1985 (produced, 1965)

Further Reading

Gomez, Joseph A., *Peter Watkins,* Boston: Twayne, 1979
Watkins, Peter, *The War Game: An Adaptation of the BBC Documentary,* New York: Avon, 1967
Welsh, James Michael, *Peter Watkins: A Guide to References and Resources,* Boston: Hall, 1986

War on Television

War on television has been the subject of both fictional accounts and extensive, often compelling news coverage. War and kindred bellicose activities have inspired television documentaries, docudramas, dramatic series, and situation comedies. Fictional accounts of war and documentary accounts of historical wars are, however, not discussed in this entry, which focuses instead on televised coverage of contemporary warfare and related martial actions.

The first noteworthy war to occur in the television age was the Korean War (1950–53). Television was in its infancy as a mass medium at the time and, as a consequence, the Korean conflict is not widely thought of as a televised war. Not only did relatively few viewers have access to television sets, but, because satellite technology was not yet developed and television film had to be transported by air to broadcasters, by the time such film arrived its immediacy was much diminished. Often, therefore, newspapers and radio remained the media of first choice for timely information. Nonetheless, in August 1950, a CBS television news announcer reported an infantry landing as it was in progress. The controversy caused by this putative security breach foreshadows conflicts that would long continue between military authorities waging war and television reporters covering warfare.

Years later, these concerns persisted and found one of their most surreal expressions in connection with the 1992 U.S.-led occupation of Somalia, when early waves of U.S. occupation forces landed on Somali beaches at night and found their landings illuminated by the television lights of international news organizations. Criticism of the security risk this illumination entailed harks back to similar criticism of the 1950 CBS report on the infantry landing in Korea, and it seems a valid military concern, as does concern during the second Gulf War that certain television correspondents reported in real time on troop movements. Other aspects of the media-military relationship, however, are less clear-cut, especially as to whether military manipulation of the media is a proper military concern or an undue intrusion into civilian politics.

In many national contexts, concerns about troop security and public perceptions have led to formal legal censorship of television war coverage, although, perhaps as frequently, physical or technological obstacles inherent to television broadcasting from theaters of war, or erected by military personnel at the scene of a conflict, have often served a similar censorship purpose. While debates about formal censorship raged during many of the 20th century's wars, informal censorship was, presumably, even more frequent, as early on when during the 1956 Suez expedition British media were requested to refrain from reporting certain information but were not forced to do so under penalty of law. Or, as almost half a century later, when U.S. military authorities, as a prelude to the second Gulf War, purchased all available time on orbiting photo-satellites to make their images publicly unavailable, and unavailable also to besieged Iraqi forces.

Other post–World War II conflicts notwithstanding, television coverage of the U.S. war with Vietnam (1962–75) seems to have inspired the most controversy worldwide. Despite clear evidence that the U.S. war effort was less than successful in objective terms, U.S. popular opinion and much expert military opinion continue to regard the Vietnam War as one that could have brought victory to the United States on the battlefield but was lost in the living room (where viewers watched their television sets and many eventually withdrew their support for the effort). Reporters who themselves covered the Vietnam War in the early 1960s remember, however, that most of that early coverage was laudatory and, in the words of Bernard Kalb, who would later join the Cable News Network (CNN), that there was "an awful lot of jingoism...on the part

The troubles of Northern Ireland: British soldier chasing a demonstrator during a riot in Londonderry, Northern Ireland, 1972.
Courtesy of the Everett Collection/CSU Archives

of the press in which it celebrated the American involvement in Vietnam." Methodical scholarly accounts of televised coverage also report that television coverage was inclined overall to highlight positive aspects of the Vietnam War and that viewers exposed to the most televised coverage were also those most inclined to view the military favorably. Nonetheless, domestic social schisms attributed to controversy about the Vietnam War and that war's ultimate failure to sustain a noncommunist regime in Vietnam are often blamed on television and other media.

Whether the public turned against the Vietnam War because television, in particular, and the media, in general, presented it unfavorably, or whether the public turned against the war because the media accurately depicted its horrors and television did so most graphically of all remains an open and hotly contested question. There is, however, no historic evidence to prove that a graphic portrayal of war disinclines a viewing public to engage in a war. Some scholars even suggest that the opposite may be the case when a public considers a war justified and that public is exposed to images of its side enduring great—and presumably righteous—suffering.

Despite a still less-than-definitive understanding of the relationship between television coverage and popular support for war efforts, military strategists continued to integrate domestic public relations (PR) strategy into overall military strategy during and after the U.S.-Vietnam War. As the war progressed, analysts

Two soldiers comfort each other under the strain of combat in Pleiku, South Vietnam, 5/26/67.
Courtesy of the Everett Collection/CSU Archives

continued to debate whether it was appropriate for the military itself—rather than some other government agency—to attempt to influence civilian public policy through such efforts. Within military circles in the wake of that war, most such debates were left behind and the military's media relations strategies began moving far beyond censorship and toward a full-fledged engagement (some say co-optation) of televised media. This trend remained strong through the second Gulf War as documented most recently by PR experts who authored *Weapons of Mass Deception: The Uses of Propaganda in Bush's War on Iraq.*

Hints of this new military strategy surfaced soon after the U.S.-Vietnam War. During 1976 naval conflicts between Britain and Iceland over fishing rights, for example, various strategies to influence televised coverage were used by the Icelandic side to depict Britain as the aggressive party, while the British Navy (then less media savvy) refused to allow television crews on its ships. As late as the 1982 Falklands/Malvinas War, during which Great Britain successfully reclaimed South Atlantic islands that Argentina's military dictatorship had occupied, British military strategists had yet to develop a comprehensive media strategy. Although by then the British Navy did allow television

and other media personnel to travel aboard its ships to the South Atlantic, the British did not systematically endeavor to control the content of the war coverage by influencing television media.

The following year, when the United States invaded Grenada, concerns regarding less-than-favorable television coverage prompted military planners to exclude civilian camera crews entirely in favor of military television crews. Sensitivity to unfavorable television coverage was heightened at that time by the deaths of 230 U.S. Marine and 50 French peacekeepers in a bomb attack during operations in Beirut. But in 1989, when the United States invaded Panama, the exclusion of civilian television crews was not feasible, and thanks to satellite technology and round-the-clock CNN coverage, television viewers were able to watch the progress of military operations with much immediacy. As had been the case, however, during the early 1960s in Vietnam, the television media were generally inclined to stress the salutary aspects of the Panama invasion, and U.S. planners also did a more effective job of controlling the public perception of the invasion.

The very short duration of the Panama, Grenada, and Falklands/Malvinas operations may have forestalled adverse reactions among the civilian populations who watched their governments wage war on television. This led some observers to argue that short-lived military engagements are suited to the television age, as they are less likely to generate adverse television coverage and public opposition. Yet a surfeit of short-lived military endeavors notwithstanding, long-term warfare is still waged in the television age. Still other observers suggest that a lack of widely available independent television coverage, especially in developing nations, was what long made extended warfare in certain regions palatable to the international community. The rise in the rest of the world of major television networks dedicated to independent coverage of news, such as Al Jazeera, is bound to factor into that equation in the coming years.

Meanwhile, no clear relationship between television coverage and a war's intensity or duration seems apparent. On the one hand, for example, the Iran-Iraq War (1980–88) received often negligible international television coverage and lasted years; on the other, civil wars in various parts of the former Yugoslavia (1991–98) continued for years as well, despite often extensive international coverage. Other extended or particularly brutal conflicts, terrorist campaigns, coups d'état, civil wars, and genocidal endeavors also received widely varying levels of television coverage. Such latter-day wars have been waged in Algeria, Angola, Armenia, Azerbaijan, Cambodia, Chad, Chechnya, El Salvador, Ethiopia, Georgia, Guatemala,

Liberia, Nigeria, Peru, Rwanda, the Sudan, Yemen, the former Zaire, and in other places far too numerous to mention. Through these myriad conflicts, horrific imagery also found its way to television screens, sometimes leading to calls for and the deployment of peacekeeping missions, sometimes not. The Balkan wars of the 1990s, in particular, featured horrific scenes of emaciated prisoners of war and poignant images of civilians shot down in the street—notably, images televised for days of corpses belonging to Admira Ismic and Bosko Brckic, Romeo-and-Juliet-type lovers from opposite sides of the Bosnian conflict shot down by snipers during a clandestine rendezvous atop a Sarajevo bridge. Broadcast scenes of those sorts led ultimately to international intervention in the Balkans, though similar scenes of civilians, both adults and children, shot by automatic gunfire in the Occupied Territories of Palestine led to no such intervention. Disturbing televised images from that conflict include those of 12-year-old Muhammad Al-Dura being shot dead, while Jamal, his father, attempted in vain to shelter him from a hail of automatic fire (television cameras captured the Al-Dura shooting in almost its every detail, and as of this writing, a video of the event is available through the BBC website, news.bbc.co.uk).

Other campaigns of mass armed atrocity, such as those in Rwanda and the Democratic Republic of the Congo (formerly Zaire), received less televised coverage or none at all. It is noteworthy, however, that conflicts in Liberia and other parts of Africa received major televised coverage when European and U.S. troops became involved as peacekeepers. *The Zanzibar Chest,* by a Reuter's reporter who covered Africa's many wars during the 1990s, and *Charlie Wilson's War,* about covert U.S. support to one-half-million Afghan and other Muslim troops fighting Soviet occupation in the 1980s, both provide vivid details about warfare not prominently televised; but, especially as regards Afghanistan, it is unfair to suggest that those struggles were entirely ignored by Western television. Most famously, Dan Rather, head anchor of the *CBS Evening News,* donned disguises and reported from among the Afghan troops on two occasions. Other Western television journalists also habitually burnish their reputations by covering certain major wars on location.

Nonetheless, even the example of Eastern Europe further bolsters arguments that regional conflicts removed from centers of Western interest garner significantly less coverage. The most far removed of these Eastern European conflicts, Chechnya's efforts to end Russian control over that part of the Caucasus, received less coverage than did the Balkan wars and much less than the various earlier uprisings that ended Soviet hegemony over the area.

Removed geographically but not economically from the Western sphere of influence, the two Persian Gulf Wars received the most televised coverage of any armed endeavor in recent years, with the single exception of the September 11, 2001, Al Qaeda attacks on the U.S. mainland. In the aftermath of both Gulf Wars, television and other media were criticized for having failed to provide balanced and complete accounts. Entman argues, in addition, that the media simply gave up trying to construct a coherent narrative for viewers in the long occupation of Iraq after the second Gulf War. As regards the first Gulf War, some critics, most notably Douglas Kellner in *The Persian Gulf TV War,* argued that television and other media failed to provide a balanced and complete account of the war because the corporate owners of commercial networks felt it was not in their business interests to do so. Other critics, also as regards the first Gulf War, suggested that television coverage simply reflected popular prejudices.

To a great extent, however, during the conduct of the Gulf Wars, as in almost all wars, the various national media had to rely on the military forces for access to events and for access to their broadcast networks. According to the *Wall Street Journal's* John Fialka, the central importance of military cooperation is seen in this: that U.S. Marines, despite their smaller role in the first Gulf War, received much more U.S. news coverage than the U.S. Army, in part, because U.S. Marines were more dedicated to opening the lines of communication between reporters in their operations area and the reporters' news organizations back home. Interestingly, British television coverage—benefiting from thoughtful media access policies put in place after the Falklands/Malvinas War—featured the timeliest reports on frontline action during the first war. The British military forces were at that time in the early 1990s the only ones to allow satellite uplinks near the front lines.

The second Gulf War brought new innovations to media relations with the public and the military. Critics continued to suggest that complicit media ownership constrained critical coverage during the war, but, more notable still, jingoistic attitudes fostered in the media by the 2001 Al Qaeda attacks on New York and Washington, D.C., created a strongly promilitary television audience in the United States that found FOX News coverage and other ardently promilitary television coverage very much to its liking. The major development in media relations with the military itself was the "embed" system: a military practice whereby reporters were "embedded" with specific military units for the duration of the war.

The implications of this system, as opposed to the "pool" system whereby groups of reporters in earlier wars were given tours at some distance behind the front, are still being examined as of this writing. Some critics suggest, however, that the embed system creates a kinship between reporters and the troops that precludes the critical distance some believe reporters need to report objectively on what they see. Other argue the embed system makes it difficult for reporters to glean an overview of the military situation as a whole. Meanwhile, reporters who remained in Baghdad as it was besieged were able to provide a different viewpoint to television viewers worldwide. Also, the Arabic-language news network Al Jazeera, free of close ties to the West, provided yet another alternative. Thanks to many such media developments in recent years, it has become possible to see military actions from multiple perspectives, to hear interviews with political and military leaders from all factions, to witness human interest stories from within the very combat zone, and to examine battles and shelling from civilian points of view as well as through combatant or diplomatic eyes. Many viewers have, however, decided instead to gravitate to media that parrot their prejudices.

As for televisual scenes of war, during the 1991 Gulf War, military cooperation with the media made possible that war's most striking television images. These were otherwise closed-circuit video images that emanated from camera-equipped high-tech weaponry directed against Iraqi targets. Thanks to access provided by the military, television viewers were literally able to see through the crosshairs of missiles and other weapons as these bore down on Iraqi civilian and military targets—mostly vehicles, buildings, and other inanimate infrastructure. Significantly, however, according to Fialka, videotape from cameras mounted on U.S. Army Apache helicopter-gunships "showing Iraqi soldiers being mowed down by the gunship's Gatling gun" was seen by a single *Los Angeles Times* reporter but was suppressed thereafter and made unavailable for television broadcast.

During the 2003 Gulf War, by contrast, the most striking images emanated from Baghdad itself, and not from military lenses either, but from television cameras based in the Iraqi capital city, especially from lenses equipped with night-vision equipment. That U.S. military forces could not prevent the broadcast of such televised images seems, however, not to have deterred them from pursuing their bombing—far from it, perhaps because they recognized, as several scholars have argued, that the American public had already been sold on the war.

During the second Gulf War, the U.S. military also appears to have overlooked ABC News interviews with troops in the field who criticized the U.S. secretary of defense, though a similar battlefield complaint

by a U.S. lieutenant during the U.S.-Vietnam War led to a court-martial. Yet the military leaders' relatively sanguine attitude toward such irregularities notwithstanding, the control of televised imagery still seems a goal of theirs. They seem willing now to engage the media relations aspects of warfare, as if exercising this control were just another aspect of military strategy and not a looming threat to the continued distinction between military and civilian political authority. U.S. military propagandists are, for instance, suspected of having instigated the toppling of Saddam Hussein's statue in Baghdad and of having staged the rescue of captured U.S. troops who, other reports have it, were not being guarded at all, fleeing Iraqi troops having left their captives to the care of civilian medical authorities. The U.S. military's staging of such events would, if not strictly in keeping with the highest traditions of military nonintervention in civilian affairs, at least accord with its tradition of remaining at the cutting edge of technological and tactical developments, for event management, as such dramatizations might be deemed, is indeed a cutting-edge tactic for the purposes of public relations.

Far from the contentious early days, when most military organizations considered television coverage a mere nuisance or a possible security risk, military planners today use many aspects of television to promote wars, and even to prepare for them. As Der Derian and other futurists pointed out several years ago, televised image technology is used to provide military personnel with virtual reality training using authentic images of war conditions and maneuvers; moreover, the next leg of military technological development they predicted is now in its nascent stages. This is the phase of "virtual warfare," during which military and paramilitary personnel remain safely ensconced at distant locations as televised imagery and other telemetry allow them to direct weaponry against remote targets. Remote missile attacks on suspected Al Qaeda militants in Afghanistan and Yemen are the most well-publicized recent uses of such technology. The use of such technology, now a part of our world, adds weight to the words of yet another forward thinker: the media guru Marshall McLuhan, who wrote in 1968 that "television war (will have) meant the end of the dichotomy between civilian and military."

That dichotomy did not, however, become moot exactly in the manner McLuhan predicted (i.e., thanks to televisual technology's facilitating the prosecution of war at a distance); rather it happened in precisely the opposite fashion, when war was prosecuted up close by Al Qaeda operatives flying fully-fueled jets into the World Trade Center and the Pentagon. Subsequently, every single broadcast on television has been at first or second or some further remove a broadcast of war on television.

DAVID HUMPHREYS

See also **Terrorism; Vietnam on Television**

Further Reading

Allen, Tim, *The Media of Conflict: War Reporting and Representations of Ethnic Violence,* Zed Books, 1999

Arnett, Peter, *Live from the Battlefield: From Vietnam to Baghdad, 35 Years in the World's War Zones,* Touchstone Books, 1993

Baum, Matthew A., *Soft News Goes to War: Public Opinion and American Foreign Policy in the New Media Age,* Princeton University Press, 2003

Carruthers, Susan L., *The Media at War: Communication and Conflict in the Twentieth Century,* Palgrave Macmillan, 2000

Combelles-Siegel, Pascale, *Target Bosnia: Integrating Information Activities in Peace Operations,* National Defense University Press, 1998

Crile, George, *Charlie Wilson's War: The Extraordinary Story of the Largest Covert Operation in History,* Atlantic Monthly Press, 2003

Dunnigan, James F., *Digital Soldiers: The Evolution of High-Tech Weaponry and Tomorrow's Brave New Battlefield,* St. Martin's Press, 1996

Entman, Robert M., *Projections of Power: Framing News, Public Opinion, and U.S. Foreign Policy,* Chicago: University of Chicago Press, 2004

Ferrari, Michell, *Reporting America at War: An Oral History,* Hyperion, 2003

Greenberg, Bradley S., *Desert Storm and the Mass Media,* Hampton Press, 1993

Hammond, Phil, *Degraded Capability: The Media and the Kosovo Crisis,* Pluto Press, 2000

Jeffords, Susan, *Seeing Through the Media: The Persian Gulf War,* Rutgers University Press, 1994

Katovsky, Bill, *Embedded: The Media at War in Iraq,* Globe Pequot Press, 2003

Kolar-Panov, Dona, *Video, War, and the Diasporic Imagination,* Routledge, 1997

Kurspahic, Kemal, *Prime Time Crime: Balkan Media in War and Peace,* U.S. Institute of Peace Press, 2003

McCain, Thomas A., *The 1,000 Hour War: Communication in the Gulf,* Greenwood, 1993

el-Nawawy, Mohammed, *Al Jazeera: How the Free Arab News Network Scooped the World and Changed the Middle East,* Westview Press, 2003

Neuman, Johanna, *Lights, Camera, War: Is Media Technology Driving International Politics?* St. Martin's Press, 1996

Politkovskaya, Anna, *A Dirty War: A Russian Reporter in Chechnya,* Harvill, 2001

Raine Baroody, Judith, *Media Access and the Military,* University Press of America, 1998

Shaw, Martin, *Civil Society and Media in Global Crises: Representing Distant Violence,* Pinter, 1996

Smith, Perry M., *How CNN Fought the War: A View from the Inside,* Diane, 1991

Taylor, John, *Body Horror: Photojournalism, Catastrophe, and War,* New York University Press, 1998

Thrall, Trevor, *War in the Media Age,* Hampton Press, 2000

Wiener, Robert, *Live from Baghdad: Gathering News at Ground Zero,* Doubleday, 2002

Warner Brothers Presents

U.S. Dramatic Series

Warner Brothers Presents, the first television program produced by Warner Brothers Pictures, appeared on ABC during the 1955–56 season. Hosted by Gig Young, the series featured an omnibus format with weekly episodes drawn from three rotating series based loosely on the Warner Brothers movies *King's Row, Casablanca,* and *Cheyenne.* Although a one-hour series, each weekly episode reserved the final ten minutes for a segment titled "Behind the Cameras at Warner Brothers." This segment featured behind-the-scenes footage, revealing the inner workings of a major movie studio and promoting the studio's recent theatrical releases.

This short-lived series was a hit with neither critics nor viewers, and yet it still stands as a milestone because it marked the introduction of the major Hollywood studios into television production. The 1955–56 season saw the television debut not only of *Warner Brothers Presents* but also of the *Twentieth Century-Fox Hour* on CBS and *MGM Parade* on ABC. The common inspiration for these programs was the success of *Disneyland,* which had premiered the previous season on ABC and had given Walt Disney an unprecedented forum for publicizing the movies, merchandise, and amusement park that carried the Disney trademark. Following Disney, Warner Brothers executives saw television as a vehicle for calling attention to their motion pictures. They were much less interested in producing for television than in using the medium to increase public awareness of the Warner Brothers trademark.

ABC had its own vested interests in acquiring a Warner Brothers series. By recruiting one of Hollywood's most venerable studios to television, ABC scored a valuable coup in its bid for respectability among the networks. As the perennial third-place network, ABC welcomed the glamour and prestige associated with a major Hollywood studio. The opening credits for *Warner Brothers Presents* pointedly reminded viewers of the studio's moviemaking legacy. As the screen filled with the trademark Warner Brothers logo superimposed over a soaring aerial shot of the studio, an announcer exclaimed, "From the entertainment capital of the world comes *Warner Brothers Presents*. The hour that presents Hollywood to you. Made for television by one of the great motion picture studios." Marketing the Warner Brothers' reputation, ABC signed contracts with several sponsors who had never before advertised on the network, including General Electric and the tobacco company Liggett and Myers, two of the largest advertisers in broadcasting.

The alternating series of *Warner Brothers Presents* were seen by both studio and network as an ongoing experiment in an effort to gauge the public taste for filmed television drama. *King's Row* was a pastoral melodrama about a small-town doctor (Jack Kelly) who returns home following medical school to aid the community members and play a role in various soothing tales of moral welfare. *Casablanca* reprised the Academy Award–winning movie, with Charles McGraw in the role made famous by Humphrey Bogart. Rick's Café Americain became the setting for tales of star-crossed romance and, to a much lesser extent, foreign intrigue. The only series to make a significant impression in the ratings was *Cheyenne,* a rough-and-tumble Western starring Clint Walker as a wandering hero who dispenses justice while riding through the old West.

Since the studio's objective was to reach viewers with its promotional messages, the "Behind the Cameras" segments provided a fascinating glimpse into the production process at a movie studio. They introduced viewers to the various departments at the studio, demonstrating the role played by editing, sound, wardrobe, lighting, and so forth in the production of a motion picture. Each segment featured exclusive footage and interviews with top movie stars and directors. On the set of *Giant* a wry James Dean demonstrated rope tricks and, in a rather macabre twist given his untimely death, talked about traffic safety. A gruff John Ford commanded the Monument Valley location of *The Searchers.* Director Billy Wilder and Jimmy Stewart explained how they recreated Charles Lindbergh's legendary flight in *The Spirit of St. Louis.*

When the series failed to find an audience, however, the advertisers balked at the studio's emphatic self-promotion in these segments, particularly when the studio seemed unable to create dramatically compelling episodes. Critics, sponsors, and network executives agreed that the dramatic episodes were formulaic in their writing and perfunctory in their production. In part, this reflected the economics of early telefilm production. The entire $3 million budget that ABC paid for 39 hour-long episodes of *Warner Brothers Presents* represented only a fraction of the budget for a single studio feature like *Giant* or *The Searchers.* Consequently, episodes of *Warner Brothers Presents* were written, produced, and edited on minuscule budgets at a frenetic pace unseen at the studio since the B-grade movies of the 1930s.

After considerable tinkering—including the recycling of scripts from several of the studio's western movies—*Cheyenne* emerged as the sole hit among the *Warner Brothers Presents* series. Had its ratings been calculated separately, it would have finished the season among the 20 highest-rated series. Observing the success of the bluntly conflict-driven *Cheyenne,* ABC asked the studio to heighten the dramatic tension in both *King's Row* and *Casablanca,* fearing, in the words of ABC President Robert Kintner, that neither series was "lusty and combative" enough to appeal to viewers. New scripts were written for both series, introducing murderous kidnappers and mad bombers, but neither series found an audience, and they were both canceled before the end of the season. In their place, *Warner Brothers Presents* substituted an anthology series, *Conflict,* which alternated with *Cheyenne* for the remainder of the season and for the next.

Due to the difficulties in gearing up for the rapid pace of television production, Warner Brothers lost more than a half-million dollars on *Warner Brothers Presents.* But the studio also achieved two lasting benefits. First, with the production of this initial series, Warner Brothers crossed the threshold into television production where, in just four years, it would become the largest producer of network series. Second, it launched the studio's first hit series, *Cheyenne,* which went on to have an eight-year run on ABC.

CHRISTOPHER ANDERSON

See also **Cheyenne; Western**

Host
Gig Young

Programming History
ABC
September 1955–September 1956 Tuesday 7:30–8:30

Casablanca (September 1955–April 1956)

Cast

Rick Jason	Charles McGraw
Capt. Renaud	Marcel Dalio
Sasha	Michael Fox
Sam	Clarence Muse
Ludwig	Ludwig Stossel

Cheyenne (See separate entry)

King's Row (September 1955–January 1956)

Cast

Dr. Parris Mitchell	Jack Kelly
Randy Monaghan	Nan Leslie
Drake McHugh	Robert Horton
Dr. Tower	Victor Jory
Grandma	Lillian Bronson
Dr. Gordon	Robert Burton

Further Reading

Anderson, Christopher, *Hollywood TV: The Studio System in the Fifties,* Austin: University of Texas Press, 1994

Balio, Tino, editor, *Hollywood in the Age of Television,* Boston: Unwin Hyman, 1990

Woolley, Lynn, Robert W. Malsbary, and Robert G. Strange, Jr., *Warner Brothers Television: Every Show of the Fifties and Sixties, Episode by Episode,* Jefferson, North Carolina: McFarland, 1985

Watch Mr. Wizard

U.S. Children's Science Program

Watch Mr. Wizard, one of commercial television's early educational efforts, was highly successful in making science exciting and understandable for children. Presenting scientific laboratory demonstrations and information in an interesting, uncomplicated, and entertaining format, this long-running series was a prime example of the Chicago School of Television and of quality education in a visual format. Created and hosted by Don Herbert, the show's low-key approach, casual ad lib style, and resourceful, often magiclike demonstrations led to rapid success and brought Herbert instant recognition and critical acclaim as an innovative educational broadcaster and as a teacher of science.

Donald Jeffry Herbert, a general science and English major at LaCrosse State Teachers College in Wisconsin, had originally planned to teach dramatics. Following his graduation in 1940, he acted in summer and winter stock and then traveled to New York with an eye toward Broadway. World War II interrupted his career, and the young actor entered the Army Air Forces as a private. As a B-24 bomber pilot, he flew 56 missions with the Fifteenth Air Force and subsequently participated in the invasion of Italy. Discharged as a captain in 1945, Herbert had earned the Distinguished Flying Cross and the Air Medal with three oak leaf clusters.

After the war Herbert accepted offers of radio work in Chicago. He acted in such children's programs as *Captain Midnight, Jack Armstrong,* and *Tom Mix* and sold scripts to *Dr. Christian, Curtain Time,* and *First Nighter.* In October 1949, as coproducer of the documentary health series *It's Your Life,* he was able to combine his interests in science and drama. Most importantly, his idea for *Mr. Wizard* began to take form. He became fascinated with general science experiments and studied television as a medium of presentation.

Herbert sold his idea for *Mr. Wizard* to WNBQ-TV, the Chicago outlet for NBC, and the series premiered on March 3, 1951, with Herbert as the Wizard and Bruce Lindgren as the first of his young assistants. Produced in cooperation with the Cereal Institute, Incorporated, the 30-minute show was targeted at pre-teenagers and initially broadcast on Saturdays from 4:00 to 4:30 P.M.

Within four months, the series had climbed to third place among children's programs in ARB ratings and its audience was growing. Chicago's Federated Advertising Club created an award especially for the show and the Voice of America entered a standing order for recorded transcripts of each program. Within two years, approximately 290 schools were using the series as required homework. In its quiet way, wrote *Variety*

Watch Mr. Wizard.
Photo courtesy of Don Herbert

on September 10, 1952, "this cleverly contrived TV tour into the world of science probably adds as much to NBC's prestige as some of the network's more highly touted educational ventures."

By 1954 *Watch Mr. Wizard* was seen live on 14 stations and via kinescope on an additional 77. The National Science Foundation (NSF) cited Herbert and his show for promoting interest in the sciences, and the American Chemical Society presented him its first citation ever awarded for "important contributions to science education." Three years into Herbert's network run, there were more than 5,000 Mr. Wizard Science Clubs across North America with a membership totaling in excess of 100,000.

Sensing the decline of Chicago as a production center, Herbert moved his show to New York in 1955. During this time, he would win a number of national awards including the prestigious Peabody Award and three Thomas Alva Edison National Mass Media Awards. The total number of *Mr. Wizard* fan clubs would increase nearly tenfold to 50,000. Notwithstanding these accomplishments, NBC canceled the series on September 5, 1965.

Herbert's abilities as a teacher-producer of quality televised science education led him to the National Educational Television network, where he produced a series of shows under the title *Experiment* (1966). He also produced films for junior and senior high schools, wrote a number of books on science, and developed the Mr. Wizard Science Center outside of Boston. On September 11, 1971, NBC revived *Watch Mr. Wizard,* but Herbert's old leisurely pace of the 1950s seemed outdated, and the show left the air on September 2, 1972.

Undaunted by his second cancellation, and challenged by the NSF to create an awareness of science in children, in the early 1970s Herbert and his wife, Norma, developed *Mr. Wizard Close-Ups* for broadcast on NBC's daily morning schedule. At the end of the decade, the husband and wife team also developed traveling elementary school assembly programs featuring young performers and live science demonstrations. By 1991 these tours were annually presenting programs to approximately 3,000 schools and 1.2 million students.

With the financial backing of the NSF and General Motors, in 1980 Herbert began production of *How About*—a long-running series of 80-second reports on developments in science and technology to be used as inserts in local news programs across the country. In time, the series would earn special praise from the American Association for the Advancement of Science–Westinghouse Science Journalism awards committee. Not content to rest on his laurels, in 1984 Herbert developed an updated and faster-paced *Mr. Wizard's World* that was seen three times a week on Nickelodeon, the children's cable network.

In 1991 Herbert received the Robert A. Millikan award from the American Association of Physics Teachers for his "notable and creative contributions to the teaching of physics." Three years later, in his late 70s, he developed another new series, *Teacher to Teacher with Mr. Wizard*—a series of NSF-sponsored 15-minute programs airing on Nickelodeon and highlighting exemplary elementary science teachers and projects. In addition, the seemingly indefatigable Herbert created, among other items, Mr. Wizard Science Secrets kits with clips from *Watch Mr. Wizard,* a Mr. Wizard Science Video Library with 20 videos from the *Mr. Wizard's World* series, and in 1997, Mr. Wizard's Science Assembly Programs using interactive techniques to assist in the demonstration of science principles to live audiences. Moving into the 21st century, nearly 50 years after his first telecast, Herbert and his wife launched an updated series of *Mr. Wizard's World* and the Whelmer Workshops—the latter providing instruction for teachers in techniques developed by Herbert throughout his long career.

In March 1984, Herbert told *Discover* magazine his purpose in life was not to teach but to have fun. "I just restrict myself to fun that has scientific content." Fortunately, for generations of children and adults attracted to his Mr. Wizard persona, this soft-spoken, Minnesota-born personality had the ability to communicate and inspire in others his passion for the "fun" to be had with science.

JOEL STERNBERG

See also **Children and Television**

Host (as Mr. Wizard)
Don Herbert

Producers
James Pewolar (1955–65); Del Jack (1971–72)

Programming History
NBC

May 1951–February 1952	Saturday 6:30–7:00
March 1952–February 1955	Saturday 7:00–7:30
1955–1965	various times
September 1971–September 1972	various times

Further Reading

"AAPT Recognizes Herbert, Creators of Mr. Wizard TV Series," *Physics Today* (November 1991)

Bolstad, Helen, "Mr. and Mrs. Wizard," *Radio-TV Mirror* (July 1954)

Cole, K.C., "Poof! Mr. Wizard Makes a Comeback," *Discover* (March 1984)

Dismuke, Diane, "Meet: Don 'Mr. Wizard' Herbert," *NEA Today* (April 1994)

Fischer, Stuart, *Kid's TV: The First 25 Years,* New York: Facts on File, 1983

Kramer, Carol, "His Wizardry Makes Aerodynamics Snappy," *Chicago Tribune* (October 31, 1971)

Margulies, Lee, "Mr. Wizard's Science Reports for Adults," *Chicago Sun-Times* (March 26, 1980)

Martindale, David, "Where Are They Now?" *Biography Magazine* (March 1999)

"Mr. Wizard," *Variety* (March 7, 1951)

"Mr. Wizard," *Variety* (September 10, 1952)

"Mr. Wizard Science Assembly to Visit Almond School," *Los Altos Town Crier* (April 23, 1997)

"NBC-TV 'Wizard's' Wizardry Clinches 54-Station Ride," *Variety* (March 18, 1953)

"The Robert A. Millikan Medal," *Physics Teacher* (November 1991)

" 'Wizard' Hot on Kinnies," *Variety* (January 13, 1954)

Watch with Mother

British Children's Program

Watch with Mother, the general title of a series of five individual programs, formed a central element in making television a domestic and family medium in Britain. Although the title *Watch with Mother* did not come into existence until 1952, *Andy Pandy,* the mainstay of the series, was first broadcast in July 1950. Two years later it was joined by *The Flowerpot Men;* later, these shows were scheduled alongside *Rag, Tag, and Bobtail,* in 1953, and *Picture Book* and *The Woodentops,* in 1955. Initially, *Andy Pandy* was shown in the afternoon between 3:45 and 4:00 P.M. at the end of the women's program *For Women.* In the 1960s, however, *Watch with Mother* was scheduled at lunch time. The different programs within the series were shown on specific days of the week: *Picture Book* on Monday; *Andy Pandy* on Tuesday; *The Flowerpot Men* on Wednesday; *Rag, Tag, and Bobtail* on Thursday; and *The Woodentops* on Friday. The series was eventually taken off the air and replaced by *See-Saw* in 1980.

Watch with Mother was the first television program series to address specifically a preschool audience, and along with BBC radio's *Listen with Mother,* which began in 1950, it represented a shift in BBC policy to make programs, both on radio and television, for this very young audience. Until this time, the BBC had made occasional radio programs for the very young; however, in the words of Derek McCulloch ("Uncle Mac"), director of *Children's Hour* radio, the network did not think that the young should be "catered for deliberately." This audience, according to McCulloch, came "into no real category at all." (An earlier program, *Muffin the Mule,* which was originally shown from 1946 on BBC children's television, had all the appearances of a preschool children's program but was in fact addressed to all children and was popular with adults as well.)

During the planning stages of *Andy Pandy,* there was clearly some reticence about introducing a television program for very young children, and the BBC had a special panel to advise it, consisting of representatives of the Ministry of Education, the Institute of Child Development, the Nursery Schools' Association, and some educational child psychologists. There was particular concern about children watching television on their own, leaving the "mother" free to do other things. To counter these concerns about the development of the child and the responsibilities of the mother, *Andy Pandy,* and the later programs, needed to be imagined in such a way as to allay such fears. The textual form of the program and its scheduling were important in this respect.

Created by Freda Lingstrom (head of Children's Television Programs at the BBC between 1951 and 1956) and her long-standing friend, program-maker Maria Bird, *Andy Pandy* was designed to be a program specifically directed at the preschool audience. Lingstrom, while assistant head of BBC School's Broadcasting, had been responsible for *Listen with Mother* and was asked to make a television equivalent on music and movement lines. *Andy Pandy* had no linear narrative structure. Instead, it presented a series of tableaus with no apparent overarching theme. For example, in one program, Andy starts by playing on a swing, accompanied by Maria Bird singing, "Swinging high, swinging low." He is joined by Teddy. The camera then focuses on Teddy, who enacts the movements to the nursery rhyme "Round and Round the Garden." Finally, after a scene with Andy and Teddy playing in their cart and a scene with Looby Loo singing her song, "Here we go Looby Loo," the two male characters return to their basket and wave goodbye and Maria Bird sings, "Time to go home." Lingstrom argued that the tempo was slow and there was no story so that the action could move from one situation to another in a way totally acceptable to the very young child.

The program was designed to bring three-year-olds into a close relationship with what was seen on the screen. *Andy Pandy* was intended to provide a friend for the very young viewer, and as a three-year-old actor was out of the question, a puppet was the obvious answer. The characters took part in simple movement, games, stories, nursery rhymes, and songs. The use of nursery rhymes was seen as particularly important, as it worked both to establish a relationship between the mother and the development of the child and also to connect the child to a tradition and community of preschool childhood. The children were invited not only to listen and to watch the movements of the puppets but also to respond to invitations to join in by clapping, stamping, sitting down, standing up, and so forth.

Andy Pandy drew upon the language of play in order to make itself, and also television, homely. Mary Adams, head of Television Talks at the BBC, argued that the puppet came to the child in the security of his or her own home and brought nothing alarming or contradictory to the safe routines of the family. In *Andy Pandy,* and also in *The Flowerpot Men,* the fictional world of preschool childhood was presented within the confines of the domestic. Andy, Teddy, and Looby Loo were always presented within the garden or the living room. Likewise, in *The Flowerpot Men,* the characters were presented within the garden and in close proximity to the little house that was pictured at the beginning of each program. In *Andy Pandy* we hear nothing of the outside world, whereas in *The Flowerpot Men* the only off-screen character we hear about is the gardener, whose character, neither seen nor heard, signifies the limits of this imaginary world.

Watch with Mother was never scheduled within the main bulk of children's programs between 5:00 and 6:00 P.M. When, in September 1950, there was discussion that *Andy Pandy* should be shown with the rest of children's programs, Richmond Postgate, acting head of Children's Television Programmes at the BBC, firmly responded by stating that at 5:00 P.M. three-year-olds should be thinking of bed. The program was designed to fit into the routines of both mothers and small children, and it was scheduled at different times during its early history. However, changes to its scheduling caused minor revolts, which were widely reported in the press. For example, when in 1963 the BBC planned to show *Watch with Mother* at 10:45 A.M., the *Daily Sketch* declared that "for most small children 10:45 is a time to 'Watch without Mother.' And there's not much joy in that." However, although the timing of the program was intended to provide a space especially for mother and small child, it is clear that some viewers saw it as a means to do other things.

In the 1960s and 1970s, a new stream of programs were invented for the series (e.g., *Pogles' Wood; Trumpton;* and *Mary, Mungo, and Midge*). There was still significant emotional investment in the older programs, however. For example, there was much concern in 1965 when viewers thought that *Camberwick Green* was to replace *Andy Pandy* and *The Flowerpot Men.* Doreen Stephens, head of Family Programmes, reassured the audience, stating that the familiar shows would be shown, which they were, although less frequently until 1970. It was no surprise that when a number of the older programs were released on a *Watch with Mother* video in 1986, it became a best-seller and topped the BBC's video charts.

DAVID OSWELL

See also **British Programming; Children and Television**

Producer
Freda Lingstrom

Andy Pandy

Writer-Composer
Maria Bird

Singer
Gladys Whitred

Puppeteers
Audrey Atterbury, Molly Gibson

The Flowerpot Men

Writer-Composer
Maria Bird

Puppeteers
Audrey Atterbury, Molly Gibson

Voices and Sound Effects
Peter Hawkins, Gladys Whitred, Julia Williams

Rag, Tag, and Bobtail

Story Narrator
Charles E. Stidwell

Story Writer
Louise Cochrane

Glove Puppeteers
Sam and Elizabeth Williams

The Woodentops

Writer and Music Composer
Maria Bird

Puppeteers
Audrey Atterbury, Molly Gibson

Voices
Eileen Brown, Josephina Ray, Peter Hawkins

Picture Books

Storytellers
Patricia Driscoll, Vera McKechnie

Programming History
BBC
1952–80   Various times

Further Reading

Oswell, David, "Watching with Mother in the early 1950s," in *In Front of the Children,* edited by Cary Bazelgette and David Buckingham, London: British Film Institute, 1995

Watergate

"Watergate" is synonymous with a series of events that began with a botched burglary and ended with the resignation of a U.S. president. The term itself formally derives from the Watergate building in Washington, D.C., where, on the night of June 17, 1972, five burglars were arrested in the Democratic National Committee offices. Newspaper reports from that point began revealing bits and pieces of details that linked the Watergate burglars with President Richard Nixon's 1972 reelection campaign. The president and his chief assistants denied involvement, but as evidence of White House complicity continued to grow, the U.S. Congress was compelled to investigate what role the

Watergate matter might have played in subverting or attempting to subvert the electoral process.

On February 7, 1973, the U.S. Senate, by a 77-to-0 vote, approved a resolution to impanel the Senate Select Committee on Presidential Campaign Activities to investigate Watergate. Known as the Ervin Committee for its chairperson, Senator Sam Ervin, the committee began public hearings on May 17, 1973; these hearings soon came to be known as the "Watergate Hearings."

Television cameras covered the Watergate hearings gavel-to-gavel, from day one until August 7. Three-hundred-nineteen hours of television were amassed, a record covering a single event. All three commercial television networks then in existence (NBC, CBS, and ABC) devoted an average of five hours per day covering the Watergate hearings for their first five days. The networks devised a rotation plan that, beginning on the hearings' sixth day, shifted coverage responsibility from one network to another every third day. Any of the three networks remained free to cover more of the hearings than required by their rotation agreement, but only once did the networks choose to exercise their option. All three networks elected to carry the nearly 30 hours of testimony by key witness and former White House counsel John Dean.

The noncommercial Public Broadcasting Service (PBS) aired the videotaped version of each day's Watergate hearing testimony during the evening. Many PBS station managers who were initially reluctant to carry such programming found that as a result of the carriage, station ratings as well as financial contributions increased.

As the Ervin Committee concluded its initial phase of Watergate hearings on August 7, 1973, the hearings' television audience had waned somewhat, but a majority of viewers continued to indicate a preference that the next hearing phase, scheduled to begin on September 24, also be televised. The networks, however, felt otherwise. The Ervin Committee continued the Watergate hearings until February 1974 but with only scant television coverage.

Television viewers were attracted to the Watergate hearings in impressive numbers. One survey found that 85 percent of all U.S. households had tuned in to at least some portion of the hearings. Such interest was not universal, however. In fact, Special Prosecutor Archibald Cox had argued that television's widespread coverage of Watergate testimony could endanger the rights of witnesses to a fair trial and in doing so, could deprive Americans of ever hearing the full story of Watergate. The Ervin Committee refused Cox's request to curtail coverage, saying that it was important that television be allowed to carry Watergate testimony to the American public firsthand.

On February 6, 1974, a new phase of Watergate began when the U.S. House of Representatives voted 410 to 4 to authorize the House Judiciary Committee to investigate whether sufficient grounds existed to impeach President Nixon. If so, the committee was authorized to report necessary articles of impeachment to the full House.

The Judiciary Committee spent late February to mid-July 1974 examining documents and testimony accumulated during the Senate's Watergate hearings. When this investigatory phase ended, the Judiciary Committee scheduled public deliberations on July 24–27, 29, and 30 to debate what, if any, impeachment recommen-

dations it would make to the House. Three articles of impeachment eventually were approved by the committee, recommending that the House begin formal impeachment proceedings against President Nixon.

The decision to televise Judiciary Committee meetings was not immediate, nor did it meet with overwhelming approval. Only after several impassioned pleas from the floor of the U.S. House that such an extraordinary event should be televised to the fullest extent did the House approve a resolution to allow telecast of the Judiciary Committee's impeachment deliberations. The committee itself had final say on the matter and voted 31 to 7 to concur with the decision of their House colleagues. One major requirement of the Judiciary Committee was that television networks covering the committee not be allowed to break for a commercial message during deliberations.

The Judiciary Committee began its televised public debate on the evening of July 24. The commercial networks chose to rotate their coverage in the same manner as utilized during the Senate Watergate hearings. What is more, the commercial networks telecast only the evening portions of Judiciary Committee deliberations, while PBS chose to telecast the morning and afternoon sessions as well. As a result, television viewers were provided nearly 13 hours of coverage for each of the six days of Judiciary Committee public deliberations.

Eventually, the full House and Senate voted to allow television coverage of impeachment proceedings in their respective chambers, once assurances were made that the presence of television cameras and lights would not interfere with the president's due process rights. Final ground rules were being laid and technical preparations for the coverage were under way when President Nixon's resignation, on August 9, 1974, brought the impeachment episode to an end.

RONALD GARAY

See also **Political Processes and Television; United States Congress and Television**

Further Reading

Garay, Ronald, *Congressional Television: A Legislative History,* Westport, Connecticut: Greenwood, 1984

Hamilton, James, *The Power to Probe,* New York: Random House, 1976

Kurland, Philip B., "The Watergate Inquiry, 1973," in *Congress Investigates: A Documented History, 1792–1974,* edited by Arthur M. Schlesinger and Roger Bruns, New York: Chelsea House, 1975

U.S. House Committee on the Judiciary, *Impeachment of Richard M. Nixon, President of the United States,* 93rd Congress, 2nd session, 1974

U.S. Senate Select Committee on Presidential Campaign Activities, *The Final Report,* 93rd Congress, 2nd session, 1974

Waterman, Dennis (1948–)

British Actor

Dennis Waterman has the distinction of being well known to the British television public, somewhat known in Australia, and almost completely unknown to the North American audience. As a screen character, Waterman is heavily dependent on a strong partner; in comedy, especially, he usually acts as a straight figure to the comic excesses of his counterparts. When he does play solo, as in the thriller *Circle of Deceit* (Independent Television, 1993, 1995–97), he shows himself to lack color and charisma.

Born in London in 1947, Waterman became a child actor, appearing in the feature film *Night Train for Inverness* (1960) and in a West End production of the musical *The Music Man*. In 1961 he landed the title role in the children's television series *William*, produced by the BBC. This series of 13 half-hour episodes was based on the very popular children's books by Richmal Crompton, adapted by writer C.E. Webber.

Waterman spent the following year in Hollywood working on the CBS situation comedy *Fair Exchange*. He was one of four British actors imported for the series, which concerned two families, one from New York and the other from London, who arranged to swap teenage daughters. Waterman played a younger boy in the London family who suddenly had to contend with a teenage American "sister." The series was unusual only because it extended the situation comedy format to hour-long episodes. However, it provoked only lukewarm interest and was dropped after three months. It was briefly revived in half-hour episodes but fared no better.

Waterman's voice broke; his appearance changed; and the child actor faded. In 1976 he landed the role of Detective Sergeant George Carter in the British police crime series *The Sweeney*, produced by Thames Television's Euston Films. *The Sweeney* was premised on a fictional version of Scotland Yard's Flying Squad, a police car unit concerned with major crimes such as armed robberies. (The series title came from Cockney rhyming slang: Sweeney Todd / The Flying Squad.) *The Sweeney* was well made, characterized by excellent action scenes, good stories, and fine acting from leads John Thaw as Detective Inspector Jack Regan, Waterman as his assistant, and Garfield Morgan as their boss, Detective Chief Inspector Hoskins.

The Sweeney offered Waterman not only considerable fame but also a second career. As a child actor, his accent had been middle-class and he had projected sensitivity and vulnerability. In *The Sweeney* he conveyed energy, toughness, and a gritty Cockney sense of how the world really worked. Although his character played second fiddle to Jack Regan, Waterman still managed to infuse Carter with considerable color and guts.

Waterman's career was boosted even further by his next series, the enormously popular *Minder*. This program, which introduced the character of Arthur Daley, a shady London car dealer, and Terry McCann, his ex-convict bodyguard and partner, has been described as a perfect blend of dark humor and colorful characterization. *Minder* was built around the inspired casting of George Cole as Arthur and Waterman as Terry. Cole was a veteran of British cinema, who had created a memorable forerunner to Arthur Daley in the figure of the Cockney Flash Harry, in three very funny St. Trinian films in the 1950s and 1960s. Drawing partly from the figure of Carter in *The Sweeney*, Waterman's Terry was tough and Cockney streetwise. What was new was that Waterman was playing comic straight man as the often hapless Terry, who was usually no match for Arthur. Although *Minder* was named after the figure of Terry, it was Arthur who was the mainstay of the series, a fact underlined by its revival in 1991, some six years after Waterman's departure, with Gary Webster filling the minder role.

In 1986 Waterman's on-screen woman troubles began with BBC 2's four-hour miniseries *The Life and Loves of a She Devil*. A gruesome black comedy that combined outrageous fantasy with close-to-the-bone social comment, *She Devil* was an enormous popular success. The series concerned an unfaithful husband (Waterman) whose ex-wife, the figure of the title, wreaks a truly memorable set of punishments on her hapless mate. In portraying Waterman as a womanizer who is finally unable to control the feminine forces that he has unleashed, *She Devil* added an interesting new dimension to the actor's screen persona.

In 1989 Waterman returned to comedy-drama with the series *Stay Lucky* for Yorkshire Television. The title, which referred to nothing in particular, was somewhat indicative of the series' problems as a whole. Like *The Sweeney* and *Minder*, *Stay Lucky* concerned a partnership, although in this instance one that was romantic as well as professional. Set aboard a houseboat, the series concerned a set of predictable oppositions between male and female leads, with Waterman as Thomas and Kay Francis as Sally. As a Cockney, he was streetwise and realistic; as a northerner, she was glamorous, sophisticated, and headstrong.

Stay Lucky attempted to mix the comedy of the sexes with the darker world of London crime and poverty, but the mixture did not quite gel. However, the series was at its strongest when it gravitated to the former theme, with Waterman usually generating solid comic exasperation, not at the outrageous schemes of an Arthur Daley, but at the outlandish stratagems of a willful, attractive woman.

Waterman was also featured in the BBC 1 situation comedy serial *On the Up*. Eighteen half-hour episodes were made between 1990 and 1992, and the comedy-drama blend was much more successful than in *Stay Lucky*. The series concerned a Cockney self-made millionaire, Tony (Waterman), who was less successful running both his marriage (to a beautiful, headstrong, upper-class woman) and a household of servants and friends. Waterman's appearances on television in the 1990s were otherwise somewhat limited: five times in the mid-1990s, he played John Neil, the lead in the occasional thriller series *Circle of Deceit*, and in 2001 he appeared on the small screen in a BBC 2 broadcast of *My Fair Lady* staged at the Royal National Theatre.

ALBERT MORAN

See also **British Programming;** *Minder; Sweeney, The*

Dennis Waterman. Born in London, February 24, 1948. Attended Corona Stage School. Married: 1) Penny (divorced); 2) Patricia Maynard (divorced); children: Hannah and Julia; 3) Rula Lenska. Stage debut, at the age of 11, 1959; by the age of 16 had spent a season with the Royal Shakespeare Company, Stratford-upon-Avon, and worked in Hollywood; star, *William* TV series and other productions, 1962; star, *The Sweeney* and the *Minder* series; later appeared mainly in comedy parts; has also had some success as a singer.

Television Series

1962	*William*
1962	*Fair Exchange*
1972	*The Sextet*
1975–78	*The Sweeney*
1979–85, 1988–93	*Minder*
1986	*The Life and Loves of a She Devil*
1989–91, 1993	*Stay Lucky*
1990–92	*On the Up*
1995–97	*Circle of Deceit*
1995	*Match of the Seventies* (presenter)

Made-for-Television Movies

1973	*The Common* (*British Play of the Month* series)
1974	*Joe's Ark* (*Play for Today* series)
1982	*The World Cup: A Captain's Tale* (also coproducer)
1985	*Minder on the Orient Express*
1987	*The First Kangaroos*
1988	*Mr. H. Is Late*
1993	*Circle of Deceit*

Television Specials

1959	*Member of the Wedding*
1960	*All Summer Long*
1974	*Regan*
1980	*Comedy Tonight*
1999	*Britain's Richest Lottery Winners* (narrator)
2000	*The Krays: Inside the Firm: Unfinished Business* (narrator)
2001	*My Fair Lady*

Films

Snowball, 1960; *Night Train for Inverness*, 1960; *Pirates of Blood River*, 1961; *Go, Kart, Go*, 1964; *Up the Junction*, 1967; *School for Unclaimed Girls*, 1969; *A Smashing Bird I Used to Know*, 1969; *A Promise of Bed*, 1969; *I Can't...I Can't* (*Wedding Night*), 1969; *My Lover, My Son*, 1970; *The Scars of Dracula*, 1970; *Fright*, 1971; *Man in the Wilderness*, 1971; *Alice's Adventures in Wonderland*, 1972; *The Belstone Fox*, 1973; *The Sweeney*, 1977; *The Sweeney II*, 1978; *Cold Justice*, 1989; *Vol-au-Vent*, 1996; *Arthur's Dyke*, 2001.

Recordings (selected)

Night Train to Inverness, 1958; *I Could Be So Good for You*, 1980; *What Are We Gonna Get 'er Indoors*, 1983; *Down Wind with Angels Waterman*.

Stage (selected)

The Music Man; Windy City; Cinderella; Same Time Next Year; Carving a Statue; Saved; Twelfth Night;

Serjeant Musgrave's Dance; A Slice of Saturday Night; The Winter's Tale; Taming of a Shrew; Saratoga; Alfie; Double Double; Jeffrey Bernard Is Unwell; Fools Rush In; Killing Time; Bing Bong; Don't Dress for Dinner; My Fair Lady, 2001.

Publication

ReMinder, with Jill Arlon (autobiography), 2000

Waters, Ethel (1896–1977)

U.S. Actor

Ethel Waters, one of the most influential jazz and blues singers of her time, popularized many song classics, including "Stormy Weather." Waters was also the first African-American woman to be given equal billing with white stars in Broadway shows and to play leading roles in Hollywood films. Once she had established herself as one of the highest-paid entertainers in the United States, she demanded, and won, dramatic roles. Single-handedly, Waters shattered the myth that African-American women could perform only as singers. In the early 1950s, for example, she played a leading role in the stage and screen versions of Carson McCullers's *The Member of the Wedding.* Waters played a Southern mammy, but she demonstrated with a complex and moving performance that it was possible to destroy the one-dimensional Aunt Jemima image of African-American women in American theater and cinema.

In a career that spanned almost 60 years, there were few openings for an African-American woman of Waters's class, talent, and ability. She appeared on television as early as 1939, when she made two experimental programs for NBC: *The Ethel Waters Show* and *Mamba's Daughters.* But it was her regular role as the devoted, cheerful maid in ABC's popular situation comedy *Beulah* (1950–53) that established her as one of the first African-American stars of the small screen.

Waters's dramatic roles on television were also stereotyped. Throughout the 1950s she made appearances in such series as *Favorite Playhouse, Climax, General Electric Theater, Playwrights '56,* and *Matinee Theater.* Without exception, Waters was typecast as a faithful mammy or suffering mother. In 1961 she gave a memorable performance in a *Route 66* episode, "Good Night, Sweet Blues," as a dying blues singer whose last wish is to be reunited with her old jazz band. Consequently, Waters became the first black actress nominated for an Emmy Award. She later appeared in *The Great Adventure* ("Go Down Moses"), with Ossie Davis and Ruby Dee in 1963; *Daniel Boone* ("Mamma Cooper") in 1970; and *Owen Marshall, Counselor at Law* ("Run, Carol, Run") in 1972. However, as African-American film and television historian Donald Bogle notes in *Blacks in American Films and Television* (1988):

Ethel Waters, 1930s.
Courtesy of the Everett Collection

Waters' later TV appearances lack the vitality of her great performances (she has little to work with in these programs and must rely on her inner resources and sense of self to get by), but they are part of her evolving image: now she's the weathered, ailing, grand old woman of film, whose talents are greater than the projects with which she's involved.

In the late 1950s, ill health forced Waters into semiretirement. A deeply religious woman, most of her public appearances were restricted to Billy Graham's rallies. She died in 1977 at the age of 80.

STEPHEN BOURNE

See also Beulah; **Racism, Ethnicity, and Television**

Ethel Waters. Born in Chester, Pennsylvania, October 31, 1896. Married: 1) Merritt Pernsley, c. 1910; 2) Clyde Matthews, c. 1928. Worked numerous maid, dishwasher, and waitressing jobs, 1903–17; sang and toured vaudeville circuit, 1917–30s; appeared in numerous theatrical productions, 1919–56; appeared in numerous films, 1929–63; appeared in numerous television programs, including the series *Beulah,* 1950–52; worked for the Billy Graham Crusade from the late 1950s. Recipient: New York Drama Critics Award for performance in *The Member of the Wedding,* 1950; U.S. Postal Service commemorative stamp, 1994. Died in Chatsworth, California, September 1, 1977.

Television Series

1950–53   *Beulah*

Television Special (selected)

1939   *The Ethel Waters Show*

Films

On with the Show, 1929; *Rufus Jones for President,* 1933; *Bubblin' Over,* 1934; *Tales of Manhattan,* 1941; *Cairo,* 1942; *Stage Door Canteen,* 1943; *Cabin in the Sky,* 1943; *Pinky,* 1950; *The Member of the Wedding,* 1952; *Carib Gold,* 1955; *The Sound and the Fury,* 1959.

Stage

Rhapsody in Black, 1931; *As Thousands Cheer,* 1933; *At Home Abroad,* 1935; *Mamba's Daughters,* 1939; *Cabin in the Sky,* 1940–41.

Publication

His Eye Is on the Sparrow, with Charles Samuels, 1951

Further Reading

Bogle, Donald, *Brown Sugar—Eighty Years of America's Black Female Superstars,* Prospect, Kentucky: Harmony Books, 1980

MacDonald, J. Fred, *Blacks and White TV: Afro-Americans in Television Since 1948,* Chicago: Nelson-Hall, 1983; 2nd edition, 1992

Watkins, Peter (1935–)

British Director

Peter Watkins stands as one of the most singular, committed, and powerful directors of the last 40 years. His prizewinning experimental documentaries *Diary of an Unknown Soldier* (1959) and *The Forgotten Faces* (1960), reconstructing respectively World War I and the Hungarian uprising of 1956, earned screenings and a job at the BBC, which he used to make the remarkable *Culloden,* a Brechtian deconstruction of documentary technique in an account of the bloody defeat of the 1742 Jacobin rebellion in Scotland. Culloden already exhibits hallmark techniques: handheld camera, direct-to-camera address from historical and fictional characters, and interviews with them, though the near surrealism of placing a modern on-camera reporter on the battlefield is a humorous touch rarely paralleled in his later work. Using, as he has throughout his oeuvre, the heightened naturalism of amateur actors, the program contrasts the effete figure of Bonnie Prince Charlie, actually a European adventurer, with the impoverished and still feudally bound Gaelic-speaking peasantry of the Highlands, a cruel indictment of both Scottish patriotism and the brutal British reprisals on the Highlanders. His next work, *The War Game,* "preconstructs" the effects of a nuclear attack on southern

England. Perhaps it was not just Watkins's deadpan voice-over, nor the matter-of-fact delivery of official prognostications of casualties and security measures, but his comparison of nuclear firestorms with the ever-sensitive British bombing of Dresden in 1945 (subject of two later banned programs in the United Kingdom) that saw the film banned. Reduced to fund-raising shows for nuclear disarmament groups, the program has rarely been discussed in terms other than those of its subject and its political fate. But its groundbreaking and still-powerful juxtaposition of interview, reconstruction, graphics, titles, and the collision of dry data with images of horror still shock, the grainy black-and-white imagery and use of telephoto, sudden zooms, and wavering focus creating an atmosphere of immediacy unique in British television. Fifty minutes that shook the world, it was banned for 25 years by the BBC amid storms of controversy, which were re-opened when it finally made British TV screens in a Channel 4 season of banned titles.

The War Game took the 1966 best documentary Oscar, opening the door to Hollywood. Universal bankrolled the feature film *Privilege* about a pop messiah in a near-future police state but pulled the plug on an ambitious reconstruction of the Battle of Little Big Horn and the subjugation of the Native Americans. From the late 1960s, Watkins's career is marked by projects cut, abandoned, or suppressed: Watkins himself listed 14 in a document seeking support for his 1980s film *The Journey*. *The Gladiators*, made for Swedish TV, about popular acquiescence in militarism, used the device of a fictional television program, "The Peace Game," in which generals play games of strategy, and the savage 16-millimeter allegory of Nixon's America *Punishment Park*, in which "deviants" are given their chance to survive in a nightmarish outlaw zone, both saw broadcast and theatrical release, though limited. These two titles extend Watkins's repertoire of effects by their focus on individual characters caught up in evil times, though the use of montage cutting and extreme naturalism in performances combine to minimize identification, and increase the intellectual engagement of the viewer with the narrative. Closer in technique to Brecht's practice than his theory, Watkins failed to benefit either from the vanguardism of contemporary film theory or the political clout of less challenging auteurs like Ken Loach and Denis Potter.

Other completed projects like *The Seventies People* (on suicide and the failures of social democracy) and *Evening Land* (a terrorist kidnap contrasted with the quelling of a strike in a military shipyard), both for Danish TV, were suppressed. Only the biopic of Norwegian painter Edvard Munch has had major distribution, though mainly as theatrical film, rather than the three-part series it was originated as. *Edvard Munch*'s passion derives not only from the subject and Watkins's handling, but from the identification between director and derided artist. The series is distinguished again by direct-cinema techniques, but also by complex editing around motifs, especially faces and flowers, and by multitracked sound design layering the characters' past, present, and future into a rich montage. As in his earlier documentaries, *Munch* adds voice-over to the sound mix, sometimes even over blank screens, to connect the narrative with worldwide events and political analysis. Carrying the use of natural light pioneered in his BBC projects into color, the film achieves a profoundly affecting image of a consumptive society unable to credit those who warn of its demise until it is too late. It is its political analysis and, stylistically, its use of sophisticated montage editing that distinguish *Munch* and its predecessors from the handheld stylistics of some recent U.S. cop shows.

In 1982 an attempt to remake *The War Game* with Central TV fell through, and Watkins devoted the following three years to accruing donations and help to make *The Journey*, perhaps his greatest achievement. Running at over 14 hours, the film was a rarely screened account, shot in over a dozen nations, of nuclear war and its effects. It has yet to be broadcast. *The Freethinker* (1994), an imaginative account of August Strindberg made with students, was boycotted by Swedish TV. In 2000 Watkins completed a 345-minute video, *La Commune*, recounting the 1871 Paris uprising through an imaginary community TV station, again working with amateurs, tearing across centuries to cross drama with politics. This remarkable project has again found its main audience on the festival and film school circuit. Watkins's mountain of suppressed work, his occasional embittered testament to intelligence, passion, and skill have perhaps contributed to a peripatetic life, consistently dogged by controversy. He is the most neglected and perhaps the most significant British director of his generation.

Watkins's mountain of suppressed work, his occasional embittered testament to intelligence, passion, and skill have perhaps contributed to a peripatetic life, consistently dogged by controversy.

SEAN CUBITT

See also **Director, Television;** *The War Game;* **War on Television**

Peter Watkins. Born in Norbiton, Surrey, England, October 29, 1935. Attended Christ College, Grecknockshire; studied acting at Royal Academy of Dramatic Art, London. Served with East Surrey Regiment. Began career as assistant producer of television short subjects and commercials, 1950s; assistant editor and director of documentaries, BBC, 1961; director, *The War Game,* banned by the BBC, 1966; director, feature film, *Privilege,* 1967; moved to Sweden, 1968; worked in United States, 1969–71; resides in Sweden.

Television
1964   *Culloden*

Films

The Web, 1956; *The Field of Red,* 1958; *Diary of an Unknown Soldier,* 1959; *The Forgotten Faces,* 1961; *Dust Fever,* 1962; *The War Game,* 1966; *Privilege,* 1967; *The Gladiators,* 1969; *Punishment Park,* 1971; *Edvard Munch,* 1974; *The Seventies People,* 1975; *The Trap,* 1975; *Evening Land,* 1977; *The Journey,* 1987; *The Freethinker,* 1994; *La Commune,* 2000.

Publications

Blue, James, and Michael Gill, "Peter Watkins Discusses His Suppressed Nuclear Film *The War Game*," *Film Comment* (fall 1965)

The War Game: An Adaptation of the BBC Documentary, 1967

"Left, Right, Wrong," *Films and Filming* (March 1970)

"Peter Watkins Talks About the Suppression of His Work Within Britain," *Films and Filming* (February 1971)

"*Punishment Park* and Dissent in the West," *Literature/Film Quarterly* (1976)

"*Edvard Munch:* A Director's Statement," *Literature/Film Quarterly* (winter 1977)

"Interview with S. MacDonald," *Journal of the University Film Association* (summer 1982)

Further Reading

Cunningham, Stuart, "Tense, Address, Tendenz: Questions of the Work of Peter Watkins," *Quarterly Review of Film Studies* (fall 1980)

Gomez, Joseph A., *Peter Watkins,* Boston: Twayne, 1979

Kawin, Bruce, "Peter Watkins: Cameraman at World's End," *Journal of Popular Film* (summer 1973)

MacDonald, Scott, "From Zygote to Global Cinema via Su Friedrich's Films," *Journal of Film and Video* (spring–summer 1992)

MacDonald, Scott, "Filmmaker as Global Circumnavigator: Peter Watkins' *The Journey* and Media Critique," *Quarterly Review of Film and Video* (Chur, Switzerland) (August 1993)

Nolley, Ken, "Narrative Innovation in *Edvard Munch,*" *Literature/Film Quarterly* (1987)

Welsh, James M., "The Dystopian Cinema of Peter Watkins," *Film Criticism* (fall 1982)

Welsh, James M., "The Modern Apocalypse: *The War Game,*" *Journal of Popular Film and Television* (spring 1983)

Welsh, James M., *Peter Watkins: A Guide to References and Resources,* Boston: Hall, 1986

Watson, Patrick (1929–)

Canadian Producer, Host

Patrick Watson has played a key role in the development of Canadian television, first producing, then hosting, many of the Canadian Broadcasting Corporation's (CBC's) groundbreaking public affairs series. In 1989, he was named chair of the CBC board of directors, a position he resigned in June 1994. His career in Canadian broadcasting, with several short detours into U.S. television, has been recognized by many for its innovative and substantive contribution to television journalism. He holds two honorary degrees and is an Officer of the Order of Canada for his journalistic efforts. At the same time, his career has been distinguished by well-publicized struggles with CBC

management and a number of Canadian politicians, both as producer and board chair. Lending substance to his television journalism has been his wide-ranging interest in the arts and social affairs.

Watson's first broadcast experience was as a radio actor in 1943 in a continuing CBC children's dramatic series called *The Kootenay Kid.* He has maintained his interest in dramatic television production by performing in several CBC dramas and by producing and performing in his two dramatized series of fictional encounters with great historical figures: *Titans* and *Witness to Yesterday.* In 1983, he wrote and acted in a one-man stage version of the Old Testament's *The Book of Job.*

Canadian television received its bilingual launch on Saturday, September 6, 1952, on CBFT, a CBC station in Montreal. Watson's involvement with television started in those early years, first as a freelancer in 1955, then as producer of *Close-Up,* 1957–60, and the national-affairs series *Inquiry,* 1960–64. Both shows were noted for their hard-hitting, sometimes confrontational interviews with the Canadian elite. *Inquiry* established an exciting and stimulating public affairs television show that would attract a larger audience than the typical narrow, well-educated one.

Watson's next project attracted the largest audience for a public affairs program in Canadian history and also proved to be the most controversial series of its kind. *This Hour Has Seven Days* was the creation of Watson and his coproducer from *Close-Up* and *Inquiry,* Douglas Leiterman. Broadcast before a live audience on Sunday nights from the fall of 1964 to the spring of 1966, this public affairs show became the darling of more than 3 million Canadians until its demise at the hands of CBC management, who could no longer withstand the criticism from Parliament or the insubordination of the *Seven Days* team. Shows featured satire of politicians in song and skit mixed with "bear pit" interviews, probing film documentaries, on-location stakeouts, and street interviews—all dealing with important, but often ignored, social and political issues. Critics hailed it for its freshness and probing investigations and condemned it for its sometimes sensational and "yellow" journalism. Watson was the coproducer for the first season of *Seven Days,* and he became the on-air cohost and interviewer in the second year in a move that the CBC management thought would curb some of the more controversial ideas and methods of the series. Watson and the extraordinary team of producers and writers assembled for the program (many of whom became influential documentarians and producers through the 1960s and 1970s) became even more innovative and "in your face" with their journalism, daring the CBC management to take action. In a later interview Watson admitted to the arrogance of those days, inciting his crew to "make people a little bit angry, frustrate them…come socking out of the screen." The management took the dare and canceled the show to the outrage of many, some of it orchestrated by the *Seven Days* team to try and save the show. There was an avalanche of calls and letters, public demonstrations, a parliamentary committee hearing, and a special investigation by an appointee of the prime minister—quite a response to the cancellation of a TV show. The series has taken on mythic proportions in the history of television journalism. It certainly pushed the boundaries of what was considered appropriate journalism, predated the cur-

Patrick Watson.
Photo courtesy of CBC Television/Fred Phipps

rent concern over the fine line between news and entertainment, and created a very chilly environment for CBC producers of public affairs for many years.

Because of his highly visible contribution to *Seven Days* and the aftermath to its cancellation, Watson was popularly touted for president of the CBC. He let it be known that he was interested, but he was not to reach high administrative office in the CBC until 25 years later. In the intervening years he turned his attention to a number of creative projects in and out of television. In addition to those already mentioned, he wrote, produced, hosted, and directed for *The Undersea World of Jacques Cousteau, The Watson Report, The Canadian Establishment, Lawyers,* and *The Fifty-first State* (for PBS Channel 13, New York), among others. In 1989, before being named chair of the CBC, he created, produced, and hosted the ten-part international coproduction television series *The Struggle for Democracy.* It was the first documentary ever to appear simultaneously in French and English on the CBC's two main networks with the same host. Researched in depth and reflecting the dominant values of Western democracy, this substantive and ambitious series took the viewer across the world and into history, to the sites of many experiments, successes, and failures of the democratic effort. In the years after *Seven Days,* Watson was frequently and deservedly praised for his skills as a host and interviewer.

Watson's years as chair of the CBC board of directors were difficult ones for him and the corporation. The CBC had to face many severe budget cuts, subsequent layoffs, and the closing of regional outlets. Watson was dealing with a board becoming stacked with Tory appointees, several of whom advocated the privatization of the CBC. He was expected to both manage the board and lobby Parliament. Though he toured the country speaking up for public television, he was seen by many CBC staffers and some of the public as less than effective in his efforts. In his last year, the CBC was hit with a new controversy over a public affairs series on the Canadian effort in World War II called *The Valour and the Horror*. This program challenged many standard versions of World War II history by critically examining the actions and the fallibility of military and political leaders. While the series won awards and was praised by many, it was vilified by veterans' groups and conservative politicians. After intense pressure, including a senate hearing controlled by the critics of the program, the CBC issued an ombudsman's report, supported by statements from the president of the CBC and the board, that essentially chastised the show's producers for their research, methods of presentation, and conclusions. As chair of the board, Watson was criticized for not speaking out publicly in support of the journalists and for not resigning. Insiders, including the producers of the show, credit Watson for moderating the board's and the president's response and mediating the dispute with CBC management.

Watson is the creative director and principal writer of the Historica Foundation's *The Heritage Minutes*. He is the commissioning editor, host, and narrator for History Television's *The Canadians, Biographies of a Nation*.

In 2002 Watson was awarded the Margaret Collier Award of the Gemini Awards, which is presented in recognition of a writer's body of work and significant contribution to the national and international profile of Canadian television.

WILLIAM O. GILSDORF

See also **Canadian Programming in English;** *This Hour Has Seven Days*

Patrick Watson. Born in Toronto, Ontario, Canada, 1929. Educated at University of Toronto, B.A., M.A.; studied linguistics at University of Michigan. Married: 1) Beverly (divorced, 1983), three children; 2) Caroline Bamford. Joined CBC-TV, early 1950s; founder, Patrick Watson Enterprises, 1966; cofounder, Immedia Inc., 1967; helped pioneer CBS Cable Network during 1980s; chair, CBC, 1989–94; first North American filmmaker to film in the People's Republic of China. Officer of the Order of Canada. Recipient: Bruxelles Festival Award, 1984; 12 Junos; two ACTRA Awards.

Television

1957–60	*Close-Up* (coproducer)
1960–64	*Inquiry* (producer and director)
1964–66	*This Hour Has Seven Days* (executive producer and cohost)
1967	*Search in the Deep* (producer)
1967	*The Undersea World of Jacques Cousteau* (producer)
1968	*Science and Conscience* (host)
1973–75	*Witness to Yesterday* (interviewer and writer)
1975–81	*The Watson Report* (interviewer)
1977	*The Fifty-first State* (editor and anchor)
1978	*Flight: The Passionate Affair* (host and writer)
1980	*The Canadian Establishment* (host and contributing writer)
1981	*The Chinese* (host, narrator, and contributing writer)
1981–82	*CBS Cable Service* (host)
1981	*Titans* (interviewer and writer)
1985	*Lawyers* (host)
1989	*The Struggle for Democracy* (ten parts; writer, host, and executive editor)

Television Special

1983–86	*Live from Lincoln Center* (host)

Films

Bethune (actor), 1963; *The 700 Million* (producer and director), 1964; *The Terry Fox Story* (actor),1982; *Countdown to Looking Glass* (actor), 1984; *The Land That Devours Ships* (coproducer), 1984.

Radio

The Kootenay Kid (actor), 1943.

Stage

The Book of Job (writer and performer).

Further Reading

Borowski, Andrew, "The Watson Report," interview, *Canadian Forum* (June–July 1991)

"CBC Chairman Resigns Post," *Montreal Gazette* (June 15, 1994)

"CBC 'Consultant' Watson Criticized over Sale of *Democracy* Episode," *Globe and Mail* (May 25, 1990)

"The Future of the CBC," interview, *Policy Options* (January–February 1994)

Johnson, Brian D., "Making 'Democracy,' " *Maclean's* (January 16, 1989)

Johnson, Brian D., "A Televisionary," *Maclean's* (January 16, 1989)

Koch, Eric, *Inside Seven Days,* Scarborough, Canada: Prentice Hall, 1986

"The New Men in Charge of the CBC," *Globe and Mail* (September 27, 1989)

Rutherford, Paul, *When Television Was Young: Primetime Canada, 1952–1967,* Toronto: University of Toronto Press, 1990

Stewart, Sandy, *Here's Looking at Us: A Personal History of Television in Canada,* Toronto: CBC Enterprises, 1986

"Watson's Sights Set on *Democracy* and the CBC," *Globe and Mail* (December 24, 1988)

Wayne and Shuster

Canadian Comedy Act

Wayne and Shuster, who won international acclaim for their distinctive gentle satiric sketches, were the founding fathers of English-Canadian TV comedy. Appearing fairly regularly on CBC radio and television from the 1940s until Wayne's death in 1990, they helped to pave the way for such successful Canadian acts as the *Royal Canadian Air Farce* and *Kids in the Hall.* At the same time, however, their near monopoly on the CBC's commitment to TV comedy for many years may have hindered the growth of other comedic talent in Canada. During their early years, they wrote all their own material, but later made use of other writers as well.

On television, they were initially a bigger sensation in the United States than in Canada. They made a record-setting 67 appearances on *The Ed Sullivan Show,* and edited versions of their many specials for CBC-TV were highly popular in U.S. syndication. Over the years, they also made frequent appearances on the BBC and won numerous awards, including the illustrious Silver Rose of Montreux.

The eldest of seven children of a successful clothing manufacturer who spoke several languages, Johnny Wayne was born John Louis Weingarten on May 28, 1918, in the heart of downtown Toronto. Although also born in Toronto, on September 5, 1916, Frank Shuster grew up in Niagara Falls, Ontario, where his father ran a small theater called the Colonial. Most evenings of his childhood were spent watching silent movies (and learning to read the intertitles), until his father was put out of business by a larger operation down the street. Failing to join other relatives in the United States (Frank's first cousin, Joe, who drew the *Superman* comic strip, lived in Cleveland, Ohio), the family returned to Toronto.

The future comics first met in tenth grade at Harbord Collegiate—seated in the same class alphabetically, S happened to be close to W. Under the influence of Charles Girdler, who taught ancient history at Harbord and set up the Oola Boola Club to teach students how to do sketches and variety, they wrote a series of comedy dramas for the school's dramatic guild. One of Wayne's long-standing characters, Professor Waynegartner, originated in a geometry lesson written by Girdler poking fun at one of the other teachers. To take the sting out it, Girdler suggested that it be done with a German accent.

Both men completed degrees in English at the University of Toronto, where they wrote, produced, and starred in a number of variety shows. They also edited and wrote for the university newspaper, the *Varsity.* In 1941 they began a show on Toronto radio station CFRB called *Wife Preserves,* which paid them $12.50 each per week to dispense household hints for women over a network of Ontario stations. They were then contracted to write and perform on the *Shuster and Wayne* (sic) comedy show on the CBC's Trans-Canada Network for one year.

In 1942 they left the CBC to join the infantry and were soon writing and performing for the big Army Show. They toured military bases across Canada and later, when the show was split into smaller units, took the Invasion Review into Normandy after D-Day. Later they wrote a 52-week series for veterans and spent six weeks entertaining the Commonwealth Division in Korea.

In 1946 the duo returned to CBC Radio on the *Wayne and Shuster Show,* broadcast live at 9:30 P.M. on Thursdays. It was one of the few Canadian programs to compete successfully against U.S. imports. Among their radio creations were the undefeated Mimico Mice, who competed against the Toronto Maple Leafs. Legendary radio sports announcer Foster Hewitt did the play-by-play using the names of

Wayne and Shuster.
Photo courtesy of National Archives of Canada/CBC Collection

real Leaf players, but only Wayne and Shuster played for the Mice.

Although they began appearing as guests on various U.S. TV programs as early as 1950, their biggest television success came in 1958 when Ed Sullivan, whose ratings had slipped, invited them to appear on his Sunday-night variety show. He insisted that they stick to the kind of comedy they were doing in Canada and gave them a one-year contract with complete freedom to decide on the length, frequency, content, sets, and supporting cast of all their sketches. Jack Gould of *The New York Times* described them as "the harbingers of literate slapstick." Sullivan, who became very fond of them both personally and professionally, said they were his biggest hit in ten years. In fact, his ratings shot up whenever they performed, and their contract was renewed again and again (in the end, they appeared on his show 58 times). Also renewed repeatedly was their CBC contract, which had been on the verge of being canceled before their U.S. success.

In 1961 Wayne and Shuster unwisely agreed to do a dreadful 13-week sitcom called *Holiday Lodge,* written by others as a summer replacement for Jack Benny on CBS. But they soon returned to the sophisticated sketches they did best, and in 1962 and 1963, they were ranked as the best comedy team in the United States in polls by *Motion Picture Daily* and *Television Today.*

Fearing overexposure, they avoided doing a weekly show for CBC-TV and instead contracted for a certain number of hour-long specials each year. Their style,

which consisted of a mixture of slapstick, pantomime, and groan-inducing jokes, depended heavily, at times excessively, on sets and props. Many of their early sketches were takeoffs on classic situations, such as putting Shakespearean blank verse into the mouths of baseball players. In their first appearance on *Ed Sullivan,* Wayne played a Roman detective investigating the murder of Julius Caesar in "Rinse the Blood off My Toga." His use of "martinus" as the singular of "martini" quickly became a catchphrase (some New York bars began advertising "Martinus Specials"), as did the line "I told him, 'Julie, don't go,'" uttered several times by actress Sylvia Lennick playing Caesar's wife. Even Marshall McLuhan complimented them on their word games, as when the hero of their western version of *Hamlet* refused a drink from the bar and ordered "the unkindest cut of all."

Some of the most memorable moments on their TV shows for CBC arose from tricks of the camera—they would walk down an apparently infinite number of stairs or defy gravity as painters on the Tower of Pisa. Although Shuster tended to play the straight man, both portrayed a variety of characters. In general, their comedy was literate, middlebrow, and upbeat. They always disdained cruel humor, preferring the send-up to the put-down. Wayne thought that the best description of their style was the phrase "innocent merriment" from Gilbert and Sullivan's *Mikado.*

By the late 1970s, some Canadian critics were complaining that the comic duo were merely going through the motions, that their comedy was hopelessly out of date, more sophomoric than sophisticated, and often embarrassingly bad. It was suggested that they had become too comfortable with the world, that they had lost the anger or frustration necessary for good comedy. There was also some criticism of their decision to do commercials for U.S.-owned Gulf Oil. Nonetheless, they remained quite popular, especially among the under-30 and over-55 age groups. The syndication of 80 half-hour specials in the United States, South Africa, and half a dozen other countries in 1980 was the CBC's largest dollar sale of programming to that date.

Despite several enticing offers from the United States, Wayne and Shuster always chose to stay in Toronto. In addition to giving Canadians the confidence to do their own comedy, they spoke passionately on behalf of Canadian cultural sovereignty. In 1978, for example, Wayne told a joint luncheon of the Ottawa Men's and Women's Clubs that "an imbalanced television system has made us a nation of American watchers, totally ignorant of our own way of life. We are being robbed of our national identity. We've put Dracula in charge of the blood bank."

Johnny Wayne died in Toronto in 1990. In 1995 Frank Shuster donated his records to the National Archives of Canada, including about 450 radio, TV, and stage scripts. He died in Toronto on January 13, 2002.

ROSS A. EAMAN

Further Reading

Rutherford, Paul, *When Television Was Young: Primetime Canada, 1952–1957,* Toronto: University of Toronto Press, 1990

WB Network

U.S. Network

The WB Network is widely recognized as the first television network to capitalize on the trend toward increasingly fragmented television audiences. By targeting programming specifically to teens and to young adults, the WB has established a focused and successful broadcast network in an era defined by cable television's incursion into the national television broadcast audience. The network, which reaches 88 percent of the U.S. audience through both broadcast and cable channels, airs prime-time programming Sunday through Friday and a children's lineup on weekday afternoons and Saturday mornings.

The WB had its start in 1995 as a joint venture owned by Time Warner, the Tribune Company, and the network's founder, Jamie Kellner. The network was established as a direct result of changes in the television regulatory environment that year that allowed television networks to produce and syndicate more of their own programming. Independent studios like Paramount and Warner Brothers (which at the time was the largest supplier of television series in Hollywood) were concerned that more products from the studios of NBC, CBS, ABC, and FOX would shut out the independent studios or leave them vulnerable to unfavorable deals. Forming a network of television station groups was a way for Warner Brothers to ensure a broadcast outlet for its studio's products. It also opened up the possibility that studios could benefit from the advertising revenue generated by their programs, rather than waiting for returns from their sale into syndication. Paramount established its own broadcast network at the same time for similar reasons, and thus the two fledgling networks entered into a race to become the fifth network.

The number of independent broadcast stations available was limited, however, making it a challenge for the two competing networks to develop their reach while maintaining financial solvency. In an innovative yet risky move, Kellner sought a deal that would require stations to share revenue with the studio when the network delivered increased ratings. Rival UPN followed a more traditional syndication route, paying compensation to affiliates while withholding national time within programs and allowing stations to sell the remaining time. Initially, the UPN plan was more attractive, and the WB was left with weak broadcast stations or with no outlets at all in some areas. At its launch the network included 45 broadcast stations, and although most of them were new, unestablished, and in medium-sized markets, together the channels reached nearly 55 percent of the U.S. audience. Cable heavily bolstered the WB's initial reach, as the network relied on the Tribune-owned Chicago superstation WGN to bring nearly 20 percent of the country to the potential audience. This brought the network's total reach close to 75 percent. By early in the 1995–96 season, the purchase of additional stations brought the network to coverage of 83 percent of the United States.

The WB's shared revenue policy was reversed in a 1997 deal with the Sinclair Broadcast Group that secured 14 new affiliates, which resulted in some griping from existing affiliates but no withdrawals. In 1998 the network further extended its reach when it entered another innovative joint venture with cable operators and television stations, enabling the network to reach smaller markets where the number of broadcast stations available is limited. When superstation WGN ceased its distribution of the network outside of the Chicago market in 2000, the WB encountered its first ratings slump in its then five-year history. In 2001,

Courtesy of the Everett Collection

when Time Warner merged with AOL, the WB became part of Turner Broadcasting Systems, Inc., which included almost all of the AOL Time Warner broadcast properties.

From its beginnings, WB founder and CEO Jamie Kellner believed that the success of the network would rest on its ability to create a recognizable "brand name." At the request of Warner Brothers studio, Kellner had come to the WB from the FOX Broadcasting Company, where he had successfully tapped the 18-to-34 audience with such programs as Beverly Hills, 90210 and the Simpsons. He brought with him from FOX Garth Ancier, the WB network's first head of programming, and Susanne Daniels, who succeeded Ancier to become the WB's entertainment president in 1998 (current WB entertainment president Jordan Levin joined Ancier and Daniels from Disney/Touchstone television as the network's head of comedy development and current programming). Kellner also brought to the WB some of the talent he had employed at FOX, including the producers of *Married . . . With Children* and Shawn and Marlon Wayans, brothers of *In Living Color* stars Keenen Ivory and Damon Wayans. Intent on appealing to the youthful demographic so important to advertisers, the network eschewed a more serious network logo in favor of a mascot drawn from a 1955 Warner Brothers cartoon, Michigan J. Frog.

The network launched January 11, 1995, with one night of comedy programming on Wednesday evenings, largely targeted to racial/ethnic audiences.

While the prime-time ratings were marginal, the WB's Saturday-morning kids lineup was beating the ratings of the ABC kids block by early in the 1995–96 season. That fall, the network premiered *7th Heaven,* a project executive-produced by Brenda Hampton (*Mad About You*), Aaron Spelling (*Beverly Hills, 90210*), and E. Duke Vincent. Airing on Monday nights, it directly competed with *Melrose Place,* another Spelling program airing on FOX. Featuring Stephen Collins and Catherine Hicks as a minister and his wife with five children, *7th Heaven*'s teen stars Jessica Biel and Barry Watson quickly gained a youthful following, and the program's positive messages garnered praise among parents' organizations. Despite its tepid reception among critics, the program has been one of the network's top-rated shows since its debut.

In light of the new ownership rules that originally motivated the network's inception, it is ironic that some of the WB's early successes came from programs originally produced by the studios of its rival television networks, Twentieth Century Fox and Paramount. While *7th Heaven* had come from the Paramount studio, it was the FOX-produced *Buffy the Vampire Slayer* that truly sparked the network's success streak and established the teen audience the network craved. Created by Joss Whedon, who wrote the unremarkable teen movie of the same name, the midseason replacement quickly established itself as a cult favorite and critics' darling. Buffy, played by Sarah Michelle Gellar, was hailed as a postfeminist icon and strong, positive role model for teen girls.

The network hit its stride the next year when it paired Buffy with the coming-of-age high school melodrama *Dawson's Creek* (Columbia TriStar), starring then-unknowns James Van Der Beek, Katie Holmes, Joshua Jackson, and Michelle Williams and created by screenwriter Kevin Williamson (*Scream I, II; I Know What You Did Last Summer*). WB executives gloated that *Dawson's Creek* had been rejected by FOX before finding its way to the network. As the FOX network abandoned its initial youthful identity in an attempt to "age" its network with programs like *Ally McBeal,* the WB became the number one network among teens in the U.S. just three years after its launch, enjoying a 32 percent increase in ratings among teens 12 to 17 that season.

The network continued its winning streak and its emphasis on strong teen female leads with the fall 1998 additions of the J.J. Abrams–created and critically acclaimed *Felicity,* starring Keri Russell as a soul-searching college coed, and a second Spelling program, the surprise hit *Charmed,* starring Shannon Doherty (formerly of *90210*), Holly Marie Combs, and Alyssa Milano as three sisters with supernatural powers. With these programs and the continuing strength of *Buffy* and *Dawson's,* the WB enjoyed its best ratings in its five-year history and more than doubled its advertising revenues between the 1996–97 and 1998–99 seasons. The network also strengthened its afternoon programming block, Kids WB, with the addition of the popular Japanese anime program *Pokemon.*

The next season, 1999–2000, saw the debut of *Angel* (starring David Boreanaz), the successful spin-off of *Buffy the Vampire Slayer* penned by Buffy's creator, Joss Whedon (and another product of Twentieth Century Fox Television). For its Friday-night lineup of ethnic-oriented comedies, the network also picked up Eddie Murphy's animated series *The PJ's,* dropped from FOX. Ratings stumbled that year, however, especially among the audiences for *Felicity,* who infamously cut her long tresses, and *Dawson's Creek,* which lost its creator to film projects. The loss of WGN's distribution of the network hurt ratings, as well.

The network was able to turn its slide around the following year, and for the first time in 2001, the network reached the coveted fifth place in ratings among overall TV households and in the 18-to-49 demographic. Adding to the strength of its continuing series, the WB rolled out *Gilmore Girls,* the critically acclaimed, multigenerational and multiethnic drama about a single mother and her teenage daughter (played by Lauren Graham and Alexis Bledel) created by Amy Sherman-Palladino. *Gilmore Girls* was the first program developed by the Family Friendly Forum, an initiative launched by Procter and Gamble, Johnson and Johnson, IBM, and other major advertisers in cooperation with the WB, in an effort to develop programming that families could watch together.

The 2001–02 season was another strong one for the WB despite the move of two of its programs, *Buffy the Vampire Slayer* and *Roswell,* to rival network UPN. *Gilmore Girls* and *Angel* achieved increased ratings, *7th Heaven* held its place as the network's top-rated program for the fourth year in a row, while the ratings for *Charmed* remained strong. *Smallville,* a new fall drama from Warner Brothers' own studio about Superman's teen years, quickly became the top-rated program for all teens. With the addition of *Reba,* featuring country music star Reba McEntire, the WB strengthened its Friday-night sitcom ratings, despite its controversial decision to pull the plug on its comedies featuring racial or ethnic leads. Minor roles for racial or ethnic characters in its centerpiece programs and the promise of other ethnically based comedies like *Greetings from Tucson,* a fall 2003 entry focused on a Mexican-American family, were designed to address this unfortunate turn.

In addition to its programming focus on teen angst and its strong young female leads, the good fortune of the WB can be attributed to its aggressive, innovative, and largely successful marketing ventures. Efforts were taken to new levels when *Dawson's Creek* was introduced at midseason in 1998. Before its debut the network spent $3.3 million on billboard, television, bus, and radio ads and had its stars serve as models in the latest J. Crew catalog, all in an effort to bring new viewers to the network. The WB even created a trailer for the program that was paired with teen-oriented films like *Scream II.*

The WB was also the first television network to offer music promotions in exchange for a break on licensing fees, enabling *Dawson's Creek, Buffy the Vampire Slayer,* and later WB dramas such as *Roswell* and *Smallville* to use popular new music in a much more affordable arrangement. Certain songs, featured in each episode following the style of film soundtracks, were highlighted at the conclusion of each episode with a five-second snippet accompanied by the band's CD cover. The approach gave the program credibility with its teen audience while also saving money for the network.

Naturally, the WB's appeal to the lucrative teen audience has been of interest to advertisers, and ad rates on the network's highest-rated series are triple what they were when the network launched, now besting rates from such venerated programs as CBS's *60 Minutes.* The WB has also experimented with product placement and advertiser funding for script development. Yet while *Gilmore Girls* was a successful example of the latter, not all advertiser and network innovations have been so well received. Critics and audiences roundly balked at the 2002 reality program *No Boundaries,* the title of which mirrored the slogan of its program's sponsor, the Ford Motor Company (which also provided vehicles for the program). Similarly, the Coca-Cola–sponsored 2000 summer series *Young Americans* was pilloried for its placement of Coke in the series' romantic scenes.

Regardless of these missteps, there is no doubt that the WB's parent company, AOL Time Warner, has profited from cross-promotional strategies involving other aspects of the Time Warner franchise. The theme song to *Dawson's Creek* was Paula Cole's "I Don't Want to Wait," featured on the Warner Brothers record label, and the network also regularly promotes films produced by its Warner Brothers studio. In 2000 the WB teamed up with AOL Time Warner–owned *TV Guide,* MilkPEP, and Dairy Management Inc. to create a series of television spots and posters folded into *TV Guide* that featured WB stars with milk mustaches. Moreover, TNT regularly airs repeats of *Charmed* and the after-school block of Kids' WB Programming airs on the Cartoon Network and on its partner website, while WB programs are frequently promoted on AOL, TNT, and TBS.

Despite its many successes, the WB is the only network that had not yet received a single Emmy nomination as of 2001. That same year, it was also the only network that had shown growth in every demographic when compared with the 1995–96 season when it was launched, and the only network to show an increase in up-front revenue and ad rates. The WB has launched more relative unknown actors into television and film stardom than any other network in the past few years and has also had more of its series enter syndication than any other network since its launch in 1995. Clearly, the people at the WB have been successful in meeting their goals of establishing a well-received brand identity among today's young and highly desirable consumers, and the Academy's recognition for some of its programming is sure to follow.

LYNN SCHOFIELD CLARK

See also *Buffy the Vampire Slayer;* **Kellner, Jamie; Teenagers and Television; UPN**

Network Administration

CEO of WB, 1995–2001	Jamie Kellner
Head of programming, 1995–98	Garth Ancier
WB entertainment president, 1998–2001	Susanne Daniels
WB entertainment president, 2001–	Jordan Levin
Chairman and CEO, Turner Broadcasting Systems, 2001–	Jamie Kellner
Chairman and CEO, AOL Time Warner, 2001–	Richard D. Parsons
COO, AOL Time Warner, 2001–	Robert W. Pittman

Further Reading

Collette, Larry, and Barry Litman, "The Peculiar Economics of New Broadcast Network Entry: The Case of United Paramount and Warner Bros.," *Journal of Media Economics,* 10, no. 4 (1997)

Schofield Clark, Lynn, *From Angels to Aliens: Teens, the Media, and Beliefs in the Supernatural,* New York: Oxford University Press, 2003

Marks, Rick Brian, "Targeting Families and Teens: Television Violence on the WB," master's thesis, University of Nevada, Las Vegas, 2000

Wilcox, Rhonda V., and David Lavery, editors, *Fighting the Forces: What's at Stake in Buffy the Vampire Slayer,* Lanham, Massachusetts: Rowman and Littlefield, 2002

Wearing, Michael

British Producer

Michael Wearing is one of Britain's most well-respected and successful producers of authored serial drama, responsible for developing a string of award-winning miniseries in the 1980s, including *Boys from the Blackstuff,* one of the landmarks in British television drama. His career in television began in 1976, when he was appointed script editor to the BBC's English Regions Drama Department in Birmingham. From 1980 Wearing was producing both single plays and series for the unit; he came into prominence in 1981 with the adaptation of Malcolm Bradbury's novel, *The History Man.*

In the development of single plays BBC producers have enjoyed considerable autonomy and, following the trend in contemporary theater, Wearing was keen to commission socially challenging material. However, by the early 1980s, single plays were being squeezed out of the schedule, and their potential to create a social stir had diminished accordingly. Wearing's contribution to television drama hinges on his success in carrying over the progressive tendencies of the single play into the short series/serial—an altogether more difficult format to negotiate with management because of the higher costs and risks incurred.

In Britain, the most celebrated of these programs was Alan Bleasdale's *Boys from the Blackstuff* (1982), a five-part play series, which explored the impact of unemployment on a gang of asphalt workers in Liverpool. The hard-hitting program coincided with a rocketing unemployment rate and gave voice to the despair of the 3 million people in Britain forced to go on the dole at the time. The series touched a vital nerve and stimulated a national debate on a major social issue like few other dramas before it.

Wearing moved to London to play a substantial role in producing the last season of single plays on the BBC in 1984. He then began work on *The Edge of Darkness,* a nuclear thriller serial by Troy Kennedy-Martin. Once again the moment was highly opportune, as the program's transmission in 1985 coincided with widespread anxiety about the nuclear issue in the wake of Chernobyl and the deployment of cruise missiles. Subsequently the program was sold to 26 countries and proved to be one of the BBC's most successful exports to North America. Other award-winning programs followed, including Peter Flannery's *Blind Justice* series in 1988, which exposed the inadequacies of the British criminal justice system.

Wearing became a head of department in the BBC Drama group in 1988 and was head of drama serials until 1998. The BBC serials product, much more than a conventional miniseries, is required to contribute to the prestige of the corporation. In the bureaucratic turmoil of the early 1990s, when the corporation was attempting to secure its charter renewal, there was considerable reappraisal as to how drama might best contribute. Under Wearing's stewardship the classic serial was reintroduced, and Andrew Davies's adaptations of *Middlemarch* and *Pride and Prejudice* enjoyed significant international success. However, Wearing also managed to preserve the space for socially engaged contemporary programs, such as *The Buddha of Suburbia, Family, The Final Cut,* and Peter Flannery's *Our Friends in the North,* an ambitious saga of friendship set against key moments in recent British politics.

By 1998 the transition from producer-led to consumer-led product in British TV was complete, and Wearing's position in the BBC had become untenable. He tendered his resignation, lashing out in the process at the "rampant commercialism" of top executives and their undue reliance on focus groups as a means of determining project viability. He continues to develop socially engaged contemporary material, working as an associate producer in the Anglo-Irish film industry.

BOB MILLINGTON

See also **Boys from the Blackstuff; Our Friends in the North**

Michael Wearing. Theater director; script editor, BBC's English Regions Drama Department, Birmingham, 1976–81; produced *Boys from the Blackstuff,* 1982; moved to BBC's London departments; head of department, BBC, 1988–98.

Television Series and Miniseries (selected)

1982	*Boys from the Blackstuff*
1988	*Blind Justice*
1995	*The Final Cut*
1996	*Our Friends in the North*
1996	*Hetty Wainthropp Investigates*
1997	*Born to Run*
1997	*The History of Tom Jones, a Foundling*
1998	*Our Mutual Friend*
1999	*Aristocrats*
2000	*Gormenghast*

Made-for-Television Films (selected)

1981	*The History Man*
1985	*The Edge of Darkness*
1993	*The Buddha of Suburbia*
1995	*Pride and Prejudice*
1997	*The Missing Postman*
1997	*Bright Hair*
2001	*The American*

Films (selected)

1999	*Human Traffic*
2000	*When the Sky Falls*
2001	*South West 9*
2002	*Mystics*
2004	*Red Light Runners*

Further Reading

Bignell, Jonathan, et al., *British Television Drama: Past, Present, and Future,* London: Palgrave, 2000

Brandt, George, *British Television Drama in the Nineteen Eighties,* Cambridge: Cambridge University Press, 1993

Cooke, Lez, *British Television Drama: A History,* London: British Film Institute, 2003

Millington, Bob, and Robin Nelson, *"Boys from the Blackstuff": The Making of TV Drama,* London: Comedia, 1986

Nelson, Robin, *Television Drama in Transition,* New York: Macmillan, 1997

Weaver, Sylvester (Pat) (1908–2002)

U.S. Media Executive, Programmer

Sylvester (Pat) Weaver had a well-deserved reputation as one of network television's most innovative executives. His greatest impact on the industry came during his tenure as programming head at NBC in the late 1940s and early 1950s. There he developed programming and business strategies the other networks would imitate for years to come. He is also remembered for supporting the idea that commercial television could educate as well as entertain, and he championed cultural programming at NBC under a policy he labeled Operation Frontal Lobes.

Weaver studied philosophy and classics at Dartmouth College, graduating magna cum laude. After military service in World War II, he worked in advertising at the Young and Rubicam Agency. At that time, advertisers owned the programs that were broadcast on network radio and television, and Weaver worked on program development for the agency's clients. This experience prepared him to make the move to network television.

Weaver joined NBC in 1949 to help the company develop its new television network and held several top-management positions, culminating in his appointment as chair of the board in 1956. During that time, he maintained close control over television programming at the network and shaped NBC's entire programming philosophy.

To promote growth in the fledgling network, Weaver commissioned a series of specials he called "spectaculars." These heavily promoted, live specials were designed to generate interest in the NBC schedule in particular and the television medium in general. He hoped that families would purchase their first television sets specifically to watch such events and would then develop regular viewing habits. The strategy especially promised to benefit NBC's parent company, RCA, which controlled most patents on new receiver sets. Programming events such as Mary Martin's *Peter Pan* and the 1952 Christmas Eve broadcast of *Amahl and the Night Visitors,* the first opera commissioned for television, resulted from this plan.

While overseeing NBC's growth, Weaver also worked to enhance its power in relation to advertisers. His experience at Young and Rubicam convinced him that sponsors rather than network programmers actually ran the television industry. Because sponsors owned shows outright, the networks had minimal control over what was broadcast through their services. Some sponsors could even dictate when a show would appear in the weekly schedule. Weaver moved to shift this power to the networks by encouraging NBC to produce programs and then to offer blocks of time to multiple sponsors. He developed certain programs, such as *Today* and *The Tonight Show,* to provide vehicles for this practice. Advertisers could buy the right to advertise in particular segments of such shows but could not control program content. Weaver called this the "magazine concept" of advertising, comparing it to the practice in which print advertisers bought space in magazines without exercising editorial control over the articles. His ambition was for NBC to develop a full schedule of programs and then persuade advertisers to purchase commercial time here and there throughout that schedule. Any given program would carry commercials of several different sponsors. Other networks eventually followed the NBC model, and by the 1960s it had become the television industry standard, commonly known as "participation advertising."

Weaver took pride in his classical education, and he championed the idea that commercial television had an educational mission. He proposed a series of cultural and public affairs programs for NBC, which he promoted under the banner Operation Frontal Lobes. The goal, Weaver announced in 1951, was "the enlargement of the horizon of the viewer." The campaign included a number of prime-time documentary specials. For example, Project XX was a full-time documentary production unit that made feature-length documentaries on historical events. The *Wisdom* series consisted of interviews with major artists and intellectuals (Edward Steichen, Margaret Mead). Weaver even required that educational material be mixed into the entertainment schedule. For example, the popular comedy-variety program *Your Show of Shows* might include a performance of a Verdi aria among its normal array of comic monologues and Sid Caesar skits.

Sylvester (Pat) Weaver, 1955.
Courtesy of the Everett Collection/CSU Archives

See also **Advertising; Advertising Agency; National Broadcasting Company; Sarnoff, David; Special/Spectacular;** *Tonight Show, The*

Sylvester (Pat) Weaver. Born Sylvester Laflin Weaver Jr. in Los Angeles, California, December 21, 1908. Dartmouth College, B.A. magna cum laude, 1930. Married: Elizabeth Inglis (Desiree Mary Hawkins), 1942; children: Trajan Victor Charles and Susan (Sigourney). Served in the U.S. Navy, 1942–45. Worked for Young and MacCallister, an advertising and printing firm; announcer, writer, producer, director, actor, and salesman, radio station KHJ, Los Angeles, 1932; program manager, station KFRC, San Francisco, 1934; worked for NBC and the United Cigar Company, 1935; joined Young and Rubicam advertising agency, 1935; supervisor of programs, Young and Rubicam's radio division, 1937; advertising manager, American Tobacco Company, 1938–46; associate director of communications, Office of the Coordination of Inter-American Affairs, 1941; vice president in charge of radio and television for Young and Rubicam, also serving on executive committee, 1947–49; vice president, vice chair, president, then chair, NBC, 1949–56; chair, McCann Erickson, 1958–63; president, Subscription TV, Los Angeles, 1963–66; chair, American Heart Association, 1959–63; member, board of directors, Muscular Dystrophy Association, from 1967; president, Muscular Dystrophy Association, from 1975. Member: Phi Beta Kappa. Recipient: Peabody Award, 1956; Emmy Award, 1967; named to Television Hall of Fame, 1985. Died in Santa Barbara, California, March 16, 2002.

Publication

The Best Seat in the House: The Golden Years in Radio and Television, 1994

Further Reading

Baughman, James, "Television in the 'Golden Age': An Entrepreneurial Experiment," *The Historian* (1985)
Boddy, William, " 'Operation Frontal Lobes' versus the Living Room Toy," *Media, Culture, and Society* (1987)
Kepley, Vance, Jr., "From 'Frontal Lobes' to the 'Bob-and-Bob' Show: NBC Management and Programming Strategies, 1949–1965," in *Hollywood in the Age of Television,* edited by Tino Balio, Boston: Unwin Hyman, 1990
Kepley, Vance, Jr., "The Weaver Years at NBC," *Wide Angle* (1990)

Weaver left NBC in 1956, when it became clear that the network could no longer follow his philosophy of program variety and innovation. His successor, Robert Kintner, pushed the network schedule toward more standardized series formats. Weaver's last major effort at television innovation came in the early 1960s, when he headed Subscription Television, Inc. (STV), an early venture into the pay-cable industry. His effort to set up a cable service in California was blocked by a referendum initiated by traditional broadcasters. Weaver challenged them in court, and the U.S. Supreme Court subsequently ruled the referendum unconstitutional. STV, however, was bankrupted by the process. Although Weaver's cable venture failed, the case helped remove certain barriers to the eventual development of cable television.

VANCE KEPLEY, JR.

Webb, Jack (1920–1982)

U.S. Actor, Producer

Although he will be remembered most for his physically rigid portrayal of the morally rigid cop Joe Friday on *Dragnet,* Jack Webb had one of the most varied and far-reaching careers in television history. In his four decades in broadcasting, Webb performed nearly every role imaginable in the industry: actor, director, producer, writer (under the pseudonym John Randolph), editor, owner of an independent production company, and major studio executive. Webb's importance stems not only from his endurance and versatility but also from his innovation and success.

Webb entered broadcasting as a radio announcer in 1945. After leading roles in radio dramas such as *Pat Novak for Hire,* he conceived of his own police program based on discussions with Los Angeles police officers about the unrealistic nature of most "cop" shows. *Dragnet* began on NBC Radio in 1949, based on "actual cases" from the files of the Los Angles Police Department (LAPD) and featuring Webb as director, producer, co-writer, and star in the role of the stoic Sergeant Joe Friday. Webb broke the traditional molds of both "true story" crime dramas and "radio noir" by de-emphasizing violence, suspense, and the personal life of the protagonists; he instead strove for maximum verisimilitude by using police jargon, showing "business-only" cops following dead-end leads and methodical procedures, and sacrificing spectacle for authenticity. Webb's personal ties to the LAPD (which approved scripts and production for every *Dragnet* episode) and his own admitted "ultraconservative" political beliefs tinted his version of "reality" in all of his productions, where good always triumphed over evil and the law always represented the best interests of all members of society at large.

Dragnet was a huge success, moving to television in 1951, where it became the highest-rated crime drama in broadcast history. The television version featured more Webb innovations, including passionless dialogue and acting (obtained by forcing actors to read dialogue "cold" from cue cards) and using camera and editing techniques taken from a film model. The show's success fueled Webb's career as an independent producer and director of both television and feature films. His Mark VII Limited production company produced *Dragnet* throughout its run on television, including its four-year return in the late 1960s. Webb also produced numerous other shows, including *Adam-12, Emergency,* and *General Electric True;* these met with varied degrees of success, but all Mark VII productions featured Webb's special blend of heightened realism, rapid-fire emotionless dialogue, and conservative politics. In 1954 *Dragnet* spawned one of the first in a long line of successful television-inspired films. Webb directed and produced more feature films throughout the 1950s, most notably an acclaimed version of *Pete Kelly's Blues* in 1955.

Webb's least successful venture was his brief tenure as a studio executive. Webb, whose association with Warner Brothers ran back to his mid-1950s film proj-

Dragnet, Jack Webb, 1952–59.
Courtesy of the Everett Collection

ects, was named head of production at Warner Brothers Television in early 1963. Although his previous successes created high expectations, he was only able to sell one show to a network (NBC's short-lived western *Temple Houston*), and his singular style was incompatible with Warner's only other series on the air, *77 Sunset Strip*. This "ultrahip" crime show was created in direct opposition to the grim procedural quality of *Dragnet,* but Webb pushed the already-waning show in a new direction—toward the stark realism of his previous work. *77 Sunset Strip* was canceled at the end of the season, but Webb did not last as long—he was fired in December 1963, ending a failed ten-month tenure.

Upon Webb's death in 1982, most reports and coverage focused on Joe Friday. His performance style has been parodied since his emergence in the 1950s, but Webb's impact on television has never been properly assessed. Always anomalous and bucking the tide of televisual convention, Webb's style lives on in syndicated episodes of *Dragnet,* while his innovations and creations are consistently being copied or forsaken on every crime show today.

JASON MITTELL

See also **Detective Programs;** *Dragnet;* **Police Programs**

Jack Webb. Born in Santa Monica, California, April 2, 1920. Educated at Belmont High School. Married: 1) Julie Peck (London), 1947 (divorced, 1954); children: Stacy and Lisa; 2) Dorothy Thompson, 1955 (divorced, 1957); 3) Jackie Loughery, 1958 (divorced, 1964). Served with the U.S. Army Air Force during World War II, 1942–45. Radio announcer, star, and producer, 1945–61; television producer, director, and actor, from 1951; star and director of motion pictures, from 1948; founder, production company Mark VII, Ltd., and music publishing firms of Mark VII Music and Pete Kelly Music; executive in charge of television production, Warner Brothers Studios, 1963. Member: Screen Actors Guild; Screen Directors Guild; American Society of Cinematographers; American Federation of Television and Radio Artists; United Cerebral Palsy Association (honorary chair). Recipient: Academy of Television Arts and Sciences' Best

Mystery Show, 1952–54; more than 100 commendations of merit awarded by radio and television critics. Died in Los Angeles, California, December 23, 1982.

Television Series (executive producer)

1951–59	*Dragnet* (actor, producer, and director)
1968–70	*Adam 12* (creator and producer)
1970–71	*The D.A.*
1970–71	*O'Hara, U.S. Treasury*
1971–75	*Emergency!*
1973	*Escape* (narrator only)
1973	*Chase*
1974–75	*The Rangers*
1975	*Mobile Two*
1977	*Sam*
1978	*Project U.F.O.*
1978	*Little Mo*

Films (selected; actor)

He Walked by Night, 1948; *Sunset Boulevard,* 1950; *The Men,* 1950; *Halls of Montezuma,* 1950; *You're in the Navy Now,* 1951; *Dragnet* (also director), 1954; *Pete Kelly's Blues* (also director), 1955; *The D.I.* (also director), 1957; *The Last Time I Saw Archie* (also director), 1961.

Radio

Pat Novak for Hire, 1946; *Johnny Modero Pier 23,* 1947; *Dragnet* (creator, director, producer, and star), 1949–55; *Pete Kelly's Blues* (creator), 1951; *True Series* (creator), 1961.

Further Reading

Anderson, Christopher, *Hollywood TV: The Studio System in the Fifties,* Austin: University of Texas Press, 1994
Collins, Max Allan, and John Javna, *The Best of Crime and Detective TV,* New York: Harmony, 1988
MacDonald, J. Fred, *Don't Touch That Dial,* Chicago: Nelson-Hall, 1979
Meyers, Richard, *TV Detectives,* San Diego, California: Barnes, 1981
Varni, Charles A., "Images of Police Work and Mass-Media Propaganda: The Case of 'Dragnet,' " Ph.D. dissertation, Washington State University, 1974

WebTV. *See* Convergence

Wednesday Play, The

British Anthology Series

The Wednesday Play is now nostalgically remembered as part of the legendary past of British television drama—a halcyon time in the 1960s when practitioners had the luxurious freedom of exploring the creative possibilities of the medium through the one-off television play, egged on by broadcasters and audiences alike. To many writers and directors today, it stands as a wistful beacon, a symbol of the possible, as they gaze enviously at the apparent freedoms of their forebears from the seemingly ratings-led, series-dominated wasteland of their TV dramatic present.

As with any legend, there is more than a grain of truth to this view of the past, but also a considerable amount of misty idealization. *The Wednesday Play* arose, in fact, not as a benign gift of liberal broadcasters but as a desperate attempt by the head of BBC-TV drama, Sydney Newman, to save the single play from being axed from the BBC's premier channel (BBC 1), due to poor ratings. Newman, who had been impressed by Scots director James MacTaggart's work on the earlier experimental play strands *Storyboard* (1961) and *Teletale* (1963), hired him as producer of the new BBC 1 play slot, handing him a brief to commission a popular series of plays.

Newman's stipulations were significant. He wanted a play slot that would be relevant to the lives of a mainstream popular audience and that would reflect the "turning points" of society: the relationship between a son and a father; a parishioner and his priest; a trade union official and his boss. He also wanted plays that would be fast—not only telling an exciting narrative sparely, rather than building up mood, but also hooking the audience's attention by way of an intriguing pretitles "teaser" sequence. Borrowing from the techniques of the popular series that was threatening to displace the single play in the schedules, Newman wanted the slot to have a recognizable "house style," so that audiences knew that if they tuned in each week, they could expect to see a certain type of show. Finally, mimicking his own success in commercial television several years earlier (on ITV's *Armchair Theatre* slot), Newman prioritized a search for material that would more accurately reflect the experience of the audience, by instituting a system of story editors whose task it was to bring fresh new writers to television.

MacTaggart absorbed Newman's guidelines but translated them in his own way, not least by appointing as his story editor a young writer and actor with whom he had worked on *Teletale:* Roger Smith. It was with Smith's help that the play slot soon came to acquire the reputation for "controversy" and "outrage" that would mark its subsequent history. The script commissioned for MacTaggart and Smith's very first *Wednesday Play* outing in January 1965 set the seal for what would follow. Written by a convicted murderer (James O'Connor) and depicting the cynical progress of a villain from gangster to baronet, *A Tap on the Shoulder* marked a conscious break with the conventions of the polite, "well-made" TV play.

Its determination to break new ground came to characterize *The Wednesday Play* ethos as a whole—from the first crucial season in 1965 to the last in 1970. The slot also acted as a showcase for new talent, in keeping with Newman's original vision. Many well-known practitioners gained their first big break on *The Wednesday Play,* including Tony Garnett and Kenith Trodd (recruited by Smith as assistant story editors), Dennis Potter, and Ken Loach, director of *A Tap,* whose contributions to the slot eventually numbered some of the most seminal TV plays of the 1960s: the "docudramas" *Up the Junction* (1965) and *Cathy Come Home* (1966).

As *The Wednesday Play* developed, shifts in emphasis, however, took place. Under the first season of MacTaggart and Smith, the plays were much more "expressionist" in style and concerned with exploiting the resources of the television studio, as the earlier *Teletale* had done. It is significant that the slot's first nonnaturalistic dramas, from such writers as Dennis Potter and David Mercer, were commissioned at this time. In later seasons, however, after MacTaggart and Smith had departed and Tony Garnett was named chief story editor, many of the plays became noticeably more "documentary," reflecting a determination to transcend the confines of the TV studio in order to record more faithfully the rapidly changing character of life in 1960s Britain. Having gained access to lightweight 16-millimeter filming equipment, Garnett and his collaborator Loach abandoned the studio for location shooting, and their form of filmed documentary realism became one of the most familiar hallmarks of *The Wednesday Play.*

The Loach-Garnett documentary style also became quite controversial and was criticized both outside and within the BBC for unacceptably blurring the distinctions between fictional drama and factual current affairs. Meanwhile, the play slot itself came under attack from some quarters for its general "filth" and "squalor." "Clean-Up TV" campaigner Mary Whitehouse harried it for what she saw as its gross sexual immorality, although the effect of her attacks was simply to boost publicity and the all-important ratings. Audiences climbed from 1 million to 8 million, as people tuned in each week to see for themselves the latest play trailed as "controversial" in the press. For one of the very few times in TV history, Newman's dream of a popular series of plays became reality. By the end of the 1960s, however, it was clear the slot had become a victim of its own past reputation: its perceived "permissiveness" and antiestablishment bias had inspired a negative reaction among significant proportions of the audience, who were now deliberately not tuning in. Accordingly, Newman's successor as head of drama, Shaun Sutton, tried to win new audiences by giving the BBC's contemporary play slot a new time and title. In 1970 he altered the title to become *Play for Today,* thereby inadvertently creating the legend of the lost "golden age" that *The Wednesday Play* has become.

JOHN COOK

See also **British Programming;** *Cathy Come Home;* **Garnett, Tony; Loach, Ken; Mercer, David; Potter, Dennis; Trodd, Kenith**

Programming History

172 episodes
BBC
January 1965–70

Further Reading

Cook, John R., *Dennis Potter: A Life on Screen,* Manchester, England: Manchester University Press, and New York: St. Martin's Press, 1995

Kennedy-Martin, Troy, "Nats Go Home: First Statement of a New Drama for Television," *Encore* (March–April 1964)

Kennedy-Martin, Troy, "Up the Junction and After," *Contrast* (winter–spring 1965–66)

Macmurraugh-Kavanagh, M.K., "The BBC and the Birth of the 'Wednesday Play,' 1962–66: Institutional Containment Versus 'Agitational Contemporaneity,' " *Historical Journal of Film, Radio, and Television,* 17, no. 3 (1997)

Macmurraugh-Kavanagh, M.K., " 'Drama' into 'News': Strategies of Intervention in 'The Wednesday Play,' " *Screen,* 38, no. 3 (1997)

Madden, Paul, editor, *Complete Programme Notes for a Season of British Television Drama, 1959–73,* London: British Film Institute, 1976

Shubik, Irene, *Play for Today: The Evolution of Television Drama,* London: Davis-Poynter, 1975

Williams, Raymond, "A Lecture on Realism," *Screen* (spring 1977)

Weinberger, Ed

U.S. Writer, Producer

Ed Weinberger is one of television's most respected writer-producers who, along with James L. Brooks, David Davis, Allan Burns, and Stan Daniels, made up the heart of the MTM Enterprises creative team. Weinberger has received many awards for his contributions to a number of successful or critically acclaimed series for both MTM and the John Charles Walters Company, of which he was a partner.

Weinberger's early TV experience included writing for *The Dean Martin Show,* where he was teamed with Stan Daniels, who eventually became Weinberger's writing partner at MTM. Weinberger had also been a writer for Bob Hope, traveling with him to Vietnam. In the late 1960s, Weinberger wrote a screenplay about a divorced woman who was struggling to make it on her own. Although it was never produced, *The Mary Tyler Moore Show* creators James L. Brooks and Allan Burns saw a copy of the script and hired Weinberger during the series' second season.

In addition to his Emmy Award–winning work on *The Mary Tyler Moore Show,* Weinberger, along with Daniels, created and produced the MTM sitcoms *Phyllis, Doc,* and *The Betty White Show.* In 1977 Weinberger, Brooks, Davis, and Daniels were all wooed away by Paramount, which was looking to finance other independent production companies for ABC programming. The MTM alumni welcomed the change, if only because the cozy MTM atmosphere was being gradually replaced by a growing bureaucracy that hampered creativity. Brooks, Davis, Daniels, and Weinberger formed the John Charles Walters Company, which produced its most famous sitcom, *Taxi,* in 1978.

In *Taxi,* Weinberger and the other members of the new creative team were able to successfully echo the quality television that had become synonymous with MTM. Much like an MTM show, *Taxi* was a sophisticated example of humor derived from carefully crafted character exploration. *Taxi* also pursued the "workplace-as-family" theme so prominent in the best of MTM sitcoms. Canceled in 1982 by ABC, *Taxi* was picked up by NBC for a subsequent season. Thus, Weinberger helped deliver a second generation of quality television that extended into the 1980s.

In 1983, after NBC also canceled *Taxi,* Weinberger seemed to take a giant step backward when he coproduced *Mr. Smith,* a sitcom featuring a talking chimp for which Weinberger provided the voice. This was not the first time Weinberger had used his voice-over talents; the sigh in the John Charles Walters Company end-credit logo is Weinberger's as well. In 1984 Weinberger was back on the quality track when he co-wrote the Emmy Award–winning pilot episode for *The Cosby Show.* Weinberger's later production credits also included the disappointing-yet-successful series *Amen,* as well as the critically acclaimed yet unpopular sitcom *Dear John.*

MICHAEL B. KASSEL

See also **Amen; Cosby Show, The; Mary Tyler Moore Show, The; Taxi**

Ed Weinberger. Attended Columbia University, New York City. Married: Carlene Watkins. Writer for night-club comedians, monologues for Johnny Carson, Bob Hope in Vietnam, Dick Gregory in Mississippi, and Dean Martin specials; creator, writer, and producer of television comedy, since 1970s, working with Stan Daniels for the early part of his career. Recipient: 13 Emmy Awards; three Golden Globes; Writers Guild Foundation Career Achievement Award, 2000.

Television Series (selected)

1965	*The Tonight Show* (writer)
1965–74	*The Dean Martin Show* (writer)
1970–77	*The Mary Tyler Moore Show* (writer and producer)
1975–76	*Doc* (producer)
1975–77	*Phyllis* (writer and producer)
1977–78	*The Betty White Show* (producer)
1978–83	*Taxi* (creator, writer, and producer)
1983	*Mr. Smith* (creator and producer)
1984–92	*The Cosby Show* (co-creator and writer)
1986–91	*Amen* (creator and producer)
1989–91	*Dear John* (producer)
1991–92	*Baby Talk* (producer)
1996–98	*Sparks* (executive producer)
1997	*Good News* (creator and executive producer)

Made-for-Television Movie

| 1978 | *Cindy* (co-writer) |

Film

The Lonely Guy (writer), 1984.

Further Reading

Feuer, Jane, Paul Kerr, and Tise Vahimagi, editors, *MTM: "Quality Television,"* London: British Film Institute, 1984

Weldon, Fay (1931–)

British Writer

Most widely known in Britain and abroad as an irreverent novelist usually concerned with women's issues, Fay Weldon has also pursued a wide variety of projects for television, radio, and the stage. The daughter of a novelist, granddaughter of a *Vanity Fair* editor, and a niece of novelist–screenwriter–radio and television dramatist Selvyn Jepson, Weldon's first published novel in 1967 simply expanded on her 1966 teleplay for *The Fat Woman's Tale.* The teleplay had been written while Weldon was working as a highly successful copywriter for English print and television advertising; her previous work included the still-remembered "Get to work on an egg" campaign. Weldon remained in advertising until the 1970s, yet she still produced teleplays for productions such as *A Catching Complaint* (1966) and *Poor Cherry* (1967).

While Weldon's real progress as a writer has often been traced back to the mid-1960s, it was in the early 1970s that she began fully to establish both her name and public voice. Where Weldon fit in British culture was another matter. *The Fat Woman's Tale* had told a decidedly protofeminist story of a housewife's anger toward her philandering husband, yet Weldon's public espousal of domestic joys and the use of "Mrs." seemed to mark her as an opponent to the growing British women's rights movement. But as David Frost learned in 1971, Weldon's relation to feminism is not always what it might seem: invited onto Frost's television program to rebut feminist activists, she instead surprised everyone by publicly embracing their complaints. That same year Weldon won the best series script award from the Writers Guild of Great Britain for "On Trial," the first episode of *Upstairs, Downstairs*. She wrote only one other episode, and in many ways the series' sober, understated visual style was quite different from the satiric, reflexive, often fantastic surfaces of much of Weldon's other work, including her sedate, but still barbed, television adaptation of *Pride and Prejudice* (1980).

Perhaps it is no coincidence that the imagined recipient of Weldon's *Letters to Alice: On First Reading Jane Austen* (1984) is a punk-haired but literary niece; that juxtaposition of texts and attitudes, together with Weldon's own later televised comments on the (mis)teaching of Austen, led some critics to accuse Weldon of unjustly attacking Austen's work.

Yet the melodramatic pleasures of both *Upstairs, Downstairs* and *Pride and Prejudice* run through nearly all of Weldon's work and inform her understanding of gender. She not only won a prestigious Booker Prize nomination for *Praxis* (1978) but also chaired the prize's 1983 panel. Yet Weldon has never divorced her "serious" literary work from her own enjoyment of what she calls "that whole women's magazine area, the communality of women's interests, and the sharing of the latest eye-shadow." With such an attitude, Weldon penned the polemical prison docudrama *Life for Christine* (1980), polished the script for Joan Collins's *Sins* miniseries (1985), and turned a critical eye toward pastoral life in *The Heart of the Country* (1987).

Despite her willingness to adapt the work of others, Weldon has been protective of the rights to her own work. Nevertheless, she has been most notably repre-

Fay Weldon.
Photo courtesy of Fay Weldon and Isolde Ohlbaum

sented on television in Britain and abroad not through her own scripts, but through two popular multipart adaptations of her novels: *The Life and Loves of a She-Devil* (1983, televised 1986), which sharply satirized conventions of both heterosexual romance and the romance novel, and *The Cloning of Joanna May* (1989, televised 1991), a slightly more genteel version of *She-Devil*'s antics, this time as practiced by a devilish husband. The same creative team (including writer Ted Whitehead, director Philip Saville, and star Patricia Hodge) helmed both adaptations, but it is the highly praised *The Life and Loves of a She-Devil* that remains the strongest evocation of Weldon's own ethos, despite the intervening memory of Susan Seidelman's limp, Americanized film adaptation (*She Devil*, 1990).

Oddly enough, Seidelman's film omitted Weldon's most visually rich and outrageous portion, the fantastic surgical reconstruction of the She-Devil into her nemesis, the physical form of female romantic perfection. This excision removed what is most remarkable throughout much of Weldon's work: her Mary

Shelley–like coupling of deliberately excessive Gothic fantasy with sharp feminist perception.

Weldon has not been alone in the use of such fantastic elements. Indeed, as Thomas Elsaesser (1988) has suggested, Weldon and "New Gothic" companion Angela Carter (*The Magic Toyshop,* 1986) may present a female-centered television parallel to the male-centered and often fantastic films of Peter Greenaway, Derek Jarman, and other directors prominent in the 1980s "New British Cinema." If these filmmakers were "learning to dream" again (to quote the familiar title of James Park's study), then Weldon has been one of British television's more prominent instructors in the same task.

ROBERT DICKINSON

See also **British Programming**

Fay Weldon. Born Fay Birkinshaw in Alvechurch, Worcestershire, England, September 22, 1931. Grew up in New Zealand. Attended University of St. Andrews, M.A. in economics and psychology, 1954. Married: 1) Ron Weldon, 1962 (died, 1994); 2) Nick Fox, 1995; four sons. Writer for Foreign Office and *Daily Mirror,* London, late 1950s; worked in advertising; author of television and radio plays, dramatizations and series, and novels and stage plays. Chair, Booker McConnell Prize judges' panel, 1983. Recipient: Writers Guild Award, 1973; Giles Cooper Award, 1978; Society of Authors traveling scholarship, 1981; *Los Angeles Times* Award, 1989.

Television Series

1980	*Pride and Prejudice*
1986	*The Life and Loves of a She-Devil*
1987	*Heart of the Country*
1998	*Big Women* (miniseries)

Television Plays/Movies (selected)

1966	*The Fat Woman's Tale*
1966	*A Catching Complaint*
1967	*Poor Cherry*
1972	*Splinter of Ice*
1980	*Life for Christine*
1991	*The Cloning of Joanna May*
1991	*Growing Rich*
1992	*President's Child, The*
1992	*Growing Rich*

Film

She-Devil, 1990.

Radio

Spider, 1973; *Housebreaker,* 1973; *Mr. Fox and Mr. First,* 1974; *The Doctor's Wife,* 1975; *Polaris,* 1978; *Weekend,* 1979; *All the Bells of Paradise,* 1979; *I Love My Love,* 1981.

Stage

A Small Green Space, 1989 (libretto).

Publications (selected)

Affliction (novel), 1994
Auto da Fay: A Memoir, 2003
The Cloning of Joanna May (novel), 1989
Darcy's Utopia (novel), 1990
Down Among the Women (novel), 1971
The Fat Woman's Joke (novel), 1967; as *...and the Wife Ran Away,* 1968
Female Friends (novel), 1975
Growing Rich (novel), 1992
The Heart of the Country (novel), 1987
The Hearts and Lives of Men (novel), 1987
Leader of the Band (novel), 1988
Letters to Alice: On First Reading Jane Austen, 1984
Life Force (novel), 1992
The Life and Loves of a She-Devil (novel), 1983
Natural Love (novel), 1993
Praxis (novel), 1978
The President's Child (novel), 1982
Puffball (novel), 1980
Remember Me (novel), 1976
The Rules of Life (novella), 1987
Splitting (novel), 1995
Watching Me, Watching You (short stories), 1981
Wicked Women (short stories), 1995
Words of Advice, 1977; as *Little Sisters,* 1978
Worst Fears, 1997

Further Reading

Brandt, George W., *British Television in the 1980s,* Cambridge and New York: Cambridge University Press, 1993

Elsaesser, Thomas, "Games of Love and Death, or an Englishman's Guide to the Galaxy," *Monthly Film Bulletin* (1988)

Pearlman, Mickey, editor, *Listen to Their Voices: Twenty Interviews with Women Who Write,* New York: Norton, 1993

Welland, Colin (1934–)

British Actor, Writer

Colin Welland is widely respected both as an actor and writer for television, the cinema, and the stage. Rotund and unfailingly good-humored, he has given invaluable support in a range of plays and serials.

Welland first became a familiar face on British television when he landed the role of Constable David Graham, one of the original characters based at Newtown police station in the long-running police serial *Z Cars* in the 1960s. The series broke new ground, introducing a fresh realism to police dramas, and the regular stars all became household names. Welland stayed with the show for some time, as PC (Police Constable) Bert Lynch's second partner on the beat, before eventually leaving for new pastures. He reappeared, together with other stars from the early years of the show, when the last episode was filmed in 1978.

Thus established in television as a performer, Welland went on to star in various plays and television movies, often also contributing the scripts (he was voted Best TV Playwright in Britain in 1970, 1973, and 1974). True to his Lancashire roots, his plays often had an earthy northern humor and dealt with themes accessible to the working-class "man in the street." He also enjoyed huge success as a writer for the cinema, notably with his screenplays for *Yanks* and *Chariots of Fire,* an Oscar-winning smash that was heralded (somewhat prematurely) as signaling a new golden era in British moviemaking. Welland himself picked up an Academy Award for Best Screenplay. Among subsequent films that have garnered their share of praise have been *A Dry White Season,* a drama dwelling on the cruelties imposed by the policy of apartheid in South Africa (co-written with Euzhan Palcy), and *The War of the Buttons,* delving into the often dark and violent world of children. Also much admired were his appearances in such films as *Kes,* in which he played the sympathetic Mr. Farthing, and Willy Russell's *Dancing Through the Dark,* which was set in familiar northwestern territory, in the bars and clubs of Liverpool.

Perhaps the most memorable image from Welland's lengthy career as a television actor came in 1979, when he was one of a first-class cast that was chosen to appear in Dennis Potter's award-winning play *Blue Remembered Hills,* which recalled the long-lost days of his own childhood. In company with Helen Mirren, Michael Elphick, Colin Jeavons, and John Bird, among others, all of whom were adults playing the roles of young children, Welland cavorted gleefully around woods and fields, his bulk grotesquely crammed into a pair of boy's shorts. Potter's brilliantly realized play, exposing the native cruelty beneath the outwardly innocent world of children, was hailed as a masterpiece, and Welland himself, not for the first time in his distinguished career, was singled out for special praise.

DAVID PICKERING

See also **Z Cars**

Colin Welland. Born Colin Williams in Leigh, Lancashire, England, July 4, 1934. Attended Newton-le-Willows Grammar School; Bretton Hall College; Goldsmith's College, London, Teacher's Diploma in

Colin Welland.
Photo courtesy of Peter Charlesworth Ltd.

Art and Drama. Married: Patricia Sweeney, 1962; children: Genevieve, Catherine, Caroline, and Christie. Art teacher, 1958–62; joined Library Theatre, Manchester, 1962–64; established popular fame as PC Graham in *Z Cars,* 1962–65; has since worked as writer and actor for film, television, and theater. Recipient: Best Television Writer and Best Supporting Film Actor, British Academy of Film and Television Arts Award, 1970; Best Television Playwright, Writers Guild, 1970, 1973, and 1974; Academy Award, 1981; *Evening Standard* Award, 1981; Broadcasting Press Guild Awards, 1973, 1981.

Television Series (actor)

1962–65   *Z Cars*

Made-for-Television Movies (actor)

1976	*Machine Gunner*
1979	*Blue Remembered Hills*
1990	*The Secret Life of Ian Fleming/Spy maker: The Secret*
1993	*Femme Fatale* (also writer)
1998	*Bramwell*

Television Plays (writer)

1969	*Bangelstein's Boys* (also actor)
1970	*Say Goodnight to Grandma*

1970	*Roll on Four O'Clock* (also actor)
1973	*Kisses at Fifty* (also actor)
1974	*Leeds United* (also actor)
1974	*The Wild West Show*
1974	*Jack Point*
1976	*Your Man from Six Counties* (also actor)
1977	*Bank Holiday*
1994	*Bambino Mio*

Films (actor)

Kes, 1969; *Straw Dogs,* 1971; *Villain,* 1971; *Sweeney!,* 1977; *Dancing Through the Dark,* 1990.

Films (writer)

Yanks, 1979; *Chariots of Fire,* 1981; *Twice in a Lifetime,* 1985; *A Dry White Season,* 1989; *War of the Buttons,* 1994; *The Yellow Jersey.*

Stage (writer)

Say Goodnight to Grandma, 1973; *Roll on Four O'Clock,* 1981.

Publications

A Roomful of Holes (play), 1972
Say Goodnight to Grandma (play), 1973
Anthology of Northern Humour, 1982

Wendt, Jana (1956–)

Australian Broadcast Journalist

Jana Wendt is Australian television's best-known female current-affairs reporter and presenter. She is also widely regarded as one of Australian commercial television's most skilled interviewers.

The daughter of Czech immigrants, Melbourne-born Wendt began her career in journalism researching documentaries for the government-funded Australian Broadcasting Commission in 1975. After completing an arts degree at Melbourne University, she accepted a job in commercial television, joining Ten Network as an on-camera news reporter in its Melbourne newsroom. Shortly after moving into the role of news presenter at Ten Network, Wendt was offered a position as

a reporter on Nine Network's new prime-time current-affairs show, *60 Minutes.*

Under the guidance of executive producer Gerald Stone, an American with broad experience in both Australian and U.S. news and current-affairs programming, *60 Minutes* proceeded to set the standard for quality commercial current affairs in Australia both in terms of content and production values. The youngest correspondent to join the *60 Minutes* team, Wendt quickly established a reputation for her aggressive interviewing style and glamorous, ice-cool on-camera demeanor. It was this combination of acuity and implacability that earned Wendt her nickname "the perfumed steamroller."

In 1987 Wendt left *60 Minutes* to anchor another Nine Network program, the nightly prime-time half-hour current-affairs show, *A Current Affair,* where she cemented her journalistic reputation with a series of incisive and revealing interviews with national and international political figures. Her subjects included Libya's Colonel Gaddafi, U.S. vice president Dan Quayle, former U.S. secretary of state Henry Kissinger, former Philippines president Ferdinand Marcos, and media barons Rupert Murdoch and Conrad Black. In 1994 Wendt returned to *60 Minutes* to fill the newly created role of anchor.

Wendt's departure from *A Current Affair* the previous year followed accelerating criticism of the program for its increasingly tabloid accent. The trend, evidenced for critics by *A Current Affair*'s frequent use of hidden cameras, walk-up interviews, and stories with a voyeuristic, sexual theme, was at odds with Wendt's image as a guarantor of dispassionate investigative reporting. While she declined to criticize the program on her departure, she did register her general professional objections to the "tabloidization" of Australian current affairs on her return to Nine Network in 1994. The first *60 Minutes* she hosted was an hour-long studio debate on journalistic ethics and the tabloidization of news and current affairs.

A traditionalist who endorses the notions of journalistic objectivity and the watchdog role of the media in the public sphere, Wendt is an icon of an era many media analysts believe to be passing in Australian commercial current-affairs television. The approach of pay television, as well as the debt burdens many network owners inherited in the 1980s, caused Australian broadcast networks to look carefully at their production budgets and demand that news and current-affairs divisions show increasing profitability. The result has been an attempt to move the focus of such programs away from public sphere issues such as politics, economics, and science and concentrate on domestic matters such as relationships, consumer issues, sexuality, and family life. In many instances, this shift in focus has been accompanied by a more melodramatic, emotional approach on the part of journalists and hosts. It is a trend that Wendt has consistently resisted and that has led her to become a respected, but somewhat isolated figure in today's commercial current-affairs landscape.

CATHARINE LUMBY

See also **Australian Programming**

Jana Wendt. Born in Melbourne, Australia, 1956. Educated at Melbourne University. Researcher, Australian Broadcasting Corporation (ABC) TV documentaries, 1975–77; field reporter, ATV-10 News, 1979, coanchor, 1980; reporter, Nine Network's *60 Minutes,* 1983–87, 1994; host, Nine's *A Current Affair,* 1988–93; host and reporter, *60 Minutes,* from 1994; host, Seven Network's current-affairs program *Witness,* 1995–97, ABC-TV's *Uncensored,* 1997–98, and SBS-TV's *Dateline,* from 1999.

Television Series

1988–93	*A Current Affair*
1983–87, 1994	*60 Minutes*
1995–97	*Witness*
1997–98	*Uncensored*
1999–	*Dateline*

Western

The western has always been a dusty rear-view mirror for reflecting back on the U.S. experience. Whether celebrating the pioneering spirit of the Scotch-Irish invading class or lamenting the genocidal whitewashing of the continent under the banner of "manifest destiny," the western has operated as an instrument for navigating through the fog of contemporary political, social, and cultural anxieties by reinterpreting and rewriting the nation's mythic past. In the 1930s, during the most desperate days of the Great Depression, singing cowboys sporting white hats offered hopeful visions of good guys finishing first to a nation starved for optimism; during the dawning of the cold war era, Hollywood's "A" westerns provided relatively safe vehicles for commenting on McCarthyism (*High Noon*) and American apartheid (*The Searchers*); prime-time westerns in the 1960s often addressed, though allegorically and indirectly, the generational discord of the decade, as well as the conflicting frustrations over U.S. involvement in an undeclared war; and in the 1980s

The Virginian, Roberta Shore, Clu Gulager, Doug McClure, Lee J. Cobb, Randy Boone, James Drury, 1962–71; 1964 episode.
Courtesy of the Everett Collection

and 1990s, revisionist westerns have taken multicultural angles on the Western Expansion (*Dances with Wolves*) or libertarian spins on the genre's longstanding infatuation with law and order (*The Unforgiven*). The western is, in other words, best understood as a "hindsight" form—a form that deploys the rich imagery of the old West in an ongoing rewriting of the pride and shame of what it means be American.

This rewriting and reinterpreting of the American experience is even evident in the first "modern" western novel, Owen Wister's *The Virginian.* Published in 1902, Wister's classic cowboy novel sparked something of a range war in the heartland of popular literature. According to contemporary literary critics, Wister's novel and the rise of the cowboy hero represented a masculinist and secular reaction to the so-called "sentimental novel" that had been so popular in the late 19th century. In the tradition of *Uncle Tom's Cabin* and *Little Women,* the sentimental novel celebrated feminine moral authority, domesticity, and religion. The 20th-century western, in stark contrast, denounced the civilized world of women and flaunted, instead, rugged images of courageous men free from the constraints of family. Ultimately, these taciturn men were more given to flirtation with death than with women, and more attached to their horses and six-shooters than they were to their mothers, sisters, sweethearts, wives, or daughters.

Although rooted in the novel, the first westerns appearing on television were more directly connected to Hollywood's mass-produced version of the genre. In television's infancy, recycled "B" westerns from marginal production companies like Mascot, Mono-

gram, PRC, Lonestar, and Republic played a prominent role in transforming television into a mass medium, by stimulating much of the initial enthusiasm for the medium especially among youngsters and rural audiences. Formulaic features and serials displaying the exploits of familiar names like Ken Maynard, Bob Steele, Hoot Gibson, and Tex Ritter were telecast locally, usually during juvenile viewing hours, in showcases with names such as *Six-Gun Playhouse, Sage-Brush Theater,* and *Saddle and Sage Theater.* Thanks to such scheduling, a survey of the programming preferences of children in New York City conducted in April 1949 ranked westerns at the top of the list, a full two percentage points ahead of *Howdy Doody.*

The astute marketing of William Boyd's Hopalong Cassidy was by far the most profitable repackaging of a B western hero in television's infancy. Performing as a romantic leading man in silent films, Boyd had trouble even mounting a horse when he first landed the role of Hopalong Cassidy in 1935. However, by 1948, after completing 66 western features, Boyd was not only at home in the saddle but also savvy enough to secure the TV rights to his Hoppy films. In 1949, as a weekly series on NBC, *Hopalong Cassidy* ranked number seven in the Nielsen ratings—and Boyd quickly cashed in on his popularity through product endorsements that included Hoppy roller skates, soap, wristwatches, and, most notably, jackknives (of which 1 million units were sold in ten days). Clearly influenced by the *Hopalong Cassidy* phenomenon, the first wave of made-for-TV westerns was targeted specifically at the juvenile market, which was a particularly appealing and expansive demographic segment because of the postwar baby boom. Some of the first western series produced expressly for television, most notably *The Gene Autry Show* and *The Roy Rogers Show,* recycled prominent stars of the B western. Others, like *The Cisco Kid* and *The Lone Ranger,* were more familiar as radio series. All featured squeaky-clean heroes who modeled what was considered positive roles for their prepubescent fans.

Perhaps the most self-conscious moralist of television's first western stars was Gene Autry, who in the early 1950s authored the Cowboy Code:

1. A cowboy never takes unfair advantage, even of an enemy.
2. A cowboy never betrays a trust.
3. A cowboy always tells the truth.
4. A cowboy is kind to small children, to old folks, and to animals.
5. A cowboy is free from racial and religious prejudice.

6. A cowboy is always helpful, and when anyone's in trouble, he lends a hand.
7. A cowboy is a good worker.
8. A cowboy is clean about his person, and in thoughts, word, and deed.
9. A cowboy respects womanhood, his parents, and the laws of his country.
10. A cowboy is a patriot.

With its emphasis on the work ethic and patriotism, the Cowboy Code adequately captures the seemingly benign, though unapologetically sexist values animating the juvenile westerns of America's cold war culture. But "Thou shall not kill" is noticeably missing from Autry's Ten Commandments—and this omission would later come to be the source of much public concern.

In the mid-1950s, as major powers in Hollywood stampeded into the television industry, a second wave of made-for-TV westerns would elevate the production values of juvenile programs and, more important, introduce the first of the so-called adult western series. On the kiddie frontier, Screen Gems, the TV subsidiary of Columbia Pictures, blazed the trail for tinsel town with *The Adventures of Rin Tin Tin,* which premiered on ABC in October 1954. Walt Disney Productions ventured into the territory of TV westerns with three hour-long installments of the *Disneyland* anthology show that presented Fess Parker's clean-cut portrayal of an American legend: *Davy Crockett, Indian Fighter* (first telecast on December 15, 1954); *Davy Crockett Goes to Congress* (January 26, 1955); and *Davy Crockett at the Alamo* (February 23, 1955). The merchandising hysteria that accompanied the initial broadcasting of the Crockett trilogy even surpassed the earlier Hopalong frenzy as Americans consumed around $100 million in Crockett products, including 4 million copies of the record "The Ballad of Davy Crockett" and 14 million Davy Crockett books. In the fall of 1957, Disney would branch out into series production with *Zorro,* which celebrated the heroics of a masked Robin Hood figure who was fond of slashing the letter "Z" onto the vests of his many foes.

On the adult frontier, four series premiering in September 1955 would start a programming revolution: *Gunsmoke* on CBS, *Frontier* on NBC, and on ABC, *Cheyenne* and *The Life and Legend of Wyatt Earp.* While *Cheyenne* is notable for being part of Warner Brothers Studio's first foray into television production, the most important and enduring of the original adult westerns is, without a doubt, *Gunsmoke.* Adapted from a CBS radio series in which the rotund William Conrad provided the mellifluous voice of Marshall Matt Dillon, the television version recast the

Rawhide, Clint Eastwood, Paul Brinegar, Eric Fleming, 1959–66.
Courtesy of the Everett Collection

taller, leaner, and more telegenic James Arness in the starring role. Destined to become one of the longest running prime-time series in network television history, the premiere episode of *Gunsmoke* was introduced by none other than John Wayne. Positioned behind a hitching post, Wayne directly addressed the camera, telling viewers that *Gunsmoke* was the first TV western in which he would feel comfortable appearing. Linking the program to Hollywood's prestigious, big-budget westerns, Wayne's endorsement was obviously a self-conscious attempt by CBS to legitimize *Gunsmoke* by setting it apart from typical juvenile fare.

The impact of the adult western was stunning and immediate. In the 1958–59 television season, there were 28 prime-time westerns crowding the network schedule. That year seven westerns (*Gunsmoke; Wagon Train; Have Gun, Will Travel; The Rifleman; Maverick; Tales of Wells Fargo;* and *The Life and Legend of Wyatt Earp*) ranked among the top ten most-watched network programs. But the extraordinary commercial success of the television western was not without its detractors. Although adult westerns displayed characters with more psychological complexity and plots with more moral ambiguity than their juvenile counterparts, the resolution of conflict still involved violent confrontations that left saloons, main streets, and landscapes littered with the dead and dying. The body count attracted the scorn of a number of concerned citizens—but by far the most powerful and threatening figure to speak out against such violence was Newton Minow. On May 9, 1961, soon after being appointed the chair of the Federal Communications

Dr. Quinn, Medicine Woman, Jane Seymour, 1993–98.
Courtesy of the Everett Collection

Commission (FCC) by President John F. Kennedy, Minow delivered his "vast wasteland" speech to a meeting of the National Association of Broadcasters. In this famous harangue, the FCC chairman singled out the TV western for special denunciation. After roundly condemning the "violence, sadism, murder, western badmen, western good men" on television, Minow rebuked westerns as a hindrance in the not-so-cold propaganda war with the Soviet bloc. "What will the people of other countries think of us when they see our western badmen and good men punching each other in the jaw in between the shooting?" Minow asked. "What will the Latin American or African child learn from our great communications industry? We cannot permit television in its present form to be our voice overseas."

In part because of such criticism from high places, and in part because of burnout in the mass audience, the western would, once again, be rewritten in the 1960s. As the networks attempted to de-emphasize vi-

olence, the domestic western emerged as a kinder, gentler programming trend. In contrast to action-oriented westerns dealing with the adventures of law officers (*The Deputy*), bounty hunters (*Have Gun, Will Travel*), professional gunmen (*Gunslinger*), scouts (*Wagon Train*), cowpunchers (*Rawhide*), gamblers (*Maverick*), and trail-weary loners (*The Westerner*), the domestic western focused on the familial. The patriarchal Murdoch Lancer and his two feuding sons in *Lancer,* the matriarchal Victoria Barkley and her brood in *The Big Valley,* and the Cannon clan in *The High Chaparral*—all were ranching families in talky melodramas that attempted to replicate the success of the Cartwrights of *Bonanza* fame (Lorne Greene's Ben, Pernell Roberts's Adam, Dan Blocker's Hoss, and Michael Landon's Little Joe). Television's most distinguished domestic western—and the first western series to be televised in color—*Bonanza* ranked among the top ten TV shows for ten of its 14 seasons and for three consecutive years from 1964 to 1967 was the nation's most-watched program.

Unfortunately, this gloss of the western cannot do justice to all of the interesting wrinkles in the genre. The innovations of series like *Branded* and *Kung Fu* are lost in such a brief accounting—and comedic westerns like *The Wild, Wild West* and *F Troop* can be mentioned only in passing. It is also impossible to catalog the accomplishments and contributions of the many talented artists who brought the western to life on television—whether working behind the camera (Lewis Milestone, Sam Fuller, Robert Altman, and Sam Peckinpah, for instance) or in front of it (Amanda Blake, Ward Bond, Richard Boone, Robert Culp, Clint Eastwood, Linda Evans, James Garner, Steve McQueen, Hugh O'Brian, Barbara Stanwyck, and Milburn Stone, to name a few). Suffice it to say that this dinosaur of a programming form once attracted many of television's most creative storytellers and most compelling performers.

In fact, no one was really surprised in 1987 when J. Fred MacDonald wrote the TV western's obituary in his book, *Who Shot the Sheriff?* Declaring that the western was "no longer relevant or tasteful," MacDonald noted the irony that "the generation [baby boomers] that once made the western the most prolific form of TV programming has lived to see a rare occurrence in American popular culture: the death of a genre." Indeed, between 1970 and 1988, fewer than 28 new westerns in total were introduced as regular network series. The last time a western made the top ten list of weekly prime-time programs was in 1973 when *Gunsmoke* was ranked eighth. With the exception of the strange popularity in the early 1980s of made-for-TV movies starring singer Kenny Rogers in the role of

Big Valley, Barbara Stanwyck, Linda Evans, Richard Long, Lee Majors, Peter Breck, 1965–69.
Courtesy of the Everett Collection

"The Gambler," the thunder of the western has been silenced in prime time.

Even so, after the publication of MacDonald's book, the TV western would have at least one more moment of glory when the adaptation of Larry McMurtry's epic western novel *Lonesome Dove* became the television event of the 1988–89 season. The highest-rated miniseries in five years, *Lonesome Dove* documented the final days of a lifelong partnership between two characters who represent distinctly different models of manhood: Woodrow Call and Augustus "Gus" McCrae. Call enacted the strong, silent tradition of the western hero. Like John Wayne's characters in *Red River* (Tom Dunson) and *The Searchers* (Ethan Edwards), Call was a powerful, tireless, generally humorless leader who outwardly feared no enemy, though his rugged individualism drove him toward the misery of self-imposed isolation. Call was masterfully portrayed by Tommy Lee Jones—but it was Robert Duval's performance of McCrae that stole the show. Where Call's outlook was utilitarian, Gus's was romantic. In some ways, Gus resembled the funny, spirited sidekicks of westerns past: Andy

Devine in *Stagecoach,* Walter Brennan in *Red River,* Pat Brady in *The Roy Rogers Show,* or Dennis Weaver and Ken Curtis in *Gunsmoke.* But in *Lonesome Dove,* the eccentric sidekick achieved equal status with the strong silent hero—and as a counterpoint to Call, Gus rewrote the meaning of the western hero. Valuing conversation, irony, the personal, and the passionate, Gus openly shed tears over the memory of a sweetheart. In a genre marred by misogyny since the publication of *The Virginian* in 1902, Gus was no woman-hater. Instead, Gus actively sought the company of women, not merely for sexual gratification, but for their conversation and civilization: he was as comfortable around women as he was around men. The rewriting of the western hero in the Gus character, then, goes a long way toward explaining why *Lonesome Dove* attracted a mammoth audience in which the women viewers actually outnumbered the men. For a story in a genre that has traditionally been written almost exclusively by men for men, this was no small accomplishment.

At the end of *Lonesome Dove,* Call returns to Texas after leading the first cattle drive to Montana. The quest for untamed land beyond the reach of bankers, lawyers, and women has been costly for Call. Narrow graves scattered along the trail north contain the remains of men who served with Call in the Texas Rangers, who worked with him in the Hat Creek Cattle Company, and who looked to him for friendship, leadership, and discipline. As Call surveys the ruins of the forlorn settlement that he once called his headquarters, he is approached by a young newspaper reporter from San Antonio. An agent of the expanding civilization that Call has spent a lifetime loathing and serving, the reporter presses the uncooperative Call for an interview. "They say you are a man of vision," says the reporter. Reflecting with anguish on the deaths of his friends (including Gus, whose dying words were "What a party!"), Call replies, "A man of vision, you say? Yes, a hell of a vision."

As the final words of the miniseries, "hell of a vision" spoke to Call's disillusionment with the dream of Montana as "Cattleman's Paradise"—a vision that inspired the tragic trail drive. Defeated and alone, his invading heart had, finally, been chastened. But in punctuating what appears to be the great last stand of the cowboy on the small screen, "hell of a vision" takes on even more profound connotations as an epitaph—an epitaph for the television western.

JIMMIE L. REEVES

See also **Cheyenne; Gunsmoke; Wagon Train; Warner Brothers Presents; Walt Disney Programs; Westinghouse-Desilu Playhouse; Zorro**

Further Reading

Barabas, SuzAnne, and Gabor Barabas, *Gunsmoke: A Complete History and Analysis of the Legendary Broadcast Series with a Comprehensive Episode-by-Episode Guide to Both the Radio and Television Programs,* Jefferson, North Carolina: McFarland, 1990

Buscombe, Edward, editor, *The BFI Companion to the Western,* New York: Atheneum, 1988

Fagen, Herb, *White Hats and Silver Spurs : Interviews with 24 Stars of Film and Television Westerns of the Thirties Through the Sixties,* Jefferson, North Carolina: McFarland, 1996

Fitzgerald, Michael G., and Boyd Magers, *Ladies of the Western: Interviews with Fifty-One More Actresses from the Silent Era to the Television Westerns of the 1950s and 1960s,* Jefferson, North Carolina: McFarland, c. 2002

Jackson, Ronald, *Classic TV Westerns: A Pictorial History,* Seacaucus, New Jersey: Carol, 1994

Lentz, Harris M., *Television Westerns Episode Guide: All United States Series, 1949–1996,* Jefferson, North Carolina: McFarland, 1997

MacDonald, J. Fred., *Who Shot the Sheriff?: The Rise and Fall of the Television Western,* New York: Praeger, 1987

Marsden, Michael T., and Jack Nachbar, "The Modern Popular Western: Radio, Television, Film, and Print," in *A Literary History of the American West,* Fort Worth: Texas Christian University Press, 1987

Peel, John, *Gunsmoke Years: The Behind-the-Scenes Story,* Las Vegas, Nevada: Pioneer, 1989

West, Richard, *Television Westerns: Major and Minor Series, 1946–1978,* Jefferson, North Carolina: McFarland, 1987

Yoggy, Gary A., *Riding the Video Range: The Rise and Fall of the Western on Television,* Jefferson, North Carolina: McFarland, 1994

Yoggy, Gary A., editor, *Back in the Saddle: Essays on Western Film and Television Actors,* Jefferson, North Carolina: McFarland, 1998

Westinghouse-Desilu Playhouse

U.S. Anthology Series

Westinghouse-Desilu Playhouse, an anthology series broadcast on CBS between 1958 and 1960, never received the critical acclaim of *Playhouse 90* or *Studio One;* nor did it last as long as those two dramatic programs. However, among the episodes in its brief run were two productions that, in effect, served as pilots for *The Twilight Zone* and *The Untouchables,* two of the most memorable (and most widely syndicated in reruns) television shows of the 1960s.

Westinghouse-Desilu Playhouse was produced by Desilu, a telefilm production company owned by Desi Arnaz and Lucille Ball that owed its genesis and initial success to a single series—*I Love Lucy* (CBS, 1951–57). By the late 1950s, the company was producing, through a variety of financial arrangements (wholly owning, coproducing, leasing of facilities and personnel), several situation comedies and western dramas. *Desilu Playhouse* was to be the realization of Arnaz's dream to make Desilu the most significant telefilm production company and to give himself the opportunity for creative play and control beyond his role as producer and actor on *I Love Lucy* and *The Lucy-Desi Comedy Hour* (an hour-long comedy series with the cast and characters of *I Love Lucy* that aired once a month during the 1957–58 television season). Departing from the standard practice of networks com-

mitting to series only after a sponsor had agreed to bankroll production costs, CBS bought *Desilu Playhouse* on the strength of the Desilu track record and with a promise that *The Lucy-Desi Comedy Hour* would be among the planned package of dramas, comedies, and musical spectaculars.

Westinghouse committed to sponsorship a month after the sale to CBS in early 1958, agreeing to a record of $12 million production-cost outlay. The company was already sponsor of the prestigious anthology series *Studio One,* but that show was canceled shortly after the deal with Desilu. Historians as well as former personnel of Desilu and Westinghouse suggest that it was Westinghouse president Mark Cresap's love of *I Love Lucy* and the persuasiveness of the charming Arnaz—who promised Cresap that the series would double Westinghouse's business in the first year—that encouraged the company to lay out so much money for the telefilmed anthology series.

The first episode of the *Westinghouse-Desilu Playhouse,* which aired in October 1958, was "Lucy Goes to Mexico," a *Lucy-Desi Hour* with guest star Maurice Chevalier. The following week the first dramatic hour premiered, "Bernadette" (a biography of Saint Bernadette, the young girl claiming visitation from the Virgin Mary in 19th-century Lourdes, France), starring

Pier Angeli. Despite Arnaz's claim that the series would never show anything offensive to children, its highest-rated telecasts were the two hours of "The Untouchables," featuring Robert Stack as Eliot Ness, leader of the crack FBI team who pursued Al Capone and other gangsters during Prohibition. When *The Untouchables* became a regular series on ABC in 1959, it was the subject of great controversy because of its violence and allegedly negative stereotypes of Italian Americans.

Westinghouse-Desilu Playhouse did not survive long for a variety of reasons—the show's inability to attract big-star guests every week, the waning power of the anthology series form due to cost and subject matter, the growing popularity of other dramatic programming (such as westerns and cop shows), and the divorce of Ball and Arnaz, which ended their partnership as Lucy and Ricky Ricardo as well. Although *Westinghouse-Desilu Playhouse* did prove Desilu to be multifaceted at telefilm production, Arnaz did not get a chance to expand his acting range, and the musical spectaculars he had envisioned producing for the series fell short of the quantity and quality promised to Westinghouse. The legacy of the series lies in its launching of *The Twilight Zone* and *The Untouchables* and its continuation of *The Lucy-Desi Hour*, which still appears regularly in syndicated reruns.

MARY DESJARDINS

See also **Anthology Drama; Arnaz, Desi; Ball, Lucille**

Host
Desi Arnaz

Westinghouse Spokesperson
Betty Furness

Producers
Desi Arnaz, Bert Granet

Programming History
48 episodes
CBS

October 1958–September 1959	Monday 10:00–11:00
October 1959–June 1960	Friday 9:00–10:00

Further Reading

Anderson, Christopher, *Hollywood TV: The Studio System in the Fifties,* Austin: University of Texas Press, 1994

Andrew, Bart, *The "I Love Lucy" Book,* New York: Doubleday, 1985

Sanders, Coyness Steven, and Tom Gilbert, *Desilu: The Story of Lucille Ball and Desi Arnaz,* New York: Morrow, 1993

Weyman, Ron (1915–)

Canadian Producer

The story of Ron Weyman is the story of the beginning of film drama on Canadian national television in the 1960s and early 1970s, a time when there were no full-length dramatic features being made on a regular basis in Canada. In Weyman's own words, "I was in the business of getting home-town (i.e., Canadian) writers to write films, which would in fact be feature pictures. They could then break through the artificial relationship (as I saw it) between television and the screen."

Weyman, an executive producer of film drama, took on this mission in the midst of a varied career. In the 1950s, he spent a number of years with the National Film Board of Canada (NFB) as producer, director, writer, and editor of more than 20 films. He traveled extensively and learned the craft of shooting film on location, a skill that he eventually brought back to the Canadian Broadcasting Corporation (CBC), where he was responsible for moving the CBC into the production of filmed series and encouraging a corporate commitment to dramatic film production.

Several years earlier, when technologies had improved and business had changed to the point that the U.S. model of the filmed series obliterated the live-television anthology genre, Weyman had begun to explore the possibilities offered by film in a form new to Canada—the serial. Serials were still studio-bound in Canada, but Weyman put film crews out on locations across the land to film sequences for insertion into the stories. The response was remarkable. Viewers loved to see where they lived—and other places in their sprawling country—on television. At the same time, with Weyman's support, Philip Keately was producing four or five stories in his limited series *Cariboo Country*—on film, on location in the Chilcotin.

The relationship between the National Film Board and the CBC was characterized at this time by uneasy and intermittent cooperation. Opinions on the relationship are divided. It is clear that as far as the medium of film—as opposed to kinescope copies of "live" or "live to tape"—productions were concerned, the two agencies were rivals in some areas. As in many other countries, film was considered to be the paramount medium in a hierarchy of entertainment that excluded theater but included radio and television. When the question of television drama on film was raised, the perceived wisdom was that this was the NFB's job. When both agencies were urged to coproduce fictional films for Canada's centennial year (1967), the premise was that CBC director-producers understood actors and NFB producers and directors (their roles were separate in film but not in television) understood film. Inevitably, this led to internal conflicts and overspent budgets. The result was three rather ordinary dramas on film, broadcast on the CBC flagship Sunday-night anthology *Festival*. The one remarkable color film from that period, *The Paper People*, did not involve the NFB. Physically removed from the working headquarters of the CBC (English) language division, Weyman and his crews and editors were free from middle management's interference—and were seen as a drama production unit of their own.

The result of this freedom was the hit series *Wojeck* (a concept that was run through the Hollywood blender to emerge as the bland *Quincy*) and *Corwin*, a medical series. Meanwhile, with David Gardner, Weyman also produced another hit series, *Quentin Durgens, M.P.*, about an idealistic member of Parliament. This program was shot on tape but still went on location for part of each episode and made a star of actor Gordon Pinsent. Weyman also produced a half-hour comedy program set in an 1837 pioneer settlement, *Hatch's Mill*, and *McQueen: The Actioneer*, a series about a newspaper columnist.

The common thread in all of these works, even *Hatch's Mill*, was engagement with topical social issues, an examination of the uses and abuses of power, and questions of individual and communal responsibility. Most episodes raised uncomfortable questions for the audience and often chose not to present the easy answers supplied by most television drama at that time. Within the series form, Weyman fused the documentary style and spirit of inquiry with the personalized focus of continuing characters, who were supplied with literate dialogue, and the subtext, nuance, and structural freedoms of fiction.

Weyman's influence continues to be felt in the work of producer Maryke McEwan, who began with the docudramas of *For the Record*, shaped the series *Street Legal*, and then returned to documentary and docudrama specials. Many successful series in Canada still reflect the blend of documentary and drama that Weyman and Keately created more than 30 years ago.

MARY JANE MILLER

See also **Quentin Durgens, M.P.; Wojeck**

Ron Weyman. Born in Kent, England, 1915. Studied briefly at Art Students' League in New York City. Married: Giovanna; two sons. Served as lieutenant-commander RCNVR RN, on destroyer escort duty in North Atlantic, aboard landing craft at Normandy during the D-Day invasion, and in Southeast Asia, 1940–45. Producer, writer, and director, more than 20 films, National Film Board of Canada, 1946–54; director and producer, CBC, 1954–80; author of books, since 1980. Recipient: Venice Film Festival First Award; Canadian Film Awards First Award.

Television Series (selected)

1961	*Jake and the Kid*
1965	*The Serial*
1966, 1968	*Wojeck*
1966–69	*Quentin Durgens, M.P.*
1969–71	*Corwin*
1969–70	*McQueen: The Actioneer*
1970–71	*The Manipulators*

Films (selected shorts)

The Safety Supervisor (writer and director), 1947; *After Prison, What?* (writer and director), 1951; *Inland Seaport* (writer and director), 1953; *Men in Armour* (writer and director), 1954; *Man Is a Universe* (writer and director), 1954; *The Research Director* (director), 1954; *Problem Clinic* (director), 1955; *Sable Island* (writer), 1956; *Railroad Town* (writer), 1956.

Wheel of Fortune

U.S. Game Show

With a global audience of more than 100 million and lifetime profit estimates as high as $4 billion, *Wheel of Fortune* is the most popular television game show in the world. *Daily Variety* even speculates, "*Wheel of Fortune* could indeed be the most widely watched and wildly profitable television show ever" (Frankel, p. A1). From its first airing in the United States in 1975 to its many global incarnations today, *Wheel of Fortune* has resonated the world over.

The goal of the game is for contestants (and home viewers) to solve a secret word puzzle, knowing only the category and length of the word or phrase, by guessing the letters it contains and accruing dollars and prizes for each correct guess. Play is determined by the titular Wheel of Fortune. Three contestants take turns spinning the giant wheel, which contains a set of wedges each labeled with dollar amounts, prizes, or penalties. If the contestant lands on a dollar amount or prize wedge, she chooses a consonant she hopes is in the word puzzle. If it is, she is awarded that dollar amount multiplied by the number of times the letter appears or the single prize, and gets another turn. If not, play moves on to the next contestant. It is also possible to land on such wedges as "Bankrupt" and "Lose a Turn," and contestants may choose to buy a vowel rather than spin the wheel. A contestant may solve the puzzle at any time, and if correct, he keeps the money and prizes he has accrued since the beginning of that round. The game generally goes four rounds, and whoever has accumulated the most cash and prizes at the end of those rounds is the overall winner. This contestant then plays a bonus round for an additional prize.

Wheel of Fortune first aired on the NBC daytime schedule on January 6, 1975. The program was created by Merv Griffin, who was inspired by the kids' game Hangman and added the wheel concept to make the game more exciting (and less morbid). The pilot was originally titled "Shopper's Bazaar," because contestants spent their round winnings on displayed merchandise in themed rooms, such as "Things for Outside" and "Trips." In the late 1980s, the U.S. version dropped this format when producers decided it slowed down the pacing of the show, plus contestants complained that they had to pay outrageous taxes on the merchandise and thus preferred to receive cash. However, some global versions of the show have retained the shopping element.

The hosts of *Wheel of Fortune*'s original pilot were Chuck Woolery and Edd "Kookie" Byrnes; only Woolery remained for the show's official run, however. Woolery left the show in December 1981 after a futile demand for a substantial pay hike, and Pat Sajak then joined *Wheel*, followed a year later by Vanna White, who replaced original hostess Susan Stafford in December 1982.

Wheel of Fortune.
Photo courtesy of Wheel of Fortune/Steve Crise

In 1983 *Wheel of Fortune* split into two versions: NBC kept a version of the show on its daytime schedule but sold the syndication rights to King World Productions for only $50,000, a stunning figure given how much the show has earned in syndication since. The syndicated version, which initially differed from its daytime counterpart only in offering richer prizes, began airing in the early-evening prime-time access slot on local stations across the nation.

Wheel of Fortune exploded in popularity after the move to prime time and became the top-rated syndicated show in 1984. It has largely owned that title since, sharing it only occasionally with another Griffin-created game show, *Jeopardy!* *Wheel* also achieved pop culture icon status by the mid-1980s, as Vanna White appeared on the cover of *Newsweek* in 1986, Pat Sajak was mocked on *Saturday Night Live,* and home versions of the show flew off of store shelves.

This popularity also had global dimensions. In 1981 Australia became the first country to produce its own licensed version of the show, starring hosts Ernie Sigley and Adriana Xenides. Since then, locally produced versions of *Wheel of Fortune* have appeared in more than 25 countries, including Belgium *(Rad Van Fortuin),* Brazil *(Roletrando Novelas),* Croatia *(Kolo Srece),* Denmark *(Lykkehjulet),* Finland *(Onnen Pyora),* France *(Le roué de la fortune),* Italy *(Le Ruota Della Fortuna),* Germany *(Glucksrad),* and the United Kingdom. A raft of additional countries air the syndicated U.S. version, including the Philippines and Columbia.

As this list attests, *Wheel of Fortune* has enormous global popularity. In part, this is because of the worldwide popularity of game shows in general. Such programs are relatively cheap to produce, allowing nations with less affluent television systems to satisfy their audiences' desire for indigenous programming instead of foreign imports. Further, the inherent qualities of live television and audience participation lend excitement to the genre, as does the combined display of sexuality and commodification, a factor explored by John Fiske in *Television Culture.* Finally, the allure of the television personality is provided by the host figures, as the 1980s American fascination with Vanna White and her fashions illustrates.

However, *Wheel of Fortune* has succeeded well beyond the typical game show. Partly this is because of its simplicity. It is easy for the average person to play, both on the set and at home, and especially in comparison to more knowledge-based shows like *Jeopardy!* It equally balances qualities of skill and luck. Contestant and home viewer play also strongly complement each other: contestants hope to accumulate as much money as possible in a round, so they often choose not to answer the puzzle until they have guessed most of the letters. This both raises suspense, given the possible bankruptcies and lost turns along the way, and allows the game player at home the satisfaction of shouting out the answer before the contestants do.

Finally, the format of the show is adaptable to varied cultural circumstances. As Michael Skovmand has illustrated in his study of *Wheel of Fortune* and four of its global versions (U.S., German, Scandinavian, and Danish), the show is generally homogeneous across its various versions, but there are significant differences: the European word puzzles are generally more challenging than the U.S. ones; the American version has a high level of audience participation with the on-stage contestants compared with little in the German version and none in the Danish version; and the U.S. version has a gaudy, glittery set, while the German incarnation displays matter-of-fact decor.

CHRISTINE BECKER

*See also **Jeopardy;*** **Quiz and Game Shows**

Wheel of Fortune (U.S.)

Talent

Host (daytime, 1975–81)	Chuck Woolery
Host (daytime, 1981–88)	Pat Sajak
Host (daytime, 1989)	Rolf Benirschke
Host (daytime, 1989–91)	Bob Goen
Host (syndication, 1983–)	Pat Sajak
Hostess (daytime, 1975–82)	Susan Stafford
Hostess (daytime & synd., 1982–)	Vanna White
Announcer (1975–88)	Jack Clark
Announcer (1975–82; 1989–)	Charlie O'Donnell

Producers

Creator/executive producer	Merv Griffin
Producer (1995–)	Harry Friedman
Producer (1985–95)	Nancy Jones

Programming History

NBC	
January 1975–June 1989	Weekdays
January 1991–September 1991	Weekdays
CBS	
July 1989–January 1991	Weekdays
Syndication	
1983–present	

Further Reading

Fiske, John, *Television Culture,* London: Routledge, 1987

Frankel, Daniel, "TV's Best Bet?" *Daily Variety* (November 5, 2002)

Moran, Albert, *Copycat Television: Globalisation, Program Formats, and Cultural Identity,* Luton, England: University of Luton Press, 1998

Schwartz, David, Steve Ryan, and Fred Wostbrock, *The Encyclopedia of TV Game Shows,* New York: Checkmark Books, 1988; 3rd edition, 1999

Skovmand, Michael, "Barbarous TV International: Syndicated Wheel of Fortune," in *Media Cultures: Reappraising Transnational Media,* edited by Michael Skovmand and Kim Christian Schroeder, London: Routledge, 1992

Wheldon, Huw (1916–1986)

British Producer, Media Executive

Sir Huw Wheldon was one of the leading figures among BBC television program makers in the 1960s and a top BBC administrator in the 1970s. A man of profound intellect and understanding, he inspired great loyalty among those who had the privilege of working with him.

After a distinguished war career, Wheldon became the arts council director for Wales and was awarded an OBE for his contributions to the Festival of Britain. Joining the BBC publicity department in 1952, he quickly established himself as a gifted television presenter with the children's program *All Your Own.* Wheldon's greatest contribution to modern television in Britain was his editorship of the arts program *Monitor* from 1958 to 1964. He both produced the program and appeared as its principal interviewer and anchor, surrounding himself with a brilliant team of young directors, which included David Jones, Ken Russell, and Melvyn Bragg. Wheldon was a wonderful encourager. He made a major contribution to the work of young directors like Ken Russell, whose career was boosted by his *Monitor* film on the life of Edward Elgar.

Wheldon made *Monitor* the seminal magazine program of the arts. As interviewer, he guided his audience by his readiness to learn and to inquire rather than to pontificate. His sensitivity to language and his skilled use of film sequences made *Monitor* the outstanding arts program of its day. Though some criticized his editorship as promoting a "middle culture" that was neither high art nor pop art, *Monitor* captured and held a large and varied audience. Wheldon described this group as "a small majority, the broad section of the public well-disposed to the arts."

The second part of Wheldon's career was as a manager and administrator. He became head of documen-

tary programs in 1962, a post that was enlarged the following year to head of music and documentary programs. He proved himself a good administrator who could detect and promote real talent. At that time Wheldon believed it was difficult to find superior documentary makers outside the department, and he seldom used freelancers. Three years later, however, when he became controller of programs, he accepted the value of the BBC's employing brilliant freelance filmmakers such as Jack Gold, Ken Russell, and Patrick Garland. In 1968 Wheldon succeeded Kenneth Adam as director of BBC television.

The post was later redesignated as managing director, and in that position Wheldon was committed to three conflicting objectives: to maintain and enhance standards; to secure at least half of the viewing audience in competition with ITV; and to contain costs in an era of inflation. Wheldon easily maintained and enhanced standards, but the challenge of competitive scheduling was formidable. His published paper *The British Experience in Television* revealed how the BBC television audience as a whole suffered because the ITV companies ran very popular programs such as *Coronation Street* and *Emergency Ward 10* at 7:30 P.M., thus winning the audience in the early evening and keeping it. Wheldon's solution was to fight like with like, pitting film against film, current affairs against current affairs. He wrote, "Both BBC-1 and ITV had to adopt broadly competitive policies if they were to remain, each of them in a 50–50 position. Neither could afford to be in a 20–80 position.... A 50–50 position was achieved in the sixties and, broadly speaking, has prevailed ever since."

Containing costs was an ever-harder task; the BBC employed the management consultants McKinsey to make recommendations, and as a result of their report, the corporation, through the efforts of Wheldon and others, introduced a system of total costing. Under this system, individual programs were charged a true proportion of the overheads. The prospect of employment casualization worried the broadcasting unions; every time Wheldon imposed cutbacks, the unions became restive. Wheldon believed that 70 percent of the program staff should be on permanent budget, and the other 30 percent on temporary or short-term contracts.

Sir Ian Trethowan, who succeeded Wheldon as managing director of television, described Wheldon's style of leadership as tending toward the flamboyant and inspirational. Wheldon was also a shrewd professional broadcaster, with a passion for the public-service role of the BBC. He believed it was the BBC's organizational foundation that made it possible to work well and achieve excellence. For Wheldon, the singularity of the BBC lay in its privileged position. Supported by the license fee, and armed with all the radio channels and two television channels, it could afford excellence.

Huw Wheldon was perhaps the last great leader in BBC television; none of his successors measured up to his achievements. He was described as the "last of the great actor-managers," but such a judgment underestimates a man who was much more than a performer. It is fascinating to speculate what would have happened if age had not debarred him from succeeding Charles Curran as director general. Instead, the job went to his immediate successor as managing director of television, Ian Trethowan. It was Wheldon's misfortune that his luck ran out just when he could have made his greatest contribution to the fortunes of the BBC as director general.

ANDREW QUICKE

See also **British Television; Russell, Ken**

Huw Wheldon. Born in Wales, 1916. Attended schools in Wales and Germany. Served in armed forces during World War II; Military Cross, 1944. Publicity officer, BBC, 1952; producer and presenter, various children's programs; editor and presenter, arts program *Monitor,* 1957–64, commissioning first films from Ken Russell, John Schlesinger, and Humphrey Burton; head of documentary and music programs, 1963–65, and controller of programs, 1965–68; managing director of television, BBC, 1968, deputy director general, BBC, 1976; after retirement from senior posts at the BBC, continued to work as a writer and presenter. President, Royal Television Society, 1979–85. Officer of the Order of the British Empire. Died 1986.

Television Series (presenter)

1954	*All Your Own*
1958–64	*Monitor* (also editor)
1977	*Royal Heritage* (also co-writer)

Publications

Monitor: An Anthology, 1962
"British Traditions in a World Wide Medium," 1973
"The Achievement of Television: A Lecture," 1975
"The British Experience in Television," 1976

Further Reading

Bakewell, Joan, with Nicholas Garnham, *The New Priesthood: British Television Today,* London: Allen Lane, 1970
Ferris, Paul, *Sir Huge: The Life of Huw Wheldon,* London: Joseph, 1990

Whicker, Alan (1925–)

British Broadcast Journalist

Alan Whicker is a globe-trotting television commentator without equal. For some 40 years, on behalf of both the BBC and independent British television networks, he has roamed far and wide in search of the eccentric, the ludicrous, and the socially revealing aspects of everyday life as lived by some of the more colorful of the world's inhabitants.

Since the late 1950s, when the long-running *Whicker's World* documentary series was first screened, Whicker—a former journalist and reporter for television's *Tonight* program (he was once reported dead while working as a war correspondent in Korea)—has probed and dissected the often secretive and unobserved private worlds of the rich and famous, rooting out the most implausible and sometimes ridiculous characters after gaining admittance to the places where they conduct their leisure hours. These have ranged from fabulously appointed cruise ships and the Orient Express to cocktail parties, world tours, health spas, and gentlemen's clubs. His focus has been truly international, with series from Australia, the Indian subcontinent, and Hong Kong, as well as Britain and the United States.

Whicker's satire is so subtle it is often almost undetectable. The objects of his interest are allowed to condemn or recommend themselves and their way of life almost entirely through their own words and appearances, with often little more than the odd encouraging question or aside from Whicker himself. With long-practiced ease and studied diffidence, he infiltrates the most select clubs and institutions and moves almost invisibly from person to person, seeking out the most promising individuals and generally being more than amply rewarded with the results. Never aggressive in his questioning and carefully cultivating the image of the relaxed but politely interested expatriate ready to accept the world as it comes, he has lured countless individuals into allowing him a privileged glimpse of sometimes extraordinary lives.

Over the years Whicker has on occasion concentrated his attention on a single individual, usually someone of immense influence or prestige who is rarely seen in the public eye. Attracted by the air of mystery surrounding such personages, he has drawn general conclusions about the problems and privileges of living with wealth and power through his detailed portraits of such enigmatic and sometimes deeply disturbed (and disturbing) figures as billionaire John Paul Getty, Paraguay's General Stroessner, and Haiti's greatly feared dictator "Papa Doc" Duvalier. Sometimes the tone is openly critical, but more often the viewer is allowed to draw her or his own conclusions.

Whicker's World, over the years, has consistently claimed a place in the top ten ratings, and Whicker himself has been widely recognized for his talents as a social commentator, winning numerous major awards.

DAVID PICKERING

See also **British Programming;** *Tonight*

Alan Donald Whicker. Born in Cairo, Egypt, August 2, 1925. Attended Haberdashers' Aske's School, London. Served as captain in Devonshire Regiment, World War II; director, Army Film and Photo Section with British 8th Army and U.S. 5th Army. Newspaper war correspondent in Korea; foreign correspondent, novelist, writer, and radio broadcaster; joined BBC television, 1957, and presented nightly film reports from around the world for *Tonight,* as well as studio interviews and outside broadcasts; participated in first Telstar two-way transmission at opening of United Nations, 1962; host, *Whicker's World,* BBC, 1959–60; helped launch Yorkshire Television, 1967; left BBC, 1968; producer and host, numerous television specials and documentaries and further series of *Whicker's World;* worked for BBC, 1982–92; returned to ITV, 1992. Fellow, Royal Society of Arts, 1970. Recipient: numerous awards, including Screenwriters Guild Best Documentary Script Award, 1963; Guild of Television Producers and Directors Personality of the Year, 1964; Royal Television Society Silver Medal, 1968; University of California DuMont Award, 1970; Hollywood Festival of TV Best Interview Program Award, 1973; British Academy of Film and Television Arts Dimbleby Award, 1978; *TV Times* Special Award, 1978; Royal Television Society Hall of Fame, 1993.

Television Series

1957–65	*Tonight*
1959–60	*Whicker's World*
1961	*Whicker Down Under*
1962	*Whicker on Top of the World!*
1963	*Whicker in Sweden*
1963	*Whicker in the Heart of Texas*
1963	*Whicker Down Mexico Way*
1964	*Alan Whicker Report Series: The Solitary Billionaire* (J. Paul Getty)
1965–67	*Whicker's World*
1968	*General Stroessner of Paraguay*
1968	*Count von Rosen*
1968	*Papa Doc—The Black Sheep*
1969	*Whicker's New World*
1969	*Whicker in Europe*
1970	*Whicker's Walkabout*
1971	*World of Whicker*
1972	*Whicker's Orient*
1972	*Broken Hill—Walled City*
1972	*Gairy's Grenada*
1972	*Whicker Within a Woman's World*
1973	*Whicker's South Seas*
1973	*Whicker Way Out West*
1974–77	*Whicker's World*
1976	*Whicker's World—Down Under*
1977	*Whicker's World: U.S.*
1978	*Whicker's World: India*
1979	*Whicker's World: Indonesia*
1980	*Whicker's World: California*
1980	*Peter Sellers Memorial Programme*
1982	*Whicker's World Aboard the Orient Express*
1982	*Around Whicker's World in 25 Years*

1982	*Whicker's World—The First Million Miles*
1984	*Whicker's World—A Fast Boat to China*
1984	*Whicker!*
1985	*Whicker's World—Living with Uncle Sam*
1987–88	*Whicker's World—Living with Waltzing Matilda*
1990	*Whicker's World—Hong Kong*
1992	*Whicker's World—A Taste of Spain*
1992	*Around Whicker's World—The Ultimate Package!*
1992	*Whicker's World—The Absolute Monarch*
1993	*Whicker's Miss World*
1993	*Whicker's World—The Sun King*
1994	*Whicker's World Aboard the Real Orient Express*
1994	*Whicker—The Mahatir Interview*
1994	*Pavarotti in Paradise*
1998	*Auntie's Greatest Hits*

Film

The Angry Silence, 1960.

Radio

Start the Week (chair); *Whicker's Wireless World,* 1983; *Around Whicker's World,* 1998; *Whicker's Week,* 1999; *Whicker's New World,* 1999.

Publications (selected)

Within Whicker's World: An Autobiography, 1982
Whicker's New World, 1985
Whicker's World Down Under, 1988
Whicker's World—Take 2, 2000

White, Betty (1922–)

U.S. Actor

One of television's most beloved, talented actresses, Betty White began as a local TV "personality" and then, defying convention, became star and producer of her own nationally broadcast sitcom. In a pair of very different roles on sitcom hits, in the 1970s and 1980s, her skillful acting as part of an ensemble and her way with a comic line earned her acclaim and a loving following—a following that has made her a legend.

Early on, White played leads at Beverly Hills High School. After graduation, she took on stage roles at the Bliss-Hayden Little Theater Group. She began to work as a radio actress as well; local TV quickly followed since it was a natural "option for someone just starting." In 1949 Los Angeles TV personality Al Jarvis called White and gave her her first regular TV assignment. Jarvis took to the airwaves six days a week on KLAC to act as a "disc jockey," to play records just like on radio. Between selections, he delivered commercials, performed in sketches, and conducted interviews. White was hired as his on-air "girl Friday" to do much of the same. Jarvis left in 1952, and soon after White took over full hosting duties.

While still appearing on daily Los Angeles television, White, with two male partners, cofounded Bandy Productions in 1952 to produce her own self-starring situation comedy. A direct outgrowth of some of White's daytime sketches, *Life with Elizabeth* told the story of married couple Elizabeth and Alvin (played by Del Moore). It was an unusual program in several respects, not the least of which was its 28-year-old cocreator, producer, and star. White was one of only two women in the early days of television (Gertrude Berg being the other) to wield creative control both in front of and behind the camera. A second distinctive feature of the program was its nonlinear stories—each episode consisted of three vignettes, three different plots. Leisurely paced, *Elizabeth*'s stories had a ring of *I Love Lucy* about them. While Elizabeth never launched any outrageous schemes, the comic conflicts often grew out of husband Alvin's disapproval of her logic.

Originally, *Elizabeth* aired only in the Los Angeles area, but by 1953 Guild Films began to syndicate the series nationally, and the program was in production until 1955. Afterward, the show's three-act format made it possible for each episode to be divided up and marketed to stations as fillers. As ten-minute segments,

Elizabeth ran successfully and profitably for many years. Betty White earned her first Emmy in 1952 for *Life with Elizabeth.*

While *Elizabeth* was still in production, White moved to NBC and to her own daily daytime variety show. Bandy Production's *The Betty White Show* premiered February 1954. White would appear in the two programs simultaneously for a year. The NBC daytime show ended in early 1955, and White filled the next two years working, primarily, for game show packagers Goodman and Toddson.

In 1957 White co-created the prime-time sitcom *A Date with the Angels.* She played Vicki Angel, and Bill Williams starred as her husband, Gus. More typical in its format and stories than *Life with Elizabeth,* the Angels were newlyweds and were seen fumbling through their first year of wedded bliss. The program aired on ABC for six months before the network retooled it into the comedy-variety vehicle *The Betty White Show.* Lackluster ratings, which inspired the revamping, lingered, and that program ended in April 1958.

Over the next several years, White concentrated on guest work. She was a regular visitor to *The Jack Paar Show,* where her funny, slightly risqué remarks made her an audience favorite. She also was a frequent visitor to daytime, as a game show panelist.

It was on *Password* in 1961 that White met her husband, host Allen Ludden. They were married in Las Vegas in 1963. The Luddens were good friends of actress Mary Tyler Moore and her producer husband Grant Tinker, the two powerhouses behind the hit *The Mary Tyler Moore Show.* When script number 73 for the series came along it called for an "icky sweet Betty White type," and the show's casting director eventually decided to call the genuine article. Though usually thought of as a series regular, White did not make her first appearance on *The Mary Tyler Moore Show* until the program's fourth year, and in her most active season she appeared in only 12 of 26 regularly scheduled episodes. Nevertheless, she made herself an integral part of that show's family and dynamic. As Sue Ann Nivens, the host of "The Happy Homemaker," White created a sparkling presence. Satirizing her own image, White threw herself into the role of a catty, man-chaser who hid her true self behind a gooey shell of sugar. White won Emmys in the 1974–75 and 1975–76 seasons for Best Supporting Actress. She was part of *The Mary Tyler Moore Show*'s final episode in 1977.

After its end White began her own series. The sitcom *The Betty White Show* premiered in 1977 on CBS. Critically acclaimed and costarring such pros as John Hillerman and Georgia Engel, the program faced tough competition on Monday nights, and CBS did not wait

Betty White.
Photo courtesy of Betty White

for the show to build an audience. It was canceled in early 1978.

In 1983 White joined the small, exclusive group of women to have hosted a daytime game show. *Just Men!* had White as host and seven male guest stars who tried to help two female contestants win cars. Though the program lasted only six months, White proved funny and unflappable as "femcee" and won the Emmy for best game show host that year. She remains, to date, the only female winner of that top honor. Back on prime time she took guest roles on *St. Elsewhere* and other shows.

In 1985 White, at age 63, began the biggest hit of her career. *The Golden Girls,* from Disney, reunited three of TV's greatest comediennes: White, Beatrice Arthur, and Rue McClanahan. (From the New York stage it imported Estelle Getty.) A highly anticipated show, it was the biggest hit of NBC's new fall season. At the end of the first year, all three lead actresses were nominated for Emmys. White won for her innocent, adorably ignorant Rose Nylund, whose nature bespoke of a more optimistic and trusting time.

Golden Girls ran for seven years. The program was repackaged, without Arthur, for CBS the following season. *Golden Palace,* with White, McClanahan, and Getty running a Florida hotel, aired for one year. White has continued to act in sitcoms and to do guest appearances and television commercials.

White's eagerly awaited autobiography, *Here We Go Again: My Life in Television,* was published that summer not long after it was announced that she would return to series TV. *Maybe This Time,* a Disney-produced sitcom costarring actress and singer Marie Osmond premiered in the fall of 1995. That same year saw White's induction into the Academy of Television Arts and Sciences' Hall of Fame. Inducted along with Dick Van Dyke, Bill Moyers, and Jim McKay, among others, White was the tenth woman so honored.

CARY O'DELL

See also **Golden Girls, The; Mary Tyler Moore Show, The**

Betty White. Born in Oak Park, Illinois, January 17, 1922. Attended public schools in Beverly Hills, California. Married: Allen Ludden, 1963 (died). Began career with appearances on radio shows; has appeared as star, regular, and guest in various television series, from 1950s. Recipient: Emmy Awards, 1952, 1975, 1976, and 1986. Inductee, Television Academy Hall of Fame, 1996.

Television Series (selected)

1953–55	*Life with Elizabeth*
1954–58	*The Betty White Show*
1957–58	*A Date with the Angels*
1970–77	*The Mary Tyler Moore Show*
1971	*The Pet Set*
1977–78	*The Betty White Show*
1979	*The Best Place to Be*
1980	*The Gossip Columnist*
1985–92	*The Golden Girls*
1992–93	*The Golden Palace*
1993	*Bob*
1995–96	*Maybe This Time*
1998–99	*Disney's Hercules*
1999–2001	*Ladies' Man*

Television Specials and Movies (selected)

1982	*Eunice*
1986	*Walt Disney World's 15th Birthday Celebration* (cohost)
1991	*The Funny Women of Television* (cohost)
1996	*The Story of Santa Claus*
1996	*A Weekend in the Country*
2003	*Stealing Christmas*

Film (selected)

Advice and Consent, 1962; *Dennis the Menace Strikes Again,* 1998; *Hard Rain,* 1998; *Lake Placid,* 1999; *The Story of Us,* 1999.

Stage (selected)

Summer stock presentations from late 1960s: *Guys and Dolls; Take Me Along; The King and I; Who Was That Lady?; Critic's Choice; Bells Are Ringing.*

Publications

Betty White in Person, 1987
Here We Go Again: My Life in Television, 1995

Further Reading

O'Dell, Cary, *Women Pioneers in Television,* Jefferson, North Carolina: McFarland, 1996

Whitfield, June (1925–)

British Comedy Actor

June Whitfield is a durable comedy actor whose entire career has been spent providing excellent support to virtually every major British comedian on radio and television. In the 1950s, she became a radio favorite, playing the perennially engaged Eth in the famous Jimmy Edwards comedy series *Take It from Here,* but her lasting stardom can be attributed to a remarkable succession of television appearances supporting Britain's best-loved comedians and to her long-running sitcom series, *Terry and June.* The list of male comedians with whom Whitfield has worked reads like a *Who's Who* of British comedy talent and includes

June Whitfield.
Photo courtesy of June Whitfield

Benny Hill, Tony Hancock, Frankie Howerd, Morecambe and Wise, and Dick Emery. However, she is most closely associated with Jimmy Edwards, with whom she costarred in a number of comedy playlets under the generic title *Faces of Jim* (*Seven Faces of Jim,* 1961; *Six More Faces of Jim,* 1962; and *More Faces of Jim,* 1963; all BBC). She also appeared in many series with Terry Scott, including *Scott on...* (BBC, 1964–74) and *Terry and June* (BBC, 1979–87), which was a continuation of an earlier series, *Happy Ever After* (BBC, 1974–78).

Whitfield made her debut on television in 1951 in *The Passing Show* (BBC), and later appeared as support to Bob Monkhouse and Derek Goodwin in *Fast and Loose* (BBC, 1954). After guesting in various sitcoms for 12 years, she landed a starring role in *Beggar My Neighbour* (1966–68), a show about ill-matched neighbors.

Terry and June was Whitfield's most famous vehicle, and while her portrayal of a typical long-suffering wife (June Fletcher) with a perennially adolescent husband (Terry Fletcher, played by Terry Scott) did not stretch her talent as an actor, it nevertheless demon-

strated her amazing consistency and willingness to bring the best out of any material. Throughout the 1980s and into the 1990s, she also reestablished herself as a radio star, working with comedian Roy Hudd in *The News Huddlines,* where she demonstrated a hitherto unknown talent for impersonation, particularly with her imitation of Margaret Thatcher.

The "new wave" of comedy that began to make serious inroads into British television in the 1980s provided Whitfield with further opportunities. Comedians Dawn French and Jennifer Saunders used the actor in their sketch show, *French and Saunders* (BBC, 1987–), and Jennifer Saunders later chose her for the role of Mother in *Absolutely Fabulous* (BBC, 1992–96, 2001–).

Absolutely Fabulous was a groundbreaking British sitcom of the 1990s, with a dazzling mix of the politically incorrect, outrageousness, and savage wit. The clever casting of Whitfield as Mother allowed Saunders to utilize the actor's housewife persona in a subversive way, employing dialogue and plot to investigate areas of the character never glimpsed in *Terry and June.* When *Absolutely Fabulous* came to a premature end in 1996, writer Jennifer Saunders used the cast (including Whitfield) in a new, equally outrageous comedy, *Mirrorball* (BBC, 2000), which was intended as a pilot to a series but which actually just convinced Saunders that there was more mileage in the *Absolutely Fabulous* format, to which she returned in 2001.

Absolutely Fabulous and similar shows written by and starring women are no longer rarities on British television, but the majority of Whitfield's career has been spent supporting male comedians who dominated the medium, with most of the programs on which she worked bearing the name of the male star (*The Benny Hill Show* and *The Dick Emery Show,* among others). She is not the only funny woman of British television to have had such a comedy-support career, but she is arguably one of the busiest. One can only lament that it has never been considered viable in British television to produce *The June Whitfield Show.*

DICK FIDDY

*See also **Absolutely Fabulous;** **British Programming***

June Rosemary Whitfield. Born in London, November 11, 1925. Attended Streatham High School; Royal Academy of Dramatic Art, diploma 1944. Married: Timothy John Aitchison, 1955; child: Suzy. Has appeared in revue, musicals, pantomime, films, radio, and television, from 1950s; formed long-running situation comedy partnership with Terry Scott, 1969–88. Officer of the Order of the British Empire, 1985; Commander of the British Empire, 1998. Freeman, City of London, 1982. Recipient: British Comedy Awards' Lifetime Achievement Award, 1994.

Television Series

1954	*Fast and Loose*
1961–63	*Faces of Jim*
1964–74	*Scott on...*
1966–68	*Beggar My Neighbour*
1967	*Hancock's Hour*
1969	*The Best Things in Life*
1969	*The Fossett Saga*
1974–78	*Happy Ever After*
1979–87	*Terry and June*
1990	*Cluedo*
1992–96, 2001–	*Absolutely Fabulous*
1994–95	*What's My Line?*
2000	*Mirrorball* (pilot)

Made-for-Television Movie

2000	*Last of the Blonde Bombshells*

Films (selected)

Carry on Nurse, 1959; *The Spy with a Cold Nose*, 1966; *Carry on Abroad*, 1972; *Bless This House*, 1972; *Carry on Girls*, 1973; *Carry on Columbus*, 1992.

Radio

Take It from Here, 1953–60; *The News Huddlines*, 1984– ; *JW Radio Special*, 1992; *Murder at the Vicarage*, 1993; *A Pocketful of Rye*, 1994; *At Bertram's Hotel*, 1995.

Stage (selected)

A Bedful of Foreigners; Not Now, Darling; An Ideal Husband, 1987; *Ring Round the Moon*, 1988; *Over My Dead Body*, 1989; *Babes in the Wood*, 1990, 1991, 1992; *Cinderella*, 1994.

Publication

...And June Whitfield (autobiography), 2000

Who Wants to Be a Millionaire

U.K. and U.S. Game Show

Who Wants to Be a Millionaire premiered in the United Kingdom on September 4, 1998, produced there by the U.K.-based company Celador, which is also in charge of *Millionaire*'s production in the United States. The American version first appeared on television screens in the summer of 1999 and immediately caused something of a programming sensation. The program uses a combination of trivia questions and educational knowledge to test its contestants, who are preselected in telephone contests. Contestants who answer one question correctly remain in a pool of contenders. This group is further reduced through luck and their success in live rehearsals, where selections are also made based on the on-screen appearance of contestants. Once in the studio, all contestants compete to correctly arrange four answers to a single question. The winner of this round—the contestant who correctly arranges the answers in the shortest possible time—goes on to sit in the "hot seat" facing the host (Regis Philbin in the first U.S. version) and competes for up to $1 million in prize money. As with many game shows, the prizes rise in value as questions rise in difficulty, beginning at the $100 level and going to $200, $300, $500, and $1,000. Questions leading up to the $1,000 level are not particularly difficult and are often played for humor. The $1,000 level also marks a "milestone"; despite incorrect answers above this level, contestants still keep the $1,000. The next tier, in which the prize doubles five times from $1,000 to $32,000, is considerably more difficult and constitutes a more serious level of the game. At $32,000, contestants reach a second milestone, and many contestants consider reaching this level as their primary goal—the following five questions, leading up to the million-dollar peak, are of such difficulty that many contestants fail.

Another distinctive aspect of *Who Wants to Be a Millionaire* is that the game allows its contestants to use outside help in the form of three "lifelines." In the first lifeline, called "50/50," a computer erases two of the four multiple-choice questions. Another lifeline, "ask the audience," polls the audience regarding the correct answer to a question. While the audience guesses are often correct, in some instances contestants have relied on the audience and answered a question incorrectly. The final lifeline, "phone a friend," allows contestants to make a call to one of five preselected friends who posses expertise in an area relevant to the question. These lifelines provide an interesting link between the contestant, the studio audience, and the home audience. Besides the role the lifelines play in the competition itself, they create a close involvement for both the studio and the home audience. This participatory aspect creates a distinctive text-audience relationship that sets *Millionaire* apart from most other shows of its kind.

Millionaire is also particularly pleasurable in its use of contestants considered average or "common people." This seems to create easy identification with on-air contestants and also allows audience members to imagine that they might be in the hot seat rather than the current contestant. This impression is further enhanced by the easy access to the initial selection process via telephone and by the availability of an online version of *Millionaire* hosted by ABC.go.com. Ideologically, the easy identification with highly successful contestants reinforces the myth that within U.S. capitalist culture it is possible for everyone to become successful and rich, the belief that everyone can become a millionaire.

While the structure of the show is generally the same in both the British and U.S. versions, the difficulty level seems to have been lowered in the United States to allow more contestants to win high amounts of prize money and create additional public attention. At the same time, publicity surrounding the program often emphasizes the intellectual capabilities of the most successful contestants. The first $1 million winner, John Carpenter, appeared on *Millionaire* on November 19, 1999, and received significant media attention highlighting his superior mental abilities. Perhaps to generate particularly high ratings for *Millionaire,* host Regis Philbin announced this event on his other show, *Live with Regis and Kelly,* on the morning of the November 19 broadcast.

The fall 1999 and spring 2000 season of *Millionaire* marked the highest ratings for the show, peaking at an audience share of 30 percent. By the fall of 2001, the ratings of *Millionaire* had dropped significantly. While the show had been broadcast up to four times a week at its peak of success, it was reduced to two broadcasts on Monday and Thursday, scheduled against other highly competitive shows. Some of *Millionaire's* ratings in the fall 2001 season were as low as a 10 percent share. While the future of *Who Wants to Be a Millionaire* as a prime-time network show might be in doubt, a syndicated daytime version, with

Regis Philbin.
Photo courtesy of ABC Photo Archives

Meredith Viera as host, has been highly successful in the United States.

OLAF HOERSCHELMANN

See also **Philbin, Regis; Quiz and Game Shows**

Who Wants to Be a Millionaire (U.S.)

Talent

Host (1998–)	Regis Philbin
Host (daytime syndication, 2002–)	Meredith Viera

Creator
Michael P. Davies

Executive Producers
Michael P. Davies, Paul Smith

Supervising Producers
Ann Miller, Michael Binkow, Tiffany Trigg

Director
Mark Gentile

Co–Executive Producer
Leigh Hampton

Senior Producer
Patrick Sheridan

Coordinating Producer
Susan A. Claxton

Programming History
ABC
Thursday, 9:00

Further Reading

Caldwell, John Thornton, *Televisuality: Style, Crisis, and Authority in American Television,* New Brunswick, New Jersey: Rutgers University Press, 1995

DeLong, Thomas A., *Quiz Craze: America's Infatuation with Game Shows,* New York: Praeger, 1991

Fiske, John, "The Discourses of TV Quiz Shows, or School 1 Luck 5 Success 1 Sex," in *Television Criticism: Approaches and Applications,* edited by Leah Vande Berg and Lawrence Wenner, New York: Longman, 1990

Fiske, John, *Television Culture,* London: Routledge, 1987

Holbrook, Morris, *Daytime Television Gameshows and the Celebration of Merchandise: The Price Is Right,* Bowling Green, Ohio: Bowling Green State University Press, 1993

Widows

British Crime Drama

Widows, a drama series of six 52-minute episodes written by Lynda La Plante, was first broadcast on British television in the spring of 1983. The series had a simple, effective conceit, which was initially condensed into the opening credits, in which viewers saw a carefully planned robbery of a security van go badly wrong, with the apparent death of all participants. The widows of the title are the three women left alone by this catastrophe that has befallen Harry's gang. The women decide, under the leadership of Harry's widow, Dolly (Ann Mitchell), to follow through the already-laid plans for the next robbery—which they will conduct themselves after recruiting another recently widowed woman, Bella (Eva Mottley). This simple variation on a traditional crime-story formula—the gang of robbers planning and carrying out a raid under the surveillance of the police—offered a series of pleasures for both male and female viewers in what is traditionally a men's genre.

The series' production company, Euston Films, a wholly owned subsidiary of Thames Television, was set up in 1971 to make high-quality films and film series for television and had a strong track record with the crime genre, being responsible for *Special Branch, The Sweeney, Out,* and *Minder.* Characteristics of the Euston series included London location shooting in a "fast" realist style, working-class and often semicriminal milieus, and sharp scripts. *Widows* offered these familiar pleasures but also engaged with changing ideas of appropriate feminine behavior by audaciously presenting the widows of the title tutoring themselves in criminality so they could be agents, not victims. In this sense, the series, which had Verity Lambert as executive producer and Linda Agran as producer, was clearly a Euston product; the series also must be understood in relation to earlier shows that had tried to insert women into the crime genre—such as *Cagney and Lacey, The Gentle Touch,* and *Juliet Bravo.* The difference with *Widows* was that the women were on the wrong side of the law.

Following the success of the first series of *Widows*—which had six episodes and a continuous narrative—a second series was commissioned, and the two were broadcast together in 1985. Again, the narrative was continuous over the two series, and at the end of *Widows II,* the central character, Dolly Rawlins, was imprisoned. Some years later, in 1995, La Plante, the writer of the first series, produced the final part to what had become a trilogy, *She's Out,* in which Dolly returns. *She's Out* reprises *Widows I* to some extent, in that its climax was a carefully planned train robbery—conducted, spectacularly, by women on horseback—but the general critical consensus was that neither of the sequels quite matched *Widows I.* (La Plante also adapted and produced a remake of *Widows* for a 2002 ABC miniseries of the same name, with Mercedes Ruehl as Dolly and also starring Brooke Shields and Rosie Perez.)

Widows.
Courtesy of ©FremantleMedia Enterprises

Retrospectively, *Widows* is now perhaps most interesting as La Plante's first successful foray into a territory she has made peculiarly her own, the hard world of women in the television crime genre. Her subsequent projects, which include the internationally successful *Prime Suspect,* in which Helen Mirren plays a chief inspector on a murder case, and *The Governor,* in which Janet McTeer plays an inexperienced governor given a prison to run, have tended to place their central female characters within a male hierarchy and visual repertoire. Here the women must both confront the prejudice of their colleagues and successfully inhabit and wield power in the context of law enforcement and criminal justice. In contrast, *Widows,* the first of La Plante's "women in a man's world" dramas, was set explicitly in a criminal milieu, with the women attempting to support themselves through robbery rather than learning how to occupy masculine positions of power. This approach had a series of interesting consequences.

First, the representation of female criminality in the crime series is strongly focused around the figures of the prostitute and the shoplifter, not the ambitious and successful bank robbers viewers find in *Widows.* Thus, the series shook up expectations about what women in crime series can do. Second, because the women are having to learn to perform as men, femininity is "made strange" and becomes a mode of behavior that the women consciously turn on when they need to escape detection. Finally, it should be noted that the heroes of this series, three white, one black, were all working class in origin—although Dolly, well-off from the proceeds of Harry's crimes, listens to opera—and the series thus has a place in the history of honorable endeavor by both Euston Films and La Plante to depict working-class life as diverse and contradictory—and more than comic.

CHARLOTTE BRUNSDON

See also **British Programming; La Plante, Lynda;** *Prime Suspect*

Cast

Dolly Rawlins	Ann Mitchell
Bella O'Reilly	Eva Mottley
Linda Perelli	Maureen O'Farrell
Shirley Miller	Fiona Hendley
Det. Inspector George Resnick	David Calder
Det. Sergeant Alec Fuller	Paul Jesson
Det. Constable Andrews	Peter Machin
Eddie Rawlins	Stanley Meadows
Harry Rawlins	Maurice O'Connell

Producers

Verity Lambert, Linda Agran

Programming History

Six 52-minute episodes
March 16, 1983–April 20, 1983

Further Reading

Alvarado, Manuel, and John Stewart, editors, *Made for Television: Euston Films Limited,* London: British Film Institute, 1985
Baehr, Helen, and Gillian Dyer, editors, *Boxed In: Women and Television,* London: Pandora, 1987

Wild Kingdom

U.S. Wildlife/Nature Program

Mutual of Omaha's Wild Kingdom (also titled *Wild Kingdom*) was one of television's first wildlife/nature programs and stands among the genre's most popular and longest-running examples. *Wild Kingdom* premiered in a Sunday-afternoon time slot on NBC in January 1963 and remained a Sunday-afternoon staple until the start of the 1968–69 television season, when it was moved to Sunday evenings. NBC dropped *Wild Kingdom* from its regular series lineup altogether in April 1971, as part of the programming changes and cutbacks each of the three networks were making at that time in response to the newly created Prime-Time Access Rule. Interestingly, *Wild Kingdom* found its largest audience as a prime-access syndicated program, playing to an estimated 34 million people on 224 stations by 1974, and beating out the likes of *The Lawrence Welk Show* and *Hee Haw* to top the American Research Bureau ratings for syndicated series in October of that year. Many of the episodes airing after 1971 were repackaged reruns from earlier network days, but new episodes continued to be produced and included in the syndicated program packages as well. *Wild Kingdom* was produced and distributed in first-run syndication until the fall of 1988.

The perennial host and figurehead of *Wild Kingdom* was zoologist Marlin Perkins. Perkins began his zoological career as reptile curator at the St. Louis Zoo (Missouri) in 1926. He served as director of the Buffalo Zoo (New York) in the late 1930s and early 1940s, the Lincoln Park Zoo (Chicago) through the 1950s, and finally the St. Louis Zoo, a position he held from 1962 until his death on June 14, 1986. Throughout his career, Perkins was drawn to the medium of television as a means of promoting a conservationist ethic and popularizing a corresponding understanding of wildlife and the natural world.

Perkins initiated his involvement in the production of nature programming in 1945, when television itself was only beginning to work its way into the fabric of American life. Having recently been named director of Lincoln Park Zoo, Perkins began hosting a wildlife television program on a small, local Chicago station, WBKB. He then became the host of *Zoo Parade* in 1949, which began its eight-year run on Chicago station WNBQ before becoming an NBC network show

early in 1950. A precursor of sorts to the regularly featured animal segments on *The Tonight Show* and other late-night talk shows, *Zoo Parade* was a location-bound production (filmed in the reptile house basement) in which Perkins would present and describe the life and peculiarities of Lincoln Park Zoo animals. Soon after his move to the St. Louis Zoo in 1962, Perkins and *Zoo Parade*'s producer-director Don Meier were convinced by representatives of the Mutual of Omaha Insurance Company to create *Wild Kingdom*. Perkins remained involved with the production of *Wild Kingdom* until a year before his death in 1986.

Unlike *Zoo Parade*, *Wild Kingdom* was shot on film almost entirely in the field and featured encounters with wild animals in their natural habitats. Indeed, one of the program's signature features was the footage of Marlin Perkins, or his assistants Jim Fowler and later Stan Brock, pursuing and at times physically engaging with the wildlife-of-the-week, whether that meant mud-wrestling with alligators, struggling to get free from the viselike grip of a massive water snake, running from unexpectedly awakened elephants or seemingly angered sea lions, or jumping from a helicopter onto the back of an elk in the snows of Montana. Edited to emphasize the dangerous, dramatic, or comedic interplay between man and beast, accompanied by the appropriate soundtrack mix of music and natural sound, and always punctuated by the familiar voice-overs of Marlin or Jim, the popular narrative conceit of *Wild Kingdom* was criticized at times by some zoologists and environmentalists for putting entertainment values before those of ecological education. Yet *Wild Kingdom* reflected in precisely these ways many of the dominant ecophilosophical and ecological tenets of its day. Set "out in nature," as one reviewer put it, and structured around the actions of protagonists who have left the ordered world of the zoo to explore the unpredictable and often alien natural landscape, *Wild Kingdom* echoed the conservationist idea of the natural world and the human world as, at best, separate but equal kingdoms.

Many wildlife/nature series since *Wild Kingdom* have developed different and less human-centered narrative strategies with which to represent the natural

Mutual of Omaha's Wild Kingdom, Marlin Perkins feeding a lion cub, 1963–85.
Courtesy of the Everett Collection

world, strategies that may themselves reflect a contemporary shift away from the anthropocentric essence of conservationism toward a more ecocentrically defined environmentalism. In their day, however, Marlin Perkins and Jim Fowler were, in the words of Charles

Seibert, "television's cowboy naturalists," and their weekly rides proved to be among the most popular in television history.

JIM WEHMEYER

Hosts
Marlin Perkins
Jim Fowler
Stan Brock

Programming History
NBC

January 1963–December 1968	Sunday non–prime time
January 1968–June 1968	Sunday 7:00–7:30
January 1969–June 1969	Sunday 7:00–7:30
September 1969–June 1970	Sunday 7:00–7:30
September 1970–April 1971	Sunday 7:00–7:30
1971–1988	First-run syndication

Further Reading

Cimons, Marlene, "It's Not Easy to Deceive a Grebe," *TV Guide* (October 26, 1974)
"How to Capture a Live Fur Coat," *TV Guide* (February 15, 1964)
Kern, J., "Marlin Perkins' Wild Wild Kingdom," *TV Guide* (April 20, 1963)
"Marlin Perkins," in *Variety Obituaries,* New York: Garland, 1988
Rouse, Sarah, and Katharine Loughrey, compilers, *Three Decades of Television: The Catalog of Television Programs Acquired by the Library of Congress, 1949–1979,* Washington, D.C.: Library of Congress, 1989
Siebert, Charles, "The Artifice of the Natural," *Harper's* (February 1993)
Walsh, Patrick, "Television's Dr. Dolittle Returns to the Air," *TV Guide* (February 17, 1968)

Wildlife and Nature Programs

Television has long capitalized on a cultural fascination with the nonhuman, the mysterious, the unknown, the exotic, and the remote aspects of the natural world in the form of programs devoted to the study and presentation of wildlife, geography, and other features of the biological universe. The past decade, however, has seen even greater expansion in wildlife and nature programming. Entire cable channels such as Discovery's

Animal Planet and the National Geographic channel are heavily invested in the genre. Watching such offerings, viewers can "go" to locations normally inaccessible because of physical and fiscal limitations. While there is certainly an entertainment value to such programs, they also play an important educational role. And, like all such offerings, while entertaining and educating, they also construct their own interpretation of

The Wonderful World of Disney: King of the Grizzlies, Wahb the grizzley bear, John Yesno, 1973.
Courtesy of the Everett Collection

"nature" or "the wild" or "the animal kingdom." Indeed, wildlife and nature presentations are among the most prominent in emphasizing television's capacity for "framing" and "constructing" particular points of view, while omitting others.

Current debates over the cinematic, cultural, ethical, and industrial foundations of wildlife and nature programs can be traced to its roots in early questions surrounding developments in visual media. Among the first subjects captured on continuous-motion film during the late 1800s were animals. These early wildlife and nature films were more often perceived as anthropological and ethnographic documents than as entertaining or educational narratives. The cinematic records of distant cultures and wildlife also served as souvenirs for wealthy travelers who embarked on tourist-as-ethnographer safaris. Continuing into the 20th century, cultural and social elites found documenting primitive nature a chic sign of modernity. It was not until the popular masses flooded movie theaters to see these first wildlife films, however, that they were established as a distinct and significant cinematic genre.

The popularity of wildlife and nature programming certainly continued to grow as television entered the American home during the 1950s. During those formative television years, two large categories of wildlife and nature programs emerged, and though they still exist, they are neither mutually exclusive nor exhaustive. The first branch, the nature documentary, follows the conventions of direct-cinema documentary filmmaking. These films involve little to no interference with the subject and focus on simple, scientific documentation of the subject being filmed. The goal of such films is to enlighten audiences about some animal, culture, or environment. Thus, their entertainment value serves merely as a means to the primary goal of elucidation. Although any cinematic or videographic presentation involves selection and editing, these programs generally emphasize information and education over entertainment and sensationalism. The second type of wildlife and nature programming, the wildlife film, is more grounded in a "Hollywood model." These films employ narrative strategies, storytelling codes, and constructed dramatic structures to examine the subject being filmed. They provide little if any social commentary.

Most wildlife and nature programs of either type are presented as and certainly fit basic documentary formats and can be further roughly subdivided into three related categories: tourism, scientific discovery, and environmental preservation. Of these categories, the first may be distinguished from purely educational or scientific inquiry because of its commercial connection. The last is also distinct because of its political motivation.

Regardless of approach or type, most wildlife and nature programs, like other documentaries, have narrative elements. In the case of nature documentaries, the narrative elements rarely take precedence over the information or content being presented, while conversely, the content or information presented in wildlife films is often shaped to fit a narrative structure conceived prior to filming. In general, there are at least three narrative elements typically present in most wildlife and nature programs: (1) characterization and personification of animals; (2) the presence of struggle; and (3) the use of traditional, rather than experimental or innovative, narrative techniques. These elements are not mutually exclusive or exhaustive, and programs can apply several in a single episode.

The characterization and personification of animals often occurs when programs give them "character names" or compare the animal's attributes with those of humans. Programs also frequently present and dramatize struggle in the wild. This struggle is intended to illustrate the constant battling forces of "brute nature." These accounts often uncover one or more of the following types of struggle: (1) protagonist versus antagonist; (2) hunter versus hunted; and (3) animals (protagonist) versus elements. The protagonist versus antagonist struggle presents one creature as the innocent (e.g., a naturally occurring species of bee) being attacked by another, unwelcome creature (e.g., the foreign killer bee, which is decimating bees native to the area). The hunter versus the hunted illustrates the "eternal" struggle between predator (e.g., fox) and prey (e.g., rabbit). Conflicts between wild animals and the environment may reveal how creatures adapt to continuing human encroachment on nature. Such programs usually present some ecological message concerning the importance of managed growth and respect for wildlife.

Many programs also use a variety of traditional narrative techniques to construct their stories. A common device is the use of narrators not only to provide information but to add dramatic highlights and to help the story flow in a conventional manner. Programs also use audio tracks to emphasize action. Music often builds in intensity to underscore climactic moments, as when a predator seizes its prey. Slow motion, freeze-framing, cross-cutting between "characters" in a dramatic narrative—all these add qualities and evoke emotional and cognitive responses often associated with fiction and familiar from viewer knowledge of fictional presentations.

Since most documentaries are shot on location, production costs are relatively high and grants or sponsorship of some kind are necessary to sustain them. On location, film crews are kept small and efficient to minimize costs. The director often doubles as stand-up and voice-over narrator. Equipment usually consists of a single camera, microphone, sound recorder, and lighting kit, where necessary.

Wildlife and nature programming first appeared on U.S. television in 1948 with the success of a 15-minute science program called *The Nature of Things*. The series' success lasted until 1954 and paved the way for a host of nature programs to follow. From the start, the introduction of nature and wildlife programming attracted audiences as a "great escape." These programs were fun and exhilarating to watch and had viewers on the edge of their seats waiting for the commercial breaks to end and the show to resume. Programs such as *Zoo Parade* (1950–57), a half-hour Sunday-afternoon series that looked at animals and animal behavior, included travel footage from such locations as the Amazon jungles. Another such program, *Expedition* (1960–63), documented journeys to various remote regions of the world and became known for presenting exciting and sometimes controversial places around the globe: one episode presented a tribe in New Guinea ruled by Tambaran—the cult of the ghost that venerated the sweet potato. In another episode, *Expedition* presented an aboriginal Indian tribe that had never before seen a white man.

After the success of adult-oriented programs such as *Zoo Parade* and *Expedition,* nature and wildlife shows changed strategies and focused attention on attracting younger audiences. Programs were often set up in a format designed to "introduce" the phenomena of wildlife and nature. *Exploring* (1962–66) targeted children ages five to 11 by using methods such as storytelling, mathematics, music, science, and history. *Discovery* (1962–71) searched the world over for natural wonders, as did *Zoo Parade* and *Expedition,* but with the aim of attracting a younger audience. The *Discovery* series was designed to stimulate the cultural, historical, and intellectual curiosity of 7- to 12-year-olds regarding nature. Young people were piloted through a spectrum of wonders including how animals use their tails, dramatized essays on the history of dance, the voyage of Christopher Columbus, and a visit to a Texas ranch, and they were introduced to the desert Native Americans. In keeping with the same format, *First Look: Wonders of the World* (1965–66) was designed to provide young children with an introduction to natural history, science, and the various inventions of the world. *First Look's* topics varied from exploring sea life to experiencing a simulated prehistoric expedition during the dinosaur period.

From the 1960s through the 1970s, wildlife and nature programming introduced a new format designed to give audiences an "untamed" and "dangerous" view into the world of nature. Programs became more "adventurous" in their presentational style. Perhaps the best known and successful of such series was *Wild Kingdom* (1963–71), sponsored by Mutual of Omaha and hosted for most of its duration by Marlin Perkins. *Wild Kingdom* traveled to out-of-the way places in Africa, South America, the Arctic, Alaska, the continental United States, Canada, and the Soviet Union in search of unusual creatures and wild adventures. The series covered such diverse topics as animal survival in the wilds, treatment of animals in captivity, and the lives and habitats of animals and primitive people and their struggle for survival. Similar documentary series followed that focused on animals and their struggle for survival, including *The Untamed World* (1969–71); *Wild, Wild World of Animals* (1973–76); *The World of Survival* (1971); *Safari to Adventure* (1971–73); and *Animal World* (*Animal Kingdom*) (1968–80). Another such program was *Jane Goodall and the World of Animal Behavior* (1973–74). ABC aired several nature documentaries featuring Miss Goodall, who came to national attention as a scientist who lived among the apes. Here the scientist as "adventurer-hero" became a central narrative focus. Two successful efforts in her ABC series were "The Wild Dogs of Africa" (1973) and the "Baboons of Gombe" (1974), which attracted audiences with their "realism" and intimate visual portraits.

To give audiences an alternative to the harsh realities of nature, wildlife programs added a sophisticated approach with the airing of such programs as the *National Geographic Specials* (1965–). Produced in cooperation with the National Geographic Society, this long-running series of specials on anthropology, exploration, and biological, historical, and cultural subjects first aired on CBS (1965–73), then on ABC (1973–74), and currently can be seen on PBS (1975–). The *National Geographic Specials,* in keeping with the traditions of the journal and the society that stand behind them, are noted for exceptional visual qualities. Another such program was *Animal Secrets* (1966–68), which disclosed the mysteries of wildlife behavior in an appealing nature series and explored such phenomena as how bees buzz, how fish talk, and why birds migrate. An episode titled "The Primates," filmed in Kenya, presented a study of baboons; their social order and living patterns were observed to find clues to the development of man. The high-quality film series *Nova* (1974–) also relies on detailed productions with exceptional production values. *Nova* is noted for examining complex scientific questions in a manner comprehensible to the layperson and in a relatively entertaining fashion. For the most part, the series concerns itself with the effects on nature and society of new developments in science. The close connection of this program with the Public Broadcasting Service has almost reached "brand" identification, and the program is often cited as an example of what PBS is and can do.

For a short period of time, wildlife documentaries added a new frontier to the nature of inquiry by examining oceans and marine worlds. With the appearance of such programs as *Water World* (1972–75) and the very popular *Undersea World of Jacques Cousteau,* a new market was opened and added to the previous audience. *The Undersea World* centered around the scientific expeditions of Captain Jacques Cousteau and the crew of his specially equipped vessel, the *Calypso.* The first show began on ABC in 1968 and continued for nearly eight years. ABC dropped the series in 1976, but it continued on PBS with underwriting by the Atlantic Richfield Corporation. Since 1981, Cousteau's environmental series and specials have been produced for Turner Broadcasting System (TBS) in a number of short series.

As the decade of the 1970s closed there was a movement toward bringing back traditional methods of presenting wildlife and nature programming—as if reintroducing the areas would stir up an interest in the subject. One such program, *Animals, Animals, Animals* (1976–81), explored the relationship of animals and man in order to help youngsters and inquiring adults understand various wildlife phenomena and the interrelated scheme of nature. An entertainment focus was combined with an introduction to the world of science, zoology, and biology, and each episode focused on a particular animal in an exciting, yet simplistic manner. By the 1980s, a few wildlife and nature programs such as *Nature* (1982–) and *Wild America* (1982–) sustained the "adventurous" format that marked the era of the 1960s and 1970s. For the most part, however, 1980s programming appeared to make great strides when the focus was on ecology and "saving the planet." During this period, programs such as *Universe* (*Walter Cronkite's Universe*) (1980–82) and *Life on Earth* (1982) often focused on space—the solar system and beyond—in order to understand the phenomena of nature and society.

Another major advancement in wildlife and nature programming occurred in 1985 when the Discovery

Channel, an all-documentary cable network, was launched into homes across the nation. This network was devoted chiefly to presenting documentaries on nature, science-technology, travel, history, and human adventure—finally, there was something for everyone. In 1990 the Discovery Channel's penetration passed the 50 million mark, making it one of the fastest growing cable networks of all time. Today, the Discovery Channel has become an alternative outlet for the kind of nature and wildlife programming that in the 1980s had to depend on public television for exposure. With the success of Discovery Channel, another cable network has joined the nature campaign. Nickelodeon (1979–), a children's programming network, recently teamed with Sea World of Florida to educate young people about the importance of conserving Earth's natural resources, protecting endangered species, preventing pollution, and recycling. In the 1990s, Nickelodeon's Cable in the Classroom service and Sea World's Shamu TV: Sea World Video Classroom service began providing hands-on programs about sea life and ecology for audiences from preschoolers to college postgraduates.

A number of programs focused on nature and wildlife have stepped beyond the most common U.S. television goals of entertaining and informing. They have attempted not only to support the preservation of species and environments but to hold corporations and government agencies accountable for acts of pollution and destruction. Films of this type often record dramatic confrontations between those who seek to conserve and those who seek to exploit the environment. The environmental activist group Greenpeace, for example, adopts as part of its policy the need to identify and protest callous indifference toward animals and the environment, and it has used such films to great advantage. It remains to be seen whether television will eventually be used in a similar manner, whether "nature" will continue to be presented either as an entertaining commodity or as an exotic topic for popular education.

As of the beginning of the 21st century, some cable and satellite channels are fully dedicated to the study of animals and nature, namely, the Discovery Channel and Animal Planet. BBC America also provides access to magnificent documentaries on a variety of environmental and nature topics. The audience segmentation reflected by the growth of such channels has given wildlife and nature programs a stature and importance of their own and has led to further subdivisions within the general categories.

The increasing popularity of "reality television" also seems to be causing a shift in the content of some nature genres. There is a movement away from objec-
tive, unobtrusive observation of nature (from a safe distance) to subjective or invasive involvement with nature (dangerously close at hand). In the first kind, as we have seen above, the recorded drama usually consists of conflict between animals themselves; in the second, the recorded drama consists of conflict between naturalist and quarry. Sadly, the more dangerous the exposure or risky the involvement, the more fascinating it is to the audience.

The entertaining wildlife format, for example, has led to development of a new subgenre of wildlife and nature programming that can be called the "extreme" wildlife program. Extreme wildlife programming began with Marty Stouffer's *Wild America,* which ran on PBS for 12 years. *Wild America* featured Stouffer's treks into nature and his encounters with wildlife and emphasized the more violent aspects of nature, including a high ratio of attack and hunting scenes. Stouffer's show faced criticism in the 1990s for being too violent and for staging some of the predator-versus-prey scenes, and it was eventually canceled by PBS, though reportedly for unrelated reasons.

Perhaps the most successful example of extreme wildlife programming is the Animal Planet's *Crocodile Hunter.* This show features Australian zoo director Steve Irwin and his excursions in the wilderness, aggressively chasing down and capturing extremely dangerous animals, such as cobras, scorpions, rattlers, and, of course, crocodiles. The growing popularity of extreme wildlife programs like *Crocodile Hunter*— which hosts a fan club, sells videos and other related merchandise, and has even been turned into a fictional, full-length motion picture—seems to demonstrate audiences' craving for this new, exciting subgenre. Such programs also illustrate a new trend in wildlife and nature programming, toward increasing use of interaction and interference with wildlife rather than documentation in an observational mode. It should be noted that Animal Planet's parent channel, the Discovery Channel, offers a tamer version of *Crocodile Hunter,* which also features an Aussie and his outdoor adventures, titled *Nigel's Wild, Wild World.*

Hosts of the more extreme shows, such as Irwin or Jeff Corwin, prove their bravery and daring by capturing animals in the wild and holding them up to the camera for close inspection. There is no doubt that the close encounter with the animals provides a more intimate knowledge of them, but the exposure seems of lesser importance than the human struggle to capture them. The "bravery" that is involved, no matter how well intended, borders on foolhardiness, for hosts are often bitten or stung or clawed in the process. In the older type of nature films (for example, David Attenborough's documentaries) the host was generally a spectator who hardly ever placed himself or herself in danger. It was a matter of principle not to interfere with the natural processes being filmed for aesthetic and scientific reasons.

Thus, in spite of audience demand for more wildlife and nature programming, questions regarding the accuracy, the purpose, and even the veracity of the programming have emerged. Because these programs have the potential to influence millions of viewers with their interpretations of nature, their accuracy stands as an important point of contention. At the core of the discussion is a central question: Are wildlife and nature programs documentaries, with a primary goal of documentation and education, or are they carefully constructed narratives with a primary goal of entertaining audiences rather than educating them? Within this context the definition, description, and classification of wildlife and nature programs continue to be examined within the television industries as well as in commentary surrounding the forms.

Though the newer breed of naturalists' enthusiasm for their quest, and their admiration of the beauty of nature, can hardly be questioned, the risks they take seem to border on sensationalism and contrived heroism, rather than love of nature or dispassionate observation. It can only be hoped that the public's fascination with such reality television will diminish and be replaced with a renewed interest in the natural world and its conservation.

LISA JONIAK AND RICHARD WORRINGHAM

See also **Animal Planet; Discovery Channel**

Further Reading

Bovet, Susan F., "Teaching Ecology: A New Generation Influences Environmental Policy," *Public Relations Journal* (April 1994)

Brooks, Tim, and Earle Marsh, *The Complete Directory to Prime-Time Network TV Shows: 1946–Present*, New York: Ballantine, 1979

Brown, Les, *Les Brown's Encyclopedia of Television*, New York: Times Books, 1977; reprint, Detroit: Gale, 1992

McNeil, Alex, *Total Television: A Comprehensive Guide to Programming from 1948 to the Present*, New York: Penguin, 1984

Woolery, George W., *Children's Television: The First Thirty-Five Years, 1946–81*, New Jersey: Scarecrow Press, 1985

Wildmon, Donald (1938–)

U.S. Minister, Media Reformer

As social mores have evolved in the United States in recent years, outspoken "media reformers" such as Donald Wildmon, the chair of the American Family Association (AFA), have expressed increasing concern about the role of the media, particularly that of television, in American culture. Wildmon is regarded by some as a self-appointed censor. To others, he is a minister whose congregation crosses the nation and comprises followers upset with the kinds of material seen on television.

Wildmon, a soft-spoken fundamentalist Methodist minister from Tupelo, Mississippi, graduated from Emory University's Divinity School. He has spoken often of the roots for his current cause: in 1977, when his family of young children were gathered around the TV set, he found nothing for them to watch that was not marked by sex, violence, adultery, and swearing. He vowed to his family that he would do something about it.

At the time he was the pastor of a Methodist church in Mississippi. He asked his congregation to go without television for one week and found such a striking reaction to the content of programming and to this action taken against the medium that he formed the National Federation for Decency (NFD; renamed American Family Association in 1988). From that time he never reentered the regular ministry.

Early on, Wildmon discovered that preaching to network chiefs, advertisers, and programmers was not an easy task. By 1980 he had joined with the Reverend Jerry Falwell, leader of the Moral Majority, to form the Coalition for Better Television (CBTV). Members began to observe and record, with a form of "content analysis," the numbers of sexual references, instances of episodes ridiculing Christian characters, and other aspects of programming deemed offensive. Armed with statistics that, to him, demonstrated the erosion of Christian principles by television programs, Wildmon visited corporate heads. On one occasion he convinced the chairman of Procter and Gamble to withdraw advertising from approximately 50 TV shows.

Disputes between Wildmon and Falwell broke up CBTV, and Wildmon started another group, Christian Leaders for Responsible Television (CLEAR-TV). His concern spread from television to movies to the distribution of adult magazines. He targeted movie studios such as MCA-Universal, distributor of *The Last Temptation of Christ,* with its "blasphemous depiction" of biblical accounts. He organized campaigns against retail chains 7-Eleven and Kmart (parent company of Waldenbooks), where adult magazines were sold. Also, he protested against hotel chains such as Holiday Inn for carrying adult movies on in-house cable systems.

Wildmon's boycotting strategies have been both direct, going to the heads of companies to request that they not sponsor anti-Christian materials, and indirect, asking media users to not buy those products advertised on questionable programs. In some cases, he seems to have been successful. Pepsico was persuaded to cancel commercials in which the pop singer Madonna's uses of religious imagery appeared. Mazda Motor of America withdrew advertising from NBC's *Saturday Night Live* because of its "indecent, vulgar, and offensive" nature. When Burger King was found advertising on TV shows containing "sex, violence, profanity, and anti-Christian bigotry," it was induced to run a newspaper ad, an "Open Letter to the American People," declaring its support of "traditional American family values on TV." Some of Wildmon's critics question whether such persuasion by Wildmon is a form of censorship. Others, including Wildmon, insist that such boycotts and public pressure are "as American as the Boston tea party."

To communicate with its supporters and encourage their activism, the AFA uses a variety of media, including a journal, a radio network, print and electronic newsletters, the Internet, and videotapes. The *AFA Journal* (which is available in print and online) and the association's website regularly present descriptions of "troublesome" TV programs and identify the advertisers supporting the shows. Accompanying this material are the names and addresses of the offending corporations and their chief executive officers, so AFA followers can lodge their complaints and pressure sponsors and producers to change their ways. The AFA also uses its journal and website to link individuals to their representatives in Congress, thereby promoting active citizen participation in the lawmaking process. Articles in the journal cover a number of topics, such as the National Endowment for the Arts' funding of "anti-Christian" art; legal and legislative contests over

Rev. Donald Wildmon with Hodding Carter on *Inside Story Special Edition: Eye of the Beholder,* 1981. *Courtesy of the Everett Collection/CSU Archives*

prayer in public schools, abortion, and gay rights; advice for families and individuals seeking to live according to moral precepts upheld by the AFA; and the activities of politicians and others who support or oppose the AFA's priorities. Supporters can sign up for the AFA's e-mail "Action Alerts," outlining issues and appropriate actions to take. The AFA also distributes the *Fight Back Book* (a directory of television advertisers and products) and sells video exposés of forces seeking to undermine the AFA's vision of a Christian America. One such video, titled *MTV Examined,* was described as a "comprehensive—and sometimes shocking—look at the destructive effects of MTV and how the programming often crosses the line from entertainment to promotion of illicit sex, violence, drug abuse, immorality, profanity, and liberal politics."

More liberal forms of media have been outspoken critics of these efforts. *Playboy* has regularly lashed out against Wildmon, presumably because of his attacks on retail outlets that sell the magazine. Other media outlets often simply ignore him.

In 1994 Wildmon's attacks hit a crescendo and gained national attention when he brought to public attention, before its airing on ABC, the controversial cop show *NYPD Blue.* The show's producer, Steven

Bochco, had indicated that he would push the frontier of what would be seen on prime-time TV with a series that included controversial language, adult situations, and brief scenes of nudity. This would be television akin to what might be seen in R-rated movies. Wildmon called for a boycott. Amid Bochco's promotions and Wildmon's protests, the show attracted viewers and received good ratings, as well as many positive critical notices. A number of ABC affiliates chose not to carry the show, however, and there was some controversy surrounding its advertisers. However, the viewing public soon became acclimated; the show did not seem strikingly indecent to many, and it continued to employ strong language, sexual imagery, and mature themes into the early 2000s. Although Wildmon later conceded that his vigorous protests against the show probably attracted attention to it, he remains convinced that he can improve American culture by voicing his objections to other programs that do not meet his moral standards. For example, when ABC broadcast *Ellen,* a sitcom in which the title character came out as a lesbian, Wildmon and the AFA again targeted the network and the program's sponsors, and the association took credit when the show was later canceled. AFA likewise pressures advertisers to make "moral" commercials, free of overt sexual references and imagery that the AFA deems disrespectful to Christianity. For instance, in 2002 the AFA urged Americans to boycott Hellmann's/Best Foods because it featured male strippers in a mayonnaise spot.

While the idea of consumer activism and consumer boycotting originated with liberals in the 1960s and 1970s, in ensuing decades such causes and tactics frequently came from the political right. Wildmon, as leader of the forces attacking the media and television in particular, brought to many people the idea that they were not helpless in countering media influences. In doing so, he has taken a prominent place in a long line of advocates addressing the social and cultural role of television.

VAL E. LIMBURG

See also **Advertising; Censorship; Religion on Television**

Donald Wildmon. Born in Dumas, Mississippi, January 18, 1938. Attended Mississippi State University, graduated from Millsaps College, Jackson, Mississippi, 1960; Emory University, Atlanta, Georgia, master of divinity. Married: Lynda Lou Bennett, 1961; two daughters and two sons. Served in U.S. Army, 1961–63. Ordained as minister, 1964; quit pastorate to protest pornography and violence in media, 1977; founded National Federation for Decency, 1977 (changed name to American Family Association, 1988); founded Coalition for Better Television, 1981 (disbanded, 1982); organized Christian Leaders for Responsible Television, 1982; widened scope of protests by submitting lists of sellers of pornographic magazines and books to Attorney General Edwin Meese's commission on pornography, 1986; convinced Federal Communications Commission to issue warning to radio personality Howard Stern, 1987; protested release of film *The Last Temptation of Christ,* 1988; protested video for and advertising use of Madonna's song "Like a Prayer," 1989; has protested National Endowment for the Arts policies, since 1989.

Publications (selected)

Thoughts Worth Thinking, 1968
Practical Help for Daily Living, 1972
Stand Up to Life, 1975
The Home Invaders, 1985

Further Reading

Kinsley, Michael, "Sour Grapes," *New Republic* (December 10, 1990)

Lafayette, Jon, "Protesting via Post Card: Wildmon Group Reminds Agencies of Product Boycotts," *Advertising Age* (July 15, 1991)

LaMarche, Gara, "Festival Furor," *Index on Censorship* (July–August 1992)

Mendenhall, Robert Roy, "Responses to Television from the New Christian Right: The Donald Wildmon Organizations," Ph.D. diss., University of Texas at Austin, 1994

"*Playboy,* Others Take Offense Against Product Boycotters," *Broadcasting* (November 6, 1989)

Stafford, Tim, "Taking on TV's Bad Boys," *Christianity Today* (August 19, 1991)

"Weighing the Wildmon Effect," *Advertising Age* (August 28, 1989)

Will & Grace. *See* **Family on Television;** *Queer as Folk;* **Sexual Orientation and Television**

Williams, Raymond (1921–1988)

British Media Critic

Raymond Williams was one of Britain's greatest postwar cultural historians, theorists, and polemicists. A distinguished literary and social thinker in the Left-Leavisite tradition, he sought to understand literature and related cultural forms not as the outcome of an isolated aesthetic adventure, but as the manifestation of a deeply social process that involved a series of complex relationships between authorial ideology, institutional process, and generic/aesthetic form. Pioneering in the context of the British literary academy, these concerns are heralded in the brief-lived postwar journal *Politics and Letters,* which he cofounded. Williams's theories are perhaps best summarized in his *Culture and Society, 1780–1950* (1958; 2nd edition, 1983), his critical panorama of literary tradition from the romantics to George Orwell, predicated on the key terms "industry," "democracy," "class," "art," and "culture." This ideological sense of cultural etymology became the basis of his influential pocket dictionary *Keywords: A Vocabulary of Culture and Society* (1976).

Marked by a commitment to his class origins and his postwar experiences of adult education, Williams's efforts to expand the traditional curriculum for English also entailed an early engagement with the allied representational pressures of drama and cinema, in books such as *Drama from Ibsen to Eliot* (1952; 2nd revised edition as *Drama from Ibsen to Brecht,* 1968), *Preface to Film* (1954), *Drama in Performance* (1954; revised edition, 1968), and *Modern Tragedy* (1966; revised edition, 1979). His perception of the links between film and drama remains evident in his 1977 *Screen* essay on the politics of realism in Loach's TV film *The Big Flame* (1969), and in his historical introduction to James Curran and Vincent Porter's *British Cinema History* (1983).

Williams's preoccupation with the relationships between ideology and culture, and the development of socialist perspectives in the communicative arts, was to continue in such works as *The Long Revolution* (1961; revised edition, 1966), *May Day Manifesto 1968* (1968), *The English Novel from Dickens to Lawrence* (1970), *The Country and the City* (1973), *Marxism and Literature* (1977), *Problems in Materialism and Culture: Selected Essays* (1980), *Culture* (1981), *Towards 2000* (1982), *Writing in Society* (1983), *Resources of Hope: Culture, Democracy, Socialism* (1989), and *The Politics of Modernism: Against the New Conformists* (1989). The Williams collection *Politics and Letters: Interviews with New Left Review* (1981) provides a useful retrospective on his work.

In the 1960s, Williams's work took on new dimensions. In 1960 he published his first, autobiographical novel, *Border Country,* which was to be followed by other works of fiction: *Second Generation* (1964), *The Volunteers* (1978), and *The Fight for Manod* (1979). In 1962, he published his first book to address directly the new world of contemporary mass media, *Communications,* an informative volume in the early history of media studies that has been influential in Great Britain and internationally. He moved to the center of left cultural politics, in the crucible of 1968, with his chairmanship of the Left National Committee and his edition of the *May Day Manifesto 1968.*

Throughout the 1960s, Williams participated in what he remembered as innumerable TV discussion programs, as the young medium found its style. Two of his novels became TV plays, now sadly lost—a "live" version of *A Letter from the Country* (1966) and *Public Inquiry* (1967), filmed in his native Wales.

From 1968 to 1972, Williams contributed a weekly column on TV to the BBC magazine *The Listener.* Now collected as *Raymond Williams on Television: Selected Writings* (1989), these writings illustrate his response to a wide range of TV themes and pleasures—from an enthusiasm for television sport to a distrust in the medium's stress on "visibility," to arguments about the economic and political relationships between production and transmission.

Williams went on to develop these ideas more formally in the book *Television: Technology and Cultural Form* (1974), one of the first major theoretical studies of the medium, which he wrote largely while on a visiting professorship at Stanford University in 1972. There he soaked up American TV, developed his influential concept of TV "flow," and encountered the newly emerging technologies of satellite and cable.

In 1970 he had contributed a personal documentary, "Border Country," to the BBC series *One Pair of Eyes,* which was to be followed at the end of the decade by

"The Country and The City: A Film with Raymond Williams," the last of five programs in the series *Where We Live Now: Five Writers Look at Our Surroundings* (1979). In the 1980s, he contributed to a trio of Open University/BBC programs—*Language in Use: "The Widowing of Mrs Holroyd"* (1981), *Society, Education, and the State: Worker, Scholar, and Citizen* (1982), and *The State and Society in 1984* (1984). He also appeared in *Identity Ascendant: The Home Counties* (1988), an episode in the HTV/Channel 4 series *The Divided Kingdom,* and in *Big Words, Small Worlds* (1987), Channel 4's record of the Strathclyde Linguistics of Writing Conference.

Williams's contribution to cultural thinking was that of a Cambridge professor who never forgot the Welsh village of his childhood. He was a theorist of literature who himself wrote novels; a historian of drama who was also a playwright; and a commentator on TV and the mass media who himself regularly contributed to the television medium in a variety of ways. For him, unlike so many academics, the medium of television was a crucial cultural form, as relevant to education as the printed word. When Channel 4 began transmission in Great Britain in 1982, it was entirely appropriate that this innovative channel's opening feature film should be *So That You Can Live,* Cinema Action's elegy for the industrial decay of the Welsh valleys, explicitly influenced by the work of Williams, from whose work the film offers us readings.

The Second International Television Studies Conference, held in London in 1986, was honored to appoint Williams as its copresident, alongside Hilde Himmelweit. However, by the time the next event came round in 1988, the conference sadly honored not Williams's presence, but his passing. The breadth of his impact in the U.K. cultural arena can be gauged from the British Film Institute monograph *Raymond Williams: Film/TV/Cinema* (edited by David Lusted; 1989), produced to accompany a Williams memorial season at the National Film Theatre and containing a contribution by his widow.

PHILLIP DRUMMOND

See also **Television Studies**

Raymond (Henry) Williams. Born in Llanfihangel Crocorney, Wales, August 31, 1921. Attended Abergavenny Grammar School, 1932–39; Trinity College, Cambridge, M.A., 1946. Served in Anti-Tank Regiment, Guards Armoured Division, 1941–45. Married: Joyce Marie Dalling, 1942; children: one daughter and two sons. Editor, *Politics and Letters,* 1946–47; extramural tutor in literature, Oxford University, 1946–61; fellow, Jesus College, Cambridge, from 1961; reader, Cambridge University, 1967–74; professor of drama, Cambridge University, 1974–83; visiting professor of political science, Stanford University, 1973; general editor, *New Thinkers Library,* 1962–70; reviewer, *The Guardian,* from 1983; adviser, John Logie Baird Centre for Research in Television and Film, from 1983; president, Classical Association, 1983–84. Litt.D.: Trinity College, Cambridge, 1969; D.Univ.: Open University, Milton Keynes, 1975; D.Litt.: University of Wales, Cardiff, 1980. Member: Welsh Academy. Died in Cambridge, January 26, 1988.

Television Plays

1966   *A Letter from the Country*
1967   *Public Inquiry*
1979   *The Country and the City*

Publications (selected)

Reading and Criticism, 1950
Drama from Ibsen to Eliot, 1952; 2nd revised edition as *Drama from Ibsen to Brecht,* 1968
Drama in Performance, 1954; revised edition, 1968
Preface to Film, with Michael Orram, 1954
Culture and Society, 1780–1950, 1958; second edition, 1983
Border Country (novel), 1960
The Long Revolution, 1961; revised edition, 1966
Communications, 1962; 3rd edition, 1976
Second Generation (novel), 1964
Modern Tragedy, 1966; revised edition, 1979
May Day Manifesto 1968 (editor), 1968
The Pelican Book of English Prose: From 1780 to the Present Day (editor), 1970
The English Novel from Dickson to Lawrence, 1970
Orwell, 1971; 3rd edition, 1991
D.H. Lawrence on Education (editor, with Joy Williams), 1973
The Country and the City, 1973
Television: Technology and Cultural Form, 1974
George Orwell: A Collection of Critical Essays (editor), 1974
Keywords: A Vocabulary of Culture and Society, 1976; revised edition, 1983
English Drama: Forms and Development: Essays in Honour of Muriel Clara Bradbrook (editor, with Marie Axton), 1977
Marxism and Literature, 1977
The Volunteers (novel), 1978
The Fight for Manod (novel), 1979
Problems in Materialism and Culture: Selected Essays, 1980
Politics and Letters: Interviews with New Left Review, 1981

Contact: Human Communication and Its History (editor), 1981

Culture, 1981; U.S. edition as *The Sociology of Culture,* 1982

Cobbett, 1983

Towards 2000, 1983

Writing in Society, 1983

Gabriel Garcia Marquez, 1984

Loyalties (fiction), 1985

People of the Black Mountains (fiction), 1989

The Politics of Modernism: Against the New Conformists, edited by Tony Pinkney, 1989

Raymond Williams on Television: Selected Writings, edited by Alan O'Connor, 1989

Resources of Hope: Culture, Democracy, Socialism, edited by Robin Gale, 1989

What I Came to Say, edited by Neil Belton, Francis Mulhern, and Jenny Taylor, 1989

Further Reading

Eagleton, Terry, editor, *Raymond Williams: Critical Perspectives,* Cambridge: Polity, and Boston: Northeastern University Press, 1989

Eldridge, J.E.T., and Lizzie Eldridge, *Raymond Williams: Making Connections,* London and New York: Routledge, 1994

Gorak, Jan, *The Alien Mind of Raymond Williams,* Columbia: University of Missouri Press, 1988

Inglis, Fred, *Raymond Williams,* London and New York: Routledge, 1995

Lusted, David, editor, *Raymond Williams: Film/TV/Culture,* London: NFT/BFI, 1989

O'Connor, Alan, *Raymond Williams: Writing, Culture, Politics,* Oxford and New York: Blackwell, 1989

Pinkney, Tony, editor, *Raymond Williams,* Bridgend, Mid Glamorgan, Wales: Seren Books, and Chester Springs, Pennsylvania: Dufour Editions, 1991

Stevenson, Nick, *Culture, Ideology, and Socialism: Raymond Williams and E.P. Thompson,* Aldershot, England, and Brookfield, Vermont: Avebury, 1995

Wilson, Flip (1933–1988)

U.S. Comedian

In the early 1970s, Flip Wilson was among a group of rising black comics that included Bill Cosby, Nipsey Russell, and Dick Gregory. Wilson is best remembered as the host of the variety program *The Flip Wilson Show*—the first variety series since *The Nat "King" Cole Show* (1956–57) to be hosted by and named after an African American—and for his role in renewing stereotype comedy.

With a keen wit developed during his impoverished youth, Clerow Wilson rose quickly to fame as a stand-up comic and television show host. Under the stage name "Flip," given to him by Air Force pals who joked he was "flipped out," Wilson began performing in cheap clubs across the United States. His early routines featured black stereotypes of the controversial *Amos 'n' Andy* type. After performing in hallmark black clubs such as the Apollo in Harlem and the Regal in Chicago, Wilson made a successful appearance on *The Ed Sullivan Show.* Recommended by Redd Foxx, Wilson also performed on *The Tonight Show* to great accolades, becoming a substitute host.

After making television guest appearances on such shows as *Love, American Style* and *That's Life,* and starring in his own 1969 NBC special, Wilson was offered an hour-long prime-time NBC show, *The Flip Wilson Show,* which saw a remarkable four-year run. Only Sammy Davis Jr. had enjoyed similar success with his song-and-dance variety show; comparatively, earlier shows hosted by Nat "King" Cole and Bill Cosby were quickly canceled, owing to lack of sponsorship and narrow appeal. At the high point of *The Flip Wilson Show,* advertising rates swelled to $86,000 per minute, and by 1972 the series was rated the most popular variety show, and the second-most popular show overall in the United States.

Wilson's television success came from his unique combination of "new" stereotype comedy and his signature stand-up form. His style combined deadpan delivery and dialect borrowed from his role models, Foxx and Cosby, but Wilson replaced their humorous puns with storytelling. His fluid body language, likened to that of silent-screen actor Charlie Chaplin, gave Wilson's act a dynamic and graceful air. The show benefited from his intensive production efforts, unprecedented for a black television performer; he wrote one-third of the show's material, heavily edited the work of writers, and demanded a five-day workweek from his staff and guests to produce each one-

Flip Wilson.
Photo courtesy of Flip Wilson

hour segment. Audiences appreciated the show's innovative style elements, such as the intimate theater-in-the-round studio and the use of medium-long shots, which replaced close-ups in order to capture fully Wilson's expressive movements.

Wilson altered his club act for television in order to accommodate family viewing, relying on descriptive portraits of black characters and situations rather than ridicule. Still, his show offended many African Americans and civil rights activists who believed Wilson's humor depended on race. A large multiethnic television audience, however, found universal humor in the routines, and others credited Wilson with subtly ridiculing the art of stereotyping itself. Wilson denied this claim, strongly denouncing suggestions that his race required that his art convey anti-bias messages.

In fact, these divergent interpretations reflect the variety among Wilson's characters. Some were rather offensive, such as the money-laundering Reverend Leroy and the smooth swinger, Freddy the Playboy. Others, such as Sonny, a White House janitor and the "wisest man in Washington," were positive black portraits. The show's most popular character, Geraldine, exemplifies Wilson's intention to produce "race-free" comedy. Perfectly coifed and decked out in designer clothes and chartreuse stockings, Geraldine demanded respect and, in Wilson's words, "Everybody knows she don't take no stuff." Liberated yet married, outspoken yet feminine, ghetto-born yet poised, Geraldine was neither floozy nor threat. This colorful black female image struck a positive chord with viewers; her one-liners—"The devil made me do it," and "When you're hot, you're hot"—became national fads. Social messages were imparted indirectly through Wilson's characters; the well-dressed and self-respecting Geraldine, for example, countered the female-degrading acts of other popular stand-up comics. Through Geraldine, Wilson also negotiated racial and class biases by positively characterizing a working-class black female, in contrast to the absence of female black images on 1970s television (with the exception of the middle-class black nurse of the 1969 sitcom *Julia*).

Wilson sometimes did address race more directly through story and theme; one skit, for example, featured Native American women discourteously greeting Christopher Columbus and crew on their arrival in North America. Such innovative techniques enabled Wilson's humorous characters and themes to suggest racial and gender tolerance.

Wilson's career lost momentum when his show was canceled in 1974. Although he was the recipient of a 1970 Emmy Award for Outstanding Writing and a 1971 Grammy for Best Comedy Record, Wilson's career never rekindled. He continued to make television specials and TV guest appearances; made his film debut in Sidney Poitier's successful post-blaxploitation movie *Uptown Saturday Night;* and performed in two subsequent unsuccessful films. His 1985 television comeback, *Charlie and Company*—a sitcom following *The Cosby Show*'s formula—had a short run.

Wilson saw himself first as an artist, and humor was more prominent than politics in his comic routines. This style, however, allowed him to impart successfully occasional social messages into his act. Moreover, he achieved unprecedented artistic control of his show, pressing the parameters for black television performers and producers. Through Geraldine, Wilson created one of 1970s television's few respectful images of black women, who were generally marginalized by both the civil rights and women's movements of that era. Finally, although no regular black variety show took up where Wilson left off, the success of his program paved the way for the popularity of later sitcoms featuring middle- and working-class black families, situations, and dialect, shows such as *Sanford and Son, The Jeffersons,* and *Good Times.*

PAULA GARDNER

See also **Flip Wilson Show, The; Racism, Ethnicity, and Television**

Flip Wilson. Born Clerow Wilson in Jersey City, New Jersey, December 8, 1933. Married: Cookie MacKenzie, 1957 (divorced, 1967); four children: Kevin, David, Stephanie, Stacey. Served in U.S. Air Force, 1950–54. Bellhop and part-time entertainer, Manor Plaza Hotel, San Francisco, 1954; traveled United States performing in night clubs, late 1950s; regular act at New York City's Apollo Theater, early 1960s; appearances on *The Tonight Show,* from 1965; appeared in numerous television shows, including *Rowan and Martin's Laugh-In,* 1967–68; recorded comedy records, 1967–68; star, *The Flip Wilson Show,* 1970–74; appeared in films, from 1970s; appeared in television series *Charlie and Company,* 1985–86. Recipient: Emmy Award, 1970; Grammy Award, 1971. Died in Malibu, California, November 25, 1998.

Television Series

1970–74	*The Flip Wilson Show*
1984	*People Are Funny*
1985–86	*Charlie and Company*

Television Specials

1974	*Flip Wilson...Of Course*
1974	*The Flip Wilson Special*
1975	*The Flip Wilson Special*
1975	*The Flip Wilson Special*
1975	*Travels with Flip*
1975	*The Flip Wilson Comedy Special*

Films

Uptown Saturday Night, 1974; *Skatetown, U.S.A.,* 1979; *The Fish That Saved Pittsburgh,* 1979.

Recordings

Cowboys and Colored People, 1967; *Flippin',* 1968; *Flip Wilson, You Devil You,* 1968; *The Devil Made Me Buy This Dress,* 1970.

Further Reading

Davidson, B., "Many Faces of Flip," *Good Housekeeping* (1971)
Robinson, Louie, "The Evolution of Geraldine," *Ebony* (1970)
"When You're Hot You're Hot," *Time* (1972)

Winant, Ethel (1925–2003)

U.S. Network Executive

Ethel Winant's career as a casting director, producer, program developer, and network executive spanned the history of television, and she was among the most important and influential women ever to have worked in the television industry.

Winant's television work began after she watched the anthology program *Studio One.* She was struck by the quality of the show, wrote the producers to inquire about the production, and was subsequently invited to watch a rehearsal of the program. She shrewdly parlayed that meeting into a job running errands for the crew. Not long thereafter, when one actor failed to appear for a particular episode, Winant quickly managed to track down a replacement for him, thus launching her career as a casting director.

Winant subsequently went to work for Talent Associates in 1953, casting episodes of such anthology programs as *Armstrong Circle Theater* and *Philco Playhouse,* and she continued to distinguish herself within the anthology genre while employed as a casting director at CBS. For Rod Serling's *The Twilight Zone,* Winant cast such beloved episodes as "Eye of the Beholder" and "Long Distance Call," and she both cast and helped produce episodes of *General Electric Theater* and *Playhouse 90,* working alongside some of the most important creative figures in early television, including John Frankenheimer, John Houseman, Arthur Penn, George Roy Hill, and Sidney Lumet.

For *Playhouse 90,* Winant developed a casting strategy that added to the show's reputation as one of the most prominent and prestigious programs on television. Throughout its run, *Playhouse 90* strove for all of the markers of high culture available in television. Winant recalled of the show, "Everything we had learned the previous ten years came with that show. It was the best of *Philco [TV Playhouse]* and *U.S. Steel,* the best writers and directors. It all came together and produced this magical moment. That was *Playhouse 90*" (Kisseloff, p.

230). The producers had hoped to cast big-name Hollywood stars to underscore the show's prestige, but the highest tier of film stars refused to do television, and only fading and lesser-known stars would agree to appear. As a result, Winant utilized a strategy she called "stunt casting," or off-casting the star and then publicizing that performance as prestigious and artistic because of its uniqueness and creativity, no matter the status of the featured actor. Examples of stunt casting on *Playhouse 90* included teen idol Tab Hunter playing a Soviet spy, comedian Ed Wynn portraying an embattled boxing trainer, and affable actor Mickey Rooney depicting an egomaniacal, destructive, and crass television comedian, a role for which he received an Emmy nomination. This successful strategy illustrated that Winant's talents lay not just in choosing actors, but also in matching them with perceptive programming decisions.

These combined abilities helped Winant ascend through the ranks at CBS, and in 1973 she became the first female network executive in the television industry after a promotion to a vice presidency position, which gave her the power to cast all network pilots, series, and specials, as well as responsibilities for program development. Winant said of this advancement:

I'm not really sure why they made me vice president. I guess someone in corporate decided they wanted a woman, which probably had to do with the Women's Movement.... It never occurred to me that I'd be a vice president. I wasn't interested in climbing the corporate ladder. I just wanted to make shows. (Gregory, p. 11)

She did precisely that through the 1970s. She cast the principle actors for *The Mary Tyler Moore Show*, left CBS in 1975, and went on to produce the 1977 PBS miniseries *The Best of Families* for the Children's Television Workshop. She subsequently moved to NBC in 1978 as a vice president of talent and later a senior vice president of miniseries and novels, developing such notable miniseries as *Shogun, Murder in Texas,* and *Little Gloria ...Happy at Last.*

Winant's career was briefly derailed after she went blind from macular degeneration in the mid-1980s, but she persevered in learning Braille, mastering it so thoroughly that she subsequently taught it to others. She then returned to a steady career of producing and consulting, working on such projects as *World War II: When Lions Roared* and *Fail Safe,* and reteaming with John Frankenheimer on the Emmy-nominated *Andersonville* and *George Wallace,* as well as the 1998 feature film, *Ronin.*

Known for her tenaciousness, liberal spirit, and high energy, Winant let her creative passions guide her entire career. She died December 2, 2003.

CHRISTINE BECKER

Ethel Winant. Born Ethel Wald in Worcester, Massachusetts, August 5, 1925. Education: B.A., University of California, Berkeley; Pasadena Playhouse; M.T.A., Whittier College. Married: H.N. Winant (divorced); three children (William, Bruce, Scott). Head of casting, Talent Associates, New York City, 1953–56; various casting and program development positions, CBS, 1960–73; vice president of talent and director of program development, CBS, 1973–75; vice president, Children's Television Workshop, 1975–77; vice president of talent, NBC, 1978; vice president of miniseries and novels for TV, NBC, 1979–81; senior vice president of creative affairs, Metromedia Producers Corp., 1981. Inducted into the Women in Film Hall of Fame in 1992 and the Television Hall of Fame in 1999. Died December 2, 2003.

Television Series: Casting (selected)
1953–55	*Armstrong Circle Theater*
1953–55	*Philco Playhouse*
1956–60	*Playhouse 90*
1960	*The Twilight Zone*
1965	*The Wild Wild West*
1967	*He & She*
1968	*Hawaii Five-O*
1970	*The Mary Tyler Moore Show*
1972	*The Waltons*
1972	*The Bob Newhart Show*

Television Production and Program Development (selected)
1956–60	*Playhouse 90* (associate producer)
1963–65	*The Great Adventure* (producer)
1974	*The Migrants*
1975	*Benjamin Franklin*
1976	*Bicentennial Minutes*
1977	*The Best of Families* (executive producer)
1980	*Shogun*
1981	*Murder in Texas*
1982	*Little Gloria ...Happy at Last*
1986	*A Time to Triumph* (executive producer)
1987	*Media Access Awards* (executive producer)
1994	*World War II: When Lions Roared* (executive producer)
1996	*Andersonville* (executive producer)
1997	*George Wallace* (executive producer)
2000	*Fail Safe* (executive consultant)

Feature Films
1962	*All Fall Down* (associate producer)
1962	*Two Weeks in Another Town* (associate producer)
1998	*Ronin* (associate producer)

Publications

"Event Programming," *Journal of the Caucus for Television Producers, Writers, and Directors,* 1993

Further Reading

Auletta, Ken, *Three Blind Mice: How the TV Networks Lost Their Way,* New York: Vintage Books, 1991

Brown, Irby, and Robert S. Alley, *Women Television Producers: Transformation of the Male Medium,* Rochester, New York: University of Rochester Press, 2002

Gitlin, Todd, *Inside Prime Time,* Berkeley: University of California Press, 2000

Gregory, Mollie, *Women Who Run the Show,* New York: St. Martin's Press, 2002

Kisseloff, Jeff, *The Box: An Oral History of Television,* New York: Penguin, 1997

Wind at My Back

Canadian Family Drama

A successful family drama from Canadian producer Sullivan Entertainment, *Wind at My Back* followed the winning formula of Sullivan's previous hit *Road to Avonlea,* combining period setting and episodic family drama broadcast during the Canadian Broadcasting Corporation's (CBC's) Sunday-evening family-hour slot, with *Wind at My Back* running five seasons, from 1996 to 2001. A one-off reunion television movie, *A Wind at My Back Christmas,* was produced in 2001 and broadcast in December of that year, again on the CBC. There are many similarities between *Wind at My Back* and *Road to Avonlea,* both in industrial/production terms and in textual/formal terms, with *Wind at My Back* apparently designed with the successful aspects of *Road to Avonlea* in mind. Like *Road, Wind at My Back* was a commercially successful production both domestically and internationally, initially securing strong audiences for the CBC's Sunday 7:00 P.M. time slot and with robust international sales to 40 countries, including the United States, France, and Australia.

Set in the fictitious town New Bedford, Ontario, during the Great Depression of the 1930s, *Wind at My Back* was a one-hour episodic program chronicling the ups and downs of the lives of the Bailey family as they endured the hardships characteristic of rural Canada in the 1930s. Loosely based on characters, settings, and locations created by Canadian novelist Max Braithwaite (best known for *Who Has Seen the Wind,* which was adapted into a successful Canadian film) in his book *Never Sleep Three on a Bed,* among other 1930s-set fictions, the program's narrative structure turned on relationship between the various generations of the Bailey family and the other residents of New Bedford.

The story begins as Honey Bailey's husband, Jack, dies suddenly, causing Honey to lose her home and the family business. Her domineering mother-in-law, May Bailey, matriarch of the town's wealthy mining family, is unsupportive, takes custody of Honey's two boys, "Hub" (Hubert) and "Fat" (Henry), in the family mansion, and sees that Honey's baby daughter, Violet, is sent to live with distant relatives. Eventually remarrying, this time to school teacher Max Sutton, Honey manages to forge a new life for herself in New Bedford, a town dominated by the influence of her late husband's family.

Just as *Road to Avonlea* did, *Wind at my Back* constructed a predominately nostalgic world, not simply through costume-period depictions of family struggle during the Depression, but also through the evolving children's relationships (particularly Hub and Fat) to their elders and their gradual transformation by the later seasons into boys maturing into adolescence, providing further avenues for exploring the coming-of-age themes so common to family entertainment of this kind. The Depression-era setting provided many opportunities to celebrate family bonds and community spirit by confronting characters with difficulties that were only satisfactorily resolved with the help of kin or community. Family crises intertwined with the presence and influence of other citizens of the town (Ollie Jefferson [Neil Crane], owner of Jefferson's Garage, and Archie Attenborough [Richard Blackburn], who ran Stutts Pharmacy, for example) and in certain instances with larger social issues. Like *The Waltons* before it, *Wind at my Back* created a liberal-humanist view of the world in which the global financial crisis of the Depression provided a suitable backdrop of difficulty on which was painted a warm canvass of cross-generational familial and community struggle and co-operation.

Wind at My Back can be seen as a representative example of the recent successes of state intervention in the Canadian television industries. Produced by a private production company, the program was made in association not only with the CBC, the national broadcaster, but also with the participation of several of the nation's industrial incentive programs for television including the Canadian Television Fund (a partnership between the Canadian government and the Canadian cable television companies), Telefilm Canada's Equity Investment Program, the Canadian Television Fund's License Fee Program, and the Government of Canada Film or Video Production Tax Credit Program. Through these various instruments of incentive, the Canadian government has largely achieved the goals of cultural policy, as programs such as *Wind at My Back* illustrate, by creating indigenous, relatively popular, nationally specific entertainment programs, and the goals of industrial policy, by generating capital, contributing to the establishment of a sufficiently large and capably trained workforce for the specialized needs of television production, and creating exportable, internationally salable cultural commodities.

The series and the Christmas special have been re-run on the CBC, and the series ran on Encore's WAM! Channel in the United States and Disney Channels in France and Australia.

PETER URQUHART

See also **Road to Avonlea**

Cast

Honey Bailey (seasons 1–3)	Cynthia Belliveau
Honey Bailey (seasons 4–5)	Laura Bruneau
"Hub" Bailey	Dylan Provencher
"Fat" Bailey	Tyrone Savage
May Bailey	Shirley Douglas
Grace Bailey	Kathryn Greenwood
Max Sutton	James Carroll
Toppy Bailey	Robin Craig

Producers

Kevin Sullivan and Trudy Grant

Programming History

65 one-hour episodes and one two-hour special
CBC

December 1996–April 2001	Sunday nights

Christmas special, December 2001

Windsor, Frank (1927–)

British Actor

Frank Windsor is one of the best-known stalwarts of British police drama serials, having costarred in several such productions since the 1960s. His career as a television performer started in radically different shows from those with which he was destined to become most closely associated, with appearances in the Shakespearean anthology *An Age of Kings* and subsequently in the science fiction series *A for Andromeda*, in which he played scientist Dennis Bridger. In 1962, however, he made his debut in the role with which he became virtually synonymous—that of Newtown's Detective Sergeant John Watt. As one of the crime-busting team crewing *Z Cars*, Watt was right-hand man to Detective Inspector Barlow (Stratford Johns) and was often placed in the role of the "nice guy" to

Stratford John's more aggressive, often bullying senior officer. The two actors formed a dynamic, absorbing partnership that survived well beyond their departure from the series in 1965.

The two stars resumed the same screen personas in their own follow-up series, *Softly, Softly,* a year after leaving the Newtown force. With Barlow raised to the rank of detective chief superintendent and Watt detective chief inspector, the pair continued to hunt down criminals in their "nice and nasty" partnership, though now based in the fictional region of Wyvern, which appeared to be somewhere near Bristol. Three years into the series, the pair were relocated to Thamesford Constabulary's CID Task Force, and the program itself was retitled *Softly, Softly—Task Force.* Barlow

Frank Windsor.
Photo courtesy of Frank Windsor

in supporting roles in a number of established series (including *All Creatures Great and Small, Boon,* and *Casualty*), participated in quiz shows, and also accumulated a number of film and stage credits.

DAVID PICKERING

See also Z Cars

Frank Windsor. Born in Walsall, Staffordshire, England, July 12, 1927. Attended St. Mary's School, Walsall. Married: Mary Corbett; children: Amanda and David. Began career as performer on radio; founding member, Oxford and Cambridge Players, later the Elizabethan Players; acted classical roles on British stage; television actor as Detective Sergeant Watt in the series *Z Cars;* has since appeared in additional police series and other productions.

Television Series

1960	*An Age of Kings*
1961	*A for Andromeda*
1962–65	*Z Cars*
1966–70, 1970–76	*Softly, Softly*
1976	*Second Verdict*

Made-for-Television Movies (selected)

1981	*Dangerous Davies—The Last Detective*
1982	*Coming Out of the Ice*

Films

This Sporting Life, 1963; *Spring and Port Wine,* 1970; *Sunday, Bloody Sunday,* 1971; *Hands of the Ripper,* 1971; *The Dropout,* 1973; *Barry MacKenzie Holds His Own,* 1974; *Assassin,* 1975; *Who Is Killing the Great Chefs of Europe?* 1978; *The London Connection,* 1979; *Night Shift,* 1979; *The Shooting Party,* 1984; *Revolution,* 1985; *Oedipus at Colonus,* 1986; *First Among Equals,* 1987; *Out of Order,* 1987.

Stage (selected)

Androcles and the Lion; Brand; Travesties; Middle-Age Spread; Mr. Fothergill's Murder.

Further Reading

Corner, John, editor, *Popular Television in Britain: Studies in Cultural History,* London: British Film Institute, 1991

disappeared from the series in 1969, when he left for his own series, *Barlow at Large,* leaving Watt to continue the battle with new partners for another seven years.

Barlow and Watt were brought together again in 1973, when they disinterred the case files connected with the real-life Jack the Ripper murders of the 1880s. They pored over the various theories concerning the identity of the murderer, including the possibility that he might have been a member of the royal family, but in the end even television's two most celebrated police detectives could draw no firm conclusion. Along similar lines was *Second Verdict,* another short series in which the two characters investigated unsolved murder cases from real life.

The extent to which Windsor became linked to just one role has subsequently militated against his taking parts that would challenge public perceptions of his original persona. He has, however, appeared as a guest

Winfrey, Oprah (1954–)

U.S. Talk Show Host

Oprah Winfrey, known primarily as the host of the nationally and internationally syndicated American talk show *The Oprah Winfrey Show,* has successfully charted and navigated a career that has built on the television industry as a form of public therapy. On *The Oprah Winfrey Show,* both ordinary people and guest celebrities are there to reveal their inner truths, and it is these revelations that create in the audience the dual sentiments that have been critical to the success of *Oprah:* there is a voyeuristic pleasure in hearing about what is normally hidden by others, and there is the cathartic sensation that the public revelation will lead to social betterment.

One of the key features of Winfrey's television persona is that her own private life has been an essential element of her talk show format of public therapy. Her accounts of growing up as a poor black child and of her past and current problems with child abuse, men, and weight have made Winfrey an exposed public personality on television and have allowed her loyal audience to feel that they "know" her quite well. This televisual familiarity is part of the power of Oprah Winfrey.

Winfrey's path into the profession was partially connected to her success in two beauty pageants. At 16, Winfrey was the first black Miss Fire Prevention for Nashville. From that position, and with her obvious and demonstrated abilities in public speaking, she was invited to be the newsreader on a local black radio station, WVOL. Later, she maintained her public profile by winning the Miss Black Tennessee pageant and gained a scholarship to Tennessee State University. In her final year of studying speech, drama, and English, Winfrey was offered a position as coanchor on the television news program of the CBS affiliate WVTF. She has described her early role model for news broadcasting as Barbara Walters.

Although not entirely comfortable with her role as news journalist/anchor, Winfrey gained a more lucrative coanchor position at WJZ, the ABC affiliate in Baltimore, Maryland, in 1977. She struggled for several months in the position; her greatest weaknesses derived from not reading the news copy before airtime and from her penchant for extensive ad-libbing. She was pulled from the anchor position and given the role of cohosting a morning chat show, *People Are Talking.* Able to be relaxed and natural on air, Winfrey excelled in this position. By the end of her run, her local morning talk show had transformed into a program dealing with more controversial issues, and Winfrey's presence helped the show outdraw the nationally syndicated talk show *Donahue* in the local Baltimore market.

In 1983 Winfrey followed her associate producer Debra Di Maio to host *A.M. Chicago,* a morning talk show on Chicago station WLZ-TV. By 1985 the name was changed to *The Oprah Winfrey Show,* and once again Winfrey's program was drawing a larger audience than *Donahue* in the local market. Winfrey also gained a national presence through her Oscar-nominated role in Steven Spielberg's *The Color Purple* (1985). The large television program syndicator King World, realizing the earning potential of Winfrey, took over production of her show in 1986 and reproduced the daily program for the national market. Within weeks of the launch in September 1986, *The Oprah Winfrey Show* became the most-watched daytime talk show in the United States.

The deal struck with King World in 1986 instantly made Winfrey the highest-paid performer in the entertainment industry, with estimated earnings from the program of $31 million in 1987. She has continued to be one of the wealthiest women in the entertainment industry and has used that power to establish her own production company, Harpo Productions. Harpo's presence on television has been evident in a number of arenas. First, in dramatic programming, Harpo produced the miniseries *The Women of Brewster Place* (1989) and the follow-up situation-drama/comedy *Brewster Place* (1990). Winfrey both starred in and produced these programs. She has produced and hosted several prime-time documentaries, including one specifically on children and abuse. In recent years, she has sometimes supplanted Walters in securing one-off interviews with key celebrities. Winfrey's prime-time interview of Michael Jackson in February 1993 (ABC) garnered a massive television audience both nationally and internationally. Similarly, her interview with basketball star Michael Jordan in October 1993 reaffirmed Winfrey's omnipresence and power in tele-

Oprah Winfrey, 1987.
Courtesy of the Everett Collection

vision. In the late 1990s, Winfrey continued to operate as producer with many special programs, films, and series, including Jonathan Demme's feature film *Beloved* (1998), in which she also played a part; the television miniseries *The Wedding* (1998); and the made-for-television movie *Tuesdays with Morrie* (1999), based on a best-selling book Winfrey had featured on her talk show.

The centerpiece of both Winfrey's wealth and her public presence continues to be her daily talk show, which is also broadcast successfully internationally. Borrowing the "run and microphone thrust" device from Donahue, she makes the television audience part of the performance. With this and other techniques, Winfrey has managed to create an interesting public forum that transforms the feminist position that "the personal is political" into a vaguely political television program. Themes range from the bizarre ("Children Who Abuse Parents") to the titillating ("How Important Is Size in Sex?"), from the overtly political ("Women of the Ku Klux Klan") to the personal trials and tribulations of her own weight loss/gain and the "problems" of fellow celebrities.

In direct counterpoint to programs such as the talk shows hosted by Jerry Springer and Ricki Lake, Winfrey has consolidated an older, and perhaps more middle-class, audience as she has moved to edify her audience. One effort to distance her program from the more scandal-driven talk shows, the "Oprah's Book Club" feature, has had a significant impact on the book industry, as Winfrey's endorsements of particular titles have become the harbinger of success for the authors of those works. Winfrey's role in book sales has become so important as to frequently spark debate. In particular, Jonathan Frantzen's decision in 2001 to decline an invitation to have his novel *The Corrections* discussed on air in her book club, and Winfrey's own announcement in 2002 that she intended to end the feature because she could not find enough satisfactory works, inspired many pundits to comment on the state of contemporary literature. In 2003 Winfrey resuscitated her book club, with John Steinbeck's *East of Eden.*

In 2001, through Harpo Productions, Winfrey successfully launched the lifestyle magazine *O,* the cover of which is almost exclusively a photo of her. Her website, oprah.com, consolidates the wealth of material that now is circulated by Winfrey and her loyal and large audience and is associated with the larger media entity Oxygen Media. Thus, Winfrey continues to represent a televisual and now multimedia path to self-actualization.

P. DAVID MARSHALL

See also **Talk Show;** *Women of Brewster Place, The*

Oprah Winfrey. Born in Kosciusko, Mississippi, January 29, 1954. Educated at Tennessee State University, B.A. in speech and drama, 1987. Began career as news reporter for WVOL Radio, Nashville, Tennessee, 1971–72; reporter, news anchorperson, WTVF-TV, Nashville, 1973–76; news anchorperson, WJZ-TV, Baltimore, Maryland, 1976–77; host, morning talk show, *People Are Talking,* 1977–83; host, *A.M. Chicago* talk show, WLS-TV, Chicago, 1984; host, *The Oprah Winfrey Show,* locally broadcast in Chicago, 1985–86, nationally syndicated, since 1986; received Oscar and Golden Globe nominations for dramatic film debut in *The Color Purple,* 1985; owner and producer, Harpo Productions, since 1986; moved to television acting with *Brewster Place* miniseries on ABC, 1990; host, series of television specials, including *Oprah: Behind the Scenes,* from 1992. Recipient: Woman of Achievement Award, National Organization of Women, 1986; numerous Emmy Awards; named Broadcaster of the Year, International Radio and TV Society, 1988; America's Hope Award, 1990; Industry Achievement Award, Broadcast Promotion Marketing

Executives/Broadcast Design Association, 1991; Image Awards, National Association for the Advancement of Colored People (NAACP), 1989, 1990, 1991, and 1992; Entertainer of the Year Award, NAACP, 1989; CEBA Awards, 1989, 1990, and 1991.

Television Series

1977–83	*People Are Talking*
1984	*A.M. Chicago*
1986–	*The Oprah Winfrey Show*
1990	*Brewster Place* (actor and producer)

Made-for-Television Movies

1989	*The Women of Brewster Place* (actor and producer)
1992	*Overexposed* (executive producer)
1993	*There Are No Children Here* (actor and producer)
1997	*Before Women Had Wings* (actor and producer)
1998	*David and Lisa* (producer)
1999	*Tuesdays with Morrie* (producer)
2001	*Amy and Isabelle* (producer)

Television Miniseries

1998	*The Wedding*

Television Specials

1991–93	*ABC Afterschool Special* (host and supervising producer)

1992	*Oprah: Behind the Scenes* (host and supervising producer)
1992	*Lincoln* (voice)
1993	*Michael Jackson Talks...to Oprah: 90 Prime-Time Minutes with the King of Pop*
1997	*About Us: The Dignity of Children* (host and producer)

Films

The Color Purple, 1985; *Native Son,* 1986; *Beloved,* 1998.

Further Reading

Barthel, Joan, "Here Comes Oprah! From *The Color Purple* to TV Talk Queen," *Ms.* (August 1986)

Gillespie, Marcia Ann, "Winfrey Takes All," *Ms.* (November 1988)

Haag, Laurie L., "Oprah Winfrey: The Construction of Intimacy in the Talk Show Setting," *Journal of Popular Culture* (spring 1993)

Harrison, Barbara Grizzuti, "The Importance of Being Oprah," *New York Times Magazine* (June 11, 1989)

King, Norman, *Everybody Loves Oprah!: Her Remarkable Life Story,* New York: Morrow, 1987

Mair, George, *Oprah Winfrey: The Real Story,* Secaucus, New Jersey: Carol, 1994

Marshall, P. David, *Celebrity and Power,* Minneapolis: University of Minnesota Press, 1997

Mascariotte, Gloria-Jean, " 'C'mon Girl': Oprah Winfrey and the Discourse of Feminine Talk," *Genders* (fall 1991)

Waldron, Robert, *Oprah!* New York: St. Martin's Press, 1988

White, Mimi, *Tele-Advising: Therapeutic Discourse in American Television,* Chapel Hill: University of North Carolina Press, 1992

Winters, Jonathan (1925–)

U.S. Comedian

Jonathan Winters began his career in radio as a disc jockey on station WING (Dayton, Ohio) and then moved to television at WBNS (Columbus, Ohio), where he hosted a local program for three years. He moved to New York in the 1950s and performed in night clubs on Broadway. But it is TV that has made Winters both famous and familiar to a huge and grateful U.S. audience for more than four decades. Known for his numerous characters and voices, his stream-of-consciousness humor has influenced countless other performers, a prime example being the contemporary comic actor Robin Williams.

Winters's first network television appearances came during the 1950s, with enormously successful guest spots on talk-variety shows such as *The Jack Paar Show, The Steve Allen Show,* and *The Tonight Show.* He went on to appear in many television programs, including *Omnibus* (where he was the show's first stand-up comedian), *Playhouse 90, Twilight Zone,* and *Here's the Show* (a summer replacement for *The*

Jonathan Winters.
Photo courtesy of Jonathan Winters

confined to a character, yet somehow managed to work many of his other personae into the stories. His performance earned an Emmy for Best Supporting Actor in a Comedy. In addition to on-camera roles, Winters frequently provides the voice for commercials and cartoons. These performances are usually wedded to his distinctive style, allowing audiences the pleasure of recognition for yet another Jonathan Winters moment.

WILLIAM RICHTER

Jonathan Winters. Born in Dayton, Ohio, November 11, 1925. Educated at Kenyon College, Gambier, Ohio, 1946; Dayton Art Institute, B.F.A., 1950. Married: Eileen Schauder, 1948; one daughter and one son. Served in U.S. Marine Corps Reserve, 1943–46. Began career at radio station WING, Dayton, Ohio, 1949; disc jockey, station WBNS-TV, Columbus, Ohio, 1950–53; nightclub comedian, New York, 1953; successful in film and as author and painter; recorded 12 albums for Verve. Honorary chair, National Congress of American Indians. Recipient: Emmy Award, 1991.

Television Series (selected)

1956–57	*The Jonathan Winters Show*
1967–69	*The Jonathan Winters Show*
1972–74	*The Wacky World of Jonathan Winters*
1975–80	*Hollywood Squares*
1978–82	*Mork and Mindy*
1991–92	*Davis Rules*

Made-for-Television Movies

1968	*Now You See It, Now You Don't*
1980	*More Wild, Wild West*
1985	*Alice in Wonderland*
1987	*The Little Troll Prince* (voice only)

Television Specials (selected)

1964	*The Jonathan Winters Special*
1965	*The Jonathan Winters Show*
1965	*The Jonathan Winters Show*
1967	*Guys 'n' Geishas*
1970	*The Wonderful World of Jonathan Winters*
1976	*Jonathan Winters Presents 200 Years of American Humor*
1977	*Yabba Dabba Doo! The Happy World of Hanna-Barbera* (cohost)
1986	*King Kong: The Living Legend* (host)
1991	*The Wish That Changed Christmas* (voice)

George Gobel Show). *The NBC Comedy Hour,* originally designed as a Sunday showcase for new talent, was revamped to feature Gail Storm as the hostess and Winters as the show's comedian. He also hosted his own program, *The Jonathan Winters Show,* in 1956–57. Aired on NBC from 7:30 to 7:45 P.M. to fill a 15-minute spot following the NBC evening news, the show was structured around Winters's sketches, blackouts, and monologues. The program was revived by CBS in a one-hour format for two seasons beginning in December 1967 and featured the famous Maude Frickert, as well as the Willard "From the Couple up the Street" sketch. In some ways, these shows indicated that Winters's comedy was almost too unpredictable for conventional network television, and he was allowed more freedom in *The Wacky World of Jonathan Winters,* a syndicated program that focused on his bravura improvisations.

Younger viewers may remember Winters from *Mork and Mindy,* where he played the role of Mork and Mindy's son. Paired with Robin Williams in the role of Mork, Winters was wildly inventive. The comedy in this show was at times truly explosive, with one improvisational genius playing off the other. In the more conventional sitcom, *Davis Rules,* Winters was

Films

It's a Mad, Mad, Mad, Mad World, 1963; *The Loved One*, 1964; *The Russians Are Coming! The Russians Are Coming!* 1966; *Penelope*, 1967; *The Midnight Oil*, 1967; *8 on the Lam*, 1967; *Oh Dad, Poor Dad, Mama's Hung You in the Closet and I'm Feeling So Sad*, 1968; *Viva Max*, 1969; *The Fish That Saved Pittsburgh*, 1979; *The Longshot*, 1986; *Say Yes*, 1986; *Moon over Parador*, 1988; *The Shadow*, 1994; *The Flintstones*, 1994; *The Adventures of Rocky and Bullwinkle*, 2000.

Publications

Mouse Breath, Social Conformity, and Other Ills, 1965
Winters' Tales: Stories and Observations for the Unusual, 1987; revised edition, 2001
Hang Ups: Paintings by Jonathan Winters, 1988

Further Reading

Adir, Karin, *The Great Clowns of American Television*, Jefferson, North Carolina: McFarland, 1988
Sanoff, Alvin P., "The Stand-Up Art of Jonathan Winters," *U.S. News and World Report* (December 5, 1988)

Wiseman, Frederick (1930–)

U.S. Documentary Filmmaker

Since the late 1960s, Frederick Wiseman has arguably been the most important American documentary filmmaker. A law professor turned filmmaker in 1967, Wiseman, in his most dramatically powerful documentaries, has poignantly chronicled the exercise of power in American society by focusing on the everyday travails of the least fortunate Americans caught in the tangled webs of social institutions operating at the community level. An underlying theme of many of these documentaries is the individual's attempt to preserve his or her humanity and dignity while struggling against laws and dehumanizing bureaucratic systems. Wiseman functions as producer, director, and editor of the films, which numbered 32 by 2001. Most of the documentaries have been broadcast on public television in the United States, presented by New York station WNET, and have regularly marked the opening of the new PBS season. Wiseman's documentaries have won numerous awards, including three Emmys and a Dupont Award. Wiseman was awarded the prestigious MacArthur Prize Fellows Award in 1982, and he has received a Peabody Award for his contribution to documentary film.

Wiseman's aesthetic falls squarely in the "direct cinema" tradition of documentary filmmaking, which emphasizes continued filming, as unobtrusively as possible, of human conversation and the routines of everyday life, with no music, no interviews, no voice-over narration, and no overt attempt to interpret or explain the events unfolding before the camera.

Wiseman calls his films "reality-fictions," reflecting his tight thematic structuring of the raw footage in the editing process. Eschewing "leading characters," Wiseman skillfully interweaves many small stories to provide contrast and thematic complexity.

Wiseman's debut as a documentarian was both auspicious and highly controversial. His first film, *Titicut Follies* (1967), was shot in the Massachusetts State Hospital for the Criminally Insane at Bridgewater. Here we see the impact of a social institution—a publicly funded mental hospital—on society's rejects. Often described as an "exposé" (a description Wiseman rejects), *Titicut Follies* chronicled the indignities suffered by the inmates, many of whom were kept naked and force-fed through nasal tubes. *Titicut Follies* caused a public outcry and demands for institutional reform. The film was officially barred from general public showings until 1993 by order of a U.S. court, on grounds that it violated an inmate's privacy.

A succession of critically acclaimed documentaries quickly followed. In *High School* (1968), Wiseman examined a largely white and middle-class Philadelphia high school and the authoritarian, conformist value system inculcated in students by teachers and administrators. The official ideology reflected in the educational power structure was largely seen as an expression of the value framework of the surrounding community.

Law and Order (1969) was filmed in Kansas City, Missouri. Here, Wiseman cast his gaze on the daily

Frederick Wiseman.
Courtesy of the Everett Collection

routine of police work in the Kansas City police department. Most of the sequences were filmed in the black district of the city. Examples of police brutality and insensitivity were juxtaposed with other examples of sympathetic patrol officers attempting to assist citizens with a variety of minor, and sometimes humorous, problems. On the whole, however, police behavior was depicted as symptomatic of deeper social crises, including racism, poverty, and the resultant pervasive violence in the inner city.

His next film, *Hospital* (1969), for which Wiseman won two Emmys for Best News Documentary, was set in the operating room, emergency ward, and outpatient clinics of New York City's Metropolitan Hospital. As in *Law and Order*, Wiseman used an institutional setting to examine urban ills. Stabbing and drug-overdose victims, abused children, the mentally disturbed, and the abandoned elderly pass through the public hospital. But unlike the authority figures in *Titicut Follies*, the doctors, nurses, and orderlies at Metropolitan come off as much more humane, responding to patients with sympathy and understanding.

In *Juvenile Court* (1973), as in *Hospital*, Wiseman reveals the compassionate side of authority. The court officials in the Memphis, Tennessee, juvenile court discuss, with evident concern, the futures of young offenders accused of crimes such as child abuse and armed robbery.

Welfare (1975) is one of the most provocative and understated of Wiseman's institutional examinations. Shot in a New York City welfare office, the documentary, in seemingly interminable shots, chronicles the frustration and pain of abject welfare recipients who spend their time sitting and waiting, or being shunted from office to office, as the degrading milieu of the welfare system grinds on. Welfare bureaucrats are largely seen as agents of dehumanization.

The Store (1983), Wiseman's first color film, at first glance appears to depart from the typical "weighty" subject matter of most of his previous films. That, however, is deceptive. For while the institution under scrutiny, the world-famous Neiman-Marcus department store in Dallas, Texas, may seem to be lightweight material, Wiseman's treatment of the activities of store employees and the mostly wealthy customers ultimately reveals the shallow lives of the United States' economic elite and those who service them. Conspicuous consumption is everywhere in evidence. The clientele while away days in the store's dressing rooms, trying on expensive gowns and furs. A compliant group of saleswomen are led in smile exercises as they prepare to meet their condescending customers. The bourgeoisie and proletariat are complicit in this sordid dance of money and unproductive leisure. *The Store* stands in stark and powerful contrast to the despair depicted in *Welfare*.

The ethics of Wiseman's filmmaking have been criticized by some as invading the privacy of the films' subjects (*Titicut Follies* is the clearest case in point). Wiseman's response is unequivocal. He argues that if an institution receives public tax support, citizens are entitled to observe its operation. Reportorial access, Wiseman adds, is a constitutional right with regard to public institutions. In his early documentaries, if any subject objected at the time of shooting to being filmed, Wiseman eliminated the footage in question from the final cut. Later, however, he denied subjects veto rights. Some subjects, while initially pleased with their portrayals, later became upset with others' negative reactions to those portrayals. This may be one of Wiseman's major contributions to the documentary form, to permit subjects to examine their own behavior—to confront the consequences of their own social actions—as seen through the eyes of others.

HAL HIMMELSTEIN

Frederick Wiseman. Born in Boston, Massachusetts, January 1, 1930. Educated at Williams College, Williamstown, Massachusetts, B.A., 1951; LL.B., Yale

University, New Haven, Connecticut, 1954. Worked as law professor; turned to television documentary film-making, 1967. Recipient: Emmy Awards, 1969 (twice), and 1970; John Simon Guggenheim Memorial Foundation Fellowship, 1980–81; John D. and Catherine T. MacArthur Fellowship, 1982–87; International Documentary Association Career Achievement Award, 1990; Peabody Award, Personal Award, 1991.

Television Documentaries (all as producer, director, and editor)

1967	*Titicut Follies*
1968	*High School*
1969	*Law and Order*
1970	*Hospital*
1971	*Basic Training*
1972	*Essene*
1973	*Juvenile Court*
1974	*Primate*
1975	*Welfare*
1976	*Meat*
1977	*Canal Zone*
1978	*Sinai Field Mission*
1979	*Manoeuvre*
1980	*Model*
1982	*Seraphita's Diary*
1983	*The Store*
1985	*Racetrack*
1986	*Blind*
1986	*Deaf*
1986	*Adjustment and Work*
1986	*Multi-Handicapped*
1987	*Missile*
1989	*Near Death*
1989	*Central Park*
1991	*Aspen*
1993	*Zoo*
1994	*High School II*
1995	*Ballet*
1996	*La Comedie Francaise*
1997	*Public Housing*
1999	*Belfast, Maine*
2001	*Domestic Violence*

Further Reading

Arlen, Michael J., *The Camera Age: Essays on Television,* New York: Penguin, 1982

Atkins, Thomas R., "Frederick Wiseman's America: *Titicut Follies* to *Primate,*" in *The Documentary Tradition,* edited by Lewis Jacob, New York: Hopkinson and Blake, 1971; 2nd edition, New York: Norton, 1979

Barnouw, Erik, *Documentary: A History of the Nonfiction Film,* New York: Oxford University Press, 1974; revised edition, 1983

Denby, David, "Documentary in America," *Atlantic Monthly* (March 1970)

Rifkin, Glenn, "Wiseman Looks at Affluent Texans," *New York Times* (December 11, 1983)

Rosenthal, Alan, editor, *New Challenges in Documentary,* Berkeley: University of California Press, 1988

Witt, Paul Junger (1941–)

U.S. Producer

Native New Yorker Paul Junger Witt took his first television position with Screen Gems in Los Angeles immediately following his graduation from the University of Virginia. At Screen Gems, one of Hollywood's most active television production companies, he worked as an associate producer and director of *The Farmer's Daughter* and *Occasional Wife.* In 1971 Witt produced the enormously successful and influential—and Emmy-winning—made-for-television movie *Brian's Song.* On that project he worked for the first time with his future partner, Tony Thomas. He then assumed producer-director duties on *The Partridge Family.*

In 1971 he moved on to become a producer with Spelling-Goldberg Productions, where he was involved in several films. A year later, he joined Danny Thomas Productions as president, serving as executive producer of five movies for television and two series, including *Fay,* which was created and written by Susan Harris.

In 1975 Witt joined with Tony Thomas (son of the legendary comedian Danny Thomas) to form Witt/Thomas Productions. A year later, the two men teamed up with Susan Harris to form Witt/Thomas/ Harris Productions. Their first venture, *Soap,* was both a critical and popular success, although it was roundly attacked by religious and cultural conservatives. Witt found the

Paul Junger Witt.
Photo courtesy of Witt-Thomas-Harris Productions

See also **Benson; Golden Girls;** **Harris, Susan;** *Soap;* **Thomas, Tony**

Paul Junger Witt. Born in New York City, March 20, 1941. Educated at the University of Virginia, Charlottesville, Virginia, B.A. in fine arts, 1963. Married: Susan Harris; one son, Oliver; one daughter and two sons from a previous marriage. Associate producer and director, Screen Gems, Hollywood, California, 1965–67, producer and director, 1967–71; producer, Spelling/Goldberg Productions, Hollywood, 1971–73; president and executive producer, Danny Thomas Productions, Hollywood, 1973–74; founder and executive producer, Witt/Thomas/Harris Productions, Hollywood, 1976–81, executive producer, since 1975; executive producer, Witt/Thomas/Harris Productions, Witt/Thomas Productions, Witt/Thomas Films, 1992. Recipient: Emmy Awards, 1972, 1985, and 1986. Member: Board of Directors, Environmental Defense Fund; National Board, Medicine Sans Frontiers; Directors Guild of America; Writers Guild of America.

Television Series (selected)

1972–76	*The Rookies*
1977–81	*Soap*
1980–81	*I'm a Big Girl Now*
1980–82	*It's a Living*
1982–83	*It Takes Two*
1983	*Condo*
1985	*Hail to the Chief*
1985–92	*The Golden Girls*
1987–90	*Beauty and the Beast*
1988–95	*Empty Nest*
1991–95	*Blossom*
1991	*Good and Evil*
1991–93	*Herman's Head*
1991–93	*Nurses*
1993	*Whoops*
1993–96	*The John Larroquette Show*
1995	*Muscle*
1996	*Local Heroes*
1996–97	*Pearl*
1996	*Common Law*
1998	*The Secret Lives of Men*
1999	*Everything's Relative*

Made-for-Television Movies

1972	*Brian's Song*
1972	*No Place to Run*
1972	*Home for the Holidays*
1973	*A Cold Night's Death*
1973	*The Letters*
1973	*Bloodsport*

criticisms particularly disturbing since no one in the groups making the attacks had ever seen the series. Yet several ABC affiliates responded to the critiques and either refused to air *Soap* or relegated it to late hours. It is Witt's belief that the unfair depictions of the show by those bent on removing it from the air continued to have a chilling effect on advertisers for all the remaining years that the program was on ABC.

A unique television event, *Soap* set in motion a long string of major television hits for the three partners, including *Benson, The Golden Girls,* and *Empty Nest.* Of these series, *Soap* and *Golden Girls* reflected a continuing emphasis on strong female characters. The company also produced at least five other shows with modest success that focused on women. In addition, Witt/Thomas produced *Beauty and the Beast, Blossom, The John Larroquette Show, The Secret Lives of Men,* and *Everything's Relative.*

The huge success of the company solidified Witt/Thomas/Harris as a powerful force in the television industry. Witt observed that their reputation gave them significant access to network time slots. In 1984, Witt/Thomas also began production of feature films including *Dead Poets Society* and *Three Kings.*

ROBERT S. ALLEY

1974	*Remember When*
1974	*The Gun and the Pulpit*
1975	*Satan's Triangle*
1976	*Griffin and Phoenix*
1976	*High Risk*
1980	*Trouble in Big Timber Country*
1996	*Radiant City*

Films

Firstborn, 1984; *Dead Poets Society,* 1988; *Final Analysis,* 1992; *Mixed Nuts,* 1994; *Three Kings,* 1999; *Insomnia,* 2002.

Wojeck

Canadian Drama Series

First aired on the anglophone network of the Canadian Broadcasting Corporation (CBC) for two seasons (1966 and 1968), *Wojeck* was a magnificent aberration: a popular, homegrown dramatic series made for the pleasure of English-Canadian viewers. Early on, francophone producers in Montreal had developed a particular genre of social melodrama, known as the *téléroman,* that captivated the imagination of French-Canadian viewers. Their anglophone counterparts had no such history of success. The record of domestic dramatic series in English Canada had been short and dismal, a collection of failures, or at best partial successes, usually modeled on U.S. hits but lacking either the inspiration or the funding necessary to succeed. Audiences much preferred watching the originals, the stories Hollywood had made, until *Wojeck* arrived. Early in its first season, *Wojeck* was purportedly attracting more viewers than many U.S. imports, and it received even higher ratings when rebroadcast in the summer of 1967.

Part of the success of *Wojeck* rested on its visual style. It was the first time the CBC had produced a filmed dramatic series for its national audience. Executive producer Ronald Weyman drew on his experience at the National Film Board to deliver stories that had the look of authenticity. This was especially true in the first season, when each episode was in black and white and scenes were sometimes shot with a handheld camera, giving the productions a gritty, realistic quality that at times suggested the news documentary. The look of authenticity was less apparent in the second season, when the series was shot in color.

Success, however, had as much to do with the subject, the script, and above all the acting. *Wojeck* told stories about a big city coroner and his quest for justice. The character and setting were novel twists on the very popular 1960s U.S. genre of workplace dramas that focused on the exploits of such professionals as lawyers, doctors, and even teachers and social workers. A decade later, the hit U.S. series *Quincy,* which began its long run on NBC in 1976, made the notion of a crusading coroner much more familiar to North American audiences. But at the time that it aired, *Wojeck* was an original, possibly inspired by the much-publicized exploits of an actual coroner of the city of Toronto.

The show did conform nonetheless to the formula of such U.S. hits as *Ben Casey* (1961–66) and *Mr. Novak* (1963–65). All of the episodes of *Wojeck* (written in the first season by Philip Hersch) center on the seamy side of life: racism, ageism, discrimination (one program deals with male prostitution and homosexuality), and other species of injustice. Often the "heavy" is society itself, whose indifference or intolerance has bred evil. *Wojeck* was a kind of "edutainment," since viewers were supposed to absorb some sort of moral lesson about the country's social ills while enjoying their hour of diversion. The first show, an outstanding episode titled "The Last Man in the World," looks at why an Indian committed suicide in the big city, exposing "Canada's shame": its mistreatment of its native peoples.

Wojeck features a strong male lead, Dr. Steve Wojeck, superbly played by John Vernon, who is backed up by a "team" that includes his wife (the understanding helpmate), an assistant (efficient but unobtrusive), and a sometimes reluctant crown attorney (the well-meaning bureaucrat). Wojeck is emphatically masculine: big and rough, aggressive, short-tempered, and domineering. These qualities are most apparent when

Wojeck.
Photo courtesy of National Archives of Canada/CBC Collection

he deals with the police and other authorities. He is easily moved to anger and moral outbursts but is much more understanding when he deals with society's outcasts. Wojeck is the engaged liberal: an advocate for the powerless committed to reforming the practices of the system so that it ensures justice for all. Like his Hollywood counterparts, Wojeck embodied the 1960s myth of the professional as hero who will turn his talents and skills to making our sadly flawed world a better place.

Wojeck had no real successors. Weyman and others did produce a number of forgettable dramas in the next few years, but none could match the appeal of the imports. Ironically, the very success of Wojeck had spelled trouble for CBC's drama department. John Vernon was lured away to Hollywood, where he came to specialize in playing villains. Indeed, Weyman later claimed that much of the talent that had contributed to the appeal of *Wojeck* was drawn away to the greener pastures down south. The memory of that brief, glorious moment was sufficient to justify replaying some of the episodes of *Wojeck* on the CBC network more than 20 years later.

PAUL RUTHERFORD

See also **Canadian Programming in English; Weyman, Ron**

Cast

Dr. Steve Wojeck	John Vernon
Marty Wojeck	Patricia Collins
Crown Attorney Bateman	Ted Follows
Byron James	Carl Banas

Producer
Ronald Weyman

Programming History
20 episodes
CBC

September 1966–November 1966	
January 1968–March 1968	Tuesday 9:00–10:00
	Tuesday 9:00–10:00

Further Reading

Miller, Mary Jane, *Turn Up the Contrast: CBC Television Drama Since 1952,* Vancouver: University of British Columbia Press, 1987

Rutherford, Paul, *When Television Was Young: Primetime Canada, 1952–1967,* Toronto: University of Toronto Press, 1990

Wolfe, Morris, *Jolts: The TV Wasteland and the Canadian Oasis,* Toronto: Lorimer, 1985

Wolf, Dick (1946–)

U.S. Writer, Producer

Artist and entrepreneur Dick Wolf revitalized television drama in the nineties with the artistic success and popularity of his *Law & Order* franchise. Combining savvy business acumen with an acute storytelling sense, Wolf devised a paradigm for a television series in the age of fragmentation and erosion of the network audience. His fascination with real-life crime inspired an almost documentary approach to the police and legal genre, complete with intricate story structure and fully realized characters, which became a model for future network programming.

Following in his father's footsteps, Richard A. Wolf began his career as an advertising copywriter and producer, responsible for more than 100 commercials in the early seventies. He helped launch campaigns for Crest toothpaste ("You can't beat Crest for fighting cavities") and National Airlines ("I'm Cheryl, fly me"), learning the power of the brand in the process. During the mid-1970s, he pursued screenwriting, but few of his scripts became finished films. Wolf himself produced his first film, *Skateboard* (1978), a teenage story starring Leif Garrett. The failure of his second film, *Gas* (1981), about phony fuel shortages, led to writing stories for the seminal police series *Hill Street Blues,* whose creator Steven Bochco was a childhood friend. During this period he changed his screen credit to the more casual Dick Wolf. He also wrote scripts for the stylish *Miami Vice,* later becoming story editor and executive producer of the Michael Mann series. Wolf continued his movie career, writing such diverse films as *No Man's Land* (1987), an undercover police adventure with Charlie Sheen; *Masquerade* (1988), a romantic thriller in the tradition of Hitchcock starring Rob Lowe; and *School Ties* (1992), a teenage drama about anti-Semitism featuring early appearances by Brendan Fraser, Matt Damon, and Ben Affleck. Throughout his career Wolf would experiment with a variety of genres, but his affinity is clearly for the traditional crime drama.

Tackling his own television projects, Wolf eschewed the serialized narrative of *Hill Street Blues* and drew inspiration in the self-contained stories of such 1950s staples as *Dragnet* and *Perry Mason.* In the crowded television universe Wolf wanted to create a recognizable landscape where plots are resolved each week with a distinct, formulaic pacing so that viewers could tune in any time and still understand what was transpiring. Wolf created a series with four lead characters, two detectives and two lawyers. *Law & Order,* a hybrid police and legal series with a complex perspective on the criminal justice system, was rejected by two networks before NBC took a chance in 1990 when such comedies as *Roseanne* and *The Cosby Show* ruled the airwaves. Wolf himself hedged his bets, thinking his hour-long drama could be sold as two half-hours in syndication. *Law & Order* started slowly, but it was on cable, first on A&E and then TNT, that the series, seen as an hour program repeated throughout the day, reached cult status.

Starting with *Law & Order,* Wolf developed several production strategies that would define his best series. He based episodes on actual events in the news. With this "ripped from the headlines" approach, Wolf and his writers could turn real life into fiction faster than any television movie or theatrical film. Wolf also carried on the legacy of *Naked City* and *The Defenders* by filming in the streets of New York City. The multicultural diversity and surreal insanity of urban life became constant motifs in Wolf's work. Wolf has also consciously made action as important as character in his core series, making sure that any changes in the cast, for whatever reason, would not disrupt the pleasure of his narrative.

One of Wolf's major ambitions is to head an independent production company responsible for quality programming, very much in the tradition of Grant Tinker's MTM. As *Law & Order* developed a critical and popular momentum in the early 1990s, Wolf attempted other projects, but they were short-lived and largely forgettable, including the futuristic cop show *Mann & Machine* (1992) and a reformed con artist drama, *South Beach* (1993). He was more successful with *New York Undercover* (1994–98), a FOX series that combined his gritty, *cinéma vérité* visuals with the beat of the emerging hip-hop culture. When other excursions into the crime genre failed (*Feds,* 1997, and *Players,* 1997–98), Wolf, with his adman sensibility, decided to brand *Law & Order,* creating other series with the same contained story formula and similar dramatic beats. In 1999 *Law & Order: Special Victims Unit* debuted, with an emphasis on the investigation of sex crimes. In 2001 Wolf extended the franchise with *Law & Order: Criminal Intent,* a journey into the deviant mind led by a modern-day Sherlock Holmes. The original *Law & Order* is signed through 2005, which will make it the longest-running hour drama in television history.

As the *Law & Order* brand extends into books, computer games, and DVDs, Wolf continued the search for another hit series. He has tested the reality genre several times, including *Arrest & Trial* (2000), a first-run syndication series following criminal cases from investigation through the final verdict, and *Crime & Punishment* (2002), a "drama-mentary" spotlighting actual trials, organized around Wolf's patented four-act structure. Wolf tried to revive the newspaper genre with *Deadline* (2000), about a crusading columnist who recruits graduate students to take on New York's power brokers. He was more successful in resurrecting a police show that inspired him: *Dragnet,* with Ed O'Neil as Joe Friday.

As head of the independent company he founded in association with Universal Television, Wolf likens himself to a CEO whose main role is to hire the right people to keep his productions running smoothly. He has taken on the role of an industry leader, speaking out against the V-chip and the ratings system. Although his shows are concerned with the consequences of crime, and not the gruesome act, he is outspoken against any regulation of violent content. His "media juggernaut" *Law & Order* was one of the crown jewels in the Vivendi Universal corporation that was pur-

chased by NBC, the network Wolf helped to sustain well over a decade. But business aside, it has been Wolf's uncommonly keen sense of storytelling that has kept several media giants thriving.

RON SIMON

See also **Law and Order**

Wolper, David L. (1928–)

U.S. Producer

David L. Wolper is arguably the most successful independent documentary producer to have ever worked in television. Through a career span of nearly 50 years, this prolific filmmaker has left his imprint with documentary specials, documentary series, dramatic miniseries, movies made for theatrical release, movies made for television, television sitcoms, entertainment specials, and entertainment special events.

Wolper began his career in the late 1940s by selling B movies, English-dubbed Soviet cartoons, and film serials, including *Superman,* to television stations. Interested in producing television documentaries, in 1958 he established Wolper Productions. Working with exclusive Russian space program footage and NASA cinematography of U.S. missile launches, within two years his first film, *The Race for Space,* was completed and had attracted a sponsor. Wolper offered the film to all three networks, but an unofficial rule of the time dictated that only news programs and documentaries produced by network personnel were allowed on the air. Not to be discouraged, the young producer fell back on his sales experience and syndicated the film to 104 local stations across the United States—the overwhelming majority of these stations network affiliates willing to preempt other programming for the Wolper show. For the first time in television history, a nonnetwork documentary special achieved near-national audience coverage. Having been released to theaters prior to television, *The Race for Space* also received an Academy Award nomination in the Best Documentary category—another first for a television film.

Wolper's notoriety helped to launch a significant number of documentary projects that found their way

to network time slots. Utilizing a basic compilation technique, these early films consisted of editing photo stills and film clips to narration and music, with occasional recreations of footage, minimal editorial viewpoint, and high-information, high-entertainment value. Increasingly successful, within four years of establishing Wolper Productions, Wolper's method would place him on a level with NBC and CBS as one of the three largest producers of television documentaries and documentary specials.

A major turning point in Wolper's career occurred in 1960 when he bought the rights to Theodore H. White's book *The Making of the President.* Aired on ABC, Wolper's potentially controversial film presented an incisive look at the American political process, won four Emmy Awards including 1963 Program of the Year, and guaranteed Wolper's celebrity.

In 1964 Wolper sold his documentary production unit to Metromedia but stayed on as the company's chief of operations. With this media giant's backing, Wolper's projects grew in scope and substance. He became a regular supplier of documentary programs to all three commercial networks creating such memorable series as *The March of Time,* in association with Time, Inc., and a series of nature specials in collaboration with the National Geographic Society. For the latter, he introduced American audiences to French oceanographer Jacques Cousteau. This in turn led to the first-ever documentary spin-off, *The Undersea World of Jacques Cousteau.*

Breaking away from Metromedia in 1967, Wolper continued his documentary work but also tried his hand at theatrical release motion pictures. He created a number of unexceptional films including *The Bridge at*

David L. Wolper.
Photo courtesy of Wolper Organization, Inc

Remagen (1968), *If It's Tuesday, This Must be Belgium* (1969), and *Willy Wonka and the Chocolate Factory* (1971). In fiction television, he found more success with regularly scheduled television series that included *Get Christie Love!* (1974–75) featuring the first black policewoman character in television history, *Chico and the Man* (1974–78), and *Welcome Back, Kotter* (1975–79).

Perhaps Wolper's most significant accomplishment was his developmental work with the television nonfiction drama miniseries. In the mid-1970s, after bypass heart surgery and sale of his company to Warner Brothers, he helped to invent the docudrama genre with his award-winning production of Alex Haley's acclaimed family saga, *Roots*. Reconstructing history in an unprecedented 12-hour film, the series was broadcast in one- and two-hour segments over an eight-day period in January 1977. Contrary to initial concerns over the high-risk nature of the venture, the series brought ABC a 44.9 rating and 66 percent share of audience to set viewership records that place it among the most-watched programs in the history of television.

In 1984 Wolper stepped out of his usual role as film producer to orchestrate the opening and closing ceremonies for the Summer Olympics in Los Angeles. The first ever to be staged by a private group, the ceremonies received a 55 percent share of audience, outranking all other Olympic coverage. For his efforts, Wolper was rewarded with a special Emmy and the Jean Hersholt Humanitarian Award at the Oscar ceremony in 1985. The following year he was recruited to produce the Liberty Weekend 100th anniversary celebration for the Statue of Liberty. The four-day event was viewed by 1.5 billion people worldwide.

In 1999 Wolper's *Celebrate the Century,* a ten-hour CNN documentary on the defining moments of the 20th century, was broadcast in May and June. In the same year, his *Great People of the 20th Century* aired on the Discovery cable network. As reported in the November 13, 2000, issue of *Broadcasting & Cable,* Wolper is excited about the opportunities offered by cable. "It's been tough for independent documentary filmmakers," he said. "Here comes cable; and the whole world opens. I am jealous; I wish I was starting now."

As a producer, filmmaker, entrepreneur, historian, and visionary, David Wolper's career has been one of taking risks and continually breaking new ground. Most important, through his more than 600 films, his innovative and creative spirit has educated and entertained millions.

JOEL STERNBERG

See also **Documentary; Roots**

David Lloyd Wolper. Born in New York City, January 11, 1928. Studied at Drake University, 1946; University of Southern California, 1948. Married: 1) Margaret Davis Richard, 1958 (divorced, 1969); one daughter and two sons; 2) Gloria Diane Hill, 1974. Began career as vice president, then treasurer, Flamingo Films, TV sales company, 1948–50; vice president, West Coast Operations, 1954–58; chair and president, Wolper Productions, Los Angeles, since 1958; president, Fountainhead International, since 1960; president, Wolper TV Sales Company, since 1964; vice president, Metromedia, Inc., 1965–68; president and chair, Wolper Pictures Limited, since 1968; consultant and executive producer, Warner Brothers, Inc., since 1976. Member: U.S. Olympic Team Benefit Committee; advisory committee, National Center for Jewish Film; Academy of Motion Picture Arts and Sciences; Producers Guild of America; Caucus for Producers, Writers, and Directors. Trustee: Los Angeles County Museum of Art, 1984; American Film Institute; Los Angeles Thoracic and Cardiovascular Foundation.

Board of directors: Amateur Athletic Association of Los Angeles, 1984; Los Angeles Heart Institute; Southern California Committee for the Olympic Games, 1977; Academy of Television Arts and Sciences Foundation, 1983; University of Southern California Cinema/Television Department. Recipient: Award for documentaries, San Francisco International Film Festival, 1960; Distinguished Service Award, U.S. Junior Chamber of Commerce; Monte Carlo International Film Festival Award, 1964; Cannes Film Festival Grand Prix for TV Programs, 1964; Academy Award: Jean Hersholt Humanitarian Award, 1985; named to TV Hall of Fame, 1988; Medal of Chevalier, French National Legion of Honor, 1990; Lifetime Achievement Award, Producers Guild of America, 1991; Honorary Doctor of Fine Arts, University of Southern California (USC), 1997; USC School of Cinema-Television's Mary Pickford Award, 1999; eight Globe Awards; five Peabody Awards; 40 Emmy Awards; numerous other awards.

Television Series (selected)

1961–64, 1979	Biography
1962–65	Story of...
1963–64	Hollywood and the Stars
1965–66	March of Time
1965–76	National Geographic
1968–76	The Undersea World of Jacques Cousteau
1971–73	Appointment with Destiny
1972–73	Explorers
1974–78	Chico and the Man
1974–75	Get Christie Love!
1975–79	Welcome Back, Kotter

Television Miniseries (selected)

1976	Victory at Entebbe
1977	Roots
1979	Roots: The Next Generations
1983	The Thorn Birds
1985	North and South, Book I
1986	North and South, Book II
1987	Napoleon and Josephine
1996	The Thorn Birds: The Missing Years
1999	Celebrate the Century

Made-for-Television Movies (selected)

1973	500 Pound Jerk
1974	Men of the Dragon
1974	Unwed Father
1974	The Morning After
1974	Get Christie Love
1976	Brenda Starr
1982	Agatha Christie Movie: Murder Is Easy
1983	Agatha Christie Movie: Sparkling Cyanide
1984	Agatha Christie Movie: Caribbean Mystery
1987	The Betty Ford Story
1988	Roots: The Gift
1989	The Plot to Kill Hitler
1989	Murder in Mississippi
1990	Dillinger
1990	When You Remember Me
1991	Bed of Lies
1992	Fatal Deception: Mrs. Lee Harvey Oswald
1993	Queen
1993	The Flood: Who Will Save our Children?
1994	Without Warning

Television Specials (selected)

1958	The Race for Space
1959	Project: Man in Space
1960	Hollywood: The Golden Years
1960, 1964, 1968	The Making of the President
1961	Biography of a Rookie
1961	The Rafer Johnson Story
1962	D-Day
1962	Hollywood: The Great Stars
1963	Hollywood: The Fabulous Era
1963	Escape to Freedom
1963	The Passing Years
1963	Ten Seconds That Shook the World
1963	Krebiozen and Cancer
1963	December 7: Day of Infamy
1963	The American Woman in the 20th Century
1964	The Legend of Marilyn Monroe
1964	The Yanks Are Coming
1964	Berlin: Kaiser to Khrushchev
1964	The Rise and Fall of American Communism
1964	The Battle of Britain
1964	Trial at Nuremberg
1965	France: Conquest to Liberation
1965	Korea: The 38th Parallel
1965	Prelude to War
1965	Japan: A New Dawn over Asia
1965	007: The Incredible World of James Bond
1965	Let My People Go

1965	October Madness: The World Series
1965	Race for the Moon
1965	The Bold Men
1965	The General
1965	The Teenage Revolution
1965	The Way Out Men
1965	In Search of Man
1965	Mayhem on a Sunday Afternoon
1966	The Thin Blue Line
1966	Wall Street: Where the Money Is
1966	A Funny Thing Happened on the Way to the White House
1967	China: Roots of Madness
1967	A Nation of Immigrants
1967	Do Blondes Have More Fun?
1968	The Rise and Fall of the Third Reich
1968	On the Trail of Stanley and Livingstone
1970	The Unfinished Journey of Robert F. Kennedy
1970–72	George Plimpton
1971	Say Goodbye
1971	They've Killed President Lincoln
1971–73	Appointment with Destiny
1973–74	American Heritage
1973–75	Primal Man
1974	Judgment
1974	The First Woman President
1974–75	Smithsonian
1975–76	Sandburg's Lincoln
1976	Collision Course
1980	Moviola
1984	Opening and Closing Ceremonies, 1984 Olympic Games
1986	Liberty Weekend
1988	What Price Victory
1999	Great People of the 20th Century
2001	Roots: Celebrating 25 Years

Films (selected)

Four Days in November, 1964; *Devil's Brigade,* 1967; *The Bridge at Remagen,* 1968; *If It's Tuesday, This Must Be Belgium,* 1968; *I Love My Wife,* 1970; *The Helstrom Chronicle,* 1971; *Willy Wonka and the Chocolate Factory,* 1971; *King, Queen, Knave!* 1972; *One Is a Lonely Number,* 1972; *Wattstax,* 1973; *Visions of Eight, 1973; Birds Do It...Bees Do It...,* 1974; *The Animal Within,* 1974; *Victory at Entebbe,* 1976; *The Man Who Saw Tomorrow,* 1980; *This Is Elvis,* 1981; *Imagine: John Lennon,* 1988; *Murder in the First,* 1994; *Surviving Picasso,* 1996; *L.A. Confidential,* 1997.

Further Reading

Angelo, Bonnie, "Liberty's Ringmaster of Ceremonies," *Time* (July 7, 1986)

Arar, Yardena, "And the Show Goes On," *Los Angeles Daily News* (May 2, 1990)

Bluem, A. William, *Documentary in American Television: Form, Function, Method,* New York: Hastings House, 1965

Berlin, Joey, "David Wolper's *Imagine* Takes a Documentary Approach," *New York Post* (October 5, 1988)

"David L. Wolper," *Broadcasting and Cable* (November 13, 2000)

Goldenson, Leonard H., with Martin J. Wolf, *Beating the Odds: The Untold Story Behind the Rise of ABC: The Stars, Struggles, and Egos That Transformed Network Television by the Man Who Made It Happen,* New York: Scribner's, 1991

Harvey, Alec, "Tragedy Is Tale of Hope, Says Wolper," *Birmingham News* (February 2, 1990)

"Hollywood Fights Back," in *Television Today: A Close-Up View Readings from TV Guide,* edited by Barry Cole, Oxford: Oxford University Press, 1981

Marc, David, and Robert J. Thompson, *Prime Time, Prime Movers: From I Love Lucy to L.A. Law—America's Greatest TV Shows and the People Who Created Them,* Boston: Little, Brown, 1992

O'Connor, Colleen, with Martin Kasindorf, "Wolper: Impresario of the Big Event," *Newsweek* (July 7, 1986)

Peterson, Brian, "David L. Wolper: L.A. Influential," *USC Trojan Family Magazine* (autumn 1999)

Peterson, Brian, "The Producer as a Trojan," *USC Trojan Family Magazine* (autumn 1999)

"Wolper, David L.," in *1993 International Television and Video Almanac,* edited by Barry Monush, New York: Quigley, 1993

"Wolper, David L(loyd),"in *Current Biography Yearbook,* edited by Charles Moritz, New York: Wilson, 1987

"Wolper Performs Hat Trick Again: Documentaries on All 3 Webs," *Variety* (May 11, 1966)

"Young King David," *Newsweek* (November 23, 1964)

Women of Brewster Place, The

U.S. Miniseries

The Women of Brewster Place, a miniseries based on the novel by Gloria Naylor, was produced in 1989 by Oprah Winfrey's firm Harpo, Inc. Winfrey served as executive producer and starred along with noted actors Mary Alice, Jackee, Lynn Whitfield, Barbara Montgomery, Phyllis Yvonne Stickney, Robin Givens, Olivia Cole, Lonette McKee, Paula Kelly, Cicely Tyson, Paul Winfield, Moses Gunn, and Douglas Turner Ward. The story, spanning several decades, includes a cast of characters that depict the constant battles fought by African-American women against racism, poverty, and sexism. Interpersonal struggles and conflicts also pepper the storyline, often revolving around black men who may be fathers, husbands, sons, or lovers.

The Winfrey character, Mattie, opens the drama. Her road to Brewster Place begins when she refuses to reveal the name of her unborn child's father to her parents (Mary Alice and Paul Winfield). Milestones for Mattie include living in the home of Eva Turner (Barbara Montgomery) until she dies and wills the house to Mattie; then forfeiting the house when her son, Basil, jumps bail after Mattie uses their home as collateral for his bond. The other characters' journeys to the tenement on Brewster Place are just as unpredictable and crooked. Kiswana, portrayed by Robin Givens, moves to the neighborhood to live with her boyfriend. They work to organize the neighbors, to plan special activities for the neighborhood, and to protest their excessive rent. One of the most powerful scenes in the drama occurs between Kiswana and her mother, Mrs. Browne (Cicely Tyson). When Tyson comes for a visit, she and Givens begin a conversation that progresses into a heated argument regarding Kiswana's name change. Mrs. Browne reveals why she named her daughter Melanie (after her grandmother) and in a powerful soliloquy tells the story of that grandmother's strength and fearlessness when facing a band of angry white men.

Other women from the building reveal bruises inflicted either by the men in their lives or by the world in general. Cora Lee (Phyllis Stickney) continues to have children because she wants the dependency of infants; once they become toddlers, her interest in them falters. By the end of the series, however, she begins to see the importance of all her children, and after being prodded by Kiswana, she attends the neighborhood production of an African-American adaptation of a Shakespearean play. Through this experience and her children's reaction to it, the audience sees a change in Cora Lee.

Miss Sophie (Olivia Cole), an unhappy woman and the neighborhood busybody, spreads vicious gossip about her neighbors in the tenement. Etta Mae (Jackee), Mattie's earthy, flamboyant, and loyal childhood friend, moves to Brewster Place for refuge from her many failed romances. Lucielia Louise Turner (Lynn Whitfield), housewife and mother, lives a somewhat happy life with her husband, Ben (Moses Gunn), and daughter, Serena, in one of the tenement apartments until Ben loses his job and leaves home. Lucielia then aborts their second child, and Serena is electrocuted when she uses a fork to chase a roach into a light socket. Theresa and Lorraine (Paula Kelly and Lonette McKee) decide to reside on Brewster Place because as lesbians they are seeking some place where they can live without ridicule and torment. Their relationship, soon discovered by their neighbors, becomes the backdrop for the drama's finale.

Criticism of the miniseries began before the drama aired. The National Association for the Advancement of Colored People requested review of the scripts before production to determine whether the negative images of the African-American male present in the Naylor book appeared in the television drama. This request was denied, but Winfrey, also concerned with the image of black men in the novel, altered several of the male roles. Ben Turner, the tenement's janitor and a drunk in Naylor's novel, was revamped for the teleplay and, in a scene created especially for the series, explains why he felt pressed into desertion. The producers also attempted to cast actors who could bring a level of sensitivity to the male roles and create characters who were more than one-dimensional villains.

Still, in a two-part series for the *Washington Post,* newspaper columnist Dorothy Gilliam criticized the

Women of Brewster Place, Jackee, Paula Kelly, Lonette Mc-Kee, Phyllis Yvonne Stickney, Oprah Winfrey, Lynn Whitfield, Olivia Cole, Robin Givens, Cicely Tyson, 1989.
Courtesy of the Everett Collection

drama as one of the most stereotype-ridden polemics against black men ever seen on television, a series that, she claimed, trotted out nearly every stereotype of black men that had festered in the mind of the most feverish racist. In spite of such criticism, the series won its time period Sunday and Monday nights against heavy competition, *The Wizard of Oz* on CBS and the *Star Wars* sequel *Return of the Jedi* on NBC.

Though criticized for its portrayal of African-American men and women, *The Women of Brewster Place* offered its audience a rare glimpse of the United States' black working class and conscientiously attempted to probe the personal relationships, dreams, and desires of a group of women who cared about their children and friends, worked long hours at jobs they

may have hated in order to survive, and moved forward despite their disappointments. A spin-off of the miniseries titled *Brewster Place,* also produced by Harpo, Inc., aired for a few weeks in 1990 on ABC but was canceled because of low ratings. The original miniseries continues to air, as a feature film, on cable television channels such as Encore, Lifetime, and BET.

BISHETTA D. MERRITT

See also **Racism, Ethnicity, and Television; Winfrey, Oprah**

Cast

Mattie Michael	Oprah Winfrey
Etta Mae Johnson	Jackee
Mrs. Browne	Cicely Tyson
Kiswana Browne	Robin Givens
Lorraine	Lonette McKee
Cora Lee	Phyllis Stickney
Ben	Moses Gunn
Butch Fuller	Clark Johnson
Ciel	Lynn Whitfield
Basil	Eugene Lee
Mattie's father	Paul Winfield
Mattie's mother	Mary Alice
Eva Turner	Barbara Montgomery
Reverend Wood	Douglas Turner Ward
Miss Sophie	Olivia Cole

Producers

Oprah Winfrey, Carole Isenberg

Programming History

ABC
March 19–20, 1989   9:00–11:00

Further Reading

Bobo, Jacqueline, and Ellen Seiter, "Black Feminism and Media Criticism: *The Women of Brewster Place,*" *Screen* (autumn 1991)
Kort, Michele, "Lights, Camera, Affirmative Action," *Ms.* (November 1988)

Wonder Years, The

U.S. Domestic Comedy

The Wonder Years, a gentle, nostalgic look at "baby-boom" youth and adolescence, told stories in weekly half-hour installments presented entirely from the point of view of the show's main character, Kevin Arnold. Fresh-faced Fred Savage portrayed young Kevin on screen, while adult Kevin, whose voice was furnished by unseen narrator Daniel Stern, commented on the events of his youth with grown-up wryness, 20 years after the fact. The series traced Kevin's development in suburban America from 1968, when he was 11 years old, until the summer of 1973, his junior year in high school.

A typical week's plot involved Kevin facing some rite of passage on the way to adulthood. His first kiss, a fleeting summer love, his first day at high school, the struggle to get Dad to buy a new, color TV—these are the innocuous narrative problems of *The Wonder Years.* The resolutions seem simple but often are surprising. Kevin the narrator always conveys the unsettling knowledge that, in our struggle toward maturity, we make decisions that prevent us from going back to the comfortable places of youth. For example, when pubescent Kevin stands up to his mother's babying, he takes pride in his new independence, but his victory is bittersweet—he realizes that he has hurt his mother, Norma, by reacting harshly to her well-meaning mothering, and that he has lost a piece of the relationship forever.

On the program, mundane situations that would resonate with most Americans' youth experiences are played out against the backdrop of everyday life in the late 1960s and early 1970s. Hip-hugger pants, army-surplus gear, and toilet-paper-strewn yards helped to place the show in the collective memory of the baby boomers who were watching it (and whose dollars advertisers were vigorously seeking). Attention to period detail was often thorough, but occasional anachronisms managed to slip through, such as the use of a television remote control device in the Arnold home in about 1970. Episodes often open with TV news clips from the era—showing a war protest, President Nixon waving good-bye at the White House, or some other instantly recognizable event—accompanied by a classic bit of rock music. Joe Cocker's rendition of "I Get By with a Little Help from My Friends" was the show's theme song, played over a montage of home movie clips depicting a harmonious Arnold family and Kevin's friends Paul and Winnie.

Much of the series' historical identification has to do with oblique references to hippie counterculture and the Vietnam War. Kevin's older sister, Karen, is a hippie, but Kevin is not, and his observation of the counterculture is from the sidelines. While Karen struggles to define her identity against the grain of her parents' traditions, Kevin, for the most part, accepts the world around him. He is portrayed as an average kid, personally uninvolved with most of the larger cultural events swirling about him. One serious treatment of the Vietnam War does intrude in Kevin's personal experience, however, when Brian Cooper, older brother of his neighbor and girlfriend, Winnie, is killed. Kevin struggles to support Winnie, first in the loss of her brother and, later, after her parents' separation results from the brother's death.

Episodes of *The Wonder Years* often center on challenges in Kevin's relationship with a family member, friend, authority figure, or competitor. Kevin's father, Jack; mother, Norma; sister, Karen; brother, Wayne; neighborhood best friend, Paul Pfeiffer; and childhood sweetheart, Winnie Cooper, are heavily involved in the storyline. Much of the action takes place in and around the middle-class Arnold home or at Kevin's school (Robert F. Kennedy Junior High and, later, William McKinley High School).

While each episode is self-contained, Kevin's struggles and changes are evident as the series develops. In one episode, Kevin's older sister becomes estranged from their father because of her involvement in the hippie culture. Other episodes reflect that estrangement, and, in a later season, the program depicts Karen's reconciliation with her father. Kevin's observations and feelings, of course, remain central to exploring such issues. Although episodes sometimes show how characters' perspectives shift, the emphasis is on Kevin's own observation of his world. This acknowledgment of the character's egocentrism melds with a major program theme—adolescent self-involvement.

The Wonder Years.
Photo courtesy of New World Entertainment

Sometimes, the primary point of the program is the effect of another character's struggle on the egocentric Kevin. He watches as father Jack quits a stultifying middle-manager's job at the Norcom corporation and as frustrated homemaker Norma enrolls in college classes and launches her own career. Often, Kevin spends much of his time reacting to the personal impact of such events, then feeling guilty about expressing his selfish thoughts. At the end of each episode, relations, although marked by change, typically become harmonious once again.

As an example of a "hybrid genre," the half-hour dramedy, *The Wonder Years* never amassed the runaway ratings of a show such as *Cheers* (although it did wind up in the Nielsen top ten for two of its five seasons). After a time, it was apparent to producers and the television audience that Kevin Arnold's wonder years were waning. Creative differences between producers and ABC began to spring up from such plot elements as Kevin's touching a girl's breast during the 8 o'clock hour usually reserved for "family viewing." Economic pressures, including rising actor salaries and the need for more location shooting after Kevin acquired a driver's license, also helped to end the show. During its 115-episode run, however, *The Wonder Years* generated intensely loyal fans and collected important notices from critics.

The final episode, on May 12, 1993, exercised a luxury few series have when they conclude their runs: tying up loose ends. Bob Brush, executive producer of the show after creators Neal Marlens and Carol Black left in the second season, took a cue from sagging ratings when the last episode was shot. In it, Kevin quits his job working in Jack Arnold's furniture store and strikes out on his own. Sadly, for some viewers, he and Winnie Cooper do not wind up together. Unfortunately, the show's resolution occurs in the summer following Kevin's junior year in high school, so the formal finality of graduation, a rite of passage so familiar to much of the audience, is missing.

Among the awards bestowed on *The Wonder Years* were an Emmy for Best Comedy Series in 1988 (after only six episodes had aired) and the George Foster Peabody Award in 1990. *TV Guide* named the show one of the 1980s' 20 best.

KAREN E. RIGGS

See also **Comedy, Domestic Settings**

Cast

Kevin Arnold (as adolescent)	Fred Savage
Kevin (as adult; voice only)	Daniel Stern
Wayne Arnold	Jason Hervey
Karen Arnold	Olivia d'Abo
Norma Arnold	Alley Mills
Jack Arnold	Dan Lauria
Paul Pfeiffer	Josh Saviano
Winnie (Gwendolyn) Cooper	Danica McKellar
Coach Cutlip	Robert Picardo
Becky Slater	Crystal McKellar
Mrs. Ritvo (1988–89)	Linda Hoy
Kirk McCray (1988–89)	Michael Landes
Carla Healy (1988–90)	Krista Murphy
Mr. DiPerna (1988–91)	Raye Birk
Mr. Cantwell (1988–91)	Ben Stein
Doug Porter (1989)	Brandon Crane
Randy Mitchell (1989)	Michael Tricario
Craig Hobson (1989–90)	Sean Baca
Ricky Halsenback (1991–93)	Scott Nemes
Jeff Billings (1992–93)	Giovanni Ribisi
Michael (1992)	David Schwimmer

Producers

Neal Marlens, Carol Black, Jeffrey Silver, Bob Brush

Programming History

115 episodes
ABC

March 1988–April 1988	Tuesday 8:30–9:00
October 1988–February 1989	Wednesday 9:00–9:30

February 1989–August 1990   Tuesday 8:30–9:00
August 1990–August 1991   Wednesday 8:00–8:30
August 1991–February 1992   Wednesday 8:30–9:00
March 1992–September 1993   Wednesday 8:00–8:30

Further Reading

Blum, David, "Where Were You in '68?" *New York Times* (February 27, 1989)

Gross, Edward A., *The Wonder Years,* Las Vegas, Nevada: Pioneer Books, 1990

Kaufman, Peter, "Closing the Album on *The Wonder Years,*" *New York Times* (May 9, 1993)

Kinosian, Janet, "Fred Savage: Having Fun," *Saturday Evening Post* (January–February 1991)

Wood, Robert (1925–1986)

U.S. Media Executive

Robert Wood moved network prime-time programming out of TV's adolescent phase into adulthood. As president of CBS, in 1971 he broke with patterned success by jettisoning long-lived popular shows in order to attract younger audiences coveted by advertisers. At the same time, he set aside traditional standards of gentle and slightly vacuous comedy for "in your face" dialogue and contemporary situations that delighted masses, offended some, and pulled network entertainment into the post–assassination/civil rights/Vietnam era.

Wood's strategy in 1970 was to cancel rural and older-skewed classic series (*Green Acres, Beverly Hillbillies, Petticoat Junction,* and *Hee Haw*) and veteran stars (Red Skelton, Jackie Gleason, Ed Sullivan, and Andy Griffith) in favor of more contemporary, urban-oriented programming. He scheduled the challenging comedy *All in the Family,* developed by producer Norman Lear, which ABC had twice rejected. After a weak initial half season, in the spring of 1971, the series built a strong viewership during summer reruns and became a sensation by the fall season. Attracting massive audiences, including sought-after younger adults, and critical praise, *All in the Family* helped CBS to decide to add to its schedule a number of other programs from Lear's production company, including *The Jeffersons, Maude, Good Times, Sanford and Son,* and *One Day at a Time.* Rather than farcical situation comedies (sitcoms), these shows were based on issues affecting characters as interacting persons, thus becoming "character comedies."

Wood presided over the entertainment revolution that changed what Americans watched on evening television. Other networks emulated the move, some-times outpacing CBS's entries in teasing audience acceptability with double entendre. But the nation's TV screens had moved to a new plateau (some cynics would claim a lower one) with Wood's determined risk taking. TV and cable in the following decades pushed forward dramatic and comedic themes from that position.

Wood was energetic, optimistic, thoughtful, and shrewd. But his strategies never undercut people as he formed policies for the stations he managed (KNXT, Los Angeles; the CBS television stations division of owned-and-operated outlets) and the network he led (CBS-TV) from 1969 to 1976. He was the longest-lived and last executive totally in command of the national television fortunes of CBS Inc.

As the industry grew more complex, he advocated shifting the programming department from network headquarters in New York City to the West Coast, where most entertainment programming was developed. After he retired from the network, his position was eventually divided into several presidencies, including TV network, entertainment (programming—on the West Coast), sports, affiliate relations, sales, and marketing. Competing networks had already begun splitting network executives' responsibilities, after Wood had proposed such a structure within CBS.

Wood was the rare network executive who was respected and liked, often with genuine affection, by broadcast colleagues, executives, staff members, local station managers, program producers, and talented actors. He dealt with each person graciously and with good cheer, caring for those with whom he worked and not taking himself too seriously. He was totally committed to his top-management responsibilities, which

Robert D. Wood, 1974.
Courtesy of the Everett Collection/CSU Archives

he handled skillfully and with enormous success. After a brief stint as an independent producer, he became president of Metromedia Producers Corporation in 1979. He died in 1986.

JAMES A. BROWN

See also **Columbia Broadcasting System; Demographics**

Robert Wood. Born in Boise, Idaho, April 17, 1925. Educated at the University of Southern California, B.S. in advertising, 1949. Married: Nancy Harwell, 1949; children: Virginia Lucile and Dennis Harwell. Served in U.S. Naval Reserve, 1943–46. Worked as sales service manager, KNXT, Los Angeles, California, 1949; account executive, KTTV, c. 1950–51; account executive, CBS-owned-and-operated KNXT-TV station, Los Angeles, 1952–54; account executive, CBS television stations division's national sales department, 1954; general sales manager, KNXT-TV, 1955–60; vice president and general manager, KNXT-TV, 1960–66; executive vice president, CBS television stations division, 1966–67; president, CBS television stations division, 1967–69; president, CBS, 1969–1976; later headed own TV production company. Died in Santa Monica, California, May 20, 1986.

Further Reading

Halberstam, David, *The Powers That Be,* New York: Knopf, 1979
Metz, Robert, *CBS: Reflections in a Bloodshot Eye,* Chicago: Playboy Press, 1975
Paley, William S., *As It Happened: A Memoir,* Garden City, New York: Doubleday, 1979
Paper, Lewis J., *Empire: William S. Paley and the Making of CBS,* New York: St. Martin's Press, 1987
Slater, Robert, *This... Is CBS: A Chronicle of 60 Years,* Englewood Cliffs, New Jersey: Prentice Hall, 1988
Smith, Sally Bedell, *In All His Glory: The Life of William S. Paley: The Legendary Tycoon and His Brilliant Circle,* New York: Simon and Schuster, 1990

Wood, Victoria (1953–)

British Comedy Actor, Writer, Singer

Victoria Wood is a talented comedy actor, writer, and singer who has built a national reputation following a string of self-written TV plays, films, and sketch shows. Born in 1953 in Lancashire, in northern England, she first had small-screen exposure on the TV talent search show *New Faces,* where she sang comedy songs of her own composition. Accompanying herself on the piano, she scored heavily with viewing audiences with her jaunty tunes, which often belied her sharp, poignant lyrics. Her regular themes of unrequited love, tedium, mismatched couples, and suburban living, as well as her ability to find humor in the minutiae of modern life, stood her in good stead when she moved into writing plays for the stage and later for television.

Talent, her first play adapted for television (Granada,

August 5, 1979), reunited her with Julie Walters, whom she had met while studying at Manchester Polytechnic. Their partnership would launch both their careers. *Talent* dealt with a mismatched couple: the ambitious would-be cabaret singer Julie Stephens (Walters) and the eternally sniffing Maureen, her plump, dull, but loyal friend (played by Wood), who had accompanied Julie to a talent contest. The bittersweet comedy explored themes of desperation, dashed hopes, lost ambition, and hopeless romances. The fact that *Talent* managed to be both funny and truthful demonstrated Wood's skill as a writer and the pair's acting ability. A sequel, *Nearly a Happy Ending* (Granada, June 1, 1980), appeared the following year. This time the couple were going out for a night on the town, pausing en route at a slimming club. Wood was then quite portly, and occasionally her material dealt with what being overweight meant to oneself and others. Later in her career, she slimmed down considerably.

Following *Nearly a Happy Ending,* Wood and Walters appeared in a one-off special, *Wood and Walters: Two Creatures Great and Small* (Granada, January 1, 1981), which led to the series *Wood and Walters* (Granada, 1982). It was the series *Victoria Wood: As Seen on TV* (BBC), however, that truly established Wood as a major TV star. A sketch show introduced by a stand-up routine from Wood, the program also featured a musical interlude. Julie Walters, Patricia Routledge, Susie Blake, Duncan Preston, and Celia Imrie provided strong support, and one favorite section of the show was "Acorn Antiques," a spoof of cheaply made soap operas.

As Walters's film career blossomed, Wood's comedic talent continued to mature, and by the end of the 1980s she was a big draw on the live circuit. Her stand-up routine relied on observational humor as she drew laughs from finding the idiosyncrasies of normal modern life. She followed a long line of (male) northern comedians with her style of taking her storylines into surreal areas, as well as her character inventions, especially the gormless Maureen. On television she remained determined to try something new and not merely revamp winning ideas. To this end, she wrote and starred in a number of half-hour comedy playlets under the generic title *Victoria Wood* (BBC, 1989), her first series not to attract universal acclaim. She also appeared in a number of solo stand-up shows, and in a one-off spoof of early-morning television news magazine programs, *Victoria Wood's All Day Breakfast* (BBC, December 31, 1992).

The feature-length TV film *Pat and Margaret* (BBC, September 11, 1994), Wood's most ambitious project to date, was her most accomplished reworking of her mismatched couple theme. In this context, Pat (Julie

Victoria Wood.
Courtesy of Victoria Wood

Walters) was a successful English actor in a hit U.S. soap (à la Joan Collins), who was reunited with her sister Margaret (Wood) on a TV chat show. The pair had not been in touch for 27 years, and neither was happy about the meeting. Once again, bittersweet themes of escape and despair were explored; once again, despite this tone, Wood's comedic ability triumphed.

After *Pat and Margaret,* Wood returned to live performance, and many of her subsequent TV appearances have been recordings of her live acts. She returned to the sketch show format for seasonal specials before turning to that hardest of genres, the sitcom. Anticipation was high when it was announced that Wood was working on a sitcom, as the genre had been laboring at the time in the United Kingdom, and viewers and professionals alike thought that Wood might have the magic touch sadly missing elsewhere. *dinnerladies* (BBC, 1998–2000) was set in the works canteen of a north-of-England firm and was full of the sort of well-drawn, earthy characters that inhabited much of Wood's work. The program provided another memorable role for Wood's long-term sparring partner Walters, here playing Wood's character's mad mother. Initially, the reaction to *dinnerladies* was somewhat muted. It did not seem to live up to the great expectations, but the number of viewers was consistently high. With the second series, however, it was as if everybody suddenly "got" the idea, and the show soared to stratospheric viewing figures and attracted critical kudos. Wood said from the start there would only be two series of *dinnerladies,* and she was as good as her word, neatly rounding up all the loose ends in the final couple of episodes. She confessed that the sitcoms were the hardest writing she had ever attempted, but once again she had risen to the challenge.

DICK FIDDY

See also **British Programming**

Victoria Wood. Born in Prestwich, Lancashire, England, May 19, 1953. Attended Bury Grammar School for Girls; University of Birmingham, B.A. in drama and theater arts. Married: Geoffrey Durham, 1980; one son and one daughter. Worked on regional television and radio, 1974–78; theater writer; formed television comedy partnership with Julie Walters; star of her own series and one-woman stage shows, writing her own material; appeared in numerous television series; author of several books. D.Litt: University of Lancaster, 1989, University of Sunderland, 1994. Recipient: Pye Colour Television Award, 1979; Broadcasting Press Guild Award, 1985; British Academy of Film and Television Arts Awards, 1985 (twice), 1986, 1987, and 1988 (twice); Variety Club BBC Personality of the Year Award, 1987; Writers Guild Award, 1992; Broadcasting Press Guild Award, 1994; Monte Carlo Best Single Drama Critics' Award, 1994; Monte Carlo Nymphe d'Or Award, 1994; British Comedy Awards for Best Female Comedy Performance, 1995, and Writer of the Year, 2000. Received Order of the British Empire, 1997.

Television Series

1976	*That's Life!*
1981–82	*Wood and Walters*
1984, 1986	*Victoria Wood: As Seen on TV*
1989	*Victoria Wood*
1994	*Victoria Wood Live in Your Own Home*
1998–2000	*dinnerladies*

Made-for-Television Movie

| 1994 | *Pat and Margaret* |

Television Specials (selected)

1979	*Talent*
1980	*Nearly a Happy Ending*
1981	*Happy Since I Met You*
1988	*An Audience with Victoria Wood*
1992	*Victoria Wood's All Day Breakfast*
2000	*Victoria Wood with All the Trimmings*
2001	*Victoria Wood's Sketch Show Story*

Stage (selected)

Talent, 1980; *Good Fun,* 1980; *Funny Turns,* 1982; *Lucky Bag,* 1984; *Victoria Wood,* 1987; *Victoria Wood Way up West,* 1990; *Victoria Wood: At It Again,* 2001.

Publications (selected)

Up to You, Porky, 1985
Good Fun and Talent, 1988
Mens Sana in Thingummy Doodah, 1990
Barmy: The Second Victoria Wood Sketch, 1993
Pat and Margaret, 1994
Chunky, 1996
Wood Plays I, 1998
Dinnerladies: First Helpings, 1999

Further Reading

Lewisohn, Mark, *The Radio Times Guide to TV Comedy,* London: BBC Worldwide, 1998

Woodward, Edward (1930–)

British Actor

Edward Woodward has enjoyed a long and varied career since he first became a professional performer in 1946. A graduate of the Royal Academy of Dramatic Art, he has acted in England, Scotland, Australia, and the United States, and on both London and Broadway stages, appearing in a wide range of productions from Shakespeare to musicals. Despite being known for dramatic roles, he can also sing and has made more than a dozen musical recordings. In recent years, his distinctive, authoritative voice has narrated a number of audio books.

Although he has played supporting roles in such prestigious films as *Becket* (1964) and *Young Winston* (1972), Woodward is best known for two hit television series, *Callan* in Britain and *The Equalizer* in the United States. Despite the fact that the series were made more than a decade apart, Woodward played essentially the same character in each—a world-weary spy with a conscience.

Woodward's definitive screen persona of an honorable gentleman struggling to maintain his own personal morality in an amoral, even corrupt, world was prefigured in two motion pictures in which the actor starred, *The Wicker Man* (1974) and *Breaker Morant* (1980). In *The Wicker Man* Woodward played a priggish Scottish policeman investigating a child's disappearance; he stumbles upon an island of modern-day pagans led by Christopher Lee. In *Breaker Morant* Woodward starred as the title character, a British Army officer well respected by his men, who is arrested with two other soldiers for war crimes and tried in a kangaroo court during the Boer War. In both cases, Woodward's character's life is sacrificed, a victim of larger hostile social and political forces he is too decent to understand or control.

Callan, an hour-long espionage series that ran in Britain on Thames Television from 1967 to 1973, starred Woodward as David Callan, an agent who carries a license to kill, working for a special secret section of British Intelligence. The section's purpose is "getting rid of" dangerous or undesirable people through bribery, blackmail, frame-ups, or, in the last resort, death. Described in one episode as "a dead shot with the cold nerve to kill," Callan is the section's best operative, and indeed, killing seems to be his main occupation. The character pays a high moral and emotional price for his expertise—he is brooding, solitary, and friendless except for a grubby petty thief named Lonely (Russell Hunter), and his only hobby is collecting toy soldiers. Callan also has two personal weaknesses: he is rebellious and he cares. Although he always does what his bosses tell him, he inevitably argues with or defies them, particularly as he becomes concerned or involved with those whose paths he crosses during the course of his assignments. Despite its bleak subject matter, *Callan* was a hit in Britain. It spawned both a theatrical film (*Callan*, 1974) and later a television special (*Wet Job,* 1981), in which loyal viewers learned of Callan's ultimate fate.

On one *Callan* episode, "Where Else Could I Go?," a psychiatrist working for British Intelligence says that Callan is "brave, aggressive, and can be quite ruthless

Edward Woodward, c. mid-1980s.
Courtesy of the Everett Collection

when he believes in the justice of his cause." This description could also be applied to Robert McCall, the lead character of *The Equalizer,* which ran in the United States on CBS from 1985 to 1989. McCall was a retired espionage agent who had been working for an American agency (probably the Central Intelligence Agency). After forcing the agency to let him go, he decides to use his professional skills to aid helpless people beset by human predators in the urban jungle, usually free of charge. His ad running in the New York classifieds reads, "Got a problem? Odds against you? Call the Equalizer." Although McCall's clients come from all walks of life, they share one thing in common: they all have problems that conventional legal authorities, such as the courts and the police, cannot handle. McCall has an ambivalent relationship with his ex-superior, Control (Robert Lansing), but often borrows agency personnel (Mickey Kostmayer, played by Keith Szarabajka, was a frequent supporting player) to assist in the " problem solving."

In a time of rising crime rates, *The Equalizer* was a potent paranoiac fantasy, made more so because Woodward as McCall cut a formidable figure. He seemed the soul of decency, always polite and impeccably dressed, but one could also detect determination in his steely-eyed gaze and danger in his rueful laugh. To many critics familiar with *Callan*, McCall seemed to be just an older, grayer version of the same character. However, there were significant differences. Like Callan, McCall suffered from a crisis of conscience, but unlike the earlier character, McCall found a way to expiate his sins. Whereas Callan was the instrument and even the victim of his superiors, McCall was the master of his fate.

A year after *The Equalizer*'s run, Woodward starred in another detective drama, *Over My Dead Body*. An attempt by producer William Link to create a male version of his successful *Murder, She Wrote*, the show paired Woodward as a cranky crime novelist with a young reporter-turned-amateur-sleuth, played by Jessica Lundy. However, there was a lack of chemistry between the stars, and the series lasted barely a season.

In 1994 Woodward returned to England to lend his authoritative voice and presence to a real-life crime series called *In Suspicious Circumstances*, a sort of British version of the American show *Unsolved Mysteries*. That same year, he also starred in a British series that explored working-class themes, the comedy-drama *Common as Muck*. The lead role was rather uncharacteristic for Woodward—that of a "binman" (trash collector) from the "up-North" town of Hepworth. By 1995, however, Woodward was back in a role better suited to his on-screen persona. In two TV movies filmed in Toronto, *The Shamrock Conspiracy* and *Harrison: Cry of the City*, Woodward played Edward Harrison, a retired Scotland Yard inspector who is as cynical and world-weary, but also as tenacious and deeply moral, as Robert McCall. In 1998 Woodward was recruited to play Harry Malone, the gruff "controller" of a team of operatives combating crime and terror around the world in *CI5: The New Professionals*. This updated version of the British cult series *The Professionals* was aired in the United Kingdom, New Zealand, and Australia, but it neither pleased fans of the original nor found a new audience and ended after 13 episodes. Still, Woodward continued to play the role of spy boss when he joined the USA Network cable series *La Femme Nikita* in its fifth and final season, as the Head of Center, the real "Mr. Jones." Woodward also guest-starred on *Babylon5: Crusade*, another short-lived series, on which his son, Peter, was a cast regular.

Woodward has also appeared in several other television movies both in Britain and the United States. His roles have been offbeat, to say the least, including most notably Merlin in *Arthur the King,* a strange version of the Camelot legend told by way of Lewis Carroll; the Ghost of Christmas Present in the very fine 1984 production of *A Christmas Carol,* starring George C. Scott as Scrooge; and as the Lilliputian Drunlo in the award-winning 1996 version of *Gulliver's Travels.*

CYNTHIA W. WALKER

Edward Woodward. Born in Croydon, Surrey, England, June 1, 1930. Attended Eccleston Road and Sydenham Road School, Croydon; Elmwood School, Wallingford; Kingston College; Royal Academy of Dramatic Art. Married: 1) Venetia Mary Collett, 1952 (divorced); children: Sarah, Tim, and Peter; 2) Michele Dotrice, 1987; child: Emily Beth. Began career as stage actor at the Castle Theatre, Farnham, 1946; worked in repertory companies throughout England and Scotland; first appeared on the London stage, 1955; continued stage work in London over next four decades, occasionally appearing in New York as well; has appeared in numerous films and in more than 2,000 television productions, including *Callan,* 1967–73, and *The Equalizer,* 1985–89; has recorded albums of music (vocals), albums of poetry, and books on tape. Officer of the Order of the British Empire, 1978. Recipient: Television Actor of the Year, 1969, 1970; Sun Award for Best Actor, 1970, 1971, 1972; Golden Globe Award; numerous other awards.

Television Series

1967	*Sword of Honour*
1967–73, 1981	*Callan*
1972	*Whodunnit?* (host)
1977–78	*1990*
1978	*The Bass Player and the Blonde*
1981	*Winston Churchill: The Wilderness Years*
1981	*Nice Work*
1985–89	*The Equalizer*
1987	*In Suspicious Circumstances*
1991–92	*America at Risk*
1994	*Common as Muck*
1998	*CI5: The New Professionals*
2000	*Dark Realm*
2001	*La Femme Nikita*

Made-for-Television Movies

1983	*Merlin and the Sword* (U.S. title, *Arthur the King*)

1983	*Love Is Forever*
1984	*A Christmas Carol*
1986	*Uncle Tom's Cabin*
1988	*The Man in the Brown Suit*
1990	*Hands of a Murderer*
1993	*A Christmas Reunion*
1995	*The Shamrock Conspiracy*
1996	*Harrison: Cry of the City*

Television Specials

1969	*Scott Fitzgerald*
1970	*Bit of a Holiday*
1971	*Evelyn*
1979	*Rod of Iron*
1980	*The Trial of Lady Chatterley*
1981	*Wet Job*
1980	*Blunt Instrument*
1986	*The Spice of Life*
1988	*Hunted*
1990	*Hands of a Murderer, or The Napoleon of Crime*
1991	*In My Defence*
1995	*Cry of the City*
1996	*Gulliver's Travels*
2000	*Messiah*

Films

Where There's a Will, 1955; *Inn for Trouble*, 1960; *Becket*, 1964; *File on the Golden Goose*, 1968; *Incense for the Damned*, 1970; *Charley One-Eye*, 1972; *Young Winston*, 1972; *Hunted*, 1973; *Sitting Target*, 1974; *The Wicker Man*, 1974; *Callan*, 1974; *Three for All*, 1975; *Stand Up Virgin Soldiers*, 1977; *Breaker Morant*, 1980; *The Appointment*, 1981; *Comeback*, 1982; *Who Dares Wins*, 1982; *Champions*, 1983; *King David*, 1986; *Mister Johnson*, 1990; *Deadly Advice*, 1993; *The House of Angelo*, 1997; *Marcie's Dowry*, 1999.

Stage (selected)

Where There's a Will, 1955; *Romeo and Juliet*, 1958; *Hamlet*, 1958; *Rattle of a Simple Man*, 1962; *Two Cities*, 1968; *Cyrano de Bergerac*, 1971; *The White Devil*, 1971; *The Wolf*, 1973; *Male of the Species*, 1975; *On Approval*, 1976; *The Dark Horse*, 1978; *The Beggar's Opera* (also director), 1980; *Private Lives*, 1980; *The Assassin*, 1982; *Richard III*, 1982; *The Dead Secret*, 1992.

Further Reading

Jefferson, Margo, "The Equalizer," *Ms.* (September 1986)

Woodward, Joanne (1930–)

U.S. Actor

Joanne Woodward has been recognized as an exceptional television performer from the beginning of her career in 1952, when she appeared on *Robert Montgomery Presents* in a drama titled "Penny." She performed in more than a dozen live New York productions from 1952 to 1958 and was also active on the stage during that period, a vocation she has pursued throughout her career. In those early years Woodward made appearances on *Goodyear Playhouse, Omnibus, Philco Television Playhouse, Studio One, Kraft Television Theatre, U.S. Steel Hour, Playhouse 90,* and *The Web,* in which she played opposite her future husband Paul Newman in 1954. Woodward remembers those experiences as "marvelous days."

In 1957 Woodward was cast in her first starring role in a feature film, *The Three Faces of Eve,* for which she received an Academy Award as Best Actress. Since then, Woodward has been recognized primarily as a feature film actress; however, her television roles have been numerous and highly memorable.

Woodward received an Emmy Award for her starring performance in *See How She Runs* on CBS in 1978. In 1985 she won a second Emmy for her role in *Do You Remember Love?*, a provocative and moving drama about the impact of Alzheimer's disease. In 1990 she received her third Emmy Award for producing and hosting a PBS special, *American Masters.* In addition, she has been nominated three times for other performances on television.

Her roles in television drama have frequently addressed social issues. Her 1981 performance as Elizabeth Huckaby in the CBS drama *Crisis at Central*

Joanne Woodward, c. late 1950s.
Courtesy of the Everett Collection

High is an example of her unique ability to draw the audience into the character by becoming that character.
ROBERT S. ALLEY

Joanne Gignilliat Woodward. Born in Thomasville, Georgia, February 27, 1930. Attended Louisiana State University, 1947–49; graduated from Neighborhood Playhouse Dramatic School, New York City. Married: Paul Newman, 1958; three daughters. Made first television appearance in "Penny" for *Robert Montgomery Presents,* 1952; numerous appearances in specials and television movies; appeared in numerous stage plays and films. Recipient: Kennedy Center Honors for Lifetime Achievement in the Performing Arts (with Paul Newman); Academy Award, 1957; Foreign Press Award, 1957; Cannes Film Festival Award, 1972; New York Film Critics Award, 1968, 1973, and 1990; Emmy Awards, 1978, 1985, 1990.

Made-for-Television Movies (selected)

1952	*Robert Montgomery Presents:* "Penny"
1976	*All the Way Home*
1976	*Sybil*
1977	*Come Back, Little Sheba*
1978	*See How She Runs*
1979	*Streets of L.A.*
1980	*The Shadow Box*
1981	*Crisis at Central High*
1985	*Do You Remember Love?*
1989	*Foreign Affairs*
1993	*Blind Spot*
1994	*Hallmark Hall of Fame: Breathing Lessons*

Television Specials

1989	*Broadway's Dreamers:* "The Legacy of the Group Theater"
1990	*American Masters*
1996	*Great Performances:* "Dance in America: A Renaissance"

Films (actress; selected)

Count Three and Pray, 1955; *A Kiss Before Dying,* 1956; *The Three Faces of Eve,* 1957; *No Down Payment,* 1957; *Rally Round the Flag Boys,* 1958; *The Long Hot Summer,* 1958; *The Sound and the Fury,* 1959; *The Fugitive Kind,* 1960; *Paris Blues,* 1961; *The Stripper,* 1963; *A New Kind of Love,* 1963; *A Big Hand for the Little Lady,* 1965; *A Fine Madness,* 1965; *Rachel, Rachel,* 1968; *Winning,* 1969; *WUSA,* 1970; *They Might Be Giants,* 1971; *The Effect of Gamma Rays on Man-in-the-Moon Marigolds,* 1972; *Summer Wishes, Winter Dreams,* 1973; *The Drowning Pool,* 1975; *The End,* 1978; *Harry and Son,* 1984; *The Glass Menagerie,* 1987; *Mr. and Mrs. Bridge,* 1990; *Philadelphia,* 1993; *The Age of Innocence* (narrator/voice only), 1993; *My Knees Were Jumping: Remembering the Kindertransports* (narrator), 1998.

Films (director)

Come Along with Me, 1982; *The Hump Back Angel,* 1984.

Stage (selected)

Picnic (understudy), 1953; *Baby Want a Kiss,* 1964; *Candida,* 1982; *The Glass Menagerie,* 1985; *Sweet Bird of Youth,* 1988.

Further Reading

McGillivray, David, "Joanne Woodward," *Films and Filming* (October 1984)

Morella, Joe, and Edward Z. Epstein, *Paul and Joanne: A Biography of Paul Newman and Joanne Woodward,* New York: Delacorte, 1988

Netter, Susan, *Paul Newman and Joanne Woodward,* London: Piatkus, 1989

Stern, Stewart, *No Tricks in My Pocket: Paul Newman Directs,* New York: Grove Press, 1989

Workplace Programs

U.S. television, from its earliest years, has developed prime-time programs that focus on the workplace. This trend is understandable enough, given TV's essential investment in the "American work ethic" and in consumer culture, although it also evinces TV's basic domestic impulse. By the 1970s and 1980s, in fact, TV's most successful workplace programs effectively merged the medium's work-related and domestic imperatives in sitcoms like *The Mary Tyler Moore Show, M*A*S*H, Taxi,* and *Cheers,* and in hour-long dramas like *Hill Street Blues, St. Elsewhere,* and *LA Law.* While conveying the working conditions and the professional ethos of the workplace, these programs also depicted coworkers as a loosely knit but crucially interdependent quasi-family within a "domesticated" workplace. This strategy was further refined in 1990s sitcoms like *Murphy Brown* and *Frasier,* and even more notably in hour-long dramas like *ER, NYPD Blue, Picket Fences, Chicago Hope, Ally McBeal, The Practice,* and *Homicide: Life in the Streets.* These latter series not only marked the unexpected resurgence of hour-long drama in prime time, but in the view of many critics evinced a new "golden age" of American television.

This integration of home and work was scarcely evident in 1950s TV, when the domestic arena and the workplace remained fairly distinct. The majority of workplace programs were male-dominant law-and-order series that generally focused less on the workplace itself than on the professional heroics of the cops, detectives, town marshals, and bounty hunters, who dictated and dominated the action. *Dragnet,* TV's prototype cop show, did portray the workaday world of the L.A. police, albeit in uncomplicated and superficial terms. The rise of the hour-long series in the late 1950s brought a more sophisticated treatment of the workplace in courtroom dramas like *Perry Mason,* detective shows like *77 Sunset Strip,* and cop shows like *Naked City* (which ran as a half-hour show in the 1958–59 season and then returned as an hour-long drama in 1960). More than simply a "home base" for the protagonists, the workplace in these programs was a familiar site of personal and professional interaction.

The year 1961 saw three important new hour-long workplace dramas: *Ben Casey, Dr. Kildare,* and *The Defenders.* The latter was a legal drama whose principals spent far less time in the courtroom and more time in the office than did Perry Mason. And while Mason's cases invariably were murder mysteries, with Mason functioning as both lawyer and detective, *The Defenders* treated the workaday legal profession in more direct and realistic terms. Both *Ben Casey* and *Dr. Kildare,* meanwhile, were medical dramas set in hospitals, and they too brought a new degree of realism to the depiction of the workplace setting—and to the lives and labors of its occupants. As *Time* magazine noted in reviewing *Ben Casey,* the series "accurately captures the feeling of sleepless intensity of a metropolitan hospital."

Another important and highly influential series to debut in 1961 was a half-hour comedy, *The Dick Van Dyke Show,* which effectively merged the two dominant sitcom strains—the workplace comedy with its ensemble of disparate characters and the domestic comedy centering on the typical (white, middle-class) American home and family. At the time, most workplace comedies fell into three basic categories: school-based sitcoms like *Mr. Peepers* and *Our Miss Brooks;* working-girl sitcoms like *Private Secretary* and *Oh Suzanna;* and military sitcoms like *The Phil Silvers Show* and *McHale's Navy.* The vast majority of half-hour comedies were domestic sitcoms extolling (or affectionately lampooning) the virtues of home and family. These occasionally raised work-related issues—via working stiffs like Chester Riley (*The Life of Riley*) lamenting an American Dream just out of reach, for instance, or an "unruly" housewife like Lucy Ricardo (*I Love Lucy*) comically resisting her domestic plight. And some series like *Hazel* centered on "domestic help" (maids, nannies, etc.), thus depicting the home itself as a workplace.

The Dick Van Dyke Show created a hybrid of sorts by casting Van Dyke as Rob Petrie, an affable suburban patriarch and head writer on the fictional Alan Brady Show. Setting the trend for workplace comedies of the next three decades, *The Dick Van Dyke Show* featured a protagonist who moved continually between home and work, thus creating a format amenable to both the domestic sitcom and the workplace comedy. The series' domestic dimension was quite conventional, but its treatment of the workplace was innovative and influential. The work itself involved television production (as would later workplace sitcoms like *The Mary Tyler Moore Show, Buffalo Bill,* and *Murphy Brown*), and thus the program carried a strong self-reflexive dimension. More important, *The Dick Van Dyke Show* developed the prototype for the domesticated workplace and the work-family ensemble—Rob and his staff writers Buddy (Morey Amsterdam) and Sally (Rose Marie); oddball autocrat Alan Brady (Carl Reiner, the creator and executive producer of *The Dick Van Dyke Show*); and Alan's producer and brother-in-law, the ever-flustered and vaguely maternal Mel (Richard Deacon). Significantly, Rob was the only member of the workplace ensemble with a stable and secure home life, and thus he served as the stabilizing, nurturing, mediating force in the comic-chaotic and potentially dehumanizing workplace.

The influence of *The Dick Van Dyke Show* on TV's workplace programs was most obvious and direct in the sitcoms produced by MTM Enterprises in the early 1970s, particularly *The Mary Tyler Moore Show* and *The Bob Newhart Show.* While these and other MTM sitcoms featured a central character moving between home and work, *The Mary Tyler Moore Show* was the most successful in developing the workplace (the newsroom of a Minneapolis TV station, WJM) as a site not only of conflict and comedic chaos but of community and kinship as well. And although Moore, who had played Rob's wife on *The Dick Van Dyke Show,* was cast here as an independent single woman, her nurturing instincts remained as acute as ever in the WJM newsroom.

While the MTM series maintained the dual focus on home and work, another crucial workplace comedy from the early 1970s, *M*A*S*H,* focused exclusively on the workplace—in this case a military surgical unit in war-torn Korea in the early 1950s (with obvious pertinence to the then-current Vietnam War). Alan Alda's Hawkeye Pierce was in many ways the series' central character and governing sensibility, especially in his caustic disregard for military protocol and his fierce commitment to medicine. Yet *M*A*S*H* was remarkably democratic in its treatment of the eight principal characters, developing each member of the ensemble, as well as the collective itself, into a functioning work-family. While ostensibly a sitcom, the series often veered into heavy drama in its treatment of both the medical profession and the war; in fact, the laugh track was never used during the scenes set in the operating room. And more than any previous workplace program, whether comedy or drama, *M*A*S*H* was focused closely on the professional "code" of its ensemble, on the shared sense of duty and commitment that both defined their medical work and created a nagging sense of moral ambiguity about the military function of the unit—that is, patching up the wounded so that they might return to battle.

A domestic sitcom hit from the early 1970s, *All in the Family,* also is pertinent here for several reasons. First, in Archie Bunker (Carroll O'Connor), the series created the most compelling and comic-pathetic working stiff since Chester Riley. Second, parenting on the series involved two grown "children," with the generation-gap squabbling between Archie and son-in-law Mike (Rob Reiner) frequently raising issues of social class and work. Moreover, their comic antagonism was recast in other generation-gap sitcoms set in the workplace, notably *Sanford and Son* and *Chico and the Man.* And third, *All in the Family* itself evolved by the late 1970s into a workplace sitcom, *Archie Bunker's Place,* with the traditional family replaced by a work-family ensemble.

The trend toward workplace comedies in the early 1970s was related to several factors both inside and outside the industry. One factor was the sheer popularity of the early-1970s workplace comedies, and their obvious flexibility in terms of plot and character development. These series also signaled TV's increasing concern with demographics and its pursuit of "quality numbers"—the upscale urban viewers coveted by sponsors. Because these series often dealt with topical and significant social issues, they were widely praised by critics, thus creating an equation of sorts between quality demographics and "quality programming." And in a larger social context, this programming trend signaled the massive changes in American lifestyles that accompanied a declining economy and runaway inflation, the sexual revolution and women's movement, the growing ranks of working wives and mothers, and rising divorce rates.

Thus, the domestic sitcom, with its emphasis on the traditional home and family, all but disappeared from network schedules in the late 1970s and early 1980s, replaced by workplace comedies like *Alice, WKRP in Cincinnati, Taxi, Cheers, Newhart, Night Court,* and *Welcome Back, Kotter.* The domestic sitcom did rebound in the mid-1980s with *The Cosby Show* and *Family Ties,* and by the 1990s the domestic and workplace sitcoms had formed a comfortable alliance, with series like *Murphy Brown, Coach,* and *Frasier* sustaining the MTM tradition of a central, pivotal character moving between home and the workplace.

TV's hour-long workplace dramas underwent a transformation as well in the 1970s, which was a direct outgrowth, in fact, of MTM's workplace sitcoms. In 1977 MTM Enterprises retired *The Mary Tyler Moore Show* and created a third and final spin-off of that series, *Lou Grant,* which followed Mary's irascible boss (Ed Asner) from WJM-TV in Minneapolis to the *Los Angeles Tribune,* where he took a job as editor. *Lou Grant* was created by two of MTM's top comedy writer-producers, James Brooks and Allan Burns, along with Gene Reynolds, the executive producer of *M*A*S*H*. It marked a crucial new direction for MTM, not only because it was an hour-long drama, but also because of its primary focus on the workplace (à la *M*A*S*H*) and its aggressive treatment of "serious" social and work-related issues. In that era of Vietnam, Watergate, and *All the President's Men, Lou Grant* courted controversy week after week, with Lou and his work-family of investigative journalists not only pursuing the truth, but agonizing over their personal lives and professional responsibilities as well.

MTM's hour-long workplace dramas hit their stride in the 1980s with *Hill Street Blues* and *St. Elsewhere,* which effectively revitalized two of television's oldest genres, the police show and the medical show. Each shifted the dramatic focus from the all-too-familiar heroics of a series star to an ensemble of coworkers and to the workplace itself—not simply as a backdrop, but as a social-service institution located in an urban-industrial war zone with its own distinctive ethos and sense of place. Each also used serial story structure and documentary-style realism, drawing viewers into the heavily populated and densely plotted programs through a heady, seemingly paradoxical blend of soap opera and cinéma vérité. Documentary techniques—location shooting, handheld camera, long takes and reframing instead of cutting, composition in depth, and multiple-track sound recording—gave these series (and the workplace itself) a "look" and "feel" that was utterly unique among police and medical dramas.

Hill Street Blues and *St. Elsewhere* also emerged alongside prime-time soap operas like *Dallas* and *Falcon Crest* and shared with those series a penchant for "continuing drama." While this serial dimension enhanced both the Hill Street precinct and St. Eligius hospital as a "domesticated workplace," the genre requirements of each series (solving crimes, healing the sick) demanded action, pathos, jeopardy, and a dramatic payoff within individual episodes. Thus, a crucial component of MTM's workplace dramas was their merging of episodic and serial forms. The episodic dimension usually focused on short-term, work-related conflicts (crime, illness), while the serial dimension involved the more "domestic" aspects of the characters' lives—and not only their personal lives, since most of the principals were "married to their work," but also the ongoing interpersonal relationships among the coworkers.

Hill Street co-creator Steven Bochco left MTM in the mid-1980s and developed *LA Law,* which took the ensemble workplace drama "upscale" into a successful big-city legal firm. While a solid success, this focus on upscale professionals marked a significant departure from *Hill Street* and *St. Elsewhere*—and from most workplace dramas in the 1990s as well. Indeed, prime-time network TV saw a remarkable run of MTM-style ensemble dramas in the 1990s, notably *ER, Homicide, Law and Order, Chicago Hope,* and another Bochco series, *NYPD Blue.* Most of these were set, like *Hill Street* and *St. Elsewhere,* in decaying inner cities, and they centered on coworkers whose commitment to their profession and to one another was far more important than social status or income. Indeed, a central paradox in these programs is that their principal characters, all intelligent, well-educated professionals, eschew material rewards to work in underfunded social institutions where commitment outweighs income, where the work is never finished nor the conflicts satisfactorily resolved, and where the work itself, finally, is its own reward.

Despite these similarities to *Hill Street* and *St. Elsewhere,* the 1990s workplace dramas differed in their emphasis. Those earlier MTM series carried a strong male-management focus, privileging the veritable "patriarch" of the work-family—Captain Frank Furillo and Dr. Donald Westphall, respectively—whose role (like Lou Grant before them) was to uphold the professional code and the familial bond of their charges. The 1990s dramas, conversely, concentrated mainly on the workers in the trenches, whose shared commitment to one another and to their work defines the ethos of the workplace and the sense of kinship it engendered.

More conventional hour-long workplace programs have been developed alongside these MTM-style dramas, of course, from 1970s series like *Medical Center, Ironside,* and *Baretta* to more recent cop, doc, and lawyer shows like *Matlock, T.J. Hooker,* and *Quincy.* In the tradition of *Dragnet* and *Marcus Welby,* the lead characters in these series are little more than heroic plot functions, with the plots themselves satisfying the generic requirements in formulaic doses and the workplace setting as mere backdrop. Two recent hour-long dramas more closely akin to the MTM-style workplace programs are *Northern Exposure* and *Picket Fences.* Both are successful ensemble dramas created by MTM alumni who took the workplace form into more upbeat and offbeat directions—the former a duck-out-of-water doc show set in small-town Alaska that veered into magical realism, the latter a hybrid cop-doc-legal-domestic drama set in small-town Wisconsin. But while both are effective ensemble dramas with an acute "sense of place," they are crucially at odds with urban-based medical dramas like *ER* and *Chicago Hope* and police dramas like *Homicide* and *NYPD Blue,* whose dramatic focus is crucially wed to the single-minded professional commitment of the ensemble and is deeply rooted in the workplace itself.

Indeed, *ER* and *Homicide* and the other MTM-style ensemble dramas posit the workplace as home and work itself as the basis for any real sense of kinship we are likely to find in the contemporary urban-industrial world. As Charles McGrath writes in *The New York Times Magazine,* "The Triumph of the Prime-Time Novel," such shows appeal to viewers because "they've remembered that for a lot of us work is where we live more of the time; that, like it or not, our job relationships are often as intimate as our family relationships, and that work is often where we invest most of our emotional energy." McGrath is one of several critics who view these workplace dramas as ushering in a renaissance of network TV programming, due to their Dickensian density of plot and complexity of character, their social realism and moral ambiguity, and their portrayal of workers whose heroics are simply a function of their everyday lives and labors.

The workplace in these series ultimately emerges as a character unto itself, and one that is both harrowing and oddly inspiring to those who work there. For the characters in *ER* and *NYPD Blue* and the other ensemble workplace dramas, soul-searching comes with the territory, and they know the territory all too well. They are acutely aware not only of their own limitations and failings but of the inadequacies of their own professions to cure the ills of the modern world. Still, they maintain their commitment to one another and to a professional code that is the very lifeblood of the workplace they share.

In the mid- to late 1990s, the shows of producer David E. Kelly especially exemplified this trend of replacing the home with the workplace, and positing coworkers as, essentially, family. His two legal dramas, *The Practice* and *Ally McBeal,* approached this development in markedly different ways. In *The Practice* a small firm of defense lawyers develop deep, familial bonds. Professional and personal relationships often overlap. The primary example of this is the relationship between the firm founder, Bobby Donnell (Dylan McDermott), and associate Lindsay Dole (Kelli Williams). The two married at the end of season four, only to separate in the seventh season. Prior to their separation, Lindsay had left the practice to form her own firm.

Kelly's other lawyer program, *Ally McBeal,* elevated the personal relationships among the staff members over their professional ones. Ally McBeal (Calista Flockhart) joined the firm of Cage/Fish & Associates, where her fellow employees included childhood sweetheart Billy Thomas (Gil Bellows) and his wife, Georgia (Courtney Thorne-Smith). The romantic entanglements of the lawyers at the firm—both with each other, with lawyers at other firms, and with those outside the legal realm—were the primary focus of the show. The actual court cases, which were generally based around unrealistic or whimsical premises, were generally notable only as they supported or reflected the personal relationships among the lawyers. In programs such as these, distinctions between the home and the workplace became essentially meaningless.

THOMAS SCHATZ

*See also **All in the Family; Ally McBeal; Cheers; Detective Programs; Dick Van Dyke Show, The; Hill Street Blues; LA Law; Lou Grant; Mary Tyler Moore Show, The; M*A*S*H; Murphy Brown; Police Programs; St. Elsewhere; Taxi***

Further Reading

Brooks, Tim, and Earle Marsh, *The Complete Directory to Prime Time Network TV Shows,* New York: Ballantine, 1979; 5th edition, 1992

Feuer, Jane, Paul Kerr, and Tise Vahimagi, editors, *MTM: "Quality Television,"* London: British Film Institute, 1984

Gitlin, Todd, *Inside Prime Time,* New York: Pantheon, 1983

McGrath, Charles, "The Triumph of the Prime-Time Novel," *New York Times Magazine* (October 22, 1995)

Schatz, Thomas, "*St. Elsewhere* and the Evolution of the Ensemble Series," in *Television: The Critical View,* edited by Horace Newcomb, New York: Oxford University Press, 1976; 4th edition, 1987

Williams, Betsy, " 'North to the Future': *Northern Exposure* and Quality Television," in *Television: The Critical View,* edited by Horace Newcomb, New York: Oxford University Press, 1976; 5th edition, 1994

World at War, The

U.K. Documentary Series

The World at War is a British historical documentary series made by the ITV company Thames Television and first broadcast in 1973. A hugely ambitious 26-episode history of World War II, combining archive film with interviews with war veterans, the series was the brainchild of producer Jeremy Isaacs, who first proposed the idea to Thames Television in the autumn of 1970. The company bravely approved the project and a team of experts assembled by Isaacs started work early in 1971.

Isaacs was determined that the series would be the most comprehensive history of the war yet attempted, based on extensive research, and would aim to meet the highest standards. Operating in no less than 18 countries over a period of four years, the team was faced with a massive task, trawling through 3 million feet of archive film (much of it unseen since the war) and adding to this a further 1 million feet of material comprising interviews and location filming. Everything the researchers viewed was carefully cataloged and recorded in a central log book to facilitate future reference. The checking of historical accuracy was placed in the hands of the academic Dr. Noble Frankland.

The interviews with surviving veterans were considered a crucial element of the project, and much effort was devoted to obtaining the recollections of a wide selection of veterans, ranging from key military and political personalities to ordinary soldiers and civilians caught up in the conflict. Among the interviewees were such notable (and sometimes controversial) figures as Hitler's personal secretary, Traudl Junge; U-boat commander and head of the German Navy Karl Donitz; German armaments minister Albert Speer; Himmler's adjutant, Karl Wolff; British foreign secretary (and later prime minister) Anthony Eden; Winston Churchill's parliamentary private secretary, John Colville; head of RAF Bomber Command Arthur "Bomber" Harris; U.S. ambassador to Russia Averill Harriman; and Hollywood film star and USAAF bomber pilot James Stewart. Some of the most telling interviews, however, were those made with the ordinary people of all nationalities who found themselves overtaken by the war, ranging from fighter pilots and shipwrecked seamen to Russian housewives and concentration camp survivors. Their testimony brought vivid realism to the unfolding of the events that took place between the rise of the Nazis in prewar Germany and the Japanese surrender following the bombing of Hiroshima and Nagasaki.

There were many technical challenges to be met. As well as having to combine color with monochrome film and amateur with professionally filmed footage, the team also had to do extensive work on the soundtrack, much of the original film being silent. Every effort was made to ensure that the soundtrack for the series was as authentic as possible, with recordings being specially made of the various armaments depicted. To provide an appropriately grave tone the duty of narrating the series was entrusted to the most celebrated figure on the contemporary stage, the British actor Sir Laurence Olivier, whose masterly delivery added both authority and humanity to the series. Other important finishing touches included the compilation of a striking title sequence (18 months in the preparation) to a memorable score by Carl Davis.

Shot on 16 millimeter, the first episode of the finished series (which cost in all around £1 million), titled *A New Germany,* went out on Wednesday, October 31, 1973, at 9 P.M.—although a television station in Houston had in fact already started showing the series some three weeks earlier. The whole series was broadcast as 26 one-hour episodes over a period of six months and met with immediate acclaim. The program attracted huge audiences, and one episode titled *Morning,* covering the D-Day landings, appeared in the top 10 audience ratings—an unprecedented success for a documentary program. The series was universally recognized as one of the most ambitious television documentary projects ever undertaken and won awards all round the world, among them an International Emmy and the George Polk Memorial Award.

Only one-hundredth of the material originally gathered by the research team was used in the final series. Selections of what remained was used for six *World at War* specials made three years later (1975), with another Shakespearean actor, Eric Porter, succeeding Olivier as narrator. The original series has been screened in nearly 100 countries and was repeated on BBC 2 in 1994 (and again in 2000). The program has aged well and remains unrivalled as a televisual source on the war, if only because many of the eyewitnesses interviewed are no longer living and available for further questioning. The account of events and the analysis offered in the narration have never been seriously challenged by experts on the period. The accompanying book to the series sold half a million copies and was translated into 14 languages, and the original 26 episodes have also been made available on videotape.

Many of the people involved in producing the series went on to further success in the British media. Writer Charles Douglas-Home was appointed editor of *The Times,* while producer and director David Elstein became director of programmes at Thames and chief executive of Channel 5 in the United Kingdom. Another producer, Ted Childs, carved a reputation as an influential maker of British television drama, with such series as *The Sweeney, Inspector Morse,* and *Kavanagh QC.* Jeremy Isaacs, the prime mover behind the whole undertaking, became founding chief executive of Channel 4 and subsequently general director of the Royal Opera House.

DAVID PICKERING

See also **Documentary; War on Television**

Creator/Producer
Jeremy Isaacs

Programming History
ITV
Produced by Thames Television

1973
26 one-hour episodes
Repeat airings:
BBC 2
1994, 2000

World in Action

British News Documentary

World in Action, Britain's long-running and most illustrious current-affairs program, goes out in prime time on ITV (the main commercial channel) and is produced by Granada Television, a company with a reputation for innovation and "quality" programming. First launched in 1963, with Tim Hewat, an ex-*Daily Express* reporter, as its editor, *World in Action* was the first weekly current-affairs program in Britain to pioneer pictorial journalism on film and to risk taking an independent editorial stance. In comparison with *Panorama,* the BBC's rival current-affairs program, which was studio based and featured several items, *World in Action* was, in the words of Gus McDonald, "born brash." It devoted each half-hour episode to a single issue and, abandoning the studio and presenter, put the story itself up-front. The lightweight film equipment gave the production team the mobility to follow up the stories firsthand and to bring raw images of the world into the living room. A conspicuous and influential style evolved with interviewees framed in close-up talking directly to camera, cross-cut with fast-edited observation of relevant action and environmental detail. The hard-hitting approach compelled attention and made complex social issues accessible to a mass audience for the first time.

Having firmly established the idea of picture journalism on TV, *World in Action* consolidated its position in 1967 under David Plowright when an investigative bureau was set up, and it is on the quality of its investigative journalism that the program's reputation chiefly rests. Award-winning episodes have included "The Demonstration" (1968) observing the mass protest outside the U.S. embassy against the

bombing of North Vietnam; "Nuts and Bolts of the Economy" (1976), a series exploring different aspects of the world economy; and an investigation into "The Life and Death of Steve Biko" (1978). The program has been equally wide ranging with domestic topics, covering the exposure of police corruption in "Scotland Yard's Cocaine Connection" (1985), revealing the British Royal Family's tax loophole (1991), and investigating the dangers of different types of contraceptive pill (1995). Over the years, the program has fearlessly and impartially pursued the truth, exposing injustice and falsehood, and frequently running at odds with the powers that be. In this respect the program's long-standing, but eventually successful, fight to secure the release of the six men wrongfully convicted for the IRA pub bombing in Birmingham provides the outstanding example.

World in Action stands as one of the finest achievements of public service television in Britain—of programming driven by the desire to inform and educate viewers as much as to entertain them. In the course of its long run it has provided the training ground for some of the most distinguished names in British broadcasting, as well as pioneering innovative program approaches such as undercover and surveillance work and drama documentary. How it will continue to fare in the more competitive broadcast market following deregulation remains to be seen. However, it is possible that to maintain its prime-time slot the emphasis will shift away from costly long-term investigations and international stories to focus on populist health and consumer issues that can be guaranteed to deliver large audiences.

JUDITH JONES AND BOB MILLINGTON

Programming History
ITV
1963–1965
1967–

Further Reading

Corner, John, *The Art of Record,* Manchester: Manchester University Press, 1996
Granada: The First Twenty-Five Years, London: British Film Institute, 1988

Worrell, Trix

British Writer

Trix Worrell has lived in Britain for most of his life, having moved there from St. Lucia when he was five. When he began his acting career, he also started writing because there were so few good parts for black actors to play. As a teenager, Worrell worked with the Albany Theatre in South London, where he wrote and directed his first play, *School's Out,* in 1980. Eventually, he enrolled at the National Film and Television School (NFTS), initially as a producer, but soon decided to concentrate on writing and directing. Even before his NFTS course, he had achieved recognition as a writer.

In 1984 Worrell won Channel 4 Television's Debut New Writers competition with his play *Mohicans,* which was broadcast on Channel 4 as *Like a Mohican* in 1985. At that time, the young Worrell was a more modest individual, and it was a colleague rather than Worrell himself who sent in the script to the competition. When he won, his pleasure was somewhat dulled when he realized that despite his success, the small print of the competition meant that Channel 4 did not actually have to broadcast his work. Showing the determination that would stand him in good stead for subsequent battles with commissioning editors, Worrell fought to have his play broadcast and successfully challenged Channel 4's insistence that single dramas were too expensive to produce. Having leapt that first hurdle, he then argued forcefully for the play to keep its original language, including the ubiquitous swearing that is an intrinsic part of polyglot London's authentic voice. Fortunately, his persistence paid off, and after this success he went on to coauthor (with Martin Stellman) the feature film *For Queen and Country* (1989) before returning again to the small screen.

In the late 1980s, Channel 4 was interested in commissioning a new sitcom, and Worrell contacted the producer Humphrey Barclay with a view to working up an idea. Though he had never written television comedy before, he had penned various satirical works for the theater and felt confident, if slightly anxious, about entering this extremely difficult terrain. Worrell has recounted that he was on his way to meet Barclay to talk through possibilities when his bus pulled up at a traffic light and he saw a barber shop with three barbers peering through the shop window to ogle the women going past: suddenly he had found his comedy situation. The subsequent show, *Desmond's,* was one of Channel 4's most successful programs, producing seven series in five years, from 1989 to 1994. As with all good sitcoms, *Desmond's* was organized around a particular location, in this case, the inside of the barber shop, with occasional shoots in the world outside or scenes set in the flat over the shop, which served as home for the eponymous Desmond and his family.

Although this was not the first British comedy series about a black family, Worrell was keen to work through a number of complex issues and important features of black migrant experiences in Britain in ways that would make sense to both black and white viewers. *Desmond's* was always intended for a mixed audience, and Worrell wanted to expose white audiences to an intact black family whose members experienced precisely the same problems and joys as those of white families. At the same time, he wanted to reflect a positive and realistic black family for black viewers as an antidote to the routinely stereotypical portraits that more usually characterize programs about black people in Britain.

In talking about the production of *Desmond's,* Worrell has revealed the considerable antagonisms he faced from black colleagues who regarded writing sitcoms as an act of betrayal, or at the very least as a soft-option sellout. But this type of criticism misses the point: powerful sentiment and subversive commentary can be made by comedy characters precisely because their comedic tone and domesticated milieu are unthreatening—the viewer is invited to laugh and empathize *with* the characters, not to scorn them. In later episodes of *Desmond's,* program narratives were pushed into more controversial areas such as racism because identification and loyalty had already been secured from the audience and more risks could be taken.

Worrell is very aware of the limited opportunities that exist for black writers wanting to break into television. By the third series of *Desmond's,* he had brought together a new team to work on the show, enabling him to concentrate more on directing as well as providing valuable production experience to a cohort of black writers, many of whom were women. Despite the considerable success of *Desmond's,* Worrell has contended that he still has to fight much harder than white colleagues to get new program ideas accepted. There are significant problems in trying to negotiate new and challenging territory that questions the cozy prejudices of the status quo, and British broadcasters now tend toward the conservative rather than the innovative in their relentless battle to retain market share. While there is a continued interest in series that reflect the assumptions and preconceptions that white editors have about black communities, Worrell is keen to explore the diversities of life as it is actually lived by Britain's blacks. His work breaks out of the suffocating straightjacket of dismal (racist) stereotypes, instead examining the complex realities of black experiences, which are as much about living, loving, and working within strongly multicultural environments as about the hopeless crack-heads, pimps, and villains who inhabit London's ghetto slums. There is no one story—there are many.

In late 1994, Worrell teamed up with Paul Trijbits to create the film and TV production company, Trijbits-Worrell. Although Worrell is quite pessimistic about the future for black writers, producers, and directors trying to penetrate the industry, the continued success of his own work ensures that there is at least one act to follow.

KAREN ROSS

See also **British Programming;** *Desmond's*

Trix Worrell. Born in St. Lucia; immigrated to Britain at the age of five. Educated at the National Film and Television School, London. Writer and actor, Albany Youth Theatre, Deptford, South East London; winner of Channel 4's Debut '84 New Writers competition for *Mohicans; Like a Mohican* aired on Channel 4, 1985; writer and director, *Desmond's,* Channel 4 situation comedy, 1989–94, *Porkpie,* 1995–96, and *Dad,* 1997–99; executive producer, science fiction film, *Hardware,* 1990; cofounder, with Paul Trijbits, Trijbits-Worrell, film and television production company, 1994.

Television Series
1989–94	*Desmond's*
1995–96	*Porkpie*
1997–99	*Dad*

Television Miniseries
| 1999 | *Laughter in the House: The Story of British Sitcom* |

Television Play
| 1985 | *Like a Mohican* |

Films
For Queen and Country (with Martin Stellman), 1989; *Hardware* (executive producer), 1990.

Stage
School's Out, 1980.

Further Reading

Pines, Jim, editor, *Black and White in Colour: Black People in British Television Since 1936,* London: British Film Institute, 1992

Wrather, Jack (1918–1984)

U.S. Media Executive, Producer

Born in Amarillo, Texas, Jack Wrather became an oil "wildcatter" who eventually rose to be president of an oil company founded by his father. He later expanded his resources into real estate, hotels, motion pictures, and broadcast properties. Following service in the U.S. Marine Corps during World War II, Wrather relocated

Producer Jack Wrather with fellow producer and wife Bonita Granville, 1947.
Courtesy of the Everett Collection

to California, where he diversified his holdings in the movie business, creating Jack Wrather Pictures, Inc., and Freedom Productions. Between 1946 and 1955, Wrather produced feature films for Eagle Lion, Warner Brothers, Allied Artists, and United Artists, including *The Guilty, High Tide, Perilous Waters, Strike It Rich, Guilty of Treason, The Lone Ranger and the Lost City of Gold, The Magic of Lassie,* and *The Legend of the Lone Ranger.*

During the 1950s, Wrather, a true entrepreneur, established such television syndication services as Television Programs of America and Independent Television Corporation. He was also co-owner of television stations licensed to Wrather-Alvarez Broadcasting Company in Tulsa, Oklahoma, and San Diego and Bakersfield, California.

Wrather is perhaps most noted for several of the television series he produced: *The Lone Ranger, Lassie,* and *Sergeant Preston of the Yukon.* These programs, which were standards among early syndicated television offerings, served stations affiliated with networks as well as independent stations, and they demonstrated that formulaic, filmed entertainment could attract audiences while providing a resalable product. In many ways, Wrather's operations foreshadowed some of the most significant developments in the economic support structure for the next generation of television, a fact he obviously recognized.

After paying $3 million to George W. Trendle for rights to *The Lone Ranger,* Wrather considered his purchase an important part of American history. The 221-episode half-hour western series, licensed through the years to ABC, CBS, and NBC, remains in syndication today. In the 1950s, Wrather also produced the popular weekly *Lassie* adventure series and 78 episodes of *Sergeant Preston.*

Among other Wrather holdings were the ship *Queen Mary* and Howard Hughes's transport aircraft, the *Spruce Goose.* He also owned Disneyland Hotel and served as board director or board chair for Continental Airlines, TelePrompTer, Muzak, Inc., and the Corporation for Public Broadcasting.

Wrather was among several prominent business executives who became members of Ronald Reagan's original transition committee when Reagan became president in 1981. Jack Wrather died of cancer in 1984 at age 66.

DENNIS HARP

See also Lassie; Lone Ranger, The; Syndication

Jack Wrather. Born John Devereaux Wrather Jr. in Amarillo, Texas, May 24, 1918. Educated at the University of Texas at Austin, B.A., 1939. Married: Bonita Granville, 1947; children: Molly, Jack, Linda, and Christopher. Served in U.S. Marine Corps Reserves, 1942–53. Independent oil producer in Texas, Indiana, and Illinois; president, Evansville Refining Company, 1938–40, Overton Refining Company, Amarillo Producers, and Refiners Corporation, Dallas, 1940–49; owner, Jack Wrather Pictures, Inc., 1947–49, and Freedom Productions Corporation, from 1949; president, Western States Investment Corporation, from 1949; president, Wrather Television Productions, Inc., from 1951; Wrather-Alvarez Broadcasting, Inc.; Lone Ranger, Inc.; Lassie, Inc.; and Disneyland Hotel, Anaheim, California; owner, KFMB, KERO, and KEMB-TV in San Diego; owner, KOTY-TV in Tulsa, Oklahoma; part owner, WNEW, New York City; chair, Muzak, Inc., Independent Television Corporation and Television Programs of America, Inc., Stephens Marine, Inc.; president and chair, Wrather Corporation; director, TelePrompTer Corporation, Continental Airlines, Transcontinent Television Corporation, Jerold Electronics Corporation, Capitol Records, Inc.; board of directors, Community Television of Southern California, Corporation for Public Broadcasting, 1970. Member: development board, University of Texas; board of counselors for performing arts, University of Southern California; Independent Petroleum Association of America; International Radio and Television Society; Academy of Motion Picture Arts and Sciences; National Petroleum Council, 1970. Died in Santa Monica, California, November 12, 1984.

Television Series (producer)

1949–57	*The Lone Ranger*
1957–74	*Lassie*
1955–58	*Sergeant Preston of the Yukon*

Films (producer)

The Guilty, 1946; *High Tide,* 1947; *Perilous Water,* 1947; *Strike It Rich,* 1948; *Guilty of Treason,* 1949; *The Lone Ranger and the Lost City of Gold,* 1958; *The Magic of Lassie,* 1978; *The Legend of the Lone Ranger,* 1981.

Wrestling on Television

At the end of the 19th century, professional wrestling was as "authentic"—as genuinely competitive—as the NFL is today. Similar to modern amateur wrestling in terms of style, holds, and strategy, professional matches during this "authentic" stage frequently lasted for hours in one- and two-hold stalemates. Although it is not clear exactly how wrestling's transformation to stage-managed spectacle was accomplished, by the 1930s its essential redefinition was complete. The economic imperatives associated with luring crowds back to the arena resulted in stylistic, promotional, and structural modification of the sport form. In this radical reformation, the ethic of competition was discarded and replaced by a new set of codes and values associated with "kayfabe." An old carnie term, kayfabe is akin to "honor among thieves." A kind of swindler's agreement, the unwritten laws of kayfabe dictate that insiders always maintain the illusion of a confidence game even when confronted by outsiders with overwhelming evidence that the con is all an act. It is important to note, here, that the kayfabe era in professional wrestling, with its gymnastic moves, theatrical contrivances, and control by flamboyant promoters, was established decades before the introduction of television. So, while professional wrestling has thrived during the age of television, sport purists cannot hold the medium accountable for wrestling's theatrical transformation.

Even so, professional wrestling performed an especially prominent role in television's early history as a mass medium. During the age of live programming, wrestling's choreographed violence and grand pantomime made it an entertainment form that was particularly well-suited to the limitations of primitive television sets. Although the faux sport was most closely associated with the ABC and Dumont networks, between 1948 and 1955 (during what is now known as the "golden era" of the sport), wrestling programs appeared at one time or another on the prime-time schedules of all four major national broadcast networks. Chicago was home to the two longest-running wrestling shows of this period. On almost every Wednesday night for six years, ABC telecast matches from the Windy City's Rainbow Arena with Wayne Griffin performing as announcer. On Saturday nights during roughly the same time span, Marigold Gardens was the setting for Dumont's "Wrestling from Chicago" with Jack Brickhouse providing the commentary. But the most noteworthy of the early announcers, Dennis James, appeared on another Dumont production that originated from various arenas in and around New York City. Remembered for the catchphrase "Okay, Mother," James's enthusiasm for the sport was both legendary and infectious.

During this golden era of kayfabe wrestling, matches pitted fan favorites like Verne Gagne, Lou Thesz, and Bruno "The Italian Superman" Sammartino against larger-than-life villains like "Classy" Freddie Blassie, Killer Kowalski, and "Nature Boy" Buddy Rogers. But by far the most significant wrestling star of this period was George Wagner—millions knew (and hated) him as Gorgeous George. After ten years of wrestling in obscurity, Wagner became something of an alchemist when he discovered how to turn homophobia into gold. In a day when most wrestlers and their male fans sported crew cuts and flattops, Gorgeous George's long, curly, platinum blond locks made him stand out. His many theatrical innovations included deploying a supporting cast/entourage and playing provocative theme music: male valets named Geoffrey and Thomas Ross would spray Wagner's corner of the ring with perfume before George, with "Pomp and Circumstance" blaring on the loud speakers, made a grand entrance that might last longer than his actual match. Wagner's showmanship would have a lasting impact on the sport, inspiring generations of imitators like Adrian Street, "Superstar" Billy Graham, Ric Flair, "Adorable" Adrian Adonis, Goldust, and Randy "Macho Man" Savage (whose theme song was also "Pomp and Circumstance"). The importance of Gorgeous George Wagner, then, is that he was the first of TV's sports performers to establish that personality, character, and color are as interesting to audiences and as crucial to television stardom as run-of-the-mill competitive superiority.

The golden era of pro wrestling would end in 1955, when wrestling vanished from all of the networks' prime-time schedules. Surviving in the ghetto time-slots of local late-night and weekend schedules, wrestling programming during the next 25 years was largely produced and distributed by regional promoters who developed a cast of heroes and villains that replicated and exploited prevailing cultural conflicts and ethnic rivalries. In Lubbock, Texas, for example, "Rapid" Ricky Romero was a popular "good guy" who appealed to the area's large Mexican-American population, while the Funks (a ranching family made up of father Dory and sons Dory Jr. and Terry) catered to Anglo fans. Where Gorgeous George exploited homophobia, many of the wrestling villains of the 1960s and 1970s capitalized on the xenophobia of cold war America. Lord Alfred Hayes, "Russian Bear" Ivan Koloff, Baron Mikel Scicluna, Baron von Raschke, The Sheik, Professor Toru Tanaka, Mr. Fuji: all were portrayed as foreign-born villains.

Another notable trend of this period was the emergence of masked wrestlers who seemed to be refugees from pages of comic books. In the United States, masked wrestlers like the Destroyer, the Bolos, Dr. X, Mr. Wrestling, and Mr. Wrestling II achieved moderate success as villains. But south of the U.S. border, colorful masked men dominated the character cosmos of what is called *Lucha Libre* (literally, free-form fighting). From the legendary El Santo and Blue Demon through the flamboyant Mil Mascaras to such contemporary young superstars as Rey Mysterio Jr. and Juventud Gurrera, the masked *luchador* is the defining figure in Mexican professional wrestling.

Back in the United States, the fragmentation of wrestling in the 1960s and 1970s is perhaps best illus-

WWF Smackdown. Rikishi Fhatu (Solofa Fatu), with 2Cool, Grandmaster Sexay (Brian Lawler) and Scotty 'Too Hotty' Taylor. Season 2.
Courtesy of the Everett Collection

trated by the contested object that motivated the main line of action in the always-developing masculine melodrama: the championship belt. The smallest wrestling circuits attached grandiose titles to belts that made the huge buckles of rodeo hardware look puny. Even so, the three most prestigious "World" heavyweight titles during this era were sanctioned by what were then the three largest wrestling associations: the American Wrestling Association (AWA), the National Wrestling Alliance (NWA), and the World Wide Wrestling Federation (WWWF). First awarded to Frank Gotch in 1904, the NWA's World Wrestling Championship was the oldest belt recognized in the United States.

In keeping with a familiar business trend in the entertainment industry, it would not be one of the three established powers that propelled professional wrestling into a hyper-golden age of global proportions. Instead, the seeds of wrestling's postmodern future would take root in a small East Coast operation known as the Capitol Wrestling Federation. In 1982, Vincent Kenneth McMahon Jr. and his wife, Linda, acquired the marginal enterprise from a partnership headed by Vincent Kenneth McMahon Sr. for $1 million divided into four quarterly payments. Like his main rival, Ted Turner, McMahon understood the economic opportunities afforded by the satellite/cable revolution. Renaming his company the World Wrestling

Federation (WWF), McMahon signed a deal with the USA Network that enabled him to cultivate a national cable audience.

McMahon was not concerned with maintaining the so-called "credibility" of the sport form. Dropping any pretense that pro wrestling was an authentic sport, McMahon violated kayfabe when he freely admitted that matches were rigged. In fact, discarding the burden of credibility enabled McMahon to connect wrestling to another superhistrionic spectacle: rock music. With the aid of pop stars (most notably, Cyndi Lauper), McMahon forged a rock-wrestling connection that successfully pitched his pyrotechnic productions to the MTV generation. McMahon's targeting of the youth market was also apparent in the WWF's new line of wrestling superstars. Hulk Hogan, Andre the Giant, and Randy "Macho Man" Savage would become internationally known names in the rapidly expanding culture of global telecommunications technology.

McMahon's greatest achievements have been in pay-per-view television. The 1985 debut of McMahon's Wrestlemania was a headline-grabbing experiment. The first Wrestlemania was staged in New York's Madison Square Garden. With Muhammad Ali serving as guest referee, Liberace keeping time, and baseball's Billy Martin performing as ring announcer, Wrestlemania I's marquee event was a grudge tag-team match that partnered Hulk Hogan and the *A Team*'s Mr. T against Rowdy Roddy Piper and Paul "Mr. Wonderful" Orndorff. The outcome of the match is, of course, not as important as the fact that the experiment *almost* made money.

Two years later, Wrestlemania III erased any lingering doubts about the profitability of pay-per-view wrestling. A record 93,173 spectators jammed the Pontiac Silverdome to make Wrestlemania's third installment rank then as the "largest indoor sports event or entertainment event of all time" (the previous indoor attendance record was for a 1981 Rolling Stones concert in New Orleans at the Superdome). Producing $1.7 million in ticket sales and $30 million more in pay-per-view and merchandising receipts, Wrestlemania III established McMahon as the architect of a new media synergy that went beyond the way professional wrestling had traditionally used televised matches to hype live events. Whether distributed on a major broadcast network (NBC's *Saturday Night's Main Event*), a minor broadcast network (UPN's *Smackdown!*), or a basic cable network (USA's *Raw*), McMahon's "free" wrestling shows—though highly rated and profitable—would come to represent relatively modest revenue streams compared with their promotional value for building anticipation and expectations

for the orgy of excess and profit taking that is Wrestlemania.

In the world of pro wrestling, McMahon now reigns supreme, having finally vanquished his only serious rival, Ted Turner. This accomplishment is even more impressive considering Turner's ten-year head start in the wrestling business. Though Turner is better known for his ownership of the Atlanta Braves, professional wrestling was actually his first venture into the world of sports programming. Soon after purchasing a money-losing UHF station in Atlanta in 1970, Turner enlisted the aid of a former girlfriend (who was married to one of Atlanta's top wrestling promoters) to help him steal a popular wrestling show from the local ABC affiliate. Outfitting Channel 17's small studio with a full-sized ring, Turner scheduled wrestling three times a week—and the station's ratings started moving upward. That small independent station would eventually become WTBS. For the next three decades, wrestling would be a key programming ingredient of Turner's cable empire. However, in the 1980s, when McMahon was taking wrestling to new heights with Wrestlemania, Turner was preoccupied with other matters: establishing CNN, trying to buy CBS, launching the Goodwill Games, acquiring MGM's film archive, and fighting off creditors. In the mid-1990s, though, Turner would go on the offensive. Changing the name of his wrestling property from the National Wrestling Alliance to World Class Wrestling (WCW), Turner retooled its programming with higher production values and more convoluted, melodramatic storylines. Beginning in July 1996, for 83 straight weeks, Turner's WCW attracted larger television audiences than McMahon's WWF fare.

McMahon mounted a counteroffensive with a makeover of the WWF that included hiring writers from MTV and the *Conan O'Brien Show* to dream up sleazy plots and odious stunts. One Thanksgiving installment, for instance, featured two women grappling in gravy. Though such tasteless gimmickry resulted in Coca Cola pulling its ads from *SmackDown!*, McMahon's strategy would bring viewers flooding back to the WWF. By 2000, WWF programming had doubled the ratings of WCW. And in March 2001, McMahon acquired the WCW from AOL Time Warner for $10 to $20 million. After the takeover, the WCW's top stars, Goldberg and Ric Flair, would go on to share the WWF spotlight with Stone Cold Steve Austin, Dwayne "The Rock" Johnson, and Mick "Mankind" Foley.

But there was something hollow about McMahon's ringing victory over his old enemy, for the WCW was not the only sport/entertainment enterprise to fold in the spring of 2001. On May 10 of that memorable year, a little over a month after the WWF-WCW merger, McMahon and his collaborators at NBC were forced to also pull the plug on the XFL, a new football league that failed to catch on with the public. Just before the launch of the XFL, McMahon had himself achieved billionaire status when a share of WWF stock was trading at $22; soon after the XFL failure, the price of WWF stock was cut in half—and it would dip as low as $7.43 in 2002.

Despite the XFL debacle, the man who brought the world Wrestlemania still stands as an impresario whose showmanship rivals that of the legendary P.T. Barnum. In addition to being associated with a low-brow cultural form, McMahon's legend is stigmatized by the widely held belief that his sizable personal fortune has been built on the blood, sweat, and tears (and chemical enhancement) of others. In fact, years before the demise of the XFL damaged McMahon's reputation, his public persona had been tainted by skullduggery. In the late 1980s and early 1990s, a steroid scandal tarnished not only McMahon's name but also the wholesome good-guy credentials of Hulk Hogan. Later, McMahon settled for a reported $18 million in a wrongful death suit filed by the family of Owen Hart. Hart, a journeyman wrestler, was fatally injured on May 23, 1999, when he fell 78 feet during an aerial stunt at a WWF show in Kansas City. And, more recently, deaths of at least two children have been attributed to juvenile violence inspired by the WWF. In the most publicized of these cases, Lionel Tate was given life in prison by a Florida court after being found guilty of body-slamming and kicking six-year-old Tiffany Eunick to death. Tate was 14 years old at the time of his sentencing.

McMahon's advice to parents concerned that his crude, misogynist, and violent programming is not suitable for children is to "Chill!" As he told Matt Meagher of *Inside Edition,* "We're not trying to corrupt the public.... We're trying to do one thing only: Entertain you! And based upon our TV ratings, that's what we're doing." On May 5, 2002, McMahon renamed his outfit World Wrestling Entertainment, Inc. (WWE). McMahon's wife, Linda, who was speaking as CEO of WWE, declared, "Our new name puts an emphasis on the 'E' for entertainment, what our company does best. WWE provides us with a global identity that is distinct and unencumbered, which is critical to our U.S. and international growth plans." Putting the emphasis on the "E" also speaks to the chief economic motive behind Vince McMahon's rejection of the pretense that pro wrestling is a sport—it provides him with a strategy for disowning the negative consequences of his business. His well-rehearsed and oft-spoken defense of his product basically boils down to a verbal shell game that equates and conflates "harmlessness" with "entertainment"—a semantic move that covers a multitude of sins and makes one nostalgic for the good old-fashioned dishonesty of kayfabe.

JIMMIE REEVES

See also **Sports and Television; Turner, Ted**

Wright, Robert C. (1943–)

U.S. Media Executive

Robert C. Wright succeeded the legendary Grant Tinker as president of NBC in 1986 when the "Peacock Network" was acquired by General Electric (GE) for $6.3 billion. Under General Electric chief executive officer Jack Welch, Wright immediately began to shape a new NBC, moving it out of radio altogether and headlong into cable television. In 1988 Wright allied with Cablevision Systems, Inc., in a $300 million deal that led in the following year to the start up of a 24-hour cable network, CNBC. He also acquired shares of the cable channel CourtTV, and of Visnews,

an international video news service. Following these acquisitions, he immediately initiated selling NBC News products to hundreds of clients overseas.

The first half of the 1990s was equally busy for Wright. The Australian Television Network became NBC's first overseas affiliate. In 1991 NBC bought out CNBC's chief rival, the Financial News Network, for well in excess of $100 million, closed it down, and merged its core components into CNBC. Wright invested in the Super Channel, an advertising-supported satellite service based in London; began NBC Asia;

and poured millions into NBC's News Channel, a TV wire service based in Charlotte, North Carolina. But the biggest deal during the first half of the 1990s came when Wright and Bill Gates announced a multimillion-dollar alliance of NBC and Microsoft to create an all-news channel, MSNBC, to rival CNN around the world.

Wright, under the tutelage of Jack Welch, remade NBC within ten years and has served as the longest-reigning NBC head since David Sarnoff. Like his mentor Welch, Wright comes from a Catholic household, is the son of an engineer, did not go to an Ivy League college, is devoted to GE, and is no fan of television. Wright had entered the GE corporate ladder as a staff attorney but quickly moved to the decision-making side, running GE's plastic sales division (1978–80), working as the head of the housewares and audio equipment division (1983–84), and being promoted to the presidency of GE Financial Services (1984–86).

Wright's first ten years at NBC were not without failure. Most notably he led NBC to well in excess of $50 million in losses by way of its pay-per-view venture Triplecast during the 1992 Olympics. But his years with NBC have also been filled with triumphs. He turned the cable news channels CNBC and MSNBC into profitable ventures and helped make A&E and the History Channel into popular cable networks. Because of such successes, GE promoted him in June 2001 to chairman and chief executive officer of NBC and a vice president of the GE board, as the company pushed beyond the Jack Welsh era. In 2003 Wright managed GE's and NBC's purchase of Vivendi-Universal, taking the network into a new era of studio ownership and tighter vertical and horizontal integration.

DOUGLAS GOMERY

See also **National Broadcasting Company; United States: Networks**

Robert Charles Wright. Born in Hempstead, New York, April 23, 1943. Holy Cross College, B.A. in history, 1965; University of Virginia, LL.B., 1968. Married: Suzanne Werner, 1967; children: Kate, Christopher, and Maggie. Served in U.S. Army Reserve. Admitted to Bar: New York, 1968; Virginia, 1968; Massachusetts, 1970; New Jersey, 1971. Attorney, General Electric Company, 1969–70 and 1973–79; general manager, plastics sales department, 1976–80; law secretary to chief judge, U.S. District Court, New Jersey, 1970–73; president, Cox Cable Communications, Atlanta, Georgia, 1979–83; executive vice president, Cox Communications, 1980–83; vice president and general manager, GE housewares, electronics, and cable TV operations, 1983–84; president and chief executive officer, GE Financial Services, Inc., 1984–86; president and chief executive officer, NBC, New York City, from 1986; chief executive officer and chairman, NBC, and vice chairman of GE board since 2001. Recipient: Steven J. Ross Humanitarian of the Year award from the UJA-Federation of New York; Gold Medal Award from the International Radio and Television Society Foundation. Inductee into the Broadcasting and Cable Hall of Fame.

Further Reading

Auletta, Ken, *Three Blind Mice: How the TV Networks Lost Their Way*, New York: Random House, 1991

Goldberg, Robert, and Gerald Jay Goldberg, *Anchors: Brokaw, Jennings, and Rather and the Evening News*, New York: Birch Lane, 1990

Tichy, Noel M., and Stratford Sherman, *Control Your Own Destiny or Someone Else Will: How Jack Welch Is Making General Electric the World's Most Competitive Corporation*, New York: Doubleday, 1993

Writer in Television

A commonplace in the television industry is that "it all begins with the script." In part, this notion recognizes the centrality of writers in the early days of live television, when authors such as Reginald Rose, Paddy Chayevsky, and Rod Serling established the medium as an arena for the exploration of character, psychology, and moral complexity in close intimate settings.

With the television industry's move to Hollywood in the 1950s, and its increasing reliance on filmed, formulaic, studio factory productions, writers were often reduced to "hack" status, churning out familiar material that was almost interchangeable across genres. This week's western could be reformatted for next week's crime drama. This view oversimplifies, of course, and ignores extraordinary work in television series such as *Naked City, The Defenders, Route 66,* and others. But it does capture conventional assumptions and expectations.

In the 1970s, with the rise of socially conscious situation comedy often identified with producer Norman Lear and the "quality" comedies associated with MTM Productions, writers once again moved to positions of prominence. Lear himself was a writer-producer, one of the many "hyphenates" who would follow into positions of authority and control. And Grant Tinker, head of MTM, sought out strong writers and encouraged them to create new shows—and new types of shows—for television. Indeed, the legacy of MTM stands strong in today's television industry. Names such as James Brooks, Allan Burns, Steven Bochco, David Milch, and others can trace their careers to that company.

At the present time almost every major producer in American television is also a writer. Writers oversee series development and production, create new programs, and see to the coordination and conceptual coherence of series in progress. Their skills are highly valued and, for the very successful few, extremely highly rewarded. Nevertheless, the role of the writer is affected by many other issues and despite new respect and prominence, remains a complex, often conflicted position in the television industry.

The film and television industries, for example, have been until quite recently very separate entities. Even in the early years of television writers were recruited not from film but from radio and the theater. In many ways, the environment for writers in television still remains distinct from that of the film industry. TV writers are quick to remark that it is nearly impossible to start out in television and move on to film, but that there are no barriers to moving in the other direction—it is, rather, a fact that writers in the film industry will not write television "unless they are starving." This belief summarizes a power relationship in which writers are clearly identified as *either* "television" or "film," or even by genre, early in their careers. One important difference lies in the common perception that writers in television have more clout, simply because there is a well-defined career path by which writers can move up through the ranks of a production company to become a senior producer and therefore control their work in ways typically denied to film scriptwriters.

An interesting aspect of writing for television is the hierarchical organization of the profession. Many production companies now employ "staff writers," although most TV writers work as freelancers competing for a diminishing number of assignments. At the bottom of the pyramid are the outside freelancers who may write no more than two or three episodes a season for various shows. At the top are the producers and executive producers. In between are readers, writer's assistants, a handful of junior staff writers (with contracts of varying lengths), and assistant and associate producers. Producer titles are often given to writers and are usually associated with seniority and supervisory responsibilities for a writing team. The desirable career path, then, involves moving from freelancer to staff writer to associate producer to supervising producer to executive producer. Executive producers are given sole responsibility for controlling a television series, are usually owners or part owners of the series, and may work on several series at once.

Writers usually become executive producers by creating their own series. But this generally occurs only after writing successfully in other positions, and after being recognized by studio and network executives as someone with the potential to create and control a series. Only in the rarest of circumstances are new program ideas purchased or developed from freelancers or beginning writers.

Readers are a critical element in a freelance television writer's working life, because they control whether or not one's work reaches senior staff with hiring authority. Readers analyze samples of a writer's work and evaluate the appropriateness of a writer's skills, experience, and background for the series, and they are used routinely as a "first cut" mechanism throughout the industry. The criteria used by readers is often very specific, sometimes seemingly arbitrary, but because of their importance TV writers learn to "write to the reader" in order to advance to the next assessment level. An entire subordinate industry exists in Los Angeles to educate writers about the process and criteria reviewers employ, even though readers describe themselves as without significant influence.

Agents are also a fact of a television writer's life because production companies and their readers generally will not consider any work from a writer unless it is submitted by an agent, preferably an agent known to that production company. A common frustration for writers is that agents refuse to represent writers without credits but credits cannot be earned without agent representation.

The Writers Guild of America (WGA), founded in 1912, is the official trade union and collective bargaining unit for writers in the film and television industries and actively monitors working conditions for writers. The WGA has warned that contemporary writers face a hostile environment with ageism and sexism a common complaint. Hollywood is enamored with youth culture and consequently producers and network executives often seek creative talent they feel will be capable of addressing that audience. According to WGA statistics, a definite bias toward younger writers has emerged in the industry. In addition, the WGA and another organization, Women in Film, recently released reports showing that although women make up 25 percent of the Hollywood writing pool they receive a smaller share of assignments proportional to their number. Although there are several prominent female writers and producers in television, many industry observers believe there exist structural and cultural barriers to the advancement of women throughout the industry that cannot be easily removed.

Because the production of most television shows (prior to syndication sales) must be "deficit financed" (network payment for the rights to the series is less than the cost to produce the episodes), writers often bear the brunt of the resulting financial insecurity, taking less cash up-front in salary or per-episode fees and hoping for healthy residuals if the series becomes successful. Although the WGA sets minimum payments for each type of writing assignment, writers are often seen at the popular "Residuals Bar" in Van Nuys where a residuals check for $1 or less earns the bearer a free drink. Seventy percent of television writers earn less than $50,000 a year through their efforts in this field. In spite of this harsh reality, hundreds of aspiring writers write thousands of new scripts each year, hoping for the chance to write the next huge hit.

In other television systems writers continue to enjoy a similar sort of prestige. Television authors such as Dennis Potter and Lynda La Plante have offered audiences outstanding, formally challenging work for this medium. Because of their work as well as because of the American system's financial and aesthetic rewards, television writing is now perhaps recognized as a truly legitimate form of creativity and has taken its place alongside the novel, the stage play, and the film screenplay as one of the most significant expressive forms of the age.

CHERYL HARRIS

See also **Chayefsky, Paddy; Bochco, Steven; Huggins, Roy; La Plante, Lynda; Mercer, David; Potter, Dennis; Rose, Reginald; Serling, Rod; Silliphant, Sterling; Tarses, Jay**

Further Reading

Berger, Arthur Asa, *Scripts: Writing for Radio and Television,* Newbury Park, California: Sage, 1990

Bielby, William T., and Denise D. Bielby, *The 1989 Hollywood Writers' Report: Unequal Access, Unequal Pay,* West Hollywood, California: Writers Guild of America, West, 1989

Blum, Richard A., *Television Writing: From Concept to Contract,* Boston: Focal Press, 1995

Brady, Ben, *The Understructure of Writing for Film and Television,* Austin: University of Texas Press, 1988

Di Maggio, Madeline, *How to Write for Television,* New York: Prentice Hall, 1990

DiTillio, Lawrence G., " 'I Hate Stories.' Script Is Easy. Story Is Hard," *Writer's Digest* (June 1994)

DiTillio, Lawrence G., "Scripting a Sample 'Seinfeld,' " *Writer's Digest* (December 1993)

Macak, Jim, "How Writers Survive," *The Journal* (January 1994)

Potter, Dennis, *Seeing the Blossom: Two Interviews, a Lecture, and a Story,* London and Boston: Faber and Faber, 1994

Root, Wells, *Writing the Script: A Practical Guide for Films and Television,* New York: Holt, Rinehart, and Winston, 1980

Stempel, Tom, *Storytellers to the Nation: A History of American Television Writing,* New York: Continuum, 1992

Straczynski, J. Michael, "The TV Commandments," *Writer's Digest* (April 1992)

Walter, Richard, *Screenwriting: The Art, Craft, and Business of Film and Television Writing,* New York: New American Library, 1988

Wyman, Jane (1916–)

U.S. Actor, Producer

Jane Wyman is one of the few Hollywood movie stars to have had an equally successful television career. She was at the height of her film career in the mid-1950s when she launched her first television series, *Jane Wyman Theater.* Modeled after the successful *The Loretta Young Show,* the prime-time filmed anthology series presented a different drama each week, with Wyman as host, producer, and sometimes actress. Between 1958 and 1980, Wyman appeared occasionally as a guest star on television series and in made-for-TV movies. Then, in 1981, she scored another series success with her portrayal of ruthless matriarch Angela Channing on CBS's prime-time soap opera *Falcon Crest.*

Wyman broke into movies in the early 1930s as a Goldwyn Girl and continued to play chorus girls until the mid-1940s. By 1948, when she won the Best Actress Academy Award for *Johnny Belinda,* her image was that of a capable dramatic actress. In the early 1950s, her success continued with romantic comedies such as *Here Comes the Groom* (1951) and such melodramas as *Magnificent Obsession* (1954). She was considered a "woman's star," mature yet glamorous, a woman with whom middle-class, middle-aged women could identify. Amid speculation as to why a currently successful film star would want to do series television, Wyman started work on her own anthology drama series. According to her, television seemed like the right thing to do at that time. The movie industry was changing, and she wanted to try the new medium. Moreover, film roles for fortyish female stars were in short supply.

Procter and Gamble's *Fireside Theatre,* a filmed anthology series, had been a fixture on NBC since 1949, but by the end of the 1954–55 season, ratings had slipped. The show was overhauled in 1955 and became Wyman's series. Her production company, Lewman Productions (co-owned with MCA's Revue Productions), produced the series. As host, she was glamorous Jane Wyman. As producer, she chose the stories. As actress, she chose her occasional roles. Presentations were dramas or light comedies, with Wyman acting in about half of the episodes. The series carried on the tradition established by *Fireside Theatre* and *The Loretta Young Show*—filmed, half-hour anthology dramas that attracted substantial audiences, while critics praised live, 60- and 90-minute anthology dramas such as *Studio One* and *Playhouse 90.*

Wyman's series was initially titled *Jane Wyman Presents the Fireside Theatre,* but the title was later shortened to *Jane Wyman Theater.* (It was called *Jane Wyman Presents* when ABC aired reruns in 1963.) Like *The Loretta Young Show,* Wyman's series was rerun on network daytime schedules (to target women audiences) and in syndication. (The aspiring writer Aaron Spelling found work with *Jane Wyman Theater* and later became one of television's most successful producers.) Wyman also hosted a summer series that featured teleplays originally shown on other anthology dramas. This 1957 program was called *Jane Wyman's Summer Playhouse.*

In the years following the cancellation of *Jane Wyman Theater,* Wyman guest-starred on television programs, made a few feature films (with starring roles in two Disney films), and appeared in a made-for-TV movie. In 1971 Wyman guest-starred on an episode of *The Bold Ones* as Dr. Amanda Fallon. This production provided the basis for a series pilot but never became a

Jane Wyman.
Photo courtesy of Jane Wyman

series. In 1979 she received attention for her supporting role in the made-for-TV movie *The Incredible Journey of Dr. Meg Laurel.* She then made appearances on two of Aaron Spelling's series, *The Love Boat* and *Charlie's Angels.*

The spotlight really returned in 1981. As the ex-wife of newly elected President Ronald Reagan, Wyman was sought out by the media. Her publicity value did not escape Lorimar Productions' Earl Hamner and CBS. Seeking to capitalize on their success with *Dallas* and *Knots Landing,* Lorimar and CBS launched *Falcon Crest* in 1981, with Wyman starring as a female version of *Dallas*'s ruthless and manipulative J.R. Ewing. For nine seasons, she portrayed Angela Channing, the powerful matriarch of a wealthy, winemaking family. Wyman thus made a successful return to series television, but in a role quite different from her earlier work. As Angela Channing, she was not the likable, clean-cut woman she had so often portrayed in the past, but she played the part of Channing to perfection. In 1984 she won a Golden Globe Award for her *Falcon Crest* performances and was reported to be the highest-paid actress on television at that time.

Jane Wyman's television career began in the mid-1950s, after she had already achieved stardom in the movies. Like Loretta Young and Lucille Ball, she was one of the few film stars and one of relatively few women to have her own successful television series. She also was one of the few women to star in her own anthology drama series. Thirty years later, in the 1980s, Wyman accomplished something even more unusual: as an actor of old Hollywood and early television, she starred in another, even more successful series, *Falcon Crest*.

MADELYN M. RITROSKY-WINSLOW

See also **Fireside Theater; Gender and Television; Melodrama; Young, Loretta**

Jane Wyman. Born Sarah Jane Fulks in St. Joseph, Missouri, January 4, 1916. Attended the University of Missouri, Colombia, 1935. Married: 1) Myron Futterman, 1937 (divorced, 1939); 2) Ronald Reagan, 1940 (divorced, 1948); children: Maureen and Michael; 3) Freddie Karger, 1952 (divorced, 1955) and 1963–65. Actress in films, from 1932; debuted as Sarah Jane Fulks in *The Kid from Spain;* radio singer under the name of Jane Durrell; contract with Warner Brothers, 1936–49; host and actor in television series *Jane Wyman Theater,* 1955–58; starring role in *Falcon Crest,* 1981–90. Recipient: Best Actress Academy Award, 1948; Golden Globe Award, 1984.

Television Series

1955–58   *Jane Wyman Theater*
1957   *Jane Wyman's Summer Playhouse*
1981–90   *Falcon Crest*

Made-for-Television Movies

1971   *The Failing of Raymond*
1979   *The Incredible Journey of Dr. Meg Laurel*

Films

(as Sarah Jane Fulks) *The Kid from Spain,* 1932; *Elmer the Great,* 1933; *College Rhythm,* 1934; *Rumba,* 1935; *All the King's Horses,* 1935; *Stolen Harmony,* 1935; *King of Burlesque,* 1936; *Anything Goes,* 1936; *My Man Godfrey,* 1936; (as Jane Wyman) *Stage Struck,* 1936; *Cain and Mabel,* 1936; *Polo Joe,* 1936; *Smart Blonde,* 1936; *Gold Diggers of 1937,* 1937; *Ready, Willing, and Able,* 1937; *The King and the Chorus Girl,* 1937; *Slim,* 1937; *The Singing Marine,* 1937; *Mr. Dodd Takes the Air,* 1937; *Public Wedding,* 1937; *The Spy Ring,* 1938; *Fools for Scandal,* 1938; *She Couldn't Say No,* 1938; *Wide Open Faces,* 1938; *The Crowd Roars,* 1938; *Brother Rat,* 1938; *Tail Spin,* 1939; *Private Detective,* 1939; *The Kid from Kokomo,* 1939; *Torchy Plays with Dynamite,* 1939; *Kid Nightingale,* 1939; *Brother Rat and a Baby,* 1940; *An Angel from Texas,* 1940; *Flight Angels,* 1940; *My Love Came Back,* 1940; *Tugboat Annie Sails Again,* 1940; *Gambling on the High Seas,* 1940; *Honeymoon for Three,* 1941; *Bad Men of Missouri,* 1941; *You're in the Navy Now,* 1941; *The Body Disappears,* 1941; *Larceny, Inc.,* 1942; *My Favorite Spy,* 1942; *Footlight Serenade,* 1942; *Princess O'Rourke,* 1943; *Make Your Own Bed,* 1944; *Crime by Night,* 1944; *The Doughgirls,* 1944; *Hollywood Canteen,* 1944; *The Lost Weekend,* 1945; *One More Tomorrow,* 1946; *Night and Day,* 1946; *The Yearling,* 1946; *Cheyenne,* 1947; *Magic Town,* 1947; *Johnny Belinda,* 1948; *A Kiss in the Dark,* 1949; *The Lady Takes a Sailor,* 1949; *It's a Great Feeling,* 1949; *Stage Fright,* 1950; *The Glass Menagerie,* 1950; *Three Guys Named Mike,* 1951; *Here Comes the Groom,* 1951; *The Blue Veil,* 1951; *Starlift,* 1951; *The Story of Will Rogers,* 1952; *Just for You,* 1952; *Let's Do It Again,* 1953; *So Big,* 1953; *Magnificent Obsession,* 1954; *Lucy Gallant,* 1955; *All That Heaven Allows,* 1955; *Miracle in the Rain,* 1956; *Holiday for Lovers,* 1959; *Pollyanna,* 1960; *Bon Voyage,* 1962; *How to Commit Marriage,* 1969; *The Outlanders.*

Further Reading

Bawden, J., "Jane Wyman: American Star Par Excellence," *Films in Review* (April 1975)
Morella, Joe, and Edward Z. Epstein, *Jane Wyman: A Biography,* New York: Delacorte, 1985
Parish, James Robert, and Don E. Stanke, *The Forties Gals,* Westport, Connecticut: Arlington House, 1980
Quirk, Lawrence J., *Jane Wyman: The Actress and the Woman,* New York: December, 1980

Xena: Warrior Princess

U.S. Drama

"In a time of ancient gods, warlords, and kings, the world cried out for a hero. She was Xena, a mighty princess forged in the heat of battle.... Her courage will change the world." This description of the hero of the syndicated television series *Xena: Warrior Princess,* recited over the opening credits of each episode, aptly lays out the basic premise of this popular show. Filmed on location in New Zealand, *Xena* emerged in 1995 as a spin-off of the syndicated series *Hercules: The Legendary Journey,* and like that show, it is immersed in Greek mythology, with many plots centered on well-known myths and legends. Xena had previously appeared in three episodes of *Hercules* as a cruel female warrior, infamous for her evil actions throughout ancient Greece. By the end of her sojourn with Hercules, Xena decided to change her evil ways and set off on her own to begin atoning for her past sins. In a short time, *Xena* overtook *Hercules* in terms of its popularity as a cult show, both in the Unites States and abroad.

However, *Xena* is about much more than a formerly evil woman making up for her past. While redemption remains a major theme in the series, the more predominant focus in the show is the deep and meaningful bond between Xena (Lucy Lawless) and her "sidekick," a young woman named Gabrielle (Renee O' Connor). In the premiere episode of the series, Xena helps to free Gabrielle and her female companions from slavery. Later, Gabrielle decides that she is not cut out for the life her family has planned for her—marriage and children, continuing to live in her home village—and sets out in search of Xena. The two women begin to travel together, with Xena fighting evil people, gods, and creatures, and Gabrielle recording their exploits in what becomes known as "The Xena Scrolls."

What sustained *Xena* as a hit (the series has a remarkable following on the Internet and generated a profitable convention-going circuit) was the intense and ambiguous relationship that developed between Xena and Gabrielle. Fans of the series soon began speculating that Xena and Gabrielle were, in fact, a loving lesbian couple. The show developed a substantial lesbian fan base, and viewers delighted in the rather obvious lesbian subtext, which became a hallmark trait of the series. One of the most famous "subtext episodes," "A Day in the Life," showed Xena and Gabrielle naked in a hot tub together, and much of the dialogue contained comical double entendres. Numerous episodes created reasons for the two women to kiss and caress each other, from people being trapped in others' bodies to the need for CPR to be administered to Xena and Gabrielle "playing lesbian" to seduce evil men into letting their guards down. In the show's final season, the episode "You Are There" featured a tabloid TV reporter intent on discovering "the truth" about the two women's relationship; when he finally obtains an on-air interview and asks them if they are lovers, the feed is cut and the viewers never get to hear the answer to the question.

The presence of a tabloid TV reporter in ancient Greece is just one example of what made *Xena* generically distinctive. While Xena and Gabrielle travel as action heroes in a world dominated by Greek gods and mythological creatures, the series plays with Greek legends and unhesitatingly rewrites history as well. In addition, the show's use of fantasy (and some science fiction) makes historical impossibilities a regular part of the series. Sometimes this element of the show is used to create humor. Ares (Kevin Smith) is constantly present, trying to get Xena to return to her evil ways by playing tricks on her and Gabrielle (and at other times respecting her choices because of a deep love he has for her). Aphrodite (Alexandra Tydings) loves to pull magical jokes on Xena and Gabrielle and develops a strong friendship with Gabrielle in particular. When Aphrodite makes an evil warlord from Xena's past fall in love with Gabrielle, his attempts to steal a magical lyre to woo Gabrielle lead to a "battle of the bands" episode in which various contestants perform rap, disco, heavy metal, and R&B numbers ("Lyre, Lyre"). In another episode ("Here She Comes, Miss Amphipolis"), Xena and Gabrielle go undercover at a beauty pageant where contestants are being attacked; in the end, Miss Artyphys, a male transvestite, wins the pageant. The characters of Joxer (a hapless warrior in love with Gabrielle, played by Ted Raimi) and Autolycus (a smarmy thief played by Bruce Campbell) also support the show's humorous tone.

While such occurrences made *Xena* regularly funny and campy (especially with the use of acrobatic fight scenes in which the laws of physics are suspended), the series also had many melodramatic storylines, some of which lasted for a full season or longer. In those narratives, Greek mythology continued to play a role, but Nordic and Christian mythology, and also Eastern Asian religions and philosophies, were used as well. For example, throughout the show, the Amazon community plays a large part in the more serious stories, especially after Gabrielle becomes an Amazon queen. In the third season, a demon spirit rapes Gabrielle, leading to the creation of Stonehenge. She later gives birth to a demon child who kills Xena's son, setting the two women against each other. (Their anger and grief is dealt with in a lavish musical episode, "The Bitter Suite.") The following year, Julius Caesar (Karl Urban), a former lover of Xena, crucifies Xena and Gabrielle when they aid a religious revolutionary; in heaven the women meet the archangel Michael and are brought back to a life. While in heaven, Xena and Callisto (who has died) reconcile and Callisto is reborn as Xena's "virgin birth" child, a child destined to end the reign of the Greek gods and introduce monotheism to the world (Eve, played by Adrienne Wilkinson).

Xena ended in 2001 after six seasons. The final year introduced Lucifer/Satan, Xena's past as a Valkyrie, and even two episodes set in 2001 that focused on fans of *Xena* in relation to the "real" Xena and Gabrielle. In the two-hour series finale, Xena and Gabrielle travel to Japa (Japan) to help Xena atone for having accidentally killed 40,000 people in her past. Xena becomes a ghost in order to kill the demon tormenting the 40,000 souls, and she leaves Gabrielle alive (after an otherworldly "kiss," of course) to continue their legendary journeys on her own. *Xena*'s remarkable success in no small measure paved the way for later action series featuring women. Shows such as *La Femme Nikita, Buffy the Vampire Slayer, Dark Angel,* and *Alias* are part of a lineage that owes much to *Xena: Warrior Princess.*

SHARON MARIE ROSS

See also **Buffy the Vampire Slayer; La Femme Nikita; Gender and Television; Sexual Orientation and Television**

Cast

Xena	Lucy Lawless
Gabrielle	Renee O'Connor
Ares	Kevin Smith
Callisto (1996–2000)	Hudson Leick
Joxer (1996–2001)	Ted Raimi
Julius Caesar (1996–2001)	Karl Urban
Autolycus (1996–99)	Bruce Campbell
Aphrodite (1997–2001)	Alexandra Tydings
Eve (2000–01)	Adrienne Wilkinson

Producers

Sam Raimi and Rob Tapert

Programming History

134 episodes
(Syndicated on local stations, afternoons and prime time, 1995–2001)

Further Reading

Journal of International Association of Xenoid Studies, www.whoosh.org

Ross, Sharon, "Funny Fantasies: Extraordinary Female Friendships in Television of the 1990s," Ph.D. diss., University of Texas at Austin, forthcoming

Weisbrot, Robert, *The Official Guide to the Xenaverse,* New York: Doubleday, 1998

X-Files, The

U.S. Science Fiction Program

Created and produced by Chris Carter, *The X-Files* was a strange brew of the science fiction, horror, and detective genres in which D.C.-based FBI agents Fox Mulder (David Duchovny) and Dana Scully (Gillian Anderson), the only two regulars for seven seasons, staffed a much-maligned unit devoted to investigating paranormal phenomena. Interspersed with these stand-alone X-File cases were episodes constituting the serialized "mythology arc" typically featured during ratings sweeps periods. The "mytharc" chronicled the brooding, iconoclastic Mulder's search for the truth behind his sister's disappearance and the extraterrestrial colonizers and government conspirators he believed culpable. Anderson's real-life pregnancy prompted a season-two plot in which Scully was herself briefly abducted, thereby integrating her character into this ongoing narrative.

Recurring characters included the agents' superiors, Walter Skinner (Mitch Pileggi) and Alvin Kersh (James Pickens Jr.), the sinister conspirator "Cigarette Smoking Man" (William B. Davis), the renegade agent Alex Krycek (Nicholas Lea), a trio of Mulder's computer-nerd buddies referred to as the "Lone Gunmen" (Tom Braidwood, Bruce Harwood, and Dean Haglund), his shady informants "Deep Throat" (Jerry Hardin), "X" (Steven Williams), and Marita Covarrubias (Laurie Holden), and Scully's steadfast mother, Maggie (Sheila Larken).

The X-Files reached a creative and commercial pinnacle in its fourth season when, in addition to accruing international renown, it moved from Friday to Sunday nights as part of a male-oriented lineup that included *The Simpsons* and FOX's afternoon football broadcasts. In the summer of 1998, it became the first U.S. series to sprout a successful feature film, *X-Files: Fight the Future,* while its prime-time run was still in full swing. Production shifted from Vancouver, British Columbia, to Los Angeles in season seven, and it was at the end of that year that Duchovny left to pursue other projects amid controversy over a lawsuit, eventually settled out of court, in which he charged FOX with undercutting his contracted profit share by noncompetitively selling the series' syndication rights to its own outlets. He agreed to appear in a handful of episodes in season eight, during which two new regulars, Agents John Doggett (Robert Patrick) and Monica Reyes

(Annabeth Gish), were introduced. The series limped into a ninth season without its original male lead, but the ratings, which had been slipping from their zenith in the top 20 since season five, soon guaranteed that the series finale, for which Duchovny would return, was close at hand.

The paranormal entities investigated by forensic pathologist Scully and psychologist/profiler Mulder, many of which could take human form, generate both literal and metaphorical meanings. Whatever a viewer's bogeyman or paranoia in the millennial, post–cold war era—corporate power, government conspiracies, "alien" others, or the dehumanizing encroachment of technology—the series was perfectly calibrated to exploit it. From a psychic who predicts his own bizarre death in "Clyde Bruckman's Final Repose" to a liver-eating mutant who slithers through ventilation systems in "Squeeze" to a criminal who mentally induces others to commit murder in "Pusher," little is as it first appears. Like the agents' emblematic flashlights, two slogans headlined in the series, "the truth is out there" and "trust no one," guide both characters and audience on their journey.

The X-Files inspired a cult following that developed along with the Internet itself and soon rivaled that of the *Star Trek* franchise. "X-philes" created fan fiction, websites, and bulletin boards that eventually reflected factionalism that might be attributed to the show's postmodern tenor, especially the innovative yet schizophrenic narrative structure in which plot-driven "monster-of-the-week" episodes were periodically suspended in favor of the sprawling and often nebulous mythology. Some fans preferred the former, while others relished the character arcs dominating the latter: Scully's abduction and the cancer and supposed infertility that resulted; and Mulder's search for his sister and the discovery of his "alien" DNA.

Carter bucked the network in hiring the quietly attractive Anderson for the female lead rather than an archetypal "bombshell." As many women as men approved and flocked to the show, also savoring the gender role reversal in which skeptical Scully furnished the scientific counterpoint to Mulder's intuitive leaps to paranormal (but usually valid) solutions. Fans split over the related issue of whether the agents, who exuded unresolved sexual tension, should become an

The X-Files, Gillian Anderson, David Duchovny, 1993–2002.
©*20th Century Fox / Courtesy of the Everett Collection*

"item." Those intrigued by the character arcs tended to answer yes, while most plot-focused fans replied nay. Carter vowed that fans would "never see" a romance and, on a technicality, he kept his word. It wasn't until Mulder's parting scene in season eight that it seemed at all plausible that Scully's newborn could have been conceived the old-fashioned way. The agents sealed the deal with a nonplatonic kiss but, otherwise, little of the romance's progression occurred on-screen for viewers to actually "see." Baby William later exhibited "otherworldly" traits and, like Clark Kent or Luke Skywalker, was farmed off for safekeeping in order to reappear, perhaps, in a sequel series.

The program is the recipient of myriad awards and nominations, including three Golden Globes for Best Drama Series, as well as laurels for such contributions as acting, directing, writing, cinematography, special effects, sound, music, and makeup. Carter, Frank Spotnitz, Vince Gilligan, Darin Morgan, Glen Morgan, and James Wong proved to be some of the series' most prolific and oft-nominated writers, with an occasional as-

sist from several of the actors and such notables as Stephen King and William Gibson.

CHRISTINE SCODARI

See also **Science Fiction Programs**

Cast

Fox Mulder (1993–2002)	David Duchovny
Dana Scully (1993–2002)	Gillian Anderson
John Doggett (2000–02)	Robert Patrick
Monica Reyes (2001–02)	Annabeth Gish
Walter Skinner (1994–2002)	Mitch Pileggi
John Byers (1994–2002)	Bruce Harwood
Melvin Frohike (1994–2002)	Tom Braidwood
Richard Langly (1994–2002)	Dean Haglund
Cigarette Smoking Man (1993– 2002)	William B. Davis
Alex Krycek (1994–2002)	Nicholas Lea
Maggie Scully (1994–2002)	Sheila Larken
Alvin Kersh (1998–2002)	James Pickens, Jr.
X (1994–2002)	Steven Williams
Marita Covarrubias (1995– 2002)	Laurie Holden
Deep Throat (1993–99)	Jerry Hardin
Billy Miles (1993–2001)	Zachary Ansley
Scott Blevins (1993–97)	Charles Cioffi
Melissa Scully (1994–97)	Melinda McGraw
Chuck Burks (1995–2001)	Bill Dow
Teena Mulder (1995–2000)	Rebecca Toolan
Alien Bounty Hunter (1995– 2000)	Brian Thompson
Bill Mulder (1995–99)	Peter Donat
Samantha Mulder (1995–99)	Megan Leitch
Albert Hosteen (1995–99)	Floyd "Red Crow" Westerman
Agent Pendrell (1995–97)	Brendan Beiser
Well-Manicured Man (1995–96)	John Neville
Jeremiah Smith (1996–2001)	Roy Thinnes
Michael Kritschgau (1996–99)	John Finn
Bill Scully, Jr. (1997)	Pat Skipper
Morris Fletcher (1998–2002)	Michael McKean
Gibson Praise (1998–2002)	Jeff Gulka
Jeffrey Spender (1998–2002)	Chris Owens
Cassandra Spender (1998–99)	Veronica Cartwright
Diana Fowley (1998–99)	Mimi Rogers
First Elder (1998–99)	Don S. Williams
Second Elder (1998–99)	George Murdock
Agent Crane (2000–01)	Kirk B.R. Woller
Brad Follmer (2001–02)	Cary Elwes
Knowle Rohrer (2001–02)	Adam Baldwin

Producers

Chris Carter, Vince Gilligan, R.W. Goodwin, Howard Gordon, Frank Spotnitz

Programming History
201 Episodes
FOX

September 1993–May 1996	Friday 9:00–10:00
October 1996–May 2002	Sunday 9:00–10:00

Further Reading

Badley, Linda, "Scully Hits the Glass Ceiling: Postmodernism, Postfeminism, Posthumanism," in *Fantasy Girls: Gender in the New Universe of Science Fiction and Fantasy Television,* edited by Elyce Helford, Lanham, Maryland: Rowman and Littlefield, 2000

Bellon, Joe, "The Strange Discourse of *The X-Files:* What It Is, What It Does, and What Is at Stake," *Critical Studies in Mass Communication,* 16, no. 2 (1999)

Delasara, Jan, *PopLit, PopCult, and "The X-Files,"* Jefferson, North Carolina: McFarland, 2000

Kellner, Douglas, "*The X-Files* and the Aesthetics and Politics of Postmodern Pop," *Journal of Aesthetics and Art Criticism,* 52, no. 3 (1998)

Knight, Peter, *Conspiracy Culture: From Kennedy to "The X-Files,"* New York and London: Routledge, 2000

Lavery, David, Angela Hague, and Marla Cartwright, editors, *Deny All Knowledge: Reading "The X-Files,"* Syracuse, New York: Syracuse University Press, 1996

McLean, Adrienne, "Media Effects: Marshall McLuhan, Television Culture, and *The X-Files,*" *Film Quarterly,* 51, no. 4 (1998)

Scodari, Christine, and Jenna L. Felder, "Creating a Pocket Universe: 'Shippers,' Fan Fiction, and *The X-Files* Online," *Communication Studies,* 51, no. 3 (2000)

Soter, Tom, *Investigating Couples: A Critical Analysis of "The Thin Man," "The Avengers," and "The X-Files,"* Jefferson, North Carolina: McFarland, 2001

Wildermuth, Mark, "The Edge of Chaos: Structural Conspiracy and Epistemology in *The X-Files,*" *Journal of Popular Film and Television,* 26, no. 4 (1999)

XYY Man, The

British Police/Crime Drama

Based on a series of novels by Kenneth Royce first published in 1970, this collection of two- and three-part serial stories within a series was developed around a reformed cat burglar, "Spider" Scott (Stephen Yardley), who was manipulated by British Intelligence to carry out various less-than-legitimate undercover tasks.

By way of clarifying the enigmatic title, the backstory in the series' opening episode informs us that when burglar William "Spider" Scott emerged from prison he knew something about himself that he had been unaware of before. His body chemistry bore an extra male chromosome. The normal chromosome structure is known as XY, but Scott was an XYY man, which often marks a genetic compulsion toward crime.

This short-lived cops-crooks-spies series had its antecedents in the 1960s British espionage-escapist genre of such series as *The Avengers, The Man in Room 17* (ITV, 1965–66), and *The Corridor People* (ITV, 1966). It would have passed by without great interest if not for the presence of a secondary character, Scott's sinister police adversary, Sergeant George Bulman, a tough bullying cop determined to nail him as a common criminal. Rather surprisingly, the obnoxious Bulman (with a penchant for constantly wearing wool

gloves) became something of an overnight favorite with both viewers and critics. Perhaps it was because Bulman was clearly the most interesting character in the series and was someone the viewer could associate with amid the complex, serialized plotting. The craft in developing the characterization belonged to actor Don Henderson, a former Royal Shakespeare Company player who had appeared in such television productions as *Warship* (BBC, 1973–77; in which he was a regular), *Poldark, Ripping Yarns,* and *The Onedin Line* before being signed by Granada for *The XYY Man.*

In view of the Bulman character's sudden popularity, *XYY Man* producers Granada Television decided to develop a completely new series based around this most unexpected of characters. The police drama *Strangers* saw Detective Sergeant Bulman and his colleague Detective Constable Willis (actor Dennis Blanch continuing his role from the previous series) transferred from London's Metropolitan Police to a northern city as part of a new racket-busting squad. Bulman was made noticeably less menacing here and was provided with a set of characteristic peculiarities: he always wore a pair of worn string gloves (something of a carryover from *The XYY Man*), carried a plastic carrier-bag stuffed with Open University papers, constantly used a nasal inhaler, and was often given to literary quotations and classical allusions.

At a time when tough, violent British cop series such as *The Sweeney* (ITV, 1975–78) and *Target* (BBC, 1977–78) had reached the peak of their popularity, *Strangers,* as a slightly less aggressive alternative, presented a singular police detective drama, full of quirky, often humorous characters and colorful dialogue ("Johnny thinks you are as genuine as a nun in a tartan hat"), and taking an unorthodox approach to its storylines. Midway through the series, Bulman was promoted to the rank of detective chief inspector and his energetic Inter-City Squad, as they were known, fought crime around different parts of Britain, spanning the underworld milieus from London to Edinburgh.

While producer Richard Everitt (who had also produced *Man in Room 17* and *Corridor People*) was responsible for the overall style and visual texture of *Strangers,* at times employing some very unusual camera angles for a prime-time British television series (which was also a visual characteristic of *The XYY Man*), it was Murray Smith, the principal author of the scripts, who fashioned the offbeat, scruffy Bulman character into a figure attaining cult status. However, much of the credit for the character's popularity and celebrity was due still to Henderson's delightfully idiosyncratic performance.

Henderson and Bulman returned in 1985, this time in his own series, *Bulman.* The character had retired from the police force and had established his own south London antiques-cum-junk shop as a repairer of antique clocks. Much to his reluctance, he is coerced by new colleague Lucy McGinty (Siobhan Redmond), a university dropout-turned-criminologist, to try his hand at the private detective business. Granada Television, hoping that the character was still something of an appealing enigma, decided to extend Bulman's eccentricities into virtual caricature. Acquiring now the affectionate nickname "Old GBH" (for Grievous Bodily Harm) and sporting an ankle-length wool scarf, he also wears a t-shirt bearing a head of Shakespeare and the slogan "Will Power."

While the first series of *Bulman* (13 episodes) enjoyed the interest of observing the outlandish character as, basically, one-half of a male-female private eye team, the program contributed very little to the small-screen gumshoe genre. Inexplicably, the second series was not broadcast until some two years later and, of an anticipated 13-episode run, only seven stories were transmitted. Despite the acceptable ratings (by U.K. standards) and an average of 14 million viewers, Granada Television had lost interest in *Bulman* and was now focusing its production energies (and bud-

gets) on the drug-running thriller serial *Floodtide* (ITV, 1987–88) and the comedy-drama series *Small World* (ITV, 1988).

Nevertheless, George Bulman remains one of the few fascinating British television characters to have spanned three different series. From his first appearance in *The XYY Man* as the grim detective sergeant to the chief inspector of the crime-busting unit in *Strangers,* and finally as eccentric private investigator *Bulman,* Don Henderson's quirky character creation was hailed as a national TV favorite. At the height of his fame there were fan clubs and fanzines idolizing the character, and even a pop song was written about him. Henderson himself recorded a song called "Strangers" in 1982.

TISE VAHIMAGI

Cast

William "Spider" Scott	Stephen Yardley
Sergeant/Detective Sergeant	
George Bulman	Don Henderson
Detective Constable Derek Willis	Dennis Blanch

Producer

Richard Everitt

Creator

Richard Everitt, from the novels by Kenneth Royce

Programming History

1976	3 one-hour episodes
1977	10 one-hour episodes
ITV	
July 1976	Saturday 9:30–10:30
June–August 1977	Monday 9:00–10:00

Strangers

Cast

Detective Sergeant/Detective Chief Inspector George Bulman	Don Henderson
Detective Constable/Detective Sergeant Derek Willis	Dennis Blanch
Detective Sergeant Singer	John Ronane
Detective Constable Linda Doran (1978–79)	Frances Tomelty
Detective Constable Frances Bennett (1979–82)	Fiona Mollison
Detective Chief Superintendent Lambie (1980–82)	Mark McManus
Security Chief Bill Dugdale (recurring guest role, 1980–82)	Thorley Walters

Producer
Richard Everitt

Creators
Richard Everitt, Murray Smith, based on characters
    created by Kenneth Royce

Programming History

1978	7 one-hour episodes
1979	5 one-hour episodes
1980	7 one-hour episodes
1981	6 one-hour episodes
1982	7 one-hour episodes
ITV	
June–July 1978	Monday 9:00–10:00
January–February 1979	Tuesday 9:00–10:00
October–November 1980	Tuesday 9:00–10:00
September–October 1981	Friday 9:00–10:00
September–October 1982	Wednesday 9:00–10:00

Bulman

Cast

George Bulman	Don Henderson
Lucy McGinty	Siobhan Redmond
Security Chief Bill Dugdale (recurring guest role)	Thorley Walters
Detective Chief Superintendent Lambie (1985)	Mark McManus
Detective Sergeant Derek Willis (1985)	Dennis Blanch

Executive Producer
Richard Everitt

Producers
Steve Hawes (1985), Sita Williams (1987)

Programming History

1985	13 one-hour episodes
1987	7 one-hour episodes
ITV	
June–August 1985	Wednesday 9:00–10:00
June–August 1987	Saturday 9:30–10:30

Further Reading

Harris, Mark, "Glove Story," *Primetime* (winter 1990–91)

Yentob, Alan (1947–)

British Producer, Executive

British television history is littered with examples of outstanding program makers who have been promoted to executive positions that have been less suited to their talents. Nobody personifies this trend more than Alan Yentob, although, unlike David Attenborough and others, he did not quickly abandon this career path in favor of a return to direct program making.

Yentob's television career has been entirely at the BBC, which he joined in 1968 as a general trainee, the way into the industry taken by many talented personalities. His main interests were in the field of the arts, and he quickly established himself as a director and producer of arts programming in the early 1970s, concentrating on popular culture and the avant-garde rather than the more traditional approach. The program that most clearly defined his style was "Cracked Actor: A Film About David Bowie," which Yentob produced and directed for the mainstream arts series *Omnibus* in 1975. This was the first time a traditional arts program had tackled a rock musician as a subject, though Bowie was the perfect artist to demonstrate the validity of the approach. Yentob found himself very much at home in the company of creative artists. His ability to share and develop their vision of how they should be presented on television was to produce many valuable collaborative partnerships. Bowie became a subject to whom Yentob would return throughout his career.

Yentob's next main move was to the program with which he is most associated: BBC 2's *Arena*. Origi-

nally split into strands on cinema, theater, and art and design, *Arena* became a byword for innovation and provocation under Yentob's direction. Though he was series editor from 1978 to 1985, he was also a highly active producer, director, and interviewer for the program, which became a home for those interested in the serious analysis of popular culture, cinema, and music, as well as for the presentation of the avant-garde and for the sort of quirky concept programs that themselves aspired to be works of art. Typical of the postmodernist investigations of everyday art was "The Private Life of the Ford Cortina" (1982), examining the impact of a particular make of car on British cultural life. Yentob himself produced another program that typified the program's style: "My Way" (1979), which presented and analyzed different interpretations of the famous Frank Sinatra song. Musicians profiled included Lene Lovich, Dire Straits, the Everly Brothers, and Jerry Lee Lewis, while the cinema was represented by the likes of Marcel Carne, Mel Brooks, and Luis Buñuel, theater by Robert Wilson and Joe Orton, and literature by Milan Kundera and Kurt Vonnegut, among many others.

Yentob continued to use his rapport with artists toward program-making ends, persuading Orson Welles to give a career-summarizing interview, which he produced as a three-part special in 1982, and exploring the television work of Dennis Potter in another memorable *Arena* interview conducted by himself. Talented arts program makers who flourished under Yentob's regime included Nigel Finch, Leslie Megahey, and Anthony Wall. *Arena* won six British Academy of Film and Television Arts (BAFTA) awards under Yentob's editorship.

The next step up the ladder for Alan Yentob was a promotion to head of music and arts at BBC Television, a post he held from 1985 to 1988. Though the main thrust of the job was directing the work of others, Yentob did not entirely withdraw from the program development process in this period, conducting the Dennis Potter interview mentioned earlier and also interviewing Arthur Miller for *Omnibus*. Indeed, Yentob was very much at home in this job, and he was the obvious choice in 1988 for the controllership of BBC 2, the BBC's more serious-minded television channel.

One of Yentob's first acts as channel controller was to set a regular end to each weekday evening on BBC 2. The highly influential daily current-affairs program *Newsnight* was for the first time given a regular 10:30 start time (where it can still be found), and it was followed every day from 11:15 to midnight (or beyond) by an innovative arts, discussion, and review program, *The Late Show,* edited by Michael Jackson, who was later to follow in Yentob's footsteps as BBC 2 controller.

Among Yentob's most successful commissions for BBC 2 were the topical news quiz show *Have I Got News for You* and the innovative comedy *Absolutely Fabulous,* both of which later transferred to BBC 1, as did Yentob himself, becoming controller of the BBC's mainstream television channel in 1993. Never a populist, this was not really the right job for him, and his

years in charge of BBC 1 and thereafter as BBC director of television (1996) and director of drama, entertainment, and children's television (2000) showed that the BBC did not really know what to do with one of its greatest talents. Many were reported to be frustrated by his lack of decisiveness, and although ultimately considered for the top job of BBC director-general, his further elevation was never really likely.

In the meantime, he maintained his links with the world of the arts through a series of cultural directorships, including chairing the Institute of Contemporary Arts. The BBC, however, came under fire for a serious decline in this area and was accused of "dumbing down" its arts coverage. To counter that, in 2003 Alan Yentob returned to program making, first as the writer and presenter of a three-part series on Leonardo da Vinci, and then as editor and presenter of a new mainstream arts series, *Imagine...,* on BBC 1.

STEVE BRYANT

See also **British Television;** *Have I Got News for You*

Alan Yentob. Born in London, March 11, 1947. One son and one daughter by Philippa Walker. Joined the BBC as a general trainee in 1968. Thereafter, producer/director arts programming, 1970–78; editor, *Arena,* 1978–85; head of music and arts, BBC-TV, 1985–88; controller, BBC 2, 1988–93; controller, BBC 1, 1993–96; director of programs, BBC-TV, 1996–2000; director of drama, entertainment, and children's programs, BBC-TV, 2000– .

Yes, Minister

British Situation Comedy

Yes, Minister, a classic situation comedy exposing the machinations of senior politicians and civil servants in Great Britain, was first broadcast by the BBC in 1980. Such was the standard of scripts and performance and the accuracy of the satire that the program became required viewing for politicians, journalists, and the general public alike, and both the initial three-season series and the two-season sequels that were made in the 1980s under the title *Yes, Prime Minister* were consistently among the top-rated shows.

The idea for the series was developed by writer Antony Jay and former *Doctor in the House* star

Jonathan Lynn while both were on the payroll of the video production company set up by John Cleese in the mid-1970s. The BBC bought the rights to the pilot episode, and work on a full series finally got under way in 1979.

The humor of each episode revolved around the maneuverings of the Right Honourable James Hacker, M.P., the idealistic and newly installed minister for administrative affairs (and ultimately prime minister), and his cynical and wily permanent undersecretary, Sir Humphrey Appleby, who was committed to seeing that his ministerial charge never meddled too much in the

Yes, Minister, Paul Eddington, 1980–82.
Courtesy of the Everett Collection

business of the department and that the real power remained securely in the hands of the civil service. Every time Hacker conceived some notion aimed at reform of the ministry, Sir Humphrey and Private Secretary Bernard Woolley were there to thwart him by various ingenious means. If Hacker inquired too closely into the reasons why he was not going to get his way about something, Sir Humphrey was more than able to throw up a smokescreen of obfuscation and technical jargon, which as often as not discouraged further questioning and persuaded the civil servant that his charge was now nearly "house-trained." This was not to say that Sir Humphrey always got his way, however: sometimes a last-minute development would deliver him into the minister's hands, leaving the civil servant speechless with rage and indignation.

The script of *Yes, Minister* was both perceptive and hugely funny, and the casting of the main roles was perfect. Paul Eddington was completely convincing as the gullible and idealistic Hacker, while Nigel Hawthorne was masterly as the Machiavellian Sir Humphrey, assisted by Derek Fowlds as the genial Bernard Woolley. The show was an immediate success and was showered with numerous awards. Among its many devotees were such distinguished figures as Margaret Thatcher, who named it as her favorite program and saw to it that writer Antony Jay received a knighthood (Eddington and Hawthorne both were appointed Commander of the British Empire in the 1986 New Year's Honours list). Also connected with the program, providing invaluable insights into the operations of Whitehall behind the scenes, was Harold Wilson's one-time secretary, Lady Marcia Falkender.

DAVID PICKERING

Cast

Rt. Hon. James Hacker	Paul Eddington
Sir Humphrey Appleby	Nigel Hawthorne
Bernard Woolley	Derek Fowlds

Producers
Stuart Allen, Sydney Latterby, Peter Whitmore

Programming History
37 30-minute episodes; 1 special
BBC 2

February 1980–April 1980	7 episodes
February 1981–April 1981	7 episodes
November 1982–December 1982	7 episodes
December 17, 1984	Christmas special
January 1986–February 1986	8 episodes
December 1987–January 1988	8 episodes

Young, Loretta (1914–2000)

U.S. Actor

Loretta Young was one of the first Hollywood actors to move successfully from movies to a television series. She made that transition in 1953 with *Letter to Loretta* (soon retitled *The Loretta Young Show*), an anthology drama series. Anthology dramas were a staple of 1950s programming, presenting different stories with different characters and casts each week. Young hosted and produced the series and acted in more than half the episodes as well. Capitalizing on her glamorous movie star image, her designer fashions became her television trademark. The show's success spurred other similar series, but Young's was the most successful. She was one of the few women who had control of her own successful series, the first woman to have her own dramatic anthology series on network television, and the first person to win both an Academy Award and an Emmy Award.

Loretta Young began her acting career with bit parts as a child extra in silent films. By the mid-1930s, fashion and glamour were important components of her star image. By 1948, after more than 20 years in films, she was recognized for her acting when she won the Best Actress Academy Award for her performance in *The Farmer's Daughter,* a romantic comedy. In 1952 she made her last feature film (released in 1953) and jumped eagerly into television. For older movie actors, television offered new opportunities, and at 40 Young was considered "older" when she began her series. Following her lead with prime-time anthology dramas were actors Jane Wyman, June Allyson, and Barbara Stanwyck.

Loretta Young.
Courtesy of the Everett Collection

As a movie star and as a woman, Young realistically had two options for a television series in 1953. CBS, the situation comedy network, home of Lucille Ball and *I Love Lucy,* suggested a sitcom. NBC offered an anthology drama. Not a zany comedian like Ball or Martha Raye (who appeared in comedy-variety shows), Young went for the anthology drama. In doing so, she would follow film actor Robert Montgomery (*Robert Montgomery Presents*) to prime-time success as host and actor in her own dramatic anthology series. She wanted—and the anthology format afforded—acting variety, a format for conveying moral messages, and a showcase for her glamorous, fashionable movie star image. Though many anthology dramas were broadcast live, Young, like most movie stars trying series TV, chose telefilm production, a mode that was not only more familiar but also able to bring future profit through syndication.

Young and husband Thomas Lewis (who was instrumental in setting up Armed Forces Radio during World War II and developed numerous radio programs) created Lewislor Enterprises to produce the series. Although Young and Lewis both functioned as executive producers, it was Lewis who was initially credited as

the official executive producer. When he left the series by the end of the third season, Young became the sole executive producer. However, her name never appeared in the credits as a producer of the show. When her five-year contract with NBC was up, Young formed a new company, Toreto Enterprises, which produced the series' last three seasons.

Religious and moral questions had long concerned Young. Known for her religious faith and work on behalf of Catholic charities, the stories she selected for production in her series carried upbeat messages about family, community, and personal conviction, and every story was summed up with a quotation from the Bible or some other recognized source. Concerned about postwar changes in American society, Young advocated TV entertainment with a message. Scripts hinged on the resolution of moral dilemmas. Numerous civic and religious groups honored her for this. She also won three Emmys, the first in 1955 as Best Dramatic Actress in a Continuing Series.

Fashion had also been an important component of Young's star image and was central to her television program. Indeed, fashion may be the most memorable feature of *The Loretta Young Show.* Every episode opened with Young making a swirling entrance showcasing her designer dresses, a move that became her television trademark. Many of the dresses she wore on the show were designed by Dan Werle, and some were marketed under the label Werle Originals. Young's strong feelings about fashion were publicized again in the early 1970s, when she won a suit against NBC for allowing her then-dated fashion introductions to be shown in syndication. While this emphasis on fashion actually served Young's conviction that women had to maintain their femininity, as a star she epitomized a supposed paradox: she was beautiful and feminine, but she was also a strong-willed woman with a career.

While the star and her fashions often attracted reviewers, some complained that Young and her show were sentimental, lowbrow women's entertainment, a typical criticism of women's fiction, where stories focus on the relationships and emotions constituting women's traditional sphere of home and family. The criticism was also typical of a 1950s conceit that filmed television series were inferior to prestigious live anthology dramas such as *Studio One* and *Philco Television Playhouse.*

Young's anecdotal and philosophical book, *The Things I Had to Learn,* was published in 1961, the same year her prime-time series went off the air. Her philosophies about life, success, and faith were the basis of the book, just as they had been for *The Loretta Young Show.* However, it should be noted that Helen

Ferguson, Young's publicist, really wrote most, if not all, of the book.

She returned to series television in the 1962–63 season with *The New Loretta Young Show*, a situation comedy, and formed LYL Productions to produce the series. The story originally centered on her as a widowed writer-mother, but her character was married by the end of the season. This new series lasted only one season, and Young did not return to television again until 1986, when she appeared in a made-for-TV movie, *Christmas Eve*. She won a Golden Globe Award for that performance. Her last television performance and dramatic role was in another made-for-TV movie, *Lady in the Corner* (1989), in which she played the publisher of a fashion magazine. In August 2000, Loretta Young's long career finally came to an end when she succumbed to ovarian cancer.

Loretta Young is probably most important to television's history as a woman who blazed a path for other women as both an actor and a producer, who succeeded with her own prime-time show in a format that was not a situation comedy, and who was able to transfer success in film to success in television. Few film stars have made this transition, and certainly none have done so with more glamour or grace than the inimitable Loretta Young.

MADELYN M. RITROSKY-WINSLOW

See also **Anthology Drama; Gender and Television;** *Loretta Young Show, The;* **Wyman, Jane**

Loretta Young. Born Gretchen Michaela Young in Salt Lake City, Utah, January 6, 1914. Attended Immaculate Heart College, Los Angeles, California. Married: 1) Grant Withers, 1930 (divorced, 1931); child: Judy; 2) Thomas H.A. Lewis, 1940; children: Christopher Paul and Peter. Debuted as an extra in *The Only Way*, 1919; contract with First National film company, late 1920s; contract with Twentieth Century Fox, 1933–40; host, producer, and often actor in anthology series, *The Loretta Young Show*, 1953–61; star of series *The New Loretta Young Show*, 1962–63. Recipient: Emmy Awards, 1955, 1956, 1959; Special Prize, Cannes Film Festival; Academy Award, 1947; Golden Globe Award, 1986. Died in Los Angeles, California, August 12, 2000.

Television Series

1953–61	*The Loretta Young Show* (titled *Letter to Loretta*, 1953–February 1954)
1962–63	*The New Loretta Young Show*

Made-for-Television Movies

1986	*Christmas Eve*
1989	*Lady in the Corner*

Films

The Only Way, 1919; *Sirens of the Sea*, 1919; *The Son of the Sheik*, 1921; *Naughty but Nice*, 1927; *Her Wild Oat*, 1928; *The Whip Woman*, 1928; *Laugh, Clown, Laugh*, 1928; *The Magnificent Flirt*, 1928; *The Head Man*, 1928; *Scarlett Seas*, 1928; *The Squall*, 1929; *The Girl in the Glass Cage*, 1929; *Fast Life*, 1929; *The Careless Age*, 1929; *The Show of Shows*, 1929; *The Forward Pass*, 1929; *The Man from Blankley's*, 1930; *The Second-Story Murder*, 1930; *Loose Ankles*, 1930; *Road to Paradise*, 1930; *Kismet*, 1930; *The Truth About Youth*, 1930; *The Devil to Pay*, 1930; *Bea Ideal*, 1931; *The Right of Way*, 1931; *Three Girls Lost*, 1931; *Too Young to Marry*, 1931; *Big Business Girl*, 1931; *I Like Your Nerve*, 1931; *Platinum Blonde*, 1931; *The Ruling Voice*, 1931; *Taxi*, 1932; *The Hatchet Man*, 1932; *Play Girl*, 1932; *Weekend Marriage*, 1932; *Life Begins*, 1932; *They Call It Sin*, 1932; *Employee's Entrance*, 1933; *Grand Slam*, 1933; *Zoo in Budapest*, 1933; *The Life of Jimmy Dolan*, 1933; *Midnight Mary*, 1933; *Heroes for Sale*, 1933; *The Devil's in Love*, 1933; *She Had to Say Yes*, 1933; *A Man's Castle*, 1933; *The House of Rothschild*, 1934; *Born to Be Bad*, 1934; *Bulldog Drummond Strikes Back*, 1934; *Caravan*, 1934; *The White Parade*, 1934; *Clive of India*, 1935; *Shanghai*, 1935; *Call of the Wild*, 1935; *The Crusades*, 1935; *The Unguarded Hour*, 1936; *Private Number*, 1936; *Ramona*, 1936; *Ladies in Love*, 1936; *Love Is News*, 1937; *Café Metropole*, 1937; *Love Under Fire*, 1937; *Wife, Doctor, and Nurse*, 1937; *Second Honeymoon*, 1937; *Four Men and a Prayer*, 1938; *Three Blind Mice*, 1938; *Suez*, 1938; *Kentucky*, 1938; *Wife, Husband, Friend*, 1939; *The Story of Alexander Graham Bell*, 1939; *Eternally Yours*, 1939; *The Doctor Takes a Wife*, 1940; *The Lady from Cheyenne*, 1941; *The Men in Her Life*, 1941; *Bedtime Story*, 1942; *A Night to Remember*, 1943; *China*, 1943; *Ladies Courageous*, 1944; *And Now Tomorrow*, 1944; *Along Came Jones*, 1945; *The Stranger*, 1946; *The Perfect Marriage*, 1947; *The Farmer's Daughter*, 1947; *The Bishop's Wife*, 1947; *Rachel and the Stranger*, 1948; *The Accused*, 1949; *Mother Is a Freshman*, 1949; *Come to the Stable*, 1949; *Key to the City*, 1950; *Cause for Alarm*, 1951; *Half Angel*, 1951; *Paula*, 1952; *Because of You*, 1952; *It Happens Every Thursday*, 1953.

Stage

An Evening with Loretta Young, 1989.

Publication

The Things I Had to Learn, as told to Helen Ferguson, 1961

Further Reading

Anderson, Joan Wester, *Forever Young: The Life, Loves, and Enduring Faith of a Hollywood Legend: The Authorized Biography of Loretta Young,* Allen, Texas: More, 2000

Atkins, J., "Young, Loretta," in *International Dictionary of Films and Filmmakers,* Vol. 3, *Actors and Actresses,* edited by N. Thomas, Detroit, Michigan: St. James Press, 1992

Bowers, R.L., "Loretta Young: Began as a Child-Extra and Exuded Glamour for Forty Years," *Films in Review* (1969)

Morella, Joe, and Edward Z. Epstein, *Loretta Young: An Extraordinary Life,* New York: Delacorte, 1986

Siegel, S., and B. Siegel, *The Encyclopedia of Hollywood,* New York: Facts on File, 1990

Young, Robert (1907–1998)

U.S. Actor

Robert Young came to television out of film and radio, and for nearly 30 years he was revered as television's quintessential father figure. In his role as Jim Anderson in the domestic melodrama *Father Knows Best* and as the title character in the long-running medical drama *Marcus Welby, M.D.,* he was admired as a strict but benevolent patriarch. Gentle, moralistic, and highly interventionist, Young's television persona corrected and guided errant behavior, initially in a family setting, then as an omnipotent doctor, and, perhaps most self-consciously, when he portrayed "himself" in a decade-long series of commercials for decaffeinated coffee. With a simple raised eyebrow and a tilt of the head, Young's character convinced even the most hedonistic of costars to relinquish their selfish ways for a greater noble purpose.

Young began his career as a second lead in Hollywood films. Displaying a generally unrecognized versatility, Young portrayed villains, best buddies, and victims with equal aplomb and performed for many of Hollywood's finest directors, including Alfred Hitchcock, Frank Borzage, and Edward Dmytryk. Frustrated with his secondary status (he described his parts as those refused by Robert Montgomery), Young ventured in 1949 into radio, where he coproduced (with his good friend and business partner Eugene Rodney) and starred in a family comedy, *Father Knows Best?* Running for five years, the program was a soft-hearted look at a family in which the benevolent head of the family was regarded with love but skepticism and in which mother generally supplied the wisdom. At the time, most family comedies were characterized by wisecracking moms and inept fathers. Young took the role on the condition that the father, in his words, not be "an idiot. Just make it so he's unaware. He's not running the ship, but he thinks he is."

In 1954 Young and Rodney were approached by Screen Gems to bring the program to television. While Young was hesitant at first, a promise of joint ownership in the program convinced him to make the move. Upon network insistence, the question mark was dropped (they thought it demeaning), and *Father Knows Best* premiered on CBS, under the sponsorship of Kent cigarettes. Because of advertising and network time-franchises, the program was placed too late in the evening to attract a family audience and quickly died in the ratings. A fan-letter campaign and the personal intervention of Thomas McCabe, president of the Scott Paper Company, resurrected the program, which was to become an NBC staple for the next five years.

The television series was quite different from the radio version. Most significantly, the radio program's ambivalence about the father's wisdom was removed and replaced by an emphatic belief that Jim Anderson was the sole possessor of knowledge and child-rearing acumen. Although the original head writer, Roswell Rogers, remained with the program, most of the radio scripts had to be rewritten or completely scrapped for the visual television medium. With the exception of Robert Young, the Anderson family was completely recast, with Jane Wyatt signing on after a yearlong search. Many of the episodes were based on the real-life exploits of Young's daughter Kathy, while Wyatt was described as an amalgamation of the wives of Young, Rodney, and Rogers.

The program was heralded by the popular press and audiences alike as a refreshing change from "dumb Dad" shows. With near-irritating consistency, Jim Anderson resolved his family's dilemmas through a pattern of psychic intimidation, guilt, and manipulation, causing the errant family member to recant his or her selfish desires and put the good of the community, family, and society ahead of personal pleasure. The wife and the three children, played by Elinor Donahue, Billy Gray, and Laurin Chapin, were lectured with equal severity by the highly exalted father, whose virtues were often the focus for episodic tribute.

The program won numerous awards and spawned a host of domestic melodramas that were to dominate the television schedule (including *The Donna Reed Show* and *Leave It to Beaver*). So popular was the program and so powerful its verisimilitude that viewers came to believe the Anderson family really existed. Women wrote to star Jane Wyatt with questions about cooking and advice about home decorating or child rearing. Young was named Mount Sinai "father of the year" and gathered similar honors throughout the series' run. In one of the stranger blends of fact and fiction, the producers were approached to do a U.S. Savings Bond benefit for the American Federation of Labor and the Treasury Department. "Twenty-four Hours in Tyrant Land" depicted the Anderson's fictional Springfield community caught in the clutches of a tyrannical despot. Never aired on television, the episode toured the country's town halls and churches.

By 1960 the personal difficulties of both Young and the teenage cast members, and the creative fatigue of Rogers, prompted the producers to cease first-run production, although reruns continued to air in prime time on ABC for two more years.

Despite a couple of television films, Young's career was basically dormant during the 1960s until the highly acclaimed television movie, *Marcus Welby, M.D.* The pilot film, revolving around the heroic efforts of a kindly general practitioner and his "anti-establishment" young assistant (played by James Brolin), became a hit television series that was to air on ABC for the next seven years. Each phenomenally slow-moving episode, featured Welby, his partner Dr. Steven Kiley, and the friendly (but usually confused) nurse, Consuella, treating a single patient whose disease functioned as some sort of personal or familial catastrophe. Even for the 1970s, the program was anachronistic—Welby practiced out of his well-appointed Brentwood home, and both he and Kiley made house calls. Significantly, the show did try to bring public attention to current health crises or recent medical discoveries. Thus, episodes dealt with Tay-Sach's disease, amniocentesis, and abortion rights (when abortion was still illegal). With kindly didacticism, Welby would lecture the guest star (and the television viewer) on the importance of consistent medical care, early detection, immunization, and the like.

By the mid-1970s, Young grew weary of the program, and this along with Brolin's career ambitions and a post-Watergate viewership hostile toward elderly male authority figures contributed to the program's demise. With the end of the program, Young continued to work in television, starring in a couple of *Welby* movies and a *Father Knows Best* reunion. He gained critical acclaim in a television film dealing with Alzheimer's disease and euthanasia. His bitterness toward Hollywood casting practices never diminished, however, and in the early 1990s Young attempted suicide, revealing a vulnerability and despair totally at odds with his carefully constructed patriarchal persona.

NINA C. LEIBMAN

*See also **Father Knows Best; Marcus Welby, M.D.***

Robert (George) Young. Born in Chicago, Illinois, February 22, 1907. Attended Lincoln High School, Los Angeles. Married: Elizabeth Louise Henderson, 1933; children: Carol Anne, Barbara Queen, Elizabeth Louise, and Kathleen Joy. Earned living as clerk, salesman, reporter, and loan company collector during four years of studies and acting with the Pasadena Playhouse; toured with stock company production *The Ship,* 1931; contract with MGM, 1931–45; on radio program *Good News of 1938,* and on *Maxwell House Coffee Time,* 1944; cofounder, with Eugene Rodney, of Cavalier Productions, 1947; star of radio series *Father Knows Best?,* 1949–54; star of television version of same, 1954–61; star of *Marcus Welby, M.D.,* 1969–76. Recipient: Emmy Awards: 1956, 1957. Died in Westlake, California, July 22, 1998.

Television Series

1954–60	*Father Knows Best*
1961–62	*The Window on Main Street*
1969–76	*Marcus Welby, M.D.*
1979	*Little Women*

Made-for-Television Movies

1969	*Marcus Welby, M.D.: A Matter of Humanities*
1971	*Vanished*
1972	*All My Darling Daughters*
1973	*My Darling Daughters' Anniversary*
1977	*The Father Knows Best Reunion*
1978	*Little Women*
1984	*The Return of Marcus Welby, M.D.*
1987	*Mercy or Murder?*
1989	*Conspiracy of Love*

Films

The Black Camel, 1931; *The Sin,* 1931; *The Guilty Generation,* 1931; *The Wet Parade,* 1931; *New Morals for Old,* 1932; *Unashamed,* 1932; *Strange*

Interlude, 1932; *The Kid from Spain*, 1932; *Men Must Fight*, 1933; *Today We Live*, 1933; *Hell Below*, 1933; *Tugboat Annie*, 1933; *Saturday's Children*, 1933; *The Right to Romance*, 1933; *La Ciudad de Carton*, 1933; *Carolina*, 1934; *Spitfire*, 1934; *The House of Rothschild*, 1934; *Lazy River*, 1934; *Hollywood Party*, 1934; *Whom the Gods Destroy*, 1934; *Paris Interlude*, 1934; *Death on the Diamond*, 1934; *The Band Plays On*, 1934; *West Point of the Air*, 1935; *Vagabond Lady*, 1935; *Calm Yourself*, 1935; *Red Salute*, 1935; *Remember Last Night*, 1935; *The Bride Comes Home*, 1935; *Three Wise Guys*, 1936; *It's Love Again*, 1936; *The Bride Walks Out*, 1936; *Secret Agent*, 1936; *Sworn Enemy*, 1936; *The Longest Night*, 1936; *Stowaway*, 1936; *Dangerous Number*, 1937; *I Met Him in Paris*, 1937; *Married Before Breakfast*, 1937; *The Emperor's Candlesticks*, 1937; *The Bride Wore Red*, 1937; *Navy Blue and Gold*, 1937; *Paradise for Three*, 1938; *Josette*, 1938; *The Toy Wife*, 1938; *Three Comrades*, 1938; *Rich Man—Poor Girl*, 1938; *The Shining Hour*, 1938; *Honolulu*, 1939; *Bridal Suite*, 1939; *Miracles for Sale*, 1939; *Maisie*, 1939; *Northwest Passage*, 1940; *Florian*, 1940; *The Mortal Storm*, 1940; *Sporting Blood*, 1940; *Dr. Kildare's Crisis*, 1940; *The Trial of Mary Dugan*, 1941; *Lady Be Good*, 1941; *Unmarried Bachelor*, 1941; *H.M. Pulham, Esq.*, 1941; *Joe Smith—American*, 1942; *Cairo*, 1942; *Journey for Margaret*, 1942; *Slightly Dangerous*, 1943; *Claudia*, 1943; *Sweet Rosie O'Grady*, 1943; *The Canterville Ghost*, 1944; *The Enchanted Cottage*, 1945; *Those Endearing Young Charms*, 1945; *Lady Luck*, 1946; *The Searching Wind*, 1946; *Claudia and David*, 1946; *They Won't Believe Me*, 1947; *Crossfire*, 1947; *Relentless*, 1948; *Sitting Pretty*, 1948; *Adventure in Baltimore*, 1949; *Bride for Sale*, 1949; *That Forsyte Woman*, 1949; *And Baby Makes Three*, 1949; *The Second Woman*, 1951; *Goodbye, My Fancy*, 1951; *The Half Breed*, 1952; *Secret of the Incas*, 1954; *Born Free*, 1966.

Radio

Good News of 1938; Father Knows Best?, 1949–53.

Publication

"How I Won the War of the Sexes by Losing Every Battle," *Good Housekeeping* (January 1962)

Further Reading

Parish, James Robert, and Gregory W. Mank, *The Hollywood Reliables*, Westport, Connecticut: Arlington House, 1980

Your Hit Parade

U.S. Music Variety

Your Hit Parade was a weekly network television program that aired from 1950 to 1959. The program enjoyed some popularity but was never as successful as its radio predecessor, which began in 1935 and ran for 15 years before moving to television. Both the radio and television versions featured the most popular songs of the previous week, as determined by a national "survey" of record and sheet-music sales. The methodology behind this survey was never revealed, but most audience members were willing to accept the tabulations without question. Both the TV and radio versions were sponsored by the American Tobacco Company's Lucky Strike cigarettes.

Original cast members for the TV program included Eileen Wilson, Snooky Lanson, Dorothy Collins, and a wholesome array of young fresh-scrubbed "Hit Parade Singers and Dancers." Gisele MacKenzie joined the cast in 1953.

The TV version featured the top seven tunes of the week and several Lucky Strike extras. These extras were older, more established popular songs that were very familiar to audiences. The top seven tunes were presented in reverse order, not unlike the various popular music countdowns currently heard on radio. The top three songs were presented with an extra flourish, and audience members would speculate among themselves as to which tunes would climb to the top three positions and how long they would stay there.

The continuing popularity of certain songs over a multiple-week period had never been a problem for the radio version of the program with its top ten list. Regular listeners were willing to hear a repeat performance of last week's songs, perhaps with a different vocalist than the previous week to provide variation. The television *Hit Parade* attempted to dramatize each song with innovative skits, elaborate sets, and a large entourage of performers. Creating new skits for longer-running popular songs proved much more difficult on television, particularly when we recall such hits from the period as "How Much Is That Doggie in the Window" and "Shrimp Boats Are Coming."

A much more serious problem facing the program was the changing taste in American popular music. Rock 'n' roll was displacing the syrupy ballads that had been the mainstay of popular music during the 1930s and 1940s. The earlier music had a multigenerational appeal, and the radio version of *Your Hit Parade* catered to a family audience. The rock music of the 1950s was clearly targeted to younger listeners and actually thrived on the disdain of its older critics.

Further, much of the popularity of the faster-paced rock hits was dependent on complex instrumental arrangements and the unique styling of a particular artist or group. Rock music's first major star, the brooding, sensuous Elvis Presley, was a sharp contrast to the sedate styles of Snooky Lanson and Dorothy Collins. As rock (and Presley) gained in popularity, the ratings for *Your Hit Parade* plummeted. The cast was changed in 1957, and the show was temporarily canceled in 1958, then revived under new management with Dorothy Collins and Johnny Desmond. Despite these changes, the program was simply out of touch with the current musical scene, and the last program was broadcast on April 24, 1959.

NORMAN FELSENTHAL

See also **Music on Television**

Announcers
Andre Baruch (1950–57)
Del Sharbutt (1957–58)

Vocalists
Eileen Wilson (1950–52)
Snooky Lanson (1950–57)
Dorothy Collins (1950–57, 1958–59)
Sue Bennett (1951–52)
June Valli (1952–53)
Russell Arms (1952–57)
Gisele MacKenzie (1953–57)
Tommy Leonetti (1957–58)
Jill Corey (1957–58)
Alan Copeland (1957–58)
Virginia Gibson (1957–58)
Johnny Desmond (1958–59)
Kelly Garrett (1974)
Chuck Woolery (1974)
Sheralee (1974)

Dancers
The Hit Paraders (chorus and dancers) (1950–58)
Peter Gennaro Dancers (1958–59)
Tom Hansen Dancers (1974)

Orchestra
Raymond Scott (1950–57)
Harry Sosnik (1958–59)
Milton Delugg (1974)

Producers
Dan Lounsberry, Ted Fetter

Programming History
NBC

July 1950–August 1950	Monday 9:00–9:30
October 1950–June 1958	Saturday 10:30–11:00
CBS	
October 1958–April 1959	Friday 7:30–8:00
August 1974	Friday 8:00–8:30

Further Reading

Williams, John R., *This Was Your Hit Parade,* Camden, Maine: n.p., 1973

Youth Television

Canadian Youth Specialty Channel

Youth TV (YTV) is a Canadian specialty television channel aimed at young people up to the age of 18 years. Since its launch in September 1988, YTV has proven remarkably successful, far surpassing even its most optimistic economic and audience projections. As of 2001, it reached 8.2 million Canadian homes (out of 11 million TV households). An important part of YTV's success is predicated upon its ownership structure. It was originally majority owned by two cable firms, CUC Ltd. and Rogers Communications, the latter being Canada's largest cable operator. Their financial interest helped make YTV available in the vast majority of Canadian homes with cable. Its historically high rate of penetration in turn made it an attractive advertising vehicle for products and services aimed at a youth demographic.

By 1996 another cable firm, Shaw, the second largest in Canada and a leading satellite operator, had acquired full control of YTV. In 2000, Shaw spun off its entertainment assets, including YTV, to a new subsidiary, Corus Entertainment. YTV is part of Corus's full range of youth-oriented media including Treehouse TV (for preschoolers), edgy radio stations (directed at teenagers and young adults), and niche digital channels (Discovery Kids, YTV Pow!, EdgeTV) for teens and preteens.

YTV has successfully inserted itself into a traditional area of Canadian programming strength, children's and young people's programming. This has been an area of strength because (a) children's programming was relatively inexpensive; (b) it could easily be exported; and (c) it tended to be neglected by more powerful U.S. production companies. As a result, YTV has been able to draw on a considerable catalog of Canadian children's programming and to provide opportunities for the expansion of this traditional area of expertise.

Finally, YTV has proven very successful in attracting its target audience. It engages in extensive polling of young people to determine their aspirations and concerns, buying patterns, and political views, and to spot trends. As a result, YTV has crafted a schedule mixing old, familiar shows with new, highly targeted programs. YTV has therefore very rapidly emerged not only as a leading showcase but also as an important producer of children's programming. It has produced or coproduced such shows as *ReBoot, Shadowraiders,* and *Freaky Stories,* some of which have received wide international distribution. Additionally, YTV regularly exceeds the programming and spending commitments imposed by the Canadian Radio-television and Telecommunications Commission (CRTC).

YTV has also emerged as a socially conscious broadcaster that contributes to numerous charities and fund-raisers (National Kids' Day, The Children's Charity, United Way, Children's Wish Foundation, etc.) and that provides educational grants. YTV has received numerous national and international awards for excellence in programming, for promoting international human rights, for aiding the cause of literacy, and for work in other areas of social concern.

Ironically, YTV's greatest problems have come not from the marketplace or from viewers but from the CRTC. The regulatory commission determined that YTV should not appeal to audience members or age groups beyond its mandated audience, since a wider appeal would threaten the market of established broadcasters; therefore, the CRTC instituted the "protagonist clause," also known as the "Little Joe" rule. This clause requires that 100 percent of YTV's drama programming broadcast in the evening feature "a major protagonist that is a child, youth under the age of 18 years, puppet, animated character, or creature of the animal kingdom."

The clause acquired its nickname when YTV discovered that Little Joe, a main character of *Bonanza,* which it had purchased to strip in prime time, actually celebrated his 19th birthday in one of the early episodes. The CRTC ordered *Bonanza* off the air, and YTV has since lobbied to have the clause removed or altered.

YTV complains that the protagonist clause prevents it from showing material that legitimately appeals to its target audience: characters such as Superman, Batman, and Robin Hood, who are all well over 18; programming featuring hockey superstar Wayne Gretzky; works of classic literature such as *Great Expectations,* in which the hero starts as a child but grows past 18;

the life stories of most musical groups; and so on. YTV claims that it is difficult to coproduce or sell internationally if a major protagonist must be "a puppet, animated character, or creature of the animal kingdom."

YTV's efforts met with some success when the CRTC amended the protagonist clause in 1992 to include comic book characters, folk and superheroes, and classical or historical heroes. Despite the CRTC's restrictions, YTV has generally managed to reach a loyal audience, produce hundreds of hours of original content, and ensure its financial success while also meeting public service and social responsibility objectives.

PAUL ATTALLAH

See also **Children and Television**

Z

Z Cars

British Police Series

Z Cars was the innovative, long-running BBC police series of the 1960s, which programmed more episodes (667) than any other weekly crime program on British television. Created by Troy Kennedy-Martin and Elwyn Jones, and produced by David Rose, the series brought a new realism to the genre as it featured day-to-day policing in Newtown, a fictitious town to the north of Liverpool. At the spearhead of operations were four police constables: "Jock" Weir, "Fancy" Smith, Bob Steele, and Bert Lynch. They occupied the two radio crime cars called Z-Victor 1 and Z-Victor 2, from which the series gained its title. Supervising operations via a VHF radio operator in the station, and securing prosecutions in the interrogation room, were Detective Sergeant Watt and the formidable Detective Inspector Barlow. Watched by nearly 14 million viewers in its first season, *Z Cars* rapidly captured the public imagination, and the leading characters became household names. Although in later seasons new characters might be brought in as replacements and the crime cars updated, the same basic formula applied. Bert Lynch, played by James Ellis, remained throughout the program's run. Promoted to station sergeant in 1966, he was still in place at the desk when the doors on the cars were finally closed for good in 1978.

In terms of program aesthetics, *Z Cars* attempted to counter the film appeal of early U.S. cop programs, such as *Highway Patrol,* with "gritty" realism. This was achieved by close attention to authentic police procedure, observation of working-class behavior, and, most especially, the adoption of regional speech. "Northern" working-class subject matter was prominent in 1960s culture, exemplified in feature films like *Saturday Night and Sunday Morning* and *A Taste of Honey.* However, *Z Cars* had more in common with the dialogue-led drama and actor-centered performances of ATV's *Armchair Theatre* and the early years of Granada's *Coronation Street.* Although later series were able to make more use of film and locations, the look of *Z Cars* was constructed almost entirely in the television studio. The 50 minutes of continuous recorded performance provided the space for displays of male comradeship and teamwork, sharp verbal exchanges with members of the community, and, most characteristic of all, intense drama in the interrogation room as Barlow bullied and coaxed confessions from his suspects.

Overall, *Z Cars* succeeded in presenting a more human and down-to-earth image of the police than had been previously created on British television. Major crime remained at the periphery of the series, and the emphasis was placed instead on domestic and juvenile crime. The program adopted the social-democratic view of society so prevalent in 1960s Britain, and at times the police constables (PCs) behaved more like social workers than policemen, as criminal behavior was explained in terms of social deprivation. The liberal approach, however, was showing signs of exhaustion. Barlow upheld the law with a fierce authoritarianism in the station, and the PCs needed all their ingenuity and skill to enforce it effectively in the community. An ongoing theme was the personal cost of securing law and order, and most of the police characters had unsatisfactory family relationships. In one episode, for instance, Watt was shown agreeing to a divorce, and in another Steele beat up his wife. The image of policemen as fallible human beings created some controversy, and for a time the chief inspector of Lancashire withdrew his support from the program, apprehensive that it might undermine public confidence in the police.

In the course of its long run, the program established the reputations of many production participants, including actors such as Stratford Johns, Frank Windsor, Colin Welland, Brian Blessed, and James Ellis; producers and directors such as Shaun Sutton, David Rose, and John McGrath; and writers such as Troy Kennedy-Martin, John Hopkins, Alan Plater, and Allan Prior. *Z Cars* has been a major influence on the course of TV police fiction in Britain. The long-running CID (Criminal Investigation Department) series *Softly Softly* (1966–75) was a direct spin-off from it, achieved by promoting Barlow to the rank of chief inspector, transferring him to a regional crime squad, and replacing the squad car with a dog-handling unit. More recent British programs about community policing as different as *The Bill* and *Heartbeat* have continued to draw from the *Z Cars* idea. One of the most interesting reworkings of the program's basic format was the BBC's *Juliet Bravo* (1980–88), which, in keeping with 1980s gender politics, transferred the power from male CID officers to a uniformed female inspector.

BOB MILLINGTON

See also **Welland, Colin; Windsor, Frank**

Cast

Charlie Barlow	Stratford Johns
John Watt	Frank Windsor
Bert Lynch	James Ellis
Fancy Smith	Brian Blessed
Jock Weir	Joseph Brady
Bob Steele	Jeremy Kemp
Sgt. Twentyman	Leonard Williams
Ian Sweet	Terence Edmond
Insp. Dunn	Dudley Foster
David Graham	Colin Welland
Sgt. Blackitt	Robert Keegan
Sally Clarkson	Diane Aubrey
Insp. Bamber	Leonard Rossiter
PC Robbins	John Philips
Insp. Millar	Leslie Sands
Ken Baker	Geoffrey Whitehead
Arthur Boyle	Edward Kelsey
PC Foster	Donald Webster
PC Boland	Michael Grover
Ray Walker	Donald Gee
Sam Hudson	John Barrie
Tom Stone	John Slater
Steve Tate	Sebastian Breaks
Alec May	Stephen Yardley
Owen Calshaw	David Daker
Jane Shepherd	Luanshya Greer
Insp. Brogan	George Sewell
PC Newcombe	Bernard Holley
Insp. Todd	Joss Ackland
PC Jackson	John Wreford
Insp. Witty	John Woodvine
PC Roach	Ron Davies
PC Bannerman	Paul Angelis
Insp. Goss	Derek Waring
Joe Skinner	Ian Cullen
Mick Quilley	Douglas Fielding
PC Culshaw	John Challis
Sgt. Moffat	Ray Lonnen
Jill Howarth	Stephanie Turner
PC Covill	Jack Carr
PC Lindsay	James Walsh
PC Scatliff	Geoffrey Hayes
PC Render	Alan O'Keefe
PC Hicks	Godfrey James
PC Logie	Kenton Moore
PC Birch	John Woodnutt
Sgt. Hagger	John Collin
WPC (Woman Police Constable) Cameron	Sharon Duce
Insp. Connor	Gary Watson
PC Yates	Nicholas Smith
WPC Bayliss	Alison Steadman
DC (Detective Constable) Braithwaite	David Jackson
Sgt. Knell	John Dunn-Hill
PC Preston	Michael Stirrup
Sgt. Chubb	Paul Stewart
DC Bowker	Brian Grellis
Insp. Maddan	Tommy Boyle
WPC Beck	Victoria Plucknett

Producers

David Rose, Colin Morris, Ronald Travers, Richard Benyon, Ron Craddock, Roderick Graham

Programming History

291 50-minute episodes; 376 25-minute episodes
BBC

January 1962–July 1962	31 episodes

September 1962–July 1963	42 episodes
September 1963–June 1964	42 episodes
September 1964–June 1965	43 episodes
October 1965–December 1965	12 episodes
March 1967–April 1971	334 episodes
August 1971–March 1972	28 25-minute episodes, one 50-minute episode
April 1972–August 1972	14 25-minute episodes; 11 50-minute episodes
September 1972–July 1973	28 episodes
September 1974–May 1975	31 episodes
January 1976–March 1976	12 episodes
April 1977–July 1977	13 episodes
June 1978–September 1978	13 episodes

Further Reading

"Allen Prior and John Hopkins Talking About the *Z Cars* Series," *Screen Education* (September–October 1963)

Casey, A., "Blood Without Thunder," *Screen Education* (September–October 1962)

Hurd, Geoffrey, "The Television Presentation of the Police," in *Popular Television and Film,* edited by Tony Bennett et al., London: British Film Institute, 1981

Laing, Stuart, "Banging in Some Reality: The Original *Z Cars,*" in *Popular Television in Britain: Studies in Cultural History,* edited by John Corner, London: British Film Institute, 1991

Vahimagi, Tise, editor, *British Television: An Illustrated Guide,* Oxford: Oxford University Press, 1994; revised edition, 1996

"*Z Cars* and Their Impact: A Conference Report," *Screen Education* (September–October 1963)

Zapping

Zapping is the use of a remote control device (RCD) to avoid commercials by switching to another channel. The process is often paired with "zipping," fast-forwarding through the commercials in recorded programs. Although zapping and zipping have received much attention, viewers have always avoided commercials by changing channels, leaving the viewing area, or simply shifting their attention away from the set. When the penetration of RCDs increased to about 90 percent and that of videocassette recorders (VCRs) increased to more than 75 percent of U.S. households by the early 1990s, advertiser concern over zapping and zipping accelerated. RCDs and VCRs, combined with a multitude of viewing options on cable and digital satellite systems, have led to the zapping or zipping of 10 to 20 percent of all commercials, according to some industry studies. Cable networks specializing in short-form programming (music videos, news stories, comedy shorts) are well suited to filling commercial breaks. Thus, the once "captive" audience of television is exercising its option to zap or zip boring or annoying commercials. Indeed, several studies of RCD gratifications have consistently identified commercial avoidance as a major motivation to use remote control devices.

In the 1980s, RCDs and VCRs proliferated, while the advertising and television industries debated the relative impact of zapping and zipping. Advertisers argued that program ratings did not reflect decreasing audience attention to commercials, while broadcasters cited studies that minimized the increase in channel changing during commercials. Several studies showed that the content of a commercial greatly affected the degree of zapping, encouraging many advertisers to restructure their television commercials by focusing on more entertaining content, fast-paced editing, or high-quality special effects. When research showed that commercials placed during sports programming were particularly susceptible to zapping, some advertisers responded with commercials that combined both program and advertising elements. For example, IBM's "You make the call" commercials inserted an advertising message between question-and-answer segments of a sports quiz. Advertisers also tried to thwart the RCD's impact through more careful audience targeting and by reducing the length of some commercials. As the decade wore on, advertisers increased their use of place-based advertising and integrated marketing to replace the ad exposures lost to zapping and zipping.

Although some observers see RCD-enhanced zapping as a modest intensification of the television audience's long-standing urge to avoid bad commercials, others have argued that zapping and zipping will lead to gradual structural changes in the commercial television industry. Refinements in RCDs and VCRs may make zapping and zipping even easier, whereas the introduction of personal video recorders (PVRs) sold under brand names such as Tivo and Ultimate TV have made commercial zipping much more likely. These devices record 30 or more hours of programming on a computer hard drive. The commercials embedded in this programming can be easily zipped using an RCD that can be upgraded, adding new functions. Research on early PVR users shows that as much as 80 percent of the advertising is skipped. As these sources of commercial avoidance decrease the value of commercially sponsored programming, advertisers may continue to shift resources to other advertising media and marketing approaches, or they may begin to offer compensation to viewers for simply watching commercials. Program providers may need to seek other revenue streams such as pay-per-view and subscriber fees to replace the lost revenue from advertisers. The result of these structural changes may be fewer viewing options

for those unable or unwilling to pay these new charges and a wider gap between the information and entertainment "haves" and "have nots."

JAMES R. WALKER

See also **Remote Control Device**

Further Reading

Ainslie, Peter, "Commercial Zapping: TV Tapers Strike Back: VCR Owners Are Skipping Station Breaks, and Advertisers Are Getting Worried," *Rolling Stone* (February 28, 1985)

Bellamy, Robert V., Jr., and James R. Walker, *Grazing on a Vast Wasteland: The Remote Control and Television's Second Generation,* New York: Guilford, 1996

Walker, James R., and Robert V. Bellamy Jr., editors, *The Remote Control in the New Age of Television,* Westport, Connecticut: Praeger, 1993

Zipping. *See* Zapping

Ziv Television Programs, Inc.

U.S. Production and Syndication Company

As the most prolific producer of programming for the first-run syndication market during the 1950s, Ziv Television Programs occupies a unique niche in the history of U.S. television. Bypassing the networks and major national sponsors, Ziv rose to prominence by marketing its series to local and regional sponsors, who placed the shows on local stations, generally in time slots outside of prime time. Using this strategy, Ziv produced several popular and long-lived series, including *The Cisco Kid* (1949–56), *Highway Patrol* (1955–59), and *Sea Hunt* (1957–61).

Frederick W. Ziv, the company's founder, was born in Cincinnati, Ohio, in 1905. The son of immigrant parents, he attended the University of Michigan, where he graduated with a degree in law. Returning to his native Cincinnati, Ziv chose not to practice the legal profession, but instead opened his own advertising agency. His corporate strategies and his vision of the

broadcasting business developed from this early experience in the Midwest.

During the radio era, Cincinnati was a surprisingly active regional center for radio production. Clear-channel station WLW, owned by the local Crosley electronics firm, broadcast a powerful signal that could be heard over much of the Midwest. Due to its regional influence, WLW became a major source of radio programming that offered local stations an alternative to network-originated programming. Cincinnati was also home to Procter and Gamble, the most influential advertiser in the radio industry at a time when most radio programming was produced by sponsors. Consequently, Procter and Gamble was directly responsible for developing many of radio's most lasting genres, including the soap opera.

Ziv's small advertising agency gained valuable experience in this fertile regional market. Ziv produced several programs for WLW, where he met John L. Sinn, a writer who would become his right-hand man. In 1937 the two men launched the Frederick W. Ziv Company into the business of program syndication. From his experience in a regional market, Ziv recognized that local and regional advertisers could not compete with national-brand sponsors because they could not afford the budget to produce network-quality programs. In an era dominated by live broadcasts, Ziv produced prerecorded programs, "transcriptions" recorded onto acetate discs, bypassing the networks and selling his programs directly to local advertisers on a market-by-market basis. Programs were priced according to the size of each market; this gave local sponsors a chance to break into radio with affordable quality programming that could be scheduled in any available slot on a station's schedule.

Ziv produced a wide range of programming for radio, including sports, music, talk shows, soap operas, anthology dramas, and action-adventure series such as *Boston Blackie, Philo Vance,* and *The Cisco Kid.* By 1948 he was the largest packager and syndicator of radio programs—the primary source of programming outside the networks.

In 1948 Ziv branched into the television market by creating the subsidiary Ziv Television Programs. His fortunes in television were entirely tied to the market for first-run syndication, which grew enormously during the first half of the 1950s before going into a steep decline by the end of the decade. In the early years of U.S. television, local stations needed programming to fill the time slots outside of prime time that were not supplied by the networks. More important, local and regional sponsors needed opportunities to advertise their products on television. As in radio, Ziv supplied this market with inexpensive, prerecorded programs that could be scheduled on a flexible basis. In 1948 the first Ziv series, *Yesterday's Newsreel* and *Sports Album,* featured 15-minute episodes of repackaged film footage.

In 1949 Ziv branched into original programming with his first dramatic series, *The Cisco Kid,* starring Duncan Renaldo as the Cisco Kid and Leo Carillo as his sidekick, Pancho. Ziv's awareness of the long-term value of filmed programming was signaled by his decision to shoot *The Cisco Kid* in color several years before color television sets were even available. *The Cisco Kid* remained in production until 1956, but its 156 episodes had an extraordinarily long life span in syndication thanks to the decision to shoot in color. In its first decade of syndication, the series grossed $11 million.

During the 1950s, Ziv produced more than 25 different series, all of which were half-hour dramas based on familiar male-oriented, action-adventure genres. His output included science fiction series such as *Science Fiction Theater* (1955–57), *Men into Space* (1959–60), and *The Man and the Challenge* (1959–60); westerns such as *Tombstone Territory* (1957–60), *Rough Riders* (1958–59), and *Bat Masterson* (1958–61); and courtroom dramas such as *Mr. District Attorney* (1954–55) and *Lockup* (1959–61).

In order to carve out a unique market niche, Ziv tried to spin variations on these familiar genres. In the crime genre, for instance, he produced few series that could be considered typical cop shows. His most notorious crime series, *I Led Three Lives* (1953–56), featured Richard Carlson as Herbert Philbrick, an undercover FBI agent sent to infiltrate communist organizations throughout the United States. While the major networks generally avoided the subject of the Red Scare, preferring to blacklist writers and performers while barely alluding to the perceived communist threat in their programming, Ziv attacked the issue with an ultraconservative zeal. By organizing the series around Philbrick's fight against the menace of communism, the series implied that communism was every bit as threatening and ubiquitous as urban crime.

Another crime series, *Highway Patrol,* starring Broderick Crawford, moved the police out of the familiar urban landscape, placing them instead on an endless highway—an important symbolic shift in a postwar America obsessed with automobile travel as a symbol of social mobility. *Sea Hunt,* which was produced for Ziv by Ivan Tors (who would go on to produce *Flipper* and *Daktari*), took the crime series onto the sea, where star Lloyd Bridges as Mike Nelson solved crimes and found adventure under the ocean's surface. The undersea footage added a touch of low-budget spectacle to the crime genre.

The market for first-run syndication swelled through the mid-1950s, and Ziv rode the wave with great success. The watchword for Ziv productions was "economy," and the company even formed a subsidiary called Economee TV in 1954. Production budgets were held to $20,000 to $40,000 per episode, which were generally shot in two to three days. As the demand for syndicated programming grew, Ziv expanded rapidly. In 1953 Ziv opened an international division to sell its series overseas. The operation proved to be such a success in England that Ziv found itself with revenues frozen by protectionist British legislation designed to force U.S. companies to spend their profits in Great Britain. In order to make use of these frozen funds, in 1956–57 Ziv produced two series in England: *The New Adventures of Martin Kane* and *Dial 999.*

With production at the studio booming, Ziv stopped leasing space from other studios and purchased its own

Frederick W. Ziv (right).
Photo courtesy of Wisconsin Center for Film and Theater Research

Hollywood studio in 1954. By 1955 the company's annual revenues were nearly doubling every year. Ziv was then producing more than 250 half-hour TV episodes annually, with a production budget that exceeded $6 million—a figure that surpassed virtually every other television producer in Hollywood.

But the tide was turning in the market for first-run syndication. By 1956 the networks had begun to syndicate reruns of their older prime-time programs. Since these off-network reruns—with their established audience appeal—had already earned money during the initial run in prime time, networks were able to sell them to local markets at deep discounts. As a consequence, the market for first-run syndication began to shrink dramatically. In 1956 there were still 29 first-run syndicated series on television, with the number

dropping to ten by 1960. By 1964 there was only one such series left on the air.

As the networks extended their influence beyond prime time and the market for first-run syndication dwindled, Ziv began to produce series specifically for network use—a decision that the company had actively avoided for more than two decades. Ziv's first network series was *West Point* (1956–57) for CBS, followed by four other network programs: *Tombstone Territory, Bat Masterson, Men into Space,* and *The Man and the Challenge.*

In 1959 Ziv elected to sell 80 percent of his company to an alliance of Wall Street investment firms for $14 million. "I sold my business," he explained,

> because I recognized the networks were taking command of everything and were permitting independent

producers no room at all. The networks demanded a percentage of your profits, they demanded script approval and cast approval. You were just doing whatever the networks asked you to do. And that was not my type of operation. I didn't care to become an employee of the networks.

In 1960 United Artists (UA) purchased Ziv Television Programs, including the 20 percent share still held by chair of the board Frederick Ziv and president John L. Sinn for $20 million. The newly merged production company was renamed Ziv-United Artists. United Artists had never been very successful in television, having placed only two series in prime time, *The Troubleshooters* (1959–60) and *The Dennis O'Keefe Show* (1959–60). This pattern continued after the merger. Ziv-UA produced 12 pilots during the first year and failed to sell any of them. In 1962, the company phased out Ziv Television operations and changed its

name to United Artists Television. Frederick Ziv left the board of directors at this time to return to Cincinnati, where he spent his retirement years.

CHRISTOPHER ANDERSON

See also **Syndication**

Further Reading

Balio, Tino, *United Artists: The Company That Changed the Film Industry,* Madison: University of Wisconsin Press, 1987

Boddy, William, *Fifties Television: The Industry and Its Critics,* Urbana: University of Illinois Press, 1990

Moore, Barbara, "The Cisco Kid and Friends: The Syndication of Television Series from 1948 to 1952," *Journal of Popular Film and Television* (Spring 1980)

Rouse, Morleen Getz, "A History of the F.W. Ziv Radio and Television Syndication Companies, 1930–1960," Ph.D. diss., University of Michigan, 1976

Znaimer, Moses (1942–)

Canadian Media Producer, Executive

Moses Znaimer, an internationally known Canadian broadcaster and producer, is the executive producer and president of CityTV, one of Canada's leading commercial media production organizations. There he guides program services such as MuchMusic, Bravo!, and MusiquePlus. Znaimer's work in forging a distinctive style of television within Canada, and internationally, identifies him as a clear auteur in television production, and he can rightfully claim that he is the visionary of Canadian television. His early work in broadcasting was as a co-creator and producer of the CBC national radio program *Cross-Country Check-up* in the 1960s (a first in the world) and in television as a cohost and producer of the CBC afternoon talk show *Take-Thirty* with Adrienne Clarkson. After being denied the opportunity to remake the radio phone-in program into a national television program, Znaimer quit the CBC and launched into private broadcasting. With no VHF licenses available, Znaimer began Toronto's first UHF station, Channel 57, known as CityTV, on a limited budget in offices on Queen Street in Toronto in 1972. The unique programming of CityTV has been Znaimer's central contribution to the world of broadcasting. The station originally created a sensation in

the 1970s for its late-night, soft-core porn-movie stripping, Baby Blue Movies, which shocked Toronto. But its inner-city focus, its celebration of a cosmopolitan ethnic diversity in its choice of personalities and reporters, its transformation of news into something that was decidedly less formal, more identifiably urban, and generally more positive, and its programming mix of just news, movies, and music all clearly made the station distinctive. Indeed, Znaimer and his small UHF station served as the real-life starting point for David Cronenberg's dystopic film *Videodrome* (1983).

Through the platform of CityTV, Znaimer has successfully produced a number of programs, many of which have gained national and international distribution. *The New Music* (1978–), designed as a *Rolling Stone*–style magazine of the air, was widely sold in Canada and internationally. More recently, Znaimer has broadcast and distributed two fashion-related programs, *Fashion Television* and *Ooh-La-La,* both nationally and internationally. *Movie Television,* an interview and news program about Hollywood in particular, has also been well syndicated throughout Canada's independent stations. The success of CityTV under Znaimer's direction allowed the company that bought the station in 1981, CHUM Limited, to launch Canada's first satellite-to-cable music specialty channel, MuchMusic. What was clear about the look of MuchMusic was that it emulated Citytv. Its style was irreverent; its use of handheld cameras at often canted angles was unending; its dependence on the "liveness" of television and its possibility for spontaneity and its transformation of the studio "backstage" into the foreground were signatures of Znaimer's work as executive producer.

Znaimer has contributed specific forms of television that celebrate the potential spontaneity of the medium. His Toronto ChumCity building (1987), the home of Citytv, MuchMusic, and Bravo!, is described as the first "studioless" television station. With complete cabling and wiring through 35 exposed "hydrants," any part of the building can be converted into an exhibition site for broadcast. Several conceptual approaches to television have been registered trademarks developed by Znaimer. The building itself is trademarked as the "Streetfront, Studioless, Television Operating System" and is marketed internationally. The vox populi box at the front of the building is trademarked "The Speaker's Corner," where anyone who drops a dollar into the slot can speak on any issue and the message will be broadcast.

Recent ventures of Znaimer, both nationally and internationally, have met with more mixed success. His involvement (along with Thames Television and Time Warner) with a 1992 bid to set up a similar inner-city style of television for Britain for the proposed Channel 5 was in the end not accepted. His recent launch of another specialty channel, Bravo!, which rebroadcasts past Canadian television programs and films, has had limited appeal and financial viability. Znaimer was involved in setting up a third television network in New Zealand, which once again built on his tried programming flow strategies developed at Citytv. His launch of a Spanish version of MuchMusic, MuchMusica, in Buenos Aires, in 1994 has gained access to more than 1.5 million viewers via cable and thousands of others via satellite in South America. The launch of MuchMusic into the U.S. cable market in 1994 has also produced access to a further 4 million viewers. By 2000 Znaimer had helped set up versions of his Citytv style of programming in both Barcelona and Bogota. He had also reformed a collection of independent channels in both Ontario and British Columbia with similar formatting.

Znaimer's versatility within the arts has occasionally led to on-camera performances. He has been an on-and-off actor, with film credits including *Atlantic City* (1980), and, more regularly, an on-air narrator/interviewer in a number of programs, most notably *The Originals*. His most recent large-scale production for the CBC is a clear acknowledgment of his role in pioneering a unique style of television. A four-part series titled *TVTV: The Television Revolution* (1995) was hosted and produced by Znaimer.

Znaimer's style of television represents a unique contribution to broadcasting. He has developed a localized style with up to 40 hours a week of local content that, because of its connection to the particular urban landscape, has gained a certain resonance and exportability to other urbanized cultures. In addition, Znaimer has emphasized the concept of the flow of television in various formats. Rather than a focus on narrative conclusion, Znaimer's programming style identifies how television can attempt to capture—however partially—the becoming aspect of contemporary life. He has been able to achieve this vision of interactive, urban, hip television through repeated financial success in Toronto, generally recognized as one of the most competitive television markets in North America. The apparent cost of his studioless studio is roughly one-quarter that of regular television stations. Portions of this style have been copied throughout North American television and, to a lesser degree, internationally.

P. David Marshall

See also **Citytv; MuchMusic**

Moses Znaimer. Born in Kulab, Tajikistan, 1942; family fled to Shanghai, arrived in Canada in 1948 and settled in Montreal. Educated at McGill University, Montreal, B.A. in philosophy and politics; Harvard University, M.A. in government. Joined the Canadian Broadcasting Corporation as radio and TV producer/director/host of several shows, from 1965 to 1969; vice president, T'ang Management Ltd. and Helix Investments; cofounder, president, chief executive officer, and executive officer, Citytv, 1972, MuchMusic, 1984, Musique Plus, 1986, Bravo!, 1995, SPACE, 1997, Cable Plus 24, 1998, MuchMore Music, 1998, Canadian Learning Television, 1999, Star!, 1999. Founder, MZTV Museum. Recipient: Canadian Association of Broadcasters CAB Gold Ribbon, 1998.

Television Series (selected)

1962	Take Thirty (producer, cohost)
1969	The Way It Is (cohost)

The Originals (on-air presenter)
Originals in Space (on-air presenter)
Originals in Art (on-air presenter)

Television Special

1995	*TVTV: The Television Revolution*

Radio

Cross-Country Checkup (coproducer), 1960s.

Films (actor)

Atlantic City, 1980; *The Last Chase,* 1981; *The Best Revenge,* 1982.

Further Reading

"Access Boys Ready for Opposition to Moses Znaimer's Access Network Deal with Alberta Government," *Calgary Herald* (March 12, 1995)

"The Gospel According to Moses: The Bad Boy of Canadian Broadcasting," *Maclean's* (May 8, 1995)

"Looking for Meaning in TV's 'Flow,' " *Globe and Mail* (May 3, 1995)

"The Masque of Moses Znaimer's Medium—Drainie," *Globe and Mail* (April 13, 1995)

"Moses Disposes Formal Launch of Bravo!" *Globe and Mail* (March 28, 1995)

Robins, Max, "Toronto's Citytv to Export Its Savvy," *Variety* (July 26,1993)

"Wholly Moses: Znaimer Takes on TV," *Montreal Gazette* (April 7, 1995)

Zorro

U.S. Western

The television version of *Zorro,* like its previous movie incarnations, was based on stories written by Johnston McCulley. These stories recounted exploits of the swashbuckling alter ego of Don Diego de la Vega in colonial California.

The most popular and recognizable TV version of *Zorro* was the Disney Studios production for ABC. The two organizations had entered into a joint production agreement in 1954, an agreement that bore immediate fruit with *Disneyland* and *The Mickey Mouse Club.* Walt Disney had purchased the rights to the Zorro stories in the early 1950s, but pilot production stalled while Walt focused on construction of his Disneyland theme park. *Zorro* went into production in 1957 and enjoyed immense popularity on ABC for two years, from October 1957 to September 1959.

Guy Williams played Zorro, the mysterious hero who righted wrongs perpetrated on the common people by the evil Captain Monastario (Britt Lomond), commandant of the Fortress de Los Angeles. Don Diego's father, Don Alejandro (George J. Lewis), persuaded his son to return to California from Spain and do his utmost to foil Monastario and his dimwitted underling, Sergeant Garcia (Henry Calvin). Zorro's true identity was known only to his deaf-mute servant, Bernardo (Gene Sheldon). Depending on the situation, Zorro rode one of two trusty mounts, one black (Tornado) and one white (Phantom). Each episode began with Zorro sticking a message on the commandant's door, "My sword is a flame to right every wrong, so heed well my name—Zorro."

Though it used almost all Caucasian actors, the story of Zorro stands out in the television landscape of 1957 for featuring a Hispanic hero figure. Roles and role models for Hispanic Americans were absent from the television productions of the era, and this acknowledgment of the Hispanic culture and the heroism of many of its constituents was considered a forward step.

The characters, however, were broadly drawn and often stereotypical. The conflict in *Zorro* was a simple distillation: a decadent, militaristic monarchy that exercised a corrupt, greedy rule over simple, God-loving folk versus the mysterious, altruistic defender of honesty and virtue. The archetypal characters of Monastario, Garcia, and Zorro provided easy markers of good and evil for the children of *Zorro*'s target audience. Evil was effeminate, devious, slovenly, and doltish. Good was decisive and (in the words of another Disney Studios product) "brave, truthful, and unselfish." Even as the prime-time western genre was approaching the end of its cycle by reinventing itself as "adult," the western genre for children remained a comfortable and predictable haven of values championed by Walt Disney and, in turn, the middle class.

By the late 1950s and early 1960s, the relationship between ABC and Disney Studios had soured. *The Mickey Mouse Club* was dropped after its fourth season. Though the network claimed this was due to flagging sponsorship, Walt Disney believed it was because of excessive commercial minutes. *Zorro,* still quite popular, was also canceled. ABC now owned enough

Zorro, Guy Williams, 1957–59.
Courtesy of the Everett Collection

shows to make the purchase of programs from independent producers less necessary. To make matters worse, ABC forbade Disney Studios from selling its product to a competing network, and while legal wrestling changed that restriction, it was clear that Disney Studios had become a casualty of the fledgling network's success.

Zorro also serves as an early example of what can happen to the popularity of a show when it is extensively merchandised. Because it was a Disney Studios product, *Zorro* had the benefit of the studio's massive merchandising machinery. During the run of the show, and for many years thereafter, *Zorro* spawned a huge number of items—hats, knives, masks, capes, pencil cases, and lunch boxes—sold with the *Zorro* logo. The original theme was recorded for the opening of the show by Henry Calvin, who played Sergeant Garcia, and made into a hit record by the musical group called the Chordettes. During the two years that *Zorro* ran on ABC, the Disney merchandising juggernaut generated millions of dollars in additional income and kept the profile of the program high, especially with children. Even years after the popularity of Disney Studios and ABC's *Zorro* had waned, the merchandising contin-

ued. When *Zorro* became a children's cartoon in the 1970s, a PEZ candy dispenser capped with Zorro's masked visage enjoyed healthy sales.

In some ways, *Zorro* serves as a model for much that is right and much that is wrong with children's television. It often propounded positive values and altruistic behavior, but it was ultimately one of the first of a long line of productions used solely to deliver a huge number of children to advertisers.

The image of Zorro remains prevalent today. From McCulley's original stories, through the movie with Tyrone Power and the serial with Clayton Moore, the Disney version for ABC, the Saturday-morning cartoon, the cable remake on the Family Channel in 1988, and the 1998 feature film *The Mask of Zorro*, Zorro still has appeal. Even today, colorized versions of the original black-and-white episodes shot by Disney air on cable, introducing the next wave of children to "a horseman known as Zorro."

JOHN COOPER

See also **Walt Disney Programs; Westerns**

Cast

Don Diego de la Vega ("Zorro")	Guy Williams
Don Alejandro	George J. Lewis
Bernardo	Gene Sheldon
Captain Monastario	Britt Lomond
Sergeant Garcia	Henry Calvin
Nacho Torres	Jan Arvan
Elena Torres	Eugenia Paul
Magistrate Galindo	Vinton Hayworth
Anna Maria Verdugo (1958–59)	Jolene Brand
Senor Gregorio Verdugo (1958–59)	Eduard Franz
Corporal Reyes (1958–59)	Don Diamond

Producers

Walt Disney, William H. Anderson

Programming History

ABC
October 1957–September 1959   Thursday 8:00–8:30

Further Reading

Hollis, Richard, *The Disney Studio Story,* London: Octopus Books, 1989

Schnider, Cy, *Children's Television,* Chicago: NTC Books, 1987

West, Richard, *Television Westerns: Major and Minor Series, 1946–1978,* Jefferson, North Carolina: McFarland, 1987

Zwick, Edward (1952–), and Marshall Herskovitz (1952–)

U.S. Producers, Writers, Directors

Marshall Herskovitz and Edward M. Zwick met as students at the American Film Institute in the mid-1970s and soon after their graduation started their television careers. Their series television work acknowledges the collective force that family represents in American culture, and as such, their authorial presence is felt through their primary themes, striving for authentic representations of the modern American family.

In 1983 Herskovitz and Zwick teamed up to coproduce an award-winning television movie, *Special Bulletin,* which brought them each their first Emmy Award. In 1985 they formed their production company, Bedford Falls, named for George Bailey's hometown of Bedford Falls in Frank Capra's *It's a Wonderful Life.*

Herskovitz and Zwick have been called the first baby boomers to depict their own lives so openly in a television series. Their drama series *thirtysomething* (1987–91) reflected the so-called self-centered dilemmas of the 1980s "thirtyish" professionals. Called a "yuppie" drama by some, the series featured a strong ensemble cast led by Ken Olin, Mel Harris, Timothy Busfield, and Patricia Wettig. Critics were divided about the show's self-exploration into relationships. Herskovitz and Zwick, however, took an unapologetic look at married and single life, which became a cultural touchstone for a generation. Their work on the 1987 season gained them each another Emmy Award.

Their series *My So-Called Life* (1994–95) was an emotionally raw look at the teenage years. Running only 19 episodes, it followed a 15-year-old girl through the sometimes dark, sometimes tender pains of identity exploration. *My So-Called Life* was a departure from cute teen entertainment, and series star Claire Danes was praised for reaching honest and profound levels of teenage experience. *Relativity* (1996–97) was a romantic comedy/drama centering on two 20-year-olds exploring the paradoxes that come when children mature and separate. While not series creators, Herskovitz and Zwick served as executive producers on *Relativity.* As with *My So-Called Life,* this show struggled to find its audience.

Most recently, *Once and Again* (1999–2002), sometimes called "fortysomething," explored the changing face of an American family faced with the realities of divorce, single parenting, and blending with other divorced families. The series also poignantly portrayed the struggles faced by children often unsettled by divorce—struggles that included anorexia, depression, and sexual identification. Winning an Emmy for her portrayal of Lily Manning, Sela Ward led an ensemble cast praised for their unflinching and uncompromising performances. *Once and Again* became part of an unusual deal that allowed ABC to replay episodes on Lifetime cable within the same week of ABC's airdate. The week before its premiere, Lifetime signed an exclusive agreement with ABC and Touchstone Television (Disney) in what was called one of the fastest network-to-cable deals ever.

Each of these series offered complex and textured sites for negotiating the shifting cultural phenomena of identity and family. The Herskovitz and Zwick narratives tend to avoid the easy answers and quick fixes. These same qualities were also the sites of profuse criticism, however. Some critics accused Herskovitz and Zwick of navel gazing, while others criticized network impatience for not letting the series' audiences build. While this may be true for *My So-Called Life* and *Relativity,* there is widespread agreement that *Once and Again* was mishandled, having been moved seven times in two and a half years.

SHERRA SCHICK

See also Family; thirtysomething

Edward M. Zwick. Born in Chicago, Illinois, October 8, 1952. Married Lynn Liberty Godshall; two children. Education: Harvard University, B.A., 1974; American Film Institute, M.F.A., 1976. Writer, producer, director associated with quality television programming centering on family (*thirtysomething, Relativity, My So-Called Life, Once and Again*); cofounder (with Marshall Herskovitz) of Bedford Falls Production Company. Recipient of Humanitas Prize Award, 1980,

1983, 1988, 2001; Emmy Award, 1983, 1988; Writers Guild Award, 1983; Directors Guild Award, 1984; Bronze Wrangler, 1995; Lone Star Film and Television Award, 1997; Oscar, 1999; BAFTA, 1999; Golden Satellite Award, 1999; Stanley Kramer Award, 2002.

Marshall Herskovitz. Born in Philadelphia, Pennsylvania, February 23, 1952. Married Susan Amanda Shilladay (divorced); children: Elizabeth Gray, May Myles. Education: Brandeis University, B.A., 1973; American Film Institute, M.F.A., 1975. Writer, producer, director associated with quality television programming centering on family (*Family, thirtysomething, Relativity, My So-Called Life, Once and Again*); cofounder (with Edward M. Zwick) of Bedford Falls Production Company. Recipient of DGA Award, 1988, 1989; Emmy Award, 1983, 1988; Humanitas Prize, 1983, 1988, 2001; Stanley Kramer Award, 2002.

Television Series: Herskovitz and Zwick, Producers

1987–1991	*thirtysomething*
1989	*Dream Street*
1994–95	*My So-Called Life*
1996–97	*Relativity*
1999–2002	*Once and Again*

Television Series: Zwick, Producer

| 1976–80 | *Family* |

Television Specials, Movies: Herskovitz and Zwick, Producers

1983	*Special Bulletin*
1990	*Extreme Close-Up*
1987	*Sawdust, CBS Summer Playhouse*
1992	*Rock the Vote*
2002	*Oooph!*

Television Movies: Zwick, Director

| 1982 | *Paper Dolls* |
| 1982 | *Having It All* |

Television Series: Herskovitz, Writer (Episodic)

1970	*Family*
1970–80	*The White Shadow*
1980	*CHiPs*
1982–83	*Seven Brides for Seven Brothers*
1987	*thirtysomething*

| 1989 | *Dream Street* |
| 1999–2002 | *Once and Again* |

Television Series: Herskovitz, Director (Episodic)

1976	*Family*
1985	*The Best Times*
1985–86	*The Insiders*
1987–91	*thirtysomething*
1999–2002	*Once and Again*
1994	*My So-Called Life*

Television Series: Zwick, Writer (Episodic)

1976	*Family*
1987	*thirtysomething*
1999–2002	*Once and Again*

Television Series: Zwick, Director (Episodic)

1985	*The Insiders*
1985	*The Best Times*
1996	*Relativity*
1994	*My So-Called Life*

Films (selected) Zwick, Director

About Last Night, 1986; *Glory,* 1989; *Leaving Normal,* 1992; *Legends of the Fall,* 1994; *Courage Under Fire,* 1995; *The Siege,* 1998. Producer: *Legends of the Fall,* 1994; *Dangerous Beauty,* 1998; *The Siege,* 1998, *Shakespeare in Love,* 1998; *Executive Search,* 1999; *Traffic,* 2000; *I Am Sam,* 2001; *Abandon,* 2002; *Lone Star State of Mind,* 2002.

Films (selected) Herskovitz, Director

Jack the Bear, 1993; *Dangerous Beauty,* 1998. Producer: *Legends of the Fall,* 1994; *Dangerous Beauty,* 1998; *Executive Search,* 1999; *Traffic,* 2000; *I Am Sam,* 2001; *Lone Star State of Mind,* 2002.

Further Reading

"A Show That Evades Easy Resolutions," *calendarlive,* www.latimes.com (May 2, 2001)

Carter, Bill, "ABC Plans Speedy Encore for New Drama," *New York Times* (September 27, 1999)

Kitman, Marvin, "Never Again for 'Once and Again,'" *Newsday* (April 7, 2002)

"*Once and Again* on Cable," *Newsday* (September 27, 1999)

Sweeney, Terrance, "Fortysomething," *Written By* (May 2000)

Weinraub, Bernard, "After 40, Letting Go of Happily Ever After," *New York Times* (August 1, 1999)

Zworykin, Vladimir (1889–1982)

U.S. Inventor

For his fundamental and crucial work in creating the iconoscope and the kinescope, inventor Vladimir Zworykin is often described as "the father of television." These basic technologies revolutionized television and led to the worldwide adoption of electronic television rather than mechanical television, a device that used synchronized moving parts to generate rudimentary pictures.

At the St. Petersburg Institute of Technology, Zworykin studied electrical engineering with Boris Rosing, who believed cathode-ray tubes would be useful in television's development because they could shoot a steady stream of charged particles. After graduating from St. Petersburg in 1912, Zworykin studied X-ray technology with well-known French physicist Paul Langevin at the College de France in Paris. Both experiences influenced Zworykin's later work after he emigrated to the United States in 1919.

In 1920 Zworykin joined Westinghouse to work on the development of radio tubes and photocells. While there, he earned his Ph.D. in physics at the University of Pittsburgh and wrote his dissertation on improving photoelectric cells. However, electronic television's development captured his attention, and in December 1923 he applied for a patent for the iconoscope, which produced pictures by scanning images. Within the year, he applied for a patent for the kinescope, which reproduced those scanned images on a picture tube. Electronic television was now possible. After Zworykin demonstrated his new system to Westinghouse executives, they decided not to pursue his research.

He found a more receptive audience in 1929 at the Radio Corporation of America (RCA), where he was hired as associate research director for RCA's electronic research laboratory in Camden, New Jersey. This same year, he filed his first patent for color television. Reportedly, Zworykin told RCA president David Sarnoff that it would take $100,000 to perfect television. Sarnoff later told the *New York Times,* "RCA spent $50 million before we ever got a penny back from TV."

In 1930 Zworykin's experiments with G.A. Morton on infrared rays led to the development of night-seeing devices. He also began to apply television technology to microscopy, which led to RCA's development of the electron microscope. His work also led to text readers, electric eyes used in security systems and garage door openers, and electronically controlled missiles and vehicles. During World War II, he advised several defense organizations, and immediately after the war, he worked with Princeton University professor John von Neumann to develop computer applications for accurate weather forecasting.

After retiring from RCA in 1954, Zworykin was named an honorary vice president of the corporation and its technical consultant. He was also appointed director of the Medical Electronics Center at Rockefeller

Vladimir Zworykin.
Photo courtesy of Broadcasting & Cable

Institute and worked on electronically based medical applications.

Zworykin received numerous awards related to these inventions, especially television. They included the Institute of Radio Engineers' Morris Liebmann Memorial Prize in 1934; the American Institute of Electrical Engineers' highest honor, the Edison Medal, in 1952; and the National Academy of Sciences' National Medal of Science in 1967.

LOUISE MARGARET BENJAMIN

See also **Television Technology**

Vladimir Kozma Zworykin. Born in Mourom, Russia, July 30, 1889. Degree in engineering from St. Petersburg Institute of Technology (Russia), 1912; attended College de France, 1912–14; University of Pittsburgh, Pennsylvania, Ph.D., 1926. Married: 1) Tatiana Vasilieff, 1916 (divorced); two children; 2) Katherine Polevitsky, 1951. Served in Signal Corps, Russian Army, World War I. Immigrated to U.S., 1919; naturalized, 1924. Bookkeeper, financial agent, Russian Embassy, Washington, D.C., 1919–20; electronics researcher, Westinghouse Electric and Manufacturing Company, Pittsburgh, 1920, 1922, 1923–29; researcher, electronics development firm, Kansas, 1922–23; filed first of 120 patents, for electronic camera tube called an "iconoscope," 1923; patented kinescope, 1924; patented color television, 1929; director of electronics research lab, Radio Corporation of America (RCA), Camden, New Jersey, 1929–42; sponsored development of early version of electron microscope, 1940; associate research director, RCA Labs, Princeton, New Jersey, 1942–45, director of electronic research, 1946–54; vice president, from 1947; honorary vice president and consultant, 1954–82; director, Medical Electronics Research Center, Rockefeller Institute (now Rockefeller University), New York City, from 1954; developed radio endosonde, 1957; developed ultraviolet color-translating television microscope, 1957; researcher, Princeton University, 1970s; visiting professor, Institute for Molecular and Cellular Evolution, University of Miami, 1970–82; contributed numerous papers concerning electronics to scientific journals. National chair, Professional Group on Medical Electronics, Institute of Radio Engineers; founder and president, International Federation for Medical Electronics and Biological Engineering; officer of the Academy, French Ministry of Education; governor, International Institute for Medical Electronics and Biological Engineering, Paris. Fellow: American Association for the Advancement of Science; American Institute of Physics; American Physical Society; Institute of Electrical and Electronics Engineers. Member: American Academy of Arts and Sciences; American Philosophical Society; charter member, Electron Microscope Society of America; National Academy of Engineering; National Academy of Sciences; charter member, Society of Television Engineers; charter member, Society of Television Pioneers; Sigma Xi. Honorary fellow: Instituto Internazionale delle Comunicazione, Italy; Television Society, England. Honorary member: British Institute of Radio Engineers; Société Française des Électriciens et des Radioélectriciens; Television Engineers of Japan. Eminent member, Eta Kappa Nu Association. Recipient: Liebman Memorial Prize, 1934; Overseas Award, 1939; National Association of Manufacturers Modern Pioneer Award, 1940; American Academy of Arts and Sciences Rumford Medal, 1941; U.S. War Department Certificate of Appreciation, 1945; U.S. Navy Certificate of Commendation, 1947; Franklin Institute Potts Medal, 1947; Presidential Certificate of Merit, 1948; chevalier, Légion d'Honneur, 1948; American Institute of Electrical Engineers (AIEE) Lamme Medal, 1949; Poor Richard Club Gold Medal of Achievement, 1949; Society of Motion Picture and Television Engineers Progress Medal, 1950; Medal of Honor, 1951; establishment of Television Prize in his name by the Institute of Radio Engineers, 1952; AIEE Edison Medal, 1952; Union Française des Inventeurs Gold Medal, 1954; University of Liege Trasenster Medal, 1959; Christoforo Columbo Award and Order of Merit, Italy, 1959; Broadcast Pioneers Award, 1960; American Society of Metals Sauveur Award, 1963; University of Liege Medical Electronics Medal, 1963; British Institution of Electrical Engineers Faraday Medal, 1965; DeForest Audion Award, 1966; National Medal of Science, 1966; American Academy of Achievement Golden Plate Award, 1967; National Academy of Engineering Founders Medal, 1968; named to National Inventor's Hall of Fame, 1977; Eduard Rhein Foundation ring, 1980. Died in Princeton, New Jersey, July 29, 1982.

Publications

Photocells and Their Applications, with E.D. Wilson, 1930

Television: The Electronics of Image Transmission, with G.A. Morton, 1940

Electron Optics and the Electron Microscope, with G.A. Morton, E.G. Ramberg, and others, 1945

Photoelectricity and Its Application, with E.G. Ramberg, 1949

Television: The Electronics of Image Transmission in Color and Monochrome, with G.A. Morton, 1954

Television in Science and Industry, with E.G. Ramberg and L.E. Flory, 1958

Further Reading

Abramson, Albert, *Zworykin, Pioneer of Television,* Urbana: University of Illinois Press, 1995

Cheek, Dennis W., and A. Kim, "Vladimir Zworykin," *Notable Twentieth-Century Scientists,* Vol. 4, edited by Emily J. McMurray, Detroit, Michigan: Gale, 1995

Parker, Sybil P., editor, *McGraw-Hill Modern Scientists and Engineers,* Vol. 3, New York: McGraw-Hill, 1980

Thomas, Robert M., Jr., "Vladimir Zworykin, Television Pioneer, Dies at 92," *New York Times Biographical Service* (August 1982)

Notes on Contributors

ABBOTT, Gina.

ABRAM, Daniel. Masters Candidate, Department of Radio Television Film, University of Texas at Austin.

ABRAMSON, Bram. Montreal, Quebec, Canada. Contributor to Canadian Review of Sociology & Anthropology, 1998; International Journal of Cultural Policy, 1999; Telecommunications Policy, 2000; Critical Perspectives on the Internet, 2001, edited by Greg Elmer; International Journal of Cultural Studies, 2001; Global Media Policy in the New Millennium, 2001, edited by Marc Raboy; and Media, Culture & Society, 2001.

ACLAND, Charles. Associate Professor, Department of Communication Studies, Concordia University, Montreal, Canada. Author, *Youth, Murder, Spectacle: The Cultural Politics of Youth in Crisis,* 1995; articles in *Wide Angle, Communication,* and *Canadian Journal of Film Studies.* Member, editorial board, *Cultural Studies.*

ALDRIDGE, Henry B. Professor, Communication & Theatre Arts, Eastern Michigan University.

ALEXANDER, Alison. Professor and department head, Telecommunications, Grady College of Journalism and Mass Communications, University of Georgia. Has served as president of the Association for Communication Administration and president of the Eastern Communication Association, and as editor of the Journal of Broadcasting & Electronic Media.

ALLEN, Erika Tyner.

ALLEN, Robert C. Godfrey Professor of American Studies, University of North Carolina at Chapel Hill. Author, *Speaking of Soap Operas* and *Horrible Prettiness: Burlesque and American Culture.* Coauthor, with Douglas Gomery, *Film History: Theory and Practice.* Editor, *To Be Continued...Soap Operas Around the World,* and of two editions of *Channels of Discourse.*

ALLEY, Robert S. Professor Emeritus, Humanities, University of Richmond. Coauthor, *Murphy Brown: Anatomy of a Sitcom,* 1990; *Love is All Around: The Making of the Mary Tyler Moore Show,* 1989; *The Producer's Medium: Conversations with Creators of American TV,* 1983. Author, *Television: Ethics for Hire,* 1977; also numerous books and essays on the relation of American religion to the First Amendment, free speech, the presidency, and the Supreme Court.

ALLOR, Martin. Associate Professor, Department of Communication Studies, Concordia University, Canada. Coauthor, *L'Etat de Culture: Généalogie Discursives des Politiques Culturelles Québécoises,* 1994. Codirector, Research Group on Cultural Citizenship.

ALVARADO, Manuel. Research fellow, Media Arts, Luton University, U.K.; editorial director, John Libbey

Media Publications. Coauthor, *Made for Television: Euston Films Limited,* 1985; *Doctor Who: The Unfolding Text,* 1983; *Hazell: The Making of a TV Series,* 1978. Coeditor, *Media Education: An Introduction: The Workbook,* 1992; *East of Dallas: The European Challenge to American Television,* 1988; editor; *Video Worldwide: An International Study,* 1988.

ALVEY, Mark. Administrator, the Field Museum, Chicago. Unaffiliated writer and researcher with interests in television, film, and other forms of popular culture. His work has appeared in *The Road Movie Book,* 1997; *The Revolution Wasn't Televised: Sixties Television and Social Conflict,* 1997; and *Screen,* 45:1, spring 2004.

AMIN, Hussein Y. Professor and Chair, Journalism and Mass Communication, American University in Cairo, Egypt. Coauthor, "Global TV News in Developing Countries: CNN's Expansion to Egypt," in *Ecquid Novi, Journal of Journalism in Southern Africa,* 1993; "The Impact of Home Video Cassette Recorder on Egyptian Film and Television Consumption Pattern," in *The European Journal of Communication,* 1993. Member, board of trustees, Egyptian Radio and Television Union; General Assembly, Egyptian Ministry of Information; advisory board, *Journal of International Communication.*

ANDERSON, Christopher. Associate Professor, Department of Communication and Culture, Indiana University-Bloomington. Author, *Hollywood TV: The Studio System in the Fifties,* 1994.

ARON, Danielle. Counterpoint Research, U.K.

ASTHANA, Sanjay. Assistant Professor, College of Mass Communication, School of Journalism, Middle Tennessee University.

ATTALLAH, Paul. Associate Director, Mass Communication, Carleton University, Toronto, Canada. Author, "Broadcasting and Narrowcasting: VCRs, Home Video, DBS," in *Cultural Studies: Into the 21st Century,* 1995; "Reconstructing North American Television Audiences," in *New Researcher,* 1992; "Trends and Developments in Canadian Television," in *Media Information Australia,* 1991; *Theories de la Communication: Sens, Sujets, Savoirs,* 1991; *Theories de la Communication: Histoire, Contexte, Pouveir,* 1989. Member, editorial board, *MIA,* from 1991; *La Revue Communication,* from 1987.

AUFDERHEIDE, Patricia. Professor and Codirector, Center for Social Media, School of Communication, American University, Washington, D.C.

AUSTER, Albert. Associate Professor, Communication and Media Studies, Fordham University.

AUTER, Philip J. Assistant Professor, Department of Communication, University of Louisiana at Lafayette.

AVERY, Robert K. Professor, Communication, University of Utah. Author, *Public Service Broadcasting in a Multichannel Environment,* 1993; *Critical Perspectives on Media and Society,* 1991; articles in *Journal of Communication, Journal of Broadcasting and Electronic Media, Communication Education,* and *Western Journal of Communication.* Founding editor, *Critical Studies in Mass Communication.*

BABE, Robert. Chair, Communications Studies Masters Program, University of Windsor, Canada.

BAL, Vidula V.

BALIO, Tino. Professor, Communication Arts, University of Wisconsin, Madison. Executive director, Arts Institute.

BANKS, Miranda. Graduate student, Department of Film, Television, and Digital Media, University of California at Los Angeles.

BAREISS, Warren. Assistant Professor, Department of Communication, University of Scranton.

BARRERA, Eduardo. Assistant Professor, Communication, El Colegio de la Frontera Norte, Mexico, and University of Texas at El Paso.

BARTONE, Richard. Associate Professor, Communication Department, William Paterson University, Wayne, New Jersey. Associate Editor of *Film & History: An Interdisciplinary Journal of Film and Television Studies.*

BATES, John. Lecturer, Polish Language and Literature, Department of Slavonic Studies, University of Glasgow. Author of *Censorship: An International Encyclopedia,* 2001; "Making Approaches: Official Attitudes and Practice in People's Poland towards Polish Emigre Literature after 1956," *Canadian-American Slavic Studies,* 33, Nos. 2–4, 1999; and "Freedom of the Press in Inter-War Poland: The System of Control," in *Poland Between the Wars, 1918–1939,* 1998.

BEASLEY, Vanessa B. Assistant Professor, Southern Methodist University.

BECHELLONI, Giovanni. Professor, Faculty of Political Science. Director, MA in Media Studies, University of Florence, Italy. Author of numerous books and articles on journalism, mass media, and television in Italy.

BECKER, Christine. Assistant Professor, Film, Television, and Theatre Department, University of Notre Dame. Author of "A Syndicated Show in a Network World: Frederic Ziv's Favorite Story," *Journal of Ra-*

dio Studies, Summer 2001. Contributor to *The Encyclopedia of Radio* (Fitzroy Dearborn, 2003).

BELLAMY, Robert V., Jr. Associate Professor, Communication, Duquesne University. Coauthor, *Grazing on a Vast Wasteland: The Remote Control and Television's Second Generation,* 1996; articles and chapters in *Journal of Communication, Journal of Broadcasting and Electronic Media, Journalism Quarterly, The Cable Networks Handbook,* and *Media, Sports, Society.* Coeditor, *The Remote Control and the New Age of Television,* 1993. Member, editorial board, *Journal of Sport and Social Issues* and *NINE.*

BENJAMIN, Louise. Associate Director, George Foster Peabody Awards. Associate Professor, Telecommunications, Grady College of Journalism and Mass Communication, University of Georgia. Author of articles on communication history and law and policy in the *Journal of Broadcasting and Electronic Media, Free Speech Yearbook, Journalism Quarterly,* and the *Historical Journal of Film, Radio, and Television.*

BENSHOFF, Harry M. Assistant Professor, Department of Radio, Television, Film, University of North Texas. Author, *Monsters in the Closet: Homosexuality and the Horror Film,* 1997. Coauthor, *America on Film: Representing Race, Class, Gender, and Sexuality at the Movies,* 2004. Coeditor, *Queer Cinema: The Film Reader,* 2004.

BERGER, Arthur Asa. Professor Emeritus, Broadcast and Electronic Communication Arts, San Francisco State University.

BERNARDI, Daniel. Assistant Professor, Department of Media Arts, University of Arizona.

BERNSTEIN, Alina. Lecturer, Film and Television Department, Tel Aviv University, Israel. Head, Media and Sport section, the International Association for Media and Communication Research (IAMCR). Coeditor, with Neil Blain, *Sport, Media, Culture: Global and Local Dimensions,* 2003; and the "Representation, Identity, and the Media" section in *The Media Book,* 2002.

BILTEREYST, Daniel. Professor, Film, Television, and Cultural Media Studies, and International Communication, at Gent University, Belgium. Author of articles in various European and international journals, including *Asian Journal of Communication, European Journal of Communication, Communicatio, Communications, European Journal of Cultural Policy, Journal of International Communication, Media, Culture, and Society, Media Perspektiven,* and *Northern Lights.*

BIRD, J. B. Freelance writer.

BIRD, William L., Jr. Curator, Political History Collection, National Museum of American History, Smithsonian Institution. Author, "Television in the Ice Age," in *Hail to the Candidate,* 1992; "From the Fair to the Family," in New Museum of Contemporary Art, *From Receiver to Remote Control: The TV Set,* 1990; "Enterprise and Meaning: Sponsored Film, 1939–49," *History Today,* December 1989. Curator, Smithsonian exhibit, "American Television from the Fair to the Family, 1939–1989."

BIRK, Thomas A. Learning Environment and Internet Services/ITS. University of Nebraska Medical Center.

BLASINI, Gilberto M. Assistant Professor, Film and Television Studies, English Department, University of Wisconsin, Milwaukee.

BLEICHER, Joan. Research team member, television program research, University of Hamburg, Germany. Author of several articles on television aesthetics and the history of German television.

BLUMLER, Jay G. Professor Emeritus, Communication, University of Leeds, U.K., and University of Maryland. Research advisor to the Broadcast Standards Commission.

BODDY, William. Professor, Department of Communication Studies, Baruch College, City University of New York. Author, "The Amateur, the Housewife, and the Salesroom Floor: Promoting Postwar US Television," *International Journal of Cultural Studies,* 1: 1 (1998); "Sixty Million Viewers Can't Be Wrong: The Rise and Fall of the TV Western," in *Back in the Saddle: New Approaches to the Western,* 1998; "Senator Dodd Goes to Hollywood: Investigating Video Violence," in *The Revolution Wasn't Televised: Sixties Television and Social Transition,* 1997.

BODROGHKOZY, Aniko. Assistant Professor, Media Studies, Department of English, University of Virginia.

BORTHWICK, Stuart. Lecturer, Media and Cultural Studies, Liverpool John Moores University, U.K.

BOUNDS, J. Dennis. Associate Professor, Cinema-Television, School of Communication and the Arts, Regent University. Author, *Perry Mason: The Authorship and Reproduction of a Popular Hero,* 1996; and "Noble Counselor: Perry Mason and Its Impact on the Legal Profession," in *The Lawyer in Popular Culture,* 1993.

BOURNE, Stephen. Author and television archivist. Contributor, *Black and White in Colour—Black People in British Television Since 1936,* 1992; *The Colour Black—Black Images in British Television,* 1989.

BREDIN, Marian. Department of Communications, Popular Culture and Film, Brock University, Ontario, Canada. Author of "Transforming Images: Communication Technologies and Cultural Identity in Nishnawbe-Aski," *Cross-cultural Consumption,* 1996; and "Ethnography and Communication: Approaches to Aboriginal Media," *Canadian Journal of Communication,* 1993.

BREEN, Myles P. Professor Emeritus, Communication, Charles Stuart University, Bathurst, Australia. Author of articles in *Communication Monographs, Journalism Quarterly, Journal of Communication, Media Information, Australia and Washington Journalism Review,* and the electronic journal *APEX-J (Asia-Pacific Exchange Journal).*

BROOKS, Dwight. Associate Professor, Telecommunications, Grady College of Journalism & Mass Communication, University of Georgia.

BROOKS-HARRIS, Carolyn N. Student Academic Services. Colleges of Arts & Sciences, University of Hawaii at Manoa.

BROWER, Sue. Freelance writer and editor. Author, "Fans as Tastemakers: Viewers for Quality Television," in *The Adoring Audience: Fan Culture and Popular Media,* 1992.

BROWN, James A. Professor Emeritus, Telecommunication and Film, University of Alabama.

BRUNSDON, Charlotte. Professor, Department of Film and Television Studies, University of Warwick, U.K. Author, *Screen Tastes,* 1997; *Feminist Television Criticism* (coedited with Julie D'Acci and Lynn Spigel), 1997; *The National Television Studies* (with David Morley), 1998; and *The Feminist, the Housewife, and the Soap Opera,* 2000.

BRYANT, Steve. Keeper of Television, National Film and Television Archive, British Film Institute, U.K.

BURNS, Gary. Assistant Chair, Professor, Media Studies, Department of Communication, Northern Illinois University. Editor, *Popular Music and Society.*

BUTCHER, Mary Margaret. Communication Studies, Fort Hays State University, Kansas.

BUTLER, Jeremy G. Professor, Telecommunication and Film, University of Alabama, Tuscaloosa. Author, *Television: Critical Methods and Applications, 2nd edition,* 2001. Editor, *Star Texts: Image and Performance in Film and Television,* 1991. Contributor to *Journal of Popular Film and Television,* 1985; *The Steinbeck Question,* 1993; *Oxford Guide to Film Studies.* 1998;

Screen, 2001; *The New Media Book,* 2002; and *Cinema Journal,* 1986, 1991. Member of editorial board for *Journal of Film and Video* and *Cinema Journal.*

BUTSCH, Richard. Professor, Sociology Department, Rider University. Author, "Bowery B'hoys and Matinee Ladies: The Regendering of Nineteenth Century American Theatre Audiences," *American Quarterly,* September 1994; "Class and Gender in Four Decades of Television Situation Comedies: Plus ça Change Plus C'est Le Meme Chose," *Critical Studies in Mass Communication,* December 1992; *For Fun and Profit: The Transformation of Leisure into Consumption,* 1990.

BUXTON, Rodney A. Associate Professor, Department of Mass Communications and Journalism Studies, University of Denver.

CALDWELL, John Thornton. Associate Professor, Department of Film, Television, and Digital Media, University of California, Los Angeles.

CARR, Steven. Associate Professor, Department of Communication, Indiana University-Purdue, University Fort Wayne.

CASTONGUAY, James. Associate Professor and Chair, Department of Media Studies and Digital Culture, Sacred Heart University. Author, "The Political Economy of the 'Indie Blockbuster': Intermediality, Fandom, and *The Blair Witch Project,*" in *Nothing That Is: Millennial Cinema and the Blair Witch Controversies,* 2002; "Hollywood Goes to Washington: Scandal, Politics, and Contemporary Media Culture," in *Headline Hollywood,* 2001; and articles on the media in journals including *The Velvet Light Trap: A Critical Journal of Film and Television, Discourse: Journal for Theoretical Studies in Media and Culture, Bad Subjects: Political Education for Everyday Life,* and *The Hitchcock Annual.*

CATRON, Christine R. Head, Media Studies, Department of English, St. Mary's College, San Antonio, Texas.

CHORBA, Frank J. Professor, Department of Mass Media, Washburn University.

CHRISTENSEN, Miyase. Assistant Professor, Faculty of Communication, Bahcesehir University, Istanbul, Turkey. Author, "Digital Divide," in *Encyclopedia of Informatics in Turkey,* 2004.

CIRKSENA, Kathryn. Research Investigator, Center for Political Studies, University of Michigan.

CLARK, Kevin A. Assistant Instructor, Speech Communication, University of Texas at Austin.

CLARK, Lynn Schofield. Assistant Research Professor, School of Journalism and Mass Communication, University of Colorado. Author, *From Angels to Aliens: Teenagers, the Media, and the Supernatural,* 2003. Coauthor, *Media, Home, and Family,* 2004.

COLLINS, Kathleen. Freelance researcher and editor.

COOK, John. Senior Lecturer, Mass Media, Glasgow Caledonian University, Scotland, U.K.

COOKE, Lez. Principal Lecturer, Media Studies, School of Humanities and Social Sciences, Staffordshire University, U.K. Author, *British Television Drama: A History,* 2002.

COOPER, John G. Assistant Professor, Telecommunications and Film, Eastern Michigan University. Author, *The Fugitive: A Complete Episode Guide,* 1994.

CORNER, John. Professor, School of Politics and Communications, University of Liverpool, U.K. Author, *Television Form and Public Address,* 1995; *The Art of Record,* 1996; *Studying Media: Problems of Theory and Method,* 1998; and *Critical Ideas in Television Studies,* 1999. Editor, *Media and Political Style,* 2003.

COUZENS, Michael. Communications attorney, Oakland, California. Federal Communications Commission staff attorney, 1978–1981; Network Inquiry special staff and Low Power Television Inquiry staff.

CRAIG, Robert. Professor, Department of Broadcast & Cinematic Arts, Central Michigan University.

CUBITT, Sean. Professor, Screen and Media Studies, University of Waikato, New Zealand. Author, *Digital Aesthetics,* 1998; and *Simulation and Social Theory,* 2001.

ČULIK, Jan. Lecturer in Czech, Slavonic Studies, School of Modern Languages and Cultures, Glasgow University, U.K.

CULLUM, Paul. Freelance writer.

CUNNINGHAM, Stuart O. Professor and Director, Creative Industries Research and Applications Centre, Queensland University of Technology, Australia.

CURTHOYS, Ann. Manning Clark Professor of History, Australian National University

CURTIN, Michael. Professor, Media and Cultural Studies, Department of Communication Arts, University of Wisconsin, Madison. Author, *Redeeming the Wasteland: Television Documentary and Cold War Politics,* 1995. Coeditor, *Making and Selling Culture,*

1996; and *The Revolution Wasn't Televised: Sixties Television and Social Conflict,* 1997.

D'ALESSANDRO, Kathryn C. Assistant Professor, Media Arts, New Jersey City University.

DAYAN, Daniel. Fellow, Laboratoire Communication et Politique, Centre National de la Recherche Scientifique, Paris, France, and External Professor of Communication, University of Oslo, Norway.

DE LA GARDE, Roger. Professor, Communication, Laval University, Quebec City, Canada. Author, "De la télévision à la vision télé," in *Traité de la culture,* 2002; "Le téléroman québécois: une aventure américaine," in *Ciberlegenda,* 2002. Coauthor, "Coming of Age: Communication Studies in Quebec," in *Mediascapes. New Patterns in Canadian Communication,* 2002; "Star Wars. Canadian TV Fiction," in *Eurofiction. Television Fiction in Europe,* 2001. Coeditor, *Small Nations, BIG Neighbour: Denmark and Quebec/Canada Compare Notes on American Popular Culture,* 1993; *Les pratiques culturelles de grande consommation. Le marché francophone,* 1992.

DEANE, Pamala S. Lecturer and writer/researcher of broadcast and film history.

DeANGELIS, Michael. Member of the Resident Faculty of the School for New Learning. Director, Undergraduate Program, Loop Campus, DePaul University.

DESJARDINS, Mary. Assistant Professor, Film and Television Studies, Dartmouth College.

DESSART, George. Professor, Television and Radio, and Executive Director, Center for the Study of World Television, Brooklyn College, City University of New York.

DICKINSON, Robert. Instructor, University of Southern California, Los Angeles. Author, "Hearing the Body of Bruce Weber's Work: *Let's Get Lost* and *Broken Noses,*" *The Spectator,* Spring 1993; "The Unbearable Weight of Winning: Garci's Trilogy of Melancholy and the Foreign Language Oscar," *The Spectator,* Spring 1991.

DOCKER, John. Australian Research Council, Research Fellow, Humanities Research Centre, Australian National University. Author, *Postmodernism and Popular Culture: A Cultural History,* 1994.

DOHERTY, Thomas. Chair, Film Studies, Brandeis University.

DONNELLY, David F. Associate Dean, School of Communications, Quinnipiac University.

DOW, Bonnie J. Associate Professor, Speech Communication, University of Georgia. Author, *Prime-*

Time Feminism: Television, Media, Culture, and the Women's Movement Since 1970, 1996. Coeditor (with Celeste Condit), *Critical Studies in Media Communication.*

DOWLER, Kevin. Assistant Professor, Communication Studies, Division of Social Science, and coresearcher, Culture of Cities Project, York University, Canada.

DOWNING, John D. H. Director, Global Media Research Center, College of Mass Communication and Media Arts, Southern Illinois University.

DRUMMOND, Phillip. School of Culture, Language, and Communication, Institute of Education, University of London.

DUGUID, Mark. British Film Institute. Content Editor of the British film and television history Web site "screenonline" (www.screenonline.org.uk).

DUNN, J. A. Head, Department of Slavonic Studies, and Lecturer, Russian, School of Modern Languages and Cultures, University of Glasgow, U.K.

EAMAN, Ross A. Supervisor, Graduate Studies, Mass Communication, Carleton University, Canada.

EDGERTON, Gary R. Professor and Chair, Communication and Theatre Arts, Old Dominion University. Author, *Ken Burns's America,* 2001; *Television Histories: Shaping Collective Memory in the Media Age,* 2001; *In the Eye of the Beholder: Critical Perspectives in Popular Film and Television,* 1997; *Film and the Arts in Symbiosis: A Resource Guide,* 1988; and *American Film Exhibition,* 1983.

ELMER, Greg. Associate Professor, Department of Communication, Florida State University.

EMMANUEL, Susan. Translator. Contributor to British publications on British and American television.

EPSTEIN, Michael. Practicing attorney. Doctoral Candidate, American Culture, University of Michigan. Regular contributor to *Television Quarterly* and for popular magazines.

EVERETT, Anna. Doctoral Candidate, Critical Studies, University of Southern California.

EVERETT, Robert. Assistant Secretary of the university, York University, Canada.

FALKENHEIM, Jaqui Chmielewski.

FANG, Irving. Professor Emeritus, University of Minnesota.

FELSENTHAL, Norman. Professor, Communications and Theater, Temple University.

FERGUSON, Robert. Senior Lecturer, Education, and course leader, MA in Media, Culture, and Communication, Institute of Education, University of London.

FERRÉ, John P. Professor, Department of Communication, University of Louisville.

FIDDY, Dick. Freelance television researcher and scriptwriter.

FINNEY, Robert G. Professor Emeritus, Film and Electronic Arts, California State University, Long Beach.

FLETCHER, Frederick J. Professor, Department of Political Science and Director, Communications and Culture Graduate Program, York University, Canada.

FLETCHER, James E. Professor, Telecommunications, University of Georgia. Author of articles in *Quarterly Journal of Speech, Western Speech, Journal of Broadcasting, Jewish Social Studies, Journal of Advertising Research, Tobacco Control,* and *Psychophysiology.* Coeditor, *Music and Program Research,* 1986; *Broadcast Research Methods,* 1985. Editor, *Handbook of RadioTV: Research Procedures,* 1981, *Feedback.*

FLEW, Terry. Senior Lecturer and discipline head, Media and Communications, and course coordinator, Creative Industries postgraduate coursework degree program, Queensland University of Technology, Australia. Author, *New Media: An Introduction,* 2002; *Understanding Global Media,* 2005.

FOSTER, Nicola. Researcher.

FREEDMAN, Eric. Assistant Professor, Department of Communication, Florida Atlantic University.

FRY, Katherine. Associate Professor, Department of Television and Radio, Brooklyn College, City University of New York.

GANZ-BLAETTLER, Ursula. Researcher, Mass Media Department, University of Zurich, Switzerland.

GARAY, Ronald. Professor and Associate Dean, Undergraduate Studies and Administration, Manship School of Mass Communication, Louisiana State University.

GARDNER, Paula. Visiting Assistant Professor, College of Communication, Florida State University.

GATEWARD, Frances K. Program in Film and Video, and the Center for Afro-American and African Studies, University of Michigan.

GIBBERMAN, Susan R. Head of Reader Services, Schaumburg Township District Library, Schaumburg, Illinois. Author, *Star Trek: An Annotated Guide to Resources on the Development, the Phenomenon, the People, the Television Series, the Films, the Novels, and the Recordings,* 1991.

GIBSON, Mark. Lecturer, Cultural Studies and Director, Centre for Everyday Life, Murdoch University, Perth, Western Australia.

GIGLIONE, Joan. Lecturer, Entertainment Studies, College of Communications, California State University, Fullerton.

GILSDORF, William O. Professor and chairperson, Department of Communication Studies, Concordia University, Montreal, Canada.

GLENNON, Ivy. Associate Professor and Director of Advising, College of Communications, University of Illinois at Urbana-Champaign.

GLYNN, Kevin. Department of American Studies, University of Canterbury, Christchurch, New Zealand.

GODDARD, Peter. Lecturer, School of Politics and Communications, University of Liverpool, U.K.

GODFREY, Donald G. Professor, Walter Cronkite School of Journalism and Mass Communication, Arizona State University.

GOMERY, Douglas. Professor, Journalism, University of Maryland. Senior researcher, Media Studies Project of the Woodrow Wilson International Center for Scholars, 1988–1992. Author, *The Future of News,* 1992; *Shared Pleasures,* 1992; *American Media,* 1989; and *The Hollywood Studio System,* 1986; over 400 articles in other sources including *Modern Maturity.*

GOURGEY, Hannah. Community Technology and Training Center, Austin, Texas.

GOVIL, Nitin. Coauthor (with Toby Miller, Richart Maxwell, and John McMurria), *Global Hollywood,* 2001.

GRANT, August. Newsplex Academic Liaison, College of Mass Communications and Information Studies, Carolina Coliseum, University of South Carolina.

GRIFFIN, Sean. Doctoral Candidate, Cinema-Television, University of Southern California, Los Angeles.

GRIFFITHS, Alison. Assistant Professor, media studies, documentary film, and media and technology, Department of Communication Studies, The Mildred and George Weissman School of Arts and Sciences, Baruch College, City University of New York.

GROSS, Lynne Schafer. Professor, Department of Radio, Television, Film, California State University, Fullerton.

GUNZERATH, David. Vice President, Research and Information Group, National Association of Broadcasters.

GUSTAFSON, Karen. Doctoral Candidate, Department of Radio Television Film, University of Texas at Austin.

HAGGINS, Bambi L. Assistant Professor, Film and Video Studies, University of Michigan.

HAGINS, Jerry. Freelance writer and researcher.

HALLIN, Daniel C. Professor, Department of Communication, University of California, San Diego. Author, *We Keep America on Top of the World: Television Journalism and the Public Sphere,* 1994; *The 'Uncensored War': The Media and Vietnam,* 1986.

HAMMILL, Geoffrey. Associate Professor, Department of Telecommunications and Film, Eastern Michigan University.

HAMOVITCH, Susan. Independent producer. Author, "The Talking Dream: A Case Study Using Video in the Public Schools," *Television Quarterly,* 1997.

HAMPSON, Keith C. Department of Sociology, Ryerson University, Canada.

HARP, Denis. Professor, Telecommunications, School of Mass Communications, Texas Tech University.

HARRIS, Cheryl. Principal, Grapentine Company.

HART, Roderick P. Professor, Department of Communication Studies, College of Communication, University of Texas at Austin.

HARTLEY, John. Dean and Professor, Creative Industries Faculty, Queensland University of Technology, Australia. Author, *A Short History of Cultural Studies,* 2003; *Communication, Cultural & Media Studies: The Key Concepts,* 2002; *The Indigenous Public Sphere* (coauthor, 2000); *American Cultural Studies: A Reader* (coeditor, 2000); *Uses of Television,* 1999; *Popular Reality: Journalism, Modernity, Popular Culture, 1996, The Politics of Pictures: The Creation of the Public in the Age of Popular Media,* 1992; *Tele-ology: Studies in Television,* 1992; *Making Sense of the Media* (coauthor, 1985); *Understanding News,* 1982; *Reading Television* (coauthor, 1978).

HASSANPOUR, Amir. Assistant Professor, Department of Near and Middle Eastern Civilizations, University of Toronto, Canada.

HAVENS, Tim. Author, "'The Biggest Show in the World': Race and the Global Popularity of The Cosby Show," *Media, Culture and Society* 22.4 (2000); "Subtitling Rap: Appropriating The Fresh Prince of Bel-Air for Youthful Identity Formation in Kuwait," *Gazette: The International Journal for Communication Studies* 63.1 (2001);and "African American Television in a Global World," in *Planet Television,* 2001.

HAWKINS-DADY, Mark. British freelance editor. Contributor, *John Osborne: A Casebook,* 1996; *New Theatre Quarterly.* Editor, *Reader's Guide to Literature in English,* 1996; series editor, *International Dictionary of Theatre,* 1992–1995.

HAY, James. Associate Professor, Speech Communication, University of Illinois at Urbana-Champaign.

HAYNES, Richard. Lecturer and Director, MSc in Media Management, Online Learning, Film and Media Studies, University of Stirling, U.K.

HILMES, Michele. Professor, Media and Cultural Studies, Director, Wisconsin Center for Film and Theater Research, University of Wisconsin, Madison. Author of several books on broadcasting history, including *Radio Voices: American Broadcasting 1922–1952* and *Only Connect: A Cultural History of Broadcasting in the United States.* Coeditor (with Jason Loviglio), *The Radio Reader: Essays in the Cultural History of Broadcasting.*

HIMMELSTEIN, Hal. Professor, Television and Radio, Brooklyn College, City University of New York. Author, *Television Myth and the American Mind,* 1994; *On the Small Screen,* 1981. Member, editorial board, *Critical Studies in Mass Communication,* 1990–1992.

HOERSCHELMANN, Olaf. Assistant Professor, Department of Speech Communication, Eastern Illinois University.

HOLDEN, Todd. Professor, Mediated Sociology, and Chair, Department of Multi-Cultural Societies, Graduate School of International Cultural Studies (GSICS), Tohoku University, Sendai, Japan. Author, "Color Coding: globalization, semiosis, and the ad," *The International Scope Review* (April 2003); "Japan's Mediated 'Global' Identities," in *Globalization, Culture and Inequality in Asia;* "Advertising: a synthetic approach," in *Handbook of Media Studies* (forthcoming); "The Overcooked and Underdone: Masculinity in Japanese Food Programming" in *Food and Foodways* (forthcoming); medi@sia: *Communication and Society In and Out of Global Cultural Context* (forthcoming). Coauthor, *Globalization, Culture and Inequality in Asia,* 2003; "Deai kei: Japan's New Culture of Encounter," (with Takako Tsuruki) in *Japanese Cybercultures,* 2003.

HOLT, Jennifer. Faculty member, Department of Cinema-Television arts, California State University-Northridge. Author, "In Deregulation We Trust: The Synergy of Politics and Industry in Reagan-Era Hollywood," *Film Quarterly,* V. 55, No. 2 (Winter 2001–02); "Vertical Vision: Deregulation, Industrial Economy and Prime Time Design," in *Quality Popular Television: Cult TV, Industry and Fans,* 2003.

HONG, Junhao. Associate Professor, Department of Communication, State University of New York at Buffalo.

HOOVER, Stewart M. Professor, School of Journalism and Mass Communication, University of Colorado at Boulder.

HUFF, W.A. Kelly. Honors Faculty, Department of Speech Communication, University of Georgia.

HUGETZ, Ed. Director, University of Houston System, Texas. Cohost and coproducer, *The Territory,* a television program devoted to presentation and discussion of new film and video.

HULTÉN, Olof. Swedish Television Company.

HUMPHREYS, David. Author, "Lessons Unlearned: An Historical Sketch of Governmental English-Spanish Translation and Interpretation in South-Central Texas," in *Vistas: Proceedings of the Thirty-Fifth Annual Conference of the American Translators Association,* 1994.

HUNT, Darnell M. Director, Center for African American Studies and Professor, Department of Sociology, University of California, Los Angeles.

JACKA, Elizabeth. Author, *The ABC of Drama,* 1990; coauthor, *The Screening of Australia,* Vols. I and II, 1987 and 1988. Editor, *Continental Shift: Globalisation and Culture,* 1993. Editor and book review editor, *Media Information Australia,* from 1991. Coeditor, *The Imaginary Industry,* 1988.

JACKSON, Matt. Assistant Professor, Communications, Pennsylvania State University.

JACOBS, Jason J. Senior Lecturer, School of Arts, Media, and Culture, Griffith University (Nathan Campus), Queensland, Australia.

JACOBS, Randy. Associate Professor, School of Communication, University of Hartford, West Hartford, Connecticut. Adjunct Lecturer, Department of Communication Sciences, University of Connecticut, West Hartford.

JARVIS, Sharon. Assistant Professor, Department of Communication Studies, College of Communication, University of Texas at Austin.

JENKINS, Henry. Director, Comparative Media Studies Program, Codirector, Media in Transition, and Professor, Literature and Comparative Media Studies, Massachusetts Institute of Technology.

JENNINGS, Ros. Author, "Desire and Design: Ripley Undressed," in *Immortal, Invisible,* 1995.

JOHNSON, Victoria E. Assistant Professor, Department of Film and Media Studies, University of California, Irvine. Author, articles in anthologies and journals including *The Revolution Wasn't Televised: Sixties Television and Social Conflict,* 1997; *Spike Lee's Do the Right Thing,* 1997; *Film Quarterly, The Velvet Light Trap,* and *Continuum: Journal of Media and Cultural Studies.*

JONES, Jeffrey P. Assistant Professor, Communication and Theatre Arts, Old Dominion University.

JONES, Judith. Lecturer, Liverpool John Moores University, Liverpool, U.K. Freelance production assistant.

JONIAK, Lisa. Assistant Professor, Broadcasting, Department of Communications and Visual Arts, University of North Florida.

JOWETT, Garth. Professor, School of Communication, University of Houston.

JOWETT, Guy. Researcher, British Film Institute, U.K.

KACKMAN, Michael. Assistant Professor, Department of Radio, Television, Film, University of Texas at Austin. Author, *Citizen Spy: Television, Espionage, and Cold War Nationalism,* 2004.

KAID, Lynda Lee. Senior Associate Dean, Graduate Studies and Research, and Professor, College of Journalism and Communications, University of Florida.

KAMERER, David. Assistant Professor, Department of Mass Media, Washburn University.

KARIITHI, Nixon K. Pearson Chair of Economics Journalism, Rhodes University, South Africa.

KASSEL, Michael B. Adjunct faculty, Department of History, University of Michigan-Flint.

KAYE, Janice. Doctoral Candidate, Critical Studies, Cinema-Television, University of Southern California.

KEARNEY, Mary Celeste. Assistant Professor, Department of Radio Television Film, University of Texas at Austin.

KELLNER, C. A.

KELLNER, Douglas. Professor, George F. Kneller Philosophy of Education Chair, Social Sciences and Comparative Education, University of California, Los Angeles. Author, *From 9/11 to Terror War: The Dangers of the Bush Legacy,* 2003.

KENNY, Brendan.

KEPLEY, Vance, Jr. Professor and Chair, Department of Communication Arts, University of Wisconsin, Madison. Author, *The End of St. Petersburg: The Film Companion,*2003, "The Weaver Years at NBC," in *Wide Angle;* "From 'Frontal Lobes' to the 'Bob-and-Bob Show': NBC Management and Programming, 1949–65," in *Hollywood in the Age of Television,* 1990.

KESSLER, Kelly. Doctoral Candidate, Department of Radio Television Film at the University of Texas at Austin. Recent publications can be found in *Film Quarterly* and the *Encyclopedia of Masculinity.*

KIM, Lahn S. School of Social & Behavioral Sciences, Chaffey College.

KIM, Won-Yong. Associate Professor, Division of Digital Media Studies, Ewha Womans University, Seoul, Korea. Author, "New Governance and Deliberative Polling," *Journal of Seoul Metropolitan Studies,* 2003; "New Digital Broadcasting Services," report prepared for Korean Broadcsting Commission, 2003. Coauthor, *Data Broadcasting in Korea,* 2003.

KLEIMAN, Howard M. Professor, Mass Communication, Miami University, Oxford, Ohio. Author, "Content Diversity and the FCC's Minority and Gender Licensing Policies," in *Journal of Broadcasting and Electronic Media,* 1991. Fellow, Cable News Network, 1994.

KOMPARE, Derek. Radio Television Film, College of Communication, Texas Christian University.

KRACKLAUER, Beth. Research Editor, *Gourmet* magazine. Writes frequently on film and television.

KUBEY, Robert. Director, Center for Media Studies, Department of Journalism and Media Studies, Rutgers University. Author, *Creating Television: Conversations with the People Behind 50 Years of American TV,*

2004. Coauthor, *Television and the Quality of Life*, 1990. Editor, *Media Literacy in the Information Age*, 1997, 2001.

La PASTINA, Antonio. Assistant Professor, Department of Communication, Texas A&M University.

LAMONTAGNE, Manon. Writer and researcher.

LANE, Christina. Assistant Professor, Motion Picture Program, University of Miami. Author, *Feminist Hollywood: From Born in Flames to Point Break*. Contributor, *The West Wing: The American Presidency as TV Drama*.

LEACH, Jim. Chair, Department of Communications, Popular Culture, and Film, Faculty of Social Sciences Brock, University, Canada. Author, *Claude Jutra, Filmmaker*, 1999. Coauthor (with Louis Giannetti), *Understanding Movies*, 1998.

LEE, Stephen. Chair and Associate Professor, Department of Communication, Santa Clara University. Author of articles in *Popular Music* and *Journal of Media Economics*.

LEIBMAN, Nina C. Author, *Living Room Lectures: The Fifties Family in Film and Television*, 1995; "Leave Mother Out: The Family in Film and TV," *Wide Angle*; "Decades and Retro-decades: Historiography in the Case of *Easy Rider* and *Shampoo*," *Mid-Atlantic Almanac*; "The Family Spree of Film Noir," *Journal of Popular Film and Television*.

LEMIEUX, Debra A. Museum Education Consultant, Docemus Museum Education, Westminster, Maryland.

LEMIEUX, Robert. Associate Professor, Communication, McDaniel College.

LEWIS, Lisa Anne. Independent scholar and film producer. Author, *Gender Politics and MTV: Voicing the Difference*, 1990. Editor, *The Adoring Audience: Fan Culture and Popular Media*, 1992.

LIEBES, Tamar. Professor and Chair, Department of Communication, The Hebrew University of Jerusalem. Author, *American Dreams, Hebrew Subtitles: Globalization from the Receiving End*, 2002; *Reporting the Arab Israeli Conflict: How Hegemony Works*, 1997; "Covering the Palestinian Israeli Conflict," in *The Vortex of Terror*, 2003. Coeditor, (with Elihu Katz and John Peters) *Canonic Texts in Media Research*, 2002; (with James Curran), *Media, Identity, Ritual*, 1998.

LIGGETT, Lucy A. Professor, Telecommunications and Film, Eastern Michigan University. Coauthor, *Audio/Video Production: Theory and Practice*, 1990. Author, *Ida Lupino as Film Director, 1940–1953*, 1979.

Executive secretary, Michigan Association of Speech Communication, 1988–1994.

LIMBURG, Val E. Professor Emeritus, Edward R. Murrow School of Communication, Washington State University.

LIVINGSTONE, Sonia. Professor, Social Psychology, Department of Media and Communications, London School of Economics and Political Science. Author *of Making Sense of Television*, 1998; *Young People and New Media*, 2002. Coauthor, *Mass Consumption and Personal Identity*, 1992; *Talk on Television*, 1994. Coeditor, *Children and Their Changing Media Environment*, 2001; *The Handbook of New Media*, 2002. Having worked for some years on adult audiences's reception of television, her current research is on children and young people's uses of new media, especially the Internet (www.children-go-online.net).

LOMETTI, Guy E. Dean, School of Communication and the Arts, Marist College. Author of chapters in *New Research Toward Better Understanding of Children as Consumers*, 1993; *Television and Nuclear Power: Making the Public Mind*, 1992; articles in *Journal of Broadcasting and Electronic Media*, *Society*, *Human Communication Research*, *Communication Research*, *Journalism Quarterly*, *The Public Perspective*, and *Television and Children*.

LOOMIS, Amy W. Author of articles in *Visual Communication Quarterly*, *CommOddities*, and *Moving Images*. Editorial assistant, *Journal of Broadcasting and Electronic Media*.

LOTZ, Amanda. Assistant Professor, Communication, Denison University. Author, "Textual (Im)Possibilities in the U.S. Post-Network Era: Negotiating Production and Promotion Processes on Lifetime's Any Day Now," *Critical Studies in Media Communication*, 2004; "Communicating Third-Wave Feminism and New Social Movements: Challenges for the Next Century of Feminist Endeavor," *Women and Language*, 2003; "Barricaded Intersections: Any Day Now and the Struggle to Examine Ethnicity AND Gender" *Race/Gender/Media: Considering Diversity Across Audiences, Content, and Producers*, 2003; "Postfeminist Television Criticism: Rehabilitating Critical Terms and Identifying Postfeminist Attributes," *Feminist Media Studies*, 2001; "Assessing Qualitative Television Audience Research: Incorporating Feminist and Anthropological Innovation," *Communication Theory*, 2000.

LOVDAL, Lynn T. Lecturer, Ohio University.

LUCAS, Chris. Doctoral Candidate, College of Communication, University of Texas at Austin.

LUCKETT, Moya. Assistant Professor, English, University of Pittsburgh. Author of articles in *The Velvet Light Trap,* 1995; *Disney Discourse,* 1994. Editor, *The Velvet Light Trap,* 1991–1993.

LUCKEY, Kathleen. Senior Television Acquisitions Assistant, National Film and Television Archive (NFTVA), British Film Institute, U.K.

LUMBY, Catharine. Media and Communications Program, University of Sydney, Australia.

MAGDER, Ted. Associate Professor, Media Ecology, Department of Culture and Communications, New York University. Author, *Canada's Hollywood: Feature Films and the Canadian State* and *Franchising the Candy Store: Split-Run Magazines and a New International Regime for Trade in Culture.*

MALIK, Sarita. Independent writer, researcher, and arts programmer.

MALIN, Brent. Media and Cultural Studies, Communications Arts and Theatre Department, Allegheny College.

MANN, Chris. Newspaper writer and editor, *The Tulsa World, The Tulsa Sentinel, The University of Tulsa Collegian,* and *The New York Times.* Editor and publisher, *The Roomie Report,* and quarterly *Three's Company* fanzine.

MARC, David. Adjunct Professor, S.I. Newhouse School of Public Communications, Syracuse University.

MARSHALL, P. David. Professor and Chair, Communication Studies, Northeastern University. Author, *Celebrity and Power,* 1997; *New Media Cultures,* 2004. Coauthor, *Web Theory,* 2003; *Fame Games,* 2001. Coeditor, *The Celebrity Culture Reader,* 2004.

MARTIN, William. Chavanne Professor of Religion and Public Policy, Chair of Sociology, Rice University.

MASCARO, Tom. Assistant Professor, Department of Telecommunications, Bowling Green State University. Author, "The Peril of the Unheeded Warning: Robert F. Rogers' Vietnam: It's a Mad War," *Journalism History,* winter 2003; "Crossing Over: How Celebrity Newsmagazines Pushed Entertainment Shows Out of Prime Time," *Popular Culture Review,* 2002; "FRONTLINE Documentaries on Terrorism," *Television Quarterly,* 2002.

MASHON, Michael. Motion Picture, Broadcasting, and Recorded Sound Division, Library of Congress. Author of articles in *Wide Angle* and *Historical Journal of Film, Radio, and Television.* Former editor, *The Velvet Light Trap.*

MASSEY, Kimberly B. Associate Professor, Media Studies, Department of Television, Radio, Film, and Theatre, San Jose State University. Coauthor, *Introduction to Radio: Production and Programming,* 1995; *Television Criticism: Reading, Writing, and Analysis,* 1994.

MAXWELL, Richard. Professor and Chair, Department of Media Studies, Queens College, City University of New York. Author, *The Spectacle of Democracy: Spanish Television, Nationalism, and Political Transition,* 1995.

MAZZARELLA, Sharon R. Associate Professor and Chair, Department of Television-Radio, Ithaca College.

McALLISTER, Matthew P. Associate Professor, Communication Studies, and Director, Graduate Studies, Virginia Polytechnic Institute and State University. Author, "Selling *Survivor:* The use of TV news to promote commercial entertainment," in *The Blackwell Companion to Media Studies,* 2003; "Is commercial culture popular culture?: A question for popular communication scholars," *Popular Communication,* 2003; "Television news plugola and the last episode of Seinfeld," *Journal of Communication,* 2002.

McCARTHY, Anna. Associate Professor, Department of Cinema Studies, New York University. Author, *Ambient Television: Visual Culture and Public Space,* 2001. Coeditor (with Nick Couldry), *MediaSpace: Place, Scale, and Culture in a Media Age,* 2004.

McCOURT, Tom.

McDERMOTT, Mark R. Freelance writer.

McKEE, Alan. Senior Lecturer in Television, Queensland University of Technology, Australia. Chief Investigator, *Understanding pornography in Australia* research project. Consulting Editor, *Continuum: Journal of Media and Cultural Studies.*

McKINNON, Lori Melton. Associate Professor, Department of Advertising and Public Relations, University of Alabama. Author of articles in numerous journals, including *Journalism and Mass Communication Quarterly, Journal of Broadcasting and Electronic Media, Harvard International Journal of Press/Politics, Political Communication, Argumentation and Advocacy,* and the *Electronic Journal of Communication.*

McLELAND, Susan. Author, "Re-shaping the Grotesque Body: Roseanne, *Roseanne,* Breast Reduction and Rhinoplasty," *The Spectator,* 1993. Cocoordinating editor, *The Velvet Light Trap,* Spring 1995.

McLUSKIE, Peter. Freelance lecturer and media projects manager.

McMURRIA, John. Doctoral Candidate, Department of Cinema Studies, New York University. Author, "Transnational Contexts to Long-Format Special-Event Television: Branding Networks in a Multichannel Era," *Must-See Television,* forthcoming. Coauthor (with Toby Miller, Nitin Govil, and Richard Maxwell), *Global Hollywood,* 2001.

MEERS, Philippe. Department of Communication, Ghent University, Belgium.

MERRITT, Bishetta D. Associate Professor, Department of Radio, Television, and Film, Howard University. Author, "The Debbie Allen Touch," in *Women and the Media: Content, Careers, and Criticism,* 1995; "Illusive Reflections: African American Women on Primetime Television," in *Our Voices: Essays in Culture, Ethnicity, and Communications,* 1993; "Black Family Imagery and Interactions on Television," *Journal of Black Studies,* 1993; "Bill Cosby: TV Auteur?" *Journal of Popular Culture,* 1992.

MESSERE, Fritz J. Professor, Broadcasting and Telecommunications, State University of New York at Oswego. Coauthor, *Broadcasting, Cable, the Internet and Beyond; Modern Radio Production; Announcing: Broadcast Communicating Today; Introduction to the Internet for Electronic Media.* Coeditor, *Pro/Con Media.*

METZ, Walter C. Assistant Professor, Media and Theatre Arts, Montana State University in Bozeman. Contributor to *Journal of Contemporary Thought, Literature/Film Quarterly, Film Criticism, The Velvet Light Trap, Journal of Film and Video, Film and History, Film Quarterly,* and *Rocky Mountain Review of Language and Literature.*

MEYERS, Cynthia. Doctoral Candidate, New York University.

MILLER, Andrew. Assistant Professor, Department of Media Studies and Digital Culture, Sacred Heart University.

MILLER, Mary Jane. Director, Dramatic Literature and Theatre, Brock University, Canada. Author, *Rewind and Search: Conversations with Makers and Decision-Makers in Television Drama,* 1996; *Turn Up the Contrast: CBC Television Drama since 1952,* 1987; articles and chapters in *Canadian Drama* and *Beyond Quebec: Taking Stock of Canada.* Book review editor, *Theatre History in Canada.*

MILLER, Toby. Associate Professor, Cinema Studies, New York University. Author, *The Well-Tempered Self:*

Citizenship, Culture and the Postmodern Subject, 1993; *The Avengers,* 1997; *Technologies of Truth: Cultural Citizenship and the Popular Media,* 1997. Coauthor (with Stuart Cunningham), *Contemporary Australian Television,* 1994.

MILLINGTON, Bob. Senior Lecturer, School of Media, Critical, and Creative Arts, Liverpool John Moores University, U.K. Author, "Myths of Creation: Theatre on the Southbank Show," *Boxed Sets,* 1996.

MITTELL, Jason. Assistant Professor, American Civilization, and Film & Media Culture, Middlebury College. Author, *Genre and Television: From Cop Shows to Cartoons in American Culture,* forthcoming. Author, essays in *Cinema Journal, The Velvet Light Trap, Television and New Media, Film History, Journal of Popular Film and Television,* and a number of anthologies.

MONTGOMERIE, Margaret. Community Historian, The Burton Street Project, Sheffield, U.K.

MOODY, Nickianne. Media and Cultural Studies Department, Liverpool John Moores University, U.K.

MORAN, Albert. Senior Lecturer, School of Film, Media, and Cultural Studies, Griffith University, Australia. Author, *Public Voices, Private Interests,* 1995; *Film Policy,* 1994; *Moran's Guide to Australian TV Series,* 1993; *Stay Tuned,* 1992; *Projecting Australia,* 1991.

MORAN, James. Writer and teacher based in Los Angeles.

MORETTI, Anthony. Assistant Professor, School of Mass Communications, Texas Tech University.

MOREY, Anne. Assistant Professor, Film, English and Performance Studies departments, Texas A&M University.

MORGAN, Michael. Professor, Department of Communications, University of Massachusetts–Amherst. Coauthor, *Democracy Tango: Television, Adolescents, and Authoritarian Tensions in Argentina,* 1995; numerous articles on television and cultivation theory.

MORLEY, David. Professor, Communications, Department of Media and Communications, Goldsmiths College, University of London. Author, *Home Territories: media, mobility and identity,* 2000. Coauthor, *The Nationwide Television Studies* (with C. Brunsdon), 1999; *Spaces of Identity* (with K. Robins), 2000.

MORSE, Margaret. Assistant Professor, Theater Arts-Film-Video, University of California, Santa Cruz. Author, "What Do Cyborgs Eat? Oral Logic in an Information Society," in *Culture on the Brink: Ideologies* *of Technology,* 1994. Member, advisory board, *Convergence* and *Quarterly Review of Film and Video.*

MULLEN, Megan. Associate Professor, Department of Communication, and Director, Humanities Program. Author, *The Rise of Cable Programming in the United States: Revolution or Evolution?,* 2003; "The Simpsons and the Hanna-Barbera Legacy" in *Leaving Springfield: The Simpsons and the Possibility of Oppositional Culture,* 2003; "The Fall and Rise of Cable Narrowcasting," *Convergence,* 2002; "The Pre-History of Pay-Cable: An Overview and Analysis," *Historical Journal of Film, Radio, and Television,* 1999.

MUN, Seung-Hwan. Doctoral Candidate, Department of Radio-Television-Film, University of Texas at Austin.

MURDOCK, Graham. Reader in the Sociology of Culture, Department of Social Sciences, Loughborough University. U.K.

MURRAY, Matthew. Department of Speech Communication and Theatre, North Central College.

MURRAY, Susan. Assistant Professor, Culture and Communication, New York University. Coeditor (with Laurie Ouellette), *Reality TV: Remaking Television Culture,* 2004. Upcoming books are *Gender & Television: A History of Theory and Method* and a book on stardom and early television.

NEGRA, Diane M. Teaches film and television, School of English and American Studies, University of East Anglia, U.K. Author, *Off-White Hollywood: American Culture and Ethnic Female Stardom,* 2001. Coeditor, *A Feminist Reader in Early Cinema,* 2002.

NEWCOMB, Horace. Director, George Foster Peabody Awards Program and Lambdin Kay Distinguished Professor for the Peabody Awards, Grady College of Journalism and Mass Communication, University of Georgia. Author, *TV: The Most Popular Art,* 1974. Coauthor, *The Producer's Medium,* 1983. Editor of six editions of *Television: The Critical View,* 1976–2000.

NEWTON, Darrell Mottley. Assistant Professor, Department of Communication and Theater Arts, Salisbury University.

NICHOLS-PETHICK, Jonathan. Associate Instructor, Department of Communication and Culture, Indiana University.

NICKS, Joan. Associate Professor, Department of Communications, Brock University, Canada. Author, "Sex, Lies and Landscape: Meditations on Vertical Tableaus in Joyce Wieland's *The Far Shore* and Jean

Beaudin's *J.A. Martin, Photographe,*" *Canadian Journal of Film Studies;* "Crossing into Eden's Storehouse," in *Textual Studies in Canada 2.*

NIELSEN, Poul Erik. Assistant Professor, University of Aarhus, Denmark. Author, "Film og TV-Produktion I USA og Danmark," *Mediekultur,* 1995; "Bag Hollywoods Dromme Fabrik," *Foreningen af Nye Medier,* 1993.

NILL, Dawn Michelle. Department of Communication, Dixie State College.

NORDENSTRENG, Kaarle. Department of Journalism and Mass Communications, University of Tampere, Finland.

O'DELL, Cary. Discovery Channel.

ORLIK, Peter B. Professor, Broadcast & Cinematic Arts, Central Michigan University. Author, *Broadcast/Cable Copywriting, 5th ed.,* 1994; *Electronic Media Criticism,* 1994; *The Electronic Media: An Introduction to the Profession,* 1992; *Critiquing Radio and Television Content,* 1988; numerous articles and book chapters.

OSWELL, David. Lecturer, Sociology Department, Goldsmiths College, University of London, U.K. Author, "Suburban Tales: Television, Masculinity and Textual Geographies" in *City Visions,* 2000; "Ethics and Techno-Childhood" in *Childhood, Technology and Culture,* 2001; *Television, Childhood and the Home: The Making of an Audience,* 2001.

PACK, Lindsy E. Assistant Professor, Communication and Theatre Arts, Frostburg State University.

PARKS, Lisa. Associate Professor, Department of Film Studies, University of California, Santa Barbara. Author, *Cultures in Orbit: Satellites and the Televisual,* 2003. Coeditor, *Planet TV: A Global Television Studies Reader,* 2002 and *Red Noise: Television Studies and Buffy the Vampire Slayer,* 2004.

PATERSON, Chris. Assistant Professor, Department of Media Studies, University of San Francisco.

PEARSON, Tony. Senior Lecturer (retired), University of Glasgow, Scotland, U.K.

PERREN, Alisa. Doctoral Candidate, University of Texas at Austin. Author, "New US Networks in the 90s," in *The Television History Book,* 2003; "*sex, lies and marketing:* Miramax and the Development of the 'Quality Indie Blockbuster," *Film Quarterly,* 54, no. 2 (Winter 2001–2002). Coauthor (with Thomas Schatz), "US Cinema Past and Present, Hollywood and Independent," in *The Handbook of Media Studies* (forthcoming).

PETTITT, Lance. Department of Media and Popular Culture, Leeds Metropolitan University, U.K.

PHILLIPS, JENNIE L. Graduate student, Department of Radio Television Film, University of Texas at Austin.

PICKERING, David. British freelance writer and editor of arts and general reference books. Editor, *Dictionary of Abbreviations,* 1995; *Dictionary of Superstitions,* 1995; *International Dictionary of Theatre 3,* 1995; *Brewer's 20th Century Music,* 1994; *Encyclopedia of Pantomime,* 1993. Assistant editor, Market House Books, Ltd., 1984–92.

PLOEGER, Joanna. Department of Communication Studies, University of Iowa.

POHL, Gayle M. Associate Professor, Public Relations Program, Department of Communication Studies, University of Northern Iowa. Author, *Public Relations: Designing Effective Communication* and articles in *Communication Reports, Popular Culture Review,* and *International Society for Exploring Teaching Alternatives.*

POLSTON, Robbie. Visiting Assistant Professor, College of Charleston.

POPELNIK, Rodolfo B. Professor, Communication, University of Puerto Rico, United States. Author, "The Problem of the Social Problem Film: A Review and a Proposal," *Memorias del Congreso Internacional de Cine y Literatura,* 1994. Coeditor, *IMAGINES,* 1985–90.

PORTER, Vincent. Director, Media, Arts, and Design Graduate Center, University of Westminster, U.K. Author, "Methodism versus the Marketplace. The Rank Organisation and British Cinema," in *The British Cinema Book* (second edition), 2001; "The Construction of an Ante-Hollywood Film Aesthetic; The Film Criticism of Walter Mycroft in the 1920s," in *Crossing the Pond. Anglo-American Film Relations Before 1930,* 2002. Coauthor (with Sue Harper), *British Cinema of the 1950s: The Decline of Deference,* 2003.

PRINCE, Julie. Freelance writer.

QUICKE, Andrew. Professor and Chair, Cinema Arts, School of Communication and the Arts, Regent University. Author, "Documentary as Pedagogy: Al Pacino's *Richard III*" *Journal of Film and Video,* Fall 1999. Coauthor, (with Karen Robinson) "Keeping the Promise of the Moral Majority? A historical/critical comparison of the Promise Keepers and the Christian Coalition, 1989–97" *The Promise Keepers: Studies in Masculinity and Christianity,* 1999; (with Andrew

Laszlo) *Every Frame a Rembrandt: The Art and Practice of Cinematography,* 2000.

RABOY, Marc. Professor, Department of Communication, University of Montreal, Canada. Author, *Media, Crisis and Democracy,* 1992; *Missed Opportunities: The Story of Canada's Broadcasting Policy,* 1990.

REAL, Michael. Professor, Communication, E. W. Scripps School of Journalism, Ohio University. Author, *Exploring Media Culture: A Guide,* 1996.

REEVES, Jimmie L. Assistant Professor, School of Mass Communications, Texas Tech University. Coauthor (with Richard Campbell), *Cracked Coverage: Television News, the Anti-Cocaine Crusade, and the Reagan Legacy,* 1994.

RICHARDS, Jef. Professor, Advertising Department, University of Texas at Austin.

RICHTER, William. Professor and Chair, School of Communication and Literature, Lenoir-Rhyne College.

RIDGMAN, Jeremy. Senior Lecturer and Convener, Film and Television Studies, University of Surrey Roehampton.

RIGGS, Karen E. Director, School of Telecommunications, Ohio University.

RING, Trudy. Senior news reporter, Lambda Publications. freelance editor and writer.

RITROSKY-WINSLOW, Madelyn. Adjunct Professor, Radio-TV Center, Department of Telecommunications, Indiana University-Bloomington.

RODRIGUEZ, America. Associate Professor, Department of Radio Television Film, University of Texas at Austin. Author, "Made in the USA: The Production of the Noticiero Univision," in *Journalism Monographs,* Winter 1995; "The Control of National Newsmaking," in *Questioning the Media,* 1995.

ROSENBERG, Stacy. Masters Degree Candidate, Department of Culture and Communication, New York University.

ROSS, Karen. Reader in Mass Communication and Director, Centre for Communication, Culture and Media Studies, Coventry School of Art and Design, Coventry University, U.K.

ROSS, Robert. Author, *Benny Hill: The Complete Companion; The Complete Goodies; The Complete Sid James; The Complete Frankie Howerd; Last of the*

Summer Wine: The Finest Vintage; Fawlty Towers: Fully Booked; The Monty Python Encyclopedia; The Carry On Companion; Carry On Uncensored; The Lost Carry Ons; and *Mr. Carry On.*

ROSS, Sharon. Department of Television, Columbia College (Chicago). Editor, *Reading Women's Lives: An Introduction to Women's Studies,* 1996. Author, "Dangerous Demons: *Buffy the Vampire Slayer*'s Feminist Rhetoric and Feminist Recuperation" in *femspec,* (forthcoming); "Talking Sex: Comparison Shopping Through Female Conversation in HBO's *Sex and the City* " in *Sitcoms* (forthcoming); "Dormant Dormitory Friendships: The Continuing Saga of Race and Gender on *Felicity*" in *Teen TV: Isolation, Inclusion and Identity* (forthcoming).

ROSTRON, Pamela. Assistant Keeper of Television, National Film and Television Archive, British Film Institute, U.K. Author, (as Pamela W. Logan) *Jack Hylton Presents.*

ROTH, Lorna. Associate Professor and Chair, Communication Studies Department, Concordia University, Canada. Author, *Something New in the Air: A History of First Peoples Television in Canada,* 2004.

ROTHENBUHLER, Eric. Director, Graduate Media Studies, New School University.

ROWE, David. Associate Professor, Media and Cultural Studies, and Director of the Cultural Industries and Practices Research Center (CIPS), The University of Newcastle, Australia. Author, *Sport, Culture and the Media: The Unruly Trinity* (second edition), 2004; *Popular Cultures: Rock Music, Sport and the Politics of Pleasure,* 1995. Editor, *Critical Readings: Sport, Culture and the Media,* 2004. Coauthor, *Globalization and Sport: Playing the World,* 2001. Coeditor, *Tourism, Leisure, Sport: Critical Perspectives,* 1998.

RUNYON, Steven C. Director, KUSF-FM, University of San Francisco. Author, "Wanda Ramey: KPIX's Girl on the Beat," in *Indelible Images: Women of Local Television,* 2001; various entries (15) in *Historical Dictionary of American Radio,* 1998; "The West's Coast's First Television Station: KCBS, Los Angeles," and "San Francisco's First Television Station: KPIX," in *Television in America: Local Station History from Across the Nation,* 1997.

RUTHERFORD, Paul. Professor, Department of History, University of Toronto, Canada. Author, *The New Icons?: The Art of Television Advertising,* 1994; *When Television Was Young: Primetime Canada 1952–1967,* 1990.

SAENZ, Michael. Advisor, Division of Teacher Education, California State University, San Bernardino.

SANTO, Avi. Assistant Instructor, Department of Radio Television Film, University of Texas at Austin.

SCHAEFER, Eric. Associate Professor, Department of Visual and Media Arts, Emerson College. Author, *"Bold! Daring! Shocking! True!": A History of Exploitation Films, 1919–1959,* 1999 and *Massacre of Pleasure: A History of Sexploitation Films, 1960–1979* (forthcoming).

SCHATZ, Thomas. Philip G. Warner Regents Professor of Communication & Associate Dean, Department of Radio, Television, Film, University of Texas at Austin.

SCHICK, Sherra. Visiting Lecturer, Department of English, Indiana University Purdue University Indianapolis. Author, entry on "Oprah Winfrey," the *Encyclopedia of the Midwest,* 2005.

SCODARI, Christine. Associate Professor, Department of Communications, Florida Atlantic University. Author, "'No Politics Here': Age and Gender in Soap Opera 'Cyberfandom'." *Women's Studies in Communication* 21 (Fall 1998); "Possession, Attraction and the Thrill of the Chase: Gendered Myth-Making in Film and Television Comedy of the Sexes." *Critical Studies in Mass Communication* 12 (Winter 1995).

SCONCE, Jeffrey. Associate Professor, Radio/Television/Film, School of Communication, and Graduate Director, program in Media, Technology and Society, Northwestern University. Author, *Haunted Media: Electronic Presence from Telegraphy to Television,* 2000.

SEATON, Elizabeth. Acting Director, Communication & Culture, Faculty of Graduate Studies, York University, Canada.

SEEL, Peter B. Associate Professor, Department of Journalism and Technical Communication, Colorado State University.

SEN, Krishna. Professor of Asian Media, Curtin University of Technology, Perth Australia. Author, *Indonesian Cinema: Framing The New Order,* 1994. Coauthor (with David T. Hill), *Internet and Democracy in Indonesia,* forthcoming (2004); (with David T. Hill), *Media, Culture and Politics in Indonesia,* 2000. Coeditor (with Maila Stivens), *Gender and Power in Affluent Asia,* 1998.

SERVAES, Jan. Professor and department head, Department of Communication at the Katholieke Universiteit van Brussel (KUB), Director of the research center Communication for Social Change (CSC), President of the European Consortium for Communications Research (ECCR), and Vice-President of the International Association of Media and Communication Research, in charge of Research and Academic Publications. Author, *Communication for Development. One World, Multiple Cultures,* 2002; "The European Information Society: Much ado about nothing?" *Gazette: The International Journal for Communication Studies,* 64, 5, (2002). Editor, *The European Information Society: A reality check,* 2003; *Approaches to Development. Studies on Communication for Development,* 2003. Coauthor, (with F. Heinderyckx), "The 'new' ICTs environment in Europe: Closing or widening the gaps?" *Telematics and Informatics,* vol. 19, no. 2, May 2002; (with R. Lie) "Media, globalization and culture: issues and trends" *Communicatio.* Vol. 29 (1–2).

SHAMP, Scott. Associate Professor, Director of the New Media Institute, Director of the Mobile Media Consortium, Grady College of Journalism and Mass Communication, University of Georgia.

SHAPIRO, Mitchell E. Professor, University of Miami, Florida. Author, chapter in "Network Non-prime Time Programming," in *Broadcast/Cable Programming,* 1993; *Television Network Weekend Programming 1959–1990,* 1992; *Television Network Daytime and Late Night Programming 1959–1989,* 1990; articles in *Journalism Quarterly, Television Quarterly, Newspaper Research Journal, Mass Communication Review, Current Research in Film,* and *Florida Communication Journal.*

SHELTON, Marla L. Doctoral Candidate, Cinema-Television, University of Southern California, Los Angeles.

SHIMPACH, Shawn. Doctoral Candidate, Department of Cinema Studies, New York University. Teaches courses on film, television, and media in NYU's Tisch School of the Arts.

SHIRES, Jeff. Assistant Professor, Department of Communications, Purdue University North Central.

SIERRA, Mayra Cue. Assistant Professor, Communication and Organizational Culture, Social Communication Faculty, La Habana University, Cuba.

SILLARS, Jane. Teaching Fellow, Department of Film and Media Studies, University of Stirling, Scotland, U.K.

SILVO, Ismo. Director of Programs, YLE Teema/Finnish Broadcasting Company.

SIMON, Ron. Curator, Museum of Television and Radio, New York. Author of numerous articles and exhibition notes related to television.

SINHA, Nikhil. Associate Professor, Department of Radio Television Film, and Associate Dean of Academic Affairs, College of Communication, University of Texas at Austin.

SLONIOWSKI, Jeannette. Associate Professor, Department of Communications, Popular Culture and Film, Brock University, Canada. Author, "Las Hurdes and the Political Efficacy of the Grotesque," *Canadian Journal of Film Studies* vol. 7 #2 (Autumn 1998). Coauthor (with B. Grant), *Documenting the Documentary,* 1996. Coeditor (with Bohdan Szuchewycx), Canadian *Communications: Issues in Contemporary Media and Culture* (revised 2nd edition), 2002.

SMITH, B. R. Associate Professor, Department of Broadcast and Cinematic Arts, Central Michigan University, United States.

SMITH, Christopher. Visiting Assistant Professor, Annenberg School for Communication, University of Southern California.

SOUKUP, Paul A. Associate Professor, Communication, Santa Clara University, California, United States. Author, *Christian Communication,* 1989. Coeditor, *Mass Media and the Moral Imagination,* 1994; *Media, Consciousness, and Culture,* 1991.

SPICER, Nigel. Victoria and Albert Museum, London, U.K.

SPIGEL, Lynn. Professor, School of Communications, Northwestern University

SRAGOW, Michael. Senior Writer, *Seattle Weekly,* United States. Contributor, *The New Yorker* and *The Atlantic.* Editor, *Produced and Abandoned: The National Society of Film Critics Write on the Best Films You've Never Seen,* 1990.

STAIGER, Janet. William P. Hobby Centennial Professor of Communication, Department of Radio Television Film, University of Texas at Austin. Director, Center for Women's Studies. Author, *Blockbuster TV: Must-See Sitcoms in the Network Era,* 2000; *Perverse Spectators: The Practices of Film Reception,* 2000. Coeditor, *Authorship and Film,* 2002.

STEIN, Laura. Assistant Professor, Department of Radio Television Film, University of Texas at Austin.

STERLING, Christopher H. School of Media and Public Affairs, and School of Public Policy and Public Administration, George Washington University.

STERNBERG, Joel B. Professor, Department of Communication, Saint Xavier University. Contributor to *Dictionary of Literary Biography Volume 171: Twentieth-Century American Sportswriters.* (1996),

Encyclopedia of Television (1997), *Quarterly Review of Film and Video* (1999), *Dictionary of Literary Biography, Volume 241: American Sportswriters and Writers on Sport* (2001), *Women Building Chicago 1790–1990: A Biographical Dictionary.* (2001), *Research Strategies: A Journal of Library Concepts and Instruction* (Summer, 1995), and *Nine: A Journal of Baseball History and Social Policy Perspectives* (Spring, 1995).

STRANGE, Nicola. Production coordinator, Independent Television Productions, U.K.

STRAUBHAAR, Joseph. Amon G. Carter Centennial Professor of Communication, Department of Radio, Television, Film, University of Texas at Austin.

STREIBLE, Dan G. Associate Professor, Film Studies, University of South Carolina.

STROVER, Sharon. Professor and Chair, Department of Radio, Television, Film, University of Texas at Austin.

SULLIVAN, John. Associate Professor, Rhetoric, American Studies, English Department, University of Virginia. Coauthor (with Steve Frantzich), *The C-SPAN Revolution,* 1996.

SYVERTSEN, Trine. Professor, Department of Media and Communication, Subdean, Faculty of Arts, University of Oslo. Author, *Mediemangfold. Styring av mediene i et globalisert marked.* [Media pluralism: Governance of the media in a globalized market], 2004; "Challenges to Public Television in the Era of Convergence and Commercialization," *Television and New Media* 4(2), 2003; "Ordinary People in Extraordinary Circumstances: a Study of Participants in Television Dating Games," *Media, Culture and Society* 23(3), 2001. Coeditor, *Et hjem for oss—et hjem for deg? Analyser av TV 2 1992–2002.* [A home for us—a home for you? Analyses of TV 2 1992–2002] (with Gunn Enli and Susanne Østby Sæther), 2002; *Sjekking på TV* [TV-dating] (With Eva Bakøy), 2000.

TAN, Zoe. Director of Research, SRT Nielsen Media Services, Taipei, Taiwan. Author, "The Role of Mass Media in Insurgent Terrorism: Issues and Perspectives," 1989, *Gazette* (Amsterdam); "Mass Media and Insurgent Terrorism: A Twenty-year Balance Sheet," 1988, *Gazette* (Amsterdam).

TAUB-PERVIZPOUR, Lora. Assistant Professor, Department of Communication, Muhlenberg College. Author, "Class" in *Television Studies,* 2003. Coauthor (with D. Schiller), "Networking the North American Higher Education Industry," in *Continental Order? Integrating North America for Cybercapitalism,* 2001.

TAYLOR, Julia. Freelance editor, Toronto, Canada.

TCHOUNGUI, Gisèle.

TEDESCO, John C. Assistant Professor, Department of Communication, Virginia Tech University. Author, "Issue and strategy agenda-setting in the 2000 presidential primaries." *American Behavioral Scientist,* 44(2), 2001; "Televised political advertising effects: Evaluating responses during the 2000 Robb-Allen Senatorial Election." *Journal of Advertising,* 31(1), 2002; "Network news coverage of campaign 2000: The public voice in context," in *The 2000 presidential campaign: A communication perspective,* 2002.

TETZLAFF, David J. Assistant Professor, Film Studies, Connecticut College.

THOMPSON, Robert J. Professor and Director, Center for the Study of Popular Television, Trustee Professor, Television and Popular Culture, S.I Newhouse School of Public Communications, Syracuse University. Author or editor, *Television's Second Golden Age,* 1996; *Prime Time, Prime Movers,* 1992; *Adventures on Prime Time,* 1990; and *Television Studies,* 1989.

THORBURN, David. Professor, Literature and Director, MIT Communications Forum, Massachusetts Institute of Technology. Author, *Conrad's Romanticism,* and many essays on literature and media. Editor in chief of the MIT Press book series, *Media in Transition.*

TIMBERG, Bernard M. Writer, media consultant, and historian.

TORRE, Paul J. Doctoral Candidate, School of Cinema-Television, University of Southern California.

TOVARES, Raul D. Chair, Department of Communication, Trinity College, Washington, DC.

TREVIÑO, Liza.

TULLOCH, John. Center for Communication and Information Services, University of Westminster, U.K.

TULLOCH, Marian. School of Social Sciences and Liberal Studies, Charles Stuart University, Australia. Author, "Evaluating Aggression: School Student's Responses to Television Portrayals of Institutionalized Violence," in *Journal of Youth and Adolescence,* 1995; coauthor, "Understanding TV Violence: A Multifaceted Cultural Analysis," in *Nation, culture, text: Australian Cultural and Media Studies,* 1993.

TURNER, J. C. Associate Dean, Learning Resources and Technology Services, St. Cloud State University.

TURNOCK, Rob. Lecturer, Media Theory, Bournemouth University, U.K. Author, *Interpreting Diana: Television Audiences and the Death of a Princess,*

2000; *Television and Consumer Culture: Britain and the Transformation of Modernity* (forthcoming).

TUROW, Joseph. Professor, Annenberg School for Communication, University of Pennsylvania, United States. Author, *Playing Doctor: Television, Storytelling, and Media Power,* 1989; *Entertainment, Education, and the Hard Sell: Three Decades of Network Children's Television,* 1981; numerous articles and book chapters.

URQUHART, Peter. Lecturer, Institute of Film Studies, School of American and Canadian Studies, University of Nottingham, U.K. Author, "The Glace Bay Miners' Museum/ Margaret's Museum: Adaptation and Resistance." *CineAction* 49 (July 1999); "You Should Know Something—Anything—About this Movie. You Paid For It." *Canadian Journal of Film Studies* 12:2 (Fall 2003); "Film Policy/Film History: From the Canadian Film Development Corporation to Telefilm Canada," in *Self Portrait II: New Essays on the Canadian and Quebec Cinemas,* 2004.

VAHIMAGI, Tise. Television database editor, Filmographic Services, British Film Institute, U.K. Compiler, *British Television: An Illustrated Guide,* 1994.

VALSDOTTIR, Hanna Bjork. MA in Media Ecology, Department of Culture and Communication, New York University.

VANDE BERG, Leah R. Professor, Communication Studies, California State University, Sacramento.

WAITE, Clayland H. Professor, Media Studies Department, Radford University.

WALKER, Cynthia W. Lecturer, Communication, Rutgers University. Author, *The Teacher's Guide to Star Trek,* 1994.

WALKER, James R. Professor, Mass Communications, Department of Communication, Saint Xavier University. Coauthor, *Grazing on a Vast Wasteland: The Remote Control and The Second Generation of Television,* 1995; *The Remote Control in the New Age of Television,* 1993; articles in *Journalism Quarterly* and *Journal of Broadcasting and Electronic Media.* Member, editorial board, *The Journal of Broadcasting and Electronic Media.*

WALSH, Kay.

WARNER, Charles. Associate Professor, Broadcast and Leonard H. Goldenson Endowed Professor of Local Broadcasting, University of Missouri School of Journalism. Coauthor, *Broadcast and Cable Selling,*

1993. Editor, *Media Management Review,* 1995.

WATERS, Jody. Assistant Professor, Department of Mass Communication, Carleton University, Canada. Author, "Power and Praxis in Development Communication Discourse and Method" *Redeveloping Communication for Social Change: Theory Practice and Power,* 2000. Coauthor (with K. Wilkins), "International News Discourse on Alternative Development Strategies" in *Encyclopedia of Life Support Systems,* 2003; (with K. Wilkins), "Current Discourse on New Technologies in Development Communication." *Media Development XLVII,* 2000.

WATSON, Mary Ann. Professor, Department of Telecommunications, Eastern Michigan University. Author, "From *My Little Margie* to *Murphy Brown:* Women's Lives on the Small Screen," in *Television Quarterly,* 1994; *The Expanding Vista: American Television in the Kennedy Years,* 1990.

WEHMEYER, James.

WEISBLAT, Tinky "Dakota." Independent writer, historian, and singer.

WHANNEL, Gary. Professor, Media Cultures, and Director, Centre for International Media Analysis, University of Luton, U.K. Author, "From Pig's Bladders to Ferraris: Media Discourses of Masculinity and Morality in Obituaries of Stanley Matthews" in *Sport, Media, Society,* 2002; *Media Sport Stars, Masculinities and Moralities,* 2001; "The Lads and The Gladiators: Traditional Masculinities in a Post-Modern Televisual Landscape" in *British Television: A Reader,* 2000. Editor, *Consumption and Participation: Leisure, Culture and Commerce,* 2000. Coauthor (with John Horne and Alan Tomlinson), *Understanding Sport: An Introduction to the Sociological and Cultural Analysis of Sport,* 1999.

WHITE, Mimi. Associate Professor, Department of Radio/Television/Film, Northwestern University. Author, *Tele:Advising: Therapeutic Discourse in American Television,* 1992; coauthor, *Media Knowledge: Popular Culture, Pedagogy, and Critical Citizenship,* 1992; articles in *Screen, Cinema Journal, Cultural Studies,* and *Wide Angle.*

WICKHAM, Phil. Information Officer, British Film Institute, U.K. Author, *Producing the Goods? British Film Production 1991–2001.* Contributor to *bfi Screen Online* and *bfi TV100.*

WIGGINS, D. Joel. Director, Austin Technology Incubator, IC2 Institute, The University of Texas at Austin. Coauthor (with David V. Gibson), "Overview of US Incubators and the Case of the Austin Technology Incubator," *Int. J. Entrepreneurship and Innovation Management,* Vol. 3, Nos. 1/2, 2003.

WILKINS, Karin Gwinn. Associate Professor and Graduate Advisor, Department of Radio Television Film, University of Texas at Austin.

WILLIAMS, Carol Traynor. Author, *"It's Time for My Story"*: *Soap Opera, Sources, Structure, and Responses,* 1992.

WILLIAMS, Kevin D. Graduate student, University of Georgia, Grady College of Journalism and Mass Communication, University of Georgia.

WILLIAMS, Mark. Department Chair and Associate Professor, Film and Television Studies, Dartmouth College.

WILLIAMS-RAUTIOLLA, Suzanne. Associate Professor, Department of Communication, Trinity University (San Antonio). Has published articles and presented papers on cultural values, particularly as they relate to children's television. Has video experience and has produced promotional and training videos.

WILSON, Pamela. Associate Professor, Department of Communication, Reinhardt College.

WINSTON, Brian. Dean, Faculty of Media and Humanities, University of Lincoln, U.K.

WORRINGHAM, Richard. Chair, Media Studies Department, Radford University.

ZAHAROPOULOS, Thimios. Professor and Chair, Department of Mass Media, Washburn University. Author, "Television viewing and the perception of the United States by Greek teenagers," in *U.S. Image Around the World: A Multicultural Perspective,* 1998. Coauthor (with M. Paraschos), *Mass Media in Greece: Power, Politics, and Privatization,* 1993.

ZAJACZ, Rita. Doctoral Candidate, Department of Telecommunications, Indiana University.

ZECHOWSKI, Sharon. Communication Arts, Indiana University South Bend.

ZUBERI, Nabeel. Senior Lecturer, Department of Film, Television and Media Studies, University of Auckland, New Zealand.

Index

The page numbers for the main discussion of a topic are in bold type. The page numbers for photographs are italicized.

Index